Marketing Management

Knowledge and Skills

Eighth Edition

J. Paul Peter
University of Wisconsin–Madison

James H. Donnelly, Jr.
University of Kentucky

Boston   Burr Ridge, IL   Dubuque, IA   Madison, WI   New York   San Francisco   St. Louis
Bangkok   Bogotá   Caracas   Kuala Lumpur   Lisbon   London   Madrid   Mexico City
Milan   Montreal   New Delhi   Santiago   Seoul   Singapore   Sydney   Taipei   Toronto

McGraw-Hill
Irwin

MARKETING MANAGEMENT: KNOWLEDGE AND SKILLS

Published by McGraw-Hill/Irwin, a business unit of The McGraw-Hill Companies, Inc., 1221 Avenue of the Americas, New York, NY, 10020. Copyright © 2007 by The McGraw-Hill Companies, Inc. All rights reserved. No part of this publication may be reproduced or distributed in any form or by any means, or stored in a database or retrieval system, without the prior written consent of The McGraw-Hill Companies, Inc., including, but not limited to, in any network or other electronic storage or transmission, or broadcast for distance learning.

Some ancillaries, including electronic and print components, may not be available to customers outside the United States.

This book is printed on acid-free paper.

1 2 3 4 5 6 7 8 9 0 DOW/DOW 0 9 8 7 6

ISBN-13: 978-0-07-313763-6
ISBN-10: 0-07-313763-4

Editorial director: *John E. Biernat*
Publisher: *Andy Winston*
Editorial coordinator: *Amy Luck*
Executive marketing manager: *Dan Silverburg*
Media producer: *Benjamin Curless*
Project manager: *Dana M. Pauley*
Senior production supervisor: *Sesha Bolisetty*
Senior designer *Adam Rooke*
Photo research coordinator: *Kathy Shive*
Senior media project manager: *Susan Lombardi*
Typeface: *10/12 Times New Roman*
Compositor: *Carlisle Publishing Services*
Printer: *R. R. Donnelley*

Library of Congress Cataloging-in-Publication Data

Peter, J. Paul
    Marketing management: knowledge and skills/J. Paul Peter, James H. Donnelly, Jr.—
8th ed.
      p. cm.
    Includes bibliographical references and index.
    ISBN-13: 978-0-07-313763-6 (alk. paper)
    ISBN-10: 0-07-313763-4 (alk. paper)
    1. Marketing—Management. 2. Marketing—Management—Case studies. I. Donnelly.
James H. II. Title
HF5415.13.P387 2007
658.8—dc22
                                       2005056244

www.mhhe.com

To Gayla

To Rose and Angie

Jim Donnelly

J. Paul Peter

About the Authors

J. Paul Peter

is the James R. McManus-Bascom Professor of Marketing at the University of Wisconsin–Madison. He was a member of the faculty at Indiana State, Ohio State, and Washington University before joining the Wisconsin faculty in 1981. While at Ohio State, he was named Outstanding Marketing Professor by the students and has won the John R. Larson Teaching Award at Wisconsin. He has taught a variety of courses including Marketing Management, Marketing Strategy, Consumer Behavior, Marketing Research, and Marketing Theory, among others.

Professor Peter's research has appeared in the *Journal of Marketing,* the *Journal of Marketing Research,* the *Journal of Consumer Research,* the *Journal of Retailing,* and the *Academy of Management Journal,* among others. His article on construct validity won the prestigious William O'Dell Award from the *Journal of Marketing Research,* and he was a finalist for this award on two other occasions. Recently, he was the recipient of the Churchill Award for Lifetime Achievement in Marketing Research, given by the American Marketing Association and the Gaumnitz Distinguished Faculty Award from the School of Business, University of Wisconsin-Madison. He is an author or editor of over 30 books, including *A Preface to Marketing Management,* ninth edition; *Marketing Management: Knowledge and Skills,* eighth edition; *Consumer Behavior and Marketing Strategy,* seventh edition; *Strategic Management: Concepts and Applications,* third edition; and *Marketing: Creating Value for Customers,* second edition. He is one of the most cited authors in the marketing literature.

Professor Peter has served on the review boards of the *Journal of Marketing, Journal of Marketing Research, Journal of Consumer Research,* and *Journal of Business Research* and was measurement editor for *JMR* and professional publications editor for the American Marketing Association. He has taught in a variety of executive programs and consulted for several corporations as well as the Federal Trade Commission.

James H. Donnelly, Jr.,

is the Thomas C. Simons Professor in the Gatton College of Business and Economics at the University of Kentucky. In 1990 he received the first Chancellor's Award for Outstanding Teaching given at the University. Previously, he had twice received the UK Alumni Association's Great Teacher Award, an award one can only be eligible to receive every 10 years. He has also received two Outstanding Teacher awards from Beta Gamma Sigma, national business honorary. In 1992 he received an Acorn Award recognizing "those who shape the future" from the Kentucky Advocates for Higher Education. In 2001 and 2002 he was selected as "Best University of Kentucky Professor." In 1995 he became one of six charter members elected to the American Bankers Association's Bank Marketing Hall of Fame. He has also received a "Distinguished Doctoral Graduate Award" from the University of Maryland.

During his career he has published in the *Journal of Marketing Research, Journal of Marketing, Journal of Retailing, Administrative Science Quarterly, Academy of Management Journal, Journal of Applied Psychology, Personnel Psychology, Journal of Business Research,* and *Operations Research* among others. He has served on the editorial review board of the *Journal of Marketing.* He is the author of more than a dozen books, which include widely adopted academic texts as well as professional books.

Professor Donnelly is very active in the banking industry where he has served on the board of directors of the Institute of Certified Bankers and the ABA's Marketing Network. He has also served as academic dean of the ABA's School of Bank Marketing and Management.

Preface

From the outset, we have strived to make *Marketing Management: Knowledge and Skills* a complete student resource for marketing management education. Our vision for this, the eighth edition, remains the same. As the resources students and instructors need have changed, the book has changed. This edition is no exception. However, our overriding goal remains the same: to enhance students' *knowledge* of marketing management and to advance their *skills* in using this knowledge to develop and maintain successful marketing strategies.

The Eighth Edition

The basic structure of our text continues to evolve and has been expanded, particularly during this and the two previous editions. Some important changes include the following:

1. Because the text chapters are an integral part of the book, they have been completely updated and revised in this edition. Each chapter has been updated and contains additional references that students can use for writing projects and case presentations.

   New content has been added throughout the text portion of the book. There are new discussions of the major types of marketing, marketing's role in cross-functional strategic planning, a comparison of data collection techniques in marketing research, the North American Industry Classification System (NAICS), product adoption and diffusion, product life cycles, important new product decisions, criteria for determining perceptions of quality, strategic goals of marketing communication, push versus pull strategies in marketing communication, the unique characteristics that distinguish services from goods, and organizing the sales force.

   A popular feature of the text chapters that has received very positive feedback from both students and teachers is the occasional "marketing highlight" that appears throughout. Not the usual "news items" found in other texts, this feature emphasizes important information and handy tools for analyzing marketing cases and problems. We have revised and replaced many in this edition.

2. The search for new cases is an unending one because finding relevant new cases is a challenge. But we have been fortunate to continue to locate truly outstanding new cases. We have added 11 new ones to this edition. Our emphasis continues to be on well-known companies whenever possible, including both domestic and global companies, high-tech companies, consumer and organizational products, small and large businesses, products and services, and manufacturers and channel members.

   We believe that many of the popular cases we retain in the book can truly be considered "classics." But whether set in 2005 or 1995, these "snapshots in time" enable students to analyze the situation within the time period the case was written and/or bring the situation up-to-date with their own research and analysis.

3. A useful resource updated in this edition is an annotated bibliography of the major online databases used in marketing. It is an up-to-date resource for students to use in the analysis of cases, the development of marketing plans, and the analysis of Internet exercises. It is included in Section IV immediately following the Internet exercises. The Internet exercises have also been revised and updated.

4. Some of the cases include in-class exercises that provide the instructor with additional means of enhancing student learning, participation, and team building.

5. A number of the cases include video instructions and discussion questions to enhance student interest, thinking, and analysis.

We have experimented over many years with various teaching philosophies. The structure of this book evolved and continues to evolve from these experiments. Currently, our six-stage learning approach includes (1) learning basic marketing principles, (2) learning approaches and tools for performing marketing analyses, (3) analyzing Internet exercises, (4) analyzing marketing management cases, (5) analyzing strategic marketing cases, and (6) developing marketing plans.

Our six-stage learning approach is the focus of the seven book sections. Each section has as its objective either *knowledge enhancement,* or *skill development,* or both. The framework and structure of our book is presented in the diagram below and will be used throughout the text to integrate various sections.

Stage 1: Learning Basic Marketing Principles

It is clearly necessary for students to learn and understand basic definitions, concepts, and marketing logic before they can apply them in the analysis of marketing problems or development of marketing plans. Section I of the book contains 13 chapters that present the essentials of marketing management. One problem we continually face in more advanced case-oriented courses is that most students have long ago discarded or sold their basic marketing texts. Consequently, when they are faced with case problems they have nothing to rely on but their memories. We believe this seriously detracts from the usefulness of case analysis. Thus, we include this section as a reference source for key marketing concepts. Our objective in this section is to focus on material that is relevant primarily for analyzing marketing problems and cases.

Stage 2: Learning Approaches and Tools for Problem Analysis

The second stage in our approach involves offering students basic tools and approaches for solving marketing problems. Section II, "Analyzing Marketing Problems and Cases," is a widely praised approach to analyzing, writing, and presenting case analyses. Section III, "Financial Analysis for Marketing Decisions," presents some important financial calculations that can be useful in evaluating the financial position of a firm and the financial impact of various marketing strategies. Section IV includes an annotated bibliography of some of the most widely used marketing databases. It will assist students in researching a particular industry or firm and can greatly improve the analysis of cases.

Stage 3: Analyzing Internet Exercises

As a way of introducing students to the challenges of case analysis, some instructors utilize Internet exercises. They find that these exercises are an especially useful way to integrate text material with case work. Accordingly, Section IV provides 12 such exercises. Other instructors, especially those with more advanced marketing students, find their students are fully prepared to tackle case analyses. For these instructors, this section is optional.

Stage 4: Analyzing Marketing Management Cases

It has been our experience that few students have the confidence and experience necessary to analyze complex strategic marketing cases in their first exposure to this type of learning. We believe it is far better for them to apply their skills by analyzing cases for which traditional marketing principles can be applied somewhat directly before they attempt more challenging problems. Accordingly, Section V of the book includes 30 marketing management cases, organized into six groups: market opportunity analysis, product strategy, promotion strategy, distribution strategy, pricing strategy, and social and ethical issues in marketing management. Within each group, cases are sequenced so that later cases contain more information and typically require higher levels of marketing management analysis skills than earlier ones.

Stage 5: Analyzing Strategic Marketing Cases

Once students have developed sufficient skills to provide thoughtful analyses of marketing management cases, they are prepared to tackle strategic marketing cases. These cases go beyond traditional marketing principles and focus on the role of marketing in cross-functional business or organization strategies. Section VI of our book contains 10 such cases. They are sequenced so that the latter cases contain more information and require higher skill levels to analyze them properly.

Stage 6: Developing Marketing Plans

The final stage in our approach involves the development of an original marketing plan. We believe that after a two-course sequence in marketing management, students should be able to do one thing very well and should know that they can do it well: Students should be able to construct a quality marketing plan for any product or service. Section VII provides a framework for developing such a plan. Instructors can consult the *Instructors Manual* that accompanies this book for alternative ways to incorporate this stage into their course.

We have found that this six-stage process is very flexible and can easily be adapted to student needs and instructor objectives. For example, if the course is the first learning experience in marketing, then emphasis could be placed on the first four stages. If students progress well through these stages, then marketing management cases can be assigned on an individual or group basis.

If the course is for students with one or more previous courses in marketing or is the capstone marketing management course, then major attention should shift to stages 2 through 6. In this instance, Section I becomes a resource for review and reference and the course focuses more on skill development.

Finally, the text can be used for a two-course sequence in marketing management. The first course can emphasize stages 1 through 4 and the second can concentrate on stages 5 and 6.

Acknowledgments

Our appreciation and thanks go to all of the case and exercise writers who contributed their work to help others better educate marketing students. Each of the contributors' names and affiliations appear in the Contents and at the point in the book where their contribution appears.

Many thanks to the users who responded to our survey. Your responses were valuable because they were used in planning this edition and in making the hard choices involved in replacing cases, selecting new cases, and deciding on which of the "classic" cases remain. Again, thank you for your help.

We also want to acknowledge those colleagues who provided detailed reviews of previous editions:

Sammy G. Amin
Frostburg State University

Andrew Bergstein
Pennsylvania State University

David Bourff
Boise State University

Brad Brooks
Queens College

Carol Bruneau
University of Montana

Daniel P. Chamberlin
Regent University

V. Glenn Chappell
Meredith College

Henry Chen
University of West Florida

Newell Chiesl
Indiana State University

Pravat K. Choudhury
Howard University

John Considine
LeMoyne College

Denver D'Rozario
Howard University

Mike Dailey
University of Texas, Arlington

Carl Dresden
Coastal Carolina University

Patricia Duncan
Harris-Stowe State College

Adel I. El-Ansary
University of North Florida

Randall Ewing
Ohio Northern University

Renee Foster
Delta State University

John Gauthier
Gateway Technical College

David Griffith
University of Oklahoma

Jack Healey
Golden State University

JoAnne S. Hooper
Western Carolina University

Jarrett Hudnall
Mississippi University for Women

Patricia Humphrey
Texas A&M University

Arun K. Jain
University at Buffalo

Wesley H. Jones
University of Indianapolis

Benoy Joseph
Cleveland State University

Anne B. Lowery
University of Mobile

Steven Lysonski
Marquette University

Gregory Martin
University of West Florida

Wendy Martin
Judson College

Mary K. McManamon
Lake Erie College

Donald J. Messmer
College of William & Mary

Hudson Nwakanma
Florida A&M University

Thomas L. Parkinson
Moravian College

Hatash Sachdev
Eastern Michigan University

Chris Samfilippo
University of Michigan—Dearborn

William F. Schoell
University of Southern Mississippi

Anusorn M. Singhapakdi
Old Henry Dominion University

Jean Shaneyfelt
Edicon Community College

John Shaw
Providence College

Charlotte Smedberg
Florida Metropolitan University System

R. Mark Smith
Campbell University

Joseph R. Stasio
Merrimack College

Albert J. Taylor
Austin Peay State University

Dillard Tinsley
Austin State University

Joanne Trotter
Gwynedd-Mercy College

David J. Vachon
CSUN

Kevin Webb
Drexel University

Paula Welch
Mansfield University

Dale Wilson
Michigan State University

Mark Young
Winona State University

We want to acknowledge three colleagues who provided valuable market feedback for this edition:

Amy Beattie
Champlain College

Richard Campbell
California State University–Bakersfield

Clare Comm
University of Massachusetts–Lowell

Robert Cosenza
University of Mississippi

Larry Crowson
University of Central Florida

Robert Cutler
Cleveland State University

Angela Hausman
University of Texas–Pan American

Dee Anne Larson
Mississippi University for Women

Brian Little
Marshall University

Elaine Notarantonio
Bryant University

Alphonso Ogbuehi
Bryant University

Amit Saini
University of Nebraska–Lincoln

Andy Winston, publisher; Amy Luck and Jill O'Malley, editorial coordinators; Dana Pauley, project manager; Adam Rooke, designer; Sesha Bolisetty, production supervisor; and Susan Lombardi, media project manager made it a pleasure to be McGraw-Hill authors and helped us immensely.

Michael Knetter, Dean of the School of Business at the University of Wisconsin, and Devanthan Sudharshan, Dean of the Gatton College of Business and Economics at the University of Kentucky, support our efforts and we are very grateful to them.

Finally, thanks to Charles Heath of the University of Kentucky and Geoffrey Gordon of Northern Illinois University who have contributed to this edition and its predecessors.

J. Paul Peter

James H. Donnelly, Jr.

Contents

Section I

Essentials of Marketing Management

Section I Essentials of Marketing Management		Section IV Internet Exercises and Sources of Marketing Information
Section II Analyzing Marketing Problems and Cases	Knowledge Enhancement → Skill Development	Section V Marketing Management Cases
Section III Financial Analysis for Marketing Decisions	Section VII Developing Marketing Plans	Section VI Strategic Marketing Cases

Introduction

Chapter 1

Strategic Planning and the Marketing Management Process

The purpose of this introductory chapter is to present the marketing management process and outline what marketing managers must *manage* if they are to be effective. In doing so, it will also present a framework around which the remaining chapters are organized. Our first task is to review the organizational philosophy known as the marketing concept, since it underlies much of the thinking presented in this book. The remainder of this chapter will focus on the process of strategic planning and its relationship to the process of marketing planning.

The Marketing Concept

Simply stated, the marketing concept means that *an organization should seek to make a profit by serving the needs of customer groups*. The concept is very straightforward and has a great deal of commonsense validity. Perhaps this is why it is often misunderstood, forgotten, or overlooked.

The purpose of the marketing concept is to rivet the attention of marketing managers on serving broad classes of customer needs (customer orientation), rather than on the firm's current products (production orientation) or on devising methods to attract customers to current products (selling orientation). Thus, effective marketing starts with the recognition of customer needs and then works backward to devise products and services to satisfy these needs. In this way, marketing managers can satisfy customers more efficiently in the present and anticipate changes in customer needs more accurately in the future. This means that organizations should focus on building long-term customer relationships in which the initial sale is viewed as a beginning step in the process, not as an end goal. As a result, the customer will be more satisfied and the firm will be more profitable.

The principal task of the marketing function operating under the marketing concept is not to manipulate customers to do what suits the interests of the firm, but rather to find effective and efficient means of making the business do what suits the interests of customers. This is not to say that all firms practice marketing in this way. Clearly, many firms still emphasize only production and sales. However, effective marketing, as defined in this text, requires that consumer needs come first in organizational decision making.

One qualification to this statement deals with the question of a conflict between consumer wants and societal needs and wants. For example, if society deems clean air and water as necessary for survival, this need may well take precedence over a consumer's want for goods and services that pollute the environment.

What Is Marketing?

Everyone reading this book has been a customer for most of his or her life. Last evening you stopped into a local supermarket to graze at the salad bar, pick up some bottled water and a bag of Fritos corn chips. While you were there, you snapped a $1.00 coupon for a new flavor salad dressing out of a dispenser and tasted some new breakfast potatoes being cooked in the back of the store. As you sat down at home to eat your salad, you answered the phone and someone suggested that you need to have your carpets cleaned. Later on in the evening you saw TV commercials for tires, soft drinks, athletic shoes, and the dangers of smoking and drinking during pregnancy. Today when you enrolled in a marketing course, you found that the instructor has decided that you must purchase this book. A friend has already purchased the book on the Internet. All of these activities involve marketing. And each of us knows something about marketing because it has been a part of our life since we had our first dollar to spend.

Since we are all involved in marketing, it may seem strange that one of the persistent problems in the field has been its definition.[1] The American Marketing Association defines marketing as "an organizational function and a set of processes for creating, communicating, and delivering value to customers and for managing customer relationships in ways that benefit the organization and its stakeholders."[2] This definition takes into account all parties involved in the marketing effort: members of the producing organization, resellers of goods and services, and customers or clients. While the broadness of the definition allows the inclusion of nonbusiness exchange processes, the primary emphasis in this text is on marketing in the business environment. However, this emphasis is not meant to imply that marketing concepts, principles, and techniques cannot be fruitfully employed in other areas of exchange as is clearly illustrated in Figure 1.1.

FIGURE 1.1
Major Types of Marketing

Type	Description	Example
Product	Marketing designed to create exchange for tangible products.	Strategies to sell Gateway computers.
Service	Marketing designed to create exchanges for intangible products.	Strategies by Allstate to sell insurance.
Person	Marketing designed to create favorable actions toward persons.	Strategies to elect a political candidate.
Place	Marketing designed to attract people to places.	Strategies to get people to vacation in national or state parks.
Cause	Marketing designed to create support for ideas, causes, or issues or to get people to change undesirable behaviors.	Strategies to get pregnant women not to drink alcohol.
Organization	Marketing designed to attract donors, members, participants, or volunteers.	Strategies designed to attract blood donors.

1. Companywide managerial awareness and appreciation of the consumer's role as it is related to the firm's existence, growth, and stability. As renowned management scholar Peter Drucker has noted, business enterprise is an organ of society; thus, its basic purpose lies outside the business itself. And the valid definition of business purpose is the creation of customers.

2. Active, companywide managerial awareness of, and concern with, interdepartmental implications of decisions and actions of an individual department. That is, the firm is viewed as a network of forces focused on meeting defined customer needs and comprising a system within which actions taken in one department or area frequently result in significant repercussions in other areas of the firm. Also, it is recognized that such actions may affect the company's equilibrium with its external environment, for example, its customers, its competitors.

3. Active, companywide managerial concern with innovation of products and services designed to solve selected consumer problems.

4. General managerial concern with the effect of new products and service introduction on the firm's profit position, both present and future, and recognition of the potential rewards that may accrue from new product planning, including profits and profit stability.

5. General managerial appreciation of the role of marketing intelligence and other fact-finding and reporting units, within and adjacent to the firm, in translating the general statements presented above into detailed statements of profitable market potentials, targets, and action. Implicit in this statement is not only an expansion of the traditional function and scope of formal marketing research, but also assimilation of other sources of marketing data, such as the firm's distribution system and its advertising agency counsel, into a potential marketing intelligence service.

6. Companywide managerial effort, based on participation and interaction of company officers, in establishing corporate and departmental objectives that are understood by and acceptable to these officers and that are consistent with enhancement of the firm's profit position.

Source: For an up-to-date discussion of the marketing concept, see Frederick E. Webster, Jr., "Defining the New Marketing Concept," *Marketing Management 2*, no. 4 (1994), pp. 22–31. For a classic discussion, see Robert L. King, "The Marketing Concept: Fact or Intelligent Platitude," *The Marketing Concept in Action*, Proceedings of the 47th National Conference (Chicago: American Marketing Association, 1964), p. 657.

What Is Strategic Planning?

Before a production manager, marketing manager, and personnel manager can develop plans for their individual departments, some larger plan or blueprint for the *entire* organization should exist. Otherwise, on what would the individual departmental plans be based?

In other words, there is a larger context for planning activities. Let us assume that we are dealing with a large business organization that has several business divisions and several product lines within each division (e.g., General Electric, Philip Morris). Before any marketing planning can be implemented by individual divisions or departments, a plan has to be developed for the entire organization.[3] This means that senior managers must look toward the future and evaluate their ability to shape their organization's destiny in the years and decades to come. The output of this process is objectives and strategies designed to give the organization a chance to compete effectively in the future. The objectives and strategies established at the top level provide the context for planning in each of the divisions and departments by divisional and departmental managers.

Strategic Planning and Marketing Management

Some of the most successful business organizations are here today because many years ago they offered the right product at the right time to a rapidly growing market. The same can also be said for nonprofit and governmental organizations. Many of the critical decisions of the past were made without the benefit of strategic thinking or planning. Whether these decisions were based on wisdom or were just luck is not important; they worked for these organizations. However, a worse fate befell countless other organizations. Over three-quarters of the 100 largest U.S. corporations of 70 years ago have fallen from the list. These corporations at one time dominated their markets, controlled vast resources, and had the best-trained workers. In the end, they all made the same critical mistake. Their managements failed to recognize that business strategies need to reflect changing environments and emphasis must be placed on developing business systems that allow for continuous improvement. Instead, they attempted to carry on business as usual.

Present-day managers are increasingly recognizing that wisdom and innovation alone are no longer sufficient to guide the destinies of organizations, both large and small. These same managers also realize that the true mission of the organization is to provide value for three key constituencies: customers, employees, and investors. Without this type of outlook, no one, including shareholders, will profit in the long run.

Strategic planning includes all the activities that lead to the development of a clear organizational mission, organizational objectives, and appropriate strategies to achieve the objectives for the entire organization. The form of the process itself has come under criticism in some quarters for being too structured; however, strategic planning, if performed successfully, plays a key role in achieving an equilibrium between the short and the long term by balancing acceptable financial performance with preparation for inevitable changes in markets, technology, and competition, as well as in economic and political arenas. Managing principally for current cash flows, market share gains, and earnings trends can mortgage the firm's future. An intense focus on the near term can produce an aversion to risk that dooms a business to stagnation. Conversely, an overemphasis on the long run is just as inappropriate. Companies that overextend themselves betting on the future may penalize short-term profitability and other operating results to such an extent that the company is vulnerable to takeover and other threatening actions.

The strategic planning process is depicted in Figure 1.2. In the strategic planning process the organization gathers information about the changing elements of its environment. Managers from all functional areas in the organization assist in this information-gathering process. This information is useful in aiding the organization to adapt better to these changes through the process of strategic planning. The strategic plan (s)[4] and supporting plan are then implemented in the environment. The end results of this implementation are fed back as new information so that continuous adaptation and improvement can take place.

The Strategic Planning Process

The output of the strategic planning process is the development of a strategic plan. Figure 1.2 indicates four components of a strategic plan: mission, objectives, strategies, and portfolio plan. Let us carefully examine each one.

Organizational Mission

The organization's environment provides the resources that sustain the organization, whether it is a business, a college or university, or a government agency. In exchange for these resources, the organization must supply the environment with quality goods and services at an acceptable price. In other words, every organization exists to accomplish something in the larger environment and that purpose, vision, or mission usually is clear at the organization's inception. As time passes, however, the organization expands, and the environment and

FIGURE 1.2 **The Strategic Planning Process**

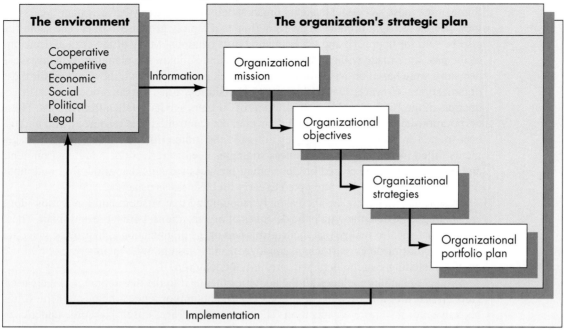

managerial personnel change. As a result, one or more things are likely to occur. First, the organization's original purpose may become irrelevant as the organization expands into new products, new markets, and even new industries. For example, Levi Strauss began as a manufacturer of work clothes. Second, the original mission may remain relevant, but managers begin to lose interest in it. Finally, changes in the environment may make the original mission inappropriate, as occurred with the March of Dimes when a cure was found for polio. The result of any or all three of these conditions is a "drifting" organization, without a clear mission, vision, or purpose to guide critical decisions. When this occurs, management must search for a purpose or emphatically restate and reinforce the original purpose.

The mission statement, or purpose, of an organization is the description of its reason for existence. It is the long-run vision of what the organization strives to be, the unique aim that differentiates the organization from similar ones and the means by which this differentiation will take place. In essence, the mission statement defines the direction in which the organization is heading and how it will succeed in reaching its desired goal. While some argue that vision and mission statements differ in their purpose, the perspective we will take is that both reflect the organization's attempt to guide behavior, create a culture, and inspire commitment.[5] However, it is more important that the mission statement comes from the heart and is practical, easy to identify with, and easy to remember so that it will provide direction and significance to all members of the organization regardless of their organizational level.

The basic questions that must be answered when an organization decides to examine and restate its mission are, What is our business? Who is the customer? What do customers value? and What will our business be?[6] The answers are, in a sense, the assumptions on which the organization is being run and from which future decisions will evolve. While such questions may seem simplistic, they are such difficult and critical ones that the major responsibility for answering them must lie with top management. In fact, the mission statement remains the most widely used management tool in business today. In developing a statement of mission, management must take into account three key elements: the organization's history, its distinctive competencies, and its environment.[7]

Organization	Mission
Community bank	To help citizens successfully achieve and celebrate important life events with education, information, products, and services.
Skin care products	We will provide luxury skin-care products with therapeutic qualities that make them worth their premium price.
Hotel chain	Grow a worldwide lodging business using total-quality-management (TQM) principles to continuously improve preference and profitability. Our commitment is that *every guest leaves satisfied.*
Mid-size bank	We will become the best bank in the state for medium-size businesses by 2010.

1. *The organization's history.* Every organization—large or small, profit or nonprofit—has a history of objectives, accomplishments, mistakes, and policies. In formulating a mission, the critical characteristics and events of the past must be considered.

2. *The organization's distinctive competencies.* While there are many things an organization may be able to do, it should seek to do what it can do best. Distinctive competencies are things that an organization does well—so well in fact that they give it an advantage over similar organizations. For Honeywell, it's their ability to design, manufacture, and distribute a superior line of thermostats.[8] Similarly, Procter & Gamble's distinctive competency is its knowledge of the market for low-priced, repetitively purchased consumer products. No matter how appealing an opportunity may be, to gain advantage over competitors, the organization must formulate strategy based on distinctive competencies.

3. *The organization's environment.* The organization's environment dictates the opportunities, constraints, and threats that must be identified before a mission statement is developed. For example, managers in any industry that is affected by Internet technology breakthroughs should continually be asking, How will the changes in technology affect my customers' behavior and the means by which we need to conduct our business?

However, it is extremely difficult to write a useful and effective mission statement. It is not uncommon for an organization to spend one or two years developing a useful mission statement. When completed, an effective mission statement will be *focused on markets rather than products, achievable, motivating, and specific.*[9]

Focused on Markets Rather than Products   The customers or clients of an organization are critical in determining its mission. Traditionally, many organizations defined their business in terms of what they made ("our business is glass"), and in many cases they named the organization for the product or service (e.g., American Tobacco, Hormel Meats, National Cash Register, Harbor View Savings and Loan Association). Many of these organizations have found that, when products and technologies become obsolete, their mission is no longer relevant and the name of the organization may no longer describe what it does. Thus, a more enduring way of defining the mission is needed. In recent years, therefore, a key feature of mission statements has been an *external* rather than *internal* focus. In other words, the mission statement should focus on the broad class of needs that the organization is seeking to satisfy (external focus), not on the physical product or service that the organization is offering at present (internal focus). These market-driven firms stand out in their ability to continuously anticipate market opportunities and respond before their competitors. This has been clearly stated by Peter Drucker:

A business is not defined by the company's name, statutes, or articles of incorporation. It is defined by the want the customer satisfies when he buys a product or service. To satisfy the customer is the mission and purpose of every business. The question "What is our business?" can, therefore, be answered only by looking at the business from the outside, from the point of view of customer and market.[10]

While Drucker was referring to business organizations, the same necessity exists for both nonprofit and governmental organizations. That necessity is to state the mission in terms of serving a particular group of clients or customers and meeting a particular class of need.

Achievable   While the mission statement should stretch the organization toward more effective performance, it should, at the same time, be realistic and achievable. In other words, it should open a vision of new opportunities but should not lead the organization into unrealistic ventures far beyond its competencies.

Motivational   One of the side (but very important) benefits of a well-defined mission is the guidance it provides employees and managers working in geographically dispersed units and on independent tasks. It provides a shared sense of purpose outside the various activities taking place within the organization. Therefore, such end results as sales, patients cared for, students graduated, and reduction in violent crimes can then be viewed as the result of careful pursuit and accomplishment of the mission and not as the mission itself.

Specific   As we mentioned earlier, public relations should not be the primary purpose of a statement of mission. It must be specific to provide direction and guidelines to management when they are choosing between alternative courses of action. In other words, "to produce the highest-quality products at the lowest possible cost" sounds very good, but it does not provide direction for management.

Organizational Objectives

Organizational objectives are the end points of an organization's mission and are what it seeks through the ongoing, long-run operations of the organization. The organizational mission is distilled into a finer set of specific and achievable organizational objectives. These objectives must be *specific, measurable, action commitments* by which the mission of the organization is to be achieved.

As with the statement of mission, organizational objectives are more than good intentions. In fact, if formulated properly, they can accomplish the following:

1. They can be converted into specific action.
2. They will provide direction. That is, they can serve as a starting point for more specific and detailed objectives at lower levels in the organization. Each manager will then know how his or her objectives relate to those at higher levels.
3. They can establish long-run priorities for the organization.
4. They can facilitate management control because they serve as standards against which overall organizational performance can be evaluated.

Organizational objectives are necessary in all areas that may influence the performance and long-run survival of the organization. As shown in Figure 1.3 objectives can be established in and across many areas of the organization. The list provided in Figure 1.3 is by no means exhaustive. For example, some organizations are specifying the primary objective as the attainment of a specific level of quality, either in the marketing of a product or the providing of a service. These organizations believe that objectives should reflect an organization's commitment to the customer rather than its own finances. Obviously, during the strategic planning process conflicts are likely to occur between various functional departments in the organization. The important point is that management must translate the organizational mission into specific objectives that support the realization of the mission. The objectives may flow directly from the mission or be considered subordinate necessities

Functions	What They May Want to Deliver	What Marketers May Want Them to Deliver
Research and development	Basic research projects	Products that deliver customer value
	Product features	Customer benefits
	Few projects	Many new products
Production/operations	Long production runs	Short production runs
	Standardized products	Customized products
	No model changes	Frequent model changes
	Long lead times	Short lead times
	Standard orders	Customer orders
	No new products	Many new products
Finance	Rigid budgets	Flexible budgets
	Budgets based on return on investment	Budgets based on need to increase sales
	Low sales commissions	High sales commissions
Accounting	Standardized billing	Custom billing
	Strict payment terms	Flexible payment terms
	Strict credit standards	Flexible credit standards
Human resources	Trainable employees	Skilled employees
	Low salaries	High salaries

for carrying out the mission. As discussed earlier, the objectives are specific, measurable, action commitments on the part of the organization.

Organizational Strategies

Hopefully, when an organization has formulated its mission and developed its objectives, it knows where it wants to go. The next managerial task is to develop a "grand design" to get there. This grand design constitutes the organizational strategies. Strategy involves the choice of major directions the organization will take in pursuing its objectives. Toward this end, it is critical that strategies are consistent with goals and objectives and that top management ensures strategies are implemented effectively. As many as 60 percent of strategic

FIGURE 1.3
Sample Organizational Objectives (manufacturing firm)

Area of Performance	Possible Objective
1. Market standing	To make our brands number one in their field in terms of market share.
2. Innovations	To be a leader in introducing new products by spending no less than 7 percent of sales for research and development.
3. Productivity	To manufacture all products efficiently as measured by the productivity of the workforce.
4. Physical and financial resources	To protect and maintain all resources—equipment, buildings, inventory, and funds.
5. Profitability	To achieve an annual rate of return on investment of at least 15 percent.
6. Manager performance and responsibility	To identify critical areas of management depth and succession.
7. Worker performance and attitude	To maintain levels of employee satisfaction consistent with our own and similar industries.
8. Social responsibility	To respond appropriately whenever possible to societal expectations and environmental needs.

FIGURE 1.4
**Organizational
Growth Strategies**

Products Markets	Present Products	New Products
Present customers	Market penetration	Product development
New customers	Market development	Diversification

plans have failed because the strategies in them were not well defined and, thus, were unable to be implemented effectively.[11] What follows is a discussion of various strategies organizations can pursue. We discuss three approaches: (1) strategies based on products and markets, (2) strategies based on competitive advantage, and (3) strategies based on value.

Organizational Strategies Based on Products and Markets   One means to developing organizational strategies is to focus on the directions the organization can take in order to grow. Figure 1.4, which presents the available strategic choices, is a product-market matrix.[12] It indicates that an organization can grow by better managing what it is presently doing or by finding new things to do. In choosing one or both of these paths, it must also decide whether to concentrate on present customers or to seek new ones. Thus, according to Figure 1.4, there are only four paths an organization can take in order to grow.

Market Penetration Strategies   These strategies focus primarily on increasing the sale of present products to present customers. For example:

- Encouraging present customers to use more of the product: "Orange Juice Isn't Just for Breakfast Anymore."
- Encouraging present customers to purchase more of the product: multiple packages of Pringles, instant winner sweepstakes at a fast-food restaurant.
- A university directs a fund-raising program at those graduates who already give the most money.

Tactics used to implement a market penetration strategy might include price reductions, advertising that stresses the many benefits of the product (e.g., "Milk Is a Natural"), packaging the product in different-sized packages, or making it available at more locations. Other functional areas of the business could also be involved in implementing the strategy in addition to marketing. A production plan might be developed to produce the product more efficiently. This plan might include increased production runs, the substitution of pre-assembled components for individual product parts, or the automation of a process that previously was performed manually.

Market Development Strategies   Pursuing growth through market development, an organization would seek to find new customers for its present products. For example:

- Arm & Hammer continues to seek new uses for its baking soda.
- McDonald's continually seeks expansion into overseas markets.
- As the consumption of salt declined, a book appeared: "101 Things You Can Do with Salt Besides Eat It."

Market development strategies involve much, much more than simply getting the product to a new market. Before deciding on marketing techniques such as advertising and packaging, companies often find they must establish a clear position in the market, sometimes spending large sums of money simply to educate consumers as to why they should consider buying the product.

Product Development Strategies   Selecting one of the remaining two strategies means the organization will seek new things to do. With this particular strategy, the new products developed would be directed primarily to present customers. For example:

- Offering a different version of an existing product: mini-Oreos, Ritz with cheese.
- Offering a new-improved version of their product: Gillette's latest improvement in shaving technology.
- Offering a new way to use an existing product: Vaseline's Lip Therapy.

Diversification   This strategy can lead the organization into entirely new and even unrelated businesses. It involves seeking new products (often through acquisitions) for customers not currently being served. For example:

- Philip Morris, originally a manufacturer of cigarettes, is widely diversified in financial services, Post cereals, Sealtest dairy, and Kraft cheese, among others.
- Brown Foreman Distillers acquired Hartmann Luggage, and Sara Lee acquired Coach Leather Products.
- Some universities are establishing corporations to find commercial uses for faculty research.

Organizational Strategies Based on Competitive Advantage   Michael Porter developed a model for formulating organizational strategy that is applicable across a wide variety of industries.[13] The focus of the model is on devising means to gain competitive advantage. Competitive advantage is an ability to outperform competitors in providing something that the market values. Porter suggests that firms should first analyze their industry and then develop either a *cost leadership strategy* or a *strategy based on differentiation*. These general strategies can be used on marketwide bases or in a niche (segment) within the total market.

Using a cost leadership strategy, a firm would focus on being the low-cost company in their industry. They would stress efficiency and offer a standard, no-frills product. They could achieve this through efficiencies in production, product design, manufacturing, distribution, technology, or some other means. The important point is that to succeed, the organization must continually strive to be the cost leader in the industry or market segment it competes in. It must also offer products or services that are acceptable to customers when compared to the competition. Wal-Mart, Southwest Airlines, and Timex Group Ltd. are companies that have succeeded in using a cost leadership strategy.

Using a strategy based on differentiation, a firm seeks to be unique in its industry or market segment along particular dimensions that the customers value. These dimensions might pertain to design, quality, service, variety of offerings, brand name, or some other factor. The important point is that because of uniqueness of the product or service along one or more of these dimensions, the firm can charge a premium price. L. L. Bean, Rolex, Coca Cola, and Microsoft are companies that have succeeded using a differentiation strategy.

Organizational Strategies Based on Value   As competition increases, the concept of "customer value" has become critical for marketers as well as customers. It can be thought of as an extension of the marketing concept philosophy that focuses on developing and delivering superior value to customers as a way to achieve organizational objectives. Thus, it focuses not only on customer needs, but also on the question, How can we create value for them and still achieve our objectives?

It has become pretty clear that in today's competitive environment it is unlikely that a firm will succeed by trying to be all things to all people.[14] Thus, to succeed firms must seek to build long-term relationships with their customers by offering a unique value that only they can offer. It seems that many firms have succeeded by choosing to deliver superior customer value using one of three value strategies—best price, best product, or best service.

Dell Computers, Price/Costco, and Southwest Airlines are among the success stories of offering customers the best price. Rubbermaid, Nike, Starbucks, and Microsoft believe they offer the best products on the market. Airborne Express, Roadway, Cott Corporation, and Lands' End provide superior customer value by providing outstanding service.

Choosing an Appropriate Strategy

On what basis does an organization choose one (or all) of its strategies? Of extreme importance are the directions set by the mission statement. Management should select those strategies consistent with its mission and capitalize on the organization's distinctive competencies that will lead to a sustainable competitive advantage. A sustainable competitive advantage can be based on either the assets or skills of the organization. Technical superiority, low-cost production, customer service/product support, location, financial resources, continuing product innovation, and overall marketing skills are all examples of distinctive competencies that can lead to a sustainable competitive advantage. For example, Honda is known for providing quality automobiles at a reasonable price. Each succeeding generation of Honda automobiles has shown marked quality improvements over previous generations. Likewise, VF Corporation, manufacturer of Wrangler and Lee jeans, has formed "quick response" partnerships with both discounters and department stores to ensure the efficiency of product flow. The key to sustaining a competitive advantage is to continually focus and build on the assets and skills that will lead to long-term performance gains.

Organizational Portfolio Plan

The final phase of the strategic planning process is the formulation of the organizational portfolio plan. In reality, most organizations at a particular time are a portfolio of businesses, that is, product lines, divisions, schools. To illustrate, an appliance manufacturer may have several product lines (e.g., televisions, washers and dryers, refrigerators, stereos) as well as two divisions, consumer appliances and industrial appliances. A college or university will have numerous schools (e.g., education, business, law, architecture) and several programs within each school. Some widely diversified organizations such as Philip Morris are in numerous unrelated businesses, such as cigarettes, food products, land development, and industrial paper products.

Managing such groups of businesses is made a little easier if resources are plentiful, cash is plentiful, and each is experiencing growth and profits. Unfortunately, providing larger and larger budgets each year to all businesses is seldom feasible. Many are not experiencing growth, and profits and resources (financial and nonfinancial) are becoming more and more scarce. In such a situation, choices must be made, and some method is necessary to help management make the choices. Management must decide which businesses to build, maintain, or eliminate, or which new businesses to add. Indeed, much of the recent activity in corporate restructuring has centered on decisions relating to which groups of businesses management should focus on.

Obviously, the first step in this approach is to identify the various divisions, product lines, and so on that can be considered a "business." When identified, these are referred to as *strategic business units* (SBUs) and have the following characteristics:

- They have a distinct mission.
- They have their own competitors.
- They are a single business or collection of related businesses.
- They can be planned independently of the other businesses of the total organization.

Thus, depending on the type of organization, an SBU could be a single product, product line, or division; a college of business administration; or a state mental health agency. Once the organization has identified and classified all of its SBUs, some method must be established to determine how resources should be allocated among the various SBUs. These methods are known as *portfolio models*. For those readers interested, the appendix of this chapter presents two of the most popular portfolio models, the Boston Consulting Group model and the General Electric model.

The Complete Strategic Plan

Figure 1.2 indicates that at this point the strategic planning process is complete, and the organization has a time-phased blueprint that outlines its mission, objectives, and strategies. Completion of the strategic plan facilitates the development of marketing plans for each product, product line, or division of the organization. The marketing plan serves as a subset of the strategic plan in that it allows for detailed planning at a target market level. This important relationship between strategic planning and marketing planning is the subject of the final section of this chapter.

The Marketing Management Process

Marketing management can be defined as "the process of planning and executing the conception, pricing, promotion, and distribution of goods, services, and ideas to create exchanges with target groups that satisfy customer and organizational objectives."[15] It should be noted that this definition is entirely consistent with the marketing concept, since it emphasizes the serving of target market needs as the key to achieving organizational objectives. The remainder of this section will be devoted to a discussion of the marketing management process according to the model in Figure 1.5.

Situation Analysis

With a clear understanding of organizational objectives and mission, the marketing manager must then analyze and monitor the position of the firm and, specifically, the marketing

FIGURE 1.5
Strategic Planning and Marketing Planning

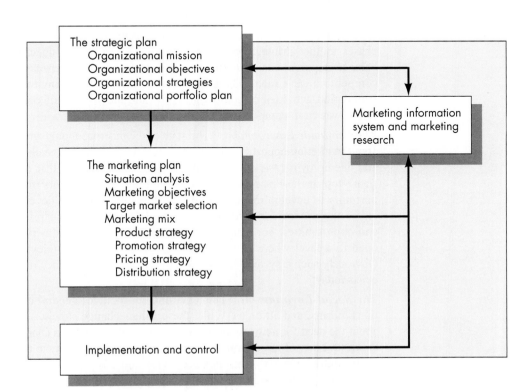

department, in terms of its past, present, and future situation. Of course, the future situation is of primary concern. However, analyses of past trends and the current situation are most useful for predicting the future situation.

The situation analysis can be divided into six major areas of concern: (1) the cooperative environment; (2) the competitive environment; (3) the economic environment; (4) the social environment; (5) the political environment; and (6) the legal environment. In analyzing each of these environments, the marketing executive must search both for opportunities and for constraints or threats to achieving objectives. Opportunities for profitable marketing often arise from changes in these environments that bring about new sets of needs to be satisfied. Constraints on marketing activities, such as limited supplies of scarce resources, also arise from these environments.

The Cooperative Environment   The cooperative environment includes all firms and individuals who have a vested interest in the firm's accomplishing its objectives. Parties of primary interest to the marketing executive in this environment are (1) suppliers, (2) resellers, (3) other departments in the firm, and (4) subdepartments and employees of the marketing department. Opportunities in this environment are primarily related to methods of increasing efficiency. For example, a company might decide to switch from a competitive bid process of obtaining materials to a single source that is located near the company's plant. Likewise, members of the marketing, engineering, and manufacturing functions may use a teamwork approach to developing new products versus a sequential approach. Constraints consist of such things as unresolved conflicts and shortages of materials. For example, a company manager may believe that a distributor is doing an insufficient job of promoting and selling the product, or a marketing manager may feel that manufacturing is not taking the steps needed to produce a quality product.

The Competitive Environment   The competitive environment includes primarily other firms in the industry that rival the organization for both resources and sales. Opportunities in this environment include such things as (1) acquiring competing firms; (2) offering demonstrably better value to consumers and attracting them away from competitors; and (3) in some cases, driving competitors out of the industry. For example, one airline purchases another airline, a bank offers depositors a free checking account with no minimum balance requirements, or a grocery chain engages in an everyday low-price strategy that competitors can't meet. The primary constraints in these environments are the demand stimulation activities of competing firms and the number of consumers who cannot be lured away from competition.

The Economic Environment   The state of the macroeconomy and changes in it also bring about marketing opportunities and constraints. For example, such factors as high inflation and unemployment levels can limit the size of the market that can afford to purchase a firm's top-of-the-line product. At the same time, these factors may offer a profitable opportunity to develop rental services for such products or to develop less-expensive models of the product. In addition, changes in technology can provide significant threats and opportunities. For example, in the communications industry, technology has developed to a level where it is now possible to provide cable television using phone lines. Obviously such a system poses a severe threat to the existence of the cable industry as it exists today.

The Social Environment   This environment includes general cultural and social traditions, norms, and attitudes. While these values change slowly, such changes often bring about the need for new products and services. For example, a change in values concerning the desirability of large families brought about an opportunity to market better methods of birth control. On the other hand, cultural and social values also place constraints on marketing activities. As a rule, business practices that are contrary to social values become

Speed of the Process. There is the problem of either being so slow that the process seems to go on forever or so fast that there is an extreme burst of activity to rush out a plan.

Amount of Data Collected. Sufficient data are needed to properly estimate customer needs and competitive trends. However, the law of diminishing returns quickly sets in on the data-collection process.

Responsibility for Developing the Plan. If planning is delegated to professional planners, valuable line management input may be ignored. If the process is left to line managers, planning may be relegated to secondary status.

Structure. Many executives believe the most important part of planning is not the plan itself but the structure of thought about the strategic issues facing the business. However, the structure should not take precedence over the content so that planning becomes merely filling out forms or crunching numbers.

Length of the Plan. The length of a marketing plan must be balanced between being so long that it is ignored by both staff and line managers and so brief that it ignores key details.

Frequency of Planning. Too frequent reevaluation of strategies can lead to erratic firm behavior. However, when plans are not revised frequently enough, the business may not adapt quickly enough to environmental changes and thus suffer a deterioration in its competitive position.

Number of Alternative Strategies Considered. Discussing too few alternatives raises the likelihood of failure, whereas discussing too many increases the time and cost of the planning effort.

Cross-Functional Acceptance. A common mistake is to view the plan as the proprietary possession of marketing. Successful implementation requires a broad consensus, including other functional areas.

Using the Plan as a Sales Document. A major but often overlooked purpose of a plan and its presentation is to generate funds from either internal or external sources. Therefore, the better the plan, the better the chance of gaining desired funding.

Source: Donald R. Lehmann and Russell S. Winer, *Analysis for Marketing Planning*, 5th ed., chap. 1. © Richard D. Irwin, Inc., 2002.

political issues, which are often resolved by legal constraints. For example, public demand for a cleaner environment has caused the government to require that automobile manufacturers' products meet certain average gas mileage and emission standards.

The Political Environment   The political environment includes the attitudes and reactions of the general public, social and business critics, and other organizations, such as the Better Business Bureau. Dissatisfaction with such business and marketing practices as unsafe products, products that waste resources, and unethical sales procedures can have adverse effects on corporation image and customer loyalty. However, adapting business and marketing practices to these attitudes can be an opportunity. For example, these attitudes have brought about markets for such products as unbreakable children's toys, high-efficiency air conditioners, and more economical automobiles.

The Legal Environment   This environment includes a host of federal, state, and local legislation directed at protecting both business competition and consumer rights. In past years, legislation reflected social and political attitudes and has been primarily directed at constraining business practices. Such legislation usually acts as a constraint on business behavior, but again can be viewed as providing opportunities for marketing safer and more efficient products. In recent years, there has been less emphasis on creating new laws for constraining

Poorly Stated Objectives	Well-Stated Objectives
Our objective is to be a leader in the industry in terms of new product development.	Our objective is to spend 12 percent of sales revenue between 2001 and 2002 on research and development in an effort to introduce at least five new products in 2002.
Our objective is to maximize profits.	Our objective is to achieve a 10 percent return on investment during 2001, with a payback on new investments of no longer than four years.
Our objective is to better serve customers.	Our objective is to obtain customer satisfaction ratings of at least 90 percent on the 2001 annual customer satisfaction survey, and to retain at least 85 percent of our 2001 customers as repeat purchasers in 2002.
Our objective is to be the best that we can be.	Our objective is to increase market share from 30 percent to 40 percent in 2001 by increasing promotional expenditures by 14 percent.

Source: Charles W. Lamb, Jr., Joseph F. Hair, Jr., and Carl McDaniel, *Marketing*, 6th ed. (Cincinnati, OH: South-Western Publishing Co., 2002), p. 35.

business practices. As an example, deregulation has become more common, as evidenced by recent events in the airlines, financial services, and telecommunications industries.

Marketing Planning

In the previous sections it was emphasized that (1) marketing activities must be aligned with organizational objectives and (2) marketing opportunities are often found by systematically analyzing situational environments. Once an opportunity is recognized, the marketing executive must then plan an appropriate strategy for taking advantage of the opportunity. This process can be viewed in terms of three interrelated tasks: (1) establishing marketing objectives, (2) selecting the target market, and (3) developing the marketing mix.

Establishing Objectives   Marketing objectives usually are derived from organizational objectives; in some cases where the firm is totally marketing oriented, the two are identical. In either case, objectives must be specified and performance in achieving them should be measurable. Marketing objectives are usually stated as standards of performance (e.g., a certain percentage of market share or sales volume) or as tasks to be achieved by given dates. While such objectives are useful, the marketing concept emphasizes that profits rather than sales should be the overriding objective of the firm and marketing department. In any case, these objectives provide the framework for the marketing plan.

Selecting the Target Market   The success of any marketing plan hinges on how well it can identify customer needs and organize its resources to satisfy them profitably. Thus, a crucial element of the marketing plan is selecting the groups or segments of potential customers the firm is going to serve with each of its products. Four important questions must be answered:

1. What do customers want or need?
2. What must be done to satisfy these wants or needs?
3. What is the size of the market?
4. What is its growth profile?

1. Do they know what the strategy is?
2. Do they understand how their actions can make the strategy work?
3. Do they have the capabilities to act on it?
4. Do they have the incentive to act on it?

Source: Gordon A. Wyner, "The Effective Organization," *Marketing Management*, November/December
2003, pp. 6–7.

Present target markets and potential target markets are then ranked according to (*a*) prof-itability; (*b*) present and future sales volume; and (*c*) the match between what it takes to appeal successfully to the segment and the organization's capabilities. Those that appear to offer the greatest potential are selected. One cautionary note on this process involves the importance of not neglecting present customers when developing market share and sales strategies. In a recent study, it was found that for every 10 companies that develop strategies aimed at increasing the number of first-time customers, only four made any serious effort to develop strategies geared toward retaining present customers and increasing their purchases.[16] Chapters 3, 4, and 5 are devoted to discussing consumer behavior, industrial buyers, and market segmentation.

Developing the Marketing Mix   The marketing mix is the set of controllable variables that must be managed to satisfy the target market and achieve organizational objectives. These controllable variables are usually classified according to four major decision areas: product, price, promotion, and place (or channels of distribution). The importance of these decision areas cannot be overstated, and in fact, the major portion of this text is devoted to analyzing them. Chapters 6 and 7 are devoted to product and new product strategies; Chapters 8 and 9 to promotion strategies in terms of both nonpersonal and personal selling; Chapter 10 to distribution strategies; and Chapter 11 to pricing strategies. In addition, marketing mix variables are the focus of analysis in two chapters on marketing in special fields, that is, the marketing of services (Chapter 12) and international marketing (Chapter 13). Thus, it should be clear to the reader that the marketing mix is the core of the marketing management process.

The output of the foregoing process is the marketing plan. It is a formal statement of decisions that have been made on marketing activities; it is a blueprint of the objectives, strategies, and tasks to be performed.

Implementation and Control of the Marketing Plan

Implementing the marketing plan involves putting the plan into action and performing marketing tasks according to the predefined schedule. Even the most carefully developed plans often cannot be executed with perfect timing. Thus, the marketing executive must closely monitor and coordinate implementation of the plan. In some cases, adjustments may have to be made in the basic plan because of changes in any of the situational environments. For example, competitors may introduce a new product. In this event, it may be desirable to speed up or delay implementation of the plan. In almost all cases, some minor adjustments or fine tuning will be necessary in implementation.

Controlling the marketing plan involves three basic steps. First, the results of the implemented marketing plan are measured. Second, these results are compared with objectives. Third, decisions are made on whether the plan is achieving objectives. If serious deviations exist between actual and planned results, adjustments may have to be made to redirect the plan toward achieving objectives.

Marketing Information Systems and Marketing Research

Throughout the marketing management process, current, reliable, and valid information is needed to make effective marketing decisions. Providing this information is the task of the marketing information system and marketing research. These topics are discussed in detail in Chapter 2.

The Strategic Plan, The Marketing Plan, and Other Functional Area Plans

Strategic planning is clearly a top-management responsibility. In recent years, however, there has been an increasing shift toward more active participation by marketing managers in strategic analysis and planning. This is because, in reality, nearly all strategic planning questions have marketing implications. In fact, the two major strategic planning questions— What products should we make? and What markets should we serve?—are clearly marketing questions. Thus, marketing executives are involved in the strategic planning process in at least two important ways: (1) They influence the process by providing important inputs in the form of information and suggestions relating to customers, products, and middlemen; and (2) they must always be aware of what the process of stategic planning involves as well as the results because everything they do, the marketing objectives and strategies they develop, must be derived from the strategic plan. In fact, the planning done in all functional areas of the organization should be derived from the strategic plan.

Marketing's Role in Cross-Functional Strategic Planning

More and more organizations are rethinking the traditional role of marketing. Rather than dividing work according to function (e.g., production, finance, technology, human resources), they are bringing managers and employees together to participate in *cross-functional teams.* These teams might have responsibility for a particular product, line of products, or group of customers.

Because team members are responsible for all activities involving their products and/or customers, they are responsible for strategic planning. It means that all personnel working in a cross-functional team will participate in creating a strategic plan to serve customers. Rather than making decisions independently, marketing managers work closely with team members from production, finance, human resources, and other areas to devise plans that address all concerns. Thus, if a team member from production says, "That product will be too difficult to produce," or if a team member from finance says, "We'll never make a profit at that price," the team members from marketing must help resolve the problems. This approach requires a high degree of skill at problem solving and gaining cooperation.

Clearly the greatest advantage of strategic planning with a cross-functional team is the ability of team members to consider a situation from a number of viewpoints. The resulting insights can help the team avoid costly mistakes and poor solutions. Japanese manufacturers are noted for using cross-functional teams to figure out ways to make desirable products at given target costs. In contrast, U.S. manufacturers traditionally have developed products by having one group decide what to make, another calculate production costs, and yet another predict whether enough of the product will sell at a high enough price.

Thus, in well-managed organizations, a direct relationship exists between strategic planning and the planning done by managers at all levels. The focus and time perspectives will, of course, differ. Figure 1.6 illustrates the cross-functional perspective of strategic planning. It indicates very clearly that all functional area plans should be derived from the strategic plan while at the same time contributing to the achievement of it.

FIGURE 1.6   **The Cross-Functional Perspective in Planning**

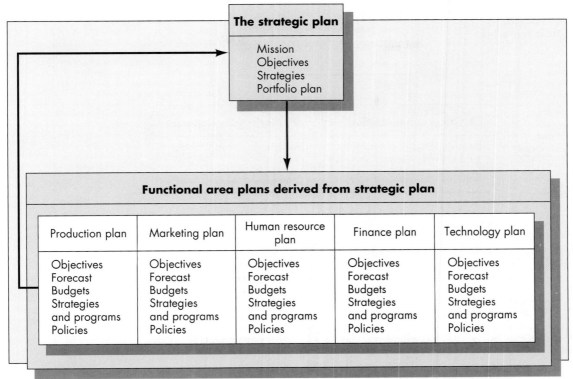

If done properly, strategic planning results in a clearly defined blueprint for management action in all functional areas of the organization. Figure 1.7 clearly illustrates this blueprint using only one organizational objective and two strategies from the strategic plan (above the dotted line) and illustrating how these are translated into elements of the marketing department plan and the production department plan (below the dotted line). Note that in Figure 1.7, all objectives and strategies are related to other objectives and strategies at higher and lower levels in the organization: That is, a hierarchy of objectives and strategies exists. We have illustrated only two possible marketing objectives and two possible production objectives. Obviously, many others could be developed, but our purpose is to illustrate the cross-functional nature of strategic planning and how objectives and strategies from the strategic plan must be translated into objectives and strategies for all functional areas including marketing.

Conclusion

This chapter has described the marketing management process in the context of the organization's overall strategic plan. Clearly, marketers must understand their cross-functional role in joining the marketing vision for the organization with the financial goals and manufacturing capabilities of the organization. The greater this ability, the better the likelihood is that the organization will be able to achieve and sustain a competitive advantage, the ultimate purpose of the strategic planning process.

At this point it would be useful to review Figures 1.5, 1.6, and 1.7 as well as the book's Table of Contents. This review will enable you to better relate the content and progression of the material to follow to the marketing management process.

FIGURE 1.7 A Blueprint for Management Action: Relating the Marketing Plan to the Strategic Plan and the Production Plan

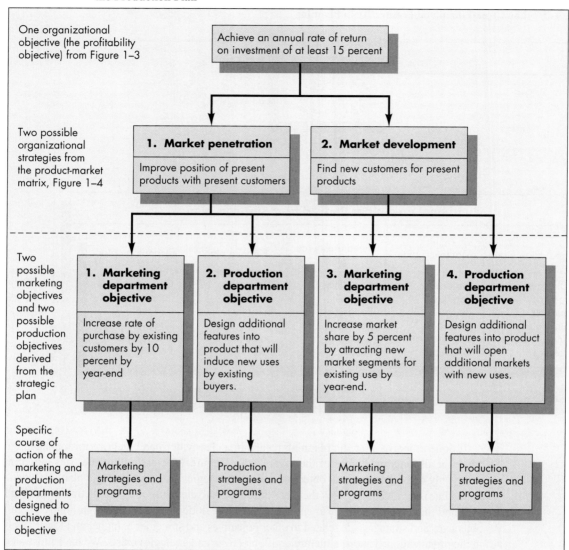

Additional Readings

Band, William, and John Guaspari. "Creating the Customer-Engaged Organization." *Marketing Management,* July/August 2003, pp. 35–39.

Best, Roger J. *Market-Based Management: Strategies for Growing Customer Value and Profitability.* 3rd ed. Upper Saddle River, N.J.: Prentice Hall, 2004.

Day, George S. "Feeding the Growth Strategy." *Marketing Management,* November/December 2003, pp. 15–21.

Goodwin, Ross, and Brad Ball. "What Marketing Wants the CEO to Know." *Marketing Management,* September/October 2003, pp. 18–23.

Lenskold, James D. "Customer Centric Marketing ROI." *Marketing Management,* January/February 2004, pp. 26–31.

Lusch, Robert F. "Creating Long-Term Marketing Health." *Marketing Management,* Spring 2000, pp. 17–24.

Reichheld, Frederick F. *The Loyalty Effect.* Boston: HBS Press, 1996.

Slywotzky, Adrian J. *Value Migration: How to Think Several Moves Ahead of the Competition.* Boston: HBS Press, 1996.

Appendix

Portfolio Models

Portfolio models remain a valuable aid to marketing managers in their efforts to develop effective marketing plans. The use of these models can aid managers who face situations that can best be described as "more products, less time, and less money." More specifically, (1) as the number of products a firm produces expands, the time available for developing marketing plans for each product decreases; (2) at a strategic level, management must make resource allocation decisions across lines of products and, in diversified organizations, across different lines of business; and (3) when resources are limited (which they usually are), the process of deciding which strategic business units (SBUs) to emphasize becomes very complex. In such situations, portfolio models can be very useful.

Portfolio analysis is not a new idea. Banks manage loan portfolios seeking to balance risks and yields. Individuals who are serious investors usually have a portfolio of various kinds of investments (common stocks, preferred stocks, bank accounts, and the like), each with different characteristics of risk, growth, and rate of return. The investor seeks to manage the portfolio to maximize whatever objectives he or she might have. Applying this same idea, most organizations have a wide range of products, product lines, and businesses, each with different growth rates and returns. Similar to the investor, managers should seek a desirable balance among alternative SBUs. Specifically, management should seek to develop a business portfolio that will ensure long-run profits and cash flow.

Portfolio models can be used to classify SBUs to determine the future cash contributions that can be expected from each SBU as well as the future resources that each will require. Remember, depending on the organization, an SBU could be a single product, product line, division, or a distinct business. While there are many different types of portfolio models, they generally examine the competitive position of the SBU and the chances for improving the SBU's contribution to profitability and cash flow.

There are several portfolio analysis techniques. Two of the most widely used are discussed in this appendix. To truly appreciate the concept of portfolio analysis, however, we must briefly review the development of portfolio theory.

A Review of Portfolio Theory

The interest in developing aids for managers in the selection of strategy was spurred by an organization known as the Boston Consulting Group (BCG) over 25 years ago. Its ideas, which will be discussed shortly, and many of those that followed were based on the concept of experience curves.

Experience curves are similar in concept to learning curves. Learning curves were developed to express the idea that the number of labor hours it takes to produce one unit of a particular product declines in a predictable manner as the number of units produced increases. Hence, an accurate estimation of how long it takes to produce the 100th unit is possible if the production times for the 1st and 10th units are known.

The concept of experience curves was derived from the concept of learning curves. Experience curves were first widely discussed in the ongoing Profit Impact of Marketing Strategies (PIMS) study conducted by the Strategic Planning Institute. The PIMS project studies 150 firms with more than 1,000 individual business units. Its major focus is on determining which environmental and internal firm variables influence the firm's return on investment (ROI) and cash flow. The researchers have concluded that seven categories of variables appear to influence the return on investment: (1) competitive position, (2) industry/market environment, (3) budget allocation, (4) capital structure, (5) production processes, (6) company characteristics, and (7) "change action" factors.[17]

The experience curve includes all costs associated with a product and implies that the per-unit costs of a product should fall, due to cumulative experience, as production volume increases. In a given industry, therefore, the producer with the largest volume and corresponding market share should have the lowest marginal cost. This leader in market share should be able to underprice competitors, discourage entry into the market by potential competitors, and, as a result, achieve an acceptable return on investment. The linkage of experience to cost to price to market share to ROI is

FIGURE A.1   **Experience Curve and Resulting Profit**

exhibited in Figure A.1. The Boston Consulting Group's view of the experience curve led the members to develop what has become known as the BCG Portfolio Model.

The BCG Model

The BCG is based on the assumption that profitability and cash flow will be closely related to sales volume. Thus, in this model, SBUs are classified according to their relative market share and the growth rate of the market the SBU is in. Using these dimensions, products are either classified as stars, cash cows, dogs, or question marks. The BCG model is presented in Figure A.2.

- *Stars* are SBUs with a high share of a high-growth market. Because high-growth markets attract competition, such SBUs are usually cash users because they are growing and because the firm needs to protect their market share position.
- *Cash cows* are often market leaders, but the market they are in is not growing rapidly. Because these SBUs have a high share of a low-growth market, they are cash generators for the firm.
- *Dogs* are SBUs that have a low share of a low-growth market. If the SBU has a very loyal group of customers, it may be a source of profits and cash. Usually, dogs are not large sources of cash.

FIGURE A.2
**The Boston
Consulting Group
Portfolio Model**

Relative Market Share

	High	Low
High	Stars	Question marks
Low	Cash cows	Dogs

**Market
Growth
Rate**

- *Question marks* are SBUs with a low share of a high-growth market. They have great potential but require great resources if the firm is to successfully build market share.

As you can see, a firm with 10 SBUs will usually have a portfolio that includes some of each of the above. Having developed this analysis, management must determine what role each SBU should assume. Four basic objectives are possible:

1. *Build share.* This objective sacrifices immediate earnings to improve market share. It is appropriate for promising question marks whose share has to grow if they are ever to become stars.
2. *Hold share.* This objective seeks to preserve the SBU's market share. It is very appropriate for strong cash cows to ensure that they can continue to yield a large cash flow.
3. *Harvest.* Here, the objective seeks to increase the product's short-term cash flow without concern for the long-run impact. It allows market share to decline in order to maximize earnings and cash flow. It is an appropriate objective for weak cash cows, weak question marks, and dogs.
4. *Divest.* This objective involves selling or divesting the SBU because better investment opportunities exist elsewhere. It is very appropriate for dogs and those question marks the firm cannot afford to finance for growth.

There have been several major criticisms of the BCG Portfolio Model, revolving around its focus on market share and market growth as the primary indicators of preference. First, the BCG model assumes market growth is uncontrollable.[18] As a result, managers can become preoccupied with setting market share objectives instead of trying to grow the market. Second, assumptions regarding market share as a critical factor affecting firm performance may not hold true, especially in international markets.[19] Third, the BCG model assumes that the major source of SBU financing comes from internal means. Fourth, the BCG matrix does not take into account any interdependencies that may exist between SBUs, such as shared distribution.[20] Fifth, the BCG matrix does not take into account any measures of profits and customer satisfaction.[21] Sixth, and perhaps most important, the thrust of the BCG matrix is based on the underlying assumption that corporate strategy begins with an analysis of competitive position. By its very nature, a strategy developed entirely on competitive analysis will always be a reactive one.[22] While the above criticisms are certainly valid ones, managers (especially of large firms) across all industries continue to find the BCG matrix useful in assessing the strategic position of SBUs.[23]

The General Electric Model

Although the BCG model can be useful, it does assume that market share is the sole determinant of an SBU's profitability. Also, in projecting market growth rates, a manager should carefully analyze the factors that influence sales and any opportunities for influencing industry sales.

Some firms have developed alternative portfolio models to incorporate more information about market opportunities and competitive positions. The GE model is one of these. The GE model emphasizes all the potential sources of strength, not just market share, and all of the factors that influence the long-term attractiveness of a market, not just its growth rate. As Figure A.3 indicates, all SBUs are classified according to

FIGURE A.3
The General Electric Portfolio Model

Industry Attractiveness	Business Strength
	Market position
Market size	Domestic market share
Market growth	World market share
Profitability	Share growth
Cyclicality	Share compared with leading competitor
Ability to recover from inflation	
World scope	Competitive strengths
	Quality leadership
	Technology
	Marketing
	Relative profitability

business strength and *industry attractiveness*. Figure A.4 presents a list of items that can be used to position SBUs in the matrix.

Industry attractiveness is a composite index made up of such factors as those listed in Figure A.4. For example: *market size*—the larger the market, the more attractive it will be; *market growth*—high-growth markets are more attractive than low-growth markets; *profitability*—high-profit-margin markets are more attractive than low-profit-margin industries.

Business strength is a composite index made up of such factors as those listed in Figure A.4. For example: *market share*—the higher the SBU's share of market, the greater its business strength; *quality leadership*—the higher the SBU's quality compared to competitors, the greater its business strength; *share compared with leading competitor*—the closer the SBU's share to the market leader, the greater its business strength.

Once the SBUs are classified, they are placed on the grid (Figure A–3). Priority "A" SBUs (often called *the green zone*) are those in the three cells at the upper left, indicating that these are SBUs high in both industry attractiveness and business strength, and that the firm should "build share." Priority "B" SBUs (often called *the yellow zone*) are those medium in both industry attractiveness and business strength. The firm will usually decide to "hold share" on these SBUs. Priority "C" SBUs are those in the three cells at the lower right (often called the *red zone*). These SBUs are low in both industry attractiveness and business strength. The firm will usually decide to harvest or divest these SBUs.

Whether the BCG model, the GE model, or a variation of these models is used, some analyses must be made of the firm's current portfolio of SBUs as part of any strategic planning effort. Marketing must get its direction from the organization's strategic plan.

Marketing Information, Research, and Understanding the Target Market

Section I Essentials of Marketing Management

Marketing Research: Process and Systems for Decision Making

Marketing managers require current, reliable, useful information to make effective decisions. In today's highly competitive global economy, marketers need to exploit opportunities and avoid mistakes if they are to survive and be profitable. Not only is sound marketing research needed, but also a system that gets current, valid information to the marketing decision maker in a timely manner.

This chapter is concerned with the marketing research process and information systems for decision making. It begins by discussing the marketing research process that is used to develop useful information for decision making. Then, marketing information systems are briefly discussed. The chapter is intended to provide a detailed introduction to many of the important topics in the area, but it does not provide a complete explanation of the plethora of marketing research topics.

The Role of Marketing Research

Marketing research is the process by which information about the environment is generated, analyzed, and interpreted for use in marketing decision making.[1] It cannot be overstated that *marketing research is an aid to decision making and not a substitute for it.* In other words, marketing research does not make decisions, but it can substantially increase the chances that good decisions are made. Unfortunately, too many marketing managers view research reports as the final answer to their problems; whatever the research indicates is taken as the appropriate course of action. Instead, marketing managers should recognize that (1) even the most carefully executed research can be fraught with errors; (2) marketing research does not forecast with certainty what will happen in the future; and (3) they should make decisions in light of their own knowledge and experience, since no marketing research study includes all of the factors that could influence the success of a strategy.

Although marketing research does not make decisions, it can reduce the risks associated with managing marketing strategies. For example, it can reduce the risk of introducing new products by evaluating consumer acceptance of them prior to full-scale introduction. Marketing research is also vital for investigating the effects of various marketing strategies after they have been implemented. For example, marketing research can examine the effects of a change in any element of the marketing mix on customer perception and behavior.

At one time, marketing researchers were primarily engaged in the technical aspects of research, but were not heavily involved in the strategic use of research findings. Today, however, many marketing researchers work hand-in-hand with marketing managers throughout the research process and have responsibility for making strategic recommendations based on the research.

The Marketing Research Process

Marketing research can be viewed as systematic processes for obtaining information to aid in decision making. There are many types of marketing research, and the framework illustrated in Figure 2.1 represents a general approach to the process. Each element of this process is discussed next.

Purpose of the Research

The first step in the research process is to determine explicitly why the research is needed and what it is to accomplish. This may be much more difficult than it sounds. Quite often a situation or problem is recognized as needing research, yet the nature of the problem is not clear or well defined nor is the appropriate type of research evident. Thus, managers and researchers need to discuss and clarify the current situation and develop a clear understanding of the problem. At the end of this stage, managers and researchers should agree on (1) the current situation involving the problem to be researched, (2) the nature of the problem, and (3) the specific question or questions the research is designed to investigate. This step is crucial since it influences the type of research to be conducted and the research design.

FIGURE 2.1
The Five Ps of the Research Process

Plan of the Research

Once the specific research question or questions have been agreed on, a research plan can be developed. A research plan spells out the nature of the research to be conducted and includes an explanation of such things as the sample design, measures, and analysis techniques to be used. Figure 2.2 presents a sample research plan. Three critical issues that influence the research plan are (1) whether primary or secondary data are needed, (2) whether qualitative or quantitative research is needed, and (3) whether the company will do its own research or contract with a marketing research specialist.

Primary versus Secondary Data

Given the information needed and budget constraints, a decision must be made as to whether primary data, secondary data, or some combination of the two is needed. *Primary data* are data collected specifically for the research problem under investigation; *secondary data* are those that have previously been collected for other purposes but can be used for the problem at hand. For example, if a company wanted to know why users of a competitive brand didn't prefer its brand, it may have to collect primary data to find out. On the other hand, if a company wanted to know the population size of key global markets that it might enter, it could find this information from secondary sources. Secondary information has the advantage of usually being cheaper than primary data, although it is not always available for strategy-specific research questions.

There are many sources of secondary data for use in marketing research. Research services such as A.C. Nielsen Co, Arbitron Co., IMS International, and Information Resources, Inc., sell a variety of useful data to companies. Business and industry publications such as the *Million Dollar Directory* or the *Encyclopedia of Associations* provide useful information for decision making, as do government reports such as *Statistical Abstracts of the United States* or the *Survey of Current Business*. Trade groups such as the American Medical Association or the National Association of Retail Dealers of America can also be contacted for information relevant to their industries.[2]

Qualitative versus Quantitative Research

Given a research question, a decision must be made whether qualitative or quantitative research would be a better approach. Qualitative research typically involves face-to-face interviews with respondents designed to develop a better understanding of what they think and feel concerning a research topic, such as a brand name, a product, a package, or an advertisement. The two most common types of qualitative research in marketing are focus groups and long interviews. *Focus groups* involve discussions among a small number of individuals led by an interviewer; they are designed to generate insights and ideas. *Long interviews* are conducted by an interviewer with a single respondent for several hours. They are designed to find out such things as the meanings various products or brands have for an individual or how a product influences a person's life.

Quantitative research involves more systematic procedures designed to obtain and analyze numerical data. Four common types of quantitative research in marketing are observation, surveys, experiments, and mathematical modeling.

Observational research involves watching people and recording relevant facts and behaviors. For example, retail stores may use observational research to determine what patterns customers use in walking through stores, how much time they spend in various parts of the store, and how many items of merchandise they examine. This information can be used to design store layouts more effectively. Similarly, many retail marketers do traffic counts at various intersections to help determine the best locations for stores.

Survey research involves the collection of data by means of a questionnaire either by mail, phone, or in person. Surveys are commonly used in marketing research to investigate

FIGURE 2.2   Sample Sections of a Research Plan

I. **Tentative projective title**

II. **Statement of the problem**
One or two sentences describing the general problem under consideration.

III. **Define and delimit the problem**
Here the writer states the purpose(s) and scope of the problem. *Purpose* refers to goals or objectives. Closely related to this is *justification*. Sometimes this is a separate step, depending on the urgency of the task. *Scope* refers to the limits of the research effort: in other words, what *is* and *is not* going to be investigated. Here is the point where the researcher spells out the various hypotheses to be investigated or the questions to be answered.

IV. **Outline**
Generally, this is a tentative framework for the entire project. It should be flexible enough to accommodate unforeseen difficulties, show statistical tables in outline form, and also show planned graphs.

V. **Method and data sources**
The types of data to be sought (primary, secondary) are briefly identified. A brief explanation of how the necessary information or data will be gathered (e.g., surveys, experiments, library sources) is given. *Sources* refer to the actual depositories for the information, whether from government publications, company records, actual people, and so forth. If measurements are involved, such as consumers' attitudes, the techniques for making such measurements are stated. The relevance of all techniques (qualitative and quantitative) should be discussed. The nature of the problem will probably indicate the types of techniques to be employed, such as factor analysis, depth interviews, or focus groups.

VI. **Sample design**
This provides a description of the population to be studied and how it will be defined. The researcher specifies the population, states the desired sample size, and discusses how nonresponse and missing data are to be handled. If a nonrandom sample is to be used, the justification and type of sampling strategy to be employed, such as convenience sample, are stated.

VII. **Data collection forms**
The forms to be employed in gathering the data are discussed here. For surveys, this involves either a questionnaire or an interview schedule. For other research, the forms could include inventory forms, psychological tests, and so forth. The plan should state how these instruments have been or will be validated, and the reader should be given any evidence of their reliability and validity.

VIII. **Personnel requirements**
This provides a complete list of all personnel who will be required, indicating exact jobs, time duration, and expected rate of pay. Assignments should be made indicating each person's responsibility and authority.

IX. **Phases of the study with a time schedule**
This is a detailed outline of the plan to complete the study. The study should be divided into workable pieces. Then, considering the persons involved in each phase, their qualifications and experience, and so forth, the time for the job is estimated. Some jobs may overlap. This plan will help in estimating the time required.
  Illustration:
  1. Preliminary investigation—two weeks.
  2. Final test of questionnaire—one week.
  3. Sample selection—one week.
  4. Mail questionnaires, field follow-up, and so forth—two months.
  5. Additional tasks.

X. **Analysis plans**
This is a discussion of editing and proofreading of questionnaires, coding instructions, and the type of data analysis. An outline of some of the major tables that will appear in the report should be presented.

XI. **Cost estimate for doing the study**
Personnel requirements are combined with time on different phases to estimate total personnel costs. Estimates on travel, materials, supplies, drafting, computer charges, and printing and mailing costs must also be included. If an overhead charge is required, it should be calculated and added to the subtotal of the above items.

Founded in 1941 in a SoHo loft in New York City, Coach built a reputation for quality leather purses in classic styles. By 1995, however, sales declines had CEO Lew Frankfurt well aware that the company was about to hit the wall. Upscale consumers preferred the offerings of companies like Louis Vuitton, Chanel, Gucci, and newcomer Kate Spade. Coach purses were viewed as conservative, traditional bags, the kind women carried to country clubs, rather than as fun, exciting, sexy, or modern.

To turn the company around, Coach selected new designs using fabric, nylon, and lighter-weight leathers to make the bags trendier. Instead of offering a new collection twice a year, Coach began offering a new collection every month. The company also redesigned its stores and expanded its distribution. It priced its bags at an average of about $200, making them an accessible luxury that appeals both to consumers who have to stretch their budgets to get one and to those who think nothing of spending $700 for Yves Saint Laurent's hot Mombasa bag.

Perhaps the most important change the company made was to select styles based on what consumers thought was cool rather than have designers decide what consumers *should* want. The company spends about $2 million a year on consumer surveys alone. A year before rolling out a product, Coach talks to hundreds of customers, asking for their opinions on every feature of a purse from comfort and strap length to style and color. It asks consumers to rank new designs against existing items. Coach test markets new products in a cross-section of stores around the country. This focus on consumers and understanding what they want sets the company apart in the fashion industry.

Using marketing research and focusing marketing efforts on what consumers want obviously paid off handsomely for Coach. Coach stores have annual sales per square foot of $865 compared to traditional retailers, like the Gap, which average $200 to $300. Coach's net income rose over 400 percent from 1999 to 2002.

Sources: LouAnn Lofton, "Coach's Success Story," Fool.com (June 12, 2003); Amy Tsao, "It's in the Bag for Coach," *Business-Week Online* (April 23, 2003); Julia Boorstin, "How Coach Got Hot," *Fortune,* October 28, 2002, pp. 131–134.

customer beliefs, attitudes, satisfaction, and many other issues. Mail surveys are useful for reaching widely dispersed markets but take more time to get responses than telephone surveys; personal surveys involving structured questions are useful but expensive.

Experimental research involves manipulating one variable and examining its impact on other variables. For example, the price of a product in one test store could be changed, while left the same in other stores. Comparing sales in the test store with those in other stores can provide evidence about the likely impact of a price change in the overall market. Experiments are useful for getting a better idea of the causal relationships among variables, but they are often difficult to design and administer effectively in natural settings. Thus, many marketing research experiments are conducted in laboratories or simulated stores to carefully control other variables that could impact results.

Mathematical modeling research often involves secondary data, such as scanner data collected and stored in computer files from retail checkout counters. This approach involves the development of equations to model relationships among variables and uses econometric and statistical techniques to investigate the impact of various strategies and tactics on sales and brand choices. Math modeling is useful because it provides an efficient way to study problems with extremely large secondary data sets.

Which of these types of research is best for particular research questions requires considerable knowledge of each of them. Often, qualitative research is used in early stages of investigating a topic to get more information and insight about it. Then, quantitative approaches are used to investigate the degree to which the insights hold across a larger sample

FIGURE 2.3   **A Comparison of Data Collection Methods Used in Marketing Research**

Method	Advantages	Disadvantages
Focus groups	• Depth of information collected. • Flexibility in use. • Relatively low cost. • Data collected quickly.	• Requires expert moderator. • Questions of group size and acquaintanceships of participants. • Potential for bias from moderator. • Small sample size.
Telephone surveys	• Centralized control of data collection. • More cost-effective than personal interviews. • Data collected quickly.	• Resistance in collecting income, financial data. • Limited depth of response. • Disproportionate coverage of low-income segments. • Abuse of phone by solicitors. • Perceived intrusiveness.
Mail surveys	• Cost-effective per completed response. • Broad geographic dispersion. • Ease of administration. • Data collected quickly.	• Refusal and contact problems with certain segments. • Limited depth of response. • Difficult to estimate nonresponse biases. • Resistance and bias in collecting income, financial data. • Lack of control following mailing.
Personal (in-depth) interviews	• More depth of response than telephone interviews. • Generate substantial number of ideas compared with group methods.	• Easy to transmit biasing cues. • Not-at-homes. • Broad coverage often infeasible. • Cost per contact high. • Data collection time may be excessive.
Mall intercepts	• Flexibility in collecting data, answering questions, probing respondents. • Data collected quickly. • Excellent for concept tests, copy evaluations, other visuals. • Fairly high response rates.	• Limited time. • Sample composition or representativeness is suspect. • Costs depend on incidence rates. • Interviewer supervision difficult.
Internet surveys	• Inexpensive, quickly executed. • Visual stimuli can be evaluated. • Real-time data processing possible. • Can be answered at convenience of respondent.	• Responses must be checked for duplication, bogus responses. • Respondent self-selection bias. • Limited ability to qualify respondents and confirm responses. • Difficulty in generating sample frames for probability sampling.
Projective techniques	• Useful in word association tests of new brand names. • Less threatening to respondents for sensitive topics. • Can identify important motives underlying choices.	• Require trained interviewers. • Cost per interview high.
Observation	• Can collect sensitive data. • Accuracy of measuring overt behaviors. • Different perspective than survey self-reports. • Useful in studies of cross-cultural differences.	• Appropriate only for frequently occurring behaviors. • Unable to assess opinions of attitudes causing behaviors. • May be expensive in data-collection-time costs.

Source: William O. Bearden, Thomas N. Ingram, and Raymond W. LaForge, *Marketing,* 4th ed. (Burr Ridge, IL: McGraw-Hill/Irwin, 2004), p. 131.

or population. Figure 2.3 provides a comparison of a variety of qualitative and quantitative data collection methods.

Company versus Contract Research

Most large consumer goods companies have marketing research departments that can perform a variety of types of research. However, there are many marketing research firms, advertising agencies, and consulting companies that do marketing research on a contract

A. Planning
1. Segmentation: What kinds of people buy our products? Where do they live? How much do they earn? How many of them are there?
2. Demand estimation: Are the markets for our products increasing or decreasing? Are there promising markets that we have not yet reached?
3. Environmental assessment: Are the channels of distribution for our products changing? What should our presence on the Internet be?

B. Problem Solving
1. Product
   a. In testing new products and product-line extensions, which product design is likely to be the most successful? What features do consumers value most?
   b. What kind of packaging should we use?
   c. What are the forecasts for the product? How might we reenergize its life cycle?
2. Price
   a. What price should we charge for our products?
   b. How sensitive to price changes are our target segments?
   c. Given the life-time value assessments of our segments, should we be discounting or charging a premium to our most valued customers?
   d. As production costs decline, should we lower our prices or try to develop higher-quality products?
   e. Do consumers use price as a cue to value or a cue to quality in our industry?
3. Place
   a. Where, and by whom, are our products being sold? Where, and by whom, should our products be sold?
   b. What kinds of incentives should we offer the trade to push our products?
   c. Are our relationships with our suppliers and distributors satisfactory and cooperative?
4. Promotion
   a. How much should we spend on promotion? How should it be allocated to products and to geographic areas?
   b. Which ad copy should we run in our markets? With what frequency and media expenditures?
   c. What combination of media—newspapers, radio, television, magazines, Internet ad banners—should we use?
   d. What is our consumer coupon redemption rate?

C. Control
1. What is our market share overall? In each geographic area? By each customer type?
2. Are customers satisfied with our products? How is our record for service? Are there many returns? Do levels of customer satisfaction vary with market? With segment?
3. Are our employees satisfied? Do they feel well trained and empowered to assist our customers?
4. How does the public perceive our company? What is our reputation with the trade?

Source: Gilbert A. Churchill, Jr., and Dawn Iacobucci, *Marketing Research: Methodological Foundations,* 9th ed. (Cincinatti: South-Western, 2005), p. 9.

basis. Some marketing research suppliers have special expertise in a particular type of research that makes them a better choice than doing the research internally. A decision has to be made as to whether the marketing research department has the ability to do a particular type of research itself or whether all or part of the research should be contracted with a research supplier. In either case, schedules for task completion, the exact responsibilities of all involved parties, and cost need to be considered.

Traditional marketing research often involves developing hypotheses about the effect of a change in a marketing mix variable on customers, collecting data, and examining the likely impact of the change. For example, a marketer may want to investigate what impact a change in price would have on sales or the likely success of adding a new product to a product mix.

However, many companies now have large databases with volumes of information about their customers and have the computer hardware and software to analyze them. Data mining is the process of searching through these data sets looking for insights to improve marketing strategies. Catalog companies such as Lands' End, Fingerhut, and Spiegel use data mining to find statistical links that suggest marketing actions. For example, Fingerhut studies about 3,500 variables over the lifetime of a customer's relationship. It has found that customers who change residences are three times as likely as regular customers to buy tables, fax machines, and decorative products but no more likely to buy jewelry or footwear. So Fingerhut has created a catalog especially targeted at consumers who have recently moved.

Some of these purchase patterns are common sense: Peanut butter and grape jelly purchases link and might suggest a joint promotion between Skippy peanut butter and Welch's grape jelly. Other patterns link seemingly unrelated purchases: Supermarkets mined checkout data from scanners and discovered men buying diapers in the evening sometimes buy a six-pack of beer as well. So they placed diapers and beer near each other. Placing potato chips between them increased sales on all three.

Still the success in data mining ultimately depends on humans—the judgments of the marketing managers and researchers in how to select, analyze, and interpret the information.

Source: Roger A. Kerin, Eric N. Berkowitz, Steven W. Hartley, and William Rudelius, *Marketing,* 7th ed. (Burr Ridge, IL: McGraw-Hill/Irwin, 2003), pp. 224–25.

Performance of the Research

Performance of the research involves preparing for data collection and actually collecting them. The tasks at this stage obviously depend on the type of research that has been selected and the type of data needed. If secondary data are to be used, they must be located, prepared for analysis, and possibly paid for. If primary data are to be collected, then observational forms, questionnaires, or other types of measures must be designed, pretested, and validated. Samples must be drawn and interviews must be scheduled or preparations must be made for mailing or phoning selected individuals.

In terms of actual data collection, a cardinal rule is to obtain and record the maximal amount of useful information, subject to the constraints of time, money, and respondent privacy. Failure to obtain and record data clearly can obviously lead to a poor research study, while failure to consider the rights of respondents raises both practical and ethical problems. Thus, both the objectives and constraints of data collection must be closely monitored.

Processing of Research Data

Processing research data includes the preparation of data for analysis and the actual analysis of them. Preparations include such things as editing and structuring data and coding them for analysis. Data sets should be clearly labeled to ensure they are not misinterpreted or misplaced.

The appropriate analysis techniques for collected data depend on the nature of the research question and the design of the research. Qualitative research data consist of interview records that are content analyzed for ideas or themes. Quantitative research data may be analyzed in a variety of ways depending on the objectives of the research.

A critical part of this stage is interpreting and assessing the research results. Seldom, if ever, do marketing research studies obtain findings that are totally unambiguous. Usually, relationships among variables or differences between groups are small to moderate, and judgment and insight are needed to draw appropriate inferences and conclusions. Marketing researchers should always double-check their analysis and avoid overstating the strength of their findings. The implications for developing or changing a marketing strategy should be carefully thought out and tempered with judgment about the overall quality of the study.

Preparation of the Research Report

The research report is a complete statement of everything done in a research project and includes a write-up of each of the previous stages as well as the strategic recommendations from the research. The limitations of the research should be carefully noted. Figure 2.4 illustrates the types of questions marketing researchers and managers should discuss prior to submitting the final research report.

Research reports should be clear and unambiguous with respect to what was done and what recommendations are made. Often research reports must trade off the apparent precision of scientific jargon for everyday language that managers can understand. Researchers should work closely with managers to ensure that the study and its limitations are fully understood.

Limitations of the Research Process

Although the foregoing discussion presented the research process as a set of simple stages, this does not mean that conducting quality marketing research is a simple task. There are many problems and difficulties that must be overcome if a research study is to provide valuable information for decision making.[3] For example, consider the difficulties in one type of marketing research, *test marketing.*

The major goal of most test marketing is to measure new product sales on a limited basis where competitive retaliation and other factors are allowed to operate freely. In this way, future sales potential can often be estimated reasonably well. Listed below are a number of problems that could invalidate test marketing study results.

1. Test market areas are not representative of the market in general in terms of population characteristics, competition, and distribution outlets.
2. Sample size and design are incorrectly formulated because of budget constraints.
3. Pretest measurements of competitive brand sales are not made or are inaccurate, limiting the meaningfulness of market share estimates.
4. Test stores do not give complete support to the study such that certain package sizes may not be carried or prices may not be held constant during the test period.

FIGURE 2.4

Eight Criteria for Evaluating Marketing Research Reports

1. Was the type of research appropriate for the research questions?
2. Was the research well designed?
   a. Was the sample studied appropriate for the research questions?
   b. Were measures well developed, pretested, and validated?
   c. Were the data analysis techniques the best ones for the study?
3. Was there adequate supervision of data collection, editing, and coding?
4. Was the analysis conducted according to standards accepted in the field?
5. Do the findings make sense, given the research question and design, and were they considered in light of previous knowledge and experience?
6. Are the limitations of the study recognized and explained in detail?
7. Are the conclusions appropriately drawn or are they over- or understated?
8. Are the recommendations for marketing strategy clear and appropriate?

Marketing researchers have ethical responsibilities to the respondents who provide them primary data, clients for whom they work, and subordinates who work under them. Below are a number of ethical responsibilities to these groups.

RESPONSIBILITIES TO RESPONDENTS

1. *Preserving respondent anonymity.* Marketing researchers should ensure that respondents' identities are safe from invasion of privacy.
2. *Avoiding mental stress for respondents.* Marketing researchers should minimize the mental stress placed on respondents.
3. *Avoiding questions detrimental to respondents.* Marketing researchers should avoid asking questions for which the answers conflict with the self-interest of the respondents.
4. *Avoiding the use of dangerous equipment or techniques.* Physical or reputational harm to respondents based on their participation in marketing research should not occur. Respondents should be informed of any other than minimal risks involved in the research and be free to self-determine their participation.
5. *Avoiding deception of respondents.* Respondents should not be deceived about the purpose of the study in most cases. Many consider deception acceptable in research where it is needed to obtain valid results, there is minimal risk to respondents, and respondents are debriefed explaining the real purpose of the study.
6. *Avoiding coercion of respondents.* Marketing researchers should avoid coercing or harassing people to try to get them to agree to be interviewed or fill out questionnaires.

RESPONSIBILITIES TO CLIENTS

1. *Providing confidentiality.* Marketing researchers are obliged not to reveal information about a client to competitors and should carefully consider when a company should be identified as a client.
2. *Providing technical integrity.* Marketing researchers are obliged to design efficient studies without undue expense or complexity and accurately report results.
3. *Providing administrative integrity.* Marketing researchers are obliged to price their work fairly without hidden charges.
4. *Providing guidance on research usage.* Marketing researchers are obliged to promote the correct usage of research and to prevent the misuse of findings.

RESPONSIBILITIES TO SUBORDINATE EMPLOYEES

1. *Creating an ethical work environment.* Marketing research managers are obliged to create an ethical work environment where unethical behavior is not encouraged or overlooked.
2. *Avoiding opportunities for unethical behavior.* Marketing research managers are obliged to avoid placing subordinates in situations where unethical behavior could be concealed but rewarded.

5. Test-market products are advertised or promoted beyond a profitable level for the market in general.
6. The effects of factors that influence sales, such as the sales force, season, weather conditions, competitive retaliation, shelf space, and so forth, are ignored in the research.
7. The test-market period is too short to determine whether the product will be repurchased by customers.

A list of such problems could be developed for any type of marketing research. However, careful research planning, coordination, implementation, and control can help reduce such problems and increase the value of research for decision making.

Marketing Information Systems

Most marketers use computer-based systems to help them gather, sort, store, and distribute information for marketing decisions.[4] A popular form of marketing information system is the marketing decision support system, which is a coordinated collection of data, tools, and techniques involving both computer hardware and software by which marketers gather and interpret relevant information for decision making. These systems require three types of software:

1. Database management software for sorting and retrieving data from internal and external sources.
2. Model base management software that contains routines for manipulating data in ways that are useful for marketing decision making.
3. A dialog system that permits marketers to explore databases and use models to produce information to address their decision-making needs.

Marketing decision support systems are designed to handle information from both internal and external sources. Internal information includes such things as sales records, which can be divided by territory, package size, brand, price, order size, or salesperson; inventory data that can indicate how rapidly various products are selling; or expenditure data on such things as advertising, personal selling, or packaging. Internal information is particularly important for investigating the efficiency and effectiveness of various marketing strategies.

FIGURE 2.5   Global Information Sources for Marketing Information Systems

Information Source	Types of Data
The Export Connection, a national trade databank service of the U.S. Department of Commerce (Washington, DC)	Monthly series of CD-ROM discs containing data from 15 U.S. government agencies, including marketing research reports, information about specific countries and their economies, and a listing of foreign importers of U.S. products.
Global Market Surveys	Detailed surveys for given industries such as graphics, computers, medical equipment, industrial equipment.
Dun & Bradstreet's *Principal International Business*	Names, addresses, number of employees, products produced, and chief executive officer, up to 6 SIC classifications (4-digit) for each organization; over 144,000 business units classified by 4-digit SIC and alphabetical order.
Moody's International Manual	Company histories, descriptions of business, financial statistics, management personnel.
Overseas Business Reports	Monthly reports provide information for marketing to specific countries (e.g., "Marketing in Pakistan," "Marketing in Nigeria").
The Exporter's Guide to Federal Resources for Small Business (Washington, DC: U.S. Government Printing Office)	Reference guide to export assistance available from the U.S. government.
Automated Trade Locator Assistance System (district offices of the Small Business Administration)	Results of current marketing research about world markets.
Small Business Foundation of America, export opportunity hotline: 800-243-7232	Answers to questions from small businesses interested in exporting.
Hotline sponsored by AT&T and seven other organizations: 800-USA-XPORT	Free exporter's kit and data on 50 industries and 78 countries.
International trade fairs (sponsored by many industry organizations and national governments, including the U.S. Small Business Administration)	Products and needs of existing and potential buyers and competitors from around the world.

External information is gathered from outside the organization and concerns changes in the environment that could influence marketing strategies. External information is needed concerning changes in global economies and societies, competitors, customers, and technology. Figure 2.5 lists a sample of sources of external information that could help global marketers make better decisions. Of course, information from marketing research studies conducted by an organization is also put into marketing information systems to improve marketing strategy development.

Conclusion

This chapter emphasized the importance of marketing research for making sound marketing strategy decisions. The chapter discussed marketing research as a process involving several stages, which include determining the purpose of the research, designing the plan for the research, performing the research, processing the research data, and preparing the research report. Then, marketing information systems were discussed and one type, the marketing decision support system, was explained. Such systems provide decision makers with the right information, at the right time in the right way, to make sound marketing decisions.

Additional Readings

Aaker, David A.; V. Kumar; and George S. Day. *Marketing Research*. 7th ed. New York: John Wiley, 2001.

Churchill, Gilbert A., Jr., and Dawn Iacobucci. *Marketing Research: Methodological Foundations*. 9th ed. Cincinatti, OH: South-Western, 2005.

———, and Tom J. Brown. *Basic Marketing Research*. 5th ed. Cincinatti, OH: South-Western, 2004.

Malhotra, Naresh K. *Marketing Research*. 4th ed. Upper Saddle River, NJ: Pearson Education, 2004.

Zikmund, William G. *Exploring Marketing Research*. 8th ed. Cincinatti, OH: South-Western, 2003.

3

Consumer Behavior

The marketing concept emphasizes that profitable marketing begins with the discovery and understanding of consumer needs and then develops a marketing mix to satisfy these needs. Thus, an understanding of consumers and their needs and purchasing behavior is integral to successful marketing. Unfortunately, there is no single theory of consumer behavior that can totally explain why consumers behave as they do. Instead, there are numerous theories, models, and concepts making up the field. In addition, the majority of these notions have been borrowed from a variety of other disciplines, such as sociology, psychology, anthropology, and economics, and must be integrated to understand consumer behavior.

In this chapter, consumer behavior will be examined in terms of the model in Figure 3.1. The chapter begins by reviewing social, marketing, and situational influences on consumer decision making. These provide information that can influence consumers' thoughts and feelings about purchasing various products and brands. The degree to which this information influences consumers' decisions depends on a number of psychological influences. Two of the most important of these are product knowledge and product involvement, which will then be discussed. The chapter concludes by discussing the consumer decision-making process.

FIGURE 3.1   An Overview of the Buying Process

Value	General Features	Relevance to Marketing
Achievement and success activity	Hard work is good; success flows from hard work.	Acts as a justification for acquisition of goods ("You deserve it").
	Keeping busy is healthy and natural.	Stimulates interest in products that are time-savers and enhance leisure time.
Efficiency and practicality	Admiration of things that solve problems (e.g., save time and effort).	Stimulates purchase of products that function well and save time.
	People can improve themselves; tomorrow should be better than today.	Stimulates desire for new products that fulfill unsatisfied needs; ready acceptance of products that claim to be "new" or "improved."
Material comfort	"The good life."	Fosters acceptance of convenience and luxury products that make life more enjoyable.
Individualism	Being oneself (e.g., self-reliance, self-interest, self-esteem).	Stimulates acceptance of customized or unique products that enable a person to "express his or her own personality."
Freedom	Freedom of choice.	Fosters interest in wide product lines and differentiated products.
External conformity	Uniformity of observable behavior; desire for acceptance.	Stimulates interest in products that are used or owned by others in the same social group.
Humanitarianism	Caring for others, particularly the underdog.	Stimulates patronage of firms that compete with market leaders.
Youthfulness	A state of mind that stresses being "young at heart" and having a youthful appearance.	Stimulates acceptance of products that provide the illusion of maintaining or fostering youthfulness.
Fitness and health	Caring about one's body, including the desire to be physically fit and healthy.	Stimulates acceptance of food products, activities, and equipment perceived to maintain or increase physical fitness.

Source: Leon G. Schiffman and Leslie Lazar Kanuck, *Consumer Behavior,* 8th ed., p. 432, 2004. Reprinted by permission of Prentice Hall, Inc., Upper Saddle River, NJ.

Social Influences on Consumer Decision Making

Behavioral scientists have become increasingly aware of the powerful effects of the social environment and personal interactions on human behavior. In terms of consumer behavior, culture, social class, and reference group influences have been related to purchase and consumption decisions. It should be noted that these influences can have both direct and indirect effects on the buying process. By direct effects we mean direct communication between the individual and other members of society concerning a particular decision. By indirect effects we mean the influence of society on an individual's basic values and attitudes as well as the important role that groups play in structuring an individual's personality.

Culture and Subculture

Culture is one of the most basic influences on an individual's needs, wants, and behavior, since all facets of life are carried out against the background of the society in which an individual lives. Cultural antecedents affect everyday behavior, and there is empirical support for the notion that culture is a determinant of certain aspects of consumer behavior.

Cultural values are transmitted through three basic organizations: the family, religious organizations, and educational institutions; and in today's society, educational institutions are playing an increasingly greater role in this regard. Marketing managers should adapt the marketing mix to cultural values and constantly monitor value changes and differences in both domestic and global markets. To illustrate, one of the changing values in America is the increasing emphasis on achievement and career success. This change in values has been recognized by many business firms that have expanded their emphasis on timesaving, convenience-oriented products.

In large nations such as the United States, the population is bound to lose a significant amount of its homogeneity, and thus subcultures arise. In other words, there are subcultures in the American culture where people have more frequent interactions than with the population at large and thus tend to think and act alike in some respects. Subcultures are based on such things as geographic areas, religions, nationalities, ethnic groups, and age. Many subcultural barriers are decreasing because of mass communication, mass transit, and a decline in the influence of religious values. However, age groups, such as the teen market, baby boomers, and the mature market, have become increasingly important for marketing strategy. For example, since baby boomers (those born between 1946 and 1962) make up about a third of the U.S. population and soon will account for about half of discretionary spending, many marketers are repositioning products to serve them. Snickers candy bars, for instance, used to be promoted to children as a treat but are now promoted to adults as a wholesome between-meals snack.

Social Class

While many people like to think of America as a land of equality, a class structure can be observed. Social classes develop on the basis of such things as wealth, skill, and power. The single best indicator of social class is occupation. However, interest at this point is in the influence of social class on the individual's behavior. What is important here is that different social classes tend to have different attitudinal configurations and values that influence the behavior of individual members. For marketing purposes, four different social classes have been identified.[1]

Upper Americans comprise 14 percent of the population and are differentiated mainly by having high incomes. This class remains the group in which quality merchandise is most prized and prestige brands are commonly sought. Spending with good taste is a priority as are products such as theater; books; investments in art; European travel; household help; club memberships for tennis, golf, and swimming; and prestige schooling for children.

The *middle class* comprises 34 percent of the population, and these consumers want to do the right thing and buy what is popular. They are concerned with fashion and buying what experts in the media recommend. Increased earnings have led to spending on more "worthwhile experiences" for children, including winter ski trips, college education, and shopping for better brands of clothes at more expensive stores. Appearance of the home is important. This group emulates the upper Americans, which distinguishes it from the working class.

The *working class* comprises 38 percent of the population and are "family folk" who depend heavily on relatives for economic and emotional support. The emphasis on family ties is only one sign of how much more limited and different working-class horizons are socially, psychologically, and geographically compared to those of the middle class. For them, "keeping up with the times" focuses on the mechanical and recreational, and thus, ease of labor and leisure are what they continue to pursue.

Lower Americans comprise 16 percent of the population and are as diverse in values and consumption goals as are other social levels. Some members of this group are prone to every form of instant gratification known to humankind when the money is available.

However, others are dedicated to resisting worldly temptations as they struggle toward what some believe will be a "heavenly reward" for their earthly sacrifices.

For the marketing manager, social class offers some insights into consumer behavior and is potentially useful as a market segmentation variable. However, there is considerable controversy as to whether social class is superior to income for the purpose of market segmentation.

Reference Groups and Families

Groups that an individual looks to (uses as a reference) when forming attitudes and opinions are described as reference groups.[2] Primary reference groups include family and close friends, while secondary reference groups include fraternal organizations and professional associations. A buyer may also consult a single individual about decisions, and this individual would be considered a reference individual.

A person normally has several reference groups or reference individuals for various subjects or different decisions. For example, a woman may consult one reference group when she is purchasing a car and a different reference group for lingerie. In other words, the nature of the product and the role the individual is playing during the purchasing process influence which reference group will be consulted. Reference group influence is generally considered to be stronger for products that are "public" or conspicuous—that is, products that other people see the individual using, such as clothes or automobiles.

As noted, the family is generally recognized to be an important reference group, and it has been suggested that the household, rather than the individual, is the relevant unit for studying consumer behavior.[3] This is because within a household the purchaser of goods and services is not always the user of these goods and services. Thus, it is important for marketing managers to determine not only who makes the actual purchase but also who makes the decision to purchase. In addition, it has been recognized that the needs, income, assets, debts, and expenditure patterns change over the course of what is called the *family life cycle*. The family life cycle can be divided into a number of stages ranging from single, to married, to married with children of different age groups, to older couples, to solitary survivors. It may also include divorced people, both with and without children. Because the life cycle combines trends in earning power with demands placed on income, it is a useful way of classifying and segmenting individuals and families.[4]

Marketing Influences on Consumer Decision Making

Marketing strategies are often designed to influence consumer decision making and lead to profitable exchanges. Each element of the marketing mix (product, price, promotion, place) can affect consumers in various ways.

Product Influences

Many attributes of a company's products, including brand name, quality, newness, and complexity, can affect consumer behavior. The physical appearance of the product, packaging, and labeling information can also influence whether consumers notice a product in-store, examine it, and purchase it. One of the key tasks of marketers is to differentiate their products from those of competitors and create consumer perceptions that the product is worth purchasing.

Price Influences

The price of products and services often influences whether consumers will purchase them at all and, if so, which competitive offering is selected. Stores, such as Wal-Mart, which are

People begin lining up in the wee hours of the morning in darkness, some still in their pajamas. When dawn breaks and the ribbon is cut, they rush through the doors, screaming, "Krispy Kreme doughnuts, yowweeee!"

This scene has happened in cities all over North America and will happen again in the years to come. Why do some people have such intensely strong attitudes toward a simple and seemingly insignificant doughnut? Well, Krispy Kreme fans will tell you this is not an ordinary doughnut. The original glazed version is best served hot, and it tastes amazingly good (like a glazed fluffy cloud, according to one five-year-old).

Still, Krispy Kreme is relatively small, with 292 stores (in 2003) compared to 3,600 Dunkin' Donuts stores in the United States alone. Sales were $492 million in 2002, with earnings of $33 million and a very strong stock performance. Same-store sales are increasing, on average, by more than 11 percent per year, but there are some signs that sales in new stores are leveling off.

The brand Krispy Kreme is not as recognizable as Coke or McDonald's, but it is a very hot brand and enjoys highly positive attitudes. All types of people seem to have very positive attitudes toward Krispy Kreme as well as strong intentions to buy and eat them.

Some analysts think attitudes toward Krispy Kreme are based on its association with the "American dream." From its beginnings as a regional icon in the South, Krispy Kreme went through some hard times before CEO Scott Livengood got control of the production processes. Another reason may be that even in hard times, with unemployment relatively high and military altercations around the globe, people still can enjoy the simple pleasure of an indulgent snack.

But there is more to it than that. Shrewd, if unconventional, marketing also has an influence. For instance, the company does very little advertising, relying instead on promotional strategies. For example, Krispy Kreme once delivered several boxes of doughnuts to the *Today Show,* where they were eaten and commented on, garnering huge national exposure for the brand. Instead of spending huge sums on national advertising, the company gives away millions of doughnuts to charitable organizations that sell them for fund-raising projects. All of this creates exposure and goodwill that further enhance consumers' attitudes toward Krispy Kreme.

The big question is whether the positive attitudes and purchase intentions of many American consumers for Krispy Kreme can be maintained. After all, they aren't exactly health food!

Source: Andy Serwer, "The Hole Story: How Krispy Kreme Became the Hottest Brand in America," *Fortune,* July 7, 2003, pp. 53–62. © 2003 Time Inc. All rights reserved. Reprinted by permission; website: **www.krispykreme.com.**

perceived to charge the lowest prices, attract many consumers based on this fact alone. For some offerings, higher prices may not deter purchase because consumers believe that the products or services are higher quality or are more prestigious. However, many of today's value-conscious consumers may buy products more on the basis of price than other attributes.

Promotion Influences

Advertising, sales promotions, salespeople, and publicity can influence what consumers think about products, what emotions they experience in purchasing and using them, and what behaviors they perform, including shopping in particular stores and purchasing specific brands. Since consumers receive so much information from marketers and screen out a good deal of it, it is important for marketers to devise communications that (1) offer consistent messages about their products and (2) are placed in media that consumers in the target market are likely to use. Marketing communications play a critical role in informing consumers about products and services, including where they can be purchased, and in creating favorable images and perceptions.

Place Influences

The marketer's strategy for distributing products can influence consumers in several ways. First, products that are convenient to buy in a variety of stores increase the chances of consumers finding and buying them. When consumers are seeking low-involvement products, they are unlikely to engage in extensive search, so ready availability is important. Second, products sold in exclusive outlets such as Nordstrom may be perceived by consumers as having higher quality. In fact, one of the ways marketers create brand equity—that is, favorable consumer perceptions of brands—is by selling them in prestigious outlets. Third, offering products by nonstore methods, such as on the Internet or in catalogs, can create consumer perceptions that the products are innovative, exclusive, or tailored for specific target markets.

Situational Influences on Consumer Decision Making

Situational influences can be defined as all those factors particular to a time and place of observation that have a demonstrable and systematic effect on current behavior. In terms of purchasing situations, five groups of situational influences have been identified.[5] These influences may be perceived either consciously or subconsciously and may have considerable effect on product and brand choice.

1. *Physical features* are the most readily apparent features of a situation. These features include geographical and institutional location, decor, sounds, aromas, lighting, weather, and visible configurations of merchandise or other material surrounding the stimulus object.

2. *Social features* provide additional depth to a description of a situation. Other persons present, their characteristics, their apparent roles and interpersonal interactions are potentially relevant examples.

3. *Time* is a dimension of situations that may be specified in units ranging from time of day to season of the year. Time also may be measured relative to some past or future event for the situational participant. This allows such conceptions as time since last purchase, time since or until meals or paydays, and time constraints imposed by prior or standing commitments.

4. *Task features* of a situation include an intent or requirement to select, shop for, or obtain information about a general or specific purchase. In addition, task may reflect different buyer and user roles anticipated by the individual. For instance, a person shopping for a small appliance as a wedding gift for a friend is in a different situation than when shopping for a small appliance for personal use.

5. *Current conditions* make up a final feature that characterizes a situation. These are momentary moods (such as acute anxiety, pleasantness, hostility, and excitation) or momentary conditions (such as cash on hand, fatigue, and illness) rather than chronic individual traits. These conditions are further stipulated to be immediately antecedent to the current situation to distinguish the states the individual brings to the situation from states of the individual resulting from the situation. For instance, people may select a certain motion picture because they feel depressed (an antecedent state and a part of the choice situation), but the fact that the movie causes them to feel happier is a response to the consumption situation. This altered state then may become antecedent for behavior in the next choice situation encountered, such as passing a street vendor on the way out of the theater.

Psychological Influences on Consumer Decision Making

Information from group, marketing, and situational influences affects what consumers think and feel about particular products and brands. However, there are a number of psychological factors that influence how this information is interpreted and used and how it impacts the consumer decision-making process. Two of the most important psychological factors are product knowledge and product involvement.[6]

Product Knowledge

Product knowledge refers to the amount of information a consumer has stored in her or his memory about particular product classes, product forms, brands, models, and ways to purchase them. For example, a consumer may know a lot about coffee (product class), ground versus instant coffee (product form), Folgers versus Maxwell House (brand), and various package sizes (models) and stores that sell it (ways to purchase).

Group, marketing, and situational influences determine the initial level of product knowledge as well as changes in it. For example, a consumer may hear about a new Starbucks opening up from a friend (group influence), see an ad for it in the newspaper (marketing influence), or see the coffee shop on the way to work (situational influence). Any of these increases the amount of product knowledge, in this case, a new source for purchasing the product.

The initial level of product knowledge may influence how much information is sought when deciding to make a purchase. For example, if a consumer already believes that Folgers is the best-tasting coffee, knows where to buy it, and knows how much it costs, little additional information may be sought.

Finally, product knowledge influences how quickly a consumer goes through the decision-making process. For example, when purchasing a new product for which the consumer has little product knowledge, extensive information may be sought and more time may be devoted to the decision.

Product Involvement

Product involvement refers to a consumer's perception of the importance or personal relevance of an item. For example, Harley-Davidson motorcycle owners are generally highly involved in the purchase and use of the product, brand, and accessories. However, a consumer buying a new toothbrush would likely view this as a low-involvement purchase.

Product involvement influences consumer decision making in two ways. First, if the purchase is for a high-involvement product, consumers are likely to develop a high degree of product knowledge so that they can be confident that the item they purchase is just right for them. Second, a high degree of product involvement encourages extensive decision making by consumers, which likely increases the time it takes to go through the decision-making process.

Consumer Decision Making

The process by which consumers make decisions to purchase various products and brands is shown in Figure 3.2. In general, consumers recognize a need for a product, search for information about alternatives to meet the need, evaluate the information, make purchases, and evaluate the decision after the purchase. There are three types of decision making, which vary in terms of how complex or expensive a product is and how involved a consumer is in purchasing it.

Extensive decision making requires the most time and effort since the purchase involves a highly complex or expensive product that is important to the consumer. For example,

FIGURE 3.2   **The Consumer Decision-Making Process**

the purchase of a car, house, or computer often involves considerable time and effort comparing alternatives and deciding on the right one. In terms of the number of purchases a consumer makes, extensive decision making is relatively rare, but it is critical for marketers of highly complex or expensive products to understand that consumers are willing to process considerable information to make the best choice. Thus, marketers should provide consumer factual information that highlights competitive advantages for such high-involvement products.

Limited decision making is more moderate but still involves some time and effort searching for and comparing alternatives. For example, when buying shirts or shorts, consumers may shop several stores and compare a number of different brands and styles. Marketers of products for which consumers usually do limited decision making often use eye-catching advertising and in-store displays to make consumers aware of their products and encourage consumers to consider buying them.

Routine decision making is the most common type and the way consumers purchase most packaged goods. Such products are simple, inexpensive, and familiar; and consumers often have developed favorite brands that they purchase without much deliberation. For example, consumers often make habitual purchases of soft drinks, candy bars, or canned soup without carefully comparing the relative merits of different brands. Marketers of such products need to have them readily available for purchase in a variety of outlets and price them competitively if price is an important criterion to consumers. Marketers of these low-involvement products often use celebrity spokespeople and other non-product-related cues to encourage purchases.

Need Recognition

The starting point in the buying process is the recognition of an unsatisfied need by the consumer. Any number of either internal or external stimuli may activate needs or wants and recognition of them. Internal stimuli are such things as feeling hungry and wanting some food, feeling a headache coming on and wanting some Excedrin, or feeling bored and looking for a movie to go to. External stimuli are such things as seeing a McDonald's sign and then feeling hungry or seeing a sale sign for winter parkas and remembering that last year's coat is worn out.

It is the task of marketing managers to find out what needs and wants a particular product can and does satisfy and what unsatisfied needs and wants consumers have for which a new product could be developed. In order to do so, marketing managers should understand what types of needs consumers may have. A well-known classification of needs was developed many years ago by Abraham Maslow and includes five types.[7] Maslow's view is that lower-level needs, starting with physiological and safety, must be attended to before higher-level needs can be satisfied. Maslow's hierarchy is described below.

Physiological needs. This category consists of the primary needs of the human body, such as food, water, and sex. Physiological needs will dominate when all needs are unsatisfied. In such a case, none of the other needs will serve as a basis for motivation.

Safety needs. With the physiological needs met, the next higher level assumes importance. Safety needs consist of such things as protection from physical harm, ill health, and economic disaster and avoidance of the unexpected.

Belongingness and love needs. These needs are related to the social and gregarious nature of humans and the need for companionship. This level in the hierarchy is the point of departure from the physical or quasi-physical needs of the two previous levels. Nonsatisfaction of this level of need may affect the mental health of the individual.

Esteem needs. These needs consist of both the need for the self-awareness of importance to others (self-esteem) and actual esteem from others. Satisfaction of these needs leads to feelings of self-confidence and prestige.

Self-actualization needs. This need can be defined as the desire to become more and more what one is, to become everything one is capable of becoming. This means that the individual will fully realize the potentialities of given talents and capabilities. Maslow assumes that satisfaction of these needs is only possible after the satisfaction of all the needs lower in the hierarchy.

While the hierarchical arrangement of Maslow presents a convenient explanation, it is probably more realistic to assume that the various need categories overlap. Thus, in affluent societies, many products may satisfy more than one of these needs. For example, gourmet foods may satisfy both the basic physiological need of hunger as well as esteem and status needs for those who serve gourmet foods to their guests.

Alternative Search

Once a need is recognized, the individual then searches for alternatives for satisfying the need. There are five basic sources from which the individual can collect information for a particular purchase decision.

1. *Internal sources.* In most cases the individual has had some previous experience in dealing with a particular need. Thus, the individual will usually "search" through whatever stored information and experience is in his or her mind for dealing with the need. If a previously acceptable product for satisfying the need is remembered, the individual may purchase with little or no additional information search or evaluation. This is quite common for routine or habitual purchases.

2. *Group sources.* A common source of information for purchase decisions comes from communication with other people, such as family, friends, neighbors, and acquaintances. Generally, some of these (i.e., relevant others) are selected that the individual views as having particular expertise for the purchase decision. Although it may be quite difficult for the marketing manager to determine the exact nature of this source of information, group sources of information often are considered to be the most powerful influence on purchase decisions.

3. *Marketing sources.* Marketing sources of information include such factors as advertising, salespeople, dealers, packaging, and displays. Generally, this is the primary source of information about a particular product. These sources of information will be discussed in detail in the promotion chapters of this text.

4. *Public sources.* Public sources of information include publicity, such as a newspaper article about the product, and independent ratings of the product, such as *Consumer Reports*.

The marketing profession has long recognized the need to uphold its integrity, honor, and dignity. Part of this obligation is to treat customers fairly and honestly. In the American Marketing Association Code of Ethics, a number of issues are concerned with this obligation. Below is a list of some of the Code of Ethics responsibilities that bear directly or indirectly on exchanges with consumers and organizational buyers.

PRODUCT DEVELOPMENT AND MANAGEMENT AREA

Products and services offered should be safe and fit for their intended use.

All substantial risks associated with product or service usage should be disclosed.

Product component substitutions that might materially change the product or impact the buyer's decision should be disclosed.

Extra-cost-added features should be identified.

PROMOTION AREA

Communication about offered products and services should not be deceptive.

False and misleading advertising should be avoided.

High-pressure manipulation or misleading sales tactics should be avoided.

Sales promotions that use deception or manipulation should be avoided.

DISTRIBUTION AREA

The availability of a product should not be manipulated for the purpose of exploitation.

Coercion in the marketing channel should not be used.

Undue influence over the resellers' choice to handle products should be avoided.

PRICING AREA

Pricing fixing should not be practiced.

Predatory pricing should not be practiced.

The full price associated with any purchase should be disclosed.

Source: Adapted from the American Marketing Association Code of Ethics.

Here product quality is a highly important marketing management consideration, since such articles and reports often discuss such features as dependability and service requirements.

5. *Experiential sources.* Experiential sources refer to handling, examining, and perhaps trying the product while shopping. This usually requires an actual shopping trip by the individual and may be the final source consulted before purchase.

Information collected from these sources is then processed by the consumer.[8] However, the exact nature of how individuals process information to form evaluations of products is not fully understood. In general, information processing is viewed as a four-step process in which the individual is (1) exposed to information, (2) becomes attentive to the information, (3) understands the information, and (4) retains the information.[9]

Alternative Evaluation

During the process of collecting information or, in some cases, after information is acquired, the consumer evaluates alternatives on the basis of what he or she has learned. One approach to describing the evaluation process is as follows:

1. The consumer has information about a number of brands in a product class.

2. The consumer perceives that at least some of the brands in a product class are viable alternatives for satisfying a recognized need.

3. Each of these brands has a set of attributes (color, quality, size, and so forth).

4. A set of these attributes is relevant to the consumer, and the consumer perceives that different brands vary in how much of each attribute they possess.

5. The brand that is perceived as offering the greatest number of desired attributes in the desired amounts and desired order will be the brand the consumer will like best.

6. The brand the consumer likes best is the brand the consumer will intend to purchase.[10]

Purchase Decision

If no other factors intervene after the consumer has decided on the brand that is intended for purchase, the actual purchase is a common result of search and evaluation. Actually, a purchase involves many decisions, which include product type, brand, model, dealer selection, and method of payment, among other factors. In addition, rather than purchasing, the consumer may make a decision to modify, postpone, or avoid purchase based on an inhibitor to purchase or a perceived risk.

Traditional risk theorists believe that consumers tend to make risk-minimizing decisions based on their *perceived* definition of the particular purchase. The perception of risk is based on the possible consequences and uncertainties involved. Consequences may range from economic loss, to embarrassment if a new food product does not turn out well, to actual physical harm. Perceived risk may be either functional (related to financial and performance considerations) or psychosocial (related to whether the product will further one's self- or reference-group image). The amount of risk a consumer perceives in a particular product depends on such things as the price of the product and whether other people will see the individual using it.

The perceived risk literature emphasizes that consumers generally try to reduce risk in their decision making. This can be done by either reducing the possible negative consequences or by reducing the uncertainty. The possible consequences of a purchase might be minimized by purchasing in small quantities or by lowering the individual's aspiration level to expect less in the way of results from the product. However, this cannot always be done. Thus, reducing risk by attempting to increase the certainty of the purchase outcome may be the more widely used strategy. This can be done by seeking additional information regarding the proposed purchase. In general, the more information the consumer collects prior to purchase, the less likely postpurchase dissonance is to occur.

Postpurchase Evaluation

In general, if the individual finds that a certain response achieves a desired goal or satisfies a need, the success of this cue-response pattern will be remembered. The probability of responding in a like manner to the same or similar situation in the future is increased. In other words, the response has a higher probability of being repeated when the need and cue appear together again, and thus it can be said that learning has taken place. Frequent reinforcement increases the habit potential of the particular response. Likewise, if a response does not satisfy the need adequately, the probability that the same response will be repeated is reduced.

For some marketers this means that if an individual finds that a particular product fulfills the need for which it was purchased, the probability is high that the individual will repurchase the product the next time the need arises. The firm's promotional efforts often act as the cue. If an individual repeatedly purchases a product with favorable results, loyalty may develop toward the particular product or brand. This loyalty can result in habitual purchases, and such habits are often extremely difficult for competing firms to alter.

Although many studies in the area of buyer behavior center on the buyer's attitudes, motives, and behavior before and during the purchase decision, emphasis has also been given

Influencing Factor	Increasing the Influencing Factor Causes the Search to:
I. Market characteristics	
A. Number of alternatives	Increase
B. Price range	Increase
C. Store concentration	Increase
D. Information availability	Increase
1. Advertising	
2. Point-of-purchase	
3. Sales personnel	
4. Packaging	
5. Experienced consumers	
6. Independent sources	
II. Product characteristics	
A. Price	Increase
B. Differentiation	Increase
C. Positive products	Increase
III. Consumer characteristics	
A. Learning and experience	Decrease
B. Shopping orientation	Mixed
C. Social status	Increase
D. Age, gender, and household life cycle	Mixed
E. Product involvement	Mixed
F. Perceived risk	Increase
IV. Situational characteristics	
A. Time availability	Increase
B. Purchase for self	Decrease
C. Pleasant surroundings	Increase
D. Social surroundings	Mixed
E. Physical/mental energy	Increase

Source: Del I. Hawkins, Kenneth A. Coney, and Roger Best, Jr., *Consumer Behavior: Implications for Marketing Strategy*, 9th ed. (Burr Ridge, IL: Irwin/McGraw-Hill, 2004), p. 539.

to study of behavior after the purchase. Specifically, studies have been undertaken to investigate postpurchase dissonance, as well as postpurchase satisfaction.

The occurrence of postdecision dissonance is related to the concept of *cognitive dissonance*. This theory states that there is often a lack of consistency or harmony among an individual's various cognitions, or attitudes and beliefs, after a decision has been made—that is, the individual has doubts and second thoughts about the choice made. Further, it is more likely that the intensity of the anxiety will be greater when any of the following conditions exist:

1. The decision is an important one psychologically or financially, or both.

2. There are a number of forgone alternatives.

3. The forgone alternatives have many favorable features.

These factors can relate to many buying decisions. For example, postpurchase dissonance might be expected to be present among many purchasers of such products as automobiles, major appliances, and homes. In these cases, the decision to purchase is usually an important one both financially and psychologically, and there are usually a number of favorable alternatives available.

These findings have much relevance for marketers. In a buying situation, when a purchaser becomes dissonant, it is reasonable to predict such a person would be highly receptive to advertising and sales promotion that support the purchase decision. Such communication presents favorable aspects of the product and can be useful in reinforcing the buyer's wish to believe that a wise purchase decision was made. For example, purchasers of major appliances or automobiles might be given a phone call or sent a letter reassuring them that they have made a wise purchase.

As noted, researchers have also studied postpurchase consumer satisfaction. Much of this work has been based on what is called the *disconfirmation paradigm*. Basically, this approach views satisfaction with products and brands as a result of two other variables. The first variable is the expectations a consumer has about a product before purchase. These expectations concern the beliefs the consumer has about the product's performance.

The second variable is the difference between expectations and postpurchase perceptions of how the product actually performed. If the product performed as well as expected or better than expected, the consumer will be satisfied with the product. If the product performed worse than expected, the consumer will be dissatisfied with it.

One implication of this view for marketers is that care must be taken not to raise prepurchase expectations to such a level that the product cannot possibly meet them. Rather, it is important to create positive expectations consistent with the product's likely performance.[11]

Conclusion

This chapter presented an overview of consumer behavior. Social, marketing, and situational influences on consumer decision making were discussed first, followed by a discussion of two important psychological factors: product knowledge and product involvement. Consumer decision making, which can be extensive, limited, or routine, was viewed as a series of stages: need recognition, alternative search, alternative evaluation, purchase decision, and postpurchase evaluation. Clearly, understanding consumer behavior is a prerequisite for developing successful marketing strategies.

Additional Readings

Hawkins, Del; Kenneth A. Coney; and Roger Best, Jr. *Consumer Behavior: Building Marketing Strategy*. 9th ed. Burr Ridge, IL: Irwin/McGraw-Hill, 2004.

Hoyer, Wayne D., and Deborah J. MacInnis. *Consumer Behavior*. Boston: Houghton Mifflin, 1997.

Kardes, Frank R. *Consumer Behavior and Managerial Decision Making*. Reading, MA: Addison-Wesley, 1999.

Mowen, John C., and Michael Minor. *Consumer Behavior*. 5th ed. New York: Macmillan Publishing, 1998.

Peter, J. Paul, and Jerry C. Olson. *Consumer Behavior and Marketing Strategy*. 7th ed. Burr Ridge, IL: Irwin/McGraw-Hill, 2005.

Schiffman, Leon G., and Leslie Kanuck. *Consumer Behavior*. 8th ed. Englewood Cliffs, NJ: Prentice Hall, 2004.

Solomon, Michael R. *Consumer Behavior*. 6th ed. Boston: Allyn & Bacon, 2004.

Appendix

Selected Consumer Behavior Data Sources

1. Demographic Information
   U.S. Census of Population,
   http://www.census.gov.
   Marketing Information Guide.
   A Guide to Consumer Markets.
   State and city government publications.
   Media (newspapers, magazines, television, and radio
   stations) make demographic data about their readers or
   audiences available.

2. Consumer Research Findings
   Advances in Consumer Research
   American Demographics
   Journal of the Academy of Marketing Science
   Journal of Advertising
   Journal of Advertising Research
   Journal of Applied Psychology
   Journal of Consumer Psychology
   Journal of Consumer Research
   Journal of Marketing
   Journal of Marketing Research
   Marketing Science

3. Marketing Applications
   Advertising Age
   BusinessWeek
   Forbes
   Fortune
   Marketing Communications
   Nation's Business
   Sales & Marketing Management

Chapter

Business, Government, and Institutional Buying

In the previous chapter we discussed consumer behavior and the decision-making process used to purchase products and services. However, final consumers are not the only purchasers of products and services. Rather, businesses, government agencies, and other institutions buy products and services to maintain their organizations and achieve their organizational objectives. These organizations are major customers for many marketers. In this chapter we discuss the nature of these organizations and offer a general model of the buying process for them. The chapter begins by discussing four categories of organizational buyers and then presents an overview of the organizational buying process.

Categories of Organizational Buyers

Organizational buyers can be classified in many ways. For example, the U.S. government classifies organizations in similar lines of business in the North American Industry Classification System (NAICS, pronounced "nakes"). NAICS provides information about the number of establishments, sales volume, and number of employees in each industry broken down by geographic area. Information on NAICS codes is available online at www.naics.com. In addition, a commercial source, Dun's Business Locator, provides information on over 10 million U.S. businesses. Both of these can provide useful information for organizational marketers seeking organizational buyers. However, for the purpose of this text, it is useful to classify organizational buyers into four categories: These include producers, intermediaries, government agencies, and other institutions. Taken collectively, marketing to producers and intermediaries is called *business-to-business* or *b2b marketing*. Business-to-business marketing has become a topic of increasing interest because it is the major area where Internet marketing has been done profitably.

Producers

These organizational buyers consist of businesses that buy goods and services in order to produce other goods and services for sale. For example, Dell Computer buys computer chips from Intel in order to make computers to be sold to consumers and other organizations. Producers are engaged in many different industries, ranging from agriculture to manufacturing, from construction to finance. Together they constitute the largest segment of organizational buyers. Producers of goods tend to be larger and more geographically concentrated than producers of services.

Intermediaries

Marketing intermediaries or resellers purchase products to resell at a profit. This group includes a number of types of resellers such as wholesalers (Grainger) and retailers (Wal-Mart) that buy products from manufacturers and distribute them to consumers and other organizational buyers. Intermediaries also purchase products and services to run their own businesses, such as office supplies and maintenance services. Given their importance to marketing, intermediaries will be discussed in detail in Chapter 10.

Government Agencies

In the United States, government agencies operate at the federal, state, and local levels; there are over 86,000 governmental agencies in this country that purchase machinery, equipment, facilities, supplies, and services. Government agencies account for trillions of dollars worth of buying, and over half of this amount represents purchases by the federal government, making it the world's biggest customer. The governments of other countries also are huge customers for marketers. Marketing to government agencies can be complex since they often have strict purchasing policies and regulations.

Other Institutions

Besides businesses and government agencies, marketers also sell products and services to a variety of other institutions, such as hospitals, museums, universities, nursing homes, and churches. Many of these are nonprofit organizations that purchase products and services to maintain their operations and serve their clientele.

The Organizational Buying Process

Regardless of the type of organization, a buying process is needed to ensure that products and services are purchased and received in a timely and efficient manner. In general, organizations develop a buying process to serve their purchasing needs. Figure 4.1 presents a model of organizational buying that represents some of the common influences and stages in the process.

FIGURE 4.1 **A Model of the Organizational Buying Process**

Purchase-Type Influences on Organizational Buying

A major consideration that affects the organizational buying process is the complexity of the purchase that is to be made. Three types of organizational purchase based on their degree of complexity include the straight rebuy, modified rebuy, and new task purchase.[1]

Straight Rebuy

The simplest and most common type of purchase is called a *straight rebuy*. This type of purchase involves routinely reordering from the same supplier a product that has been purchased in the past. Organizations use a straight rebuy when they are experienced at buying the product, have an ongoing need for it, and have regular suppliers of it. In many cases, organizations have computer systems that automatically reorder certain commonly used products. Organizations use this simple approach to purchasing because it is fast and requires relatively few employees.

Straight rebuys are common among organizations that practice *just-in-time inventory,* which is a system of replenishing parts or goods for resale just before they are needed. Such buyers do not have time to hunt around for potential suppliers and solicit bids. Instead they regularly place their orders with a supplier whose quality and timely delivery can be counted on. If a supplier delivers items that are late or of unacceptable quality, these buyers will not have a reserve in inventory to draw on. Therefore, organizations that use just-in-time inventory tend to favor suppliers with a strong commitment to quality.

To retain customers who use straight rebuys, the marketer needs to maintain high-quality products and reliable service so that the customers will continue to be satisfied with their purchases.

Modified Rebuy

When some aspects of the buying situation are unfamiliar, the organization will use a *modified rebuy*. This type of purchase involves considering a limited number of alternatives before making a selection. Organizational buyers follow this approach rather than a straight rebuy when a routine purchase changes in some way; for example, a supplier discontinues a product or stops satisfying the customer, the price of a usual product rises, or a new product becomes available to meet the same need.

In such situations, the organizational buyer considers the new information and decides what changes to make. If the change proves satisfactory and the product is one needed routinely, the buyer may then make it a straight rebuy. Marketers seek to win new organizational customers by giving them reasons to change from a straight rebuy to a modified rebuy in which the marketer's products are considered.

New Task Purchase

Organizations purchase some products only occasionally, especially in the case of large investments such as machinery, equipment, and real estate. In these cases, the organization may use a *new task purchase*. This type of purchase involves an extensive search for information and a formal decision process.

New task purchases are most often used for big-ticket items, so the cost of a mistake is great. Therefore, a new task purchase is time consuming and involves a relatively large number of decision makers, who may consider many alternatives. This is the type of purchase decision that is most likely to involve joint decision making because many kinds of expertise are required to make the best decision.

FIGURE 4.2   **Differences in Types of Organizational Purchases**

Purchase Type	Complexity	Time Frame	Number of Suppliers	Applications
Straight rebuy	Simple	Short	One	Frequently purchased, routine products, such as printer paper and toner.
Modified rebuy	Moderate	Medium	Few	Routine purchase that has changed in some way, such as air travel (new fares, flights, destinations).
New task purchase	Complex	Long	Many	Expensive, seldom-purchased products, such as a new location for a department store.

A new task purchase is an opportunity for the marketer to learn about the needs of the organizations in its target market and to discuss ways to meet organizational needs, such as through the use of new products and technology. Figure 4.2 summarizes the differences in the three types of purchases.

Structural Influences on Organizational Buying

The term *structural influences* refers to the design of the organizational environment and how it affects the purchasing process. Three important structural influences on organizational buying are purchasing roles, organization-specific factors, and purchasing policies and procedures.

Purchasing Roles

It is common in organizational buying for purchases to be made cross-functionally with representatives from different functional departments playing various roles in the process. Taken collectively, these are called *the buying center* and include the following roles:

1. *Initiators,* who start the purchasing process by recognizing a need or problem in the organization. For example, an executive might see a need for faster computers.
2. *Users,* who are the people in the organization who actually use the product, for example, an assistant who would use a new word processor.
3. *Influencers,* who affect the buying decision, usually by helping define the specifications for what is bought. For example, an information systems manager would be a key influencer in the purchase of a new computer system.
4. *Buyers,* who have the formal authority and responsibility to select the supplier and negotiate the terms of the contract. For example, in the purchase of a computer system, the *purchasing agent* would likely perform this role.
5. *Deciders,* who have the formal or informal power to select or approve the supplier that receives the contract. For important technical purchases, deciders may come from R&D, engineering, or quality control.
6. *Gatekeepers,* who control the flow of information in the buying center. Purchasing personnel, technical experts, and assistants can all keep marketers and their information from reaching people performing the other four roles.[2]

When several persons are involved in the organizational purchase decision, marketers may need to use a variety of means to reach each individual or group. Fortunately, it is often easy to find which individuals in organizations are involved in a purchase because such information is provided to suppliers. Organizations do this because it makes suppliers more

How Marketing to Organizational Buyers Differs	Example
More variation in buyer-seller relationships	Relationships can be deep and involve several layers of the industry: BASF partners with Gaskell and GM, for example.
Shorter distribution channels	BASF sells fibers *direct* to DuPont for the manufacture of carpet; through distributors to smaller companies—consumer goods sold through distributors, wholesalers, and retailers.
Greater emphasis on personal selling	BASF salespeople work directly with fire departments to sell the latest fire-fighting chemicals and ensure that they are used properly.
Greater Web integration	BASF uses its *cc-markets* Web site to create a communication space with special customers.
Unique promotional strategies	BASF exhibits at trade shows such as Powder Coatings Europe, a show held every January in Amsterdam.

Source: F. Robert Dwyer and John F. Tanner, *Business Marketing,* 2nd ed. (Burr Ridge, IL: McGraw-Hill/Irwin, 2002), p. 11.

knowledgeable about purchasing practices, thus making the purchasing process more efficient.[3] Also, a number of firms have developed closer channel relationships that facilitate these transactions.

Organization-Specific Factors

Three primary organization-specific factors influence the purchasing process: orientation, size, and degree of centralization. First, in terms of orientation, the dominant function in an organization may control purchasing decisions. For example, if the organization is technology oriented, it is likely to be dominated by engineering personnel, and buying decisions will be made by them. Similarly, if the organization is production oriented, production personnel may dominate buying decisions.

Second, the size of the organization may influence the purchasing process. If the organization is large, it will likely have a high degree of joint decision making for other than straight rebuys. Smaller organizations are likely to have more autonomous decision making.

Finally, the degree of centralization of an organization influences whether decisions are made individually or jointly with others. Organizations that are highly centralized are less likely to have joint decision making. Thus, a privately owned, small company with technology or production orientations will tend toward autonomous decision making, while a large-scale public corporation with considerable decentralization will tend to have greater joint decision making.

Purchasing Policies and Procedures

Organizations typically develop a number of policies and procedures for various types of purchases. These policies and procedures are designed to ensure that the appropriate products and services are purchased efficiently and that responsibility for buying is assigned appropriately. Often a purchasing department will be assigned the task of centralized buying for the whole organization, and individuals within this department will have authority to purchase particular types of products and services in a given price range.

A current trend in many organizations is *sole sourcing,* in which all of a particular type of product is purchased from a single supplier. Sole sourcing has become more popular because organizational buyers have become more concerned with quality and timely delivery and less likely to purchase only on the basis of price. Sole sourcing is advantageous for suppliers because it provides them with predictable and profitable demand and allows them to build long-term relationships with organizational buyers. It is advantageous for organizational buyers because it not only increases timely delivery and quality of supplies but also allows the buyers to work more closely with suppliers to develop superior products that meet their needs and those of their customers. The use of sole sourcing also simplifies the buying process and can make what were formerly modified rebuys into simpler straight rebuys.

Of course, many organizational purchases are more complicated and require policies and procedures to direct the buying process. In many cases, organizations will develop a list of approved vendors from which buyers have authorization to purchase particular products. The buyer's responsibility is to select the vendor that will provide the appropriate levels of quality and service at the lowest cost. These policies and procedures also specify what positions in the purchasing department or buying center have authority to make purchases of different types and dollar amounts.

For large one-time projects, such as the construction of a building, organizations may seek competitive bids for part or all of the project. The development of policies and procedures for handling such purchases is usually complex and involves a number of criteria and committees.

Behavioral Influences on Organizational Buying

Organizational buyers are influenced by a variety of psychological and social factors. We will discuss two of these, personal motivations and role perceptions.

Personal Motivations

Organizational buyers are, of course, subject to the same personal motives or motivational forces as other individuals. Although these buyers may emphasize nonpersonal motives in their buying activities, it has been found that organizational buyers often are influenced by such personal factors as friendship, professional pride, fear and uncertainty (risk), trust, and personal ambitions in their buying activities.

For example, professional pride often expresses itself through efforts to attain status in the firm. One way to achieve this might be to initiate or influence the purchase of goods that will demonstrate a buyer's value to the organization. If new materials, equipment, or components result in cost savings or increased profits, the individuals initiating the changes have demonstrated their value at the same time. Fear and uncertainty are strong motivational forces on organizational buyers, and reduction of risk is often important to them. This can have a strong influence on purchase behavior. Marketers should understand the relative strength of personal gain versus risk-reducing motives and emphasize the more important motives when dealing with buyers.

Thus, in examining buyer motivations, it is necessary to consider both personal and nonpersonal motivational forces and to recognize that the relative importance of each is not a fixed quantity. It will vary with the nature of the product, the climate within the organization, and the relative strength of the two forces in the particular buyer.

Role Perceptions

A final factor that influences organizational buyers is their own perception of their role. The manner in which individuals behave depends on their perception of their role, their

1. Is the need or problem pressing enough that it must be acted on now? If not, how long can action be deferred?
2. What types of products or services could conceivably be used to solve our need or problem?
3. Should we make the item ourselves?
4. Must a new product be designed, or has a vendor already developed an acceptable product?
5. Should a value analysis be performed?
6. What is the highest price we can afford to pay?
7. What trade-offs are we prepared to make between price and other product/vendor attributes?
8. Which information sources will we rely on?
9. How many vendors should be considered?
10. Which attributes will be stressed in evaluating vendors?
11. Should bids be solicited?
12. Should the item be leased or purchased outright?
13. How far can a given vendor be pushed in negotiations? On what issues will that vendor bend the most?
14. How much inventory should a vendor be willing to keep on hand?
15. Should we split our order among several vendors?
16. Is a long-term contract in our interest?
17. What contractual guarantees will we require?
18. How shall we establish our order routine?
19. After the purchase, how will vendor performance be evaluated?
20. How will we deal with inadequate product or vendor performance?

Source: Michael H. Morris, Leyland F. Pitt, and Earl D. Honeycutt, Jr., *Business-to-Business Marketing,* 3rd ed. (Thousand Oaks, CA: Sage Publications, 2001), p. 74.

commitment to what they believe is expected of their role, the "maturity" of the role type, and the extent to which the institution is committed to the role type.

Different buyers will have different degrees of commitment to their buying role, which will cause variations in role behavior from one buyer to the next. By *commitment* we mean willingness to perform their job in the manner expected by the organization. For example, some buyers seek to take charge in their role as buyer and have little commitment to company expectations. The implication for marketers is that such buyers expect, even demand, that they be kept constantly advised of all new developments to enable them to more effectively shape their own role. On the other hand, other buyers may have no interest in prescribing their role activities and accept their role as given to them. Such a buyer is most concerned with merely implementing prescribed company activities and buying policies with sanctioned products. Thus, some buyers will be highly committed to play the role the firm dictates (i.e., the formal organization's perception of their role), while others might be extremely innovative and uncommitted to the expected role performance. Obviously, roles may be heavily influenced by the organizational climate existing in the particular organization.[4]

Organizations can be divided into three groups based on differences in degree of employee commitment. These groups include innovative, adaptive, and lethargic firms. In

1. Avoid the intent and appearance of unethical or compromising practice in relationships, actions, and communications.
2. Demonstrate loyalty to the employer by diligently following the lawful instructions of the employer, using reasonable care and only the authority granted.
3. Refrain from any private or professional business activity that would create a conflict between personal interests and the interests of the employer.
4. Refrain from soliciting or accepting money, loans, credits, or prejudicial discounts and the acceptance of gifts, entertainment, favors, or services from past or potential suppliers that might influence or appear to influence purchasing decisions.
5. Handle confidential or proprietary information belonging to employers or suppliers with due care and proper consideration of ethical and legal ramifications and government regulations.
6. Promote positive supplier relationships through courtesy and impartiality throughout all phases of the purchasing cycle.
7. Refrain from reciprocal agreements that restrain competition.
8. Know and obey the letter and spirit of laws governing the purchasing function and remain alert to the legal ramifications of purchasing decisions.
9. Encourage all segments of society to participate by demonstrating support for small, disadvantaged, and minority-owned businesses.
10. Discourage purchasing's involvement in employer-sponsored programs of personal purchases that are not business related.
11. Enhance the proficiency and stature of the purchasing profession by acquiring and maintaining current technical knowledge and the highest standards of ethical behavior.
12. Conduct international purchasing in accordance with the laws, customs, and practices of foreign countries, consistent with U.S. laws, your organization's policies, and these Ethical Standards and Guidelines.

Source: National Association of Purchasing Managers as reported in F. Robert Dwyer and John F. Tanner, *Business Marketing,* 2nd ed. (Burr Ridge, IL: McGraw-Hill/Irwin, 2002), p. 88.

innovative firms, individuals approach their occupational roles with a weak commitment to expected norms of behavior. In an *adaptive organization,* there is a moderate commitment. In a *lethargic organization,* individuals express a strong commitment to traditionally accepted behavior and behave accordingly. Thus, a buyer in a lethargic firm would probably be less innovative in order to maintain acceptance and status within the organization and would keep conflict within the firm to a minimum.

Buyers' perception of their role may differ from the perception of their role held by others in the organization. This difference can result in variance in perception of the actual purchase responsibility held by the buyer. One study involving purchasing agents revealed that, in every firm included in the study, the purchasing agents believed they had more responsibility and control over certain decisions than the other influential purchase decision makers in the firm perceived them as having. The decisions were (1) design of the product, (2) cost of the product, (3) performance life, (4) naming of the specific supplier, (5) assessing the amount of engineering help available from the supplier, and (6) reduction of rejects. This variance in role perception held true regardless of the size of the firm or the significance of the item purchased to the overall success of the firm. It is important, therefore, that the marketer be aware that such perceptual differences may exist and to determine as accurately as possible the amount of control and responsibility over purchasing decisions held by each purchase decision influencer in the firm.

Stages in the Organizational Buying Process

As with consumer buying, most organizational purchases are made in response to a particular need or problem. Ideally, the products or services purchased will meet the organizational need and improve the organization's efficiency, effectiveness, and profits. The organizational buying process can be analyzed as a series of four stages: organizational need, vendor analysis, purchase activities, and postpurchase evaluation.

Organizational Need

Organizations have many needs for products and services to help them survive and meet their objectives. For example, a manufacturer may need to purchase new machinery to increase its production capacity and meet demand; a retailer may need to purchase services from a marketing research firm to better understand its market; a government agency may need to purchase faster computers to keep up with growing demand for its services; a hospital may need to purchase more comfortable beds for its patients. Recognizing these needs, and a willingness and ability to meet them, often results in organizational purchases. For straight rebuys, the purchase process may involve little more than a phone call or a few clicks on a computer to order products and arrange payment and delivery. For modified rebuys or new task purchases, the process may be much more complex.

Vendor Analysis

Organizational buyers must search for, locate, and evaluate vendors of products and services to meet their needs. Searching for and locating vendors is often easy since they frequently make sales calls on organizations that might need their products. Vendors also advertise in trade magazines or on the Internet and have displays at industry trade shows to increase their visibility to organizational buyers. For products and services that the organization has previously purchased, a list of approved vendors may have already been developed by the organization.

Organizational buyers often use a vendor analysis to evaluate possible suppliers. A *vendor analysis* is the process by which buyers rate each potential supplier on various performance measures such as product quality, on-time delivery, price, payment terms, and use of modern technology. Figure 4.3 presents a sample vendor analysis form that lists a number of purchase criteria and the weights one organization used to compare potential suppliers.

A formal vendor analysis can be used for at least three purposes. First, it can be used to develop a list of approved vendors, all of which provide acceptable levels of products and services. Organizational buyers can then select any company on the list, simplifying the purchase process. Second, a vendor analysis could be used to compare competing vendors; the buyers then select the best one on the basis of the ratings. This could help the organization pare down vendors to a single supplier for which a long-term, sole-sourcing relationship could be developed. Third, a vendor analysis can be done both before and after purchases to compare performance on evaluation criteria and evaluate the process of vendor selection.

Purchase Activities

Straight rebuys may involve a quick order to an approved vendor or sole-source supplier. However, other types of organizational purchases can involve long time periods with extensive negotiations on price and terms and formal contracts stating quality, delivery, and service criteria. The complexity of the product or service, the number of suppliers available, the importance of the product to the buying organization, and pricing all influence the number of purchase activities to be performed and their difficulty. For example, an airline buying a fleet of jumbo jets or a car rental agency buying a fleet of cars may take months or years to negotiate and make purchases. While such buyers may have considerable

FIGURE 4.3   Sample Vendor Analysis Form

	5 Excellent	4 Good	3 Satisfactory	2 Fair	1 Poor	0 N/A

Supplier Name: _____   Type of Product: _____

Shipping Location: _____   Annual Sales Dollars: _____

	5 Excellent	4 Good	3 Satisfactory	2 Fair	1 Poor	0 N/A
Quality (45%)						
Defect rates	—	—	—	—	—	—
Quality of sample	—	—	—	—	—	—
Conformance with quality program	—	—	—	—	—	—
Responsiveness to quality problems	—	—	—	—	—	—
Overall quality	—	—	—	—	—	—
Delivery (25%)						
Avoidance of late shipments	—	—	—	—	—	—
Ability to expand production	—	—	—	—	—	—
Performance in sample delivery	—	—	—	—	—	—
Response to changes in order size	—	—	—	—	—	—
Overall delivery	—	—	—	—	—	—
Price (20%)						
Price competitiveness	—	—	—	—	—	—
Payment terms	—	—	—	—	—	—
Absorption of costs	—	—	—	—	—	—
Submission of cost savings plans	—	—	—	—	—	—
Overall price	—	—	—	—	—	—
Technology (10%)						
State-of-the-art components	—	—	—	—	—	—
Sharing research & development capability	—	—	—	—	—	—
Ability and willingness to help with design	—	—	—	—	—	—
Responsiveness to engineering problems	—	—	—	—	—	—
Overall technology	—	—	—	—	—	—

Buyer: _____   Date: _____

Comments: _____

leverage in negotiating, it should be remembered that these organizations need the products just as badly as the sellers need to sell them. Thus, there is often more collaboration among organizational buyers and sellers than in the consumer market.

Postpurchase Evaluation

Organizational buyers must evaluate both the vendors and the products they purchase to determine whether the products are acceptable for future purchases or whether other sources of supply should be found. A comparison of the performance of the vendor and products with the criteria listed on the prior vendor analysis can be useful for this purpose. If the purchase process goes smoothly and products meet price and quality criteria, then the

FIGURE 4.4
Functional Areas and Their Key Concerns in Organizational Buying

Source: Michael H. Morris, Leyland F. Pitt, and Earl D. Honeycutt, Jr., *Business-to-Business Marketing*, 3rd ed. (Thousand Oaks, CA: Sage Publications, 2001), p. 66.

Functional Areas	Key Concerns
Design and development engineering	Name reputation of vendor; ability of vendors to meet design specifications.
Production	Delivery and reliability of purchases such that interruption of production schedules is minimized.
Sales/marketing	Impact of purchased items on marketability of the company's products.
Maintenance	Degree to which purchased items are compatible with existing facilities and equipment; maintenance service offered by vendor; installation arrangements offered by vendor.
Finance/accounting	Effects of purchases on cash flow, balance sheet, and income statement positions; variances in costs of materials over estimates; feasibility of make-or-buy and lease options to purchasing.
Purchasing	Obtaining lowest possible price at acceptable quality levels; maintaining good relations with vendors.
Quality control	Assurance that purchased items meet prescribed specifications and tolerances, governmental regulations, and customer requirements.

vendor may be put on the approved list or perhaps further negotiations can be made to sole-source with the supplier.

One problem in judging the acceptability of suppliers and products is that different functional areas may have different evaluation criteria. Figure 4.4 presents several functional areas of a manufacturing company and their common concerns in purchasing. Clearly, these concerns should be considered both prior to purchasing from a particular supplier and after purchasing to ensure that every area's needs are being met as well as possible.

Conclusion

Organizational buyers include individuals involved in purchasing products and services for businesses, government agencies, and other institutions and agencies. The organizational buying process is influenced by whether the purchase is a straight rebuy, modified rebuy, or new task purchase. It is also influenced by people in various purchasing roles, the orientation, size, and degree of centralization of the organization, the organization's purchasing policies and procedures, and individuals' motivations and perceived roles. The organizational buying process can be viewed as a series of four stages ranging from organizational need, to vendor analysis, to purchase activities, to postpurchase evaluation. It is important for companies marketing to organizations to understand the influences and process by which organizations buy products and services so that their needs can be met fully and profitably.

Additional Readings

Anderson, James C., and James A. Narus. *Business Market Management*. Upper Saddle River, NJ: Prentice Hall, 1999.

Dwyer, F. Robert, and John F. Tanner. *Business Marketing*. 2nd ed. Burr Ridge, IL: McGraw-Hill/Irwin, 2002.

Morris, Michael H; Leyland F. Pitt; and Earl D. Honeycutt. *Business-to-Business Marketing*. 3rd ed. Thousand Oaks, CA: Sage Publications, 2001.

Reid, David A., and Richard E. Plank. "Business Marketing Comes of Age: A Comprehensive Review of the Literature." *Journal of Business-to-Business Marketing* 7 (213), 2000, pp. 9–185.

Chapter 5

Market Segmentation

Market segmentation is one of the most important concepts in marketing. In fact, a primary reason for studying consumer and organizational buyer behavior is to provide bases for effective segmentation, and a large portion of marketing research is concerned with segmentation. From a marketing management point of view, selection of the appropriate target market is paramount to developing successful marketing programs.

The logic of market segmentation is quite simple and is based on the idea that a single product item can seldom meet the needs and wants of *all* consumers. Typically, consumers vary as to their needs, wants, and preferences for products and services, and successful marketers adapt their marketing programs to fulfill these preference patterns. For example, even a simple product like chewing gum has multiple flavors, package sizes, sugar contents, calories, consistencies (e.g., liquid centers), and colors to meet the preferences of various consumers. While a single product item cannot meet the needs of all consumers, it can almost always serve more than one consumer. Thus, there are usually *groups of consumers* who can be served well by a single item. If a particular group can be served *profitably* by a firm, it is a viable market segment. In other words, the firm should develop a marketing mix to serve the group or market segment.

In this chapter we consider the process of market segmentation. We define *market segmentation* as the process of dividing a market into groups of similar consumers and selecting the most appropriate group(s) for the firm to serve. The group or market segment that a company selects to focus on is called a *target market*. We break down the process of market segmentation into six steps, as shown in Figure 5.1. While we recognize that the order of these steps may vary, depending on the firm and situation, there are few if any times when market segmentation analysis can be ignored. In fact, even if the final decision is to "mass market" and not segment at all, this decision should be reached only *after* a market segmentation analysis has been conducted. Thus, market segmentation analysis is a cornerstone of sound marketing planning and decision making.

Delineate the Firm's Current Situation

As emphasized in Chapter 1, a firm must do a complete situational analysis when embarking on a new or modified marketing program. At the marketing planning level, such an analysis aids in determining objectives, opportunities, and constraints to be considered when selecting target markets and developing marketing mixes. In addition, marketing managers must have a clear idea of the amount of financial and other resources that will be available for developing and executing a marketing plan. Thus, the inclusion of this first step in the market segmentation process is intended to be a reminder of tasks to be performed prior to marketing planning.

FIGURE 5.1
A Model of the Market Segmentation Process

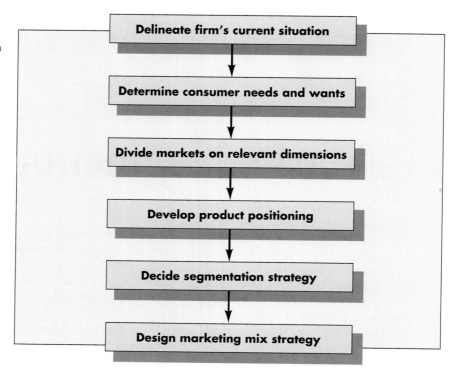

Delineate firm's current situation

Determine consumer needs and wants

Divide markets on relevant dimensions

Develop product positioning

Decide segmentation strategy

Design marketing mix strategy

Determine Consumer Needs and Wants

As emphasized throughout this text, successful marketing strategies depend on discovering and satisfying consumer needs and wants. In some cases, this idea is quite operational. To illustrate, suppose a firm has a good deal of venture capital and is seeking to diversify its interest into new markets. A firm in this situation may seek to discover a broad variety of unsatisfied needs. However, in most situations, the industry in which the firm operates specifies the boundaries of a firm's need satisfaction activities. For example, a firm in the communication industry may seek more efficient methods for serving consumers' long-distance telephone needs.

As a practical matter, new technology often brings about an investigation of consumer needs and wants for new or modified products and services. In these situations, the firm is seeking the group of consumers whose needs could best be satisfied by the new or modified product. Further, at a strategic level, consumer needs and wants usually are translated into more operational concepts. For instance, consumer attitudes, preferences, and benefits sought, which are determined through marketing research, are commonly used for segmentation purposes.

Divide Markets on Relevant Dimensions

In a narrow sense, this step is often considered to be the whole of market segmentation (i.e., consumers are grouped on the basis of one or more similarities and treated as a homogeneous segment of a heterogeneous total market). There are three important questions to be considered here:

1. Should the segmentation be a priori or post hoc?
2. How does one determine the relevant dimensions or bases to use for segmentation?
3. What are some bases for segmenting consumer and organizational buyer markets?

Forrester Research Inc. and NPD Group conducted marketing research to determine the profiles of customers in the market for high-tech products. The study polled 131,000 people about their motivations, buying habits, and financial ability to purchase high-tech products. The study identified 10 market segments. Marketers of high-tech products could use these to select the best target markets for their offerings.

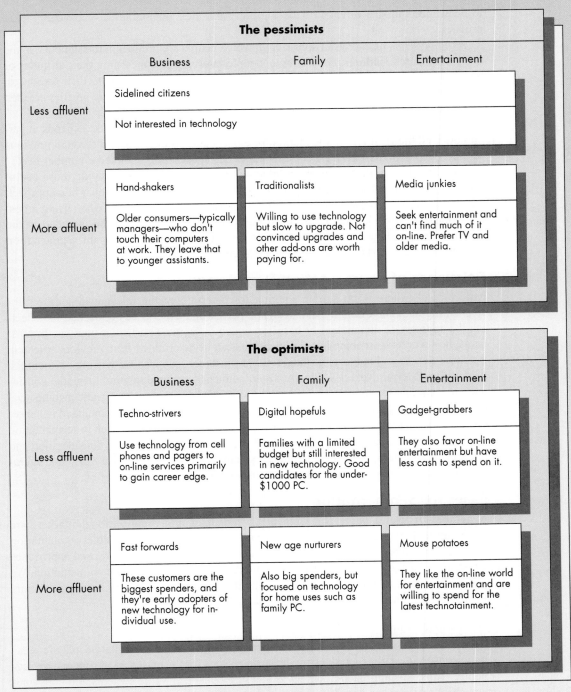

The pessimists

	Business	Family	Entertainment
Less affluent	Sidelined citizens — Not interested in technology		
More affluent	**Hand-shakers** — Older consumers—typically managers—who don't touch their computers at work. They leave that to younger assistants.	**Traditionalists** — Willing to use technology but slow to upgrade. Not convinced upgrades and other add-ons are worth paying for.	**Media junkies** — Seek entertainment and can't find much of it on-line. Prefer TV and older media.

The optimists

	Business	Family	Entertainment
Less affluent	**Techno-strivers** — Use technology from cell phones and pagers to on-line services primarily to gain career edge.	**Digital hopefuls** — Families with a limited budget but still interested in new technology. Good candidates for the under-$1000 PC.	**Gadget-grabbers** — They also favor on-line entertainment but have less cash to spend on it.
More affluent	**Fast forwards** — These customers are the biggest spenders, and they're early adopters of new technology for individual use.	**New age nurturers** — Also big spenders, but focused on technology for home uses such as family PC.	**Mouse potatoes** — They like the on-line world for entertainment and are willing to spend for the latest technotainment.

Source: Jakki Mohr, *Marketing of High-Technology Products and Innovations* (Upper Saddle River, NJ: Prentice Hall, 2001), p. 135, and adapted from Paul Judge, "Are Tech Buyers Different?" *BusinessWeek*, January 26, 1998, pp. 64–66.

A Priori versus Post Hoc Segmentation

Real-world segmentation has followed one of two general patterns. An *a priori segmentation* approach is one in which the marketing manager has decided on the appropriate basis for segmentation in advance of doing any research on a market. For example, a manager may decide that a market should be divided on the basis of whether people are nonusers, light users, or heavy users of a particular product. Segmentation research is then conducted to determine the size of each of these groups and their demographic or psychographic profiles.

Post hoc segmentation is an approach in which people are grouped into segments on the basis of research findings. For example, people interviewed concerning their attitudes or benefits sought in a particular product category are grouped according to their responses. The size of each of these groups and their demographic and psychographic profiles are then determined.

Both of these approaches are valuable, and the question of which to use depends in part on how well the firm knows the market for a particular product class. If through previous research and experience a marketing manager has successfully isolated a number of key market dimensions, then an a priori approach based on them may provide more useful information. In the case of segmentation for entirely new products, a post hoc approach may be useful for determining key market dimensions. However, even when using a post hoc approach, some consideration must be given to the variables to be included in the research design. Thus, some consideration must be given to the relevant segmentation dimensions regardless of which approach is used.

Relevance of Segmentation Dimensions

Unfortunately, there is no simple solution for determining the relevant dimensions for segmenting markets. Certainly, managerial expertise and experience are needed for selecting the appropriate dimensions or bases on which to segment particular markets. In most cases, however, at least some initial dimensions can be determined from previous research, purchase trends, and managerial judgment. For instance, suppose we wish to segment the market for all-terrain vehicles. Clearly, several dimensions come to mind for initial consideration, including sex (male), age (18 to 35 years), lifestyle (outdoorsman), and income level (perhaps $30,000 to $80,000). At a minimum, these variables should be included in subsequent segmentation research. Of course, the most market-oriented approach to segmentation is on the basis of what benefits the potential consumer is seeking. Thus, consideration and research of sought benefits are a strongly recommended approach in the marketing literature. This approach will be considered in some detail in the following section.

Bases for Segmentation

A number of useful bases for segmenting consumer and organizational markets are presented in Figure 5.2. This is by no means a complete list of possible segmentation variables but represents some useful bases and categories. Two commonly used approaches for segmenting markets include benefit segmentation and psychographic segmentation. We will discuss these two in some detail. We will also discuss geodemographic segmentation, a recent development with a number of advantages for marketers.

Benefit Segmentation

The belief underlying this segmentation approach is that the benefits that people are seeking in consuming a given product are the basic reasons for the existence of true market segments.[1] Thus, this approach attempts to measure consumer value systems and consumer perceptions of various brands in a product class. To illustrate, the classic example of a benefit segmentation was provided by Russell Haley and concerned the toothpaste market.

FIGURE 5.2 Useful Segmentation Bases for Consumer and Organizational Buyer Markets

Consumer Markets

Segmentation Base	Examples of Market Segments
Geographic:	
Continents	Africa, Asia, Europe, North America, South America
Global regions	Southeast Asia, Mediterranean, Caribbean
Countries	China, Canada, France, United States, Brazil
Country regions	Pacific Northwest, Middle Atlantic, Midwest
City, county, or SMSA size	Under 5,000 people, 5,000–19,999, 20,000–49,999, 50,000+
Population density	Urban, suburban, rural
Climate	Tropical, temperate, cold
Demographic:	
Age	Under 6 years old, 6–12, 13–19, 20–29, 30–39, 40–49, 50+
Gender	Male, female
Family size	1–2 persons, 3–4 persons, more than 4 persons
Family life cycle	Single, young married, married with children, sole survivor
Income	Under $10,000 per year, $10,000–$19,999, $20,000–$29,999, $30,000–$39,999, $40,000–$49,999, $50,000+
Education	Grade school or less, some high school, graduated from high school, some college, graduated from college, some graduate work, graduate degree
Marital status	Single, married, divorced, widowed
Social:	
Culture	American, Hispanic, African, Asian, European
Subculture	
Religion	Jewish, Catholic, Muslim, Mormon, Buddhist
Race	European American, Asian American, African American, Hispanic American
Nationality	French, Malaysian, Australian, Canadian, Japanese
Social class	Upper class, middle class, working class, lower class
Thoughts and feelings:	
Knowledge	Expert, novice
Involvement	High, medium, low
Attitude	Positive, neutral, negative
Benefits sought	Convenience, economy, prestige
Innovativeness	Innovator, early adopter, early majority, late majority, laggards, nonadopter
Readiness stage	Unaware, aware, interested, desirous, plan to purchase
Perceived risk	High, moderate, low
Behavior:	
Media usage	Newspaper, magazine, TV, Internet
Specific media usage	*Sports Illustrated, Life, Cosmopolitan*
Payment method	Cash, Visa, MasterCard, American Express, check
Loyalty status	None, some, total
Usage rate	Light, medium, heavy
User status	Nonuser, ex-user, current user, potential user
Usage situation	Work, home, vacation, commuting
Combined approaches:	
Psychographics	Achievers, strivers, strugglers
Person/situation	College students for lunch, executives for business dinner
Geodemography	Blue Blood Estates, Towns and Gowns, Hispanic Mix

Organizational Buyer Markets

Segmentation Base	Examples of Market Segments
Company size	Small, medium, large relative to industry
Purchase quantity	Small, medium, large account
Product application	Production, maintenance, product component
Organization type	Manufacturer, retailer, government agency, hospital
Location	North, south, east, west sales territory
Purchase status	New customer, occasional purchaser, frequent purchaser, nonpurchaser
Attribute importance	Price, service, reliability of supply

FIGURE 5.3   **Toothpaste Market Benefit Segments**

	Sensory Segment	Sociable Segment	Worrier Segment	Independent Segment
Principal benefit sought	Flavor and product appearance	Brightness of teeth	Decay prevention	Price
Demographic strengths	Children	Teens, young people	Large families	Men
Special behavioral characteristics	Users of spearmint-flavored toothpaste	Smokers	Heavy users	Heavy users
Brands disproportionately favored	Colgate	Macleans, Ultra Brite	Crest	Cheapest brand
Lifestyle characteristics	Hedonistic	Active	Conservative	Value-oriented

Haley identified five basic segments, which are presented in Figure 5.3. Haley argued that this segmentation could be very useful for selecting advertising copy, media, commercial length, packaging, and new product design. For example, colorful packages might be appropriate for the sensory segment, perhaps aqua (to indicate fluoride) for the worrier group, and gleaming white for the social segment because of this segment's interest in white teeth.

Calantone and Sawyer also used a benefit segmentation approach to segment the market for bank services.[2] Their research was concerned with the question of whether benefit segments remain stable across time. While they found some stability in segments, there

FIGURE 5.4
VALS™ Framework and Segments

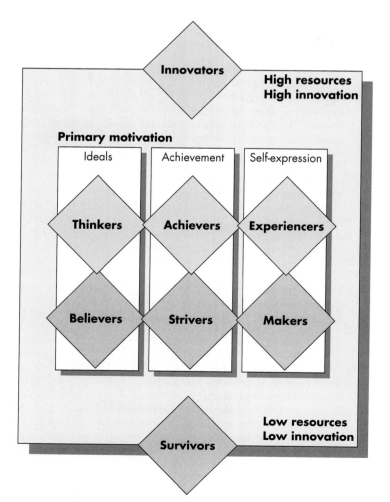

were some differences in attribute importance, size, and demographics at different times. Thus, they argue for ongoing benefit segmentation research to keep track of any changes in a market that might affect marketing strategy.

Benefit segmentation is clearly a market-oriented approach to segmentation that seeks to identify consumer needs and wants and to satisfy them by providing products and services with the desired benefits. It is clearly very consistent with the approach to marketing suggested by the marketing concept.

Psychographic Segmentation

Whereas benefit segmentation focuses on the benefits sought by the consumer, psychographic segmentation focuses on consumer lifestyles. Consumers are first asked a variety of questions about their lifestyles and then grouped on the basis of the similarity of their responses. Lifestyles are measured by asking consumers about their *activities* (work, hobbies, vacations), *interests* (family, job, community), and *opinions* (about social issues, politics, business). The activity, interest, and opinion (AIO) questions are very general in some studies but in others, at least some of the questions relate to specific products.[3]

The best-known psychographic segmentation is called VALS,™ which stands for "values and lifestyles." Originally developed in the 1970s, it has been redone several times to enhance its ability to explain changing lifestyles and predict consumer behavior. Segmentation research based on VALS™ is a product of SRI Consulting Business Intelligence.

As shown in Figure 5.4, there are eight psychographic groups arranged in a rectangle based on two dimensions. The vertical dimension segments people based on the degree to

**FIGURE 5.4
(continued)**

Sources: SRI Consulting Business Intelligence, **www.sric-bi.com,** July 27, 2003; Martha Farnsworth Riche, "Psychographics for the 1990s," *American Demographics,* July 1989, pp. 24–26ff. Copyright 1989, PRIMEDIA Business Magazines & Media Inc. All rights reserved.

Innovators. These consumers are on the leading edge of change, have the highest incomes, and such high self-esteem and abundant resources that they can indulge in any or all self-orientations. They are located above the rectangle. Image is important to them as an expression of taste, independence, and character. Their consumer choices are directed toward the "finer things in life."

Thinkers. These consumers are the high-resource group of those who are motivated by ideals. They are mature, responsible, well-educated professionals. Their leisure activities center on their homes, but they are well informed about what goes on in the world and are open to new ideas and social change. They have high incomes but are practical consumers and rational decision markers.

Believers. These consumers are the low-resource group of those who are motivated by ideals. They are conservative and predictable consumers who favor American products and established brands. Their lives are centered on family, church, community, and the nation. They have modest incomes.

Achievers. These consumers are the high-resource group of those who are motivated by achievement. They are successful work-oriented people who get their satisfaction from their jobs and families. They are politically conservative and respect authority and the status quo. They favor established products and services that show off their success to their peers.

Strivers. These consumers are the low-resource group of those who are motivated by achievement. They have values very similar to achievers but have fewer economic, social, and psychological resources. Style is extremely important to them as they strive to emulate people they admire.

Experiencers. These consumers are the high-resource group of those who are motivated by self-expression. They are the youngest of all the segments, with a median age of 25. They have a lot of energy, which they pour into physical exercise and social activities. They are avid consumers, spending heavily on clothing, fast foods, music, and other youthful favorites, with particular emphasis on new products and services.

Makers. These consumers are the low-resource group of those who are motivated by self-experession. They are practical people who value self-sufficiency. They are focused on the familiar—family, work, and physical recreation—and have little interest in the broader world. As consumers, they appreciate practical and functional products.

Survivors. These consumers have the lowest incomes. They have too few resources to be included in any consumer self-orientation and are thus located below the rectangle. They are the oldest of all the segments, with a median age of 61. Within their limited means, they tend to be brand-loyal consumers.

You can find your VALS classification by filling out a questionnaire on the Internet. The Web address is www.sric-bi.com. The questionnaire takes about 10 minutes to complete, and your lifestyle will take about 10 seconds to compute. You will get a report that includes both your primary and secondary VALS type. The VALS Web site has a lot of information describing the program and different types of VALS segments.

which they are innovative and have resources such as income, education, self-confidence, intelligence, leadership skills, and energy. The horizontal dimension represents primary motivations and includes three different types. Consumers driven by knowledge and principles are motivated primarily by *ideals*. These consumers include the Thinkers and Believers groups. Consumers driven by a goal of demonstrating success to their peers are motivated primarily by *achievement.* These consumers include Achievers and Strivers. Consumers driven by a desire for social or physical activity, variety, and risk taking are motivated primarily by self-expression. These consumers include both the Experiencers and Makers. At the top of the rectangle are the Innovators, who have such high resources that they could have any of the three motivations. At the bottom of the rectangle are the Survivors, who live complacently and within their means without a strong primary motivation of the types listed above. Figure 5.4 gives more details about each of the eight groups.[4]

Marketers can purchase research data that show which VALS™ groups are the primary buyers of specific products and services. This information can be used to better focus elements of the marketing mix, such as promotion, on the best target markets.

Geodemographic Segmentation

One problem with many segmentation approaches is that while they identify types or categories of consumers, they do not identify specific individuals or households within a market. *Geodemographic segmentation* does identify specific households in a market by focusing on local neighborhood geography (such as zip codes) to create classifications of actual, addressable, mappable neighborhoods where people live and shop. One geodemographic system created by Claritas, Inc., is called PRIZM, which stands for Potential Ranking Index by Zip Markets. This system classifies every U.S. neighborhood into one of 62 distinct types or clusters of consumers. Each PRIZM cluster is based on zip codes, demographic information from the U.S. census, and information on product usage, media usage, and lifestyle preferences to create profiles of the people who live in specific neighborhoods. Figure 5.5 shows a sample cluster profile. The PRIZM system includes maps of different areas that rank neighborhoods on their potential to purchase specific products or services.

The PRIZM system is based on the assumptions that consumers in particular neighborhoods are similar in many respects and that the best prospects are those who actually use a product or other consumers like them. Marketers use PRIZM to better understand consumers in various markets, what they're like, where they live, and how to reach them. These data help marketers with target market selection, direct-marketing campaigns, site selection, media selection, and analysis of sales potential in various areas.

Develop Product Positioning

By this time, the firm should have a good idea of the basic segments of the market that could potentially be satisfied with its product. The current step is concerned with positioning the product favorably in the minds of customers relative to competitive products. There are

FIGURE 5.5
Claritas PRIZM Cluster 36—Towns and Gowns

Source: Valarie Walsh and J. Paul Peter, "Claritas Inc.: Using Compass and PRIZM," in *Marketing Management: Knowledge and Skills,* 7th ed., eds. J. Paul Peter and James H. Donnelly, Jr. (Burr Ridge, Il.: Irwin/McGraw-Hill, 2004), p. 289.

The "towns and gowns" cluster describes most of our college towns and university campus neighborhoods. With a typical mix of half locals (towns) and half students (gowns), it is wholly unique, with thousands of penniless 18- to 24-year-old kids, plus highly educated professionals, all with a taste for prestige products beyond their evident means.

Predominant Characteristics

- Households (% U.S.):   1,290,200 (1.4%)
- Population: 3,542,500
- Demographic caption: College-town singles
- Ethnic diversity: Dominant white, high Asian
- Family type: Singles
- Predominant age ranges: Under 24, 25–34
- Education: College graduates
- Employment level: White collar/service
- Housing type: Renters/multiunit 10+
- Density percentile: 58 (1 = sparse, 99 = dense)

More Likely to:

Lifestyle	Products and Services
Go to college football games	Have a personal education loan
Play racquetball	Use an ATM card
Go skiing	Own a Honda
Play billiards/pool	Buy 3+ pairs of jeans annually
Use cigarette rolling paper	Drink Coca-Cola Classic
Use a charter/tour bus	Eat Kraft Macaroni and Cheese

Radio/TV	Print
Watch VH1	Read *Self*
Listen to alternative rock music	Read newspaper comics section
Watch "Jeopardy"	Read *Rolling Stone*
Listen to variety radio	Read *GQ*
Watch "The Simpsons"	

several different positioning strategies that can be used. First, products can be positioned by focusing on their superiority to competitive products based on one or more attributes. For example, a car could be positioned as less expensive (Hyundai), safer (Volvo), higher quality (Toyota), or more prestigious (Lexus) than other cars. Second, products can be positioned by use or application. For example, Campbell's soup is positioned not only as a lunch item but also for use as a sauce or dip or as an ingredient in main dishes. Third, products can be positioned in terms of particular types of product users. For example, sales for Johnson's Baby Shampoo increased dramatically after the company positioned the product not only for babies but also for active adults who need to wash their hair frequently. Fourth, products can be positioned relative to a product class. For example, Caress soap was positioned by Lever Brothers as a bath oil product rather than as a soap. Finally, products can be positioned directly against particular competitors. For example, Coke and Pepsi and McDonald's and Burger King commonly position directly against each other on various criteria, such as taste. The classic example of positioning is of this last type: Seven-Up positioned itself as a tasty alternative to the dominant soft drink, colas.

FIGURE 5.6
**Positioning Map for
Automobiles**

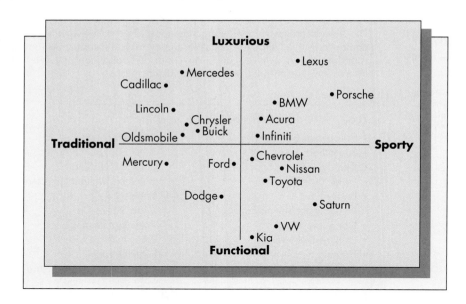

One way to investigate how to position a product is by using a *positioning map,* which is a visual depiction of customer perceptions of competitive products, brands, or models. It is constructed by surveying customers about various product attributes and developing dimensions and a graph indicating the relative position of competitors. Figure 5.6 presents a sample positioning map for automobiles that offers marketers a way of assessing whether their brands are positioned appropriately. For example, if Chrysler or Buick wants to be positioned in the minds of consumers as serious competitors to Lexus, then their strategies need to be changed to move up on this dimension. After the new strategies are implemented, a new positioning map could be developed to see if the brands moved up as desired.

Some experts argue that different positioning strategies should be used depending on whether the firm is a market leader or follower and that followers usually should not attempt to position directly against the industry leader.[5] The main point here is that in segmenting markets, some segments might have to be forgone because a market-leading competitive product already dominates in sales and in the minds of customers. Thus, a smaller or less desirable target market may have to be selected since competing with market leaders is costly and not often successful.

Decide Segmentation Strategy

The firm is now ready to select its segmentation strategy. There are four basic alternatives. First, the firm may decide not to enter the market. For example, analysis to this stage may reveal there is no viable market niche for the firm's offering. Second, the firm may decide not to segment but to be a mass marketer. There are at least three situations when this may be the appropriate decision for the firm:

1. The market is so small that marketing to a portion of it is not profitable.
2. Heavy users make up such a large proportion of the sales volume that they are the only relevant target.

Dividing markets into segments and then selecting the best ones to serve is one of the cornerstones of sound marketing practice. However, there are situations when target marketing has been criticized as being unethical.

- R. J. Reynolds Tobacco Company planned to target African American consumers with a new brand of menthol cigarettes, Uptown. This brand was to be advertised with suggestions of glamour, high fashion, and night life. After criticism for targeting a vulnerable population, the company canceled plans for the brand.
- RJR planned to target white, 18- to 24-year-old "virile" females with a new cigarette brand, Dakota. It was criticized for targeting young, poorly educated, blue-collar women; and although it expanded the market to include males, Dakota failed in test markets and was withdrawn.
- Heileman Brewing Company planned to market a new brand of malt liquor called PowerMaster. Malt liquor is disproportionately consumed by African Americans and in low-income neighborhoods. Criticism of this strategy led the brand to be withdrawn.

One study suggests that whether targeting a group of consumers is unethical depends on two dimensions. The first is the degree to which the product can harm the consumers, and the second is the vulnerability of the group. Thus, to market harmful products to vulnerable target markets is likely to be considered unethical and could result in boycotts, negative word of mouth, and possibly litigation or legislation.

Source: N. Craig Smith and Elizabeth Cooper-Martin, "Ethics and Target Marketing: The Role of Product Harm and Consumer Vulnerability," *Journal of Marketing*, July 1997, pp. 1–20.

3. The brand is the dominant brand in the market, and targeting to a few segments would not benefit sales and profits.

Third, the firm may decide to market to one segment. And fourth, the firm may decide to market to more than one segment and design a separate marketing mix for each. In any case, the firm must have some criteria on which to base its segmentation strategy decisions. Three important criteria on which to base such decisions are that a viable segment must be (1) measurable, (2) meaningful, and (3) marketable.

1. *Measurable.* For a segment to be selected, the firm must be capable of measuring its size and characteristics. For instance, one of the difficulties with segmenting on the basis of social class is that the concept and its divisions are not clearly defined and measured. Alternatively, income is a much easier concept to measure.
2. *Meaningful.* A meaningful segment is one that is large enough to have sufficient sales and growth potential to offer long-run profits for the firm.
3. *Marketable.* A marketable segment is one that can be reached and served by the firm in an efficient manner.

Figure 5.7 offers a list of questions marketing managers should answer when deciding whether a market segment meets these criteria. Segments that do so are viable target markets for the firm's offering. The firm must now give further attention to completing its marketing mix.

FIGURE 5.7
Selecting Target Markets: Some Questions Marketing Managers Should Answer

In order to select the best target markets, marketing managers must evaluate market segments on a number of dimensions. Below is a list of questions managers should answer before selecting target markets.

Measurability Questions

1. What are the appropriate bases for segmenting this market and are these bases readily measurable?
2. Are secondary data available on these bases so that the market segment can be identified and measured inexpensively?
3. If primary data are needed, is there sufficient return on investment to do the research?
4. Are specific names and addresses of people in this market segment needed; or is general knowledge of their existence, number, and geographic location sufficient?
5. Can purchases of people in this market segment be readily measured and tracked?

Meaningfulness Questions

1. How many people are in this market segment and how frequently will they purchase our product?
2. What market share can we expect in this segment?
3. What is the growth potential of this segment?
4. How strong is competition for this market segment and how is it likely to change in the future?
5. How satisfied are customers in this market segment with current product offerings?

Marketability Questions

1. Can this market segment be reached with our current channels of distribution?
2. If new channels are needed, can we establish them efficiently?
3. What specific promotion media do these people read, listen to, or watch?
4. Can we afford to promote to these people in the appropriate media to reach them?
5. Are people in this market segment willing to pay a price that is profitable for the company?
6. Can we produce a product for this market segment and do so profitably?

Design Marketing Mix Strategy

The firm is now in a position to complete its marketing plan by finalizing the marketing mix or mixes to be used for each segment. Clearly, selection of the target market and designing the marketing mix go hand in hand, and thus many marketing mix decisions should have already been carefully considered. To illustrate, the target market selected may be price sensitive, so some consideration has already been given to price levels, and clearly product positioning has many implications for promotion and channel decisions. Thus, while we place marketing mix design at the end of the model, many of these decisions are made in *conjunction* with target market selection. In the next six chapters of this text, marketing mix decisions will be discussed in detail.

Conclusion

The purpose of this chapter was to provide an overview of market segmentation. Market segmentation was defined as the process of dividing a market into groups of similar consumers and selecting the most appropriate group(s) for the firm to serve. Market segmentation was analyzed as a six-stage process: (1) to delineate the firm's current situation, (2) to determine consumer needs and wants, (3) to divide the market on relevant dimensions, (4) to develop product positioning, (5) to decide segmentation strategy, and (6) to design marketing mix strategy.

Additional Readings

Bolton, Ruth N., and Matthew B. Myers."Price-Based Global Market Segmentation for Services," *Journal of Marketing,* July 2003, pp. 108–128.

Dickson, Peter R., and James L. Ginter. "Market Segmentation, Product Differentiation, and Marketing Strategy." *Journal of Marketing,* April 1987, pp. 1–10.

Green, Paul E., and Abba M. Krieger. "Segmenting Markets with Conjoint Analysis." *Journal of Marketing,* October 1991, pp. 20–31.

Myers, James H. *Segmentation and Positioning for Strategic Marketing Decisions*. Chicago: American Marketing Association, 1996.

The Marketing Mix

Part C

Product Strategy

Product strategy is a critical element of marketing and business strategy, since it is through the sale of products and services that companies survive and grow. This chapter discusses four important areas of concern in developing product strategies. First, some basic issues are discussed, including product definition, product classification, product quality and value, product mix and product line, branding and brand equity, and packaging. Second, the product life cycle and its implications for product strategy are explained. Third, the product audit is reviewed, and finally, three ways to organize for product management are outlined. These include the marketing manager system, brand manager system, and cross-functional teams.

Basic Issues in Product Management

Successful marketing depends on understanding the nature of products and basic decision areas in product management. In this section, we discuss the definition and classification of products, the importance of product quality and value, and the nature of a product mix and product lines. Also considered is the role of branding and packaging.

Product Definition

The way in which the product variable is defined can have important implications for the survival, profitability, and long-run growth of the firm. For example, the same product can be viewed at least three different ways. First, it can be viewed in terms of the *tangible product*—the physical entity or service that is offered to the buyer. Second, it can be viewed in terms of the *extended product*—the tangible product along with the whole cluster of services that accompany it. For example, a manufacturer of computer software may offer a 24-hour hotline to answer questions users may have or to offer free or reduced-cost software updates, free replacement of damaged software, and a subscription to a newsletter that documents new applications of the software. Third, it can be viewed in terms of the *generic product*—the essential benefits the buyer expects to receive from the product. For example, many personal care products bring to the purchaser feelings of self-enhancement and security in addition to the tangible benefits they offer.

From the standpoint of the marketing manager, to define the product solely in terms of the tangible product is to fall into the error of "marketing myopia." Executives who are guilty of committing this error define their company's product too narrowly, since they overemphasize the physical object itself. The classic example of this mistake can be found in railroad passenger service. Although no amount of product improvement could have staved off its decline, if the industry had defined itself as being in the transportation business, rather than the railroad business, it might still be profitable today.

1. An audit of the firm's actual and potential resources
   a. Financial strength
   b. Access to raw materials
   c. Plant and equipment
   d. Operating personnel
   e. Management
   f. Engineering and technical skills
   g. Patents and licenses
2. Approaches to current markets
   a. More of the same products
   b. Variations of present products in terms of grades, sizes, and packages
   c. New products to replace or supplement current lines
   d. Product deletions
3. Approaches to new or potential markets
   a. Geographical expansion of domestic sales
   b. New socioeconomic or ethnic groups
   c. Overseas markets
   d. New uses of present products
   e. Complementary goods
   f. Mergers and acquisitions
4. State of competition
   a. New entries into the industry
   b. Product imitation
   c. Competitive mergers or acquisitions

On the positive side, toothpaste manufacturers have been willing to exercise flexibility in defining their product. For years toothpaste was an oral hygiene product in which emphasis was placed solely on fighting tooth decay and bad breath (e.g., Crest with fluoride). More recently, many manufacturers have recognized the need to market toothpaste as a cosmetic item (to clean teeth of stains), as a defense against gum disease (to reduce the buildup of tartar above the gumline), as an aid for denture wearers, and as a breath freshener. As a result, special-purpose brands have been designed to serve these particular needs, such as Ultra Brite, Close-Up, Aqua-Fresh, Aim, Dental Care, and the wide variety of baking soda, tartar-control formula, and gel toothpastes offered under existing brand names.

In line with the marketing concept philosophy, a reasonable definition of product is that it is *the sum of the physical, psychological, and sociological satisfactions the buyer derives from purchase, ownership, and consumption*. From this standpoint, products are customer-satisfying objects that include such things as accessories, packaging, and service.

Product Classification

A product classification scheme can be useful to the marketing manager as an analytical device to assist in planning marketing strategy and programs. A basic assumption underlying such classifications is that products with common attributes can be marketed in a similar fashion. In general, products are classed according to two basic criteria: (1) end use or market, and (2) degree of processing or physical transformation.

1. *Agricultural products and raw materials*. These are goods grown or extracted from the land or sea, such as iron ore, wheat, and sand. In general, these products are fairly homogeneous, sold in large volume, and have low value per unit or in bulk weight.
2. *Organizational goods*. Such products are purchased by business firms for the purpose of producing other goods or for running the business. This category includes the following:
   a. Raw materials and semifinished goods.
   b. Major and minor equipment, such as basic machinery, tools, and other processing facilities.
   c. Parts or components, which become an integral element of some other finished good.

    d. Supplies or items used to operate the business but that do not become part of the final product.

3. *Consumer goods.* Consumer goods can be divided into three classes:

    a. Convenience goods, such as food, which are purchased frequently with minimum effort. Impulse goods would also fall into this category.

    b. Shopping goods, such as appliances, which are purchased after some time and energy are spent comparing the various offerings.

    c. Specialty goods, which are unique in some way so the consumer will make a special purchase effort to obtain them.

In general, the buying motive, buying habits, and character of the market are different for organizational goods vis-à-vis consumer goods. A primary purchasing motive for organizational goods is, of course, profit. As mentioned in a previous chapter, organizational goods are usually purchased as means to an end and not as an end in themselves. This is another way of saying that the demand for organizational goods is a derived demand. Organizational goods are often purchased directly from the original source with few middlemen, because many of these goods can be bought in large quantities; they have high unit value; technical advice on installation and use is required; and the product is ordered according to the user's specifications. Many organizational goods are subject to multiple-purchase influence, and a long period of negotiation is often required.

The market for organizational goods has certain attributes that distinguish it from the consumer goods market. Much of the market is concentrated geographically, as in the case of steel, auto, or shoe manufacturing. For certain products there are a limited number of buyers; this is known as a *vertical market,* which means that (1) it is narrow, because customers are restricted to a few industries; and (2) it is deep, in that a large percentage of the producers in the market use the product. Some products, such as desktop computers, have a *horizontal market,* which means that the goods are purchased by all types of firms in many different industries. In general, buyers of organizational goods are reasonably well informed. As noted previously, heavy reliance is often placed on price, quality control, and reliability of supply source.

In terms of consumer products, many marketing scholars have found the convenience, shopping, and specialty classification inadequate and have attempted either to refine it or to derive an entirely new typology. None of these attempts appears to have met with complete success. Perhaps there is no best way to deal with this problem. From the standpoint of the marketing manager, product classification is useful to the extent that it assists in providing guidelines for developing an appropriate marketing mix. For example, convenience goods generally require broadcast promotion and long channels of distribution as opposed to shopping goods, which generally require more targeted promotion and somewhat shorter channels of distribution.

Product Quality and Value

Quality can be defined as the degree of excellence or superiority that an organization's product possesses.[1] Quality can encompass both the tangible and intangible aspects of a firm's products or services. In a technical sense, quality can refer to physical traits such as features, performance, reliability, durability, aesthetics, serviceability, and conformance to specifications. Although quality can be evaluated from many perspectives, the customer is the key perceiver of quality because his or her purchase decision determines the success of the organization's product or service and often the fate of the organization itself.

Many organizations have formalized their interest in providing quality products by undertaking total-quality management (TQM) programs. TQM is an organizationwide commitment to satisfying customers by continuously improving every business process involved in delivering products or services. Instead of merely correcting defects when they occur, organizations that practice TQM train and commit employees to continually look for ways to do things better so defects and problems don't arise in the first place. The result of this process is higher-quality products being produced at a lower cost. Indeed, the emphasis on quality has risen to such a level that over 70 countries have adopted the ISO 9000 quality system of standards, a standardized approach for evaluating a supplier's quality system, which can be applied to virtually any business.[2]

The term *quality* is often confused with the concept of value. Value encompasses not only quality but also price. *Value* can be defined as what the customer gets in exchange for what the customer gives. In other words, a customer, in most cases, receives a product in exchange for having paid the supplier for the product. A customer's perception of the value associated with a product is generally based both on the degree to which the product meets his or her specifications and the price that the customer will have to pay to acquire the product. Some organizations are beginning to shift their primary focus from one that solely emphasizes quality to one that also equally encompasses the customer's viewpoint of the price/quality trade-off. Organizations that are successful at this process derive their competitive advantage from the provision of customer value. In other words, they offer goods and services that meet or exceed customer needs at a fair price. Recall that Chapter 1 described various strategies based on value.

Product Mix and Product Line

A firm's *product mix* is the full set of products offered for sale by the organization; A product mix may consist of several *product lines,* or groups of products that share common characteristics, distribution channels, customers, or uses. A firm's product mix is described by its width and depth. *Width* of the product mix refers to the number of product lines handled by the organization. For example, one division of General Mills has a widespread mix consisting of five different product lines: ready-to-eat cereals, convenience foods, snack foods, baking products, and dairy products. *Depth* refers to the average number of products in each line. In its ready-to-eat cereals line, General Mills has eight different products. It has five different products in its line of convenience foods. Thus, the organization has a wide product mix and deep product lines.

An integral component of product line planning revolves around the question of how many product variants should be included in the line.[3] Manufacturing costs are usually minimized through large-volume production runs, and distribution costs tend to be lower if only one product is sold, stocked, and serviced. At a given level of sales, profits will usually be highest if those sales have been achieved with a single product. However, many product variants are offered by many firms.

There are three reasons organizations offer varying products within a given product line. First, potential customers rarely agree on a single set of specifications regarding their "ideal product," differing greatly in the importance and value they place on specific attributes. For example, in the laundry detergent market, there is a marked split between preferences for powder versus liquid detergent. Second, customers prefer variety. For example, a person may like Italian food but does not want to only eat spaghetti. Therefore, an Italian restaurant will offer the customer a wide variety of Italian dishes to choose from. Third, the dynamics of competition lead to multiproduct lines. As competitors seek to increase market share, they find it advantageous to introduce new products that subsegment an existing market segment by offering benefits more precisely tailored to the specific needs of a portion of that segment. For example, Proctor & Gamble offers Jif peanut butter in a low-salt version to target a specific subsegment of the peanut butter market.

A. CLASSES OF CONSUMER GOODS—SOME CHARACTERISTICS AND MARKETING CONSIDERATIONS

Characteristics and Marketing Considerations	Type of Product		
	Convenience	Shopping	Specialty
Characteristics			
Time and effort devoted by consumer to shopping	Very little	Considerable	Cannot generalize; consumer may go to nearby store and buy with minimum effort or may have to go to distant store and spend much time and effort
Time spent planning the purchase	Very little	Considerable	Considerable
How soon want is satisfied after it arises	Immediately	Relatively long time	Relatively long time
Are price and quality compared?	No	Yes	No
Price	Usually low	High	High
Frequency of purchase	Usually frequent	Infrequent	Infrequent
Importance	Unimportant	Often very important	Cannot generalize
Marketing considerations			
Length of channel	Long	Short	Short to very short
Importance of retailer	Any single store is relatively unimportant	Important	Very important
Number of outlets	As many as possible	Few	Few; often only one in a market
Stock turnover	High	Lower	Lower
Gross margin	Low	High	High
Responsibility for advertising	Producer	Retailer	Joint responsibility
Importance of point-of-purchase display	Very important	Less important	Less important
Brand or store name important	Brand name	Store name	Both
Importance of packaging	Very important	Less important	Less important

Source: Michael J. Etzel, Bruce J. Walker, and William J. Stanton, *Fundamentals of Marketing*, 13th ed. © 2004, New York, McGraw-Hill, Inc., pp. 211, 214. Reproduced by permission of The McGraw-Hill Companies.

All too often, organizations pursue product line additions with little regard for consequences.[4] However, in reaching a decision on product line additions, organizations need to evaluate whether (1) total profits will decrease or (2) the quality/value associated with current products will suffer. If the answer to either of the above is yes, then the organization should not proceed with the addition. Closely related to product line additions are issues associated with branding. These are covered next.

Branding and Brand Equity

For some organizations, the primary focus of strategy development is placed on brand building, developing, and nurturing activities.[5] Factors that serve to increase the strength of a brand include[6] (1) product quality when products do what they do very well (e.g., Windex and Easy-Off); (2) consistent advertising and other marketing communications in which brands tell their story often and well (e.g., Pepsi and Visa); (3) distribution intensity

B. CLASSES OF ORGANIZATIONAL PRODUCTS—SOME CHARACTERISTICS AND MARKETING CONSIDERATIONS

Characteristics and Marketing Considerations	Type of Product				
	Raw Materials	Fabricating Parts and Materials	Installations	Accessory Equipment	Operating Supplies
Example	Iron ore	Engine blocks	Blast furnaces	Storage racks	Paper clips
Characteristics					
Unit price	Very low	Low	Very high	Medium	Low
Length of life	Very short	Depends on final product	Very long	Long	Short
Quantities purchased	Large	Large	Very small	Small	Small
Frequency of purchase	Frequent delivery; long-term purchase contract	Infrequent purchase, but frequent delivery	Very infrequent	Medium frequency	Frequent
Standardization of competitive products	Very much; grading is important	Very much	Very little; custom made	Little	Much
Quantity of supply	Limited; supply can be increased slowly or not at all	Usually no problem	No problem	Usually no problem	Usually no problem
Marketing considerations					
Nature of channel	Short; no middlemen	Short; middlemen for small buyers	Short; no middlemen	Middlemen used	Middlemen used
Negotiation period	Hard to generalize	Medium	Long	Medium	Short
Price competition	Important	Important	Not important	Not main factor	Important
Presale/postsale service	Not important	Important	Very important	Important	Very little
Promotional activity	Very little	Moderate	Sales people very important	Important	Not too important
Brand preference	None	Generally low	High	High	Low
Advance buying contract	Important; long-term contracts used	Important; long-term contracts used	Not usually used	Not usually used	Not usually used

whereby customers see the brand wherever they shop (e.g., Marlboro); and (4) brand personality where the brand stands for something (e.g., Disney). The strength of the Coca-Cola brand, for example, is widely attributed to its universal availability, universal awareness, and trademark protection, which came as a result of strategic actions taken by the parent organization.[7]

The brand name is perhaps the single most important element on the package, serving as a unique identifier. Specifically, a *brand* is a name, term, design, symbol, or any other

85

feature that identifies one seller's good or service as distinct from those of other sellers. The legal term for brand is *trademark*.[8] A good brand name can evoke feelings of trust, confidence, security, strength, and many other desirable characteristics.[9] To illustrate, consider the case of Bayer aspirin. Bayer can be sold at up to two times the price of generic aspirin due to the strength of its brand image.

Many companies make use of manufacturer branding strategies in carrying out market and product development strategies. The *line extension* approach uses a brand name to facilitate entry into a new market segment (e.g., Diet Coke and Liquid Tide). An alternative to line extension is brand extension. In *brand extension,* a current brand name is used to enter a completely different product class (e.g., Jello pudding pops, Ivory shampoo).[10]

A third form of branding is *franchise extension* or *family branding,* whereby a company attaches the corporate name to a product to enter either a new market segment or a different product class (e.g., Honda lawnmower, Toyota Lexus). A final type of branding strategy that is becoming more and more common is dual branding. A *dual branding* (also known as joint or cobranding) strategy is one in which two or more branded products are integrated (e.g., Bacardi rum and Coca-Cola, Long John Silver's and A&W Root Beer, Archway cookies and Kellogg cereal, US Airways and Bank of America Visa). The logic behind this strategy is that if one brand name on a product gives a certain signal of quality, then the presence of a second brand name on the product should result in a signal that is at least as powerful as, if not more powerful than, the signal in the case of the single brand name. Each of the preceding four approaches is an attempt by companies to gain a competitive advantage by making use of its or others' established reputation, or both.

Companies may also choose to assign different brand names to each product. This is known as *multibranding* strategy. By doing so, the firm makes a conscious decision to allow the product to succeed or fail on its own merits. Major advantages of using multiple brand names are that (1) the firm can distance products from other offerings it markets; (2) the image of one product (or set of products) is not associated with other products the company markets; (3) the product(s) can be targeted at a specific market segment; and (4) should the product(s) fail, the probability of failure impacting on other company products is minimized. For example, many consumers are unaware that Dreft, Tide, Oxydol, Bold, Cheer, and Dash laundry detergents are all marketed by Procter & Gamble. The major disadvantage of this strategy is that because new names are assigned, there is no consumer brand awareness and significant amounts of money must be spent familiarizing customers with new brands.

Increasingly, companies are finding that brand names are one of the most valuable assets they possess. Successful extensions of an existing brand can lead to additional loyalty and associated profits. Conversely, a wrong extension can cause damaging associations, as perceptions linked to the brand name are transferred back from one product to the other.[11] *Brand equity* can be viewed as the set of assets (or liabilities) linked to the brand that add (or subtract) value.[12] The value of these assets is dependent upon the consequences or results of the marketplace's relationship with a brand. Figure 6.1 lists the elements of brand equity. Brand equity is determined by the consumer and is the culmination of the consumer's assessment of the product, the company that manufactures and markets the product, and all other variables that impact on the product between manufacture and consumer consumption.

Before leaving the topic of manufacturer brands, it is important to note that, as with consumer products, organizational products also can possess brand equity. However, several differences do exist between the two sectors.[13] First, organizational products are usually branded with firm names. As a result, loyalty (or disloyalty) to the brand tends to be of a more global nature, extending across all the firm's product lines. Second, because firm versus brand loyalty exists, attempts to position new products in a manner differing from existing products may prove to be difficult, if not impossible. Finally, loyalty to organizational

FIGURE 6.1
Elements of Brand Equity

Source: David A. Aaker, *Managing Brand Equity.* © 1991, New York, by David A. Aaker. Reprinted with the permission of Free Press, a division of Simon & Schuster.

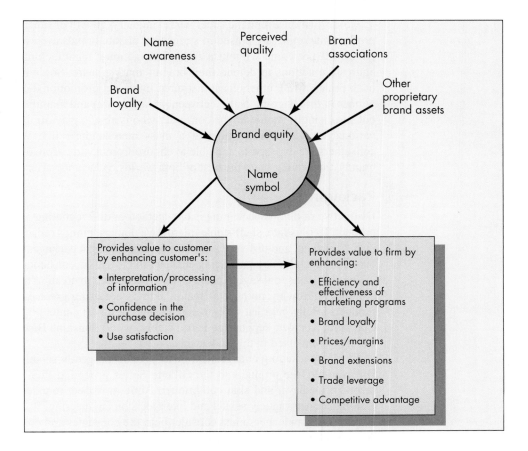

products encompasses not only the firm and its products but also the distribution channel members employed to distribute the product. Therefore, attempts to establish or change brand image must also take into account distributor image.

As a related branding strategy, many retail firms produce or market their products under a so-called private label. For example, Kmart has phased in its own store-brand products to compete with the national brands. There's Nature's Classics, a line of fancy snacks and cookies; Oral Pure, a line of dental care products; Prevail house cleaners; B.E., a Gap-style line of weekend wear; and Benchmark, a line of "made in the U.S.A." tools. Such a strategy is highly important in industries where middlemen have gained control over distribution to the consumer. The growth of the large discount and specialty stores, such as Kmart, Wal-Mart, Target, The Gap, Limited, and others, has accelerated the development of private brands. If a manufacturer refuses to supply certain middlemen with private branded merchandise, the alternative is for these middlemen to go into the manufacturing business, as in the case of Kroger supermarkets.

Private label products differ markedly from so-called generic products that sport labels such as "beer," "cigarettes," and "potato chips." Today's house brands are packaged in distinctively upscale containers. The quality of the products used as house brands equals and sometimes exceeds those offered by name brands. While generic products were positioned as a means for consumers to struggle through recessionary times, private label brands are being marketed as value brands, products that are equivalent to national brands but are priced much lower. Private brands are rapidly growing in popularity. For example, it only took JC Penney Company, Inc., five years to nurture its private-label jeans, the Arizona brand, into a powerhouse with annual sales surpassing $500 million.

Consolidation within the supermarket industry, growth of super centers, and heightened product marketing are poised to strengthen private brands even further.[14] However, these gains will not come without a fight from national manufacturers who are undertaking aggressive actions to defend their brands' market share. Some have significantly rolled back prices, while others have instituted increased promotional campaigns. The ultimate winner in this ongoing battle between private (store) and manufacturer (national) brands, not surprisingly, should be the consumer who is able to play off these store brands against national brands. By shopping at a mass merchandiser like Wal-Mart or Walgreens, consumers are exposed to and able to choose from a wide array of both national and store brands, thus giving them the best of both worlds: value and variety.

Packaging

Distinctive or unique packaging is one method of differentiating a relatively homogeneous product. To illustrate, shelf-stable microwave dinners, pumps rather than tubes of toothpaste or bars of soap, and different sizes and designs of tissue packages are attempts to differentiate a product through packaging changes and to satisfy consumer needs at the same time.

In other cases, packaging changes have succeeded in creating new attributes of value in a brand. A growing number of manufacturers are using green labels or packaging their products totally in green wrap to signify low- or no-fat content.[15] Frito-Lay, Quaker Oats, ConAgra, Keebler, Pepperidge Farm, Nabisco, and Sunshine Biscuits are all examples of companies involved in this endeavor.

Finally, packaging changes can make products urgently salable to a targeted segment. For example, the products in the Gillette Series grooming line, including shave cream, razors, aftershave, and skin conditioner, come in ribbed, rounded, metallic-gray shapes, looking at once vaguely sexual and like precision engineering.[16]

Marketing managers must consider both the consumer and costs in making packaging decisions. On one hand, the package must be capable of protecting the product through the channel of distribution to the consumer. In addition, it is desirable for packages to have a convenient size and be easy to open for the consumer. For example, single-serving soups and zip-lock packaging in cereal boxes are attempts by manufacturers to serve consumers better. Hopefully, the package is also attractive and informative, capable of being used as a competitive weapon to project a product's image. However, maximizing these objectives may increase the cost of the product to such an extent that consumers are no longer willing to purchase it. Thus, the marketing manager must determine the optimal protection, convenience, positioning, and promotional strengths of packages, subject to cost constraints.

Product Life Cycle

A firm's product strategy must take into account the fact that products have a life cycle. Figure 6.2 illustrates this life-cycle concept. Products are introduced, grow, mature, and decline. This cycle varies according to industry, product, technology, and market. Marketing executives need to be aware of the life-cycle concept because it can be a valuable aid in developing marketing strategies.

During the introduction phase of the cycle, there are usually high production and marketing costs, and since sales are only beginning to materialize, profits are low or nonexistent. Profits increase and are positively correlated with sales during the growth stage as the market begins trying and adopting the product. As the product matures, profits for the initiating firm do not keep pace with sales because of competition. Here the seller may be forced to "remarket" the product, which may involve making price concessions, increasing

FIGURE 6.2
The Product Life Cycle

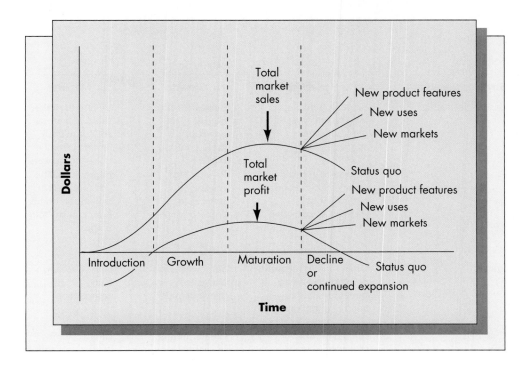

product quality, or expanding outlays on advertising and sales promotion just to maintain market share. At some point sales decline, and the seller must decide whether to (1) drop the product, (2) alter the product, (3) seek new uses for the product, (4) seek new markets, or (5) continue with more of the same.

The usefulness of the product life-cycle concept is primarily that it forces management to take a long-range view of marketing planning. In doing so, it should become clear that shifts in phases of the life cycle correspond to changes in the market situation, competition, and demand. Thus, the astute marketing manager should recognize the necessity of altering the marketing mix to meet these changing conditions. It is possible for managers to undertake strategies that, in effect, can lead to a revitalized product life cycle. For example, past advancements in technology led to the replacement of rotary dial telephones by touch-tone, push-button phones. Today, even newer technology has enabled the cordless and cellular phone to replace the traditional touch-tone, push-button phone. When applied with sound judgment, the life-cycle concept can aid in forecasting, pricing, advertising, product planning, and other aspects of marketing management. However, the marketing manager must also recognize that the life cycle is purely a tool for assisting in strategy development and not let the life cycle dictate strategy development.[17]

As useful as the product life cycle can be to managers, it does have limitations that require it to be used cautiously in developing strategy. For one thing, the length of time a product will remain in each stage is unknown and can't be predicted with accuracy. Thus, while each stage will likely occur for a successful product, marketers can't forecast when one stage will end and another will begin in order to adapt their strategies at the appropriate time. Also, they may misjudge when a stage is ending and implement an inappropriate strategy. For example, marketers who believe their products are ending the maturity stage may cut promotion costs and thus push the product into decline, whereas the product might have continued to sell if promotion had been maintained and altered.

Another limitation is that not all products go through the product life cycle in the same way. For example, many products are failures and do not have anything approaching a

	Life-Cycle Stage			
Strategy Dimension	**Introduction**	**Growth**	**Maturity**	**Decline**
Basic objectives	Establish a market for product type; persuade early adopters to buy	Build sales and market share; develop preference for brand	Defend brand's share of market; seek growth by luring customers from competitors	Limit costs or seek ways to revive sales and profits
Product	Provide high quality; select a good brand; get patent or trademark protection	Provide high quality; add services to enhance value	Improve quality; add features to distinguish brand from competitors' brands	Continue providing high quality to maintain brand's reputation; seek ways to make the product new again
Pricing	Often high to recover development costs; sometimes low to build demand rapidly	Somewhat high because of heavy demand	Low, reflecting heavy competition	Low to sell off remaining inventory or high to serve a niche market
Channels	Limited number of channels	Greater number of channels to meet demand	Greater number of channels and more incentives to resellers	Limited number of channels
Promotion	Aimed at early adopters; messages designed to educate about product type; incentives such as samples and coupons to induce trial	Aimed at wider audience; messages focus on brand benefits; for consumer products, emphasis on advertising	Messages focus on differentiating brand from its competitors' brands; heavy use of incentives such as coupons to induce buyers to switch brands	Minimal, to keep costs down

complete life cycle. Several variations of the life cycle also exist, two of which are fashions and fads.

Fashions are accepted and popular product styles. Their life cycle involves a distinctiveness stage in which trendsetters adopt the style, followed by an emulation stage in which more customers purchase the style to be the trendsetters. Next is the economic stage, in which the style becomes widely available at mass-market prices. Many fashions, such as skirt length and designer jeans, lose popularity, then regain it and repeat the fashion of cycle. The fashion cycle is clearly visible in clothing, cosmetics, tattoos, and body piercing.

Fads are products that experience an intense but brief period of popularity. Their life cycle resembles the basic product life cycle but in a very compressed form. It is usually so brief that competitors have no chance to capitalize on the fad. Some fads may repeat their popularity after long lapses.

Product Adoption and Diffusion

Obviously not all customers immediately purchase a product in the introductory stage of the product life cycle. The shape of the life-cycle curve indicates that most sales occur after the product has been available for awhile. The spread of a product through the population

FIGURE 6.3
Adopter Categories

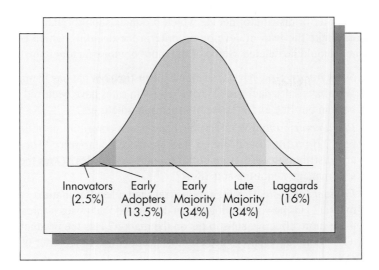

is known as the diffusion of innovation, as illustrated in Figure 6.3 which presents five adopter categories.

The first category is *innovators,* those who are the first to buy a new product. When innovators are consumers, they tend to be people who are venturesome and willing to take risks. When innovators are organizational buyers, they tend to be organizations that seek to remain at the cutting edge through the use of the latest technology and ideas.

If the experience of innovators is favorable, *early adopters* begin to buy. These buyers, who are respected social leaders and above average in education, influence the next group. Influenced by what early adopters have, the rest of the market begins to get interested in the product. The biggest category of buyers is divided into groups called the early majority and late majority. Members of the *early majority* tend to avoid risk and to make purchases carefully. They also have many informal contacts. Members of the *late majority* not only avoid risks, but are cautious and skeptical about new ideas. Eventually, the product becomes commonplace, and even laggards are ready to buy. *Laggards* are reluctant to make changes and are comfortable with traditional products. They also have a fear of debt, but may eventually purchase a well-established brand.

The Product Audit

The product audit is a marketing management technique whereby the company's current product offerings are reviewed to ascertain whether each product should be continued as is, improved, modified, or deleted. The audit is a task that should be carried out at regular intervals as a matter of policy. Product audits are the responsibility of the product manager unless specifically delegated to someone else.

Deletions

In today's environment, there are a growing number of products being introduced each year that are competing for limited shelf space. This growth is primarily due to (1) new knowledge being applied faster, and (2) the decrease in time between product introductions (by a given organization).[18] In addition, companies are not consistently removing products from the market at the same time they are introducing new products. The result is a situation in which too many products are fighting for too little shelf space. One of the main purposes of the product audit is to detect sick products and then bury them. Rather than let the retailer or distributor decide which products should remain, organizations themselves should take the lead in developing criteria for deciding which products should stay and which should be deleted. Some of the more obvious factors to be considered are

Sales trends. How have sales moved over time? What has happened to market share? Why have sales declined? What changes in sales have occurred in competitive products both in our line and in those of other manufacturers?

Profit contribution. What has been the profit contribution of this product to the company? If profits have declined, how are these tied to price? Have selling, promotion, and distribution costs risen out of proportion to sales? Does the product require excessive management time and effort?

Product life cycle. Has the product reached a level of maturity and saturation in the market? Has new technology been developed that poses a threat to the product? Are there more effective substitutes on the market? Has the product outgrown its usefulness? Can the resources used on this product be put to better use?

Customer migration patterns. If the product is deleted, will customers of this product switch to other substitute products marketed by our firm? In total, will profits associated with our line increase due to favorable switching patterns?

The above factors should be used as guidelines for making the final decision to delete a product. Deletion decisions are very difficult to make because of their potential impact on customers and the firm. For example, eliminating a product may force a company to lay off some employees. There are other factors to consider, such as keeping consumers supplied with replacement parts and repair service and maintaining the goodwill of distributors who have an inventory of the product. The deletion plan should provide for clearing out of stock in question.

Product Improvement

One of the other important objectives of the audit is to ascertain whether to alter the product in some way or to leave things as they are. Altering the product means changing one or more of its attributes or marketing dimensions. *Attributes* refer mainly to product features, design, package, and so forth. *Marketing dimensions* refer to such things as price, promotion strategy, and channels of distribution.

It is possible to look at the product audit as a management device for controlling the product strategy. Here, control means feedback on product performance and corrective action in the form of product improvement. Product improvement is a top-level management decision, but the information needed to make the improvement decision may come from the consumer or the middlemen. Suggestions are often made by advertising agencies or consultants. Reports by the sales force should be structured in a way to provide management with certain types of product information; in fact, these reports can be the firm's most valuable product-improvement tool. Implementing a product improvement decision will often require the coordinated efforts of several specialists, plus some research. For example, product design improvement decisions involve engineering, manufacturing, accounting, and marketing. When a firm becomes aware that a product's design can be improved, it is not always clear how consumers will react to the various alterations. To illustrate, in blind taste tests, the Coca-Cola Company found that consumers overwhelmingly preferred the taste of a reformulated, sweeter new Coke over old Coke. However, when placed on the market in labeled containers, new Coke turned out to be a failure due to consumers' emotional attachments to the classic Coke. Consequently, it is advisable to conduct some market tests in realistic settings.

A discussion of product improvement would not be complete without taking into account the benefits associated with benchmarking, especially as they relate to the notion of

Instead of abandoning or harvesting an older, mature product, many companies are looking instead to rejuvenate that product and extend its life cycle. The advantages of product rejuvenation include the following:

Less risk. Past experience in all phases of the product's life cycle permits the company to focus on improving business practices instead of formulating completely new, untested methods.

Lower costs. Most, if not all, of the product's start-up costs are now avoided. Plus, prior experience in both marketing and producing the product makes spending more efficient.

Less time. Because the beginning stages of product development have already occurred, the time involved in rejuvenating a product is significantly less than a new venture.

Cheaper market share. The money new products need to invest to create initial brand recognition as well as the lower costs mentioned above can be saved, used to enhance the product offering, or enable the product to be offered at a lower price.

Higher profits. Efficiency, brand recognition, superior product quality, and the ability to have a narrow focus all contribute to lower costs or increased sales, or both, thus increasing the potential for higher profits.

Source: Conrad Berenson and Iris Mohr-Jackson, "Product Rejuvenation: A Less Risky Alternative to Product Innovation," *Business Horizons*, November–December 1994, pp. 51–57. © 1994 by the Foundation for the School of Business at Indiana University. Used with permission.

the extended product, the tangible product along with the whole cluster of services that accompany it.[19] The formal definition of *benchmarking* is the continuous process of measuring products, services, and practices against those of the toughest competitors or companies renowned as leaders. In other words, benchmarking involves learning about best practices from best-performing companies—how they are achieving strong performance. It is an effective tool being used by organizations to improve on existing products, activities, functions, or processes. Major corporations such as IBM, AT&T, DuPont, Ford, Eastman Kodak, Miliken, Motorola, and Xerox all have numerous benchmarking studies in progress. For example, IBM has already performed more than 500 benchmarking studies. Benchmarking can assist companies in many product improvement efforts, including (1) boosting product quality, (2) developing more user-friendly products, (3) improving customer order-processing activities, and (4) shortening delivery lead times. In the case of benchmarking, companies can achieve great success by copying others. Thus, by its very nature, benchmarking becomes an essential element in the ongoing product auditing process.

Organizing for Product Management

Whether managing existing products or developing new products (the subject of the next chapter), organizations that are successful have one factor in common: They actively manage both types. Obviously, if a firm has only one product, it gets everyone's attention. But as the number of products grow and the need to develop new products becomes evident, some rational management system is necessary.

Under a *marketing-manager system,* one person is responsible for overseeing an entire product line with all of the functional areas of marketing such as research, advertising, sales promotion, sales, and product planning. This type of system is popular in organizations with a line or lines of similar products or one dominant product line. Sometimes referred to as category management, the marketing manager system is seen as being superior to a brand manager system because one manager oversees all brands within a particular line, thus avoiding brand competition. Organizations such as PepsiCo, Purex, Eastman Kodak, and Levi Strauss use some form of marketing-manager system.

Under a *brand-manager system,* a manager focuses on a single product or a very small group of new and existing products. Typically, this person is responsible for everything from marketing research and package design to advertising. Often called a product-management system, the brand-manager system has been criticized on several dimensions. First, brand managers often have difficulty because they do not have authority commensurate with their responsibilities. Second, they often pay inadequate attention to new products. Finally, they are often more concerned with their own brand's profitability than with the profitability of all of the organization's brands. These criticisms are not aimed at people but at the system itself, which may force brand managers into the above behaviors. Despite its drawbacks, organizations such as RJR Nabisco and Black & Decker have used that system.

Successful *new* products often come from organizations that try to bring all of the capabilities of the organization to bear on the problems of customers. Obviously, this requires the cooperation of all of the various functional departments in the organization. Thus, the use of *cross-functional teams* has become an important way to manage the development of new products. A *venture team* is a popular method used in such organizations as Xerox, Polaroid, Exxon, IBM, Monsanto, and Motorola. A venture team is a cross-functional team responsible for all the tasks involved in the development of a new product. Once the new product is already launched, the team may turn over responsibility for managing the product to a brand manager or product manager or it may manage the new product as a separate business.

The use of cross-functional teams in product management and new product development is increasing for a very simple reason: Organizations need the contributions of all functions and therefore require their cooperation. Cross-functional teams operate independently of the organization's functional departments but include members from each function. A team might include a member from engineering, marketing, finance, service, and designers. Some organizations even include important outsiders (e.g., parts suppliers) on cross-functional teams. Figure 6.4 presents some important prerequisites for the use of cross-functional teams in managing existing products and developing new products.

FIGURE 6.4

Some Requirements for the Effective Use of Cross-Functional Teams in Product Management and New Product Development

A growing number of organizations have begun using cross-functional teams for product management and new product development. Having representatives from various departments clearly has its advantages, but most important, effective teams must have the nurture and support of management. Some requirements for effective teams are

1. *Commitment of top management and provision of clear goals.* Organizations that successfully use cross-functional teams in product management or development have managers who are deeply committed to the team concept. As a result, high-performance teams have a clear understanding of the product management and development goals of the organization. The importance of these goals encourages individuals to defer their own functional or departmental concerns to team goals.

2. *Trust among members.* For cross-functional teams to work, a high level of trust must exist among members. The climate of trust within a team seems to be highly dependent on members' perception of management's trust of the group as a whole.

3. *Cross-functional cooperation.* If a team is to take responsibility and assume the risk of product development, its members will need detailed information about the overall operation of the organization. It often requires that functional units be willing to share information that previously was not shared with other departments.

4. *Time and training.* Effective cross-functional teams need time to mature. They require massive planning and intense and prompt access to resources, financial and other. Because members have to put aside functional and departmental loyalties and concerns, training is usually necessary.

Conclusion

This chapter has been concerned with a central element of marketing management—product strategy. The first part of the chapter discussed some basic issues in product strategy, including product definition and classification, product quality and value, product mix and product lines, branding and brand equity, and packaging. The product life cycle was discussed as well as the product audit. Finally, three methods of organizing for product management were presented. Although product considerations are extremely important, remember that the product is only one element of the marketing mix. Focusing on product decisions alone, without consideration of the other marketing mix variables, would be an ineffective approach to marketing strategy.

Additional Readings

Butscher, Stephen A., and Michael Laker. "Market Driven Product Development." *Marketing Management,* Summer 2000, pp. 48–53.

Crawford, C. Merle, and Anthony DeBenedetto. *New Products Management,* Burr Ridge, IL: McGraw-Hill/Irwin, 2001.

Jain, Dipak. "Managing New Product Development for Strategic Competitive Advantage." In *Kellogg on Marketing,* ed. Dawn Iacobucci, New York: John Wiley, 2001.

Kuczmarski, Thomas D. "Measuring Your Return on Innovation." *Marketing Management,* Spring 2000, pp. 25–34.

Moser, Mike. *United We Brand*. Boston: HBS Press, 2003.

Rust, Roland T.; Valarie Zeithaml; and Katherine N. Lemon. *Driving Customer Equity*. New York: The Free Press, 2000.

Sobek, Durwood K.; Jeffrey K. Liker; and Allen C. Ward. "Another Look at How Toyota Integrates Product Development." *Harvard Business Review,* July–August 1998, pp. 36–48.

New Product Planning and Development

New products are a vital part of a firm's competitive growth strategy. Leaders of successful firms know that it is not enough to develop new products on a sporadic basis. What counts is a climate of product development that leads to one triumph after another. It is commonplace for major companies to have 50 percent or more of their current sales in products introduced within the last 10 years. For example, the 3M Company derives 30 percent of its revenues from products less than four years old.[1]

Some additional facts about new products are:

- Many new products are failures. Estimates of new product failures range from 33 percent to 90 percent, depending on industry.
- New product sales grow far more rapidly than sales of current products, potentially providing a surprisingly large boost to a company's growth rate.
- Companies vary widely in the effectiveness of their new product programs.
- A major obstacle to effectively predicting new product demand is limited vision.
- Common elements appear in the management practices that generally distinguish the relative degree of efficiency and success between companies.

In one recent year, almost 22,000 products were introduced in supermarkets, drugstores, mass merchandisers, and health food stores.[2] Of these, only a small percentage (less than 20 percent) met sales goals. The cost of introducing a new brand in some consumer markets can range from $50 million to hundreds of millions of dollars. In addition to the outlay cost of product failures, there are also opportunity costs. These opportunity costs refer not only to the alternative uses of funds spent on product failures but also to the time spent in unprofitable product development.

Product development can take many years. For example, Hills Brothers (now owned by Nestlé) spent 22 years in developing its instant coffee, while it took General Foods (now owned by Philip Morris) 10 years to develop Maxim. However, the success of one new product is no guarantee that the way will be paved for additional and successful low-cost brand extensions. For example, on the positive side, Gillette was able to leverage the research and monies spent on the original Sensor to successfully develop and launch the Sensor razor for women and the Sensor Excel razor. On the negative side, Maxwell House (Philip Morris), Folgers (Procter & Gamble), and Nestlé are still struggling to develop commercially successful lines of fresh whole bean coffee, having been beaten to the punch by smaller companies such as Starbucks, Millstone Coffee, Inc., and Brothers Gourmet Coffees.[3]

Since successful new product development is of vital importance to an organization, corporations are searching for numerous methods to improve the NPD process. However, in the mad rush, managers can overlook their greatest ally, common sense. What follows are three misconceptions that are commonly held by managers involved in the new product development process.

1. *It worked there; it will work here.* What works well at one company may not be as easily transferable with equal success to another company. There is no one common formula to the new product development process.
2. *It worked once; it will work again.* There will be peaks and valleys in every new product development process. Failure, as well as success, should be viewed as a common outcome.
3. *The cart can come before the horse.* Successful implementation of a means to improve the new product development process is heavily dependent on assumed conditions already existing within the corporation. Before the process can be improved, other organizational changes may have to be implemented.

Source: Adapted from Geoffrey Gordon, Douglas Ayers, Nessim Hanna, and Rick Ridnour, "The Product Development Process: Three Misconceptions which Can Derail Even the 'Best-Laid' Plans," *Journal of Product and Brand Management* 4, no. 1 (1995), pp. 7–17.

Good management, with heavy emphasis on planning, organization, and interaction among the various functional units (e.g., marketing, manufacturing, engineering, R&D), seems to be the key factor contributing to a firm's success in launching new products. The primary reason found for new product failure is an inability on the part of the selling company to match up its offerings to the needs of the customer. This inability to satisfy customer needs can be attributed to three main sources: inadequacy of upfront intelligence efforts, failure on the part of the company to stick close to what the company does best, and the inability to provide better value than competing products and technologies.

New Product Strategy

In developing new products, the first question a marketing manager must ask is, In how many ways can a product be new? C. Merle Crawford and Anthony DiBenedetto developed a definition of new products based on the following five different categories:[4]

1. *New-to-the-world products.* Products that are inventions: for example, Polaroid camera, the first car, rayon, the laser printer, in-line skates.
2. *New category entries.* Products that take a firm into a category new to it, but that are not new to the world: for example, P&G's first shampoo, Hallmark gift items, AT&T's Universal Card.
3. *Additions to product lines.* Products that are line extensions, flankers, and so on, to the firm's current markets, for example, Tide Liquid detergent, Bud Light, Apple's Power Mac.
4. *Product improvements.* Current products made better; virtually every product on the market has been improved, often many times.
5. *Repositionings.* Products that are retargeted for a new use or application; a classic case is Arm & Hammer baking soda, which was repositioned several times as drain deodorant, refrigerator freshener, toothpaste, deodorant, and so on.

The new product categories listed on the previous page raise the issue of imitation products, strictly me-too or improved versions of existing products. If a firm introduces a form of dry beer that is new to them but is identical or similar to other beers on the market, is it a new product? The answer is yes, because it is new to the firm. Managers should not get the idea that to imitate is bad and to innovate is good, for most of the best-selling products on the market today are improvements over another company's original invention. The best strategy is the one that will maximize company goals. It should be noted that Crawford and DiBenedetto's categories don't encompass variations such as, new to a country, new channel of distribution, packaging improvement, and different resources or method of manufacture, which they consider to be variations of the five categories, especially as these variations relate to additions to product lines.

A second broader approach to the new product question is the one developed by H. Igor Ansoff in the form of growth vectors.[5] This is the matrix first introduced in Chapter 1 that indicates the direction in which the organization is moving with respect to its current products and markets. It is shown again in Figure 7.1.

Market penetration denotes a growth direction through the increase in market share for present product markets. *Product development* refers to creating new products to replace existing ones. Firms using either market penetration or product development strategies are attempting to capitalize on existing markets and combat competitive entry and/or further market incursions. *Market development* refers to finding new customers for existing products. *Diversification* refers to developing new products and cultivating new markets. Firms using market development and diversification strategies are seeking to establish footholds in new markets or preempt competition in emerging market segments.

As shown in Figure 7.1, market penetration and market development strategies use present products. A goal of these types of strategies is to either increase frequency of consumption or increase the number of customers using the firm's product(s). A strategic focus is placed on altering the breadth and depth of the firm's existing product lines. Product development and diversification can be characterized as product mix strategies. New products, as defined in the growth vector matrix, usually require the firm to make significant investments in research and development and may require major changes in its organizational structure. Firms are not confined to pursuing a single direction. For example, Miller Brewing Co. has decided four key strategies should dictate its activities for the next decade, including (1) building its premium-brand franchises through investment spending, (2) continuing to develop value-added new products with clear consumer benefits, (3) leveraging local markets to build its brand franchise, and (4) building business globally.[6] Success for Miller depends on pursuing strategies that encompass all areas of the growth vector matrix.

It has already been stated that new products are the lifeblood of successful business firms. Thus, the critical product policy question is not whether to develop new products but in what direction to move. One way of dealing with this problem is to formulate standards or norms that new products must meet if they are to be considered candidates for launching. In other words, as part of its new product policy, management must ask itself the basic question, What is the potential contribution of each anticipated new product to the company?

FIGURE 7.1
Organizational Growth Strategies

Products Markets	Present	New
Present	Market penetration	Product development
New	Market development	Diversification

1. *Product superiority/quality.* The competitive advantage the product has by virtue of features, benefits, quality, uniqueness, and so on.
2. *Economic advantage to user.* The product's quality for the customer's money.
3. *Overall company/project fit.* The product's synergy with the company—marketing, managerial, business fit.
4. *Technological compatibility.* The product's technological synergy with the company—R&D, engineering, production fit.
5. *Familiarity to the company.* How familiar or "close to home" the product is to the company's current products and markets (as opposed to being targeted at new customers or markets).
6. *Market need, growth, and size.* The magnitude of the market opportunity.
7. *Competitive situation.* How easy the market is to penetrate from a competitive standpoint.
8. *Defined opportunity.* Whether the product has a well-defined category and established market to enter.
9. *Market-driven process.* The new product process is well planned and executed, receiving adequate resources suited to the customer's needs, wants, and buying behavior.
10. *Customer service.* The product is supported by friendly, courteous, prompt, and efficient customer service.

Source: Based on research conducted by Robert G. Cooper, "What Distinguishes the Top Performing New Products in Financial Services," *Journal of Product Innovation Management,* September 1994, pp. 281–99; and "The NewProd System: The Industry Experience," *Journal of Product Innovation Management,* June 1992, pp. 113–27.

Each company must answer this question in accordance with its long-term goals, corporate mission, resources, and so forth. Unfortunately, some of the reasons commonly given to justify the launching of new products are so general that they become meaningless. Phrases such as *additional profits, increased growth,* or *cyclical stability* must be translated into more specific objectives. For example, one objective may be to reduce manufacturing overhead costs by using plant capacity better. This may be accomplished by using the new product as an off-season filler. Naturally, the new product proposal would also have to include production and accounting data to back up this cost argument.

In every new product proposal some attention must be given to the ultimate economic contribution of each new product candidate. If the argument is that a certain type of product is needed to keep up with competition or to establish leadership in the market, it is fair to ask, Why? To put the question another way, top management can ask: What will be the effect on the firm's long-run profit picture if we do not develop and launch this or that new product? Policy-making criteria on new products should specify (1) a working definition of the profit concept acceptable to top management, (2) a minimum level or floor of profits, (3) the availability and cost of capital to develop a new product, and (4) a specified time period in which the new product must recoup its operating costs and begin contributing to profits.

It is critical that firms not become solely preoccupied with a short-term focus on earnings associated with new products. For example, in some industrial markets, a 20-year spread has been found between the development and wide-spread adoption of products, on average. Indeed, an advantage that some Japanese firms appear to possess is that their management is free from the pressure of steady improvement in earnings per share that plagues American managers who emphasize short-term profits. Japanese managers believe that market share will lead to customer loyalty, which in turn will lead to profits generated from repeat purchases. Through a continual introduction of new products, firms will succeed in building share. This share growth will then ultimately result in earnings growth and profitability that will be supported by the stock market in terms of higher share prices over the long term.

New Product Planning and Development Process

Ideally, products that generate a maximum dollar profit with a minimum amount of risk should be developed and marketed. However, it is very difficult for planners to implement this idea because of the number and nature of the variables involved. What is needed is a systematic, formalized process for new product planning. Although such a process does not provide management with any magic answers, it can increase the probability of new product success. Initially, the firm must establish some new product policy guidelines that include the product fields of primary interest, organizational responsibilities for managing the various stages in new product development, and criteria for making go-ahead decisions. After these guidelines are established, a process such as the one shown in Figure 7.2 should be useful in new product development.

Idea Generation

Every product starts as an idea. But all new product ideas do not have equal merit or potential for economic or commercial success. Some estimates indicate that as many as 60 or 70 ideas are necessary to yield one successful product. This is an average figure, but it serves to illustrate that new product ideas have a high mortality rate. In terms of

FIGURE 7.2
The New Product Development Process

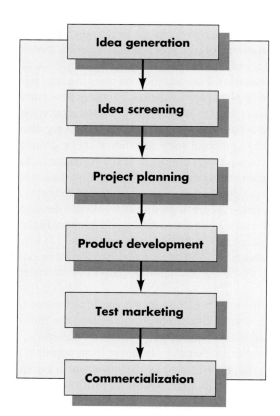

money, almost three-fourths of all the dollars of new product expense go to unsuccessful products.

The problem at this stage is to ensure that all new product ideas available to the company at least have a chance to be heard and evaluated. Ideas are the raw materials for product development, and the whole planning process depends on the quality of the idea generation and screening process. Since idea generation is the least costly stage in the new product development process (in terms of investment in funds, time, personnel, and escalation of commitment), it makes sense that an emphasis be placed first on recognizing available sources of new product ideas and then on funneling these ideas to appropriate decision makers for screening.

Top-management support is critical to providing an atmosphere that stimulates new product activity. Many times, great ideas come from some very unusual sources. A top-management structure that is unwilling to take risks will avoid radical new product and other innovation activities and instead concentrate solely on minor areas of improvement such as line extensions. To facilitate top-management support, it is essential that new product development be focused on meeting market needs.

Both technology push and market pull research activities play an important role in new product ideas and development. By taking a broad view of customer needs and wants, basic and applied research (technology push) can lead to ideas that will yield high profits to the firm. For example, Compaq bet millions (and won) on PC network servers in the early 1990s even though business customers said they would never abandon their mainframes. In a similar vein, Chrysler forged ahead with the original minivan despite research showing people disliked the odd-looking vehicle.[7] Marketing, on the other hand, is more responsible for gathering and disseminating information gained from customers and other contacts. This information relates mainly to specific features and functions of the product that can be improved upon or market needs that current products are not satisfying (market pull). For example, product ideas at Rubbermaid often come from employees roaming the aisles at hardware stores and conversations with family and friends.[8] Both technology push and market pull approaches are essential to the generation of new product ideas.

Some firms use mechanisms such as "out-rotation," outsider involvement, and rewards to foster cooperation between design engineers and marketers.[9] Out-rotation involves placing employees in positions that require direct contact with customers, competitors, and other key outside groups. For example, Hewlett-Packard regularly rotates design engineers to retail sales positions on a temporary basis. Other organizations actively involve "outsiders" in planning or reward engineers for making external customer contacts. Regardless of method used, the primary lesson is to keep the communications flow going in all directions throughout the organization.

Idea Screening

The primary function of the idea screening process is twofold: first, to eliminate ideas for new products that could not be profitably marketed by the firm, and second, to expand viable ideas into full product concepts. New product ideas may be eliminated either because they are outside the fields of the firm's interest or because the firm does not have the necessary resources or technology to produce the product at a profit. Generally speaking, the organization has to consider three categories of risk (and its associated risk tolerance) in the idea screening phase prior to reaching a decision. These three risk categories are:[10]

1. *Strategic risk.* Strategic risk involves the risk of not matching the role or purpose of a new product with a specific strategic need or issue of the organization. If an organization feels it necessary to develop certain types of radical innovations or products new to the

1. Customers
   a. Customer requests
   b. Customer complaints/compliments
   c. Market surveys
   d. Focus groups
2. Competitors
   a. Monitoring competitors' developments
   b. Monitoring testing of competitors' products
   c. Monitoring industry movements
3. Distribution channels
   a. Suppliers
   b. Distributors
   c. Retailers
   d. Trade shows
4. Research and engineering
   a. Product testing
   b. Product endorsement
   c. Brainstorming meetings
   d. Accidental discovery
5. Other internal sources
   a. Management
   b. Sales force
   c. Employee suggestions
   d. Innovation group meetings
   e. Stockholders
6. Other external sources
   a. Consultants
   b. Academic journals
   c. Periodicals and other press

company in order to carry out long-term strategies, then management must be willing to dedicate necessary resources and time to pursue these type projects.

2. *Market risk.* Market risk is the risk that a new product won't meet a market need in a value-added, differentiated way. As products are being developed, customer requirements change and new technologies evolve. Management must be willing and able to shift its new product efforts to keep pace with change.

3. *Internal risk.* Internal risk is the risk that a new product won't be developed within the desired time and budget. Up front, management must decide the level of commitment it will extend in terms of time and budgetary expenditures to adequately ensure the completion of specific projects. Concurrently, progress goals must be established so that "proceed" or "do not proceed" decisions can be reached regarding continuation of projects.

In evaluating these risks, firms should not act too hastily in discounting new product ideas solely because of a lack of resources or expertise. Instead, firms should consider forming joint or strategic alliances with other firms. A strategic alliance is a long-term partnership between two organizations designed to accomplish the strategic goals of both parties. Potential benefits to be gained from alliances include (1) increased access to technology, funding, and information; (2) market expansion and greater penetration of current markets; and (3) de-escalated competitive rivalries. Motorola is a company that has prospered by forming numerous joint ventures with both American and foreign companies.[11]

Ideas that appear to have adequate profit potential and offer the firm a competitive advantage in the market should be accepted for further study.

Project Planning

This stage of the process involves several steps. It is here that the new product proposal is evaluated further and responsibility for the project is assigned to a project team. The proposal is analyzed in terms of production, marketing, financial, and competitive factors. A development budget is established, and some preliminary marketing and technical research is undertaken. The product is actually designed in a rough form. Alternative product features and component specifications are outlined. Finally, a project plan is written up, which includes estimates of future development, production, and

Leader
Full-time
Experienced
Facilitator

Core members
May be full-time
Key function
Permanent
Fuse into a group

Support members
In and out, as needed
Scores of functions:
Legal, sales,
accounting, PR,
HRM, advertising,
customer service inside/
outside the firm
All stakeholders
Liaison, not on team
Reached via network

Support Members

Core Members

R&D   Manufacturing

Leader

**New Products
Manager**

Design   Marketing

Market research   Finance

Source: C. Merle Crawford, *New Products Management,* 5th ed. (Burr Ridge, IL: Irwin, 1997), p. 31.

marketing costs along with capital requirements and manpower needs. A schedule or timetable is also included. Finally, the project proposal is given to top management for a go or no-go decision.

Various alternatives exist for creating and managing the project teams. Two of the better-known methods are the establishment of a *skunkworks,* whereby a project team can work in relative privacy away from the rest of the organization, and a *rugby* or *relay approach,* whereby groups in different areas of the company are simultaneously working on the project.[12] The common tie that binds these and other successful approaches together is the degree of interaction that develops among the marketing, engineering, production, and other critical staff. The earlier in the process that interactive, cooperative efforts begin, the higher the likelihood is that development efforts will be successful. A key component contributing to the success of many companies' product development efforts relates to the emphasis placed on creating *cross-functional teams* early in the development process. Both of the above methods use cross-functional teams. Members from many different departments come together to jointly establish new product development goals and priorities and to develop new product development schedules. Frequently, marketing and/or sales personnel are called in to lead these teams.[13]

FINANCIAL CRITERIA

Return on investment (ROI)

Various profit margin measures

Sales and sales growth

Various profit measures

Payback and payback period

Internal rate of return (IRR)

Return on assets (ROA)

Return on equity (ROE)

Breakeven and breakeven point

Share and market share

Return on sales

Net present value (NPV)

NONFINANCIAL CRITERIA

Performance of new products

Market share achieved

Satisfaction of customer needs

Other market-related benefits

Strategic issues/fit/synergy

Technical aspects of production

Uniqueness of the new products

Source: Albert L. Page, "Assessing New Product Development Practices and Performance: Establishing Crucial Norms," *Journal of Product Innovation Management,* September 1993, pp. 273–90. 1993 by Elsevier Science Inc. Reprinted by permission of the publisher.

Product Development

At this juncture, the product idea has been evaluated from the standpoint of engineering, manufacturing, finance, and marketing. If it has met all expectations, it is considered a candidate for further research and testing. In the laboratory, the product is converted into a finished good and tested. A development report to management is prepared that spells out in fine detail: (1) results of the studies by the engineering department, (2) required plan design,(3) production facilities design, (4) tooling requirements, (5) marketing test plan; (6) financial program survey, and (7) estimated release date.[14]

Test Marketing

Up until now the product has been a company secret. Now management goes outside the company and submits the product candidate for customer approval. Test-market programs are conducted in line with the general plans for launching the product. Test marketing is a controlled experiment in a limited geographical area to test the new product or in some cases certain aspects of the marketing strategy, such as packaging or advertising.

The main goal of a test market is to evaluate and adjust, as necessary, the general marketing strategy to be used and the appropriate marketing mix. Additionally, producers can use the early interaction with buyers, occurring in test markets, to begin exploration of issues related to the next generation of product development.[15] Especially in cases where new technologies and markets are emerging, firms can benefit greatly from knowledge gained in test markets. Throughout the test market process, findings are being analyzed and forecasts of volume developed. In summary, a well-done test market procedure can reduce the risks that include not only lost marketing and sales dollars but also capital—the expense of installing production lines or building a new factory. Upon completion of a successful test market phase, the marketing plan can be finalized and the product prepared for launch.

Commercialization

This is the launching step in which the firm commits to introducing the product into the marketplace. During this stage, heavy emphasis is placed on the organization structure and

When specialized knowledge is needed to satisfy the needs of customers, cross-functional teams can greatly improve product development success. Such teams bring together complementary skills in one of three areas: technical or functional expertise, problem-solving and decision-making skills, and interpersonal skills.

1. *Technical or functional skills.* It would make little sense for a marketer to design technical specifications for a new type of cellular phone. Likewise, it would make little sense for an engineer to try to guess what features consumers find most important in choosing what type of phone to purchase. In this case, a product development group that consists solely of marketers or engineers would be less likely to succeed than a cross-functional team using the complementary skills of both.

2. *Problem-solving and decision-making skills.* Cross-functional teams possess the ability to identify problems and opportunities the entire organization faces, identify feasible new product alternatives, and make the necessary choices quicker. Most industrial functional units are not able to perform all of these tasks effectively. However, it is likely that the necessary skills are present in a well-chosen cross-functional team and that these skills can be used in the organization's best interests.

3. *Interpersonal skills.* Common understanding and knowledge of problems faced and decisions needed for effective product development cannot arise without effective communication and constructive conflict. What is needed is risk-taking, helpful criticism, objectivity, active listening, support, and recognition of the interests and achievements of others. An effective, cross-functional team is made up of members who, in total, possess all of these skills. Individual members, at various times, will be called on to use their interpersonal skill to move the team forward. The use of the complementary interpersonal skills of team members can lead to extraordinary results for organizations.

management talent needed to implement the marketing strategy. Emphasis is also given to following up on such things as bugs in the design, production costs, quality control, and inventory requirements. Procedures and responsibility for evaluating the success of the new product by comparison with projections are also finalized.

The Importance of Time

Over the course of the last five years, companies have placed an increasing emphasis on shortening their products' time to market. *Time to market* can be defined as the elapsed time between product definition and product availability. It has been well documented that companies that are first in bringing their products to market enjoy a competitive advantage both in terms of profits and market share.[16] Successful time-based innovations can be attributed to the use of short production runs, whereby products can be improved on an incremental basis, and the use of cross-functional teams, decentralized work scheduling and monitoring, and a responsive system for gathering and analyzing customer feedback.

Several U.S. companies, including Procter & Gamble, have taken steps to speed up the new product development cycle by giving managers, at the product class and brand family level, more decision-making power. Increasingly, companies are bypassing time-consuming regional test markets, when feasible, in favor of national launches. It is becoming important, more than ever, that firms do a successful job of developing new products right the first time. To accomplish this, companies must have the right people with the right skills and talents in key positions within the new product framework.

Some Important New Product Decisions

In the development of new products, marketers have several important decisions to make about the characteristics of the product itself. These include quality level, product features, product design, and product safety levels.

Quality Level

Both consumers and organizational buyers consider the level of product quality when making purchase decisions for both new and existing products. At a minimum, buyers want products that will perform the functions they are supposed to and do so reasonably well. Some customers are willing to accept lower quality if product use is not demanding and the price is lower. Some homeowners might prefer Sears brand hand tools over the higher-quality Craftsman brand since they are lower priced and may be used only occasionally. Industrial buyers of nuts and bolts for automobiles seldom use the highest quality used in aircraft since cars are used in less demanding situations.

In designing new products, marketers must consider what criteria potential customers use to determine their perceptions of quality. While these will vary by product, Figure 7.3 presents eight general criteria.

An important indicator of a number of the criteria listed in Figure 7.3 is the presence and extent of a new product *warranty*. A warranty is the producer's statement of what it will do to compensate the buyer if the product is defective or does not work properly. In many instances, the courts also hold that businesses have implied warranties or unstated promises to compensate buyers if their products fail to perform up to the basic standards of the industry or to the level promised. Certainly an organization that wants to emphasize high quality will offer customers more than implied warranties enforced by the courts.

Finally, many marketers offer a guarantee instead of or in addition to a warranty on new products. A *guarantee* is an assurance that the product is as represented and will perform properly. Typically if the product fails to perform, the organization making the guarantee replaces the product or refunds the customer's money. Guarantees imply to some buyers that the manufacturer is confident of the new products' quality.

Product Features

A *product feature* is a fact or particular specification about a product (e.g., "less calories than all other soft drinks," "more vitamin C than any other multiple vitamin"). Marketers select new product features by determining what it is that customers want their products

FIGURE 7.3
Some Criteria for Determining Perceptions of Quality

Source: Adopted from David A. Garvin, "Competing on the Eight Dimensions of Quality," *Harvard Business Review,* November–December 1987.

1. *Performance*—How well does the product do what it is supposed to do?
2. *Features*—Does the product have any unique features that are desirable?
3. *Reliability*—Is the product likely to function well and not break down over a reasonable time period?
4. *Conformance*—Does the product conform to established standards for such things as safety?
5. *Durability*—How long will the product last before it will be worn out and have to be replaced?
6. *Serviceability*—How quickly and easily can any problems be corrected?
7. *Aesthetics*—How appealing is the product to the appropriate senses of sight, taste, smell, feel, and/or sound?
8. *Overall Evaluation*—Considering everything about the product, including its physical characteristics, manufacturer, brand image, packaging, and price, how good is this product?

to offer. Effective marketers attempt not only to ask potential customers what they want, but to learn what these customers are likely to need. Such marketers may identify a need for new features that target markets have not yet thought of and may not yet even understand.

Product Design

Many well-designed products are easy to use as intended and pleasing to the senses. Designing new products with both ease of use and aesthetic appeal can be difficult, but it can clearly differentiate a new product from competitors. Good design can add great value to a new product. A well-designed product can please customers without necessarily costing more to make. This is especially likely to happen when the organization uses cross-functional teams to develop its products. If employees from engineering, marketing, and manufacturing work together on what the product will look like and how it will operate, they are more likely to create a design that is easy and economical to make as well as use.

Product Safety

Clearly, new products must have a reasonable level of safety. Safety is both an ethical and practical issue. Ethically, customers should not be harmed by using a product as intended. The practical issue is that when users get harmed by a product, they may stop buying, tell others about their experience, or sue the company that made or sold it.

Some products are inherently dangerous and can result in injury to users. However, it may be so expensive to make them safer that buyers could not afford to buy them. Such products include automobiles, farm equipment and other machinery, and guns. Other products such as patented medicines can harm a small portion of users. Hopefully, the benefits such products offer outweigh their risks.

Causes of New Product Failure

Many new products with satisfactory potential have failed to make the grade. Many of the reasons for new product failure relate to execution and control problems. What follows is a brief list of some of the more important causes of new product failures after the products have been carefully screened, developed, and marketed.[17]

1. No competitive point of difference, unexpected reactions from competitors, or both.
2. Poor positioning.
3. Poor quality of product.
4. Nondelivery of promised benefits of product.
5. Too little marketing support.
6. Poor perceived price/quality (value) relationship.
7. Faulty estimates of market potential and other marketing research mistakes.
8. Faulty estimates of production and marketing costs.
9. Improper channels of distribution selected.
10. Rapid change in the market (economy) after the product was introduced.

Some of these problems are beyond the control of management, but it is clear that successful new product planning requires large amounts of reliable information in diverse areas. Each department assigned functional responsibility for product development automatically becomes an input to the information system needed by the new product decision maker. For example, when a firm is developing a new product, it is wise for both engineers and marketers to consider both the kind of market to be entered (e.g., consumer, organizational, international) and specific target segments. These decisions will be of paramount influence on the design and cost of the finished good, which will, of course, directly influence price, sales, and profits.

Need for Research

In many respects it can be argued that the keystone activity of any new product planning system is research—not just marketing research, but technical research as well. Regardless of the way in which the new product planning function is organized in the company, new product development decisions by top management require data that provide a base for making more intelligent choices. New product project reports ought to be more than a collection of "expert" opinions. Top management has a responsibility to ask certain questions, and the new product planning team has an obligation to generate answers to these questions based on research that provides marketing, economic, engineering, and production information. This need will be more clearly understood if some of the specific questions commonly raised in evaluating product ideas are examined:

1. What is the anticipated market demand over time? Are the potential applications for the product restricted?
2. Can the item be patented? Are there any antitrust problems?
3. Can the product be sold through present channels and sales force? What will be the number of new salespersons needed? What additional sales training will be required?
4. At different volume levels, what will be the unit manufacturing costs?
5. What is the most appropriate package to use in terms of color, material, design, and so forth?
6. What is the estimated return on investment?
7. What is the appropriate pricing strategy?

While this list is not intended to be exhaustive, it serves to illustrate the serious need for reliable information. Note also that some of the essential facts required to answer these questions can be obtained only through time-consuming and expensive marketing research studies. Other data can be generated in the engineering laboratories or pulled from accounting records. Certain types of information must be based on assumptions, which may or may not hold true, and on expectations about what will happen in the future, as in the case of anticipated competitive reaction or the projected level of sales.

Conclusion

This chapter has focused on the nature of new product planning and development. Attention has been given to the management process required to have an effective program for new product development. It should be obvious that this is one of the most important and difficult aspects of marketing management. The problem is so complex that, unless management develops a plan for dealing with the problem, it is likely to operate at a severe competitive disadvantage in the marketplace.

Additional Readings

Chaudhuri, Arjun, and Morris B. Holbrook. "The Chain of Effects from Brand Trust and Brand Affect to Brand Performance: The Role of Brand Loyalty." *Journal of Marketing,* April 2001, pp. 81–93.

Chiagouris, Larry, and Brant Wansley. "Branding on the Internet." *Marketing Management,* Summer 2000, pp. 34–39.

Duckler, Mitch. "Testing Your Brand Limits." *Marketing Management,* November/December 2003, pp. 28–33.

Keller, Kevin Lane. *Strategic Brand Management: Building, Measuring, and Managing Brand Equity.* 2nd ed. Upper Saddle River, N.J.: Prentice Hall, 2003.

Lehman, Donald R., and Russell S. Winer. *Product Management,* 4th ed. Burr Ridge, IL; McGraw Hill/Irwin, 2005.

Schultz, Don D. "The New Branding Lingo." *Marketing Management,* November/December 2003, pp. 8–9.

Chapter 8

Integrated Marketing Communications: Advertising, Sales Promotion, Public Relations, and Direct Marketing

Communicating with customers will be the broad subject of the next two chapters that focus on various elements of promotion. To simplify our discussion, the topic has been divided into two basic categories: nonpersonal communication (Chapter 8) and personal communication (Chapter 9). This chapter also discusses the necessity to integrate the various elements of marketing communication.

Strategic Goals of Marketing Communication

Marketers seek to communicate with target customers for the obvious goal of increased sales and profits. Accordingly, they seek to accomplish several strategic goals with their marketing communications efforts.

Create Awareness

Obviously, we cannot purchase a product if we are not aware of it. An important strategic goal must be to generate awareness of the firm as well as its products. Marketing communications designed to create awareness are especially important for new products and brands in order to stimulate trial purchases. As an organization expands globally, creating awareness must be a critical goal of marketing communications.

Build Positive Images

When products or brands have distinct images in the minds of customers, the customers better understand the value that is being offered. Positive images can even create value for customers by adding meaning to products. Retail stores and other organizations also use communications to build positive images. A major way marketers create positive and distinct images is through marketing communications.

Identify Prospects

Identifying prospects is becoming an increasingly important goal of marketing communications because modern technology makes information gathering much more practical, even in large consumer markets. Marketers can maintain records of consumers who have expressed an interest in a product, then more efficiently direct future communications. Technology now enables marketers to stay very close to their customers. Web sites are used to gather information about prospects and supermarkets use point-of-sale terminals to dispense coupons selected on the basis of a customer's past purchases.

Build Channel Relationships

An important goal of marketing communications is to build a relationship with the organization's channel members. When producers use marketing communications to generate awareness, they are also helping the retailers who carry the product. Producers may also arrange with retailers to distribute coupons, set up special displays, or hold promotional events in their stores, all of which benefit retailers and wholesalers. Retailers support manufacturers when they feature brands in their ads to attract buyers. Because of such efforts, all members of the channel benefit. Cooperating in these marketing communication efforts can build stronger channel relationships.

Retain Customers

Loyal customers are a major asset for every business. It costs far more to attract a new customer than to retain an existing customer. Marketing communications can support efforts to create value for existing customers. Interactive modes of communication—including salespeople and Web sites—can play an important role in retaining customers. They can serve as sources of information about product usage and new products being developed. They can also gather information from customers about what they value, as well as their experiences using the products. This two-way communication can assist marketers in increasing the value of what they offer to existing customers, which will influence retention.

The Promotion Mix

The promotion mix concept refers to the combination and types of nonpersonal and personal communication the organization puts forth during a specified period.[1] There are five elements of the promotion mix, four of which are nonpersonal forms of communication (advertising, sales promotion, public relations, and direct marketing), and one, personal selling, which is a personal form of communication. Let's briefly examine each one.

1. *Advertising* is a paid form of nonpersonal communications about an organization, its products, or its activities that is transmitted through a mass medium to a target audience. The mass medium might be television, radio, newspapers, magazines, outdoor displays, car cards, or directories.

2. *Sales promotion* is an activity or material that offers customers, sales personnel, or resellers a direct inducement for purchasing a product. This inducement, which adds value to or incentive for the product, might take the form of a coupon, sweepstakes, refund, or display.

3. *Public relations* is a nonpersonal form of communication that seeks to influence the attitudes, feelings, and opinions of customers, noncustomers, stockholders, suppliers, employees, and political bodies about the organization. A popular form is *publicity,* which is a nonpaid form of nonpersonal communication about the organization and its products that is transmitted through a mass medium in the form of a news story. Obviously, marketers seek positive publicity.

4. *Direct marketing* uses direct forms of communication with customers. It can take the form of direct mail, online marketing, catalogs, telemarketing, and direct response advertising. Similar to personal selling, it may consist of an interactive dialog between the marketer and the customer. Its objective is to generate orders, visits to retail outlets, or requests for further information. Obviously, personal selling is a form of direct marketing, but because it is a very personal form of communication, we place it in its own category.

5. *Personal selling* is face-to-face communication with potential buyers to inform them about and persuade them to buy an organization's product. It will be examined in detail in the next chapter.

Obviously, marketers strive for the right mix of promotional elements to ensure that their product is well received. For example, if the product is a new soft drink, promotional effort is likely to rely more on advertising, sales promotion, and public relations (publicity) in order to (1) make potential buyers aware of the product, (2) inform these buyers about the benefits of the product, (3) convince buyers of the product's value, and (4) entice buyers to purchase the product. If the product is more established but the objective is to stabilize sales during a nonpeak season, the promotion mix will likely contain short-run incentives (sales promotions) for people to buy the product immediately. Finally, if the product is a new complex technology that requires a great deal of explanation, the promotional mix will likely focus heavily on personal selling so that potential buyers can have their questions answered.

As seen by the previous examples, a firm's promotion mix is likely to change over time. The mix will need continual altering and adapting to reflect changes in the market, competition, the product's life cycle, and the adoption of new strategies. In essence, the firm should take into account three basic factors when devising its promotion mix: (1) the role of promotion in the overall marketing mix, (2) the nature of the product, and (3) the nature of the market. Figure 8.1 provides an overview of the major strengths and weaknesses associated with the elements of the promotion mix.

Integrated Marketing Communications

In many organizations, elements of the promotion mix are often managed by specialists in different parts of the organization or, in some cases, outside the organization when an advertising agency is used. For example, advertising plans might be done jointly by the advertising department and the advertising agency; plans for the sales force might be done by managers of the sales force; and sales promotions might be developed independently of the advertising and sales plans. Thus, it is not surprising that the concept of *integrated marketing communications* has evolved in recent years.

FIGURE 8.1
**Some Strengths and
Weaknesses of the
Major Promotion
Elements**

Element	Strengths	Weaknesses
Advertising	Efficient for reaching many buyers simultaneously; effective way to create image of the brand; flexible; variety of media to choose from.	Reaches many people who are not potential buyers; ads are subject to much criticism; exposure time is usually short; people tend to screen out advertisements; total cost may be high.
Personal selling	Salespeople can be persuasive and influential; two-way communication allows for questions and other feedback; message can be targeted to specific individuals.	Cost per contact is high; salespeople may be hard to recruit and motivate; presentation skills may vary among salespeople.
Sales promotion	Supports short-term price reductions designed to stimulate demand; variety of sales promotion tools available; effective in changing short-term behavior; easy to link to other communications.	Risks inducing brand-loyal customers to stock up while not influencing others; impact may be limited to short term; price-related sales promotion may hurt brand image; easy for competitors to copy.
Public relations	Total cost may be low; media-generated messages seen as more credible than marketer-sponsored messages.	Media may not cooperate; heavy competition for media attention; marketer has little control over message.
Direct marketing	Message can be customized and prepared quickly; can facilitate a relationship with customer.	Managing and maintaining up-to-date database can be costly; often low customer response.

The idea of integrated marketing communications is easy to understand and certainly has a great deal of commonsense validity. But like so many concepts in marketing, it is difficult to implement. The goal of integrated marketing communications is to develop marketing communications programs that coordinate and integrate all elements of promotion—advertising, sales promotion, personal selling, and publicity—so that the organization presents a consistent message. Integrated marketing communication seeks to manage all sources of brand or company contacts with existing and potential customers. Marketing Highlight 8–1 presents the critical aspects of integrated marketing communications and how they differ from the way traditional marketing communications efforts have been managed.

The concept of integrated marketing communication is illustrated in Figure 8.2. It is generally agreed on that potential buyers usually go through a process of (1) *awareness* of the product or service, (2) *comprehension* of what it can do and its important features, (3) *conviction* that it has value for them, and (4) *ordering* on the part of a sufficient number of potential buyers. Consequently, the firm's marketing communication tools must encourage and allow the potential buyer to experience the various stages. Figure 8.2 illustrates the role of various marketing communication tools for a hypothetical product.

The goal of integrated marketing communication is an important one, and many believe it is critical for success in today's crowded marketplace. As with many management concepts, implementation is slower than many would like to see. Internal "turf" battles within organizations and the reluctance of some advertising agencies to willingly broaden their role beyond advertising are two factors that are hindering the successful implementation of integrated marketing communication.

There is wide agreement about the importance of integrating marketing communication efforts. While organizations differ on just how fully integrated their efforts are, it is clear that integrated marketing communications is an idea whose time has come. The following are some important differences between a traditional approach to marketing communications and an integrated approach.

Traditional Approach	**Integrated Approach**
Focus on:	Focus on:
1. Making transactions.	1. Building and nourishing relationships.
2. Customers.	2. All stakeholders in the organization.
3. Independent brand messages.	3. Strategic consistency on brand messages.
4. Mass media—monologue with customers.	4. Interactivity—dialogue with customers.
5. Product claims.	5. Corporate mission marketing.
6. Adjusting prior year's plan.	6. Zero-based campaign planning.
7. Functional department planning and monitoring.	7. Cross-functional planning and monitoring.
8. Communication specialists.	8. Creating core competencies.
9. Mass marketing and customer acquisition.	9. Building and managing databases to retain customers.
10. Stable of agencies.	10. One communication management agency.

Source: Adapted from Tom Duncan and Sandra Moriarity, *Driving Brand Value: Using Integrated Marketing to Manage Profitable Stakeholder Relationships* (New York: McGraw-Hill, 1997), pp. 16–19.

FIGURE 8.2

How Various Promotion Tools Might Contribute to the Purchase of a Hypothetical Product

Advertising: Planning and Strategy

Advertising seeks to promote the seller's product by means of printed and electronic media. This is justified on the grounds that messages can reach large numbers of people and make them aware and persuade and remind them about the firm's offerings.

From a marketing management perspective, advertising is an important strategic device for maintaining a competitive advantage in the marketplace. Advertising budgets represent a large and growing element in the cost of goods and services. In a year it is possible for large multiproduct firms to spend $1.5 to $2 billion advertising their products, and it is common to spend $74 to $100 million on one individual brand. Clearly, advertising must be carefully planned.

Objectives of Advertising

There are at least three different viewpoints taken in attempts to evaluate the contribution of advertising to the economic health of the firm. The generalist viewpoint is primarily concerned with sales, profits, return on investment, and so forth. At the other extreme, the specialist viewpoint is represented by advertising experts who are primarily concerned with measuring the effects of specific ads or campaigns; here primary attention is given to organizations that offer services that measure different aspects of the effects of advertising such as the Nielsen Index, Starch Reports, Arbitron Index, and Simmons Reports. A middle view, one that might be classified as more of a marketing management approach, understands and appreciates the other two viewpoints but, in addition, sees advertising as a competitive weapon. Emphasis in this approach is given to the strategic aspects of the advertising function.[2]

Building on what was said earlier, objectives for advertising can be assigned that focus on creating *awareness,* aiding *comprehension,* developing *conviction,* and encouraging *ordering.* Within each category, more specific objectives can be developed that take into account time and degree of success desired. Obviously, compared to the large number of people that advertising makes aware of the product or service, the number actually motivated to purchase is usually quite small.

In the long run and often in the short run, advertising is justified on the basis of the revenue it produces. Revenue in this case may refer to either sales or profits. Economic theory assumes that firms are profit maximizers, and the advertising outlays should be increased in every market and medium up to the point where the additional cost of gaining more business equals the incremental profits. Since most business firms do not have the data required to use the marginal analysis approach, they usually employ less-sophisticated decision-making models. There is also evidence to show that many managers advertise to maximize sales on the assumption that higher sales mean more profits (which may or may not be true).

The point to be made here is that the ultimate objective of the business advertiser is to make sales and profits. To achieve this objective, the actions taken by customers must encompass purchase and continued repurchases of the advertised product. Toward this end, an approach to advertising is needed that provides for intelligent decision making. This approach must recognize the need for measuring the results of advertising, and these measurements must be as valid and reliable as possible. Marketing managers must also be aware that advertising not only complements other forms of communication but is subject to the law of diminishing returns. This means that for any advertised product, it can be assumed a point is eventually reached at which additional advertising produces little or no additional sales.

Advertising Decisions

In line with what has just been said, the marketing manager must make two key decisions. The first decision deals with determining the size of the advertising budget, and the second deals with how the advertising budget should be allocated. Although these decisions are highly interrelated, we deal with them separately to achieve a better understanding of the problems involved. Today's most successful brands of consumer goods were built by heavy advertising and marketing investment long ago. Many marketers have lost sight of the connection between advertising spending and market share. They practice the art of discounting: cutting ad budgets to fund price promotions or fatten quarterly earnings. Companies employing these tactics may benefit in the short term but may be at a severe competitive disadvantage in the long term.

Marketers at some companies, however, know that brand equity and consumer preference for brands drive market share. They understand the balance of advertising and promotion expenditures needed to build brands and gain share, market by market, regardless of growth trends in the product categories where they compete. For example, Procter & Gamble has built its Jif and Folger's brands from single-digit shares to being among category leaders. In peanut butter and coffee, P&G invests more in advertising and less in discounting than its major competitors. What P&G and other smart marketers such as Kellogg, General Mills, Coke, and PepsiCo hold in common is an awareness of a key factor in advertising: consistent investment spending. They do not raid their ad budgets to increase earnings for a few quarters, nor do they view advertising as a discretionary cost.

The Expenditure Question

Most firms determine how much to spend on advertising by one of the following methods:

Percent of Sales

This is one of the most popular rule-of-thumb methods, and its appeal is found in its simplicity. The firm simply takes a percentage figure and applies it to either past or future sales. For example, suppose next year's sales are estimated to be $1 million. Using a 2-percent-of-sales criterion, the ad budget would be $20,000. This approach is usually justified by its advocates in terms of the following argument: (1) Advertising is needed to generate sales; (2) a number of cents (i.e., the percentage used) out of each dollar of sales should be devoted to advertising in order to generate needed sales; and (3) the percentage is easily adjusted and can be readily understood by other executives. The percent-of-sales approach is popular in retailing.

Per-Unit Expenditure

Closely related to the above technique is one in which a fixed monetary amount is spent on advertising for each unit of the product expected to be sold. This method is popular with higher-priced merchandise, such as automobiles or appliances. For instance, if a company is marketing color televisions priced at $500, it may decide that it should spend $30 per set on advertising. Since this $30 is a fixed amount for each unit, this method amounts to the same thing as the percent-of-sales method. The big difference is in the rationale used to justify each of the methods. The per-unit expenditure method attempts to determine the retail price by using production costs as a base. Here the seller realizes that a reasonably competitive price must be established for the product in question and attempts to cost out the gross margin. All this means is that, if the suggested retail price is to be $500 and manufacturing costs are $250, there is a gross margin of $250 available to cover certain

1. Does the advertising aim at *immediate sales?* If so, objectives might be:

   - Perform the complete selling function.
   - Close sales to prospects already partly sold.
   - Announce a special reason for buying now (price, premium, and so forth).
   - Remind people to buy.
   - Tie in with special buying event.
   - Stimulate impulse sales.

2. Does the advertising aim at *near-term sales?* If so, objectives might be:

   - Create awareness.
   - Enhance brand image.
   - Implant information or attitude.
   - Combat or offset competitive claims.
   - Correct false impressions, misinformation.
   - Build familiarity and easy recognition.

3. Does the advertising aim at building a *long-range consumer franchise?* If so, objectives might be:

   - Build confidence in company and brand.
   - Build customer demand.
   - Select preferred distributors and dealers.
   - Secure universal distribution.
   - Establish a "reputation platform" for launching new brands or product lines.
   - Establish brand recognition and acceptance.

4. Does the advertising aim at helping *increase sales?* If so, objectives would be:

   - Hold present customers.
   - Convert other users to advertiser's brand.
   - Cause people to specify advertiser's brand.
   - Convert nonusers to users.
   - Make steady customers out of occasional ones.
   - Advertise new uses.
   - Persuade customers to buy larger sizes or multiple units.
   - Remind users to buy.
   - Encourage greater frequency or quantity of use.

5. Does the advertising aim at some specific step that leads to a sale? If so, objectives might be:

   - Persuade prospect to write for descriptive literature, return a coupon, enter a contest.
   - Persuade prospect to visit a showroom, ask for a demonstration.
   - Induce prospect to sample the product (trial offer).

6. How important are supplementary benefits of advertising? Objectives would be:

   - Help salespeople open new accounts.
   - Help salespeople get larger orders from wholesalers and retailers.
   - Help salespeople get preferred display space.
   - Give salespeople an entrée.
   - Build morale of sales force.
   - Impress the trade.

7. Should the advertising impart information needed to consummate sales and build customer satisfaction? If so, objectives may be to use:

   - "Where to buy it" advertising.
   - "How to use it" advertising.
   - New models, features, package.
   - New prices.
   - Special terms, trade-in offers, and so forth.
   - New policies (such as guarantees).

8. Should advertising build confidence and goodwill for the corporation? Targets may include:

   - Customers and potential customers.
   - The trade (distributors, dealers, retail people).
   - Employees and potential employees.
   - The financial community.
   - The public at large.

9. What kind of images does the company wish to build?

   - Product quality, dependability.
   - Service.
   - Family resemblance of diversified products.
   - Corporate citizenship.
   - Growth, progressiveness, technical leadership.

Source: William Arens, *Contemporary Advertising,* 7th ed. (Burr Ridge, IL: Irwin/McGraw-Hill, 2004), p. RL 8–3.

expenses, such as transportation, personal selling, advertising, and dealer profit. Some of these expense items are flexible, such as advertising, while others are nearly fixed, as in the case of transportation. The basic problem with this method and the percentage-of-sales method is that they view advertising as a function of sales, rather than sales as a function of advertising.

All You Can Afford

Here the advertising budget is established as a predetermined share of profits or financial resources. The availability of current revenues sets the upper limit of the ad budget. The only advantage to this approach is that it sets reasonable limits on the expenditures for advertising. However, from the standpoint of sound marketing practice, this method is undesirable because there is no necessary connection between liquidity and advertising opportunity. Any firm that limits its advertising outlays to the amount of available funds will probably miss opportunities for increasing sales and profits.

Competitive Parity

This approach is often used in conjunction with other approaches, such as the percent-of-sales method. The basic philosophy underlying this approach is that advertising is defensive. Advertising budgets are based on those of competitors or other members of the industry. From a strategy standpoint, this is a "followership" technique that assumes that the other firms in the industry know what they are doing and have similar goals. Competitive parity is not a preferred method, although some executives feel it is a safe approach. This may or may not be true depending in part on the relative market share of competing firms and their growth objectives.

The Research Approach

Here the advertising budget is argued for and presented on the basis of research findings. Advertising media are studied in terms of their productivity by the use of media reports and research studies. Costs are also estimated and compared with study results. A typical experiment is one in which three or more test markets are selected. The first test market is used as a control, either with no advertising or with normal levels of advertising. Advertising with various levels of intensity is used in the other markets, and comparisons are made to see what effect different levels of intensity have. The marketing manager then evaluates the costs and benefits of the different approaches and intensity levels to determine the overall budget. Although the research approach is generally more expensive than some other models, it is a more rational approach to the expenditure decision.

The Task Approach

Well-planned advertising programs usually make use of the task approach, which initially formulates the advertising goals and defines the tasks to accomplish these goals. Once this is done, management determines how much it will cost to accomplish each task and adds up the total. This approach is often in conjunction with the research approach.

The Allocation Question

This question deals with the problem of deciding on the most effective way of spending advertising dollars. A general answer to the question is that management's choice of strategies and objectives determines the media and appeals to be used. In other words, the firm's or product division's overall marketing plan will function as a general guideline for answering the allocation question.

From a practical standpoint, however, the allocation question can be framed in terms of message and media decisions. A successful ad campaign has two related tasks: (1) say the

Effective advertising should follow a plan. There is no one best way to go about planning an advertising campaign, but in general, marketers should have good answers to the following eight questions:

1. *The management question:* Who will manage the advertising program?
2. *The money question:* How much should be spent on advertising as opposed to other forms of communication?
3. *The market question:* To whom should the advertising be directed?
4. *The message question:* What should the ads say about the product?
5. *The media question:* What types and combinations of media should be used?
6. *The macroscheduling question:* How long should the advertising campaign be in effect before changing ads or themes?
7. *The microscheduling question:* At what times and dates would it be best for ads to appear during the course of the campaign?
8. *The measurement question:* How will the effectiveness of the advertising campaign be measured and how will the campaign be evaluated and controlled?

right things in the ads themselves, and (2) use the appropriate media in the right amounts at the right time to reach the target market.

Message Strategy

The advertising process involves creating messages with words, ideas, sounds, and other forms of audiovisual stimuli that are designed to affect consumer (or distributor) behavior. It follows that much of advertising is a communication process. To be effective, the advertising message should meet two general criteria: (1) It should take into account the basic principles of communication, and (2) it should be predicated upon a good theory of consumer motivation and behavior.

The basic communication process involves three elements: (1) the sender or source of the communication, (2) the communication or message, and (3) the receiver or audience. Advertising agencies are considered experts in the communications field and are employed by most large firms to create meaningful messages and assist in their dissemination. Translating the product idea or marketing message into an effective ad is termed *encoding*. In advertising, the goal of encoding is to generate ads that are understood by the audience. For this to occur, the audience must be able to *decode* the message in the ad so that the perceived content of the message is the same as the intended content of the message. From a practical standpoint, all this means is that advertising messages must be sent to consumers in an understandable and meaningful way.

Advertising messages, of course, must be transmitted and carried by particular communication channels commonly known as advertising media. These media or channels vary in efficiency, selectivity, and cost. Some channels are preferred to others because they have less "noise," and thus messages are more easily received and understood. For example, a particular newspaper ad must compete with other ads, pictures, or stories on the same page. In the case of radio or TV, while only one firm's message is usually broadcast at a time, there are other distractions (noise) that can hamper clear communications, such as driving while listening to the radio.

The relationship between advertising and consumer behavior is quite obvious. For many products and services, advertising is an influence that may affect the consumer's decision to purchase a particular product or brand. It is clear that consumers are subjected to many selling influences, and the question arises about how important advertising is or can be. In this case, the advertising expert must operate on some theory of consumer behavior. The reader will recall from the discussion of consumer behavior that the buyer was viewed as progressing through various stages from an unsatisfied need through and beyond a purchase decision. The end goal of an advertisement and its associated campaign is to move the buyer to a decision to purchase the advertised brand. By doing so, the advertisement will have succeeded in moving the consumer to the trial and repeat purchase stage of the consumer behavior process, which is the end goal of advertising strategy.

The planning of an advertising campaign and the creation of persuasive messages require a mixture of marketing skill and creative know-how. Relative to the dimension of marketing skills, some important pieces of marketing information are needed before launching an ad campaign. Most of this information must be generated by the firm and kept up-to-date. Listed below are some of the critical types of information an advertiser should have.

1. *Who* the firm's customers and potential customers are; their demographic, economic, and psychological characteristics; and any other factors affecting their likelihood of buying.
2. *How many* such customers there are.
3. *How much* of the firm's type and brand of product they are currently buying and can reasonably be expected to buy in the short-term and long-term future.
4. *Which* individuals, other than customers and potential customers, *influence* purchasing decisions.
5. *Where* they buy the firm's brand of product.
6. *When* they buy, and frequency of purchase.
7. *Which* competitive brands they buy and frequency of purchase.
8. *How* they use the product.
9. *Why* they buy particular types and brands of products.

Media Mix

Media selection is no easy task. To start with, there are numerous types and combinations of media to choose from. Marketing Highlight 8–4 presents a brief summary of the advantages and disadvantages of some of the major advertising media.

In the advertising industry, a common measure of efficiency or productivity is cost per thousand, or CPMs. This figure generally refers to the dollar cost of reaching 1,000 prospects, and its chief advantage lies in its simplicity and allowance for a common base of comparison between differing media types. The major disadvantage of the use of CPMs also relates to its simplicity. For example, the same commercial placed in two different television programs, having the same viewership and the same audience profile, may very well generate different responses depending on the level of viewer involvement. This "positive effects" theory states that the more the viewers are involved in a television program, the stronger they will respond to commercials. In essence, involving programs produce engaged respondents who demonstrate more favorable responses to advertising messages.

Generally, such measures as circulation, audience size, and sets in use per commercial minute are used in the calculation. Of course, different relative rankings of media can occur, depending on the measure used. A related problem deals with what is meant by "effectively reaching" the prospect.[3] *Reach,* in general, is the number of different targeted audience members exposed at least once to the advertiser's message within a

NEWSPAPERS

Advantages

1. Flexible and timely.
2. Intense coverage of local markets.
3. Broad acceptance and use.
4. High believability of printed word.

Disadvantages

1. Short life.
2. Read hastily.
3. Small "pass-along" audience.

RADIO

Advantages

1. Mass use (over 25 million radios sold annually).
2. Audience selectivity via station format.
3. Low cost (per unit of time).
4. Geographic flexibility.

Disadvantages

1. Audio presentation only.
2. Less attention than TV.
3. Chaotic buying (nonstandardized rate structures).
4. Short life.

OUTDOOR

Advantages

1. Flexible.
2. Relative absence of competing advertisements.
3. Repeat exposure.
4. Relatively inexpensive.

Disadvantages

1. Creative limitations.
2. Many distractions for viewer.
3. Public attack (ecological implications).
4. No selectivity of audience.

TELEVISION

Advantages

1. Combination of sight, sound, and motion.
2. Appeals to senses.
3. Mass audience coverage.
4. Psychology of attention.

Disadvantages

1. Nonselectivity of audience.
2. Fleeting impressions.
3. Short life.
4. Expensive.

MAGAZINES

Advantages

1. High geographic and demographic selectivity.
2. Psychology of attention.
3. Quality of reproduction.
4. Pass-along readership.

Disadvantages

1. Long closing periods (six to eight weeks prior to publication).
2. Some waste circulation.
3. No guarantee of position (unless premium is paid).

DIRECT MAIL

Advantages

1. Audience selectivity.
2. Flexible.
3. No competition from competing advertisements.
4. Personalized.

Disadvantages

1. Relatively high cost.
2. Consumers often pay little attention and throw it away.

INTERNET

Advantages

1. Interactive.
2. Low cost per exposure.
3. Ads can be placed in interest sections.
4. Timely.
5. High information content possible.
6. New favorable medium.

Disadvantages

1. Low attention getting.
2. Short message life.
3. Reader selects exposure.
4. May be perceived as intruding.
5. Subject to download speeds.

PROCEDURES FOR EVALUATING SPECIFIC ADVERTISEMENTS

1. *Recognition tests.* Estimate the percentage of people claiming to have read a magazine who recognize the ad when it is shown to them (e.g., Starch Message Report Service).
2. *Recall tests.* Estimate the percentage of people claiming to have read a magazine who can (unaided) recall the ad and its contents (e.g., Gallup and Robinson Impact Service, various services for TV ads as well).
3. *Opinion tests.* Potential audience members are asked to rank alternative advertisements as most interesting, most believable, best liked.
4. *Theater tests.* Theater audience is asked for brand preferences before and after an ad is shown in context of a TV show (e.g., Schwerin TV Testing Service).

PROCEDURES FOR EVALUATING SPECIFIC ADVERTISING OBJECTIVES

1. *Awareness.* Potential buyers are asked to indicate brands that come to mind in a product category. A message used in an ad campaign is given and buyers are asked to identify the brand that was advertised using that message.
2. *Attitude.* Potential buyers are asked to rate competing or individual brands on determinant attributes, benefits, characterizations using rating scales.

PROCEDURES FOR EVALUATING MOTIVATIONAL IMPACT

1. *Intention to buy.* Potential buyers are asked to indicate the likelihood they will buy a brand (on a scale from "definitely will not" to "definitely will").
2. *Market test.* Sales changes in different markets are monitored to compare the effects of different messages, budget levels.

Source: Joseph Guiltinan and Gordon Paul, *Marketing Management,* 6th ed., © 1997, New York, McGraw-Hill, Inc., p. 274. Reproduced by permission of The McGraw-Hill Companies.

predetermined time frame. Just as important as the number of different people exposed (reach) is the number of times, on average, that they are exposed to an advertisement within a given time period. This rate of exposure is called *average frequency.* Since marketers all have budget constraints, they must decide whether to increase reach at the expense of average frequency or average frequency at the expense of reach. In essence, the marketer's dilemma is to develop a media schedule that both (1) exposes a sufficient number of targeted customers (reach) to the firm's product and (2) exposes them enough times (average frequency) to the product to produce the desired effect. The desired effect can come in the form of reaching goals associated with any or all of the categories of advertising objectives (prospect becomes aware of the product, takes action, etc.) covered earlier in the chapter.

Sales Promotion

Over the past two decades, the popularity of sales promotion has been increasing. Two reasons for this increased popularity are undoubtedly the increased pressure on management for short-term results and the emergence of new purchase tracking technology. For example, many supermarket cash registers are now equipped with a device that dispenses coupons to a customer at the point of purchase. The type, variety, and cash amount of the coupon will vary from customer to customer based on their purchases. In essence, it is

WHEN DIRECTED AT CONSUMERS

1. To obtain the trial of a product.
2. To introduce a new or improved product.
3. To encourage repeat or greater usage by current users.
4. To bring more customers into retail stores.
5. To increase the total number of users of an established product.

WHEN DIRECTED AT SALESPEOPLE

1. To motivate the sales force.
2. To educate the sales force about product improvements.
3. To stabilize a fluctuating sales pattern.

WHEN DIRECTED AT RESELLERS

1. To increase reseller inventories.
2. To obtain displays and other support for products.
3. To improve product distribution.
4. To obtain more and better shelf space.

now possible for the Coca-Cola Company to dispense coupons only to those customers who purchase Pepsi Cola, thus avoiding spending promotional dollars on already-loyal Coke drinkers. Figure 8.3 presents some popular targets of sales promotion and the methods used.

Push versus Pull Marketing

Push and pull marketing strategies comprise the two options available to marketers interested in getting their product into the hands of customers. They are illustrated in Figure 8.4. *Push strategies* involve aiming promotional efforts at distributors, retailers, and sales personnel to gain their cooperation in ordering, stocking, and accelerating the sales of a

FIGURE 8.3   **Example of Sales Promotion Activities**

Source: William D. Perreault, Jr. and E. Jerome McCarthy, *Basic Marketing: A Global Managerial Approach,* 14th ed. Irwin/McGraw-Hill, 2002, Chap. 14.

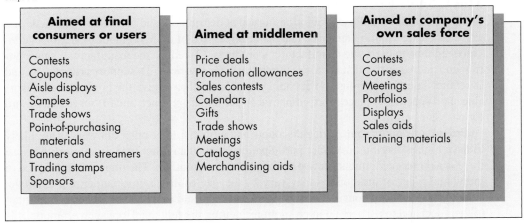

Aimed at final consumers or users	Aimed at middlemen	Aimed at company's own sales force
Contests	Price deals	Contests
Coupons	Promotion allowances	Courses
Aisle displays	Sales contests	Meetings
Samples	Calendars	Portfolios
Trade shows	Gifts	Displays
Point-of-purchasing materials	Trade shows	Sales aids
Banners and streamers	Meetings	Training materials
Trading stamps	Catalogs	
Sponsors	Merchandising aids	

FIGURE 8.4 **Push versus Pull Strategies in Marketing Communications**

product. For example, a local rock band may visit local DJs seeking air play for their record, offer distributors special prices to carry the CD, and offer retailers special allowances for putting up posters or special counter displays. These activities, which are usually in the form of price allowances, distribution allowances, and advertising dollar allowances, are designed to "push" the CD toward the customer.[4]

Pull strategies involve aiming promotional efforts directly at customers to encourage them to ask the retailer for the product. In the past few years drug manufacturers have begun to advertise prescription drugs directly to consumers. Customers are encouraged to "Ask Your Doctor" about Viagra or Paxil. These activities, which can include advertising and sales promotion, are designed to "pull" a product through the channel from manufacturer to buyer.

Trade Sales Promotions

Trade promotions are those promotions aimed at distributors and retailers of products who make up the distribution channel. The major objectives of trade promotions are to (1) convince retailers to carry the manufacturer's products, (2) reduce the manufacturer's inventories and increase the distributor's or retailer's inventories, (3) support advertising and consumer sales promotions, (4) encourage retailers either to give the product more favorable shelf space or to place more emphasis on selling the product, and (5) serve as a reward for past sales efforts.

Promotions built around price discounts and advertising or other allowances are likely to have higher distributor/retailer participation levels than other type promotions because there is a direct economic incentive attached to the promotion.[5] The importance attached to individual types of promotions may vary by the size of distributor/retailer. For example, small retailers do not consider contests, sweepstakes, and sales quotas as being important to their decision to participate in promotions; getting the full benefit of such promotions is

FIGURE 8.5
Some Commonly Used Forms of Consumer Promotions

• *Sampling.*	Customers are offered regular trial sizes of the product either free or at a nominal price.
• *Price deals.*	Customers are offered discounts from the product's regular price.
• *Bonus packs.*	Additional amounts of the product are given to buyers when they purchase the product.
• *Rebates and refunds.*	Customers are given reimbursements for purchasing the product either on the spot or through the mail.
• *Sweepstakes and contests.*	Prizes are available either through chance selection or games of skill.
• *Premiums.*	A reward or gift can come from purchasing a product.
• *Coupons.*	Probably the most familiar and widely used of all consumer promotions, now often available at point of purchase.

difficult due to their size. Marketers must keep in mind that not all distributors or retailers will have the same reaction to promotions offered. Differences in attitudes need to be carefully considered by the manufacturer when designing and implementing trade promotion programs.

Consumer Promotions

Consumer promotions can fulfill several distinct objectives for the manufacturer. Some of the more commonly sought-after objectives include: (1) inducing the consumer to try the product, (2) rewarding the consumer for brand loyalty, (3) encouraging the consumer to trade up or purchase larger sizes of a product, (4) stimulating the consumer to make repeat purchases of the product, (5) reacting to competitor efforts, and (6) reinforcing and serving as a complement to advertising and personal selling efforts.

Figure 8.5 presents a brief description of some of the most commonly used forms of consumer promotion activities.

What Sales Promotion Can and Can't Do

Advocates of sales promotion often point to its growing popularity as a justification for the argument that we don't need advertising; sales promotion itself will suffice. Marketers should bear in mind that sales promotion is only one part of a well-constructed integrated marketing communications program. While sales promotion is proven to be effective in achieving the objectives listed in the previous sections, there are several compelling reasons why it should not be used as the sole promotional tool. These reasons include sales promotion's inability (1) to generate long-term buyer commitment to a brand in many cases; (2) change, except on a temporary basis, declining sales of a product; (3) to convince buyers to purchase an otherwise unacceptable product; and (4) to make up for a lack of advertising or sales support for a product. In addition, promotions can often fuel the flames of competitive retaliation far more than other marketing activities. When the competition gets drawn into the promotion war, the effect can be a significant slowing of the sharp sales increases predicted by the initiator of the promotion. Worse yet, promotions can often devalue the image of the promoted brand in the consumer's eyes.

The dilemma faced by marketers, as shown in Figure 8.6, is how to cut back on sales promotions without losing market share to competitors. In an effort to overcome this problem, some consumer products companies are instituting new pricing policies to try to cut back on the amount of sales promotions used. For example, Procter & Gamble and General Mills have instituted everyday low-price strategies for many of their products. The intent of this type of policy is to give retailers a lower list price in exchange for the cutting of trade promotions. While the net cost of the product to retailers remains

FIGURE 8.6   The Sales Promotion Dilemma

Source: George E. Belch and Michael A. Belch, *Introduction to Advertising and Promotion: An Integrated Communications Perspective,* 6th ed. (Burr Ridge, IL: Irwin/McGraw-Hill, 2004), p. 557.

unchanged, retailers are losing promotional dollars that they controlled. In many situations, although trade allowances are supposed to be used for encouraging retail sales, it is not uncommon for retailers to take a portion of the trade allowance money as profit. The rationale behind companies' (such as Procter & Gamble and General Mills) efforts to cut back on trade and other promotions is (1) not to force brand-loyal customers to pay unusually high prices when a product isn't on special; (2) to allow consumers to benefit from a lower average shelf price, since retailers will no longer have discretion over the use of allowance dollars; and (3) to improve efficiencies in manufacturing and distribution systems because retailers will lose the incentive to do heavy forward buying of discounted items.

In addition to developing pricing policies to cut back on short-term promotions, some consumer products companies are starting to institute *frequency marketing programs* in which they reward consumers for purchases of products or services over a sustained period of time.[6] These programs are not technically considered sales promotions due to their ongoing nature. Frequency marketing originated in 1981 when American Airlines launched its frequent-flyer program with the intention of securing the loyalty of business travelers.

Public Relations

As we noted earlier in the chapter, public relations is a nonpersonal form of communication that tries to influence the overall image of the organization and its products and services among its various stakeholder groups. Public relations managers prefer to focus on communicating positive news about the organization, but must also be available to minimize the negative impacts of a crisis or problem. We have already noted that the most popular and frequently used public relations tool is publicity. There are several forms of publicity:

1. *News release.* An announcement regarding changes in the organization or the product line, sometimes called a *press release.* The objective is to inform members of the media of a newsworthy event in the hope that they will convert it into a story.

2. *News conference.* A meeting held for representatives of the media so that the organization can announce major news events such as new products, technologies, mergers,

acquisitions, and special events, or, in the case of a crisis or problem, present its position and plans for dealing with the situation.

3. *Sponsorship.* Providing support for and associating the organization's name with events, programs, or even people such as amateur athletes or teams. Besides publicity, sponsorship can also include advertising and sales promotion activities. Many organizations sponsor sporting events, art festivals, and public radio and television programs.

4. *Public service announcements.* Many nonprofit organizations rely on the media to donate time for advertising for contributions and donors. Many nonprofit organizations cannot afford the cost of advertising or in some cases are prohibited from doing so.

Direct Marketing

We already know that with direct marketing the organization communicates directly with customers either online, through direct mail, catalogs, direct response advertising, or personal selling (the subject of the next chapter).

Direct marketing methods are certainly not new. In fact, several of them will be discussed later in the book as methods of nonstore retailing. What is new is the ability to design and use them more efficiently and effectively because of the availability of computers and databases. Technology has clearly been the catalyst in the tremendous growth in direct marketing activities in the last decade. Because of technology, it is now possible for marketers to customize communication efforts and literally create one-to-one connections and dialogues with customers. This would be especially true for those organizations that have successfully implemented an integrated marketing communications program.

Another obvious catalyst for growth in direct marketing has been the increased use of the Internet by consumers for purchasing many types of products. And the projected growth rates for online expenditures continue to rise. As growth continues in the number of households with Internet access and in the number of businesses with web sites and product or service offerings via the Internet, it will likely fuel even greater growth in direct marketing.

For the American consumer facing a "poverty of time," direct marketing offers many benefits. In addition to saving time, consumers often save money, get better service, and enjoy increased privacy; many even find it entertaining. For the marketer, sales revenues are the obvious benefit but not the only one. Direct marketing activities are often very effective in generating sales leads when a customer asks for more information about a product or service and can also increase store traffic when potential buyers are encouraged to visit a dealership or retail store.

Conclusion

This chapter has been concerned with integrated marketing communications. Remember that advertising and sales promotion are only two of the ways by which sellers can affect the demand for their product. Advertising and sales promotion are only part of the firm's promotion mix, and in turn, the promotion mix is only part of the overall marketing mix. Thus, advertising and sales promotion begin with the marketing plan and not with the advertising and sales promotion plans. Ignoring this point can produce ineffective and expensive promotional programs because of a lack of coordination with other elements of the marketing mix.

Additional Readings

Duncan, Tom, and Sandra Moriority. *Driving Brand Value: Using Integrated Marketing to Manage Profitable Stakeholder Relationships.* New York: McGraw-Hill, 1997.

Fombrun, Charles J., and Cees B. M. Van Riel. *Fame and Fortune: How Successful Companies Build Winning Reputations.* Upper Saddle River, N.J.: Prentice Hall, 2004.

Manning, Jeff, and Kevin Lane Keller. "Got Advertising That Works?" *Marketing Management,* January/February 2004, pp. 16–20.

Miller, Robin. *The Online Rules of Successful Companies.* Upper Saddle River, N.J.: Prentice Hall, 2003.

McArthur, D. N., and T. Griffin. "A Marketing Management View of Integrated Marketing Communications." *Journal of Advertising Research,* September–October 1997, pp. 19–26.

Peterman, John. "The Rise and Fall of the J. Peterman Company." *Harvard Business Review,* September–October 1999, pp. 58–66.

Sternthal, Brian. "Advertising Strategy." In *Kelloggon Marketing,* ed. Dawn Iacobucci. New York: John Wiley, 2001, pp. 215–46.

Appendix

Major Federal Agencies Involved in Control of Advertising

Agency	Function
Federal Trade Commission	Regulates commerce between states; controls unfair business practices; takes action on false and deceptive advertising; most important agency in regulation of advertising and promotion.
Food and Drug Administration	Regulatory division of the Department of Health, Education, and Welfare; controls marketing of food, drugs, cosmetics, medical devices, and potentially hazardous consumer products.
Federal Communications Commission	Regulates advertising indirectly, primarily through the power to grant or withdraw broadcasting licenses.
Postal Service	Regulates material that goes through the mails, primarily in areas of obscenity, lottery, and fraud.
Alcohol and Tobacco Tax Division	Part of the Treasury Department; has broad powers to regulate deceptive and misleading advertising of liquor and tobacco.
Grain Division	Unit of the Department of Agriculture responsible for policing seed advertising.
Securities and Exchange Commission	Regulates advertising of securities.

Information Source	Description
Patent Office	Regulates registration of trademarks.
Library of Congress	Controls protection of copyrights.
Department of Justice	Enforces all federal laws through prosecuting cases referred to it by other government agencies.

Chapter 9

Personal Selling, Relationship Building, and Sales Management

Personal selling, unlike advertising or sales promotion, involves direct relationships between the seller and the prospect or customer. In a formal sense, personal selling can be defined as a two-way flow of communication between a potential buyer and a salesperson that is designed to accomplish at least three tasks: (1) identify the potential buyer's needs; (2) match those needs to one or more of the firm's products or services; and (3) on the basis of this match, convince the buyer to purchase the product.[1] The personal selling element of the promotion mix can encompass diverse forms of direct interaction between a salesperson and a potential buyer, including face-to-face, telephone, written, and computer communication. The behavioral scientist would most likely characterize personal selling as a type of personal influence. Operationally, it is a complex communication process, one still not fully understood by marketers.

Importance of Personal Selling

The importance of the personal selling function depends partially on the nature of the product. As a general rule, goods that are new and different, technically complex, or expensive require more personal selling effort. The salesperson plays a key role in providing the consumer with information about such products to reduce the risks involved in purchase and use. Insurance, for example, is a complex and technical product that often needs significant amounts of personal selling. In addition, many organizational products cannot be presold, and the salesperson has a key role to play in finalizing the sale.

It is important to remember that, for many companies, the salesperson represents the customer's main link to the firm. In fact, to some, the salesperson is the company. Therefore, it is imperative that the company take advantage of this unique link. Through the efforts of the successful salesperson, a company can build relationships with customers that continue long beyond the initial sale. It is the salesperson who serves as the conduit through which information regarding product flaws, improvements, applications, or new uses can pass from the customer to the marketing department. To illustrate the importance of using salespeople as an information resource, consider this fact: In some industries, customer information serves as a major source for up to 90 percent of new product and process ideas.

Along with techniques described in the previous chapter, personal selling provides the push needed to get middlemen to carry new products, increase their amount of goods purchased, and devote more effort in merchandising a product or brand.

In summary, personal selling is an integral part of the marketing system, fulfilling two vital duties (in addition to the core sales task itself): one for customers and one for companies.[2] First, the salesperson dispenses knowledge to buyers. Lacking relevant information, customers are likely to make poor buying decisions. For example, computer users would not learn about new equipment and new programming techniques without the assistance of computer sales representatives. Doctors would have difficulty finding out about new drugs and procedures were it not for pharmaceutical salespeople. Second, salespeople act as a source of marketing intelligence for management. Marketing success depends on satisfying customer needs. If present products don't fulfill customer needs, then profitable opportunities may exist for new or improved products. If problems with a company's product exist, then management must be quickly apprised of the fact. In either situation, salespeople are in the best position to act as the intermediary through which valuable information can be passed back and forth between product providers and buyers.

The Sales Process

Personal selling is as much an art as it is a science. The word *art* is used to describe that portion of the selling process that is highly creative in nature and difficult to explain. This does not mean there is little control over the personal selling element in the promotion mix. It does imply that, all other things equal, the trained salesperson can outsell the untrained one.

Before management selects and trains salespeople, it should have an understanding of the sales process. Obviously, the sales process will differ according to the size of the company, the nature of the product, the market, and so forth, but there are some elements common to almost all selling situations that should be understood. For the purposes of this text, the term *sales process* refers to two basic factors: (1) the objectives the salesperson is trying to achieve while engaged in selling activities; and (2) the sequence of stages or steps the salesperson should follow in trying to achieve the specific objectives (the relationship-building process).

Objectives of the Sales Force

Much like the concepts covered in the previous chapter, personal selling can be viewed as a strategic means to gain competitive advantage in the marketplace. For example, most organizations include service representatives as part of their sales team to ensure that customer concerns with present products are addressed and remedied at the same time new business is being solicited.

In a similar manner, marketing management understands that while, ultimately, personal selling must be justified on the basis of the revenue and profits it produces, there are other categories of objectives generally assigned to the personal selling function as part of the overall promotion mix.[3] These objectives are:

1. *Information provision.* Especially in the case of new products or customers, the salesperson needs to fully explain all attributes of the product or service, answer any questions, and probe for additional questions.

2. *Persuasion.* Once the initial product or service information is provided, the salesperson needs to focus on the following objectives:

   - Clearly distinguish attributes of the firm's products or services from those of competitors.
   - Maximize the number of sales as a percent of presentations.

a. Problems with current products.
b. Cost-reduction needs of customer.
c. Unmet needs or wishes of customer.
d. Superior features of competitive products.
e. Changes in technology/industry standards.
f. Additions needed for service(s) accompanying the product.
g. Changes in the regulatory environment.
h. Other manufacturers' (competitors') products currently used by customer.
i. Customer's level of satisfaction with products currently used.
j. Product features evaluated by customers in choosing another manufacturer's product.
k. Customer's ideal products according to relevant choice criteria.
l. Customer's criteria for rating products.
m. Customer's order of preference for competing products.
n. Customer's likely demand for products in the future.

Source: Adapted from Geoffrey Gordon, Denise Schoenbachler, Peter Kaminski, and Kimberly Brouchous, "The Use of the Sales Force in the Opportunity Identification Phase of the New Product Development Process," *Journal of Business and Industrial Marketing* 12, no. 1 (1997), pp. 33–48.

- Convert undecided customers into first-time buyers.
- Convert first-time customers into repeat purchasers.
- Sell additional or complementary items to repeat customers.
- Tend to the needs of dissatisfied customers.

3. *After-sale service.* Whether the sale represents a first-time or repeat purchase, the salesperson needs to ensure the following objectives are met:

- Delivery or installation of the product or service that meets or exceeds customer expectations.
- Immediate follow-up calls and visits to address unresolved or new concerns.
- Reassurance of product or service superiority through demonstrable actions.

The Sales Relationship-Building Process

For many years, the traditional approach to selling emphasized the first-time sale of a product or service as the culmination of the sales process. As emphasized in Chapter 1, the marketing concept and accompanying approach to personal selling view the initial sale as merely the first step in a long-term relationship-building process, not as the end goal. As we shall see later in this chapter, long-term relationships between the buyer and seller can be considered partnerships because the buyer and seller have an ongoing, mutually beneficial affiliation, with each party having concern for the other party's well-being.[4] The relationship-building process, which is designed to meet the objectives listed in the previous section, contains six sequential stages (Figure 9.1). These stages are (1) prospecting, (2) planning the sales call, (3) presentation, (4) responding to objections, (5) obtaining commitment/closing the sale, and (6) building a long-term relationship. What follows is a brief description of each of the stages.

Prospecting

The process of locating potential customers is called *prospecting.* The prospecting activity is critical to the success of organizations in maintaining or increasing sales volume.

FIGURE 9.1
The Sales Relationship-Building Process

Source: Adapted from material discussed in Barton A. Weitz, Stephen B. Castleberry, and John F. Tanner, *Selling: Building Partnerships,* 5th ed. (Burr Ridge, IL: Irwin/McGraw-Hill, 2004), p. 181.

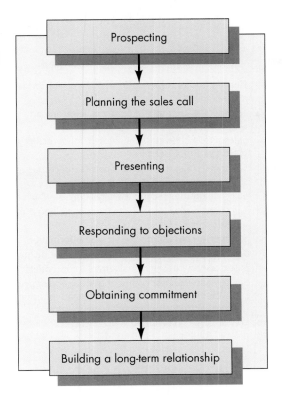

Continual prospecting is necessary for several reasons, including the fact that customers (1) switch to other suppliers, (2) move out of the organization's market area, (3) go out of business because of bankruptcy, (4) are acquired by another firm, or (5) have only a one-time need for the product or service. In addition, the organization's buying contracts with present customers may be replaced and organizations who wish to grow must increase their customer base. Prospecting in some fields is more important than in others. For example, a stockbroker, real estate agent, or partner in an accounting firm with no effective prospecting plan usually doesn't last long in the business. In these positions, it may take as many as 100 contacts to gain 10 prospects who will listen to presentations from which one to two sales may result. On the other hand, a Procter & Gamble sales representative in a certain geographic area would likely know all the potential retailers for Crest toothpaste.

The prospecting process usually involves two major activities that are undertaken on a continual, concurrent basis. First, prospects must be located. When names and addresses of prospects are not available, as is usually the case when firms enter new markets or a new salesperson is hired, they can be generated by randomly calling on businesses or households or by employing mass appeals (through advertising). This process, called *random lead generation,* usually requires a high number of contacts to gain a sale. A *lead* is a potential prospect that may or may not have the potential to be a true prospect, a candidate, to whom a sale could be made.

For most professional, experienced salespeople, a more systematic approach to generating leads from predetermined target markets is used. This approach, aptly named *selected-lead searching,* uses existing contacts and knowledge to generate new prospects. In general, the best source of prospects is referrals from satisfied customers. The more satisfied one's customers are, the higher the quality of leads a salesperson will receive from

Source	How Used
Satisfied customers	Current and previous customers are contacted for additional business and leads.
Endless chain	Salesperson attempts to secure at least one additional lead from each person he or she interviews.
Center of influence	Salesperson cultivates well-known, influential people in the territory who are willing to supply lead information.
Promotional activities	Salesperson ties into the company's direct mail, telemarketing, and trade shows to secure and qualify leads.
Lists and directories	Salesperson uses secondary data sources, which can be free or fee-based.
Canvassing	Salesperson tries to generate leads by calling on totally unfamiliar organizations.
Spotters	Salesperson pays someone for lead information.
Telemarketing	Salesperson uses phone and/or telemarketing staff to generate leads.
Sales letters	Salesperson writes personal letters to potential leads.
Other sources	Salesperson uses noncompeting salespeople, people in his or her own firm, social clubs, and so forth, to secure lead information.

Source: Adapted from material discussed in Barton A. Weitz, Stephen B. Castleberry, and John F. Tanner, *Selling: Building Partnerships,* 5th ed. (Burr Ridge, IL: Irwin/McGraw-Hill, 2004), p. 185.

them. Marketing highlight 9–2 lists some common sources of leads and how they are used to generate new contacts.

The second step in the prospecting process involves screening. Once leads are generated, the salesperson must determine whether the prospect is a true prospect. This qualifying process usually entails gathering information, which leads to answering five questions:

1. Does the lead have a want or need that can be satisfied by the purchase of the firm's products or services?
2. Does the lead have the ability to pay?
3. Does the lead have the authority to pay?
4. Can the lead be approached favorably?
5. Is the lead eligible to buy?

Depending on the analysis of answers to these questions, the determination of whether a lead is a true prospect can be made. In seeking and qualifying leads, it is important to recognize that responsibility for these activities should not be totally assumed by individual salespeople. Rather, companies should develop a consistent, organized program, recognizing that the job of developing prospects belongs to the entire company, not just the sales force.

Planning the Sales Call

Salespeople will readily admit that their number one problem is getting through the door for an appointment with a prospect. Customers have become sophisticated in their buying strategies. Consequently, salespeople have to be equally sophisticated in developing their selling strategies.

	Production	Sales	Marketing	Partnering
Time Period	Before 1930	1930 to 1960	1960 to 1990	After 1990
Objective	Making sales	Making sales	Satisfying customer needs	Building relationships
Orientation	Short-term seller needs	Short-term seller needs	Short-term customer needs	Long-term customer and seller needs
Role of Salesperson	Provider	Persuader	Problem solver	Value creator
Activities of Salespeople	Taking orders, delivering goods	Aggressively convincing buyers to buy products	Matching available offerings to buyer needs	Creating new alternatives, matching buyer needs with seller capabilities

Source: Barton A. Weitz, Stephen B. Castleberry, and John F. Tanner, *Selling: Building Relationships,* 5th ed. (Burr Ridge, IL: McGraw-Hill/Irwin, 2004), p. 33.

While a full discussion on the topic of planning sales calls is beyond the scope of this text, what follows are brief descriptions of some key areas of knowledge salespeople should possess prior to embarking on sales calls.

1. They should have thorough knowledge of the company they represent, including its past history. This includes the philosophy of management as well as the firm's basic operating policies.
2. They should have thorough knowledge of their products and/or product lines. This is particularly true when selling organizational products. When selling very technical products, many firms require their salespeople to have training as engineers.
3. They should have good working knowledge of competitors' products. This is a vital requirement because the successful salesperson will have to know the strengths and weaknesses of those products that are in competition for market share.
4. They should have in-depth knowledge of the market for their merchandise. *The market* here refers not only to a particular sales territory but also to the general market, including the economic factors that affect the demand for their goods.
5. They should have accurate knowledge of the buyer or the prospect to whom they are selling. Under the marketing concept, knowledge of the customer is a vital requirement.

Presenting

Successful salespeople have learned the importance of making a good impression. One of the most important ways of improving the buyer's impression is for the salesperson to be well prepared in the knowledge areas discussed above. Some salespeople actually develop a checklist of things to take to the presentation so that nothing is forgotten. Just as important is the development of good interpersonal skills; they are a key ingredient of effective selling. Salespeople who can adapt their selling style to individual buyer needs and styles have a much stronger overall performance than less-flexible counterparts.

Responding to Objections

To assume the buyer will passively listen and positively respond to a sales presentation by placing an immediate order would be unrealistic. Salespeople can expect to hear objections (issues or concerns raised by the buyer) at any time during the presentation and subsequent relationship. Objections can be raised when the salesperson attempts to secure appointments, during the presentation, when the salesperson attempts to obtain commitment, or during the after-sale follow-up.

When sales prospects raise an objection, it is a sign that they are not ready to buy and need an acceptable response to the objection before the buying decision can be made. In response to an objection, the salesperson should not challenge the respondent. Rather, the salesperson's objective should be to present the necessary information so that the prospect is able to make intelligent decisions based on that information.

Obtaining Commitment

At some point, if all objections have been resolved, the salesperson must ask for commitment. It's a rare moment when a customer will ask to buy. Consequently, knowing how and when to close a sale is one of a salesperson's most indispensable skills.

It should be noted that not all sales calls end in commitment, a successful closing. If commitment is not obtained, salespeople should analyze the reasons and determine whether (1) more sales calls are necessary to obtain commitment; or (2) currently, there just does not exist a good match between customer needs and seller offerings. If the salesperson determines that more calls are necessary, then he or she should leave the meeting with a clear action plan, which is agreeable to the customer, for the next visit.

Building a Long-Term Relationship

Focusing on building and maintaining long-term relationships with customers has become an important goal for salespeople. As marketers realize that it can take five times as much to acquire a new customer than to service an existing one, the importance of customer retention and relationship building has become very clear.[5] Terry Vavra focuses on the value of current customers to the organization and has developed the concept of *aftermarketing,* which focuses the organization's attention on providing continuing satisfaction and reinforcement to individuals or organizations that are past or current customers. The goal of aftermarketing is to build lasting relationships with customers.[6] Successful aftermarketing efforts require that many specific activities be undertaken by the salesperson and others in the organization. These activities include:

1. Establishing and maintaining a customer information file.
2. Monitoring order processing.
3. Ensuring initial proper use of the purchased product or service.
4. Providing ongoing guidance and suggestions.
5. Analyzing customer feedback and responding quickly to customer questions and complaints.
6. Continually conducting customer satisfaction research and responding to it.

1. *Improved sales productivity.* When the product or system being purchased is for the whole organization, different specialists handle different parts of the job. This usually results in a more effective and efficient sales process.

2. *More flexibility and quicker decisions.* To thrive in today's increasingly competitive markets, buying organizations often require selling organizations to produce small runs of tailored products on a very tight schedule. Cross-functional sales teams enable sellers to be more flexible because all functional units are involved in the sales process, which also enables the seller to make quicker decisions in response to buyer demands.

3. *Better decisions.* In most cases, the use of cross-functional teams composed of individuals with varied backgrounds in the company will lead to more innovative forms of thought and superior decisions than would be the case of an individual acting alone. Improved decisions would benefit both the buyer and the seller.

4. *Increased customer satisfaction.* The ultimate measure of the success of cross-functional sales teams comes with increased customer satisfaction, cemented relationships, and repeat business. The energy, flexibility, and commitment associated with cross-functional sales teams have led many organizations to adopt the approach.

As seen by the preceding discussion, there are no magic secrets of successful selling. The difference between good salespeople and mediocre ones is often the result of training plus experience. Training is no substitute for experience; the two complement each other. The difficulty with trying to discuss the selling job in terms of basic principles is that experienced, successful salespeople will always be able to find exceptions to these principles.

Relationships Can Lead to Partnerships

When the interaction between a salesperson and a customer does not end with the sale, the beginnings of a relationship are present. Many salespeople are finding that building relationships and even partnering with customers is becoming increasingly important.

When a buyer and a salesperson have a close personal relationship, they both begin to rely on each other and communicate honestly. When each has a problem, they work together to solve it. Such market relationships are known as *functional relationships.* An important trust begins to exist between each party. As with any relationship, each often gives and takes when the situation calls for it in order to keep the relationship intact. The reader may have such a relationship with a long-term medical or dental practitioner or hair cutter.

When organizations move beyond functional relationships, they develop *strategic partnerships,* or *strategic alliances.* These are long-term, formal relationships in which both parties make significant commitments and investments in each other in order to pursue mutual goals and to improve the profitability of each other. While a functional relationship is based on trust, a strategic partnership or alliance moves beyond trust. The partners in the relationship actually invest in each other. Obviously, the reasons for forming strategic partnerships vary. Some do it to create joint opportunities (banks, insurance companies, and brokerage firms), to gain access to new markets (United Parcel Service of America and Mail Boxes Etc.), to develop new technology or exploit joint opportunities (IBM and Apple), or to gain a marketing advantage over competitors (United Airlines and Starbucks Coffee, American Airlines and Career Track).

People Who Support the Sales Force

In many instances, sales personnel will require some assistance at various stages of the sales process. These support personnel do not seek the order. Their purpose is to focus on the long-term relationship and increase the likelihood of sales in the long run.

Missionary salespeople are used in certain industries such as pharmaceuticals to focus solely on promotion of existing products and introduction of new products. They may call on physicians to convince them to prescribe a new drug or on pharmacies to convince them to promote a new cold remedy with a large display during the cold and flu season.

A *technical sales specialist* supports the sales staff by providing training or other technical assistance to the prospect. This individual may follow up an expression of interest to the salesperson from a prospect, especially when the product is to be used to solve certain technical problems of the buyer. Some organizations will provide training to the front-line staff of the buying organization who will be expected to sell the product to their customers.

Finally, when the product is extremely high priced and is being sold to the whole organization, *cross-functional sales teams* are often used. Since products increase in technical complexity, and specialized knowledge is required by units of the buying organization before a buying decision can be made, team selling has increased in popularity. For example, a manufacturer's sales team might be made up of people from sales, engineering, customer service, and finance, depending on the needs of the customer. A bank's sales team might consist of people from the commercial lending, investments, small business, and trust departments.

Managing the Sales and Relationship-Building Process

Every personal sale can be divided into two parts: the part done by the salespeople and the part done for the salespeople by the company. For example, from the standpoint of the product, the company should provide the salesperson with a product skillfully designed, thoroughly tested, attractively packaged, adequately advertised, and priced to compare favorably with competitive products. Salespeople have the responsibility of being thoroughly acquainted with the product, its selling features, and points of superiority and possess a sincere belief in the value of the product. From a sales management standpoint, the company's part of the sale involves the following:

1. Efficient and effective sales tools, including continuous sales training, promotional literature, samples, trade shows, product information, and adequate advertising.
2. An efficient delivery and reorder system to ensure that customers will receive the merchandise as promised.
3. An equitable compensation plan that rewards performance, motivates the salesperson, and promotes company loyalty. It should also reimburse the salesperson for all reasonable expenses incurred while doing the job.
4. Adequate supervision and evaluation of performance as a means of helping salespeople do a better job not only for the company but for themselves as well.

The Sales Management Task

Marketing managers and sales managers must make some very important decisions regarding how the sales force should be organized. Most companies organize their sales efforts either by geography, product, or customer. These are illustrated in Figure 9.2.

In a *geographic structure,* individual salespeople are assigned geographic territories to cover. A salesperson calls on all prospects in the territory and usually represents all of the

FIGURE 9.2
Organizing the Sales Force

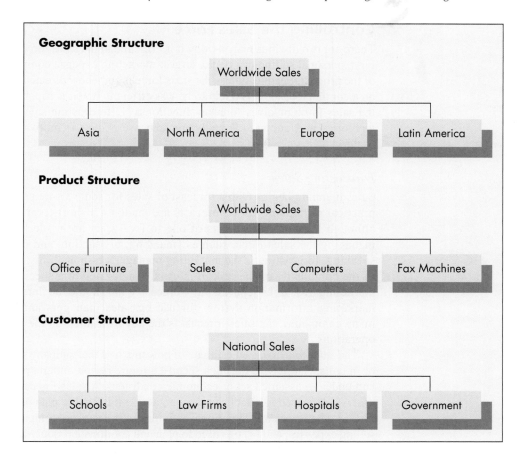

company's products. A geographic structure provides the practical benefit of limiting the distance each salesperson must travel to see customers and prospects.

In a *product structure,* each salesperson is assigned to prospects and customers for a particular product or product line. A product structure is useful when the sales force must have specific technical knowledge about products in order to sell effectively. However, this structure can result in a duplication of sales efforts because more than one salesperson can call on the same customer. Consequently, it tends to be expensive.

A *customer structure* assigns a salesperson or selling team to serve a single customer or single type of customer. This structure works best when different types of buyers have large or significantly different needs. When this structure involves devoting all of a salesperson's time to a single customer, it is expensive but can result in large sales and satisfied customers.

In a variation of the customer structure, a company may employ *major account management,* or the use of team selling to focus on major customers to establish long-term relationships.[7] Procter & Gamble, whose sales force used to be organized by product, has shifted to major account management. Assigning resources to particular customers has proved to be more flexible and customer focused for the company.

The customer-organized structure is well suited for the use of cross-functional teams. However, geographic and product territories can also be effective. The key is that sales management and the sales force must concentrate on learning and meeting customers' wants and needs better than competitors do.

Controlling the Sales Force

There are two obvious reasons why it is critical that the sales force be properly controlled. First, personal selling can be the largest marketing expense component in the final price of the product. Second, unless the sales force is somehow directed, motivated, and audited on a continual basis, it is likely to be less efficient than it is capable of being. Controlling the sales force involves four key functions: (1) forecasting sales, (2) establishing sales territories and quotas, (3) analyzing expenses, and (4) motivating and compensating performance.

Forecasting Sales

Sales planning begins with a forecast of sales for some future period or periods. From a practical standpoint, these forecasts are made on a short-term basis of a year or less, although long-range forecasts of one to five years are made for purposes other than managing the sales force, such as financing, production, and development. Generally speaking, forecasting is the marketing manager's responsibility. In large firms, because of the complexity of the task, it is usually delegated to a specialized unit, such as the marketing research department. Forecast data should be integrated into the firm's marketing information system for use by sales managers and other executives. For many companies, the sales forecast is the key instrument in the planning and control of operations.

The *sales forecast* is an estimate of how much of the company's output, either in dollars or in units, can be sold during a specified future period under a proposed marketing plan and under an assumed set of economic conditions. A sales forecast has several important uses: (1) It is used to establish sales quotas; (2) it is used to plan personal selling efforts as well as other types of promotional activities in the marketing mix; (3) it is used to budget selling expenses; and (4) it is used to plan and coordinate production, logistics, inventories, personnel, and so forth.

Sales forecasting has become very sophisticated in recent years, especially with the increased availability of computer software. It should be mentioned, however, that a forecast is never a substitute for sound business judgment. At the present time there is no single method of sales forecasting known that gives uniformly accurate results with infallible precision. Outlined next are some commonly used sales forecasting methods.[8]

1. *Jury of executive opinion method.* This combines and averages the views of top management representing marketing, production, finance, purchasing, and administration.
2. *Sales force composite method.* This is similar to the first method in that it obtains the combined views of the sales force about the future outlook for sales. In some companies all salespeople, or district managers, submit estimates of the future sales in their territory or district.
3. *Customer expectations method.* This approach involves asking customers or product users about the quantity they expect to purchase.
4. *Time-series analysis.* This approach involves analyzing past sales data and the impact of factors that influence sales (long-term growth trends, cyclical fluctuations, seasonal variations).
5. *Correlation analysis.* This involves measuring the relationship between the dependent variable, sales, and one or more independent variables that can explain increases or decreases in sales volumes.
6. *Other quantitative techniques.* Numerous statistical and mathematical techniques can be used to predict or estimate future sales. Two of the more important techniques are

(*a*) growth functions, which are mathematical expressions specifying the relationship between demand and time; and (*b*) simulation models, in which a statistical model of the industry is developed and programmed to compute values for the key parameters of the model.

Establishing Sales Territories and Quotas

The establishment of sales territories and sales quotas represents management's need to match personal selling effort with sales potential (or opportunity). Soundly designed sales territories can improve how the market is served.[9] It is much easier to pinpoint customers and prospects and to determine who should call on them when the market is geographically divided than when the market is considered a large aggregate of potential accounts. The geographic segments should represent small clusters of customers or prospects within some physical proximity. Implied here is the notion that there are some distinct economic advantages to dividing the market into smaller segments. Salespeople restricted to a geographic area are likely to get more sales in the territory. Instead of simply servicing the "easy" and larger accounts, they are prone to develop small accounts. Of course, there are criteria other than geography for establishing territories. One important criterion is product specialization. In this case, salespeople are specialists relative to particular product or customer situations.

The question of managing sales territories cannot be discussed meaningfully without saying something about sales quotas. In general, quotas represent goals assigned to salespeople. As such, quotas provide three main benefits. First, they provide incentives for salespeople. For example, the definite objective of selling $500,000 worth of computer equipment is more motivating to most salespeople than the indefinite charge to go out and sell computer equipment. Sales bonuses and commissions based on quotas can also be motivational. Second, quotas provide a quantitative standard against which the performance of individual sales representatives or other marketing units can be measured. They allow management to pinpoint individuals and units that are performing above average and those experiencing difficulty. Third, quotas can be used not only to evaluate salespersons' performances but also to evaluate and control their efforts. As part of their job, salespeople are expected to engage in various activities besides calling on established accounts. These activities might include calling on new accounts, collecting past-due accounts, and planning and developing sales presentations. Activity quotas allow the company to monitor whether salespeople are engaging in these activities to the extent desired.

Sales quotas represent specific sales goals assigned to each territory or unit over a designated time period. The most common method of establishing quotas for territories is to relate sales to forecasted sales potential. For example, if the Ajax Drug Company's territory M has an estimated industry sales potential for a particular product of $400,000 for the year, the quota might be set at 25 percent of that potential, or $100,000. The 25 percent figure represents the market share Ajax estimates to be a reasonable target. This $100,000 quota may represent an increase of $20,000 in sales over last year (assuming constant prices) that is expected from new business.

In establishing sales quotas for its individual territories or sales personnel, management needs to take into account three key factors. First, all territories will not have equal potential and, therefore, compensation must be adjusted accordingly. Second, all salespeople will not have equal ability and assignments may have to be made accordingly. Third, the sales task in each territory may differ from time period to time period. For instance, the nature of some territories may require that salespeople spend more time seeking new accounts, rather than servicing established accounts, especially in the case of so-called new territories. The point to be made here is that quotas can vary, not only by territory but also by assigned

In today's information-driven business environment, companies are looking to their sales force as a vital souce of customer information. The image of salespeople carrying a sample case and making random sales calls is quickly fading. Today's salespeople use technology to gather information about and communicate with prospects and customers. They also use it internally to bring the resources of their organization together to solve the problems of customers. Following are the percentage of sales forces surveyed that use a particular form of technology and some of the tangible and intangible benefits companies are experiencing from technology.

| Cell phones | E-mail | Desktop PCs |
| 89% | 85% | 68% |

| Notebook computers | Presentation software | Contact management software |
| 63% | 85% | 55% |

Tangible Benefits

- Better business results.
- Increased time spent with customer/ clients.
- Increased customer satisfaction.
- Increased number of promising prospects.
- Consistent and prompt follow-up correspondence.
- Increased revenue per salesperson.
- Improved customer service.
- Better time management by salespeople and managers.
- Improved internal communication.

Intangible Benefits

- Improved employee motivation and satisfaction.
- Better-trained salespeople and marketing personnel.
- More recent and pertinent information with easier access.
- Improved responsiveness to customer and prospect needs.
- Smoother organizational change.
- Improved control and understanding of selling expenses.

Source: The results of sales forces surveyed is from Ginger Conlan, "Plug and Play," *Sales and Marketing Management*, December 1998, pp. 64–66. Adapted from Barton A. Weitz, Stephen B. Castleberry, and John F. Tanner, *Selling: Building Partnerships*, 5th ed. (Burr Ridge, IL: Irwin/McGraw-Hill, 2004), p. 6.

EFFORT-ORIENTED MEASURES

1. Number of sales calls made.
2. Number of MRO (maintenance-repairs-operations) calls made.
3. Number of complaints handled.
4. Number of checks on reseller stocks.
5. Uncontrollable lost job time.
6. Number of inquiries followed up.
7. Number of demonstrations completed.

RESULTS-ORIENTED MEASURES

1. Sales volume (total or by-product or model).
2. Sales volume as a percentage of quota.
3. Sales profitability (dollar gross margin or contribution).
4. Number of new accounts.
5. Number of stockouts.
6. Number of distributors participating in programs.
7. Number of lost accounts.
8. Percentage volume increase in key accounts.
9. Number of customer complaints.
10. Distributor sales-inventory ratios.

Source: Adapted from Thomas N. Ingram, Raymond W. Laforge, and Charles H. Schwepker, Jr., *Sales Management: Analysis and Decision Making,* 3d ed. (Fort Worth, TX: The Dryden Press, 1997), Chap. 15; and Thayer C. Taylor, "SFA: The Newest Orthodoxy," *Sales and Marketing Management,* February 1993, pp. 26–28.

tasks. The effective sales manager should assign quotas not only for dollar sales but also for each major selling function. Figure 9.3 is an example of how this is done for the Medi-test Company, where each activity is assigned a quota and a weight reflecting its relative importance.

FIGURE 9.3
Medi-test Company Sales Activity Evaluation

Territory: Southern
Salesperson: Marsha Smith

Functions	(1) Quota	(2) Actual	(3) Percent (2 ÷ 1)	(4) Weight	(5) Score (3 × 4)
Sales volume					
Old business	$380,000	$300,000	79	0.7	55.7
New business	$ 20,000	$ 20,000	100	0.5	50.0
Calls on prospects					
Doctors	20	15	75	0.2	15.0
Druggists	80	60	75	0.2	15.0
Wholesalers	15	15	100	0.2	20.0
Hospitals	10	10	100	0.2	20.0
				2.0	175.7

Performance index = 175.7

Analyzing Expenses

Sales forecasts should include a sales expense budget. In some companies, sales expense budgets are developed from the bottom up. Each territorial or district manager submits estimates of expenses and forecasted sales quotas. These estimates are usually prepared for a period of a year and then broken down into quarters and months. The sales manager then reviews the budget requests from the field offices and from staff departments.

Motivating and Compensating Performance

An important task for the sales manager is motivating and compensating the sales force. These two tasks are major determinants of sales force productivity. Managing people is always a challenge and involves personal interaction with members of the sales force, time in the field visiting customers, free-flowing communication with the sales force, either by e-mail or telephone, and providing feedback on a regular basis as well as coaching and developing incentive programs through which job promotions or increased earnings can be achieved.[10]

There are two basic types of compensation: salary and commission. *Salary* usually refers to a specific amount of monetary compensation at an agreed rate for definite time periods. *Commission* is usually monetary compensation provided for each unit of sales and expressed as a percentage of sales. The base on which commissions are computed may be volume of sales in units of product, gross sales in dollars, net sales after returns, sales volume in excess of a quota, or net profits. Very often, several compensation approaches are combined. For example, a salesperson might be paid a base salary, a commission on sales exceeding a volume figure, and a percentage share of the company's profits for that year.

In addition to straight dollar compensation, there are numerous other forms of incentives that can be used to motivate the sales force. Some of these types of incentives and their potential performance outcomes are listed in Figure 9.4.

FIGURE 9.4
Types of Incentives and Their Possible Performance Outcomes

Source: Some of the material was adapted from Gilbert A. Churchill Jr., Neil M. Ford, and Orville C. Walker, *Sales Force Management,* 5th ed. (Burr Ridge, IL: Irwin/McGraw-Hill, 1997), p. 490.

Types of Incentives

- Positive feedback on salesperson performance evaluation.
- Company praise (e.g., recognition in a newsletter).
- Bonus (e.g., cash, merchandise, or travel allowances).
- Salary increase.
- Pay for performance for specific new product idea.
- Paid educational allowance.
- Earned time off.
- Fringe benefits.
- Stock options.
- Vested retirement plan.
- Profit sharing.

Performance Outcomes

- Sell a greater dollar volume.
- Increase sales of more profitable products.
- Push new products.
- Push selected items at designated seasons.
- Achieve a higher degree of market penetration by products, kinds of customers, or territories.
- Increase the number of calls made.
- Secure large average orders.
- Secure new customers.
- Service and maintain existing business.
- Reduce turnover of customers.
- Achieve full-line (balanced) selling.
- Reduce direct selling costs.
- Submit reports and other data promptly.

Conclusion

This chapter has attempted to outline and explain the personal selling aspect of the promotion mix. An emphasis was placed on describing the importance of the relationship-building aspect of the personal selling process. For organizations that wish to continue to grow and prosper, personal selling plays an integral part in the marketing of products and services. As long as production continues to expand through the development of new and highly technical products, personal selling will continue to be an important part of marketing strategy.

Additional Readings

Crosby, Lawrence A., and Sheree L. Johnson. "Customer Relationship Management." *Marketing Management,* Fall 2000, pp. 4–5.

Cravens, David W.; Greg W. Marshall; Felicia Lassk; and George S. Law. "The Control Factor." *Marketing Management,* January/February 2004, pp. 39–44.

Fram, Eugene H., and Michael S. McCarthy. "For the Sales Function, Is E-Commerce Friend or Foe?" *Marketing Management,* Fall 2000, pp. 24–33.

Kissan, Joseph. "On the Optimality of Delegating Price Authority to the Sales Force." *Journal of Marketing,* January 2001, pp. 62–70.

Lemon, Katherine N.; Roland T. Rust; and Valarie Zeithaml. "What Drives Customer Loyalty." *Marketing Management,* Spring 2001, pp. 20–25.

Vavra, Terry G. *Aftermarketing.* Burr Ridge, IL: McGraw-Hill, 1995.

Chapter 10

Distribution Strategy

Channel of distribution decisions involve numerous interrelated variables that must be integrated into the total marketing mix. Because of the time and money required to set up an efficient channel, and since channels are often hard to change once they are set up, these decisions are critical to the success of the firm.

This chapter is concerned with the development and management of channels of distribution and the process of goods distribution in complex, highly competitive, and specialized economies. It should be noted at the outset that channels of distribution provide the ultimate consumer or organizational buyer with time, place, and possession utility. Thus, an efficient channel is one that delivers the product when and where it is wanted at a minimum total cost.

The Need for Marketing Intermediaries

A *channel of distribution* is the combination of institutions through which a seller markets products to the user or ultimate consumer. The need for other institutions or intermediaries in the delivery of goods is sometimes questioned, particularly since the profits they make are viewed as adding to the cost of the product. However, this reasoning is generally fallacious, since producers use marketing intermediaries because the intermediary can perform functions more cheaply and more efficiently than the producer can. This notion of efficiency is critical when the characteristics of advanced economies are considered.

For example, the U.S. economy is characterized by heterogeneity in terms of both supply and demand. In terms of numbers alone, there are over 7 million establishments with employees comprising the supply segment of the economy, and there are nearly 110 million households making up the demand side. Clearly, if each of these units had to deal on a one-to-one basis to obtain needed goods and services, and there were no intermediaries to collect and disperse assortments of goods, the system would be totally inefficient. Thus, the primary role of intermediaries is to bring supply and demand together in an efficient and orderly fashion.

Classification of Marketing Intermediaries and Functions

There are a great many types of marketing intermediaries, many of which are so specialized by function and industry that they need not be discussed here. Figure 10.1 presents the major types of marketing intermediaries common to many industries. Although there

FIGURE 10.1
Major Types of Marketing Intermediaries

Source: Based on Peter D. Bennett, ed., *Dictionary of Marketing Terms,* 2d ed. (Chicago: American Marketing Association, 1995).

Middleman—an independent business concern that operates as a link between producers and ultimate consumers or organizational buyers.

Merchant middleman—a middleman who buys the goods outright and takes title to them.

Agent—a business unit that negotiates purchases, sales, or both but does not take title to the goods in which it deals.

Wholesaler—a merchant establishment operated by a concern that is primarily engaged in buying, taking title to, usually storing and physically handling goods in large quantities, and reselling the goods (usually in smaller quantities) to retailers or to organizational buyers.

Retailer—a merchant middleman who is engaged primarily in selling to ultimate consumers.

Broker—a middleman who serves as a go-between for the buyer or seller. The broker assumes no title risks, does not usually have physical custody of products, and is not looked upon as a permanent representative of either the buyer or the seller.

Manufacturers' agent—an agent who generally operates on an extended contractual basis, often sells within an exclusive territory, handles noncompeting but related lines of goods, and possesses limited authority with regard to prices and terms of sale.

Distributor—a wholesale middleman especially in lines where selective or exclusive distribution is common at the wholesaler level in which the manufacturer expects strong promotional support; often a synonym for wholesaler.

Jobber—a middleman who buys from manufacturers and sells to retailers; a wholesaler.

Facilitating agent—a business firm that assists in the performance of distribution tasks other than buying, selling, and transferring title (i.e., transportation companies, warehouses, etc.)

is some overlap in this classification, these categories are based on the marketing functions performed; that is, various intermediaries perform different marketing functions and to different degrees. Figure 10.2 is a listing of the more common marketing functions performed in the channel.

It should be remembered that whether or not a manufacturer uses intermediaries to perform these functions, the functions have to be performed by someone. In other words, the managerial question is not whether to perform the functions, but who will perform them and to what degree.

FIGURE 10.2
Major Functions Performed in Channels of Distribution

Source: Roger A. Kerin, Eric N. Berkowitz, Steven W. Hartley, and William Rudelius, *Marketing,* 7th ed. (Burr Ridge, IL: McGraw-Hill/Irwin, 2003).

Transactional Function

Buying: Purchasing products for resale or as an agent for supply of a product.
Selling: Contacting potential customers, promoting products, and soliciting orders.
Risk taking: Assuming business risks in the ownership of inventory that can become obsolete or deteriorate.

Logistical Function

Assorting: Creating product assortments from several sources to serve customers.
Storing: Assembling and protecting products at a convenient location to offer better customer service.
Sorting: Purchasing in large quantities and breaking into smaller amounts desired by customers.
Transporting: Physically moving products to customers.

Facilitating Function

Financing: Extending credit to customers.
Grading: Inspecting, testing, or judging products, and assigning them quality grades.
Marketing information and research: Providing information to customers and suppliers, including competitive conditions and trends.

Channels of Distribution

As previously noted, a channel of distribution is the combination of institutions through which a seller markets products to the user or ultimate consumer. Some of these links assume the risks of ownership; others do not. The conventional channel of distribution patterns for consumer goods markets are shown in Figure 10.3.

Some manufacturers use a *direct channel,* selling directly to a market. For example, Gateway 2000 sold computers through the mail without the use of other intermediaries. Using a direct channel, called *direct marketing,* increased in popularity as marketers found that products could be sold directly using a variety of methods. These include direct mail, telemarketing, direct-action advertising, catalog selling, cable selling, online selling, and direct selling through demonstrations at home or place of work. These will be discussed in more detail later in this chapter.

In other cases, one or more intermediaries may be used in the distribution process. For example, Hewlett-Packard sells its computers and printers through retailers such as Best Buy and Office Max. A common channel for consumer goods is one in which the manufacturer sells through wholesalers and retailers. For instance, a cold remedy manufacturer may sell to drug wholesalers who, in turn, sell a vast array of drug products to various retail outlets. Small manufacturers may also use agents, since they do not have sufficient capital for their own sales forces. Agents are commonly used intermediaries in the jewelry industry. The final channel in Figure 10.3 is used primarily when small wholesalers and retailers are involved. Channels with one or more intermediaries are referred to as *indirect channels.*

In contrast to consumer products, the direct channel is often used in the distribution of organizational goods. The reason for this stems from the structure of most organizational markets, which often have relatively few but extremely large customers. Also, many organizational products, such as computer systems, need a great deal of presale and postsale service. Distributors are used in organizational markets when there is a large number of buyers but each purchases a small amount of a product. As in the consumer market, agents are used

FIGURE 10.3   Conventional Channels of Distribution of Consumer Goods

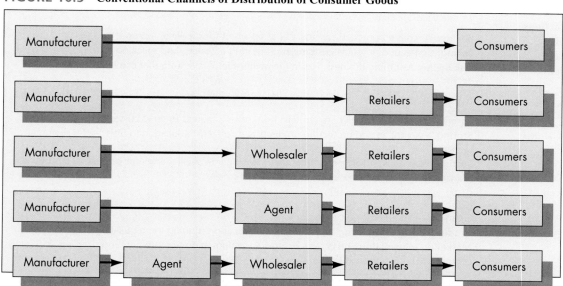

FIGURE 10.4   **Conventional Channels of Distribution for Organizational Goods**

in organizational markets in cases where manufacturers do not wish to have their own sales forces. Such an arrangement may be used by small manufacturers or when the market is geographically dispersed. The final channel arrangement in Figure 10.4 may also be used by a small manufacturer or when the market consists of many small customers. Under such conditions, it may not be economical for sellers to have their own sales organization.

Selecting Channels of Distribution

Given the numerous types of channel intermediaries and functions that must be performed, the task of selecting and designing a channel of distribution may at first appear to be overwhelming. However, in many industries, channels of distribution have developed over many years and have become somewhat traditional. In such cases, the producer may be limited to this type of channel to operate in the industry. This is not to say that a traditional channel is always the most efficient and that there are no opportunities for innovation. But the fact that such a channel is widely accepted in the industry suggests it is highly efficient. A primary constraint in these cases and in cases where no traditional channel exists is that of *availability* of the various types of middlemen. All too often in the early stages of channel design, executives map out elaborate channel networks only to find out later that no such independent intermediaries exist for the firm's product in selected geographic areas. Even if they do exist, they may not be willing to accept the seller's products. In general, there are six basic considerations in the initial development of channel strategy. These are outlined in Figure 10.5.

It should be noted that for a particular product any one of these characteristics greatly influences choice of channels. To illustrate, highly perishable products generally require direct channels, or a firm with little financial strength may require intermediaries to perform almost all of the marketing functions.

Specific Considerations

The above characteristics play an important part in framing the channel selection decision. Based on them, the choice of channels can be further refined in terms of (1) distribution

FIGURE 10.5   General Considerations in Channel Planning

1. **Customer characteristics.**
   a. Number.
   b. Geographic dispersion.
   c. Preferred channels and outlets for purchase.
   d. Purchasing patterns.
   e. Use of new channels (e.g., online purchasing).
2. **Product characteristics.**
   a. Unit value.
   b. Perishability.
   c. Bulkiness.
   d. Degree of standardization.
   e. Installation and maintenance services required.
3. **Intermediary characteristics.**
   a. Availability.
   b. Willingness to accept product or product line.
   c. Geographic market served.
   d. Marketing functions performed.
   e. Potential for conflict.
   f. Potential for long-term relationship.
   g. Competitive products sold.
   h. Financial condition.
   i. Other strengths and weaknesses.
4. **Competitor characteristics.**
   a. Number.
   b. Relative size and market share.
   c. Distribution channels and strategy.
   d. Financial condition and estimated marketing budget.
   e. Size of product mix and product lines.
   f. Overall marketing strategy employed.
   g. Other strengths and weaknesses.
5. **Company characteristics.**
   a. Relative size and market share.
   b. Financial condition and marketing budget.
   c. Size of product mix and product lines.
   d. Marketing strategy employed.
   e. Marketing objectives.
   f. Past channel experience.
   g. Marketing functions willing to perform.
   h. Other strengths and weaknesses.
6. **Environmental characteristics.**
   a. Economic conditions.
   b. Legal regulations and restrictions.
   c. Political issues.
   d. Global and domestic cultural differences and changes.
   e. Technological changes.
   f. Other opportunities and threats.

coverage required, (2) degree of control desired, (3) total distribution cost, and (4) channel flexibility.

Distribution Coverage Required

Because of the characteristics of the product, the environment needed to sell the product, and the needs and expectations of the potential buyer, products will vary in the intensity of distribution coverage they require. Distribution coverage can be viewed along a continuum ranging from intensive to selective to exclusive distribution.

Intensive Distribution   Here the manufacturer attempts to gain exposure through as many wholesalers and retailers as possible. Most convenience goods require intensive distribution based on the characteristics of the product (low unit value) and the needs and expectations of the buyer (high frequency of purchase and convenience).

Selective Distribution   Here the manufacturer limits the use of intermediaries to the ones believed to be the best available in a geographic area. This may be based on the service organization available, the sales organization, or the reputation of the intermediary. Thus, appliances, home furnishings, and better clothing are usually distributed selectively. For appliances, the intermediary's service organization could be a key factor, while for better clothing and home furnishings, the intermediary's reputation would be an important consideration.

Exclusive Distribution   Here the manufacturer severely limits distribution, and intermediaries are provided exclusive rights within a particular territory. The characteristics of the product are a determining factor here. Where the product requires certain specialized

THE PERFECT INTERMEDIARY

1. Has access to the market that the manufacturer wants to reach.
2. Carries adequate stocks of the manufacturer's products and a satisfactory assortment of other products.
3. Has an effective promotional program—advertising, personal selling, and product displays. Promotional demands placed on the manufacturer are in line with what the manufacturer intends to do.
4. Provides services to customers—credit, delivery, installation, and product repair—and honors the product warranty conditions.
5. Pays its bills on time and has capable management.

THE PERFECT MANUFACTURER

1. Provides a desirable assortment of products—well designed, properly priced, attractively packaged, and delivered on time and in adequate quantities.
2. Builds product demand for these products by advertising them.
3. Furnishes promotional assistance to its middlemen.
4. Provides managerial assistance for its middlemen.
5. Honors product warranties and provides repair and installation service.

THE PERFECT COMBINATION

1. Probably doesn't exist.

Source: Adapted from William J. Stanton, Michael J. Etzel, and Bruce J. Walker, *Fundamentals of Marketing*, 9th ed. © New York, McGraw-Hill, 1991, p. 305. Reproduced by permission of The McGraw-Hill Companies.

selling effort or investment in unique facilities or large inventories, this arrangement is usually selected. Retail paint stores are an example of such a distribution arrangement.

Degree of Control Desired

In selecting channels of distribution, the seller must make decisions concerning the degree of control desired over the marketing of the firm's products. Some manufacturers prefer to keep as much control over their products as possible. Ordinarily, the degree of control achieved by the seller is proportionate to the directness of the channel. One Eastern brewery, for instance, owns its own fleet of trucks and operates a wholly owned delivery system direct to grocery and liquor stores. Its market is very concentrated geographically, with many small buyers, so such a system is economically feasible. However, all other brewers in the area sell through distributors.

When more indirect channels are used, the manufacturer must surrender some control over the marketing of the firm's product. However, attempts are commonly made to maintain a degree of control through some other indirect means, such as sharing promotional expenditures, providing sales training, or other operational aids, such as accounting systems, inventory systems, or marketing research data on the dealer's trading area.

Total Distribution Cost

The total distribution cost concept has developed out of the more general topic of systems theory. The concept suggests that a channel of distribution should be viewed as a total system composed of interdependent subsystems, and that the objective of the system (channel) manager should be to optimize total system performance. In terms of distribution costs, it generally is assumed that the total system should be designed to minimize costs, other things being equal. The following is a representative list of the major distribution costs to be minimized.

1. Transportation.
2. Order processing.
3. Cost of lost business (an opportunity cost due to inability to meet customer demand).
4. Inventory carrying costs, including:
   a. Storage-space charges.
   b. Cost of capital invested.
   c. Taxes.
   d. Insurance.
   e. Obsolescence and deterioration.
5. Packaging.
6. Materials handling.

The important qualification to the total-cost concept is the statement "other things being equal." The purpose of the total-cost concept is to emphasize total system performance to avoid suboptimization. However, other important factors must be considered, not the least of which are level of customer service, sales, profits, and interface with the total marketing mix.

Channel Flexibility

A final consideration relates to the ability of the manufacturer to adapt to changing conditions. To illustrate, much of the population has moved from inner cities to suburbs, and thus buyers make most of their purchases in shopping centers and malls. If a manufacturer had long-term exclusive dealership with retailers in the inner city, the ability to adapt to this population shift could have been severely limited.

Managing a Channel of Distribution

Once the seller has decided on the type of channel structure to use and selected the individual members, the entire coalition should operate as a total system. From a behavioral perspective, the system can be viewed as a social system since each member interacts with the others, each member plays a role vis-à-vis the others, and each has certain expectations of the other. Thus, the behavioral perspective views a channel of distribution as more than a series of markets or participants extending from production to consumption.

Relationship Marketing in Channels

For many years in theory and practice, marketing has taken a competitive view of channels of distribution. In other words, since channel members had different goals and strategies, it was believed that the major focus should be on concepts such as power and conflict. Research interests focused on issues concerning bases of power, antecedents and consequences of conflict, and conflict resolution.

More recently, however, a new view of channels has developed. Perhaps because of the success of Japanese companies in the 1980s, it was recognized that much could be gained by developing long-term commitments and harmony among channel members. This view is called *relationship marketing,* which can be defined as "marketing with the conscious aim to develop and manage long-term and/or trusting relationships with customers, distributors, suppliers, or other parties in the marketing environment."[1]

It is well documented in the marketing literature that long-term relationships throughout the channel often lead to higher-quality products with lower costs. These benefits may account for the increased use of vertical marketing systems.[2]

Vertical Marketing Systems

To this point in the chapter the discussion has focused primarily on conventional channels of distribution. In conventional channels, each firm is relatively independent of the other members in the channel. However, one of the important developments in channel management in recent years is the increasing use of vertical marketing systems.

Vertical marketing systems are channels in which members are more dependent on one another and develop long-term working relationships in order to improve the efficiency and effectiveness of the system. Figure 10.6 shows the major types of vertical marketing systems, which include administered, contractual, and corporate systems.[3]

Administered Systems

Administered vertical marketing systems are the most similar to conventional channels. However, in these systems there is a higher degree of interorganizational planning and management than in a conventional channel. The dependence in these systems can result from the existence of a strong channel leader such that other channel members work closely with this company in order to maintain a long-term relationship. While any level of channel member may be the leader of an administered system, Wal-Mart, Kmart, and Sears are excellent examples of retailers that have established administered systems with many of their suppliers.

Contractual Systems

Contractual vertical marketing systems involve independent production and distribution companies entering into formal contracts to perform designated marketing functions. Three major types of contractual vertical marketing systems are the retail cooperative organization, wholesaler-sponsored voluntary chain, and various franchising programs.

In a retail cooperative organization, a group of independent retailers unite and agree to pool buying and managerial resources to improve competitive position. In a wholesaler-sponsored voluntary chain, a wholesaler contracts with a number of retailers and performs channel functions for them. Usually, retailers agree to concentrate a major portion of their purchasing with the sponsoring wholesaler and to sell advertised products at the same price. The most visible type of contractual vertical marketing systems involves a variety of franchise programs. Franchises involve a parent company (the franchisor) and

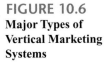

FIGURE 10.6
Major Types of Vertical Marketing Systems

Marketing Highlight   Franchising: An Alternative to Conventional
Channels of Distribution
       10–2

A franchise is a means by which a producer of products or services achieves a direct channel of distribution without wholly owning or managing the physical facilities in the market. In effect, the franchisor provides the franchisee with the franchisor's knowledge, manufacturing, and marketing techniques for a financial return.

INGREDIENTS OF A FRANCHISED BUSINESS

Six key ingredients should be included within a well-balanced franchise offered to a franchisee. These are given in order of importance.

- *Technical knowledge* in its practical form is supplied through an intensive course of study.
- *Managerial techniques* based on proven and time-tested programs are imparted to the franchisee on a continuing basis, even after the business has been started or taken over by the franchisee.
- *Commercial knowledge* involving prescribed methods of buying and selling is explained and codified. Most products to be obtained, processed, and sold to the franchisee are supplied by the franchisor.
- *Financial instruction* on managing funds and accounts is given to the franchisee during the indoctrination period.
- *Accounting controls* are set up by the franchisor for the franchisee.
- *Protective safeguards* are included in the intensive training of the franchisee for employees and customers, including the quality of the product, as well as the safeguards for assets through adequate insurance controls.

ELEMENTS OF AN IDEAL FRANCHISE PROGRAM

- *High gross margin.* In order for the franchisee to be able to afford a high franchise fee (which the franchisor needs), it is necessary to operate on a high gross margin percentage. This explains the widespread application of franchising in the food and service industries.
- *In-store value added.* Franchising works best in those product categories in which the product is at least partially processed in the store. Such environments require constant on-site supervision—a chronic problem for company-owned stores using a hired manager. Owners simply are willing to work harder over longer hours.
- *Secret processes.* Concepts, formulas, or products that the franchisee can't duplicate without joining the franchise program.
- *Real estate profits.* The franchisor uses income from ownership of property as a significant revenue source.
- *Simplicity.* The most successful franchises have been those that operate on automatic pilot: All the key decisions have been thought through, and the owner merely implements the decisions.

Source: Partially adapted from Philip D. White and Albert D. Bates, "Franchising Will Remain Retailing Fixture, but Its Salad Days Have Long Since Gone," *Marketing News*, February 17, 1984, p. 14; and Scott Shane and Chester Spell, "Factors for New Franchise Success," *Sloan Management Review*, Spring 1998, pp. 43–50. Also see Stephen Spinelli, Jr., Robert M. Rosenberg, and Sue Birley, *Franchising* (Upper Saddle River, NJ: Prentice-Hall PTR, 2004).

an independent firm (the franchisee) entering into a contractual relationship to set up and operate a business in a particular way. Many products and services reach consumers through franchise systems, including automobiles (Ford), gasoline (Mobil), hotels and motels (Holiday Inn), restaurants (McDonald's), car rentals (Avis), and soft drinks (Pepsi). In fact, some analysts predict that within the next 10 years, franchises will account for 50 percent of all retail sales.

Corporate Systems

Corporate vertical marketing systems involve single ownership of two or more levels of a channel. A manufacturer's purchasing wholesalers or retailers is called *forward integration.* Wholesalers or retailers' purchasing channel members above them is called *backward integration.* Firms may choose to develop corporate vertical marketing systems in order to compete more effectively with other marketing systems, to obtain scale economies, and to increase channel cooperation and avoid channel conflict.

Wholesaling

As noted, wholesalers are merchants that are primarily engaged in buying, taking title to, usually storing and physically handling goods in large quantities, and reselling the goods (usually in smaller quantities) to retailers or to industrial or business users.[4] Wholesalers are also called *distributors* in some industries, particularly when they have exclusive distribution rights, such as in the beer industry. Other wholesalers that do not take title to goods are called *agents, brokers,* or *manufacturers' representatives* in various industries. There are over 520,000 wholesalers in the United States.

Wholesalers create value for suppliers, retailers, and users of goods by performing distribution functions efficiently and effectively. They may transport and warehouse goods, exhibit them at trade shows, and offer advice to retailers concerning which lines of products are selling best in other areas. Producers use wholesalers to reach large markets and extend geographic coverage for their goods. Wholesalers may lower the costs for other channel members by efficiently carrying out such activities as physically moving goods to convenient locations, assuming the risk of managing large inventories of diverse products, and delivering products as needed to replenish retail shelves.

While producers may actively seek out wholesalers for their goods, wholesalers also try to attract producers to use their services. To do so, they may offer to perform all the distribution functions or tailor their services to include only the functions that producers do not have the ability to perform effectively. Naturally, wholesalers especially seek producers of major brands for which sales and profit potential are likely to be the greatest. Wholesalers may compete with other wholesalers to attract producers by offering lower costs for the functions they perform. Wholesalers with excellent track records that do not carry directly competing products and brands, that have appropriate locations and facilities, and that have relationships with major retail customers can more easily attract manufacturers of successful products. Also, wholesalers that serve large markets may be more attractive since producers may be able to reduce the number of wholesalers they deal with and thereby lower their costs. Long-term profitable producer-wholesaler relationships are enhanced by trust, doing a good job for one another, and open communication about problems and opportunities.

Wholesalers also need to attract retailers and organizational customers to buy from them. In many cases, wholesalers have exclusive contracts to distribute products in a particular trading area. For popular products and brands with large market shares, the wholesaler's task is simplified because retailers want to carry them. For example, distributors of Coke and Pepsi can attract retailers easily because the products sell so well and consumers expect to find them in many retail outlets. Retail supermarkets and convenience stores would be at a competitive disadvantage without these brands.

However, for new or small market-share products and brands, particularly those of less well-known manufacturers, wholesalers may have to do considerable marketing to get retailers to stock them. Wholesalers may get placement for such products and brands in retail stores because they have previously developed strong long-term working

BENEFITS FOR MANUFACTURERS

- Provide the ability to reach diverse geographic markets cost effectively.
- Provide information about retailers and end users in various markets.
- Reduce costs through greater efficiency and effectiveness in distribution functions performed.
- Reduce potential losses by assuming risks and offering expertise.

BENEFITS FOR RETAILERS

- Provide potentially profitable products otherwise unavailable for resale in retail area.
- Provide information about industries, manufacturers, and other retailers.
- Reduce costs by providing an assortment of goods from different manufacturers.
- Reduce costs through greater efficiency in distribution functions performed.

BENEFITS FOR END USERS

- Increase the product alternatives available in local markets.
- Reduce retail prices by the efficiency and effectiveness contributed to the channel.
- Improve product selection by providing information to retailers about the best products to offer end users.

relationships with them. Alternatively, wholesalers may have to carefully explain the marketing plan for the product, why it should be successful, and why carrying the product will benefit the retailer.

While there are still many successful wholesalers, the share of products sold by them is likely to continue to decrease. This is because large retail chains such as Wal-Mart have gained such market power that they can buy directly from manufacturers and bypass wholesalers altogether. The survival of wholesalers depends on their ability to meet the needs of both manufacturers and retailers by performing distribution functions more efficiently and effectively than a channel designed without them.

Store and Nonstore Retailing

As noted, retailers are merchants that are primarily engaged in selling to ultimate consumers. The more than 1.5 million retailers in the United States can be classified in many ways. For example, they are broken down in the North American Industry Classification System (NAICS) codes into eight general categories and a number of subcategories based on the types of merchandise they sell.[5]

Marketers have a number of decisions to make to determine the best way to retail their products. For example, decisions have to be made about whether to use stores to sell merchandise, and if so, whether to sell through company-owned stores, franchised outlets, or independent stores or chains. Decisions have to be made about whether to sell through nonstore methods, such as the Internet, and if so, which methods of nonstore retailing should be used. Each of these decisions brings about a number of others such as what types of stores to use, how many of them, what locations should be selected, and what specific types of nonstore retailing to use.

Store Retailing

Over 90 percent of retail purchases are made through stores. This makes them an appropriate retail method for most types of products and services. Retailers vary not only in the types of merchandise they carry but also in the breadth and depth of their product assortments and the amount of service they provide. In general, *mass merchandisers* carry broad product assortments and compete on two bases. Supermarkets (Kroger), department stores (Marshall Fields), and catalog showrooms (Service Merchandise) compete with other retailers on the basis of offering a good selection in a number of different product categories, whereas superstores (Cub Foods), hypermarkets (Bigg's), discount stores (Wal-Mart), warehouse stores (Price Club), variety stores (Woolworth), and off-price retailers (T. J. Maxx) compete more on the basis of offering lower prices on products in their large assortments. Manufacturers of many types of consumer goods must get distribution in one or more types of mass merchandisers to be successful.

Specialty stores handle deep assortments in a limited number of product categories. Specialty stores include limited-line stores that offer a large assortment of a few related product lines (The Gap), single-line stores that emphasize a single product (Batteries Plus), and category killers (Circuit City), which are large, low-priced limited-line retail chains that attempt to dominate a particular product category. If a product type is sold primarily through specialty stores and sales are concentrated in category killer chains, manufacturers may have to sell through them to reach customers.

Convenience stores (7-Eleven) are retailers whose primary advantages to consumers are location convenience, close-in parking, and easy entry and exit. They stock products that consumers want to buy in a hurry, such as milk or soft drinks, and charge higher prices for the purchase convenience. They are an important retail outlet for many types of convenience goods.

In selecting the types of stores and specific stores and chains to resell their products, manufacturers (and wholesalers) have a variety of factors to consider. They want stores and chains that reach their target market and have good reputations with consumers. They want stores and chains that handle distribution functions efficiently and effectively, order large quantities, pay invoices quickly, display their merchandise well, and allow them to make good profits. Selling products in the right stores and chains increases sales, and selling in prestigious stores can increase the equity of a brand and the price that can be charged. The locations of retail stores, the types of people who shop at them, and the professionalism of the salespeople and clerks who work in them all affect the success of the stores and the products they sell. In addition to the merchandise offered, store advertising, and price levels, the characteristics of the store itself—including layout, colors, smells, noises, lights, signs, and shelf space and displays—influence the success of both the stores and the products they offer.

Nonstore Retailing

Although stores dominate sales for most products, there are still opportunities to market products successfully in other ways. Five nonstore methods of retailing include catalogs and direct mail, vending machines, television home shopping, direct sales, and electronic exchanges.[6]

Catalogs and Direct Mail

As shown in Figure 10.7, catalogs and direct mail dominate nonstore retailing. The advantages of this type of nonstore retailing for marketers are that consumers can be targeted effectively and reached in their homes or at work, overhead costs are decreased, and

In 2003, Wal-Mart became the first company to be not only the largest company in the world but also the most admired in *Fortune*'s annual poll of 10,000 executives. Wal-Mart has been so successful in marketing to consumers that it had sales of over $244 billion in 2002, accounting for an estimated 2.3 percent of the total U.S. GNP. It has redefined what it means to be a big marketer! Some other startling facts about Wal-Mart's success include the following:

- It employs 1.3 million people.
- It is the biggest employer in 21 states, with more people in uniform than the U.S. Army.
- Some 70 million consumers shop in Wal-Mart stores each week.
- Wal-Mart's sales on a single day in Fall 2002, $1.42 billion, were larger than the GDPs of 36 countries.
- Its losses to theft each year, estimated at $2 billion, are equivalent to the size of the revenues of the 694th company on the Fortune 1000.
- It accounts for 39 percent of sales of Tandy Brands, 23 percent of Clorox, 20 percent of Revlon, 20 percent of RJR Tobacco, and 17 percent of Procter & Gamble.
- Its U.S. market share is 36 percent for dog food, 32 percent for disposable diapers, 30 percent for photographic film, 26 percent for toothpaste, and 21 percent for pain remedies.

Wal-Mart is so influential in the economy that its low prices are considered a key reason inflation has stayed low in recent years. Apparently Wal-Mart understands consumers well and delivers value to them.

Sources: Jerry Useem, "One Nation under Wal-Mart," *Fortune,* March 3, 2003, pp. 64–78; Nicholas Stein, "America's Most Admired Companies," *Fortune,* March 3, 2003, pp. 81–85; **www.walmart.com.**

FIGURE 10.7
Annual Nonstore Retail Sales

Source: Adapted from Michael Levy and Barton A. Weitz, *Retailing Management,* 5th ed. (Burr Ridge, IL: McGraw-Hill/Irwin. 2004), pp. 57–62. Reproduced with permission from The McGraw-Hill Companies.

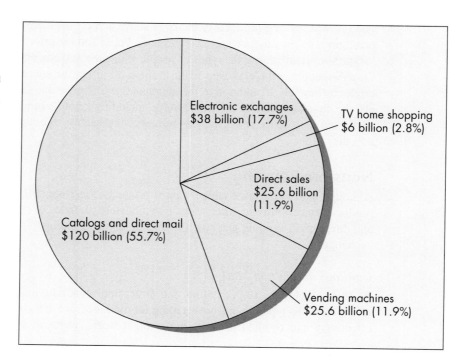

Electronic exchanges $38 billion (17.7%)

TV home shopping $6 billion (2.8%)

Direct sales $25.6 billion (11.9%)

Catalogs and direct mail $120 billion (55.7%)

Vending machines $25.6 billion (11.9%)

assortments of specialty merchandise can be presented with attractive pictures and in-depth descriptions of features and benefits. Catalogs can also remain in homes or offices for a lengthy time period, making available potential sales. Catalogs can offer specialty products for unique markets that are geographically dispersed in a cost-effective manner. Although consumers cannot experience products directly as they can in stores, catalog retailers with reputations for quality and generous return policies can reduce consumers' risks. For example, Levenger, which sells pens, desks, and "other tools for serious readers," sends consumers a postage-paid label to return unwanted merchandise. Many consumers enjoy the time savings of catalog shopping and are willing to pay higher prices to use it.

Vending Machines

Vending machines are a relatively limited method of retail merchandising, and most vending machine sales are for beverages, food, and candy. The advantages for marketers include the following: They are available for sales 24 hours a day, they can be placed in a variety of high-traffic locations, and marketers can charge higher prices. While uses of vending machines for such things as airline insurance and concert and game tickets are not unusual, this method has limited potential for most products.

Television Home Shopping

Television home shopping includes cable channels dedicated to shopping, infomercials, and direct-response advertising shown on cable and broadcast networks. Home Shopping Network and QVC are the leaders in this market, and the major products sold are inexpensive jewelry, apparel, cosmetics, and exercise equipment. While this method allows better visual display than catalogs, potential customers must be watching at the time the merchandise is offered; if not, they have no way of knowing about the product or purchasing it.

Direct Sales

Direct sales are made by salespeople to consumers in their homes or offices or by telephone. The most common products purchased this way are cosmetics, fragrances, decorative accessories, vacuum cleaners, home appliances, cooking utensils, kitchenware, jewelry, food and nutritional products, and educational materials. Avon, Mary Kay, and Tupperware are probably the best-known retail users of this channel. Salespeople can demonstrate products effectively and provide detailed feature and benefit information. A limitation of this method is that consumers are often too busy to spend their time this way and do not want to pay the higher prices needed to cover the high costs of this method of retailing.

Electronic Exchange

Electronic exchanges or Internet marketing involves customers collecting information, shopping, and purchasing from Web sites on the Internet. Electronic exchange has had its greatest success in business-to-business marketing, although it accounts for only about 10 percent of business-to-business commerce. In the business-to-consumer market, electronic exchange is the fastest-growing type of nonstore retailing. However, sales in this market are still a small portion of the sales in traditional retail stores. In fact, Wal-Mart's sales in its traditional stores are far greater than the total of all business-to-consumer exchanges on the Internet taken collectively.

Initially, many analysts thought that electronic exchange would become a leading source of commerce because of its potential to reduce costs for marketers and prices for

Many companies spend heavily to develop effective Web sites. One study found that 32 percent of the companies it polled were spending from $500,000 to over $5 million to create a commerce-based Web site. Like most marketing strategies, designing successful Web sites requires careful analysis of consumers. Below are six recommendations for designing Web sites that customers will be able to use efficiently and effectively.

1. Make sure the site has contact information that is accurate and complete. Many Web sites lack basics such as postal address, phone and fax numbers, and e-mail addresses. Don't hide this stuff five levels deep in a back corner; make it easy to find.

2. Don't make factual information, such as product updates and prices, hard to come by. Someone other than the Webmaster should be responsible for tracking this information and keeping it up-to-date.

3. Make sure users can find the site with straightforward key words. Make it simple to find the site via the various search engines. Work on improving the search function on the site itself.

4. Make it just as easy for customers to exit the site as it is for them to find and use it. The layout and design of the site should be fairly obvious to viewers no matter where they land inside.

5. Create a good table of contents and index. Most customers do not want to start at the front door and proceed in an orderly fashion through the entire site. Keep the number of screens and subscreens for contents and site organization down to a bare minimum. Put links both to the table of contents and to an index on the front page so that consumers can find them quickly.

6. Overall, design Web sites from the customers' point of view, to serve their needs as well as to market products and brands effectively.

To find more information about site usability, see the Alertbox written by Jakob Nielsen of SunSoft (www.useit.com/alertbox/) or read *Understanding Electronic Commerce* by David Kosiur available through www.Amazon.com.

Sources: Adapted from Larry Chiagouris and Conrad Nankin, "Strategic Plans to Solidify Branding on Net," *Marketing News,* June 1, 2004, pp. 29–30; Mark Harper, "So Does Your Web Site Pay?" *Forbes ASAP,* August 25, 1997, pp. 117–118; David Strom, "Five Steps for Site Success," *Forbes ASAP,* August 25, 1997, p. 118.

customers. However, these analysts may have overestimated the ability of electronic exchange to do so; marketing functions in a channel still have to be performed although, admittedly, some of them can be done more efficiently using this method. For example, order-taking and processing can be done more efficiently and accurately by electronic means.

Figure 10.8 lists some of the advantages and disadvantages of the electronic exchange for marketers. In examining this figure, it is important to recognize that there are some differences in the advantages and disadvantages depending on whether the marketer is a small, entrepreneurial venture or a large, established company. Since electronic exchange offers low-entry barriers, this is an advantage for a small company that wants to get into a market and compete for business with less capital. However, for large, established companies, this is less of an advantage since they have the capital to invest; low-entry barriers create more competition for them from smaller companies.

Similarly, large companies with established names and brand equity can more easily market products that customers would ordinarily want to examine before purchase (touch-and-feel products) than can smaller companies with less brand equity. For

FIGURE 10.8
Electronic Commerce: Advantages and Disadvantages for Marketers

Advantages for Marketers

Reduces the need for stores, paper catalogs, and salespeople; can be cost efficient.

Allows good visual presentation and full description of product features and benefits.

Allows vast assortments of products to be offered efficiently.

Allows strategic elements, such as product offerings, prices, and promotion appeals to be changed quickly.

Allows products to be offered globally in an efficient manner.

Allows products to be offered 24 hours a day, 365 days a year.

Fosters the development of one-on-one, interactive relationships with customers.

Provides an efficient means for developing a customer database and doing online marketing research.

Disadvantages for Marketers

Strong price competition often squeezes profit margins.

Low entry barriers led some e-marketers to overemphasize order-taking and not develop sufficient infrastructure for order fulfillment.

Customers must go to the Web site rather than having marketers seek them out via salespeople and advertising; advertising their Web sites is prohibitively expensive for many small e-marketers.

Limits the market to customers who are willing and able to purchase electronically; many countries still have a small population of computer-literate people.

Not as good for selling touch-and-feel products as opposed to look-and-buy products unless there is strong brand/store/site equity (Dell computers/Wal-Mart/Amazon.com) or the products are homogeneous (books, CDs, plane tickets, etc.).

Often less effective and efficient in business-to-consumer markets than in business-to-business markets.

example, companies like Lands' End, J.C. Penney, and Wal-Mart are more successful in attracting customers electronically because customers know the companies and their offerings better and perceive less risk in purchasing from them than from a new or unknown electronic marketer. This does not mean that newer companies that sell only by electronic means cannot compete for business. Companies such as Amazon.com and Priceline.com have created well-known Web sites and have generated considerable sales. However, as with most dot.com businesses, generating profits has been difficult for them.

In sum, while electronic exchange has not met the growth expectations of many marketers, it is an established alternative for marketing some products and services. It does provide customers with a wealth of product information and product assortments that are readily available. Many electronic marketers will have to find ways to deliver superior customer value in order to become profitable and survive in the long run.[7]

Conclusion

This chapter introduced the distribution of goods and services in a complex, highly competitive, highly specialized economy. It emphasized the vital need for marketing intermediaries to bring about exchanges between buyers and sellers in a reasonably efficient manner. The chapter examined various types of intermediaries and the distribution functions they perform as well as topics in the selection and management of distribution channels. Finally, both wholesaling and store and nonstore retailing were discussed.

Additional Readings

Burt, David N.; Donald W. Dobler; and Stephen L. Starling. *World Class Supply Management.* Burr Ridge: McGraw-Hill, 2003.

Chopra, Sunil, and Peter Meindl. *Supply Chain Management.* 2nd ed. Upper River Saddle, NJ: Prentice Hall, 2004.

Coughlin, Anne T.; Erin Anderson; Louis W. Stern; and Adel I. El-Ansary. *Marketing Channels.* 6th ed. Upper Saddle River, NJ: Prentice Hall, 2001.

Levy, Michael, and Burton A. Weitz. *Retailing Management.* 5th ed. Burr Ridge, IL: Irwin/McGraw-Hill, 2004.

Pelton, Lou E.; David Strutton; and James R. Lumpkin. *Marketing Channels: A Relationship Management Approach.* Burr Ridge, IL: Irwin, 1997.

Rosenbloom, Bert. *Marketing Channels: A Management View.* 6th ed. Fort Worth: Dryden Press, 1999.

Chapter

11

Pricing Strategy

One of the most important and complex decisions a firm has to make relates to pricing its products or services. If consumers or organizational buyers perceive a price to be too high, they may purchase competitive brands or substitute products, leading to a loss of sales and profits for the firm. If the price is too low, sales might increase, but profitability may suffer. Thus, pricing decisions must be given careful consideration when a firm is introducing a new product or planning a short- or long-term price change.

This chapter discusses demand, supply, and environmental influences that affect pricing decisions and emphasizes that all three must be considered for effective pricing. However, as will be discussed in the chapter, many firms price their products without explicitly considering all of these influences.

Demand Influences on Pricing Decisions

Demand influences on pricing decisions concern primarily the nature of the target market and expected reactions of consumers to a given price or change in price. There are three primary considerations here: demographic factors, psychological factors, and price elasticity.

Demographic Factors

In the initial selection of the target market that a firm intends to serve, a number of demographic factors are usually considered. Demographic factors that are particularly important for pricing decisions include the following:

1. Number of potential buyers, and their age, education, and gender.
2. Location of potential buyers.
3. Position of potential buyers (organizational buyers or final consumers).
4. Expected consumption rates of potential buyers.
5. Economic strength of potential buyers.

These factors help determine market potential and are useful for estimating expected sales at various price levels.

Psychological Factors

Psychological factors related to pricing concern primarily how consumers will perceive various prices or price changes. For example, marketing managers should be concerned with such questions as:

1. Will potential buyers use price as an indicator of product quality?
2. Will potential buyers be favorably attracted by odd pricing?

Small changes in the price received by marketers can lead to large differences in net income. For example, at Coca-Cola, a 1 percent improvement in the price received for its products would result in a net income boost of 6.4 percent; at Fuji Photo, 16.7 percent; at Nestlé, 17.5 percent; at Ford, 26 percent; and at Philips, 28.7 percent. In some companies, a 1 percent improvement in the price received would be the difference between a profit and a significant loss. Given the cost structure of large corporations, a 1 percent boost in realized price yields an average net income gain of 12 percent. In short, when setting pricing objectives and developing pricing strategies, it's worth the effort to do pricing research to see what prices consumers are willing to pay and still feel they are receiving good value.

Source: Based on Robert J. Dolan and Hermann Simon, *Power Pricing: How Managing Price Transforms the Bottom Line* (New York: Free Press, 1996), p. 4. Also see Kent B. Monroe, *Pricing: Making Profitable Decisions,* 3d ed. (Burr Ridge, IL: McGraw-Hill/Irwin, 2003), Chapter 12.

3. Will potential buyers perceive the price as too high relative to the service the product gives them or relative to competition?

4. Are potential buyers prestige oriented and therefore willing to pay higher prices to fulfill this need?

5. How much will potential buyers be willing to pay for the product?

While psychological factors have a significant effect on the success of a pricing strategy and ultimately on marketing strategy, answers to the above questions may require considerable marketing research. In fact, a review of buyers' subjective perceptions of price concluded that very little is known about how price affects buyers' perceptions of alternative purchase offers and how these perceptions affect purchase response.[1] However, some tentative generalizations about how buyers perceive price have been formulated. For example, research has found that persons who choose high-priced items usually perceive large quality variations within product categories and see the consequences of a poor choice as being undesirable. They believe that quality is related to price and see themselves as good judges of product quality. In general, the reverse is true for persons who select low-priced items in the same product categories. Thus, although information on psychological factors involved in purchasing may be difficult to obtain, marketing managers must at least consider the effects of such factors on their desired target market and marketing strategy.[2]

There are three types of psychological pricing strategies. First there is *prestige pricing,* in which a high price is charged to create a signal that the product is exceptionally fine. Prestige pricing is commonly used for some brands of cars, clothing, perfume, jewelry, cosmetics, wine and liquor, and crystal and china. Second, there is *odd pricing,* or odd-even pricing, in which prices are set a few dollars or a few cents below a round number. For example, Frito-Lay's potato chips are priced at 69 cents a bag rather than 70 cents to encourage consumers to think of them as less expensive (60 some-odd cents) rather than 70 cents. Hertz economy cars are rented for $129 rather than $130 to appear less expensive. Third, there is *bundle pricing,* in which several products are sold together at a single price to suggest a good value. For example, travel agencies offer vacation packages that include travel, accommodations, and entertainment at a single price to connote value and convenience for customers.

Price Elasticity

Both demographic and psychological factors affect price elasticity. Price elasticity is a measure of consumers' price sensitivity, which is estimated by dividing relative changes in the quantity sold by the relative changes in price:

$$e = \frac{\text{Percent change in quantity demanded}}{\text{Percent change in price}}$$

Although price elasticity is difficult to measure, there are two basic methods commonly used to estimate it. First, price elasticity can be estimated from historical data or from price/quantity data across different sales districts. Second, price elasticity can be estimated by sampling a group of consumers from the target market and polling them concerning various price/quantity relationships. Both of these approaches provide estimates of price elasticity; but the former approach is limited to the consideration of price changes, whereas the latter is often expensive and there is some question as to the validity of subjects' responses. However, even a crude estimate of price elasticity is a useful input to pricing decisions.[3]

Supply Influences on Pricing Decisions

For the purpose of this text, supply influences on pricing decisions can be discussed in terms of three basic factors. These factors relate to the objectives, costs, and nature of the product.

Pricing Objectives

Pricing objectives should be derived from overall marketing objectives, which in turn should be derived from corporate objectives. Since it is traditionally assumed that business firms operate to maximize profits in the long run, it is often thought that the basic pricing objective is solely concerned with long-run profits. However, the profit maximization norm does not provide the operating marketing manager with a single, unequivocal guideline for selecting prices. In addition, the marketing manager does not have perfect cost, revenue, and market information to be able to evaluate whether or not this objective is being reached. In practice, then, many other objectives are employed as guidelines for pricing decisions. In some cases, these objectives may be considered as operational approaches to achieve long-run profit maximization.

Research has found that the most common pricing objectives are (1) pricing to achieve a target return on investment, (2) stabilization of price and margin, (3) pricing to achieve a target market share, and (4) pricing to meet or prevent competition.

Cost Considerations in Pricing

The price of a product usually must cover costs of production, promotion, and distribution, plus a profit for the offering to be of value to the firm. In addition, when products are priced on the basis of costs plus a fair profit, there is an implicit assumption that this sum represents the economic value of the product in the marketplace.

Cost-oriented pricing is the most common approach in practice, and there are at least three basic variations: markup pricing, cost-plus pricing, and rate-of-return pricing. *Markup pricing* is commonly used in retailing, where a percentage is added to the retailer's invoice price to determine the final selling price. Closely related to markup pricing is *cost-plus pricing,* where the costs of producing a product or completing a project are totaled and a profit amount or percentage is added on. Cost-plus pricing is most often used to describe the pricing of jobs that are nonroutine and difficult to "cost" in advance, such as construction and military weapon development.

Rate-of-return or *target pricing* is commonly used by manufacturers. With this method, price is determined by adding a desired rate of return on investment to total costs. Generally, a break-even analysis is performed for expected production and sales levels and a rate

There are two common pricing strategies at the retail level: EDLP, which stands for "everyday low pricing," and high/low, which means that the retailer charges prices that are sometimes above competitors' but promotes frequent sales that lower prices below them. Four of the most successful U.S. retailers—Home Depot, Wal-Mart, Office Depot, and Toys 'R' Us—have adopted EDLP, while many fashion, grocery, and drug stores use high/low. Below is a list of the advantages of each of these pricing strategies.

ADVANTAGES OF EDLP

1. *Reduces price wars*—If consumers believe that the store's prices are low, the retailer can avoid getting into price wars with competitors.
2. *Reduces advertising*—Since prices are relatively stable using EDLP, weekly advertisements promoting sales are unnecessary.
3. *Improves customer service*—Since customer flow is more steady without sales-stimulating throngs of shoppers, in-store salespeople and clerks can spend more time with each customer.
4. *Reduces stockouts and improves inventory management*—Since large variations in demand created by sales are eliminated, necessary inventory can be kept on the shelf to avoid stockouts; inventory ordering, delivery, and handling are more efficient.
5. *Increases overall profit margins*—Even though prices are generally lower using EDLP, overall profit margins can increase since merchandise is no longer sold at large price reductions and some costs are reduced.

ADVANTAGES OF HIGH/LOW

1. *Helps segment the market*—Since different groups of customers are willing to pay different prices for products, high/low allows stores to receive higher prices from the first people to buy and still serve hard-core bargain hunters at the end of the fashion cycle.
2. *Creates excitement*—Sales can draw crowds and create an exciting buying experience for shoppers. This exciting experience may bring shoppers back for other sales.
3. *Moves merchandise*—Frequent sales enable retailers to move merchandise, even though profits are lower on sale merchandise.
4. *Emphasizes product quality and store service*—The high initial price sends a signal to customers that a product is high quality or the store provides excellent service, or both.
5. *Is easier to use*—Most retailers have a difficult time using EDLP because they must convince customers that the store's prices are relatively low on most products. High/low, on the other hand, offers customers a means of assessing how low prices are since the original and sale prices are readily available and can be compared.

Source: Based on Michael Levy and Barton A. Weitz, *Retailing Management*, 5th ed. (Burr Ridge, IL: Irwin/McGraw-Hill, 2004), pp. 478–9.

of return is added on. For example, suppose a firm estimated production and sales to be 75,000 units at a total cost of $300,000. If the firm desired a before-tax return of 20 percent, the selling price would be $(300,000 + 0.20 \times 300,000) \div 75,000 = \$4.80$.

Cost-oriented approaches to pricing have the advantage of simplicity, and many practitioners believe that they generally yield a good price decision. However, such approaches have been criticized for two basic reasons. First, cost approaches give little or no consideration to demand factors. For example, the price determined by markup or cost-plus methods has no necessary relationship to what people will be willing to pay for the product. In the case of rate-of-return pricing, little emphasis is placed on estimating sales volume. Even if it were, rate-of-return pricing involves circular reasoning, since unit cost depends on

The following formulas are used to calculate break-even points in units and in dollars:

$$BEP_{(in\ units)} = \frac{FC}{(SP - VC)}$$

$$BEP_{(in\ dollars)} = \frac{FC}{1 - (VC/SP)}$$

where

  FC = Fixed cost
  VC = Variable cost
  SP = Selling price

If, as is generally the case, a firm wants to know how many units or sales dollars are necessary to generate a given amount of profit, profit (P) is simply added to fixed costs in the formulas. In addition, if the firm has estimates of expected sales and fixed and variable costs, the selling price can be solved for. (A more detailed discussion of break-even analysis is provided in the financial analysis section of this book.)

sales volume but sales volume depends on selling price. Second, cost approaches fail to reflect competition adequately. Only in industries where all firms use this approach and have similar costs and markups can this approach yield similar prices and minimize price competition. Thus, in many industries, cost-oriented pricing could lead to severe price competition, which could eliminate smaller firms. Therefore, although costs are a highly important consideration in price decisions, numerous other factors need to be examined.

Product Considerations in Pricing

Although numerous product characteristics can affect pricing, three of the most important are (1) perishability, (2) distinctiveness, and (3) stage in the product life cycle.

Perishability

Goods that are very perishable in a physical sense must be priced to promote sales without costly delays. Foodstuffs and certain types of raw materials tend to be in this category. Products can be considered perishable in two other senses. High fashion, fad, and seasonal products are perishable not in the sense that the product deteriorates but that demand for the product is confined to a specific time period. Perishability also relates to consumption rate, which means that some products are consumed very slowly, as in the case of consumer durables. Two important pricing considerations here are that (1) such goods tend to be expensive because large amounts of service are purchased at one time; and (2) the customer has a certain amount of discretionary time available in making replacement purchase decisions.

Distinctiveness

Products can be classified in terms of how distinctive they are. Homogeneous goods are perfect substitutes for each other, as in the case of bulk wheat or whole milk, while most manufactured goods can be differentiated on the basis of certain features, such as package, trademark, engineering design, and chemical features. Thus, few consumer goods are perfectly homogeneous, and one of the primary marketing objectives of most firms is to make their products and brands distinctive in the minds of buyers. Large sums of money are often invested to accomplish this task, and one of the payoffs for such investments is the seller's ability to charge higher prices for distinctive products.

Life Cycle

The stage of the life cycle that a product is in can have important pricing implications. With regard to the life cycle, two approaches to pricing are skimming and penetration price policies. A *skimming* policy is one in which the seller charges a relatively high price on a new product. Generally, this policy is used when the firm has a temporary monopoly and when demand for the product is price inelastic. In later stages of the life cycle, as competition moves in and other market factors change, the price may then be lowered. Digital watches and calculators are examples of this. A *penetration* policy is one in which the seller charges a relatively low price on a new product. Generally, this policy is used when the firm expects competition to move in rapidly and when demand for the product is, at least in the short run, price elastic. This policy is also used to obtain large economies of scale and as a major instrument for rapid creation of a mass market. A low price and profit margin may also discourage competition. In later stages of the life cycle, the price may have to be altered to meet changes in the market.

Environmental Influences on Pricing Decisions

Environmental influences on pricing include variables that are uncontrollable by the marketing manager. Two of the most important of these are competition and government regulation.

Competition

In setting or changing prices, the firm must consider its competition and how competition will react to the price of the product. Initially, consideration must be given to such factors as:

1. Number of competitors.
2. Size of competitors.
3. Strengths and weaknesses of each competitor.
4. Likely entry of new firms into the industry.
5. Degree of vertical integration of competitors.
6. Number of products sold by competitors.
7. Cost structure of competitors.
8. Historical reaction of competitors to price changes.

These factors help determine whether the firm's selling price should be at, below, or above competition. Pricing a product at competition (i.e., the average price charged by the industry) is called *going-rate pricing* and is popular for homogeneous products, since this approach represents the collective wisdom of the industry and is not disruptive of industry harmony. An example of pricing below competition can be found in *sealed-bid pricing,* in which the firm is bidding directly against competition for project contracts. Although cost and profits are initially calculated, the firm attempts to bid below competitors to obtain the job contract. A firm may price above competition because it has a superior product or because the firm is the price leader in the industry.

Government Regulations

Prices of certain goods and services are regulated by state and federal governments. Public utilities are examples of state regulation of prices. However, for most marketing managers, federal laws that make certain pricing practices illegal are of primary consideration in pricing decisions. The following list is a summary of some of the more important legal constraints on pricing. Of course, since most marketing managers are not trained as lawyers, they usually seek legal counsel when developing pricing strategies to ensure conformity to state and federal legislation.

1. Price fixing is illegal per se. Sellers must not make any agreements with competitors or distributors concerning the final price of the goods. The Sherman Antitrust Act is the primary device used to outlaw horizontal price fixing. Section 5 of the Federal Trade Commission Act has been used to outlaw price fixing as an unfair business practice.

2. Deceptive pricing practices are outlawed under Section 5 of the Federal Trade Commission Act. An example of deceptive pricing would be to mark merchandise with an exceptionally high price and then claim that the lower selling price actually used represents a legitimate price reduction.

3. Price discrimination that lessens competition or is deemed injurious to it is outlawed by the Robinson-Patman Act (which amends Section 2 of the Clayton Act). Price discrimination is not illegal per se, but sellers cannot charge competing buyers different prices for essentially the same products if the effect of such sales is injurious to competition. Price differentials can be legally justified on certain grounds, especially if the price differences reflect cost differences. This is particularly true of quantity discounts.

4. Promotional pricing, such as cooperative advertising, and price deals are not illegal per se; but if a seller grants advertising allowances, merchandising service, free goods, or special promotional discounts to customers, it must do so on proportionately equal terms. Sections 2(d) and 2(e) of the Robinson-Patman Act are designed to regulate such practices so that price reductions cannot be granted to some customers under the guise of promotional allowances.[4]

A General Pricing Model

It should be clear that effective pricing decisions involve considerations of many factors, and different industries may have different pricing practices. Although no single model will fit all pricing decisions, Figure 11.1 presents a general model for developing prices for products and services.[5] While all pricing decisions cannot be made strictly on the basis of this model, it does break pricing strategy into a set of manageable stages that are integrated into the overall marketing strategy.

Set Pricing Objectives

Given a product or service designed for a specific target market, the pricing process begins with a clear statement of the pricing objectives. These objectives guide the pricing strategy and should be designed to support the overall marketing strategy. Because pricing strategy has a direct bearing on demand for a product and the profit obtained, efforts to set prices must be coordinated with other functional areas. For example, production will have to be able to meet demand at a given price, and finance will have to manage funds flowing in and out of the organization at predicted levels of production.

Evaluate Product-Price Relationships

As noted, the distinctiveness, perishability, and stage of the life cycle a product is in all affect pricing. In addition, marketers need to consider what value the product has for customers and how price will influence product positioning. There are three basic value positions. First, a product could be priced relatively high for a product class because it offers value in the form of high quality, special features, or prestige. Second, a product could be priced at about average for the product class because it offers value in the form of good

FIGURE 11.1
**A General Pricing
Model**

quality for a reasonable price. Third, a product could be priced relatively low for a product class because it offers value in the form of acceptable quality at a low price. A Porsche or Nike Air Jordans are examples of the first type of value; a Honda Accord or Keds tennis shoes are examples of the second; and Hyundai cars and private label canvas shoes are examples of the third. Setting prices so that targeted customers will perceive products to offer greater value than competitive offerings is called *value pricing.*

In addition, research is needed to estimate how much of a particular product the target market will purchase at various price levels—price elasticity. This estimate provides valuable information about what the target market thinks about the product and what it is worth to them.

Estimate Costs and Other Price Limitations

The costs to produce and market products provide a lower bound for pricing decisions and a baseline from which to compute profit potential. If a product cannot be produced and

1. *Base pricing strategies on sound research.* Although a recent study found that few companies do serious pricing research, it is a must for sound pricing strategies. Research is needed to understand the factors that influence supply and demand.

2. *Continuously monitor pricing decisions.* Pricing should be treated as a process of developing prices and changing them as needed rather than an annual budgeting exercise. Price decisions define an organization's value image in the eyes of customers and competitors.

3. *Recognize that buyers may have difficulty in computing price differences.* Buyers do not constantly monitor the prices of many products and will not necessarily quickly recognize the value in a price deal.

4. *Recognize that customers evaluate prices comparatively.* Behavioral pricing research suggests that customers compare prices and price deals relative to internal or external reference prices rather than just evaluating them in an absolute sense. An internal reference price is the price a customer has in mind for a product and an external reference price is one the customer has seen in advertising, a catalog, or on a store sign or price tag.

5. *Recognize that buyers typically have a range of acceptable prices.* Buyers often have an upper and lower threshold or range of acceptable prices rather than only one acceptable price they are willing to pay.

6. *Understand the importance of relative price to buyers.* The relative price of a product compared to competitive offerings or to what a buyer previously paid for it may be more important than the absolute price asked.

7. *Understand the importance of price information.* Price information can affect preferences and choices for different models in a product line or for competitive offerings, particularly when buyers cannot easily evaluate product quality.

8. *Recognize that price elasticities vary.* Price elasticities vary according to the direction of a price change, and buyers are generally more sensitive to price increases than to price decreases. Thus, it is easier to lose sales to current customers by increasing prices than it is to gain sales from new buyers by reducing them.

Source: Based on Kent B. Monroe and Jennifer L. Cox, "Pricing Practices That Endanger Profits," *Marketing Management,* September/October 2001, pp. 42–46.

---

marketed at a price to cover its costs and provide reasonable profits in the long run, then it should not be produced in its designed form. One possibility is to redesign the product so that its costs are lower. In fact, some companies first determine the price customers are willing to pay for a product and then design it so that it can be produced and marketed at a cost that allows targeted profits.

Other price limitations that need to be considered are government regulations and the prices that are charged by competitors for similar and substitute products. Also, likely competitive reactions that could influence the price of a new product or a price change in an existing one need to be considered.

Analyze Profit Potential

Analysis in the preceding stages should result in a range of prices that could be charged. Marketers must then estimate the likely profit in pricing at levels in this range. At this stage, it is important to recognize that it may be necessary to offer channel members quantity discounts, promotional allowances, and slotting allowances to encourage them to actively market the product. *Quantity discounts* are discounts for purchasing a large number of units. *Promotional allowances* are often in the form of price reductions in exchange for the channel member performing various promotional activities, such as featuring the product in store advertising or on in-store displays. *Slotting allowances* are payments to retailers to get them to stock items on their shelves. All of these can increase sales but also add marketing cost to the manufacturer and affect profits.

Set Initial Price Structure

Since all of the supply, demand, and environmental factors have been considered, a marketer can now set the initial price structure. The price structure takes into account the price to various channel members, such as wholesalers and retailers, as well as the recommended price to final consumers or organizational buyers.

Change Price as Needed

There are many reasons why an initial price structure may need to be changed. Channel members may bargain for greater margins, competitors may lower their prices, or costs may increase with inflation. In the short term, discounts and allowances may have to be larger or more frequent than planned to get greater marketing effort to increase demand to profitable levels. In the long term, price structures tend to increase for most products as production and marketing costs increase.

Conclusion

Pricing decisions that integrate the firm's costs with marketing strategy, business conditions, competition, demand, product variables, channels of distribution, and general resources can determine the success or failure of a business. This places a very heavy burden on the price maker. Modern-day marketing managers cannot ignore the complexity or the importance of price management. Pricing strategies must be continually reviewed and must take into account that the firm is a dynamic entity operating in a very competitive environment. There are many ways for money to flow out of a firm in the form of costs, but often there is only one way to bring in revenues and that is by the price-product mechanism.

Additional Readings

Dolan, Robert J., and Hermann Simon. *Power Pricing*. New York: Free Press, 1996.

Monroe, Kent B. *Pricing: Making Profitable Decisions*. 3d ed. New York: McGraw-Hill, 2003.

Nagle, Thomas T., and Reed K. Holden. *The Strategy and Tactics of Pricing*. 3d ed. Englewood Cliffs, NJ: Prentice Hall, 2002.

Simon, Hermann, and Robert J. Dolan. "Price Customization." *Marketing Management,* Fall 1998, pp. 11–17.

Part D

Marketing in Special Fields

Chapter

12

The Marketing of Services

Over the course of the past 40 years, the fastest-growing segment of the American economy has not been the production of tangibles but the performance of services. Spending on services has increased to such an extent that today it captures more than 50 cents of the consumer's dollar. In addition, the service sector in the United States produces a balance-of-trade surplus and is expected to be responsible for all net job growth through the year 2005.[1] And the dominance of the service sector is not limited to the United States. The service sector accounts for more than half the GNP and employs more than half the labor force in most Latin American and Caribbean countries. Over the course of the next decade, the service sector will spawn whole new legions of doctors, nurses, medical technologists, physical therapists, home health aids, and social workers to administer to the needs of an aging population, along with armies of food servers, child care providers, and cleaning people to cater to the wants of two-income families. Also rising to the forefront will be a swelling class of technical workers, including computer engineers, systems analysts, and paralegals.

Many marketing textbooks still devote little attention to program development for the marketing of services, especially those in the rapidly changing areas of health care, finance, and travel. This omission is usually based on the assumption that the marketing of products and services is basically the same, and, therefore, the techniques discussed under products apply as well to the marketing of services. Basically, this assumption is true. Whether selling goods or services, the marketer must be concerned with developing a marketing strategy centered on the four controllable decision variables that comprise the marketing mix: the product (or service), the price, the distribution system, and promotion. In addition, the use of marketing research is as valuable to service marketers as it is to product marketers. However, because services possess certain distinguishing characteristics, the task of determining the marketing mix ingredients for a service marketing strategy may raise different and more difficult problems than those encountered in marketing products.

The purpose of this chapter is fourfold. First, the reader will become acquainted with the special characteristics of services and their strategy implications. Second, key concepts associated with providing quality services will be discussed. Third, obstacles will be described that in the past impeded and still continue to impede development of services marketing. Finally, current trends and strategies of innovation in services marketing will be explored. With this approach, the material in the other chapters of the book can be integrated to give a better understanding of the marketing of services.

Before proceeding, some attention must be given to what we refer to when using the term *services*. Probably the most frustrating aspect of the available literature on services is that the definition of what constitutes a service remains unclear. The fact is that no common definition and boundaries have been developed to delimit the field of services. The American Marketing Association has defined services as follows:[2]

1. *Service products,* such as a bank loan or home security, that are intangible, or at least substantially so. If totally intangible, they are exchanged directly from producer to user, cannot be transported or stored, and are almost instantly perishable. Service products are often difficult to identify, since they come into existence at the same time they are bought and consumed. They are composed of intangible elements that are inseparable; they usually involve customer participation in some important way, cannot be sold in the sense of ownership transfer, and have no title. Today, however, most products are partly tangible and partly intangible, and the dominant form is used to classify them as either goods or services (all are products). These common, hybrid forms, whatever they are called, may or may not have the attributes just given for totally intangible services.

2. *Services,* as a term, is also used to describe activities performed by sellers and others that accompany the sale of a product and that aid in its exchange or its utilization (e.g., shoe fitting, financing, an 800 number). Such services are either presale or postsale and supplement the product but do not comprise it.

The first definition includes what can be considered almost pure services, such as insurance, banking, entertainment, airlines, health care, telecommunications, and hotels; the second definition includes such services as wrapping, financing an automobile, providing warranties on computer equipment, and the like, because these services exist in connection with the sale of a product or another service. This suggests that marketers of goods are also marketers of services. For example, one could argue that McDonald's is not in the hamburger business. Its hamburgers are actually not very different from those of the competition. McDonald's is in the service business.

More and more manufacturers are also exploiting their service capabilities as standalone revenue producers. For example, General Motors, Ford, and Chrysler all offer financing services. Ford and General Motors have extended their financial services offerings to include a MasterCard, which offers discounts on purchases of their automobiles.

The reader can imagine from his or her own experience that some purchases are very tangible (a coffeemaker) while others are very much intangible (a course in marketing). Others have elements of both (lunch on a flight from New York to Chicago). In other words, in reality there is a goods-service continuum, with many purchases including both tangible goods and intangible services. Figure 12.1 illustrates such a continuum. On the goods side of the continuum, the buyer owns an object after the purchase. On the services side of the continuum, when the transaction is over, the buyer leaves with an experience and a feeling. When the course in marketing is over or the flight from New York to Chicago is completed, the student or passenger leaves with a feeling.

The examples of services on the right side of Figure 12.1 are mostly or entirely intangible. They do not exist in the physical realm. They cannot appeal to the five senses.

FIGURE 12.1
The Goods-Service Continuum

Tangible	← ——————— Mixed ——————— →	Intangible
Golf clubs	Green fees with sleeve of balls included	Green fees
Car	Oil change	Taxi ride
Suit	Suit with alterations	Alterations
Airplane	Air flight with lunch	Air flight

Important Characteristics of Services

Services possess several unique characteristics that often have a significant impact on marketing program development. These special features of services may cause unique problems and often result in marketing mix decisions that are substantially different from those found in connection with the marketing of goods. Some of the more important of these characteristics are intangibility, inseparability, perishability and fluctuating demand, a client relationship, customer effort, and uniformity. They are presented in Figure 12.2.

Intangibility

The obvious basic difference between goods and services is the intangibility of services, and many of the problems encountered in the marketing of services are due to intangibility. To illustrate, how does an airline make tangible a trip from Philadelphia to San Francisco? These problems are unique to service marketing.

The fact that many services cannot appeal to a buyer's sense of touch, taste, smell, sight, or hearing before purchase places a burden on the marketing organization. For example, hotels that promise a good night's sleep to their customers cannot actually show this service in a tangible way. Obviously, this burden is most heavily felt in a firm's promotional program, but, as will be discussed later, it may affect other areas. Depending on the type of service, the intangibility factor may dictate use of direct channels because of the need for personal contact between the buyer and seller. Since a service firm is actually selling an idea or experience, not a product, it must tell the buyer what the service will do because it is often difficult to illustrate, demonstrate, or display the service in use. For example, the hotel must somehow describe to the consumer how a stay at the hotel will leave the customer feeling well rested and ready to begin a new day.

The above discussion alludes to two strategy elements firms should employ when trying to overcome the problems associated with service intangibility. First, tangible aspects associated with the service should be stressed. For example, advertisements for airlines should emphasize (through text and visuals) the newness of the aircraft, the roominess of the

FIGURE 12.2   Unique Characteristics Distinguishing Services from Goods

Characteristic	Services	Goods
Intangibility	The customer owns only memories, outcomes, or feelings such as an airline flight, greater knowledge or styled hair.	The customer owns objects that can be used, resold, or given to others.
Inseparability	Services often cannot be separated from the person providing them. They are often produced and consumed at the same time.	Goods are usually produced and sold by different people.
Perishability	Services can be used only at the time they are offered. They cannot be inventoried, stored, or transported.	Goods can be placed in inventory for use at another time.
Client Relationship	Services often involve a long-term personal relationship between buyer and seller.	Goods often involve an impersonal short-term relationship although in many instances relationship strength and duration are increasing.
Customer Effort	Customers are often heavily involved in the production.	Customer's involvement may be limited to buying completed product and using it.
Uniformity	Because of inseparability and high involvement on the part of the buyer, each service may be unique, with the quality likely to vary.	Variations in quality and variance from standards can be corrected before customers purchase products.

PRODUCTS

1. The customer owns an object.
2. The goal of producing a product is uniformity—all widgets are alike.
3. A product can be put into inventory; a sample can be sent in advance for the customer to review.
4. The customer is an end user who is not involved in the production process.
5. One conducts quality control by comparing output to specifications.
6. If improperly produced, the product can be pulled off the line or recalled.
7. The morale of production employees is important.
8. Customer can determine level of quality by comparing product to other products.
9. There is a low level of collaboration between the buyer and the seller.
10. Greater number and variety of product brands are available to customer.

SERVICES

1. The customer owns a memory. The experience cannot be sold or passed on to a third party.
2. The goal of service is uniqueness; each customer and each contact is special.
3. A service happens at the moment. It cannot be stockpiled or saved to be used at a later date.
4. The customer is a coproducer who is a partner in creating the service.
5. Customer conducts quality control by comparing expectations to experience.
6. If improperly performed, apologies and reparations are the only means of recourse.
7. The morale of service employees is critical.
8. Customer can determine level of quality throughout the delivery of the service.
9. There is a high level of collaboration between the buyer and the seller.
10. Fewer brands of services are available to customer.

Sources: Ron Zemke, "The Emerging Art of Service Management," *Training,* January 1992, pp. 36–42; and Ralph W. Jackson, Lester A. Neidell, and Dale A. Lunsford, "An Empirical Investigation of the Differences in Goods and Services as Perceived by Organizational Buyers," *Industrial Marketing Management* 24 (1995), pp. 99–108.

cabin, and the friendliness of the flight attendants. Second, end benefits resulting from completion of the service encounter should be accentuated. In the case of air travel, an individual's ability to make an important meeting or arrive home in time for a special occasion could be the derived benefit.

Inseparability

In many cases, a service cannot be separated from the person of the seller. In other words, the service must often be produced and marketed simultaneously. Because of the simultaneous production and marketing of most services, the main concern of the marketer is usually the creation of time and place utility. For example, the bank teller produces the service of receiving a deposit and markets other appropriate bank services at the same time. Many services, therefore, are tailored and not mass produced. Often, because a company's employees are "the company" at the point of contact, they must be given wide latitude and assistance in determining how best to tailor a specific service to meet customer needs.

The implication of inseparability on issues dealing with the selection of channels of distribution and service quality is quite important. Inseparable services cannot be inventoried, and thus direct sale is the only feasible channel of distribution. Service quality is sometimes unable to be completely standardized due to the inability to completely mechanize the service encounter. However, some industries, through innovative uses of technology, have been able to overcome or, at least, alleviate challenges associated with the inseparability characteristic.

For example, in the financial services industry, automated teller machines (ATMs) and home banking, through use of computers and telephones, have contributed greatly to eliminating the need for the customer to directly interact with a bank teller. Further, many banks are developing computer applications to allow tellers and other service representatives to think like expert problem solvers. These applications allow for platform banking, a means of enabling bank representatives in any location to bring up on a screen all the information the bank has about the customer. Every face-to-face contact with a customer can mean an opportunity to make a sale and, more importantly, further the relationship with the customer. Of course, the bank representative is still of critical importance as the one who might recognize by the customer's expression or words that this visit is not the appropriate time to be marketing additional services.

In addition to technology, tangible representations of the service can serve to overcome the inseparability problem. For example, in the insurance industry, a contract serves as the tangible representation of the service. The service itself remains inseparable from the seller (insurance provider), but the buyer has a tangible representation of the service in the form of a policy. This enables the use of intermediaries (agents) in the marketing of insurance. Another example is in the use of a credit card—the card itself is a tangible representation of the service that is being produced and consumed each time the card is being used.

Perishability and Fluctuating Demand

Services are perishable and markets for most services fluctuate either by season (tourism), days (airlines), or time of day (movie theaters). Unused telephone capacity and electrical power; vacant seats on planes, trains, buses, and in stadiums; and time spent by catalog service representatives waiting for customers to reach them all represent business that is lost forever.

The combination of perishability and fluctuating demand has created many problems for marketers of services. Specifically, in the areas of staffing and distribution, avenues must be found to have the services available for peak periods, and new strategies need to be developed to make use of the service during slack periods. Some organizations are attempting to cope with these problems through the use of pricing strategy. *Off-peak pricing* consists of charging different prices during different times or days in order to stimulate demand during slow periods. Discounts given for weekend calling, Saturday night stay-overs, early-bird dinners, or winter cruises are all examples of efforts made by service providers to redistribute demand.

Other organizations are dealing with issues related to peak period demand through the use of technology. To illustrate, a well-designed voice mail system allows companies and callers to cut down on missed phone calls, eliminates long waits on hold, and delivers clear, consistent messages. In the catalog industry, automated call routing (ACR) is used to route incoming calls to available service representatives in the order in which they were received. Finally, in the utilities industry, many electric utilities no longer have to generate capacity that will meet peak electrical demand. Instead, they rely on buying unused power from other utilities in other regions of the country.

Client Relationship

In the marketing of a great many services, a client relationship, as opposed to a customer relationship, exists between the buyer and the seller. In other words, the buyer views the seller as someone who has knowledge that is of value. Examples of this type of relationship

Type of Service	Type of Customer	Principal Expectations
Automobile repair	Consumers	*Be competent.* Fix it right the first time.
		Explain things. Explain why the customer needs the suggested repairs—provide an itemized list.
		Be respectful. "Don't treat me like an idiot."
Automobile insurance	Consumers	*Keep me informed.* "I shouldn't have to learn about insurance law changes from the newspaper."
		Be on my side. "I don't want them to treat me like I am a criminal just because I have a claim."
		Play fair. "Don't drop me when something goes wrong."
		Protect me from catastrophe. "Make sure my estate is covered in the event of a major accident."
		Provide prompt service. "I want fast settlement of my claims."
Hotel	Consumers	*Provide a clean room.* "Don't have a deep-pile carpet that can't be completely cleaned . . . You can literally see germs down there."
		Provide a secure room. Good bolts and a peephole on the door.
		Treat me like a guest. "It is almost like they're looking you over to decide whether or not they're going to let you have a room."
		Keep your promise. "They said the room would be ready at the promised time, but it wasn't."
Property and casualty insurance	Business customers	*Fulfill obligations.* Pay up.
		Learn my business and work with me. "I expect them to know me and my company."
		Protect me from catastrophe. Cover risk exposure so there is no single big loss.
		Provide prompt service. Fast claim service.
Equipment repair	Business customers	*Share my sense of urgency.* Speed of response. "One time I had to buy a second piece of equipment because of the huge downtime with the first piece."
		Be prepared. Have all the parts ready.
Truck and tractor rental/leasing	Business customers	*Keep the equipment running.* Have equipment working all the time—that is the key.
		Be flexible. "The leasing company should have the leasing flexibility to rent us equipment when we need it."
		Provide full service. Get rid of all the paperwork and headaches.

Source: A. Parasuraman, Leonard L. Berry, and Valarie A. Zeithaml, "Understanding Customer Expectations of Service," *Sloan Management Review,* Spring 1991, pp. 39–48.

are the physician-patient, college professor–student, accountant–small business owner, and broker-investor. The buyer, many times, abides by the advice offered or suggestions provided by the seller, and these relationships may be of an ongoing nature. Also, since many service firms are client-serving organizations, they may approach the marketing function in a more professional manner, as seen in health care, finance, and legal, governmental, and educational services.

There appear to be at least two marketing challenges that professionals face. First, in many cases, fear or hostility is brought to the transaction because the customer is uncertain about how genuine the professional's concern for his or her satisfaction is. For example, many unpleasant reasons exist for consulting doctors, lawyers, bankers, or even visiting a college professor. These could include having surgery, being sued, having to take out a loan, or doing poorly on an exam. Second, even high-quality service delivery by the professional can lead to dissatisfied customers. For a physician, the ability to provide high-quality medical care may be overshadowed by a brusque, unfriendly personality. For a college professor, the demand on students to contact or visit him or her only during office hours, coupled with students' own hectic work schedules, can diminish the impact of the professor's classroom presentations. It is vitally important that the professional service provider strive to build long-term positive relationships with clients.

Customer Effort

Customers are often involved to a relatively great degree in the production of many types of service. In some restaurants you clean your table. You may carry your luggage to a cart parked next to a baggage compartment of the plane. If you wish to enjoy an exhibit at a local art museum, you must walk around the facility and pay careful attention to what is on display. If an organization purchases the services of an advertising agency, employees will have to work with the agency, review its ideas, and make the final selections.

Obviously, not every service requires the same degree of customer effort. Your effort with a credit card service may be little beyond taking it from your wallet to make a purchase and writing a check once a month to pay the bill.

Uniformity

The quality of services can vary more than the quality of goods. Producers of goods have procedures to prevent, identify, and correct defects. If these procedures are working, customers are unlikely to purchase defective products. This is not the case with most services. Because they are often human performances and often customized to the needs of the buyer, quality can vary. Each trip to the bank or airline flight or university course can be a different experience. Many service jobs such as nursing, teaching, and career counseling require a positive attitude; how employees feel influences their performance.

Providing Quality Services

In today's increasingly competitive environment, quality service is critical to organizational success. Unlike products in which quality is often measured against standards, service quality is measured against performance.[3] Since services are frequently produced in the presence of a customer, are labor intensive, and are not able to be stored or objectively examined, the definition of what constitutes good service quality can be difficult and, in fact, continually changes in the face of choices.[4] Customers determine the value of service quality in relation to available alternatives and their particular needs. In general, problems in the determination of good service quality are attributable to differences in the expectations, perceptions, and experiences regarding the encounter between the service provider and consumer. These gaps can be classified as follows:

1. The gap between consumer expectations and management perceptions of consumer expectations.
2. The gap between management perceptions of consumer expectations and the firm's service quality specifications.

3. The gap between service quality specifications and actual service quality.

4. The gap between actual service delivery and external communications about the service.

In essence, the customer perceives the level of service quality as being a function of the magnitude and direction of the gap between expected service and perceived service. Management of a company may not even realize that they are delivering poor-quality service due to differences in the way managers and consumers view acceptable quality levels. To overcome this problem and to avoid losing customers, firms must be aware of the determinants of service quality. A brief description of these determinants follows.

1. *Tangibles* include the physical evidence of the service. For example, employees are always visible in a hotel lobby dusting, emptying ash trays, or otherwise cleaning up. Likewise, clean, shiny, up-to-date medical equipment or aircraft are examples of tangible elements.

2. *Reliability* involves the consistency and dependability of the service performance. For example, does a bank or phone company always send out accurate customer statements? Likewise, does the plumber always fix the problem on his or her first visit?

3. *Responsiveness* concerns the willingness or readiness of employees or professionals to provide service. For example, will a physician see patients on the same day they call in to say they are ill? Will a college professor return a student's call the same day?

4. *Assurance* refers to the knowledge and competence of service providers and the ability to convey trust and confidence. This determinant encompasses the provider's name and reputation; possession of necessary skills; and trustworthiness, believability, and honesty. For example, a bank will guarantee same-day loan processing; a doctor is highly trained in a particular specialty.

5. *Empathy* refers to the service provider's efforts to understand the customer's needs and then to provide, as best as possible, individualized service delivery. For example, flight attendants on a customer's regular route learn what type of beverages the customer drinks and what magazines the customer reads.

Each of the determinants on the previous page plays an important role in how the customer views the service quality of a firm. Turning service quality into a powerful competitive weapon requires continuously striving for service superiority—consistently performing above the adequate service level and capitalizing on opportunities for exceeding the desired service level. Relentless efforts to continually improve service performance may well be rewarded by improvements in customer attitudes toward the firm: from customer frustration to customer preference to customer loyalty. What should be obvious is that to be successful, a service firm must have both an effective means to measure customer satisfaction and dedicated employees to provide high-quality service.

Customer Satisfaction Measurement

As mentioned above, satisfied customers can become loyal customers. Service quality and customer satisfaction are of growing concern to business organizations throughout the world, and research on these topics generally focuses on two key issues: (1) understanding the expectations and requirements of the customer, and (2) determining how well a company and its major competitors are succeeding in satisfying these expectations and requirements.[5]

As such, an organization's approach to measuring service quality through customer satisfaction measurement (CSM) and effectively implementing programs derived from results of such studies can spell the difference between success and failure. Research on market leaders' CSMs found they had the following aspects in common:

1. Marketing and sales employees were primarily responsible (with customer input) for designing CSM programs and questionnaires.

2. Top management and the marketing function championed the programs.

3. Measurement involved a combination of qualitative and quantitative research methods that primarily included mail questionnaires, telephone surveys, and focus groups.

4. Evaluations included both the company's and competitors' satisfaction performance.

5. Results of all research were made available to employees, but not necessarily to customers.

6. Research was performed on a continual basis.

7. Customer satisfaction was incorporated into the strategic focus of the company via the mission statement.

8. There was a commitment to increasing service quality and customer satisfaction from employees at all levels within the organization.

The Importance of Internal Marketing

Properly performed customer satisfaction research can yield a wealth of strategic information about customers, the sponsoring company, and competitors. However, service quality goes beyond the relationship between a customer and company. Rather, as shown by the last aspect listed, it is the personal relationship between a customer and the particular employee that the customer happens to be dealing with at the time of the service encounter that ultimately determines service quality. The importance of having customer-oriented, frontline people cannot be overstated.[6] If frontline service personnel are unfriendly, unhelpful, uncooperative, or uninterested in the customer, the customer will tend to project that same attitude to the company as a whole. The character and personality of an organization reflects the character and personality of its top management. Management must develop programs that will stimulate employee commitment to customer service. To be successful, these programs must contain five critical components:

1. *A careful selection process in hiring frontline employees.* To do this, management has to clearly define the skills the service person must bring to the job.[7] For example, Fairfield Inn often considers as many as 25 candidates for each housekeeping or front-desk position.[8]

2. *A clear, concrete message* that conveys a particular service strategy that frontline people can begin to act on. People delivering service need to know how their work fits in the broader scheme of business operations.[9] They need to have a cause because servicing others is just too demanding and frustrating to be done well each day without one.[10]

3. *Significant modeling by managers,* that is, managers demonstrating the behavior that they intend to reward employees for performing. For example, some airline executives regularly travel economy class to talk to customers and solicit ideas for improvement.[11]

4. *An energetic follow-through process,* in which managers provide the training, support, and incentives necessary to give the employees the capability and willingness to provide quality service. For example, AT&T Universal Card Services has set up an umbrella organization, aptly called Universal Card University, to give all of its employees a single point of reference in their training.[12]

5. *An emphasis on teaching employees to have good attitudes.* This type of training usually focuses on specific social techniques, such as eye contact, smiling, tone of voice, and standards of dress.

However, organizing and implementing such programs will only lead to temporary results unless managers practice a strategy of internal marketing. We define *internal marketing* as the continual process by which managers actively encourage, stimulate, and support employee commitment to the company, the company's goods and services, and the company's customers. Emphasis should be placed on the word *continual.* Managers who consistently pitch in to help when needed, constantly provide encouragement and words of praise to employees, strive to help employees understand the benefits of performing their jobs well, and emphasize the importance of employee actions on both company and employee results are practitioners of internal marketing. In service marketing, successful internal marketing efforts, leading to employee commitment to service quality, are a key to success.

Federal Express serves as a prime example of the benefits accruing to a company that successfully practices internal marketing.[13] Federal Express is the first service organization to win the Malcolm Baldrige National Quality Award. The company's motto is "people, service, and profits." Behind its purple, white, and orange planes and uniforms are self-managing work teams, gainsharing plans, and empowered employees seemingly consumed with providing flexible and creative services to customers with varying needs. Federal Express is a high-involvement, horizontally coordinated organization that encourages employees to use their judgment above and beyond the rulebook.

Overcoming the Obstacles in Service Marketing

The factors of intangibility and inseparability, as well as difficulties in coming up with objective definitions of acceptable service quality, make comprehension of service marketing difficult. However, in view of the size and importance of services in our economy, considerable innovation and ingenuity are needed to make high-quality services available at convenient locations for consumers as well as businesspeople. In fact, the area of service marketing probably offers more opportunities for imagination and creative innovation than does goods marketing. Unfortunately, many service firms still lag in the area of creative marketing. Even today, those service firms that have done a relatively good job have been slow in recognizing opportunities in all aspects of their marketing programs. Four reasons, connected to past practices, can be given for the lack of innovative marketing on the part of service marketers: (1) a limited view of marketing, (2) a lack of strong competition, (3) a lack of creative management, and (4) no obsolescence.

Limited View of Marketing

Because of the nature of their service, many firms depended to a great degree on population growth to expand sales. A popular example here is the telephone company, which did not establish a marketing department until 1955. It was then that the company realized it had to be concerned not only with population growth but also with meeting the needs of a growing population. Increases in educational levels and the standard of living also bring about the need for new and diversified services.

Service firms must meet these changing needs by developing new services and new channels and altering existing channels to meet the changing composition and needs of the population. For many service industries, growth has come as a result of finding new channels of distribution. For example, some banks and other financial service companies were able to grow and tap into new markets by establishing limited-service kiosks in malls and supermarkets. Airlines have successfully brought in a whole new class of travelers by offering advance-purchase discounted fares. Traditionally, users of these fares either drove or used other means of transportation in order to reach their destination.

While many service firms have succeeded in adopting a marketing perspective, others have been slow to respond. It was not until deregulation of the telecommunications industry took place in 1984 that the telephone companies began taking a broadened view of marketing. Even today, critics point to the obsession with inventing new technology versus using current technology in meeting customer needs as a weakness of these companies.

On the Internet, you cannot have a more convenient location than your competition. Everyone is just a click away. It is critical that it is easy to do business with your company in order to attract and retain customers. Following are some ways to improve e-service.

1. A customer should be able to buy something in seven clicks or less beginning from the home page. Many experts believe the ideal should be four clicks.

2. Shorten the time it takes for images to load. Research shows that eight seconds is the longest people will wait before they move on to another site.

3. From a product section of your site, customers should be able to get from your home page to a product page in that section in one click.

4. Shopping should be easy. Searching, browsing, checking out, returning items, and getting assistance from a live person must be easy.

5. Customers should have the choice to register their personal information (e.g., address and credit card information) or to enter this information each time they purchase.

6. A customer should be able to check out in no more than three steps.

7. Delivery should be on time.

Source: Ron Zemke, *E-Service: 24 Ways to Keep Your Customers—When the Competition Is Just a Click Away* (New York: Amazon, 2001).

Limited Competition

A second major cause of the lack of innovative marketing in many service industries was the lack of competition. Many service industries such as banking, railroads, and public utilities have, throughout most of their histories, faced very little competition; some have even been regulated monopolies. Obviously, in an environment characterized by little competition, there was not likely to be a great deal of innovative marketing. However, two major forces have changed this situation. First, in the past two decades the banking, financial services, railroad, cable, airline, telecommunications industries, and utilities have all been deregulated in varying degrees. With deregulation has come a need to be able to compete effectively. For example, AT&T was once the sole provider of long-distance telephone service. Now, AT&T has to compete not only against such companies as MCI and Sprint but also against the regional Bell operating companies such as Ameritech and US West, which once were part of AT&T. Second, service marketing has taken on an international focus. Today, many foreign companies are competing in domestic service markets. Foreign interests own several banks, many hotels (including Holiday Inn), and shares in major airlines (including Northwest and US Airways). Likewise, American companies are expanding overseas as markets open up. For example, Merrill Lynch & Co. purchased Smith New Court PLC, a large British security firm, to become the world's largest brokerage firm.

Noncreative Management

For many years, the managements of service industries have been criticized for not being progressive and creative. Railroad management was criticized for many years for being slow to innovate. More recently, however, railroads have become leading innovators in the field of freight transportation, introducing such innovations as piggyback service and containerization, and in passenger service, introducing luxury overnight accommodations on trains with exotic names such as the Zephyr. Some other service industries, however, have been slow to develop new services or to innovate in the marketing of their existing services. In fact, as a whole, U.S. firms lag behind their Japanese and German competitors not only in collecting customer satisfaction data but also in designing services that address customers' needs.[14]

No Obsolescence

A great advantage for many service industries is the fact that many services, because of their intangibility, are less subject to obsolescence than goods. While this is an obvious advantage, it has also led some service firms to be sluggish in their approach to marketing. Manufacturers of goods may constantly change their marketing plans and seek new and more efficient ways to produce and distribute their products. Since service firms are often not faced with obsolescence, they often failed to recognize the need for change. This failure has led to wholesale changes in many industries as new operators, who possessed marketing skills, revolutionized the manner in which the service is performed and provided. Many barbershops and hair dressers have gone out of business due to an inability to compete against hairstyling salons. Many accountants have lost clients to tax preparation services, such as H&R Block, that specialize in doing one task well and have used technology, including computerized filing services, to their advantage. Likewise, the old, big movie house has become a relic of the past as entrepreneurs realized the advantages to be gained from building and operating theater complexes that contain several minitheaters in or near suburban malls.

The Service Challenge

Despite traditional thinking and practices on the part of many marketing managers and writers concerning the similarities between the operation of manufacturing and services organizations, the past decade has seen the growth of many innovative ways of meeting the service challenge. The service challenge is the quest to (1) constantly develop new services that will better meet customer needs, (2) improve on the quality and variety of existing services, and (3) provide and distribute these services in a manner that best serves the customer. This next section illustrates the challenges facing companies in various service industries and examples of marketing strategies employed by them to meet the service challenge.

Banking

"Banking is vital to a healthy economy. Banks are not." This is the message that a banking expert delivered to a group of his peers.[15] Needless to say, the days when banking was considered a dead-end career, but one that offered stable employment for marketers, are long gone. Perhaps banking best exemplifies the changes that are taking place as service organizations strive to become practitioners of the "marketing concept." Buy or be bought is the new watchword in the banking industry, which is experiencing the biggest wave of consolidation in its history.

Banking is becoming an increasingly technology-driven business. The main reason is that more and more financial services, from loans to credit cards, are being marketed through computers and telephones instead of through branches. Banks large enough to afford big technology investments can reach customers nationwide even though their physical franchise may be limited. For example, most consumers possess credit cards from banks they have never physically visited. Further, the advent of new electronic delivery systems (via computer) for consumer and small-business banking could, within the next decade, greatly reduce the number of branch banks needed. To prevent a loss of a large portion of their customer base, many of the leading banks, such as Chase Manhattan and Citibank, are aligning themselves with software and hardware manufacturers to develop home banking systems.

Banks have also learned the value of bundling services. Many now offer an account that combines checking, savings, credit card, and auto loan features. Benefits to the customer include free ATM transactions, interest-bearing checking accounts, no-fee credit cards, and the convenience of one-stop banking. In addition, they offer preapproved auto loans and cash-flow statements. Most banks also target some marketing activities toward senior citizens, which may include discount coupons for entertainment, travel newsletters, and lower monthly minimum required balances.

Competition between banks and other financial institutions will continue to intensify. The survivors will be those that have best mastered the art of services marketing.

Health Care

The distribution of health care services is of vital concern. In health care delivery, the inseparability characteristic presents more of a handicap than in other service industries because users (patients) literally place themselves in the hands of the seller. Although direct personal contact between producer and user is often necessary, new and more efficient means of distribution seem to be evolving.

Up until the past few decades, medical care has been traditionally associated with the solo practice, fee-for-service system. Recently, several alternative delivery systems have been developed, most notably the health maintenance organization (HMO). This type of delivery system stresses the creation of group health care clinics using teams of salaried health practitioners (physicians, pharmacists, technicians, and so forth) that serve a specified, enrolled membership on a prepaid basis. The primary benefits to the customer (patient) from membership in an HMO are (1) the ability to have all ailments treated at one facility, (2) payment of a fixed fee for services, and (3) the encouragement of preventive versus remedial treatments. The success of the HMO concept in traditional medical care has inspired similar programs to be developed for dental and eye care.

In the pharmaceutical field, Chronimed of Minnetonka, Minnesota, has focused on providing great customer service as its avenue to success.[16] The company supplies 100,000 patients across the United States with specialized medications that local pharmacies can't afford to stock. Chronimed's skill is twofold. First, it provides needed drugs by mail to organ transplant recipients and patients with diabetes or AIDS. Second, it employs a team of 50 pharmacists and assistants who provide much-needed information about the medications they dispense, such as details about drug interaction and side effects. As evidenced by the above examples, health care companies, regardless of what specific area in which they compete, are becoming more and more market oriented as they try to differentiate their offerings from those of the competition.

Insurance

In recent years, the insurance industry has exploded with new product and service offerings. Not too long ago, customers were faced with limited options in choosing life, hospital, or auto insurance. Now there is a wide array of insurance policies to choose from, including universal life policies, which double as retirement savings; nursing care insurance; reversible mortgages, which allow people to take equity from their house while still living in it; and other offerings aimed at serving an aging population. To illustrate, Prudential Insurance Company offers a program whereby terminally ill policyholders are allowed to withdraw funds against the face value of their policy while still alive. In addition to insurance services, most insurance companies now offer a full range of financial services, including auto loans, mortgages, mutual funds, and certificates of deposit.

Distribution of insurance services has also been growing. The vending machines found in airports for flight insurance have been finding their way into other areas. Travel auto insurance is now available in many motel chains and through the AAA. Group insurance written through employers and labor unions also has been extremely successful. In each instance, the insurance industry has used intermediaries to distribute its services.

1. Customers do not buy your services—they buy solutions to their problems.
2. There are only two conditions under which customers will change their behavior: (*a*) when it's a matter of life and death (and then not in every case), and (*b*) if they want to—if they are given a reason to change.
3. The most important parts of employees' contributions to the goals of your organization are being made at their discretion.
4. Management and leadership are exercised outside, not inside the office.
5. Quality service means never having to say "that's not my job."
6. How your employees feel is eventually how your customers will feel.
7. Customers should never be required to restate their request or complain to several employees before having it resolved.
8. If you establish negative expectations for your customers, you will always meet them.
9. The delivery of quality service is never the customer's job.
10. If you are an underdog, only compete in market segments where you have or can develop strengths, avoid head-to-head competition with dominant competitors, emphasize profits rather than volume, and focus on specialization rather than diversification.

Source: Adapted from James H. Donnelly, Jr., *25 Management Lessons from the Customer's Side of the Counter* (Burr Ridge, IL: McGraw-Hill, 1996).

Travel

The travel industry, most notably the airlines, has been a leader in the use of technology. Computerized reservation systems allow customers to book plane tickets from home or work. Nearly all airlines are using Internet sites to dispense flight and fare information. Airlines are in the midst of implementing ticketless travel programs in which passengers purchase tickets, select their seats, and pick up boarding passes and luggage tags at machines resembling ATMs.[17] Technology has also allowed airlines to make strategic pricing decisions through the use of yield management. In yield management, certain seats on aircraft are discounted and certain ones aren't. Through the use of elaborate computer programs, managers are able to determine who their customer segments are and who is likely to purchase airline tickets when and to where.

Despite its success in employing technology to attract additional customers and offer added convenience, the airline industry has operated in somewhat dire straits, plagued by problems associated with over-capacity, high labor costs, and low perceived service quality. The decade of the 90s could be considered the most turbulent ever encountered by U.S. commercial airlines.[18] During this time, some airlines either went out of business (Midway, Eastern, and Pan Am) or were in and out of bankruptcy proceedings (Continental, America West, and TWA); and most others operated at a loss. Fortunately, in recent years, good news came to the industry in the form of decreased fuel prices, the abandoning of some hub-and-spoke operations, and other events leading to cost decreases.

A notable exception to the fate that befell most carriers is Southwest Airlines, which has finally convinced its peers that a carrier can be consistently profitable by offering cheap fares on short-distance routes. Now, big carriers such as Continental and United have created their own Southwest look-alikes to supplement their long-haul, full-service, high-fare operations. Southwest's secret to success (which other airlines may or may not be able to imitate) is the high level of employee morale exhibited by everyone associated with the company. This has come as a direct result of upper management's internal marketing efforts.

Implications for Service Marketers

The preceding sections emphasized the use of all components of the marketing mix. Many service industries have been criticized for an overdependence on advertising. The overdependence on one or two elements of the marketing mix is a mistake that service marketers cannot afford. The sum total of the marketing mix elements represents the total impact of the firm's marketing strategy. The slack created by severely restricting one element cannot be compensated by heavier emphasis on another, since each element in the marketing mix is designed to address specific problems and achieve specific objectives.

Services must be made available to prospective users, which implies distribution in the marketing sense of the word. The revised concept of the distribution of services points out that service marketers must distinguish conceptually between the production and distribution of services. The problem of making services more widely available must not be ignored.

The above sections also pointed out the critical role of new service development. In several of the examples described, indirect distribution of the service was made possible because "products" were developed that included a tangible representation of the service. This development facilitates the use of intermediaries, because the service can now be separated from the producer. In addition, the development of new services paves the way for companies to expand and segment their markets. With the use of varying service bundles, new technology, and alternative means of distributing the service, companies are now able to practice targeted marketing.

Conclusion

This chapter has dealt with the complex topic of service marketing. While the marketing of services has much in common with the marketing of products, unique problems in the area require highly creative marketing management skills. Many of the problems in the service area can be traced to the intangible and inseparable nature of services and the difficulties involved in measuring service quality. However, considerable progress has been made in understanding and reacting to these difficult problems, particularly in the area of distribution. In view of the major role services play in our economy, it is important for marketing practitioners to better understand and appreciate the unique problems of service marketing.

Additional Readings

Berry, Leonard T. *Discovering the Soul of Service,* New York: Free Press, 2000.

Gronroos, Christian. *Service Management and Marketing.* 2nd ed. New York: John Wiley and Sons, 2000.

Matanovich, Tim. "Pricing Services vs. Pricing Products." *Marketing Management,* July/August 2003, pp. 12–13.

Price, B. Joseph, III, and James Gilmore. "Welcome to the Experience Economy." *Harvard Business Review,* July–August 1998, pp. 97–105.

Wood, Stephen D. "Getting More and Better Business from Service Customers." *Marketing Management,* Fall 2000, pp. 10–11.

Chapter 13

Global Marketing

A growing number of U.S. corporations have transversed geographical boundaries and become truly multinational in nature. For most other domestic companies, the question is no longer, Should we go international? Instead, the questions relate to when, how, and where the companies should enter the international marketplace. The past 15 years have seen the reality of a truly world market unfold.

Firms invest in foreign countries for the same basic reasons they invest in their own country. These reasons vary from firm to firm but fall under the categories of achieving offensive or defensive goals. Offensive goals are to (1) increase long-term growth and profit prospects; (2) maximize total sales revenue; (3) take advantage of economies of scale; and (4) improve overall market position. As many American markets reach saturation, American firms look to foreign markets as outlets for surplus production capacity, sources of new customers, increased profit margins, and improved returns on investment. For example, the ability to expand the number of locations of McDonald's restaurants in the United States is becoming severely limited. Yet, on any given day, only 0.5 percent of the world's population visits McDonald's. Indeed, in the recent past, of the 50 most profitable McDonald's outlets, 25 were located in Hong Kong. For PepsiCo, the results are similar. Its restaurant division operates over 10,000 Kentucky Fried Chicken, Pizza Hut, and Taco Bell outlets abroad.

Multinational firms also invest in other countries to achieve defensive goals. Chief among these goals are the desire to (1) compete with foreign companies on their own turf instead of in the United States, (2) have access to technological innovations that are developed in other countries, (3) take advantage of significant differences in operating costs between countries, (4) preempt competitors' global moves, and (5) not be locked out of future markets by arriving too late.

Such well-known companies as Zenith, Pillsbury, A&P, Shell Oil, CBS Records, and Firestone Tire & Rubber are now owned by non-U.S. interests. Since 1980, the share of the U.S. high-tech market held by foreign products has grown from less than 8 percent to over 25 percent. In such diverse industries as power tools, tractors, television, and banking, U.S. companies have lost the dominant position they once held. By investing solely in domestic operations or not being willing to adapt products to foreign markets, U.S. companies are more susceptible to foreign incursions. For example, there has been a great uproar over Japan's practice of not opening up its domestic automobile market to U.S. companies. However, as of the end of the 90s, a great majority of the American cars shipped to Japan still had the steering wheel located on the left side of the vehicle—the opposite of where it should be for the Japanese market.

In many ways, marketing globally is the same as marketing at home. Regardless of which part of the world the firm sells in, the marketing program must still be built around a sound product or service that is properly priced, promoted, and distributed to a carefully analyzed target market. In other words, the marketing manager has the same controllable decision variables in both domestic and nondomestic markets.

Although the development of a marketing program may be the same in either domestic or nondomestic markets, special problems may be involved in the implementation of marketing programs in nondomestic markets. These problems often arise because of the environmental differences that exist among various countries that marketing managers may be unfamiliar with.

In this chapter, marketing management in a global context will be examined. Methods of organizing global versus domestic markets, global market research tasks, methods of entry strategies into global markets, and potential marketing strategies for a multinational firm will be discussed. In examining each of these areas, the reader will find a common thread—knowledge of the local cultural environment—that appears to be a major prerequisite for success in each area.

With the proper adaptations, many companies have the capabilities and resources needed to compete successfully in the global marketplace. To illustrate, companies as diverse as Kellogg's, Avon, Eli Lilly, and Sun Microsystems all generate a large percentage of their sales from foreign operations. Smaller companies can also be successful. For example, Nemix, Inc., of Bell Gardens, California, is a franchisee of Church's Fried Chicken. Small by world standards, this company has succeeded in developing a fully vertical operation in Poland, doing everything from raising chickens to operating restaurants.[1]

Organizing for Global Marketing

When compared with the tasks it faces at home, a firm attempting to establish a global marketing organization faces a much higher degree of risk and uncertainty. In a foreign market, management is often less familiar with the cultural, political, and economic situation. Many of these problems arise as a result of conditions specific to the foreign country. Managers are also faced with the decisions concerning how to organize the multinational company.

Problems with Entering Foreign Markets

While numerous problems could be cited, attention here will focus on those that firms most often face when entering foreign markets.

Cultural Misunderstanding

Differences in the cultural environment of foreign countries may be misunderstood or not even recognized because of the tendency for marketing managers to use their own cultural values and priorities as a frame of reference. Some of the most common areas of difference lie in the way dissimilar cultures perceive time, thought patterns, personal space, material possessions, family roles and relationships, personal achievement, competitiveness, individuality, social behavior, and other interrelated issues.[2] Another important source of misunderstandings is in the perceptions of managers about the people with whom they are dealing. Feelings of superiority can lead to changed communication mannerisms.

American managers must make the necessary efforts to learn, understand, and adapt to the cultural norms of the managers and customers they deal with in other parts of the world. Failure to do so will result in missed market opportunities. Marketing Highlight 13–1 provides further examples of cultural differences that could lead to marketing problems.

BODY LANGUAGE

- Standing with your hands on your hips is a gesture of defiance in Indonesia.
- Carrying on a conversation with your hands in your pockets makes a poor impression in France, Belgium, Finland, and Sweden.
- Shaking your head from side to side means yes in Bulgaria and Sri Lanka.
- Crossing your legs to expose the sole of your shoe is really taboo in Muslim countries. In fact, to call a person a "shoe" is a deep insult.

PHYSICAL CONTACT

- Patting a child on the head is a grave offense in Thailand or Singapore, since the head is revered as the location of the soul.
- In an Oriental culture, touching another person is considered an invasion of privacy; in Southern European and Arabic countries, it is a sign of warmth and friendship.

PROMPTNESS

- Be on time when invited for dinner in Denmark or in China.
- In Latin countries, your host or business associate would be surprised if you arrived at the appointed hour.

EATING AND COOKING

- It is rude to leave anything on your plate when eating in Norway, Malaysia, or Singapore.
- In Egypt, it is rude *not* to leave something.
- In Italy and Spain, cooking is done with oil.
- In Germany and Great Britain, margarine and butter are used.

OTHER SOCIAL CUSTOMS

- In Sweden, nudity and sexual permissiveness are quite all right, but drinking is really frowned on.
- In Spain, there is a very negative attitude toward life insurance. By receiving insurance benefits, a wife feels that she is profiting from her husband's death.
- In Western European countries, many consumers still are reluctant to buy anything (other than a house) on credit. Even for an automobile, they will pay cash.

Source: William J. Stanton, Michael J. Etzel, and Bruce J. Walker, *Fundamentals of Marketing,* 11th ed. © 1997. New York, McGraw-Hill, Inc., p. 544. Reproduced by permission of The McGraw-Hill Companies.

On the other hand, companies should not shy away from attempting to enter global markets because conventional wisdom says that products and service will not succeed in some regions purely due to cultural reasons. For example, PepsiCo's Pepsi division entered into a $500 million offensive to try to grab a larger share of the $6 billion Brazilian soft-drink market.[3] Understanding the dramatic changes that had taken place in Brazil, Pepsi repositioned itself as the choice of a new Brazil. Advertisements for the Pepsi brand feature young people enumerating recent changes in Brazil, such as perhaps the devaluation of its currency in 1999. Does this campaign sound familiar? It should since it's a takeoff on the popular "Pepsi, the choice of a new generation" theme used in the United States. Actions taken by PepsiCo's Frito-Lay unit serve as another example of a successful adaptation to cultural differences.[4] In China, Frito-Lay recently introduced its popular Cheetos snack food. The twist to this effort lies in the fact that the Chinese are not big consumers of dairy products. In China, Cheetos are cheeseless, instead consisting of flavors such as "Savory American Cream" and "Zesty Japanese Steak." As a result of these and other adaptations, it's no wonder that PepsiCo ranks among the leaders in the global food and beverage industry.

Political Uncertainty

Governments are unstable in many countries, and social unrest and even armed conflict must sometimes be reckoned with. Other nations are newly emerging and anxious to seek their independence. These and similar problems can greatly hinder a firm seeking to establish its position in foreign markets. For example, at the turn of the century, firms scaled back their investment plans in Russia due to, among other reasons, (1) a business environment plagued by mobsters, (2) politics badly corrupted by the botched invasion of Chechnya, and (3) an economy troubled by runaway inflation and a plummeting ruble.[5] This is not to say investment in Russia is a poor choice. Rather, in situations like this, caution must be used and companies must have a keen understanding of the risks involved in undertaking sizable investments.

Import Restrictions

Tariffs, import quotas, and other types of import restrictions hinder global business. These are usually established to promote self-sufficiency and can be a huge roadblock for the multinational firm. For example, a number of countries, including South Korea, Taiwan, Thailand, and Japan, have placed import restrictions on a variety of goods produced in America, including telecommunications equipment, rice, wood products, automobiles, and produce. In other cases, governments may not impose restrictions that are commonly adhered to in the United States. For example, Chrysler pulled out of a proposed investment deal in China, worth billions of dollars, because the Chinese government refused to protect its right to limit access to technological information.

Exchange Controls and Ownership Restrictions

Some nations establish limits on the amount of earned and invested funds that can be withdrawn from it. These exchange controls are usually established by nations that are experiencing balance-of-payment problems. In addition, many nations have a requirement that the majority ownership of a company operating there be held by nationals. These and other types of currency and ownership regulations are important considerations in the decision to expand into a foreign market. For example, up until a few years ago, foreign holdings in business ventures in India were limited to a maximum of 40 percent. Once this ban was lifted, numerous global companies such as Sony, Whirlpool, JVC, Grundig, Panasonic, Kellogg's, Levi Strauss, Pizza Hut, and Domino's rushed to invest in this market.[6]

Economic Conditions

As noted earlier, nations' economics are becoming increasingly intertwined, and business cycles tend to follow similar patterns. However, there are differences, mainly due to political upheaval or social changes, and these may be significant. In determining whether to invest, marketers need to perform in-depth analyses of a country's stage of economic development, the buying power of its populace, and the strength of its currency. For example, when the North American Free Trade Agreement (NAFTA) was signed, many American companies rushed to invest in Mexico, building production facilities and retail outlets. These companies assumed that the signing of the agreement would stabilize Mexico's economy. In the long term, these investments may pay off. However, many companies lost millions of dollars there due to the devaluation of the peso. Indeed, the crash of the peso caused the retail giant Wal-Mart to scale back a $1 billion investment project to open stores throughout Mexico.

Organizing the Multinational Company

There are two kinds of global companies—the multidomestic corporation and the global corporation.[7] The *multidomestic company* pursues different strategies in each of its foreign markets. It could have as many different product variations, brand names, and advertising campaigns as countries in which it operates. Each overseas subsidiary is autonomous. Local managers are given the authority to make the necessary decisions and are held accountable for results. In effect, the company competes on a market-by-market basis. Honeywell and General Foods are U.S. firms that have operated this way.

The *global company,* on the other hand, views the world as one market and pits its resources against the competition in an integrated fashion. It emphasizes cultural similarities across countries and universal consumer needs and wants rather than differences. It standardizes marketing activities when there are cultural similarities and adapts them when the cultures are different. Since there is no one clear-cut way to organize a global company, three alternative structures are normally used: (1) worldwide product divisions, each responsible for selling its own products throughout the world; (2) divisions responsible for all products sold within a geographic region; and (3) a matrix system that combines elements of both of these arrangements. Many organizations, such as IBM, Caterpillar, Timex, General Electric, Siemens, and Mitsubishi, are structured in a global fashion.

Most companies are realizing the need to take a global approach to managing their businesses. However, recognizing the need and actually implementing a truly global approach are two different tasks. For some companies, industry conditions dictate that they take a global perspective. The ability to actually implement a global approach to managing international operations, however, largely depends on factors unique to the company. Globalization, as a competitive strategy, is inherently more vulnerable to risk than a multidomestic or domestic strategy, due to the relative permanence of the organizational structure once established.

In determining whether or not to globalize a particular business, managers should look first at their industry.[8] Market, economic, environmental, and competitive factors all influence the potential gains to be realized by following a global strategy. Factors constituting the external environment that are conducive to a global strategy are:

1. *Market factors.* Homogeneous market needs, global customers, shortening product life cycles, transferable brands and advertising, and the ability to globalize distribution channels.

2. *Economic factors.* Worldwide economies of scale in manufacturing and distribution, steep learning curves, worldwide sourcing efficiencies, rising product development costs, and significant differences in host-country costs.

3. *Environmental factors.* Improving communications, favorable government policies, and the increasing speed of technological change.

4. *Competitive factors.* Competitive interdependencies among countries, global moves of competitors, and opportunities to preempt a competitor's global moves.[9]

Many of the reasons given in the first part of the chapter about why a domestic company should become a multinational can also be used to support the argument that a firm should take a global perspective. This is because the integration of markets is forcing companies that wish to remain successful not only to become multinationals but also to take a global perspective in doing so. In the past, companies had the option of remaining domestic or going multinational due to the separation of markets. This is no longer the case.

Several internal factors can either facilitate or impede a company's efforts to undertake a global approach to marketing strategies. These factors and their underlying dimensions are:

1. *Structure.* The ease of installing a centralized global authority and the absence of rifts between present domestic and international divisions or operating units.

Growth in global markets has created opportunities for building global brands. The advantages are many and so are the pitfalls. Here are 10 commandments that marketers can use when planning a global branding campaign.

1. *Understand similarities and differences in the global branding landscape.* The best brands retain consistency of theme and alter specific elements to suit each country.
2. *Don't take shortcuts in brand building.* Build brands in new markets from the "bottom up."
3. *Establish marketing infrastructure.* Most often, firms adopt or invest in foreign partners for manufacturing and distribution.
4. *Embrace integrated marketing communications.* Because advertising opportunities may be more limited, marketers must use other forms of communication such as sponsorship and public relations.
5. *Establish brand partnerships.* Most global brands have marketing partners ranging from joint venture partners, franchisees, and distributors who provide access to distribution.
6. *Balance standardization and customization.* Know what to standardize and what to customize.
7. *Balance global and local control.* This is very important in the following areas: organization structure, entry strategies, coordination processes, and mechanisms.
8. *Establish operable guidelines.* Set the rules about how the brand will be positioned and marketed.
9. *Implement a global brand equity measurement system.* The ideal measurement system provides complete, up-to-date information on the brand and on all its competitors to the appropriate decision makers.
10. *Leverage brand elements.* If the meanings of the brand name and all related trademarked identifiers are clear, they can be an invaluable source of brand equity worldwide.

Source: Kevin Lane Keller, "The Ten Commandments of Global Branding," *MBA Bullet Point*, October 3–16, 2000, p. 3.

2. *Management processes.* The capabilities and resources available to perform global planning, budgeting, and coordination activities, coupled with the ability to conduct global performance reviews and implement global compensation plans.
3. *Culture.* The ability to project a global versus national identity, a worldwide versus domestic commitment to employees, and a willingness to tolerate interdependence among business units.
4. *People.* The availability of employable foreign nationals and the willingness of current employees to commit to multicountry careers, frequent travel, and having foreign superiors.

Overall, whether a company should undertake a multidomestic or global approach to organizing its international operations will largely depend on the nature of the company and its products, how different foreign cultures are from the domestic market, and the company's ability to implement a global perspective. Many large brands have failed in their quest to go global. The primary reason for this failure is rushing the process. Successful global brands carefully stake out their markets, allowing plenty of time to develop their overseas marketing efforts and evolve into global brands.

Indeed, in many cases, firms do not undertake either purely multidomestic or global approaches to marketing. Instead, a hybrid approach is developed whereby these global brands carry with them the same visual identity, the same strategic positioning, and the same advertising. In addition, local characteristics are factored in. Regardless of the approach undertaken, management and organizational skills that emphasize the need to handle diversity are the critical factors that determine the long-term success of any company's endeavors in the global marketplace.

Programming for Global Marketing

In this section of the chapter, the major areas in developing a global marketing program will be examined. As was mentioned at the outset, marketing managers must organize the same controllable decision variables that exist in domestic markets. However, many firms that have been extremely successful in marketing in the United States have not been able to duplicate their success in foreign markets.

Global Marketing Research

Because the risks and uncertainties are so high, marketing research is equally important in foreign markets and in domestic markets and probably more so. Many companies encounter losing situations abroad because they do not know enough about the market.[10] They don't know how to get the information or find the cost of collecting the information too high. To be successful, organizations must collect and analyze pertinent information to support the basic go/no-go decision before getting to the issues addressed by conventional market research. Toward this end, in attempting to analyze foreign consumers and markets, at least four organizational issues must be considered.

Population Characteristics

Population characteristics are one of the major components of a market, and significant differences exist between and within foreign countries. If data are available, the marketing manager should be familiar with the total population and with the regional, urban, rural, and interurban distribution. Other demographic variables, such as the number and size of families, education, occupation, and religion, are also important. In many markets, these variables can have a significant impact on the success of a firm's marketing program. For example, in the United States, a cosmetics firm can be reasonably sure of the desire to use cosmetics being common among women of all income classes. However, in Latin America the same firm may be forced to segment its market by upper-, middle-, and lower-income groups, as well as by urban and rural areas. This is because upper-income women want high-quality cosmetics promoted in prestige media and sold through exclusive outlets. In some rural and less prosperous areas, cosmetics must be inexpensive; in other rural areas, women do not accept cosmetics.

Ability to Buy

To assess the ability of consumers in a foreign market to buy, four broad measures should be examined: (1) gross national product or per capita national income, (2) distribution of income, (3) rate of growth in buying power, and (4) extent of available financing. Since each of these vary in different areas of the world, the marketing opportunities available must be examined closely.

Willingness to Buy

The cultural framework of consumer motives and behavior is integral to the understanding of the foreign consumer. If data are available, cultural values and attitudes toward the material culture, social organizations, the supernatural, aesthetics, and language should be analyzed for their possible influence on each of the elements in the firm's marketing program.

Many consumer goods companies have sought growth by expanding into global markets. For U.S. companies, this is sound strategy since 95 percent of the world's population and two-thirds of its purchasing power are located outside their country. The potential for success in global markets is enhanced when companies carefully research and analyze consumers in foreign countries, just as it is in domestic markets. Below are some suggestions for companies seeking to successfully market to global consumers.

- Research the cultural nuances and customs of the market. Be sure that the company and brand name translate favorably in the language of the target country, and if not, consider using an abbreviation or entirely different brand name for the market. Consider using marketing research firms or ad agencies that have detailed knowledge of the culture.
- Determine whether the product can be exported to the foreign country as is or whether it has to be modified to be useful and appealing to targeted consumers. Also, determine what changes need to be made to packaging and labeling to make the product appealing to the market.
- Research the prices of similar products in the target country or region. Determine the necessary retail price to make marketing it profitable in the country, and research whether a sufficient number of consumers would be willing to pay that price. Also, determine what the product has to offer that should make consumers willing to pay a higher price.
- On the basis of research, decide whether the targeted country or region will require a unique marketing strategy or whether the same general strategy can be used in all geographic areas.
- Research the ways consumers purchase similar products in the targeted country or region and whether the company's product can be sold effectively using this method of distribution. Also, determine if a method of distribution not currently being used in the country could create a competitive advantage for the product.
- Pretest integrated marketing communication efforts in the targeted country to ensure not only that messages are translated accurately but also that subtle differences in meaning are not problematic. Also, research the effectiveness of planned communication efforts.

Marketing consumer goods successfully in global markets requires a long-term commitment because it may take time to establish an identity in new markets. However, with improving technology and the evolution of a global economy, both large and small companies have found global marketing both feasible and profitable.

Source: Dom Del Prete, "Winning Strategies Lead to Global Marketing Success," *Marketing News,* August 18, 1997, pp. 1, 2.

It is easy to see that such factors as the group's values concerning acquisition of material goods, the role of the family, the positions of men and women in society, and the various age groups and social classes can have an effect on marketing, because each can influence consumer behavior.

In some areas there appears to be a convergence of tastes and habits, with different cultures becoming more and more integrated into one homogeneous culture, although still separated by national boundaries. This appears to be the case in Western Europe, where consumers are developing into a mass market. This obviously will simplify the task for a marketer in this region. However, cultural differences still prevail among many areas of the world and strongly influence consumer behavior. Marketing organizations may have to do primary research in many foreign markets to obtain usable information about these issues.

Differences in Research Tasks and Processes

In addition to the dimensions mentioned above, the processes and tasks associated with carrying out the market research program may also differ from country to country. Many market researchers count on census data for in-depth demographic information. However, in foreign countries the market researcher is likely to encounter a variety of problems in using census data. These include[11]

1. *Language.* Some nations publish their census reports in English. Other countries offer census reports only in their native language; some do not take a census.

2. *Data content.* Data contained in a census vary from country to country and often omit items of interest to researchers. For example, most foreign nations do not include an income question on their census. Others do not include such items as marital status or education levels.

3. *Timeliness.* The United States takes a census every 10 years. Japan and Canada conduct one every five years. However, some northern European nations are abandoning the census as a data-collection tool and instead are relying on population registers to account for births, deaths, and changes in marital status or place of residence.

4. *Availability in the United States.* If a researcher requires detailed household demographics on foreign markets, the cost and time required to obtain the data will be significant. Unfortunately, census data for many countries do not exist. For some it will be difficult to obtain, although others can be found on the Internet.

Global Product Strategy

Global marketing research can help determine whether (1) there is an unsatisfied need for which a new product could be developed to serve a foreign market or (2) there is an unsatisfied need that could be met with an existing domestic product, either as is or adapted to the foreign market. In either case, product planning is necessary to determine the type of product to be offered and whether there is sufficient demand to warrant entry into a foreign market.

Most U.S. firms would not think of entering a domestic market without extensive product planning. However, some marketers have failed to do adequate product planning when entering foreign markets. An example of such a problem occurred when American manufacturers began to export refrigerators to Europe. The firms exported essentially the same models sold in the United States. However, the refrigerators were the wrong size, shape, and temperature range for some areas and had weak appeal in others—thus failing miserably. Although adaptation of the product to local conditions may have eliminated this failure, this adaptation is easier said than done. For example, even in the domestic market, overproliferation of product varieties and options can dilute economies of scale. This dilution results in higher production costs, which may make the price of serving each market segment with an adapted product prohibitive.

The solution to this problem is not easy. In some cases, changes need not be made at all or, if so, can be accomplished rather inexpensively. In other cases, the sales potential of the particular market may not warrant expensive product changes. For example, Pepsi's Radical Fruit line of juice drinks was introduced without adaptation on three continents. On the other hand, U.S. companies wishing to market software in foreign countries must undertake painstaking and costly efforts to convert the embedded code from English to foreign languages. This undertaking severely limits the potential markets where individual software products can be profitably marketed. In any case, management must examine these product-related problems carefully prior to making foreign market entry decisions.

Global Distribution Strategy

The role of the distribution network in facilitating the transfer of goods and titles and in the demand stimulation process is as important in foreign markets as it is at home. Figure 13.1 illustrates some of the most common channel arrangements in global marketing. The continuum ranges from no control to almost complete control of the distribution system by manufacturers.

The channel arrangement where manufacturers have the least control is shown at the left in Figure 13.1. These are the most indirect channels of distribution. Here manufacturers sell to resident buyers, export agents, or export merchants located in the United States. In reality, these are similar to some domestic sales, since all of the marketing functions are assumed by intermediaries.

Manufacturers become more directly involved and, hence, have greater control over distribution when agents and distributors located in foreign markets are selected. Both perform similar functions, except that agents do not assume title to the manufacturers' products, while distributors do. If manufacturers should assume the functions of foreign agents or distributors and establish their own foreign branch, they greatly increase control over their global distribution system. Manufacturers' effectiveness will then depend on their own administrative organization rather than on independent intermediaries. If the foreign branch sells to other intermediaries, such as wholesalers and retailers, as is the case with most consumer goods, manufacturers again relinquish some control. However, since the manufacturers are located in the market area, they have greater potential to influence these intermediaries. For example, Volkswagen, General Motors, Anheuser-Busch, and Procter & Gamble have each made substantial investments in building manufacturing facilities in Brazil. These investments allow the companies to begin making direct sales to dealers and retailers in the country.

The channel arrangement that enables manufacturers to exercise a great deal of control is shown at the right in Figure 13.1. Here, manufacturers sell directly to organizational buyers or ultimate consumers. Although this arrangement is most common in the sale of organizational goods, some consumer goods companies have also pursued this arrangement.

Global Pricing Strategy

In domestic markets, pricing is a complex task. The basic approaches used in price determination in foreign markets are the same as those discussed earlier in the chapter on pricing.

FIGURE 13.1

Common Distribution Channels for Global Marketing

Source: Betty J. Punnett and David A. Ricks, *International Business,* p. 257. Reproduced with the permission of South-Western College Publishing. Copyright © 1992 PWS-Kent Publishing Co. All rights reserved.

However, the pricing task is often more complicated in foreign markets because of additional problems associated with tariffs, antidumping laws, taxes, inflation, and currency conversion.

Import duties are probably the major constraint for global marketers and are encountered in many markets. Management must decide whether import duties will be paid by the firm, by the foreign consumer, or shared by both. This and similar constraints may force the firm to abandon an otherwise desirable pricing strategy or may force the firm out of a market altogether.

Another pricing problem arises because of the rigidity in price structures found in many foreign markets. Many foreign intermediaries are not aggressive in their pricing policies. They often prefer to maintain high unit margins at the expense of low sales volume rather than develop large sales volume by means of lower prices and smaller margins per unit. Many times this rigidity is encouraged by legislation that prevents retailers from cutting prices substantially at their own discretion. These are only a few of the pricing problems encountered by foreign marketers.

Global Advertising and Sales Promotion Strategy

When expanding their operations into the world marketplace, most firms are aware of the language barriers that exist and realize the importance of translating their messages into the proper idiom. However, numerous other issues must be resolved, such as selecting appropriate media and advertising agencies in foreign markets.

There are many problems in selecting media in foreign markets. Often the media that are traditionally used in the domestic market are not available. For example, it was not until recently that national commercial TV became a reality in the former Soviet Union. If media are available, they may be so only on a limited basis or they may not reach the potential buyers. In addition to the problem of availability, other difficulties arise from the lack of accurate media information. There is no rate and data service or media directory that covers all the media available throughout the world. Where data are available, their accuracy is often questionable.

Another important promotion decision that must be made is the type of agency used to prepare and place the firm's advertisements. Along with the growth in multinational product companies, more multinational advertising agencies are available. Among the top 15 global advertising agencies, less than half are U.S. owned. Alliances and takeovers have served to stimulate growth in the formation of global agencies. For the U.S. company, there are two major approaches to choosing an agency. The first is to use a purely local agency in each area where the advertisement is to appear. The rationale for this approach is that a purely local agency employing only local nationals can better adapt the firm's message to the local culture.

The other approach is to use either a U.S.–based multinational agency or a multinational agency with U.S. offices to develop and implement the ad campaign. For example, the Coca-Cola Company uses one agency to create ads for the 80 nations in which Diet Coke is marketed. The use of these so-called super agencies is increasing (annual growth rates averaging over 30 percent in the last decade). By using global advertising agencies, companies are able to take advantage of economies of scale and other efficiencies. However, global agencies are not without their critics. Many managers believe that small, local agencies in emerging markets take a more entrepreneurial and fresher approach to advertising than do global agencies. Much discussion has developed over which approach is best, and it appears that both approaches can be used successfully by particular firms.

The use of sales promotion can also lead to opportunities and problems for marketers in foreign markets. Sales promotions often contain certain characteristics that are more attractive than other elements of the promotion mix.[12] In less-wealthy countries, consumers

OVERALL ECONOMIC AND POLITICAL CONDITIONS

- What is the foreign debt service expense as a percentage of hard currency foreign exchange earnings?
- What is the inflation rate? If hyperinflation exists, are appropriate fiscal and monetary policies being implemented to bring it under control?
- How substantial are raw material reserves that can be converted to hard currency?
- Are state subsidies, cheap credits, and tax concessions for state enterprises being phased out?
- Does the government intend to sell stakes in state enterprises to foreign investors?
- Is there an emerging capital market based on real interest rates?
- What progress is being made toward developing a code of company law?
- Is political decision-making authority centralized or fragmented?
- How rapid and sustainable is continued progress toward democracy and a free market economy? Is there any historical tradition to support such trends?

CLIMATE FOR FOREIGN INVESTMENT

- What percentage ownership may foreign companies have in joint ventures? Is government approval required, and if so, how long does it take to obtain?
- Is private ownership of property recognized?
- Are intellectual property rights upheld?
- Can foreign investors obtain premises easily? Can they own real estate?
- Can an initial capital investment by a foreign company be held in hard currency?
- Can a foreign investor sell its stake in a joint venture?
- Can hard currency be used to pay for imported raw materials or to repatriate profits?
- What is the tax rate on business enterprise profits?

MARKET ATTRACTIVENESS

- What is the sales potential in this country?
- Do the country's geographical location and political relations permit it to serve as a gateway to other East European markets?
- How well developed are the necessary managerial and technical skills?
- How skilled is the labor pool? What are labor costs?
- Can continued supply of the raw materials required for production be assured?
- What is the quality of the transportation and telecommunications infrastructure?
- Will Western executives accept being located in the country?
- To what degree have government officials developed a familiarity with Western business practices?

Source: John A. Quelch, Erich Joachimsthaler, and Jose Luis Nueno, "After the Wall: Marketing Guidelines for Eastern Europe," *Sloan Management Review,* Winter 1991, p. 85.

tend to be even more interested in saving money through price discounts, sampling, or premiums. Sales promotion can also be used as a strategy for bypassing restrictions on advertising placed by some foreign governments. In addition, sales promotion can be an effective means for reaching people who live in rural locations where media support for advertising is virtually nonexistent.

Entry and Growth Strategies for Global Marketing

A major decision facing companies that desire either to enter a foreign market or pursue growth within a specific market relates to the choice of entry or growth strategy. What type of strategy to employ depends on many factors, including the analysis of market opportunities, company capabilities, the degree of marketing involvement and commitment the company is willing to make, and the amount of risk that the company is able to tolerate.[13] A company can decide to (1) make minimal investments of funds and resources by limiting its efforts to exporting; (2) make large initial investments of resources and management effort to try to establish a long-term share of global markets; or (3) take an incremental approach whereby the company starts with a low-risk mode of entry that requires the least financial and other resource commitment and gradually increases its commitment over time. All three approaches can be profitable. In general, there are six ways by which a company can initially enter a global market and, subsequently, pursue growth in the global marketplace:

1. *Exporting.* Exporting occurs when a company produces the product outside the final destination and then ships it there for sale. It is the easiest and most common approach for a company making its first international move. Exporting has two distinct advantages. First, it avoids the cost of establishing manufacturing operations in the host country; second, it may help a firm achieve experience-curve and location economies. By manufacturing the product in a centralized location and exporting it to other national markets, the firm may be able to realize substantial scale economies from its global sales volume. This method is what allowed Sony to dominate the global TV market. The major disadvantages related to exporting include (1) the sometimes higher cost associated with the process, (2) the necessity of the exporting firm to pay import duties or face trade barriers, and (3) the delegation of marketing responsibility for the product to foreign agents who may or may not be dependable.

2. *Licensing.* Companies can grant patent rights, trademark rights, and the right to use technological processes to foreign companies. This is the most common strategy for small and medium-size companies. The major advantage to licensing is that the firm does not have to bear the development costs and risks associated with opening up a foreign market. In addition, licensing can be an attractive option in unfamiliar or politically volatile markets. The major disadvantages are that (1) the firm does not have tight control over manufacturing, marketing, and strategy that is required for realizing economies of scale; and (2) there is the risk that the licensed technology may be capitalized on by foreign companies. RCA Corporation, for example, once licensed its color TV technology to a number of Japanese firms. These firms quickly assimilated the technology and used it to enter the U.S. market.

3. *Franchising.* Franchising is similar to licensing but tends to involve longer-term commitments. Also, franchising is commonly employed by service firms, as opposed to manufacturing firms. In a franchising agreement, the franchisor sells limited rights to use its brand name in return for a lump sum and share of the franchisee's future profits. In contrast to licensing agreements, the franchisee agrees to abide by strict operating procedures. Advantages and disadvantages associated with franchising are primarily the same as with licensing except to a lesser degree. In many cases, franchising offers an effective mix of centralized and decentralized decision making.

4. *Joint ventures.* A company may decide to share management with one or more collaborating foreign firms. Joint ventures are especially popular in industries that call for large investments, such as natural gas exploration and automobile manufacturing. Control of the joint venture may be split equally, or one party may control decision making. Joint

ventures hold several advantages. First, a firm may be able to benefit from a partner's knowledge of the host country's competitive position, culture, language, political systems, and so forth. Second, the firm gains by sharing costs and risks of operating in a foreign market. Third, in many countries, political considerations make joint ventures the only feasible entry mode. Finally, joint ventures allow firms to take advantage of a partner's distribution system, technological know-how, or marketing skills. For example, General Mills teamed up with CPC International in an operation called International Dessert Partners to develop a major baking and dessert-mix business in Latin America. The venture combines General Mills' technology and Betty Crocker dessert products with CPC's marketing and distribution capabilities in Latin America. The major disadvantages associated with joint ventures are that (1) a firm may risk giving up control of proprietary knowledge to its partner; and (2) the firm may lose the tight control over a foreign subsidiary needed to engage in coordinated global attacks against rivals.

5. *Strategic alliances.* Although strategic alliances are considered by some to be a form of joint venture, we consider them to be a distinct entity for two reasons. First, strategic alliances are normally partnerships entered into by two or more firms to gain a competitive advantage on a worldwide versus local basis. Second, strategic alliances are usually of a much longer-term nature than are joint ventures. In strategic alliances, the partners share long-term goals and pledge almost total cooperation. Strategic alliances can be used to reduce manufacturing costs, accelerate technological diffusion and new product development, and overcome legal and trade barriers.[14] The major disadvantage associated with formation of a strategic alliance is the increased risk of competitive conflict between the partners.

6. *Direct ownership.* Some companies prefer to enter or grow in markets either through establishment of a wholly owned subsidiary or through acquisition. In either case, the firm owns 100 percent of the stock. The advantages to direct ownership are that the firm has (1) complete control over its technology and operations, (2) immediate access to foreign markets, (3) instant credibility and gains in the foreign country when acquisitions are the mode of entry or growth, and (4) the ability to install its own management team. Of course, the primary disadvantages of direct ownership are the huge costs and significant risks associated with this strategy. These problems may more than offset the advantages depending upon the country entered.

Regardless of the choice of methods used to gain entry into and grow within a foreign marketplace, companies must somehow integrate their operations. The complexities involved in operating on a worldwide basis dictate that firms decide on operating strategies. A critical decision that marketing managers must make relates to the extent of adaptation of the marketing mix elements for the foreign country in which the company operates. Depending on the area of the world under consideration and the particular product mix, different degrees of standardization/adaptation of the marketing mix elements may take place. As a guideline, standardization of one or more parts of the marketing mix is a function of many factors that individually and collectively affect companies in their decision making.[15] It is more likely to succeed under the following conditions:

- When markets are economically similar.
- When worldwide customers, not countries, are the basis for segmenting markets.
- When customer behavior and lifestyles are similar.
- When the product is culturally compatible across the host country.
- When a firm's competitive position is similar in different markets.
- When competing against the same competitors, with similar market shares, in different countries, rather than competing against purely local companies.

- When the product is an organizational and high-technology product rather than a consumer product.
- When there are similarities in the physical, political, and legal environments of home and host countries.
- When the marketing infrastructure in the home and host countries is similar.

The decision to adapt or standardize marketing should be made only after a thorough analysis of the product-market mix has been undertaken. The company's end goal is to develop, manufacture, and market the products best suited to the actual and potential needs of the local (wherever that may be) customer and to the social and economic conditions of the marketplace. There can be subtle differences from country to country and from region to region in the ways a product is used and what customers expect from it.

Conclusion

The world is truly becoming a global market. Many companies that avoid operating in the global arena are destined for failure. For those willing to undertake the challenges and risks necessary to become multinational corporations, long-term survival and growth are likely outcomes. The purpose of this chapter was to introduce the reader to the opportunities, problems, and challenges involved in global marketing.

Additional Readings

Aaker, David, and Erich Joachimsthaler. "The Lure of Global Branding." *Harvard Business Review,* November–December 1999, pp. 137–44.

Bartlett, Christopher A., and Sumuntra Ghoshal. "Going Global: Lessons from Late Movers." *Harvard Business Review,* March–April 2001, pp. 132–42.

Hise, Richard T. "Overcoming Exporting Barriers to Mexico." *Marketing Management,* Spring 2001, pp. 52–54.

Kaikati, Jack G., and Andrew M. Kaikati. "Identity Crisis: The Dos and Don'ts of Brand Rechristening." *Marketing Management,* January/February 2004.

Montgomery, David B., and George S. Yip. "The Challenge of Global Customer Management." *Marketing Management,* Winter 2000, pp. 22–29.

Section II

Analyzing Marketing Problems and Cases

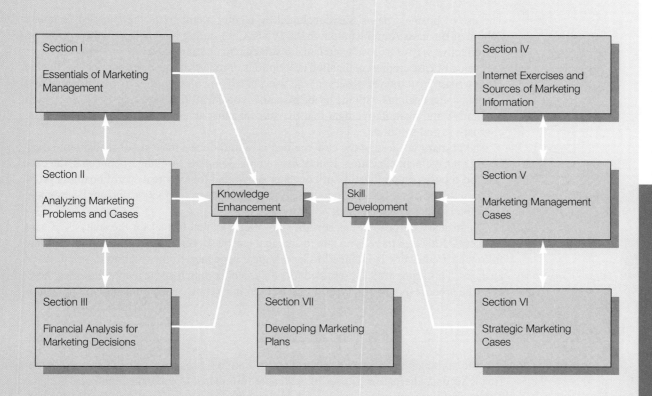

Case studies help bridge the gap between classroom learning and the practice of marketing management. They provide us with an opportunity to develop, sharpen, and test our analytical skills at:

- Assessing situations.
- Sorting out and organizing key information.
- Asking the right questions.
- Defining opportunities and problems.
- Identifying and evaluating alternative courses of action.
- Interpreting data.
- Evaluating the results of past strategies.
- Developing and defending new strategies.
- Interacting with other managers.
- Making decisions under conditions of uncertainty.
- Critically evaluating the work of others.
- Responding to criticism.

Source: David W. Cravens, Charles W. Lamb, Jr., and Victoria L. Crittenden, *Strategic Marketing Management Cases,* 7th ed., (Burr Ridge, IL: McGraw-Hill/Irwin, 2002), p. 671.

The use of business cases was developed by faculty members of the Harvard Graduate School of Business Administration in the 1920s. Case studies have been widely accepted as one effective way of exposing students to strategic marketing processes.

Basically, cases represent detailed descriptions or reports of business problems. They are often written by a trained observer who was actually involved in the firm or organization and had some dealings with the problems under consideration. Cases generally entail both qualitative and quantitative data that the student must analyze to determine appropriate alternatives and solutions.

The primary purpose of the case method is to introduce a measure of realism into marketing management education. Rather than emphasizing the teaching of concepts, the case method focuses on application of concepts and sound logic to real-world business problems. In this way, students learn to bridge the gap between abstraction and application and to appreciate the value of both.

The primary purpose of this section is to offer a logical format for the analysis of case problems. Although there is no one format that can be successfully applied to all cases, the following framework is intended to be a logical sequence from which to develop sound analyses. This framework is presented for analysis of comprehensive marketing cases; however, the process should also be useful for shorter marketing cases, incidents, and problems.

A Case Analysis Framework

A basic approach to case analysis involves a four-step process. First, the problem is defined. Second, alternative courses of action are formulated to solve the problem. Third, the alternatives are analyzed in terms of their strengths and weaknesses. And fourth, an alternative is accepted and a course of action is recommended. This basic approach is quite useful for students well versed in case analysis, particularly for shorter cases or incidents. However, for the newcomer, this framework may be oversimplified. Thus, the following expanded framework and checklists are intended to aid students in becoming proficient in case and problem analysis.

1. Analyze and Record the Current Situation

Whether the analysis of a firm's problems is done by a manager, student, or paid business consultant, the first step is to analyze the current situation. This does not mean writing up a history of the firm but entails the type of analysis described below. This approach is useful not only for getting a better grip on the situation but also for discovering both real and potential problems—central concerns of any case analysis.

Phase 1: The Environment

The first phase in analyzing a marketing problem or case is to consider the environment in which the firm is operating. The environment can be broken down into a number of different components such as the economic, social, political, and legal areas. Any of these may contain threats to a firm's success or opportunities for improving a firm's situation.

Phase 2: The Industry

The second phase involves analyzing the industry in which the firm operates. A framework provided by Michael Porter includes five competitive forces that need to be considered to do a complete industry analysis.[1] The framework is shown in Figure 1 and includes rivalry among existing competitors, threat of new entrants, and threat of substitute products. In addition, in this framework, buyers and suppliers are included as competitors because they can threaten the profitability of an industry or firm.

While rivalry among existing competitors is an issue in most cases, analysis and strategies for dealing with the other forces can also be critical. This is particularly so when a firm is considering entering a new industry and wants to forecast its potential success. Each of the five competitive forces is discussed below.

Rivalry among Existing Competitors   In most cases and business situations a firm needs to consider the current competitors in its industry in order to develop successful strategies. Strategies such as price competition, advertising battles, sales promotion offers, new product

FIGURE 1   **Competitive Forces in an Industry**

Source: Adapted from Michael E. Porter, "Industry Structure and Competitive Strategy: Keys to Profitability," *Financial Analysts Journal,* July–August 1980, p. 33.

introductions, and increased customer service are commonly used to attract customers from competitors.

To fully analyze existing rivalry, it is important to determine which firms are the major competitors and what are their annual sales, market share, growth profile, and strengths and weaknesses. Also, it is useful to analyze their current and past marketing strategies to try to forecast their likely reactions to a change in a competitive firm's strategy. Finally, it is important to consider any trends or changes in government regulation of an industry or changes in technology that could affect the success of a firm's strategy.

Threat of New Entrants   It is always possible for firms in other industries to try to compete in a new industry. New entrants are more likely in industries that have low entry barriers. *Entry barriers* include such things as a need for large financial resources, high brand equity for existing brands in an industry, or economies of scale obtained by existing firms in an industry. Also, existing firms in an industry may benefit from experience curves; that is, their cumulative experience in producing and marketing a product may reduce their per-unit costs below those of inexperienced firms. In general, the higher the entry barriers, the less likely outside firms are to enter an industry. For example, the entry barriers for starting up a new car company are much higher than for starting up an online software company.

Threat of Substitute Products   In a broad sense, all firms in an industry compete with industries producing substitute products. For example, in cultures where bicycles are the major means of transportation, bicycle manufacturers compete with substitute products such as motor scooters and automobiles. Substitutes limit the potential return in an industry by placing a ceiling on the prices a firm in the industry can profitably charge. The more attractive the price-performance alternative offered by substitutes, the tighter the lid on industry profits. For example, the price of candy, such as Raisinets chocolate-covered raisins, may limit the price that can be charged for granola bars.

Bargaining Power of Suppliers   Suppliers can be a competitive threat in an industry because they can raise the price of raw materials or reduce their quality. Powerful suppliers can reduce the profitability of an industry or firm if companies cannot raise their prices to cover price increases by suppliers. Also, suppliers may be a threat because they may forward integrate into an industry by purchasing a firm that they supply or other firms in the industry.

Bargaining Power of Buyers   Buyers can compete with an industry by forcing prices down, bargaining for higher quality or more services, and playing competitors off against each other. All of these tactics can lower the profitability of a firm or industry. For example, because Wal-Mart sells such a large percentage of many companies' products, it can negotiate for lower prices than smaller retailers can. Also, buyers may be a threat because they may backward integrate into an industry by purchasing firms that supply them or other firms in the industry.

Phase 3: The Organization

The third phase involves analysis of the organization itself not only in comparison with the industry and industry averages but also internally in terms of both quantitative and qualitative data. Key areas of concern at this stage are such factors as objectives, constraints, management philosophy, financial condition, and the organizational structure and culture of the firm.

Phase 4: The Marketing Strategy

Although there may be internal personnel or structural problems in the marketing department that need examination, typically an analysis of the current marketing strategy is the next phase. In this phase, the objectives of the marketing department are analyzed in comparison with those of the firm in terms of agreement, soundness, and attainability. Each element of the marketing mix as well as other areas, such as marketing research and

A common criticism of prepared cases goes something like this: "You repeated an awful lot of case material, but you really didn't analyze the case." Yet, at the same time, it is difficult to verbalize exactly what *analysis* means—that is, "I can't explain exactly what it is, but I know it when I see it!"

This is a common problem since the term *analysis* has many definitions and means different things in different contexts. In terms of case analysis, one thing that is clear is that analysis means going beyond simply describing the case information. It includes determining the implications of the case information for developing strategy. This determination may involve careful financial analysis of sales and profit data or thoughtful interpretation of the text of the case.

One way of thinking about analysis involves a series of three steps: synthesis, generalizations, and implications. A brief example of this process follows.

The high growth rate of frozen pizza sales has attracted a number of large food processors, including Pillsbury (Totino's), Quaker Oats (Celeste), American Home Products (Chef Boy-ar-dee), Nestlé (Stouffer's), General Mills (Saluto), and H. J. Heinz (La Pizzeria). The major independents are Jeno's, Tony's, and John's. Jeno's and Totino's are the market leaders, with market shares of about 19 percent each. Celeste and Tony's have about 8 to 9 percent each, and the others have about 5 percent or less.

The frozen pizza market is a highly competitive and highly fragmented market.

In markets such as this, attempts to gain market share through lower consumer prices or heavy advertising are likely to be quickly copied by competitors and thus not be very effective.

Lowering consumer prices and spending more on advertising are likely to be poor strategies. Perhaps increasing freezer space in retail outlets could be effective (this might be obtained through trade discounts). A superior product, for example, better-tasting pizza, microwave pizza, or increasing geographic coverage of the market, may be better strategies for obtaining market share.

Note that none of the three analysis steps includes any repetition of the case material. Rather, they involve abstracting a meaning of the information and, by pairing it with marketing principles, coming up with the strategic implications of the information.

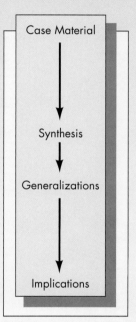

Case Material

Synthesis

Generalizations

Implications

information systems, is analyzed in terms of whether it is internally consistent, synchronized with the goals of the department and firm, and focused on specific target markets. Although cases often are labeled in terms of their primary emphasis, such as "pricing" or "advertising," it is important to analyze the marketing strategy and entire marketing mix, since a change in one element will usually affect the entire marketing program.

In performing the analysis of the current situation, the data should be analyzed carefully to extract the relevant from the superfluous. Many cases contain information that is not relevant to the problem; it is the analyst's job to discard this information to get a clearer picture of the current situation. As the analysis proceeds, a watchful eye must be kept on each phase to determine (1) symptoms of problems, (2) current problems, and (3) potential problems. Symptoms of problems are indicators of a problem but are not problems in and of themselves. For example, a symptom of a problem may be a decline in sales in a particular sales territory. However, the problem is the root cause of the decline in sales—perhaps the field representative quit making sales calls and is relying on phone orders only.

The following is a checklist of the types of questions that should be asked when performing the analysis of the current situation.

Checklist for Analyzing the Current Situation

Phase 1: The Environment

1. What is the state of the economy and are there any trends that could affect the industry, firm, or marketing strategy?
2. What are current trends in cultural and social values and how do these affect the industry, firm, or marketing strategy?
3. What are current political values and trends and how do they affect the industry, firm, or marketing strategy?
4. Is there any current or pending federal, state, or local legislation that could change the industry, firm, or marketing strategy?
5. Overall, are there any threats or opportunities in the environment that could influence the industry, firm, or marketing strategy?

Phase 2: The Industry

1. What industry is the firm in?
2. Which firms are the major competitors in the industry and what are their annual sales, market share, and growth profile?
3. What strategies have competitors in the industry been using and what has been their success with them?
4. What are the relative strengths and weaknesses of competitors in the industry?
5. Is there a threat of new competitors coming into the industry and what are the major entry barriers?
6. Are there any substitute products for the industry and what are their advantages and disadvantages compared to this industry's products?
7. How much bargaining power do suppliers have in this industry and what is its impact on the firm and industry profits?
8. How much bargaining power do buyers have in this industry and what is its impact on the firm and industry profits?

Phase 3: The Organization

1. What are the objectives of the organization? Are they clearly stated? Attainable?
2. What are the strengths of the organization? Managerial expertise? Financial? Copyrights or patents?
3. What are the constraints and weaknesses of the organization?
4. Are there any real or potential sources of dysfunctional conflict in the structure of the organization?
5. How is the marketing department structured in the organization?

Phase 4: The Marketing Strategy

1. What are the objectives of the marketing strategy? Are they clearly stated? Are they consistent with the objectives of the firm? Is the entire marketing mix structured to meet these objectives?
2. What marketing concepts are at issue in the current strategy? Is the marketing strategy well planned and laid out? Is the strategy consistent with sound marketing principles? If the strategy takes exception to marketing principles, is there a good reason for it?

3. To what target market is the strategy directed? Is it well defined? Is the market large enough to be profitably served? Does the market have long-run potential?

4. What competitive advantage does the marketing strategy offer? If none, what can be done to gain a competitive advantage in the marketplace?

5. What products are being sold? What are the width, depth, and consistency of the firm's product lines? Does the firm need new products to fill out its product line? Should any product be deleted? What is the profitability of the various products?

6. What promotion mix is being used? Is promotion consistent with the products and product images? What could be done to improve the promotion mix?

7. What channels of distribution are being used? Do they deliver the product at the right time and right place to meet customer needs? Are the channels typical of those used in the industry? Could channels be made more efficient?

8. What pricing strategies are being used? How do prices compare with similar products of other firms? How are prices determined?

9. Are marketing research and information systematically integrated into the marketing strategy? Is the overall marketing strategy internally consistent?

The relevant information from this preliminary analysis is now formalized and recorded. At this point the analyst must be mindful of the difference between facts and opinions. Facts are objective statements, such as financial data, whereas opinions are subjective interpretations of facts or situations. The analyst must make certain not to place too much emphasis on opinions and to carefully consider any variables that may bias such opinions.

Regardless of how much information is contained in the case or how much additional information is collected, the analyst usually finds that it is impossible to specify a complete framework for the current situation. At this point, assumptions must be made. Clearly, since each analyst may make different assumptions, it is critical that assumptions be explicitly stated. When presenting a case, the analyst may wish to distribute copies of the assumption list to all class members. In this way, confusion is avoided in terms of how the analyst perceives the current situation, and others can evaluate the reasonableness and necessity of the assumptions.

2. Analyze and Record Problems and Their Core Elements

After careful analysis, problems and their core elements should be explicitly stated and listed in order of importance. Finding and recording problems and their core elements can be difficult. It is not uncommon when reading a case for the first time for the student to view the case as a description of a situation in which there are no problems. However, careful analysis should reveal symptoms, which lead to problem recognition.

Recognizing and recording problems and their core elements is most critical for a meaningful case analysis. Obviously, if the root problems are not explicitly stated and understood, the remainder of the case analysis has little merit, because the true issues are not being dealt with. The following checklist of questions is designed to assist in performing this step of the analysis.

Checklist for Analyzing Problems and Their Core Elements

1. What is the primary problem in the case? What are the secondary problems?

2. What proof exists that these are the central issues? How much of this proof is based on facts? On opinions? On assumptions?

3. What symptoms are there that suggest these are the real problems in the case?

4. How are the problems, as defined, related? Are they independent or are they the result of a deeper problem?

5. What are the ramifications of these problems in the short run? In the long run?

3. Formulate, Evaluate, and Record Alternative Courses of Action

This step is concerned with the question of what can be done to resolve the problem defined in the previous step. Generally, a number of alternative courses of action are available that could potentially help alleviate the problem condition. Three to seven are usually a reasonable number of alternatives to work with. Another approach is to brainstorm as many alternatives as possible initially and then reduce the list to a workable number.

Sound logic and reasoning are very important in this step. It is critical to avoid alternatives that could potentially alleviate the problem, but would create a greater new problem or require greater resources than the firm has at its disposal.

After serious analysis and listing of a number of alternatives, the next task is to evaluate them in terms of their costs and benefits. Costs are any output or effort the firm must exert to implement the alternative. Benefits are any input or value received by the firm. Costs to be considered are time, money, other resources, and opportunity costs; benefits are such things as sales, profits, brand equity, and customer satisfaction. The following checklist provides a guideline of questions to be used when performing this phase of the analysis.

Checklist for Formulating and Evaluating Alternative Courses of Action

1. What possible alternatives exist for solving the firm's problems?
2. What limits are there on the possible alternatives? Competence? Resources? Management preference? Ethical responsibility? Legal restrictions?
3. What major alternatives are now available to the firm? What marketing concepts are involved that affect these alternatives?
4. Are the listed alternatives reasonable, given the firm's situation? Are they logical? Are the alternatives consistent with the goals of the marketing program? Are they consistent with the firm's objectives?
5. What are the financial and other costs of each alternative? What are the benefits? What are the advantages and disadvantages of each alternative?
6. Which alternative best solves the problem and minimizes the creation of new problems, given the above constraints?

4. Select and Record the Chosen Alternative and Implementation Details

In light of the previous analysis, the alternative is now selected that best solves the problem with a minimum creation of new problems. It is important to record the logic and reasoning that precipitated the selection of a particular alternative. This includes articulating not only why the alternative was selected but also why the other alternatives were not selected.

No analysis is complete without an action-oriented decision and plan for implementing the decision. The accompanying checklist indicates the type of questions that should be answered in this stage of analysis.

Checklist for Selecting and Implementing the Chosen Alternative

1. What must be done to implement the alternative?
2. What personnel will be involved? What are the responsibilities of each?
3. When and where will the alternative be implemented?
4. What will be the probable outcome?
5. How will the success or failure of the alternative be measured?

Pitfalls to Avoid in Case Analysis

Following is a summary of some of the most common errors analysts make when analyzing cases. When evaluating your analysis or those of others, this list provides a useful guide for spotting potential shortcomings.

1. *Inadequate definition of the problem.* By far the most common error made in case analysis is attempting to recommend courses of action without first adequately defining or understanding the core problems. Whether presented orally or in a written report, a case analysis must begin with a focus on the central issues and problems represented in the case situation. Closely related is the error of analyzing symptoms without determining the root problem.

2. *The search for "the answer."* In case analysis, there are usually no clear-cut solutions. Keep in mind that the objective of case studies is learning through discussion and exploration. There is usually no one "official" or "correct" answer to a case. Rather, there are usually several reasonable alternative solutions.

3. *Not enough information.* Analysts often complain there is not enough information in some cases to make a good decision. However, there is justification for not presenting *all* of the information in a case. As in real life, a marketing manager or consultant seldom has all the information necessary to make an optimal decision. Thus, reasonable assumptions have to be made, and the challenge is to find intelligent solutions in spite of the limited information.

4. *Use of generalities.* In analyzing cases, specific recommendations are necessarily not generalities. For example, a suggestion to increase the price is a generality; a suggestion to increase the price by $1.07 is a specific.

5. *A different situation.* Considerable time and effort are sometimes exerted by analysts contending that "If the situation were different, I'd know what course of action to take" or "If the marketing manager hadn't already fouled things up so badly, the firm wouldn't have a problem." Such reasoning ignores the fact that the events in the case have already happened and cannot be changed. Even though analysis or criticism of past events is necessary in diagnosing the problem, in the end, the present situation must be addressed and decisions must be made based on the given situations.

6. *Narrow vision analysis.* Although cases are often labeled as a specific type of case, such as "pricing," "product," and so forth, this does not mean that other marketing variables should be ignored. Too often analysts ignore the effects that a change in one marketing element will have on the others.

7. *Realism.* Too often analysts become so focused on solving a particular problem that their solutions become totally unrealistic. For instance, suggesting a $1 million advertising program for a firm with a capital structure of $50,000 is an unrealistic solution.

8. *The marketing research solution.* A quite common but unsatisfactory solution to case problems is marketing research; for example, "The firm should do this or that type of marketing research to find a solution to its problem." Although marketing research may be helpful as an intermediary step in some cases, marketing research does not solve problems or make decisions. In cases where marketing research is recommended, the cost and potential benefits should be fully specified in the case analysis.

9. *Rehashing the case material.* Analysts sometimes spend considerable effort rewriting a two- or three-page history of the firm as presented in the case. This is unnecessary since the instructor and other analysts are already familiar with this information.

10. *Premature conclusions.* Analysts sometimes jump to premature conclusions instead of waiting until their analysis is completed. Too many analysts jump to conclusions upon first reading the case and then proceed to interpret everything in the case as justifying their conclusions, even factors logically against it.

A useful approach to gaining an understanding of the situation an organization is facing at a particular time is called *SWOT analysis.* SWOT stands for the organization's strengths and *weaknesses* and the *opportunities* and *threats* it faces in the environment. Below are some issues an analyst should address in performing a SWOT analysis.

POTENTIAL RESOURCE STRENGTHS AND COMPETITIVE CAPABILITIES

- A powerful strategy.
- Core competencies in _____.
- A distinctive competence in _____.
- A product that is strongly differentiated from those of rivals.
- Competencies and capabilities that are well matched to industry key success factors.
- A strong financial condition; ample financial resources to grow the business.
- Strong brand-name image/company reputation.
- An attractive customer base.
- Economy of scale and/or learning and experience curve advantages over rivals.
- Proprietary technology/superior technological skills/important patents.
- Superior intellectual capital relative to key rivals.
- Cost advantages over rivals.
- Strong advertising and promotion.
- Product innovation capabilities.
- Proven capabilities in improving production processes.
- Good supply chain management capabilities.
- Good customer service capabilities.
- Better product quality relative to rivals.
- Wide geographic coverage and/or strong global distribution capability.
- Alliances/joint ventures with other firms that provide access to valuable technology, competencies, and/or attractive geographic markets.

POTENTIAL RESOURCE WEAKNESSES AND COMPETITIVE DEFICIENCIES

- No clear strategic direction.
- Resources that are not well matched to industry key success factors.
- No well-developed or proven core competencies.
- A weak balance sheet; too much debt.
- Higher overall unit costs relative to key competitors.
- Weak or unproven product innovation capabilities.
- A product/service with ho-hum attributes or features inferior to those of rivals.
- Too narrow a product line relative to rivals.
- Weak brand image or reputation.
- Weaker dealer network than key rivals and/or lack of adequate global distribution capability.

Communicating Case Analyses

The final concern in case analysis deals with communicating the results of the analysis. The most comprehensive analysis has little value if it is not communicated effectively. There are two primary media through which case analyses are communicated—the written report and the oral presentation.

- Behind on product quality, R&D, and/or technological know-how.
- In the wrong strategic group.
- Losing market share because _____.
- Lack of management depth.
- Inferior intellectual capital relative to leading rivals.
- Subpar profitability because _____.
- Plagued with internal operating problems or obsolete facilities.
- Behind rivals in e-commerce capabilities.
- Short on financial resources to grow the business and pursue promising initiatives.
- Too much underutilized plant capacity.

POTENTIAL MARKET OPPORTUNITIES

- Openings to win market share from rivals.
- Sharply rising buyer demand for the industry's product.
- Serving additional customer groups or market segments.
- Expanding into new geographic markets.
- Expanding the company's product line to meet a broader range of customer needs.
- Utilizing existing company skills or technological know-how to enter new product lines or new businesses.
- Online sales.
- Integrating forward or backward.
- Falling trade barriers in attractive foreign markets.
- Acquiring rival firms or companies with attractive technological expertise or capabilities.
- Entering into alliances or joint ventures that can expand the firm's market coverage or boost its competitive capability.
- Openings to exploit emerging new technologies.

POTENTIAL EXTERNAL THREATS TO A COMPANY'S WELL-BEING

- Increasing intensity of competition among industry rivals—may squeeze profit margins.
- Slowdowns in market growth.
- Likely entry of potent new competitors.
- Loss of sales to substitute products.
- Growing bargaining power of customers or suppliers.
- A shift in buyer needs and tastes away from the industry's product.
- Adverse demographic changes that threaten to curtail demand for the industry's product.
- Vulnerability to industry driving forces.
- Restrictive trade policies on the part of foreign governments.
- Costly new regulatory requirements.

Source: Arthur A. Thompson, Jr., A. J. Strickland III, and John E. Gamble, *Crafting and Executing Strategy,* 14th ed. (Burr Ridge, IL: McGraw-Hill/Irwin, 2005), p. 95.

The Written Report

Since the structure of the written report will vary by the type of case analyzed, the purpose of this section is not to present a "one and only" way of writing up a case. The purpose of this section is to present some useful generalizations to aid analysts in case write-ups.

A good written report starts with an outline that organizes the structure of the analysis in a logical manner. The following is a general outline for a marketing case report.

1. Read the case quickly to get an overview of the situation.
2. Read the case again thoroughly. Underline relevant information and take notes on potential areas of concern.
3. Review outside sources of information on the environment and the industry. Record relevant information and the source of this information.
4. Perform comparative analysis of the firm with the industry and industry averages.
5. Analyze the firm.
6. Analyze the marketing program.
7. Record the current situation in terms of relevant environmental, industry, firm, and marketing strategy parameters.
8. Make and record necessary assumptions to complete the situational framework.
9. Determine and record the major issues, problems, and their core elements.
10. Record proof that these are the major issues.
11. Record potential courses of action.
12. Evaluate each initially to determine constraints that preclude acceptability.
13. Evaluate remaining alternatives in terms of costs and benefits.
14. Record analysis of alternatives.
15. Select an alternative.
16. Record alternative and defense of its selection.
17. Record the who, what, when, where, how, and why of the alternative and its implementation.

   I. **Title Page**
  II. **Table of Contents**
 III. **Executive Summary** (one- to two-page summary of the analysis and recommendations)
  IV. **Situation Analysis**
       A. *Environment*
          1. Economic conditions and trends
          2. Cultural and social values and trends
          3. Political and legal issues
          4. Summary of environmental opportunities and threats
          5. Implications for strategy development
       B. *Industry*
          1. Classification and definition of industry
          2. Analysis of existing competitors
          3. Analysis of potential new entrants
          4. Analysis of substitute products
          5. Analysis of suppliers
          6. Analysis of buyers
          7. Summary of industry opportunities and threats
          8. Implications for strategy development
       C. *Organization*
          1. Objectives and constraints
          2. Financial condition
          3. Management philosophy
          4. Organizational structure

     5. Organizational culture

     6. Summary of the firm's strengths and weaknesses

     7. Implications for strategy development

   D. *Marketing strategy*

     1. Objectives and constraints

     2. Analysis of sales, profits, and market share

     3. Analysis of target market(s)

     4. Analysis of marketing mix variables

     5. Summary of marketing strategy's strengths and weaknesses

     6. Implications for strategy development

V. Problems Found in Situation Analysis

   A. *Statement of primary problem(s)*

     1. Evidence of problem(s)

     2. Effects of problem(s)

   B. *Statement of secondary problem(s)*

     1. Evidence of problem(s)

     2. Effects of problem(s)

VI. Strategic Alternatives for Solving Problems

   A. *Description of strategic alternative 1*

     1. Benefits of alternative 1

     2. Costs of alternative 1

   B. *Description of strategic alternative 2*

     1. Benefits of alternative 2

     2. Costs of alternative 2

   C. *Description of strategic alternative 3*

     1. Benefits of alternative 3

     2. Costs of alternative 3

VII. Selection of Strategic Alternative and Implementation

   A. *Statement of selected strategy*

   B. *Justification for selection of strategy*

   C. *Description of implementation of strategy*

VIII. Summary

  IX. Appendices

   A. *Financial analysis*

   B. *Technical analysis*

Writing the case report entails filling out the details of the outline in prose form. Of course, not every case report requires all the headings listed above, and different headings may be required for some cases. Like any other skill, it takes practice to determine the appropriate headings and approach for writing particular cases. However, good case reports flow logically from topic to topic, are clearly written, are based on solid situation analysis, and demonstrate sound strategic thinking.

The Oral Presentation

Case analyses are often presented by an individual or team. As with the written report, a good outline is critical, and it is often useful to hand out the outline to each class member. Although there is no best way to present a case or to divide responsibility between team members, simply reading the written report is unacceptable because it encourages boredom and interferes with all-important class discussion.

The use of visual aids can be quite helpful in presenting class analyses. However, simply presenting financial statements contained in the case is a poor use of visual media. On the other hand, graphs of sales and profit curves can be more easily interpreted and can be quite useful for making specific points.

Oral presentation of cases is particularly helpful to analysts for learning the skill of speaking to a group. In particular, the ability to handle objections and disagreements without antagonizing others is a skill worth developing.

Conclusion

From the discussion it should be obvious that good case analyses require a major commitment of time and effort. Individuals must be highly motivated and willing to get involved in the analysis and discussion if they expect to learn and succeed in a course where cases are used. Persons with only passive interest who perform "night before" analyses cheat themselves out of valuable learning experiences that can aid them in their careers.

Additional Readings

Aaker, David A. *Strategic Market Management.* 7th ed. Hoboken, NJ: Wiley, 2005.

Anderson, Carol H., and Julian W. Vincze. *Strategic Marketing Management.* 2nd ed. Boston: Houghton Mifflin, 2004.

Cravens, David W; Charles W. Lamb, Jr.; and Victoria L. Crittenden. *Strategic Marketing Management Cases.* 7th ed. Burr Ridge, IL: McGraw-Hill/Irwin, 2002, Appendix B.

Kevin, Roger A., and Robert A. Peterson. *Strategic Marketing Problems.* 9th ed. Upper Saddle River, NJ: Prentice Hall, 2001, pp. 693–708.

Section III

Financial Analysis for Marketing Decisions

Financial Analysis

Financial analysis is an important aspect of strategic marketing planning and should be an integral part of marketing problem and case analysis. In this section, we present several financial tools that are useful for analyzing marketing problems and cases. First, we investigate break-even analysis, which is concerned with determining the number of units or dollar sales, or both, necessary to break even on a project or to obtain a given level of profits. Second, we illustrate net present value analysis, which is a somewhat more sophisticated tool for analyzing marketing alternatives. Finally, we investigate ratio analysis, which can be a useful tool for determining the financial condition of the firm, including its ability to invest in a new or modified marketing program.

Break-Even Analysis

Break-even analysis is a common tool for investigating the potential profitability of a marketing alternative. The *break-even point* is that level of sales in either units or sales dollars at which a firm covers all of its costs. In other words, it is the level at which total sales revenue just equals the total costs necessary to achieve these sales.

To compute the break-even point, an analyst must have or be able to obtain three values. First, the analyst needs to know the selling price per unit of the product (SP). For example, suppose the Ajax Company plans to sell its new electric car through its own dealerships at a retail price of $5,000. Second, the analyst needs to know the level of fixed costs (FC). Fixed costs are all costs relevant to the project that do not change regardless of how many units are produced or sold. For instance, whether Ajax produces and sells 1 or 100,000 cars, Ajax executives will receive their salaries, land must be purchased for a plant, a plant must be constructed, and machinery must be purchased. Other fixed costs include such things as interest, lease payments, and sinking fund payments. Suppose Ajax has totaled all of its fixed costs and the sum is $1.5 million. Third, the analyst must know the variable costs per unit produced (VC). As the name implies, variable costs are those that vary directly with the number of units produced. For example, each car Ajax produces involves costs for raw materials and components to build the car, such as batteries, electric motors, steel bodies, and tires; labor costs for operating employees; and machine costs, such as electricity and welding rods. Suppose these are totaled by Ajax and the variable costs for each car produced equal $3,500. With this information, the analyst can now determine the break-even point, which is the number of units that must be sold to just cover the cost of producing the cars. The break-even point is determined by dividing total fixed costs by the *contribution margin*. The contribution margin is simply the difference between the selling price per unit (SP) and variable costs per unit (VC). Algebraically,

$$BEP_{\text{(in units)}} = \frac{\text{Total fixed costs}}{\text{Contribution margin}}$$

$$= \frac{FC}{SP - VC}$$

Substituting the Ajax estimates,

$$BEP_{\text{(in units)}} = \frac{1,500,000}{5,000 - 3,500}$$

$$= \frac{1,500,000}{1,500}$$

$$= 1,000 \text{ units}$$

In other words, the Ajax Company must sell 1,000 cars to just break even (i.e., for total sales revenue to cover total costs).

Alternatively, the analyst may want to know the break-even point in terms of dollar sales volume. Of course, if the preceding analysis has been done, one could simply multiply the $BEP_{\text{(in units)}}$ times the selling price to determine the break-even sales volume (i.e., 1,000 units $\times$ \$5,000/unit = \$5 million). However, the $BEP_{\text{(in dollars)}}$ can be computed directly, using the formula below:

$$BEP_{\text{(in dollars)}} = \frac{FC}{1 - \dfrac{VC}{SP}}$$

$$= \frac{1,500,000}{1 - \dfrac{3,500}{5,000}}$$

$$= \frac{1,500,000}{1 - .7}$$

$$= \$5,000,000$$

Thus, Ajax must produce and sell 1,000 cars, which equals \$5 million sales, to break even. Of course, firms do not want to just break even but want to make a profit. The logic of break-even analysis can easily be extended to include profits (P). Suppose Ajax decided that a 20 percent return on fixed costs would make the project worth the investment. Thus, Ajax would need 20% $\times$ \$1,500,000 = \$300,000 before-tax profit. To calculate how many units Ajax must sell to achieve this level of profits, the profit figure (P) is added to fixed costs in the above formulas. (We will label the break-even point as BEP' to show that we are now computing unit and sales levels to obtain a given profit level.) In the Ajax example:

$$BEP'_{\text{(in units)}} = \frac{FC + P}{SP - VC}$$

$$= \frac{1,500,000 + 300,000}{5,000 - 3,500}$$

$$= \frac{1,800,000}{1,500}$$

$$= 1,200 \text{ units}$$

In terms of dollars,

$$BEP'_{\text{(in dollars)}} = \frac{FC + P}{1 - \dfrac{VC}{SP}}$$

$$= \frac{1,500,000 + 300,000}{1 - \dfrac{3,500}{5,000}}$$

$$= \frac{1,800,000}{1 - .7}$$

$$= \$6,000,000$$

Thus, Ajax must produce and sell 1,200 cars (sales volume of $6 million) to obtain a 20 percent return on fixed costs. Analysis must now be directed at determining whether a given marketing plan can be expected to produce sales of at least this level. If the answer is yes, the project would appear to be worth investing in. If not, Ajax should seek other opportunities.

Net Present Value Analysis

The profit-oriented marketing manager must understand that the capital invested in new products has a cost. It is a basic principle in business that whoever wishes to use capital must pay for its use. Dollars invested in new products could be diverted to other uses—to pay off debts, pay dividends to stockholders, or buy U.S. Treasury bonds that would yield economic benefits to the corporation. If, on the other hand, all of the dollars used to finance a new product have to be borrowed from lenders outside the corporation, interest has to be paid on the loan.

One of the best ways to analyze the financial aspects of a marketing alternative is *net present value* analysis. This method employs a discounted cash flow, which takes into account the time value of money and its price to the borrower. The following example will illustrate this method.

To compute the net present value of an investment proposal, the cost of capital must be estimated. The cost of capital can be defined as the required rate of return on an investment that would leave the owners of the firm as well off as if the project was not undertaken. Thus, it is the minimum percentage return on investment that a project must make to be worth undertaking. There are many methods of estimating the cost of capital. However, because these methods are not the concern of this text, we will simply assume that the cost of capital for the Ajax Corporation has been determined to be 10 percent.[1] Again, it should be noted that once the cost of capital is determined, it becomes the minimum rate of return required for an investment—a type of cutoff point. However, some firms in selecting their new product investments select a minimum rate of return that is above the cost of capital figure to allow for errors in judgment or measurement.

The Ajax Corporation is considering a proposal to market instant-developing movie film. After conducting considerable marketing research, sales were projected to be $1 million per year. In addition, the finance department compiled the following information concerning the projects:

New equipment needed	$700,000
Useful life of equipment	10 years
Depreciation	10% per year
Salvage value	$100,000
Cost of goods and expenses	$700,000 per year
Cost of capital	10%
Tax rate	50%

To compute the net present value of this project, the net cash flow for each year of the project must first be determined. This can be done in four steps:

1. Sales − Cost of goods and expenses = Gross income or

$$\$1,000,000 - 700,000 = \$300,000$$

2. Gross income − Depreciation = Taxable income or

$$\$300,000 - (10\% \times 600,000) = \$240,000$$

3. Taxable income − Tax = Net income or

$$\$240,000 - (50\% \times 240,000) = \$120,000$$

4. Net income + Depreciation = Net cash flow or

$$\$120,000 + 60,000 = \$180,000 \text{ per year}$$

Because the cost of capital is 10 percent, this figure is used to discount the net cash flows for each year. To illustrate, the $180,000 received at the end of the first year would be discounted by the factor $1/(1 + 0.10)$, which would be $180,000 \times 0.9091 = \$163,638$; the $180,000 received at the end of the second year would be discounted by the factor $1/(1 + 0.10)$,[2] which would be $180,000 \times 0.8264 = \$148,752$, and so on. (Most finance textbooks have present value tables that can be used to simplify the computations.) The table that follows shows the present value computations for the 10-year project. It should be noted that the net cash flow for year 10 is $280,000 because there is an additional $100,000 inflow from salvage value.

Thus, at a discount rate of 10 percent, the present value of the net cash flow from new product investment is greater than the $700,000 outlay required, and so the decision can be considered profitable by this standard. Here the net present value is $444,560, which is the difference between the $700,000 investment outlay and the $1,144,560 discounted cash

Year	Net Cash Flow	0.10 Discount Factor	Present Value
1	$ 180,000	0.9091	$ 163,638
2	180,000	0.8264	148,752
3	180,000	0.7513	135,234
4	180,000	0.6830	122,940
5	180,000	0.6209	111,762
6	180,000	0.5645	101,610
7	180,000	0.5132	92,376
8	180,000	0.4665	83,970
9	180,000	0.4241	76,338
10	280,000	0.3855	107,940
Total	$1,900,000		$1,144,560

flow. The *present value ratio* is nothing more than the present value of the net cash flow divided by the cash investment. If this ratio is 1 or larger than 1, the project would be profitable for the firm to invest in.

There are many other measures of investment worth, but only one additional method will be discussed. It is the very popular and easily understood payback method. *Payback* refers to the amount of time required to pay back the original outlay from the cash flows. Staying with the example, the project is expected to produce a stream of cash proceeds that is constant from year to year, so the payback period can be determined by dividing the investment outlay by this annual cash flow. Dividing $700,000 by $180,000, the payback period is approximately 3.9 years. Firms often set a maximum payback period before a project will be accepted. For example, many firms refuse to take on a project if the payback period exceeds three years.

This example should illustrate the difficulty in evaluating marketing investments from a profitability or economic worth standpoint. The most challenging problem is that of developing accurate cash flow estimates because there are many possible alternatives, such as price of the product and channels of distribution, and the consequences of each alternative

Years	8%	10%	12%	14%	16%	18%
1	.9259	.9091	.8929	.8772	.8621	.8475
2	.8573	.8264	.7972	.7695	.7432	.7182
3	.7938	.7513	.7118	.6750	.6407	.6086
4	.7350	.6830	.6355	.5921	.5523	.5158
5	.6806	.6209	.5674	.5194	.4761	.4371
6	.6302	.5645	.5066	.4556	.4104	.3704
7	.5835	.5132	.4523	.3996	.3538	.3139
8	.5403	.4665	.4039	.3506	.3050	.2660
9	.5002	.4241	.3606	.3075	.2630	.2255
10	.4632	.3855	.3220	.2697	.2267	.1911

must be forecast in terms of sales volumes, selling costs, and other expenses. In spite of all the problems, management must evaluate the economic worth of new product and other decisions, not only to reduce some of the guesswork and ambiguity surrounding marketing strategy development but also to reinforce the objective of making profits.

Ratio Analysis

Firms' income statements and balance sheets provide a wealth of information that is useful for developing marketing strategies. Frequently, this information is included in marketing cases, yet analysts often have no convenient way of interpreting the financial position of the firm to make sound marketing decisions. Ratio analysis provides the analyst an easy and efficient method for investigating a firm's financial position by comparing the firm's ratios across time or with ratios of similar firms in the industry or with industry averages.

Ratio analysis involves four basic steps:

1. Choose the appropriate ratios.
2. Compute the ratios.
3. Compare the ratios.
4. Check for problems or opportunities.

1. Choose the Appropriate Ratios

The five basic types of financial ratios are (1) liquidity ratios, (2) asset management ratios, (3) profitability ratios, (4) debt management ratios, and (5) market value ratios.[2] While calculating ratios of all five types is useful, liquidity, asset management, and profitability ratios provide information that is most directly relevant for marketing decision making. Although many ratios can be calculated in each of these groups, we have selected two of the most commonly used and readily available ratios in each group to illustrate the process.

Liquidity Ratios   One of the first considerations in analyzing a marketing problem is the liquidity of the firm. *Liquidity* refers to the ability of the firm to pay its short-term obligations. If a firm cannot meet its short-term obligations, there is little that can be done until this problem is resolved. Simply stated, recommendations to increase advertising, to do marketing research, or to develop new products are of little value if the firm is about to go bankrupt.

1. http://finance.yahoo.com/. Input the company symbol to receive financial ratios and other useful information. Under the "Company" heading, "Key statistics," "Competitors," and "Industry" are most useful for comparative ratio analyses.
2. *Annual Statement Studies.* Published by Robert Morris Associates, this work includes 11 financial ratios computed annually for over 150 lines of business. Each line of business is divided into four size categories.
3. *Industry Norms and Key Business Ratios.* Published by Dun & Bradstreet, this work provides a variety of industry ratios.
4. *Almanac of Business and Industrial Financial Ratios.* The almanac, published by Prentice Hall, Inc., lists industry averages for 22 financial ratios. Approximately 170 businesses and industries are listed.
5. *Quarterly Financial Report for Manufacturing Corporations.* This work, published jointly by the Federal Trade Commission and the Securities and Exchange Commission, contains balance-sheet and income-statement information by industry groupings and by asset-size categories.
6. Trade associations and individual companies often compute ratios for their industries and make them available to analysts.

The two most commonly used ratios for investigating liquidity are the *current ratio* and the *quick ratio* (or "acid test"). The current ratio is determined by dividing current assets by current liabilities and is a measure of the overall ability of the firm to meet its current obligations. A common rule of thumb is that current ratio should be about 2:1.

The quick ratio is determined by subtracting inventory from current assets and dividing the remainder by current liabilities. Since inventory is the least liquid current asset, the quick ratio deals with assets that are most readily available for meeting short-term (one-year) obligations. A common rule of thumb is that the quick ratio should be at least 1:1.

Asset Management Ratios   Asset management ratios investigate how well the firm handles its assets. For marketing problems, two of the most useful asset management ratios are concerned with *inventory turnover* and *total asset utilization.* The inventory turnover ratio is determined by dividing sales by inventories.[3] If the firm is not turning its inventory over as rapidly as other firms, it suggests that too much money is being tied up in unproductive or obsolete inventory. In addition, if the firm's turnover ratio is decreasing over time, it suggests that there may be a problem in the marketing plan, because inventory is not being sold as rapidly as it had been in the past. One problem with this ratio is that, since sales usually are recorded at market prices and inventory usually is recorded at cost, the ratio may overstate turnover. Thus, some analysts prefer to use cost of sales rather than sales in computing turnover. We will use cost of sales in our analysis.

A second useful asset management ratio is total asset utilization. It is calculated by dividing sales by total assets and is a measure of how productively the firm's assets have been used to generate sales. If this ratio is well below industry figures, it suggests that the firm's marketing strategies are less effective than those of competitors or that some unproductive assets need to be eliminated.

Profitability Ratios   Profitability is a major goal of marketing and is an important measure of the quality of a firm's marketing strategies. Two key profitability ratios are *profit margin on sales* and *return on total assets.* Profit margin on sales is determined by dividing profit before tax by sales. Serious questions about the firm and marketing plan should be raised if profit margin on sales is declining across time or is well below other firms in

FIGURE 1   Balance Sheet and Income Statement for Ajax Home Computer Company

Ajax Home Computer Company
Balance Sheet
March 31, 2005
(in thousands)

Assets		Liabilities and Stockholders' Equity	
Cash . . . .$ 30		Trade accounts payable . . . .$ 150	
Marketable securities 40		Accrued 25	
Accounts receivable 200		Notes payable 100	
Inventory 430		Accrued income tax 40	
Total current assets 700		Total current liabilities 315	
Plant and equipment 1,000		Bonds 500	
Land 500		Debentures 85	
Other investments 200		Stockholders' equity 1,500	
Total assets $2,400		Total liabilities and stockholders' equity $2,400	

Ajax Home Computer Company
Income Statement
for the 12-Month Period Ending March 31, 2005
(in thousands)

Sales $3,600	
Cost of sales	
Labor and materials 2,000	
Depreciation 200	
Selling expenses 500	
General and administrative expenses 80	
Total cost 2,780	
Net operating income 820	
Less interest expense	
Interest on notes 20	
Interest on debentures 200	
Interest on bonds 300	
Total interest 520	
Profit before tax 300	
Federal income tax (@40%) 120	
Net profit after tax . . . .$ 180	

the industry. Return on total assets is determined by dividing profit before tax by total assets. This ratio is the return on the investment for the entire firm.

2. Compute the Ratios

The next step in ratio analysis is to compute the ratios. Figure 1 presents the balance sheet and income statement for the Ajax Home Computer Company. These six ratios can be calculated from the Ajax balance sheet and income statement as follows:

Liquidity ratios:

$$\text{Current ratio} = \frac{\text{Current assets}}{\text{Current liabilities}} = \frac{700}{315} = 2.2$$

$$\text{Quick ratio} = \frac{\text{Current assets} - \text{Inventory}}{\text{Current liabilities}} = \frac{270}{315} = .86$$

Asset management ratios:

$$\text{Inventory turnover} = \frac{\text{Cost of sales}}{\text{Inventory}} = \frac{2{,}780}{430} = 6.5$$

$$\text{Total asset utilization} = \frac{\text{Sales}}{\text{Total assets}} = \frac{3{,}600}{2{,}400} = 1.5$$

Profitability ratios:

$$\text{Profit margin on sales} = \frac{\text{Profit before tax}}{\text{Sales}} = \frac{300}{3{,}600} = 8.3\%$$

$$\text{Return on total assests} = \frac{\text{Profit before tax}}{\text{Total assets}} = \frac{300}{2{,}400} = 12.5\%$$

3. Compare the Ratios

While rules of thumb are useful for analyzing ratios, it cannot be overstated that comparison of ratios is always the preferred approach. The ratios computed for a firm can be compared in at least three ways. First, they can be compared over time to see if there are any favorable or unfavorable trends in the firm's financial position. Second, they can be compared with the ratios of other firms of similar size in the industry. Third, they can be compared with industry averages to get an overall idea of the firm's relative financial position in the industry.

Figure 2 provides a summary of the ratio analysis. The ratios computed for Ajax are presented along with the median ratios for firms of similar size in the industry and the industry median. The median is often reported in financial sources, rather than the mean, to avoid the strong effect of outliers.[4]

4. Check for Problems or Opportunities

The ratio comparison in Figure 2 suggests that Ajax is in reasonably good shape financially. The current ratio is above the industry figures, although the quick ratio is slightly below them. However, the high inventory turnover ratio suggests that the slightly low quick ratio should not be a problem, since inventory turns over relatively quickly. Total asset utilization is slightly below industry averages and should be monitored closely. This, coupled with the slightly lower return on total assets, suggests that some unproductive assets should be eliminated or that the production process needs to be made more efficient. While the problem could be ineffective marketing, the high profit margin on sales suggests that marketing effort is probably not the problem.

FIGURE 2
Ratio Comparison for Ajax Home Computer Company

	Ajax	Industry Firms Median ($1–10 Million in Assets)	Overall Industry Median
Liquidity ratios			
Current ratio	2.2	1.8	1.8
Quick ratio	.86	.9	1.0
Asset management ratios			
Inventory turnover	6.5	3.2	2.8
Total assets utilization	1.5	1.7	1.6
Profitability ratios			
Profit margin	8.3%	6.7%	8.2%
Return on total assets	12.5%	15.0%	14.7%

Conclusion

This section has focused on several aspects of financial analysis that are useful for marketing decision making. The first, break-even analysis, is commonly used in marketing problem and case analysis. The second, net present value analysis, is quite useful for investigating the financial impact of marketing alternatives, such as new product introductions or other long-term strategic changes. The third, ratio analysis, is a useful tool sometimes overlooked in marketing problem solving. Performing a ratio analysis as a regular part of marketing problem and case analysis can increase the understanding of the firm and its problems and opportunities.

Additional Readings

Brealey, Richard A., and Stewart C. Myers. *Fundamentals of Corporate Finance.* 4th ed. New York: McGraw-Hill, 2004.

Ross, Stephen A.; Randolph W. Westerfield; and Jeffrey F. Jaffe. *Corporate Finance.* 7th ed. Burr Ridge, IL: Irwin/McGraw-Hill, 2005.

Ross, Stephen A.; Randolph W. Westerfield; and Bradford D. Jordan. *Fundamentals of Corporate Finance.* 6th ed. Burr Ridge, IL: Irwin/McGraw-Hill, 2003.

Section IV

Internet Exercises and Sources of Marketing Information

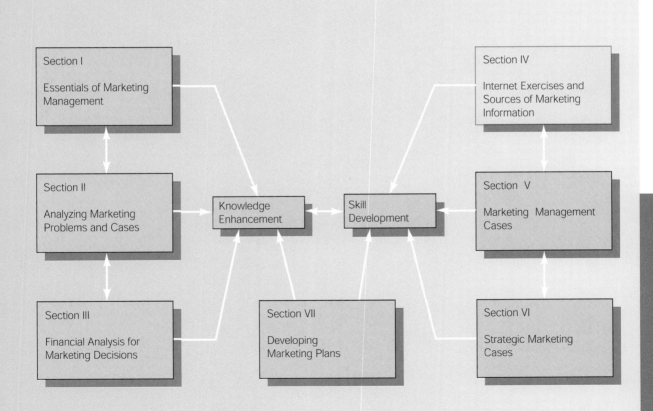

Internet Exercises

Charles Heath *University of Kentucky*

Exercise 1: Corporate Websites

Every major corporation has a corporate website. For the most part, the primary purpose of the corporate website is to communicate with their current and potential customers, investors, and channel partners. Because they are used to attracting new business, corporate websites are a good place to determine what they see as their mission and primary purpose.

IBM [www.ibm.com]	Cisco Systems [www.cisco.com]
Microsoft [www.microsoft.com]	Ben and Jerry's [www.benjerry.com]

For this assignment, visit the corporate websites listed above and look for the following pieces of business information.

1. Look for a statement of mission.
2. Investigate their history and changes.
3. Look for what they claim to be strengths (what are they selling to their investors) and distinctive competencies.
4. Organizational objectives—do they make statements resembling those in Highlight 1–2?
5. Look at their product lines and business units.

Exercise 2: Online vs. Offline Retail Experiences

The growth of e-commerce has brought about a whole new shopping experience. It is easy to see that shopping online is different from shopping at a traditional "brick and mortar" store. But how is it different? What are companies doing to make the shopping experience similar and/or different?

Find two retail sites on the World Wide Web (WWW) that have famous "real world" counterparts.

For example:

Barnes and Noble [www.bn.com]	Macy's [www.macys.com]
Best Buy [www.bestbuy.com]	Nordstroms [www.nordstrom.com/Shop/]
Bloomingdales [www.bloomingdales.com]	Robinsons–May [www.shopmay.com]
Circuit City [www.circuitcity.com]	Sears [www.sears.com]
CVS Pharmacy [www.cvs.com]	Target Stores [www.target.com]
Eddie Bauer [www.eddiebauer.com]	Toys Я Us [www.toysrus.com]
The Gap Online [www.gap.com]	Victoria's Secret [www.victoriassecret.com]
Kroger [www.kroger.com]	Wal-Mart [www.wal-mart.com]

1. Compare shopping at the virtual retailer to the physical version. What about the shopping experience is similar?
2. Now, contrast the two experiences. What does the online store offer that the "brick and mortar" store cannot? What does the "brick and mortar" store offer that the virtual store cannot?
3. What value does the online site add to the retailer as a corporation?
4. Will the online site ever completely replace the "brick and mortar" store? Why or why not?

Exercise 3: Consumer Decision-Making Process

When consumers make a purchase, they progress through a series of behaviors. The consumer decision-making process describes those behaviors and the activities that take place at each stage. In order to increase sales, marketers are looking at the five stages and trying to find ways to influence the consumers as they progress through the CDM process.

The Internet is the most recent tool that marketers are using to influence consumers. Discuss the impact of the Internet on the five stages of the CDM process. What happens differently, or how does the Internet use these processes to sell more efficiently?

Need Recognition—During the first stage, the consumer recognizes a need that can be satisfied by a purchase. What are ways that Internet marketers are attempting to trigger consumers' recognition of needs? What are some things that Amazon.com [www.amazon.com] is doing to activate need recognition?

Alternative Search—Once consumers realize a need, they begin to search for potential ways to satisfy that need that provides details about the alternatives. There are five primary sources of information: internal, group, marketing, public, and experimental sources. How can the Internet provide information for consumers? Which of the sources can the Internet influence? What impact does the information available at Edmunds [www.edmunds.com] have on consumers' alternative search?

Alternative Evaluation—All the viable alternatives that can satisfy the need are evaluated and compared against each other. Consumers select the brand which best satisfies the need as their intended purchase. Many times comparing products is difficult because of complex product features, numerous available choices, and physical distance between products in stores. Visit iQVC [www.iqvc.com] and select any product category of your choice. How does this website help consumers compare product alternatives?

Purchase Decision—The consumer decides to make a purchase of the intended brand, purchase a different brand, or postpone the purchase. The Internet plays a major role in consumers' purchase decisions. What are some Internet features that influence the purchase decisions? Revisit Amazon.com and discuss some of the ways they influence the consumer's purchase decision. What role does UPS [www.ups.com] play in the purchase decision? Visit the site of Paypal [www.paypal.com]; discuss the role of digital cash, credit cards, cash, and checking accounts on the purchase decision.

Post-purchase Evaluation—The consumer reviews the purchase and the entire purchase process of the product. If consumers have doubts or second thoughts about a purchase, they experience postpurchase dissonance. What are Internet marketers doing online to help customers avoid dissonance? Go to the Ford website [www.ford.com]. If you had a problem with the purchase of a Ford Explorer, what does the site do to help you alleviate or avoid dissonance? How does eBay.com [www.ebay.com] allow consumers to review the purchase process?

Exercise 4: Discovering Product Assortments Online

Most companies manufacture a wide range of products that they then offer to consumers. How companies that offer multiple products and product lines manage those offerings is of extreme importance to the overall success of the company.

Procter & Gamble [www.pg.com]

Kraft Foods [www.kraft.com]

Gillette.com [www.gillette.com]

General Motors [www.gm.com]

General Mills [www.generalmills.com]

Using the Internet, visit one of the corporate sites listed above. Browse through the site and find where they discuss their product offerings. How have they defined their product mix? How many different product lines do they offer? Discuss both the breadth and depth of the product mix. Pick three of their products and tell which type of product they are (convenience, shopping, or specialty) and why the company produces that type of product.

Exercise 5: Brand Equity on the Internet

Branding issues are of extreme importance to manufacturers, traditional retailers, and customers. The growth of the Internet has lead to the increased importance of a strong product brand name. The brand name is used to differentiate products in both traditional and online retail situations. Online, there is increased importance because of trust and security issues. Pick a company from the list below and write a few words that describe your thoughts about the company whose website you are about to visit.

Apple [www.apple.com]

Baldwin Pianos [www.baldwinpiano.com/]

Ben and Jerry's [www.benjerry.com]

Coke [www.coke.com]

Fender Guitars [www.fender.com]

IBM [www.ibm.com]

L.L. Bean [www.llbean.com]

McDonald's [www.mcdonalds.com]

Metropolitan Museum of Art [www.metmuseum.org]

MTV [www.mtv.com]

Ragu [www.eat.com]

Reebok [www.reebok.com]

Target [www.target.com]

Now, browse the company's website and get a good feeling for what information is presented at the site, how the site is organized, how the designers have chosen the theme, color scheme, images, etc.

1. What is the main purpose for the website?
2. Briefly discuss what messages the website is trying to convey.
3. Compare what you thought about the company before visiting the website to the message that was conveyed by the material on the website. Does the web material match what you thought or is it different?
4. What is it about the company's website that is helping them build brand equity?

Exercise 6: The Impact of Communities on Marketing

Communities are areas online where consumers who share interests gather and interact. There are a number of virtual areas that function as a community including discussion lists, chat rooms, and message boards. The unique properties of online communities offer marketers a number of opportunities to reach their customers in ways that never existed before.

1. Go to the Amazon.com [www.amazon.com] homepage and click on the "Friends & Favorites" button (especially the purchase circles section). Discuss how Amazon uses reference groups to influence consumers at their website.

2. Visit the message boards at iVillage.com [www.ivillage.com] and pick a topic. How might a sponsor benefit by being associated with a community?

3. Take a tour of GM's Owner Center at the GM website [www.gm.com] by clicking on the Owner Center link on the navigation bar at the top of the page. What are some ways that a company can use community to develop new products or change existing ones?

Exercise 7: Branding for Pure Plays

Barnes & Noble.com (BN.com) entered the e-commerce arena in 1997 and has grown to become the fifth largest online retailer. When it began to operate online, Barnes & Noble already had an established brand name while Amazon.com, a pure play (a company that exists only in an online form), did not.

Brand equity is determined by the consumer and is the sum of all of the consumer's assessment of the product. Visit both Amazon.com [www.amazon.com] and BN.com [www.bn.com]. Describe the different elements of each of their brand equity (see Figure 6–1 for help). How did Amazon develop such a strong brand name? What issues will B&N have to deal with that Amazon did not?

"Brick and Mortar" Retailer		"Pure Play" Retailer
Sam Goody [www.samgoody.com]	VS.	CDNow [www.cdnow.com]
Joseph-Beth [www.josephbeth.com]	VS.	Amazon.com [www.amazon.com]
Blockbuster Video [www.blockbuster.com]	VS.	Reel.com [www.reel.com]

Pick a pair of retailers from the list above and answer the following questions.

1. Compare the purpose of the two sites. How are they similar/different?
2. Which of the two do you think has the advantage in the future and why?
3. What strategic advantage does the "brick and mortar" retailer have that the "pure play" retailer does not?
4. Does the "pure play" retailer have any strategic advantages that the "brick and mortar" retailer does not?

Exercise 8: Pricing Issues on the Internet

One of the easiest places to see the impact of the Internet on marketing is by looking at its effect on pricing decisions and consumers' perceptions of prices. Over just the last five years, the WWW has developed the reputation as being *the* place to shop to get the lowest prices.

1. Why has this reputation developed?
2. Why might it be possible to charge lower prices online?
3. Are products really cheaper?

To answer this last question, choose two products and find them for sale online (books, CDs, and software work very well). Calculate the total price that would be charged to your credit card; then go to a "brick and mortar" retailer and find prices for the same product there. Make your comparisons.

1. Where is the cheapest place to buy the products that you have selected?
2. What costs go into determining which place you buy your product?
3. Are there any nonfinancial costs to shopping online? To offline shopping?

Exercise 9: Selecting the Internet as a Distribution Channel

One very important decision that marketers need to make is which channel of distribution to use for their products or services. Four primary considerations need to be analyzed before making the distribution choice.

Distribution coverage required

Degree of control desired

Total distribution cost

Channel flexibility

Discuss the implications of using the Internet on these four considerations. To help analyze the possible implications of the Internet on these elements, visit the following sites and consider how they distribute their products differently than traditional manufacturers.

Dell Computers [www.dell.com]   Peapod Groceries [www.peapod.com]

Gateway Computers [www.gateway.com]   Amazon.com [www.amazon.com]

Also visit these sites and think about the role that they play in the new breed of channel intermediaries.

Federal Express (FedEx) [www.fedex.com]   Yahoo.com [www.yahoo.com]

United Parcel Service (UPS) [www.ups.com]   IBM eBusiness

Roadway Express [www.roadway.com]   [www.ibm.com/ebusiness/]

Exercise 10: Internet Advertising

Marketers need to decide the best possible way to get the message about their products to those consumers who would be interested in making a purchase. Advertising is one of the most popular methods for companies to use to deliver their product messages. However, not only must the marketing communications manager decide where to advertise but also how to communicate that message. There are four primary objectives that marketers wish to accomplish with advertising.

Awareness

Comprehension

Conviction

Ordering

Discuss how Internet advertising can be used to accomplish these four objectives.

Awareness—Visit both Buy.com [www.buy.com] and Amazon.com [www.amazon.com]. What features of their homepages are attempting to trigger awareness in the consumer?

Comprehension—Go to the Sony website [www.sony.com], select electronics, electronics again, and then choose televisions from the drop-down list. How does this site help comprehension of the product offering?

Conviction—Go to Cdnow.com [www.cdnow.com] and select the artist and title of your choice. What does CDnow do to try to convince customers to purchase a CD?

Ordering—Go to Google.com [www.google.com] and search for glasses. Notice the different ways that Google sells advertising space. How are sponsored links different from TV ads and magazine ads for a consumer that wants to order the product?

Exercise 11: The Adaptation of Services to the Internet

The way that services are offered to consumers is changing drastically because of the impact of the Internet. How have the following industries had to change to adapt to this technological change?

Banking—Go to the US Bank homepage [www.usbank.com] and select internet banking from the homepage. Take a look at Citibank [www.citibank.com], eMortgages.com [www.emortgages.com], and Lending Tree [www.lendingtree.com].

Healthcare—Visit one of the following prescription drug sites: Viagra [www.viagra.com], Rogaine [www.rogaine.com], or Prozac [www.prozac.com]. Try one of these sites: Dentists.com [www.dentists.com], Ask a Nurse [www.askanurse.com], or WebMD.com [www.Webmd.com].

Insurance—Log onto Instant Quote [www.instantquote.com] and click on "how it works." How does this compare to the "old" way of buying insurance?

Travel—Visit one of the following travel sites: Cheaptickets.com [www.cheaptickets.com], Travelocity.com [www.travelocity.com], Expedia [www.expedia.com]. How have the growth of these online reservation sites affected the travel agencies? What role do travel agencies *now* play in the marketplace?

Exercise 12: Marketing Communications Techniques in the Internet Age

A blog (weblog) is a personal, contemporary, and sometimes interactive publishing of information on the Internet. Blogging has become an extremely popular activity on the Internet today. Blogs exist for every interest, for every product, and every company. Many major companies have actively incorporated blogging into their marketing communications strategies.

Visit these corporate blogs:

Google [googleblog.blogspot.com/]
Microsoft [blogs.msdn.com/]
Harvard Law School [blogs.law.harvard.edu/]
Stonyfield Farms Dairy [www.stonyfield.com/weblog/]

Visit these consumer-based blogs:

Gizmodo, the gadgets weblog [Gizmodo.com/]
Fast Food News [www.foodfacts.info/blog/]
Digital Music [digitalmusic.weblogsinc.com/]
Cars! Cars! Cars! [carscarscars.blogs.com/]

1. How can the content of consumer blogs affect companies?
2. What marketing communications purposes would a company-supported blog serve?
3. How can companies use the content of blogs to help accomplish corporate objectives?
4. How might blogging by employees adversely affect a company?

Internet Sources of Marketing Information

Part B

Charles Heath *University of Kentucky*

When doing research on a company, there are thousands of sites on the World Wide Web (WWW) that can contain information about your company of choice. For example, a search conducted on Google in June 2005 found 47,200,000 web pages that contained the word "Microsoft"! A similar search found 338,000 pages for Monsanto, a life sciences company. Though far fewer results, it would be impossible to search 338,000 websites for information about the company you are writing your marketing plan about. In fact, a very small percentage of those pages found would contain information that would be of any use!

This section is designed to provide you with a list of sources that would be helpful when uncovering the information necessary to write an insightful case analysis or marketing plan. The list is not in any order, and each company will have different levels of information available at some of these sites. In addition, there are plenty of business resources that are not listed here. The business resource librarian at your university's library will be another *very* valuable resource! Please look beyond this list during your research as well as utilizing these sources. Hopefully this list will help you save hours of time and eliminate the frustration sometimes associated with searching the Internet! Some of these sites may require you to register in order to use the useful parts of their sites.

Search Engines and Directories

The enormous growth of the web has placed a growing strain on the ability of search engines to adequately represent the total number of web pages. In fact, search engines only cover 42 percent of the Web pages that exist online, and the best search engines only retrieve information about 16 percent of them![1] Despite all this, the search engine can be your friend if you use very specific queries. For help don't hesitate to visit the help section that each search site offers!

www.altavista.com—Provides tons of possible results and has an easy-to-use search tool.

www.google.com—Started as a project at Stanford, it is now the web's leading search destination!

www.hotbot.com—Relevance-related results that are usually very relevant!

www.yahoo.com—Best directory with categorized and indexed results.

Corporate Websites

When looking for information, you have to look at the company's own website! It can provide a wealth of information about what they are currently doing in the marketplace. Remember that corporate websites are also designed to lure investors and often provide a great deal of investment-level information just for that purpose. Don't expect to find any company secrets though!

The vast majority of corporate sites have bought their own corporation domain name [**www.microsoft.com, www.abc.com, www.ibm.com**].

Others use abbreviated versions of their company name [Procter & Gamble is **www.pg.com** and Ben and Jerry's is **www.benjerry.com**].

Government

The government, both federal and state levels, collects a great deal of information about companies and industries. This information has always been available in the government references section of your university library. Now, the government has done an admirable

---

[1]Sirapyan, Nancy. Search Sites. ZDNet.com.

job of creating access to this information via Internet sources! Here are a few of the useful government sites.

www.census.gov—The Census Bureau details economic and social descriptors. Includes a handy population tool on the front page.

www.doc.gov—The Commerce Department website contains useful legislative information pertinent to the external environment.

www.dol.gov—The Department of Labor homepage links to labor information, including the Bureau of Labor Statistics.

www.fedstats.gov—Fedstats offers statistics from over 100 federal agencies at one location!

www.loc.gov—The Library of Congress is a vault of information about a great deal of subjects.

www.odci.gov—The CIA website features the *World Factbook,* an excellent resource for international information.

www.sec.gov—Access to the EDGAR database, which has quarterly and annual financial reports that must be filed with the SEC.

Business Publications

Some publications focus their reporting eyes on the business world and are excellent sources of information about companies and today's marketplace. Almost all the major business publications have websites that include stories from the current issue as well as some archives that can be searched. A few of the sites do require a membership to search their archives.

www.adage.com—The world of advertising is at your mouse click with *Advertising Age's* website.

www.adweek.com—Home of *Adweek* and linked to its partners *Brandweek* and *Mediaweek.*

www.barrons.com—*Barrons* online presents some market information for free and full text versions of the print version to subscribers.

www.brandweek.com—Information covering the top brands—the strategies and the people who create them.

www.business2.com—Internet-related issues are featured in the web version of the e-commerce magazine.

www.businessweek.com—Some of the articles are subscription only, but there is some good free information as well.

www.demographics.com—*American Demographics* magazine and its wealth of statistical data can be found here.

www.forbes.com—Access to the type of news, articles, and information that *Forbes* is known for!

www.pathfinder.com—Links to the *Time* magazine homepage, but also links to the *Fortune* and *Money* homepages.

www.salesandmarketing.com—The popular sales publication offers articles online. However, a magazine subscription is needed to search the archieves.

www.sportsbusinessjournal.com—Street & Smith's *Sports Business Journal* is the leading edge of sports marketing information if you are a subscriber or register.

www.thomasregister.com—Information about thousands of U.S. companies, including contact information.

www.usnews.com—More than just college rankings, the online version of *US News & World Report* is a wealth of information!

Newspapers

Major newspapers have also made their presence known on the World Wide Web. Since they focus exclusively on news, they are an excellent online source of business information. While the major newspapers carry a good deal of national information, more regionalized newspapers focus on the business news in their immediate geographic region. Matching a company's headquarters with their local newspaper may result in more information than looking only at the large national papers.

National Papers

www.usatoday.com—America's newspaper has a user-friendly site that contains all the major business news.

www.wsj.com—The business newspaper is a subscription-based service that has archives of its articles online. It might be a good idea to subscribe while you are in college.

www.newsindex.com—This news only search engine looks through more than 250 newspapers online and retrieves all matches to your search request.

Large City Papers

www.nyt.com—The *New York Times* maintains its class and informative content online.

www.chicagotribune.com—The Windy City's newspaper makes it easy to search and find corporate information.

www.washingtonpost.com—From the nation's capital, the *Washington Post* is rich in politically based business news.

International Papers

www.sunday-times.co.uk—Get an international flavor by searching through London's source of business information.

www.financialtimes—If you want international business information, you must look at the *Financial Times.*

Regional Papers

dir.yahoo.com/News_and_Media/Newspapers/By_Region/U_S_States/—Regional newspapers are listed by the state in which they are published.

General Business Sites

In addition to print media and newspapers, there are a number of websites that provide researchers and investors with very timely and in-depth business information. These sites provide news headlines and also allow the researcher to search the site using keywords.

cbs.marketwatch.com—CBS provides business- and investment-based news.

www.cnnmoney.com—A joint venture between the news network CNN and *Money* magazine provides up-to-the-minute information about the marketplace and companies.

www.dailystocks.com—The web's first and largest stock research site is a great way to get a feel for a company and their activities. Tons of additional links that track stock movements and news

globaledge.msu.edu—The Michigan State University–Center for International Business Education and Research (CIBER) maintains a directory of international web resources.

www.hoovers.com—Possibly the best business information site on the Web. Great information from their business search function plus a business directory that links the researcher to even more business information!

www.fool.com—Home of the Motley Fool. Once you register, you have access to tons of information.

knowledge.wharton.upenn.edu—Access to articles and studies about many business topics—after you sign up for free.

www.msnbc.com—This joint venture between Microsoft and NBC television has both event news and business information.

www.reuters.com—Reuters is a leading source of business information with a market focus.

Yahoo! Industry News—If you are doing a report on a specific industry, this page will guide you to all the recent news stories.

Internet Marketing Reference Sites

This collection of sites provides information about Internet marketing or e-commerce issues both B-to-B (business to business) and B-to-C (business to consumer).

www.ClickZ.com—ClickZ has numerous articles that focus on business use of the Internet. The stats page is particularly useful.

www.cnet.com—CNET central is an online information mecca. Information includes personal technology reviews, corporate news stories, downloads, and more.

www.ecommercetimes.com—The E-Commerce Times front page has everything you need to know about doing business online.

www.emarketer.com—eMarketer.com offers tons of good ecommerce focused information.

www.fastcompany.com—Fast Company and its magazine counterpart focus on the e-commerce field.

www.interactiveage.com—Interactive Age provides information about the technical side of the Internet.

www.jupiterresearch.com—Home of Jupiter's research projects. Most of the good information is tantalizingly offered, but registration and even purchase is necessary to reach it.

www.netb2b.com—Business-to-business-based information for marketing and e-commerce strategists.

www.redherring.com—Business information with a tech twist. Some free information, but more in-depth information requires subscription.

www.websense.com—Websense analyzes the use of the Internet in the workplace and offers consultative solutions. Follow the Resources Center link.

wired.com/news/—Wired News contains information about business, culture, politics, and technology.

www.zdnet.com—ZDNet provides business information that focuses on technology firms and advances.

Compilation Sites

The following are sites that have been created and maintained as resources for business-based research.

www.lib.umich.edu/govdocs/stats.html—The University of Michigan's Document Center maintains a listing of web-based statistical resources, including housing, labor, consumers, agriculture, and more.

www.executivelibrary.com/—The Wall Street Executive Library is a compilation of business websites even larger than *this* one.

Section V

Marketing Management Cases

Section I

Essentials of Marketing Management

Section II

Analyzing Marketing Problems and Cases

Section III

Financial Analysis for Marketing Decisions

Knowledge Enhancement

Skill Development

Section VII

Developing Marketing Plans

Section IV

Internet Exercises and Sources of Marketing Information

Section V

Marketing Management Cases

Section VI

Strategic Marketing Cases

Note to the Student

The primary emphasis of the cases in this section is on marketing as a functional business or organizational area. As such, much of the analysis in these cases involves research and selection of appropriate target markets and the development and management of marketing mix variables.

We have divided these cases into six groups to help focus your analysis. These six groups include cases dealing with market opportunity analysis, product strategy, promotion strategy, distribution strategy, pricing strategy, and selected issues in marketing management. However, keep in mind that regardless of how the case is classified, you should not become too focused on a single issue or marketing mix variable and ignore other elements of marketing strategy.

Case Group A

Marketing Opportunity Analysis

Case

1

Abercrombie & Fitch— Early 2005

Jerry C. Olson *Pennsylvania State University*

As you stroll into the store you are greeted by blaring music, racy photos, and a cooler-than-cool "sales force" that doesn't actually try to sell you anything. And if you're over 25, there is a decent chance you are the oldest person in the place. To borrow a phrase from another company's marketing compaign, Abercrombie & Fitch is definitely not your father's clothing store. Although, interestingly, it may have been your grandfather's.

A&F is one of a handful of retail chains that has done a masterful job of appealing to fashion conscious teens and college students. The challenge for A&F, Gap, J. Crew, and others is how to remain relevant to the notoriously fickle youth subculture.

Founded in 1892, A&F was originally an outlet for camping gear. Early in its history, in fact, it outfitted former U.S. President Theodore Roosevelt's African safaris. Later it established a niche selling conservative menswear to an older clientele, but eventually sales plummeted and A&F filed for bankruptcy. The Limited purchased the chain in 1988 and four years later hired Michael Jeffries to oversee A&F operations. Jeffries wanted to shift the company's focus away from, as he describes it, the "70 to death" demographic toward a much younger and faster-growing group—consumers between the ages of 14 and 24. The tweed suits came off the racks, replaced by jeans and T-shirts. It worked. By the time The Limited spun off A&F in 1998, the company was already a hit. Sales exploded from $165 million in 1994 to $2.02 billion in 2004. The number of stores jumped from 36 in 1992 to 351 in 2005. The chain also includes 167 Abercrombie, 271 Hollister, and 5 Ruehl stores.

Jerry C. Olson is the Earl P. Strong Executive Education Professor of Marketing at Pennsylvania State University and a founding partner of Olson-Zaltman Associates.

A recent survey showed A&F to be the sixth coolest brand in the world among kids, out-ranking Levi's and Nintendo. A&F's spot in the pantheon of youth culture was solidified in a hit pop song by the group LFO, who sang about how much they liked girls who "look like Abercrombie and Fitch."

A&F and its direct competitors are appealing to the so-called "echo boom" generation—people born between 1977 and 1994. By 2010 it is estimated that in the United States there will be 34 million people between the ages of 12 and 19. And, unlike previous generations, most of these youths have money to spend and because most of them live at home and have few financial responsibilities, much of that money goes toward clothing.

At an A&F store there is no such thing as a minor detail. According to an analyst at Goldman, Sachs, & Co, "they are very single-minded and very driven. Everything they do is directed to making sure they are truly representative of the lifestyle of their core college-age consumer." A&F unabashedly admits it hires employees based less on skill than on how they look and act. In fact, because A&F believes young people don't like being told what to buy, the sales staff doesn't actually offer sales help. Their job is to greet customers, walk around, and look beautiful. "We're not interested in salespeople or clerks," declared Lonnie Fogel, the director of investor relations. "We're interested in finding people who represent the brand's lifestyle . . . who portray the image of the brand." And management makes certain employees don't deviate from that image. For example, employees can wear only certain kinds of shirts with certain styles of pants. And black shoes are completely forbidden because the company believes they project an undesirable urban street image.

A&F's reach is not limited to its storefront. It is one of only a handful of clothing companies that have successfully targeted young buyers via catalogs. Alloy and the very-hip Delia's also have a large catalog customer base. But A&F's publication, the Quarterly, is more than just a catalog. It has become required reading for people who consider themselves cool. The catalog is filled with erotic photographs of scantily clad co-eds and buff frat boys cavorting on the beach or caught in compromising positions. A recent Christmas catalog included a fake interview with a mall Santa purported to be a pedophile along with sexual advice from a renowned porn star. Older folks—including the Michigan attorney general—expressed their concern and A&F agreed to distribute the publication only to those over 18. But one can assume the controversy and establishment outrage probably made the catalog (and the brand) all the more appealing to A&F's younger clientele.

How does any company remain popular and keep up with what fashions young people consider cool? It's not easy. Thanks to the Internet and MTV the concept of "fashionable" has become a constantly moving target. Wet Seal is a company that specializes in "club" clothing. Its president Ed Thomas says, "The market is all about change. You have to constantly reinvent yourself to attract people to your store and that's constantly a challenge." The Limited, A&F's former sister chain, was once hailed for its skill at keeping pace with youth fashion trends. But somewhere along the line it lost its touch. In 1998 a $40 million operating loss forced The Limited to close stores. A&F is trying to keep pace with its customers by filling its merchandising and design staffs with people right out of college—young people who already live the A&F lifestyle. Plus, the company employs a team of "field editors"—college students from all over the United States who provide weekly reports on the latest fashion and lifestyle trends.

Despite A&F's success, it is wrong to assume it has a monopoly on the youth market. Some elements of that subculture don't find the A&F lifestyle or clothing to be very appealing. "A lot of my friends think Abercrombie's kind of silly, between the way they advertise with magazines and their high prices," says Erik Lappinen, a high school senior from New Jersey. Another New Jersey high school student, Kristen Ricciardi, agrees. "I'd rather buy the same clothes from The Gap or American Eagle and not have the company's name on my shirt." Gap, Inc.'s Old Navy stores—with their $8 T-shirts and $25 cargo pants—appeal to those who want to keep pace with fashion, but who won't pay A&F's prices. Of course, there are some young people who want to get as far away as possible from the A&F lifestyle and sense of fashion. At the 270-store Hot Topic chain you can buy patent leather military boots, hair dye, vinyl pants, and even jewelry for your pierced tongue.

Why have A&F and other companies been so successful marketing to teens and college students? It is largely because they appeal to a sense of belonging that is especially important to people in this age group. "These young people want to be with one another," says the 60-year-old Jeffries. "That is totally different. My generation grew up as loners." So while the definition of what is fashionable may vary from person to person, most young people do feel social pressure to wear clothes and live a lifestyle that others in their peer group consider to be cool.

Of course, there is a catch-22. How cool is too cool? Airwalk initially marketed its shoes to teens who were part of a more alternative subculture. But eventually so many people were wearing Airwalks that the brand was perceived as being mainstream and therefore not appropriate footwear for someone truly avant-garde. Now the company is trying to reshape its image to become more relevant to those in its original target market. So, somewhat paradoxically, while young people seek social acceptance, they also want to retain some sense of individuality. As one teen said about A&F, "No one wants to admit they shop at a store because it's cool."

In sum, it is a never-ending battle for companies like A&F. Cultural tastes change, fashions change, established competitors redouble their efforts, and new competitors spring up seemingly out of nowhere. To remain a major player in the youth clothing market for the long haul requires an intelligent marketing strategy and an accurate feel for the ever-changing lifestyles of young consumers.

Discussion Questions

1. Companies like J. Crew (**http://www.jcrew.com**) and Banana Republic (**http://www. bananarepublic.com)** are targeting many of the same consumers as Abercrombie & Fitch. Visit their websites and discuss how their marketing strategies are different from those of A&F. Would you suggest any changes in these strategies that would allow these two companies to better position themselves in the minds of consumers?

2. The success of specialty clothing stores has come at the expense of large department stores like Sears and J.C. Penney. What can department stores do to make themselves more relevant to the youth subculture?

3. Check out the Hot Topic website (**http://www.hottopic.com**). Compare the submarkets (subsubcultures) Hot Topic is aiming for with those of Abercrombie & Fitch. Identify the behaviors, affective responses, and cognitions most important in shopping at each store.

4. How can A&F guard against becoming too mainstream and experiencing a customer backlash? Do you believe it is possible for A&F to remain popular with young shoppers for a span of many years?

5. Both A&F and The Gap are trying to use their brand names to market clothing to different age groups. For example, A&F has opened a chain of children's stores called abercrombie (lowercase "a"), while Gap, Inc. has had success with GapKids and BabyGap. Discuss the advantages and potential disadvantages of such a diversification strategy.

Sources: Robert Berner, "Flip-Flops, Torn Jeans—and Control," *BusinessWeek,* May 30, 2005, pp. 68–70. Lauren Goldstein, "The Alpha Teenager," *Fortune,* December 20, 1999, pp. 201–204; Rebecca Quick, "Is Ever-So-Hip Abercrombie & Fitch Losing Its Edge With Teens?" *The Wall Street Journal,* February 22, 2000, pp. B1, B4; Abigail Goldman, "Store Most Likely to Succeed: A&F," *Los Angeles Times,* April 3, 1999, p. 3; Stephanie Stoughton, "Listening to the 'Echo Boom,'" *Washington Post,* March 6, 1999, pp. E1, E3; abercrombie.com.

2

McDonald's Corporation in the New Millennium

J. Paul Peter and Ashish Gokhale *University of Wisconsin–Madison*

Jack Greenberg, CEO of McDonald's Corporation, stared into the clear September skies thinking about the "Big Mac Attack." At one time, the term was an advertising slogan referring to a craving for a McDonald's Big Mac burger. However, "Big Mac Attack" now referred to McDonald's earnings declines in the late 1990s and early 2000s. Dynamic market expansion, new products, and special promotional strategies had made McDonald's Corporation a leader of the fast-food industry. However, sales growth in the United States had slowed to below the industry average in recent years. Jack Greenberg was trying to decide on a set of appropriate strategies for the future in order to reverse the declines and to stay ahead of competition.

The Fast-Food Industry

Years of profit drains and flat sales are driving fast-food chains to find new marketing strategies to compete in a mature market. While McDonald's and most other hamburger chains continue discounting and offering a variety of new products to attract customers, they also seek to shed their "cheap and greasy" image with new store designs. Major competitors in the hamburger segment of the fast-food industry in order of annual sales are McDonalds, Burger King, Wendy's, and Hardees.

Since these chains recognize the importance of drive-through customers (65 percent of sales), they are all trying to increase the speed of drive-through delivery. Strategies include using timers to encourage employees to prepare and deliver food faster, training employees in faster food preparation methods, having separate kitchens and food preparation facilities for drive-through customers, and even windshield responders that automatically bill customers. Drive-through sales are expected to grow three times faster than on-premise sales. It is estimated that increasing drive-through efficiency by 10 percent increases average fast-food restaurant sales by $54,000. The average fast-food restaurant has sales of about $560,000 per year.

J. Paul Peter is James R. McManus–Bascom Professor in Marketing and Ashish Gokhale was a Project Assistant at the University of Wisconsin–Madison.

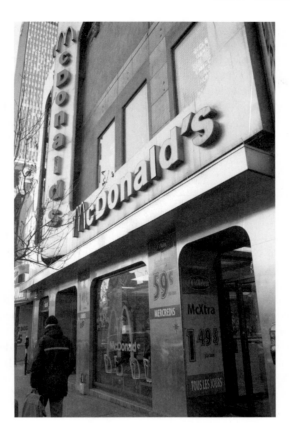

Another segment of the fast-food industry is comprised of a number of non-hamburger fast-food restaurants. Major players in this segment include Pizza Hut, KFC (Kentucky Fried Chicken), and Taco Bell. Sales in these restaurants have grown faster than hamburger chains in recent years. A growing trend is the move by customers to non-hamburger sandwiches. Subway dominates the market with more than 13,200 U.S. outlets. Prepared meals and sandwiches available in supermarkets, convenience stores, and gas stations are competitors as are the variety of microwave meals available to consumers.

Another trend is the recognition of the importance of heavy users of fast-food restaurants. It is estimated that heavy users comprise 20 percent of customers but account for 60 percent of all visits. Some of these customers visit fast-food restaurants 20 times per month and spend up to $40 per day in them. Heavy users have been described as single males, under 30 years of age, who have working class jobs, love loud music, don't read much and hang out with friends.

A major change in the fast-food industry is the increase in the fast-casual segment that includes restaurants like Boston Market, Panera Bread Company and Atlanta Bread Company. These chains offer deli sandwiches and meals that are more upscale than traditional fast food, served in nicer restaurants with more comfortable surroundings, but faster than in traditional restaurants. It is estimated that the fast-casual sector is growing from 15 to 20 percent per year, while growth in the quick service sector is only about 2 percent a year. "People are willing to pay a couple dollars more for a better dining experience, yet don't want to sacrifice the convenience of quick service. Fast-casual combines all the elements for what the on-the-go consumer—which seems to be almost everyone these days—is looking for," said one analyst.[1]

[1]Mitchell Speiser, analyst at Lehman Brothers

Americans are eating out less often compared to previous years and eating habits are changing.[2] Though the recession is a major reason why folks aren't eating out as much at upscale restaurants, it's another story at fast-food restaurants. Many younger consumers are getting tired of fast food and are thinking about their health. There seems to be a growing dissatisfaction with the quality aspect of the McDonald's and Burger Kings of the world. It's not just young adults who are turning away from fast food. Baby boomers are also looking for "better" alternatives and fast food is not as appealing to this large group who frequently eat out.

McDonald's Corporation

McDonald's systemwide sales for 2001 were over $40 billion, but net income shrunk 17 percent to $1.64 billion, as shown in the exhibit. McDonald's U.S. market share remained above that of competitors, but grew more slowly. Its share was up 2.2 percent in 2000 compared to 2.7 percent growth for Burger King Corp. and 2.5 percent for Wendy's International.[3]

Looking for hits to reverse earnings declines, McDonald's accelerated plans for "New Tastes Menu" items.[4] Products for limited-time offers included a fried chicken sandwich of tenderloin strips under the Chicken Selects name, a new grilled chicken sandwich, a brownie, a pork tenderloin sandwich, and a Philly cheese steak sandwich. Facing competitors' chicken sandwiches, like Wendy's Spicy Chicken Filet and Burger King's Chicken Whopper, McDonald's put chicken menu items at the forefront of its offerings. The chain

EXHIBIT **McDonald's Corporation Summary of Financial Data 1997–2001**

Dollars in Millions, Except per Share Data	2001	2000	1999	1998	1997
Franchised sales	$ 24,838	24,463	23,830	22,330	20,863
Company-operated sales	$ 11,040	10,467	9,512	8,895	8,136
Affiliated sales	$ 4,752	5,251	5,149	4,754	4,639
Total Systemwide Sales	$ 40,630	40,181	38,491	35,979	33,638
Total revenues	$ 14,870	14,243	13,259	12,421	11,409
Operating Income	$ 2,697	3,330	3,320	2,762	2,808
Income before taxes	$ 2,330	2,882	2,884	2,307	2,407
Net income	$ 1,637	1,977	1,948	1,550	1,642
Cash provided by operations	$ 2,688	2,751	3,009	2,766	2,442
Capital expenditures	$ 1,906	1,945	1,868	1,879	2,111
Free cash flow	$ 782	806	1,141	887	331
Treasury stock purchases	$ 1,090	2,002	933	1,162	765
Financial position at year end					
Total assets	$ 22,535	21,684	20,983	19,784	18,242
Total debt	$ 8,918	8,474	7,252	7,043	6,463
Total shareholders' equity	$ 9,488	9,204	9,639	9,465	8,852
Shares outstanding IN MILLIONS	1,280.7	1,304.9	1,350.8	1,356.2	1,371.4
Total Systemwide Restaurants	30,093	28,707	26,309	24,513	22,928

[2]Harris Interactive, December 2001

[3]*Advertising Age;* Chicago; Mar 18, 2002; Kate MacArthur

[4]*Brandweek;* New York; Mar 11, 2002; Bob Sperber

also added a chicken-honey biscuit item to its menu. Other entries included a breakfast steak burrito similar to an existing sausage version, hot dog McNuggets for kids, and an Italian-style burger similar to the Chicken Parmesan. The McRib sandwich was reintroduced.

McDonald's advertising message focused on tasty and nutritious food, friendly folks, and fun. The company invested heavily in advertising its product and improving its public image. McDonald's annual Charity Christmas Parade in Chicago and its Ronald McDonald House charity provide the company with a positive corporate image. Much of its promotional budget was spent on games, giveaways and deals, including Monopoly II, Scrabble, a Kraft salad dressing give-away, Happy Meals, plush toys, in-store kid videos, and various Big Mac-related deals.

McDonald's opened its first domestic McCafe with the expectation that the gourmet coffee shop would move it closer to its goal of doubling sales at existing U.S. restaurants over the next decade.[5] The 32-seat McCafe occupies a 900-square-foot space that shares an entrance with a traditional McDonald's restaurant. The menu features a selection of specialty drinks, including cappuccinos, lattes, teas and fruit smoothies served via a limited service front counter. Enhancing the coffee bar is a glass display case filled with a variety of high-end cakes, pastries, cookies and soft pretzels. Customers can place carryout orders that are packaged in disposable containers. If patrons opt to dine in the cafe, all drinks and food items are served on china with stainless steel flatware. McCafe originated in Australia in 1993 and has grown to more than 300 units in 17 countries. The gourmet coffee concept was created to be placed within or adjacent to existing McDonald's restaurants. McDonald's estimates that the new concept will boost sales by 15 percent. At McCafe, cappuccino drinks start at $2.49 featuring a coffee imported from Italy. The drink menu includes specialty coffees, listed as "Caramel Cream Steamer," "French Vanilla" and "Milky Way." The pastries, including tiramisu, cheesecake, apple tart and muffins, range in price from $1.59 to $2.59. Many of the items are baked on-site and the others are prepared daily by various local suppliers. In addition to three on-premise bakers, the cafe has a staff of 15 with about six employees working each shift. Created to enhance an upscale coffee shop environment, the cafe's decor features lace curtains, mahogany accents, a leather couch, an antique mirror, wall sconces and fresh flowers.

Major Competitors in the Hamburger Segment

McDonald's has three major competitors in the hamburger segment. These include Burger King, Hardee's and Wendy's. Both Burger King and Wendy's have had small gains in market share while Hardee's lost share.

Burger King Corp.

Burger King Corp., in its ongoing effort to increase sales and market share, offered a new salad line and a permanent array of value-priced offerings, endeavors already under way at its fast-food competitors. The nation's No. 2 burger chain, hoping to show signs of a turnaround in order to expedite its pending separation from parent Diageo PLC of London, debuted more than 10 new or improved products, including the Chicken Whopper, which officials said stimulated sales growth. The menu overhaul is one part of a major turnaround strategy engineered by Burger King's chairman and chief executive, John Dasburg, who joined the chain in 2000.

As part of BK's sweeping transformation program, restaurant operators had to make extensive kitchen and drive-through upgrades. The Chicken Whopper, which debuted in 2001,

[5]*Nation's Restaurant News;* New York; May 14, 2001

generated "an enormous amount of trial" that led to double-digit same-store-sales growth at restaurants. Burger King is developing a more permanent marketing strategy and moving away from its previous tactical approach, which revolved around the monthly changes in menu items and deals.

Hardee's

Hardee's parent, CKE Restaurants Inc., owns or franchises 2,784 Hardee's and 112 Taco Bueno restaurants and showed a 15-percent decline in net income in a recent quarter. The chain posted year-to-year quarterly declines of 4.8 percent in company-owned same-store sales. The efforts to reverse slowing but continuing sales erosion at Hardee's, the industry's No. 4 burger chain, had dominated management's attention in its conversion of Hardee's to a format called "Star Hardee's."

The company attempted to reverse sliding sales by introducing new items on the menu and joining the price-promotion burger wars. The company tested individual item discounts at most of Hardee's company-owned units. Franchisees in selected markets offered sandwiches bundled with regular-sized French fries and a soft drink for $2.99. Other new Hardee's sales-spiking tactics included its mid-priced sandwich option, the Famous Bacon Cheeseburger for $1.59, and a new Croissant Sunrise breakfast sandwich for $1.79. The chain hoped to increase breakfast sales by at least 2 percent; currently breakfast items account for approximately 10 percent of Hardee's sales.

CKE also owns or franchises 878 upscale fast-food chains, Carl's Jr. It rolled out a premium sandwich product that had first debuted on the Hardee's menu in 1994 and recently was second only to the Carl's Jr.'s $3.99 sirloin steak sandwich in trial markets.

Wendy's International

Wendy's has had the strongest same-store-sales gains of the major burger chains in recent years. Chain officials and Wall Street analysts attributed at least part of the growth to Wendy's line of four upscale salads called "Garden Sensations." The nation's No. 3 burger chain holds an enviable position—analysts consistently rank it ahead of chief rivals in quality, customer satisfaction, innovation, and unit-level sales. Citing Wendy's planned 30 percent boost in media outlays to an estimated $308 million in 2002 and its strong focus on in-store operations, one analyst stated, "This one-two punch looks like a formidable foe for rival chains to face this year."[6] Wendy's same-store sales were expected to grow 3 percent in 2002, eclipsing the 2 percent projections for Tricon Global Restaurants' Taco Bell and KFC, and a 1 percent to 2 percent projection for McDonald's Corp.

Wendy's product line includes four core menu items: burgers, chicken sandwiches, its value menu, and its Garden Sensations salads. The salad line is designed to provide custom taste comparable to salads offered by casual-dining chains and includes the $3.99 Chicken BLT, Taco Supremo, Mandarin Chicken and $2.99 Spring Mix salads. The Garden Sensations line was expected to contribute 5 percent to total Wendy's sales.[7]

Major Competition in the Non-hamburger Segment

The gradual shift of consumer preference toward hamburger substitutes has created strong competitors for McDonald's. Three of the major competitors offering non-hamburger fast foods are Pizza Hut, Kentucky Fried Chicken and Taco Bell.

---

[6] Mark Kalinowski, restaurant analyst for Salomon Smith Barney
[7] Merrill Lynch analyst Peter Oakes, January 2002

Pizza Hut

Pizza Hut dominates the pizza segment with 22 percent of all restaurant pizza sales in the country, with Domino's lagging far behind with about 11 percent of sales. Papa John's has steadily expanded to the point where it is the country's 4th largest pizza chain behind Little Caesars.

Pizza Hut is owned by Tricon Global Restaurants, which also owns KFC and Taco Bell. It scored a major success with its P'Zone, a portable, calzone-like item that company officials call "the pizza that actually sold out in test market."[8] The $70 million national product launch featured the P'Zone for $5.99, or two for $10.99. Each pie is made with a 12-inch traditional crust, a layer of sliced mozzarella cheese and a choice of three different ingredient combinations: pepperoni; a mixture of meats that includes pepperoni, sausage, beef and ham; or sausage with green peppers and red onions. The P'Zone exceeded expectations and drove same-store sales up 7 percent to 8 percent. Pizza Hut's latest effort was called "a well-executed, differentiated, yet value-oriented product that would drive traffic and sales over the next several periods"[9] by one industry analyst.

KFC

KFC (Kentucky Fried Chicken) operates 11,000 global outlets of which 5,400 are in the U.S. Its recent strategies included a "Kids Lap Top Pack" meal program, to attract more kids and families to its food offerings. KFC planned to introduce the meals as part of its new product lineup for 2002.[10] Roughly 80 percent of KFC's domestic stores signed up to offer the kids' meals, which featured more food and variety of choices. The meals are priced at $2.99 and offer 18 different food combinations. The kids' meal containers, designed to open as a laptop computer, featured colorfully illustrated interactive puzzles and games. The idea builds upon the latest batch of kids' meals launched previously, which introduced an education theme with crossword puzzles, word searches and mazes. KFC took away the staple of most kids meals—the plastic toy—after company research found that children, especially older ones, were not interested in them. Instead, the new meals included stickers or a paper-based prize. The chain doesn't expect the new meal to generate substantial returns immediately. "This is about brand building; it's not about building sales today,"[11] said a company spokesperson.

Other new products at KFC for 2002 included a meal of three spicy Blazin' Crispy Strips with a choice of side and a biscuit priced at $2.99 and the Blazin' Buffalo Twister sandwich and a beverage in the price range of $2.29 to $2.79. In fiscal 2001, KFC led its sister brands, Pizza Hut and Taco Bell, in same-store sales at U.S. company-owned stores, posting growth of 3 percent.

Taco Bell

The dramatic rebound in sales at Taco Bell and a 19 percent increase in 2001 profits were due to a strategy shift to higher-priced products, like the Grilled Stuft Burrito and Chicken Quesadilla.[12] Taco Bell's success with high-priced offerings proved that the brand could leverage its strengths to bring up the average meal price, as well as appeal to light and medium users.[13] Taco Bell planned to add more grilled extensions with higher quality tortillas, beef and beans, and sell them at non-discounted prices. Officials said Taco Bell would continue to experiment with ingredients, such as fish and pork, that are unique to fast food.

---

[8] *Nation's Restaurant News;* New York; Feb 11, 2002; Amy Zuber

[9] John Ivankoe of J. P Morgan Securities in New York

[10] Cynthia Koplos, KFC's director of marketing.

[11] Cynthia Koplos, KFC's director of marketing.

[12] *Nation's Restaurant News;* New York; Feb 25, 2002; Amy Zuber

[13] Salomon Smith Barney analyst Mark Kalinowski

McDonald's Future

Jack Greenberg recognized the difficult task the company faced in trying to grow sales, market share and profits in a fiercely competitive industry. He recognized the strengths of competitors in the burger segment but also knew that other providers of fast food and other meals were quick to take advantage of changes in customer preferences and tastes. He knew he had to counter attack the "Big Mac Attack" and find market opportunities for McDonald's.

Discussion Questions

1. How are customer tastes changing in the fast-food industry? What impact do these changes have on McDonald's?
2. How well are these changes in customer tastes and preferences being reflected in competitive strategies in the industry?
3. What are McDonald's strengths and weaknesses and what conclusions do you draw about its future?
4. Should McDonald's develop a separate strategy for the heavy user segment of the fast food industry?
5. What should Jack Greenberg do to grow sales, profits, and market share at McDonald's?

Case 3

Campus Calendar

William R. Wynd *Eastern Washington University*

Eastern Washington University is one of four regional universities in Washington State. Operated on a quarter system, enrollment is around 8,200 students, most of whom are residents of Spokane County. Academic programs at Eastern feature liberal arts, education, business, and science.

Spokane, Washington's second largest city, is 16 miles east. The county is a metro area with over 356,000 people. It is a banking, health care, and distribution center for a portion of three states designated as the "Inland Empire."

As part of a class in basic marketing, eight junior students became so interested in marketing that they banded together for the purpose of applying what they were learning. With the help of their instructor they formed a partnership called CI (Collegiate Images). They sought to develop and market a product for the express purpose of making enough money to fund their senior year tuition of $500 per quarter and gain some practical experience in business.

Over a period of several weeks in the fall quarter they sought to narrow a list of potential products. Three limitations helped purge their list almost immediately. First, each could raise no more than $500 for start-up capital. Second, the venture could require no more than an average of about 15 hours per week per student. Third, if they were to market a product the following fall, only nine months remained for planning and production. Applying these criteria they screened a list and determined that a calendar featuring Eastern students posed in campus settings would be a likely candidate.

The idea of a campus calendar is not new. Several other schools in the Pacific Northwest had produced calendars at one time or another. Since the marketing research section of their beginning course had taught them to start by finding out what others had done, they developed a questionnaire and conducted a telephone survey; the results of that survey are in Table 1. Based on the results of the survey, the students concluded that quality was particularly important. Visual inspection of sample calendars sent by the survey respondents emphasized that the quality of printing, paper, and photography contributed greatly to the product image. The size of the calendar varied from a folded size of $8\frac{1}{2}'' \times 11''$, which was considered small, to $12'' \times 12''$, which was considered large. The large size calendar

This case was prepared by William R. Wynd of Eastern Washington University as a basis for class discussion rather than to illustrate either effective or ineffective handling of a managerial situation.

TABLE 1   Comparison of Calendars

Questions	U of M	OSU	U of O	USC
1. Size of market	18,000	15,000	18,000	International Market
2. What type of calendar did you produce? M—Male F—Female B—Both on same page.	F	F	F	M & F
3. Was it a: B—full-body shot S—swimsuit M—mixed	M	M	M	F—swimsuit M—head
4. Did you produce in: B/W—blk/white C—color	C	C	B/W	C
5. Who did your photography? T—themselves C—contracted out	C	C	T	C
6. What calendar year did you use? S—school year C—calendar year	C	C	C	C
7. Did you put advertising on the calendar?	Yes	No	Yes	No
8. What was your unit price?	$3–$4	$6.95	$5–$6	$7.95 $8.95–$9.95
9. How many did you sell?	3,300	6,500	1,000	International Market
10. How did you sell them? R—retail W—wholesale B—both	W	W	W	B
11. Sponsor?	Miller Beer	Several Businesses	Coors Beer	No sponsor

produced at USC on heavyweight stock was the most attractive. But the survey left many unanswered questions about what was wanted in a product and what information was needed to develop strategies for pricing, promotion, and distribution.

Several focus groups were held to determine how students use a calendar and what they wanted in terms of quality, price, and character of poses. The focus groups revealed that students need a place to write notes and reminders. Normally they try to find a calendar with a date page that is large enough for this purpose. However, most students receive free calendars and so may not specifically purchase a calendar with a large date page. In addition most students, particularly full-time students living on campus or off campus in Cheney, said they would be interested in a calendar featuring Eastern students indicating some school spirit. Older students and many of those who commuted, however, were not interested. They came to Eastern for an education, worked in their spare time, and did not come to the campus except for their classes.

Women said they would like a calendar featuring men, and men said they would like a calendar featuring women in swimsuits. Most said they would prefer a fairly large calendar, especially if it featured attractive pictures.

Information from the focus groups was used to generate a measurement instrument. This one-page questionnaire was administered to 329 students in classes selected at random at a time and on a day when most students attended classes. Results of the survey are shown in Exhibit 1. A check with records in the Office of the Registrar indicated that the proportion

EXHIBIT 1 Questionnaire

We are students in a marketing class at Eastern Washington University. We are conducting a survey to decide the possibility of a campus calendar. We would appreciate your answer to the following questions. Please answer fully and honestly; all information is anonymous. Thank you for your time and trouble.

1. We would like to produce a quality E.W.U. campus calendar. We plan to use students from the campus as models. Would you be interested in a calendar with only E.W.U. students in it?
   253 (a) yes   76 (b) no
2. What kind of models would you prefer in a single calendar?
   49 (a) all male   62 (c) alternating males and females
   110 (b) all female   108 (d) male & female on the same page
3. What kind of photo poses would you prefer? (Check all that apply):
   107 (a) fully clothed body shot   36 (c) face and chest shot
   12 (b) swimsuit body shot   86 (d) partially clothed
4. What starting date would you prefer?
   132 (a) a calendar year, starting in January
   181 (b) school year, starting in September
5. Would you buy the calendar?
   105 (a) for yourself   32 (b) as a gift   192 (c) not at all
6. If we produce a calendar which is pleasing to you what is the most you would be willing to pay?
   0 (a) $12   19 (b) $10   48 (c) $8   70 (d) $6
7. What is your age?
   135 (a) 18–21   80 (b) 22–24   54 (c) 25–29   60 (d) over 29
8. What is your sex?
   150 (a) male   179 (b) female
9. Where do you reside?
   161 (a) off campus, commute   61 (b) on campus
   107 (c) off campus (Cheney)
10. What is your class standing?
    41 (a) freshman   55 (b) sophomore   82 (c) junior   151 (d) senior

of sexes, ages, and class standings in the sample closely matched that of the student body. Ninety-three percent of the student body was classified as full time.

Several cross tabulations were run on the data. These revealed that 54 percent of the students who expressed interest in the calendar were male. In addition, 68 percent of those who said they were interested lived on campus or in Cheney. Seniors were less interested than underclassmen. Student preferences for poses are shown in Table 2. Most males preferred females in swimsuits, whereas most females preferred males with their clothes on.

Several printers were contacted to obtain quotes. There were variations in both price and quality. Production quotes for the best quality and price combination are shown in Table 3.

There was a minimum order of 2,000, and 15 percent for each additional 500. Production costs included paper, printing, and binding. Typesetting was an extra $1,000.

Since the pictures were the central part of the product they had to be of good quality. A number of professional photographers were asked to submit their portfolios. The best work was far ahead of the rest. Their charge was $250 per setting with a minimum of 12 settings. This price included travel, set-up charges, several negatives, and a final camera-ready print.

Selecting the students to pose for the pictures was a problem. One idea was to have students nominate whom they wanted in the pictures. One of the student partners in Collegiate Images was an amateur photographer and agreed to take the preliminary snapshots that would later be screened by another group of students. Film and developing costs were estimated at $75.

TABLE 2   **Student Preferences for Poses**

Pose	Male	Female
Fully clothed body shot	42	63
Swimsuit body shot	70	52
Face and chest shot	21	14
Partially clothed shot	45	38

TABLE 3   **Production Costs**

Weight of Cover Stock	Size of Calendar	
	Small	Large
Light	$6,920	$ 9,829
Heavy	8,000	12,040

Distribution was also a problem. The campus bookstore offered to take 1,000 calendars at a markup on the cost of 40 percent. A booth in a high traffic area of the Student Union Building could be rented for $2 per day as long as it was connected with a student project. A booth could also be set up in the stadium at the homecoming football game. There were other possibilities but a strategy decision would have to be made about intensive, selective, or exclusive distribution before outlets could be selected.

Promotion possibilities included interviews with the local student newspaper and announcements in the *FOCUS,* a daily flyer available to all students in all buildings on campus. A member of Collegiate Images could also appear as a guest on a talk show aired by the student radio station. None of these activities cost money. On the other hand, an ad in the student newspaper about the size of the date page of the large-size calendar would cost $140. The *Easterner* is published weekly with a press run of 6,000. Flyers about the same size were estimated to cost about $2.50 in quantities of 100.

By this time it was evident that there was not enough money available to meet start-up costs even at the minimum order of 2,000. Someone suggested that an advertiser might be interested in sponsoring a portion of the calendar. Three of the other universities surveyed had sponsors. Advertising consisted of a corporate logo in the background of the date page. Students felt that if accepted, advertisements should be tasteful.

There was a lot of work to be done before attempting to secure sponsorship. A business plan would have to be made on how many calendars to produce, the exact composition of poses, the calendar start date, price, distribution, and promotion strategy. A price for advertising sponsorship for all or a portion of the calendar would have to be established. Everyone knew that the success of the project depended on the amount of creativity used in developing and implementing a marketing strategy.

Case **4**

3DV-LS:[1] Assessing Market Opportunity in the Computer Visualization Market

Robin Habeger *Iowa State University*

Kay M. Palan *Iowa State University*

As Pat Patterson, director of the 3DV Litigation Services business unit, was reviewing the second quarter sales numbers, he sighed heavily and rubbed his temples in an attempt to avert an impending migraine blooming behind his eyes. The sales numbers were disappointing, to say the least. In fact, sales had been low over the last four quarters. Sales had dried up on the east and west coasts because of increased competition, resulting in an alarming 16% average sales decline each of the last four quarters. 3DV had recently reorganized several of its business units, closing some and combining others. To avoid a similar fate, it was imperative that Litigation Services post increasing sales and profits. The decline in sales, Pat knew, put the business unit in jeopardy.

Pat sighed again as his mind ran through the available options. He could give the marketing and sales efforts more time to increase sales. A new Web page, giving the unit improved Internet presence, would soon be implemented, which might spark some sales activity. But, as he pondered the situation, Pat believed that it would take more than this to reverse the declining sales trend. When he joined the company in the mid-1990s as a salesman, he shared a cubicle with three other people. He remembered the lean days when it was touch and go as to whether or not he would even get a paycheck. Now, in December 2000, he had his own corner office. He had helped build the Litigation Services unit into the nationwide competitor it now was. Pat was determined to overcome the recent sales decline. He had invested too much of his own time and energy into the business unit to let it fail now.

[1]The name of the company and the principal players in this case were disguised to protect the competitive interests of 3DV-LS.

Reprinted by permission from the *Case Research Journal*, volume 22, issue 1. Copyright 2002 by Robin Habeger, Kay M. Palan, and the North American Research Association. All rights reserved.

Just then, Pat heard a knock on his door. Glancing up, he saw Lance Wolffe, one of 3DV-LS's project managers. Lance had an air of excitement about him. "Pat, I've got to show you this magazine article I came across last night!" He tossed the magazine into Pat's hands and continued, "The article discusses how some construction and transportation projects are beginning to use computer-generated models to help clients visualize finished projects—that's something we could be doing, only better!"

Pat briefly looked at the civil engineering trade magazine turned to the article Lance had marked. Pat, too, could see that the kind of computer visualization process used by 3DV might be transferable to other industries such as the construction and transportation industries illustrated in the article. But any enthusiasm Pat shared with Lance was tempered by the realization that entering a new market would take time and resources, and, in the end, might not be any more fruitful than improving the unit's marketing efforts.

To Lance, he said, "It certainly does look like there's some potential for us to expand our efforts into other markets, but there's a lot of information we need to know before we make such a decision. Let's make a list of questions we need to answer."

Pat and Lance created a list of questions to answer regarding this new market opportunity. The list addressed issues such as quantifying market potential, determining 3DV-LS's competitive advantage, and identifying threats and weaknesses to market entry.

As the list grew longer, Lance observed, "What we essentially need to do is a cost/benefit analysis."

Pat agreed, but added, "We need to focus our analysis just on the construction and transportation industries, but we also need to compare the results of the cost/benefit analysis to maintaining the status quo. If we can't demonstrate that entry into this new market will be profitable in a reasonable period of time, then we just won't be able to do it."

Lance felt his bubble burst. He really felt in his gut that expanding 3DV-LS's technological capabilities to the construction and transportation industries was the right thing to do. He grew quiet for a few minutes, trying to settle his desire for immediate market entry.

Finally he said, "We do need to go into this with our eyes open and that means finding as much information as we can. Where do you want me to start?"

"At the beginning," Pat replied. "Find out everything you can about the customers and competitors in the construction and transportation industries, the costs and profits, the attractiveness of the market. You should probably ask Sandy to help you. Since she is in charge of marketing she will have some idea where to find the information you need. Let's plan to meet again in a couple of weeks to review the situation."

As Lance turned to leave, Pat allowed himself a momentary glimmer of hope—could this be the break 3DV-LS needed to improve sales and profitability?

3DV: History of the Company

3DV, founded in 1988 for the purpose of accurately creating 3-D accident reconstructions, used a revolutionary programming code developed by the founders. Attorneys, representing automobile manufacturers, hired 3DV to construct visual animations of automobile accidents. These visualizations were used in court cases to demonstrate how an automobile accident had most likely occurred.

Although the company's primary focus in the early years was accident reconstruction for automobile manufacturers, by 1999 3DV had several distinct products and services, each targeting a select market. For example, using the basis of the original programming code, 3DV developed several different types of software packages that allowed manufacturing companies to use the Internet for project collaboration and visualization. That is, the software enabled employees in different locations to view, modify, and work with the same 3-D model simultaneously, while at the same time maintaining secure online access. Another product helped companies in various industries improve the ergonomics of product designs and workplace tasks. Companies could use still other 3DV software to cost-effectively model and view an entire 2-D/3-D manufacturing facility by designing optimal factory floor plans and testing efficiency through virtual simulation. 3DV provided software support and training and implementation services for all of its software products.

3DV's software had revolutionized the visualization industry. Relative to other companies that provided computer visualization, 3DV produced animation and 3-D models that were the highest quality visualizations available. Consequently, although 3DV had once been fairly unknown, it now enjoyed an international reputation, having served such customers as General Motors, Ford, Toyota, Honda, Eastman Kodak, Lockheed Martin, Johnson & Johnson, Dow Chemical Company, and Motorola. Moreover, 3DV had benefited from the public trading frenzy accorded to high-tech companies in the mid-90s.

But 3DV's fortunes in the last few years had not been good. The stock price had reached a high of $72, but it was currently trading under $20, and the company as a whole had reported a net operating loss of over $40 million in 1999. As a result, 3DV had gone through two major restructurings within the last two years. It closed several business units that fell outside of its core competencies. A second reduction in support staff (human resources, technical support, etc.) followed the first by approximately six to eight months. Although 3DV still employed approximately 600 people worldwide, managers were aware that additional staff reductions were possible in unprofitable business units.

3DV: The Litigation Services Business Unit

From the outset, 3DV had created a specialized business unit, known as 3DV Litigation Services, to focus specifically on litigation visualization services. 3DV Litigation Services (3DV-LS) specialized in animation and 3-D models for attorneys to use as displays or demonstrative evidence in court cases. 3DV-LS offered some additional visualization services, including secure on-line project management workspace, DVD presentation systems, digitally altered photographs for use as before versus after displays, videotape production, and visuals needed for presentation materials. 3DV-LS differentiated itself from other visualization providers by using computers to hardware render the frames (individual pictures) used to make an animation (see Exhibit 1). This method, relative to the more commonly used software rendering,

EXHIBIT 1   **Definitions for Computer Visualization Terms**

Term	Definition
Animation	A group of computer-rendered frames shown in a sequential manner to portray movement or show a specific angle. It takes 1,800 frames to make one minute of animation.
3-D model	A computer-generated picture of a virtual 3-D object usually created in a CAD package that contains all the spatial information (x, y, z, and scale) of a real object.
Rendered frame	A 3-dimensional photograph of the subject material created by a computer, i.e., a picture of a building from a specific angle.
Software render	A computer image rendered using a software program. The speed is restricted by the central processing unit (CPU) processing speed and available RAM. The rendering of one frame is completed in several minutes to several days depending on image complexity. Ongoing programming throughout the development of a visualization is required.
Hardware render	A computer image rendered directly by computer hardware with preprogrammed construction sets. The rendering of an average frame can be completed in approximately 5 to 10 seconds using this process. Some highly complex images may take up to 30 seconds to render. Visualizations take less time to develop because ongoing programming with software is not required.

created customized animations faster and with more precision and greater detail. For clients, the primary advantage of hardware rendered animations was the ability to make changes to animations within days, whereas software rendering processes required weeks to make similar changes. In particular, in the litigation industry, attorneys sometimes requested changes right up to the day before the animations were used in a trial. Hardware rendering, unlike software rendering, accommodated these last-minute changes.

However, the process, and, consequently, the advantage of hardware rendering was not well understood by potential clients. Simply put, hardware rendered visualizations were created directly by computer hardware, while software rendered visualizations were created from software packages. Pat liked to explain the difference between hardware and software rendering to clients as analogous to how the brain functioned in humans. The brain (the "hardware") was programmed to tell the lungs when to breathe, the eyes to blink, or the heart to beat. It did not require any conscious thought to do these functions and, therefore, no conscious thought ("processing power") was required to complete the tasks. In contrast, Pat would continue, a human activity such as playing chess required a great deal of concentration and conscious thought, thereby slowing down or replacing all brain functions except the preprogrammed tasks like breathing. Software rendering was, therefore, similar to playing chess in that it required the computer to perform higher level processing that required more time and effort than did hardware coded functions. Software rendering required ongoing programming throughout the development of a visualization, but hardware rendering was preprogrammed.

Despite the advantages of hardware rendering, more and more firms were using software rendering to create computer visualizations. As one salesperson had reported to Pat, "We've been losing lots of cases to small mom and pop shops that are located in the same cities as the law firms. The law firms seem to think that it's important for the visualization firm to be geographically close, so they use local firms that do software rendering. They don't seem to 'get it' that our animation and modeling process is more precise and faster." This was directly impacting 3DV-LS's sales.

Financial Position

By 1999, 3DV-LS had created visualizations and reconstructions for thousands of cases involving patent infringement, product liability, medical malpractice, insurance defense, and aviation and automobile accident reconstruction. In 1998 alone, it produced more than 10,000 minutes of litigation animation. 3DV-LS was the giant in the litigation visualization services market. Despite this success, however, the litigation services unit had slowly lost its place of importance within the company as 3DV developed other areas of specialization. The unit's financial position was also worrisome. While sales were decreasing, operating expenses remained the same, including the annual $10,000 marketing budget. At the current level of operations, Pat calculated that 3DV-LS needed to generate at least $2.4 million in yearly sales for the unit to break even. If 3DV-LS entered a new market, there was the possibility of additional costs, such as the training and hiring of salespeople. The cost of hiring just one salesperson was $50,000. Revenues in FY2000 (January 1–December 31) were expected to be $2.7 million.

Contracts for litigation visualizations varied greatly based on the depth and breadth of the case. For example, the animations created for biomedical cases tended to be longer than those created for ground/vehicle accident projects because the information was less common and harder to understand. On average, though, the typical project required approximately 6 to 12 minutes of animation at an average cost of $26,000 to $60,000. For smaller projects, such as still models or storyboards that did not require animation, the cost of the project averaged $5,000 to $15,000. Prices were set at rates that covered variable costs plus a 25–30% profit margin.

Organization Structure and Culture

3DV-LS had 33 employees, most of whom worked on-site. Nearly all of the employees on-site had engineering or technical backgrounds. Pat Patterson, who reported directly to a 3DV vice-president, had a Ph.D. in construction engineering and a law degree. Five project managers reported directly to Pat. Two managers had Ph.D.'s in mechanical engineering, one had a Ph.D. in biological medicine, one had a master's degree in engineering mechanics, and one had a degree in architecture. The qualifications of the project managers gave 3DV-LS an advantage in the litigation market because attorneys preferred dealing with doctorate-prepared managers.

Underneath the project managers were production crews. These employees were either engineers with bachelor's degrees or "technical animators" who had either a two- or four-year degree in graphics art design. Rounding out the on-site group was an administrative assistant who did secretarial tasks and a marketing coordinator who performed a variety of marketing functions. However, most of the marketing efforts required by the unit were performed or controlled by 3DV, which also handled 3DV-LS's accounting and human resource management needs.

3DV-LS employed five field salespeople. These people were dispersed across the country in large metropolitan centers (two in Chicago and one each in New York, Texas, and California). None of the salespeople had backgrounds in the computer or technology industries, but they all had extensive experience in working with and selling to attorneys. The salespeople reported directly to Pat.

The litigation services unit was different from the rest of the company. Whereas 3DV's culture was formal, 3DV-LS's was markedly informal. There were frequent informal meetings among the production staff and project managers to exchange ideas on individual projects. The project managers also talked informally with Pat on a daily basis and kept him apprised of progress on the various projects. Project managers met weekly to allocate the production staff. Every two weeks, the entire business unit met informally over lunch. Nicknamed 'Lit Lunch' (for 'Litigation Lunch'), it was a time to catch up on personal news as well as to informally discuss projects.

In sharp contrast, however, to this free-flowing exchange of technical and creative ideas was the lack of communication between the production section of the business and the marketing coordinator. The marketing coordinator, Sandy Clarke, had been relocated to headquarters from a remote office during one of the reorganizations about two years earlier. The 3DV-LS director tightly controlled and supervised her activities and did not promote interaction with the other employees. About a year later, when Pat Patterson became the 3DV-LS director, his attempts to integrate marketing activities with production failed. Neither the project managers nor the sales staff knew what Sandy did and rarely talked to her about projects. Salespeople independently made decisions about what kind of marketing efforts to use in their region—only rarely would they ask Sandy for help or ideas. Even Sandy, who had extensive experience marketing in the legal industry, was confused about her job responsibilities. Any efforts she made to influence the unit's marketing decisions were ignored.

Marketing Communications

Salespeople generally used either e-mail or direct mail campaigns to generate sales leads. Qualified sales leads then received personal sales calls at which the salesperson showed product demos. The marketing coordinator also maintained a customer database and identified sales leads by staying current with various industry publications.

3DV-LS was dependent on 3DV for publicity, advertising, and marketing support. Publication of marketing materials, which had been designed by Sandy Clarke, had to be approved by and contracted by 3DV. News releases were submitted to 3DV's publicity department for release. Unfortunately, as 3DV-LS's favored status within the company declined, so did the marketing support it received.

A recent addition to 3DV-LS's communications package was development of a Web site, which potential clients could access to view all its products. In addition, the site included a feature that allowed viewers to contact a project manager via the Web site. Other than including information about the Web site in all client contacts, 3DV-LS did not develop any specific strategy detailing how to use the site to develop new business.

Assessing the Market Opportunity

Lance hurried to his desk to start compiling the information he would need to complete the analysis. He had worked at 3DV-LS as a project manager for two years, but had yet to complete a task such as this. His usual duties included discussing project-specific concepts and issues with the attorneys that hired 3DV-LS, monitoring the progress of the modeling and animations, and dealing with the production crew. Completing an analysis of the construction and transportation industries in a two-week period would be difficult considering that some of his projects were reaching drop-dead dates.[2]

Lance decided that this was definitely a situation that required more help. He grabbed his list and went to see Sandy Clarke, the marketing coordinator. Lance knew Sandy, but had never worked with her on a project. Because the market and this type of technology were so new, finding accurate and relevant information would be difficult; he was hopeful that Sandy would be able to help. After Lance shared his list with her, Sandy took a deep breath.

"Whew," Sandy said, when Lance finished, "that's a lot of information to find and make sense of in two weeks."

"But is it possible?" Lance queried. "If it helps," he continued, "I've been doing some research on my own, so I already know a little about what's happening in the construction and transportation industries."

"Well, that's a start," Sandy replied, "tell me what you know."

The Construction and Transportation Industries

The transportation and construction industries utilized hand-drawn renderings (pictures) of buildings and landscapes in the development of projects. These hand-drawn renderings provided general concept ideas in a washed-out, two-dimensional picture, but they did not allow stakeholders and the public to grasp how the finished project would look in the surrounding environment. Several companies released computer applications that created computer-generated two-dimensional pictures conveying aesthetics and design concepts. However, because many of these computer software programs relied on software rendering, they were not capable of creating complicated or highly detailed pictures in a short period of time. Using the software required high-end computer equipment and an experienced user who was familiar with Computer Aided Drafting (CAD).

Lance learned that certain aspects of construction and transportation projects differed depending on whether or not they were publicly or privately funded. Both types of funded projects used a bidding process, starting with RFPs (Requests for Proposals), to select project consultants. In turn, consultants were responsible for hiring subcontractors, such as 3DV-LS. Any firm could submit bids in response to an RFP, but for public agencies, contracts would only be awarded to firms that had been preapproved by the governing agency.

---

[2]A drop-dead date was the date that visualizations and materials were due to attorneys. Material that did not arrive by the drop-dead date could not legally be admitted into evidence.

Moreover, the pre-approval process extended to subcontractors. In contrast, privately funded large-scale construction projects did not require a pre-approval process.

Publicly funded and privately funded projects also differed in the project design phase. Publicly funded designs had to go through a public participation process, while privately funded designs used a marketing process. The public participation process, required by all government agencies for any type of construction project, consisted of several meetings at which the public asked questions and provided input to the governing agency. Frequently, the public had very strong opinions concerning these projects, especially those dealing with land acquisition or condemnation. The government agency's role was often to educate the public about the necessity and value of the project.

In contrast, private large-scale development projects were promoted to governing agencies, the public, and investors. This process was mainly concerned with convincing officials and the public that the project was beneficial to the community and would not have any negative impact. For investors, the promotion process centered on the project design issues and associated costs. For either process, accurate visualization of the finished project enhanced the participants' ability to understand the proposed project, and, consequently, could be very important to securing project approval.

In addition to needing computer visualizations of construction and transportation projects, the construction and transportation industries also needed to study human factors in the design of construction and transportation projects. For example, human reaction time to construction zone signing was a concern, as were potential weather effects. The merging of 3-D visualization with Geographical Information Systems (GIS) was a hot topic in many trade publications. GIS was a mapping technology that was the norm in the transportation industry. Light Detection and Ranging (LIDAR) technology, a revolutionary laser scanning system, could also revolutionize the industry. In fact, Lance had been looking into purchasing LIDAR technology for 3DV-LS, but with a price tag of $250,000 he thought it was cost prohibitive. However, purchase of the technology might be justified if 3DV-LS expanded into the transportation industry.

After Lance briefed Sandy on what he knew, they decided to spend the next several days contacting and questioning firms that had won construction and transportation consulting contracts. As Sandy put it, "We need to know more about the size of the market, whether or not it's growing, and more specific information on the use of computer visualization."

Use of Computer Visualization in Construction and Transportation Projects

Firms reported that computer-generated pictures were beginning to replace the hand-rendered sketches that had been the industry standard. However, after talking with several consultants, Lance and Sandy found that only large consultants were heavy users (there was a reluctance to use animations for anything but large-scale projects, i.e., those involving hundreds of millions of dollars) because acquiring the hardware, software, and personnel capable of creating quality models or pictures was extremely expensive. Even those consultants who subcontracted for visualization services were concerned about the cost of computer-generated pictures. "Unless computer visualizations are required, I avoid using them because they add unnecessary expense to an already expensive project," one consultant observed.

Nonetheless, some of the consultants Lance and Sandy talked to mentioned that the benefit of computer visualizations, though not immediately obvious, was still significant. As one consultant put it, "I can show a group of investors a hand-drawn sketch of how a building will look like when it's done, or I can show them a computer-generated picture of the finished building that's about as close to a real picture of the finished building as possible without actually erecting the building. They're always much more impressed with the computer-generated pictures. It saves a lot of time in securing final project approval. I figure the time I save by using computer-generated pictures more than outweighs the expense of creating the pictures." Another consultant stated that computer visualizations made it easier to respond to "what if " scenarios frequently requested by customers.

Growth in Construction and Transportation Industries

As Sandy delved deeper into the market trends she found a report released by the American Institute of Architects (AIA). In this report, she found several pieces of interesting information. The AIA projected:

- 1% increase in building activity paralleling population growth, as compared to levels in the first half of the 1990s.
- A 13.91% increase in the average annual volume of contract awards (see Exhibit 2).
- An emphasis on growth in construction spending in the commercial and industrial categories, especially for office buildings.
- A growing share of construction spending for building renovations over the next fifteen years. By 2010, building renovations would exceed new building construction.

The AIA report also reported preliminary results indicating that approximately $24 billion was billed for architectural services in 1999. Roughly one-third of that amount related to the commercial/industrial sector, whereas institutional billings accounted for almost one-half of the billed services.

From a contact in the Department of Transportation, Lance learned that transportation projects would also continue to become available due to the federal government's commitment to rehabilitating the nation's road infrastructure. Billions of dollars were allocated annually for road enhancement projects and large-scale interstate construction.

Perceptions of Computer Visualization

Next, Sandy put together a list of questions and spent several hours on the phone talking to potential clients. Sandy found that consultants networked through a variety of conferences, most held in conjunction with trade organizations. Consultants usually worked on projects in teams, with the same three or four consultants completing several different types of projects for the same government agency or private developer. Often, the consultants who designed projects for government-initiated projects were the same consultants who designed large-scale commercial projects. The designated primary consultant changed depending on the project but had the same subcontractors. Most consultants decided who to work with based on experience, quality, past working relationship, availability, and price.

EXHIBIT 2 **Average Volume of Contract Awards (in billions of 2000 dollars)**

Source: American Institute of Architects 2000 Firm Survey. Originally given in 1987 dollars, converted to 2000 dollars.

	1991 to 1995	1996 to 2010	% Change
Educational Facilities	$24.3	$24.1	−1%
Health Care Facilities	13.3	13.3	0
Public Buildings	7.1	7.9	10%
Retail Facilities	23.2	22.7	−2%
Office Buildings	16.4	28.1	42%
Industrial Facilities	19.1	21.7	12%
Total	$103.5	$117.9	

The consultants Sandy talked to also shared with her some of their perceptions of 3DV-LS. For example, one consultant told her that 3DV-LS had a reputation of charging high fees for standard services. Another reported a concern that 3DV-LS's prices were too high, since it did not provide any expertise concerning design issues. Sandy was surprised by this, because her research showed 3DV-LS's prices, even with a 25–30% profit margin, to be competitive in the litigation market. She was afraid that the perception of high prices derived from the early years in computer visualization when any type of computer-generated models or animation had been extremely expensive.

Sandy also queried the consultants on whether or not the visualizations they contracted for were software or hardware rendered. Most were uncertain. "I didn't know that there was more than one way to get pictures," was a typical response.

Pricing

The consultants were reluctant to share what they were paying for visualization services in the construction and transportation industries. However, after some digging, Lance was able to identify the going rates for animation and photo simulations in the transportation industry. The rates did not specify what kind of process was used (i.e., hardware or software rendering) to create the visualizations. But, because Lance knew of no other companies who did hardware rendering besides 3DV-LS, he assumed the prices reflected software rendered visualizations.

- Animation—$3,000 to $6,000 per minute
- Digitally altered photographs—$5,000 to $7,000 per image
- Photo-images or 3D models—$800 to $1,500 per image

In the transportation industry, most of the projects were large-scale transportation projects funded by government agencies. The government agency often specified the amount of money to be spent on visualizations. For example, the allowable costs for visualization on a recently approved $500 million transportation project ranged from $70,000 to $150,000.

Neither Sandy nor Lance was able to find a range of prices in the construction industry, but assumed that the rates were most likely comparable to those in the transportation industry. Moreover, because many construction projects were also funded by the government, Lance and Sandy surmised that the government would specify the computer visualization budgets for those projects, also.

Competition

After talking to several consultants, Sandy looked into how competitive the market was. She identified two types of competitors and profiled each of these.

The first competitor was typically a large firm that provided a full complement of services desired by the construction and transportation industries. These firms had the ability to design a project, conduct marketing campaigns and public participation workshops, and manage the implementation or construction of the project. Competitors in this group, such as Howard, Needles, Tammen, and Bergendoff (HNTB), the 8th largest architecture firm nationwide and 4th largest in transportation design, had national brand recognition and many years of extensive and varied experience. Not surprisingly, these firms rarely hired subcontractors, relying, instead, on in-house technology departments for their visualization needs. For example, HNTB's Technology Group employed content planners, media designers, 3-D animators, and networking and programming professionals to provide high-tech communication and information solutions to the architecture, transportation, environmental engineering, and construction services industries. However, HNTB relied on software rendering for its visualization projects.

Another firm that fit this competitor profile was Parsons Brinckerhoff, Inc., a global engineering giant. This firm provided planning, engineering, construction management, and operations and maintenance services to a wide variety of clients around the world. Similar to HNTB, Parsons Brinckerhoff had started Parsons and Brinckerhoff 4D Imaging (PB4D) in 1988 as an advanced computer visual simulation business unit. While PB4D was the industry leader for the visualization of transportation projects, it was also a large-scale multimedia and Internet business unit. Like HNTB, PB4D also relied on software rendering.

The second type of competitor was characterized as firms specializing in design visualization services. Typically, these firms were smaller than 3DV and had regional brand recognition. Although these firms' staffs were small, they also had specific experience with architects, landscape architects, planners, and civil engineers. Consequently, these competitors knew how to communicate with these professionals using industry jargon. Interestingly, most of these firms also relied on software rendering and did not provide extensive product or service lines. One firm typical of this type of competitor was Newlands & Co., a consulting firm located in Portland, Oregon that specialized in design visualization, 3D animation and Web development services. Newlands & Company, Inc. produced high-quality visual simulations, animations, Web and multimedia presentations for transportation, urban design and architecture. Its mission was to employ the best in art and technology to facilitate communication between designers and their clients. Its services included photography, 3-D modeling, photo simulation, animation, multimedia presentation creation, Web development, and training.

The Future

Lance met with Pat two weeks later to present the information he and Sandy had uncovered about the construction and transportation industries. When Lance finished the brief overview, he handed over a complete written report of the findings to Pat. "So," Pat said, "based on what you've learned, what do you think we should do?"

Lance, expecting this question, carefully formulated his response. "I think there's an excellent opportunity for 3DV-LS in this new market. The construction and transportation industries are growing, and there's increasing use of computer visualizations on projects. Plus, I think the advantage of hardware rendering—that is, being able to quickly create and change visualizations—will be just as important to the construction and transportation industries as it has proven to be in the litigation industry. But we'll have to convince consultants of this fact and at the same time compete against companies that are already firmly established in this market. It won't be easy."

Pat thanked Lance for all his hard work. Left alone with his thoughts, Pat pondered his options. One option was to hire and train one to two new salespeople to focus on developing business in the construction and transportation industries. This would require some investment, but would allow the current salesforce to stay focused on the litigation industry. Another option was to allocate the time and efforts of one or two current salespeople to developing small scale bids for regional projects in the construction and transportation industries. This option was less risky financially, but might further affect sales in the litigation industry.

Pat couldn't help but speculate. What if the sales decline in the last year was just temporary? What if the Web site proved to be an effective tool in cultivating sales? Several times over the last few months, Pat had wondered whether the declining sales were a direct effect of poorly communicating the advantages of hardware rendering relative to software rendering. At especially low moments, he worried that, to the average client, the advantages of hardware rendering were not tangible enough to clearly differentiate it from software rendering.

With respect to the new market opportunity, Pat had other nagging questions. Did 3DV-LS have the necessary skills and resources to enter the construction and transportation market while at the same time maintaining its litigation business? In particular, could the current five salespeople adapt their skills, honed in the litigation market, to the construction and transportation market? Could 3DV-LS successfully differentiate its hardware rendering visualization method from the more commonly used software rendering in the new market? Would entry into the new market pull necessary attention from the litigation industry? While Pat appreciated Lance's opinion, he knew that whether or not 3DV-LS should enter the construction and transportation market depended on the answers to these questions.

South Delaware Coors, Inc.

James E. Nelson and Eric J. Karson *University of Colorado*

Larry Brownlow was just beginning to realize the problem was more complex than he thought. The problem, of course, was giving direction to Manson and Associates regarding which research should be completed by February 20, 1989, to determine market potential of a Coors beer distributorship for a two-county area in southern Delaware. With data from this research, Larry would be able to estimate the feasibility of such an operation before the March 5 application deadline. Larry knew his decision on whether or not to apply for the distributorship was the most important career choice he had ever faced.

Larry Brownlow

Larry was just completing his M.B.A. and, from his standpoint, the Coors announcement of expansion into Delaware could hardly have been better timed. He had long ago decided the best opportunities and rewards were in smaller, self-owned businesses and not in the jungles of corporate giants. Because of a family tragedy some three years ago, Larry found himself in a position to consider small business opportunities such as the Coors distributorship. Approximately $500,000 was held in trust for Larry, to be dispersed when he reached age thirty. Until then, Larry and his family lived on an annual trust income of about $40,000. It was on this income that Larry decided to leave his sales engineering job and return to graduate school for his M.B.A.

The decision to complete a graduate program and operate his own business had been easy to make. While he could have retired and lived off investment income, Larry knew such a life would not be to his liking. Working with people and the challenge of making it on his own, Larry thought, were far more preferable to enduring an early retirement.

Larry would be thirty in July, about the time money would actually be needed to start the business. In the meantime, he had access to about $15,000 for feasibility research. While

This case was written by Professor James E. Nelson and doctoral student Eric J. Karson, University of Colorado. This case is intended for use as a basis for class discussion rather than to illustrate either effective or ineffective administrative decision making. Some data are disguised. © by the Business Research Division, College of Business and Administration and the Graduate School of Business Administration, University of Colorado, Boulder, Colorado 80309–0419.

there certainly were other places to spend the money, Larry and his wife agreed the opportunity to acquire the distributorship could not be overlooked.

Coors, Inc.

Coors's history dates back to 1873, when Adolph Coors built a small brewery in Golden, Colorado. Since then, the brewery has prospered and become the fourth-largest seller of beer in the country. Coors's operating philosophy could be summed up as "hard work, saving money, devotion to the quality of the product, caring about the environment, and giving people something to believe in." Company operation is consistent with this philosophy. Headquarters and most production facilities are still located in Golden, Colorado, with a new Shenandoah, Virginia, facility aiding in nationwide distribution. Coors is still family operated and controlled. The company issued its first public stock, $127 million worth of nonvoting shares, in 1975. The issue was received enthusiastically by the financial community despite its being offered during a recession.

Coors's unwillingness to compromise on the high quality of its product is well known both to its suppliers and to its consuming public. Coors beer requires constant refrigeration to maintain this quality, and wholesalers' facilities are closely controlled to ensure proper temperatures are maintained. Wholesalers are also required to install and use aluminum can recycling equipment. Coors was one of the first breweries in the industry to recycle its cans.

Larry was aware of Coors's popularity with many consumers in adjacent states. However, Coors's corporate management was seen by some consumers to hold antiunion beliefs (because of a labor disagreement at the brewery some ten years ago and the brewery's current use of a nonunion labor force). Some other consumers perceived the brewery to be somewhat insensitive to minority issues, primarily in employment and distribution. The result of these attitudes—plus many other aspects of consumer behavior—meant that Coors's sales in Delaware would depend greatly on the efforts of the two wholesalers planned for the state.

Manson Research Proposal

Because of the press of his studies, Larry had contacted Manson and Associates in January for their assistance. The firm was a Wilmington-based general research supplier that had conducted other feasibility studies in the south Atlantic region. Manson was well known for the quality of its work, particularly with respect to computer modeling. The firm had developed special expertise in modeling population and employment levels for cities, counties, and other units of area for periods of up to ten years into the future.

Larry had met John Rome, senior research analyst for Manson, and discussed the Coors opportunity and appropriate research extensively in the January meeting. Rome promised a formal research proposal (Exhibits 1 and 2) for the project, which Larry now held in his hand. It certainly was extensive, Larry thought, and reflected the professionalism he expected. Now came the hard part, choosing the more relevant research from the proposal, because he certainly couldn't afford to pay for it all. Rome had suggested a meeting for Friday, giving Larry only two more days to decide.

Larry was at first overwhelmed. All the research would certainly be useful. He was sure he needed estimates of sales and costs in a form allowing managerial analysis, but what data in what form? Knowledge of competing operations' experience, retailer support, and consumer acceptance also seemed important for feasibility analysis. For example, what if consumers were excited about Coors and retailers indifferent or the other way around? Finally, several of the studies would provide information that could be useful in later months of operation in the

EXHIBIT 1   Manson and Associates Research Proposal

Mr. Larry Brownlow   January 16, 1989
1198 West Lamar
Chester, PA 12345

Dear Larry:

It was a pleasure meeting you last week and discussing your business and research interests in Coors wholesaling. After further thought and discussion with my colleagues, the Coors opportunity appears even more attractive than when we met.

Appearances can be deceiving, as you know, and I fully agree some formal research is needed before you make application. Research that we recommend would proceed in two distinct stages and is described below:

Stage One Research Based on Secondary Data and Manson Computer Models:

Study A: National and Delaware per Capita Beer Consumption for 1988–1992.
  Description: Per capita annual consumption of beer for the total population and population aged
     21 and over is provided in gallons.
  Source: Various publications, Manson computer model
  Cost: $1,000

Study B: Population Estimates for 1985–1995 for Two Delaware Counties in Market Area.
  Description: Annual estimates of total population and population aged 21 and over is provided for
     the period 1985–1995.
  Source: U.S. Bureau of Census, Sales Management Annual Survey of Buying Power, Manson
  computer model
  Cost: $1,500

Study C: Coors Market Share Estimates for 1990–1995.
  Description: Coors market share for the two-county market area based on total gallons consumed
     is estimated for each year in the period 1990–1995. This data will be projected from Coors's
     nationwide experience.
  Source: Various publications, Manson computer model
  Cost: $2,000

Study D: Estimated Liquor and Beer Licenses for the Market Area, 1990–1995.
  Description: Projections of the number of on-premise sale operations and off-premise sale
     operations is provided.
  Source: Delaware Department of Revenue, Manson computer model
  Cost: $1,000

Study E: Beer Taxes Paid by Delaware Wholesalers for 1987 and 1988 in the Market Area.
  Description: Beer taxes paid by each of the six presently operating competing beer wholesalers is
     provided. This can be converted to gallons sold by applying the state gallonage tax rate (6 cents
     per gallon).
  Source: Delaware Department of Revenue
  Cost: $200

Study F: Financial Statement Summary of Wine, Liquor, and Beer Wholesalers for Fiscal Year 1986.
  Description: Composite balance sheets, income statements, and relevant measures of performance
     provided for 510 similar wholesaling operations in the United States is provided.
  Source: Robert Morris Associates Annual Statement Studies 1987 ed.
  Cost: $49.50

(continued)

EXHIBIT 1   Manson and Associates Research Proposal   (*concluded*)

Stage Two Research Based on Primary Data:

Study G: Consumer Study
   Description: Study G involves focus group interviews and a mail questionnaire to determine
      consumer past experience, acceptance, and intention to buy Coors beer. Three focus
      group interviews would be conducted in the two counties in the market area. From these
      data, a mail questionnaire would be developed and sent to 300 adult residents in the
      market area, utilizing direct questions and semantic differential scale to measure attitudes
      toward Coors beer, competing beers, and an ideal beer.
   Source: Manson and Associates
   Cost: $6,000

Study H: Retailer Study
   Description: Group interviews would be conducted with six potential retailers of Coors beer in
      one county in the market area to determine their past beer sales and experience and their
      intention to stock and sell Coors. From these data, a personal interview questionnaire would
      be developed and executed at all appropriate retailers in the market area to determine
      similar data.
   Source: Manson and Associates
   Cost: $4,800

Study I: Survey of Retail and Wholesale Beer Prices
   Description: Study I involves in-store interviews with a sample of 50 retailers in the market area
      to estimate retail and wholesale prices for Budweiser, Miller Lite, Miller, Busch, Bud Light,
      Old Milwaukee, and Michelob.
   Source: Manson and Associates
   Cost: $2,000

Examples of the form of final report tables are attached [Exhibit 2]. This should give you a better idea of the data you will receive.

As you can see, the research is extensive and, I might add, not cheap. However, the research as outlined will supply you with sufficient information to make an estimate of the feasibility of a Coors distributorship, the investment for which is substantial.

I have scheduled 9:00 next Friday as a time to meet with you to discuss the proposal in more detail. Time is short, but we firmly feel the study can be completed by February 20, 1989. If you need more information in the meantime, please feel free to call.

Sincerely,

John

John Rome

Senior Research Analyst

EXHIBIT 2 Examples of Final Research Report Tables

(A) National and Delaware Resident Annual Beer Consumption per Capita, 1988–1992 (Gallons)

Year	U.S. Consumption		Delaware Consumption	
	Based on Entire Population	Based on Population over Age 21	Based on Entire Population	Based on Population over Age 21
1988				
1989				
1990				
1991				
1992				

Source: Study A.

(B) Population Estimates for 1986–1996 for Two Delaware Counties in Market Area

Entire Population

County	1986	1988	1990	1992	1994	1996
Kent						
Sussex						

Population Age 21 and Over

County	1986	1988	1990	1992	1994	1996
Kent						
Sussex						

Source: Study B.

(C) Coors Market Share Estimates for 1990–1995

Year	Market Share (%)
1990	
1991	
1992	
1993	
1994	
1995	

Source: Study C.

(D) Liquor and Beer License Estimates for Market Area for 1990–1995

Type of License	1990	1991	1992	1993	1994	1995
All beverages						
Retail beer and wine						
Off-premises beer only						
Veterans beer and liquor						
Fraternal						
Resort beer and liquor						

Source: Study D.

(E) Beer Taxes Paid by Beer Wholesalers in the Market Area, 1987 and 1988

Wholesaler	1987 Tax Paid ($)	1988 Tax Paid ($)
A		
B		
C		
D		
E		
F		

Source: Study E.

Note: Delaware beer tax is 6 cents per gallon.

(continued)

EXHIBIT 2   Examples of Final Research Report Tables   *(continued)*

(F) Financial Statement Summary for 510 Wholesalers of Wine, Liquor, and Beer in Fiscal Year 1986			
Assets		**Percentage**	
Cash and equivalents			
Accounts and notes receivable net			
Inventory			
All other current			
Total current			
Fixed assets net			
Intangibles net			
All other noncurrent	_____		
Total	100.0	*Ratios*	
		Quick	
		Current	
		Debts/worth	
Liabilities		**Percentage**	
Notes payable—short-term		Sales/receivables	
Current maturity long-term debt		Cost sales/inventory	
Accounts and notes payable—trade		Percentage profit before taxes	
Accrued expenses		based on total assets	
All other current			
Total current			
Long-term debt			
All other noncurrent			
Net worth	_____		
Total liabilities and net worth	100.0		
Income Data			
Net sales	100.0		
Cost of sales			
Gross profit			
Operating expenses			
Operating profit			
All other expenses net	_____		
Profit before taxes			

Source: Study F (Robert Morris Associates, © 1987)

Interpretation of Statement Studies Figures

RMA recommends that Statement Studies data be regarded only as general guidelines and not as absolute industry norms. There are several reasons why the data may not be fully representative of a given industry:

1. The financial statements used in the *Statement Studies* are not selected by any random or statistically reliable method. RMA member banks voluntarily submit the raw data they have available each year, with these being the only constraints: (a) The fiscal year-ends of the companies reported may not be from April 1 through June 29, and (b) their total assets must be less than $100 million.

2. Many companies have varied product lines; however, the *Statement Studies* categorize them by their primary product Standard Industrial Classification (SIC) number only.

3. Some of our industry samples are rather small in relation to the total number of firms in a given industry. A relatively small sample can increase the chances that some of our composites do not fully represent an industry.

4. There is the chance that an extreme statement can be present in a sample, causing a disproportionate influence on the industry composite. This is particularly true in a relatively small sample.

5. Companies within the same industry may differ in their method of operations which in turn can directly influence their financial statements. Since they are included in our sample, too, these statements can significantly affect our composite calculations.

6. Other considerations that can result in variations among different companies engaged in the same general line of business are different labor markets; geographical location; different accounting methods; quality of products handled; sources and methods of financing; and terms of sale.

For these reasons, RMA does not recommend the Statement Studies figures be considered as absolute norms for a given industry. Rather the figures should be used only as general guidelines and in addition to the other methods of financial analysis. RMA makes no claim as to the representativeness of the figures printed in this book.

(continued)

EXHIBIT 2   Examples of Final Research Report Tables   (*continued*)

(G) Consumer Questionnaire Results

	Yes	No
Consumed Coors in the Past:	%	%
Attitudes toward Coors:	%	
Strongly like		
Like		
Indifferent/no opinion		
Dislike		
Strongly dislike		
Total	100.0	

Weekly Beer Consumption:	%
Less than 1 can	
1–2 cans	
3–4 cans	
5–6 cans	
7–8 cans	
9 cans and over	
Total	100.0

Intention to Buy Coors:	%
Certainly will	
Maybe will	
Not sure	
Maybe will not	
Certainly will not	
Total	100.0

	Yes	No
Usually Buy Beer at:		%
Liquor stores		
Taverns and bars		
Supermarkets		
Corner grocery		
Total		100.0

Features Considered Important When Buying Beer:	%
Taste	
Brand Name	
Price	
Store location	
Advertising	
Carbonation	
Other	
Total	100.0

Semantic Differential Scale—Consumers*

	Extremely	Very	Somewhat	Somewhat	Very	Extremely	
Masculine	___	___	___	___	___	___	Feminine
Healthful	___	___	___	___	___	___	Unhealthful
Cheap	___	___	___	___	___	___	Expensive
Strong	___	___	___	___	___	___	Weak
Old-fashioned	___	___	___	___	___	___	New
Upper-class	___	___	___	___	___	___	Lower-class
Good taste	___	___	___	___	___	___	Bad taste

Source: Study G.
*Profiles would be provided for Coors, three competing beers, and an ideal beer.

(H) Retailer Questionnaire Results

Brands of Beer Carried:	%
Budweiser	
Miller Lite	
Miller	
Busch	
Bud Light	
Old Milwaukee	
Michelob	

Beer Sales:	%
Budweiser	
Miller Lite	
Miller	
Busch	
Bud Light	
Old Milwaukee	
Michelob	
Others	
Total	100.0

(*continued*)

EXHIBIT 2   Examples of Final Research Report Tables   (concluded)

Semantic Differential Scale—Retailers*

	Extremely	Very	Somewhat	Somewhat	Very	Extremely	
Masculine	____	____	____	____	____	____	Feminine
Healthful	____	____	____	____	____	____	Unhealthful
Cheap	____	____	____	____	____	____	Expensive
Strong	____	____	____	____	____	____	Weak
Old-fashioned	____	____	____	____	____	____	New
Upper-class	____	____	____	____	____	____	Lower-class
Good taste	____	____	____	____	____	____	Bad taste

Intention to Sell Coors: _____ %

Certainly will	
Maybe will	
Not sure	
Maybe will not	
Certainly will not	_____
Total	100.0

Source: Study G.

*Profiles would be provided for Coors, three competing beers, and an ideal beer.

(I) Retail and Wholesale Prices for Selected Beers in the Market Area

Beer	Wholesale* Six-Pack Price (dollars)	Retail† Six-Pack Price (dollars)
Budweiser		
Miller Lite		
Miller		
Busch		
Bud Light		
Old Milwaukee		
Michelob		

Source: Study I.
*Price that the wholesaler sold to retailers.
†Price that the retailer sold to consumers.

areas of promotion and pricing, for example. The problem now appeared more difficult than before!

It would have been nice, Larry thought, to have had some time to perform part of the suggested research himself. However, there was just too much in the way of class assignments and other matters to allow him that luxury. Besides, using Manson and Associates would give him research results from an unbiased source.

Investing and Operating Data

Larry was not completely in the dark regarding investment and operating data for the distributorship. In the past two weeks he had visited two beer wholesalers in his hometown of Chester, Pennsylvania, who handled Anheuser-Busch and Miller beer, to get a feel for their operations and marketing experience. It would have been nice to interview a Coors wholesaler, but Coors management had strictly informed all of their distributors to provide no information to prospective applicants.

While no specific financial data was discussed, general information had been provided in a cordial fashion because of the noncompetitive nature of Larry's plans. Based on his conversations, Larry made the following estimates:

Inventory		$240,000
Equipment		
Delivery trucks	$150,000	
Forklift	20,000	
Recycling and miscellaneous equipment	20,000	
Office equipment	10,000	
Total equipment		200,000
Warehouse		320,000
Land		40,000
Total investment		$800,000

A local banker had reviewed Larry's financial capabilities and saw no problem in extending a line of credit on the order of $400,000. Other sources also might loan as much as $400,000 to the business.

As a rough estimate of fixed expenses, Larry planned on having four route salespeople, a secretary, and a warehouse manager. Salaries for these people and himself would run about $160,000 annually plus some form of incentive compensation he had yet to determine. Other fixed or semifixed expenses were estimated at:

Equipment depreciation	$35,000
Warehouse depreciation	15,000
Utilities and telephone	12,000
Insurance	10,000
Personal property taxes	10,000
Maintenance and janitorial	5,600
Miscellaneous	2,400
	$90,000

According to the wholesalers, beer in bottles and cans outsold keg beer by a three-to-one margin. Keg beer prices at the wholesale level were about 45 percent of prices for beer in bottles and cans.

Meeting

The entire matter deserved much thought. Maybe it was a golden opportunity, maybe not. The only thing certain was that research was needed, Manson and Associates was ready, and Larry needed time to think. Today is Tuesday, Larry thought—only three days until he and John Rome would get together for direction.

Product Strategy

6

Starbucks—Early 2005

J. Paul Peter *University of Wisconsin–Madison*

Starbucks Corporation is the world's largest coffee retailer and has continued its phenomenal growth into 2005. In the quarter ending April 3, the company increased its net revenue 22 percent to $1.5 billion and its net earnings by 27 percent to $101 million compared to the same quarter the previous year. Starbucks was also fourth-rated on *Fortune*'s list of Most Admired

J. Paul Peter is James R. Mc Manus–Bascom Professor in Marketing at the University of Wisconsin–Madison. All information in this case is taken from public sources including starbucks.com.

EXHIBIT 1 **Starbucks Growth in Revenue, Earnings, and Number of Stores**

Source: www.Starbucks.com.

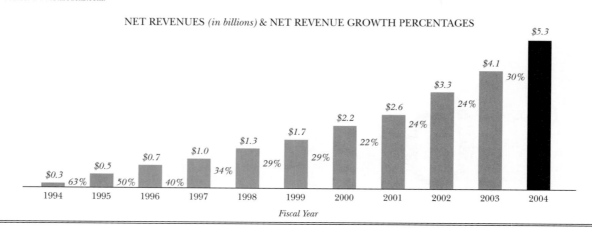

NET REVENUES *(in billions)* & NET REVENUE GROWTH PERCENTAGES

NET EARNINGS *(in millions)*

STORES OPEN AT YEAR END
(Company-operated and licensed stores)

Companies in 2004 and was awarded a gold medal from the World Environment Center for its work in setting coffee-buying guidelines that are environmentally, socially, and economically responsible. Exhibit 1 shows the impressive growth in Starbucks' revenue, earnings, and number of stores in recent years.

Starbucks was started in Seattle, Washington, in 1971 when three young men decided to try their hand at selling gourmet coffee. They were betting that consumers would pay $1.50 for a cup of their coffee compared to 40 cents for a generic coffee offered elsewhere. By 2005 there were more than 9,000 Starbucks coffeehouses in 35 countries worldwide. Of these, over 1,100 were in the Asia Pacific region and about half of these in Japan. In the Europe, Middle East, Africa region, there were 248 Starbucks. There were 161 in the western hemisphere outside the United States with 66 of these in Canada. Starbucks long-term goal is to have 30,000 stores worldwide. Store locations are selected for high traffic and high visibility. Approximately 33 million customers visit a Starbucks coffeehouse each week worldwide.

Starbucks was started in Seattle, Washington, in 1971 when three young men decided to try their hand at selling gourmet coffee. They were betting that consumers would pay $1.50 for a cup of their coffee compared to 40 cents for a generic coffee offered elsewhere. By 2005 there were more than 9,000 Starbucks coffeehouses in 35 countries worldwide. Of these, over 1,100 were in the Asia Pacific region and about half of these in Japan. In the Europe, Middle East, Africa region, there were 248 Starbucks. There were 161 in the western hemisphere outside the United States with 66 of these in Canada. Starbucks long-term goal is to have 30,000 stores worldwide. Store locations are selected for high traffic and high visibility. Approximately 33 million customers visit a Starbucks coffeehouse each week worldwide.

A recent study found that there are over 166 million coffee drinkers in the United States, and the number of them has increased steadily since the mid-1990s. A significant trend in U.S. coffee drinking has been the increase in the amount of coffee drinking in the out-of-home segment. For example, coffee drinkers aged 25–29 increased their out-of-home coffee consumption from 42 to 66 percent in a recent year and 30–59-year-olds from 33 to 46 percent. Coffee drinkers 60 and older increased their out-of-home consumption from 14 to 20 percent in the same year. Of the out-of-home segment, the biggest increase was among those who drink their coffee at work. However, while more consumers are drinking coffee in the workplace, they are increasingly getting their coffee from outside the office. This means the percentage of at-work coffee being sourced from within the workplace has declined dramatically.

Starbucks has made coffee drinking a social phenomenon by offering consumers a comfortable atmosphere in which to drink a premium beverage while either chatting with friends, reading a newspaper or magazine, or working on their laptops. Howard Schultz, chairman of Starbucks, believes that the company has created a "third place" between home and work where people can go for personal time out or to relax with friends. Whereas many of these people previously would have stopped in a bar for a beer, they now frequent Starbucks for coffee.

Schultz also attributes the company's success to the 96,700 employees working worldwide. Starbucks' employee training program churns out "baristas" by educating classes of 300 to 400 in courses such as "Brewing the Perfect Cup at Home" and "Coffee Knowledge." They are taught to remind customers who buy Starbucks coffee beans to brew at home to purchase new beans weekly and that tap water might not be sufficient for brewing really good coffee. They are also encouraged to share their feelings about working at Starbucks. Employees are given guidelines for maintaining and enhancing self-esteem, learning how to listen and acknowledge customer comments, and knowing when to ask for help. If the annual barista turnover of 60 percent compared to 140 percent for hourly wage earners in the fast-food industry is any indication of the quality of its training programs, Starbucks seems to have made progress in developing employee loyalty. Most of Starbucks employees have some education beyond high school, and their average age is 26. Eligible employees qualify for a comprehensive benefits package, including stock options and health, medical, dental, and vision coverage. Concern for employees is one of Starbucks guiding principles, as shown in Exhibit 2.

Starbucks product line includes more than 30 blends and single-origin coffees, handcrafted espresso and blended beverages, Tazo teas, a line of bottled Frappuccino coffee drinks and Starbucks DoubleShot. In addition it offers an exclusive line of Starbucks Barista home espresso machines, coffee brewers and grinders, freshly baked pastries, a line of super-premium ice cream, a line of premium chocolate, sandwiches, salad, coffee mugs annd coffee accessories, compact discs, and assorted gift items. It also offers a highly successful Starbucks

EXHIBIT 2 **Starbucks' Mission Statement and Guiding Principles**

Establish Starbucks as the premier purveyor of the finest coffee in the world while maintaining our uncompromising principles while we grow.

The following six guiding principles will help us measure the appropriateness of our decisions:

–Provide a great work environment and treat each other with respect and dignity.

–Embrace diversity as an essential component in the way we do business.

–Apply the highest standards of excellence to the purchasing, roasting and fresh delivery of our coffee.

–Develop enthusiastically satisfied customers all of the time.

–Contribute positively to our communities and our environment.

–Recognize that profitability is essential to our future success.

Environmental Mission Statement

Starbucks is committed to a role of environmental leadership in all facets of our business.

–We fulfill this mission by a commitment to:

–Understanding of environmental issues and sharing information with our partners.

–Developing innovative and flexible solutions to bring about change.

–Striving to buy, sell and use environmentally friendly products.

–Recognizing that fiscal responsibility is essential to our environmental future.

–Instilling environmental responsibility as a corporate value.

–Measuring and monitoring our progress for each project.

–Encouraging all partners to share in our mission.

Source: www.Starbucks.com.

Card, a reloadable stored-value card, which allows consumers to prepay the purchase of Starbucks products. The card can then be used and reloaded with funds when needed either at a Starbucks store or at Starbucks.com. This card has been hugely successful with over 37 million cards in use and over $1 billion in sales on these cards in the first 3 years. The card is so successful it is being launched internationally with initial rollouts in Japan and Greece. The card provides convenience to customers but does not offer any discount for prepayment. In fact, Starbucks does not discount any of its products or offer special prices or sales.

Starbucks also has licensing agreements for its products with a number of other companies. For example, it has an agreement with Pepsi-Cola Company to produce and distribute bottled Starbucks products and one with Kraft Foods, Inc., to distribute Starbucks coffee beans and ground coffees and packaged tea products in grocery and warehouse club stores. It has an agreement with Dreyer's Grand Ice Cream, Inc., to develop and distribute Starbucks line of superpremium ice cream and one with Jim Beam Brands Inc. to manufacture and market a Starbucks premium liqueur product. It has an alliance with SYSCO Corporation to distribute its coffee and tea products to institutional food services for health care accounts, office coffee distributors, hotels, restaurants, airlines, and other retailers. Starbucks' products were offered by nearly 14,000 food service accounts worldwide in 2005.

Discussion Questions

1. What is Starbucks' product?
2. What changes in society have helped Starbucks be successful?
3. What strategic factors account for Starbucks success in developing brand equity?
4. What opportunities and threats face Starbucks?
5. What are the advantage of the Starbucks Card to the company and to customers?
6. What should Starbucks do to continue growing its revenues and earnings?
7. Evaluate Starbucks' mission statement and guiding principles. What do they suggest about the company?

7

easyCar.com

John J. Lawrence Luis Solis *University of Idaho Instituto de Empresa*

> At easyCar we aim to offer you outstanding value for money. To us value for money means a reliable service at a low price. We achieve this by simplifying the product we offer, and passing on the benefits to you in the form of lower prices.[1]

This was the stated mission of car rental company easyCar.com. EasyCar was a member of the EasyGroup family of companies, founded by the flamboyant Greek entrepreneur Stelios Haji-Ioannou, who was known simply as Stelios to most. Stelios founded low-cost air carrier easyJet.com in 1995 after convincing his father, a Greek shipping billionaire, to loan him the £5 million (note: in January 2003, £1 = €1.52 = U.S.$1.61) needed to start the business.[2] EasyJet was one of the early low-cost, no frills air carriers in the European market. It was built upon a foundation of simple point-to-point flights, booked over the Internet, and the aggressive use of yield management policies to maximize the revenues it derived from its assets. The company proved highly successful, and as a result Stelios had expanded this business model to industries with similar characteristics as the airline industry. EasyCar, founded in 2000 on a £10 million investment on the part of Stelios, was one of these efforts.

EasyCar's approach, built on the easyJet model, was quite different from the approaches used by the traditional rental car companies. EasyCar rented only a single vehicle type at each location it operated, while most of its competitors rented a wide variety of vehicle types.

EasyCar did not work with agents—over 95% of its bookings were made through the company's website, with the remainder of bookings being made directly through the company's phone reservation system (at a cost to the customer of €0.95 per minute for the call). Most rental car companies worked with a variety of intermediaries, with their own websites accounting for less than 10% of their total booking.[3] And like easyJet, easyCar managed prices in an attempt to have its fleet rented out 100% of the time and to generate the maximum revenue from its rentals. EasyCar's information system constantly evaluated projected demand and expected utilization at each site, and adjusted price accordingly. Because of its aggressive pricing, easyCar was able to achieve a fleet

This case was prepared by John J. Lawrence of the University of Idaho and Luis solis of the Instituto de Empresa as a basis for class discussion.

[1]EasyCar.com website

[2]"The big picture—an interview with Stelios" *Sunday Herald* (UK), 16 March 2003,

[3]"Click to Fly" *Economist,* 13 May 2004.

[4]Simpkins, E. "Stelios isn't taking it easy," *Sunday Telegraph* (UK), 15 December 2002.

utilization rate in excess of 90%[4]—much higher than other major rental car companies. Industry leader Avis Europe, for example, had a fleet utilization rate of 68%.[5]

It was January 2003. EasyCar had broken even in the fiscal year ending September 2002[6] on revenues of £27 million.[7] This represented a significant improvement over 2001, when easyCar had lost £7.5 million on revenues of £18.5 million.[8] While pleased that the company had broken even in only its third year of operation, Stelios set aggressive financial goals for easyCar for the next 2 years. Plans called for a quadrupling of revenues in the next 2 years in preparation for a planned initial public offering in the second half of 2004. EasyCar's goal was to reach £100 million in revenue and £10 million in profit for the year 2004. The £100 million revenue goal and £10 million profit goal were felt necessary to obtain the desired return from an IPO. It was thought that with this level of performance, the company might be worth about £250 million.[9] In order to achieve these financial goals, the company was pushing to open an average of two new sites a week through 2003 and 2004 to reach a total of 180 sites by the end of 2004.[10]

The Rental Car Industry in Western Europe

The Western European rental car industry consisted of many different national markets that were only semi-integrated. While there were many companies that competed within this European rental car industry, a handful of companies held dominant positions, either across a number of national markets or within one or a few national markets. Industry experts saw the sector as ripe for consolidation.[11] Several international companies—notably Avis, Europcar, and Hertz—had strong positions across most major European markets. Within most countries, there was also a primarily national or regional company that had a strong position in its home market and perhaps moderate market share in neighboring markets. Sixt was the market leader in Germany, for example, while Atesa (in partnership with National) was the market leader in Spain. Generally these major players accounted for more than half of the market. In Germany, for example, Sixt, Europcar, Avis and Hertz had a combined 60% of the €2.5 billion German rental car market.[12] In Spain, the top five firms accounted for 60% of the €920 million Spanish rental car market. Generally, these top firms targeted both business and vacation travelers and offered a wide range of vehicles for rent. Exhibit 1 provides basic information on these market-leading companies.

In addition to these major companies, there were many smaller rental companies operating in each market. In Germany, for example, there were over 700 smaller companies,[13] while in Spain there were more than 1,600 smaller companies. Many of these smaller companies operated at only one or a few locations, and were particularly prevalent in tourist locations. There were also a number of brokers operating in the sector, like Holiday Autos. Brokerage companies did not own their own fleet of cars but basically managed the excess

---

[5]Avis Europe plc 2002 annual report, p. 10, at ir.avis-europe.com/avis/reports on 16 August, 2004.

[6]Simpkins, E. "Stelios isn't taking it easy," *Sunday Telegraph* (UK), 15 December 2002.

[7]"Marketing: Former eBay UK chief lands top easyCar position," *Financial Times Information Limited,* 9 January 2003.

[8]Burt, T. "EasyCar agrees deal with Vauxhall," *Financial Times,* 30 April 2002, p. 24.

[9]Hodgson, N. "Stelios plans easycar float," *Liverpool Echo,* 24 September 2002.

[10]Simpkins, E. "Stelios isn't taking it easy," *Sunday Telegraph* (UK), 15 December 2002.

[11]"Marketing Week: Don't write off the car rental industry," *Financial Times Information Limited,* 26 September 2002.

[12]"EasyCar set to shake up German car rental market," European Intelligence Wire, 22 February 2002.

[13]Ibid.

EXHIBIT 1   Information on easyCar's Major European Competitors

	easyCar	Avis Europe	Europcar	Hertz	Sixt
Number of rental outlets	46	3100	2,650	7,000	1,250
2002 fleet size	7,000	120,000	220,000	700,000	46,700
Number of countries	5	107	118	150	50
Largest market	UK	France	France	U.S.	Germany
Who owns company	EasyGroup/ Stelios Haji-Ioannou	D'Ieteren (Belgium) is majority shareholder	Volkswagen AG	Ford Motor Company	Publicly traded
European revenues	€41 million	€1.25 billion	€1.12 billion	€910 million	€600 million
Company website	www.easycar.com	www.avis-europe.com	www.europcar.com	www.hertz.com	ag.sixt.com

Source: Information in this table came from each company's website and online annual reports. European revenues are for vehicle rental in Europe and are estimated based on market share estimates for 2001 from Avis Europe's website.

inventory of other companies and matched customers with rental companies with excess fleet capacity.

Overall, the rental car market could be thought of as composed of two broad segments: a business segment and a tourist/leisure segment. Depending on the market, the leisure segment represented somewhere between 45 and 65% of the overall market, and a large part of this segment was very price conscious. The business segment made up the remaining 35 to 55% of the market. It was less price sensitive than the tourist segment and more concerned about service quality, convenience, and flexibility.

The Growth of EasyCar

EasyCar opened its first location in London, on 20 April 2000 under the name EasyRentacar. In the same week, easyCar opened locations in Glasgow and Barcelona. All three locations were popular easyJet destinations. Vehicles initially could be rented for as low as €15 per day plus a one-time car preparation fee of €8. Each of these locations had a fleet consisting entirely of Mercedes A-class vehicles. It was the only vehicle that easyCar rented at the time.

EasyCar had signed a deal with Mercedes, amidst much fanfare, at the Geneva Motor Show earlier in the year to purchase a total of 5,000 A-class vehicles. The vehicles, which came with guaranteed buy-back terms, cost easyCar's parent company a little over £6 million.[14] Many in the car rental industry were surprised by the choice, expecting easyCar to rely on less expensive models.[15] In describing the acquisition of the 5000 Mercedes vehicles, Stelios had said:

> The choice of Mercedes reflects the easyGroup brand. EasyRentacar will use brand new Mercedes cars in the same way that easyJet uses brand new Boeing aircraft. We do not compromise on the hardware, we just use innovation to substantially reduces costs. The car hire industry is where the airline industry was five years ago, a cartel feeding off the corporate client. EasyRentacar will provide a choice for consumers who pay out of their own pockets and who will not be ripped off for traveling mid-week.[16]

EasyCar quickly expanded to other locations, focusing first on those locations that were popular with easyJet customers, including Amsterdam, Geneva, Nice, and Malagra. By

[14]Hodgson, N. "Stelios plans easycar float," *Liverpool Echo,* 24 September 2002.
[15]Felsted, A. "EasyCar courts Clio for rental fleet," *Financial Times,* 11 February 2002, p. 26.
[16]EasyCar.com website news release, 1 March 2000.

July 2001, a little over a year after its initial launch, easyCar had fleets of Mercedes A-class vehicles in 14 locations in the UK, Spain, France, and the Netherlands. At this point, easy-Car secured £27 million from a consortium of Bank of Scotland Corporate Banking and NBGI Private Equity to further expand its operations. The package consisted of a combination of equity and loan stock.

While easyCar added a few sites in the second half of 2001 and early 2002, volatile demand in the wake of the September 11 attacks forced easyCar to roll out new rental locations somewhat slower than originally expected.[17] Growth accelerated, however, in spring 2002. Between May 2002 and January 2003, easyCar opened 30 new locations, to go from 18 sites to a total of 48 sites. This acceleration in growth also coincided with a change in easyCar's policy regarding the makeup of its fleet. By May 2002, easyCar's fleet consisted of 6,000 Mercedes A-class vehicles across 18 sites. Beginning in May, however, easyCar began to stock its fleet with other types of vehicles. It still maintained its policy of only offering a single vehicle at each location, but now the vehicle the customer received depended on the location. The first new vehicle easyCar introduced was the Vauxhall Corsa. According to Stelios,

> Vauxhall Corsas cost easyCar £2 a day less than Mercedes A-Class so we can pass this saving on to customers. Customers themselves will decide if they want to pay a premium for a Mercedes. EasyGroup companies benefit from economies of scale where relevant but we also want to create contestable markets among our suppliers so that we can keep the cost to our customers as low as possible.[18]

By January 2003, easyCar was also using Ford Focuses (four locations), Renault Clios (three locations), Toyota Yarises (three locations), and Mercedes Smart cars (two locations), in addition to the Vauxhall Corsas (seven locations) and the Mercedes A-class vehicles (28 locations). Plans called for a further expansion of the fleet, from the 7,000 vehicles that easyCar had in January to 24,000 vehicles across 180 rental sites by the end of 2004.[19]

In addition to making vehicles available at more locations, easyCar had also changed its policies for 2003 to allow rentals for as little as one hour, and with as little as one hour's notice of rental. By making this change, Stelios felt that easyCar could be a serious competitor to local taxis, buses, trains, and even car ownership. EasyCar expected that if it made car rental simple enough and cheap enough, that some people living in traffic-congested European cities who only use their car occasionally would give up the costs and hassles of car ownership and simply hire an easyCar when they needed a vehicle. Tapping into this broader transportation market would help the company reach its ambitious future sales goals.

Facilities

EasyCar had facilities in a total of 17 cities in 5 European countries, as shown in Exhibit 2. It primarily located its facilities near bus and train stations in the major European cities, seeking out sites that offered lower lease costs. It generally avoided prime airport locations, as the cost for space at and, in some cases, near airports was significantly higher than most other locations. When easyCar did locate near an airport, it generally chose sites off the airport, in order to reduce the cost of the lease. Airport locations also tended to require longer hours to satisfy customers arriving on late flights or departing on very early flights. Easy-Car kept its airport locations open 24 hours a day, whereas its other locations were generally only open from 7 A.M. to 11 P.M.

---

[17]Burt, T. "EasyCar agrees deal with Vauxhall," *Financial Times,* 30 April 2002, p. 24.

[18]EasyCar.com website news release, 2 May 2002.

[19]"Marketing Week: EasyCar appoints head of European marketing," *Financial Times Information Limited,* 9 January 2003.

EXHIBIT 2
**EasyCar Locations in
January 2003**

Source: EasyCar.com Web
site January 2003.

Country	City	Number	Number Near an Airport
France	Nice	1	1
France	Paris	8	0
Netherlands	Amsterdam	3	1
Spain	Barcelona	2	0
Spain	Madrid	2	0
Spain	Majorca	1	1
Spain	Malagra	1	1
Switzerland	Geneva	1	1
UK	Birmingham	2	0
UK	Bromley	1	0
UK	Croydon	1	1
UK	Glasgow	2	1
UK	Kingston-Upon-Thames	1	0
UK	Liverpool	2	1
UK	London	15	0
UK	Manchester	2	1
UK	Waterford	1	0
Total	5 Countries, 17 Cities	46	9

The physical facilities at all locations were kept to a minimum. In many locations, easy-Car leased space in an existing parking garage. Employees worked out of a small, self-contained cubicle within the garage. The cubicle, depending on the location, might be no more than 15 square meters, and included little more than a small counter and a couple of computers at which staff processed customers as they came to pick up or return their vehicles. EasyCar also leased a number of spaces within the garage for its fleet of cars. However, because easyCar's vehicles were rented 90% of the time, the number of spaces required at an average site, which had a fleet of about 150 cars, was only 15–20 spaces.[20] To speed up the opening of new sites, easyCar had equipped a number of vans with all the needed computer and telephone equipment to run a site.[21] From an operational perspective, it could open a new location by simply leasing 20 or so spaces in a parking garage, hiring a small staff, driving a van to the location, and adding the location to the company's website. Depending on the fleet size at a location, easyCar typically had only one or two people working at a site at a time.

Vehicle Pickup and Return Processes

Customers arrived at a site to pick up a vehicle within a prearranged one-hour time period. Each customer selected this time slot when he or she booked the vehicles. EasyCar adjusted the first day's rental price based on the pickup time. Customers who picked their cars up earlier in the day or at popular times were charged more compared to customers picking up their cars later in the day or at less busy times. Customers were required to bring a printed copy of their contract, along with the credit card they used to make the booking and identification. Given the low staffing levels, customers occasionally had to wait 30 minutes or more to be processed and receive their vehicles, particularly at peak times of the day. Processing a customer began with the employee accessing the customer's contract online. If the customer was a new easyCar customer to the site, the basic policies and possible additional charges were briefly explained. The employee then made copies of the customer's identification and credit

[20]Simpkins, E. "Stelios isn't taking it easy," *Sunday Telegraph* (UK), 15 December 2002.
[21]Ibid.

card and took a digital photo of the customer. The customer was charged an €80 refundable deposit, signed the contract, and was on the way.

All vehicles were rented with more or less empty fuel tanks with the exact level dependent on how much gasoline was left in the vehicle when the previous renter returned it. Customers were provided with a small map of the immediate area around the rental site, showing the location and hours of nearby gas stations. Customers could return vehicles with any amount of gas in them as long as the "low-fuel" indicator light in the vehicle was not on. Customers who returned vehicles with the low-fuel indicator light on were charged a fueling fee of €16.

Customers were also expected to return the vehicle within a prearranged one-hour time period, which they also selected at the time of booking. While customers did not have to worry about refueling the car before returning it, they were expected to thoroughly clean the car. This clean car policy had been implemented in May 2002 as a way to further reduce the price customers could pay for their vehicle. Prior to this change, all customers paid a fixed preparation fee of €11 each time they rented a vehicle (up from the €8 preparation fee when the company started operations in 2000). The new policy reduced this up-front preparation fee to €4 but required customers to either return the vehicle clean or pay an additional cleaning fee of €16. In order to avoid any misunderstanding about what it meant by a clean car, easyCar provided customers with an explicit description of what constituted a clean car, both for the interior and the exterior of the car. This included that it had to be apparent that the exterior of the car had been washed prior to returning the vehicle. The map that customers were provided when they picked up their cars that showed nearby gas stations also showed nearby car washes where they could clean the car before returning it. While easyCar had received some bad press in relation to the policy,[22] 85% of customers returned their vehicles clean as a result of the policy.

When a customer returned the vehicle, an easyCar employee would check to make sure that the vehicle was clean, undamaged, and that the low-fuel indicator light was not on. The employee would also check the kilometers driven. The customer would then be notified of any additional charges. These charges would be subtracted from the €80 deposit and the difference refunded to the customer's credit card (or, if additional charges exceeded the €80 deposit, the customer's credit card would be charged the difference).

Pricing

EasyCar clearly differentiated itself from its competitors with its low price. In addition, pricing also played a key role in easyCar's efforts to achieve high utilization of its fleet of cars. EasyCar advertised prices as low as €5 per day plus a per-rental preparation fee of €4. Prices, however, varied by the location and dates of the rental, by when the booking was made, and by what time the car was to be picked up and returned. EasyCar's systems constantly evaluated projected demand and expected utilization at each site and adjusted price accordingly. Achieving the €5 per day rate usually required customers to book well in advance, and these rates were typically only available on weekdays. Weekend rates, when booked well in advance, typically started a few euros higher than the weekday rates. As a given rental date approached, however, the price typically went up significantly as easyCar approached 100% fleet utilization for that day. Rates could literally triple overnight if there was sufficient booking activity. Generally, however, easyCar's price was less than half that of its major competitors. EasyCar, unlike most other rental car companies, required customers to pay in full at the time of booking, and once a booking was made, it was nonrefundable.

EasyCar's base price covered only the core rental of the vehicle—the total price customers paid was in many cases much higher and depended on how the customer reserved, paid for, used, and returned the vehicle. EasyCar's price was based on customers booking through the company's website and paying for their rental with their easyMoney credit card. EasyMoney was the easyGroup's credit and financial services company. Customers who chose to book through the company's phone reservation system were charged an additional €0.95 a minute for the call, and those who used other credit cards were charged €5 extra. All vehicles had to be paid for by a credit or debit card—cash was not accepted. The base rental price allowed customers to drive vehicles 100 kilometers per day—additional kilometers were charged at a rate of €0.12 per kilometer. In addition, customers were expected to return their cars clean and on time. Customers who returned cars that did not meet easyCar's standards for cleanness were charged a €16 cleaning fee. Those who returned their cars late were immediately charged €120 and subsequently charged an additional €120 for each subsequent 24-hour period in which the car was not returned. EasyCar explained the high late fee as representing the cost that it would likely incur in providing another vehicle to the next customer. Customers wishing to make any changes to their bookings were also charged a change fee of €16. Changes could be made either before the rental started or during the rental period, but were limited to changing the dates, times, and location of the rental and were subject to the prices and vehicle availability at the time the change was being made. If the change resulted in an overall lower price for the rental, however, no refund was provided for the difference.

Beginning in 2003, all customers were also required to purchase loss/damage insurance for an additional charge of €4 a day that eliminated the customer's liability for loss or damage to the vehicle (excluding damage to the tires or windshield of the vehicle). Through 2002, customers were able to choose whether or not to purchase additional insurance from easyCar to eliminate any financial liability in the event that the rental vehicle was damaged. The cost of this insurance had been €6 a day, and approximately 60% of easyCar's customers purchased this optional insurance. Those not purchasing this insurance had either assumed the liability for the first €800 in damages personally, or had their own insurance through some other means (e.g., some credit card companies provide this insurance to their cardholders at no additional charge for short-term rentals paid for with the credit card).

EasyCar's website attempted to make all these additional charges clear to customers at the time of their booking. EasyCar had received a fair amount of bad press when it first opened for business after many renters complained about having to pay undisclosed charges when they returned their cars.[23] In response, easyCar had revamped its website in an effort to make these charges more transparent to customers and to explain the logic behind many of these charges.

Promotion

EasyCar's promotional efforts had through 2002 focused primarily on posters and press advertising. Posters were particularly prevalent in metro systems and bus and train stations in cities were easyCar had operations. All this advertising focused on easyCar's low price. According to founder Stelios:

> You will never see an advert for an easy company offering an experience—it's about price. If you create expectations you can't live up to then you will ultimately suffer as a result.[24]

In 2002, easyCar spent £1.43 million on such advertising.[25]

EasyCar also promoted itself by displaying its name, phone number, and website address prominently on the doors and rear window of its entire fleet of vehicles, and took advantage

[23]Stanton, J. "The empire that's easy money," *Edinburgh Evening News,* 26 November 2002.

[24]"The big picture—an interview with Stelios" *Sunday Herald* (UK), 16 March 2003,

[25]"Marketing Week: EasyCar appoints head of European marketing," *Financial Times Information Limited,* 9 January 2003.

of free publicity when the opportunity presented itself. An example of seeking out such publicity occurred when Hertz complained that easyCar's comparative advertising campaign in the Netherlands that featured the line "The best reason to use easyCar.com can be found at hertz.nl" violated Dutch law that required comparative advertising to be exact, not general. In response, Stelios and a group of easyCar employees, dressed in orange boiler suits and with a fleet of easyCar vehicles, protested outside the Hertz Amsterdam office with signs asking "What is Hertz frightened of?"[26]

In an effort to help reach its goal of quadrupling sales in the next 2 years, easyCar had hired Jennifer Mowat for the new position of commercial director to take over responsibility for easyCar's European marketing. Mowat had previously been eBay's UK country manager and had recently completed an MBA in Switzerland. Previously, Stelios and easyCar's managing director, Andrew Fitzmaurice, had handled the marketing function themselves.[27] As part of this stepped up marketing effort, easyCar also planned to double its advertising budget for 2003, to £3 million, and to begin to advertise on television. The television advertising campaign was to feature easyCar's founder, Stelios.[28]

Legal Challenges

EasyCar faced several challenges to its approaches. The most significant dealt with a November 2002 ruling made by the Office of Fair Trading (OFT) that easyCar had to grant customers 7 days from the time they made a booking to cancel their booking and receive a full refund. The OFT was a UK governmental agency that was responsible for protecting UK consumers from unfair and/or anticompetitive business practices. The ruling against easyCar was based on the 2000 Consumer Protection Distance Selling Regulations. These regulations stipulated that companies that sell at a distance (e.g., by Internet, phone) must provide customers with a 7-day cooling-off period, during which time customers can cancel their contracts with the company and receive a full refund. The law exempted accommodation, transportation, catering, and leisure service companies from this requirement. The OFT's ruling concluded that easyCar did not qualify as a transportation service company because the consumers had to drive themselves, and as such they were not receiving a transport service, just a car.[29]

EasyCar had appealed the OFT's decision to the UK High Court on the grounds that it was indeed a transportation service company and was entitled to an exemption from this requirement. EasyCar was hopeful that it would eventually win this legal challenge. EasyCar had argued that this ruling would destroy the company's book-early-pay-less philosophy and could lead to a tripling of prices.[30] Chairman Stelios was quoted as saying:

> It is very serious. My fear is that as soon as we put in the seven-day cooling off periods our utilization rate will fall from 90% to 65%. That's the difference between a profitable company and an unprofitable one.[31]

EasyCar was also concerned that prolonged legal action on this point could interfere with its plans for a 2004 IPO.

[26]EasyCar.com website news release, 22 April 2002.

[27]"Marketing Week: EasyCar appoints head of European marketing," *Financial Times Information Limited,* 9 January 2003.

[28]"Campaigning: EasyGroup appoints Publicis for easyCar TV advertising brief," *Financial Times Information Limited,* 31 January 2003.

[29]Macintosh, J. "EasyCar sues OFT amid threat to planned flotation," *Financial Times,* 22 November 2002, p. 4.

[30]"Marketing Week: EasyCar appoints head of European marketing," *Financial Times Information Limited,* 9 January 2003.

[31]Mackintosh, J. "EasyCar sues OFT amid threat to planned flotation." *Financial Times,* 22 November, 2002, p. 4.

OFT, for its part, had also applied to the UK High Court for an injunction to make the company comply with the ruling. Other rental car companies were generally unconcerned about the ruling, as few offered big discounts for early bookings or nonrefundable bookings.[32]

EasyCar's new policy of posting the pictures of customers whose cars were 15 days or more overdue was also drawing legal criticism. EasyCar had recently received public warnings from lawyers that this new policy might violate data protection, libel, privacy, confidentiality, and human rights laws.[33] Of particular concern to some lawyers was the possibility that easyCar might post the wrong person's picture, given the large number of customers the company dealt with.[34] Such a mistake could open the company to costly libel suits. The policy of posting the pictures of overdue customers on the easyCar website, initiated in November 2002, was designed to reduce the losses associated with customers renting a vehicle and never returning it. The costs were significant, according to Stelios:

> These cars are expensive, £15,000 each, and we have 6000 of them. At any given time we are looking for as many as several tens which are overdue. If we don't get one back, it's a write-off. We are writing off an entire car, and its uninsurable.[35]

Stelios was also convinced of the legality of the new policy. In a letter to the editor responding to the legal concerns raised in the press, Stelios said:

> From a legal perspective, we have been entirely factual and objective and are merely reporting the details of the overdue car and the person who collected it. In addition, our policy is made very clear in our terms and conditions and the photo is taken both overtly and with the consent of the customer. . . . I estimate the total cost of overdue cars to be 5% of total easyCar costs, or 50p on every car rental day for all customers. In 2004, when I intend to float easyCar, this cost will amount to £5 million unless we can reduce our quantity of overdue cars.[36]

In the past, easyCar had simply provided pictures to police when a rental was 15 or more days overdue. It was hoped that posting the picture would both discourage drivers from not returning vehicles and shame those drivers who currently had overdue cars into returning them. In fact, the first person who easyCar posted to its website did indeed return his car 2 days later. The vehicle was 29 days late.[37]

The Future

At the end of 2002, Stelios had stepped down as the CEO of easyJet so that he could devote more of his time to the other easyGroup companies, including easyCar. He had three priorities for the new year. One was to turn around the money losing easyInternetCafe business, which Stelios had described as "the worst mistake of my career."[38] The 22-store chain had lost £80 million in the last 2 years. A second was to oversee the planned launch of another new easyGroup business, easyCinema, in spring 2003. And the third was to oversee the rapid expansion of the easyCar chain, so that it would be ready for an initial public offering in the second half of 2004.

[32]Ibid.

[33]Sherwood, B. & Wendlandt, A. "EasyCar may be in difficulty over naming ploy," *Financial Times,* 14 November 2002, p. 2.

[34]Ibid.

[35]"e-business: Internet fraudsters fail to steal Potter movie's magic & other news," *Financial Times Information Limited,* 19 November 2002.

[36]Haji-Ioannou, S. "Letters to the editor: Costly effect of late car return," *Financial Times,* 16 November 2002, p. 10.

[37]Hookham, M. "How Stelios nets return of his cars," *Daily Post* (Liverpool, UK), 14 November 2002.

[38]Bentley, S. "The worst mistake of my career, by Stelios" *Financial Times,* 24 December 2002.

Pfizer, Inc., Animal Health Products[1]— Industry Downturns and Marketing Strategy

Jakki Mohr *University of Montana*

Sara Streeter, MBA *University of Montana*

Gail Oss, Territory Manager of Pfizer, Inc., Animal Health Group in western Montana and southeastern Idaho, was driving back to her home office after a day of visiting cattle ranchers in her territory. The combination of the spring sunshine warming the air and the snow-capped peaks of the Bitterroot Mountains provided a stunningly beautiful backdrop for her drive. But the majestic beauty provided little relief to her troubled thoughts.

The NAFTA agreement with Canada and Mexico had hit local ranchers particularly hard. The influx of beef cattle into the U.S. market from these countries, as well as beef from other countries (e.g., Australia) that entered the U.S. via more lenient import restrictions in Mexico, had wreaked havoc over the past year. Prices of beef had declined precipitously from the prior year. Ranchers in the past had retained sufficient reserves to come back from a bad year, but this year, things were particularly bad. The prices being offered for the calves by the feedlot operators were, in many cases, less than the costs of raising those calves. Ranchers' objectives had changed from making some modest income off their cattle operations to minimizing their losses.

In this environment, ranchers were actively seeking ways to cut costs. Gail sold high-quality animal health products, oftentimes at a premium price. One way in which ranchers could cut costs was either to scrimp on animal healthcare products, such as vaccines and antibiotics, or to switch to a lower-cost alternative. The current environment posed a particu-

[1]Some of the information in this case has been modified to protect the proprietary nature of firms' marketing strategies. The case is intended to be used as a basis for class discussion rather than to illustrate either effective or ineffective marketing strategies.

larly severe threat, not only to Gail's company, but also to her very livelihood. Gail had spent a substantial amount of time and effort cultivating long-term relationships with many of these ranchers—many of whom she had had to convince of her credibility, given her gender. Given the time and effort she had spent cultivating these relationships, as well as the camaraderie she felt with her customers, she did not want to see the ranchers in her territory go under. Ranching was an important part of the history of Montana; many ranchers had ties to the land going back generations. They took pride in producing the food for many tables in the U.S. and other areas of the world. Gail felt that Pfizer could use its fairly significant resources in a very influential manner to help these ranchers. Merely lowering the price on her products (if that was even possible) was merely a band-aid solution to the problem.

As part of Gail's weekly responsibilities, she communicated via an automated computer system to her sales manager, Tom Brooks, (also in Montana) and to the marketing managers at headquarters (in Exton, Pennsylvania). She knew she needed to report the severity of the situation, but more importantly, she wanted to encourage headquarters to take the bull by the horns, so to speak. So, she was pondering the message she would write that evening from her kitchen table.

Industry Background

The supply chain (Exhibit 1) for beef begins with the cow/calf producer (the commercial rancher). Commercial ranchers are in the business of breeding and raising cattle for the purpose of selling them to feedlots. Ranchers keep a herd of cows that are bred yearly. The calves are generally born in the early spring, weaned in October, and shipped to feedlots generally in late October/early November. The ranchers' objectives are to minimize death loss in their herd and to breed cows that give birth to low birth-weight calves (for calving ease), produce beef that will grade low choice by having a good amount of marbling, and produce calves that gain weight quickly. Success measures include conception rate of cows exposed to bulls, live birth rates, birth weights, weaning weights, death loss, and profitability. By the time a rancher sells his calves to the feedlot, the name of the game is pounds. The rancher generally wants the biggest calves possible by that time.

Within a commodity market, basic laws of supply and demand are influenced by those in a position to control access to the markets. Four meatpackers controlled roughly 80% of the industry. Meatpackers have acted as an intermediary between the meat consumer and the meat producer. This situation has not facilitated a free flow of information throughout the supply chain, and therefore, the industry has not been strongly consumer focused.

Exhibit 2 traces the market share for beef, pork, and poultry from 1970–1997 and projects changes in the market through 2003. The market share for beef has fallen from 44% in 1970 to 32% in 1997, a 27% drop.

Some of the reasons for the decline included

- Changes in consumer lifestyles (less time spent in preparing home-cooked meals); an interesting statistic is that two-thirds of all dinner decisions are made on the same day and of those, three-quarters don't know what they're going to make at 4:30 PM.
- Health/nutritional issues (dietary considerations involving cholesterol, fat content, food-borne diseases, etc.).
- Switching to alternative meat products.

EXHIBIT 1
Supply Chain for Beef

Cow/Calf Producers → Feedlot → Meat Packer → Customers (food service, retail, etc.)

EXHIBIT 2 Per Capita Meat Consumption % Market Share (Retail Weight)

Source: USDA & NCBA.

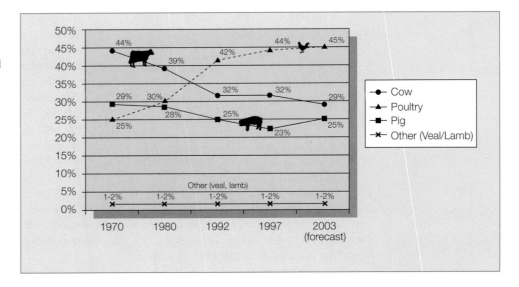

In addition, the pork and poultry industries had done a better job of marketing their products. During 1997, the number of new poultry products (for example, stuffed chicken entrees, gourmet home meal replacements) introduced to the market increased 13% from the prior year, compared to an increase of only 3.5% for new beef products. And, retail pricing for beef remained stubbornly high (although this high price did not translate into higher prices of the calves on a per-weight basis to the ranchers, as discussed subsequently).

Based upon historical data, shown in Exhibit 3, the beef production cycle spans a twelve-year period in which production levels expand and contract. As Exhibit 3 shows, the amount of beef produced (bars in the chart, millions of pounds on the left-hand scale) increased through the mid-90s—despite the declining beef consumption in the U.S. shown in the prior figure. This relationship between production and consumption is consistent with other commodity markets, where there exists an inverse relationship between supply and demand.

Some of the reasons for increased beef production in the mid-90s included

- Herd liquidation: low cattle prices, coupled with the high cost of feed, drove some producers out of business.
- Improved genetics and animal health/nutrition increased production yields; indeed, although cow numbers had decreased by 10% since 1985 (as noted by Exhibit 4), productivity per cow increased by 29%.
- Export of beef increased sevenfold since 1985 (to 2 billion pounds); key markets include Japan (54% of export volume); Canada (16%); Korea (11%), and Mexico (9%).

Exhibit 3 also shows that the price the ranchers received for their beef cattle varied inversely with production (right-hand scale). Although calf prices were expected to rise slightly through the late 90s/early 2000s, the prices paid were still far below the relatively high prices consumers paid at retail. One of the reasons given for the relatively low prices paid to ranchers on a per-pound basis for their calves was the high degree of concentration at the meat packer level of the supply chain. As noted previously, four packing houses controlled access to the market. Some ranchers believed this gave the packing houses near-monopoly power in setting prices (both for what they would pay

EXHIBIT 3   Beef Production and Price

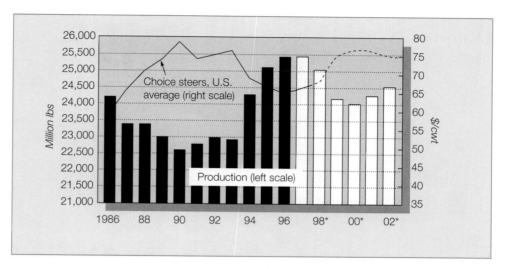

feedlot operators for the calves, and in charging prices to their downstream customers (e.g., the grocery store chains). Although the U.S. government had investigated the possibility of collusion among packers, the evidence was not sufficient to draw any firm conclusions.

To further complicate matters, the NAFTA agreement passed in 1989 had given open access to the U.S. markets from Mexican and Canadian ranchers. The lowering of trade barriers, coupled with weakness in the Canadian dollar and the Mexican peso, made imported livestock cheap, compared to U.S.-grown animals. As a result, thousands of head of cattle came streaming across the borders. The flow was heaviest from Canada.

During the summer of 1998, ranchers had been quite vocal in drawing attention to the influx of cattle from Canada. Local governments were somewhat responsive to their concerns. Indeed, trucks carrying Canadian cattle had been turned back at the U.S./Canadian border for minor infractions, such as licensing. In addition, the trucks were consistently pulled over for inspections. A private coalition of ranchers, calling itself the Ranchers-Cattlemen Action Legal Foundation (R-CALF) filed three separate petitions with the U.S. International Trade Commission (ITC) on October 1, 1998, two against Canada and one against Mexico, asking for U.S. government trade investigations. The group requested that anti-dumping duties be levied on meat or livestock imports from the two countries. The Montana Stockgrowers Association had been an early and steadfast supporter of R-CALF.

The ITC determined that there was evidence to support the charge that Canadian cattle imports are causing material injury to U.S. domestic cattle producers. The Department of Commerce began to collect information on Canadian subsidies and prices at which Canadian cattle are sold in Canada and in the United States. In the case against Mexico, the ITC determined that there was no indication that imports of live cattle from Mexico were causing "material injury" to the domestic industry in the U.S. Dissatisfied with the response, R-CALF decided to appeal the case to the Court of International Trade.

Ranchers were doing what they could to minimize the impact of the NAFTA agreement on their livelihoods; however, some could not sustain their operations in light of the lower cattle prices. The number of cattle operations was declining. In many cases, smaller ranchers were selling out to their larger neighbors. This reality was reflected in the cattle inventory statistics, shown in Exhibit 4. The number of cattle kept by U.S.

EXHIBIT 4   **Total U.S. Inventory**

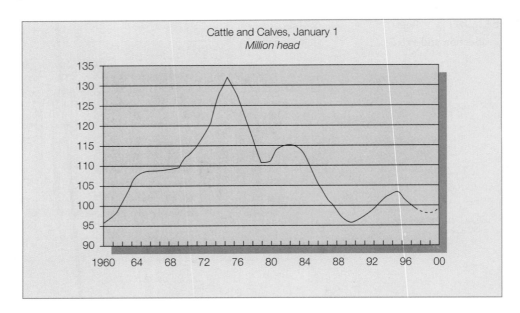

ranchers had declined from a high of approximately 132 million head in 1975, to just under 100 million head in 1998. As noted previously, improvements in genetics and animal health and nutrition allowed ranchers to increase production yields, even with fewer head.

Additional Industry Changes

Some of the changes that had occurred in the poultry and pork industries, including more ready-to-eat products and branded products, were expected to diffuse into the cattle industry. Industry analysts believed that the beef industry would need to develop products that could be more easily prepared, and to develop branded products that consumers could recognize and rely upon for quality and convenience. In addition, industry analysts believed that the beef industry would need to improve the quality of its products (in terms of more consistent taste and tenderness), as currently only 25% of the beef produced met quality targets.

The development of branded beef would require a tracking system from "birth-to-beef " in the supply chain. Such tracking would allow standardized health, quality, and management protocols, as well as improved feedback through the entire production model. This change would also necessitate the producers being more closely linked to the feedlots to improve the quality of the beef. Branded beef production would move the industry from a cost-based (production) model to a value-added model. Better coordination along the supply chain would insure an increased flow of information from the consumer to the producer. Alliances between the cow/calf producer and the feedlots would allow ranchers to better track the success of their calves (based on health and weight gain). Such data could allow the ranchers to further improve the genetics of their herd by tracking which cow/bull combinations had delivered the higher-yield calves. As part of these trends, some degree of integration or vertical coordination will occur in the beef industry. Ranchers will need to participate in order to ensure market access for their product. Ranchers will have to think beyond the boundaries of their own ranches.

EXHIBIT 5 **Pfizer Animal Health Organization**

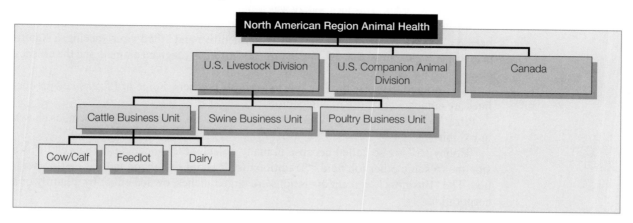

Pfizer Animal Health Group

Pfizer Inc. is a research-based, diversified health care company with global operations. Pfizer Animal Health is one of the corporation's three major business groups (the other two being the Consumer Health Care Group and U.S. Pharmaceuticals). The Animal Health Products Group accounted for roughly 12% of the company's revenues in 1998 (Pfizer Annual Report).

Pfizer Animal Health products are sold to veterinarians and animal health distributors in more than 140 countries around the world for use by livestock producers and horse and pet owners; the products are used in more than 30 animal species. Pfizer Animal Health is committed to providing high-quality, research-based health products for livestock and companion animals. The company continues to invest significant dollars for research and development. As a result, Pfizer has many new animal health products in its research pipeline, a number of which have already been introduced in some international markets and will become available in the United States in the next several years.

As Exhibit 5 shows, the Animal Health Group is divided into a North America Region with a U.S. Livestock Division, a U.S. Companion Animal Division (cats, dogs, etc.), and Canada. The Cow/Calf Division falls under the Cattle Business Unit within the Livestock Division. That Division is organized further by product type (Wood Mackenzie Report).

The marketing managers for each cattle market segment work closely with product managers and sales managers to ensure timely, accurate information back from the field. Territory managers responsible for all sales activities report to an Area Sales Manager, who in turn reports to the national sales and marketing manager. Territory managers are typically compensated on a roughly 80% salary/20% commission basis. This percentage would vary by salesperson by year: in a good year the commission might be a much higher percentage of overall earnings, while in a bad year, the salary component might be a greater percentage of the salesperson's overall earnings.

Marketing Strategy

Pfizer's Cow/Calf Division offers a full range of products to cattle ranchers, including vaccines for both newborn calves and their mothers, medications (for example, de-wormers, anti-diarrheals), and antibiotics (for pneumonia and other diseases). Pfizer's sophisticated research-and-development system resulted in a number of new and useful products for the market. For example, Pfizer developed a long-lasting de-wormer that was simply poured along the cow's back. This technology was a significant time-saver to the rancher, eliminating the need to administer either an oral medication or an injection. Moreover, Pfizer had been the first company to come up with a modified-live and killed virus vaccine, a significant technological breakthrough which provided safety in pregnant animals and the efficacy of a modified-live virus.

Pfizer offered a diverse product line to cow/calf ranchers. Some of Pfizer's key product lines are compared to those of competitors in Exhibit 6.

Pfizer segmented ranchers in the cow/calf business on the basis of herd size, as shown in Exhibit 7.

"Hobbyists" are so called because in many cases, these ranchers run their cattle as a sideline to some other job held. "Traditionalists'" main livelihood is their cattle operation. The "Business" segment operations are large ranches, owned either by a family or a corporation.

Pfizer's extensive network of field sales representatives visits the ranchers to inform them about new and existing products. Time spent with accounts was typically allocated on the basis of volume of product purchased.

Pfizer positioned its products on the combination of superior science (resulting from its significant R&D efforts) and high-quality production/quality control techniques. For example, although other companies in the market (particularly generics) used similar formulations in their products, on occasion they did not have good quality control in the production line, resulting in batches of ineffective vaccines and recalls. Pfizer backed its products completely with a Technical Services Department. If ranchers had any kind of health or nutritional problem with their herds, they could call on a team of Pfizer technical specialists who would work with the local veterinarian, utilizing blood and other diagnostics to identify the problem and suggest a solution.

Pfizer also was very involved in the cattle industry itself. Each territory manager was given an annual budget that included discretionary funds to be spent in his/her territory to sponsor industry activities such as seminars on herd health, stock shows, 4-H, and so forth. Gail Oss, for example, chose to spend a significant portion of her discretionary funds sponsoring meetings and conferences for the Montana Stockgrower's Association, which might include a veterinarian or a professor from the Extension Office of a state university speaking on issues pertinent to ranchers.

The majority of Pfizer's trade advertising was focused on specific products and appeared in cattle industry publications, such as *Beef Magazine* and *Bovine Veterinarian.* One ad read, "More veterinarians are satisfied with [Pfizer's] Dectomax Pour-On," and went on to describe veterinarians' superior satisfaction and greater likelihood of recommending Dectomax compared to a key competitor, Ivomec:

> Eighty-four percent of veterinarians who recommended Dectomax Pour-On said they were satisfied or very satisfied with its performance—compared to only 51% who were satisfied or very satisfied with Ivomec Eprinex Pour-On. . . . If choosing only between Dectomax and Ivomec, over three out of four veterinarians would choose to recommend Dectomax Pour-On.

Another ad read, "Calf Health Program Boosts Prices by Up to $21 More per Head." The data in the copy-intensive ad highlighted that "cow-calf producers enrolled in value-added programs like Pfizer Select Vaccine programs are being rewarded for their efforts with top-of-the-market prices." Such programs are based on a consistent program of vaccinating animals with specific products, and they provide optimal disease protection. The programs result in cattle that perform more consistently and predictably in terms of weight gain and beef quality—resulting in higher prices at sale time.

EXHIBIT 6 Comparison of Product Lines

Company	Pfizer	American Home Products (Fort Dodge)	Bayer	Merial
Sales and Profitability	10-year average annual sales growth increase of 3.8%; average for global veterinary market is 6.9%. Profit rate in 1997 was 8.4%. Market share in 1997 was 15.3%	10-year average annual sales growth increase of 7.8%; average for global veterinary market is 6.9%. Profit rate in 1997 was 11.0%; market share was 9.0%	10-year average annual sales growth increase of 10.2%; average for global veterinary market is 6.9%. Profit rate in 1997 was 16.8%; market share was 10.9%.	10-year average annual sales growth increase of 11.9%; average for global veterinary market is 6.9%. Profit rate in 1997 was 22.8%; market share was 16.4%.
Bovine Diseases Covered by Product Range	IBR; P1–3; BVD; BRSV; leptospira; rotavirus; coronavirus; campylobacter; clostridia; E.Coli; pasteurellosis; haemophilus.	Pasteurellosis; enterotoxaemia; chlamydia; salmonella; IBR; P1–3; brucellosis; rabies; E.Coli; anaplasmosis; tetanus; BVD; BRSV; leptospirosis; trichomonas; campylobacter; papilloma; haemophilus	IBR; FMD; IPV; P1–3; balanoposthitis; clostridia; haemophilus; BRSV; BVD; leptospira; E.Coli; rhinotracheitis; campylobacter.	Foot and mouth; rabies; brucellosis; paratuberculosis; rhinotracheitis; rotavirus; coronavirus; colibacciliosis; parainfluenza; BVD; aglactia; foot rot; black leg; IBR; leptospira; clostridia; pasteurella; BRSV; E.Coli.
Significant Products for Cattle	Comprehensive product line; anti-infectives have formed basis of product line for many years; vaccine businesses also very important; also sells a performance enhancer, virginiamycin; parasiticides, led by Dectomax, starting to make significant impact on sales; Valbazen anthelmintic; broad range of general pharmaceuticals.	Predominantly a vaccine company; antibiotics centered on anti-mastitis products; anti-infectives based on penicillins, tetracyclines, sulphonamides and quinolones; parasiticides led by Cydectin; main products in general pharmaceuticals are anabolic implants for muscle growth.	Product range biased towards parasiticides, particularly ectoparasiticides, and antibiotics; overall product range is diverse; some mastitis anti-microbials; wide range of pharmaceuticals, but sales value of each product is limited; focus is more towards companion animal market.	Most important product sector is parasiticides, with product range dominated by Ivermectin, which was the first endectocide to reach the market; success of Ivermectin has drawn strong competition; remainder of product range made up primarily of anthelmintics and a range of general pharmaceuticals and vaccines.
Strengths	Strong manufacturing capabilities based on fermentation expertise and capacity; global marketing coverage supported by strategic local manufacture;	Leading global vaccine business; good international exposure; comprehensive vaccine product range; potential for growth through Cydectin.	Growing market in expanding companion animal sector; solid in-house manufacturing supported by global distribution capability;	Leading veterinary vaccine company with broad product portfolio; strong line of new product introductions; good companion animal

(continued)

EXHIBIT 6 *(concluded)*

Company	Pfizer	American Home Products (Fort Dodge)	Bayer	Merial
	strong range of new products in early commercialization; broad product range with strength in companion animals.		business focused on key market areas.	business; global distribution network; strength in parasiticides and vaccines sectors.
Weaknesses	North America still dominates turnover; high proportion of sales due to off-patent products; heavily dependent on performance of livestock markets.	Business with disparate parts requiring strong central focus; except for vaccines, product range is dominated by commodity products; R&D likely to be reduced.	Underweight in USA; lack of critical mass in biologicals; no blockbuster product in North American market; narrow anti-infectives product portfolio; current R&D emphasis away from new product discovery.	Specialist pharmaceutical product line, not significantly involved in livestock sectors; aging anti-infectives portfolio; Ivermectin subject to intense competition.
% of R&D to Sales*	5	3	3	2
Position on Quality vs. Price†	5	3.5	3	3
Price Support of Distibution Channel‡	2	4	3	3

* Specific ratios are considered proprietary. Hence, a general rating scale is used where 5 means a higher percentage of R&D/Sales and 1 is a lower percentage.

† 5 = Focus on Quality only; 1 = Focus on Low Price only

‡ 5 = Strong emphasis on SPIFs (Special Promotional Incentive Funds) and price-related trade promotions; 1 = low emphasis

Source: This information is taken from the Wood MacKenzie Animal Health Market Review and its Veterinary Company Profiles, both done on a worldwide basis.

EXHIBIT 7 Pfizer Market Segments, 1998

Segment	# of Cattle	# of Operations	% of National Cattle Inventory
Hobbyist	<100	808,000	50%
Traditionalist	100–499	69,000	36%
Business	500+	5,900	14%

Although the territory managers called on ranchers (as well as the veterinarians, distributors, and dealers) in their territories, they sold no product directly to ranchers. Ranchers could buy their animal health products from either a local veterinarian or a distributor or dealer (such as a feed-and-seed store). The percentage of product flowing through vets or distributors and dealers varied significantly by region. In areas where feedlots (versus cow/calf ranchers) were the predominant customers, 95% of the product might flow through distributors. In areas where ranchers are the predominant customers, vets might sell 50% of the product, depending upon customer preferences.

Vets were particularly important given that the overwhelming majority of ranchers said that the person they trusted the most when it came to managing the health of their herd was their veterinarian. Pfizer capitalizes on this trust in the vet in its marketing program. When the vet consults and recommends a Pfizer product to a rancher, the vet gives the rancher a coded coupon which may be redeemed at either a vet clinic or supply house. When the coupon is sent back to Pfizer for reimbursement, the vet is credited for servicing that product, regardless of where the product is purchased.

Pfizer offers some trade promotions to vets and distributors, including volume rebate programs, price promotions on certain products during busy seasonal periods, and so forth. However, Pfizer's competitors oftentimes gave much more significant discounts and SPIFs to distributors. As a result, when a rancher went to a distributor to buy a product the vet had recommended, the distributor might switch the rancher to a similar product for which the distributor was making more profit. If it was a Pfizer product the vet had recommended, the distributor might switch the rancher to a competitor's product. Pfizer had historically avoided competing on the basis of such promotional tactics, feeling instead that redirecting such funds back into R&D resulted in better long-term benefits for its customers.

So, as Gail pondered these various facets of the company's market position and strategies, she decided to take a strong stance in her weekly memo. It was time to cut the bull.

Discussion Questions

1. Evaluate the trends affecting the cattle ranching industry.
2. To what degree is a high quality/premium price position a strength or a liability during an industry downturn? What are the various ways Pfizer could handle this situation?
3. Evaluate the various dimensions of Pfizer's marketing strategy: Market segmentation and positioning; product/price; distribution; trade advertising and trade promotion; personal selling; public relations and sponsorships. What makes sense and what doesn't? Why or why not?
4. Would Pfizer benefit from a relationship marketing focus? How would its marketing strategy need to be modified to take such a focus?
5. When an industry is in decline, to what extent should a supplier be involved in ensuring its customers' livelihoods?

9

Snacks to Go

JoAnn K. Linrud *Central Michigan University*

Jill Harms' half-year tenure as Assistant Category Manager for the Nuts, Natural Snacks and Cookies Category at Sathers, Inc. had been exciting. The variety of tasks in her category had been a challenge partly because Sathers management had targeted the Nuts, Natural Snacks and Cookies Category for growth, and partly because she had been given full responsibility for the category from the first day she had started at Sathers. That meant that she had direct responsibility to Mike Halverson, Director of Marketing.

Her focus on this Friday in mid-July of 1995 was the recommendation she would make to Mike on Monday concerning Snacks to Go, the snack nuts product line introduced earlier in the year. After a fast start, sales had lagged. Now, with lackluster market-monitoring reports on her desk, Jill was being asked to decide the line's fate. As she thought about possible alternatives for the product line, she knew she could commission a new round of research. But pressures were mounting to improve the line's performance—soon—or drop the line completely.

Background

History

As if the economic woes of the Great Depression weren't enough, in 1936 John Sather's grocery store in Round Lake, Minnesota, burned to the ground. With a tenacity of spirit that wouldn't allow him to give up, he instead began to distribute cookies in bulk to area grocers, adding other products as time passed. Ten years later, his son Kenneth joined the business, after serving as a bomber pilot in WWII. Kenneth implemented the philosophy of value by selling packages of cookies and other products such as almond bark, four packages for $1.00, to grocers in a five-county area. Sathers serviced their accounts with a sales force that personally took orders, delivered product, and stocked shelves. A turning point came when a number of salesmen left the organization, leaving Sathers shorthanded. As a stop-gap measure, Sathers management offered discounts to the customers who would order by telephone and stock their own shelves. Consequently, Sathers became an early entrant in the field of telephone marketing.

In the 1960s Kenneth Sather initiated the "pegboard" display: hanging cellophane bags with paper headers. Distributing product in ten states by this time, Sathers candy caught the eye of some regional Kmart managers, who were at that time responsible for making buying decisions for their own stores. Kenneth convinced these Kmarts to carry two bags of candy for $1.00, Sathers' original "Two for One." Success in these stores led to the capture of the entire Kmart account by 1972. So began national distribution of the Sathers line of packaged candy.

Still emphasizing repackaging (called "rebagging" by some in the trade), Sathers purchased a nut roasting operation in the 1960s, expanding the product line beyond cookies and candy. Further acquisitions included a New Orleans manufacturing plant from American Candy Company in 1985, and an additional candy manufacturing operation in the later 1980s. Sathers acquired Powell's Inc., a Hopkins, Minnesota, candy manufacturer and distributor with over 340 employees and revenues of about $30 million in 1991, bringing the company's total employees to 1,500 and its in-house production to fifty percent, well toward its goal of eighty percent. The Powell's acquisition also netted Sathers a film-printing business, Flex-o-Print, which would increase their packaging capabilities.

In 1992, Sathers upgraded its Round Lake packaging facility with a robotics operation. By 1993, Sathers' $135 million in sales marked the tenth straight year of sales gains. In 1994, Sathers broadened the product line produced in the Hopkins operation. That year also brought the acquisition of the assets of North Star Candy Company, a Wisconsin-based niche candy marketer.

To manage the change from distributor to manufacturer, Sathers hired a professional management team, headed by Howard Kosel, who came to Sathers as President in 1980. He assumed the CEO duties when William S. Bradfield joined the organization as Executive Vice President in 1989. Bradfield became COO and President in 1991, positions he continued to hold. Michael Halverson was brought in as Director of Marketing, a newly created position, in 1992. Mr. Halverson instituted the Category Manager organizational design for his department; some Category Managers' positions were unfilled. (See Marketing organizational chart, Exhibit 1.) Over the years, ownership had passed to four grandsons of John Sather. Although their management style was "hands-off," a family atmosphere pervaded the Round Lake facility.

Operations

In 1995, Sathers manufactured and distributed bag candy, nuts, natural snacks, and cookies, sold through over 50,000 drug, convenience, grocery, variety, and discount stores worldwide. Sathers grouped its products into six categories: general candy, seasonal candy, nuts and natural snacks, cookies, international, and private label candy. (See Exhibit 2 for a description of each category.)

Hanging bag candy was Sathers' mainstay; the "Two for $1.00" Value Line generated up to fifty percent of the vertically integrated company's $150 million in revenues. Sathers employed approximately 1,500 people in its manufacturing plants in Hopkins, a Minneapolis suburb, and New Orleans, and in its distribution centers in Chattanooga, Pittston, Pennsylvania, and Round Lake, and at Flex-o-Print, at Rogers, just north of Minneapolis.

The 350,000 square foot facility at Round Lake (population 463, in the southwestern part of Minnesota) was command central for all operations, including the telemarketing arm and the fleet of trucks used for distribution in the U.S. and Canada. The plant was equipped with a $5 million robotics packaging operation, to run ten lines using the latest robotics and vision inspection system, ending with robotics palletization. The system gave Sathers state-of-the-art efficiency in packaging and quality control. Round Lake also had a computerized telemarketing system for calling each customer every three weeks to track existing accounts, take orders, and monitor new business efforts.

EXHIBIT 1   Marketing Organizational Chart

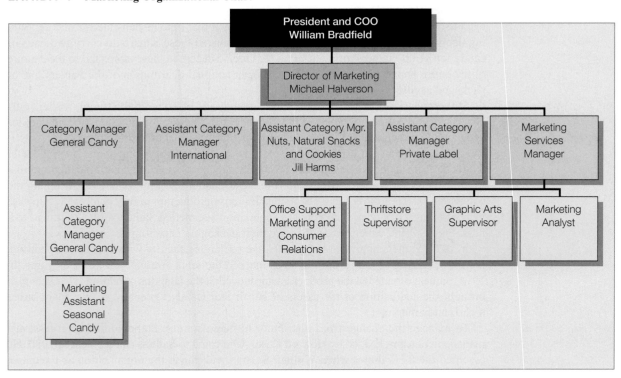

EXHIBIT 2   Sathers Product Categories

Category	Description
General Candy	• 119 items in the 2/$1.00 line (chocolate candy, licorice, jelly/gummy candy, mint candy, kiddie candy, coconut candy, hard candy, caramel candy, traditional candy, sugar-free candy, Hispanic candy); • 70 items in the profit-advantage line; • 25 items in the 2/$3.00 line in the traditional "peg board" hanging bags; • 85 different candy products offered in bulk; • other package alternatives including prepacked shippers and large lay-down bag candy.
Seasonal Candy	• Many products in the general candy lines, offered in special packages and priced for seasonal product movement.
Nuts and Natural Snacks	• 24 items in the 2/$1.00 line (such as Salted-in-the-shell, Sunflower Seeds and Peanuts, Spanish Peanuts, Banana Chips, Mixed Nuts, Aloha Mix, Trail Mix, Pineapple Tidbits, Red and Natural Pistachios, etc.); • 23 items in the profit-advantage line; • over 30 items offered in bulk.
Cookies	• 16 items in the 2/$1.00 line (such as Chocolate Covered Regal Graham Cookies, Coco Chip Cookies, Oatmeal Raisin Cookies, Fig Bars, Striped Shortbread Cookies, sandwich crèmes, etc.); • sugar-free wafers in four flavors with separate counter and floor displays.
International	• Sales of candy, nuts, and natural snacks to thirty accounts in countries such as Mexico, Canada, Saudi Arabia, Panama, Uruguay, and countries in the Caribbean.
Private Label Candy	• Sales of candy, nuts, and natural snacks to twelve accounts of national and regional drug and discount stores.

The Sathers truck fleet capped its distribution system with over 300 trucks running at almost 100 percent efficiency, carrying finished product out and supplies in. The system enabled Sathers to complete delivery in about half the time of typical truck delivery, allowing customers to minimize inventory. Sales were to confections distributors, retail chain distribution centers, and some direct store-door delivery accounts. And, while Sathers did very little consumer promotions, it heavily supported retailers and distributors' efforts to sell to retailers. For example, Sathers provided point-of-purchase signage and racks, product reorder tags, product samples, and detailed instructions for product display, order and reorder. Sathers paid no slotting allowances.

Candy Market

Candy consumption, in general, was on the rise in the U.S., from 16 pounds per capita in 1986 to almost 22 pounds in 1994, with a retail market of $12 to $15 billion. Reasons for the growth varied. Candy was often treated as a reward, even in (and because of) troubled economic times. Value lines were likely to do better in recessions. Some experts believed that the growth had occurred at a time of increasing health-consciousness because people were eating better overall, so they were more willing to reward themselves. About eighty percent of consumer candy decisions were made at the retail store.

The candy market could be divided into two parts: chocolate and nonchocolate. Since chocolate candy made up sixty percent of all confection sales, Sathers competed with other nonchocolate producers for the remaining shelf space. "[The nonchocolate category] is a tough game," according to Jan Kitt, a sales and marketing consultant who specializes in candy. "Good hard candy tastes the same no matter who makes it. It's very difficult to get a point of difference . . . Since candy is a commodity business, distribution is the name of the game. If the product is out there, it will be purchased. The more it's available, the more people will buy it. That stands more true for confection than for any other category." Of all suppliers of confections, gum, and snacks to U.S. convenience stores in 1991, Sathers ranked twelfth, according to the *ICC/Accutracks Convenience Store Report,* ahead of Cornnuts, Inc., and E. J. Brach Corp. And, Sathers ranked seventh of all nonchocolate brands, ahead of Tootsie Roll. After-tax profit margins in the candy industry ranged from two to five percent.

Sathers' Strategy for Success

Competitors and the trade recognized Sathers' competitive advantages. "There are a lot of rebaggers, but Sathers' strength is in distributing the product," according to Kenneth McCarley, of the Winona Division of Brock Candy Company of Chattanooga, a competitor. Another competitor, Ron Meyer of Shari Candies, Inc. (Mankato, Minnesota) recognized Sathers as a "very well-run company whose business has been built on service." Keith Canning of Pine State Tobacco and Candy (Augusta, Maine) called Sathers "the single most successful company we've brought on in the last five years. The penetration they've had in the East has been nothing short of phenomenal. You can't go into a store in this area and not see it." And Dave McElhatten, a candy buyer for Kmart, pointed to Sathers' creativity: "They're always looking for new products. They're very good at innovation."[1]

Sathers' strategy for success was built on offering a price point, exemplified by the "Two for $1.00" Value Line, and building a distribution network based on service. Sathers President William Bradfield pointed out that value, to Sathers, "doesn't only mean more product for the money. It includes product quality, variety, availability, price, packaging, and

[1]Fink, Laurie (1992), "Sweet Success," *Corporate Report—Minnesota,* (March), pp. 28–32.

quantity. . . . The consumer value is the driving force of the company. We have a very real mindset that whatever we do has to add value for the customer."[2]

Vice President of Operations Charlie Mayer echoed the idea. "The path we've taken has been a tremendous advantage because we control the product from start to finish. Everything in this company revolves around service to the customer first because that's what distribution is. That has been the cornerstone of the development of this company."[3]

Building on that cornerstone, William Bradfield identified Sathers' goals. "We have a very simple formula—be profitable, continue to grow, with a focus on candy." Sathers' strategy for the twenty-first century will be to "continue to develop our position in nuts, natural snacks and cookies, but we will dominantly be a candy manufacturer."

The Snacks to Go Product Line

Development of Snacks to Go

When Jill arrived at Sathers as an Assistant Category Manager and was given responsibility for the Snacks to Go line in January of 1995, progress in developing the line was well underway. The idea for a snack nuts product in a ziplock package for "on the go" consumers was initiated in early 1994. The aim in developing the line was to become one of the first in the industry to introduce a ziplock package filled with nuts and natural snacks, while achieving Sathers' company objective of developing the nuts and natural snacks category.

To explore the feasibility of using a ziplock bag closing for snack nuts, Sathers had contacted Zip-Pak, the originator of the ziplock zipper bag closing, to learn more about ziplock zippers. Zip-Pak provided information from a 1989 Food Packaging Research Study of 300 food shoppers in four U.S. cities conducted by an independent research firm. The study revealed that most consumers who preferred resealable packaging would switch brands and pay more for the food protection, convenience, and freshness that resealable packaging offered. Over half of the respondents preferred nuts in resealable packaging, and of those who ate nuts often, most believed that it was important to preserve the freshness of the food, to keep it from drying out and becoming stale, and that the package should be easy to open and close.

In general, consumers appeared to have positive responses to the idea of resealable packages. With that information, the next step was to gain knowledge of consumers' snack nuts consumption. To do that, Sathers commissioned a nationally recognized marketing research firm to conduct focus groups and personal interviews. Sathers believed such analysis would offer greater depth about usage patterns than other research types, such as mail or telephone surveys, for instance.

1. Focus Groups—Phase 1   The firm conducted two focus groups in June, 1994, to explore positioning and package themes. Qualifying participants for these focus groups, conducted in Chicago, had purchased nuts for snacking within the past three months, at a drug, convenience, or discount store, from a stand-up display, pouch, or hanging bag, jar or can, and were between 18 and 44 years old. Objectives of the research included determining attitudes toward snacking and the role of nuts in snacking; attitudes toward and usage of packaged nuts; awareness, attitudes, and imagery of packaged nut brands; opinions regarding packaging formats; reactions to the ziplock concept and execution; reactions to three selected positionings: "freshness," "convenience," and "health"; reactions

---

[2]"It's in the bag: hanging bag candy manufacturer Sathers, Inc." (1994), *U.S. Distribution Journal,* (July 15), pp. 42–43.
[3]Tiffany, Susan (1995), "Sathers secures niche as manufacturer," *Candy Industry,* (July), pp. 51–57.

to three package designs; and interest in a microwaveable snack nut product sold in convenience stores.

Results revealed that these focus group participants snacked every day, eating both salty and sweet snacks. While snacking, for them, was often solitary, nuts were associated with parties, as well as with routine snacking, and were chosen for their taste, convenience, and protein. Disadvantages of nuts as a snack included being fattening, greasy, more expensive, and containing harmful oils. There was no "right time" for snacking on nuts; purchase was often driven by mood and a coupon or sale, and included a variety of nut types, rather than just one type. Snack nuts were purchased in discount, grocery, and convenience stores, as planned and impulse purchases.

In terms of package format, the advantage of cans and jars was their resealability, while bags were more portable, more appropriate for one or several snacks, and more easily disposed when finished. However, they were often easy to spill and not resealable. A ziplock closing for snack nuts was seen as a clear advantage, with a primary benefit of preventing spilling. A larger bag that could be resealed for a later snack could also yield a cost savings. The "convenience" positioning, therefore, captured the essence of the portability concept. While "freshness" was an appealing concept, most of these respondents did not have problems with stale nuts. Because of their high fat content, snack nuts were not seen as being "healthy." Consequently, the ideal packaged snack nuts product would be convenient, easy to open and seal, fresh, portable, and a healthier alternative to "typical" snacks. A microwaveable snack nut product was not appealing to these consumers.

Packaging designs viewed by these focus groups corresponded with the three positioning alternatives, "freshness," "convenience," and "health." These packages were larger and more colorful than the traditional Sathers "Two for $1.00" header package. Participants seemed to prefer the new lively package, considering it to be more eye-catching, communicating a better quality, fresher product, and perhaps more successful at upgrading the image of the "Two for $1.00" package.

While Planters, Fisher and Evon's were the most recognized, better quality brands, the respondents exhibited little brand loyalty within the snack nuts category. Purchase of an unknown brand was more likely, however, if the consumer could see the product through a film or cellophane "window." The participants' attitudes towards brands revealed that Sathers was either not well recognized or was known for candy. Respondents' perceptions were drawn from the Sathers' "Two for $1.00" package, Planters' Mr. Peanut, and Fisher's colorful foil packages and advertising. A projective technique used to ascertain brand impressions resulted in the following profiles.

Sathers: unsophisticated, plain, common, not necessarily downscale, but thrifty/frugal;

Planters: conservative/traditional/classic, stable, ranging between affluent and middle class, aged 50s;

Fisher: trendy, sophisticated, affluent, aged 30s to 40s.

2. Focus Groups—Phase 2   The research firm conducted a second set of two focus groups in Tampa in August, 1994, to gauge reactions to revised positioning and packaging designs and to assess ziplock packaging for Sathers. The qualifying characteristics for these participants were the same as before; the purposes were the same, except for the addition of an objective about attitudes toward salt, and the omission of the "microwaveable" objective.

Tampa participants' responses about snacking in general and snack nuts in particular were very similar to the Chicago groups' responses. However, brand was more important for these consumers. They purchased from a small set of "known" brands (Planters, Eagle, and Fisher, most often) partly because of their confidence that better-known brands were fresher, a concern in the hot, humid Florida climate. Planters' quality image was favored for its duration in the marketplace, availability, and advertisements. Brand impressions resulting from a projective technique included:

> Sathers (based on the traditional "Two for $1.00" package): Younger group members suggested a teenaged, downscale male. Older members suggested a 20–40 year old male or female, unsophisticated and nondescript;
>
> Planters: older gentleman who enjoys the finer things in life and has finances to pay for them;
>
> Fisher: upscale, young, trendy male or female.

Members of these groups were also more particular about package format features. Determination of freshness came from a package with evidence of air in the bag (vacuum sealed) and a clear product-viewing area (more important for unknown brands). Flashy, brightly colored packages appealed more to younger respondents. Reactions to the concept and execution of a ziplock package closing were universally favorable.

Tampa respondents preferred the "freshness" positioning concept over the "convenience" concept. Ideal positioning, however, would include both, plus being easy to open and close, economical, and a healthier alternative to "typical" snacks.

The Tampa residents viewed somewhat different package executions than the Chicago groups, since the designs were modified on the basis of the Chicago groups' responses. Of four executions, all larger and more brightly colored than the traditional Sathers "Two for $1.00" package, more preferred a lively white and green Snacks to Go package with nut cartoon characters, a design that they believed to be more attention-getting and that upgraded the image of the brand. Some expressed concern that the window didn't reveal enough of the product within.

While the presence of salt was a concern, particularly among the 35–44 year old consumers, most agreed that salt was an important ingredient in snack nuts. "Lightly salted" nuts were viewed favorably; most group members did not purchase "salt substitute" products.

3. Personal Interviews   To enhance and crystallize these findings, an additional research effort was conducted in September, 1994, by the same research firm. In this investigation, seventy-six respondents completed personal interviews at two locations in Chicago. Respondent qualifications were identical to the earlier studies, with the exception of extending the upper age limit to 54. These respondents answered questions about the ziplock features and the Snacks to Go name, and they rated three different package executions:

> green package with red letters;
>
> blue package with graduated darkening of the blue;
>
> green package with yellow letters.

The blue package rated highest on a 5-point like-dislike scale. In addition, it was also chosen as the best at gaining attention, conveying a quality product, and conveying a premium-priced product. Again, the ziplock was overwhelmingly rated as a good idea. Over eighty percent liked the Snacks to Go name. In a comparison of the blue Snacks to Go package with competitive brands' packages, Planters outperformed Sathers, but Sathers was rated higher than the Fisher package.

The Snacks to Go Program

With these three research reports to guide their decision making, Jill and Mike Halverson developed the program for introducing Snacks to Go in the spring of 1995.

Products

Products chosen for the Snacks to Go line were the top two items in the Sathers snack nuts line (Salted-in-the-shell Sunflower Seeds and Shelled Roasted Sunflower Nuts) and the top two items in their Natural Snacks line (Trail Mix and California Mix). The main selling point would be the ziplock package closing feature, which would appeal to active 18–44 year olds. To accommodate their on-the-go lifestyle, the product would be available in convenience stores. To ensure freshness, a "nitrogen flushing" procedure would be used before sealing the packages. Some products, particularly Shelled Roasted Sunflower Nuts, had a tendency to spoil when exposed to oxygen. In packaging, "nitrogen flushing" would remove the oxygen from the package, preserving freshness and ensuring a longer shelf life. The process would not be necessary for non-roasted products, such as Trail Mix, California Mix, and Salted-in-the-shell Sunflower Seeds.

Packaging for the four items, identical but for the item names, consisted of a 9.5″ by 6″ film package, bright blue in the center graduated to dark blue at the bottom. (See Exhibit 3.) A bright yellow band crossed the upper portion of the package; "Snacks to Go" was printed in large yellow letters across the center blue portion. Below the letters, on the left side were two cashew nut cartoon characters wearing helmets, one driving a sporty red cartoon car, the other on in-line skates, depicting "on the go" activities. To the right of the characters was a clear window, approximately 2″ by 1.5″ to display the contents, above which read the item name in a half-inch band, black letters on white background.

The brand name "Sathers" was emblazoned in half-inch red letters on the yellow band near the package top, beside a red banner proclaiming "NEW! Resealable Package." At the very top, a red stripe crossed the package, with the words "ZIP-PAK" and "Resealable Packaging" identifying the closing feature in white letters. The package backside contained directions for opening and resealing the zipper, nutrition facts, ingredients, distribution information, a guarantee and thank you message from Sathers, a bar code and a repeat of the cashew character in the red sports car.

These packages were designed to hang on a state-of-the-art tubular blue metal display rack approximately 5′ high by 18″ wide, in a three-by-four format: three facings of an item in a row with four rows, approximately six bags deep. The top of the display repeated the yellow-on-blue "Snacks to Go" name and art, with "Sathers" and "ZIP-PAK" in somewhat smaller letters. The rack would hold six cases of product (72 packages, 18 of each product).

Pricing

Because the ziplock closing feature required a minimum package size, the price points for the four items were chosen to remain competitive. Expected retailer and distributor combined margins for all items were around thirty percent. Suggested retail price for California Mix (6.25 oz.), Trail Mix (7.0 oz.), and Shelled Roasted Sunflower Nuts (9.0 oz.) would be $1.49, while Salted-in-the-shell Sunflower Seeds (6.25 oz.), would be sold at $.89. A $.99 price point was considered for all four packages, but it was not profitable to produce the smaller package with a ziplock closing that the $.99 price point would have required. Suggested retail prices were not printed on the packages.

Promotion and Distribution

Sathers account executives would be responsible for introducing the Snacks to Go program to convenience store distributors and large retailers with their own warehouses. Incentives included a $3.00 per rack spiff for all distributor salespeople who gained placement in stores. There was a $.20 per case allowance for distributors who met their quota, established by Sathers. The blue tubular rack (at a cost of approximately $60 each to Sathers) would be supplied free to the retailer.

Sales incentives for the account executives were designed to successfully motivate the sales force during the roll-out period of the new program. As such, both individual and regional performance would be rewarded. Each salesperson participating in the program would be provided with realistic sales quotas by his or her Regional Sales Manager. Over the four-month duration of the program, case sales by salesperson (as a percent of quota) and regional sales would be posted on a tally board. At the end of the fourth month, all salespersons

EXHIBIT 3   The
Snacks to Go Product
Line

SATHERS®

The National Value Line®

EXHIBIT 4A
**Snacks to Go Sell
Sheet**

SATHERS, has created a brand new innovation in the nut and snack market. **SATHERS**, line of fresh roasted nuts are now available in convenient resealable zip lock packages. Eat some now ... save some for later!

- Your customers will love the convenience of a resealable and spill-proof package.
- Your impulse sales will soar with the colorful and bold graphics.
- The unique and dynamic floorstand will attract consumers to the Snacks to Go™ display.
- The Snacks to Go™ zip lock package will provide a fresh snack every time you use it!
- We offer a variety of four different items: California Mix, Trail Mix, Salted-in-Shell Sunflower Seeds and Sunflower Nuts

Item Code	Description	Case Pack	SRP
5200	Shelled Roasted Sunflower Nuts	12	$1.49
5201	Trail Mix	12	$1.49
5202	California Mix	12	$1.49
5203	Salted-in-Shell Sunflower Seeds	12	$ .89
3420	Floorstand (Provided by Sathers with program participation)		

SATHERS   Round Lake, Minnesota 56167

The National Value Line,

(895)

F-191-A

achieving quota would earn a choice of a Sony Watchman TV or a Sony portable CD player. The salesperson with the highest sales, as a percentage over quota, would receive a weekend getaway package worth $500. For an entire region achieving quota, a special event, such as a team outing at an Atlanta Braves baseball game, would be offered.

To assist the sales force, supplementary support materials and a direct mail kit were provided. The printed support materials included a brochure outlining the key features of the program and the bold graphics of the packaging. In addition, a sell sheet, line art (an artist's rendering of what the display rack would look like), a planogram (a diagram of product packages to be displayed on the rack, per the contract), and a contract were designed to aid in the selling effort to distributors (see Exhibits 4a–4d). The contract was binding between

SNACKS TO GO LINE ART

Sathers and the retailer; among other specifications, it stated that the rack would be used exclusively for Snacks to Go product. The direct mail kit included a large sample of the Snacks to Go ziplock package, a sales flier, and an introduction letter to the distributor's buyer to familiarize each account with the program and prepare them for the salesperson's visit. No consumer promotions were planned.

The Roll-Out

While convenience stores throughout the nation were the eventual outlet through which Sathers would market Snacks to Go, convenience stores in the Southeast region were targeted for the March to June program roll-out. Specifically, this included Oklahoma,

EXHIBIT 4C
Snacks to Go
Planogram

Arkansas, Louisiana, Mississippi, Tennessee, Alabama, Georgia, North and South Carolina, Virginia, Florida, and part of Texas. Although the entire snack nut category's heaviest concentration of sales was in the Northeast, the Southeast was a stronger area for
the Sathers brand. Competition in the Southeast would come mostly from Planters (with
1994 market share of 35.2 percent), Fisher (3.8 percent), and Eagle (2.6 percent). Private labels accounted for 19.2 percent market share. The remainder of the market was
composed of many small, regional brands. David and Sons was known in the sunflower

EXHIBIT 4D
Snacks to Go
Contract

SATHERS® SNACKS TO GO PROGRAM

Sathers Inc. (hereinafter referred to as "Sathers") and _____
_____, the participating customer (hereinafter referred to as the "Participant"), agree to the
following:

1. Sathers will supply Participant with the merchandising floorstand attached as Exhibit A as
   specified below at no charge to the Participant.

2. Participant will order sufficient quantities of open stock Sathers Snacks to Go™ (zip lock bags) on
   an ongoing basis to fill and maintain distribution of Sathers Snacks to Go™ (zip lock bags) on the
   floorstands.

3. Participant will display only Sathers Snacks to Go™ (zip lock bags) products on the floorstand.
   The merchandising floorstands remain the property of Sathers Inc.

4. If the floorstand becomes damaged or additional stands are needed, Participant agrees to contact
   their Sathers sales representative immediately.

5. Floorstands will be set to a planogram agreed to by Participant and Sathers.

This contract becomes effective on the day signed and will remain in effect until cancelled by either the
Participant or Sathers.

Participant:
Number of stands per store:

Number of stores:

Total floorstands requested:

Signature:

Date:

Sathers Inc.

Signature:

Title:

Date:

HEADQUARTERS: WHITE COPY / SALES: YELLOW COPY / PARTICIPANT: PINK COPY   S-221 (295)

seeds and sunflower nuts categories. The Snacks to Go line would be competitively
priced (see Exhibit 5). There was some seasonality in the snack food market. Generally,
presentations to distributors were made six months in advance to obtain seasonally-ap-
propriate distribution. Snack food presentations often began in January.

One hundred ten distributor accounts in the southeast region were selected, to be sold
by seven account executives and a Regional Sales Manager. The goal for this region was
to have 10,000 cases and 1,200 display racks placed by June 30, with sales of $650,000
by December 1, 1995. The initial presentation to the Sathers sales force occurred February 27, at the American Wholesale Marketers Association trade show. Through March
and April the sales force introduced the Snacks to Go program to their targeted accounts.
All accounts had been presented by the end of May, with product completely placed by
the end of June.

EXHIBIT 5
Price Comparisons

Brand	Weight in Oz.	Price	Price per Oz.
Sunflower Seeds			
Planters	2.0	.33	.11
SATHERS	6.25	.89	.1424
David & Son*	6.25	.89	.1424
Evons	2.75	.50	.1818
Fisher	3.25	.69	.212
Sunflower Kernels			
SATHERS	9.0	1.49	.1655
David & Son*	10.0	1.99	.199
Planters	3.75	.75	.20
Trail Mix			
SATHERS	7.0	1.49	.2128
Evons	2.0	.50	.25
Planters (Fruit & Nut)*	3.0	1.09	.3633
California Mix			
Golden Stream	12.0	2.59	.2158
SATHERS	6.25	1.49	.2384
Harmony	4.0	.99	.2475
Evons*	2.0	.50	.25
Fisher	2.5	.97	.388

*Dominant brand in category, nationwide.

Performance

Beginning with initial placement, the sales force tracked sales of the targeted accounts with weekly performance checks, usually on Monday. The Snacks to Go line had achieved good distributor placement at the outset, building upon the strength of the Sathers distribution network. Of the 110 targeted accounts, fifty percent took initial placement. And while weekly case sales showed slow movement in March and into April, by mid-April sales picked up and showed dramatic increases through May. By June, however, case sales had slowed again. While initial placement with distributors had been good, none of the distributors took the program for all their stores. Just twenty-six distributors placed reorders.

The June sales report showed that sales had slowed to five to six packages per week per store, very slow movement indeed compared to about twenty-five packages per week for Sathers "Two for $1.00" brand. Fewer than 8,000 cases had been sold, and fewer than 800 racks had been placed. (See Exhibit 6 for sales charts.) In consultation with Mike Halverson, Jill had extended the promotional program for another month.

June's slow sales were doubly disappointing when added to the packaging problem Jill had faced. In April, she had been alerted to a problem with the Shelled Roasted Sunflower Nuts package. After carefully inspecting the packages, she'd discovered that the film package had air leaks, which allowed oxygen to mix with the product, causing the product to spoil and the shelf life, which had originally been one year, to deteriorate. While all new product had been packaged with a new, more resilient film, and distributed, about 2,000 cases of the old product had already been sold.

So, at the end of June, seeking specific reasons for the declining sales, Jill had asked for a quick internal study of snack nuts consumers in convenience stores where Snacks to Go had been distributed, and a poll of distributors in the Southeast region. The results, which she'd just reviewed, were not encouraging (see Exhibits 7 and 8).

EXHIBIT 6
**Weekly Case Sales
Patterns for Snacks
to Go Products**

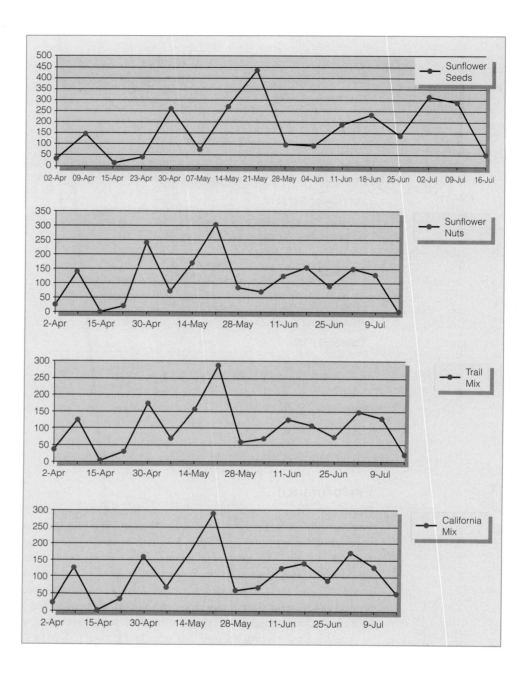

EXHIBIT 7
**Convenience Store
Survey Results***

Demographics: (Of 57 labeled surveys)					
	White male	White female	Black male	Black female	Hispanic female
Teenager	6	3			
20s and 30s	14	7	6		3
40s+	9	6	1	2	

Results: (Of 72 total respondents)

Percent who did not recognize the ziplock closing feature: 69%

Percent who wanted a change in the variety of products: 21

Percent who thought the ziplock was worth paying more money for: 65

EXHIBIT 7
(concluded)

Interviewer's Comments:
It seems to be the teenagers and the travelers who are most likely to buy this package.
Everyone liked the colorful graphics and were attracted mostly by the bright colors.
A lot of people mentioned that they would like to see candy in a ziplock bag.
It was mentioned several times that the top of the package was sort of boring.
The product in the window seems to be drowning out the characters, hard to see them.

*This was a mall-intercept survey of consumers in one convenience store where the Snacks to Go line was sold.

EXHIBIT 8
Comments from Distributors' Surveys*

Positive comments:

- Packaging, nice rack system.
- Likes package, likes rack.
- Rack and packaging looked very good at spring show.
- The rack was very nice, packaging was nice, looked good.
- Ziplock/unpriced.
- Ziplocks, rack system.
- Graphics/rack and unpriced.
- Good concept, but not sure if its niche is drug outlets, perhaps better in food stores.
- New concept.
- All the items are top selling items.
- Ziplock bag.
- Package stands out, is attractive.
- Love the package.
- Rack was easy to put together, and had all contents needed.
- Love the ziplock feature; attraction is the graphics and design of the display; very bright graphics is eye catching.
- Chain retailers feel ziplock differentiates program from others and helps sales.

Negative comments:

- Too many facings on racks, because it is selling so slow retailers are putting other items on the rack. Need more items to fill rack.
- $1.49 too high, $1.29 better. Rack too large for 4 items.
- Consumer doesn't realize it is a resealable bag. Resealable needs to be more prominent.
- It is not selling.
- Market is very competitive, thus hard to get good selling numbers. Program is average selling at best.
- Add pistachios.
- If Sathers were a guaranteed product everyone would order more when a new product is introduced, and avoid running out of a good selling item.
- $.89 OK, $1.49 too high, should be $.99.
- Package geared towards kids, but good package.
- $.89 OK, $1.49 too high, recommend $.99.
- Would like one retail price; would like to see different variety, some candy in the bags; already so many nut/snack competitors. Other suggestions: banana chips, sesame sticks, chocolates.
- Add ziplock gummies to mix.

*These comments were offered by the twenty-one distributors who returned the survey. Additionally, they reported that some convenience stores utilized the rack, while others placed the Snacks to Go products "in line," on the shelf with other snack products. Of those that did use the rack, some placed it near the front of the store, some near the back, some near the pop cooler, and some in other locations within the store.

Mike Halverson was anticipating her review and recommendation. What would she tell him? She could commission a new round of research, which should include store tests at grocery and drug stores, in addition to convenience stores, to monitor case sales by product type. But this would take ten weeks, at a minimum, and cost approximately $30,000. Or, she could suggest a different approach to marketing the product. She'd have to give more thought to exactly what she would change: additional trade promotions? price changes? additional design changes? How about a product change—a switch to candy? But, would that be consistent with the Snacks to Go concept and William Bradfield's charge to develop the snack nuts category? Finally, she knew she could recommend dropping the line completely. That would be a tough decision; would it be giving up too soon?

It was a mixed blessing that the company was closing at 2:30 this Friday, Jill thought, as she packed the sales and research study reports into her briefcase. It was going to be a long weekend of careful thinking about what she'd recommend to Mike on Monday morning for the future of the Snacks to Go product line.

Callaway Golf Company

John E. Gamble *University of South Alabama*

As Ely Callaway walked through the sea of drivers, irons, putters, golf apparel, golf bags, and training devices displayed at the 2000 PGA Merchandise Show in Orlando, Florida, and toward Callaway Golf Company's booth, he noted that the eyes cast toward him seemed to express a greater sense of anticipation and curiosity than usual. As one of the most recognizable figures in the golf equipment industry, he had grown accustomed to his celebrity status among the golfing world and was aware that both rivals and retailers alike anxiously awaited the new products his company typically launched at the industry's premier annual trade show. However, the drama and suspense surrounding Callaway's new products at the February 2000 show were very different from usual. Callaway had gone ahead and introduced its innovative Big Bertha X-14 irons and Big Bertha Steelhead Plus metal woods in January. The PGA Merchandise Show had been saved for the introduction of the company's highly touted and much-anticipated Callaway golf ball.

Callaway Golf Company had become the leader in the golf equipment industry by developing technologically advanced golf clubs that compensated for the poor swing characteristics of most amateur golfers. During a golf swing, the clubhead travels in an arc around the golfer's body, making contact with the ball for 300 to 500 milliseconds. During this very brief period of contact, inertia is transferred from the clubhead to the ball, and the ball is propelled forward at a speed of up to 150 miles per hour. There are an infinite number of variations in a golfer's swing that can alter the swing path, causing the clubhead to strike the ball not squarely but somewhat off-center, at an angle. The more that a golfer's swing path deviates from square contact with the ball, the greater the loss of accuracy and distance. A golfer loses approximately 12.5 yards of distance for every millimeter that the ball is struck off the clubhead's center.

Ely Callaway, the founder of Callaway Golf Company, understood the importance of the physics of golf, so much so that he made the phrase, "You can't argue with physics," an early company slogan. Callaway Golf revolutionized the golf industry in 1990 by introducing an oversized clubhead called the Big Bertha that was more forgiving of golfers' swing imperfections. A Callaway executive stated in a 1995 *Fortune* interview that the company's objective was to design a club that would allow golfers to "miss [the center of the clubhead] by an inch" and still achieve distance and accuracy.

The company's high-tech golf clubs became so popular with golfers in the 1990s that Callaway Golf's revenues and profits grew by 1,239 percent and 1,907 percent, respectively, between 1991 and year-end 1996. With the company's competitive position securely rooted and a line of innovative new clubs ready for a 1997 launch, Ely Callaway retired as CEO in mid-1996 and turned to Callaway Golf Company president Donald Dye to become the new CEO. Soon after Ely Callaway's retirement, Callaway Golf Company's fortunes reversed due to a variety of factors, including the Asian financial crisis, poor global weather conditions, strategic miscues on the part of Callaway's executives, and the introduction of innovative clubs by rivals. The reversal led to nearly an 18 percent sales decline in 1998. Callaway Golf also broke its string of 24 consecutive quarters of growth in net income in early 1998 and went on to record a net loss of $26.5 million for the entire 1998 fiscal year.

Ely Callaway returned as CEO in November 1998 to launch a vast turnaround effort that included the development of new models of golf clubs and a $54.2 million restructuring program, which brought a number of operational improvements and cost-reduction initiatives. Callaway Golf Company returned to profitability and recaptured a great deal of its lost market share in 1999, but on February 4, 2000, the entire golf industry watched intently as Ely Callaway launched the company's new Rule 35 golf ball. Callaway's entry into the golf ball market had been vigilantly anticipated since mid-1996 when Ely Callaway announced the formation of the Callaway Golf Ball Company, and was considered by many industry participants to be the biggest event in the golf equipment industry since the debut of the Big Bertha. Callaway's managers and investors expected the entry to become a catalyst for the company's future growth. Exhibit 1 presents a summary of Callaway Golf Company's financial performance between 1989 and 1999.

Company History

When Ely (rhymes with *feely*) Reeves Callaway Jr. graduated from Emory University in Atlanta, his father said, "Don't go to work for the family."[1] Ely Callaway Sr. and almost everyone else in La Grange, Georgia, worked for the younger Callaway's uncle, Fuller Callaway. Fuller Callaway owned a number of farms, 23 cotton mills, the local bank, and the local department store. Heeding his father's advice, Ely Callaway Jr. decided to join the army just prior to World War II. By the age of 24, he had achieved the rank of major and had become one of the army's top five procurement officers responsible for purchasing cotton clothing for the U.S. armed forces. At the peak of World War II, Callaway's apparel procurement division of the U.S. Army purchased 70 percent of all cotton clothing manufactured by the U.S. apparel industry.

After the war, Callaway was hired as a sales representative with textile manufacturer Deering, Millikin & Company. He rose quickly through the company's ranks by selling textiles to the manufacturers from which he had purchased apparel while in the Army. Callaway was later hired away from Deering, Millikin by Textron, which subsequently sold its textile business to Burlington Industries—at that time the largest textile manufacturer in the world. Ely Callaway was promoted to president and director of Burlington Industries, but he left the company in 1973 after losing a bid to become its chief executive officer.

Callaway had long believed that Burlington Industries' success was a result of its ability to provide customers with unique, superior-quality products. When Callaway left Burlington and the textile industry, he decided to launch his own business founded on that same philosophy. In 1974 he established Callaway Vineyard and Winery outside of San Diego. The well-known northern California vineyards scoffed at Callaway's entry into the industry and predicted a rapid failure of the venture. Not only did Callaway have no experience running a winery but, additionally, no vineyard had ever been successful in the San Diego area. Ely Callaway understood the risks involved and was much better prepared to run a start-up vine-

[1]*Inc.,* December 1994, p. 62.

EXHIBIT 1 **Callaway Golf Company, Financial Summary, 1989–99 (In thousands, except per share amounts)**

Source: Callaway Golf Company annual reports.

	1999	1998	1997	1996	1995	1994	1993	1992	1991	1990	1989
Net sales	$714,471	$697,621	$842,927	$678,512	$553,287	$448,729	$254,645	$132,058	$54,753	$21,518	$10,380
Pretax income	$85,497	($38,899)	$213,765	$195,595	$158,401	$129,405	$69,600	$33,175	$10,771	$2,185	$329
Estimated ranking within industry—sales	1st	1st	1st	1st	1st	1st	1st	2nd	6th	14th	23rd
Pretax income as a percent of sales	12%	−6%	25%	29%	29%	29%	27%	25%	20%	10%	3%
Net income	$55,322	($25,564)	$132,704	$122,337	$97,736	$78,022	$42,862[a]	$19,280	$6,416	$1,842	$329
Net income as a percent of sales	8%	−4%	16%	18%	18%	17%	17%[a]	15%	12%	9%	3%
Fully diluted earnings per share[c]	$0.78	($0.38)	$1.85	$1.73	$1.40	$1.07	$0.62	$0.32	$0.11	$0.04	$0.01
Shareholders' equity	$499,934	$453,096	$481,425	$362,267	$224,934	$186,414	$116,577	$49,750	$15,227	$8,718	$6,424
Market capitalization at Dec. 31	$1,349,595	$769,725	$2,120,813	$2,094,588	$1,604,741	$1,127,823	$901,910	$245,254	—[b]	—[b]	—[b]

[a]Includes cumulative effect of an accounting change of $1,658,000.
[b]The company's stock was not publicly traded until February 1992.
[c]Adjusted for all stock splits through February 10, 1995, not adjusted for February 10, 1995, stock split.

yard than skeptics believed. He began by transplanting the very best grape vines from Italy to California and hired winemaking experts to manage the day-to-day operations of the vineyard. Callaway's strategy was to focus on a narrow segment of the wine market where competition with the established wineries was not as strong and barriers to entry were relatively low. Callaway Vineyard and Winery limited distribution of its products to exclusive restaurants that chose to stock only the highest-quality wines. The company made no attempt to distribute its high-quality wines through traditional retail channels. In 1981, Ely Callaway sold the company to Hiram Walker & Sons, Inc., for a $14 million profit.

In late 1982, Ely Callaway decided to enter the golf club industry and, once again, apply his concept of "providing a product that is demonstrably superior to what's available in significant ways and, most importantly, pleasingly different."[2] Callaway purchased Hickory Stick USA, a manufacturer and marketer of replicas of old-fashioned hickory-shafted clubs, for $400,000. From the outset, Callaway grasped the limitations of the company's hickory-shafted product line and realized that the company would have to extend its offerings beyond replicas of antique golf clubs to provide an acceptable return on his investment.

Callaway noticed that most golf equipment had changed very little since the 1920s and believed that many golfers would purchase technologically advanced golf equipment if it would improve their game. Ely Callaway and Richard C. Helmstetter—Callaway Golf's senior executive vice president and chief club designer—put together a team of five aerospace and metallurgical engineers to develop the S2H2 (short, straight, hollow hosel) line of irons. The S2H2 line was introduced in 1988 and was well received by golfers. The following year the company introduced S2H2 traditional-sized metal woods, and in 1990 it introduced the Big Bertha driver—named after the World War I German long-distance cannon. The Big Bertha was revolutionary in that it was much larger than conventional woods and lacked a hosel so that the weight could be better distributed throughout the clubhead. This innovative design gave the clubhead a larger sweet spot, which allowed a player to mis-hit or strike the golf ball off-center of the clubhead and not suffer much loss of distance or accuracy. By 1992 Big Bertha drivers were number one on the Senior PGA, the LPGA, and Hogan Tours. Callaway Golf Company became a public company on February 28, 1992. By year-end 1992 its annual revenues had doubled to $132 million, and by 1996 Callaway Golf had become the world's largest manufacturer and marketer of golf clubs, with annual sales of more than $678 million.

Ely Callaway's 1996 Retirement and the Formation of the Callaway Golf Ball Company

Callaway Golf continued to lead the golf equipment industry through the mid-1990s with innovative new lines of clubs. The company also introduced a line of golf apparel in 1996 that was available to golfers through an exclusive licensing agreement with Nordstrom. In May 1996, Ely Callaway announced that even though he would remain involved in the promotion of the Callaway Golf products, he was transferring his position as chief executive officer to the company's president, Donald Dye. Dye had been a business associate of Ely Callaway since 1974, when Callaway was in the wine business. Ely Callaway simultaneously announced that he and Charles Yash, Taylor Made Golf Company's CEO and president, would launch Callaway Golf Ball Company as a subsidiary of Callaway Golf. "We believe that there is a good and reasonable opportunity for Callaway Golf Ball Company, in due time, to create, produce and merchandise a golf ball that will be demonstrably superior to, and pleasingly different from, any other golf ball we know of," said Callaway.[3] Yash, who

---

[2]*Business Week,* September 16, 1991, p. 71.

[3]"Donald H. Dye Given CEO Duties at Callaway Golf Company." *Two-Ten Communications, Ltd.,* 1996. www.twoten.press.net:80/stories/96/05/13/headlines/appointments_callaway.html, February 6, 1997.

had been the general manager of Spalding's golf ball business and who turned around Taylor Made with the introduction of the Burner Bubble driver, resigned his post at Taylor Made to become president and CEO of the new venture. Upon announcing his decision to work with Callaway, Yash commented, "This is an exciting and most unusual opportunity to develop a new and important golf ball franchise with Ely Callaway for Callaway Golf Company. As a competitor, I have been in awe of Callaway's accomplishments. As his partner, I look forward to the exciting opportunities and challenges Ely and I are sure to find in this new venture."[4]

Callaway Golf Company's 1998 Performance and the Return of Ely Callaway as CEO

A variety of events occurred shortly after Ely Callaway's retirement that resulted in Callaway Golf's loss of market share in fairway woods and its poor financial and market performance in 1998. The U.S. and international markets for golf clubs moved from rapid growth to maturity during 1997 and 1998 after a large percentage of avid golfers purchased titanium drivers and saw little reason to upgrade again until dramatic innovations were available. Global market maturity was compounded by the Asian financial crisis that began in late 1997 and made the export of U.S.-made products, especially expensive luxury goods like Callaway golf clubs, unaffordable for many Asians. Also, heavy global rainfall caused by El Niño contributed to an overall decline in the number of rounds played around the world in 1998. In addition, many club manufacturers believed that the United States Golf Association's (USGA) discussions during 1998 to limit innovations in golf club design caused many golfers to postpone club purchases. The USGA had considered a number of limitations on club design, but ultimately decided to bar only a "spring-like effect" in golf clubs. The USGA advised Callaway Golf that none of its products violated the new regulation.

The emergence of shallow-faced fairway woods had as much to do with Callaway's downturn as any other single event. Callaway had dominated the market for fairway woods since the early 1990s, when the Big Bertha line gained in popularity. By 1996 no other manufacturer came close to Callaway in building a loyal following among fairway woods customers. Even when Callaway users experimented with a rival's new driver, they frequently stayed with Callaway for their fairway woods. However, Callaway's dominance in fairway woods was severely challenged in 1997 when relatively unknown golf manufacturers Adams Golf and Orlimar Golf each heavily promoted a line of shallow-faced fairway woods that they claimed made it easier for golfers to hit a ball off the fairway or from a poor lie. The two challengers each ran a series of highly successful infomercials that demonstrated the clubs' performance and led to phenomenal sales growth for both companies. Adams' and Orlimar's success came more or less directly at the expense of Callaway. No other golf club manufacturer sold large volumes of fairway woods, so when golfers purchased the new clubs offered by Adams and Orlimar, it was typically Callaway that lost sales and market share.

Callaway CEO Donald Dye took much of the blame for Callaway's failure to predict the popularity of shallow-faced woods and was also ultimately responsible for initiatives that took management's focus off of golf clubs. Under Dye, Callaway Golf began new ventures in golf course and driving range management, opened interactive golf sites, created a new player development project, and launched a golf publishing business with Nicholas Callaway, the youngest son of Ely Callaway and a successful publisher of tabletop books. After a record year in 1997, the company's financial and market performance suffered immensely during 1998. In October 1998, Donald Dye resigned as Callaway's CEO and Ely Callaway returned to rebuild the company.

---

[4]"Keeping His Eye on the Ball," *ParValu Stock Update,* 1996. www.golfweb.com:80/gi/parvalu/updates/03.html, February 6, 1997.

Ely Callaway's first efforts on his return to active management at Callaway Golf were to "direct [the company's] resources—talent, energy, and money—in an ever-increasing degree toward the creation, design, production, sale and service of new and better products."[5] As part of his turnaround strategy, Ely Callaway also initiated a $54.2 million restructuring program that involved a number of cost-reduction actions and operational improvements. During 1997 and 1998 the company had built up a large inventory of older model clubs that were not sold before the latest clubs were shipped to retailers. Callaway management liquidated the inventory of older generation clubs to generate cash flow and improve the company's financial position. In addition, the company divested its interest in noncore businesses began under Dye and combined the administrative and manufacturing functions of Odyssey Golf and Callaway Golf. Callaway's business restructuring eliminated a variety of job responsibilities and thus resulted in the loss of 750 positions from all functional areas of the company. Callaway Golf Company's income statements for 1993 through 1999 are presented in Exhibit 2. Exhibit 3 presents the company's balance sheets for 1993–99. The company's market performance is graphed in Exhibit 4.

The Golf Equipment Industry

In 1999, more than 26 million Americans played golf. Of these, 5.4 million were considered avid golfers, playing more than 25 rounds of golf annually. The number of U.S. golfers was expected to grow 1 to 2 percent annually through 2010 as the baby boom generation aged and had more free time and disposable income. In 1999 the typical golfer was a 39-year-old male with a household income of $66,000 who played golf about twice a month. Many women, juniors, and senior citizens also enjoyed the sport. In 1999 there were 5.7 million women and 2.1 million junior golfers aged 12 to 17 in the United States. Seniors accounted for 25 percent of all U.S. golfers in 1999. The average golf score was 97 for men and 114 for women. Only 6 percent of men and 1 percent of women golfers regularly broke a score of 80. Exhibit 5 provides the number of U.S. golfers during various years between 1986 and 1999.

Golf was popular in developed countries worldwide—especially so in Asia, where there were over 3,500 courses and 16 million golfers. Most of Europe's 2 million-plus golfers resided in England, France, Germany, Scotland, Ireland, and Sweden. The sport was becoming popular in former Soviet-bloc countries—such as Croatia, Slovenia, the Czech Republic, Poland, and Russia—but was not expected to grow dramatically until the economies of those countries stabilized. Russia's first country club opened in Moscow in 1993; by 2000, it had 550 members, who had each paid a $28,000 membership fee for the privilege to play the Robert Trent Jones–designed course. However, only 70 of the club's members were Russian. Some teaching professionals working in Russia projected that there could be 100,000 golfers in Russia by 2025, but in 2000 there were fewer than 500 Russians who could be called avid golfers.

The wholesale value of golf equipment sales in the United States had increased from $740 million in 1986 to over $2.7 billion in 1999. In 1999 the U.S. market for golf balls accounted for about 25 percent of the industry's wholesale sales. The wholesale value of the international golf ball market was estimated at $1.5 billion. Exhibit 6 provides wholesale sporting goods equipment sales for selected years during the 1986–99 period. The growth in golf equipment sales during the early 1990s was attributable not so much to an increase in the number of golfers as to the introduction of technologically advanced equipment offered by Callaway Golf and other manufacturers like Ping and Taylor Made. Many of these

[5]Callaway Golf Company 1998 annual report.

EXHIBIT 2 Callaway Golf Company, Income Statements, 1993–99 ($000, except per share amounts)

Source: Callaway Golf Company annual reports.

	1999	1998	1997	1996	1995	1994	1993
Net sales	$714,471	$697,621	$842,927	$678,512	$553,287	$448,729	$254,645
Cost of goods sold	376,405	401,607	400,127	317,353	270,125	208,906	115,458
Gross profit	338,086	296,014	442,800	361,159	283,162	239,823	139,187
Selling, general, and administrative expenses	224,336	245,070	191,313	155,177	120,201	106,913	—
Research and development costs	34,002	36,848	30,298	16,154	8,577	6,380	3,653
Restructuring and transition costs	(181)	54,235	—	—	—	—	—
Litigation settlement	—	—	12,000	—	—	—	—
Income (loss) from operations	79,909	(40,139)	209,189	189,828	154,384	126,530	68,416
Interest & other income, net	9,182	3,911	4,586	5,804	4,038	2,879	1,184
Interest expense	(3,594)	(2,671)	(10)	(37)	(21)	(4)	—
Income before income taxes and cumulative effect of accounting change	85,497	(38,899)	213,765	195,595	158,401	129,405	69,600
Provision for income taxes (benefit)	30,175	(12,335)	81,061	73,258	60,665	51,383	28,396
Cumulative effect of accounting change	n/a	n/a	n/a	n/a	n/a	n/a	(1,658)
Net income	$55,322	($26,564)	$132,704	$122,337	$97,736	$78,022	$42,862
Primary earnings per share	$0.79	($0.38)	$1.94	$1.83	$1.47	$1.14	$0.62
Fully diluted earnings per share	$0.78	($0.38)	$1.85	$1.73	$1.40	$1.07	$0.60
Common equivalent shares	71,214	69,463	71,698	70,661	69,855	73,104	68,964

EXHIBIT 3 Callaway Golf Company, Balance Sheets, 1993–99 ($000)

Source: Callaway Golf Company annual reports.

	1999	1998	1997	1996	1995	1994	1993
Assets							
Current assets							
Cash and cash equivalents	$ 112,602	$ 45,618	$ 26,204	$ 108,457	$ 59,157	$ 54,356	$ 48,996
Accounts receivable, net	54,525	73,466	124,470	74,477	73,906	30,052	17,546
Inventories, net	97,938	149,192	97,094	98,333	51,584	74,151	29,029
Deferred taxes	32,558	51,029	23,810	25,948	22,688	25,596	13,859
Other current assets	13,122	4,310	10,208	4,298	2,370	3,235	2,036
Total current assets	310,472	323,606	281,786	311,513	209,705	187,390	111,466
Property, plant, and equipment, net	142,214	172,794	142,503	91,346	69,034	50,619	30,661
Other assets	120,143	127,779	112,141	25,569	11,236	5,613	2,233
Total assets	$ 616,783	$ 665,827	$ 561,714	$ 428,428	$ 289,975	$ 243,622	$ 144,360
Liabilities and shareholders' equity							
Current liabilities							
Accounts payable and accrued expenses	$ 46,664	$ 35,928	$ 30,063	$ 14,996	$ 26,894	$ 17,678	$ 11,949
Accrued employee compensation and benefits	21,126	11,083	14,262	16,195	10,680	9,364	6,104
Accrued warranty expense	36,105	35,815	28,059	27,303	23,769	18,182	9,730
Accrued restructuring cost	1,379	7,389	—	—	—	—	—
Income taxes payable	—	9,903	—	2,558	1,491	11,374	n/a
Total current liabilities	105,274	184,008	72,384	61,052	62,834	56,598	27,783
Long-term liabilities	11,575	18,823	7,905	5,109	2,207	610	n/a
Shareholders' equity							
Common stock	763	751	743	729	709	680	676
Paid-in-capital	307,329	258,015	337,403	278,669	214,846	75,022	60,398
Unearned compensation	(2,784)	(5,653)	(3,575)	(3,105)	(2,420)	(3,670)	(2,591)
Retained earnings	288,090	252,528	298,728	238,349	131,712	114,402	58,094
Less grantor stock trust*	(93,744)	(54,325)	(151,315)	(152,375)	(119,913)	—	—
Total shareholders' equity	499,934	453,096	481,425	362,267	224,934	186,414	116,577
Total liabilities and shareholders' equity	$616,783	$ 655,827	$ 561,714	$ 428,428	$ 289,975	$ 243,622	$ 144,360

*The sale of 5,300,000 shares to the grantor stock trust had no net impact to shareholders' equity. The shares in the GST may be used to fund the company's obligations with respect to one or more of the company's nonqualified employee benefit plans.

EXHIBIT 4
Monthly Performance of Callaway Golf Company's Stock Price, 1992–March 2000
(a) Trend in Callaway Golf Company's Common Stock Price

(b) Performance of Callaway Golf Company's Stock Price versus the S&P 500 Index

EXHIBIT 5
Number of U.S. Golfers, 1986, 1991, 1993, 1995, 1997, 1999

Source: National Golf Foundation.

EXHIBIT 6   **Wholesale Sales of Sporting Goods Equipment, 1986, 1993–99 (In millions of dollars)**

Source: Sporting Goods Manufacturers Association, 1997–1999 State of the Industry Reports.

Type of Equipment	1999*	1998	1997	1996	1995	1994	1993	1986
Exercise	$ 3,635	$ 3,400	$ 3,180	$ 2,890	$ 2,510	$ 1,825	$ 1,755	$ 680
Golf	2,770	2,800	2,749	2,463	2,130	1,793	1,490	740
Camping	1,700	1,620	1,590	1,500	1,508	1,275	1,225	580
Baseball/softball	340	340	338	350	349	348	328	240
Soccer	230	220	208	200	185	175	155	90
Tennis	220	215	235	240	235	259	380	255
Total sports equipment	$17,805	$17,350	$17,064	$16,395	$15,379	$13,877	$12,433	$8,250

*Estimated

technological advances made the game much easier for beginners to learn than was possible with older equipment. Additionally, experienced players frequently looked for equipment that could help them improve their game. However, it was expected that in the early 2000s the sales of golf equipment would grow only modestly since most avid golfers had already upgraded their equipment and were unlikely to do so again unless major new innovations came about.

Key Technological Innovations

The golfing industry had come up with four major innovations that made it easier for golfers to hit better shots and improve their scores: (1) perimeter weighting in the late 1960s, (2) metal woods in the early 1980s, (3) graphite shafts in the late 1980s, and (4) oversized clubheads in the early 1990s. Perimeter weighting came about due to the poor putting of Karsten Solheim, a General Electric mechanical engineer, who took up golf at the age of 47 in 1954. Solheim designed a putter for himself that he found provided more "feel" when he struck the ball. Solheim moved much of the clubhead weight to the heel and toe, leaving a cavity at the rear and center of the club. Perimeter-weighted or cavity-back clubs had a larger "sweet spot" because of a higher moment of inertia or resistance to twisting. The resistance to twisting reduced the gear effect of the clubhead and resulted in straighter, longer shots with irons. In addition to perimeter weighting, Karsten Solheim also developed the investment-casting manufacturing process. This process allowed clubheads to be formed from molds, rather than forged from steel—the traditional manufacturing process.

Solheim made his putters by hand from 1959 until 1967, when he left GE and founded Karsten Manufacturing. By the 1970s, Karsten was manufacturing a full line of perimeter-weighted putters and irons that carried the Ping brand name. Solheim chose this name because of the sound the cavity-back clubhead made when it struck the ball. Karsten Manufacturing's line of Ping putters and irons was thought to be among the most technologically advanced throughout the 1980s and reigned as the market leader. Karsten Manufacturing was renamed Ping, Inc., in 1999. In 2000, over 95 percent of all irons and putters sold worldwide were perimeter-weighted.

Ping's investment-casting manufacturing process also made the manufacture of perimeter-weighted "metal woods" possible. Taylor Made designed the first metal wood which, like the perimeter-weighted irons, had the advantage of a larger sweet spot than traditional clubs. Although they actually had no wood components, metal woods were so named because it had been traditional to use wooden clubs for driving from the tee and for long fairway shots. The hollow metal head made it possible to move the weight to the heel and toe of the clubhead, as was done with perimeter-weighted irons. Conventional wood heads were made of solid persimmon and had a uniform weight distribution.

The characteristics of the golf club shaft affected a club's performance almost as much as the clubhead did. Distance and accuracy were largely a function of shaft characteristics. Weak or overly flexible shafts could torque as a result of the swinging action and the weight of the clubhead. The torquing of the shaft created a gear effect that resulted in a mis-hit golf ball. Additionally, the flex of the shaft had the ability to increase clubhead speed and improve accuracy. Shafts with greater flex at the tip or clubhead end were advantageous to high handicappers because they helped produce greater clubhead speed at the point of contact with the golf ball, caused the ball to have a higher trajectory, and promoted greater distance. Professional and low-handicap golfers preferred shafts that flexed a few inches higher or nearer the grip because a higher flex point produced added control of the shot.

Graphite shafts were introduced in 1969 by Shakespeare, but were not accepted by golfers because they flexed too much and overly dampened the feel of the club striking the ball. By the early 1990s, technological advances in graphite materials, shaft design, and production had eliminated the previous torsion problems, and graphite shafts quickly gained acceptance by both amateur and professional golfers. Shaft manufacturers were using aerospace technology to improve graphite shafts that had as many as 14 to 16 layers of composite materials (carbon fibers, Kevlar, boron, glass-fiber-reinforced epoxy resins, and synthetic fibers). In 1998, graphite shafts were used in 86 percent of drivers, 77 percent of fairway woods, and 46 percent of irons. Because of the higher prices commanded by graphite, the dollar volume of graphite shaft sales exceeded that of steel alloy shafts by a greater margin than the unit volume differential.

Callaway Golf was the first golf club manufacturer to actually increase the size of the hollow metal wood and make the size of the sweet spot bigger. The larger the clubhead, the bigger the sweet spot, but weight was the primary constraint in increasing clubhead size. If oversized clubheads were too heavy, golfers could not achieve as much speed as they could with lighter clubheads. Slower clubhead speeds resulted in shorter flight distances. The vice president of research and development for a golf club manufacturer described the challenge of trying to increase the size of metal wood clubheads as follows:

> The problem with a big driver is that you have to keep the total weight about the same as a normal-sized driver in order to give the same feel to the golfer. You can't build an overweight club or one that you can't swing at the same speed. A slightly bigger head pulls a little more drag through the air, but it's negligible. Making a bigger head is like blowing bubble gum. You have the same amount of gum but you've got to make a bigger bubble, so the metal walls will be thinner.[6]

Companies experimented with a number of materials, including stainless steel, titanium, silicon aluminum carbide, and thermoplastics, to find a way of increasing clubhead size without adding weight to the clubhead or diminishing its structural integrity. By 1992, most manufacturers had discovered that titanium was the best material for oversized drivers because the material was 20 percent lighter and 40 percent stronger than stainless steel. By using titanium, club manufacturers were able to increase the size of oversized drivers by about 30 percent. A golf club design engineer explained why material selection was vital to the structural integrity of the clubhead:

> Keeping weight to a minimum is the single biggest aggravation. Once you have a shape you're comfortable with, the challenge is to design a driver that will meet your weight standards. Everybody wants to go bigger, bigger, and bigger in drivers, but as you go bigger, your wall gets thinner. You could make a driver three times the normal size, but it would be like tinfoil. It would fold up and crush on impact.[7]

[6]*Machine Design,* April 23, 1992, p. 32.
[7]Ibid.

During the late 1990s, innovators like Callaway Golf and Taylor Made began to use combinations of metals in the design of oversized metal woods and irons. In 1997 Callaway introduced a line of irons that were 85 percent titanium and 15 percent tungsten. A tungsten insert was placed directly at the center of the enlarged sweet spot of the titanium clubface to add weight to the portion of the clubhead that should actually strike the ball. The addition of tungsten to the clubhead concentrated 40 percent of the clubhead weight directly at the sweet spot and made it possible to create an oversized clubhead with a weight concentration designed to maximize the energy transfer from the clubhead to the ball. Taylor Made introduced tungsten-titanium oversized clubs shortly after Callaway's introduction of its tungsten-titanium Great Big Bertha irons. In 1998 Callaway and Taylor Made introduced tungsten-titanium woods and Orlimar boasted clubheads that were made from three different metals. Cleveland Golf introduced a four-metal oversized clubhead design in 1999. In 2000 all major golf club manufacturers had at least one oversized exotic metal driver with a graphite shaft in its product line.

Competitive Rivalry in the Golf Equipment Industry

For decades, the golf equipment industry had been dominated by Wilson Sporting Goods, MacGregor Golf, Inc., and Spalding Sporting Goods. All three companies were very conservative in their approach to new product development, sticking to lines of the standard steel-shafted, forged-steel clubs that had been popular since the 1920s. They were caught completely off guard by the success of companies like Ping, Taylor Made, and Callaway Golf. Amateur golfers readily accepted the technological advances offered by the new golf companies and the market shares of the established brands of the three traditional industry leaders quickly eroded. An executive for one of the new manufacturers stated that Wilson's inability to introduce innovative products of its own had resulted in the company's market share diminishing to a "rounding error."[8]

In the late 1980s as many as 20 manufacturers accounted for about 80 percent of all golf equipment sales, but by 1997 the industry had already consolidated to the point where 6 companies commanded over 80 percent of the market for golf equipment. It was estimated that, of the more than 350 manufacturers in existence, only those 6 were profitable. During the late 1990s industry consolidation stimulated attrition as many smaller club manufacturers exited the industry. Even though longtime industry participants like Wilson, MacGregor, and Spalding were still in business and had attempted to introduce technologically advanced lines of clubs, they had all largely failed in regaining lost market share.

Manufacturing

Most club makers' manufacturing activities were restricted to club assembly, since clubhead production was contracted out to investment casting houses and shafts and grips were usually purchased from third-party suppliers. Most golf club companies offered two to four general models of irons and woods built around proprietary heads that were internally developed. Each clubhead model line was equipped with shafts of varying flex that were either proprietary designs or standard models purchased from shaft manufacturers. Grip manufacturers such as Eaton/Golf Pride and Lamkin offered a number of models, but club manufacturers usually chose to purchase a limited variety of grips from a single source, since most golfers did not have strong preferences for one brand of grip over another. Some club manufacturers used custom grips bearing the company name and logo, while others used standard grips.

The brand and type of shaft had a relatively important influence over golfers' perceptions of club quality and performance. Most golfers had a strong preference for either steel or graphite and some preference for certain manufacturers. True Temper had one of the best

---

[8]*Fortune,* June 12, 1995, p. 110.

reputations in steel shafts and had dominated that segment of the industry ever since it introduced the steel shaft in 1924. Most club manufacturers purchased standard steel shafts from a sole supplier rather than developing proprietary steel shafts or using a multiple sourcing strategy.

As the 1990s progressed, a larger and larger percentage of golfers' preferences shifted to graphite shafts for both drivers and irons. Graphite shaft manufacturers could easily produce a broad line of shafts with varying degrees of flex at a number of flexpoints. Many golfers were persuaded that the unique characteristics of graphite contributed to game improvement. Companies such as Aldila, United Sports Technologies, HST, Unifiber, and Graman USA were competent manufacturers of high-quality graphite shafts and had made it difficult for True Temper to build a dominant market share in the graphite segment as it had done in steel.

Some companies such as Callaway Golf independently designed their shafts, while others collaborated with shaft manufacturers to develop proprietary graphite shafts. Taylor Made's innovative "bubble shaft" was co-designed and manufactured by respected graphite shaft producer HST. Cobra Golf was the only golf manufacturer to vertically integrate into shaft production and produce 100 percent of its shafts in-house. Cobra Golf was acquired by American Brands (renamed Fortune Brands in 1998 when its cigarette business was divested), which also owned Foot-Joy (a leading maker of golf shoes) and Titleist (the maker of the most popular brand of golf balls and also a producer of golf clubs and other golf equipment). Cobra's golf club shaft facilities were used to produce a portion of the shafts needed for Fortune's Titleist golf clubs.

Marketing

As television networks aired increasing numbers of professional golf tournaments, endorsements by professional golfers started to play a major role in the marketing of golf equipment. The dollar volume of player endorsements was estimated to be three times greater than the projected total Professional Golfers Association (PGA) year 2000 prize money payout of $132 million.

Professional golfer endorsements had been instrumental in the success of some fledgling companies. In 1990, Cobra Golf offered Greg Norman shares of stock and Australian distribution rights to the new company's products in return for the golfer's use and endorsement of Cobra equipment. Norman accepted the offer and, after the company went public, sold 450,000 Cobra shares for $12 million. Norman received an additional $30 million from the sale of his remaining Cobra Golf shares when American Brands acquired Cobra in 1996. Norman's endorsement of Cobra golf clubs helped make Cobra Golf an almost immediately identifiable brand in the golf equipment industry and an attractive acquisition target. Fortune Brand's belief in endorsements led the company to offer Tiger Woods a $20 million five-year contract upon his professional debut in 1996 to endorse Titleist drivers, irons, and balls. Woods's endorsement of the company's newly designed lines of clubs resurrected the brand's presence in clubs, particularly so in woods, where its new 975D driver became one of the top-selling clubs of 1999. Prior to Woods's endorsement of Titleist clubs, the company was primarily thought of as a golf ball company.

Tiger Woods's entry into the PGA set a new standard for endorsement contracts—the $20 million Woods received in 1996 for endorsing Titleist golf clubs and balls was surpassed by the $40 million he received for endorsing Nike apparel and footwear for a five-year period. In 1999 Woods signed a five-year renewal with Nike for $90 million. Tiger Woods also signed a two-year, $10 to 15 million deal with Buick to appear in Buick ads and carry the Buick logo on his golf bag. Woods's five-year renewal with Titleist provided a $2 million annual fee to use Titleist balls and clubs in PGA tournaments; this contract was primarily a defensive measure for Fortune Brands since Woods's Nike and Buick contracts prevented him from appearing in Titleist advertisements or displaying the Titleist logo on his golf bag. Tiger Woods's success in landing large endorsement contracts had spilled over to other professional golfers to some degree, but in 2000 no other golfer had been able to garner contracts in the same range as those signed by Woods.

Most pro-line or high-quality golf equipment manufacturers distributed their products through on-course pro shops and a select number of off-course pro shops, such as Edwin Watts and Nevada Bob's. The off-course pro shops were quickly accounting for the largest portion of retail golf club sales because they carried a wider variety of brands and marketed more aggressively than on-course shops. Most on-course pro shops sold only to members and carried few clubs since their members purchased golf clubs less frequently than apparel and footwear. In 1997 on-course pro shops carried, on average, 4 brands of drivers, 4 brands of irons, and 6 brands of putters, while off-course pro shops carried, on average, 12 brands of drivers, 18 brands of irons, and 17 brands of putters.

Pro-line manufacturers chose to limit their channels of distribution to on-course and off-course pro shops because they believed that PGA professionals had the training necessary to properly match equipment to the customer. Manufacturers such as Taylor Made, Callaway, and Ping all provided the pro shops with inexpensive devices that gave an estimate of the golfer's swing characteristics. The pro could take the readings from these devices and then custom-fit the golfer with the proper clubs. Custom fitting could be done more precisely with more expensive, specialized computer equipment, but most pro shops had not invested in the new technology. The Sportech Swing Analyzer aided in custom fitting by recording 12 swing variables, such as clubhead speed and path, club face angle at impact, ball position, the golfer's weight distribution, ball flight pattern, and ball flight distance. The pro could use the fit data provided by the Swing Analyzer to select the appropriate club for the customer. Golf equipment manufacturers expected a larger percentage of golfers to demand more precise custom fitting from retailers in the future.

Pro shops generally chose to stock only pro-line equipment and did not carry less expensive, less technologically advanced equipment. Low-end manufacturers such as Spalding, MacGregor, and Dunlop sold their products mainly through discounters, mass merchandisers, and large sporting goods stores. These retailers had no custom-fitting capabilities and rarely had sales personnel who were knowledgeable about the performance features of the different brands and models of golf equipment carried in the store. The appeal of such retail outlets was low price, and they mainly attracted beginning golfers and occasional golfers who were unwilling to invest in more expensive equipment.

Callaway Golf Company

Callaway Golf Company's competitive strategy was rooted in Ely Callaway's philosophy that true long-term success comes from innovative products that are "demonstrably superior to, and pleasingly different from" the products offered by industry rivals. Ely Callaway believed that due to the difficulty of the game of golf (there was tremendous room for variation in *each* swing of the club and for off-center contact with the ball), serious golfers would be willing to invest in high-quality, premium-priced equipment, like the Big Bertha driver and the titanium Great Big Bertha driver, if such clubs could improve their game by being more forgiving of a less-than-optimum swing. Since the introduction of Callaway's S2H2 line of irons in 1988, the company had sought to develop, manufacture, and market the most technologically advanced golf clubs available. In addition, Richard Helmstetter and his team of engineers sought quantum leaps in club performance, rather than incremental improvements, with each new line of clubs introduced by the company.

Callaway's "Demonstrably Superior and Pleasingly Different" Value Chain

Callaway Golf Company's ability to develop "demonstrably superior and pleasingly different" golf clubs was a result of activities performed by the company throughout its value chain. Callaway's differentiation was achieved through both its unique value chain and through its ability to out-execute its rivals where value chain similarities existed.

Product Development and the Helmstetter Test Center

When Ely Callaway purchased Hickory Stick USA he believed strongly that developing "demonstrably superior and pleasingly different" golf clubs would be more closely related to the company's physics-oriented R&D than would a focus on cosmetics. Richard Helmstetter and his engineering team were critical to the execution of Callaway's competitive strategy. As of 2000 Callaway Golf had consistently outspent its rivals on R&D. In 1999 alone, the company spent $27 million on research and development related to its golf club business—more than most of its key rivals' combined R&D budgets. The company's R&D efforts allowed it to continually beat its competitors to the market with new innovations. Callaway's engineers developed the first oversize driver in 1990, were the first to make clubheads even larger by using titanium, and were the first to use a combination of materials (titanium and tungsten) in clubhead design.

Callaway Golf opened the Richard C. Helmstetter Test Center in 1994 to support its research and product development efforts. The test center was located about a mile from Callaway's main campus and included a laboratory and a golfing area. The test center laboratory was home to Helmstetter's engineers, who worked both on teams and individually to develop new models of clubheads and shafts. Callaway's products were designed on powerful workstations running computer-aided design (CAD) software similar to that used in the aerospace industry. The CAD software allowed engineers not only to design new clubheads and shafts but also to conduct aerodynamic and strength testing in a simulated environment. Actual physical models could be created from the computer-generated images through the use of numerically controlled systems. The center's "destruction and durability" laboratory used robots and air cannons to establish minimum thresholds of strength and durability for prototypes of new models of clubheads and shafts.

The club-fitting and specifications area of the test center used the company's Callaway Performance Analysis System to match equipment to a golfer's swing characteristics. The internally developed proprietary video and computer system used stereo imaging techniques to capture a sequence of eight multiple exposures of the clubhead and ball at various time intervals immediately before and after a golfer hit the ball into a net approximately 10 feet from where it was struck. Callaway's proprietary computer software analyzed the video images of the clubhead's approach to the ball and the ball's rotational patterns over its first few feet of flight to make a variety of calculations needed to project the ball's ultimate path. The projected path was displayed on a six-foot video screen that showed the ball's flight along the 18th fairway at Pebble Beach. The computer system also recorded the clubhead speed, ball velocity, side spin, back spin, attack angle, and launch angle to calculate the efficiency rating, carry, roll, total distance, and dispersion (deviation from a straight path). All of these statistics were projected on the screen, along with the image of ball's flight down the fairway. The equipment allowed the company to build a set of clubs for the touring professional that had the perfect swing weight, frequency, loft, lie, and length to maximize distance and accuracy.

The Helmstetter Test Center's golfing area was an 8.1-acre outdoor testing facility that included three putting and chipping greens, a deep pot bunker, a shallow fairway bunker, and a 310-yard fairway that was 80 yards wide at its narrowest point. Sensors located along the fairway recorded the distance and dispersion of any ball landing in the test area.

Atmospheric conditions, such as wind speed, direction, temperature, barometric pressure, humidity, and dew point were recorded by three weather stations located around the test site. The facility also included an artificial tee box and green that accurately simulated a real green. Ball reaction on the simulated green was almost identical to that on the other three greens and allowed the company to continue testing while the natural test site was being irrigated or mowed.

The Helmstetter Test Center had two primary uses: It provided an ideal place to custom-fit clubs for the touring pros who used Callaway equipment, and it allowed Callaway R&D staff to test new products during their developmental stage. Once a professional's new clubs were fitted using the video and computer capabilities of the Callaway Performance Analysis System, the touring pro could then use the golfing area to hit balls and fine-tune his or her clubs by requesting minor modifications to the clubhead or shaft. Callaway included nontouring professionals in addition to engineers among its R&D staff. The golfing staff was critical to the product development process since engineers were able to refine new prototypes based on the feedback and recommendations of Callaway's R&D staff golfers. Callaway's engineers also tested prototypes with robots to evaluate the distance and accuracy of the club, but only a human could evaluate the feel of a golf club striking a ball.

Callaway's Purchasing and Production Processes

Once its clubheads were designed on a CAD system and tested in the Helmstetter Center, stainless-steel master plates were cut by Callaway to the exact specifications called for by the system. Each clubhead mold was made by pouring liquid wax between the stainless-steel master plates. The wax clubheads were removed from the master plates and sprayed with a mixture of highly heat resistant material. The wax was melted out of these heat-resistant molds, leaving a hollow core. The hollow molds were then sent to an investment casting house, where either stainless steel or titanium was poured into the molds. The casting house then broke away the mold and welded, sanded, and painted the clubheads before sending them to Callaway for further assembly.

Callaway Golf used five investment casting houses, all of which underwent extensive screening and were closely monitored during the casting process. Callaway management believed that it was particularly important to supervise the casting process since poor casting could produce clubhead inconsistencies that could lead to poor performance or product failures. Callaway had entered into a joint venture with Sturm, Ruger & Company in 1995 to produce its clubheads but had since recognized that quality clubheads could be obtained through outsourcing. Even though Callaway Golf was certain it would obtain high-quality clubheads through its sourcing agreements, it made daily inspections of incoming clubhead shipments using the materials analysis and durability-testing capabilities of the Helmstetter Center.

Like Callaway's clubheads, all of its shafts were designed and tested at the Helmstetter Center. Callaway manufactured all prototype shafts by hand at the testing center but contracted shaft production out to independent shaft manufacturers once specifications were established for the various graphite shafts used in its product line. As with clubheads, shafts were drawn from incoming shipments and tested at the company's R&D facility. Steel shafts were contracted out and inspected in a similar fashion. Callaway had produced as much as 50 percent of its graphite shafts internally during the late 1990s but outsourced 100 percent of its shaft requirements in 2000.

Callaway Golf's cell manufacturing process allowed the company to include quality control inspections throughout each club's assembly. In addition, the assembly plant was highly automated, with all processes requiring very tight tolerances performed by computer-controlled machinery. For example, the drilling necessary to produce Callaway's tapered bore-thru hosels was done by a series of precision drill presses that ensured that each hosel was drilled at the correct angle. Once the hosel had been drilled through, the clubhead moved to a production station that checked the lie and loft angles of the club and made any necessary corrections by slightly bending the clubhead to the proper angle.

Each shaft was inspected for fractures prior to insertion into the clubhead, and then the entire assembled club was weighed to assess the swing weight. Callaway production workers could choose between medallions of four different weights to bring a finished iron to the exact specified swing weight. The chosen medallion was permanently affixed to the back of the clubhead with a press. Swing weights for assembled woods were brought to their specifications by inserting epoxy through a small hole in the rear of the clubhead.

After undergoing a baking process that dried the glue used to attach the shaft to the clubhead, each club was fitted with a grip using a laser alignment device, airbrushed with details like the club number and Callaway trademarks, and then visually inspected for blemishes or other imperfections. Each finished club was wrapped by hand to protect its finish during shipping.

Sales and Customer Service

New product development at Callaway Golf Company was a cross-functional effort that included not only the R&D staff but also the company's sales and advertising staffs. Callaway sales and advertising personnel would evaluate new designs created by the company's aerospace engineers and recommend design changes based on their knowledge of the market. Once a new design was settled on, Callaway's sales force and internal advertising staff would create a name for the new product line, an advertising campaign, and promotional materials that would accompany the product launch in parallel with the R&D staff's developmental and testing processes.

Callaway's customer service department was viewed as a critical component of the company's overall level of differentiation. The customer service staff was made up of experienced employees who were offered a generous compensation package that included commissions for superior performance in meeting the needs of Callaway's retailers and consumers. Many of Callaway's rivals viewed customer service as a low-value-adding activity and typically made customer service a place for entry-level employees to become acquainted with the business. Each of Callaway Golf's customer service representatives received eight weeks of training before being allowed to handle a customer service inquiry. No other company in the industry provided more than three weeks of training to its customer service personnel. In addition to providing extensive training, Callaway promoted a team-oriented atmosphere that allowed the company's knowledge base to expand through the mentoring of newer employees by longtime customer service employees.

The entire customer service staff was empowered to make a final decision regarding a consumer or retailer complaint or warranty claim. Callaway customer service personnel were allowed to make decisions that might be pushed to the CEO at some other golf equipment companies. For example, if a golfer was vacationing and had a problem with a club, a customer service staff member could instruct the consumer to visit a local retailer to pick up a replacement club. If the consumer was out of the country and was not near a Callaway retailer, the Callaway employee was allowed to send a new club to the customer via Federal Express. Callaway customer service staff members were also known to send a gift to club owners who had experienced problems with Callaway equipment. Callaway's two-year warranty on all of its products entitled the owner to replace any defective product with a new product rather than return the product for a repair. In addition, Callaway generally chose to replace defective or broken clubs for the life of the club rather than stick to its two-year warranty period. A Callaway sales executive remarked, "A bad experience with a Callaway product usually winds up making someone a Callaway customer for life."

Callaway Golf's Product Line

Metal Woods

Callaway Golf's Big Bertha driver was the most innovative club in the industry when it was introduced in 1990. Its key features were a bigger clubhead, a bigger sweet spot, and a longer shaft, all of which helped to improve the consistency with which a golfer could drive the ball off the tee. Callaway wasted no time in capitalizing on the explosive popularity of its new driver; company managers understood that once a driver developed a following among golfers, these golfers usually wanted other woods to match it. The company subsequently introduced a series of fairway woods—a 2 wood, a 3 wood, a 5 wood, two styles of 7 woods, a 9 wood, and an 11 wood—to complement the Big Bertha driver. Many golfers rushed to buy not only the Big Bertha driver but also the company's other Big Bertha metal woods; it was common for Big Bertha enthusiasts to have three or four of the Big Bertha fairway woods in their bag.

Four years later, the company again moved to set itself apart from rival equipment makers (most of whom had by then come out with imitative versions of the Big Bertha line) by introducing the Great Big Bertha driver, made out of strong, lightweight titanium. The driver had a clubhead 30 percent larger than the original Big Bertha driver but was still just as light because of the substitution of titanium for stainless steel in the clubhead and the use of a graphite shaft; the Great Big Bertha (GBB) was the industry's most technologically advanced golf club and retailed for $500 (a heretofore unheard-of price for a single golf club).

Callaway's introduction of its titanium Biggest Big Bertha in 1997 again caught industry rivals off guard as they moved to match the size of the GBB. The Biggest Big Bertha (BBB) was 15 percent larger than the titanium Great Big Bertha (and the titanium clubs produced by Callaway's rivals) and was equipped with a 46-inch lightweight shaft. The total weight of the BBB was less than the total weight of the titanium GBB and the stainless steel Big Bertha drivers, which had 45- and 44-inch shafts, respectively.

The size of Callaway woods began to decrease with the introduction of its Big Bertha (BB) Steelhead metal woods in 1998 and Hawk Eye titanium metal woods in 1999. The BB Steelhead line was created in response to the popularity of the shallow-faced woods introduced by Orlimar and Adams in 1998. BB Steelhead drivers and fairway woods had a lower center of gravity than GBB and BBB woods, but had a higher profile than Adams and Orlimar woods. The BB Steelhead line incorporated the best features of both competing club designs by maintaining a very low center of gravity but having a larger clubface, which prevented the golfer from hitting below the ball, as was frequently done by amateur golfers using shallow-faced woods.

The BB Steelhead Plus was introduced in January 2000 as an improvement to the BB Steelhead line of drivers and fairway woods. Like the BB Steelhead line, the BB Steelhead Plus included a precision-cast steel chip to lower the club's center of gravity but featured variable clubface thickness that optimized energy transfer between the clubhead and the ball. Callaway's Variable Face Thickness Technology, developed through computer modeling and player testing, allowed the company to vary the clubface thickness to maximize perimeter weighting while keeping an elliptical area near the center of the clubface relatively thick. This thickness directly at the sweet spot of the clubface provided more energy transfer when a ball was well struck, while the perimeter weighting and thin walls near the outside edges of the clubface provided more forgiveness if a ball was mis-hit. Callaway's BB Steelhead Plus metal woods and its Variable Face Thickness Technology are described in the Callaway print ad shown in Exhibit 7. Callaway's Great Big Bertha Hawk Eye titanium drivers and fairway woods featured a titanium body and crown plate and Callaway's exclusive tungsten gravity screw, which accounted for only 2 percent of the clubhead volume but 25 percent of its overall weight. The lightweight titanium clubhead body and crown plate allowed Call-

away to increase the overall size of the driver and the sweet spot, while the tungsten screw performed a number of functions. First, the use of tungsten low in the club created a low center of gravity, which helped the golfer produce a high trajectory. The tungsten screw also was strategically positioned in the sole of the clubhead to create Callaway's Draw Bias Technology, which drew the clubhead square at impact and reduced the likelihood of a slice. The tungsten screw also increased backspin, which helped produce greater distance. Exhibit 8 presents a print ad for Callaway's line of GBB Hawk Eye metal woods.

Irons

To capitalize on the initial popularity of the Big Bertha metal woods, Callaway Golf introduced lines of stainless-steel and graphite-shafted Big Bertha irons in 1994. In 1997 the company introduced Great Big Bertha tungsten-titanium irons, which included a tungsten insert located in the sole of the club that lowered the clubhead's center of gravity. The use of titanium allowed Callaway to increase the overall size of the clubface, creating a larger sweet spot, while the tungsten insert allowed Callaway to keep the center of gravity low and add weight to the sweet spot. This low center of gravity and concentration of weight in the sweet spot allowed the irons to hit higher, straighter shots.

Callaway's Hawk Eye tungsten-injected titanium irons, introduced in 1999, included innovative design improvements over the original GBB tungsten-titanium irons. The Hawk Eye titanium irons included a hidden cavity that ran the length of the clubhead and extended upward behind the hitting area. Small, uniform tungsten spheres were added by a computer weigh station to the cavity through a port and then covered with a dense molten metal to permanently lock them into place. Each iron contained a different number of spheres depending on the optimal center of gravity for the loft of the club. Once the appropriate number of tungsten spheres and the molten metal were added to the clubhead, the weight port was hidden by a Hawk Eye medallion. The Tungsten Weight Matrix that resulted from the addition of the spheres occupied only 27 percent of the volume of a Callaway Hawk Eye 5-iron yet accounted for 45 percent of the clubhead's weight. The weight matrix created a low center of gravity that acted much like the gravity screw used in Hawk Eye metal woods and allowed golfers to create a high shot likely to maintain a straight path.

Callaway Golf replaced its stainless-steel Big Bertha irons in 1998 with its Big Bertha X-12 irons. The X-12 line of irons included a number of improvements over the Big Bertha irons and became the best-selling iron in the company's history. The X-12 line featured a narrower sole than Big Bertha irons, which made it easier to hit shots out of the rough. Big Bertha X-12 irons also had a multilayer design effect on the back of the clubface that allowed Callaway designers to locate the center of gravity at the ideal location for each length iron. The introduction of a variable 360-degree undercut channel also aided Callaway engineers in placing the center of gravity at the best possible location on the clubhead.

Callaway replaced the X-12 line of irons in 2000 with the Big Bertha X-14 Steelhead line. The X-14 featured Callaway's Variable Face Thickness Technology, which tapered the clubface from top to bottom and from heel to toe to create better perimeter weighting than previous generations of Callaway irons. The technology also allowed Callaway engineers to move the center of gravity to the ideal location on each iron. For example, the X-14 short irons had a higher center of gravity to provide extra control on approach shots, while the midlength irons and long irons had a lower center of gravity to produce a higher ball flight. Exhibit 9 shows a sample ad for Callaway Golf's X-14 irons.

Putters

Callaway Golf Company manufactured and marketed Bobby Jones, Carlsbad, and Tuttle lines of putters and the Odyssey brand of putters. Callaway had moderate success with its own Callaway putter lines, but its acquisition of Odyssey in 1997 made it the leading producer of putters in 2000. The 12 Bobby Jones putters and four Carlsbad putters were all made from

EXHIBIT 8   **Sample Ad for Callaway Golf's New Hawk Eye Metal Woods**

stainless steel and came in blade and mallet styles. The Tuttle putter came in one model, which was unique in that it actually resembled a Big Bertha driver but was the size of a putter. Odyssey became known as an innovator in putters when it became one of the first companies to introduce polymer clubface inserts. Many golfers preferred putters with an insert since the soft material created a softer noise and provided more feel when putting a ball. Callaway's Odyssey putter was one of the two leading brands of putter in 2000 (Ping and Odyssey regularly exchanged the number one title) and was available in 26 different blade and mallet designs. Each of Odyssey's 26 models of putters featured its Stronomic polymer insert, available in three degrees of softness. In early 2000, Odyssey introduced its White Hot line of putters, which used Callaway's golf ball material as a clubface insert.

Callaway's Battle Against Patent and Trademark Infringement

Ever since the Big Bertha driver had gained mass acceptance by professional and amateur golfers, Callaway Golf had been attacked by small golf companies offering clubs that were so similar in design and appearance that they infringed on Callaway's patents and trademarks. Although they looked like the branded clubs, the knockoff clubs were of inferior quality and typically sold for as much as 75 percent less than name-brand clubs. Some knockoff brands outsold the brands offered by such well-known makers as Hogan, Cleveland, and MacGregor. Callaway Golf was extremely committed to battling the makers of knockoff and counterfeit clubs. The company hired a retired U.S. Army counterintelligence expert to investigate trademark infringement cases and also worked in this area with private investigators, U.S. Customs, and U.S. marshals. In early 2000, Callaway Golf carried out a four-state sweep against illegal club makers that netted $65,000 worth of Callaway golf clubs that had been stolen and were being sold over the Internet; officials seized 5,800 golf clubs, including Canterbury Big Bursar V-17 irons and Connection Golf Big Bernard Steel-clad metal woods. However, even when patent infringers and counterfeiters were caught and convicted, it was difficult to collect damages because such companies usually had minimal assets to seize.

Callaway Golf also aggressively protected its legal rights when it believed that a branded rival infringed on its patents or made false claims about either its own products or Callaway's products. In 1998 Callaway brought a suit against Spalding Sports Worldwide for trademark violation after Spalding created a line of System C golf balls and claimed they were specifically designed for Callaway clubs. The two parties settled in 1999, with Spalding agreeing to pull the line of golf balls. In addition, after a legal challenge from Callaway, Orlimar Golf was ordered by the court to retract advertisements falsely claiming that it was the number one metal wood used on the PGA tour. In 1999 Callaway Golf saw that the vice president of Callaway Golf Ball Company could in no way be involved with Taylor Made's golf ball operations after the Callaway employee left with company trade secrets to become Taylor Made's president and CEO. Callaway Golf also forced an apology from the CEO of La Jolla Golf after Callaway found that La Jolla's chief executive had used a fictitious name to make untrue and disparaging remarks about Callaway golf clubs on the Internet.

Endorsements and Use of Callaway Products by Golf Professionals

Callaway golf clubs were popular with both professionals and amateurs alike. Callaway drivers were endorsed by the professional golfers listed in Exhibit 10. However, many professional golfers used Callaway equipment even though they were not paid to endorse the company's products. In 1999 Callaway drivers were used in 61 wins, Callaway irons were used in 37 wins, and Odyssey putters produced 36 wins in a total of 186 PGA, LPGA, Senior PGA, Nike, and European PGA professional tournaments. A comparison of clubs used by professionals in all five tournaments is presented in Exhibit 11.

EXHIBIT 10
**Callaway Golf
Company Staff
Professionals, 2000**

Source: Callaway Golf 2000
catalog.

Tour	Staff Players
Professional Golfers Association	Stephen Ames
	Paul Azinger
	Oline Browne
	Carlos Franco
	Brian Henninger
	Rocco Mediate
	Jesper Parnevik
	Paul Stankowski
Senior Professional Golfers Association	Bob Charles
	Jim Colbert
	Jim Dent
	Dave Eichelberger
	Bruce Fleisher
	David Graham
	Orville Moody
	Walter Morgan
	Bob Murphy
Ladies Professional Golfers Association	Jane Geddes
	Rachel Hetherington
	Rosie Jones
	Emilee Klein
	Leta Lindley
	Cindy McCurdy
	Liselotte Neumann
	Alison Nicholas
	Annika Sorenstam
European Professional Golfers Association	Mark McNulty
	Colin Montgomerie
	Eduardo Romero

Callaway Golf's Major Competitors

Callaway management considered its strongest competitive rivals to be Ping and Taylor Made because of those companies' track records in product innovation and their strong brand-name recognition: Ping irons had dominated the industry during much of the 1980s and 1990s (the perimeter-weighting feature pioneered by Karsten was a major technological breakthrough and had since become the industry standard in designing irons), while Taylor Made's distinctive bubble shaft was also considered to be a high-tech innovation. Other key rivals of Callaway Golf Company were Titleist, Adams Golf, and Orlimar Golf. Exhibit 12 presents a price comparison of golf equipment produced by Callaway Golf Company and its key rivals.

Ping

Ping had not been well known for its drivers but had been one of the industry's premier manufacturers of irons since its Ping Eye 2-irons were introduced in the mid-1980s. The company's Ping Eye 3-irons that were introduced in 1999 were among the most popular irons with both professionals and amateurs. Ping Eye 3-irons were one of the two leading brands of irons sold in the United States and were frequently the most-used iron in various

EXHIBIT 11
**Golf Club Use
Comparison among
Professional Golfers
(All tours
combined), 1998–99**

Source: Callaway Golf Company annual reports and Darrell Survey.

	1999	1998
Drivers		
Callaway	38.5%	55.2%
Titleist	24.2	16.9
Ping	13.4	n.a.
Taylor Made	5.3	8.0
Orlimar	3.0	0.1
All others	15.6	17.5
Total drivers	100.0%	100.0%
Fairway woods		
Callaway	52.1%	48.3%
Orlimar	17.9	10.5
Taylor Made	8.8	13.3
Titleist	4.5	5.1
Cleveland	3.1	n.a.
All others	13.6	20.3
Total fairway woods	100.0%	100.0%
Irons		
Callaway	18.3%	19.4%
Ping	15.0	15.3
Mizuno	15.0	14.1
Titleist	14.5	12.6
Taylor Made	4.4	4.7
All others	32.8	33.9
Total irons	100.0%	100.0%
Putters		
Odyssey	28.9%	31.0%
Ping	21.8	24.8
Titleist	19.8	18.7
Never Compromise	11.2	3.7
Tear Drop	4.0	n.a.
All others	14.3	16.0
Total putters	100.0%	100.0%

n.a. = Not available.

EXHIBIT 12   **Retail Price Comparison of Equipment Produced by Leading Golf Equipment Companies, March 2000**

Source: Edwin Watts Golf Shops and International Golf Discount, March 11, 2000.

Brand	Titanium Drivers	Graphite-Shafted Stainless-Steel Irons (Set of 8)	Putters (Price Range of Most Popular Models)	Golf Balls (Price per Ball—Based on Single Sleeve)
Callaway Golf/Odyssey	$400	$900	$90–$200	$3.60
Ping	$400	$850	$80–$140	n.a.
Taylor Made	$300	$750	$100	$3.33
Titleist	$400	$870	$270	$3.33
Adams Golf	$300	Not carried	n.a.	n.a.
Orlimar Golf	$300	$800	n.a.	n.a.

n.a. = Not applicable.

professional tournaments. Ping Eye 3s were available with a compact blade-style clubhead designed for low-handicap golfers and with an oversized clubhead that had greater perimeter weighting for more forgiveness. All Ping Eye 3-irons featured a custom tuning port that was very similar in appearance to Callaway's tungsten weight matrix port, but functioned differently. Rather than acting as a port to add tungsten weights, Ping's custom tuning port allowed the company to make minor adjustments to the loft and lie of the club during custom fitting.

Ping had elected not to introduce a titanium driver until 1998, because the company's engineers believed that the material provided no advantage over stainless steel. However, in 2000 its 323-cc displacement TiSI titanium driver was actually the largest custom-fit driver available. Ping also offered Ti3 titanium fairway woods that featured a zirconium soleplate and a tungsten bottom weight that were both intended to lower the club's center of gravity. Ping also offered an i3 line of stainless-steel fairway woods in five different lofts.

Ping's greatest strength was in putters, where it alternated every quarter or so with Odyssey as the number one brand of putters in the U.S. and international markets. Depending on the tournament, Ping putters were often used by professional golfers more than any other brand. Ping had 46 models of putters that were made from either antiqued manganese bronze, stainless steel, or laminated maple. Certain Ping putters featured inserts made from an elastomer compound, aluminum pixels, or copper pixels. Ping began offering custom-fit clubs in the 1960s, and in 2000 all Ping metal woods, irons, and putters could be custom-fitted to golfers who desired that service.

Taylor Made–Adidas Golf

Taylor Made was founded in 1979 by Gary Adams, who mortgaged his home and began production of his metal woods in an abandoned car dealership building in McHenry, Illinois. Both touring pros and golf retailers were skeptical of the new club design until they found that the metal woods actually hit the ball higher and farther than persimmon woods. By 1984, Taylor Made metal woods were the number one wood on the PGA tour and the company had grown to be the third largest golf equipment company in the United States. In 1984 the company was acquired by France-based Salomon SA, which provided the capital necessary for the company to continue to develop innovative new lines of clubs. The company's sales had stalled during the late 1980s and early 1990s until it introduced its Burner Bubble drivers in 1994. The bubble shaft design allowed some of the shaft weight to be moved from underneath the grip to just below the grip. Taylor Made management claimed that this weight relocation decreased the club's inertia, which resulted in faster clubhead acceleration. The bubble shaft also featured a reinforced midsection, said to minimize any twisting of the clubhead during the swing.

Many of the company's innovations in drivers and fairway woods mirrored those of Callaway Golf. In 1996, shortly after Callaway's introduction of the Great Big Bertha, Taylor Made had come out with an oversized titanium driver that had its differentiating bubble shaft and copper-colored clubhead. Taylor Made also produced and marketed a line of irons with its patented bubble shafts and introduced a line of bubble-shafted tungsten-titanium irons and a new titanium bubble-shafted T2 driver in 1997. The T2 and Taylor Made's tungsten-titanium irons appeared in retail locations at approximately the same time that the Biggest Big Bertha and the Big Bertha tungsten-titanium irons made their debut. Also in 1997, Taylor Made and its parent were both acquired by the Germany-based sports conglomerate Adidas.

In 2000 Taylor Made offered titanium FireSole metal woods and irons that featured a tungsten sole plug and SuperSteel stainless-steel metal woods and irons. The FireSole was Taylor Made's answer to Callaway's Hawk Eye lines of metal woods and irons, while its promotion of its SuperSteel line touted many of the same benefits as Callaway's BB Steel-

Head Plus metal woods and X-14 irons. Taylor Made also offered FireSole Rescue clubs, which had a large tungsten sole attached to a reduced-size titanium clubhead that placed 75 percent of the clubhead's weight below the equator of the ball. The rescue woods had an ultralow center of gravity and could be used on either the fairway or the rough. In early 2000 Taylor Made's Rescue fairway woods were unique; no products of similar appearance were offered by other major club manufacturers. Taylor Made also had a line of putters that featured a polymer clubface. Taylor Made introduced its InterGel line of golf balls in 1999.

Fortune Brands/Acushnet (Titleist and Cobra Golf)

The Acushnet Company was a rubber deresinating company founded in 1910 in Acushnet, Massachusetts. The company opened a golf ball division in 1932 when founder Phil Young believed that a bad putt during a round of golf he was playing was a result of a faulty ball rather than his poor putting. Young took the ball to a dentist's office to have it X-rayed and found that the core of the ball was indeed off-center. Young believed that Acushnet could develop and manufacture high-quality golf balls and teamed with a fellow MIT graduate, Fred Bommer, to create the Titleist line of balls. Young and Bommer introduced their first Titleist golf ball in 1935, and by 1949 Titleist had become the most-played ball on the PGA. In 2000, Titleist was still the number one golf ball on the PGA, being used by more than 75 percent of all professional golfers in tournament play. Acushnet also manufactured and marketed a Pinnacle line of golf balls, developed in 1980 as a lower-priced alternative to Titleist branded golf balls.

Acushnet's acquisition of John Reuter, Jr., Inc., in 1958 and Golfcraft, Inc., in 1969 put Titleist into the golf club business. Titleist's Reuter Bull's Eye putter became a favorite on the PGA tour during the 1960s, and its AC-108 heel-toe weighted irons were among the most popular brands of irons during the early 1970s. In 1996 the Acushnet Company was acquired by American Brands, which had increased its presence in the golf equipment industry in 1985 when it acquired Foot-Joy, the number one seller of golf gloves and shoes. Also in 1996 American Brands acquired Cobra Golf for $715 million. The company's golf and leisure products division had an operating profit of $147 million on sales of $965 million in 1999.

Acushnet's two golf club brands maintained separate sales forces, but every other value chain activity was combined for overall cost savings whenever possible. The Titleist brand of clubs had achieved only moderate success after Ping's perimeter-weighted clubs became popular in the 1980s, but Titleist had become much more successful during the late 1990s due to Tiger Woods's endorsement of the company's irons and metal woods. In 2000 Titleist's 975D driver, used by Tiger Woods, was among the more popular drivers with both professionals and amateurs. The 975D was an oversized titanium driver designed for a flatter ball flight to help a golfer achieve greater roll once the ball hit the ground. The Titleist titanium 975R was a variation of the 975D, which had a more shallow face and a slightly smaller clubhead. Titleist also offered a line of 975F stainless-steel fairway woods in 2000.

Titleist had two lines of stainless steel irons: the DCI 990 and DCI 981. The DCI 990 was intended for low-handicap golfers and had a reduced clubface offset and more weight toward the lower portion of the heel, where better golfers were more prone to mis-hit a golf ball. The DCI 981 line, designed for higher-handicap golfers, had an offset clubface, a low center of gravity, and more weight toward the toe of the clubface of short irons. The overall design objectives of the 981 line were to produce higher trajectories and more forgiveness. The DCI 981 also was available in an SL series intended for seniors or other golfers with less clubhead speed. All Titleist irons and metal woods were available with either steel or graphite shafts. Titleist also marketed a line of 17 different Scotty Cameron putters in stainless steel, teryllium, or platinum finishes. Some Scotty Cameron putters included an elastomer membrane covering the clubface.

In 1996, Cobra Golf held the industry's number two spot in irons and was number three in drivers and fairway woods (behind Callaway and Taylor Made). Cobra's popularity was a result of Greg Norman's endorsement of the clubs and the company's strategy of reducing the loft of its irons. The reduced loft added considerable distance to each club. For example, a golfer switching to King Cobra irons might pick up 20 yards or more on each club. Cobra Golf's King Cobra drivers were also considered a long-distance club.

After its acquisition by Acushnet, Cobra began to rapidly lose market share in both irons and metal woods. The company was forced to change its marketing approach since its high-profile, aggressive marketing practices clashed with the wishes of Acushnet's managers, who preferred a conservative approach to marketing. In addition, Acushnet management believed that Cobra should redesign its clubs to promote forgiveness at the expense of distance. Loyal Cobra customers were disappointed when they found that Cobra new models of clubs did not offer any greater distance than other brands. The decline in demand forced Cobra into a practice of deep discounting, which encouraged golfers to wait for the company to cut prices before they purchased the latest Cobra products. Cobra Golf also lost a considerable number of retailers during the later 1990s. The combination of missteps by Acushnet and Cobra Golf managers had all but made Cobra an afterthought by 1999.

Cobra struggled to rebuild its image and market presence after its strategic gaffes of the late 1990s. In 1999 the company launched a Web site and print ads that promoted its products as hip, nonconformist alternatives to the more technology-based golf clubs on the market. In early 2000 Cobra had abandoned this new image and recast itself as a more mainstream golf company.

Cobra's new products for 2000 included its Gravity Back drivers and fairway metal woods, which featured a titanium clubhead with a bronze alloy backweight placed at the rear of the clubhead. The bronze alloy backweight was designed to give the club a lower center of gravity. The Gravity Back fairway woods also featured a copper-tungsten sole weight to further lower the center of gravity. Cobra's CXI stainless-steel irons featured an X-like design on the backside of the clubface to more evenly disperse weight throughout the rear of the cavity back club. In 1999 Cobra Golf introduced Cobra Dista golf balls, which came in four models.

Adams Golf

Barney Adams founded Adams Golf in 1987 in Plano, Texas, as a golf club components supplier and contract manufacturer. In 1995 the company introduced its Tight Lies line of fairway woods, which featured an innovative low-profile clubface with a very low center of gravity. The shallow clubface and low center of gravity enlarged the effective hitting area of the clubface and created shots with a higher trajectory than shots with traditional-sized metal woods of the same loft. Tight Lies fairway woods were named the "Breakthrough Product of the Year" in 1997 by the Golf Market Research Institute and were rated the "Best of the Best" fairway woods in an independent real-golfer comparison in 1998. Adams Golf went public in July 1998 at an initial offering price of $16.00. The company recorded 1998 sales and earnings of $85 million and $13 million, respectively. In 1997 Adams had revenues of $37 million and a net loss of $5 million.

Adams's success became more difficult to maintain after other leading golf club manufacturers offered new lines of fairway woods with a shallower face than their previous models. In 1999 Adams Golf's revenues had declined to $54 million and the company recorded a net loss of $11 million. The company's stock traded below $2.00 during the first three months of 2000. Adams Golf's product line for 2000 included its Tight Lies[2] fairway woods, which had a deeper clubface than the original Tight Lies fairway woods. The new Tight Lies[2] retained the key features of the original Tight Lies line, but its deeper clubface made it easier to hit from the rough. In 1999 Adams introduced a line of SC series drivers, which were available in four different clubface curvatures designed to correct either a slice, a fade, or a hook. One SC driver featured a neutral clubface curvature for golfers without swing path problems. Adams also offered Assault VMI (variable moment of inertia) irons, which were heavier than most other brands of irons and used a patented mathematical formula to determine the ideal weight of the club based on the overall club length, shaft length, grip weight, and shaft weight.

Orlimar Golf Company

Orlimar Golf Company was founded in 1960 by Lou Ortiz in the basement of a converted stable in San Francisco. The company was a little-known maker of custom clubs primarily used by professionals and had annual sales of under $1 million in 1996. The company exploded onto the broad market for golf clubs in 1998 when it introduced its Tri-Metal fairway woods. Orlimar's Tri-Metal woods were made of stainless steel, copper, and tungsten and featured a low center of gravity and a shallower clubface than Callaway's GBB fairway woods. The combination of three metals and the low profile made the Tri-Metal instantly popular with professionals and amateurs alike. By year-end 1998 the company's sales had grown to more than $50 million and it was named as the fastest-growing private company in the San Francisco Bay area.

The company added drivers and irons to its product line in 1999 as its sales of fairway woods began to decline after Callaway's fairway woods began to recapture market share lost in 1997 and 1998. Orlimar's 2000 lineup of new products included its Tri-Metal Plus fairway woods and drivers and Tri-Metal irons. Like Orlimar's original Tri-Metal woods, Tri-Metal Plus fairway woods and drivers were made from stainless steel and included a copper tungsten sole plate to lower their center of gravity, but the Plus line had a deeper clubface than the original Tri-Metals. The clubface of the Tri-Metal Plus metal woods was coated with an Alpha Maraging Face material that the company claimed was harder than titanium. Orlimar's Tri-Metal irons were made from the same materials as the company's metal woods and were designed to produce high trajectories and longer distance than competing clubs.

Callaway's Prospects for Growth and the February 2000 Launch of the Callaway Golf Ball

Callaway's introduction of its new Rule 35 golf ball had been eagerly awaited since mid-1996, when Ely Callaway announced the formation of Callaway Golf Ball Company and the move of Charles Yash from Taylor Made to the new company. Whereas Nike had entered the golf ball industry in 1999 by outsourcing its production to Bridgestone and Taylor Made chose its mode of entry by purchasing an existing plant from a competitor, Ely Callaway had chosen a more time-consuming route to enter the market for golf balls by electing to construct a new golf ball facility and internally develop an all-new ball. He noted: "This is the first time in the modern history of the industry, to our knowledge, that anyone has built a major-production golf ball business from scratch. After analyzing all of our other options, which included buying an existing company, buying an existing plant or buying a golf ball from another manufacturer and merely stamping our name on it, we decided this was the best way to go in order to create a superior product now and for the future."[9]

Callaway Golf spent three years developing in parallel its new golf ball and its state-of-the-art production facility. The company's entry into the market represented a $170 million investment in the research and development of the ball, construction of the 225,000-square-foot production facility, and development and purchase of special manufacturing equipment. Callaway's manufacturing facility and its equipment were designed specifically for the unique production requirements for the new ball.

---

[9]"Play Ball: Callaway Introduces the Rule 35," www.pgatour.com.

Ely Callaway believed that the company's custom-designed manufacturing equipment and facility would contribute to the company's competitive strength and the ball's success: "No one else has the collection of late 90s equipment that we have, everything you need to make a better ball. No one has put it together and purchased it all the way we have. Some of the companies, because of the age of some of their equipment, just can't utilize the latest equipment without going outside."[10] Callaway's competitors were so interested in the company's new golf ball facility that they took aerial photographs of the plant's foundation as it was under construction.

Callaway Golf Ball Company engineers, recruited from Du Pont and Boeing, used aerodynamic computer programs (first used by Boeing and General Electric) to evaluate more than 300 dimple patterns and more than 1,000 variations of ball cores, boundary layers, and cover materials to create the new Rule 35 ball. Callaway engineers designed only two models of the Rule 35 ball—choosing to develop a "complete-performance" ball rather than separate balls developed for spin, control, distance, and durability. Ely Callaway explained the company's product development objectives as follows: "We have combined all of the performance benefits into one ball so players no longer need to sacrifice control for distance, or feel, or durability. Each Rule 35 ball contains a unique synergy of distance, control, spin, feel and durability characteristics. This eliminates confusion and guesswork in trying to identify the golf ball that is right for each individual golfer."[11]

Callaway's production process used computers to mill the rubber core, control injection molding of a boundary layer, and deposit a proprietary urethane coating to golf balls as they were assembled. The golf balls then moved through a transparent tube to a battery of diagnostic machines that ensured that each ball was exactly the same. A laser was then used to twice measure the depth of each of the ball's 382 dimples, and an electrical process was used to bond paint to the ball securely and evenly. Each ball was then X-rayed and machine-inspected before being packed or rejected. Callaway's production process included 16,000 quality assurance checkpoints, and Callaway employees were allowed to stop the flow of balls at the first sign of defects.

Callaway's Rule 35 balls were differentiated from competing brands in a large number of ways. The name Rule 35 was a play on the 34 long-standing rules of golf published by the USGA and the Royal & Ancient Golf Club of St. Andrews. Ely Callaway suggested that there should be a 35th rule of golf—"Enjoy the game."[12] The complete-performance balls came in only two variations, whereas the golf balls offered by competitors came in as many as 10 models. The blue-logo Callaway ball was called the Softfeel and had all of the same characteristics as its red-logo Firmfeel ball but had a slightly softer feel. Ely Callaway believed the availability of only two complete-performance balls and the avoidance of a discussion of the technical aspects of the balls' design and construction would make it easier for golfers to purchase golf balls: "We know there is a lot of complex science that goes into making a golf ball, but we don't think there should be a lot of complexity to buying one."[13] Callaway later commented, "We've come up with two balls. That's it. We're not gonna tell you much about them. We have only two, you make the choice. If you like a soft feel, you try this one (blue). If you like a firm feel, you try this one (red). We don't say a damn thing about how far they go. We don't say a word about compression or the construction or the details of the cover. We just say, 'Try them.' We believe that either one of them will give you more of what you've been looking for in one ball than anything else."[14]

[10]"Long on Promises, Short on Explanation," *Golfweek,* February 5, 2000.
[11]"Callaway Enters the Ball Game," *Show News,* February 5, 2000.
[12]"Play Ball: Callaway Introduces the Rule 35."
[13]"Callaway Enters the Ball Game."
[14]"Long on Promises, Short on Explanation."

EXHIBIT 13
Estimated Manufacturing Shares of the Leading Producers of Golf Balls, 12 Months Ending September 30, 1999

Source: Callaway Golf Company.

	Dollars	Units
Titleist	36%	29%
Top-Flite/Spalding	23	27
Pinnacle	11	14
Maxfli	8	7
Wilson	7	8
Slazenger	5	3
Precept	3	2
Dunlop	2	3
Taylor Made	1	1
All others	4	6
Total	100%	100%

Callaway Golf Ball Company's CEO, Chuck Yash, discussed the company's philosophy behind offering only two models of the Rule 35 and why the company refused to comment on the ball's technology: "Our basic aim in this process was to make a ball that reflects the parent company's philosophy and vision of creating a 'demonstrably superior and pleasingly different' product. We also set out to cut through the noise regarding the performance claims by most of the competitors' products, and all of the techno-babble about various polymers and compressions and dimple patterns and claims regarding the longest distance balls. What we have in Rule 35 is a very clear message. If you prefer a firm feel, our Firm-feel ball has everything you need in performance. If you prefer a softer feel, our Softfeel ball is the choice. It's that easy."[15]

Callaway golf balls were further differentiated by their logo and packaging. The Callaway name used a stylized script rather than the Old English script used on Callaway golf clubs, and the company's logo was comprised of a letter *C* created from a rendering of the bottom of a golf cup. The balls were also packaged in sleeves of 5 and packs of 10 rather than sleeves of 3 or packs of 12 like other brands. Callaway Golf Ball Company's national sales manager explained why Callaway chose unique packaging for its golf balls: "When we were doing our research, we couldn't find a single person who could tell us why golf balls were packaged in sleeves of three or in dozens. When we discovered that the average golfer uses 4.5 balls per round, we decided the five-ball sleeve was the right way to go with packaging."[16] In addition, unlike the packaging of other brands of balls, Callaway's packaging included only the name and logo printed on a translucent plastic box rather than the name and product performance characteristics printed on a cardboard box. Callaway's use of a five-ball sleeve also allowed its golf balls to be placed away from other brands of balls since most retailers' display cases were designed for three-ball sleeves.

Even though the industry had long been dominated by Titleist and Spalding (see Exhibit 13), many analysts believed that Callaway's ability to develop technologically advanced products, its marketing expertise, and its established retailer network would allow the company to quickly gain a 2 to 3 percent share of the market and achieve $60 to $70 million in sales during 2000. Analysts also speculated that Callaway Golf Ball Company could hit sales of over $200 million within two years of the ball's launch. It was expected that Callaway's golf ball operations would considerably impact the company's net profit since profit margins in the premium segment of the golf ball market ranged between 60 and 75 percent. In addition, golf ball sales were less seasonal since they were consumable items

[15]Callaway press release, February 4, 2000.
[16]"Callaway Enters the Ball Game."

that were purchased throughout the year. Also, unlike a $500 driver, golfers could not delay the purchase of golf balls until they felt financially ready to make a large purchase. The company's objective was for the Rule 35 to capture a 10 percent share of the market within two years and ultimately become one of the two top brands of golf balls. "We have 7 million people out there playing our products, and 80 percent of them think they're the best clubs in the world," said Ely Callaway. "We have almost a guaranteed 'try' on our new products."[17] Callaway further commented, "We're going to sell a lot of balls."[18] An advertisement for the Rule 35 golf ball is shown in Exhibit 14.

In February 2000 a survey of golf equipment company executives voted Callaway's Big Bertha driver the best golf product of the century by a 2-to-1 margin. The same group of executives called Ely Callaway the most influential golf trade person of the 1990s. As he approached his 81st birthday, Ely Callaway had vowed to retire by December 31, 2000, and make Chuck Yash the new CEO and president of Callaway Golf Company as well as Callaway Golf Ball Company. Just prior to the PGA Merchandise Show, Chuck Yash commented on his growing responsibility at Callaway Golf Company and the importance of its golf ball operations to the company's future growth: "The trust and faith Ely and the board of directors and the shareholders have shown in us is extraordinary. It has allowed me to use my 20 years of golf experience to build an organization and a team that, we believe, can have a significant impact. That is the way we are looking at things now, as a long-term commitment. It will take years before we feel we can compete with the leading companies in the golf ball market. But that is our objective. If we do that right, we have the potential to continue to grow."[19]

---

[17]"Rule 35 Tees Off," *San Diego Union-Tribune,* February 4, 2000.
[18]"Play Ball: Callaway Introduces the Rule 35."
[19]"On the Spot: Chuck Yash," *Golf Product News,* January/February 2000.

EXHIBIT 14   **Sample Ad for Callaway Golf's Rule 35 Golf Ball**

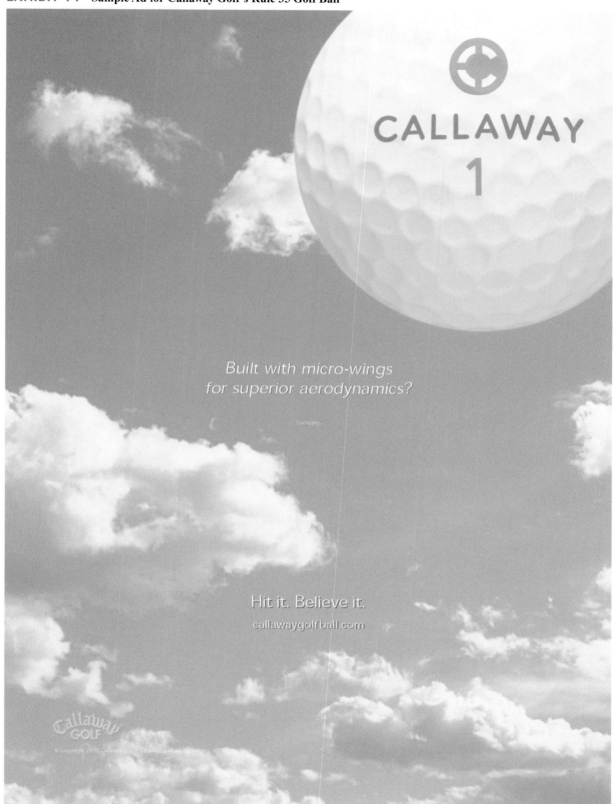

Case
Group C

Case

Promotion Strategy

11

---

harley-davidson.com and the Global Motorcycle Industry

J. Paul Peter *University of Wisconsin–Madison*

Harley-Davidson, Inc., achieved its thirteenth consecutive year of record revenue and earnings and a 74 percent increase in the value of the firm in 1998. The company had previously divested interests in other industries and focused its efforts exclusively on the motorcycle industry, including accessories and financing. It strengthened its presence in the industry by obtaining full ownership in Buell Motorcycle Company, a manufacturer of sport motorcycles based on Harley-Davidson components and previously established Eaglemark Financial Services, Inc., to provide financial services to dealers and customers.

The company completed a new 479,200-square-foot facility near Milwaukee in 1998 which manufactures engines and transmissions and finished a 330,000-square-foot facility in Kansas City, Missouri, which produces all six models of Sportsters, Harley's 833cc and 1200cc bikes. The company also introduced a new engine, the Twin Cam 88, a more powerful one to compete with the larger engines in some competitive motorcycles. Overall, it sold 157,152 motorcycles in 1998, a 15 percent increase over the previous year, achieved net sales of over $2 billion, a 17 percent increase over 1997, and gross profits of $104.5 million, a 17.8 percent increase over the previous year.

Chairman and CEO Jeffrey L. Bleustein believed that the phenomenal success of Harley could be attributed to four major factors:

• A powerful and much admired brand centered around the experiences of motorcycling; its attributes of freedom, adventure, and individuality that appeal to people across a wide variety of demographic segments.

- Strong relationships with all of its stakeholders including dealers, customers, employees, suppliers, governments, society, and shareholders.

- A proven management team and empowered employees committed to sustaining steady, manageable growth in a worldwide motorcycle market.

- Harley-Davidson's mystique . . . the ability of the brand to bring together in unique and surprising ways seemingly disparate combinations of products, people, processes, and experiences.

A final measure of the success of Harley-Davidson can be seen in the growth of its Harley Owners Group or H.O.G., started in 1983 with 33,000 members, all in the U.S. In 1997, it had 380,000 members in 105 countries and grew to 430,000 members in 115 countries by 1998. Clearly, the company had made a number of excellent management decisions and had built a large group of satisfied, involved, loyal customers around the world.

Global Competition

Exhibit 1 presents motorcycle registrations in three major regions where Harley competes. All three areas show solid growth which demonstrates, in part, the success of motorcycle manufacturers in generating demand for their products.

Exhibit 2 presents a breakdown of market shares by competitors in three regions. While Harley-Davidson dominates the market in North America, it has the smallest market share of major competitors in Europe and is fourth in the Asia/Pacific region which is dominated by Japanese brands. Part of the reason for Harley's smaller market share in Europe and the Asia/Pacific region is that the company cannot produce enough motorcycles to meet demand and its prices tend to be higher than competitive models. Overall, Harley-Davidson and Buell together achieved 25.2 percent of the global heavyweight motorcycle market.

Product quality for Harley and its major competitors is excellent although competitive bikes are often more technologically advanced. Competition in the industry is based on such things as styling, engine displacement (power), features (e.g., cruise control, fuel injection), availability, brand equity and price. Shortages of Harleys lead many consumers to purchase competitive bikes as there are two-year waiting lists for some Harley models.

EXHIBIT 1 New Heavyweight Motorcycle (651 cc+) Registrations in Three Global Regions (in 000's)

Source: Adapted from Harley-Davidson, Inc., *1998 Annual Report,* p. 52.

Year	North America[1]	Europe[2]	Asia/Pacific[3]	Total
1998	246.2	270.5	69.2	585.6
1997	205.4	250.3	58.9	514.6
1996	178.5	224.7	37.4	440.6
1995	163.1	207.2	39.4	409.7
1994	150.4	201.9	39.1	391.4

[1]Includes United States and Canada.
[2]Includes Austria, Belgium, France, Germany, Italy, Netherlands, Spain, Switzerland and United Kingdom.
[3]Includes Japan and Australia.

EXHIBIT 2 1998 Heavyweight Motorcycle (651 cc+) Market Shares by Global Regions

Source: Adapted from Harley-Davidson, Inc., *1998 Annual Report,* p. 52.

Company	North America	Europe	Asia/Pacific
BMW	2.7%	13.4%	4.3%
Harley-Davidson/Buell	48.5	6.4	15.6
Honda	20.5	24.1	28.0
Kawasaki	10.2	10.7	22.1
Suzuki	10.3	17.2	7.9
Yamaha	4.8	16.3	16.6
Other	3.0	11.9	5.5

Note: Regions defined as in Exhibit 1.

All of the major competitors produce touring and custom (cruiser) motorcycles that compete directly with Harley and sport bikes that compete with Buell's offerings. BMW's R and K series of bikes; Honda's Gold Wing, ST1100, Shadow, Valkyrie, and Pacific Coast; Kawasaki's Vulcan series and Concours; Yamaha's Venture, Road Star, Royal Star, Virago, and Vstar; and Suzuki's Marauder and Intruder series are some of the major models competing with Harley-Davidson. In addition, most of the major competitors have full lines of smaller motorcycles with engine displacements of less than 651 ccs, a market in which Harley does not compete.

New Competition

In addition to established competitors, there are a number of new competitors entering the market. Polaris, the snowmobile manufacturer, converted an assembly line in its Spirit Lake, Iowa, facility to produce the Polaris Victory Y9ZC, a retro-look, V-twin cruiser. This bike is targeted to Polaris's existing snowmobile customers, 30 percent of whom are also motorcycle enthusiasts. Excelsior-Henderson, once one of the big three motorcycle manufacturers (along with Harley and Indian), has been resurrected in Belle Plaine, Minnesota, to produce the Super X, a direct Harley competitor. A California company purchased the Indian trademark and plans to build a limited edition Indian Chief motorcycle. All of these companies are seeking to capitalize on the demand for heavyweight bikes, particularly Harleys.

Competitive Remakes and Accessories

Big Dog Motorcycles of Sun Valley, Idaho, produces the Big Dog Aerosport Cruiser, a customized Harley selling for thousands over the stock Harley price. A variety of other companies, such as Titan, Ultra Kustom, Illusion, and California Motorcycle Co., make non-Harley Harleys with their own parts. S&S Cycle produces performance parts that compete directly with Harley parts as do other manufacturers who produce seats, exhaust pipes, saddlebags, and windshields that some customers prefer over Harley offerings.

Motorcycle Buyers

The demographic profile of motorcycle buyers has changed over the years. According to the Motorcycle Industry Council, 61 percent of buyers are over 35 years old whereas in 1980, only 27 percent had reached this age. In 1980, only 2.4 percent of motorcycle buyers had incomes of $50,000 or higher, whereas in 1998, over one third were in this income group. White-collar professionals are the largest group of new bike riders, accounting for 36 percent. Many are former riders now stepping up to their dream machines and state that motorcycle riding helps reduce stress in their lives.

Motorcycle Company Websites

Harley-Davidson's management believes that the Internet is a powerful marketing tool. Its website is affectionately called the "anti-website" since it encourages visitors to get off-line and onto their Harleys. The website includes detailed information on the company and its products and had nearly 1.5 million visitors in 1997 alone.

All of Harley's major competitors have products other than motorcycles on their websites including cars (Honda, Acura, Suzuki, BMW), outboard motors (Honda, Yamaha, Suzuki), jet skis (Kawasaki), snowmobiles (Yamaha), boats (Yamaha), generators and power equipment (Honda, Yamaha). However, Harley-Davidson's website is devoted exclusively to motorcycle-related information about Harley's products, experience, and the company itself, including financial data. This may be a competitive advantage for Harley because it illustrates that the company is focused only in the motorcycle industry.

Discussion Questions

1. Why is the Internet a particularly good promotion medium for Harley-Davidson?

2. What different roles could Harley-Davidson's website play for Harley owners, for people shopping for a motorcycle, and for people just interested in motorcycles in general?

3. Visit Harley-Davidson's website (www.harley-davidson.com) and evaluate it on the following criteria:
   a. Home page quality
   b. Site map quality
   c. Ease of browsing
   d. Image speed
   e. Attractiveness
   f. Product information
   g. Dealer information
   h. Company information
   i. Ease of exiting
   j. Overall evaluation (sum of above)

   Rate each dimension on a scale from one (poor) to five (excellent). What do you conclude about the quality of Harley's website as a marketing tool?

4. Evaluate Harley-Davidson's website from a promotion strategy point of view. What role does it play in Harley's promotion mix?

5. Compare Harley-Davidson's website with those of its major competitors on the criteria listed in Question 3 above. Focus only on the motorcycle portion of these websites:

   www.bmw.com

   www.honda.com

   www.kawasaki.com

   www.suzuki.com

   www.yamaha-motor.com

   Overall, what are the strengths and weaknesses of each website?

6. Visit the Polaris website at www.victory-usa.com. What is your evaluation of this website and the Polaris Victory Y9ZC?

7. Why do you think the heavyweight motorcycle market has grown so much in recent years?

8. How many motorcycles did each company sell globally in 1998? What accounts for Honda's success?

References

Brown, Stuart F., "The Company That Out-Harleys Harley," *Fortune,* September 28, 1998, pp. 56–57.

della Cava, Marco R., "Motorcycle Maker Caters to the Continent," *USA Today,* April 22, 1998, p. 8B.

Eldridge, Earle, "Motorcycling Passion Climbs the Corporate Ladder," *USA Today,* May 7, 1999, pp. B1–B2.

Harley-Davidson, Inc., 1997 *Annual Report.*

Harley-Davidson, Inc., 1998 *Annual Report.*

Machan, Dyan, "Is the Hog Going Soft?" *Forbes,* March 10, 1997, pp. 114–119.

Melcher, Richard A., "Tune-Up Time for Harley," *Business Week,* April 8, 1996, pp. 90–94.

Motorcycle Cruiser, Los Angeles, CA: Peterson Publishing Company, April 1999.

Stevens, Karen, and Dale Kurschner, "That Vroom! You Hear May Not Be a Harley," *Business Week,* October 1997, pp. 159–160.

12

Wind Technology

Ken Manning *University of South Carolina*

Jakki J. Mohr *University of Montana*

Kevin Cage, general manager of Wind Technology, sat in his office on a Friday afternoon watching the snow fall outside his window. It was January 1991 and he knew that during the month ahead he would have to make some difficult decisions regarding the future of his firm, Wind Technology. The market for the wind profiling radar systems that his company designed had been developing at a much slower rate than he had anticipated.

The Situation

During Wind Technology's 10-year history, the company had produced a variety of weather-related radar and instrumentation. In 1986, the company condensed its product mix to include only wind-profiling radar systems. Commonly referred to as wind profilers, these products measure wind and atmospheric turbulence for weather forecasting, detection of wind direction at NASA launch sites, and other meteorological applications (i.e., at universities and other scientific monitoring stations). Kevin had felt that this consolidation would position the company as a leader in what he anticipated to be a high-growth market with little competition.

Wind Technology's advantages over Unisys, the only other key player in the wind-profiling market, included the following: (1) The company adhered stringently to specifications and quality production; (2) Wind Technology had the technical expertise to provide full system integration. This allowed customers to order either basic components or a full system including software support; (3) Wind Technology's staff of meteorologists and atmospheric scientists provided the customer with sophisticated support, including operation and maintenance training and field assistance; (4) Finally, Wind Technology had devoted all of its resources to its wind-profiling business. Kevin believed that the market would perceive this as an advantage over a large conglomerate like Unisys.

Wind Technology customized each product for individual customers as the need arose; the total system could cost a customer from $400,000 to $5 million. Various governmental

This case was prepared by Ken Manning of the University of South Carolina and Jakki J. Mohr, University of Montana. This case is intended for use as a basis for class discussion rather than to illustrate either effective or ineffective administrative decision making. Some data are disguised. All rights reserved.

entities, such as the Department of Defense, NASA, and state universities had consistently accounted for about 90 percent of Wind Technology's sales. In lieu of a field sales force, Wind Technology relied on top management and a team of engineers to call on prospective and current customers. Approximately $105,000 of their annual salaries was charged to a direct selling expense.

The Problem

The consolidation strategy that the company had undertaken in 1986 was partly due to the company being purchased by Vaitra, a high-technology European firm. Wind Technology's ability to focus on the wind-profiling business had been made possible by Vaitra's financial support. However, since 1986 Wind Technology had shown little commercial success, and due to low sales levels, the company was experiencing severe cash-flow problems. Kevin knew that Wind Technology could not continue to meet payroll much longer. Also, he had been informed that Vaitra was not willing to pour more money into Wind Technology. Kevin estimated that he had from 9 to 12 months (until the end of 1991) in which to implement a new strategy with the potential to improve the company's cash flow. The new strategy was necessary to enable Wind Technology to survive until the wind-profiler market matured. Kevin and other industry experts anticipated that it would be two years until the wind-profiling market achieved the high growth levels that the company had initially anticipated.

One survival strategy that Kevin had in mind was to spin off and market component parts used in making wind profilers. Initial research indicated that, of all the wind-profiling system's component parts, the high-voltage power supply (HVPS) had the greatest potential for commercial success. Furthermore, Kevin's staff on the HVPS product had demonstrated knowledge of the market. Kevin felt that by marketing the HVPS, Wind Technology could reap incremental revenues, with very little addition to fixed costs. (Variable costs would include the costs of making and marketing the HVPS. The accounting department had estimated that production costs would run approximately 70 percent of the selling price, and that 10 percent of other expenses—such as top management direct-selling expenses—should be charged to the HVPS.)

High-Voltage Power Supplies

For a vast number of consumer and industrial products that require electricity, the available voltage level must be transformed to different levels and types of output. The three primary types of power supplies include linears, switchers, and converters. Each type manipulates electrical current in terms of the type of current (AC or DC) and/or the level of output (voltage). Some HVPS manufacturers focus on producing a standardized line of power supplies, while others specialize in customizing power supplies to the user's specifications.

High-voltage power supplies vary significantly in size and level of output. Small power supplies with relatively low levels of output (under 3 kV)[1] are used in communications equipment. Medium-sized power supplies that produce an output between 3 and 10 kV are used in a wide range of products including radars and lasers. Power supplies that produce output greater than 10 kV are used in a variety of applications, such as high-powered X rays and plasma-etching systems.

Background on Wind Technology's HVPS

One of Wind Technology's corporate strategies was to control the critical technology (major component parts) of its wind-profiling products. Management felt that this control was important since the company was part of a high-technology industry in which confidentiality and innovation were critical to each competitor's success. This strategy also gave Wind Technology a

[1]kV (kilovolt): 1,000 volts.

differential advantage over its major competitors, all of whom depended on a variety of manufacturers for component parts. Wind Technology had successfully developed almost all of the major component parts and the software for the wind profiler, yet the development of the power supply had been problematic.

To adhere to the policy of controlling critical technology in product design (rather than purchasing an HVPS from an outside supplier), Wind Technology management had hired Anne Ladwig and her staff of HVPS technicians to develop a power supply for the company's wind-profiling systems. Within six months of joining Wind Technology, Anne and her staff had completed development of a versatile power supply which could be adapted for use with a wide variety of equipment. Some of the company's wind-profiling systems required up to ten power supplies, each modified slightly to carry out its role in the system.

Kevin Cage had delegated the responsibility of investigating the sales potential of the company's HVPS to Anne Ladwig since she was very familiar with the technical aspects of the product and had received formal business training while pursuing an MBA. Anne had determined that Wind Technology's HVPS could be modified to produce levels of output between 3 and 10 kV. Thus, it seemed natural that if the product was brought to market, Wind Technology should focus on applications in this range of output. Wind Technology also did not have the production capabilities to compete in the high-volume, low-voltage segment of the market, nor did the company have the resources and technical expertise to compete in the high-output (10 kV +) segment.

The Potential Customer

Power supplies in the 3–10 kV range could be used to conduct research, to produce other products, or to place as a component into other products such as lasers. Thus, potential customers could include research labs, large end-users, OEMs, or distributors. Research labs each used an average of three power supplies; other types of customers ordered a widely varying quantity.

HVPS users were demanding increasing levels of reliability, quality, customization, and system integration. *System integration* refers to the degree to which other parts of a system are dependent upon the HVPS for proper functioning, and the extent to which these parts are combined into a single unit or piece of machinery.

Anne had considered entering several HVPS market segments in which Wind Technology could reasonably compete. She had estimated the domestic market potential of these segments at $237 million. To evaluate these segments, Anne had compiled growth forecasts for the year ahead and had evaluated each segment in terms of the anticipated level of customization and system integration demanded by the market. Anne felt that the level of synergy between Wind Technology and the various segments was also an important consideration in selecting a target market. Exhibit 1 summarizes this information. Anne believed that if the product was produced, Wind Technology's interests would be best served by selecting only one target market on which to concentrate initially.

Competition

To gather competitive information, Anne contacted five HVPS manufacturers. She found that the manufacturers varied significantly in terms of size and marketing strategy (see Exhibit 2). Each listed a price in the $5,500–$6,500 range on power supplies with the same features and output levels as the HVPS that had been developed for Wind Technology. After she spoke with these firms, Anne had the feeling that Wind Technology could offer the HVPS market superior levels of quality, reliability, technical expertise, and customer support. She optimistically believed that a one-half percent market share objective could be achieved the first year.

EXHIBIT 1   HVPS Market Segments in the 3–10 kV Range

Application	Forecasted Annual Growth (%)	Level of Customization/ Level of System Integration*	Synergy Rating**	Percent of $237 Million Power Supply Market***
General/univ. laboratory	5.40	Medium/medium	3	8
Lasers	11.00	Low/medium	4	10
Medical equipment	10.00	Medium/medium	3	5
Microwave	12.00	Medium/high	4	7
Power modulators	3.00	Low/low	4	25
Radar systems	11.70	Low/medium	5	12
Semiconductor	10.10	Low/low	3	23
X-ray systems	8.60	Medium/high	3	10

* The level of customization and system integration generally in demand within each of the applications is defined as low, medium, or high.

** Synergy ratings are based on a scale of 1 to 5; 1 is equivalent to a very low level of synergy and 5 is equivalent to a very high level of synergy. These subjective ratings are based on the amount of similarities between the wind-profiling industry and each application.

*** Percentages total 100 percent of the $237 million market in which Wind Technology anticipated it could compete.

Note: This list of applications is not all-inclusive.

EXHIBIT 2   Competitor Profile (3–10 kV range)

Company	Gamma	Glassman	Kaiser	Maxwell*	Spellman
Approximate annual sales	$2 million	$7.5 million	$3 million		$7 million
Market share	1.00%	3.00%	1.50%		2.90%
Price**	$5,830	$5,590	$6,210	$5,000–$6,000	$6,360
Delivery	12 weeks	10 weeks	10 weeks	8 weeks	12 weeks
Product customization	No	Medium	Low	Medium	Low
System integration experience	Low	Low	Low	Medium	Low
Customer targets	Gen. lab.	Laser	Laser	Radar	Capacitors
	Space	Medical	Medical	Power mod.	Gen. lab.
	Univ. lab.	X ray	Microwave	X ray	Microwave
			Semiconductor	Medical equip.	X ray

*Maxwell was in the final stages of product development and stated that the product would be available in the spring. Maxwell anticipated that the product would sell in the $5,000–$6,000 range.

** Price quoted for an HVPS with the same specifications as the "standard" model developed by Wind Technology.

Promotion

If Wind Technology entered the HVPS market, they would require a hard-hitting, thorough promotional campaign to reach the selected target market. Three factors made the selection of elements in the promotion mix especially important to Wind Technology: (1) Wind Technology's poor cash flow, (2) the lack of a well-developed marketing department, and (3) the need to generate incremental revenue from sales of the HVPS at a minimum cost. In fact, a rule of thumb used by Wind Technology was that all marketing expenditures should be about 9 to 10 percent of sales. Kevin and Anne were contemplating the use of the following elements:

1. Collateral Material   Sales literature, brochures, and data sheets are necessary to communicate the product benefits and features to potential customers. These materials are designed to be (1) mailed to customers as part of direct-mail campaigns or in response to customer requests, (2) given away at trade shows, and (3) left behind after sales presentations.

Because no one in Wind Technology was an experienced copywriter, Anne and Kevin considered hiring a marketing communications agency to write the copy and to design the layout of the brochures. This agency would also complete the graphics (photographs and artwork) for the collateral material. The cost for 5,000 pieces (including the 10 percent markup for the agency) was estimated to be $5.50 each.

EXHIBIT 3   **Trade Publications**

Trade Publication	Editorial	Cost per Color Insertion (1 page)	Circulation
Electrical Manufacturing	For purchasers and users of power supplies, transformers, and other electrical products.	$4,077	35,168 nonpaid
Electronic Component News	For electronics OEM's. Products addressed include work stations, power sources, chips, etc.	$6,395	110,151 nonpaid
Electronic Manufacturing News	For OEM's in the industry of providing manufacturing and contracting of components, circuits, and systems.	$5,075	25,000 nonpaid
Design News	For design OEM's covering components, systems, and materials.	$8,120	170,033 nonpaid
Weatherwise	For meteorologists covering imaging, radar, etc.	$1,040	10,186 paid

Note: This is a partial list of applicable trade publications. Standard Rate and Data Service lists other possible publications.

2. Public Relations   Kevin and Anne realized that one very cost-efficient tool of promotion is publicity. They contemplated sending out new product announcements to a variety of trade journals whose readers were part of Wind Technology's new target market. By using this tool, interested readers could call or write to Wind Technology, and the company could then send the prospective customers collateral material. The drawback of relying too heavily on this element was very obvious to Kevin and Anne—the editors of the trade journals could choose not to print Wind Technology's product announcements if their new product was not deemed newsworthy.

The cost of using this tool would include the time necessary to write the press release and the expense of mailing the release to the editors. Direct costs were estimated by Wind Technology to be $500.

3. Direct Mail   Kevin and Anne were also contemplating a direct-mail campaign. The major expenditure for this option would be buying a list of prospects to whom the collateral material would be mailed. Such lists usually cost around $5,000, depending upon the number of names and the list quality. Other costs would include postage and the materials mailed. These costs were estimated to be $7,500 for a mailing of 1,500.

4. Trade Shows   The electronics industry had several annual trade shows. If they chose to exhibit at one of these trade shows, Wind Technology would incur the cost of a booth, the space at the show, and the travel and incidental costs of the people attending the show to staff the booth. Kevin and Anne estimated these costs at approximately $50,000 for the exhibit, space, and materials, and $50,000 for a staff of five people to attend.

5. Trade Journal Advertising   Kevin and Anne also contemplated running a series of ads in trade journals. Several journals they considered are listed in Exhibit 3, along with circulation, readership, and cost information.

6. Personal Selling

(a) *Telemarketing* (Inbound/Inside Sales).[2] Kevin and Anne also considered hiring a technical salesperson to respond to HVPS product inquiries generated by product announcements, direct mail, and advertising. This person's responsibilities would include answering

[2]"Inbound" refers to calls that potential customers make to Wind Technology, rather than "outbound," in which Wind Technology calls potential customers (i.e., solicits sales).

phone calls, prospecting, sending out collateral material, and following up with potential customers. The salary and benefits for one individual would be about $50,000.

(b) Field Sales. The closing of sales for the HVPS might require some personal selling at the customer's location, especially if Wind Technology pursued the customized option. Kevin and Anne realized that potentially this would provide them with the most incremental revenue, but it also had the potential to be the most costly tool. Issues such as how many salespeople to hire, where to position them in the field (geographically), and so on, were major concerns. Salary plus expenses and benefits for an outside salesperson were estimated to be about $80,000.

Decisions

As Kevin sat in his office and perused the various facts and figures, he knew that he would have to make some quick decisions. He sensed that the decision about whether or not to proceed with the HVPS spin-off was risky, but he felt that to not do something to improve the firm's cash flow was equally risky. Kevin also knew that if he decided to proceed with the HVPS, there were a number of segments in that market in which Wind Technology could position its HVPS. He mulled over which segment appeared to be a good fit for Wind Technology's abilities (given Anne's recommendation that a choice of one segment would be best). Finally, Kevin was concerned that if they entered the HVPS market, promotion for their product would be costly, further exacerbating the cash flow situation. He knew that promotion would be necessary, but the exact mix of elements would have to be designed with financial constraints in mind.

13

Lady Foot Locker: The Lobo Launch

Andrew J. Rohm *Northeastern University*

David W. Rosenthal *Miami University*

Thomas C. Boyd *Cal State Fullerton*

As he walked briskly down Broadway to the Lady Foot Locker (LFL) offices in Manhattan, Bill Wyatt recalled the newspaper headline he had seen a month ago, in early January 1997, declaring "*Lobo Signs with the WNBA's New York Liberty.*" Rebecca Lobo had played center on the University of Connecticut women's basketball team and was a member of the U.S. Women's Olympic team that had won the gold medal at the 1996 Olympic Games. Wyatt, the General Merchandise Manager responsible for overseeing footwear and apparel buying and merchandise assortment for all 650 Lady Foot Locker stores, had watched Lobo and her teammates as they played for the gold in Atlanta.

That newspaper headline had motivated Wyatt to initiate discussions with Reebok, one of LFL's primary vendors and one of Lobo's sponsors, regarding the commercial potential in a Rebecca Lobo "signature" shoe. Wyatt believed there was great potential in a signature basketball shoe and apparel collection targeting female basketball players and consumers. Lobo was about to enter the inaugural Women's National Basketball Association (WNBA) season in 1997 as one of the league's most popular athletes, particularly among 12 to 17 year-old girls.

Wyatt quickened his step. He was running late for an important merchandise meeting he held weekly with his buying staff. This morning they were going to discuss the potential

This case is based on personal interviews and field research and was written solely as a basis for class discussion rather than to illustrate either effective or ineffective retail and marketing strategy practices. The decisions, organizations, individuals, and information are real. Thus, the information presented in the case is the same information used by the decision makers. The authors acknowledge the valuable comments of three anonymous reviewers and the editor of the *Case Research Journal,* Linda Swayne. The quality of this case was greatly improved as a result of their efforts.

Lobo product launch. In the four weeks since Wyatt had proposed the Lobo idea to Reebok management, a series of negotiations had resulted in a launch plan on which Wyatt and his buying staff had to make a decision soon.

The purpose of this week's merchandise meeting with two of his footwear buyers, Mike Tilbrook and Al Ellerbroek, was to decide whether or not to move ahead with the Lobo launch. While Lobo's popularity was an advantage, LFL faced significant risks in taking a large inventory position in a product, basketball shoes designed specifically for women, targeted to a relatively underdeveloped market segment.

The Athletic Footwear Industry

During the 1970s and 1980s the athletic footwear industry focused on a few core categories—basketball, tennis, running, and fitness. As the industry grew in the early 1990s, the level of product segmentation and number of footwear categories grew as well. However, total sales were falling, so the choice of segments in which to compete was becoming more critical. Exhibits 1 and 2 illustrate dollar and unit sales in the U.S. athletic footwear industry between 1995 and 1997.

Industry Suppliers

Nike

Nike was the U.S. market share leader in both women's and men's athletic footwear. Its 1996 share of the overall U.S. athletic footwear market was 34.7%. Nike's strengths included product design and development, its Air technology, promotions of its footwear products with well-known athletes such as Michael Jordan, stand-out advertising communications, and operations. Its Swoosh icon and the Just Do It! tagline were recognized worldwide as symbols of performance and quality. In 1996, Nike's global revenues were $7.1 billion (a 35% increase from 1995), and U.S. footwear revenues were estimated at $3.1 billion, a 22% increase from 1995.

Reebok

Reebok International consisted of three principal operating units: The Reebok Division, The Rockport Company, and the Greg Norman Collection (golf apparel). Reebok designed, marketed, and distributed sports, fitness, and casual footwear, apparel, and equipment. Al-

EXHIBIT 1 **Total U.S. Athletic Footwear Market (wholesale)**

Source: Footwear Market Index 1997 (FMI)

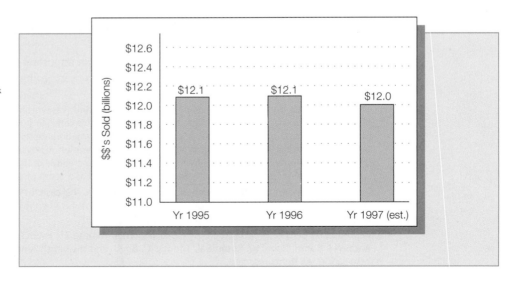

EXHIBIT 2 **Total U.S. Athletic Footwear Market**

Source: Footwear Market Index 1997 (FMI)

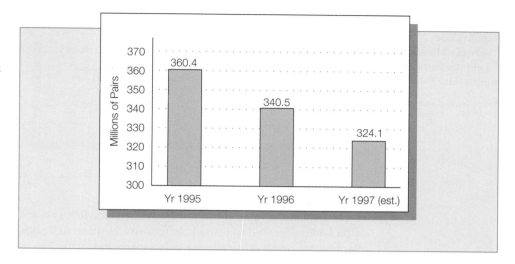

though Reebok products were sold in approximately 170 countries, the U.S. was Reebok's single largest market.

Reebok's share of the U.S. athletic footwear market in 1996 declined to 17.7% from 18.9%. Reebok's strengths included a category of casual and comfort-based shoes called "Classics" as well as shoes targeting the 25–44 year-old female in the walking, women's fitness, and aerobic categories. In the early 1990s, however, in response to Nike's growing share of the performance footwear segment in the basketball, running, and cross-training categories, Reebok began to target the male-oriented footwear categories. The company renewed product development efforts in the basketball category and signed young, up-and-coming players such as Shaquille O'Neal. In 1996, Reebok's global revenues were $3.5 billion (flat versus 1995 levels); its U.S. footwear revenues declined to $1.2 billion from $1.4 billion in 1995.

Fila

Fila's business grew during the early 1990s amongst the 12–24 year-old urban consumer. In 1996, Fila's share of the global footwear market was 5.4% and its share of the U.S. footwear market was 8.5%. Fila also began signing high-profile endorsers such as Grant Hill of the National Basketball Association (NBA) in order to promote its performance-based basketball shoes. Fila also believed that this strategy would help protect its revenue stream from the vagaries of the fashion market and a relatively fickle young consumer. In 1996, Fila's global revenues were $3.1 billion (a 59% increase from 1995), and U.S. footwear revenues were estimated at $1.3 billion (a 22% increase from 1995).

adidas

Adidas had an 11.3% share of the global footwear market and 5.4% of the overall U.S. athletic footwear market in 1996. For many years prior, however, adidas had been the leader in global athletic footwear sales. Because of this, U.S. retailers viewed adidas as a "sleeping giant" because of its relative market under-performance. In 1996, adidas' global revenues were $1.7 billion, and U.S. footwear revenues were estimated at $400 million, a 13% increase from 1995 levels.

Substitute Brands

Surf and skate footwear from the more "edgy" alternative brands like Airwalk and Vans, however, had begun to cut into the market share of the core athletic brands. Also, several

EXHIBIT 3 **Total U.S. Athletic Footwear Market (as % of total footwear units sold)**

Source: Footwear Market Index 1997 (FMI)

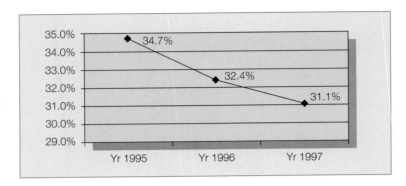

new, non-traditional competitors entered the athletic footwear and apparel market in 1996. Ralph Lauren licensed its entire Polo footwear business to Rockport, a division of Reebok International, and it was expected to introduce an athletic footwear line in 1998. Nautica had also launched its Nautica Competition athletic footwear and apparel line. Nautica distributed this line through its traditional department-store channel as well as select Foot Locker and Lady Foot Locker stores. Tommy Hilfiger's new athletic footwear line was slated for 1997 exclusive distribution within its department store accounts. Donna Karan had launched its DKNY Active line of athletic footwear and apparel within select department stores as well as Foot Locker, Lady Foot Locker, and Champs. Exhibit 3 highlights the recent unit sales trends within the U.S. athletic footwear market as a percentage of the total U.S. footwear market.

Private Label Trends

By 1997, private labels and house brands were gaining momentum within the specialty athletic retail channel. Private-label products provided greater retailer profitability and greater control of the store merchandise mix. Third-party sourcing agents produced private-label brands specifically for the retailer. By buying direct from a factory agent, the retailer was potentially able to increase selling margins from 45% to as much as 65%. Foot Locker had recently developed its In The Zone (ITZ) line of store-brand basketball footwear, signing the NBA's Bobby Hurley as ITZ spokesperson; and JC Penney was planning a line of private-label Olympic footwear displaying the trademarked Olympic rings as part of its U.S. Olympic Committee sponsorship.

Industry Competition-Marketing Mix

Product

Economies of scale and purchasing power within the channel provided advantages to companies with broad lines. Nike led the industry with breakthrough product design and technical innovations. Whereas Reebok, adidas, Fila and smaller niche brands possessed specific category strengths, none were able to match Nike's market share across multiple footwear categories. Larger brands such as Nike, Reebok, adidas, and Fila developed numerous product lines ranging from basketball and tennis to soccer and hiking/outdoor shoes. Smaller, more focused brands such as Saucony or Ryka tended to concentrate on fewer categories; for example, Ryka focused exclusively on categories with greater women's participation, such as aerobics, fitness, and walking.

Several athletic footwear brands offered proprietary technologies designed to enhance their products' performance. Technologies such as Nike Air went through frequent (annual and even bi-annual) evolutions, such as rearfoot and forefoot Air, and varying volume of Air units depending on the specific shoe and price level. Exhibit 4 highlights some of these proprietary footwear technologies.

EXHIBIT 4   **Technology Attributes by Brand**

Source: prepared by authors based on various trade publications and discussions with industry personnel

Brand	Technology	Features/Benefits	Price Range (retail)
Nike	Nike Air (introduced 1979)	Pressurized air units in heel and/or forefoot for cushioning	$60–$150
	Zoom Air (due 1997)	Lower profile, lightweight version of Nike Air	$75+
Reebok	Hexalite Viz Hex Suspended Hex Radial Hex (introduced and evolved during the 1980s/1990s)	Lightweight, honeycomb material in heel for cushioning	$50–$70 (regular Hex) $75–$90 (Viz-Hex, Suspended Hex, Radial Hex)
	DMX (due April 1997)	Ten-chambered air unit for dynamic air movement and cushioning	$110+
Asics	Gel (introduced in the mid-1980s)	Lightweight material in heel and/or forefoot for cushioning	$55+
Fila	Fila 2A (due 1997)	Lightweight cushioning unit	$75+
adidas	Feet You Wear (due 1997)	Shoe outsole designed to mimic the human foot	$100+

Air seemed to be the most widely recognized technology among both retailers and end-consumers. Reebok's DMX technology was slated for an April 1997 launch in Reebok's running category, with additional DMX product launches scheduled for later in 1997 in the cross-training and basketball categories. Reebok was confident of DMX's prospects and positioned it directly against Nike Air as a superior cushioning technology system.

Investing in the development and marketing of these technologies helped to build brand credibility and differentiation. Brand managers believed that technology delivered an important point-of-difference between the emerging fashion, or sport casual, brands and the performance brands.

As a result of growing consumer demand, consumer segmentation, and increased competition, manufacturers frequently introduced new products and shortened product life cycles. Product cycles, particularly in the more fashion-dependent basketball category, had evolved from yearly introductions to quarterly and even monthly introductions. This shift put pressure on the footwear suppliers, such as Reebok, to shorten their design and development timelines.

Pricing

Consumers paid premium prices for athletic shoes with advanced technology because they believed these products enhanced performance. Nike was the industry's product leader, in large part because of its stable of sponsored athletes, such as Michael Jordan, Scottie Pippen, and Andre Agassi, and also due to its well-known Air technology. Nike priced its Air shoes between $60 and $150 at retail, while Reebok priced its Hexalite shoes between $50 and $90. No other footwear brands were able to match Nike's ability to command premium prices for its top-end products. Pricing in the athletic footwear industry was typically based upon 30% to 55% supplier gross margins on wholesale selling price and 45% retailer markups on retail selling price.

EXHIBIT 5
**Total U.S. Athletic
Footwear Market (%
of total pairs sold by
top 10 retailers)**

Source: Footwear Market Index
1997 (FMI)

Retailer	1995	1996	1997 (est.)
Payless	11.5%	12.1%	12.4%
Wal-Mart	8.2	9.0	9.9
Foot Locker/Lady Foot Locker	**10.1**	**10.5**	**9.2**
Kmart	6.9	6.8	7.4
JC Penney	5.9	5.7	6.3
Sears	3.1	2.6	2.7
Famous Footwear	2.0	2.6	2.5
Target	2.2	2.6	2.4
Kohl's	1.2	1.4	1.9
Sports Authority	0.9	1.0	1.6

Retail Channels

Retail competition within the athletic footwear market was based upon several factors, including target consumer segment, price, merchandise assortment, store or chain reputation, store location, advertising, and customer service. For years, Foot Locker and Lady Foot Locker experienced little direct competition. Few national chains specialized in athletic footwear and even fewer specialized in women's-specific athletic footwear. Exhibit 5 shows the market shares of the ten largest athletic shoe retailers.

Although no other national retailer besides LFL concentrated solely on the women's athletic market, indirect competitors to LFL included national athletic specialty stores such as Footaction and Finish Line as well as "big box" stores such as The Sports Authority, Sneaker Stadium, and Just For Feet. Athletic footwear and apparel departments within regional and national department stores (such as JC Penney's Simply For Sports concept) also competed indirectly with LFL. The department store channel tended to focus on the female consumer. Exhibit 6 details the total U.S. women's athletic footwear market by percent of total pairs sold within the primary retail channels.

Promotion

Companies such as Reebok and Nike depended on promotions to grow market share. Promotions included celebrity endorsements and national brand and image campaigns. Industry sources estimated that adidas spent 12.5 % of its revenues on promotional activity, with much of that spending going to celebrity endorsements. The company had recently signed basketball star Kobe Bryant for $10 million, and the entire New York Yankee baseball team at a cost of $100 million.

However, Nike was the industry leader in celebrity endorsements, and its stable of athletes included Michael Jordan, Tiger Woods, and many others. Reebok spent heavily in celebrity endorsements as well, having recently signed basketball player Shaquille O'Neal for $3 million per year. Advertising expenditures for the top ten athletic shoe brands are shown in Exhibit 7. It is important to note that the costs of celebrity endorsements are not included in these figures. "Unmeasured" promotional expenditures (which would include the costs of celebrity endorsements) for Nike totaled $290 million in 1997 (est.) and $160 million in 1996. Reebok's figures were $68.1 million in 1997 (est.) and $68.2 million in 1996.

Industry Trends

As the industry matured and competition intensified, athletic footwear companies attempted to capture sales and market share through market segmentation (often by type of sport or usage category), differentiation, and branding. It was now possible to find a "sneaker" for every conceivable sport or activity, in categories such as cross-training and walking to subcategories such as Versatraining (Reebok) and Total Body Conditioning (Nike).

EXHIBIT 6
Women's U.S. Athletic Footwear Market* (% of total pairs sold by distribution channel)

Source: Footwear Market Index 1997 (FMI)

Distribution Channel	1995	1996	1997 (est.)
High-Priced			
Department Stores	10.7%	9.9%	9.2%
Apparel Specialty Shops	1.1	1.4	1.4
Sporting Goods Shops	8.0	5.9	7.7
Mail Order	2.7	2.4	2.2
Shoe Stores	7.6	7.4	6.2
Athletic Specialty Stores*	11.2	12.7	13.9
Moderate-Priced			
Sears, JC Penney, Wards	9.4	9.6	11.0
Shoe Stores	5.2	4.8	4.3
Factory Outlets	3.3	2.6	4.2
All Other	3.2	2.9	1.8
Low-Priced			
Discount Stores	24.4	26.7	25.8
Self-Service Stores	12.9	13.6	12.3
All Other	0.3	0.2	0.1
	100.0%	100.0%	100.0%

*Lady Foot Locker falls under the Athletic Specialty Store category

EXHIBIT 7
Total Advertising Expenditures of the Top 10 Athletic Footwear Brands: 1996–1997

Source: Ad Age Dataplace Reprinted by permission from the Advertising Age Data Center at www.AdAge.com. Copyright Crain Communications Inc.

Rank	Brand	Measured Advertising 1997 (in millions)	Measured Advertising 1996 (in millions)
1	Nike	$159.0	$149.0
2	Reebok	55.0	84.0
3	adidas	21.0	14.0
4	Fila	15.0	13.0
5	Converse	8.0	5.0
6	New Balance	4.0	3.0
7	Keds	3.0	3.0
8	Airwalk	2.0	9.0
9	Asics	2.0	2.0
10	Foot-Joy	2.0	2.0

The athletic footwear market had been declining for the past two years. Industry sources believed this trend resulted from a shift to alternative footwear, such as sandals and casual shoes, that they expected to continue into 1997. Total market revenue had remained flat at about $12 billion over the same time period, reflecting increasing shoe prices. Exhibit 8 shows sales by category.

The Emerging Women's Athletic Market

Both the 1972 Title IX ruling that helped to bring sex parity to intercollegiate sports and the related emergence of sports participation among pre-teen and teen-age girls had recently influenced the women's sport market. According to the Women's Sports Foundation, one in 27 girls participated in high school sports in 1971. By 1997, that figure was one in three. Also, over 13 million women aged six and over played basketball in the U.S. by 1997, compared with 11 million in 1987.

EXHIBIT 8
Total U.S. Retail Athletic Footwear Market (% of total pairs sold by footwear category)

Source: Footwear Market Index 1997 (FMI)

Footwear Category	1995	1996
Aerobic	2.3%	2.9%
Cross Training	9.9	10.0
Basketball	9.1	13.8
Tennis/Court	4.5	6.4
Running	10.4	6.3
Casual Sneakers	25.3	34.6
Walking	17.2	16.6
Infant	7.9	6.0
Other	13.3	3.3
	100.0%	100.0%

EXHIBIT 9
Women's Athletic Market Size (wholesale)

Source: Footwear Market Index 1997 (FMI)

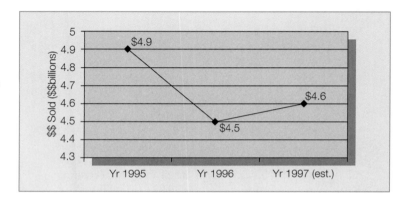

EXHIBIT 10
Women's U.S. Athletic Footwear Market

Source: Footwear Market Index 1997 (FMI)

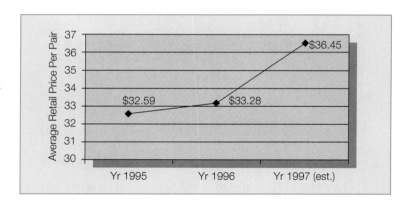

Even with the increase in women's sports participation, Wyatt observed that LFL's average sales volume was still well below that of Foot Locker and Kids Foot Locker, due to relatively greater demand for men's and children's shoes. Wyatt explained that "we're profitable and we maintain a very good sales per square foot, but nothing like Kids (Kids Foot Locker) and nothing like Foot (Foot Locker)." Exhibits 9 and 10 detail the U.S. women's athletic footwear market growth and average retail price per pair. Exhibit 11 also provides information on the primary brands competing within the women's athletic footwear market.

EXHIBIT 11

Women's U.S. Retail Athletic Footwear Market (top brand market shares by % pairs sold)

Source: Footwear Market Index 1997 (FMI)

Brand	1995	1996	1997 (est.)
Nike	17.0%	27.1%	26.8%
Reebok	17.5	16.8	17.0
Keds	8.0	5.6	5.0
Fila	1.8	3.3	4.0
Easy Spirit	1.8	2.3	2.4
adidas	2.5	1.5	2.2
New Balance	1.2	1.6	2.0
Avia	2.0	1.8	1.7
Rockport	1.4	1.1	0.9
Dr. Scholl's	0.8	1.1	0.6

LFL's Background

Woolworth Corporation

Woolworth Corporation's Athletic Group included LFL, Foot Locker, World Foot Locker, Kids Foot Locker, Champs Sports, Going To The Game!, and the Eastbay mail order catalogue (acquired by Woolworth in January 1997). The Athletic Group, Woolworth's largest and most profitable business unit, operated 3,588 stores in North America, Europe, Asia, and Australia and led the industry in sales of branded athletic footwear and apparel in the U.S., with 1996 domestic sales of $3.6 billion. In the U.S., the Athletic Group operated 3,083 stores, primarily located in shopping malls. Comparable 1996 U.S. same-store sales growth (versus 1995) within the Athletic Group was 5%.

As part of its growth strategy, the Athletic Group had continually introduced new store designs that combined trend-setting product assortments with exciting retail environments. Historically, its largest proportion of sales and net income were generated during the Back-To-School (BTS) season in August.

Lady Foot Locker

LFL's first retail store opened in 1982 in Joliet, Illinois. As of 1997, LFL operated approximately 650 stores across the United States and in Puerto Rico, primarily in shopping malls. LFL was the premier retailer of athletic footwear, apparel, and related products for women, carrying major brands of athletic footwear and apparel for a variety of sports and fitness activities, including running, fitness, and basketball. LFL prided itself on providing the best in woman-to-woman service and product selection. Its stores typically ranged from 800–1,200 square feet of selling space. Besides operating retail store sales, LFL had recently initiated a mail-order catalogue. The LFL organization chart in Exhibit 12 summarizes the retailer's management structure in early 1997.

The LFL Consumer

LFL targeted the 18–34 year-old active female. According to management, this woman was active in sports, fitness, and family life. The 12–17 year-old teen female represented an important secondary market. Management believed that sales occurred across broad age segments, and thus considered the LFL customer to be "ageless." Exhibit 13 details the U.S. athletic footwear market by percent of total pairs sold within specific age segments and Exhibit 14 highlights the percentage of pairs sold across certain women's athletic footwear categories.

EXHIBIT 12   **Lady Foot Locker Management Structure**

Source: Lady Foot Locker

EXHIBIT 13   Total U.S. Athletic Footwear Market (% of total pairs sold by consumer segment)

Source: Footwear Market Index 1997 (FMI)

Segment	1995	1996
Men (17 + years)	33.0%	35.3%
Women (17 + years)	**41.8**	**39.8**
Boys	10.2	11.2
Girls	**7.1**	**7.7**
Infants	7.9	6.0
	100.0%	100.0%

Supplier Relationships

Maintaining relationships with key suppliers was critical for athletic specialty retailers such as LFL. Close supplier relationships and partnerships benefited the retailer in many ways, including the ability to:

- Ensure that the retailer had the most current merchandise in stock;
- Provide special make-up product[1] that offered the retailer a competitive product point-of-difference;
- Increase the level of advertising or in-store marketing support from the supplier.

Until recently, the women's footwear and apparel market had been an afterthought to many LFL suppliers. Other than in categories such as walking and aerobics, women's sport-specific products constituted a small percentage of new product development. Wyatt commented:

> . . .(in the past) the desire on the retailer's part for women's product was almost nonexistent. Women were buying Ked's and canvas shoes as their leisure footwear, and other than

[1] Special make-up products were custom footwear or apparel products particularly designed for accounts that desired special colors or styles not featured in the suppliers' regular in-line collections. Typically, special make-ups were offered as semi-exclusive products to small groups of retailers or as account-exclusive products to accounts that could afford significant inventory commitments.

EXHIBIT 14
Women's U.S. Athletic Footwear Market (% of total pairs sold by footwear category)

Source: Footwear Market Index 1997 (FMI)

Footwear Category	1995	1996	1997 (est.)
Aerobic	5.0%	5.8%	5.4%
Cross Training	11.4	10.3	10.5
Basketball	2.8	9.7	9.2
Tennis / Court	4.1	5.1	4.5
Running	10.1	8.5	8.7
Casual Sneakers	25.5	33.4	34.5
Walking	26.1	24.9	25.2
Other	15.0	2.3	2.0
	100.0%	100.0%	100.0%

that they were wearing regular shoes. It wasn't until Lady Foot Locker started to develop their stores that women started becoming interested in athletic shoes. Reebok was the one that really kicked off the women's business, when they developed the Princess and Freestyle with the real soft leather uppers . . . then L.A. Gear came along and they were really a major partner with Lady Foot Locker when Lady Foot Locker was going through its growth phase, because nobody really concentrated on that kind of product. L.A. Gear had a fashion twist . . . just basic basketball shoes with a couple of feminine little treatments. Nike didn't really come on board until a few years ago . . . quite honestly, there was so much growth in the men's business that it was challenging enough for most people to concentrate on that market . . . also, many of the tests in the women's market early on were failures.

LFL management believed that its position as a national 650-store chain dedicated to the women's athletic market strengthened its relationships with its vendors such as Reebok. Marketing funds from vendors (typically around 2–3% of account sales, yet sometimes ranging as high as 10%) for advertising, in-store displays, sales associate education, and athlete and event sponsorships were critical to supporting store sales. Negotiations for marketing funds with suppliers such as Reebok and Nike were important to gaining additional merchandising and marketing resources needed to drive store sales.

Several factors determined the success or failure of a product launch. During quarterly meetings called *pre-lines,* LFL buyers, including Tilbrook and Ellerbroek, met with suppliers on issues such as shoe design, product introductions, pricing, inventory commitments, and product delivery dates. Particularly with regards to special make-up product, negotiations between LFL and its vendors centered around shoe design, materials and colors, pricing, product minimums required for account exclusivity (typically between 30,000 and 50,000 total pairs), matching apparel, marketing support such as advertising, and athlete and event tie-ins.

Recent Lady Foot Locker Product Launches

New product successes at LFL were typically measured by weekly sell-through—the inventory of a particular shoe that was sold in a given week. Successful product launches such as the Air Jordan typically resulted in 50% or more product liquidation in a single day at chains such as Foot Locker and approached 20% daily sell-through at LFL.

Recent LFL product launches included the Nike Air Jordan as well as Nike's Sheryl Swoopes (the former Texas Tech basketball star) shoe, launched in 1995 with an update introduced in 1996. Sell-through expectations at LFL for the Swoopes and similar new women's products were closer to 15% weekly "pushes" or sell-through.

The two Swoopes launches featured the industry's first marquee women's basketball product, offered at a suggested retail price of between $100 and $110. Even though Wyatt considered the initial Swoopes launch during Fall 1995 a success, LFL had bought a total of only 7,200 pairs; further, the shoe was not an LFL exclusive. According to Wyatt, it was "a very strong shoe and Lady Foot Locker sold every pair we bought."

However, the second Swoopes launch in 1996 was a different story. Sell-through of the Swoopes II ranged between 3–4% per week and the shoe was marked down after 10 weeks to liquidate the remaining inventory. Due to product quality and design issues and poor sell-through, LFL considered the 1996 Swoopes launch a failure.

Pricing Strategy

LFL typically held new footwear products at full suggested retail price for the first two weeks. Although sell-through expectations depended on the brand and type of shoe, LFL buyers typically did not begin to mark down footwear products until they fell below a 10% weekly push. Shoes were marked down in sequential 10% increments in order to liquidate remaining inventory. The number of subsequent mark-downs depended on the weekly sell-through rates, which were monitored by the buyers.

LFL's average footwear retail price per pair was approximately $60 in 1996. Its average gross margin per pair of shoes sold, before vendor discounts, was approximately 45%. LFL planned for and expected vendor discounts averaging 9%, which helped to increase its net gross margins.

Performance Measures

LFL continually evaluated its product assortment in the context of its *open-to-buy* budget (the money available for new inventory). LFL management used a metric called Gross Margin Return on Investment (GMROI) to make buying decisions and evaluate financial performance. LFL buyers considered gross margin percentage (gross margin dollars/net sales) times the sales-to-stock ratio (net sales/average inventory at cost) in their calculation of GMROI. A GMROI of 140 was typically used as a benchmark for specialty footwear retailers such as LFL, where a GMROI above 140 was considered desirable.

The WNBA and Rebecca Lobo

The WNBA

The concept of a women's professional basketball league was not a new one. The Liberty Basketball Association, which featured shorter courts, lower rims, and unitard uniforms for the players, opened in 1991 but folded after one exhibition game. The Women's World Basketball Association (WWBA) opened in 1992 with six teams, primarily in the Midwest; however, it soon folded as well.

On April 24, 1996, the National Basketball Association (NBA) Board of Governors approved the concept of a Women's National Basketball Association (WNBA). Shortly after the U.S. women's basketball team won the gold medal in Atlanta, the WNBA signed its first two players, Olympians Rebecca Lobo and Sheryl Swoopes. The WNBA was slated to begin its inaugural season in June 1997. The league selected eight cities to host the charter teams: Charlotte, Cleveland, Houston, Los Angeles, New York, Phoenix, Sacramento, and Salt Lake City. Approximately 155 LFL stores were located in these eight cities. Prior to the WNBA's planned 1997 season, the American Basketball League (ABL), another women's professional league, began its first season in October 1996 with eight teams across the U.S.

WNBA Promotional Partners
WNBA broadcast partners included NBC, ESPN, and Lifetime. Analysts projected that these network partners would reach up to 50 million people over 34 scheduled broad-

EXHIBIT 15
Rebecca Lobo
playing for the
WNBA's New York
Liberty

Source: www.wnba.com

casts during the WNBA's first season. WNBA marketing partners included Champion, Spalding, Nike, Kellogg USA, and McDonald's. Spalding planned to design and supply the official WNBA game ball, and Nike planned to produce WNBA-themed television commercials featuring its marquee players, including Sheryl Swoopes. Nike planned to conduct basketball leagues, clinics, and camps for young girls. Nike had also received the right to include Nike-sponsored WNBA players in their team uniforms in advertising and promotional programs. Kellogg planned to promote top WNBA players on cereal boxes and trading card packs available with proof-of-purchase. Total league promotional spending among the WNBA's marketing partners for 1997 was estimated to be between $25–$30 million.

Rebecca Lobo

Rebecca Lobo attended the University of Connecticut between 1992–1995 as a Political Science major. At Connecticut, she became the school's all-time leader in rebounding and blocked shots, while averaging 16.9 points per game. Playing center at Connecticut, Lobo was named the 1994 and 1995 Big East Conference Player of the Year as well as an Academic All-American. In 1995, she led Connecticut to a 35–0 record and the NCAA Championship and was named the Final Four Most Valuable Player. Lobo also received the Wade trophy in 1995 as consensus National Player of the Year. As the youngest member of the 1996 USA Women's Olympic Team, she won a gold medal at the Atlanta Games and played on the 1996 USA Basketball Women's National Team that played 52 games around the world in preparation for the Olympics. Exhibit 15 features Lobo playing with the New York Liberty.

Reebok's Lobo Endorsement

Rebecca Lobo's contract with Reebok enabled Reebok to involve her in product endorsements and advertisements, store appearances, and speaking engagements. However, because Nike (in footwear) and Champion (in apparel) were primary sponsors of the WNBA, Lobo could not appear in WNBA games with Reebok footwear unless the Reebok logo was masked on her shoes. Further, Reebok could not feature Lobo in its advertisements or in-store displays wearing her New York Liberty uniform.

The Current Situation

As their weekly merchandise meeting progressed, Wyatt, Tilbrook, and Ellerbroek outlined the key elements negotiated thus far with Reebok regarding the Lobo launch.

The Target Consumer

LFL executives believed that 12–17 year-old female consumers were increasingly critical to reach because of their present and future buying power. Traditionally, Reebok held a relatively low share of this segment compared to other brands such as Nike and adidas. How could Reebok ensure that its Lobo shoe would appeal to the young female consumer? In the past, this segment primarily bought shoes based upon fashion, styling, and brand appeal rather than performance.

Exhibits 16, 17, 18, and 19 provide information on the behavior of teen consumers, including where they shopped, what brands were cool, their sports participation, and their familiarity with and opinions of athletes.

Product Pricing

Reebok management believed that the Lobo shoe should incorporate Reebok's soon-to-be-introduced DMX technology. Reebok's DMX shoes were slated for $110 suggested retail. LFL, on the other hand, had seen Nike struggle with a $100-plus product in the Swoopes shoe. Both Tilbrook and Ellerbroek thought that a women's-specific basketball shoe from Reebok might command at most $80–85. They proposed that Reebok produce a Lobo product with a version of Hexalite technology, an existing and lower-priced Reebok footwear technology. Reebok had agreed to offer LFL the Lobo shoe with Hexalite cushioning at an $85 suggested retail price, based upon a 45% selling margin.

Product Timing and the Commercialization Process

LFL and Reebok considered two launch windows if they were to introduce a Lobo shoe: (1) introduce it in June at the start of the inaugural WNBA season, which ran from June to

EXHIBIT 16
Teen Retail Outlet Preferences

Source: 2002 Teenage Research Unlimited, Inc.

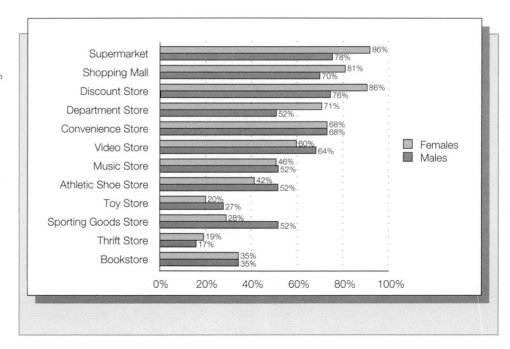

EXHIBIT 17
**Coolest Brands
According to Teens**

Source: 2002 Teenage Research
Unlimited, Inc.

The "Coolest" Brands Brands receiving a mention of 3% or more			
	Total	Male	Female
Nike	24%	28%	19%
Sony	16%	26%	6%
Abercrombie & Fitch	11%	8%	13%
adidas	11%	10%	11%
Pepsi	9%	8%	8%
American Eagle	8%	6%	9%
Old Navy	7%	6%	9%
Coke	7%	8%	5%
Chevrolet	8%	8%	4%
Tommy Hilfiger	6%	5%	6%
Ford	5%	6%	5%
Nintendo	5%	8%	2%
Gap	5%	3%	7%
Cover Girl	4%	0%	8%
Mudd	4%	-	7%
Honda	3%	4%	3%
FUBU	3%	5%	2%
L.E.I.	3%	-	6%
Mountain Dew	3%	4%	3%

EXHIBIT 18
**Sports Participation
Among Teens**

Source: 2002 Teenage Research
Unlimited, Inc.

Males		Females	
1. Basketball	66%	1. Swimming	59%
2. Football	53%	2. Exercise/Aerobics	49%
3. Swimming	47%	3. Running/Jogging	41%
4. Baseball	43%	4. Basketball	46%
5. Bicycling	39%	5. Bicycling	32%
6. Running/Jogging	36%	6. Bowling	38%
7. Billiards/Pool	37%	7. Volleyball	33%
8. Bowling	39%	8. Softball	29%
9. Weight Training	40%	9. Billiards/Pool	27%
10. Fishing	33%	10. Soccer	23%

late August 1997, or (2) in October 1997 when school basketball seasons typically began. Men's signature models, such as the Air Jordan, were typically launched during November/December for the holiday selling season.

An eighteen-month cycle, from product development to retail launch, was typical for the athletic footwear industry. In other words, it usually took 18 months to commercialize or introduce a new product at retail from the time the product first appeared as a two-dimensional drawing. The product commercialization process entailed several steps, including translating the designer's drawing to a workable blueprint and sending the blueprint to manufacturers in Asia for tooling and prototyping. After the prototype was developed, the product went through a four-step "tech" process that examined manufacturability, costing, fit-testing, and wear-testing.

Even though Wyatt preferred a June launch in order to capitalize on the hype surrounding the WNBA, he estimated that the earliest possible window in which to launch a Lobo shoe might be October '97. LFL and Reebok agreed that at this stage of the game (February

EXHIBIT 19   TRU*Score™ Athlete Ranking

TRU Score Ranking

Name	TRU* Score	Sport	Name	TRU* Score	Sport
Michael Jordan	49	Basketball	Ichiro Suzuki	30	Baseball
Vince Carter	47	Basketball	Grant Hill	30	Basketball
Kobe Bryant	45	Basketball	Bob Burnquist	30	Skateboarding
Tony Hawk	44	Skateboarding	Barry Bonds	30	Baseball
Allen Iverson	42	Basketball	Sheryl Swoopes	29	Basketball
Jason Kidd	39	Basketball	Lisa Leslie	29	Basketball
Tracy McGrady	39	Basketball	Dirk Nowitzki	29	Basketball
Jay Williams	39	Basketball	Apolo Ono	29	Speed skating
Marshall Faulk	38	Football	Ray Lewis	28	Football
Eddie George	37	Football	Steve Nash	28	Basketball
Kevin Garnett	37	Basketball	Mario Lermieux	27	Hockey
Shaquille O'Neal	37	Basketball	Dale Earnhardt, Jr.	27	NASCAR
Sammy Sosa	36	Baseball	Antoine Walker	26	Basketball
Tiger Woods	34	Golf	Brian Urlacher	25	Football
Tim Duncan	34	Basketball	Jaromir Jagr	23	Hockey
Donovan McNabb	34	Football	Alex Rodriguez	23	Baseball
Randy Moss	33	Football	Ben Wallace	20	Basketball
Venus Williams*	33	Tennis	Antawn Jamison	20	Basketball
Mat Hoffman	33	Extreme Biking	Jeff Gordon	20	NASCAR
Serena Williams*	33	Tennis	Jennifer Capriati	19	Tennis
Derek Jeter	32	Baseball	Jay Miron	16	Extreme Biking
Anna Kournikova	32	Tennis	Bode Miller	15	Skiing
Nomar Garciaparra	32	Baseball	Pau Gasol	13	Basketball
Dave Mirra	32	Extreme Biking	Anthony Thomas	12	Football
Travis Pastrana	31	Motocross	Brian Deegan	12	Motocross
Michael Vick	31	Football	David Carr	11	Football
Emmitt Smith	30	Football	Claudio Reyna	10	Soccer

Fielded in a Supplemental Sample—August '02

1997) a June 1997 target would be impossible because of product development and production timing. Since initial designs and blueprints of a women's basketball shoe had been drawn up earlier in 1996, Reebok managers believed that they could accelerate the development process in order to allow for an October 1997 delivery.

Retail Exclusivity

LFL desired retail exclusivity if it were to carry and promote a Lobo shoe and apparel collection. Even though LFL might benefit from a broad national distribution of Lobo product at additional national retailers, Wyatt believed that an exclusivity agreement would help differentiate LFL.

Reebok's management considered the opportunity costs of selling exclusively to LFL. Based upon the potential demand for the shoe at other competing retailers (estimated as high as 50,000 pairs), the companies agreed to 15,000 pairs as the inventory to which LFL would have to commit for Lobo exclusivity. Because the retailer was typically not able to return unsold inventory, inventory cost was treated as a fixed cost in the athletic footwear industry. In the past, LFL had only purchased between 5,000 and 10,000 pairs of similar women's-specific basketball products from Nike; but these products were not LFL exclusives.

Marketing Support

Wyatt and his managers had also discussed the marketing support needed behind the Lobo product if the launch were to become a reality. In LFL's view, it would provide the stores and the distribution; it was up to its partners such as Reebok to provide the launch plans and marketing funds. Manufacturers typically provided 2–10% of annual account sales for retailer-specific marketing support and merchandise funds. Promotional and launch support for past basketball products depended on the product. A national launch for a Jordan or Grant Hill product might cost several million dollars due to advertising production and media (television, print, and outdoor) costs as well as in-store merchandise displays. Television commercial production costs alone could run $500,000 and higher, while a print ad might cost as much as $50,000 to $75,000 to produce.

Every two weeks, LFL designated space in its stores for specific vendor supported merchandising (VSM) programs. Thus, Reebok could potentially support a Lobo launch with a two-week VSM within all 650 LFL stores. LFL and Reebok had agreed that if the Lobo launch were to happen, Reebok would fund the following marketing elements: a national television ad featuring the Lobo footwear and apparel as available only at LFL; Lobo/LFL "Go-cards" (postcards) distributed at retailers such as Tower Records; Lobo in-store displays; and store promotions such as an appearance by Rebecca Lobo at specially chosen LFL stores. Additionally, Reebok would conduct salesclerk training at key LFL stores. Wyatt estimated Reebok's total cost for this marketing program would be $1 million. Reebok was willing to commit this level of support as an investment in the LFL account relationship and by extension, the relationship with the entire Athletic Group.

The Decision

Wyatt played devil's advocate with his merchandise team as he thought about their decision. Wyatt began the meeting by discussing how associating a marquee athlete with an athletic shoe had proved effective in the past, particularly on the men's side of the business. "Even though the recent success of the [Nike's] Air Jordan shows the potential of a product connected to an athlete, Jordan is . . . well, Jordan is Jordan," Wyatt mused, "one-of-a-kind." Wyatt could recall only a few instances in which women's-specific shoes had been introduced that were similar to the proposed Lobo launch. "Remember the Swoopes launches . . . the first launch in 1995 was good but the 1996 launch failed miserably compared with what we've achieved on the men's side."

"You really can't compare this Lobo shoe to an Air Jordan. This isn't going to be a Jordan. You can't measure anything against a Jordan!" Ellerbroek countered.

"Yes, but the question is still whether a female athlete can drive product sales or at least create demand," Wyatt responded. "Historically, this hasn't even worked in tennis, with probably some of the most recognizable athletes such as Chris Everett and Martina [Navratilova]."

"It would be great to launch the Lobo at the start of the WNBA season this coming June to capitalize on the excitement around the league, although basketball shoes traditionally do not sell in the summer, outside of the Air Jordan," Wyatt continued. "But Reebok's development timelines won't allow us to get the product in time."

"[Well] . . . kids really don't start buying basketball shoes until September and playing hoops until October," Ellerbroek noted.

Regarding exclusivity, Tilbrook observed, "Reebok has offered us exclusivity on the Lobo shoe, and I know they could place it elsewhere if they wanted to."

"Exclusivity is a good thing but there are two sides to that coin," Wyatt countered. "We have to remember that it helps everybody, including us, if there is more exposure to the product, more exposure to the athlete, and more exposure to the Reebok brand, which would come from other retailers carrying the product as well. But, you're right, in the end we could really benefit from Lady Foot Locker exclusivity with the Lobo product."

Based upon these critical issues, Wyatt wondered if LFL should consider bringing a Lobo shoe to market in partnership with Reebok. Was there retail potential in a signature product built around an emerging professional women's player such as Lobo? Could such a product deliver a true point-of-difference for LFL? Did it make sense financially? Wyatt, Tilbrook, and Ellerbroek faced an important decision.

Was there a big enough market for another signature women's basketball shoe? Nike had both success *and* failure in this arena. Granted, Rebecca Lobo was one of the more popular players to enter the WNBA and seemed to have quite a following of young fans. Would she appeal to the young 12–17 year-old female? Should LFL try to hit an October '97 delivery or should it wait until June '98 and the start of the *next* WNBA season in order to launch the Lobo shoe?

Most important were the financial considerations LFL faced with the Lobo launch decision. Would LFL be able to liquidate the approximately 15,000 pairs it would carry, without significant markdowns? Wyatt still harbored concerns that a women's-specific product such as a Lobo signature model was a tremendous risk. Moreover, Wyatt felt that the sales in the basketball category were trending down. With these questions and more in mind, Wyatt knew they had a difficult decision on their hands—whether or not to launch a Lobo shoe with Reebok.

14

Mountain Dew: Selecting New Creative

Douglas B. Holt *Oxford University*

Standing at the front of a PepsiCo conference room, Bill Bruce gestured enthusiastically, pointing to the sketches at his side. Bruce, a copywriter and Executive Creative Director, headed up the creative team on the Mountain Dew account for PepsiCo's advertising agency, BBDO New York. In fact, it was Bruce who devised the famous "Do the Dew" campaign that had catapulted Mountain Dew to the number three position in its category. With his partner, art director Doris Cassar, Bruce had developed ten new creative concepts for Mountain Dew's 2000 advertising to present to PepsiCo management. Gathered in the room to support Bruce and Cassar were BBDO senior executives Jeff Mordos (Chief Operating Officer), Cathy Israelevitz (Senior Account Director), and Ted Sann (Chief Creative Officer). Each of the three executives had over a decade of experience working on Mountain Dew. Representing PepsiCo were Scott Moffitt (Marketing Director, Mountain Dew), Dawn Hudson (Chief Marketing Officer, and a former senior ad agency executive), and Gary Rodkin (Chief Executive Officer, Pepsi Cola North America).

Scott Moffitt scribbled notes as he listened to Bruce speak. Moffitt and the brand managers under him were charged with day-to-day oversight of Mountain Dew marketing. These responsibilities included brand strategy, consumer and sales promotions, packaging, line extensions, product changes, and sponsorships. But for Moffitt and the senior managers above him, the most important decisions of the year were made in conference rooms with BBDO creatives. Each of the ads would cost over a million dollars to produce. But the production costs were minor compared to the $55 million media budget that would be committed to air these spots. Historically, PepsiCo management had learned that selecting the right creative was one of the most critical decisions they made in terms of impact on sales and profits.

Mountain Dew had carried PepsiCo's soft drink revenues during the 1990s as cola brands struggled. But now the *Do the Dew* campaign was entering its eighth year, a long stretch by any consumer goods baseline. Many other brands were now sponsoring the same alternative sports that Mountain Dew had relied upon to boost its image. And teens were gravitating to new activities and new music that Dew's competitors had successfully exploited in their branding activities. Figuring out how to keep the campaign working hard to maintain the brand's relevance with its target consumers had become a chief preoccupation of senior management at both PepsiCo and BBDO. At the same time, key competitors were raising their ad budgets as competition in both the Carbonated Soft Drink (CSD) and noncarbonated drinks categories was heating up, sending Dew sales below targets. Choosing the right ads to maximize the impact of Mountain Dew's relatively small media budget was a make-or-break decision.

PepsiCo and BBDO

PepsiCo was widely considered to be one of the most sophisticated and aggressive marketing companies in the world. In North America, the company had three divisions, each with category-leading brands. Pepsi and Mountain Dew were the number two and three soft drinks. Frito-Lay dominated the salty-snack category with Ruffles, Lay's, Doritos, and Cheetos. And the company had recently acquired Tropicana, the leading juice brand. In 2000, PepsiCo had acquired the SoBe line of teas and "functional" drinks from South Beach Beverages, which it operated as a stand-alone subsidiary.

BBDO was one of the ten largest ad agencies in the world, with worldwide billings of about $15 billion. Of the largest full-service agencies, BBDO was particularly renowned for the quality of their creative work. The roster of the New York office, BBDO New York, included many high-powered clients such as General Electric, Visa, M&M/Mars, Charles Schwab, and FedEx. Their top 10 accounts had been BBDO clients for an average of 32 years. BBDO's relationship with PepsiCo dated to breakthrough campaigns for Pepsi in the 1960s. BBDO took over Mountain Dew from Ogilvy & Mather in 1974 and had held the account ever since. In 1998, PepsiCo hired Uniworld, the largest African-American owned ad agency in the United States, to develop a separate Mountain Dew campaign targeted to African-Americans.

The Carbonated Soft Drinks Category

Similar to most other countries, in the United States soft drink consumption was ubiquitous. And, until recently, soft drinks had meant cola. The retail carbonated soft drinks (CSD) category had long been dominated by the two cola giants, Coke and Pepsi. In the so-called cola wars of the 1960s and 70s, Pepsi directly attacked Coke with taste tests and with advertising designed to make Pepsi the hipper and more stylish "choice of the new generation," implying that Coke was a drink for older and less "with it" people. The soft drink category, and colas in particular, boomed throughout the 1970s and 1980s as people substituted away from coffee to soft drinks as a source of caffeine. The industry also consolidated as once-important brands (RC Cola, Orange Crush, A&W Root Beer) faded into the background. By the 1990s, three companies controlled all of the major national brands: The Coca-Cola Company (Coke, Diet Coke, Sprite), PepsiCo (Pepsi, Diet Pepsi, Mountain Dew), and Cadbury-Schweppes (Dr. Pepper and 7-UP).

CSDs were a promotion intensive category. In most grocery stores, Coke and Pepsi controlled a great deal of shelf space and displays. They had so much clout that their bottlers were able to choose how to stock the shelves and what to display. Impulse purchase displays had become an important source of incremental volume. A substantial and increasing share of volume came from convenience stores, where most purchases were of single servings purchased for immediate consumption. The major brands ran seasonal promotions, such as "under the cap" games in which every tenth bottle had a free bottle give-away written under the cap. More junior brand managers spent considerable time developing and implementing these promotions.

Product, promotion, packaging, and pricing innovations were constant though usually incremental, quickly diffusing throughout the category. In the last decade, one of the major innovations in the category had been the 20-ounce single serve bottle, usually priced at $.99 and sold as an impulse purchase. The margins on this bottle were higher than the twelve-packs or 2-liter bottles. Also, all of the large brands introduced 24-pack cases sold to heavy users. Brand managers worked to keep package design contemporary. For example, at PepsiCo, both Pepsi and Mountain Dew had substantial make-overs in the 1990s resulting in richer and more vibrant colors and simplified graphics. Other brands, including 7-UP and Sprite also executed similar packaging re-designs.

For most of the twentieth century, PepsiCo and The Coca-Cola Company competed fiercely, each responding in tit-for-tat fashion to the other's successes. Pepsi rolled out lemon-lime Slice in the 1980s to compete against Sprite, but soon withdrew support for that brand. Recently it was rumored that the company was plotting yet another new lemon-lime introduction. In the 1970s, Coca-Cola introduced Mr. Pibb to attack Dr. Pepper and Mello-Yello as a me-too competitor against Mountain Dew. With Mountain Dew's national success in the 1990s, Coca-Cola launched a second frontal assault, introducing another copy-cat brand called Surge. In addition, both companies had launched other new products without much success: Coke had flopped with OK Cola (the cynical retro cola), and Fruitopia (the neo-hippie fruit beverage). PepsiCo had similar problems with the introduction of Crystal Pepsi (the clear crisp cola), though was able to establish Pepsi One as a niche brand.

In the 1990s, cola growth slowed and the "flavor" CSDs did very well. Sprite, Mountain Dew, and Dr. Pepper all enjoyed great success, although 7-UP continued to struggle (See Exhibit 1). In 1999, however, all CSD sales suffered as a result of customers' sticker shock to a category-wide 5% retail price increase, and also a trend toward experimentation with noncarbonated drinks and bottled water as substitutes for soft drinks. Sports drinks were led by Gatorade, tea and juice blends by Snapple, Arizona, and SoBe, and the highly caffeinated "energy" drinks by Red Bull. These drinks, sometimes termed "functional" or "alternative," often included a stimulant (caffeine or similar substance) and plant extracts reputed to have medicinal value (ginko, guarana, St. Johns Wort, ginseng). Many of these drinks were launched by small companies with grass-roots marketing efforts focused on music and sports sponsorships, on-site promotions, and non-traditional distribution (e.g., sandwich shops for Snapple, record stores for Red Bull). Industry rumors were circulating that Coca-Cola, Anheuser-Busch, PepsiCo, and Cadbury-Schweppes were working aggressively to develop functional drinks to tap into this growing segment.

Advertising and Branding

Over many decades, Coca-Cola had become "America's drink" (and later the preferred drink in many countries around the world) through advertising that conveyed that Coke served as a social elixir. Coke promoted the idea that the drink brought people together in friendship around ideas that people in the nation cared about. From 1995 onward, Coke had struggled as it experimented with a variety of new branding ideas. Pepsi rose to the rank of Coke's loyal opposition in the 1960s with the successful "The Pepsi Generation" ad campaign, in which the brand harnessed the ideas and passions of the 1960s counterculture.

EXHIBIT 1 CSD Sales/Share (Million cases/Percent market)

Source: Maxwell Report

	1990		1991		1992		1993		1994		1995		1996		1997		1998		1999 (Est.)	
	Sales	Share	Sales	Share	Sales	Share	Sales	Share	Sales	Share	Sales	Share	Sales	Share	Sales	Share	Sales	Share	Sales	Share
Coke	1,565.5	20.1	1,597.9	20.1	1,613.9	20.1	1,680.4	20.2	1,776.7	20.4	1,868.6	20.8	1,929.2	20.8	1,978.2	20.6	2,037.5	20.6	2,018.0	20.3
Pepsi	1,370.0	17.6	1,338.0	16.9	1,327.3	16.5	1,305.9	15.7	1,310.0	15.0	1,344.3	15.0	1,384.6	14.9	1,391.5	14.5	1,399.8	14.2	1,371.8	13.8
Diet Coke	726.9	9.3	741.2	9.3	732.6	9.1	740.6	8.9	767.6	8.8	793.0	8.8	811.4	8.7	819.0	8.5	851.8	8.6	843.0	8.5
Diet Pepsi	490.0	6.3	500.0	6.3	509.5	6.4	491.5	5.9	511.2	5.9	521.4	5.8	541.5	5.8	523.5	5.5	529.7	5.4	503.0	5.1
Sprite	295.0	3.8	313.1	3.9	328.1	4.1	357.6	4.3	396.3	4.5	460.3	5.1	529.8	5.7	598.0	6.2	651.8	6.6	671.5	6.8
Dr. Pepper	364.8	4.7	385.3	4.9	414.0	5.2	445.6	5.4	485.1	5.6	515.0	5.7	536.8	5.8	566.8	5.9	599.4	6.1	630.0	6.3
Mountain Dew	300.0	3.9	327.5	4.1	351.1	4.4	387.6	4.7	455.0	5.2	509.6	5.7	535.6	5.8	605.2	6.3	665.1	6.7	705.0	7.1
7-UP	211.5	2.7	207.7	2.6	211.3	2.6	209.9	2.5	221.5	2.5	219.9	2.5	217.7	2.3	216.7	2.3	210.9	2.1	204.9	2.1
Surge															69.0		51.8		26.7	
Mello Yello	42.9		49.5		59.5		64.0		64.6		61.6		59.0		46.6		42.4		41.6	

EXHIBIT 2   Advertising Spending: Television Media
(Major CSDs, $MM)

Source: Competitive Media Reports.

	1990	1991	1992	1993	1994	1995	1996	1997	1998	1999	2000 (Est.)
Coke	$157.4	$139.9	$168.1	$131.1	$161.5	$124.7	$199.8	$156.8	$140.4	$167.7	$208.3
Pepsi	129.8	141.3	137.8	144.0	120.6	133.1	98.1	133.1	140.5	165.9	159.6
Mountain Dew	12.9	20.0	25.9	29.1	30.3	38.3	40.4	43.1	50.3	45.0	55.9
Sprite	32.0	36.1	27.5	26.9	36.0	54.6	57.9	60.6	56.2	69.9	87.7
Dr. Pepper	32.2	49.3	50.1	52.8	61.5	65.4	67.9	81.0	86.8	102.4	106.8
7-UP	38.8	37.4	23.7	29.4	27.3	23.2	33.1	38.7	27.0	38.7	45.1
Surge	0.0	0.0	0.0	0.0	0.0	0.0	0.0	15.5	21.0	19.6	0.2

More recently, Pepsi used celebrities—particularly musicians such as Michael Jackson, Madonna, Faith Hill, Ricky Martin, and Mary J. Blige—to convey the idea that Pepsi was an expression of youth attitudes. Nonetheless, the Pepsi brand also had struggled to maintain sales in the 1990s.

7-UP was successful in the 1970s branding against the colas as the "uncola" in ads that used a charismatic Jamaican actor to describe the purity and naturalness of 7-UP in a tropical setting. Similarly, the sweet cherry-cola concoction Dr Pepper challenged the audience to "be a Pepper" with well-received dance numbers that encouraged consumers to do their own thing rather than follow the masses in drinking cola. From the late 1980s onward, 7-UP faded as the brand was used as a cash cow with ever-shrinking media investments. Meanwhile, Mountain Dew rose from its regional status to become a major "flavor" brand. The three major flavor brands dominated different geographic areas: Dr Pepper dominated Texas and the rest of the deep South, Mountain Dew dominated rural areas, particularly in the Midwest and Southeast, and Sprite dominated urban-ethnic areas.

Category advertising spending exceeded $650 Million (See Exhibit 2). PepsiCo spent substantially less as a percentage of sales than its competitors. Instead, the company relied on exceptional creativity to make the advertising work harder for less cost. PepsiCo viewed the creative development process as a key organizational competency, a strategic weapon that was central to their financial success.

Mountain Dew Brand History

Mountain Dew was invented by the Hartman Beverage Company in Knoxville, Tennessee in the late 1940s. The bright yellow-green drink in the green bottle packed a powerful citrus flavor, more sugar and more caffeine than other soft drinks, and less carbonation so that it could be drunk quickly. The drink became a favorite on the Eastern seaboard, through Kentucky, Tennessee, and eventually spread up through the Great Lakes states (skirting the big cities) and into the Northern Plains of Minnesota and the Dakotas. PepsiCo, amazed by Dew's success in what brand managers would come to call the "NASCAR belt" (the stock car racing circuit that drew rural men as its primary audience), and in need of a "flavor" soft-drink to round out its line-up, purchased Mountain Dew in 1964.

PepsiCo originally assigned Mountain Dew to the Ogilvy & Mather ad agency. The strategy for the new brand extrapolated from Dew's origins and existing packaging. The beverage's heart-pumping caffeine and sugar rush were linked to its backwoods heritage to produce the idea of a comic "hillbilly" character named Willie who drank Mountain Dew to "get high" on the soft drink equivalent of moonshine liquor. The tagline, "Yahoo! Mountain Dew!" was accompanied by "Thar's a bang in ever' bottle."

In 1973 PepsiCo assigned the brand to BBDO, its agency of record for Pepsi. For two decades client and agency worked to expand the brand's reach from America's hinterlands into the suburbs and cities of the major metropolitan areas. The major campaign of the 1970s—"Hello Sunshine"—sought to tie Mountain Dew's distinctive product characteristics to a set of backcountry recreational images. The yellow-green product and strong citrus flavor are represented over and over by the gleaming sun sparkling in beautiful natural settings. The product name is represented in virtually every ad by mountains, dew drops reflecting in the sun, and condensed drops on cans to represent dew. The energizing effects of the caffeine and sugar are toned down and now are a refreshing part of an active outdoor lifestyle. Often the ads featured casual coed athletic activities that always ended in a plunge into a rural pond or creek.

This campaign pulled the Mountain Dew brand into more contemporary terrain, but it was still too rural to get much traction in the suburbs. So in the 1980s, PepsiCo directly targeted suburban teenagers with a new campaign called "Country Cool." The creative idea was to marry the popular athletic endeavors of suburban kids (cool) with Mountain Dew's active rural lifestyle (country), all punctuated by the refreshing Dew plunge. Ads featured male teens performing on skateboards, mountain bikes, and BMX bikes. A new tune was crafted for the occasion: "Being cool you'll find is a state of mind. Your refreshing attitude. Things get hot. Cool is all you got. Dewin' it country cool. So chill on out; when the heat comes on. With a cool, smooth Mountain Dew. Dewin' it Country Cool. Mountain Dew. Dewin' it Country Cool."

BBDO jettisoned the "country" component of the campaign in 1991 to build an entire campaign around athletic stunts. This advertising departed dramatically from anything that BBDO had produced in the previous sixteen years. The spots featured daredevil maneuvers of sports like windsurfing, rollerblading, motocross cycling, and paragliding. The closely framed shots, which put the viewer in the middle of the action, also suggested excitement and energy. The spots were set to aggressive rock music rather than studio jingles. In 1992, a new song called "Get Vertical" is introduced with the lyrics "Ain't no doubt about the power of dew, got the airborne thrust of rocket fuel."

Cultural Trends

PepsiCo and BBDO managers paid close attention to cultural trends. They were particularly focused on track music and sports trends since these activities were so central to youth culture.

Music

Three musical trends dominated the airwaves in the 1990s. Rap music exploded to become the most popular genre in the country. At first, gangsta rap, which flaunted misogynistic and violent lyrics, was said to represent the reality of life in the "hood" (the American ghetto). From 1992 onward, gangsta rap broke out with a lighter sound and slightly less aggressive lyrics, sometimes called gangsta-lite, that made the music much more accessible while maintaining the forbidding connotations. By 1993, media coverage of the travails of celebrity rappers like Snoop Doggy Dog and Tupac Shakur ruled not only the music magazines but *People* and *Newsweek*. Rap music, and the hip-hop lifestyle of which it was a part, permeated teen life. MTV's program *Yo! MTV Raps* and specialty magazines like *The Source* and *Vibe* became mainstream cultural venues. By 1999, rap remained very popular amongst male teens, especially in urban areas, though its Top 40 appeal had subsided somewhat.

At roughly the same time, the alternative rock music scene, which throughout the 1980s existed as a small subcultural scene found mostly on college campuses, also exploded. Two Seattle bands—Nirvana and Pearl Jam—put CDs at the top of the charts with aggressive and emotive music that combined equal parts punk and heavy metal. The media tagged this music "grunge" and anointed Seattle as grunge headquarters. Grunge was marketed heavily by the culture industries—music labels put out dozens of grunge bands, films that displayed the grunge attitude appeared, and fashion runways and J.C. Penney's stores were clogged with flannel shirts and clothes that had the look of the vintage Salvation Army gear that was the uniform of the grunge scene. Grunge faded in its influence in part due to the death of its most talented lead actor when Nirvana's Kurt Cobain committed suicide in 1995.

Later in 1990s, techno music began making significant inroads into American youth culture. Invented in the 1980s as "house music" in low-budget studios of Chicago and Detroit, this beat-driven dance music became the lifeblood of dance parties called "raves" in places like London and the Spanish island of Ibiza. Raves quickly spread throughout continental Europe and beyond. Raves were all-night dancing marathons often set up in warehouses, exotic outdoor locales, and other improvised spaces. Raves attracted young people, mostly teens, who danced for hours at a time, not in pairs, but in free-form groups. The highly rhythmic music and long-winded dancing combined to produce for some fans an ecstatic trance-like state. The music was produced almost entirely by disk jockeys sampling records with tape loops and other electronic tricks. Many sub-genres have since emerged that mix-and-match musical styles from around the world. Part of the scene was a drug called ecstasy, a drug that induces promiscuous affection, sensory overload, and euphoria. And, to keep the energy flowing all night, the dancers demanded energizing drinks. In particular, an enterprising Austrian company marketed Red Bull, a drink that was once an Asian hangover cure, as a rave stimulant. Either straight or mixed with vodka, Red Bull became the rave drink of choice. Raves diffused rather late to the United States, but proved to be most popular in the major metropolitan areas.

Sports

The so-called "alternative sports" took off in the early 1990s. Teen enthusiasts transformed casual hobby activities—mountain biking, skateboarding, paragliding, BMX biking, and in-line skating—into highly technical, creative, and often dangerous sports. Snowboarding became an overnight hit with teens. Bungee jumping was a fad that disappeared quickly. As these sports became increasingly risky and creative, they began to attract spectators. So-called extreme sports—skiing down extremely steep terrain or jumping off tall buildings with a parachute—were covered by ESPN. ESPN also aggressively promoted circuits and tournaments to professionalize these new sports, which culminated in the Extreme Games in 1994, a non-traditional Olympics of sorts. Mountain Dew was one of the founding lead sponsors of the Extreme Games, which later became the X Games. Later, NBC followed with the Gravity Games, and MTV also began to cover these sports. Grunge music, more aggressive styles of rap, and various hybrids were prominent aural expressions of these sports.

GenX Ethos

During the 1990s, teens and young adults evinced a growing cynicism toward the dominant work-oriented values of the previous generation and toward corporations more generally. They found that working hard to get ahead in terms of salary and occupational prestige was harder to swallow in an era of corporate reengineering. Their cynicism also extended to corporations themselves and their marketing efforts. As this cohort became increasingly knowledgeable about how marketing worked and increasingly jaded about why brands were popular, they were not interested in listening to "sales messages" that tried to persuade them into believing a particular brand of soft drink or beer was cool. Instead, these youth adopted a campy interest in non-trendy products, television programs, and music of previous eras.

As these odd new tastes became commercialized in programming like Nickelodeon cable channel's "Nick at Nite" series—which featured less-than-notable programming from the 1950s–1970s—"retro" was born.

The Do the Dew Campaign

In 1992, senior management at PepsiCo sensed an opportunity to increase business on Diet Mountain Dew. Diet Mountain Dew's distribution was limited mostly to the rural regions where the brand was strongest, even though regular Dew was now a national brand. Diet Mountain Dew performed very well on product tests versus other diet drinks in the category because the heavy citrus flavor did a better job of masking the undesirable taste of the artificial sweetener. So PepsiCo allocated money for incremental advertising to support an effort to expand Diet Mountain Dew distribution. Bill Bruce, then a junior copywriter working on several brands, was assigned to the project. The strategy statements that guided the initial creative idea and subsequent spots in the campaign are reported in Exhibit 3. Bruce came up with the "Do Diet Dew" tag line (which soon evolved into "Do the Dew" to support the entire brand) and several new ideas to embellish what BBDO had begun with the Get Vertical campaign.

The first breakthrough ad of the new campaign, *Done That,* features a hair-raising shot of a guy jumping off the edge of a cliff to take a free-fall toward the narrow canyon's river bottom, set to throbbing grunge music. This was the first ad to feature the "Dew Dudes"— four young guys who are witnessing the daredevil stunts presented in the ad and commenting on them. *Done That* became a huge hit, capturing the country's imagination. The ad was widely parodied and the phrase "been there, done that" entered the vernacular. For 1994 and 1995, BBDO produced three carbon-copy "pool-outs"[1] of *Done That.* By 1995, after two years of these ads, consumer interest in the creative was fading fast. According to Jeff Mordos, if the creative hadn't moved to another idea that year, consumer's flagging interest and the potential of a revolt by PepsiCo bottlers likely would have forced PepsiCo to develop an entirely new campaign.

For 1995, three of four spots produced relied upon different creative ideas. One of these spots, *Mel Torme,* became the second hit of the campaign. The spot was a parody featuring the aging Vegas lounge singer Mel Torme, tuxedo-clad atop a Vegas hotel crooning "I Get a Kick out of You," with lyrics altered to incorporate Mountain Dew references. He impresses the Dew Dudes with a base jump of his own. Similar ads followed. In *007,* a teenage James Bond engages in a frenetic pursuit scene with typical Bond stunts, accompanied by the familiar Bond theme music. The Dew Dudes are not impressed until Bond comes upon a Mountain Dew vending machine. In *Training,* brash tennis star Andre Agassi performs extreme stunts as training exercises, and then plays an extreme game of tennis with the Dew Dudes as his coaches.

In 1997, BBDO came up with two breakthrough spots. The director of Nirvana's classic music video "Smells Like Teen Spirit" was hired to direct *Thank Heaven,* which mimics a music video. The spot stars the lead singer of an alternative rock band called Ruby. She sings a punked-up version of the classic song "Thank Heaven for Little Girls," in which the grunge style suggests the "little girls" of old have been replaced by the feminine brand of

---

[1]The noun pool-out is derived from a verb that is particular to the advertising business—"to pool out." The idea is to develop a pool of ads that are all closely related derivations from the same creative idea. Some advertisers feel that pools deliver a more consistent campaign while others feel that the ads become too formulaic when they are so similar. Regardless, there is a great temptation when an ad breaks through and becomes a hit to develop pool-outs to extend the popularity.

EXHIBIT 3   Mountain Dew Brand Communications Strategies (1993–1999)

Source: PepsiCo

	Objective	Strategy	Target	Executional Direction
1993–94	Increase awareness and trial of Mountain Dew	You can have the most thrilling, exciting, daring experience but it will never compete with the experience of a Mt. Dew	Male teens/young adults	• Distinct campaign with Dew equity consistency • Leverage "full tilt taste" and "rush" as point of difference
1995	Distinguish Mt. Dew within the competitive environment through contemporary communication of the trademark's distinct, historical positioning	You can have the most thrilling, exciting, daring experience but it will never compete with the experience of a Mt. Dew	Bull's eye: 18 yr. old leading edge male Broad 12–29 year olds	• Shift to a unified trademark focus modeled after "Do Diet Dew" • Explore outdoor settings • Predominant male, mid-20's casting • Preserve balance between "outlandish" and "realistic" actions/sports
1996	Optimize Dew's positioning equity among the target in a highly relevant and contemporary manner	(You can have the most thrilling, exciting, daring experience but . . .) there's nothing more intense than slamming a Mt. Dew	Bull's eye: 18 yr. old leading edge male Broad: 12–29 year olds	• Bring "Do the Dew" trademark campaign to the next level
1997	Optimize Dew's positioning equity among the target in a highly relevant and contemporary manner • Strengthen brand perceptions among AA • Encourage product trial where familiarity is low	(You can have the most thrilling, exciting, daring experience but . . .) there's nothing more intense than slamming a Mt. Dew	Bull's eye: 18 yr. old leading edge male Broad: 12–29 year olds	• Continue "Do the Dew" trademark campaign and encompass the Mt. Dew experience
1998	Build badge value and authentic, true Icon status for Mt. Dew in the world of youth-targeted consumer goods	Associate Mt. Dew with thrilling and exhilarating adventures in a light-hearted manner	Bull's eye: 18 yr. old leading edge male Broad: 12–29 male/female	• Evolve the "Do the Dew" campaign against core target with fresh and relevant copy • Develop ethnically-targeted "cross-appeal" spot • Enhance product perception
1999	Optimize relevance of Dew's positioning among the target	Associate Mt. Dew with the exhilarating intensity of life's most exciting, fun adventures	Male Teens (16 yr. old epicenter) • Invite teen girls while continuing as male CSD • Maintain cross-over appeal among 20–39 year olds	• Develop pool of "Do the Dew" executions • Explore other metaphors beyond alternative sports to express "exhilarating intensity" • One execution should have AA/ urban relevance • Communicate quenching • Inclusion of water-greenery elements not mandatory

aggressiveness presented in the ad. *Jackie Chan* deploys the Hong Kong movie star's patented martial arts with humorous stunts into the campaign's jaded, "seen it already" motif. The ad begins in the midst of what seems like a classic chase scene from a Chan film with lots of harrowing action. When Chan faces down his enemy, the Dew Dudes magically appear as Confucian wisemen who assist Chan with cans of Mountain Dew.

Other ads produced were significantly less effective. *Scream,* a high-speed amalgam of extreme sports shots that are organized to answer the lead-in question—"What is a Mountain Dew?"—did not fare well. And *Michael Johnson,* a spot developed to broaden Dew's appeal in the African-American community, did not meet the company's expectations.

By 1998, PepsiCo managers worried that the advertising was becoming too predictable. In particular, they were concerned that the use of alternative sports was becoming less impactful due to oversaturation. Many other brands, including companies like Bagel Bites, AT&T, Gillette Extreme Deodorant, and Slim Jims beef jerky snacks, were now major sponsors of alternative sports. To keep the campaign fresh, they needed to find alternative ways to express Mountain Dew's distinctive features. *Parking Attendant,* produced in 1999, was a solid effort at advancing toward an alternative expression. The spot features a parking attendant who takes liberties when parking a BMW handed off by a stuffy businessman. The kid drives as if in a police chase, flying from one building to another, accompanied by a frenetic surf instrumental that had been featured in Quentin Tarantino's *Pulp Fiction* a few years prior.

Mountain Dew Market Research

Mountain Dew's distinctive demographic profile reflected the brand's historic popularity in the NASCAR belt (see the Brand Development Index Map in Exhibit 4 and lifestyle analysis in Exhibit 5a). And Mountain Dew had much lower penetration of the total population than its major competitors. But its consumers were the most loyal in the category. Mountain Dew had the highest "gatekeeping" rating of all CSDs—it was the drink that mothers tried the hardest to keep out of the stomachs of their children. Periodically, the PepsiCo research department fielded a major study to assess the "health" of the brand, and to direct any fine-tuning. A 1997 "brand fitness" study profiled the status of the Dew brand versus its major competitors (Exhibits 6a–d).

PepsiCo monitored both the effectiveness of individual ads, as well as the cumulative impact of advertising on the overall health of the Mountain Dew brand. The contribution made by a single ad toward building brand equity was notoriously challenging to measure. Both quantitative and qualitative research provided data from which managers make useful inferences. But Pepsi managers had yet to find a research method that was accurate enough to rely upon to provide definitive judgments on ad effectiveness. PepsiCo routinely gathered a wide variety of data that hinted at an ad's impact. In addition to formal research, managers monitored "talk value" or "buzz"—the extent to which the ad has been picked up by the mass media. In particular, *The Tonight Show* and David Letterman were useful barometers. Feedback from the Mountain Dew website, unofficial websites, and the brand's 800 number were important gauges as well. In addition, PepsiCo carefully monitored how the salesforce and bottlers responded to the ads, since they were getting direct feedback from their customers. PepsiCo managers used all these data as filters. But, ultimately, the evaluation of advertising rested on managerial judgement. Based on their past experience with the brand and with advertising across many brands, managers made a reasoned evaluation.

However, PepsiCo managers did rely on market research to assess the cumulative impact of advertising on the brand. Because many other factors—especially pricing and retail display activity—had an immediate short-term impact on sales, it was often difficult to draw causal relationships between advertising and sales. But advertising campaigns do directly

EXHIBIT 4   Mountain Dew Brand Development Index Map

MOUNTAIN DEW BDI MAP

MOUNTAIN DEW FRANCHISES

Key

	Very High BDIs	136+
	High BDIs	91–135
	Mid BDIs	46–90
	Low BDIs	0–45

Indicates strong ethnic population

EXHIBIT 5A   **Spectra Lifestyle Analysis**

Source: AC Nielsen Product Library 11/97 to 11/99.

Mountain Dew Consumption Index

Lifestage

Spectra Lifestyle	18–34 W/Kids	18–34 W/O Kids	35–54 W/Kids	35–54 W/O Kids	55–64	65+	Total Lifestyle
Upscale Suburbs	82	77	101	56	45	13	64
Traditional Families	118	121	160	79	42	35	96
Mid Upscale Suburbs	101–	111	108	71	64	18	66
Metro Elite	139	85	141	47	47	21	72
Working Class Towns	237	139	242	121	67	42	139
Rural Towns & Farms	225	153	212	141	91	39	140
Mid Urban Melting Pot	148	104	97	52	49	31	74
Downscale Rural	309	142	291	127	87	43	158
Downscale Urban	99	98	107	73	55	32	76
Total Lifestage	171	112	165	83	61	31	100

impact how the brand is perceived. And these perceptions, in turn, drive sales. So PepsiCo had assembled a set of what they termed key performance indicators (KPIs), intermediate measures that were directly impacted by advertising and that had been proven to significantly impact sales. Managers tracked KPIs, also referred to as *brand health* measures, both for teens and for 20–39 year olds. But managers were particularly concerned with brand health amongst teens because at this age soft drink consumers often moved from experimenting with a variety of drinks to becoming loyal lifetime drinkers of a single soda. The latest study, conducted in the spring of 1999, reported Mountain Dew's teen KPIs. Dew improved 6 points on "Dew Tastes Better" (to 48% versus a year ago). Unaided brand awareness had dropped 5 points (to 39%). "For someone like me" had increased 5 points (to 53%). And "Dew Drinkers are Cool" increased 5 points (to 64%).

2000 Planning

In 1999, Mountain Dew became the third largest carbonated soft drink at retail, overtaking Diet Coke. However, part of this success in gaining share had to do with the sustained weakness of Pepsi and Coke. In 1999, the problems that the colas were facing seemed to be spreading to Mountain Dew, Sprite, and Dr. Pepper. All of the leading CSDs began to show real weakness as alternative non-carbonated drinks began to attract a great deal of trial, especially amongst teens. While Mountain Dew sales began to lag, all of the "brand health" indicators remained strong. And the advertising continued to significantly outperform competition. In planning for 2000, Moffitt and his senior management were particularly concerned with two dilemmas:

• How to keep the "Do the Dew" campaign working hard to build the brand given that extreme sports were becoming overexposed

• How to respond to the growing threat of non-CSDs, especially Gatorade and the new highly-caffeinated and sugary energy drinks like Red Bull

A detailed strategy statement was developed by Moffitt's team at Pepsi-Cola North America, in conjunction with the account team at BBDO New York led by Cathy Israelevitz. This strategy was boiled down to a single sentence to focus the development of new creative: *Symbolize that drinking Mountain Dew is an exhilarating experience.* This document was used to brief Bruce and his creative team (Exhibit 7).

EXHIBIT 5B   Lifestyle Glossary

Source: AC Nielsen Product Library 11/97 to 11/99.

Upscale Suburbs

"The American Dream," a nice house in a nice suburban neighborhood. College-educated executives and professionals who index high on travel, eating out, playing golf, going to health clubs, buying imported cars, watching/reading business and news. Low African-American and Hispanic. High income.

Traditional Families

Like Upscale Suburbs, but lower socio-economic level. Mix of lower level administrators and professionals with well-paid blue-collar. Index high on: gardening, DIY home improvement, driving SUVs, camping, classic rock, sports radio. Low African-American and Hispanic. Mid-high income.

Mid/Upscale Suburbs

Live in first-generation suburbs that are now part of the urban fringe. Lower income than Traditional Families, but more college-educated and white collar. Index high on: baseball fans, casino gambling, using internet, attending live theatre, reading science and technology, listening/watching news. Low African-American and Hispanic. Mid-high income.

Metro Elite

Younger and more urban, college-educated, ethnically diverse. Very attuned to new fashions. Geographically mobile. Index high on: health clubs, bars and night clubs, fashion magazines, VH-1, music, film, computers. Middle income.

Working Class Towns

Well paid blue collar families living in suburbs of smaller cities. Index high on: auto racing, fishing, hunting, country music, camping, televised sports. Own trucks or minivans. Low African-American and Hispanic. Middle income.

Rural Towns & Farms

Small towns mostly in the middle of the country, dominated by blue-collar and agricultural work. Index high on: rodeos, fishing, woodworking, chewing tobacco, wrestling, camping, country music, TV movies, USA and TNN channels. Don't read magazines and newspapers. Low African-American. Lower income.

Mid Urban Melting Pot

Urban multi-ethnic neighborhoods. Old European ethnic enclaves and new Asian immigrants, mixed with African-American and Hispanic neighborhoods. Index high on: menthol cigarettes, dance music, boxing, pro basketball, lottery, Home Shopping Network, heavy TV viewing, urban contemporary radio. Lower income, low college, service industries.

Downscale Rural

Poor rural areas in Appalachia, throughout the South, and the Plains States. This socially conservative and religious area is sometimes called "the bible belt:" While indexing high African-American, these are very segregated neighborhoods with little racial mixing. Lowest on education, occupation, income, housing. Index high on: trucks, chewing tobacco, belonging to veteran's club, target shooting, tractor pulls, country music, fishing and hunting., daytime drama TV programs.

Downscale Urban

Same socioeconomic profile as Downscale Rural but very different cultural profile, more similar to Mid-Urban Melting Pot. Mostly African-American and Hispanic urban neighborhoods.

Super Bowl

In addition to these strategic issues, Moffitt had to consider carefully where these ads would be broadcast. Mountain Dew's national media plan focused on a younger audience. Typical buys would include MTV, *The Simpsons*, and ESPN during alternative sports broadcasts. However, with its long run of sales increases in the 1990s, Mountain Dew was becoming less of a niche brand. Partly in recognition of this expanding customer base and partly to celebrate within the company Dew's arrival as the third most popular CSD, top management decided to feature Mountain Dew rather than Pepsi during the Super Bowl.

The Super Bowl had for decades been a hugely influential event for advertisers. The game drew the biggest audience of the year and the ads received an amazing amount of attention. In recent years, the frenzy around the advertising had grown disproportionately to the game itself. The media paid almost as much attention to the ads shown as to the teams

User Imagery (54%)

Product Imagery

*Too sweet
Most entertaining ads
Fun to drink
Intense experience
Lots of flavor

When need energy boost
In mood for something different
*At a sporting event

Psychographic Imagery

Adventurous
Wild
Active
Daring
*Courageous
Exciting
Free-spirited
Rebellious
Spontaneous
Athletic
Youthful
Cool
Hip
*Out-going

EXHIBIT 6B
Brand Imagery—
Surge

Source: BBDO New York

User Imagery (49%)

Product Imagery

*Can't relate to ads
*Low quality product
*Not always available
Unique
Intense experience
*Tastes artificial

When need energy boost
In mood for something
different

Psychographic Imagery

Wild
Rebellious
Daring
Adventurous
Active
Up-to-date
Athletic
*Trendy
Youthful
*Leading-edge
Exciting
Spontaneous
Individualistic
*Powerful
Hip
In style

**Brand Imagery—
7 UP**

Source: BBDO New York

Product
Imagery

*Least fattening
Lowest calories
Low in sodium
*Too little flavor
*Not sweet enough
*Not filling
*Healthy/good for you
Most refreshing

User
Imagery
(48%)

Psychographic
Imagery

Sensitive
Relaxed
Peaceful
*Healthy
Feminine
Kind
*Nurturing

(Nice)
(Loyal)
(Cooperative)

**Brand Imagery—
Sprite**

Source: BBDO New York

Product Imagery

Lowest calories
Most refreshing
*Thirst quenching
*Goes down easy
Low in sodium

In a nice restaurant
*After exercise/sports

(In the evening)
(In the morning)

User
Imagery
(56%)

Psychographic
Imagery

Feminine
Sensitive
Peaceful
*Nice
Relaxed
Free-spirited
*Cooperative
*Friendly
*Happy
Kind

(Innovative)

EXHIBIT 7
Mountain Dew FY 2000 Brand Communications Strategy

Source: PepsiCo

Objective: Expand appeal of Mountain Dew to new users while reinforcing it among current users

Positioning: To 18 year old males, who embrace excitement, adventure and fun, Mountain Dew is the great tasting carbonated soft drink that exhilarates like no other because it is energizing, thirst-quenching, and has a one-of-a-kind citrus flavor.

Communication Strategy: Symbolize that drinking Mountain Dew is an exhilarating experience.

Target: Male Teens—18 year-old epicenter

- Ensure appeal amongst 20–39 year olds (current users)
- Drive universal appeal (white, African-American, Hispanic, and other ethnic)

Product Benefits	Emotional Benefits	Personality
Energizing	Exhilaration	Irreverent
Quenching	Excitement	Daring
Great Taste		Fun

and players. The networks interviewed the advertisers and the stars of the ads, and even replayed the ads on their programs. So a Super Bowl ad now had a huge ripple effect in free public relations. In addition, the Super Bowl was an extremely important contest for advertisers and especially for ad agencies. To "win" the Super Bowl (to be voted the top ad in the *USA Today* Ad Meter poll reported in the newspaper the following day) was a prestigious honor within the industry. Finally, Super Bowl ads provided a powerful sales tool to motivate retailers and distributors. PepsiCo and other grocery products advertisers used their annual Super Bowl advertising to sell in retail displays.

Super Bowl advertising, as a result, had become a distinctive genre within advertising. The demographically diverse audience demanded advertising with hooks that were easily understood. Insider humor did not work. While MTV ads could talk in a colloquial language to teens, Super Bowl ads could not afford this luxury. Second, the heated competition to win the affection of the audience had led to "big" productions that would stand out against an ever-more impressive set of competitors.

The New Creative

Bruce and Cassar had just finished presenting ten new ad concepts for PepsiCo to evaluate. For each concept, PepsiCo managers were given a "storyboard"—a script and a set of rough pencil sketches that depicted the most important scenes. Bruce and Cassar talked through each storyboard to help the client imagine how the ad would look if it were produced. The storyboard served as the skeletal outline of the ad. The creatives put flesh on these bones by describing in detail the characters, the action, how the scene is depicted, and the music. Of the ten new concepts, Moffitt and his senior managers hoped to select three ads to produce. The two best ads would run on the Super Bowl and then all three ads would be broadcast throughout 2000. It was already October, so there was barely enough time to produce the ads presented to get them on the Super Bowl. Asking Bruce to try again was not an option. The ten initial concepts were quickly whittled down to five finalists.

1. *Labor of Love.* A humorous spot about the birth of a Dew drinker. The doctor in the delivery room calls out "code green" and retreats to catch with a baseball mitt the baby as it shoots out of its mother like a cannon.

2. *Cheetah.* One of the Dew Dudes chases down a cheetah on a mountain bike. The cheetah, running on the African plain, has stolen his Dew and he wants it back. He tackles the cat, pulls the can out of the cat's stomach, but finds that it's empty and full of holes.

3. *Dew or Die.* The Dew Dudes are called in to foil the plot of an evil villain who is threatening to blow up the planet. Performing daredevil maneuvers down a mountain, they get

sidetracked in a ski lodge with some girls, but accidentally save the world anyway, powered by a spilled can of Dew.

4. *Mock Opera.* A parody of the Queen song *Bohemian Rhapsody* sung by the Dew Dudes who mock the cover of the original Queen album. The ad portrays the story of the altered lyrics: alternative sports action in which the athletes just miss cans of Dew as they shoot by.

5. *Showstopper.* A take-off on an extravagantly choreographed production number that mimics a Buzby Berkeley musical/dance film from the 1930s. The dancers are silver-clad BMX riders and skateboarders who perform for the Dew Dudes posing as directors.

PepsiCo viewed the evaluation of new creative as the most challenging aspect of brand management. Unlike decisions on new product ideas, consumer promotions, or product improvements, there was no market research or marketplace data to guide the decision. Junior managers typically did not sit in the agency presentations as they were not yet seasoned enough to judge creative work. PepsiCo believed that managers first had to gain knowledge of how advertising worked to build brands through years of seasoning and tutorials on several of the company's brands. So Scott Moffitt was the most junior person in the room. The skills and judgment that he demonstrated would be key to moving up the ladder at PepsiCo.

Bill Bruce finished presenting his last storyboard and scanned the room to lock eyes with the PepsiCo executives who would be deciding the fate of his ideas. Scott Moffitt didn't return the gaze. Instead he looked anxiously at his superiors, knowing that the spotlight would next focus on him. This was his chance to prove himself not only to PepsiCo senior management, but also to BBDO. BBDO's senior managers had become influential advisors, whom PepsiCo's top marketing executives routinely relied upon to help guide branding decisions. With six years of experience under his belt, this was Moffitt's chance to earn their respect as a contributing member to these critical discussions. Moffitt was eager to make a strong impression with nuanced and well-reasoned evaluations. Following long-standing protocol in packaged goods companies, the junior manager at the table gets the first crack at evaluating the creative. Moffitt cleared his throat, complimented Bruce on the high quality of the new work he had presented, and began his evaluation.

Case
Group D

Case

Distribution Strategy

15

Amazon.com

J. Paul Peter   *University of Wisconsin–Madison*

In 1994, a young senior vice president at a Wall Street investment firm, Jeff Bezos, decided that he wanted to be a part of the Internet revolution. He decided to try and sell books via the World Wide Web. Why books? Because there were about 1.3 million books in print at the time. And because he thought he would be able to provide the customer discounted prices, the opportunity to get any book wanted, and convenience. Bezos initially came up with a list of possible items he might be able to sell online, including books, music, PC hardware and software, and magazines. After eliminating all but books and music, he realized that only 250,000 music CDs were available at any one time compared to 1.5 million English book titles (3 million titles if all languages are considered). So, Bezos decided to go with books and drew up a business plan as he and his wife drove westward in search of their new home. He subsequently decided to start his new business in Seattle, and sold his first book in July 1995. And with that, **Amazon.com** began its rapid ascent toward becoming one of the most recognized businesses in the world.

While it still hasn't turned a profit, **Amazon.com** has succeeded where so many other fledgling Internet companies have failed. Bezos, who was recently named *Time* magazine's "Person of the Year" and *Advertising Age*'s 1999 "Marketer of the Year," is the first to admit that first mover advantage was instrumental in the growth of his company. He also credits the company's success to the comprehensive selection of books available. "There's no way to have a physical bookstore with 1.1 million titles," he says. "Our catalog, if you were to print it, would be the size of seven New York City phone books." In addition, **Amazon.com** is known for its ability to fulfill and deliver, thanks to large investments in nationwide warehouse distribution centers.

If you are worried that your local Barnes & Noble bookstore might be forced out of business any time soon however, don't be. **Amazon.com** cannot compete when customers want the physical presence of a bookstore. The online book behemoth cannot provide soft, comfortable couches, music, and gourmet coffee. Nor does it allow consumers the opportunity to page through a book before purchasing it, savoring the crisp new pages and the creaking of the binding when it is first opened. The company does, however, offer several advantages in the way of customer-to-customer and customer-to-author interaction. Customers can log on to the site, post a review on any book they have read, and have it permanently associated with that book's entry in the online catalog. Authors are also able to answer a variety of stock interview questions, which are then posted on the site associated with all of their books. Authors are also able to leave their e-mail addresses so that readers may e-mail their own opinions or comments. Bezos believes that his is the world's most "customer-centric" company.

Another unique feature that the company offers readers who have their own Web sites is the opportunity to set up their own specialized bookstores. For example, suppose that someone is an expert on investing. She may list several investment strategy books on her Web site and then link them from her site directly into the **Amazon.com** catalog. The company is able to track books that are purchased in this manner and gives the individual a commission on all sales. What else can customers expect when they try to purchase a book from **Amazon.com?** Discounts. But don't be fooled. Only roughly 30 percent of the book titles are discounted by 10 to 30 percent. The others are sold at list price.

The company's strategy of providing consumers with a sense of community within their Web site seems to be working. In December 1999, 15.8 million unique visitors logged on. And as the online bookselling market is projected to be worth $4.9 billion by 2003 (compared to $1.3 billion in 1999), **Amazon.com** stands to gain many more loyal customers. In the fourth quarter of 1999 alone, 73 percent of sales were from repeat buyers.

Recently, the mammoth bookseller has moved into other areas. You can now purchase books as well as toys, home improvement products, software, videos, and DVDs online. With this push into selling other products, the company faces increasing competition from traditional retailers and e-commerce startups. Some believe that the company risks diluting its brand name by expanding its business to too many lines, too quickly. But Bezos begs to differ. He says, "I get asked a lot, 'Are you trying to be the Wal-Mart of the Web?' The truth is, we're not trying to be the Anything of the Web. We're genetically pioneers." The company's former UK managing director, Simon Murdoch, adds, "It's a great name. 'Amazon' is not tied to any product category. The brand is extendible; it stands for delivery." Time will tell if the company will continue to deliver. For now, Amazon is one of the few, Internet brands recognized around the world. It is the most frequented Web site in America, and one of the top few in France, Britain, Germany and Japan. Jeff Bezos' vision has certainly become one of the great entrepreneurial success stories.

Discussion Questions

1. Why are books and CDs sold successfully online while many other products haven't sold well?

2. Do you think that consumers who buy from **Amazon.com** also shop at other Web sites for books and CDs and buy from the site that offers the lowest price?

3. What aspects of customer service have helped **Amazon.com** be successful?

4. Why do you think **Amazon.com** isn't profitable even though it generates high sales dollars?

5. What are the differences in the purchasing experience between buying a book at **Amazon.com** versus at a Barnes & Noble brick-and-mortar store?

6. What problems arise as **Amazon.com** expands its offerings to products other than books?

Sources: K. J. Bannan, "Book Battle," *Adweek,* February 28, 2000, pp. 90–94; Anonymous, "Survey: E-Commerce: Amazon's Amazing Ambition," *The Economist,* February 26, 2000, p. S24; B. Rosier, "Amazon Leads Race to Expand Web Services," *Marketing,* February 24, 2000, pp. 19–20; D. A. Williamson, "Marketer of the Year: Amazon.com—Dot-Commerce: Worlds' Biggest E-tail Brand Writes Book on Marketing Savvy," *Advertising Age,* December 13, 1999, pp. 1, 36–40; K. Brooker, "Amazon vs. Everybody," *Fortune,* November 8, 1999, pp. 120–128; M. H. Martin, "The Next Big Thing: A Bookstore?" *Fortune,* December 9, 1996, pp. 168–170; K. Southwick, "An Interview: Jeff Bezos, Amazon.com," *Upside,* October 1996, pp. 29–33.

16

IKEA's Global Strategy: Furnishing the World

Paul Kolesa

IKEA is a furniture manufacturer and retailer, well known throughout the world for its knockdown furniture. Its large retail stores in the blue-and-yellow colors of the Swedish flag are located on the outskirts of major cities, attracting shoppers who are looking for modern designs at good value. The low-cost operation relies on buyers with automobiles to carry the disassembled furniture in packaged kits and assemble the pieces at home.

The IKEA case is interesting because it shows how even retailers can go global once the key competitive advantages of the offering are standardized. The case focuses on the American entry, which posed barriers IKEA had not encountered before and which forced adaptation of some features.

IKEA, the Swedish furniture store chain virtually unknown outside of Scandinavia 25 years ago, has drawn large opening crowds to its stores as it has pushed into Europe, Asia, and North America. Along the way it has built something of a cult following, especially among young and price-conscious consumers. But the expansion was not always smooth and easy, for example, in Germany and Canada, and particularly difficult in the United States.

Company Background

IKEA was founded in 1943 by Ingvar Kamprad to serve price-conscious neighbors in the province of Smaland in southern Sweden. Early on, the young entrepreneur hit upon a winning formula, contracting with independent furniture makers and suppliers to design furniture that could be sold as a kit and assembled in the consumer's home. In return for favorable and guaranteed orders from IKEA, the suppliers were prohibited from selling to other stores. Developing innovative modular designs whose components could be mass produced and venturing early into eastern Europe to build a dedicated supplier network, IKEA could offer quality furniture in modern Scandinavian designs at very low prices. By investing profits in new stores, the company expanded throughout Scandinavia in the 1950s.

Throughout the following years, the IKEA store design and layout remained the same; IKEA was basically a warehouse store. Because the ready-to-assemble "knockdown" kits could be stacked conveniently on racks, inventory was always large, and instead of waiting for the store to deliver the furniture, IKEA's customers could pick it up themselves. Stores

This case was prepared by Paul Kolesa for class analysis and discussion.

were therefore located outside of the big cities, with ample parking space for automobiles. Inside, an assembled version of the furniture was displayed in settings along with other IKEA furniture. The purchaser could decide on what to buy, obtain the inventory tag number, and then either find the kit on the rack, or, in the case of larger pieces, have the kit delivered through the back door to the waiting car.

This simple formula meant that there were relatively few sales clerks on the floor to help customers sort through the more than 10,000 products stocked. The sales job consisted mainly of making sure that the assembled pieces were attractively displayed, that clear instructions were given as to where the kits could be found, and that customers did not have to wait too long at the checkout lines. IKEA's was a classic "cash-and-carry" approach, except that credit cards were accepted.

This approach, which trims costs to a minimum, is dependent on IKEA's global sourcing network of more than 2,300 suppliers in 67 countries. Because IKEA's designers work closely with suppliers, savings are built into all its products from the outset. Also since the same furniture is sold all around the world, IKEA reaps huge economies of scale from the size of its stores and the big production runs necessary to stock them. Therefore, IKEA is able to match rivals on quality while undercutting them up to 30 percent on price.

To draw the customers to the distant stores, the company relies on word-of-mouth, limited advertising, and its catalogues. These catalogues are delivered free of charge in the mailboxes of potential customers living in the towns and cities within reach of a store. The catalogues depict the merchandise not only as independent pieces of furniture but also together in actual settings of a living room, bedroom, children's room, and so on. This enables the company to demonstrate its philosophy of creating a "living space," not just selling furniture. It also helps the potential buyer visualize a complete room and simplifies the planning of furnishing a home. It also shows how IKEA's various components are stylistically integrated into a complete and beautiful whole. Even though furniture is hardly high-tech, the philosophy is reminiscent of the way high-tech producers, such as mobile phone makers, attempt to develop add-on features that fit their particular brand and not others.

As the company has grown, the catalogue has increased in volume and in circulation. By 2003, the worldwide circulation of the 360-page catalogue reached over 130 million, making it the world's largest printed publication distributed for free. In 2003 the catalogue was distributed in 36 countries and 28 languages, showing more than 3,000 items from storage solutions and kitchen renovation ideas to office furniture and bedroom furnishings.

EXHIBIT 1
IKEA Sales Data

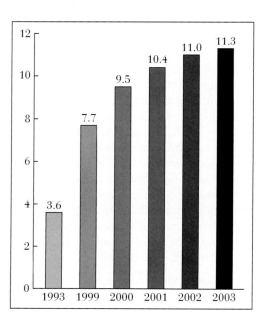

Turnover for the IKEA Group:

Sales for the IKEA Group for the financial year 2003 (1 September 2002 – 31 August 2003) totaled 11.3 billion euro (12.2 billion USD).

Sales totaled about 12.2 billion U.S. dollars in 2003, with a net profit margin around 6–7 percent. Of this, Europe accounted for over 80 percent of revenues, with Asia accounting for 3 percent, and North America 15 percent. The huge stores are relatively few in number—only 175 worldwide but growing rapidly—and the company employs about 76,000 people around the world (see Exhibits 1 and 2). Many of the stores have only one expatriate Swedish manager at the top, sufficient to instill the lean Ingvar Kamprad and IKEA ethos in the local organization.

Although the firm remains private, it continues to innovate and reorganize itself. For instance, fast decision making is aided by a management structure that is as flat as the firm's knockdown furniture kits, with only four layers separating IKEA's chief executive from its checkout workers. In 1992 IKEA abolished internal budgets and now each region must merely keep below a fixed ratio of costs to turnover.

EXHIBIT 2   **IKEA Retail Operations**

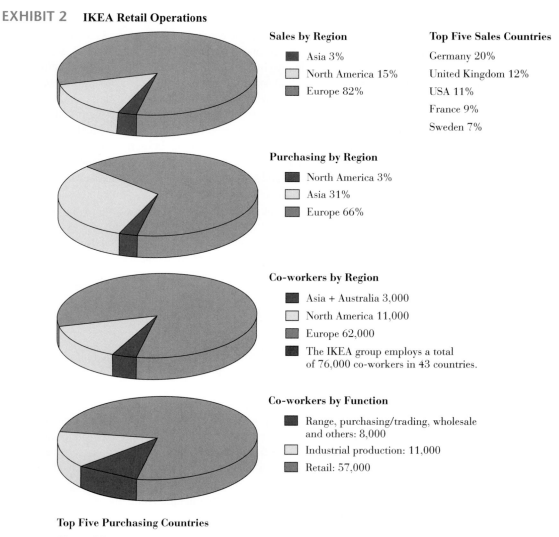

Sales by Region
- Asia 3%
- North America 15%
- Europe 82%

Top Five Sales Countries
Germany 20%
United Kingdom 12%
USA 11%
France 9%
Sweden 7%

Purchasing by Region
- North America 3%
- Asia 31%
- Europe 66%

Co-workers by Region
- Asia + Australia 3,000
- North America 11,000
- Europe 62,000
- The IKEA group employs a total of 76,000 co-workers in 43 countries.

Co-workers by Function
- Range, purchasing/trading, wholesale and others: 8,000
- Industrial production: 11,000
- Retail: 57,000

Top Five Purchasing Countries
China 18%
Poland 12%
Sweden 9%
Italy 7%

European Expansion

In the 1960s and 70s, as modern Scandinavian design became increasingly popular, expansion into Europe became a logical next step. The company first entered the German-speaking regions of Switzerland, thereby testing itself in a small region similar to Scandinavia. Yet expansion so far away from Sweden made it necessary to develop new suppliers, which meant that Kamprad traveled extensively, visiting potential suppliers and convincing them to become exclusive IKEA suppliers. Once the supply chain was established, the formula of consumer-assembled furniture could be used. After some resistance from independent furniture retailers who claimed that the furniture was not really "Swedish," since much of it came from other countries, IKEA's quality/price advantage proved irresistible even to fastidious Swiss consumers.

The next logical target was Germany, much bigger than Switzerland, but also culturally close to IKEA's roots. In Germany, well-established and large furniture chains were formidable foes opposed to the competitive entry and there were several regulatory obstacles. The opening birthday celebration of the first store in 1974 outside Cologne was criticized because in German culture birthdays should be celebrated only every 25 years. The use of the Swedish flag and the blue-yellow colors was challenged because the IKEA subsidiary was an incorporated German company (IKEA GmbH). The celebratory breakfast was mistitled because no eggs were served. Despite these rearguard actions from the established German retailers, IKEA GmbH became very successful, and was thus accepted, being voted German marketer of the year in 1979. The acceptance of IKEA's way of doing business was helped by the fact that IKEA had enlarged the entire market by its low prices, and some of the established retailers adopted the same formula in their own operations.

To get the stores abroad started, Kamprad usually sent a team of three or four managers who could speak the local language and had experience in an existing IKEA store. This team hired and trained the sales employees, organized the store layout, and established the sales and ordering routines. Although the tasks were relatively simple and straightforward, IKEA's lean organizational strategies meant that individual employees were assigned greater responsibilities and more freedom than usual in more traditional retail stores. Although this was not a problem in Europe and Japan (where its Japanese-sounding name also was an advantage), it was a problem in the United States.

Canadian Entry

To prepare for eventual entry into the United States, IKEA first expanded into Canada. The Canadian market was close to the U.S. market, and creating the supply network for Canada would lay the foundation for what was needed for the much larger U.S. market. Drawing upon a successful advertising campaign and positive word-of-mouth, and by combining newly recruited local suppliers with imports from existing European suppliers, the Canadian entry was soon a success. The advertising campaign was centered around the slogan, "IKEA: The impossible furniture store from Sweden," which was supported by a cartoon drawing of a moose's head, complete with antlers. The moose symbol had played very well in Germany, creating natural associations "with the north," and also creating an image of fun and games that played well in the younger segments the company targeted. The Canadians responded equally well to the slogan and the moose, as well as to IKEA's humorous cartoonlike ads poking fun at its Swedish heritage ("How many Swedes does it take to screw in a lightbulb? Two—one to screw in the lightbulb, and one to park the Volvo"), which became often-heard jokes.

The United States presented a much different challenge, as it offered a much larger market with its population dispersed, great cultural diversity, and strong domestic competition.

The initial problems centered around which part of the United States to attack first. While the east coast seemed more natural, with its closer ties to Europe, the California market on the west coast was demographically more attractive. But trafficking supplies to California would be a headache, and competition seemed stronger there, with the presence of established retailers of Scandinavian designs.

Then, there was the issue of managing the stores. In Canada, the European management style had been severely tested. The unusually great independence and authority of each individual employee in the IKEA system had been welcomed, but the individuals often asked for more direction and specific guidance. For example, the Swedish start-up team would say to an employee, "You are in charge of the layout of the office furniture section of the store," and consider this a perfectly actionable and complete job description. This seemed to go against the training and predisposition of some employees, who came back with questions such as, "How should this piece of furniture be displayed?" IKEA's expansion team suspected that the situation would be possibly even more difficult in the United States. The team also wondered if the same slogan and the moose symbol would be as effective in the United States as it had been in Germany and Canada.

Entry Hurdles in the United States

From the outset IKEA had succeeded despite breaking many of the standard rules of international retailing: enter a market only after exhaustive study; cater to local tastes as much as possible; and tap into local expertise through acquisitions, joint ventures, or franchising. Although breaking these rules had not hurt IKEA in Europe, the firm got into some trouble in America with its initial seven stores; six on the east coast and one in California. Many people visited the stores, looked at the furniture, and left empty-handed, citing long queues and nonavailable stock as chief complaints.

IKEA managers believed that their most pressing problem in entering the U.S. market was the creation of a stable supply chain. By taking an incremental approach, starting with a few stores on the east coast including an initial one outside Philadelphia, IKEA managers believed that they had ensured a smooth transition from the eastern United States, with its relative proximity to European suppliers, and its Canadian beachhead. Although the store in southern California was much farther away, its large market and customer demographics—young and active—favored IKEA's modern designs and assemble-it-yourself strategy. The California entry was also precipitated by the emergence of a local imitator, "Stør," which had opened ahead of IKEA, capitalizing on the word-of-mouth generated by IKEA'S new concept.

IKEA's early effort had problems because of less adaptation to the American market than customers desired. For example, IKEA decided not to reconfigure its bedroom furniture to the different dimensions used in the American market. As a result, the European-style beds sold by IKEA were slightly narrower and longer than standard American beds, and customers' existing mattresses and sheets did not fit the beds. Even though IKEA stocked European-sized sheets in the stores, bed sales remained very slow. IKEA ended up redesigning about a fifth of its American product range and sales immediately increased by around 30–40 percent.

The American suppliers, whom IKEA gradually recruited to reduce the dependence on imports, also proved in need of upgrading and instruction in IKEA's way of producing furniture. IKEA sent its people to the suppliers' plants, providing technical tips about more efficient methods and helping the suppliers shop around for better-quality or lower-price materials. Now IKEA produces about 45 percent of the furniture sold in its American stores locally, up from 15 percent just a few years earlier. In turn this has helped the firm cut prices in its American stores for three years running. The American difficulties also highlighted how growth could lead to quality problems in managing its increasingly complex global supply chain, so IKEA began conducting random checks.

Other adaptations to the American market proved just as successful. For instance, new cash registers were installed to speed throughput by 20 percent, with the goal of eliminating long checkout lines. Store layout was altered to conform more with American aesthetics and shopping styles. A more generous return policy than in Europe was instituted and a next-day delivery service was implemented.

Promotion

While some managers helped establish the supply side of the stores, IKEA's marketing staff was busy with the promotional side of the business. Store locations had generally disadvantaged IKEA relative to competitors. Because of the huge size of the stores (typically around 200,000 square feet), the need to keep a large inventory so that customers could get the purchased furniture immediately, and the amount of land needed for parking around each store, most stores were located in out-of-the-way places—next to the airport in New Jersey in one case and in a shopping mall 20 miles south of Washington, DC, in another. Thus, advertising was needed to make potential customers aware of store locations. It was thought that lower prices and selection would do the rest—positive word-of-mouth had proven the best advertising in most other markets.

But in the United States' competitive retail climate IKEA found that more focused media advertising was needed. As one manager stated: "In Europe you advertise to gain business; in the United States you advertise to stay in business." The diversity of the consumers made word-of-mouth less powerful than in ethnically more homogeneous countries. Management decided that a strong slogan and unique advertising message were going to be necessary to really bring awareness close to the levels in other countries.

The Moose symbol of IKEA (see Exhibit 3), although successful in Germany and Canada, was considered strange and too provincial for the U.S. market and would project

EXHIBIT 3

EXHIBIT 4

It's a big country.
Someone's got to furnish it.

the wrong image especially in California. Instead IKEA, in collaboration with its New York–based advertising agency Deutsch, developed a striking slogan that combined the down-home touch of the company philosophy with the humorous touch of the Moose: "It's a big country. Someone's got to furnish it" (see Exhibit 4).

Following the success of this advertising strategy, the company ventured further to establish itself as a pioneering store and to attract new kinds of customers. IKEA and Deutsch developed a series of eight TV advertising spots that featured people at different transitional stages in their lives, when they were most likely to be in the market for furniture. One spot featured a young family who had just bought a new house, another a couple whose children had just left home, and so on. IKEA even developed one spot that featured a homosexual couple, two men talking about furnishing their home. It was a daring step, applauded by most advertising experts and impartial observers. The campaign had a positive impact on IKEA's image—and on IKEA's sales. The company has continued the trend. One 30-second TV spot showed a divorced woman buying furniture for the first time on her own.

The privately held company won't reveal income figures, but it is successful in each of the market areas where it has located its U.S. stores. It is credited with being partly responsible for a shift in furniture buying behavior in the United States. Choosing furniture has become a matter of personality, lifestyle, and emotions in addition to functionality. IKEA's managers like that—they want IKEA to be associated with the "warmest, most emotional furniture in the world."

Discussion Questions

1. What are IKEA's firm-specific advantages? Country-specific advantages?
2. What are the cultural factors that make expansion abroad in retailing difficult? What has made it possible in IKEA's case?
3. Describe how IKEA's expansion has reenergized mature markets around the world and changed the competitive situation.
4. How does the TV advertising campaign initiated by IKEA overcome the entry barrier of high advertising expenditures?
5. Should IKEA expand further in the United States or focus on other countries?

Sources: Case compiled by Paul Kolesa from Rita Martenson, "Innovations in International Retailing," University of Gothenburg, Sweden: Liber, 1981; "Furnishing the world," *The Economist,* November 19, 1994, pp. 79–80; Richard Stevenson, "IKEA's New Realities: Recession and Aging Consumers," *New York Times,* April 25, 1993, p. F4; Kate Fitzgerald, "IKEA Dares to Reveal Gays Buy Tables Too," *Advertising Age,* March 12, 1994, pp. 3, 41; Vito Pilieci. "The IKEA catalogue: Swedish for massive circulation," *Calgary Herald,* August 27, 2003, p. C1.

17

Blockbuster Entertainment Corporation

James A. Kidney *Southern Connecticut State University*

Introduction

Seated at his desk in a rented two-story stucco executive office building in downtown Fort Lauderdale, Florida, H. Wayne Huizenga prepared to announce record revenues and net income for his chain of Blockbuster Video stores. His mid-April 1992 announcement would attribute those results to "increasing market penetration, gains in same-store revenue, and continued emphasis on cost control and increased productivity."[1] As Blockbuster Entertainment Corporation's Chairman of the Board and Chief Executive Officer, he also prepared to announce that it was now possible to pay a cash dividend to the company's 8,000 stockholders—something that had not been done before.

At the end of 1991, having achieved a 13 percent share of market, the company announced that its goal was to reach a 20 percent share of the U.S. home video market and have 3,000 Blockbuster Video stores operating in North America by 1995.[2] In some of its most mature markets, such as Atlanta, Chicago, Dallas, Detroit, and South Florida, that would mean market shares well in excess of 30 percent. Such a high share of market has been rare in specialty retailing. However, Blockbuster was the only U.S. video rental chain operating on a nationwide basis. Its next largest competitor was a regional chain, less than one-tenth its size.

This case was prepared by Dr. James A. Kidney, Management Department, School of Business, Southern Connecticut State University, New Haven, CT 06515.

[1]Corporate news release dated April 21, 1992.

[2]The total population of video rental stores operating throughout the U.S. ranged between 25,000 and 29,000, and turnover of individual store locations was quite high during the late 1980s and early 1990s.

External Challenges and Opportunities

As Huizenga optimistically pondered the company's strategic situation over the next five to seven years, there were several interesting external challenges and opportunities lurking on the horizon:

- With a higher market share than all of its 300 closest competitors combined, how much further could the company's market penetration grow?
- Could any significant technological changes in home entertainment alter the video rental industry's attractiveness?
- What were the future implications of Philips Electronics N.V.'s recent investment in Blockbuster stock?

Company History

David P. Cook, a 31-year-old Texas entrepreneur, founded the company in December 1982 as Cook Data Services, Inc., a provider of software and computer services to the oil and gas industries. Facing a sagging market for such services, Cook decided to switch over to a new, rapidly growing niche in specialty retailing—video rental stores. Cook's first store was opened during 1985, and the present corporate name was adopted one year later. From the outset, Cook recognized that an innovative superstore concept would draw many customers away from typical mom-and-pop rental stores and that well-designed computerized information systems would be advantageous for inventory planning and control as well as for customer information.

The typical mom-and-pop store had a spartan, nondescript atmosphere; short hours; a selection of fewer than 3,000 titles stressing recent hits; and empty boxes to be brought to a clerk who would have to find appropriate tapes—provided they were then in stock. Many mom-and-pops obtained significant rental revenues from X-rated videos, and that occasionally created an unwholesome image.

In comparison, Cook's idea was to have a family-oriented atmosphere with an extensive selection of children's videos, longer, more convenient hours, improved layout, quality service, faster check-in/check-out, state-of-the-art real time computer information systems, and a thoroughly trained professional staff.

Attracting Huizenga's Attention

After only two years of operation, Blockbuster's latent potential attracted the attention of Huizenga. By that time, Cook owned 8 stores and franchised 11 more in the Dallas area. Huizenga, then 48 years old, was restless, looking for a way to come back from early retirement, after having successfully made a small fortune from several companies.

Huizenga's previous experience had been in building up businesses in a variety of dissimilar industries, such as trash bin rentals and garbage hauling, dry cleaning, lawn care, portable toilet rentals, water cooler rentals and sale of bottled water. His most notable success was Waste Management, Inc., which he had honed into the world's largest waste collection and disposal company.

There was a common denominator running throughout his past entrepreneurial ventures. Each had rendered relatively basic services, had repeat customers, required little employee training, earned a steady cash flow, and was able to expand within an industry filled with small, undercapitalized competitors. Usually, the fragmented industries he entered were ripe for consolidation, because greater firm size led to economies of scale in marketing, distribution, computerized information systems, and/or potential clout in purchasing products and services.

Expansion and Acquisition of Store Locations

During 1987 Huizenga and a couple of close business associates bought out Blockbuster's founders and franchise holders for $18 million, and soon thereafter began acquiring small regional chains, such as Southern Video Partnership and Movies to Go. To help him run the new business, Huizenga hired several former upper level managers from McDonald's Corporation. His upper management group adopted the view that Blockbuster's target audience should be very similar to McDonald's broad-based restaurant clientele. Thus, Blockbuster's national expansion of its retail business was based upon McDonald's well-established growth philosophy, namely: blitz major markets, add stores quickly, use franchising to speed the process of obtaining managerial talent and operating capital, and never admit that the market is saturated.

Facing a rapid rise in VCR ownership, management tried to combine careful planning with opportunistic risk taking. An aggressive acquisition program was financed by new equity capital, in order to avoid burdensome long-term debt. Over the following four years, additional regional chains, such as Video Library Inc., Major Video Corp., Oklahoma Entertainment Inc., Vector Video Inc., Video Superstores Venture L.P., and Erol's Inc. were eagerly gobbled up.

A major international thrust was launched in early 1992, with the acquisition of Cityvision plc, the largest home video retailer in the U.K. Operating under the "Ritz" name and enjoying a 20 percent share of market, this firm had roughly 800 small stores and was considered to be an underperformer.

Around the same time, several Blockbuster Video stores were opened in Japan in a joint-venture with Fujita & Co., a retailer running over 800 McDonald's restaurants and holding a stake in Toys 'R' Us Japan, Ltd. Jointly they hoped to open 1,000 stores over the next ten years.

Describing the hectic, and occasionally disorganized, rush to add store locations Huizenga explained, "We felt we had to go fast because we had nothing proprietary. We had to get the locations in each area before somebody else moved in. It was a mistake, but it turned out okay. We have the locations, the people are trained, and the customers are ours. Now if somebody else comes in, they have to take it away from us."[3]

Blockbuster Video's Profile as of 1992

Blockbuster Video was a membership only club, serving more than 29 million members worldwide, who rented more than 1 million of the company's videocassettes daily. Without incurring any membership fees, patrons were provided with bar-coded membership cards which allowed for speedy computerized check-out from the issuing store. Cards were sometimes honored at other locations in the chain as well. By requiring personal photo identification and an application for membership, rather than dealing with anonymous walk-ins, the rental store was able to secure an extra measure of control over tapes which left the premises. A major credit card also had to be presented, so that the store could charge members for lost or damaged inventory.

[3] *The New York Times Business World Magazine,* June 9, 1991.

EXHIBIT 1
Blockbuster Entertainment Corporation (Number of Blockbuster video stores, by ownership type)

Source: Blockbuster's 1991 Annual Report and 1992 press releases.

Date	Company	Franchised	Total
December 31, 1985	1	0	1
December 31, 1986	19	0	19
December 31, 1987	112	126	238
December 31, 1988	341	248	589
December 31, 1989	561	518	1,079
December 31, 1990	787	795	1,582
December 31, 1991	1,025	1,003	2,028
March 31, 1992	1,805	1,024	2,829

Note: The surge in company stores during the first quarter of 1992 is attributable to the Cityvision plc acquisition.

The typical Blockbuster Video store was located in a free-standing building of approximately 6,000 square feet (560 square meters) and was open from 10:00 am to midnight, seven days per week, 365 days per year. The atmosphere was bright and wholesome. Aisles were clearly marked and divided into more than 30 categories to distribute customer traffic and encourage browsing. Video boxes with tapes inside were openly displayed within easy reach. Similar categories were placed adjacent to one another, thereby increasing the potential for increased rentals. Blockbuster's superstores typically carried a comprehensive selection of 10,000 prerecorded videocassettes, consisting of more than 8,000 titles. The strongest months for video store rentals tended to be December through March and June through August, with Hollywood's release schedule being a crucial variable.

Blockbuster Video stores proudly claimed to offer "More Movies Than Anyone in the World." Additionally, their relatively weak, fragmented rivals were seldom able to match Blockbuster's advertising clout and wide array of attractions, such as: computer-driven movie selection aids; a three-evening rental policy; an attractive overnight pricing policy for new hit releases which improved turnover and in-stock positions; a state-of-the-art management information system which tracked rentals and market trends; microwave popcorn and other snack foods; promotional tie-ins with Domino's Pizza, Pepsi-Cola, Pizza Hut, Subway, U.S. Air, and Universal Studios; drop-off boxes for fast returns; and publicity from an annual Blockbuster Bowl football game. Nevertheless, some competitors clearly differentiated themselves from Blockbuster by offering lower prices, reservations, home delivery, or hard core "adult" videos.

As of March 31, 1992, there were 2,829 Blockbuster Video stores, worldwide, up from 19 just five years earlier (Exhibit 1).

Locations and Operations

By the first quarter of 1992, 68 percent of Blockbuster's stores were located in 46 of America's 50 states, with the remaining 32 percent located in Austria, Australia, Canada, Chile, Guam, Japan, Mexico, Puerto Rico, Spain, the United Kingdom, and Venezuela. Nearly all of the company's retail, distribution, and administrative facilities were rented under non-cancellable operating leases, which in most cases contained renewal options. Blockbuster employed approximately 12,500 individuals.

There had historically tended to be a 50–50 balance between company-owned and franchised locations. Although franchising remained beneficial in foreign countries, where local partners made it easier to conduct business, franchising within the U.S. became less essential once the company had an ample cash flow and employed many competent people who could help manage ongoing growth.

The usual initial investment (i.e., franchise fee, inventory, equipment, and start-up capital) for a franchised location ranged from $700,000 to $1,000,000. Annual operating costs

EXHIBIT 2

Blockbuster Entertainment Corporation (Selected annual financial data)

Source: Blockbuster's 1991 Annual Report and Standard & Poor's Stock Report.

	1991	1990	1989	1988	1987
Income Data (Million $)					
Systemwide revenue	1,520	1,133	663	284	98
Company revenue	868	633	402	136	43
Operating costs & expenses	714	514	326	110	37
Operating income	154	119	76	26	6
Net income	94	69	44	17	3
Depreciation & amortization	189	124	76	22	5
Cash flow	283	193	120	39	8
Balance Sheet Data (Million $)					
Total assets	804	608	417	235	105
Cash & cash equivalents	48	49	40	9	7
Current assets	163	116	93	39	27
Current liabilities	164	110	83	49	17
Long-term debt	134	169	118	39	22
Shareholders' equity	483	315	208	124	59
Per Share Data ($)					
Earnings per share	.56	.42	.28	.12	.04
Tangible book value	2.35	1.65	1.18	.75	.41
Stock price—high	15.12	13.37	10.81	6.25	2.63
Stock price—low	7.75	6.75	4.87	1.06	.75
Common Stock and Equivalents (Millions)					
Average shares outstanding	168	162	155	142	75

Notes: Systemwide revenues include franchise store revenues, while company revenues do not. Operating costs and expenses include depreciation and amortization. Cash flow is net income plus depreciation and amortization. Tangible book value excludes cost of purchased businesses in excess of market value of tangible assets acquired (unamortized goodwill).

per location fell in the $400,000 to $500,000 range. Franchisees were provided extensive guidelines for site selection, store design and product selection, as well as customer service, and management training programs. In addition, the company furnished national and local advertising and promotional programs for the entire system. Franchisees paid royalties and other fees for those services and also routinely paid Blockbuster Entertainment for video-cassette inventories, computer hardware and software.

For a typical Blockbuster Video store, cash flow payback on initial store investment occurred rapidly—generally in under three years. The average new store attained monthly revenues of $70,000 within twelve months of opening date.

Systemwide revenues, for company-owned and franchise-owned operations combined, as well as other selected financial data are shown in Exhibit 2.

Sources of Revenues

During 1991, 5 percent of company revenues were derived from franchise royalties and fees, 20 percent from product sales mainly to franchisees, and 75 percent from rentals. Other than low-priced used products, outright sales of home videos were never emphasized prior to late 1991, because the largest sellers were highly competitive national discount chains like Wal-Mart and Kmart. As a growing portion of consumer spending went towards videocassette and laser disc purchases, it became logical for video rental stores to begin taking the sell-through market more seriously.

EXHIBIT 3
Estimated and Projected Annual U.S. Movie Revenues, by Viewing Method ($ billions)

Source: Blockbuster's 1991 Annual Report.

Viewing Method	1990	1995	2000
Video	10.3	15.2	19.3
Movie theater	5.1	6.9	7.4
Pay cable (premium channels)	5.1	6.2	7.6
Pay-per-view	.01	0.5	2.0
Total	20.6	28.8	36.3

Mr. Joseph Baczko, who headed the highly successful International Division of Toys 'R' Us, Inc. for eight years, was hired in 1991 as Blockbuster's new President and Chief Operating Officer. To carry out a process of "retailing" as well as internationalizing the company, he brought several executives with significant retailing experience into the firm. Promotional and display efforts to stimulate sell-through transactions were given added emphasis under Baczko's direction. Given his background in toys, he was interested in treating child oriented movies, such as *Batman, Bambi, The Little Mermaid,* and *101 Dalmatians,* mainly as sell-through rather than rental products. Blockbuster's stores also began renting Nintendo and Sega Genesis video game products.

Industry Environment

Rentals and sales of home videos in the U.S. amounted to a mere $700 million in 1982. By 1991, domestic revenue for the video rental industry reached $11 billion, and Americans were spending more than twice as much to watch movies at home as they did to watch them in movie theaters. Within the marketplace for prerecorded videocassettes, movies accounted for more than 80 percent of rental revenues and at least 50 percent of dollars spent on purchases. Blockbuster Entertainment estimated that the U.S. video rental market for movies would reach $19.3 billion by the turn of the century (Exhibit 3).

In 1980, the percentage of U.S. households owning at least one television set reached 98 percent and remained at that level thereafter. By 1995, there were expected to be almost 100 million households in the U.S., and 98 percent of them were likely to own at least one color TV set. Blockbuster Entertainment expected 91 percent of those TV owning households also to own VCRs (Exhibit 4), with more than 35 percent of them owning at least two machines.

VCR ownership in Europe also was growing rapidly, with household penetration rates in individual countries lagging behind the U.S. anywhere from two to five years. Total 1991 worldwide spending for home video rental and sales was $21.2 billion (Exhibit 5). Licensing, sale, and rental practices differed from one product/market to another, and in some countries most of the television viewing population remained unaware that movie videos could be rented instead of being purchased.

Movie Production and Distribution

Approximately 390 to 450 new feature films were released annually in the United States. Eight of the largest distributors accounted for more than 90 percent of movie theater film rentals in the United States and Canada. Most of them, such as Paramount, Universal, Warner, Fox, Columbia, and Disney, had been in business for more than 50 years. Leading producers and distributors of videos were usually subsidiaries of large companies which owned other leisure-time businesses. Large distributors also had prime access to international channels for distributing American-made films in foreign countries. Musical,

EXHIBIT 4
Estimated and Projected VCR and Cable TV Penetration among U.S. TV Owning Households (Millions of TV owning households, percent with VCRs, percent with cable TV, and percent with additional pay-per-view or pay cable services, by year)

Source: Blockbuster's 1991 Annual Report, the Universal Almanac, and author's estimates.

Year	No. of TV Owning Households	Percent with		
		VCR	Cable	Pay Cable
1980	76	1	20	7
1981	78	3	22	10
1982	82	6	30	16
1983	83	10	34	19
1984	84	17	39	24
1985	85	30	43	26
1986	86	42	46	27
1987	87	53	48	26
1988	89	62	49	27
1989	90	68	53	29
1990	92	72	56	29
1991	92	77	58	30
1992	93	82	61	31
1993	95	86	64	32
1994	96	89	67	34
1995	97	91	70	36

Note: From 1982 through 1995, it's assumed that 98 percent of all U.S. households own televisions.

EXHIBIT 5
Estimated Population, Home Video Spending, VCR Penetration and Basic Cable Penetration by Country, as of 1991

Sources: Blockbuster's 1991 Annual Report, *This Business of Television,* and 1992 *World Almanac.*

Country	Population (millions)	Video Spending ($ billions)	VCRs (% of households)	Cable (% of households)
Australia	17	0.7	70	0
Canada	27	1.2	65	69
France	56	0.7	40	10
Germany	79	0.7	46	32
Italy	58	0.6	38	1
Japan	124	2.6	70	20
United Kingdom	57	1.4	70	2
United States	250	11.0	75	57
Others	4,732	2.3	n.a.	n.a.
Worldwide total	5,400	21.2	n.a.	n.a.

Note: n.a. = not available

cultural, educational, exercise programs, instructional, and documentary videos tended to be handled by smaller distributors.

The time span from the point when work began on a new movie to the point when its revenue stream was largely realized often was five years or longer. Over that period, producers and distributors attempted to play out their products in a manner which gave them an optimum revenue stream.

By 1991, home video had become a major ancillary source of revenue for movie studios. For example, *Nothing but Trouble* (directed by Dan Aykroyd, 1991) grossed $8.5 million in box office receipts. The studio's share was roughly 50 percent. When released on videocassette, the same movie earned an additional $9.6 million in revenue for the studio.[4]

The sequence of each film's release depended on the nature of individual deals made by the distributor. Domestic release usually occurred somewhat ahead of international release.

[4]Source: Blockbuster Entertainment 1991 Corp. Annual Report.

A typical major studio's United States release tended to be rolled out in the following illustrative manner:

Theatrical showings: January through April, 1992

Home video: Mid-Summer, 1992

Airline: Mid-Summer, 1992

Pay-per-view: Late-Summer or Fall, 1992

Pay cable (premium channels): Winter, 1992–93

If attractively priced, popular movies that were developed for young children were likely to achieve a sell-through market of 1.5 million or more copies. Movies that had been adult hits at the box office within the latest year were the ones most in demand for rentals, and 100,000 to 500,000 copies of them were generally sold, mostly to video rental stores. Assuming a $3 charge per rental, it normally took anywhere from 13 to 19 rentals to recover a store's initial investment in a hit movie tape.

Distributors set high initial suggested retail prices (roughly $80 to $100 on box office hits) for videotaped films they expected consumers to rent and low prices (roughly $20 to $30) for those they expected consumers to buy. Each videocassette cost distributors about $2 to manufacture and $2 to market. Wholesale prices paid by Blockbuster were generally 55 to 65 percent of suggested retail prices.

Wholesalers

Despite the fact that movies were the mainstay of the home video business, Blockbuster Entertainment traditionally purchased its movie rental inventory from wholesalers rather than film distributors. Having achieved nationwide scope, the company could decide to bypass regional wholesalers and purchase its movies more economically directly from motion picture distributors.

Technological Threats

During the decade from 1982 through 1991 Americans purchased 1.2 billion prerecorded and 2.2 billion blank videocassettes. They also built up a $32 billion investment in VCR equipment. This burgeoning consumer commitment to VCR technology seemed to assure long-range demand for videocassettes. Nevertheless, the ease of duplicating and pirating videocassettes was a matter of some concern to movie producers. As laser discs began to attract a modest following, rentals and sales of video discs were being added to many video store's product offerings.

No one knew precisely when new types of home entertainment might begin to undermine home videotape viewing. Cable television was expected to become a more and more serious threat. Even though three out of five TV owning households subscribed to cable service as of 1991, only one third of those subscribers had access to movies on pay cable (e.g. HBO, Showtime, Cinemax, The Disney Channel, The Movie Channel) or pay-per-view channels.

Employing "addressable technology," pay-per-view service allowed customers to call in and have a movie, concert, or sporting event broadcast on their TV for a fee. Being transaction based, pay-per-view depended upon impulse buying. It was sold by direct mailings, advertisements, bill stuffers, and 24 hour "barker" promotional channels.

In 1992, sporting events generated almost twice as much pay-per-view business as other alternatives. As pay-per-view's market potential continued to develop, the Summer of 1992 was regarded as an important psychological turning point. Cable operators were seeking broadcasting rights for live coverage of the Olympic Games in Atlanta, Georgia, hoping that such coverage would significantly boost the number of new subscribers for pay-per-view services.

While viewers had to watch pay-per-view at a scheduled time, this service certainly provided greater convenience than having to make two round trips to a video store. The competitive threat was moderated by the fact that most new movies were released on videocassettes before they appeared on pay-per-view services or pay cable. However, that disparity could disappear rapidly, if movie distributors were enticed by cable's potential for licensing and revenue sharing arrangements.

Interactive Television

Over the long-term, advances in satellite and cable television technology and entry of regional telephone companies into the electronic home delivery arena were other potential concerns within the U.S. market. With new developments in fiber optics and digital signal compression, expansion to 500 channels could become feasible for video delivery systems. Thus, there was a possibility that "video-on-demand" could become a reality on cable or telephone systems by the mid 1990s.

Anticipating major advances in communications, IBM and Time Warner Corp. had begun discussing ways to combine data processing and transmitting expertise with cable TV systems, TV shows, and movies. IBM believed interactive television would eventually encroach upon a wide array of existing entertainment and information product/markets, including catalog shopping, broadcast and cable advertising, home video, information services, theater, video games, electronic messaging, videoconferencing, photography, records, tapes, and CDs. Furthermore, the Federal Communications Commission (FCC) had allocated a portion of the broadcast spectrum to interactive television and intended to award licenses to investors who could serve large markets.

Nervous Investors

Had the video rental market remained extremely fragmented, it might not have become so large and well-established. Some industry watchers predicted that Blockbuster's success in becoming a high quality specialty retail chain might impair the development of innovative competing technologies for accessing home entertainment.

Recognizing that other forms of retailing were withstanding competition from television, Baczko made the following point, "Home shopping has not taken the store away, and pay-per-view is not going to do so to video. I don't think you can ever beat a retailing environment."[5]

Nevertheless, newspaper reports of questionable depreciation accounting practices, bankruptcy filings by sizable video retailers, and media hype of future electronic home delivery systems, from time to time, stirred predictions of impending disaster for the video rental industry. Consequently, Blockbuster's common stock attracted speculators and short sellers, and the market price per share plunged every so often as frightened investors hastily bailed out to "take profits" or "stop losses." For example, the price per share reached a high of $15.125 and a low of $7.75 on the New York Stock Exchange during the first half of 1991.

[5] *The New York Times,* February 21, 1992.

EXHIBIT 6		1991	1990
Philips Electronics N.V., Net Sales by Product Sector and Geographical Area (mMillions of guilders)	**Product Sector**		
	Lighting	7,351	7,026
	Consumer products	26,861	25,856
Source: Philips' 1991 Annual Report.	Professional products and systems	12,510	12,400
	Components and semiconductors	7,844	7,953
	Miscellaneous	2,420	2,529
	Net sales	56,986	55,764
	Geographical Area		
	Netherlands	3,206	3,604
	Rest of Europe	30,433	30,366
	U.S.A. and Canada	12,833	11,819
	Latin America	3,142	3,361
	Africa	730	772
	Asia	5,565	4,770
	Australia and New Zealand	1,077	1,072
	Net sales	56,986	55,764

Note: On December 31, 1991 and 1990, respectively, one U.S. dollar equaled 1.71 and 1.69 Dutch guilders.

Strategic Alliance with Philips Electronics

During 1992, an intriguing strategic alliance began to emerge between Blockbuster Entertainment Corp. and Philips Electronics, N.V. Headquartered in the Netherlands, Philips was the world's second largest consumer electronics company after Japan's Matsushita Electric Industrial Co. Philips' decision to purchase 13 million newly issued common shares (nearly 7.2 percent of outstanding shares) suggested that the two companies might be heading toward a close working relationship.[6]

In 1991 consumer products accounted for 47 percent of Philips' $33 billion in sales revenues. The early 1990s found the U.S., Canada, Australia, the United Kingdom, and Japan all experiencing economic downturns and declining consumer confidence. Stagnant demand and bloody price wars were curbing profits throughout the consumer electronics industry. Battered by stagnant demand and stiff price competition from its Japanese competitors, Philips reported a $3 billion loss in 1990. Philips' new President, Jan D. Timmer, was struggling to slash the payroll, close inefficient plants, and divest unprofitable operations. A streamlining and restructuring process initiated by Timmer provided a $210 million profit on sales of $33 billion in 1991. Recent sales data are shown in Exhibit 6.

Some analysts, suspecting that Huizenga might be ready to move on to another new venture, speculated that Philips might be interested in acquiring a controlling interest in Blockbuster Entertainment Corp. Others expressed doubts that outright ownership and management of a captive group of rental stores would serve Philips' best interest.

Having pioneered such consumer electronics products as the videocassette recorder, audio compact disc, digital compact cassette, and high-definition television, Philips had long been a superior technological leader. Marketing agility and competitive pricing had never been Philips' strengths. Philips conceivably might be aiming for a reliable international retail base for rapid, broad distribution of future hardware and software products.

[6]These funds have been used by Blockbuster to help pay for the Cityvision plc acquisition.

Philips owned 51 percent of Super Club Holding & Finance S.A., a poorly performing music and video retail chain. With store locations in Europe and the United States, Super Club might benefit from a tie-in with Blockbuster. Philips also owned 80 percent of Polygram, one of the three largest music publishing, production, marketing, and distribution companies in the world, and a major European manufacturer of compact discs. Recognizing the increasingly complementary natures of the audio and video fields, Polygram had begun producing and distributing filmed entertainment, as part of its strategy to become a multicultural, global entertainment company.

Philips' Multimedia Systems

Potentially even more relevant were Philips' plans for a new Imagination Machine. Philips had developed a new Compact Disk Interactive (CD-I) entertainment system that could turn the family TV into a terminal through which one could play regular music CDs, view photo CD disks, and interact with programs rather than just watch them. Touted as the "VCR of the 21st century," Philips' Imagination Machine was one of the products that Timmer was counting on heavily to revive depressed earnings. Blending text, full-motion video, and stereo-quality sound, it called up sports statistics during live broadcasts, displayed digital snapshots, played karaoke sing-along disks, used Nintendo's new games and played movies and music videos. While CD-I had been promoted primarily to the consumer market, it was also highly suited to the educational market.

Philips utilized a special format for its CD-ROM, which was supported by several other electronics firms as well. Commodore, Apple, Toshiba, and Tandy were offering multimedia equipment with different CD formats. Sony and Panasonic (Matsushita) had not yet revealed the type of standard they might support. Having witnessed the VHS/Beta wars of the late 1970s, Philips recognized the need to insure that its CD-I standard won out over its rivals. Ultimately, the availability of appealing multimedia software would help determine which compact disc standard would dominate.

Potential New Undertakings

As Blockbuster entered numerous foreign markets, its employees started to acquire increasing familiarity with markets for movies and home entertainment within many different cultures and political jurisdictions. Blockbuster's increasing knowledge of ways to formalize and expand global rental markets could help foster widespread acceptance of the rental concept for expensive multimedia CDs, such as encyclopedias, music libraries, and games. Blockbuster could thus become a leading worldwide distributor of a new generation of home entertainment products, perhaps selling and/or renting Philips' Imagination Machines and CDs.

Reacting to investor skepticism a year earlier, Huizenga had optimistically asserted, "We have the best locations in town. We've got a plain vanilla box. We can sell shoes there if we want to. Maybe we'll build a music store that's green and white. We could call it Chartbusters."[7] Such remarks indicate that someday Blockbuster Entertainment Corporation could be attracted to retailing opportunities elsewhere within the diverse, yet more and more intertwined, marketplace for home entertainment products.

---

[7] *The New York Times Business World Magazine,* June 9, 1991.

18

eBay: In a League by Itself

Louis Marino *The University of Alabama*

Patrick Kreiser *The University of Alabama*

On September 20, 2000, eBay's top management surprised the financial community by announcing ambitious objectives of $3 billion in annual revenues by year-end 2005, a gross margin target above 80 percent, and target operating margins of 30–35 percent. Given that eBay's 2000 annual revenues were only $400 million, the $3 billion annual revenue target implied a compound annual growth rate of 50 percent from the end of 2000 through 2005—an objective some analysts criticized as too aggressive. Other analysts, however, wondered if the revenue target was ambitious enough, since online auction sales were forecast to reach $54.3 billion by 2007 and since eBay was far and away the dominant player in the online auction market.

But in early 2004 eBay was well on its way to meeting the 2005 goals it set for itself in 2000. In January 2004, eBay reported 2003 revenues of $2.17 billion and a gross margin of 81 percent. If the company could grow its revenues by 40 percent in 2004, it could reach its $3 billion annual revenue goal a year ahead of the 2005 target date. However, analysts were becoming increasingly concerned about whether eBay could sustain its phenomenal growth (see Exhibit 1), given that almost one-third of all U.S. Internet users were already registered on eBay and that eBay could expect stiffening competition from other ambitious online auction sites and e-tailers as it pursued its growth initiatives.

Building on the vision of its founder, Pierre Omidyar (pronounced oh-*mid*-ee-ar), eBay was initially conceived as an online marketplace that would facilitate a person-to-person trading community based on a democratized, efficient market in which everyone could have equal access through the same medium, the Internet. Leveraging a unique business model and the growing popularity of the Internet, eBay had dominated the online auction market since its beginning in the mid-1990s and had grown its business to include over 94.9 million registered users from more than 150 countries heading into 2004. The auction site's diverse base of registered users in early 2004—which ranged from high school and college students looking to make a few extra dollars, to Fortune 500 companies such as IBM selling excess inventory, to large government agencies like the U.S. Postal Service selling undeliverable parcels—differed greatly from its original user base of individuals and small companies.

EXHIBIT 1   **Selected Indicators of eBay's Growth, 1996–2003**

	1996	1997	1998	1999	2000	2001	2002	2003
Number of registered users (in millions)	0.041	0.341	2.2	10.0	22.0	42.4	61.7	94.9
Active users (in millions)	NA	NA	NA	NA	NA	18.0	27.7	41.2
Gross merchandise sales (in millions)	$7	$95	$745	$2,800	$5,400	$9,300	$14,900	$24,000
Number of auctions listed (in millions)	0.29	4.4	33.7	129	264	423	638	971

EXHIBIT 2   **Estimated Growth in Global E-Commerce 1999–2004**

	1999	2000	2001	2002	2003	2004
Estimated value of e-commerce transactions	$170 billion	$657 billion	$1.23 billion	$2.23 trillion	$3.98 trillion	$6.79 trillion

Source: Forrester Research.

The Growth of E-Commerce and Online Auctions

The concepts underlying the Internet were first conceived in the 1960s, but it wasn't until the 1990s that the Internet garnered widespread use and became a part of everyday life. The *Computer Industry Almanac* estimated that by the end of 2002 there were approximately 665 million Internet users worldwide in over 150 countries and that number would grow to over 1 billion users worldwide by 2005.[1] While the top 15 countries accounted for more than 70 percent of the computers in use, slightly less than one-fourth of these Internet users (160.7 million) resided in the United States, and the United States' share as a percentage of total Internet users worldwide was falling. The highest areas of Internet usage growth were expected to be in developing countries in Asia, Latin America, and Eastern Europe with increasing access through new technologies such as Web-enabled cell phones. However, it was expected that total growth rates would not exceed 20 percent annually in the future.

Forrester Research forecast that worldwide e-commerce revenues would be $6.79 trillion in 2004 and that online retail would grow at a 19 percent annual rate between 2003 and 2008 to reach $229.9 billion, of which 25 percent, or $57.5 billion, was expected to come from online auction sales. It was also predicted that North America would account for 51.5 percent of total e-commerce sales in 2004, with the Asia-Pacific region accounting for 24.3 percent, Western Europe accounting for 22.5 percent, and Latin America accounting for 12.1 percent of total sales. Within the business-to-consumer segment, eBay's primary area of operation, U.S. e-commerce accounted for over 65 percent of all Internet transactions in 1999 but was expected to account for only about 38 percent in 2003 and potentially less in the future, due to rapid expansion in other parts of the world. Asia was expected to grow especially rapidly following the 2001 decision to include China in the World Trade Organization. In 2002, Germany, the United Kingdom, France, and Italy accounted for 70 percent of the e-commerce revenues in Western Europe, but this share was expected to decline as business-to-business e-commerce in Europe was expected to triple from 2003 to 2006. Exhibit 2 displays the expected total growth in worldwide e-commerce between 1999 and 2004.

[1]www.c-i-a.com, press releases, April 2001 and July 2001.

Key Success Factors in Online Retailing

It was relatively easy to create a Web site that functioned like a retail store; the more significant challenge was for an online retailer to generate traffic to the site in the form of both new and returning customers. To reach new customers, some online retailers partnered with search engines—such as Google, MySimon, or StreetPrices—that allowed customers to compare prices for a given product from many retailers. Other tactics employed to build traffic included direct e-mail, online advertising at portals and content-related sites, and some traditional advertising such as print and television advertising. For customers who found their way to a site, most online retailers endeavored to provide extensive product information, include pictures of the merchandise, make the site easily navigable, and have enough new things happening at the site to keep customers coming back. (A site's ability to generate repeat visitors was known as *stickiness.*) For new Internet users, retailers had to help them overcome their nervousness about using the Internet itself to shop for items customers generally bought in stores. Web sites had to appease concerns about the possible theft of credit card numbers and the possible sale of personal information to marketing firms. Online retailing also had severe limitations in the case of those goods and services people wanted to see in person to verify their quality. From the retailer's perspective, there was the issue of collecting payment from buyers who wanted to use checks or money orders instead of credit cards.

Online Auctions

The first known auctions were held in Babylon around 500 BC. In AD 193, the entire Roman Empire was put up for auction after the emperor Pertinax was executed. Didius Julianus bid 6,250 drachmas per royal guard and was immediately named emperor of Rome. However, Julianus was executed only two months later, suggesting that he may have been the first-ever victim of the winner's curse (bidding more than the good would cost in a nonauction setting).

Auctions have endured throughout history for several reasons. First, they give sellers a convenient way to find a buyer for something they would like to dispose of. Second, auctions are an excellent way for people to collect difficult-to-find items, such as certain Beanie Babies or historical memorabilia, that have a high value to them personally. Finally, auctions are one of the "purest" markets that exist for goods, in that they bring buyers and sellers into contact to arrive at a mutually agreeable price. As technological advances led to the advent and widespread adoption of the Internet, this ancient form of trade found a new medium.

Online auctions worked in essentially the same way as traditional auctions, the only difference being that the auction process occurred over the Internet rather than at a specific geographic location with buyers and sellers physically present. There are three basic categories of online auctions:

1. Business-to-business auctions, typically involving equipment and surplus merchandise.
2. Business-to-consumer auctions, in which businesses sold goods and services to consumers via the Internet. Many such auctions involved companies interested in selling used or discontinued goods, or liquidating unwanted inventory.
3. Person-to-person auctions, which gave interested sellers and buyers the opportunity to engage in competitive bidding.

Since eBay's pioneering of the person-to-person online auction process in 1995, the number of online auction sites on the Internet had grown to well over 2,750 by the end of 2001. Forrester Research predicted that 6.5 million customers would use online auctions in 2002.

Online auction operators could generate revenue in four principal ways:

1. Charging sellers for listing their good or service.
2. Charging a commission on all sales.
3. Selling advertising on their Web sites.
4. Selling their own new or used merchandise via the online auction format.

More recently, however, online auction sites had also added a fifth revenue-generation option that allowed buyers to purchase the desired good without waiting for an auction to close:

5. Selling their own goods or allowing other sellers to offer their goods in a fixed-price format.

Most sites charged sellers either a fee or a commission and sold advertising to companies interested in promoting their goods or services to users of the auction site.

Online Auction Users

Participants in online auctions could be grouped into six categories: (1) bargain hunters, (2) hobbyist/collector buyers, (3) professional buyers, (4) casual sellers, (5) hobbyist/collector sellers and (6) corporate and power sellers.

Bargain Hunters

Bargain hunters viewed online auctions primarily as a form of entertainment; their objective usually was to find a great deal. Bargain hunters were thought to make up only 8 percent of active online users but 52 percent of eBay visitors. To attract repeat visits from bargain hunters, industry observers said, sites must appeal to them on both rational and emotional levels, satisfying their need for competitive pricing, the excitement of the search, and the desire for community.

Hobbyist and Collector Buyers

Hobbyists and collectors used auctions to search for specific goods that had a high value to them personally. They were very concerned with both price and quality. Collectors prized eBay for its wide variety of product offerings.

Professional Buyers

As the legitimacy of online auctions grew, a new type of buyer began to emerge: the professional buyer. Professional buyers covered a broad range of purchasers, from purchasing managers acquiring office supplies to antiques and gun dealers purchasing inventory. Like bargain hunters, professional buyers were looking for a way to help contain costs; and like hobbyists and collectors, some professional buyers were seeking unique items to supplement their inventory. The primary difference between professional buyers and other types, however, was their affiliation with commercial enterprises. With the growth of online auction sites dedicated to business-to-business auctions, professional buyers were becoming an increasingly important element of the online auction landscape.

Casual Sellers

Casual sellers included individuals who used eBay as a substitute for a classified ad listing or a garage sale to dispose of items they no longer wanted. While many casual sellers listed only a few items, some used eBay to raise money for some new project.

Hobbyist and Collector Sellers

Sellers who were hobbyists or collectors typically dealt in a limited category of goods and looked to eBay as a way to sell selected items in their collections to others who might want them. Items ranged from classic television collectibles, to hand-sewn dolls, to coins and stamps. The hobbyists and collectors used a range of traditional and online outlets to reach their target markets. A number of the sellers used auctions to supplement their retail operations, while others sold exclusively through online auctions and in fixed-price formats such as Half.com.

Power and Corporate Sellers

Power sellers were typically small to medium-sized businesses that favored eBay as a primary distribution channel for their goods and often sold tens of thousands of dollars' worth of goods every month on the site. One estimate suggested that while these power sellers accounted for only 4 percent of eBay's population, they were responsible for 80 percent of eBay's total business.[2] Individuals who were power sellers could often make a full-time job of the endeavor.

As with the evolution of buyers, commercial enterprises were becoming an increasingly important part of the online auction industry. These commercial enterprises generally achieved power-seller status relatively rapidly. On eBay, for example, some of the new power sellers were familiar names such as IBM, Compaq, and the U.S. Postal Service (which sells undeliverable items on eBay under the user name usps-mrc).

Pierre Omidyar and the Founding of eBay

Pierre Omidyar was born in Paris, France, to parents who had left Iran decades earlier. The family emigrated to the United States when Omidyar's father began a residency at Johns Hopkins University Medical Center. Omidyar attended Tufts University, where he met his future wife, Pamela Wesley, who came to Tufts from Hawaii to get a degree in biology. Upon graduating in 1988, the couple moved to California, where Omidyar, who had earned a bachelor of science degree in computer science, joined Claris, an Apple Computer subsidiary in Silicon Valley, and wrote a widely used graphics application, MacDraw. In 1991, Omidyar left Claris and cofounded Ink Development (later renamed eShop), which became a pioneer in online shopping and was eventually sold to Microsoft in 1996. In 1994 Omidyar joined General Magic as a developer services engineer and remained there until mid-1996, when he left to pursue full-time development of eBay.

Internet folklore has it that eBay was founded solely to allow Pamela to trade Pez dispensers with other collectors. While Pamela was certainly a driving force in launching the initial Web site, Pierre had long been interested in how one could establish a marketplace to bring together a fragmented market. Pierre saw eBay as a way to create a person-to-person trading community based on a democratized, efficient market where everyone could have equal access through the same medium, the Internet. Pierre set out to develop his marketplace and to meet both his and Pamela's goals. In 1995 he launched the first online auction under the name of Auctionwatch at the domain name of www.eBay.com. The name *eBay* stood for "electronic Bay area," coined because Pierre's initial concept was to attract neighbors and other interested San Francisco Bay area residents to the site to buy and sell items of mutual interest. The first auctions charged no fees to either buyers or sellers and contained mostly computer equipment (and no Pez dispensers). Pierre's fledgling venture generated $1,000 in revenue the first month and an additional $2,000 the second. Traffic grew rapidly, however, as word about the site spread in the Bay area and a community of collectors emerged, using the site to trade and chat—even some marriages resulted from exchanges in eBay chat rooms.[3]

By February, 1996 the traffic at Pierre Omidyar's site had grown so much that his Internet service provider informed him that he would have to upgrade his service. When

[2]Claire Tristram, " 'Amazoning' Amazon," www.contextmag.com, November 1999.
[3]Quentin Hardy, "The Radical Philanthropist," *Forbes*, May 1, 2000, p. 118.

Omidyar compensated for this by charging a listing fee for the auction, and saw no decrease in the number of items listed, he knew he was on to something. Although he was still working out of his home, Omidyar began looking for a partner and in May asked his friend Jeffrey Skoll to join him in the venture. While Skoll had never cared much about money, his Stanford master of business administration degree provided the firm with the business background that Omidyar lacked. With Omidyar as the visionary and Skoll as the strategist, the company embarked on a mission to "help people trade practically anything on earth."

Their concept for eBay was to "create a place where people could do business just like in the old days—when everyone got to know each other personally, and we all felt we were dealing on a one-to-one basis with individuals we could trust."

In eBay's early days, Omidyar and Skoll ran the operation alone, using a single computer to serve all of the pages. Omidyar served as CEO, chief financial officer, and president, while Skoll functioned as copresident and director. It was not long until Omidyar and Skoll grew the company to a size that forced them to move out of Pierre Omidyar's living room, due to the objections of Pamela, and into Skoll's living room. Shortly thereafter, the operations moved into the facilities of a Silicon Valley business incubator for a time until the company settled in its current facilities in San Jose, California. Exhibits 3 and 4 present eBay's recent financial statements.

eBay's Transition to Professional Management

From the beginning Pierre Omidyar intended to hire a professional manager to serve as the president of eBay: "[I would] let him or her run the company so . . . [I could] go play."[4] In 1997 both Omidyar and Skoll agreed that it was time to locate an experienced professional to function as CEO and president. In late 1997 eBay's headhunters came up with a candidate for the job: Margaret (Meg) Whitman, then general manager for Hasbro, Inc.'s preschool division. Whitman had received her bachelor of arts degree in economics from Princeton and her master of business administration from the Harvard Business School; her first job was in brand management at Procter & Gamble. Her experience also included serving as the president and CEO of FTD, the president of Stride Rite Corporation's Stride Rite Division, and as the senior vice president of marketing for the Walt Disney Company's consumer products division.

When first approached by eBay, Whitman was not especially interested in joining a company that had fewer than 40 employees and less than $6 million in revenues the previous year. It was only after repeated pleas that Whitman agreed to meet with Omidyar in Silicon Valley. After a second meeting, Whitman realized the company's enormous growth potential and agreed to give eBay a try. According to Omidyar, Meg Whitman's experience in global marketing with Hasbro's Teletubbies, Playskool, and Mr. Potato Head brands made her "the ideal choice to build upon eBay's leadership position in the one-to-one online trading market without sacrificing the quality and personal touch our users have grown to expect."[5] In addition to convincing Whitman to head eBay's operations, Omidyar had been instrumental in helping bring in other talented senior executives and in assembling a capable board of directors. Notable members of eBay's board of directors included Scott Cook, the founder of Intuit, a highly successful financial software company, and Fred D. Anderson, executive vice president and chief financial officer of Apple.

[4]"Billionaires of the Web," *Business 2.0,* June 1999.
[5]eBay press release, May 7, 1998.

EXHIBIT 3   eBay's Income Statements, 1996–2002 (In thousands, except per share figures)

	1996	1997	1998	1999	2000	2001	2002	2003
Net revenues	$32,051	$41,370	$86,129	$224,724	$431,424	$748,821	$1,214,100	$2,165,096
Cost of net revenues	6,803	8,404	16,094	57,588	95,453	134,816	213,876	416,058
Gross profit	$25,248	$32,966	$70,035	$167,136	$335,971	$614,005	$1,000,224	$1,749,038
Operating expenses:								
Sales and marketing	$13,139	$15,618	$35,976	$96,239	$166,767	$253,474	$349,650	$567,565
Product development	28	831	4,640	24,847	55,863	75,288	104,636	159,315
General and administrative	5,661	6,534	15,849	43,919	73,027	105,784	171,785	304,703
Patent litigation expense	—	—			—	—	—	29,965
Payroll taxes on stock options	—	—	0	0	2,337	2,442	4,015	9,590
Amortization of acquired intangibles	—	—	805	1,145	1,443	36,591	15,941	50,659
Merger-related costs	—	—	0	4,359	1,550	0	—	0
Total operating expenses	$18,828	$22,983	$57,270	$170,509	$300,977	$473,579	$646,027	$1,119,797
Income (loss) from operations	$6,420	$9,983	$12,765	$(3,373)	$34,994	$140,426	$354,197	$629,241
Interest and other income (expense), net	(2,607)	(1,951)	1,799	23,833	46,337	41,613	49,209	37,803
Interest expense	—	—	(2,191)	(2,319)	(3,374)	(2,851)	(1,492)	(4,314)
Impairment of certain equity investments	—	—	0	0	0	(16,245)	(3,781)	(1,230)
Income before income taxes and minority interest	$3,813	$8,032	$12,373	$18,141	$77,957	$162,943	$398,133	$661,500
Provision for income taxes	(475)	(971)	(4,789)	(8,472)	(32,725)	(80,009)	(145,946)	(206,738)
Minority interests in consolidated companies	—	—	(311)	(102)	3,062	7,514	(2,296)	(7,578)
Net income	$3,338	$7,061	$7,273	$9,567	$48,294	$90,448	$249,891	$447,184
Net income per share:								
Basic	$0.39	$0.29	$0.07	$0.04	$0.19	$0.34	$0.43	$0.69
Diluted	0.07	0.08	0.03	0.04	0.17	0.32	0.43	0.67
Weighted-average shares:								
Basic	8,490	24,428	104,128	217,674	251,776	268,971	574,992	638,288
Diluted	45,060	84,775	233,519	273,033	280,346	280,595	585,640	656,657

Source: Company financial documents.

EXHIBIT 4   eBay's Consolidated Balance Sheets, 1997–2003 (In thousands)

				Year Ended December 31			
	1997	1998	1999	2000	2001	2002	2003
Assets							
Current assets:							
Cash and cash equivalents	$3,723	$37,285	$219,679	$201,873	$523,969	$1,109,313	$1,381,513
Short-term investments	—	40,401	181,086	354,166	199,450	89,690	340,576
Accounts receivable, net	1,024	12,425	36,538	67,163	101,703	131,453	225,871
Funds receivable	—	—	—	—	—	41,014	79,893
Other current assets	220	7,479	22,531	52,262	58,683	96,988	118,029
Total current assets	$4,967	$97,590	$459,834	$675,464	$883,805	$1,468,458	$2,145,882
Long-term investments	—	—	—	—	286,998	470,227	934,171
Restricted cash and investments	—	—	—	—	129,614	134,644	127,432
Property and equipment, net	652	44,062	111,806	125,161	142,349	218,028	601,785
Goodwill	—	—	—	—	187,829	1,456,024	1,719,311
Investments	—	—	373,988	—	—	—	—
Deferred tax assets	—	—	5,639	—	21,540	84,218	—
Intangible and other assets, net	—	7,884	12,675	23,299	26,394	292,845	291,553
Total assets	$5,619	$149,536	$963,942	$1,182,403	$1,678,529	$4,040,226	$5,820,134
Liabilities and stockholders' equity							
Current liabilities:							
Accounts payable	$252	$9,997	$31,538	$31,725	$33,235	$47,424	$64,633
Funds payable and amounts due to customers	—	—	—	—	—	50,396	106,568
Accrued expenses and other current liabilities	—	6,577	32,550	60,882	94,593	199,323	356,491
Deferred revenue and customer advances	128	973	5,997	12,656	15,583	18,846	28,874
Debt and leases, current portion	258	4,047	12,285	15,272	16,111	2,970	2,840
Income taxes payable	169	1,380	6,455	11,092	20,617	67,265	87,870
Deferred tax liabilities, current	—	1,682	—	—	—	—	—
Other current liabilities	128	5,981	7,632	5,815	—	—	—
Total current liabilities	$1,124	$24,656	$88,825	$137,442	$180,139	$386,224	$647,276
Debt and leases, long-term portion	305	18,361	15,018	11,404	12,008	13,798	124,476
Deferred tax liabilities, long-term	—	—	—	—	3,629	27,625	79,238
Other liabilities	157	—	—	6,549	15,864	22,874	33,494
Minority interests	—	—	—	—	37,751	33,232	39,408
Total liabilities	$1,586	$48,998	$111,475	$168,643	$249,391	$483,753	$923,892
Series B redeemable convertible preferred stock and Series B warrants	3,018	—	—	—	—	—	—
Total stockholders' equity	1,015	100,538	852,467	1,013,760	1,429,138	3,556,473	4,896,242
	$5,619	$149,536	$963,942	$1,182,403	$1,678,529	$4,124,444	$5,820,134

Source: Company financial documents.

How an eBay Auction Worked

eBay endeavored to make it very simple to buy and sell goods. In order to sell or bid on goods, users first had to register at the site. Once they registered, users selected both a user name and a password. Unregistered users were able to browse the Web site but were not permitted to bid on any goods or list any items for auction.

On the Web site, search engines helped customers determine what goods were currently available. When registered users found an item they desired, they could choose to enter a single bid or to use automatic bidding (called proxy bidding). In automatic bidding the customer entered an initial bid sufficient to make him or her the high bidder, and then the bid would be automatically increased as others bid for the same object until the auction ended and either the bidder won or another bidder surpassed the original customer's maximum specified bid. Regardless of which bidding method they chose, users could check bids at any time and either bid again, if they had been outbid, or increase their maximum amount in the automatic bid. Users could choose to receive e-mail notification if they were outbid.

Once the auction had ended, the buyer and seller were each notified of the winning bid and were given each other's e-mail address. The parties to the auction would then privately arrange for payment and delivery of the good.

Fees and Procedures for Sellers

Buyers on eBay were not charged a fee for bidding on items, but sellers were charged an insertion fee and a "final value" fee; they could also elect to pay additional fees to promote their listing. Listing, or insertion, fees ranged from 30 cents for auctions with opening bids, minimum values, or reserve prices of between $0.01 and $0.99, to $4.80 for auctions with opening bids, minimum values, or reserve prices of $500 and up. Final value fees ranged from 1.25 to 5 percent of the final sale price and were computed according to a graduated fee schedule in which the percentage fell as the final sales price rose. As an example, in a basic auction with no promotion, if the item had brought an opening bid of $200 and eventually sold for $1,500, the total fee paid by the seller would be $35.48—the $3.60 insertion fee plus $31.88. The $31.88 was based on a fee structure of 5 percent of the first $25 (or $1.25), 2.5 percent of the additional amount between $25.01 and $1,000 (or $24.38), and 1.25 percent of the additional amount between $1,000.01 and $1,500 (or $6.25). Auction fees varied for special categories of goods such as passenger vehicles in eBay Motors that were charged a $40 transaction fee when the first successful bid was placed and a $100 insertion fee for residential, commercial, and other real estate.

Sellers could also customize items by adding photographs and featuring their item in a gallery. Sellers could indicate a photograph in the item's description if they posted the photograph on a Web site and provided eBay with the appropriate Web address. Items could be showcased in the Gallery section with a catalog of pictures rather than text. A seller who used a photograph in his or her listing could have this photograph included in the Gallery section for 25 cents or featured there for $19.95. A Gallery option was available in all categories of eBay, but fees varied between categories and the prominence of the gallery. For example, a simple gallery listing cost 25 cents, whereas a featured gallery listing, which included a periodic listing in the featured section above the general gallery, cost $19.95. In the eBay Motors gallery, options could cost as much as $99.95.

To make doing business on eBay more attractive to potential sellers, the company introduced several features. To receive a minimum price for an auction, the seller could specify an opening bid or set a reserve price on the auction. If the bidding did not top the reserve price, the seller was under no obligation to sell the item to the highest bidder and could relist the item at no additional cost. For items with a reserve price between $0.01 and $49.99, the fee was $1.00; between $50.00 and $199.99, the fee was $2.00; and for over $200, the fee was 1 percent of the reserve price. If the seller wished, he or she could also set a Buy It Now price that allowed bidders to pay a set amount for a listed item. The fee for this service was $1.00. If the Buy It Now price was met, the auction would end immediately.

As of June 11, 2001, new sellers at eBay were required to provide both a credit card number and bank account information to register. While eBay admitted that these requirements are extreme, it argued that they helped protect everyone in the community against fraudulent sellers and ensured that sellers were of legal age and were serious about listing the item on eBay.

How Transactions Were Completed

Under the terms of eBay's user agreement, if a seller received one or more bids above the stated minimum, or reserve, price, the seller was obligated to complete the transaction, although eBay had no enforcement power beyond suspending a noncompliant buyer or seller from using the company's service. In the event the buyer and seller were unable to complete the transaction, the seller notified eBay, which then credited the seller the amount of the final value fee.

When an auction ended, the eBay system validated that the bid fell within the acceptable price range. If the sale was successful, eBay automatically notified the buyer and seller via e-mail; the buyer and seller could then either work out the transaction details independent of eBay or use eBay's checkout and payment services to complete the transaction. In its original business model, at no point during the process did eBay take possession of either the item being sold or the buyer's payment. In an effort to increase revenues, eBay expanded its offerings to facilitate buyers' payments by first offering services that accepted credit card payments and electronic funds transfers on behalf of the seller and then purchasing PayPal, the leading third-party online payment facilitator in 2003. To make selling easier, eBay also had alliances with two leading shippers, the U.S. Postal Service and United Parcel Service (UPS). Both of these shippers had centers on eBay that would allow sellers to calculate postage and to print postage-paid labels. However, the buyer and seller still had to independently arrange shipping terms, with buyers typically paying for shipping. Items were sent directly from the buyer to the seller unless an independent escrow service was arranged to help ensure security.

To encourage sellers to use eBay's ancillary services the company offered an automated checkout service to help expedite communication, payment, and delivery between buyers and sellers.

Feedback Forum

In early 1996 eBay pioneered a feature called Feedback Forum to build trust among buyers and sellers and to facilitate the establishment of reputations within its community. Feedback Forum encouraged individuals to record comments about their trading partners. At the completion of each auction, both the buyer and seller were allowed to leave positive, negative, or neutral comments about each other. Individuals could dispute feedback left about them by annotating comments in question.

By assigning values of $+1$ for a positive comment, 0 for a neutral comment, and -1 for a negative comment, each trader earned a ranking that was attached to his or her user name. A user who had developed a positive reputation over time had a color-coded star symbol displayed next to his or her user name to indicate the amount of positive feedback. The highest ranking a trader could receive was "over 100,000," indicated by a red shooting star. Well-respected high-volume traders could have rankings well into the thousands.

Users who received a sufficiently negative net feedback rating (typically a -4) had their registrations suspended and were thus unable to bid on or list items for sale. Buyers could review a person's feedback profile before deciding to bid on an item listed by that person or before choosing payment and delivery methods. A sample user profile is shown in Exhibit 5.

EXHIBIT 5   A Sample Feedback Forum Profile

← Back to My eBay   Home > Services > Feedback Forum > **Member Profile**   Why does this page look different?

Member Profile: nuggett12 (50 ⭐)

Feedback Score:	**50**
Positive Feedback:	**100%**
Members who left a positive:	50
Members who left a negative:	0
All positive feedback received:	56

Learn about what these numbers mean.

Recent Ratings:

		Past Month	Past 6 Months	Past 12 Months
⊕	positive	0	16	21
⊙	neutral	0	0	0
⊖	negative	0	0	0

Bid Retractions (Past 6 months): 0

Member since: May-17-99
Location: United States
▪ ID History
▪ Items for Sale

[Contact Member]

All Feedback Received | From Buyers | From Sellers | Left for Others

56 feedback received by nuggett12   page 1 of 3

Comment	From	Date / Time	Item #
⊕ Super transaction! Lightning FAST payment! Thanks! Come back again soon :)	Seller fussypants (fpdotcomm@aol.com) (1382 ⭐)	Jan-06-04 18:25	2976322019
⊕ FAST PAYMENT!! GREAT EBAY'R!! THANKS!!	Seller cheribook (cheriberri5@aol.com) (645 ⭐)	Dec-11-03 10:35	2207627646
⊕ Very prompt and courteous buyer, great to deal with, Thanks!	Seller network482 (sales@shopoem.com) (11742 🖋)	Nov-28-03 01:04	3057703028
⊕ Very prompt and courteous buyer, great to deal with, Thanks!	Seller network482 (sales@shopoem.com) (11742 🖋)	Nov-28-03 01:04	3058162337
⊕ very good transaction	Seller hoefken@earthlink.net (hoefken@earthlink.net) (35 ☆) no longer a registered user	Nov-27-03 11:48	3061637655
⊕ FAST PAY!!! EXCELLENT!!! PLEASURE TO DO BUSINESS WITH! AAAAA+++++	Seller rafaelos (lancergroup@yahoo.com) (3907 ⭐)	Nov-25-03 08:22	2966729737
⊕ Very prompt and courteous buyer, great to deal with, Thanks!	Seller network482 (sales@shopoem.com) (11742 🖋)	Nov-14-03 08:38	3058162328
⊕ Very prompt and courteous buyer, great to deal with, Thanks!	Seller network482 (sales@shopoem.com) (11742 🖋)	Nov-14-03 08:38	3057561133
⊕ a+	Seller mountainairvideo (firebaseutah@aol.com) (1817 ⭐) 🎁	Nov-10-03 11:12	243650630174
⊕ Quick payment, and easy to deal with. Fine buyer!	Seller dumbells101 (91 ⭐)	Oct-27-03 06:29	2863059214
⊕ A very easy and fast transaction. Couldn't ask for a better buyer.	Seller cornshedprofits (1459 ⭐)	Oct-05-03 03:05	243633243888
⊕ Fast payment enjoed working with you.....	Seller mmddaa@msn.com (82 ⭐)	Sep-21-03 20:35	3627701979
⊕ Smooth transaction!	Seller phoenix_trading_co (23518 ☆)	Sep-02-03 13:47	3044087884
⊕ Smooth transaction!	Seller phoenix_trading_co (23518 ☆)	Sep-02-03 13:42	3044088621
⊕ Great seller! Delivered promptly! Smooth transaction.	Buyer barna-tarheels (3)	Aug-25-03 11:44	2188695578
⊕ Prompt payment and good communication	Seller rjpedigo (35 ☆)	Aug-17-03 14:53	3040479706
⊕ I highly recommend this seller.	Buyer jessievanderhoff (6)	Jul-21-03 11:48	3033456370
⊕ Customer is A+! We appreciate your business and fast payment!	Seller restaurant.com (100851 🖋)	Apr-14-03 13:14	2922961668
⊕ Customer is A+! We appreciate your business and fast payment!	Seller restaurant.com (100851 🖋)	Apr-14-03 13:14	2922958665
⊕ Worthwhile in every way. A+	Seller genuine_oem (29204 🖋)	Feb-10-03 21:41	1949802659
⊕ EXCELLENT eBayer, GREAT customer service, DEFFINATELY do bus. with again! AAAA++	Buyer brendon800 (81 ⭐)	Feb-09-03 18:01	2156921953
⊕ Very understanding. I Would have great confidence buying from this seller.	Buyer longinternational (142 ☆)	Feb-01-03 18:44	2156940759
⊕ Item as described & functioning. Shipping excellent. Will do business again!	Buyer brkidsman (11 ☆)	Dec-10-02 07:25	1789511721
⊕ AN EXAMPLE OF A GOOD EBAYER _ HIGHLY RECOMMENDED _ AAAAAAA++++++	Seller shilito34 (1338 ⭐)	Oct-03-02 15:12	1772433194
⊕ Super quick payment and very patient. My apologies for being late...	Seller dane_mel (107 ☆)	Sep-13-02 09:00	243518255865

Source: www.ebay.com, February 4, 2004.

The terms of eBay's user agreement prohibited actions that would undermine the integrity of the Feedback Forum, such as leaving positive feedback about oneself through other accounts or leaving multiple negative comments about someone else through other accounts. The Feedback Forum had several automated features designed to detect and prevent some forms of abuse. For example, feedback posted from the same account, positive or negative, could not affect a user's net feedback rating by more than one point, no matter how many comments an individual made. Furthermore, a user could make comments only about his or her trading partners in completed transactions. Prior to 2004, once a feedback comment was made, it could not be altered. However, as of February 9, 2004, the system was changed in response to suggestions by community members to all users to mutually withdraw feedback about each other. Withdrawn feedback would no longer impact a user's feedback rating.

The company believed its Feedback Forum was extremely useful in overcoming users' initial hesitancy about trading over the Internet, since it reduced the uncertainty of dealing with an unknown trading partner. However, there was growing concern among sellers and bidders that feedback might be positively skewed, as many eBayers chose not to leave negative feedback for fear of unfounded retribution that could damage their carefully built reputations.

eBay's Strategy to Sustain Its Market Dominance

Meg Whitman assumed the helm of eBay in February 1998 and began acting as the public face of the company. In an effort to stay in touch with her customers, Whitman hosted an auction on eBay herself. She found the experience so enlightening that she required all of eBay's managers to sell on eBay. Pierre Omidyar stepped back to become chairman of eBay's board of directors and focused his time and energy on overseeing eBay's strategic direction and growth, business model and site development, and community advocacy. Jeff Skoll, who became the vice president of strategic planning and analysis, concentrated on competitive analysis, new business planning and incubation, the development of the organization's overall strategic direction, and supervision of customer support operations.

The Move to Go Public

eBay's initial public offering (IPO) took place on September 24, 1998, with a starting price of $18 per share. The IPO exceeded that price and closed the day up 160 percent at $47. The IPO generated $66 million in new capital for the company and was recognized by several investing publications. The success of the September 1998 offering led eBay to issue a follow-up offering in April 1999 that raised an additional $600 million. As a qualification to the IPOs, eBay's board of directors retained the right to issue as many as 5 million additional shares of preferred stock with no further input from the current shareholders in case of a hostile takeover attempt.

eBay's Business Model

According to eBay's Meg Whitman, the company could best be described as a dynamic, self-regulating economy. Its business model was based on creating and maintaining a person-to-person trading community in which buyers and sellers could readily and conveniently exchange information and goods. The company's role was to function as a value-added facilitator of online buyer–seller transactions by providing a supportive infrastructure that enabled buyers and sellers to come together in an efficient and effective manner. Success depended not only on the quality of eBay's infrastructure but also on the quality and quantity of buyers and sellers attracted to the site; in management's view, this entailed maintaining a compelling trading environment, a number of trust and safety programs, a cost-effective and convenient trading experience, and strong community affinity.

EXHIBIT 6   **Share of eBay Transaction Revenue Growth, 2001–2008**

	2001(a)	2002(a)	2003(e)	2004(e)	2005(e)	2006(e)	2007(e)	2008(e)
U.S.	62.8%	48.0%	31.7%	39.1%	31.7%	32.5%	32.5%	32.7%
International	32.6	36.9	34.6	35.9	41.6	42.0	38.7	38.7
Payments	4.7	15.1	33.8	25.0	26.7	25.5	28.8	28.6
	100.0%	100.0%	100.0%	100.0%	100.0%	100.0%	100.0%	100.0%

By developing the eBay brand name and increasing the customer base, eBay endeavored to attract a sufficient number of high-quality buyers and sellers necessary to meet the organization's goals. The online auction format meant that eBay carried zero inventory and could operate a marketplace without the need for a traditional sales force.

eBay's business model was built around three profit centers: the domestic business (auction operations within the United States), international business (auction operations outside of the United States), and payments (e.g., PayPal). It was estimated that, in 2003, U.S. operations accounted for 31.7 percent of revenue growth, international's share was 34.6 percent, and the remaining 33.8 percent was from payments (see Exhibit 6).

Specific elements of eBay's business model that the company particularly recognized as key to its success included:[6]

1. The fact that it was the largest online trading forum, with a critical mass of buyers, sellers, and items listed for sale.

2. Its compelling and entertaining trading environment, which had strong values, established rules, and procedures that facilitated communication and trade between buyers and sellers.

3. Established trust and safety programs such as SafeHarbor. This program provided guidelines for trading, aided in resolving disputes, and warned and suspended (both temporarily and permanently) users who violated eBay's rules.

4. Cost-effective, convenient trading.

5. Strong community affinity.

6. An intuitive user interface that was easy to understand, arranged by topics, and fully automated.

In implementing its business model, eBay employed three main competitive tactics. First, it sought to build strategic partnerships in all stages of its value chain, creating an impressive portfolio of over 250 strategic alliances with companies such as America Online (AOL), Yahoo, IBM, Compaq, and Walt Disney. Second, it actively sought customer feedback and made improvements on the basis of this information. Third, it actively monitored both its external and internal environments for developing opportunities. One way eBay executives kept in touch with internal trends was by hosting online town hall meetings and by visiting cities with large local markets. The feedback gained from these meetings was used to adopt and adjust practices to keep customers satisfied.

eBay's Strategy

eBay's strategy to sustain growth rested on five key elements:[7]

1. *Broaden the existing trading platform* within existing product categories, across new product categories, through geographic expansion, both domestic and international, and through introduction of additional pricing formats such as fixed price sales.

---

[6]Company 10K filing with the Securities and Exchange Commission, March 3, 2001, pp. 4–6.
[7]eBay company 10K, filed March 28, 2001.

2. *Foster eBay community affinity* by instilling a vibrant, loyal eBay community experience, seeking to maintain a critical mass of frequent buyers and sellers with a vested interest in the eBay community.

3. *Enhance features and functionality* by continually updating and enhancing the features and functionality of the eBay and Half.com Web sites to ensure continuous improvement in the trading experience.

4. *Expand value-added services* to include end-to-end personal trading service by offering a variety of pre- and post-trade services to enhance the user experience and make trading easier.

5. *Continue to develop U.S. and international markets* that employ the Internet to create an efficient trading platform in local, national, and international markets that can be transformed into a seamless, truly global trading platform.

Broadening the Existing Trading Platform

Efforts intended to broaden the eBay trading platform concentrated on growing the content within current categories, broadening the range of products offered according to user preferences, and developing regionally targeted offerings. Growth in existing product categories was facilitated by deepening the content within the categories through the use of content-specific chat rooms and bulletin boards as well as targeted advertising at trade shows and in industry-specific publications.

To broaden the range of products offered, eBay developed new product categories, introduced specialty sites, and developed eBay stores. Over 2,000 new categories were added between 1998 and 2000, and by 2003 eBay offered over 27,000 categories of items (greatly expanded from the original 10 categories in 1995). Ten of these categories had gross merchandise sales of over $1 billion, including eBay Motors ($7.5 billion), Consumer Electronics ($2.6 billion), Computers ($2.4 billion), Books/Movies/Music ($2.0 billion), Clothing and Accessories ($1.8 billion), Sports ($1.8 billion), Collectibles ($1.5 billion), Toys ($1.5 billion), Home and Garden ($1.3 billion), and Jewelry and Gemstones ($1.3 billion).

Significant new product categories and specialty sites developed since eBay's early days included:

- eBay Motors, which began as a category and was developed when eBay noticed that an increasing number of automobile transactions were taking place on its site. In 2002, eBay Motors sold more than $3 billion worth of vehicles and parts and was the largest online marketplace for buying and selling autos as of mid-2003. According to Meg Whitman, "One month, we saw the miscellaneous category had a very rapid growth rate, and someone said we have to find out what's going on. It was the buying and selling of used cars. So we said, maybe what we should do is give these guys a separate category and see what happens. It worked so well that we created eBay Motors."[8] In partnership with AutoTrader.com this category was later expanded to a specialty site.

- The LiveAuctions specialty site, which allowed live bidding via the Internet for auctions occurring in brick-and-mortar auction houses around the world. Through an alliance with Icollector.com, eBay users had access to more than 300 auction houses worldwide. Auction houses that participated in this agreement were well rewarded, as more than 20 percent of their sales went to online bidders. One auction broadcast on the LiveAuctions site, held in February 2001, featured items from a rare Marilyn Monroe collection including a handwritten note from Monroe that listed her reasons for divorcing her first husband.

[8]"Q&A with eBay's Meg Whitman," *BusinessWeek E.Biz,* December 3, 2001.

- The eBay Business marketplace, launched in 2002, which allowed business-related items to be sold in one location. Items such as office technology, wholesale lots, and marketplace services were offered at this destination. By the end of 2002, over 500,000 items were listed in eBay Business each week and more than $1 billion in annualized gross merchandise sales occurred across these categories.
- eBay's Real Estate category, launched to foster eBay's emerging real estate marketplace. The offerings within this category were significantly enhanced by eBay's August 2001 acquisition of Homesdirect, which specialized in the sale of foreclosed properties owned by government agencies such as Housing and Urban Development and the Department of Veterans Affairs (formerly known as the Veterans Administration). The company estimated that a parcel of land was sold through the Real Estate category every 45 minutes during 2002.

Other notable moves to broaden the platform included the following:

- The Application Program Interface (API) and Developers Program was launched to allow other companies to use eBay's commerce engine and technology to build new sites.
- Starting in 1999, eBay launched over 60 regional sites to offer a more local flavor to eBay's offerings. These regional sites focused on the 50 largest metropolitan areas in the United States. Regional auction sites were intended to encourage the sale of items that were prohibitively expensive to ship, items that tended to have only a local appeal, and items that people preferred to view before purchasing. To supplement the regional sites, in mid-2001 eBay began offering sellers the option of having their items listed in a special seller's area in the classified sections of local newspapers. Sellers could highlight specific items, their eBay store, or their user ID in these classifieds.
- In June 2001 eBay introduced eBay stores to complement new offerings, to make it easier for sellers to build loyalty and for buyers to locate goods from specific sellers and to prevent sellers from driving bidders to the seller's own Web site. In an eBay store the entirety of a seller's auctions would be listed in one convenient location. These stores could also offer a fixed-price option from a seller and the integration of a seller's Half.com listings with their auction listings. While numerous sellers of all sizes moved to take advantage of eBay stores, the concept was especially appealing to large retailers such as IBM, Hard Rock Café, Sears, and Handspring that were moving to take advantage of eBay's reach and distribution power.
- In May 2002 eBay reached an agreement with Accenture to develop a service intended to allow large sellers to more efficiently sell their products. These sellers were able to use a wide range of tools, such as high-volume listing capabilities, expanded customer service and support, and payment and fulfillment processes.
- A fixed-price format was established through the acquisition of Half.com and allowed eBay to compete more directly with online sellers such as Amazon.com. Half.com was a fixed-price, person-to-person format that enabled buyers and sellers to trade books, CDs, movies and video games at prices starting at generally half of the retail price. Like eBay, Half.com offered a feedback system that helped buyers and sellers to build a solid reputation. eBay intended to eventually fully integrate both Half.com's listings and the feedback system into eBay's current site.

Fostering eBay Community Affinity

From its founding, eBay considered developing a loyal, vivacious trading community to be a cornerstone of its business model. This community was nurtured through open and honest communication and was built on five basic values that eBay expected its members to honor:

> We believe people are basically good.
>
> We believe everyone has something to contribute.

We believe that an honest, open environment can bring out the best in people.

We recognize and respect everyone as a unique individual.

We encourage you to treat others the way that you want to be treated.[9]

The company recognized that these values could not be imposed by fiat. According to Omidyar,

> As much as we at eBay talk about the values and encourage people to live by those values, that's not going to work unless people actually adopt those values. The values are communicated not because somebody reads the Web site and says, "Hey, this is how we want to treat each other, so I'll just start treating people that way." The values are communicated because that's how they're treated when they first arrive. Each member is passing those values on to the next member. It's little things, like you receive a note that says, "Thanks for your business."[10]

Consistent with eBay's desire to stay in touch with its customers and be responsive to their needs, the company flew in 10 new sellers every few months to hold group meetings known as Voice of the Customer. The company noted that 75–80 percent of new features were originally suggested by community members.

An example of eBay values in action took place when eBay introduced a feature that referred losing bidders to similar auctions from other eBay sellers, eliciting a strong outcry from the community. Sellers demanded to know why eBay was stealing their sales, and one longtime seller went so far as to auction a rare eBay jacket so that he could use the auction as a forum to complain about "eBay's new policy of screwing the folks who built them."[11] This caught the attention of Omidyar and Whitman, who met with the seller in his home for 45 minutes. After the meeting eBay changed its policy.

Recognizing that many new users might not get the most out of their eBay experience, and hoping to introduce new entrepreneurs to the community, the company created eBay University in August 2000. The university traveled across the country to hold two-day seminars in various cities. These seminars attracted between 400 and 500 people, who each paid $25 for the experience. Courses offered ranged from freshmen-level classes that introduced buying and selling on eBay to graduate-level classes that taught the intricacies of bulk listing and competitive tactics. eBay University was so successful that the company partnered with Evoke Communications to offer an online version of the classes. While community members gained knowledge from these classes, so did eBay. The company kept careful track of questions and concerns and used them to uncover areas that needed improvement.

A second important initiative to make the eBay community more inclusive was aimed at the fastest-growing segment of the U.S. population, adults 50 and older. In an effort to bridge the digital divide for seniors, eBay launched the Digital Opportunity Program for Seniors and set a goal of training and bringing online 1 million seniors by 2005. Specific elements of this plan included partnering with SeniorNet, the leading nonprofit computer technology trainer of seniors, and donating $1 million to this organization for training and establishing 10 new training facilities by 2005, developing a volunteer program for training seniors, and creating a specific area on eBay for Senior Citizens (www.ebay.com/seniors).

To foster a sense of community among eBay users, the company employed tools and tactics designed to promote both business and personal interactions between consumers, to foster trust between bidders and sellers, and to instill a sense of security among traders. Interactions between community members were facilitated through the creation of chat rooms based on personal interests. These chat rooms allowed individuals to learn about their chosen collectibles and to exchange information about items they collected.

---

[9]http://pages.ebay.com/help/community/values.html, January 1, 2002.
[10]"Q&A with eBay's Meg Whitman."
[11]Ibid.

To manage the flow of information in the chat rooms, eBay employees went to trade shows and conventions to seek out individuals who had knowledge about and a passion for either a specific collectible or a category of goods. These enthusiasts would act as community leaders or ambassadors; they were never referred to as employees but were compensated $1,000 a month to host online discussions with experts.

Although personal communication between members fostered a sense of community, as eBay's community grew from "the size of a small village to a large city" additional measures were necessary to ensure a continued sense of trust and honesty among users.[12] One of eBay's earliest trust-building efforts was the 1996 creation of the Feedback Forum, described earlier.

Unfortunately, the Feedback Forum was not always sufficient to ensure honesty and integrity among traders. eBay estimated that far less than 1 percent of the millions of auctions completed on the site involved some sort of fraud or illegal activity, but some users, like Clay Monroe, disagreed. Monroe, a Seattle-area trader of computer equipment, estimated that "ninety percent of the time everybody is on the up and up . . . [but] . . . ten percent of the time you get some jerk who wants to cheat you." Fraudulent or illegal acts perpetrated by sellers included misrepresentation of goods; trading in counterfeit goods or pirated goods that infringed on others' intellectual property rights; failure to deliver goods paid for by buyers; and shill bidding, whereby sellers would use a false bidder to artificially drive up the price of a good. Buyers could manipulate bids by placing an unrealistically high bid on a good to discourage other bidders and then withdraw their bid at the last moment to allow an ally to win the auction at a bargain price. Buyers could also fail to deliver payment on a completed auction.

Recognizing that fraudulent activities represented a significant danger to eBay's future, management took the Feedback Forum a step further in 1998 by launching the SafeHarbor program to provide guidelines for trade, provide information to help resolve user disputes, and respond to reports of misuse of the eBay service. The SafeHarbor initiative was expanded in 1999 to provide additional safeguards and to actively work with law enforcement agencies and members of the trading community to make eBay more secure. New elements of SafeHarbor included:

- Free insurance, with a $25 deductible for transactions under $200 and further protection for buyers and sellers who used PayPal.
- Cooperation with local law enforcement agencies to identify and prosecute fraudulent buyers and sellers.
- Enhancements to the Feedback Forum such as listing whether the user was a buyer or a seller in a transaction.
- A partnership with SquareTrade, an online dispute resolution service.
- A partnership with Escrow.com to promote the use of escrow services on purchases over $500.
- A new class of verified eBay users with an accompanying icon.
- Easy access to escrow services.
- Tougher policies relating to nonpaying bidders and shill bidders.
- Clarification of which items were not permissible to list for sale (such as items associated with Nazi Germany, the Ku Klux Klan, or other groups that glorified hate, racial intolerance, or racial violence).
- A strengthened antipiracy and anti-infringement program known as the Verified Rights Owner program (VeRO), and the introduction of dispute resolution services.

[12]Tristram, "'Amazoning' Amazon."

The use of verified buyer and seller accounts was viewed as especially significant because it allowed eBay to ensure that suspended users did not open new eBay accounts under different names. User information was verified through Atlanta-based Equifax, Inc. To further ensure that suspended users didn't register new accounts with different identities, eBay partnered with Infoglide to use a similarity search technology to examine new registrant information.

To implement these new initiatives, eBay increased the number of positions in its Safe-Harbor department from 24 to 182, including full-time employees and independent contractors. It also organized the department around the functions of investigations, community watch, and fraud prevention. The investigations group was responsible for examining reported trading violations and possible misuses of eBay. The fraud prevention group mediated customer disputes over such things as the quality of the goods sold. If a written complaint of fraud was filed against a user, eBay generally suspended the alleged offender's account, pending an investigation. Despite all of these initiatives, innovative thieves were developing new ways to cheat honest bidders and sellers as quickly as eBay could identify and ban them from the system, and many eBayers still viewed this as one of the most significant threats to the eBay community.

The community watch group worked with over 100 industry-leading companies, ranging from software publishers to toy manufactures to apparel makers, to protect intellectual property rights. To ensure that illegal items were not being sold and sale items listed did not violate intellectual property rights, this SafeHarbor group automated daily keyword searches on auction content. Offending auctions were closed and the seller was notified of the violation. Repeated violations resulted in suspension of the seller's account.

As eBay expanded its categories to include Great Collections and the new automobile categories, new safeguards were introduced to meet the unique needs of these areas. In the eBay Great Collections category, the company partnered with Collector's Universe to offer authentication and grading services for specific products such as trading cards, coins, and autographs. In the automobile area, one of eBay's fastest-growing segments, eBay partnered with Saturn to provide users with access to a nationwide automobile brand and offered a free limited one-month or 1,000-mile warranty, free purchase insurance up to $20,000 with a $500 deductible, and a special escrow service (Secure Pay) designed for the needs of automotive buyers and sellers.

Expanding Value-Added Services

Since its earliest days, eBay had realized that to be successful, its service had to be both easy to use and convenient to access. Recognizing this, the company continuously sought to add services to fill these needs by offering a variety of pre- and post-trade services to enhance the user experience and provide an end-to-end trading experience.

Early efforts in this direction included alliances with:

- Leading shipping services (USPS and UPS).
- Two companies that helped guarantee that buyers would get what they paid for (Trade-safe and I-Escrow).
- The world's largest franchiser of retail business, communications, and postal service centers (Mailboxes, Etc.).
- The leader in multicarrier Web-based shipping services for e-commerce (iShip.com).

To facilitate person-to-person credit card payments, eBay acquired PayPal, a company that specialized in transferring money from one cardholder to another, in October 2002. Using the newly acquired capabilities of PayPal, eBay was able to offer sellers the option of accepting credit card payments from other eBay users. At the end of 2002, PayPal was available to users in 38 countries, including the United States. eBay's objective was to make credit card payment a "seamless and integrated part of the trading experience."[13] The company expected that net revenues from the payments segment of PayPal would be approximately $300 to $310 million in 2003.

Developing U.S. and International Markets

As competition increased in the online auction industry, eBay began to seek growth opportunities in international markets in an effort to create a global trading community. While international buyers and sellers had been trading on eBay for some time, there were no facilities designed especially for the needs of these community members. In entering international markets, eBay considered three options: it could build a new user community from the ground up, acquire a local organization, or form a partnership with a strong local company. In realizing its goals of international growth, eBay employed all three strategies.

In late 1998, eBay's initial efforts at international expansion into Canada and the United Kingdom relied on building new user communities. The first step in establishing these communities was creating customized home pages for users in those countries. These home pages were designed to provide content and categories locally customized to the needs of users in specific countries, while providing them with access to a global trading community. Local customization in the United Kingdom was facilitated through the use of local management, grassroots and online marketing, and participation in local events.[14] In February 1999 eBay partnered with PBL Online, a leading Internet company in Australia, to offer a customized Australian and New Zealand eBay home page. When the site went live in October, 1999 transactions were denominated in Australian dollars and, while buyers could bid on auctions anywhere in the world, they could also search for items located exclusively in Australia. Further, local chat boards were designed to facilitate interaction between Australian users, and country-specific categories, such as Australian coins and stamps as well as cricket and rugby memorabilia, were offered.

To further expand its global reach, eBay acquired Germany's largest online person-to-person trading site, Alando.de AG, in June 1999. eBay's management handled the transition of service in a manner calculated to be smooth and painless for Alando.de AG's users. While users would have to comply with eBay rules and regulations, the only significant change for Alando.de AG's 50,000 registered users was that they would have to go to a new URL to transact their business.

To establish an Asian presence, in February 2000 eBay formed a joint venture with NEC to launch eBay Japan. According to the new CEO of eBay Japan, Merle Okawara, an internationally renowned executive, NEC was pleased to help eBay in leveraging the tried-and-trusted eBay business model to provide Japanese consumers with access to a global community of active online buyers and sellers. In customizing the site to the needs of Japanese users, eBay wrote the content exclusively in Japanese and allowed users to bid in yen. The site had over 800 categories ranging from internationally popular categories (such as computers, electronics, and Asian antiques) to categories with a local flavor (such as Hello Kitty, Pokémon, and pottery). The eBay Japan site also debuted a new merchant-to-person concept known as Supershops, which allowed consumers to bid on items listed by companies.

In 2001, eBay expanded into South Korea through an acquisition of a majority ownership position in the country's largest online trading service, Internet Auction Co. Ltd., and into Belgium, Brazil, Italy, France, the Netherlands, Portugal, Spain, and Sweden through the acquisition of Europe's largest online trading platform, iBazar. Further expansion in 2001 included the development of a local site in Singapore, and an equity-based alliance

---

[13]eBay press release, May 18, 1999.
[14]eBay 10K, filed March 30, 2000.

with the leading online auction site for the Spanish and Portuguese-speaking communities in Latin America, MercadoLibre.com, that would give eBay access to Argentina, Chile, Colombia, Ecuador, Mexico, Uruguay, and Venezuela.

At the end of 2003 eBay had a presence in 28 countries, including Australia, Austria, Belgium, Canada, China (through an investment in the Chinese company Eachnet), France, Germany, Ireland, Italy, the Netherlands, New Zealand, Singapore, South Korea, Spain, Sweden, Switzerland, Taiwan, Great Britain, and Latin America (through an investment in MercadoLibre.com) and held the top online auction position in every country except Taiwan, where it was a close number two to Yahoo. eBay perceived this rapid international expansion as one of the keys to attaining its goal of having $3 billion in annual revenues by 2005. Growth opportunities were especially appealing in Asia (due to rapid increases in Internet access) and Europe. The company's international business grew by 165 percent in 2002, and its largest international markets were Germany (where 75 percent of eBay users were classified as active users), the United Kingdom, and South Korea. At the end of 2002, the company said:

> [We are] going to invest heavily in international expansion, to tap the huge potential that appears to be the hallmark of Germany, the UK, and Korea and so many of the other markets that we've entered. And we're going to do all of this with the same financial discipline we have always shown by staying true to our strategy of balancing returns with appropriate investment to capitalize on the company's long-term opportunities.[15]

How eBay's Auction Site Compared with Those of Rivals

Auction sites varied in a number of respects: their inventory, the bidding process, extra services and fees, technical support, functionality, and sense of community. Since its inception eBay had gone to great lengths to make its Web site intuitive, easy to use by both buyers and sellers, and reliable. Efforts to ensure ease of use ranged from narrowly defining categories (to allow users to quickly locate desired products) to introducing services designed to personalize a user's eBay experience. Two specific services developed by eBay and launched in 1998 to increase personalization were My eBay and About Me. My eBay gave users centralized access to confidential, current information regarding their trading activities. From his or her My eBay page a user could view information pertaining to his or her current account balances with eBay; feedback rating; the status of any auctions in which he or she was participating, as either a buyer or a seller; and auctions in favorite categories. In October, eBay introduced the About Me service, which allowed users to create customized home pages that could be viewed by all other eBay members and could include elements from the My eBay page such as user ratings or items the user had listed for auction, as well as personal information and pictures. This service not only increased customer ease of use but also contributed to the sense of community among the traders; one seller stated that the About Me service "made it easier and more rewarding for me to do business with others."[16] New features and services added in 2000 included new listing functions that could make an auction stand out, including Highlight and Feature Plus, as well as a feature that allowed sellers to cross-list their products in two categories, a tool to set prequalification guidelines for bidders, a new imaging and photo hosting service that made it easier for sellers to include pictures of their goods, and the introduction of the Buy It Now tool.

Throughout its history eBay had struggled to balance its explosive growth with its technological infrastructure. To counter several significant service outages the company had faced in its early days, eBay hired Maynard Webb, a premier software engineer and troubleshooter who was working at Gateway Computer. Webb took swift action, forming alliances with key vendors such as Sun, IBM, and Microsoft, and outsourcing its technology

---

[15]2002 eBay annual report.

[16]Ann Pearson, in an eBay press release dated October 15, 1998.

EXHIBIT 7   **Performance Metris for Online Auction Firms**

	Customer Experience Metrics				
	Reliability	Efficiency			Consistency
	Percent Error Rate	Average Transaction Length (seconds)	Minimum Transaction Length (seconds)	Maximum Transaction Length (seconds)	Variability of Transaction Length (seconds)
Amazon Auctions	0.52	5.68	3.39	47.1	3.6
BidVille	0.62	3.90	.05	71.1	3.77
eBay	3.97	13.20	7.34	97.5	6.01
ePier	1.02	7.29	4.7	83	5.99
uBid	11.76	5.95	3.05	185	8.39
Yahoo Auctions	2.38	10.94	2.97	112	4.37

Source: Benchmark Study of Online Auction Performance August–September 2003, www.empirix.com.

and Web site operations to Exodus Communications and Abovenet. These outsourcing agreements were intended to allow Exodus and Abovenet to "manage network capacity and provide a more robust backbone" while eBay focused on its core business.[17] While eBay still experienced minor outages when it changed or expanded services (for example, a system crash coincided with the introduction of the original 22 regional Web sites), system downtime decreased. However, the stability of the system under eBay's explosive growth and continuous introduction of new features was a continuing management concern.

In 2003 Empirix conducted a benchmark study of online auction site performance that measured key performance metrics for six leading auction sites. This study included three customer experience metrics: efficiency (how long transactions were in seconds), consistency (how much the transaction lengths varied), and reliability (how often transactions were completed successfully). Results indicated that Amazon.com had the best performance, BidVille had the shortest transaction length, and eBay's Web applications were slower and more error prone than rivals' (see Exhibit 7).

eBay's Main Competitors

eBay considered the ability to attract buyers, the volume of transactions and selection of goods, customer service, and brand recognition to be the most important competitive factors in the online auction industry. In addition to these principal factors, eBay was also attempting to compete along several other dimensions: sense of community, system reliability, reliability of delivery and payment, Web site convenience and accessibility, level of service fees, and quality of search tools.[18]

Early in eBay's history the company's main rivals could be considered classified advertisements in newspapers, garage sales, flea markets, collectibles shows, and other venues such as local auction houses and liquidators. As eBay's product mix and selling techniques evolved, the company's range of competitors did as well. The broadening of eBay's product mix beyond collectibles to include practical household items, office equipment, toys, and so on brought the company into more direct competition with brick-and-mortar retailers, import/export companies, and catalog and mail order companies. Further, with the acquisition of Half.com, the introduction of eBay stores, and the growing percentage of fixed-price and Buy It Now sales as a percentage of eBay's revenue, eBay considered itself to be competing in a broad sense with a number of other online retailers, such as Wal-Mart, Kmart, Target, Sears, JCPenney, and Office Depot. In competing with these larger sellers, eBay began to adopt some of their tools, such as the use of gift certificates. The company also felt that it was

[17]eBay press release, October 8, 1999.

[18]Ibid.

EXHIBIT 8

Customer Service Rankings (Scores out of 100)

Sector/Company	1999	2000	2001	2002
E-commerce				
E-commerce retail	NA	78	77	83
Yahoo, Inc.	74	73	76	78
Amazon.com, Inc.	NA	84	84	88
Online Auctions Overall	NA	72	74	77
eBay	NA	80	82	82
uBid, Inc.	NA	67	69	70
Portals/search engines				
Yahoo, Inc.	74	73	76	78
Google, Inc.	NA	NA	80	82
Retail				
Overall retail	73.3	72.9	74.8	74.6
Target	74	73	77	78
Sears	71	73	76	75
Wal-Mart	72	73	75	74

Source: American Customer Satisfaction Index, www.theacsi.org.

competing with a number of specialty retailers, such as Christie's (antiques), KB Toys (toys), Blockbuster (movies), Dell (computers), Foot Locker (sporting goods), Ticketmaster (tickets), and Home Depot (tools).[19] In 2003 eBay begin experiencing competition from new sources, including portals (such as Yahoo) and search providers (such as Google and Overture) that sought to become primary launch pads for online shopping. Exhibit 8 displays eBay's customer service rankings as compared to a variety of rivals' customer service rankings.

eBay management saw traditional competitors as inefficient because their fragmented local and regional nature made it expensive and time-consuming for buyers and sellers to meet, exchange information, and complete transactions. Moreover, the competitors suffered from three other deficiencies: (1) They tended to offer limited variety and breadth of selection as compared to the millions of items available on eBay, (2) they often had high transaction costs, and (3) they were information inefficient in the sense that buyers and sellers lacked a reliable and convenient means of setting prices for sales or purchases. By the same token, eBay's management saw its online auction format as competitively superior to these rivals because (1) it facilitated buyers and sellers meeting, exchanging information, and conducting transactions; (2) it allowed buyers and sellers to bypass traditional intermediaries and trade directly, thus lowering costs; (3) it provided global reach to greater selection and a broader base of participants; (4) it permitted trading at all hours and provided continuously updated information; and (5) it fostered a sense of community among individuals with mutual interests.

Even with the strengthening competition, analysts estimated that eBay controlled approximately 85 percent of the consumer-to-consumer online auction market and 64 percent of total online auction revenue share. The most significant competitors to eBay's auction business included Amazon Auctions, Yahoo Auctions, and uBid. Two of the smaller competitors in the online auction industry included BidVille (an auction site with no listing fees and no final value fees) and ePier (60,000 members as of January, 2004). Both of these had closely copied eBay's look and fee structure and touted themselves as "alternatives to eBay."

Amazon.com Auctions

Amazon.com's business strategy was to "be the world's most customer-centric company where customers can find and discover anything they may want to buy online."[20] With its customer base of 35 million users in over 150 countries and a very well-known brand name, Amazon.com

---

[19]eBay 10Q annual report, November 14, 2001.

[20]2000 Amazon annual report.

EXHIBIT 9
Operating Results

Year	Income or (Loss) from Operations (in millions)
1996	$(6.2)
1997	(31.0)
1998	(124.5)
1999	(720.0)
2000	(863.9)
2001	(412.3)
2002	64.1
2003	400.0 (est)

was considered the closest overall competitive threat to eBay, especially as eBay expanded its business model beyond its traditional auction services. Analysts estimated that Amazon.com had a 5–7 percent share of all online retail sales, but Hitwise, an Internet competitive intelligence service, found that for the week ending September 20, 2003, eBay had a 93.6 percent share of all Web traffic to auction sites while Amazon.com had only a 1.1 percent share.

Amazon was created in July 1995 as an online bookseller and had rapidly transitioned into a full-line, one-stop-shopping retailer with a product offering that included books, music, toys, electronics, tools and hardware, lawn and patio products, video games, software, and a mall of boutiques (called z-shops). Amazon.com was the Internet's number one music, video, and book retailer. One of the distinctive features customers appreciated about Amazon.com was the extensive reviews available for each item. These product reviews were written both by professionals and by regular users who had purchased a specific product. The company's 2003 net sales were estimated between $6.2 and $6.7 billion, up almost 58.9 percent from 2002. In 2002 Amazon.com generated its first profit from operations—$64.1 million—and in 2003 operating profits increased substantially from 2002 (as seen in Exhibit 9). One significant weakness analysts noted in Amazon's financials was that the company's free shipping policies, put in place to draw more customers, had a significant, negative impact on net income.

By 2003 Amazon's management felt that it was time to strike a better balance between cost control and growth in executing a strategy intended to enhance Amazon's position as leader in retail e-commerce. An indication of the company's success was the rise in Amazon's customer base from 14 million to 20 million during 2000 and to 35 million by 2003. The company invested more than $300 million in infrastructure in 1999 and opened two international sites, www.amazon.co.uk (the United Kingdom) and www.amazon.de (Germany), and later added www.amazon.ca (Canada), www. amazon.co.jp (Japan) and www.amazon.fr (France). These sites, along with Amazon.com, were among the most popular online retail domains in Europe. By 2004 international sales had grown to over $2 billion from just $168 million in 1999 and accounted for 38 percent of all Internet sales.

Some analysts felt that in expanding its position both internationally and abroad Amazon had conceded the top spot in online auction to eBay and was looking to explore other avenues. Amazon often used strategic alliances to support its innovative expansion initiatives. For example, the company had agreements with Borders Books to allow customers to pick up Amazon.com book orders in-store, as well as e-commerce partnerships with Ashford.com, Drugstore.com, CarsDirect.com, and Sotheby's (a leading auction house for art, antiques, and collectibles), and opened a co-branded toy and video game store online with Toysrus.com. During 2003, the company announced an agreement with the band Pearl Jam to sell the group's music directly to fans through Amazon's Advantage program. By 2003 Amazon.com had over 550,000 active third-party sellers on its site and 350 branded sellers, most of them selling through shops rather than auctions. These third-party sellers accounted for over 22 percent of U.S. sales. To further expand the company's reach, in September 2003 Amazon established an independent unit called A9 that was charged with creating the best shopping search tool for Amazon's use and for use by other companies and third-party Web sites. To compete with eBay's fixed-price formats, Amazon began including links on product pages that allowed customers to view identical new and used items from third-party sellers.

uBid.com

uBid's mission statement was to "be the most recognized and trusted business-to-consumer marketplace, consistently delivering exceptional value and service to its customers and supplier partners."[21] According to the company, "uBid delivers to the customer both the cost savings of an auction and the customer care of popular brand name retail e-commerce sites, making uBid a destination point for consumer share of wallet as they capitalize on the benefits of this high performance hybrid business model."[22] As such, uBid considered itself to be in direct competition with eBay, although a distant second, especially to that portion of eBay's business that was derived from large corporations and smaller companies wanting to sell their products through an auction format. The company's business model centered on offering brand-name merchandise, often refurbished and closeout, at a deep discount in a relatively broad range of categories from leading brand-name manufacturers such as Sony, Hewlett-Packard, IBM, Compaq, AMD, Minolta, and over 1,000 other suppliers. Categories included Computer and Office; Consumer Electronics; Music, Movies & Games; Jewelry & Gifts; Travel & Events; Home & Garden; Sports; Toys & Hobbies; Apparel; Collectibles; and Everything Else. The merchandise was offered in both an online auction format in which prices started at $1.00 and through uBid's fixed-price superstore. The merchandise was sourced from corporate partners and from uBid's own operations, which included a 400,000-square-foot warehouse and refurbishment center, and their current parent company Petters Group Worldwide, and from small and medium-sized companies who were members of uBid's Certified Merchant Program. Although uBid had offered consumer-to-consumer auctions at one time, the company had discontinued this option as of 2002 due to the costs associated with policing fraud and concerns over product quality.

Founded in April 1997, uBid offered an initial public offering on the Nasdaq in December 1998. The company had experienced significantly increased revenues every year since its inception through 2000, but it had never captured the share of the auction market that its founders hoped was possible, although it at one time had a 14.7 percent share of revenues in the online auction market. In mid-2000 uBid was sold to CGMI Networks, and then it was sold again to Petters Group Worldwide in 2003. With each sale the number of workers employed by uBid fell and the product mix was changed in an attempt to find a niche market that would insulate the company from the competitive power of eBay.

Yahoo Auctions

Yahoo.com, the first online navigational guide to the Web, launched Yahoo Auctions in 1998. Yahoo.com offered services to nearly 200 million users every month in North America, Europe, Asia, and Latin America. The Web site was available in 24 countries and 12 languages. Yahoo reported net revenues of $1.11 billion in 2000 (up 88 percent from 1999) and net income of $290 million. Yahoo's user base grew from 120 million to over 180 million during 2000. In December 2000 Yahoo's traffic increased to an average of 900 million page views per day (up 94 percent from 1999). Yahoo had entered into numerous alliances and marketing agreements to generate additional traffic at its site and was investing in new technology to improve the site's performance and attractiveness.

Its auction services were provided to users free of charge in the early days, and the number of auctions listed on Yahoo increased from 670,000 to 1.3 million during the second

---

[21]www.ubid.com/about/companyinfo.asp.
[22]Ibid.

half of 1999. However, when Yahoo decided to start charging users a listing fee in January 2001, listings fell from over 2 million to about 200,000.[23] Yahoo Auctions also offered many extra services to its users. For example, the Premium Sellers Program was designed to reward the sellers that were consistently at the top of their category. These Premium Sellers were allowed enhanced promotions, premium placement, and direct access to customer support. In recognition of the fall in listings due to the listing fee instituted in January, Yahoo Auctions announced a revamped performance-based pricing model for its U.S. auctions in November 2001. In this system, which was relatively similar to eBay's, listing fees were reduced and sellers were charged according to the value of an item sold. In response to this change the number of listings rose to more than 500,000 by December 7, 2001.

While Yahoo had significant reach throughout the world, including over 25 local auction sites internationally, by 2004 Yahoo Auctions had reduced its international operations from 16 countries to 7 (Brazil, Canada, Hong Kong, Japan, Mexico, Singapore, and Taiwan). In 2002 alone Yahoo conceded its auction sites in France, Germany, Italy, Spain, and the United Kingdom and Ireland and promoted eBay's sites in each of those countries via banner ads and text links. In 2003 Yahoo sold its Australian site as well. However, in 2004 Yahoo began offering auctions in China through a joint venture with a dominant Chinese Web portal, Sina, indicating that it had not completely abandoned the international auction market. Further reinforcing Yahoo's commitment to online retail, in July 2003 Yahoo acquired Overture, which was the leading provider of commercial search as of the end of the first quarter of 2003 with more than 88,000 advertisers globally as well as an extensive affiliate distribution network. Many of the sellers who advertised on Overture also advertised on eBay, and some analysts estimated that the amount of sales by merchants through the combination of Yahoo's and Overture's offerings would total between one-half to two-thirds of that available on eBay.

eBay's New Challenges

Heading into 2004 eBay was the undisputed leader in the online auction industry. To reach this enviable position, eBay had to overcome a number of hurdles. Throughout its history, eBay faced each new challenge with an eye on its founding values and an ear for community members. Omidyar said, "What we do have to be cautious of, as we grow, is that our core is the personal trade, because the values are communicated person-to-person. It can be easy for a big company to start to believe that it's responsible for its success. Our success is really based on our members' success. They're the ones who have created this, and they're the ones who will create it in the future. If we lose sight of that, then we're in big trouble."[24] The company applied this perspective in response to significant customer concerns regarding the growing presence of corporate sellers on eBay.

Omidyar and Whitman recognized the importance of eBay's culture and were aware of the potential impact rapid growth and the evolution of the product line could have on this valued asset. When asked about the importance of the culture Omidyar said, "If we lose that, we've pretty much lost everything."[25] Whitman agreed with the importance of eBay's culture, but she did not see the influx of larger retailers and liquidators as a significant problem. Even as these sellers grew to account for 5 percent of eBay's total business in 2004 (from 1 percent in 2001), these large sellers received no favorable treatment. Whitman stated, "There are no special deals. I am passionate about creating this level playing field."[26]

[23]Troy Wolverton , "eBay Seeks to Sail into New Territory," CNET News.com, July 19, 2001.
[24]"Q&A with eBay's Pierre Omidyar," *BusinessWeek E.Biz*, December 3, 2001.
[25]"The People's Company," *BusinessWeek E.Biz*, December 3, 2001.
[26]"Queen of the Online Flea Market," Economist.com, December 30, 2003.

While this view was applauded by the smaller sellers, some larger sellers viewed these policies as overly restrictive.

Heading into 2004, eBay faced two fundamental challenges:

1. How could eBay continue to grow at its current pace given the maturing of its domestic market?

2. As eBay's business model evolved to include more fixed-price sales, could it transfer its competitive advantage in the online auction industry into the more general area of on-line retail?

Continued Growth

By virtually any measure, eBay's growth had been outstanding. However, this impressive track record, coupled with the progress they had made in reaching their stated goals had created high expectations among investors. These lofty expectations began to cause some concern among analysts as eBay's domestic core market of online auction sales began to show some warning signals. For example, in 2003 the average conversion rate (the number of auctions that were completed successfully) was approximately 51 percent, a rate that had held steady over the last two years. However, supply imbalances threatened this key metric. In many categories, as the number of sellers grew, supply was beginning to outstrip demand. One of the few categories in which demand outstripped supply was eBay Motors, which had an average of 11 bids from seven unique users for each sale. Further, almost half of eBay's registered users were from the United States and represented almost one-third of all U.S. Internet users. With the U.S. online auction market maturing and eBay maintaining the dominant market share, analysts were concerned with how much more penetration eBay could achieve.

In response to these concerns, eBay cited new trends indicating that even in the United States the company was reaching new customers and had room to grow. One of the trends eBay saw as particularly promising was the increasing use of eBay's 28,000 registered Trading Assistants and the emergence of drop-off eBay consignment services. Trading Assistants were experienced eBay sellers who, for a fee, would help users sell their items on eBay. Extending this service, drop-off consignment services began to spring up as early as 2000. These consignment services, such as AuctionDrop, QuickDrop, and Picture-It-Sold, would take physical possession of a customer's items, typically those with an eBay value of over $50, and sell them on eBay for a fee equal to between 30 and 40 percent of the item's final sale price. The company was encouraged by these activities because they reached sellers who would not normally use the Internet.

eBay also challenged the theory that the maturity of its markets was based on the company's total market penetration in key categories. For example, eBay argued that it had significant market opportunity in areas such as eBay Motors, where its $6.7 billion in gross merchandise sales accounted for less than 1 percent of the value of all vehicles sold in the United States. Based on this model, none of eBay's largest categories had a market penetration of 5 percent (see Exhibit 10).

Evolution of the Business Model

There was little concern that any company could seriously threaten eBay in its core auction business in the near future, but with the increasing use of tools such as gift certificates, the growing importance of fixed-price sales, the purchase of Half.com, and the growing popularity of Buy It Now, eBay came into more direct competition with retailers such as Amazon.com, with e-commerce solutions, and with the likes of Microsoft. Some analysts also thought that search engines such as Google that were directing customers to clients who paid to have their sites prominently featured in the search engine's results would also become a competitor in the near future, but Meg Whitman dismissed this possibility, saying, "We see Google and Yahoo search and MSN search . . . as actually enablers of our busi-

EXHIBIT 10

eBay's Largest
Auction Categories,
by Annualized Gross
Merchandise Sales, as
Fourth Quarter 2003
(In millions)

	Fourth-Quarter 2003	Market Penetration
Motors	$7,500	< 1%
Consumer electronics	2,600	1–4%
Computers	2,400	1–3%
Books, movies, music	2,000	~ 3%
Clothing and accessories	1,800	< 1%
Sports	1,800	2–5%
Collectibles	1,500	2–3%
Toys	1,500	~ 5%
Home and garden	1,100	< 1%

Source: Corporate reports, Lehman Brothers estimates, www.lehman.com.

ness," she said. "We think both natural search and paid search are allies of ours."[27] When asked about how the evolution of eBay's business model influenced the company's sphere of competition, Whitman said,

> If we were a retailer, we'd be the 27th-largest in the world. So our sellers are competing [with retailers] for consumer dollars. If you're thinking about buying a set of golf clubs or a tennis racket or a jacket or a pair of skis, you decide whether you're going to do that at eBay, at Wal-Mart, a sporting-goods store, or Macy's. I would define our competition more broadly than ever before.[28]

The threat of these competitors increased as fixed-price sales comprised an ever-increasing percentage of eBay's total sales and growth. By the end of 2003, fixed-price trading accounted for 28 percent of eBay's gross merchandise sales (the dollar value of merchandise sold) and was expected to experience continued growth throughout the foreseeable future.

The Future

Heading into 2004, eBay was almost certain to reach the aggressive growth targets it had set for itself in 2000—and its stock price reflected this belief (see Exhibit 11). In fact, most analysts forecast that eBay would meet these goals a year early. The main question that plagued investors was, How would the company continue its phenomenal growth rate? In considering future moves eBay had a few issues to address. First, how should it prioritize its efforts? Was additional expansion in the international markets the highest priority? If so, where? Alternatively, should eBay focus on further broadening its offerings to include more categories, more specialty sites, and more sellers? How much emphasis should be put on fixed-price options? If the company chose to continue expanding its fixed-price offerings, how could it position itself vis-à-vis established online retailers, and how could it defend itself against new, more diverse competitors such as paid search engines?

Finally, eBay was facing increasing dissatisfaction by some of its largest corporate sellers. Some corporate sellers were experiencing significant difficulty with selling a large volume of goods on the site while maintaining a sufficient profit margin. According to Walt Shill, the former chief of Return-Buy, a company that liquidated unsold merchandise for electronics retailers and manufacturers, eBay didn't have enough buyer demand to absorb significant quantities of a single good, such as a specific brand and model of a digital camera, in a short period

[27]Ben Berkowitz, "eBay to Experiment Again with Local Auction Sites," www.usatoday.com, February 24, 2004.
[28]"Meg Whitman on eBay's Self-Regulation," *BusinessWeek Online,* August 18, 2003.

EXHIBIT 11

eBay's Stock Price Performance, March 2003–February 2004

Source: www.bigcharts.com, February 9, 2004.

of time, as eBay was "two inches deep and miles wide."[29] Whitman acknowledged this problem and stated that, for sellers wishing to "move a thousand of the same computer in a day, eBay may not be one of the most effective channels."[30] This problem, coupled with eBay's fairness policy, was causing many large sellers such as Motorola and Circuit City to abandon selling on eBay and to search for additional sales outlets. According to Scott Wingo, CEO of ChannelAdvisor, a leading provider of auction and marketplace management software that was partially owned by eBay, eBay would need to reconsider its level-playing-field policy, which prohibited giving special perks or fee discounts to big sellers if it wanted to attract large businesses and keep growing at its current rate.[31]

When eBay posted its 2003 results in early 2004, it was apparent to most industry observers that it would easily reach its stated goals a year early. Perhaps the only significant concern among analysts and investors was whether eBay could continue its growth without stretching itself too thin, especially given Meg Whitman's philosophy, as evinced in the following statement:

> You really need to do things 100 percent. Better to do 5 things at 100 percent than 10 things at 80 percent. Because the devil in so much of this is in the detail and while we have to move very, very fast, I think you are not well served by moving incredibly rapidly and not doing things that well.[32]

[29]Nick Wingfield, "As eBay Grows, Site Disappoints Some Big Vendors," *The Wall Street Journal,* February 26, 2004.
[30]Ibid.
[31]Ibid.
[32]"What's Behind the Boom at eBay?" *BusinessWeek Online,* May 21, 1999.

Wal-Mart Stores, Inc.: A New Set of Challenges

Arthur A. Thompson *The University of Alabama*

In early 2004, Wal-Mart's president and CEO, H. Lee Scott, was bullish not only about Wal-Mart's growth prospects but also about its ability to deal with critics who were challenging the company's seemingly virtuous business model of relentlessly wringing cost efficiencies out of its supply chain and providing customers with everyday low prices. Scott and other members of Wal-Mart's highly regarded management team, as well as members of founder Sam Walton's family, could look with justifiable pride on the company's remarkable journey from humble beginnings in the 1960s as a folksy discount retailer in the boondocks of Arkansas to what in 2004 was a $260 billion retailing juggernaut in the early stages of globalizing its operations from its headquarters in Bentonville, Arkansas (which was now served by two daily nonstop flights to New York's LaGuardia Airport). Wal-Mart's growth over the past four decades was unprecedented:

	1962	1970	1980	1990	2000	2004
Sales	$1.4 million	$31 million	$1.2 billion	$26 billion	$191 billion	$256 billion
Profits	$112,000	$1.2 million	$41 million	$1 billion	$6.3 billion	$9.0 billion
Stores	9	32	276	1,528	4,188	4,906

Just as unprecedented was Wal-Mart's impact on general merchandise retailing and the attraction its stores had to shoppers. During 2003, about 140 million people in 11 countries shopped Wal-Mart's almost 4,700 stores every week. More than half of American shoppers visited a Wal-Mart at least once a month, and one-third went once a week—in 2002 an estimated 82 percent of American households made at least one purchase at Wal-Mart.[1] Since the early 1990s, the company had gone from dabbling in supermarket sales to taking the number one spot in grocery retailing worldwide. In the United States, Wal-Mart was the biggest employer in 21 states, and it employed 1.4 million people worldwide, far more than any other company.[2] It was the largest retailer in Canada and Mexico, as well as in the

---

[1]Anthony Bianco and Wendy Zellner, "Is Wal-Mart Too Powerful?" *BusinessWeek,* October 6, 2003, p. 102.

[2]Jerry Useem, "One Nation Under Wal-Mart," *Fortune,* March 3, 2003, p. 66.

United States and the world as a whole. On November 28, 2003, Wal-Mart set a one-day sales record of $1.52 billion in the United States and over $1.6 billion worldwide—figures bigger than the gross domestic products of 36 countries.

Wal-Mart's performance and prominence in the retailing industry had resulted in numerous awards. By the turn of the century, it had been named "Retailer of the Century" by *Discount Store News,* made the *Fortune* magazine lists of "Most Admired Companies in America" and "100 Best Companies to Work for in America," and been included on the *Financial Times'* "Most Respected in the World" list. In 2000, Wal-Mart was ranked fifth on Fortune's list of the "Global Most Admired Companies." In 2002, Wal-Mart became number one on the Fortune 500 list of the largest companies in America and also on *Fortune's* Global 500 list. Wal-Mart topped Fortune's 2003 list of "Most Admired Companies in America" and was recognized as the "Largest Corporate Cash Giver" by *Forbes* magazine based on the *Chronicle of Philanthropy*'s survey of sales and cash donations for 2002—Wal-Mart's cash contributions to some 80,000 organizations increased in 2002 to $136 million, up 17 percent from 2001; in addition, customers and associates raised another $70 million at Wal-Mart's stores and clubs. Wal-Mart received the 2002 Ron Brown Award, the highest presidential award recognizing outstanding achievement in employee relations and community initiatives. In 2003, American Veterans Awards gave Wal-Mart its "Corporate Patriotism Award."

Wal-Mart's success had made the Walton family (Sam Walton's heirs and living relatives) the wealthiest in the world—in 2003, five Walton family members controlled about 1.75 billion shares of Wal-Mart stock worth about $93 billion. Increases in the value of Wal-Mart's stock over the years had made hundreds of Wal-Mart employees, retirees, and shareholders millionaires or multimillionaires. Since 1970, when Wal-Mart shares were first issued to the public, the company's stock had split 11 times. A $1,650 investment in Wal-Mart stock in 1970 (100 shares purchased at the initial offer price of $16.50) equated to 204,800 shares worth $10.8 million as of December 2003.

Company Background

Sam Walton graduated from the University of Missouri in 1940 with a degree in economics and took a job as a management trainee at J. C. Penney Company. His career with Penney's ended with a call to military duty in World War II. When the war was over, Walton decided to purchase a franchise and open a Ben Franklin retail variety store in Newport, Arkansas, rather than return to Penney's. Five years later, when the lease on the Newport building was lost, Walton decided to relocate his business in Bentonville, Arkansas, where he bought a building and opened Walton's 5 & 10 as a Ben Franklin–affiliated store. By 1960 Walton was the largest Ben Franklin franchisee, with nine stores.

In 1961 Walton started to become concerned about the long-term competitive threat to variety stores posed by the emerging popularity of giant supermarkets and discounters. An avid pilot, he took off in his plane on a cross-country tour to study the changes in stores and retailing trends, then put together a plan for a discount store of his own. Walton went to Chicago to try to interest Ben Franklin executives in expanding into discount retailing; when they turned him down, he decided to go forward on his own because he believed deeply in the retailing concept of offering significant price discounts to expand sales volumes and increase overall profits. The first Wal-Mart Discount City opened July 2, 1962, in Rogers, Arkansas. The store was successful, and Walton quickly began to look for opportunities to open stores in other small towns and to attract talented people with retailing experience to help him grow the business. Although he started out as a seat-of-the-pants merchant, he had great instincts, was quick to learn from other retailers' successes and failures, and was adept at garnering ideas for improvements from employees and promptly trying them out. Sam Walton incorporated his business as Wal-Mart Stores in 1969. When the company went public in 1970 and sold 300,000 shares at $16.50 each to help finance its rapid growth, it had 38 stores and sales of $44.2 million. In 1979, with 276 stores, 21,000 employees, and operations in 11 states, Wal-Mart became the first company to reach $1 billion in sales in such a short time.

As the company grew, Sam Walton proved to be an effective and visionary leader. His folksy demeanor and his talent for motivating people, combined with a very hands-on management style and an obvious talent for discount retailing, produced a culture and a set of values and beliefs that kept Wal-Mart on a path of continuous innovation and rapid expansion. Moreover, Wal-Mart's success and Walton's personable style of leadership generated numerous stories in the media that cast the company and its founder in a positive light. As Wal-Mart emerged as the premier discount retailer in the United States in the 1980s, an uncommonly large cross-section of the American public came to know who Sam Walton was and to associate his name with Wal-Mart. Sam Walton's folksy personality, unpretentious manner, and interest in people and their feelings caused people inside and outside the company to hold him in high esteem. Regarded by many as "the entrepreneur of the century" and "a genuine American folk hero," he enjoyed a reputation of being not only a community-spirited man who was concerned for his employees but also a devoted family man who epitomized the American dream and demonstrated the virtues of hard work.

Just before Sam Walton's death in 1992, his vision was for Wal-Mart to become a $125 billion company by 2000. But his handpicked successor, David D. Glass, beat that target by almost two years. Under Glass's leadership (1988–2000), Wal-Mart's sales grew at an average annual compound rate of 19 percent, pushing revenues up from $20.6 billion to $165 billion. When David Glass retired in January 2000, H. Lee Scott was chosen as Wal-Mart's third president and CEO. In the four years that Scott had been CEO, Wal-Mart's sales had grown over $100 billion, matching the company's growth in its first 35 years. Even though there were Wal-Mart stores in all 50 states and 10 foreign countries in 2004, Scott and other senior executives believed there were sufficient domestic and foreign growth opportunities to permit the company to grow at double-digit rates for the foreseeable future and propel Wal-Mart's revenues past $500 billion by 2010.

Exhibit 1 provides a summary of Wal-Mart's financial and operating performance for the 1993–2004 fiscal years.

Yet, while a report by the prominent Boston Consulting Group said, "The world has never known a company with such ambition, capability, and momentum," in 2003 there were growing signs that the continued growth and influence of the "Beast of Bentonville" was breeding a backlash among competing retailers, organized labor, community activists, and so-called cultural progressives. Wal-Mart was drawing increasing flak from organized labor about the company's low wages and anti-union posture. It was confronting some 6,000 lawsuits on a variety of issues, including one claiming that it discriminated against female employees.

Wal-Mart's Strategy

The hallmarks of Wal-Mart's strategy were multiple store formats, low everyday prices, wide selection, a big percentage of name-brand merchandise, a customer-friendly store environment, low operating costs, innovative merchandising, a strong emphasis on customer satisfaction, disciplined expansion into new geographic markets, and in many cases using acquisitions to enter foreign markets. On the outside of every Wal-Mart store in big letters was the message "We Sell for Less." The company's advertising tag line reinforced the low-price theme: "Always low prices. Always." Major merchandise lines included housewares, consumer electronics, sporting goods, lawn and garden items, health and beauty aids,

EXHIBIT 1   **Financial and Operating Summary, Wal-Mart Stores, Fiscal Years 1993–2004 (In billions, except earnings per share data)**

| | \multicolumn{6}{c}{Fiscal Year Ending January 31} |
	2004	2003	2002	2001	2000	1993
Financial and operating data						
Net sales	$256.3	$244.5	$217.8	$191.3	$165.0	$55.5
Net sales increase	12%	12%	14%	16%	20%	26%
Domestic comparable store sales increase*	5%	5%	6%	5%	8%	11%
Cost of sales	198.7	191.8	171.6	150.3	129.7	44.2
Operating, selling, general and administrative expenses	44.9	41.0	36.2	31.6	27.0	8.3
Interest costs, net	0.8	0.9	1.2	1.2	0.8	0.3
Net income	$ 9.0	$ 8.0	$ 6.7	$ 6.3	$ 5.4	$ 2.0
Earnings per share of common stock (diluted)	$2.07	$1.81	$1.49	$1.40	$1.20	$0.44
Balance sheet data						
Current assets	$ 34.2	$30.5	$27.9	$26.6	$24.4	$10.2
Net property, plant, equipment, and capital leases	55.2	51.9	45.8	40.9	36.0	9.8
Total assets	104.9	94.7	83.5	78.1	70.3	20.6
Current liabilities	37.4	32.6	27.3	28.9	25.8	6.8
Long-term debt	17.5	16.6	15.7	12.5	13.7	3.1
Long-term obligations under capital leases	3.0	3.0	3.0	3.2	3.0	1.8
Shareholders' equity	43.6	39.3	35.1	31.3	25.8	8.6
Financial ratios						
Current ratio	0.9	0.9	1.0	0.9	0.9	1.5
Return on assets	8.6%	9.2%	8.5%	8.7%	9.5%	11.1%
Return on shareholders' equity	20.6%	21.6%	20.1%	22.0%	22.9%	25.3%
Other year-end data						
Number of domestic Wal-Mart Discount stores	1,478	1,568	1,647	1,736	1,801	1,848
Number of domestic Wal-Mart Supercenters	1,471	1,258	1,066	888	721	34
Number of domestic Sam's Clubs	538	525	500	475	463	256
Number of domestic Neighborhood Markets	64	49	31	19	7	—
Number of international stores	1,355	1,288	1,170	1,070	1,004	10

*Defined as sales at stores open a full year that have not been expanded or relocated in the past 12 months.

Source: Wal-Mart annual reports for 2003 and 2004.

apparel, home fashions, paint, bed and bath goods, hardware, jewelry, automotive repair and maintenance, toys and games, and groceries.

Multiple Store Formats

In 2004, Wal-Mart was seeking to meet customers' needs with four different retail concepts: Wal-Mart discount stores, Supercenters, neighborhood markets, and Sam's Clubs:

- *Discount stores*—These stores ranged from 40,000 to 125,000 square feet, employed an average of 150 people, and offered as many as 80,000 different items, including family apparel, automotive products, health and beauty aids, home furnishings, electronics, hardware, toys, sporting goods, lawn and garden items, pet supplies, jewelry, house-wares, prescription drugs, and packaged grocery items. Discount stores had sales in the $30 to $50 million range, depending on store size and location.

• *Supercenters*—Supercenters, which Wal-Mart started opening in 1988 to meet a demand for one-stop family shopping, joined the concept of a general merchandise discount store with that of a full-line supermarket. They ranged from 109,000 to 220,000 square feet, employed between 200 and 550 associates, had about 36 general merchandise departments, and offered up to 150,000 different items, at least 30,000 of which were grocery products. In addition to the value-priced merchandise offered at discount stores and a large supermarket section with 30,000+ items, Supercenters contained such specialty shops as vision centers, tire and lube expresses, a fast-food restaurant, portrait studios, one-hour photo centers, hair salons, banking, and employment agencies. Typical Supercenters had annual sales in the $80–$100 million range.

• *Sam's Clubs*—A store format that Wal-Mart launched in 1983, Sam's was a cash-and-carry, members-only warehouse that carried about 4,000 frequently used, mostly brand-name items in bulk quantities along with some big-ticket merchandise. The product lineup included fresh, frozen, and canned food products, candy and snack items, office supplies, janitorial and household cleaning supplies and paper products, apparel, CDs and DVDs, and an assortment of big-ticket items (TVs, tires, large and small appliances, watches, jewelry, computers, camcorders, and other electronic equipment). Stores were approximately 110,000 to 130,000 square feet in size, with most goods displayed in the original cartons stacked in wooden racks or on wooden pallets. Many items stocked were sold in bulk quantity (five-gallon containers, bundles of a dozen or more, and economy-sized boxes). Prices tended to be 10–15 percent below the prices of the company's discount stores and Supercenters since merchandising costs and store operation costs were lower. Sam's was intended to serve small businesses, churches and other religious organizations, beauty salons and barber shops, motels, restaurants, offices, local schools, families, and individuals looking for great prices on large-volume quantities or big-ticket items. Annual member fees were $30 for businesses and $35 for individuals—there were 46 million members in 2003. Sam's stores employed about 125 people each and had annual sales averaging $63 million. A number of Sam's stores were located adjacent to a Supercenter or discount store.

• *Neighborhood markets*—Neighborhood markets—the company newest store format, launched in 1998—were designed to appeal to customers who just needed groceries, pharmaceuticals and general merchandise. They were always located in markets with Wal-Mart Supercenters so as to be readily accessible to Wal-Mart's food distribution network. Neighborhood Markets ranged from 42,000 to 55,000 square feet, employed 80–100 people each, and featured fresh produce, deli foods, fresh meat and dairy items, health and beauty aids, one-hour photo and traditional photo developing services, drive-through pharmacies, stationery and paper goods, pet supplies, and household supplies—about 28,000 items in total.

Domestically, during 2004 Wal-Mart planned to open approximately 50 to 55 new discount stores, 220 to 230 new Supercenters, 25 to 30 new neighborhood markets, and 35 to 40 new Sam's Clubs. Relocations or expansions of existing discount stores accounted for approximately 140 of the new Supercenters, and approximately 20 of the Sam's Clubs were relocations or expansions.

Internationally, Wal-Mart planned to open 130 to 140 units in the 10 countries where it already had stores; of these, 30 were expected to be relocations or expansions. In 2004 Wal-Mart expected to spend $18 million to open three new stores in eastern China, an area where French retailer Carrefour (the world's second largest retailer behind Wal-Mart) and Germany's Metro AG had stores; Wal-Mart had opened 31 stores in 15 cities across the country since 1996.

Exhibit 2 shows the number of Wal-Mart stores in each state and country. There were still many locations in the United States that were underserved by Wal-Mart stores. Inner-city

EXHIBIT 2
Wal-Mart's Store
Count, January 2003

State	Discount Stores	Super centers	Sam's Clubs	Neighborhood Markets
Alabama	34	49	9	2
Alaska	6	0	3	0
Arizona	24	17	10	0
Arkansas	35	43	4	6
California	133	0	30	0
Colorado	17	29	14	0
Connecticut	27	2	3	0
Delaware	3	3	1	0
Florida	66	87	37	1
Georgia	42	61	20	0
Hawaii	6	0	1	0
Idaho	5	11	1	0
Illinois	81	33	27	0
Indiana	42	42	14	0
Iowa	27	24	7	0
Kansas	29	23	6	0
Kentucky	34	41	5	0
Louisiana	35	47	12	0
Maine	12	9	3	0
Maryland	32	5	13	0
Massachusetts	41	1	3	0
Michigan	48	14	22	0
Minnesota	34	9	12	0
Mississippi	21	41	5	1
Missouri	56	58	14	0
Montana	5	6	1	0
Nebraska	10	11	3	0
Nevada	11	7	5	0
New Hampshire	19	6	4	0
New Jersey	30	0	8	0
New Mexico	6	18	5	0
New York	52	22	18	0
North Carolina	47	52	17	0
North Dakota	8	0	2	0
Ohio	70	28	26	0
Oklahoma	41	40	7	12
Oregon	24	3	0	0
Pennsylvania	50	43	20	0
Rhode Island	8	0	1	0
South Carolina	22	37	9	0
South Dakota	6	4	2	0
Tennessee	33	57	15	2
Texas	117	155	68	24
Utah	6	15	7	1
Vermont	4	0	0	0
Virginia	21	52	13	0
Washington	29	6	2	0
West Virginia	8	20	3	0
Wisconsin	49	20	11	0
Wyoming	2	7	2	0
U.S. totals	1,568	1,258	525	49

(continued)

EXHIBIT 2
(concluded)

State	Discount Stores	Super centers	Sam's Clubs	Neighborhood Markets
International/ Worldwide				
Argentina	0	11	0	0
Brazil	0	12	8	2[a]
Canada	213	0	0	0
China	0	20	4	2
Germany	0	94	0	0
S. Korea	0	15	0	0
Mexico	472[b]	75	50	0
Puerto Rico	9	1	9	33[c]
United Kingdom	248[d]	10	0	0
International totals	942	238	71	37
Grand totals	2,510	1,496	596	86

[a]Brazil includes Todo Dias.

[b]Mexico includes 118 Bodegas, 50 Suburbias, 44 Superamas, 260 Vips.

[c]Puerto Rico includes 33 Amigos.

[d]United Kingdom includes 248 ASDA Stores.

sections of New York City had no Wal-Mart stores of any kind because ample space with plenty of parking was unavailable at a reasonable price. Wal-Mart's first Supercenter in all of California opened in 2003 at a three-story location in downtown Los Angeles that had escalators sized for shopping carts. There were no Supercenters in New Jersey, Rhode Island, Vermont, or Hawaii, and only 1 in Massachusetts and 2 in Connecticut (versus 155 in Texas, 87 in Florida, 58 in Missouri, 52 in North Carolina, 49 in Alabama, and 47 in Louisiana).

Wal-Mart's various domestic and international stores were served by 108 regional general merchandise and food distribution centers. Five additional distribution centers averaging over 1 million square feet of space were planned for 2004.

Wal-Mart's Geographic Expansion Strategy

One of the most distinctive features of Wal-Mart's domestic strategy was the manner in which it expanded outward into new geographic areas. Whereas many chain retailers achieved regional and national coverage quickly by entering the largest metropolitan centers before trying to penetrate less-populated markets, Wal-Mart always expanded into adjoining geographic areas, saturating each area with stores before moving into new territory. New stores were usually clustered within 200 miles of an existing distribution center so that daily deliveries could be made cost-effectively; new distribution centers were added as needed to support store expansion into additional areas. In the United States, the really unique feature of Wal-Mart's geographic strategy had involved opening stores in small towns surrounding a targeted metropolitan area before moving into the metropolitan area itself—an approach Sam Walton had termed "backward expansion." Wal-Mart management believed that any town with a shopping-area population of 15,000 or more was big enough to support a Wal-Mart Discount Store and that towns of 25,000 could support a Supercenter. Once stores were opened in towns around the most populous city, Wal-Mart would locate one or more stores in the metropolitan area and begin major market advertising.

By clustering new stores in a relatively small geographic area, Wal-Mart could spread advertising expenses for breaking into a new market across all the area stores, a tactic the company used to keep its advertising costs under 1 percent of sales (compared to 2 or 3 percent for other discount chains). Don Soderquist, Wal-Mart's retired senior vice chairman, explained why the company preferred its backward expansion strategy:

> Our strategy is to go into smaller markets first before we hit major metro areas because you've got a smaller population base to convince over. So you begin to get the acceptance in smaller markets and the word begins to travel around and people begin to travel further and further to get to your stores.[3]

In the small towns Wal-Mart entered, it was not unusual for a number of local businesses that carried merchandise similar to Wal-Mart's lines to fail within a year or two of Wal-Mart's arrival. Wal-Mart's low prices tended to attract customers away from apparel shops, general stores, pharmacies, sporting goods stores, shoe stores, hardware stores, supermarkets, and convenience stores operated by local merchants. The "Wal-Mart effect" in small communities was so potent that it had spawned sometimes fierce local resistance to the entry of a new Wal-Mart among both local merchants and area residents wanting to preserve the economic vitality of their downtown areas and protect against the invasion of what they considered to be an unsightly Wal-Mart store and parking lot. Consulting firms formed that specialized in advising local retailers on how to survive the opening of a Wal-Mart.

For the past several years, Wal-Mart had been driving hard to expand its geographic base of stores outside the United States through a combination of new store construction and acquisition. Acquisition of general merchandise or supermarket chains had been a part of Wal-Mart's entry and/or store expansion strategy in Canada, Mexico, Brazil, Japan, Puerto Rico, China, and Great Britain. International sales accounted for 16.7 percent of total sales in fiscal 2003, and the percentage was expected to rise in the coming years. Wal-Mart stores in China had some of the highest traffic counts of any stores in the world. Wal-Mart's entry into Japan via minority ownership of Japan's fifth largest supermarket chain, Seiyu, had stirred a retailing revolution among Japanese retailers to improve their merchandising, cut their costs, lower their prices, and streamline their supply chains. Prior to buying a minority stake in Seiyu in 2002 (with an option to increase its ownership to 67 percent by 2007), Wal-Mart had studied the Japanese market for four years. It planned to spend most of 2003–2004 getting Seiyu stores and its Japanese supply chain ready for a full-scale assault on penetrating the Japanese market with a lineup of both supermarket and general merchandise products. Sales at Wal-Mart's nearly 1,300 international stores averaged about $31 million per store in fiscal 2003; the company's international division had 2003 total sales of $40.7 billion (up 15 percent) and operating profits of $2.0 billion (up almost 56 percent).

But as Wal-Mart grew more global, management intended to "remain local" in terms of the goods it carried and in some of the ways it operated. Most store managers and senior managers in its foreign operations were natives of the countries where Wal-Mart operated; many had begun their careers as hourly employees. Wal-Mart did, however, have a program that allowed stores in different areas to exchange best practices.

Everyday Low Prices

While Wal-Mart did not invent the concept of everyday low pricing, it had done a better job than any other discount retailer in executing the strategy. The company was widely seen by consumers as being the lowest-priced general merchandise retailer in its market. Recent studies showed that prices of its grocery items were 8 to 27 percent below those of such leading supermarket chain competitors as Kroger (which used the City Market brand in the states west of the Mississippi), Safeway, and Albertson's, after making allowances for specials and loyalty cards. In-store services were also bargain-priced—customers could wire money for a flat $12.95 (versus a fee of $50 to wire $1,000 at Western Union) and could purchase money orders for 46 cents (versus 90 cents charged by the U.S. Postal Service).

---

[3]*Discount Store News,* December 18, 1989, p. 162.

Wal-Mart touted its low prices on its storefronts ("We Sell for Less"), in advertising, on signs inside its stores, and on the logos of its shopping bags. Some economists believed that Wal-Mart's everyday low prices had reduced inflationary pressures economywide, allowing all U.S. consumers to benefit from the Wal-Mart effect. The well-known financier Warren Buffet said, "You add it all up and they have contributed to the financial well-being of the American public more than any other institution I can think of."[4]

Merchandising Innovations

Wal-Mart was unusually active in testing and experimenting with new merchandising techniques. From the beginning, Sam Walton had been quick to imitate good ideas and merchandising practices employed by other retailers. According to the founder of Kmart, Sam Walton "not only copied our concepts; he strengthened them. Sam just took the ball and ran with it."[5] Wal-Mart prided itself on its "low threshold for change," and much of management's time was spent talking to vendors, employees, and customers to get ideas for how Wal-Mart could improve. Suggestions were actively solicited from employees. Most any reasonable idea was tried; if it worked well in stores where it was first tested, then it was quickly implemented in other stores. Experiments in store layout, merchandise displays, store color schemes, merchandise selection (whether to add more upscale lines or shift to a different mix of items), and sales promotion techniques were always under way. Wal-Mart was regarded as an industry leader in testing, adapting, and applying a wide range of cutting-edge merchandising approaches. In 2003 Wal-Mart was testing the merits of an in-store candy department featuring an assortment mainly targeted to children, with bulk candy from Brach's, Jelly Belly, and M&M, plus a wide range of novelty and licensed items and coin-operated kiddie rides.

Advertising

Wal-Mart relied less on advertising than most other discount chains did. The company distributed only one or two circulars per month and ran occasional TV ads, relying primarily on word of mouth to communicate its marketing message. Wal-Mart's advertising expenditures ran about 0.3 percent of sales revenues, versus 1.5 percent for Kmart and 2.3 percent for Target. Wal-Mart spent $676 million on advertising in fiscal 2003, $618 million in fiscal 2002, and $574 million in fiscal 2001. Wal-Mart's spending for radio and TV advertising was said to be so low that it didn't register on national ratings scales. Most Wal-Mart broadcast ads appeared on local TV and local cable channels. Wal-Mart did no advertising for its Sam's Club stores. The company often allowed charities to use its parking lots for their fund-raising activities.

Distribution

Over the years, Wal-Mart's management had turned the company's centralized distribution systems into a competitive edge—the company's low distribution costs and cost-effective supply chain management practices were a big reason why its prices were low. Wal-Mart got an early jump on competitors in distribution efficiency because of its rural store locations. Whereas other discount retailers relied on manufacturers and distributors to ship directly to their mostly metropolitan-area stores, Wal-Mart found that its rapid growth during the 1970s was straining suppliers' ability to use independent trucking firms to make frequent and timely deliveries to its growing number of rural store locations. To improve the delivery of merchandise to its stores, the company in 1980 began to build its own centralized distribution centers and to supply stores from these centers with daily deliveries by its own truck fleet. Wal-Mart added new distribution centers when new outlying stores could no longer be reliably and economically supported from an existing center.

[4]As quoted in Useem, "One Nation Under Wal-Mart," p. 68.
[5]As quoted in Bill Saporito, "What Sam Walton Taught America," *Fortune,* May 4, 1992, p. 105.

The Competitive Environment

Discount retailing was an intensely competitive business. Competition among discount retailers centered on pricing, store location, variations in store format and merchandise mix, store size, shopping atmosphere, and image with shoppers. Wal-Mart's primary competitors were Kmart and Target in general merchandise retailing, and in superstores that also included a full-line supermarket Super Target stores and Super Kmart stores. Wal-Mart also competed against category retailers like Best Buy and Circuit City in electronics; Toys "R" Us in toys; Goody's in apparel; Bed, Bath, and Beyond in household goods; and Kroger, Albertson's, and Safeway in groceries.

Surveys of households comparing Wal-Mart with Kmart and Target indicated that Wal-Mart had a strong competitive advantage. According to *Discount Store News:*

> When asked to compare Wal-Mart with Kmart and Target, the consensus of households is that Wal-Mart is as good or better. For example, of the households with a Wal-Mart in the area, 59 percent said that Wal-Mart is better than Kmart and Target; 33 percent said it was the same. Only 4 percent rated Wal-Mart worse than Kmart and Target . . . When asked why Wal-Mart is better, 55 percent of the respondents with a Wal-Mart in their area said lower/better prices . . . Variety/selection and good quality were the other top reasons cited by consumers when asked why Wal-Mart is better. Thirty percent said variety; 18 percent said good quality.[6]

The two largest competitors in the warehouse club segment were Costco and Sam's Clubs; BJ's Wholesale Club, a smaller East Coast chain, was the only other major U.S. player in this segment.[7] For the year ended August 31, 2003, Costco had U.S. sales of $34.4 billion at 312 stores versus $32.9 billion at 532 stores for Sam's. The average Costco store generated annual revenues of $112 million, almost double the $63 million average at Sam's. Costco catered to affluent households with upscale tastes and located its stores in mostly urban areas. Costco's 42 million members averaged 11.4 store visits annually and spent an average of $94 per visit, which compared favorably with averages of 8.5 visits and expenditures of $78 at Sam's. Costco was the nation's biggest retailer of fine wines ($600 million annually) and roasted chickens (55,000 rotisserie chickens a day). While its product line included food and household items, sporting goods, vitamins, and various other merchandise, its big attraction was big-ticket luxury items (diamonds and plasma TVs) and the latest gadgets at bargain prices (Costco capped its markups at 14 percent). Costco had beaten Sam's in being the first to sell fresh meat and produce (1986 versus 1989), to introduce private-label items (1995 versus 1998), and to sell gasoline (1995 versus 1997). Costco offered its workers good wages and fringe benefits (full-time hourly workers made about $40,000 after four years).

Wal-Mart's rapid climb to become the largest supermarket retailer had triggered heated price competition in the aisles of most supermarkets. Wal-Mart's three major rivals—Kroger, Albertson's, and Safeway—along with a host of smaller regional supermarket chains, were scrambling to cut costs, narrow the price gap with Wal-Mart, and otherwise differentiate themselves so as to retain their customer base and grow revenues. Continuing increases in the number of Wal-Mart Supercenters meant that the majority of rival supermarkets would be within 10 miles of a Supercenter by 2010. Wal-Mart had recently concluded that it took fewer area residents to support a Supercenter than the company had thought; management believed that Supercenters in urban areas could be as little as four miles apart and still attract sufficient store traffic. Kroger had announced plans to cut its

---

[6]*Discount Store News,* December 18, 1989, p. 168.

[7]The information in this paragraph is drawn from John Helyar, "The Only Company Wal-Mart Fears," *Fortune,* November 24, 2003, pp. 158–66.

costs by $500 million by January 31, 2004, to put it in better position to match Wal-Mart's lower prices on grocery items. Supermarket industry observers were speculating that either Albertson's (which was already closing underperforming stores and struggling to maintain current revenues) or Safeway (which had its hands full trying to digest a series of acquisitions of regional supermarket chains) would not survive a coming shakeout among the weaker supermarket competitors.

Wal-Mart's Approaches to Strategy Execution

To implement and execute its strategy, Wal-Mart put heavy emphasis on getting the lowest possible prices from its suppliers, forging close working relationships with key suppliers in order to capture win–win cost savings throughout its supply chain, keeping its internal operations lean and efficient, paying attention to even the tiniest details in store layouts and merchandising, making efficient use of state-of-the-art technology, and nurturing a culture that thrived on hard work, constant improvement, and pleasing customers, especially passing cost savings on to customers in the form of low prices.

Wal-Mart's Use of Cutting-Edge Technology

Wal-Mart began using computers to maintain inventory control on an item basis in its distribution centers and stores in 1974. Wal-Mart began testing point-of-sale scanners in 1981 and then committed to systemwide use of scanning bar codes in 1983—a move that improved checkout times by 25–30 percent. In 1984, Wal-Mart developed a computer-assisted merchandising system that allowed each store to tailor the product mix to its own market circumstances and sales patterns. Between 1985 and 1987 Wal-Mart installed the nation's largest private satellite communication network, which allowed two-way voice and data transmission between headquarters, the distribution centers, and the stores and one-way video transmission from Bentonville's corporate offices to distribution centers and to the stores; the system was less expensive than the previously used telephone network. The video system was used regularly by company officials to speak directly to all employees at once.

In 1989 Wal-Mart established direct satellite links with about 1,700 vendors supplying close to 80 percent of the goods sold by Wal-Mart; these links allowed the use of electronic purchase orders and instant data exchanges. Wal-Mart also used the satellite system's capabilities to develop a credit card authorization procedure that took five seconds, on average, to authorize a purchase, speeding up credit check-out by 25 percent compared to the prior manual system. In the early 1990s, through pioneering collaboration with Procter & Gamble, Wal-Mart instituted an automated reordering system that notified suppliers as their items moved through store checkout lanes; this allowed suppliers to track sales and inventories of their products (so they could plan production and schedule shipments accordingly).

Throughout the 1990s Wal-Mart continued to invest in information technology and online systems, usually being a first-mover among retailers in upgrading and improving its capabilities as new technology was introduced. By 2003 the company had developed and deployed sophisticated information technology systems and online capability that not only gave it real-time access to detailed figures on most any aspect of its operations but also made it a leader in cost-effective supply chain management. It could track the movement of goods through its entire value chain—from the sale of items at the cash register backward to stock on store shelves, in-store backup inventory, distribution center inventory, and shipments en route. Moreover, Wal-Mart collaborated with its suppliers to develop data-sharing capabilities aimed at streamlining the supply of its stores, avoiding both stockouts and excess inventories, identifying slow-selling items that might warrant replacement, and spotting ways to squeeze costs out of the supply chain. The company's Retail Link system allowed suppliers to track their wares through Wal-Mart's value chain, get hourly sales figures for each item, and monitor gross margins on each of their products (Wal-Mart's actual selling price less what it paid the supplier).

In mid-2003 Wal-Mart informed its suppliers that they would have to convert to electronic product code (EPC) technology based on radio frequency identification (RFID) systems by 2005. EPCs involved a new product numbering standard that went beyond identifying products. Every single item that rolled off a manufacturing line was embedded with an electronic tag containing a unique number. EPCs offered users significant time savings and enhanced their ability to update online databases—identifying where and when a case or pallet of goods arrived, for example—in supply chain logistics applications. EPC tags could be read by RFID scanners when brought into range of a tag reader—unlike bar codes, they did not have to be directly in the line of sight of the scanner. Wal-Mart's management expected EPC scanning would eventually be built into warehouse bin locations and store shelves, allowing the company to locate and track items throughout the supply chain in real time. With EPC and RFID capability, every single can of soup or DVD or screwdriver in Wal-Mart's supply chain network or on its store shelves could then be traced back to where and when it was made, where and when it arrived at the store, and where and when it was sold (or turned up missing). Further, EPCs linked to an online database provided a secure way of sharing product-specific information with supply chain partners. Wal-Mart management believed that EPC technology, in conjunction with the expanding production of RFID-capable printers/encoders, had the potential to revolutionize the supply chain by providing more accurate information about product movement, stock rotation, and inventory levels; it was also seen as a significant tool for preventing theft and dealing with product recalls. An IBM study indicated that EPC tagging would reduce stockouts by 33 percent, while an Accenture study showed that EPC/RFID technology could boost worker productivity by 5 percent and shrink working capital and fixed capital requirements by 5 to 30 percent.

The attention Wal-Mart management placed on using cutting-edge technology and the astuteness with which it deployed this technology along its value chain to enhance store operations and continuously drive down costs had, over the years, resulted in Wal-Mart's being widely regarded as having the most cost-effective, data-rich information technology systems of any major retailer in the world. So powerful had Wal-Mart's influence been on retail supply chain efficiency that its competitors (and many other retailers as well) had found it essential to follow Wal-Mart's lead and pursue "Wal-Martification" of their retail supply chains.[8]

Relationships with Suppliers

Wal-Mart was far and away the biggest customer of virtually all of its suppliers (see Exhibit 3). Wal-Mart's scale of operation allowed it to bargain hard with suppliers and get their bottom prices. It looked for suppliers who were dominant in their category (thus providing strong brand-name recognition), who could grow with the company, who had full product lines (so that Wal-Mart buyers could both cherry-pick and get some sort of limited exclusivity on the products the company chose to carry), who had the long-term commitment to R&D to bring new and better products to retail shelves, and who had the ability to become more efficient in producing and delivering what it supplied.

Procurement personnel spent a lot of time meeting with vendors and understanding their cost structure. By making the negotiation process transparent, Wal-Mart buyers soon learned whether a vendor was doing all it could to cut down its costs and quote Wal-Mart an attractively low price. Wal-Mart's purchasing agents were dedicated to getting the lowest prices they could, and they did not accept invitations to be wined or dined by suppliers. The marketing vice president of a major vendor told *Fortune* magazine:

[8]Paul Lightfoot, "Wal-Martification," *Operations and Fulfillment,* June 1, 2003, posted at www.opsandfulfillment.com.

EXHIBIT 3   **The Scale of Wal-Mart's Purchases from Selected Suppliers and its Market Shares in Selected Product Categories**

Supplier	Percent of Total Sales to Wal-Mart	Product Category	Wal-Mart's U.S. Market Share*
Tandy Brands Accessories	39%	Dog food	36%
Dial	28	Disposable diapers	32
Del Monte Foods	24	Photographic film	30
Clorox	23	Shampoo	30
Revlon	20–23	Paper towels	30
RJR Tobacco	20	Toothpaste	26
Procter & Gamble	17	Pain remedies	21
		CDs, DVDs, and videos	15–20
		Single-copy sales of magazines	15
Although sales percentages were not available, Wal-Mart was also the biggest customer of Disney, Campbell Soup, Kraft, and Gillette.		Although market shares were not available, Wal-Mart was also the biggest seller of toys, guns, diamonds, detergent, video games, socks, and bedding.	

*Based on sales through food, drug, and mass merchandisers.

Sources: Jerry Useem, "One Nation Under Wal-Mart," *Fortune,* March 3, 2003, p. 66; and Anthony Bianco and Wendy Zellner, "Is Wal-Mart Too Powerful?" *BusinessWeek,* October 6, 2003, p. 102.

They are very, very focused people, and they use their buying power more forcefully than anybody else in America. All the normal mating rituals are verboten. Their highest priority is making sure everybody at all times in all cases knows who's in charge, and it's Wal-Mart. They talk softly, but they have piranha hearts, and if you aren't totally prepared when you go in there, you'll have your ass handed to you.[9]

All vendors were expected to offer their best price without exception; one consultant that helped manufacturers sell to retailers observed, "No one would dare come in with a half-ass price."[10]

Even though Wal-Mart was tough in negotiating for absolute rock-bottom prices, the price quotes it got were still typically high enough to allow suppliers to earn a profit. Being a Wal-Mart supplier generally meant having a stable and dependable enough sales base to operate production facilities in a cost-effective manner. Moreover, once Wal-Mart decided to source from a vendor, then it worked closely with the vendor to find *mutually beneficial* ways to squeeze costs out of the supply chain. Every aspect of a supplier's operation got scrutinized—how products got developed, what they were made of, how costs might be reduced, what data Wal-Mart could supply that would be useful, how sharing of data online could prove beneficial, and so on. Nearly always, as they went through the process with Wal-Mart personnel, suppliers saw ways to prune costs or otherwise streamline operations in ways that enhanced their profit margins. In 1989 Wal-Mart became the first major retailer to embark on a program urging vendors to develop products and packaging that would not harm the environment. In addition, Wal-Mart expected its vendors to contribute ideas about how to make its stores more fun insofar as their products were concerned. The maker of Power Rangers products, for example, had created the world's largest inflatable structure— a 5,000-cubic-foot moon—which toured Wal-Mart parking lots.[11] Coca-Cola had routed its Los-Angeles-to-Atlanta Olympic Torch Run past as many Wal-Mart stores as possible. Those suppliers that were selected as "category managers" for such product groupings as lingerie or pet food or school supplies were expected to educate Wal-Mart on everything that was happening in their respective product category.

[9]As quoted in *Fortune,* January 30, 1989, p. 53.
[10]As quoted in Useem, "One Nation Under Wal-Mart," p. 68.
[11]Ibid., p. 74.

Some 200 vendors had established offices in Bentonville to work closely with Wal-Mart on a continuing basis—most were in an area referred to locally as "Vendorville." Vendors were encouraged to voice any problems in their relationship with Wal-Mart and to become involved in Wal-Mart's future plans. Top-priority projects ranged from using more recyclable packaging to working with Wal-Mart on merchandise displays and product mix to tweaking the just-in-time ordering and delivery system to instituting automatic reordering arrangements to coming up with new products with high customer appeal. Most recently, one of Wal-Mart's priorities was working with vendors to figure out how to localize the items carried in particular stores and thereby accommodate varying tastes and preferences of shoppers in different areas where Wal-Mart had stores. Most vendor personnel based in Bentonville spent considerable time focusing on which items in their product line were best for Wal-Mart, where they ought to be placed in the stores, how they could be better displayed, what new products ought to be introduced, and which ones ought to be rotated out.

A 2003 survey conducted by Cannondale Associates found that manufacturers believed Wal-Mart was the overall best retailer with which to do business—the fifth straight year in which Wal-Mart was ranked number one.[12] Target was ranked second, and Costco was ranked seventh. The criteria for the ranking included such factors as clearest company strategy, best store branding, best buying teams, most innovative consumer marketing/merchandising, best supply chain management practices, best overall business fundamentals, and best practice management of individual product categories. One retailing consultant said, "I think most [suppliers] would say Wal-Mart is their most profitable account."[13] While this might seem surprising because of Wal-Mart's enormous bargaining clout, the potentially greater profitability of selling to Wal-Mart stemmed from the practices of most other retailers to demand that suppliers pay sometimes steep slotting fees to win shelf space and their frequent insistence on supplier payment of such extras as in-store displays, damage allowances, handling charges, penalties for late deliveries, rebates of one kind or another, allowances for advertising, and special allowances on slow-moving merchandise that had to be cleared out with deep price discounts; further, most major retailers expected to be courted with Super Bowl tickets, trips to the Masters golf tournament, fancy dinners at conventions and trade shows, or other perks in return for their business. All of these extras represented costs that suppliers had to build into their prices. At Wal-Mart everything was boiled down to one price number, and no "funny-money" extras ever entered into the deal.[14]

Most suppliers viewed Wal-Mart's single bottom-line price and its expectation of close coordination as a win–win proposition, not only because of the benefits of cutting out all the funny-money costs and solidifying their relationship with a major customer but also because what they learned from the collaborative efforts and mutual data-sharing often had considerable benefit in the rest of their operations. Many suppliers, including Procter & Gamble, liked Wal-Mart's supply chain business model so well that they had pushed their other customers to adopt similar practices.[15]

Wal-Mart's Standards for Suppliers

In the 1990s Wal-Mart began establishing standards for its suppliers, with particular emphasis on foreign suppliers that had a history of problematic wages and working conditions. Management believed that suppliers' practices regarding workers' hours; child labor; discrimination based on race, religion, or other factors; workplace safety, and compliance with local laws and regulations could be attributed to Wal-Mart and could affect its reputation

---

[12]Reported in a *DSN Retailing Today Online* editorial by Tony Lisanti, November 10, 2003.
[13]As quoted in Useem, "One Nation Under Wal-Mart," p. 74.
[14]Ibid.
[15]Ibid.

with customers and shareholders. To mitigate the potential for being adversely affected by the manner in which its suppliers conducted their business, Wal-Mart had established a set of supplier standards and set up an internal group to see that suppliers were conforming to the published ethical standards and business practices of Wal-Mart itself.

The company's supplier standards had been through a number of changes as the concerns of Wal-Mart management evolved over time. Suppliers' factories were monitored regularly, and in February 2003 Wal-Mart took direct control of foreign factory audits. Wal-Mart had factory certification teams based in offices in Dubai, Singapore, India, and China; the offices were staffed with more than 100 Wal-Mart employees dedicated to monitoring foreign factory compliance with the company's supplier standards. All suppliers were asked to sign a document certifying their compliance with the standards and were required to post a version of the supplier standards in both English and the local language in each production facility servicing Wal-Mart.

Distribution Center Operations

Throughout the 1980s and 1990s, Wal-Mart had pursued a host of efficiency-increasing actions at its distribution centers. The company had been a global leader in automating its distribution centers and expediting the transfer of incoming shipments from manufacturers to its fleet of delivery trucks, which made daily deliveries to surrounding stores. Prior to automation, bulk cases received from manufacturers had to be opened by distribution center employees and perhaps stored in bins, then picked and repacked in quantities needed for specific stores, and finally loaded onto trucks for delivery to Wal-Mart stores—a manual process that was error-prone and sometimes slow. Using state-of-the-art technology, Wal-Mart had automated many of the labor-intensive tasks, gradually creating an ever-more-sophisticated and cost-efficient system of conveyors, bar-coding, and handheld computers, along with other devices with the capability to quickly sort incoming shipments from manufacturers into smaller, store-specific quantities and route them to waiting trucks to be sent to stores to replenish sold merchandise. Often, incoming goods from manufacturers being unloaded at one section of the warehouse were immediately sorted into store-specific amounts and conveyed directly onto waiting Wal-Mart trucks headed for those particular stores—a large portion of the incoming inventory was in a Wal-Mart distribution center an average of only 12 hours. Distribution center employees had access to real-time information regarding the inventory levels of all items in the center and used the different bar codes for pallets, bins, and shelves to pick up items for store orders. Handheld computers also enabled the packaging department to get accurate information about which items to pack for which store and what loading dock to convey them to.

Truck Fleet Operations

Wal-Mart operated a fleet of 3,500+ company-owned trucks to get goods from its 100+ distribution centers to its almost 5,000 stores. Wal-Mart hired only experienced drivers who had driven more than 300,000 accident-free miles with no major traffic violations. Distribution centers had facilities where drivers could shower, sleep, eat, or attend to personal business while waiting for their truck to be loaded. A truck dispatch coordinator scheduled the dispatch of all trucks according to the available time of drivers and estimated driving time between the distribution center and the designated store. Drivers were expected to pull their trucks up to the store dock at the scheduled time (usually late afternoon or early evening) even if they arrived early; trucks were unloaded by store personnel during nighttime hours, with a two-hour gap between each new truck delivery (if more than one was scheduled for the same night).

In instances where it was economical, Wal-Mart trucks were dispatched directly to a manufacturer's facilities, picked up goods for one or more stores, and delivered them directly, bypassing the distribution center entirely. Manufacturers that supplied certain high-volume items or even a number of different items sometimes delivered their products in truckload lots directly to some or many of Wal-Mart's stores.

Store Construction and Maintenance

Wal-Mart management worked at getting more mileage out of its capital expenditures for new stores, store renovations, and store fixtures. Ideas and suggestions were solicited from vendors regarding store layout, the design of fixtures, and space needed for effective displays. Managers had open-air offices that could be furnished economically, and store designs featured a maximum of display space that could be rearranged and refurbished easily. Wal-Mart claimed that the design and aisle width at its new Supercenters would accommodate 100 million shoppers a week. Because Wal-Mart insisted on a high degree of uniformity in the new stores it built, the architectural firm Wal-Mart employed was able to use computer modeling techniques to turn out complete specifications for 12 or more new stores a week. Moreover, the stores were designed to permit quick, inexpensive construction as well as to allow for low-cost maintenance and renovation. All stores were renovated and redecorated at least once every seven years. If a given store location was rendered obsolete by the construction of new roads or the opening of new shopping locations, then the old store was abandoned in favor of a new store at a more desirable site. In 2003, Wal-Mart stores were being expanded or relocated at the rate of 100–200 annually.

In keeping with the low-cost theme for facilities, Wal-Mart's distribution centers and corporate offices were also built economically and furnished simply. The offices of top executives were modest and unpretentious. The lighting, heating, and air-conditioning controls at all Wal-Mart stores were connected via computer to Bentonville headquarters, allowing cost-saving energy management practices to be implemented centrally and freeing store managers from the time and worry of trying to hold down utility costs. Wal-Mart mass-produced a lot of its displays in-house, not only saving money but also cutting the time needed to roll out a new display concept to as little as 30 days. The company also had a group that disposed of used fixtures and equipment via auctions at the store sites where the surplus existed—a calendar of upcoming auctions was posted on the company's Web site.

Wal-Mart's Approach to Providing Superior Customer Service

Wal-Mart tried to put some organization muscle behind its pledge of "Satisfaction Guaranteed" and do things that would make customers' shopping experience at Wal-Mart pleasant. Store managers challenged store associates to practice what Sam Walton called "aggressive hospitality." A "greeter" was stationed at store entrances to welcome customers with a smile, thank them for shopping at Wal-Mart, assist them in getting a shopping cart, and answer questions about where items were located. Clerks and checkout workers were trained to be courteous and helpful and to exhibit a "friendly, folksy attitude." All store associates were called on to display the "10-foot attitude" and commit to a pledge of friendliness: "I solemnly promise and declare that every customer that comes within ten feet of me, I will smile, look them in the eye, and greet them." Wal-Mart's management stressed five themes in training and supervising store personnel:

1. Think like a customer.
2. Sell what customers want to buy.
3. Provide a genuine value to the customer.
4. Make sure the customer has a good time.
5. Exceed the customer's expectations.

In all stores, efforts were made to present merchandise in easy-to-shop shelving and displays. Floors in the apparel section were carpeted to make the department feel homier and to make shopping seem easier on customers' feet. Store layouts were constantly scrutinized to improve shopping convenience and make it easier for customers to find items. Store employees wore blue vests to make it easier for customers to pick them out from a distance. Fluorescent lighting was recessed into the ceiling to create a softer impression than exposed fluorescent lighting strips. Yet nothing about the decor conflicted with Wal-Mart's low-price image; retailing consultants considered Wal-Mart to be very adept at sending out an effective mix of signals concerning customer service, low prices, quality merchandise, and friendliness. Wal-Mart's management believed that the effort the company put into making its stores more user-friendly and inviting caused shoppers to view Wal-Mart in a more positive light. A reporter for *Discount Store News* observed:

> The fact is that everything Wal-Mart does from store design to bar coding to lighting to greeters-regardless of how simple or complex—is implemented only after carefully considering the impact on the customer. Virtually nothing is done without the guarantee that it benefits the customer in some way . . . As a result Wal-Mart has been able to build loyalty and trust among its customers that is unparalleled among other retail giants.[16]

The Culture at Wal-Mart in 2003

Wal-Mart's culture in 2003 continued to be deeply rooted in Sam Walton's business philosophy and leadership style. Mr. Sam, as he had been fondly called, had been not only Wal-Mart's founder and patriarch but also its spiritual leader—and still was in many respects. Four key core values and business principles underpinned Sam Walton's approach to managing:[17]

- Treat employees as partners, sharing both the good and bad about the company so that they will strive to excel and participate in the rewards. (Wal-Mart fostered the concept of partnership by referring to all employees as "associates," a term Sam Walton had insisted on from the company's beginnings because it denoted a partnerlike relationship.)

- Build for the future, rather than just immediate gains, by continuing to study the changing concepts that are a mark of the retailing industry and be ready to test and experiment with new ideas.

- Recognize that the road to success includes failing, which is part of the learning process rather than a personal or corporate defect or failing. Always challenge the obvious.

- Involve associates at all levels in the total decision-making process.

Sam Walton practiced these principles diligently in his own actions and insisted that other Wal-Mart managers do the same. Up until his health failed badly in 1991, he spent several days a week visiting the stores, gauging the moods of shoppers, listening to employees discuss what was on their minds, learning what was or was not selling, gathering ideas about how things could be done better, complimenting workers on their efforts, and challenging them to come up with good ideas.

The values, beliefs, and practices that Sam Walton instilled in Wal-Mart's culture and that still carried over in 2003 were reflected in statements made in his autobiography:

> Everytime Wal-Mart spends one dollar foolishly, it comes right out of our customer's pockets. Everytime we save a dollar, that puts us one more step ahead of the competition—which is where we always plan to be.

> One person seeking glory doesn't accomplish much; at Wal-Mart, everything we've done has been the result of people pulling together to meet one common goal.

> I have always been driven to buck the system, to innovate, to take things beyond where they've been.

---

[16]*Discount Store News,* December 18, 1989, p. 161.

[17]Sam Walton with John Huey, *Sam Walton: Made in America* (New York: Doubleday, 1992), p. 12.

We paid absolutely no attention whatsoever to the way things were supposed to be done, you know, the way the rules of retail said it had to be done.

My role has been to pick good people and give them the maximum authority and responsibility.

I'm more of a manager by walking and flying around, and in the process I stick my fingers into everything I can to see how it's coming along . . . My appreciation for numbers has kept me close to our operational statements, and to all the other information we have pouring in from so many different places.

The more you share profit with your associates—whether it's in salaries or incentives or bonuses or stock discounts—the more profit will accrue to your company. Why? Because the way management treats the associates is exactly how the associates will then treat the customers. And if the associates treat the customers well, the customers will return again and again.

The real challenge in a business like ours is to become what we call servant leaders. And when they do, the team—the manager and the associates—can accomplish anything.

There's no better way to keep someone doing things the right way than by letting him or her know how much you appreciate their performance.

I like my numbers as quickly as I can get them. The quicker we get that information, the quicker we can act on it.

The bigger we get as a company, the more important it becomes for us to shift responsibility and authority toward the front lines, toward that department manager who's stocking the shelves and talking to the customer.

We give our department heads the opportunity to become real merchants at a very early stage of the game . . . we make our department heads the managers of their own businesses . . . We share everything with them: the costs of their goods, the freight costs, the profit margins. We let them see how their store ranks with every other store in the company on a constant, running basis, and we give them incentives to want to win.

We're always looking for new ways to encourage our associates out in the stores to push their ideas up through the system . . . Great ideas come from everywhere if you just listen and look for them. You never know who's going to have a great idea.

A lot of bureaucracy is really the product of some empire builder's ego . . . We don't need any of that at Wal-Mart. If you're not serving the customers, or supporting the folks who do, we don't need you.

I believe in always having goals, and always setting them high . . . The folks at Wal-Mart have always had goals in front of them. In fact, we have sometimes built real scoreboards on the stage at Saturday morning meetings.

You can't just keep doing what works one time, because everything around you is always changing. To succeed, you have to stay out in front of that change.[18]

Walton's success flowed from his cheerleading management style, his ability to instill the principles and management philosophies he preached into Wal-Mart's culture, the close watch he kept on costs, his relentless insistence on continuous improvement, and his habit of staying in close touch with both consumer and associates. It was common practice for Walton to lead cheers at annual shareholder meetings, store visits, managers' meetings, and company events. His favorite was the Wal-Mart cheer:

Give me a W!

Give me an A!

Give me an L!

[18]Ibid., pp. 10, 12, 47, 63, 115, 128, 135, 140, 213, 226–229, 233, 246, 249–254, and 256.

Give me a Squiggly!

   (Here, everybody sort of does the twist.)

Give me an M!

Give me an A!

Give me an R!

Give me a T!

What's that spell?

Wal-Mart!

Whose Wal-Mart is it?

My Wal-Mart!

Who's number one?

The Customer! Always!

In 2003, the Wal-Mart cheer was still a core part of the Wal-Mart culture and was used throughout the company at meetings of store employees, managers, and corporate gatherings in Bentonville to create a "whistle while you work" atmosphere, loosen everyone up, inject fun and enthusiasm, and get sessions started on a stimulating note. While the cheer seemed corny to outsiders, once they saw the cheer in action at Wal-Mart they came to realize its cultural power and significance. And much of Sam Walton's cultural legacy remained intact in 2003, most especially among the company's top decision makers and longtime managers. As a *Fortune* writer put it:

> Spend enough time inside the company—where nothing backs up a point better than a quotation from Walton scripture—and it's easy to get the impression that the founder is orchestrating his creation from the beyond.[19]

The Three Basic Beliefs Underlying the Wal-Mart Culture in 2003

Wal-Mart top management stressed three basic beliefs that Sam Walton had preached since 1962:

1. *Treat individuals with respect and dignity*—Management consistently drummed the theme that dedicated, hardworking, ordinary people who teamed together and who treated each other with respect and dignity could accomplish extraordinary things. Throughout company literature, comments could be found referring to Wal-Mart's "concern for the individual." Such expressions as "Our people make the difference," "We care about people," and "People helping People" were used repeatedly by Wal-Mart executives and store managers to create and nurture a family-oriented atmosphere among store associates.

2. *Service to customers*—Management stressed that the company was nothing without its customers. Management emphasized that, to satisfy customers and keep them coming back again and again, the company had to build their trust in its pricing philosophy—Wal-Mart customers had to always find the lowest prices with the best possible service. One of the standard Wal-Mart mantras preached to all associates was that the customer was boss. Associates in stores were urged to observe the rule regarding the "10-foot attitude."

3. *Strive for excellence*—The concept of striving for excellence stemmed from Sam Walton's conviction that prices were seldom as low as they needed to be and that product quality was seldom as high as customers deserved. The thesis at Wal-Mart was that new ideas and ambitious goals made the company reach further and try harder—the process

[19]Useem, "One Nation Under Wal-Mart," p. 72.

of finding new and innovative ways to push boundaries and constantly improve made the company better at what it did and contributed to higher levels of customer satisfaction. Wal-Mart managers at all levels spent much time and effort motivating associates to offer ideas for improvement and to function as partners. It was reiterated again and again that every cost counted and that every worker had a responsibility to be involved.

These three beliefs were supplemented by several supporting cultural themes and practices:

- Go all-out to exceed customers' expectations and make sure that customers have a good time shopping at Wal-Mart. Every associate repeatedly heard "The customer is boss and the future depends on you."

- Practice Sam Walton's 10 rules for building a business. Management had distilled much of Sam Walton's business philosophy into 10 rules (see Exhibit 4); these were reiterated

EXHIBIT 4   **Sam Walton's 10 Rules for Building a Business**

Rule 1: Commit to your business. Believe in it more than anybody else. I think I overcame every single one of my personal shortcomings by the sheer passion I brought to my work. I don't know if you're born with this kind of passion, or if you can learn it. But I do know you need it. If you love your work, you'll be out there every day trying to do it the best you possibly can, and pretty soon everybody around will catch the passion from you—like a fever.

Rule 2: Share your profits with all your Associates, and treat them as partners. In turn, they will treat you as a partner, and together you will all perform beyond your wildest expectations. Remain a corporation and retain control if you like, but behave as a servant leader in a partnership. Encourage your Associates to hold a stake in the company. Offer discounted stock, and grant them stock for their retirement. It's the single best thing we ever did.

Rule 3: Motivate your partners. Money and ownership alone aren't enough. Constantly, day-by-day, think of new and more interesting ways to motivate and challenge your partners. Set high goals, encourage competition, and then keep score. Make bets with outrageous payoffs. If things get stale, cross-pollinate; have managers switch jobs with one another to stay challenged. Keep everybody guessing as to what your next trick is going to be. Don't become too predictable.

Rule 4: Communicate everything you possibly can to your partners. The more they know, the more they'll understand. The more they understand, the more they'll care. Once they care, there's no stopping them. If you don't trust your Associates to know what's going on, they'll know you don't really consider them partners. Information is power, and the gain you get from empowering your Associates more than offsets the risk of informing your competitors.

Rule 5: Appreciate everything your Associates do for the business. A paycheck and a stock option will buy one kind of loyalty. But all of us like to be told how much somebody appreciates what we do for them. We like to hear it often, and especially when we have done something we're really proud of. Nothing else can quite substitute for a few well-chosen, well-timed, sincere words of praise. They're absolutely free—and worth a fortune.

Rule 6: Celebrate your successes. Find some humor in your failures. Don't take yourself so seriously. Loosen up, and everybody around you will loosen up. Have fun. Show enthusiasm—always. When all else fails, put on a costume and sing a silly song. Then make everybody else sing with you. Don't do a hula on Wall Street. It's been done. Think up your own stunt. All of this is more important, and more fun, than you think, and it really fools the competition. "Why should we take those cornballs at Wal-Mart seriously?"

Rule 7: Listen to everyone in your company. And figure out ways to get them talking. The folks on the front lines—the ones who actually talk to the customer—are the only ones who really know what's going on out there. You'd better find out what they know. This really is what total quality is all about. To push responsibility down in your organization, and to force good ideas to bubble up within it, you must listen to what your Associates are trying to tell you.

Rule 8: Exceed your customers' expectations. If you do, they'll come back over and over. Give them what they want-and a little more. Let them know you appreciate them. Make good on all your mistakes, and don't make excuses—apologize. Stand behind everything you do. The two most important words I ever wrote were on that first Wal-Mart sign, "Satisfaction Guaranteed." They're still up there, and they have made all the difference.

Rule 9: Control your expenses better than your competition. This is where you can always find the competitive advantage. For 25 years running—long before Wal-Mart was known as the nation's largest retailer—we ranked No. 1 in our industry for the lowest ratio of expenses to sales. You can make a lot of different mistakes and still recover if you run an efficient operation. Or you can be brilliant and still go out of business if you're too inefficient.

Rule 10: Swim upstream. Go the other way. Ignore the conventional wisdom. If everybody else is doing it one way, there's a good chance you can find your niche by going in exactly the opposite direction. But be prepared for a lot of folks to wave you down and tell you you're headed the wrong way. I guess in all my years, what I heard more often than anything was: a town of less than 50,000 population cannot support a discount store for very long.

Source: www.walmartstores.com, accessed December 18, 2003.

to associates and used at meetings to guide decision making and the crafting and executing of Wal-Mart's strategy.

- Observe the Sundown Rule: Answer requests by sundown on the day they are received. Management believed this working principle had to be taken seriously in a busy world in which people's job performance depended on cooperation from others.

Wal-Mart's culture had unusually deep roots at the headquarters complex in Bentonville. The numerous journalists and business executives who had been to Bentonville and spent much time at Wal-Mart's corporate offices uniformly reported being impressed with the breadth, depth, and pervasive power of the company's culture. Jack Welch, former CEO of General Electric and a potent culture builder in his own right, noted that "the place vibrated" with cultural energy. There was little evidence that the culture in Bentonville was any weaker in 2003 than it had been 12 years earlier when Sam Walton personally led the culture-building, culture-nurturing effort.

But Wal-Mart executives nonetheless were currently facing a formidable challenge in sustaining the culture in the company's distribution centers and especially in its stores. Annual turnover rates in Wal-Mart's stores were running about 45 percent in 2002–2003 and had run as high as 70 percent in 1999 when the economy was booming and the labor market was tight. Such high rates of turnover among the company's worldwide workforce of 1.4 million, coupled with the fact that Wal-Mart would need to add another 800,000 new employees from 2004 to 2008 (including 47,000 management positions) to staff its new stores and distribution centers, made keeping the culture intact outside Bentonville a Herculean task. No other company in all of business history had been confronted with cultural indoctrination of so many new employees in so many locations in such a relatively short time.

Soliciting Ideas from Associates

Associates at all levels were expected to be an integral part of the process of making the company better. Wal-Mart store managers usually spent a portion of each day walking around the store checking on how well things were going in each department, listening to associates' comments, soliciting suggestions, discussing how improvements could be made, and praising associates who were doing a good job. Store managers frequently asked associates what needed to be done better in their department and what could be changed to improve store operations. Associates who believed that a policy or procedure detracted from operations were encouraged to challenge and change it. Task forces to evaluate ideas and plan out future actions to implement them were common, and it was not unusual for the person who developed the idea to be appointed the leader of the group. An assistant store manager explained the importance of getting employees to suggest ways to boost sales:

> We are encouraged to be merchants. If a sales clerk, a checker or a stockman believes he can sell an item and wants to promote it, he is encouraged to go for it. That associate can buy the merchandise, feature it, and maintain it as long as he can sell it.[20]

That same assistant store manager, when he accidentally ordered four times as many Moon Pies for an in-store promotion as intended, was challenged by the store manager to be creative and figure out a way to sell the extra inventory. The assistant manager's solution was to create the first World Championship Moon Pie Eating Contest, held in the store's parking lot in the small town of Oneonta, Alabama. The promotion and contest drew thousands of spectators and was so successful that it became an annual store event.

Listening to employees was a very important part of each manager's job. All of Wal-Mart's top executives relied on a concept known as management by walking around; they visited stores, distribution centers, and support facilities regularly, staying on top of what

---

[20]*Discount Store News,* December 18, 1989, p. 83.

was happening and listening to what employees had to say about how things were going. Senior managers at Wal-Mart's Bentonville headquarters believed that visiting stores and listening to associates was time well spent because a number of the company's best ideas had come from Wal-Mart associates—Wal-Mart's use of people greeters at store entrances was one of those ideas.

Compensation and Incentives

New hourly associates at U.S. Wal-Mart stores were paid anywhere from $1 to $6 above the minimum wage, depending on the type of job, and could expect to receive a raise within the first year at one or both of the semiannual job evaluations. Typically, at least one raise was guaranteed in the first year if Wal-Mart planned to keep the individual on the staff. The other raise depended on how well the associate worked and improved during the year. At the store level, only the store manager was salaried; all other associates, including the department managers, were considered hourly employees. A 2003 study by *Forbes* found that Wal-Mart employees earned an average hourly wage of $7.50, which translated to an annual income of $18,000. Store clerks generally earned the least—one study showed that sales clerks earned an average of $8.23 an hour and $13,861 annually in 2001.[21] Workers that unloaded trucks and stocked store shelves could earn anywhere from $25,000 to $50,000.

Part-time jobs were most common among sales clerks and checkout personnel in the stores where customer traffic varied appreciably during days of the week and months of the year. New full-time and part-time associates became eligible for health care benefits after a six-month wait and a one-year exclusion for preexisting conditions. As of 2003, about 60 percent of the roughly 800,000 U.S. Wal-Mart associates signed up for coverage (compared with an average of 72 percent for the whole retailing industry); many Wal-Mart associates did not sign up for health care coverage because another household member already had family coverage at his or her place of employment. Worker premiums for coverage were as little as $13 every two weeks with an annual deductible of $1,000, but associates could opt for plans with a higher premium and a lower deductible.[22] The health care benefit package covered 100 percent of most major medical expenses above $1,750 in employee out-of-pocket expenses and entailed no lifetime cap on medical cost coverage (a feature offered by fewer than 50 percent of U.S. employers). The company's health benefits also included dental coverage, short- and long-term disability, an illness protection plan, and business travel accident insurance. But to help control its health care costs for associates, Wal-Mart's plan did not pay for flu shots, eye exams, child vaccinations, chiropractic services, and certain other treatments allowed in the plans of many companies; further, Wal-Mart did not pay any health care costs for retirees. Due to Wal-Mart management's recent efforts to control costs for health care benefits, the company's health care costs compared very favorably with those of other organizations:[23]

	Average Cost per Eligible Employee	
	2001	**2002**
U.S. employees of a cross-section of large, medium, and small companies	$4,924	$5,646
Employees of wholesale/retail stores	4,300	4,834
Wal-Mart employees (estimated)	3,000	3,500

[21]According to documents filed in a lawsuit against the company and cited in Bianco and Zellner, "Is Wal-Mart Too Powerful?" p. 102.

[22]Bernard Wysocki Jr. and Ann Zimmerman, "Wal-Mart Cost-Cutting Finds a Big Target in Health Benefits," *The Wall Street Journal*, September 30, 2003, p. A16.

[23]Ibid., p. A1.

Wal-Mart's package of fringe benefits for full-time employees (and some part-time employees) also included:

- Vacation and personal time.
- Holiday pay.
- Jury duty pay.
- Medical and bereavement leave.
- Military leave.
- Maternity/paternity leave.
- Confidential counseling services for associates and their families.
- Child care discounts for associates with children (through four national providers).
- GED reimbursement/scholarships for associates and their spouses.

Wal-Mart associates received 10 percent off selected merchandise and Sam's Club associates received a Sam's Club membership card at no cost.

According to management, some 60 percent of associates indicated that a major reason they joined Wal-Mart was the benefits. In addition to compensation and fringe benefits, Wal-Mart had installed an extensive system of incentives that allowed associates to share monetarily in the company's success.

The Profit-Sharing Plan

Wal-Mart maintained a profit-sharing plan for full- and part-time associates; individuals were eligible after one year and 1,000 hours of service. Annual contributions to the plan were tied to the company's profitability and were made at the sole discretion of management and the board of directors. Employees could contribute up to 15 percent of their earnings to their 401(k) accounts. Wal-Mart's contribution to each associate's profit-sharing account became vested at the rate of 20 percent per year beginning the third year of participation in the plan. After seven years of continuous employment the company's contribution became fully vested; however, if the associate left the company prior to that time, the unvested portions were redistributed to all remaining employees. The plan was funded entirely by Wal-Mart, and most of the profit-sharing contributions were invested in Wal-Mart's common stock. The company had contributed more than $2.7 billion toward associates' profit-sharing and 401(k) accounts since 1972. Company contributions to the plan totaled $98.3 million in 1991, $129.6 million in 1992, and $166 million in 1993 but had risen significantly over the last decade—annual contributions to 401(k) and profit-sharing worldwide amounted to $663 million in fiscal 2003, $555 million in fiscal 2002, and $486 million in fiscal 2001. Associates could begin withdrawals from their account upon retirement or disability, with the balance paid to family members upon death.

Stock Purchase and Stock Option Plans

A stock purchase plan was adopted in 1972 to allow eligible employees a means of purchasing shares of common stock through regular payroll deduction or annual lump-sum contribution. Prior to 1990, the yearly maximum under this program was $1,500 per eligible employee; starting in 1990 the maximum was increased to $1,800 annually. The company contributed an amount equal to 15 percent of each participating associate's contribution. Longtime employees who had started participating in the early years of the program had accumulated stock worth over $100,000. About one-fourth of Wal-Mart's employees participated in the stock purchase plan in 1993, but this percentage had since declined because many new employees opted not to participate.

In addition to regular stock purchases, certain employees qualified to participate in stock option plans; options expired 10 years from the date of the grant and could be exercised in nine annual installments. In 2003 there were over 59 million shares reserved for issuance under stock option plans. The value of options granted in recent years was substantial: $96 million (1990), $128 million (1991), $143 million (1992), and $235 million (1993).

Sales Contests and Other Incentive Programs

Associate incentive plans were in place in every store, club, distribution center, and support facility. Associates received bonuses for "good ideas," such as how to reduce shoplifting or how to improve merchandising. Wal-Mart instituted a shrinkage bonus in 1980. If a store held losses from theft and damage below the corporate goal, every associate in that store was eligible to receive up to $200. As a result, Wal-Mart's shrinkage ran about 1 percent, compared to an industry average of 2 percent. One of Wal-Mart's most successful incentive programs involved in-store sales contests that allowed departments within the store to do a special promotion and pricing on items they themselves wanted to feature. Management believed these contests boosted sales, breathed new life into an otherwise slow-selling item, and helped keep associates thinking about how to help bolster sales. In 1999 (the most recent year for which data were available), Wal-Mart paid $500 million in incentive bonuses based on store and individual performance to 525,000 full- and part-time employees.

On the basis of data provided by Wal-Mart associates, *Fortune* had included Wal-Mart on its list of the "100 Best Companies to Work For" for four of the six years from 1998 to 2003. Wal-Mart was the largest U.S. employer of African Americans and Hispanics.

However, in 2003, Wal-Mart was faced with a federal lawsuit filed by six female employees claiming that the company discriminated against women in pay, promotions, training, and job assignments—plaintiffs' attorneys were seeking class-action status for the lawsuit on behalf of all past and present female workers at Wal-Mart's U.S. stores and wholesale clubs. According to data from various sources, while two-thirds of Wal-Mart's hourly employees were women, less than 15 percent held store manager positions. There were also indications of pay gaps between male and female employees. The differences increased up the corporate ladder for the same positions, beginning with full-time hourly women employees making 6.2 percent less than their male counterparts, and female senior vice presidents making 50 percent less than men in the same position. According to a study conducted by the plaintiffs as part of their discrimination lawsuit and based on an analysis of Wal-Mart's payroll data, female workers at Wal-Mart between 1996 and 2001 earned 4.5 to 5.6 percent less than men doing similar jobs and with similar experience levels. The pay gap allegedly widened higher up the management ladder. The study found that male management trainees made an average of $23,175 a year, compared with $22,371 for women trainees. At the senior vice president level, the average male made $419,435 a year, whereas the four female senior vice presidents earned an average of $279,772.

Training

Top management was committed to providing all associates state-of-the-art training resources and development time to help achieve career objectives. The company had a number of training tools in place, including classroom courses, computer-based learning, distance learning, corporate intranet sites, mentor programs, satellite broadcasts, and skills assessments. In November 1985 the Walton Institute of Retailing was opened in affiliation with the University of Arkansas. Within a year of its inception every Wal-Mart manager from the stores, the distribution facilities, and the general office were expected to take part in special programs at the Walton Institute to strengthen and develop the company's managerial capabilities.

Management Training

Wal-Mart store managers were hired in one of three ways. Hourly associates could move up through the ranks from sales to department manager to manager of the check lanes into store management training—more than 65 percent of Wal-Mart's managers had started out as hourly associates. Second, people with outstanding merchandising skills at other retail companies were recruited to join the ranks of Wal-Mart managers. And third, Wal-Mart recruited college graduates to enter the company's training program. Store management trainees went through an intensive on-the-job training program of almost 20 weeks and then were given responsibility for an area of the store. Trainees who progressed satisfactorily and showed leadership and job knowledge were promoted to an assistant manager, which included further training in various aspects of retailing and store operations. Given Wal-Mart's continued store growth, above-average trainees could progress to store manager within five years. Through bonuses for sales increases above projected amounts and company stock options, the highest-performing store managers earned well into six figures annually.

Associate Training

Wal-Mart did not provide a specialized training course for its hourly associates. Upon hiring, an associate was immediately placed in a position for on-the-job-training. From time to time, training films were shown in associates' meetings. Store managers and department managers were expected to train and supervise the associates under them in whatever ways were needed. As one associate put it, "Mostly you learn by doing. They tell you a lot; but you learn your job every day."

Respect for the individual, one of the company's three core values, was reinforced throughout the training process for both managers and associates. Wal-Mart had been ranked among *Training* magazine's "Top Training 100" companies in 2001 and 2002.

Meetings and Rapid Response

The company used meetings both as a communication device and as a culture-building exercise. In Bentonville, there were Friday merchandising meetings and Saturday-morning meetings at 7:30 AM to review the week. The weekly merchandising meeting included buyers and merchandising staff headquartered in Bentonville and various regional managers who directed store operations.

David Glass, Wal-Mart's former CEO, explained the purpose of the Friday merchandise meetings:

> In retailing, there has always been a traditional, head-to-head confrontation between operations and merchandising. You know, the operations guys say, "Why in the world would anybody buy this? It's a dog, and we'll never sell it." Then the merchandising folks say, "There's nothing wrong with that item. If you guys were smart enough to display it well and promote it properly, it would blow out the doors." So we sit all these folks down together every Friday at the same table and just have at it.
>
> We get into some of the doggonedest, knock-down drag-outs you have ever seen. But we have a rule. We never leave an item hanging. We will make a decision in that meeting even if it's wrong, and sometimes it is. But when the people come out of that room, you would be hard-pressed to tell which ones oppose it and which ones are for it. And once we've made that decision on Friday, we expect it to be acted on in all the stores on Saturday. What we guard against around here is people saying, "Let's think about it." We make a decision. Then we act on it.[24]

At the Saturday-morning meetings—a Wal-Mart tradition since 1961—top officers, merchandising and regional managers, and other Bentonville headquarters' staff (about 100 people in all) gathered to exchange ideas on how well things were going and talk about any problems relating to the week's sales, store performance, special promotion items, store construction, distribution centers, transportation, supply chain activities, and so on. As with the Friday merchandise meetings, decisions were made about what actions needed to be taken.

[24]Walton with Huey, *Sam Walton,* pp. 225–26.

The store meetings and the Friday/Saturday meetings in Bentonville, along with the in-the-field visits by Wal-Mart management, created a strong bias for action. A *Fortune* reporter observed, "Managers suck in information from Monday to Thursday, exchange ideas on Friday and Saturday, and implement decisions in the stores on Monday."[25]

Wal-Mart's Future: Mounting Flak from Several Directions

Sam Walton had engineered the development and rapid ascendancy of Wal-Mart to the forefront of the retailing industry—the discount stores and Sam's Clubs were strategic moves that he directed. His handpicked successor, David Glass, had directed the hugely successful move into Supercenters and grocery retailing, as well as presiding over the company's growth into the world's largest retailing enterprise; the neighborhood market store format also came into being during his tenure as CEO. H. Lee Scott, Wal-Mart's third CEO, had the challenge of globalizing Wal-Mart operations and continuing the long-term process of saturating the U.S. market with Supercenters and adding other types of stores in those areas that were underserved.

But as 2003 unfolded, it was apparent that Scott had to deal with a growing number of issues and obstacles that were being thrown in Wal-Mart's path, some of which were embarrassing or threatening. Not only was the company faced with over 6,000 active lawsuits, ranging from antitrust and consumer issues to torts claims (like a customer suffering injury from falling in a store or being in a collision with a Wal-Mart truck). A couple of the lawsuits had potentially serious consequences—like the one alleging the company discriminated against women, which had potential to turn into the largest sex-bias class action ever, and a second alleging that associates were forced to work unpaid overtime. But Wal-Mart was also getting flak from other quarters, forcing management to devote more time and attention to putting out brushfires than to growing and operating the business (as had been the case during the David Glass era):

- Wal-Mart had to temporarily stop selling guns at its 118 stores across California following what California's attorney general said were hundreds of violations of state laws. Investigations by California authorities revealed that six Wal-Mart stores had released guns before the required 10-day waiting period, failed to verify the identity of buyers properly, sold illegally to felons, and committed other violations. Wal-Mart cooperated with governmental officials and agreed to immediately suspend firearms sales until corrective action could be taken and store associates properly trained on state firearms laws.

- In New York, Wal-Mart had run afoul of the state's 1988 toy weapons law. The toy guns Wal-Mart sold had an orange cap at the end of the barrel but otherwise looked real, thus violating New York laws banning toy guns with realistic colors such as black or aluminum and not complying with New York's requirement that toy guns have unremovable orange stripes along the barrel. Investigators from the state attorney general's office shopped 10 Wal-Marts in New York state from Buffalo to Long Island and purchased toy guns that violated the law at each of them. The president of New York's State Police Investigators Union said, "Without clear markings, it is extremely difficult to tell the difference between a toy gun and a real weapon." Wal-Mart acknowledged that its toy guns did not have all of the state-required markings, but the company maintained that it need only comply with federal law, which requires an orange cap on the end of the barrel. Wal-Mart had sold more than 42,000 toy guns in the state during the past two and a half years. If the state of New York prevailed in its halt of toy gun sales at Wal-Mart, it could seek damages equal to $1,000 for each illegal toy gun sold since April 1, 1997.

[25]Saporito, "What Sam Walton Taught America," p. 105.

- Immigration authorities were investigating certain Wal-Mart managers for knowingly hiring janitorial contractors who were using illegal immigrants to clean stores. In a series of predawn raids on October 23, 2003, federal agents had arrested nearly 250 illegal immigrants after cleaning shifts at 61 Wal-Mart stores in 21 states; agents also searched a manager's office at Wal-Mart's Bentonville headquarters and took 18 boxes of documents relating to cleaning contractors dating back to March 2000.[26] Federal officials reportedly had wiretaps showing that Wal-Mart officials knew its contractors were furnishing illegal cleaning crews. Several weeks later, Wal-Mart was notified that it had been included in a federal grand jury probe of the contractors. Wal-Mart, however, was indignant about the charges, saying that Wal-Mart managers at many levels knew about the problem of illegal workers in its stores and had been cooperating with federal authorities in the investigations for almost three years. Wal-Mart indicated that it had helped federal investigators tape conversations between some of its store managers and employees of the cleaning contractors suspected of using illegal immigrants; that it revised its written contracts with cleaning contractors in 2002 to include language that janitorial contractors were complying with all federal, state, and local employment laws (because of the information developed in 2001); and that it had begun bringing all janitorial work in-house rather than outsourcing such services in 2003 because outsourcing was more expensive—in October 2003 fewer than 700 Wal-Mart stores used outside cleaning contractors, down from almost half in 2000.

- United Food and Commercial Workers (UFCW) was exerting all the pressure it could to force Wal-Mart to raise its wages and benefits for associates to levels that would be comparable to union wages and benefits at unionized supermarket chains. A UFCW spokeswoman in Southern California, where union members were striking supermarket chains to protest efforts to trim health care costs, said:

  > Their productivity is becoming a model for taking advantage of workers, and our society is doomed if we think the answer is to lower our standards to Wal-Mart's level. What we need to do is to raise Wal-Mart to the standard we have set using the supermarket industry as an example so that Wal-Mart does not destroy our society community by community.[27]

  Wal-Mart's labor costs were said to be 20 percent less than those at unionized supermarkets.[28] In Dallas, 20 supermarkets had closed once Wal-Mart had saturated the area with its Supercenters. According to one source, for every Wal-Mart Supercenter opened in the next five years, two other supermarkets would be forced to close, thus casting some doubt on whether Wal-Mart's entry into a community resulted in a net increase in jobs and tax revenues.[29] One trade publication estimated that Wal-Mart's plans to open more than 1,000 Supercenters in the United States in the 2004–2008 period would boost Wal-Mart's grocery and related revenues from $82 billion to $162 billion, thus increasing its market share in groceries from 19 percent to 35 percent and its share of pharmacy and drugstore-related sales from 15 percent to 25 percent.[30]

- Opponents of "big-box" retailers had battled against Wal-Mart's efforts to locate new stores in such states as Vermont and California. Oakland officials had recently voted to limit stores with full-service supermarkets to 100,000 square feet or 2.5 acres—a move deliberately aimed at blocking Wal-Mart's plan to open 187,000-square-foot

---

[26]Ann Zimmerman, "After Huge Raid on Illegals, Wal-Mart Fires Back at U.S.," *The Wall Street Journal,* December 19, 2003, pp. A1, A10.

[27]As quoted in Lorrie Grant, "Retail Giant Wal-Mart Faces Challenges on Many Fronts," *USA Today,* November 11, 2003, p. B2.

[28]Bianco and Zellner, "Is Wal-Mart Too Powerful?" p. 103.

[29]Ibid.

[30]Ibid., p. 108.

Supercenters in the Oakland area. In Contra Costa County, near San Francisco, county supervisors enacted an ordinance prohibiting any retail outlet larger than 90,000 square feet from devoting more than 5 percent of its floor space to food or other non-taxable goods—Wal-Mart gathered enough signatures to force a referendum in March 2004, but the referendum lost due mainly to certain tactics Wal-Mart employed as opposed to citizens' rejection of Wal-Mart Supercenters.[31] Restrictive zoning codes, vocal opponents of big-box retailers (most of whom were desirous of protecting local businesses from the competition of Wal-Mart's everyday low prices), high land costs in urbanized areas, and combative labor unions were major reasons why in 2003 Wal-Mart had more stores in rural and less urbanized areas compared to major metropolitan areas. Saturating major metropolitan areas with Supercenters, Sam's Clubs, and neighborhood markets was crucial to Wal-Mart's strategy of sustaining its double-digit growth rate in the United States.

- An article by newspaper reporter Jon Talton in the August 17, 2003 issue of Phoenix's *Arizona Republic* slammed Wal-Mart on several fronts:

  Fair play is a heartland value. But Wal-Mart is known for clear-cutting the retail landscape. Competing national stores won't even consider locating within three miles of a Wal-Mart Supercenter, and local retailers go out of business. Suppliers are bullied for "everyday low prices," with the result being that many have been forced from business.

  Speaking of fair, you're the nation's largest employer, with a million "associates." But relatively few work 40-hour weeks, and a union cashier at Safeway or Albertson's can make twice as much as one of your checkers. Nor is it easy for someone making seven bucks an hour to afford your "pay-for-it-yourself" benefits.

- Wal-Mart had been criticized for refusing to stock CDs or DVDs with parental warning stickers (mostly profanity-laced hip-hop music) and for either pulling certain racy magazines (*Maxim, Stuff,* and *FHM*) from its shelves or obscuring their covers. Critics contended that Wal-Mart made no effort to survey shoppers about how they felt about such products but rather that it responded in ad hoc fashion to complaints lodged by a relative handful of customers and by conservative outside groups.[32] Wal-Mart had also been the only one of the top 10 drugstore chains to refuse to stock Preven, a morning-after contraceptive introduced in 1999, because company executives did not want its pharmacists to have to grapple with the moral dilemma of abortion.

- In Colorado, the UFCW accused Wal-Mart of harassing workers to keep them from joining its local in Denver and elsewhere. According to the complaint filed with the National Labor Relations Board, Wal-Mart managers at a Denver store threatened, intimidated, and illegally monitored employees who were organizing. Similar complaints had previously been filed in Florida and Texas. A Wal-Mart spokesman denied the charge concerning the Denver store and noted that similar complaints at other locations had been dismissed without a hearing. Even so, Wal-Mart, which had an official policy of being strongly opposed to unionization, had seen the number of complaints about its efforts to prevent unionization grow in recent years—so far, 17 complaints had been filed in 12 states.

A Web site called Walmartwatch.com had sprung up to collect and publicize reports of misbehavior and wrongful conduct on the part of Wal-Mart management and the company's growing economic power and influence. A union-affiliated Web site (www.nlcnet.org), run by the National Labor Committee, was also disseminating anti–Wal-Mart information.

H. Lee Scott was understandably concerned about the raft of issues that threatened to mar Wal-Mart's reputation and raise questions about the company's efforts to secure the

---

[31]Ibid.
[32]Ibid., pp. 104, 106.

lowest prices for its customers. He recognized that the company's size and market standing made it an attractive target for critics; as he put it, "In the past we were judged by our aspirations. Now, we're going to be judged by our exceptions."[33] Scott had launched his own investigations into the sex-bias claims and the use of illegal workers and vowed that there would be zero tolerance on Wal-Mart's part for misbehavior:

> Wal-Mart does not and will not tolerate illegal workers in any capacity. Whatever we find, we would be shocked if a Wal-Mart executive were ever involved in the hiring of illegal workers.
>
> What we can't do is give people the fuel to attack us. I have a responsibility that is twofold: to make sure we're not doing the wrong thing, and to make sure that we are trying to communicate that this is a quality company.[34]

However, despite concerns in some quarters over Wal-Mart's growing size and economic influence, Scott believed the company could grow to be two or three times its present size.

---

[33]Useem, "One Nation Under Wal-Mart," p. 78.
[34]Grant, "Retail Giant Wal-Mart Faces Challenges on Many Fronts," p. B1.

Pricing Strategy

20

Schwinn Bicycles

J. Paul Peter *University of Wisconsin–Madison*

Inside a plain, brown building in Boulder, Colorado, is a shrine to an American icon: the Schwinn bicycle. Some mud-caked from daily use, some shiny museum pieces—dozens of bikes stand atop file cabinets and lean against cubicles. Amid the spokes and handlebars, a group of zealots is working to pull off the turnaround of the century in the bike business. Brimming with energy, they're determined to resurrect the best known brand on two wheels. But as Schwinn celebrates its 100th anniversary, its management team faces a long uphill climb. Just two years ago, once-mighty Schwinn had a near-death experience in bankruptcy court. Now it's trying to rise to the top of the crowded mountain bike market.

For years, Schwinn was the top U.S. brand, with as much as 25 percent of the market. Now, it has less than 5 percent of the $2.5 billion annual retail bike market. The new Schwinn will sell about 400,000 redesigned bikes—many of them Asian-made models—that sell for $200 to $400 retail, the lower end of the adult bike market. Those models are catching on. But the turnaround won't be a success unless Schwinn persuades cyclists to fork over $700 or more for its newer bikes. Below are market shares of manufacturers for bikes retail-priced $400 and up:

Trek	24%
Cannondale	12%
Specialized	12%
Schwinn	7%

This case prepared by J. Paul Peter of the University of Wisconsin–Madison.
Source: Patrick McGeehan, "Biking Icon Wants to Lose Training Wheels," *USA Today,* August 8, 1995, pp. 1B, 2B; "Hard Pedaling Powers Schwinn Uphill in Sales, Toward Profits," *Chicago Tribune,* June 22, 1995, p. 2N; " 'New Schwinn' Bike Has Gone Full Cycle," *Chicago Tribune,* May 16, 1995, p. 3N.

Giant	6%
Diamondback	6%
GT	6%
Scott	4%
Mongoose	3%
Pro Flex	3%

The mass market for low-priced bikes and those made for children is dominated by three U.S. manufacturers: Huffy, Murray, and Roadmaster. The mass market accounts for about 8.5 million of the 12 million bikes sold in the nation annually.

Schwinn's history as a maker of sturdy, low-cost bikes is no longer the asset it once was. Many under-30 cyclists see Schwinns as the bikes their parents rode. They prefer trendier mountain bikes, with their padded seats, upright handlebars, fat tires and additional gears for climbing.

"We have an image challenge," admits Schwinn Marketing Director Gregg Bagni. That's clear from a walk around the University of Colorado campus a half-mile away. Outside dorms and classrooms, racks are filled with bikes made by Trek Bicycle, Specialized Bicycle Components, Cannondale and Giant. Waterloo, Wisconsin-based Trek is the leader. This year it expects about $300 million in revenue on sales of more than 900,000 bikes.

"When I was a kid, if you had a Schwinn, you were the luckiest kid in the world," says Scott Montgomery, a Cannondale marketing chief. "Ask a college kid now and they'll say, 'Oh, Schwinn? They're toast.'"

For decades, the Schwinn brand, synonymous with durability, ruled the road. Generations of kids clamored for the company's Excelsiors, Phantoms, Sting-Rays and 10-speed Varsitys. "Schwinn used to be number one and you could hardly find number two," says industry consultant Bill Fields. But in the late '70s and early '80s, cyclists veered off the road into the woods and mountains. Schwinn ignored the mountain bike craze for most of the '80s. By 1992, two-thirds of bikes sold were mountain bikes and Schwinn was in bankruptcy court. Unable to pay lenders or suppliers, the descendants of company founder Ignaz Schwinn sold the company to the Zell/Chilmark Investment fund for $43 million. Zell/Chilmark appointed new management and funded the company, Scott Sports Group, with an additional $7 million.

So far, the Schwinn turnaround is being attempted on a shoestring. Schwinn's workforce shrank from 300 employees to about 180 when the company was reorganized and moved from Chicago to Boulder. The move west was calculated to attract young workers plugged into the mountain-biking community. Once assembled, the managers focused on product design. They had inherited a Schwinn line whose only mountain bikes were priced at the low end of the bike-shop range, between $200 and $400.

"Previous management wouldn't believe anybody would buy a $1,500 mountain bike with the Schwinn name on it," one Schwinn executive stated. Now, Schwinn is emblazoned on everything from $100 kids' bikes to $2,500 mountain bikes. Its top-of-the-line, American-made Homegrown model starts at $1,750. One of its hottest products is a decidedly low-tech, retro-style, one-speed Cruiser with a wide seat and balloon tires. It's selling fast in Sunbelt states for up to $250. The Cruiser appeals to retirees and snowbirds in beach communities and to college students who call them "bar bikes" because they are ridden to bars and back.

"They want to position this company as high-end, high-tech," says Cannondale's Montgomery. "And what they've got is this traditional, old-fashioned Harley-Davidson type of product. That's their greatest marketing challenge."

Today's bike business is quite different from the one Schwinn dominated so long ago. Exclusive dealerships like Schwinn uses are disappearing, being replaced by independent bike shops. The typical bike shop carries four brands, so Schwinn bikes are subjected to side-by-side comparisons with competing products. Some of the other brands, such as Trek and Cannondale, have built reputations for cutting-edge technology. Cannondale makes aluminum-frame bikes in U.S. plants, and Trek, a pioneer in carbon fiber frames, is moving production back from Taiwan. All but a few thousand Schwinns are made in Asia.

"Handmade in the USA is a tremendous marketing feature," says Brett Hahn, manager of Yeti Cycles in Durango, Colorado. "Bottom line: Mountain biking is a U.S. sport." Yeti makes hundreds of frames for Schwinn's top-of-the-line Homegrown models. Schwinn is considering buying Yeti or another U.S. manufacturer.

Discussion Questions

1. What are the strengths and weaknesses of Schwinn?
2. What opportunities and threats face the company?
3. How important is it for mountain bikes to be made in America?
4. Evaluate Schwinn's strategy of selling bikes for prices from $100 to $2,500.
5. Evaluate Zell/Chilmark's decision to invest $50 million in Schwinn. What did it get for its money? Calculate the breakeven point and the payback period for this investment given the following assumptions: Schwinn has 4 percent of the retail bike market; Schwinn bikes are marked up an average of 20 percent at retail; Schwinn has a 25 percent profit margin on its bikes.
6. Noting that 80 percent of Trek's sales are for bikes priced $400 and over, how many bikes does Schwinn sell in this category?

21

Toyota

Brian Brenner and Chester Dawson* *BusinesssWeek*

YOI KANGAE, YOI SHINA! That's Toyota-speak for "Good thinking means good products." The slogan is emblazoned on a giant banner hanging across the company's Takaoka assembly plant, an hour outside the city of Nagoya. Plenty of good thinking has gone into the high-tech ballet that's performed here 17 hours a day. Six separate car models—from the Corolla compact to the new youth-oriented Scion xB—glide along on a single production line in any of a half-dozen colors. Overhead, car doors flow by on a conveyor belt that descends to floor level and drops off the right door in the correct color for each vehicle. This efficiency means Takaoka workers can build a car in just 20 hours.

The combination of speed and flexibility is world class (Exhibit 1). More important, a similar dance is happening at 30 Toyota plants worldwide, with some able to make as many as eight different models on the same line. That is leading to a monster increase in productivity and market responsiveness—all part of the company's obsession with what President Fujio Cho calls "the criticality of speed."

Remember when Japan was going to take over the world? Corporate America was apoplectic at the idea that every Japanese company might be as obsessive, productive, and well-managed as Toyota Motor Corp. We know what happened next: One of the longest crashes in business history revealed most of Japan Inc. to be debt-addicted, inefficient, and clueless. Today, 13 years after the Nikkei peaked, Japan is still struggling to avoid permanent decline. World domination? Hardly.

Except in one corner. In autos, the Japanese rule (Exhibit 2). And in Japan, one company—Toyota—combines the size, financial clout, and manufacturing excellence needed to dominate the global car industry in a way no company ever has. Sure, Toyota, with $146 billion in sales, may not be tops in every category. GM is bigger—for now. Nissan Motor Co. makes slightly more profit per vehicle in North America, and its U.S. plants are more efficient. Both Nissan and Honda have flexible assembly lines, too. But no car company is as strong as Toyota in so many areas.

Of course, the carmaker has always moved steadily forward: Its executives created the doctrine of *kaizen*, or continuous improvement (Exhibit 3). "They find a hole, and they plug it," says auto-industry consultant Maryann Keller. "They methodically study problems, and they solve them." But in the past few years, Toyota has accelerated these gains, raising the bar for the entire industry. Consider:

- Toyota is closing in on Chrysler to become the third-biggest carmaker in the U.S. Its U.S. share, rising steadily, is now above 11%.

*With Kathleen Kerwin in Detroit, Christopher Palmeri in Los Angeles, and Paul Magnusson in Washington

EXHIBIT 1   Global Push

Toyota's on the offensive around the globe. Here's a look at its worldwide operations:

Data: Toyota Motor, 2002 sales figures.

North America

SALES: 1.94 million

Toyota's products keep gaining on the Big Three's models, while Lexus is a luxury leader. Toyota employs 35,000 people and runs 10 factories in the region, and has 11.2% of the U.S. market.

South America

SALES: 97,000

Builds cars in Argentina, Brazil, Colombia, and Venezuela. Regionwide revenues fell 10% last year because of economic troubles in Argentina, but sales in Brazil grew after the launch of a new **Corolla.**

Europe

SALES: 756,000

Has a 4.4% market share, led by the **Yaris** compact and a new **Avensis** with a cleaner diesel engine. Plans to boost production in Britain and France. Lexus though, is struggling.

Africa

SALES: 140,000

Has manufacturing plants in Kenya and South Africa. Last year, it saw sales across the continent jump 10.5%, thanks to a new **Corolla** sedan and **Prado** SUV.

Southwest Asia

SALES: 268,000

Builds cars in Bangladesh, India, Pakistan, and Turkey. The durable **Qualis** SUV is a big hit in India, and Toyota plans to start building transmissions there in mid-2004.

China

SALES: 58,000

Playing catch-up with rivals Volkswagen and GM. In April, it agreed with FAW to make the **Land Cruiser, Corolla, and Crown.** Share today is about 1.5%, but Toyota wants 10% by 2010.

Southeast Asia

SALES: 455,000

Assembles cars in seven countries and is expanding its factories in Thailand and Indonesia. Plans to export trucks, engines, and components from the region to 80 countries.

Japan

SALES: 1.68 million

Has maintained 40% plus market share for five years running. New models this year include the **Sienta** compact minivan, the sportier **Wish** minivan, and a revamped **Harrier** SUV.

EXHIBIT 2   Way Ahead of the Pack

Data: Bloomberg Financial Markets, Harbour & Associates, J.D. Power & Associates, Toyo Keizai, Dresden Kleinwort, Burnham Securities. Research assistance by Susan Zegel.

	Market Cap*	Operating Profit*	Hours per Vehicle†	Defects‡
Toyota	$110	$12.7	21.83	196
Nissan	54	7.5	16.83	258
Honda	40	6.1	22.27	215
DaimlerChrysler	38	5.7	28.04†	311
GM	24	3.8	24.44	264
Ford	22	3.6	26.14	287

*Billions. †Average assembly time (North America). ‡Problems per 100 vehicles on year 2000 models.

- At its current rate of expansion, Toyota could pass Ford Motor Co. in mid-decade as the world's No. 2 auto maker. The No. 1 spot—still occupied by General Motors Corp., with 15% of the global market—would be the next target. President Cho's goal is 15% of global sales by 2010, up from 10% today. "They dominate wherever they go," says Nobuhiko Kawamoto, former president of Honda Motor Co. "They try to take over everything."

- Toyota has broken the Japanese curse of running companies simply for sales gains, not profit. Its operating margin of 8% plus (vs. 2% in 1993) now dwarfs those of Detroit's Big Three. Even with the impact of the strong yen, estimated 2003 profits of $7.2 billion will be double 1999's level. On Nov. 5, the company reported profits of $4.8 billion on sales of $75 billion for the six months ended Sept. 30. Results like that have given Toyota a market capitalization of $110 billion—more than that of GM, Ford, and Daimler-Chrysler combined (Exhibit 4).

- The company has not only rounded out its product line in the U.S., with sport-utility vehicles, trucks, and a hit minivan, but it also has seized the psychological advantage in the market with the Prius, an eco-friendly gasoline-electric car. "This is going to be a real paradigm shift for the industry," says board member and top engineer Hiroyuki Watanabe. In October, when the second-generation Prius reached U.S. showrooms, dealers got 10,000 orders before the car was even available.

EXHIBIT 3   Kaizen in Action

Toyota stresses constant improvement, or **kaizen,** in everything it does. Here's how the company revamped the 2004 Sienna minivan after the previous generation got disappointing reviews.

Data: Toyota Motor; *BusinessWeek*, Edmunds.com Inc.

- The 3.3-liter, 230 hp engine is bigger and more powerful than before, but it gets slightly better gas mileage.
- Now has five-speed transmission instead of four.
- The 2004 is nimbler with a turning diameter of 36.8 feet–3.2 feet shorter than the previous model.
- At $23,495, it's $920 cheaper than the 2003.
- Third-row seats fold flat into the floor. On the older model they had to be removed to maximize cargo space.
- The new model is longer and wider than the 2003, with more headroom, leg room, and 12% more cargo space.

Camry	Prius	Scion xB
Bland? Sure, as bland as the bread and butter it is to Toyota. This reliable family sedan has been America's top-selling car in five of the past six years. $19,560–$25,920	A funky-looking and earth-friendly gas-electric hybrid that gets 55 mpg–but offers the power and roominess of a midsize sedan. $20,510	An attempt to be hip and edgy included underground marketing for this new car aimed at young people. Sales have been double Toyota's forecasts. $14,165–$14,965

Yaris	Tundra	Lexus RX330
The snub-nosed compact is Toyota's top-seller in Europe. Its Euro-styling has made it a hit in Japan too, where it's known as the Vitz. $11,787–$14,317	This full-size pickup has built a loyal following as it has grown in bulk and power. A Double Cab model due in November will up the ante. $16,495–$31,705*	The first Lexus built in North America, this luxury SUV boasts a smooth, car-like ride and nimble handling. It has been Lexus' U.S. sales leader. $35,700–$37,500

*Doesn't include Double cab model, which isn't yet priced.

EXHIBIT 4
Toyota's Money Machine

Data: Toyota Motor Corp., Lehman Brothers Inc.

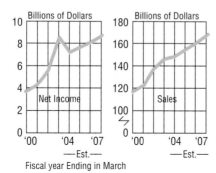

If Cho gets this transformation right, he'll end up with an automotive machine that makes the Americans and Germans quake. Cost-cutting and process redesign will chop out billions in expenses. That will keep margins strong and free up cash to develop new models and technologies such as the Prius, to invest in global manufacturing, and to invade markets such as Europe and China. New models and new plants will build share, which will build more clout. And if there's a hiccup—well, there's a cash-and-securities hoard of $30 billion. "This is a company that does not fear failure," says Cho.

- Toyota has launched a joint program with its suppliers to radically cut the number of steps needed to make cars and car parts. In the past year alone, the company chopped $2.6 billion out of its $113 billion in manufacturing costs without any plant closures or layoffs. Toyota expects to cut an additional $2 billion out of its cost base this year.
- Toyota is putting the finishing touches on a plan to create an integrated, flexible, global manufacturing system. In this new network, plants from Indonesia to Argentina will be designed both to customize cars for local markets and to shift production to quickly satisfy any surges in demand from markets worldwide. By tapping, say, its South African plant to meet a need in Europe, Toyota can save itself the $1 billion normally needed to build a new factory.

Roadblocks?

Can anything stop Toyota? There are some potential roadblocks. Toyota doesn't always get it right: Its early attempts at the youth market, minivans, and big pickup trucks all disappointed. It remains dependent on the U.S. business for some 70% of earnings. Its Lexus luxury sedans are losing ground to BMW, though Lexus' strong SUV sales are keeping the division in the game. The average Toyota owner is about 46, a number the company must lower or risk going the way of Buick. And most of Toyota's big sellers aren't exactly head-turners.

Meanwhile, Toyota's rivals are hardly sitting still. GM is finishing up a $4.3 billion revamp of Cadillac, and a revival is in the works: Overall GM quality is on an upswing too. "Toyota is a good competitor, but they're not unbeatable," says GM Chairman G. Richard Wagoner Jr. Over at Nissan, CEO Carlos Ghosn doubts Toyota's big bet on hybrids will pay off. "There will be no revolution," he predicts. And Detroit's Big Three are praying that a strong yen will batter Toyota. If the yen sticks at 110 to the dollar over the next 12 months, Toyota could see its pretax profits shrink by $900 million.

A strengthening yen might have hammered Toyota in the 1980s, and it will certainly have an impact next year. But today, three decades after starting its global push, Toyota can't be accused of needing a cheap yen to subsidize exports. Since starting U.S. production in 1986, Toyota has invested nearly $14 billion there. What's more, many of its costs are now set in dollars: Last year, Toyota's purchases of parts and materials from 500 North American suppliers came to $19 billion—more than the annual sales of Cisco Systems Inc. or Oracle Corp. The U.S. investment is an enormous natural hedge against the yen. "About 60% of what we sold here, we built here," Toyota Chairman Hiroshi Okuda said in a Sept. 10 speech in Washington.

Better for Toyota, those cars are also among the industry's biggest money-makers. Take SUVs: Ten years ago, Toyota had a puny 4% share. Today, it owns nearly 12% of that high-margin segment with eight models ranging from the $19,000 RAV4 to the $65,000 Lexus LX 470—and makes as much as $10,000 on each high-end model it sells. The company is steadily robbing Ford, Chrysler, and GM of their primacy in the cutthroat U.S. SUV market and has largely sat out the latest round of rebates: Toyota's average incentive per car this fall is just $647, compared with $3,812 at GM and $3,665 at Ford, according to market watcher Edmunds.com. This is one war of attrition where Detroit is clearly outgunned.

Toyota's charge into SUVs indicates a new willingness to play tough in the U.S., which it considers vital to its drive for a global 15% share. "The next era is full-size trucks and luxury, environmental, and youth cars," predicts James E. Press, chief operating officer at Toyota Motor Sales USA Inc. Toyota is already intent on boosting its 4.5% market share in pickups, the last profit refuge of the Big Three. Toyota is building an $800 million plant in San Antonio, Tex., that will allow it to more than double its Tundra output, to some 250,000 trucks a year by 2006, with rigs powerful and roomy enough to go head to head with Detroit's biggest models.

Toyota plans to extend its early lead in eco-cars by pushing the Prius and adding a hybrid Lexus RX 330 SUV next summer. The Lexus will get as much as 35 miles per gallon, compared with roughly 21 mpg for a conventional RX 330. And Toyota is vigorously attacking the youth market with the $14,500 Scion xB compact, which surprised Toyota-bashers with its angular, minimalist design. Since the Scion's U.S. launch in California in June, Toyota has sold nearly 7,700 of them, 30% better than forecast. Toyota Vice-President James Farley says three out of four buyers of the brand had no intention of buying a Toyota when they started looking. "That's exactly why we started the Scion," he says.

The Scion is evidence that Toyota's growing cash cushion gives it the means to revamp its lack luster designs. When Cho traveled through Germany in 1994, he recalls being asked: Why are Toyota cars so poorly styled? Part of the problem, says Cho, is that too many Toyotas were designed with Japanese consumers in mind and then exported. Some worked; some flopped.

These days, design teams on the West Coast of the U.S., in southern France, and back home compete for projects. That has paid off with models such as the Yaris, Toyota's best-seller in Europe, where the company now has a 4.4% share, compared with less than 3% a decade ago. The Yaris was designed by a Greek, Sotiris Kovos, then imported successfully to Japan because of its "European" look. "Toyota has finally recognized that buyers want to feel like they have some level of style," says Wesley Brown, a consultant with auto researcher Iceology. The redesigned Solara sports coupe is getting high grades, too: A V-shape line flowing up from the grille gives it a more muscular silhouette, and its interior is 20% roomier than before.

Toyota Man

Leading Toyota to this new level of global vigor is Cho. He's Toyota Man personified: Self-effacing, ever smiling, but an executive whose radar seems to pick up every problem and opportunity. "Cho understands as much as anyone I've ever seen what's actually happening on the factory floor," says manufacturing consultant Ronald E. Harbour, whose firm's annual report on productivity is the industry bible.

That feel for the factory didn't come naturally. The 66-year-old company lifer studied law, not business, at the prestigious University of Tokyo and could have easily ended up as a faceless bureaucrat at the Ministry of Finance. But Cho learned the car business—and clearly learned it well—at the knee of Taichi Ohno, the creator of the legendary Toyota Production System, a series of in-house precepts on efficient manufacturing that changed the industry. Ohno, a brilliant but notoriously hot-headed engineer, lectured Cho about the need to be flexible and to look forward.

That advice is something Cho found invaluable when he was tapped to oversee the 1988 launch of Toyota's key U.S. plant in Georgetown, Ky., now the company's biggest U.S. factory and the maker of the Camry sedan. The good-natured and unpretentious Cho regularly worked the plant floor, making sure to shake hands with each line worker at Christmas to show his appreciation. He spoke at Rotary Club meetings and stopped to make small talk with the folks in Georgetown.

Given Toyota's booming U.S. sales in the late 1990s, few inside the company were surprised when Cho won the top job. Yet equally few had any clue that the new president was about to unleash so many powerful changes. Like his predecessor Okuda, Cho had long been frustrated by Toyota's glacial decision-making process and cultural insularity. Those had led to missed opportunities, such as when product planners at headquarters in Japan resisted calls from their U.S. colleagues to build an eight-cylinder pickup truck. Cho is rectifying that deficiency with a vengeance with the San Antonio plant.

Then three years ago, as Ghosn—"le cost killer"—was slashing billions at rival Nissan and cutting its supplier ranks in half, Cho had a revelation: If Nissan could do it, Toyota could do it better. The resulting program, called Construction of Cost Competitiveness for the 21st Century, or CCC21, taps into the company's strengths across the board to build cars more efficiently. It's also turning many operations inside out.

No Detail Too Small

Toyota has always valued frugality. It still turns down the heat at company-owned employee dormitories during working hours and labels its photocopy machines with the cost per copy to discourage overuse. But cost-cutting was often a piecemeal affair. With CCC21, Cho set a bold target of slashing prices on all key components for new models by 30%, which meant working with suppliers and Toyota's own staff to ferret out excess. "Previously, we tried to find waste here and there," says Cho. "But now there is a new dimension of proposals coming in."

EXHIBIT 5
Deciphering Toyota-Speak
A handy glossary for understanding the company's vernacular.

Kaizen	PDCA	Obeya
Continuous improvement. Employees are given cash rewards for ferreting out glitches in production and devising solutions.	Plan, do, check, action. Steps in the development cycle aimed at quick decision-making in a task such as designing a car.	Literally, "big room," Regular face-to-face brainstorming sessions among engineers, designers, marketers, and suppliers.
Pokayoke	**CCC21**	**GBL**
Mistake-proofing. Use of sensors to detect missing parts or improper assembly. Robots alert workers to errors by flashing lights.	Construction of Cost Competitiveness for the 21st century. A three-year push to slash costs of 170 components that account for 90% of parts expenses.	Global Body Line. A manufacturing process that holds auto frames together for welding with one brace instead of the 50 braces previously required.

In implementing CCC21, no detail is too small. For instance, Toyota designers took a close look at the grip handles mounted above the door inside most cars. By working with suppliers, they managed to cut the number of parts in these handles to five from 34, which helped cut procurement costs by 40%. As a plus, the change slashed the time needed for installation by 75%—to three seconds. "The pressure is on to cut costs at every stage," says Takashi Araki, a project manager at parts maker Aisin Seiki Co.

Just as Cho believes he can get far more out of suppliers, he thinks Toyota can make its workers vastly more productive. This is classic *kaizen,* but these days it has gone into overdrive (Exhibit 5). In the middle of the Kentucky plant, for instance, a *Kaizen* Team of particularly productive employees works in a barracks-like structure. The group's sole job is coming up with ways to save time and money. Georgetown employees, for instance, recommended removing the radiator support base—the lower jaw of the car—until the last stage of assembly. That way, workers can step into the engine compartment to install parts instead of having to lean over the front end and risk straining their backs. "We used to have to duck into the car to install something," explains Darryl Ashley, 41, a soft-spoken Kentucky native who joined Toyota nine years ago.

In Cambridge, Ont., Cho is going even further: He's determined to show the world that Toyota can meet its own highest standards of excellence anywhere in its system. It was once company doctrine that Lexus could only be made in Japan. No longer. Production of the RX 330 SUV started in Cambridge on Sept. 26. If the Canadian hands can deliver the same quality as their Japanese counterparts, Toyota will be able to chop shipping costs by shifting Lexus production to the market where the bulk of those cars are sold (Exhibit 6).

The Japanese bosses put the Canadians through their paces. The 700 workers on the RX 330 line trained for 12 weeks, including stints in Japan for 200 of them. There, the Canadians managed to beat Japanese teams in quality assessment on a mock Lexus line. Cambridge has taken Toyota's focus on poka-yoke, or foolproofing measures, to another level. The plant has introduced "Circle L" stations where workers must double- and triple-check parts that customers have complained about—anything from glove boxes to suspension systems. "We know that if we can get this right, we may get to build other Lexus models," says Jason Birt, a 28-year-old Lexus line worker.

The Cambridge workers are aided by a radical piece of manufacturing technology being rolled out to Toyota plants worldwide. The system, called the Global Body Line, holds vehicle frames in place while they're being welded, using just one master brace instead of the dozens of separate braces required in a standard factory. No big deal? Perhaps, but the system is half as expensive to install. Analysts say it lets Toyota save 75% of the cost of refitting a production line to build a different car, and it's key to Toyota's ability to make multiple models on a single line. Better yet, the brace increases the rigidity of the car early

EXHIBIT 6

Lexus: Still Looking for Traction in Europe

Source: Brian Bremner and Chester Dawson, "Can Anything Stop Toyota?" *Business-Week* November 17, 2003, 114–122.

When Dirk Lindermann was looking for a new luxury sedan last summer, he considered Mercedes and BMW before settling on a $40,000, black Audi A4. Lexus, though, didn't even enter into the game. "Lexus has no personality," says the 40-year-old Berlin advertising executive.

That's a problem for Toyota Motor Corp. The company's smooth-driving Lexus sedans sprinted from zero to luxury-market leader in the U.S. during the 1990s, overtaking German rivals Mercedes and BMW—as well as Cadillac and Lincoln—by offering better quality and service at a lower price. But Lexus is going nowhere fast in Europe: After 12 years in showrooms, last year it registered sales of just 21,156 cars—down 11% from 2001—compared with more than 234,000 in the U.S.

Toyota itself is fast shedding any *arriviste* stigma in the Old World. Since it began producing cars on the Continent in the '90s, European sales are up nearly 60%, to 734,000. Now it wants to crack the high-end with a renewed push for Lexus. The goal is to triple sales of the six Lexus models Toyota offers there by 2010, to at least 65,000 cars. "The potential in

Europe for Lexus is every bit as great as in the U.S.," says Stuart McCullough, director of Lexus Europe.

To make Lexus a success, though, Toyota needs to establish it as a separate brand. Until now, the car has been sold in Europe mainly through Toyota's 250 dealerships, along with the far less lustrous Yaris, Corolla, and Avensis models. So Toyota is trying to set up dealerships that offer luxury-car buyers the kind of white-glove service they demand. "Lexus has to establish its own heritage, not just chase BMW and Mercedes," says Tadashi Arashima, president and chief executive of Toyota Motor Marketing Europe.

Will image-conscious Europeans warm up to Lexus if the cars are sold in tony showrooms? In Spain, where exclusive Lexus dealerships have been operating since 2000, sales are up 9% so far this year, though the brand sold just 969 vehicles in the country. "We've been able to show that these cars can compete with the big German brands in quality and also offer a lot more in terms of price," says Jorge Merino, head of sales at Axel, a three-year-old Lexus dealership in Madrid.

One big selling point is Lexus' six-year warranty. And the carmaker includes three years of free checkups, maintenance, and roadside assistance. That compares with a standard guarantee of two years at most luxury brands. "I like BMW and Mercedes, but I have a feeling I may get more for my money with Lexus," says Ignacio Redondo, a legal consultant in Madrid who drives a Saab 900 but is mulling a new Lexus for the first time.

Harder, though, will be conforming to the European concept of luxury. Americans love comfort, size and dependability, while Europeans think luxury means attention to detail and brand heritage. "The biggest selling point for Lexus is that it doesn't break down," says Philipp Rosengarten, analyst at Global Insight Inc.'s automotive group. That's not enough to succeed in Europe. Instead, Lexus needs to create a desire to own the car—and even with plush dealerships and extended warranties, it has kilometers to go before reaching that goal.

By Gail Edmondson in Frankfurt, and Karen Nickel Anhalt in Berlin with Paulo Prada in Madrid.

---

in production, which boosts the accuracy of welds and makes for a more stable vehicle. "The end results are improved quality, shortened welding lines, reduced capital investment, and less time to launch new vehicles," says Atsushi Niimi, president of Toyota Motor Manufacturing North America.

Cho and his managers are not just reengineering how Toyota makes its cars—they want to revolutionize how it creates products. With the rise of e-mail and teleconferencing, teams of designers, engineers, product planners, workers, and suppliers rarely all convened in the same place. Under Cho, they're again required to work face to face, in a process Toyota calls obeya—literally, "big room." This cuts the time it takes to get a car from the drawing board to the showroom. It took only 19 months to develop the 2003 Solara. That's better than 22 months for the latest Sienna minivan, and 26 months for the latest Camry—well below the industry average of about three years.

If all this sounds like Toyota is riding a powerful growth wave, well, it is. While Cho is as mild-mannered and modest as they come, the revolution he has kicked off is anything but. Toyota is in the midst of a transformative makeover—and if Cho succeeds, the entire global auto industry is in for one, too.

22

Cowgirl Chocolates

John J. Lawrence *University of Idaho*

Linda J. Morris *University of Idaho*

Joseph J. Geiger *University of Idaho*

Marilyn looked at the advertisement—a beautiful woman wearing a cowboy hat in a watering trough full of hot and spicy Cowgirl Chocolate truffles (see Exhibit 1). The ad would appear next month in the March/April edition of *Chile Pepper* magazine, the leading magazine for people who liked fiery foods. The ad, the first ever for the business, cost $3,000 to run and Marilyn wondered if it would be her big mistake for 2001. Marilyn allowed herself one $3,000–$6,000 mistake a year in trying to get her now four-year old business to profitability. Two years ago, it was the pursuit of an opportunity to get her product into Great Britain on the recommendation of the owner of a British biscuit company who loved her chocolates. Despite significant effort and expense, she could not convince anyone in Great Britain to carry her chocolates. Last year it was her attempt to use a distributor for the first time. It was a small, regional distributor, and she had provided them with $5,000 worth of product and had never gotten paid. She eventually got half her product back, but by the time she did it had limited remaining shelf life and she already had enough new stock on hand to cover demand. She ended up giving most of what she got back away.

Marilyn knew it took time to make money at something. She was now an internationally celebrated ceramicist, but it had taken 20 years for her ceramic art to turn a profit. She also knew, however, that she could not wait 20 years for her foray into chocolates to make money, especially not at the rate that she was currently losing money. Last year, despite not paying herself a salary and occasionally bartering her art for services, the small business's revenues of $30,000 did not come close to covering her $50,000+ in expenses. While her art for a long time did not make money, it did not lose that kind of money either. Her savings account was slowly being depleted as she loaned the company money. She knew that the product was excellent—it had won numerous awards from the two main fiery food competitions in the U.S.—and her packaging was also excellent and had won awards itself. She just was not sure how to turn her award winning products into a profitable business.

This case was prepared by the authors for the sole purpose of providing material for class discussion. It is not intended to illustrate either effective or ineffective handling of a managerial situation. The authors thank Marilyn Lysohir for her cooperation and assistance with this project.

Reprinted by permission from the *Case Research Journal,* volume 22, issue 1. Copyright 2002 by John L. Lawrence, Linda J. Morris, Joseph J. Geiger, and the North American Case Research Association. All rights reserved.

EXHIBIT 1 Cowgirl Chocolate Ad to Appear in *Chile Pepper* Magazine

Company History

Cowgirl Chocolates was started in Moscow, Idaho, in 1997 by Marilyn Lysohir and her husband, Ross Coates. Marilyn and Ross were both artists. Marilyn was an internationally known ceramicist and lecturer; Ross was also a sculptor and a professor of fine arts at a nearby university. They had started publishing a once a year arts magazine in 1995 called *High Ground.* *High Ground* was really a multimedia product—each edition contained more than simply printed words and pictures. For example, past editions had included such things as vials of Mount St. Helen's ash, cassette tapes, seeds, fabric art, and chocolate bunnies in addition to articles and stories. One edition was even packaged in a motion picture canister. With a total production of about 600 copies, however, *High Ground* simply would not pay for itself. But the magazine was a labor of love for Marilyn and Ross, and so they sought creative ways to fund the endeavor. One of the ways they tried was selling hot and spicy chocolate truffles.

The fact that Marilyn and Ross turned to chocolate was no random event. Marilyn's first job, at age 16, was at Daffin's Candies in Sharon, Pennsylvania. The business's owner, Pete Daffin, had been an early mentor of Marilyn's and had encouraged her creativity. He even let her carve a set of animals, including an 8-foot tall chocolate bunny, for display. Her sculptures proved irresistible to visiting youngsters, who would take small bites out of the sculptures. It was at this point that Marilyn realized the power of chocolate.

In addition to loving chocolate, Marilyn loved things hot and spicy. She also was aware that cayenne and other chilies had wonderful health properties for the heart. But it was her brother who originally gave her the idea of combining hot and spicy with chocolate. Marilyn considered her brother's idea for a while, and could see it had possibilities, so she started experimenting in her kitchen. She recruited neighbors, friends and acquaintances to try out her creations. While a few people who tried those early chocolates were not so sure that combining hot and spicy with chocolate made sense, many thought the chocolates were great. Encouraged, and still searching for funding for *High Ground,* Marilyn found a local candy company to produce the chocolates in quantity, and she and her husband established Cowgirl Chocolates.

The name itself came from one friend's reaction the first time she tasted the chocolates—the friend exclaimed "these are cowboy chocolates!" Marilyn agreed that there was a certain ruggedness to the concept of hot and spicy chocolates that matched the cowboy image, but thought that *Cowgirl* Chocolates was a more appropriate name for her company. Marilyn found the picture of May Lillie that would become the Cowgirl Chocolate logo in a book about cowgirls. May Lillie was a turn of the century, pistol-packing cowgirl, and Marilyn loved the picture of May looking down the barrel of a pistol because May looked so tough. And it certainly was not hard to envision May adopting the Cowgirl Chocolate motto—Sissies Stay Away. That motto had come to Marilyn when a group of friends told her that they really did not like her hot and spicy chocolates. Marilyn was a little disappointed and hurt, and thought to herself "well, sissies stay away, if you don't like them, don't eat them."

The Product

Cowgirl chocolate sold its hot and spicy creations in three basic forms: individually wrapped truffles, chocolate bars, and a hot caramel dessert sauce. The individually wrapped truffles were available in a variety of packaging options, with most of the packaging designed to set Cowgirl Chocolates apart. The truffles could be purchased in gift boxes, in drawstring muslin bags, and in a collectible tin. According to Marilyn, this packaging made them "more than a candy—they become an idea, an experience, a gift." The truffles were also available in a plain plastic bag over Cowgirl Chocolate's website for customers who just wanted the chocolate and did not care about the fancy packaging. The chocolate bars and truffles were offered in several flavors. The chocolate bars were available in either orange espresso or lime tequila crunch. The truffles were available in plain chocolate, mint, orange, lime tequila, and espresso. The plain chocolate, mint, and orange truffles were packaged in gold wrappers, while the lime tequila truffles were packaged in green wrappers. The espresso truffles were the hottest, about twice as hot as the other varieties, and were wrapped in a special red foil to give customers some clue that these were extra hot. Cowgirl Chocolates' full line of product offerings are described in Exhibit 2 and are shown in Exhibit 3.

EXHIBIT 2   Cowgirl Chocolate Product Offerings with Price and Cost Figures

Item	Approximate Percentage of Total Revenues	Suggested Retail Price[1]	Wholesale Price[1]	Total Item Cost (a + b)	Cost of Chocolate or Sauce (a)	Cost of Product Packaging[2] (b)
Spicy Chocolate Truffle Bars (available in 2 flavors: orange-espresso or lime tequila crunch)	50%	$2.99	$1.50	$1.16	$1.04	$0.12
1/4 pound Muslin Bag (13 truffles in a drawstring muslin bag—available in 3 flavors: assorted hot, lime-tequila, and mild-mannered)	16%	$6.95	$3.50	$2.35	$1.69	$0.66
1/2 pound Tin (assorted hot & spicy truffles in a collectable tin)	12%	$14.95	$7.50	$4.78[3]	$3.25	$1.53
Hot Caramel Dessert Sauce (9.5 oz. Jar)	10%	$5.95	$3.50	$2.50	$2.00	$0.50
Sampler Bag (4 assorted hot truffles in a small drawstring muslin bag)	7%	$2.95	$1.50	$0.97	$0.52	$0.45
1/4 pound Gift Box (assorted hot truffles or mild-mannered truffles in a fancy gift box with gift card)	~ 1%	$8.95	$4.50	$2.95	$1.69	$1.26
1 pound Gift Box (assorted hot truffles or mild-mannered truffles in a fancy gift box with gift card)	~ 1%	$24.95	$12.95	$9.05	$6.37	$2.68
Gift Bucket (tin bucket containing 1/4 pound gift box, 2 truffle bars and 1 jar of caramel sauce)	~ 1%	$39.95	$20.95	$11.02	$5.77	$5.25
Gift Basket (made of wire and branches and containing 1/2 pound tin, 2 truffle bars, 1 jar of caramel sauce and a T-shirt)	~ 1%	$59.95	$30.95	$23.06	$15.29[3]	$7.77
Nothing Fancy (one pound assorted hot truffles or mild-mannered truffles in a plastic bag)	~ 1%	$19.50	N.A.	$7.42	$6.37	$1.05

[1]Approximately 1/3 of sales were retail over the Cowgirl Chocolate website, the remaining 2/3 of sales were to wholesale accounts (i.e., to other retailers).
[2]Packaging cost includes costs of container (bags, tins, or boxes), labels, and individual truffle wrapping. Packaging cost assumes Marilyn packs the items and does not include the packing & labeling fee charged by Seattle Chocolates if they do the packing ($1.00 per 1/2 pound tin or 1 pound box; $0.75 per 1/4 pound box; $0.25 per 1/4 pound bag; $0.20 per sampler bag).
[3]This cost includes the cost of the T-shirt.

EXHIBIT 3
Picture of Cowgirl
Chocolate Products
& Packaging

Marilyn was also in the process of introducing "mild-mannered" truffles. Mild-mannered truffles were simply the same fine German chocolate that Marilyn started with to produce all of her chocolates, but without the spice. Marilyn had chosen silver as the wrapper color for the mild-mannered truffles. While she took kidding from friends about how this did not fit with the company's motto—Sissies Stay Away—which was integrated into the company's logo and printed on the back of company t-shirts and hats, she had decided that even the sissies deserved excellent chocolate. Further, she thought that having the mild-mannered chocolate might allow her to get her product placed in retail locations that had previously rejected her chocolates as being too spicy. Marilyn was the first to admit that her chocolates packed a pretty good kick that not everybody found to their liking. She had developed the hot and spicy chocolates based primarily on her own tastes and the input of friends and acquaintances. She had observed many peoples' reactions upon trying her hot and spicy chocolates at trade shows and at new retail locations, and while many people liked her chocolates, the majority found at least some of the varieties to be too hot. In general, men tended to like the hotter truffles much more than women did. Marilyn knew her observations were consistent with what information was available on the fiery foods industry—only approximately 15% of American consumers were currently eating hot and spicy foods and men were much more inclined to eat hot and spicy foods than were women. In addition to introducing "mild-mannered" chocolates, Marilyn was also thinking about introducing a chocolate with a calcium supplement aimed at woman concerned about their calcium intake.

All of Cowgirl Chocolate's chocolate products were sourced from Seattle Chocolates, a Seattle-based company that specialized in producing European-style chocolate confections wrapped in an elegant package fit for gift giving. Seattle Chocolates obtained all of its raw chocolate from world-renowned chocolate producer Schokinag of Germany. Seattle Chocolates sold its own retail brand plus provided private label chocolate products for a variety of companies including upscale retailers like Nieman Marcus and Nordstroms. Seattle Chocolates was, at least relative to Cowgirl Chocolates, a large company with annual sales in excess of $5,000,000. Seattle Chocolates took Cowgirl Chocolates on as a private label customer because they liked and were intrigued by the company's product and owners, and they had made some efforts to help Cowgirl Chocolates along the way. Seattle Chocolates provided Cowgirl Chocolates with a small amount of its table space at several important trade shows and produced in half batches for them. A half batch still consisted of 150 pounds of a given variety of chocolate, which was enough to last Cowgirl Chocolates for six months at 2000 sales rates. Marilyn hoped that she could one day convince Seattle Chocolates to manage the wholesale side of Cowgirl Chocolates, but Seattle Chocolates simply was not interested in taking this on at the present time, at least in part because they were not really sure where the market was for the product. Marilyn also knew she would need to grow sales significantly before Seattle Chocolates would seriously consider such an arrangement, although she was not sure exactly how much she would have to grow sales before such an arrangement would become attractive to Seattle Chocolates.

The chocolate bars themselves cost Cowgirl Chocolates $1.04 per bar while the individual chocolate truffles cost $0.13 per piece. Seattle Chocolates also performed the wrapping and packing of the product. The chocolate bar wrappers cost $0.06 per bar. The wrapper design of the bars had recently been changed to incorporate dietary and nutritional information. While such information was not required, Marilyn felt it helped convey a better image of her chocolates. The change had cost $35 to prepare the new printing plates. Including the materials, wrapping the individual truffles cost $0.02 per piece.

The distinctive muslin bags, collector tins and gift boxes also added to the final product cost. The muslin bags cost $0.35 each for the quarter-pound size and $0.32 each for the sampler size. The tamperproof seals for the bags cost an additional $0.05/bag. The minimum size bag order was 500 bags. As with the chocolate bar wrappers, Cowgirl Chocolate had to buy the printing plates to print the bags. The plates to print the bags, however, cost $250 per plate. Each color of each design required a separate plate. Each of her three quarter-pound bag styles (assorted, lime-tequila, and mild-mannered) had a three-color design. One plate that was used to produce the background design was common to all three styles of bags, but each bag required two additional unique plates. There was also a separate plate for printing the sampler bags. Marilyn was planning to discontinue the separate lime-tequila bag, and just include lime-tequila truffles in the assorted bag as a way to cut packaging costs. The lime-tequila bags had been introduced a year ago, and while they sold reasonably well, they also appeared to mostly cannibalize sales of the assorted bags.

The collectible tins cost $0.80 each, and the labels for these tins cost $0.19 per tin. The tape used to seal the tins cost $0.04 per tin. The minimum order for the tins was for 800 units. The company that produced the tins had recently modified the tin design slightly to reduce the chance that someone might cut themselves on the edge of the can. Unfortunately, this change had resulted in a very small change to the height of the can, which left Cowgirl Chocolate with labels too big for the can. Each label currently had to be trimmed slightly to fit on the can. The alternative to this was to switch to a smaller label. This would require purchasing a new printing plate at a cost of about $35 and might require the purchase of a new printing die (the die holds the label while it is printed), which would cost $360. Marilyn also had hopes of one day being able to get her designs printed directly on the tins. It would make for even nicer tins and save the step of having to adhere the labels to the tins. The minimum order for such tins, however, was 15,000 units.

The gift boxes, including all of the associated wrapping, ribbon, and labels, cost about $1.70 per box. The gift boxes did not sell nearly as well as the tins or bags and were available primarily through Cowgirl Chocolates website. Marilyn was still using and had a reasonable inventory of boxes from a box order she had placed three years ago.

Marilyn currently had more packaging in inventory than she normally would because she had ordered $5,000 worth in anticipation of the possibility of having her product placed in military PX stores at the end of 2000. Seattle Chocolates had been negotiating to get their product into these stores, and there had been some interest on the part of the PX stores in also having Cowgirl Chocolate products. Given the six- to eight-week lead-time on packaging, Marilyn had wanted to be positioned to quickly take advantage of this opportunity if it materialized. While Marilyn was still hopeful this deal might come about, she was less optimistic than she had been at the time she placed the packaging order.

Marilyn was concerned that the actual packing step was not always performed with the care it should be. In particular, she was concerned that not enough or too many truffles ended up in the bags and tins, and that the seals on these containers, which made the packages more tamper resistant, were not always applied correctly. Each quarter-pound bag and gift box was supposed to contain 13 individual truffles, each half-pound tin was supposed to contain 25 individual truffles, and each one-pound gift box was supposed to contain 49 individual truffles. The tins, in particular, had to be packed pretty tightly to get 25 truffles into them. Marilyn had done some of the packing herself at times, and wondered if she would not be better off hiring local college or high school students to do the packing for her to insure that the job was done to her satisfaction. It could also save her some money, as Seattle Chocolates charged her extra for packing the tins and bags. The tins, in particular, were expensive because of the time it took to apply the labels to the top and side of the tin and because of the extra care it took to get all 25 truffles into the tin. Seattle Chocolates charged $1.00 per tin for this step.

Marilyn made the caramel sauce herself with the help of the staff in a commercial kitchen in Sandpoint, Idaho, about a 2½-hour drive north of Moscow. She could make 21 cases of 12 jars each in one day, but including the drive it took all day to do. As with the chocolate, she used only the best ingredients, including fresh cream from a local Moscow dairy. Marilyn figured her costs for the caramel sauce at about $2.50 per jar, which included the cost of the ingredients, the jars, the labeling and the cost of using the Sandpoint kitchen. That figure did not include any allowance for the time it took her to make the sauce or put the labels on the jars. She was considering dropping the caramel sauce from her product line because it was a lot of work to produce and she was not sure she really made any money on it after her own time was factored in. She had sold 70 cases of the sauce in 2000, however, so she knew there was some demand for the product. She was considering the possibility of only offering it at Christmas time as a special seasonal product. She was also looking into the possibility of having a sauce company in Montana make it for her. The company produced caramel, chocolate, and chocolate-caramel sauces that had won awards from the fancy food industry trade association. Marilyn thought the sauces were quite good, although she did not like their caramel sauce as much as her own. The company would sell her 11 oz. jars of any of the sauces, spiced up to Marilyn's standards, for $2.75 per jar. Marilyn would have to provide the labels, for which she would need to have new label designs made to match the jar style the company was set up for, and she would also have to pay a shipping cost of $70–$90 per delivery. The company requested a minimum order size of 72 cases, although the company's owner had hinted that they might be willing to produce in half batches initially.

All of Cowgirl Chocolate's products had won awards, either in the annual Fiery Food Challenges sponsored by *Chile Pepper* magazine or the Scovie Award Competitions sponsored by *Fiery Foods* magazine (the Scovie awards are named after the Scovie measure of heat). All in all, Cowgirl Chocolates had won eleven awards in these two annual competitions. Further, the truffles had won first place in the latest Fiery Food Challenge and the caramel sauce won first place in the latest Scovie competition. The packaging, as distinctive as the chocolate itself, had also won several awards, including the 2000 Award for Excellence for Package Design from American Corporate Identity.

Distribution and Pricing

Marilyn's attempts to get her chocolates into the retail market had met with varying degrees of success. She clearly had been very successful in placing her product in her hometown of Moscow, Idaho. The Moscow Food Co-op was her single best wholesale customer, accounting for 10%–15% of her annual sales. The Co-op sold a wide variety of natural and/or organic products and produce. Many of its products, like Cowgirl Chocolates, were made or grown locally. The Co-op did a nice job of placing her product in a visible shelf location and generally priced her product less than any other retail outlet. The Co-op sold primarily the chocolate bars, which it priced at $2.35, and the quarter-pound muslin bags of truffles, which it priced at $5.50. This compared to the suggested retail prices of $2.99 for the bars and $6.99 for the bags. The product was also available at three other locations in downtown Moscow: Wild Women Traders, a store that described itself as a "lifestyle outfitter" and that sold high-end women's clothing and antiques; Northwest Showcase, a store that sold locally produced arts and crafts; and Bookpeople, an independent bookstore that catered to customers who liked to spend time browsing an eclectic offering of books and drinking espresso before making a book purchase.

Marilyn was unsure how many of these local sales were to repeat purchasers who really liked the product and how many were to individuals who wanted to buy a locally made product to give as a gift. She was also unsure how much the Co-op's lower prices boosted the sales of her product at that location. At the Co-op, her product was displayed with other premium chocolates from several competitors, including Seattle Chocolates' own branded chocolate bars, which were priced at $2.99. Marilyn knew the Seattle Chocolate bars were clearly comparable in chocolate quality (although without the spice and cowgirl image). Some of the other competitors' comparably sized bars were priced lower, at $1.99, and some smaller bars were priced at $1.49. While these products were clearly higher in quality than the inexpensive chocolate bars sold in vending machines and at the average supermarket checkout aisle, they were made with a less expensive chocolate than she used and were simply not as good as her chocolates. Marilyn wondered how the price and size of the chocolate bar affected the consumer's purchase decision, and how consumers evaluated the quality of each of the competing chocolate bars when making their purchase.

Outside of Moscow, Marilyn had a harder time getting her product placed onto store shelves and getting her product to move through these locations. One other Co-op, the Boise Food Co-op, carried her products, and they sold pretty well there. Boise was the capital of Idaho and the state's largest city. The Boise Museum of Fine Arts gift shop also carried her product in Boise, although the product did not turn over at this location nearly as well as it did at the Boise Co-op. Other fine art museums, gift shops in places like Missoula, Montana, Portland, Oregon, and Columbus, Ohio, carried Cowgirl Chocolates and Marilyn liked having her product in these outlets. She felt that her reputation as an artist helped her get her product placed in such locations, and the product generally sold well in these locations. She thought her biggest distribution coup was getting her product sold in the world-renowned Whitney Museum in New York City. She felt that the fact that it was sold there added to the product's panache. Unfortunately, the product did not sell there particularly well and it was dropped by the museum. The museum buyer had told Marilyn that she simply thought it was too hot for their customers. Another location in New York City, the Kitchen Market, did much better. The Kitchen Market was an upscale restaurant and gourmet food take-out business. The Kitchen Market was probably her steadiest wholesale customer other than the Moscow Co-op. The product also sold pretty well at the few similar gourmet markets where she had gotten her product placed, like Rainbow Groceries in Seattle and the Culinary Institute of America in San Francisco.

Marilyn had also gotten her product placed in a handful of specialty food stores that focused on hot and spicy foods. Surprisingly, she found, the product had never sold well in these locations. Despite the fact that the product had won the major fiery food awards, customers in these shops did not seem to be willing to pay the premium price for her product. She had concluded that if her product was located with similarly priced goods, like at the

Kitchen Market in New York City, it would sell, but that if it stood out in price then it did not sell as well. Marilyn was not sure, however, just how similarly her product needed to be priced compared to other products the store sold. It seemed clear to her that her $14.95 half-pound tins were standing out in price too much in the hot and spicy specialty stores that thrived on selling jars of hot sauce that typically retailed for $2.99 to $5.99. Marilyn wondered how her product might do at department stores that often sold half pound boxes of "premium" chocolates for as little as $9.95. She knew her half pound tins contained better chocolate, offered more unique packaging and logo design, and did not give that "empty-feeling" that the competitor's oversized boxes did, but wondered if her product would stand out too much in price in such retail locations.

Several online retailers also carried Cowgirl Chocolates, including companies like Salmon River Specialty Foods and Sam McGee's Hot Sauces, although sales from such sites were not very significant. Marilyn had also had her product available through Amazon.com for a short time, but few customers purchased her product from this site during the time it was listed. Marilyn concluded that customers searching the site for music or books simply were not finding her product, and those who did simply were not shopping for chocolates.

Marilyn also sold her products retail through her own website. The website accounted for about one-third of her sales. She liked Web-based sales, despite the extra work of having to process all the small orders, because she was able to capture both the wholesale and retail profits associated with the sale. She also liked the direct contact with the retail customers, and frequently tossed a few extra truffles into a customer's order and enclosed a note that said "a little extra bonus from the head cowgirl." Marilyn allowed customers to return the chocolate for a full refund if they found it not to their liking. Most of her sales growth from 1999 to 2000 had come from her Web site.

The website itself was created and maintained for her by a small local Internet service provider. It was a fairly simple site. It had pages that described the company and its products and allowed customers to place orders. It did not have any of the sophisticated features that would allow her to use it to capture information to track customers. Although she did not know for sure, she suspected that many of her Internet sales were from repeat customers who were familiar with her product. She included her website address on all of her packaging and had listed her site on several other sites, like saucemall.com and worldmall.com that would link shoppers at these sites to her site. Listing on some of these sites, like saucemall.com, was free. Listing on some other sites cost a small monthly fee—for the worldmall.com listing, for example, she paid $25/month. Some sites simply provided links to her site on their own. For example, one customer had told her she had found the Cowgirl Chocolate site off of an upscale shopping site called Style365.com. She was not sure how much traffic these various sites were generating on her site, and was unsure how best to attract new customers to her website aside from these efforts.

Marilyn had attempted to get her product into a number of bigger name, upscale retailers, like Dean & Delucca and Coldwater Creek. Dean and Delucca was known for its high-end specialty foods, and the buyers for the company had seemed interested in carrying Cowgirl Chocolates, but the owner had nixed the idea because he found the chocolates too spicy. One of the buyers had also told Marilyn that the owner was more of a chocolate purist or traditionalist who did not really like the idea of adding cayenne pepper to chocolate. Marilyn had also tried hard to get her product sold through Coldwater Creek, one of the largest catalog and online retailers in the country that sold high-end women's apparel and gifts for the home. Coldwater Creek was headquartered just a couple of hours north of Moscow in Sandpoint, Idaho. Like Dean & Delucca, Coldwater Creek had decided that the chocolate was too spicy. Coldwater Creek had also expressed some reservations about carrying food products other than at its retail outlet in

Sandpoint. Marilyn hoped that the introduction of mild-mannered Cowgirl Chocolates would help get her product into sites like these two.

Promotion

Marilyn was unsure how best to promote her product to potential customers given her limited resources. The ad that would appear in *Chile Pepper* magazine was her first attempt at really advertising her product. The ad itself was designed to grab readers' attention and pique their curiosity about Cowgirl Chocolates. Most of the ads in the magazine were fairly standard in format. They provided a lot of information and images of the product packed into a fairly small space. Her ad was different—it had very little product information and utilized the single image of the woman in the watering trough. It was to appear in a special section of the magazine that focused on celebrity musicians like Willie Nelson and The Dixie Chicks.

Other than the upcoming ad, Marilyn's promotional efforts were focused on trade shows and creating publicity opportunities. She attended a handful of trade shows each year. Some of these were focused on the hot and spicy food market, and it was at these events that she had won all of her awards. Other trade shows were more in the gourmet food market, and she typically shared table space at these events with Seattle Chocolates. She always gave away a lot of product samples at these trade shows, and had clearly won over some fans to her chocolate. But while these shows occasionally had led to placement of her product in retail locations, at least on a trial basis, they had as yet failed to land her what she would consider to be a really high volume wholesale account.

Marilyn also sought ways to generate publicity for her company and products. Several local newspapers had carried stories on her company in the last couple of years, and each time something like that would happen, she would see a brief jump in sales on her website. The *New York Times* had also carried a short article about her and her company. The day after that article ran, she generated sales of $1,000 through her Web site. More publicity like the *New York Times* article would clearly help. The recently released movie *Chocolat* about a woman who brings spicy chocolate with somewhat magical powers to a small French town was also generating some interest in her product. A number of customers had inquired if she used the same pepper in her chocolates as was used in the movie. Marilyn wondered how she might best capitalize on the interest the movie was creating in spicy chocolates. She thought that perhaps she could convince specialty magazines like *Art & Antiques* or regional magazines like *Sunset Magazine* or even national magazines like *Good Housekeeping* to run stories on her, her art and her chocolates. But she only had so much time to divide between her various efforts. She had looked into hiring a public relations firm, but had discovered that this would cost something on the order of $2,000/month. She did not expect that any publicity a public relations firm could create would generate sufficient sales to offset this cost, particularly given the limited number of locations where people could buy her chocolates. Marilyn was considering trying to write a cookbook as a way to generate greater publicity for Cowgirl Chocolates. She always talked a little about Cowgirl Chocolates when she gave seminars and presentations about her art, and thought that promoting a cookbook would create similar opportunities. The cookbook would also feature several recipes using Cowgirl Chocolate products.

In addition to being unsure how best to promote her product to potential customers, Marilyn also wondered what she should do to better tap into the seasonal opportunities that presented themselves to sellers of chocolate. Demand for her product was somewhat seasonal, with peak retail demand being at Christmas and Valentine's Day. But she was clearly not seeing the Christmas and Valentine sales of other chocolate companies. Seattle

Chocolates, for example, had around three-quarters of its annual sales in the fourth quarter, whereas Cowgirl Chocolate sales in the second half of 2000 were actually less than in the first half. Likewise, while Cowgirl Chocolates experienced a small increase in demand around Valentine's Day, it was nowhere near the increase in demand that other chocolate companies experienced. Marilyn did sell some gift buckets and baskets through her website, and these were more popular at Christmas and Valentine's Day. The Moscow Co-op had also sold some of these gift baskets and buckets during the 2000 Christmas season. Marilyn knew that the gift basket industry in the U.S. was pretty large, and that the industry even had its own trade publication called the *Gift Basket Review.* But she was not sure if gift baskets were the best way to generate sales at these two big holidays and thought that she could probably be doing more. One other approach to spur these seasonal sales that she was planning to try was to buy lists of e-mail addresses, that would allow her to send out several e-mails promoting her products right before Valentine's Day and Christmas. She had talked to the owners of a jewelry store about sharing the expense of this endeavor and they had tentative plans to purchase 10,000 e-mail addresses for $300.

What Next?

Marilyn looked again at the advertisement that would be appearing soon in *Chile Pepper* Magazine. The same friend who had helped her with her award winning package design had helped produce the ad. It would clearly grab people's attention, but would it bring customers to her products in the numbers she needed?

Next to the ad sat the folder with what financial information she had. Despite having little training in small business accounting and financial management, Marilyn knew it was important to keep good records. She had kept track of revenues and expenses for the year, and she had summarized these in a table (see Exhibit 4). Marilyn had shared this revenue and cost information with a friend with some experience in small business financial management, and the result was an estimated income statement for the year 2000 based upon the unaudited information in Exhibit 4. The estimated income statement, shown in Exhibit 5, revealed that Cowgirl had lost approximately $6,175 on operations before taxes. Combining the information in Exhibits 4 and 5, it appeared that the inventory had built up to approximately $16,848 by December 31, 2000. Marilyn had initially guessed she had $10,000 worth of product and packaging inventory, about twice her normal level of inventory, between what was stored in her garage turned art studio turned chocolate warehouse and what was stored for her at Seattle Chocolates. But the financial analysis indicated that she either had more inventory than she thought or that she had given away more product than she originally thought. Either way, this represented a significant additional drain on her resources—in effect cash expended to cover both the operational loss and the inventory buildup was approximately $23,000 in total (see note 3 of Exhibit 4 for a more detailed explanation). When Marilyn looked at the exhibits, she could see better why she had to loan the firm money. She also recognized that the bottom line was that the numbers did not look good, and she wondered if the ad would help turn things around for 2001.

If the ad did not have its desired affect, she wondered what she should do next. She clearly had limited resources to work with. She had already pretty much decided that if this ad did not work, she would not run another one in the near future. She was also pretty wary of working with distributors. In addition to her own bad experience, she knew of others in the industry that had bad experiences with distributors, and she did not think she could afford to take another gamble on a distributor. She wondered if she should focus more attention on her online retail sales or on expanding her wholesale business to include more retailers. If she focused more on her own online sales, what exactly should she do? If she

EXHIBIT 4
Summary of 2000
Financial
Information
(Unaudited)

Revenues:

Product Sales	$ 26,000
Revenue from Shipping	4,046 (see Note 1)
Total Revenues	**$ 30,046**

Expenses: (related to cost of sales)

Chocolate (raw material)	$16,508
Caramel (raw material)	2,647
Packaging (bags, boxes, tins)	9,120
Printing (labels, cards, etc)	3,148
Subtotal	$31,423 (see Note 2)

Other Expenses

Shipping and Postage	$ 4,046
Brokers	540
Travel (airfare, lodging, meals, gas)	5,786
Trade shows (promotions, etc.)	6,423
Website	1,390
Phone	981
Office Supplies	759
Photography	356
Insurance, Lawyers, Memberships	437
Charitable Contributions	200
Miscellaneous Other Expenses	1,071
State Taxes	35
Subtotal	$ 22,024
Total Expenses	**$ 53,447**
Cash needed to sustain operations	**$ 23,023** (see Note 3)

Estimated year-end inventory (12/31/00):

Product Inventory	$ 9,848
Extra Packaging and Labels	7,000
Total Inventory	**$16,848**

Notes (1) The $4,046 Revenue from Shipping represents income received from customers who are charged shipping and postage up front as part of the order. Cowgirl then pays the shipping and postage when the order is delivered. The offsetting operating expense is noted in "Other Expenses."

(2) Of this amount, $14,575 is attributed to product actually sold and shipped. The remaining $16,848 represents leftover inventory and related supplies (i.e., $16848 + $14575 = $31,423).

(3) Marilyn made a personal loan to the firm in the year 2000 for approximately $23,000 to sustain the business's operations.

focused on expanding her wholesale business, where should she put her emphasis? Should she continue to pursue retailers that specialized in hot and spicy foods, try to get her product placed in more Co-ops, expand her efforts to get the product positioned as a gift in museum gift shops and similar outlets, or focus her efforts on large, high-end retailers like Coldwater Creek and Dean & Delucca now that she had a nonspicy chocolate in her product mix? Or should she try to do something else entirely new? And what more should she do to create publicity for her product? Was the cookbook idea worth pursuing? As she thought about it, she began to wonder if things were beginning to spin out of control. Here she was, contemplating writing a cookbook to generate publicity for her chocolate company that she started to raise money to publish her arts magazine. Where would this end?

EXHIBIT 5   **Cowgirl Chocolates Income Statement (Accountant's unaudited estimate for Year 2000)**

			% of Sales
Revenues:			
Product Sales	$26,000		
Miscellaneous Income	$4,046		
Total Net Sales		**$30,046**	100%
Cost of Sales (shipped portion of chocolate, caramel, packaging, and printing)		$14,197	47%
Gross Margin		**$15,849**	53%
Operating Expenses:			
Advertising & Promotions:			
Trade Shows	6,423		
Website	1,390		
Charitable Contributions	200		
Subtotal		8,013	27%
Travel		5,786	19%
Miscellaneous		1,071	4%
Payroll Expense/Benefits @ 20%	(no personnel charges)	—	0%
Depreciation on Plant and Equipment	(no current owner-ship of PPE)	—	0%
Continuing Inventory (finished and unfinished)	(not included in income statement)	—	
Shipping & Postage		4,046	13%
Insurance, Lawyers, Professional Memberships		437	1.5%
Brokers		540	1.8%
Office Expenses (phone, supplies, photography, taxes)		2,131	7%
Total Operating Expenses		**22,024**	
Grand Total: All expenses		**$36,221**	
Profit before Interest & Taxes		**($6,175) [see note]**	
Interest Expense (short term)		—	
Interest Expense (long term)		—	
Taxes Incurred (Credit @ 18%, approximate tax rate)		($1,124)	
Net Profit After Taxes		**($5,051.15)**	
Net Profit After Taxes/Sales			−17%

Note: The ($6,175) loss plus the $16,848 in inventory build-up approximates the cash needed ($23,023—see Exhibit 4) to cover the total expenses for year 2000.

23

America Online (AOL)

Natalya V. Delcoure, Lawrence R. Jauch, and John L. Scott
Northeast Louisiana University

Introduction

America Online, Inc. (NYSE: AOL) was founded in 1985. This media company, with headquarters in Dulles, Virginia, has more than 10 million members and currently operates in the United States, Canada, the United Kingdom, France and Germany. AOL provides online services including electronic mail, online conferencing, Internet access, news, magazines, sports, weather, stock quotes, mutual fund transactions, software files, games, computing support and online classes.

According to the company, its mission is "to lead the development of a new interactive medium that eliminates traditional boundaries between people and places to create a new kind of interactive global community that holds the potential to change the way people obtain information, communicate with one another, buy products and services, and learn."

To accomplish this mission, the company's strategy is to continue investment in the growth of its subscriber base, pursue related business opportunities often through joint ventures and acquisitions, provide a full range of interactive services, and maintain technological flexibility.

AOL's rapid growth and community orientation have made it the most popular, easiest, and well-known way for consumers to get online. In December 1996, AOL had 8.5 million member sessions a day; 7 million e-mails sent to 12 million recipients a day; and it accounted for approximately $750,000 per day in merchandise transactions.

But AOL has not been trouble-free. On August 7, 1996, AOL threw 6 million subscribers off line for 19 hours due to software problems. America Online revealed that the glitch resulted from an error made by its working subsidiary, ANS Co., in reconfiguring software, and from a bug in router software. The error cost AOL $3 million in rebates. On January 8, 1997, America Online suffered a partial outage that forced it to shut down half of its system for four hours to find a problem. The problem was with an interface in a router device, which manages the flow of data in the network. The outage drew front-page headlines around the world, as millions of users were unable to access electronic mail, the Internet, and a variety of services and publications online for nearly a day.

America Online—Company Profile

America Online emerged from a firm founded in the early 1980s as Control Video Corp., which aimed to create an online service that specialized in games. It failed to meet strong competition from the Apple II and Commodore 64. Control Video was reorganized as Quantum Computer Services and became a custom developer of online services for other companies. Over time, Quantum managed to persuade Tandy Corp. and Apple Computers to offer a new service called Applelink Personal Edition. At the last minute, Apple withdrew from the deal and left Quantum holding software it had developed expressly for Applelink. In 1989 Quantum was only scraping by, and it did not have much money for splashy ad campaigns to attract computer users to their new service—America Online. So it came on the market with a unique approach, which was to blanket the countryside with diskettes containing America Online software. As the years went by, the company changed the way it accounted for the costs of acquiring subscribers and its pricing plans, but America Online had never actually made any money in its entire life. At the same time America Online has tried to position itself as the first "digital media company."

AOL Organization

AOL Corporation now oversees the operations of several subsidiaries and three divisions: AOL Networks, ANS Access, and AOL Studios. The Corporate Division comprises the core business functions of Finance, Human Resources, Legal Affairs, Corporate Communications, Corporate Development, and Technology. The Technology group is responsible for delivering research, development, network/data center operations, and member support to the other America Online divisions, technology licensees, and joint venture partners. The group is also responsible for support functions—including technical support, billing, and sales.

AOL Networks is responsible for extending the AOL brand into the market, developing new revenue streams, advertising, and online transactions. AOL Networks is led by Robert Pittman, President, formerly managing partner and CEO of Century 21 and co-founder of MTV Network.

ANS Access is responsible for the telecommunication network. The network consists of more than 160,000 modems connecting 472 cities in the U.S. and 152 cities internationally. Nearly 85 percent of the American population can dial into AOLNet on a local number. For America Online's members who travel, GlobalNet offers access in approximately 230 additional cities in 83 countries. The ANS technical team is responsible for architecture, design, development, installation, management and maintenance of hardware and software for the nationwide corporate data networks and Internet backbone by which communications take place.

AOL Studios runs AOL's innovative chat (iChatco), games (INN), local (Digital City), and independent (Greenhouse) programming properties. AOL Studios is the newest division in AOL. It is working on development of leading-edge technology for broadband and mid-band distribution, interactive brands that can be extended into other media properties such as TV and radio, and managing joint ventures with companies including Time-Warner and CapCities/ABC. Imagination Network Inc. is the provider of computer online entertainment services for AOL.

Digital City provides local programming, news, services, chat rooms, and commerce to AOL members as well as to the Internet at large. To date, Digital City has been launched nationally in Washington DC, Boston, Philadelphia, Atlanta, San Francisco and Los Angeles. Digital City planned to expand to over 40 cities in 1997. Digital City, Inc., is owned by Digital City LP. AOL owns a majority interest in that entity, and the Tribune Company owns the remaining interest.

Advanced CO+RE Systems, Inc., is a wholly owned subsidiary of America Online, which provides network services for AOLnet, together with Sprint Corporation and BBN Corporation. Through this subsidiary, America Online designs, develops, and operates high performance wide-area networks for business, research, education, and government organizations.

In February 1996, AOL merged with the Johnson-Grace Company, a leading developer of compression technology and multimedia development and delivery tools. Using the Johnson-Grace technology, America Online is able to deliver the data-intensive graphics and audio and video capabilities using narrow-band technologies, even over the slower speed modems currently used by most AOL members.

In fiscal 1996 AOL combined its key production areas to form AOL Productions, Inc., a wholly owned subsidiary. AOL Productions has emerged as a leading studio system with expertise in all phases of interactive content development for online, World Wide Web, Internet, and CD-ROM delivery.

2Market, Inc., is a joint venture between America Online, Apple Computer, and Medior. It provides retail catalog shopping CD-ROMs that include online ordering capabilities. In 1997 America Online, along with Netscape Communications and Disney's ABC unit, announced their plans to launch ABCNEWS.com, a 24-hour news service.

Since the beginning of 1995, the company also acquired Advanced Network and Services, Inc., Ubique, Ltd., Navisoft, Inc., Global Network Navigator, Inc., Book-Link Technologies, Inc., and Redgate Communications Corporation. AOL is also planning to go into the bookselling business in a joint venture with Barnes & Noble, but the timing is still uncertain.

AOL Marketing

The goals of the firm's consumer marketing programs are to increase the general visibility of America Online and to make it easy for customers to experiment with and subscribe to its services. AOL attracts new subscribers through independent marketing programs such as direct mail, disk inserts and inserts in publications, advertising, and a variety of co-marketing efforts. The company has entered into co-marketing agreements with numerous personal computer hardware, software, and peripheral production companies, and also with certain of its media partners. These companies bundle America Online software with their products and cater to the needs of a specific audience.

America Online has also been expanding into business-to-business markets, using AOL's network to provide customized network solutions to both individual businesses and to professional communities and industries. These private AOLs (the "PAOLs") offer the ease of use America Online is known for, as well as customized features and functionality accessible only by preauthorized users, access to the fleet of AOL distribution platforms, secure communications and information. The company offers these products using a direct sales force and direct marketing, and through resellers and system integrators.

America Online utilizes specialized retention programs designed to increase customer loyalty and satisfaction and to maximize customer subscription life. These retention programs include regularly scheduled online events and conferences; the regular addition of new content, services, and software programs; and online promotions of upcoming online events and new features. The firm also provides a variety of support mechanisms such as online technical support and telephone support services.

In May 1995 America Online introduced its Web browser, which provides integrated World Wide Web access within the AOL services. The integrated approach allows the user to seamlessly use the full suite of America Online features, including chat room, e-mail gateways and mailing lists, file transfer protocol, USENET News-groups, WAIS, and Gopher.

In the summer of 1997 America Online, Inc. planned to offer its 8 million members a three-dimensional gaming world, CyberPark. The company will try to compete with such heavyweights as Microsoft, Internet Gaming Zone site, and MCI, which will launch a service in 1997 that allows computer users to play their favorite CD-ROM games. The projected earnings are expected to reach $127 million in 1997, but there are still some technical problems to overcome and the uncertainty of how much to charge future users.

America Online has included international market expansion in its strategy to gain competitive advantage. In April 1995, AOL entered into a joint venture with Bertelsmann, one of the world's largest media companies, to offer interactive services in Europe: Germany (November 1995), the United Kingdom (January 1996), and France (March 1996). Bertelsmann agreed to contribute up to $100 million to fund the launch of the European services, provided access to its book and music club membership base of over 30 million, and offered its publishing content to the joint venture on a most favored customer basis. In addition, Bertelsmann acquired approximately a 5 percent interest in America Online and was designated a member of the company's Board of Directors. AOL contributed interactive technology and management expertise, proprietary software licenses and development services, staff training, and technical support in order to develop, test, and launch the interactive services in Europe. Subscribers to the European services enjoy access to America Online's services in the United States, and United States subscribers enjoy access to the European services.

AOL Canada, launched in January 1996, features local content and services. In October 1996, AOL Canada offered Canadian members software, thirteen local channels, billing in Canadian dollars, e-mail, message boards, and easy access to the Internet through a Web browser. AOL Canada's key partners include Citytv, an internationally renowned broadcaster and program producer; MuchMusic, Canada's first national music television channel; Shift Magazine, Canada's hottest publication in media; Intuit Canada, makers of the world's leading personal finance software, Quicken; and Southam New Media, a wholly owned subsidiary of Southam Inc., Canada's largest news organization.

In May 1996, America Online announced a partnership with Mitsui & Co., one of the world's largest international trading companies, and Nikkei, one of Japan's leading media companies with respected business and computer publications. The joint venture consists of Mitsui & Co. owning 40 percent, Nikkei 10 percent and AOL 50 percent. Japanese partners contributed more than 120 years of experience and credibility in the Japanese market, a strong management team, and $56 million to fund the launch of the Japanese service. America Online brings to the venture its ability to develop, manage, and execute interactive online services in the U.S., Europe, and Canada.

America Online's wildly successful marketing ploy of flat rate pricing in the U.S. turned out to contribute to AOL's latest problem. About 75 percent of AOL's customers took the flat-rate offer. As a result, total daily AOL customer use soared from 1.6 million hours online in October 1996 to more than 4 million hours in January 1997. (These problems are more fully described later in this case.)

Meeting Customer Needs

The company provides tools to its members so that they can control their child's or teen's experience online without cramping the adults who enjoy using AOL's services to talk to other adults. Parental controls can block or limit the use of chat, Instant Messages, e-mail, binary files, news groups, or the Web. Different online areas support different values. For instance:

- ACLU forum: encourages lively yet responsible debate. Illegal activities (harassment, distribution of illegal materials) are not permitted in this area.
- Womens' Network: is a women-friendly and safe space for chatting, learning, teaching and networking, but men are still welcome to join the communication.

- Christian Chat room: allows fellowship among Christian members. In this space, prose-lytizing is forbidden.
- Kids Only: gives children their own space online for searching help with homework, sending e-mail, and hanging out in chat rooms. Parental control can be set up in this area.

The average adult spends about an hour per day on line, but the average child spends three. Currently, there are 4.1 million kids surfing the Net. By 2000, it is expected there will be 19.2 million. Kids, who spent $307 million in 1996 on online services, will spend $1.8 billion by 2002, and that is why media and Web giants are scrambling to offer new kid-friendly sites. Fox TV features cartoons and kid shows. Disney gave AOL first crack at hosting Daily Blast, which offers kids games, comics, and stories for $4.95 per month or $39.95 per year. But, says Rob Jennings, vice-president for programming for AOL networks, "we felt we had a good mix already." Yahooligans! offers kids-friendly Web-sites for free. AOL still has partnerships with other media giants such as Disney rival Viacom Inc.'s Nickelodeon unit, for other offerings.

Since 1994, AOL has offered a Kids Only area featuring homework help, games, and online magazines, as well as the usual fare of software, games, and chat rooms. The area gets about 1 million 8- to 12-year-old visitors monthly.

In April 1996, America Online began to see the effect of seasonality in both member acquisitions and in the amount of time spent by customers using its services. The company expects that member acquisition is to be highest in the second and third fiscal quarters, when sales of new computers and computer software are highest due to holiday seasons. Customer usage is expected to be lower in the summer months, due largely to extended daylight hours and competing outdoor leisure activities.

AOL Employees

As of June 30, 1996, America Online had 5,828 employees, including 1,058 in software and content development; 3,271 in customer support; 199 in marketing; 1,099 in operations; and 291 in corporate operations. None of AOL's employees is represented by a labor union, and America Online has never experienced a work stoppage.

AOL employs numerous part-time workers around the world known as remote staff. These are volunteer staff who develop content and provide both marketing and operations functions. Remote staff write informational articles, produce graphics, host chat rooms, provide technical assistance, and fulfill various support functions. Remote staff duties vary. Some may work as little as ten hours per week or more than forty hours per week.

AOL's remote staff are compensated for these services with "community leader accounts"—a membership for which the staff members are not charged. Relatively few remote staff are paid as independent contractors.

AOL's flat rate pricing plan had a serious impact on its remote staff. Prior to the flat rate, members paid about $3 per hour of online access. Hence, a "free account" would have a value of approximately $300 for a staff member who spent three hours per day online. After the flat rate pricing plan, this account's value fell to $20. This enormous decrease in incentives led many remote staff to resign their positions. The positions hardest hit were those for which the job pressures were highest. AOL's once touted "Techlive" is now all but invisible.

AOL Finance

Exhibits 1 and 2 present the financial statements for fiscal years 1995 and 1996. About 90 percent of the firm's revenues are generated from online subscription fees. AOL's other revenues are generated from sales of merchandise, data network services, online transactions and advertising, marketing and production services and development and licensing fees. The increase of over $600 million in service revenues from 1995 to 1996 was primarily attributed to a 93 percent increase in AOL subscribers.

EXHIBIT 1
Income Statement,
Year Ended June 30
(Amounts in
thousands, except per
share data)

	1996	1995
Revenues:		
Online service revenues	$ 991,656	$344,309
Other revenues	102,198	49,981
Total revenues	1,093,854	394,290
Costs and expenses:		
Cost of revenues	627,372	229,724
Marketing	212,710	77,064
Product development	53,817	14,263
General and administrative	110,653	42,700
Acquired research and development	16,981	50,335
Amortization of goodwill	7,078	1,653
Total costs and expenses	1,028,611	415,739
Income (loss) from operations:	**65,243**	**(21,449)**
Other income (loss) from operations	(2,056)	3,074
Merger expenses	(848)	(2,207)
Income (loss) before provision for income taxes	62,339	(20,582)
Provision for income taxes	(32,523)	(15,169)
Net income (loss)	$ 29,816	$ (35,751)
Earnings (loss) per share:		
Net income (loss)	$ 0.28	$ (0.51)
Weighted average shares outstanding	108,097	69,550

This is expected to undergo radical change, due to flat rate pricing, with much less revenue coming from subscriber fees, which AOL hopes to make up by increases in the other revenue streams.

Cost of revenue, which includes network-related costs, consists of data and voice communication costs, costs associated with operating the data centers, and providing customer support. These increased almost $400 million from 1995 to 1996. This increase was related to a growth of data communication cost, customer support cost and royalties paid to information and service providers.

For fiscal 1996, marketing expenses increased 176 percent over fiscal 1995. This was primarily attributed to an increase in the size and number of marketing programs designed to expand the subscriber base.

Product development costs include research and development and the amortization of software. For fiscal 1996, these costs increased 277 percent over fiscal 1995, and increased as a percentage of total revenues from 3.6 percent to 4.9 percent. The increases in product development costs were primarily attributable to an increase in the number of technical employees. Product development costs, before capitalization and amortization, increased by 242 percent.

For fiscal 1996, general and administrative costs increased 159 percent over fiscal 1995 and decreased as a percentage of total revenues from 10.8 percent to 10.1 percent. The increase in general and administrative costs was related to higher personnel, office, and travel expenses related to an increase in the number of employees. The decrease in general and administrative costs as a percentage of total revenues was a result of the substantial growth in revenues, which more than offset the additional general and administrative costs, combined with the semi-variable nature of many of the general and administrative costs.

Acquired research and development costs relate to in-process research and development purchased with the acquisition of Ubique, Ltd., in September 1995. Acquired re-

EXHIBIT 2
**Consolidated Balance
Sheets, June 30
(Amounts in
thousands, except per
share data)**

	1996	1995
Assets		
Current assets:		
Cash and cash equivalents	$118,421	$ 45,877
Short-term investments	10,712	18,672
Trade accounts receivable	42,939	32,176
Other receivables	29,674	11,381
Prepaid expenses and other current assets	68,832	25,527
Total current assets	270,578	133,633
Property and equipment at cost, net	101,277	70,919
Other assets:		
Product development costs, net	44,330	18,949
Deferred subscriber acquisition costs, net	314,181	77,229
License rights, net	4,947	5,579
Other assets	35,878	9,121
Deferred income taxes	135,872	35,627
Goodwill, net	51,691	54,356
Total assets	$958,754	$405,413
Liabilities and Stockholders' Equity		
Current liabilities:		
Trade accounts payable	$105,904	$ 84,640
Other accrued expenses and liabilities	127,898	23,509
Deferred revenue	37,950	20,021
Accrued personnel costs	15,719	2,863
Current portion of long-term debt	2,435	2,329
Total current liabilities	289,906	133,362
Long-term liabilities:		
Notes payable	19,306	17,369
Deferred income taxes	135,872	35,627
Other liabilities	1,168	2,243
Total liabilities	$446,252	$188,601
Stockholders' Equity:		
Preferred stock, $.01 par value; 5,000,000 shares authorized; 1,000 shares issued and outstanding at June 30, 1996	1	—
Common stock, $.01 par value; 300,000,000 and 100,000,000 shares authorized, 92,626,000 and 76,728,268 shares issued and outstanding at June 30, 1996 and 1995, respectively	926	767
Additional paid-in capital	519,342	252,668
Accumulated deficit	(7,767)	(36,623)
Total stockholders' equity	512,502	216,812
Total liabilities and equity	$958,754	$405,413

search and development costs relate to in-process research and development purchased as part of the acquisitions of BookLink Technologies, Inc. ("Booklink"), and Navisoft, Inc. ("Navisoft").

The amortization of goodwill increase relates primarily to America Online's fiscal 1995 acquisitions of Advanced Network & Services, Inc., and Global Network Navigator, Inc., which resulted in approximately $56 million of goodwill. The goodwill related to these acquisitions is being amortized on a straight-line basis over periods ranging from five to ten

EXHIBIT 3
Market Price of
Common Stock

For the Quarter Ended	High	Low
September 30, 1994	$10.28	$ 6.88
December 31, 1994	14.63	7.47
March 31, 1995	23.69	12.31
June 30, 1995	24.06	16.75
September 30, 1995	37.25	21.38
December 31, 1995	46.25	28.25
March 31, 1996	60.00	32.75
June 30, 1996	71.00	36.63
September 30, 1996	37.75	34.65
December 31, 1996	33.38	32.25

years. The increase in amortization of goodwill results from a full year of goodwill recognized in fiscal 1996 compared to only a partial year of goodwill recognized in fiscal 1995.

Other income (expenses) consists of interest expense and nonoperating charges net of investment income and nonoperating gains. The change in other income (expense) was attributed to the $8 million settlement of a class action lawsuit partially offset by an increase in investment income.

Nonrecurring merger expenses totaling $848,000 were recognized in fiscal 1996 in connection with the merger of America Online with Johnson-Grace Company. Nonrecurring merger expenses totaling $2,207,000 were recognized in fiscal 1995 in connection with the mergers of AOL with Redgate Communications Corporation, Wide Area Information Servers, Inc., and Medior, Inc.

In December 1993, the company completed a public offering of 8,000,000 shares of common stock, which generated net cash proceeds of approximately $62.7 million. In April 1995, the joint venture with Bertelsmann to offer interactive online services in Europe netted approximately $54 million through the sale of approximately 5 percent of its common stock to Bertelsmann. In October 1995, AOL completed a public offering of 4,963,266 shares of common stock, which generated net cash proceeds of approximately $139.5 million. In May 1996, America Online sold convertible preferred stock to Mitsui in its joint venture with Mitsui & Co., Ltd., and Nohon Keizai Shimbun, Inc., to offer interactive online services in Japan. The preferred stock has an aggregate liquidation preference of approximately $28 million and accrues dividends at a rate of 4 percent per annum. Accrued dividends can be paid in the form of additional shares of preferred stock. Exhibit 3 shows the history of share prices of AOL's common stock.

America Online has financed its operations through cash generated from operations and the sale of its capital stock. AOL has financed its investments in facilities and telecommunications equipment principally through leasing. America Online leases the majority of its facilities and equipment under non-cancelable operating leases. The communication network requires a substantial investment in telecommunications equipment, which America Online plans to finance principally through leasing. The company has never declared, nor has it paid, any cash dividends on its common stock. AOL currently intends to retain its earnings to finance future growth.

The company uses its working capital to finance ongoing operations and to fund marketing and content programs and the development of its products and services. America Online plans to continue to invest in computing and support infrastructure. Additionally, AOL expects to use a portion of its cash for the acquisition and subsequent funding of technologies, products, or businesses complementary to the company's current business. For example, America Online is investing in the development of alternative technologies to deliver its services. AOL has entered into agreements with several manufacturers of PDAs, including Sony, Motorola, Tandy, and Casio, to bundle a palmtop edition of America Online's client software with the PDAs sold by such manufacturers. AOL is participating in early cable trials using cable as the conduit into PCs, and has announced future support of ISDN and wireless. In the paging market, AOL has entered into agreements with AT&T Wireless Services and MobileMedia to provide their paging customers who subscribe to AOL with mobile access to certain America Online services.

AOL's Environment

For a long time such companies as AT&T, Western Union, and RCA dominated the telecommunication industry. The courts deregulated the telephone industry in the 1980s. Although technology and market development made passage of new telecommunications legislation inevitable, it took about ten years to frame it. Even though the Telecommunications Reform Act of 1996 meant to remove many of the regulatory barriers and make it easier for telecom companies to invest in the information superhighway, so far it has made little difference. The Department of Commerce and the U.S. Trade Representative has pushed the World Trade Organization to open up the telecom sector to more service and equipment competition. As the result of trade negotiations in Singapore, tariffs on many telecommunications products and services will be reduced with great potential benefit to U.S. firms. Additional talks were under way in Switzerland in 1997, which may permit U.S. telecommunications companies to compete on equal footing with providers in Europe and elsewhere.

America Online must pay particular attention to changes in the regulatory environment relating to telecommunications and the media. Additional legislative proposals from international, federal, and state government bodies in the areas of content regulations, intellectual property, privacy rights and state tax issues could impose additional regulations and obligations upon all online service providers.

Telephone companies are collecting high revenues as computer and online services expand. One study found that local carriers collected revenues totaling $1.4 billion in 1995 from second phone lines used mainly for Net links, while spending only $245 million to upgrade their networks for the additional usage. Phone companies experienced 8 percent to 9 percent profit growth in 1996 since second phone line installations at homes grew 25 percent. Both local carriers and online service providers agree that there is a necessity to build higher capacity networks to satisfy the increasing demand for public phone networks to meet the growing trend in cybersurfing.

The future of technology is difficult to predict, but can affect AOL's future strategy. Some speculate that interactive TV is going to be replaced by network computers (such as those from Sun). Some argue that Internet connections should be available for people who want to use them, and that public monies should be provided to ensure access for all. There is a growing place for satellite and fiber in the new communication system. Technology trends are sometimes born of social change. Here are some of the most important trends to watch for in the next five years.

- The world phone could be a satellite wireless phone that uses digital technology. A combination of Global System for Mobilization (GSM) and satellite technologies could be the model for the world phone. Pioneers such as Wildfire Communications, Lucent Technologies, Dialogic, and VDOnet are among hundreds of alternative carriers that try to unite PCs, phone, e-mail, fax, and video into a seamless fabric. They are designing software that sends phone calls around the world on the Internet very cheaply. The line dividing computers and telephones, voice and data is blurring. Building on the union of data networks and computers, the Internet has become the new global communications infrastructure for businesses.

- Personal Communication Systems (PCS) could broadside local telecom carriers. Projections are that local exchange carriers must brace for a loss of 35 percent of high-margin business customers and 25 percent or more of their residential shares to PCS providers. Mobile subscribers could represent 17 percent of traditional wireline carrier business by 2010. VocalTec Ltd., leading maker of Internet telephone products, recently broadened the appeal by introducing gateways that connect the Internet to standard phone systems—allowing PC users to call non-PC users on their phones and vice versa. VocalTec claims it saves $10,000 a month on phone bills between the company's New Jersey and Israeli offices.

- Wireless convergence: commercial mobile wireless will include mobile satellite, and satellite communication will overlap coverage and mobility with cellular/ PCS. Cordless telephony will play major roles. Several years ago, Microsoft Corp. and Novell Inc. tried to apply computer-telephony integration technology to any desktop by creating competing standards for connecting phone systems to PC networks. But the products, TAPI and TSAPI, which allowed desktop computers to receive and manage phone calls through their PCs, went nowhere. Now, a wave of products built on TAPI and TSAPI that work with standard telecom equipment is hitting the market. Users can select a handful of names from a database and command the phone switch to set up a conference call with all of them. Pacific Bell is testing a sophisticated messaging service on 300 wireless-phone customers in San Diego. It answers incoming phone calls, screens them, and automatically routes them to wherever you are—a conference room, your home office, or a shopping mall. For a richer media experience, many companies are concentrating on desktop videoconferencing products from Intel, C-Phone, and VDOnet, among others. Those products are very cost efficient and price compatible.

- Asynchronous transfer mode: ATM carrier services are still expensive. Originally developed by Bell Laboratories for high-speed voice networks, ATM has now been adapted for data applications. They are able to move data at 155 mbps, whereas advanced modems top out at 56 kbps. The Defense Department uses a fiber-optic ATM network between the U.S. and Germany. The Mayo Clinic in Rochester, Minn., uses ATM for "tele-medicine"—doctors can video conference with patients. ATM switches account for an estimated savings of $200,000 per month for American Petroleum Institution, which uses this tool to transmit drilling-site data over satellite. This technology is moving quickly into the public phone network, which increases the speed of the global communication network.

- Residential gateways: will let customers plug in telecom carriers and cable companies' networks and give users more control.

Increased competition makes it hard to make money on selling unlimited online access. Service providers have to upgrade their equipment to handle higher modem speeds and install separate equipment and phone lines for rival technologies. Sales of new modems are expected to be huge, driven by the Internet boom. AOL signed a deal with U.S. Robotics, which was scheduled to start turning on telephone access numbers on February 27, 1997, to give subscribers log-on access at a faster speed. Currently, the only high speed (56 kbps) modems that America Online customers can use are made by U.S. Robotics, which now controls a quarter of the market. Modems from the Open 56K Forum group—available in March 1997—can't talk to those of U.S. Robotics. Most of the Open 56K group will have modems out in March 1997. The No. 2 modem maker, Hayes Microcomputer Products Inc., registered more than 40,000 people for a deal it offered on the company's Web page: customers can get their high-speed modems for $99 by sending in any brand modem. U.S. Robotics sells its superfast modems for $199 for a version that is installed into the computer, or $239 for an external model.

Use of the Net has dramatically increased the demand for techies. An estimated 760,000 people are working for Net-related companies alone. The Internet is full of companies' ads wanting programmers. A new study by the Information Technology Association of America estimates that 190,000 infotech jobs stand vacant in U.S. companies—half in the information industry. The situation can get worse, because the number of college students in computer science has fallen 43 percent in the past decade. Net-related companies are spending millions of dollars recruiting employees. In 1996, pay for info-tech workers rose by 12 percent to 20 percent, while average annual pay for software architects rose to $85,600.

The online services market is highly competitive. Major direct competitors include Prodigy Services Company, a joint venture of IBM and Sears; e-World, a service of Apple Computer, Inc.; GEnie, a division of General Electric Information Services; Delphi Internet Services Corporation, a division of News Corp.; Interchange, a service of AT&T Corp.; and Microsoft Corp., which launched its online service under the name Microsoft Network. Microsoft has been devoting considerable resources and energy to focus the firm and its products squarely on the Internet. The Internet directory services are another source of competition, including NETCOM On-Line Communication Services, Inc.; Bolt, Beranek & Newman, Inc.; Performance System International, UUNET Technologies with Internet MCI; Yahoo, Inc.; Excite, Inc.; Infoseek Corporation; and Lycos, Inc. Finally, software providers such as Intuit Inc. and Netscape Communication Corporation are another category of competitors.

America Online is, by far, the largest online service, with 10 million American members, as of September 1997. Compuserve was the second largest service prior to AOL acquiring it. The Microsoft Network is now the second largest online service, with 2.3 million subscribers. But a great deal of the competition comes from the small local Internet providers, who were the catalyst that drove AOL to the flat rate pricing plan.

The imperatives for global communications look very promising. Telecom and data networks should become a lifeline for nations, businesses, and individuals. The Internet is pushing world financial markets and the flow of goods and services. The Net has the potential to revolutionize business and human lives, but it also has the danger that the network can be a vehicle of isolation. Communication by fax, modem, wireless handset, video conferencing, or telecommuting can create personal isolation. A high-tech world may need to be counterbalanced by community, family and person-to-person contacts. The Internet and more advanced computing plus training for people to understand and participate in the network have obvious educational potential.

The Flat Rate Debacle

Through December 31, 1994, the company's standard monthly membership fee for its service, which included five hours of services, was $9.95, with a $3.50 hourly fee for usage in excess of five hours per month. Effective January 1, 1995, the hourly fee for usage in excess of five hours per month decreased from $3.50 to $2.95, while the monthly membership fee remained the same.

In October 1995, AOL launched its Internet Service, Global Network Navigator (GNN), which was aimed at consumers who wanted a full-featured Internet-based service, but without the full service quality of AOL. The monthly fee for GNN was $14.95. This fee included 20 hours of service per month with a $1.95 hourly fee for usage in excess of 20 hours per month. In May 1996, AOL announced an additional pricing plan, which was oriented to its heavier users and called "Value Plan." It became effective July 1, 1996, and included 20 hours of services for $19.95 per month, with a $2.95 hourly fee for usage in excess of 20 hours per month.

AOL usage increased dramatically when the company announced its plans to offer flat rate unlimited pricing in October 1996. AOL switched its more than 7 million members at

EXHIBIT 4
AOL System Use Before and After Flat Rate Pricing

Average AOL	January 1997	September 1996
Member daily usage	32 minutes	14 minutes
Daily sessions	10 million	6 million
Total hours daily	4.2 million	1.5 million
Total hours per month	125 million (est.), (Dec.: 102 million)	45 million
Peak simultaneous usage	260,000	140,000
Avg. minutes per session	26 minutes	16 minutes

that time to unlimited access for $19.95 a month. Its network was deluged by subscribers, many of whom could not log onto the system during peak evening hours or on weekends. Exhibit 4 shows comparative data before and after this new pricing policy.

Following the second shutdown of its system in January 1997, the company's Chairman and CEO, Steve Case, emphasized that AOL took full responsibility for the "busy signals." "When we decided . . . to introduce unlimited use pricing, we were well aware that usage would increase substantially. We did some consumer testing and operations modeling to generate usage forecast, and we began building extra capacity in advance of the December launch of unlimited pricing. We thought that there would be some problems with busy signals during our peak periods in some cities. . . . But we expected those problems to be modest, and not too long in duration."

AOL has tried to decrease the "busy signal" by increasing the size and the pace of the system capacity expansion, by bringing in new hardware, installing circuits, adding 150,000 new modems, increasing the number of customer service representatives to 4,000, offering a toll-free line, and reducing marketing efforts. Mr. Case even asked the customers for help by moderating their own use of AOL during peak hours.

Even so, AOL became fodder for comics and lawsuits. In one comic strip, the customer is shown on the telephone conversing with "customer service":

Caller: "I am not getting my money's worth with your online service."
Service: "Good news, sir! We have just cut our rates."
Caller: "Your lines are always busy . . . I can't get online!"
Service: "Don't forget you get unlimited time online for no extra charge."

A number of AOL customers filed lawsuits against the company in more than 37 states, charging the firm with civil fraud, breach of contract, negligence, and violation of state consumer-protection statutes. The negative publicity from the "busy signals" allowed other online providers the opportunity to expand their number of subscribers and increase their revenues from advertising and merchandising fees.

America Online began a refund offer to its members, and the Attorneys General in several states agreed to support its proposed plan to members. The plan gives customers a refund policy: customers had a choice of a free month online or up to $39.90—the cost of two months of its unlimited service. In addition, AOL increased customer service staffing to handle member cancellations so that calls were answered within two minutes. Also, AOL gave customers the opportunity to cancel their membership through mail, fax, or toll-free number.

In the meantime America Online was facing another legal problem, this time from its shareholders. On February 24, 1997, shareholders sued in U.S. District Court in Virginia alleging that AOL directors and outside accountants violated securities laws in the way the company did its accounting. The online giant took a $385 million charge in October 1996 for marketing expenses it had capitalized.

The various problems facing America Online raised serious doubts among analysts about its ability to meet its goal to earn $60 million in fiscal year 1998 (ending in June) without more revenues from sources outside of operations. An analyst with Smith, Barney & Company believed that the $1.7 billion company has a cash flow problem which could force AOL to raise cash through bank loans or another stock offering—which would be the company's fourth. "The worst time to go to the market—is when you need to," notes Abe Mastbaum, money manager of American Securities.

Prior to 1997, AOL was able to maintain its positive cash flow through the addition of new members. Due to overload of the system, brought on by flat-rate pricing, new members cannot be added as aggressively as needed. The company will have to develop new sources of revenue, such as online advertising and fees on electronic transfers, or charge additional fees for premium channels. AOL launched its first premium channel in July of 1997. Its premium games channel allows people from around the world to play both traditional games, such as hearts, and new games against each other. It charges $2 per hour for the premium games channel.

Since AOL did not have the infrastructure in place to handle the increased usage that came with the revised pricing structure, America Online planned to hold its membership at 8 million and spend $350 million to expand system capacity and customer support. At least that was the plan before the Compuserve acquisition.

In April 1997, rumors were heard about AOL acquiring CompuServe from H&R Block. America Online declined to comment. CompuServe said the company is in "external discussions" regarding a deal. Buying CompuServe would add much-needed network capacity to AOL's strained system. Those speculations gave a boost to both companies' stock: CompuServe's shares jumped 12 percent to $11; AOL's stock was up 7.6 percent to $45.75. A month before, CompuServe Corp. had quietly cut 500 jobs, or 14 percent of its work force, which was the latest evidence of the online company's troubles as it lost members in an intense competition with America Online and other rivals. The cuts left CompuServe's home office in Columbus, Ohio, with about 3,200 employees who are primarily online content and service specialists. At the same time CompuServe posted a $14 million quarterly loss and three days later the company's president and chief executive, Robert J. Massey, resigned. In September 1997, AOL traded ANS Access from Worldcom for CompuServe's online service.

24

Sun Microsystems: A High Growth, Loosely Organized Giant in a Constrained, Technology Intensive Environment

Walter E. Greene *University of Texas Pan American*
William C. House *University of Arkansas–Fayetteville*

Introduction

In 1982, four individuals, who were 27 years old, combined forces to found Sun Microsystems, with the objective of producing and marketing computer workstations to scientists and engineers. Two of the four were Stanford MBA graduates—Michigan born Scott McNealy, and Vinod Khosla, a native of India. They were joined by Andreas Bechtolsheim, a Stanford engineering graduate who had constructed a computer workstation with spare parts in order to perform numerical analysis, and Unix software expert William Joy from the Berkeley campus. Sun's founders believed there was demand for a desktop computer workstation costing between $10,000 and $20,000 in a market niche ignored by minicomputer makers IBM, Data General, DEC, and Hewlett-Packard.

Sun Microsystems is the market leader in the fast-growing workstation industry, expecting sales revenue growth of 30 percent annually during the next five years compared to

The research and written case information was prepared by Wm. C. House of the University of Arkansas–Fayetteville, and Walter E. Greene, Professor, University of Texas Pan American for presentation at the North American Case Research Association Symposium (Atlanta, 1991).

5 to 10 percent for the personal computer industry. Workstations can be used in standalone fashion or as part of networked configurations. The product lines produced range from low priced diskless units to higher powered graphics oriented stations at the top of the line.

In contrast to personal computers, workstations are characterized by 32-bit instead of 16-bit microprocessors, a strong tendency to use the UNIX operating system instead of MS/DOS, more sophisticated software and graphics capabilities, larger storage capacities, faster processing speeds and the ability to function effectively in a networking environment. The principal users of workstations have been engineers and scientists. However, price reductions and technological improvements have broadened the appeal of workstations so that they are finding use in financial trading, desktop publishing, animation, mapping, and medical imaging applications.

Sun, the fastest growing company in the computer hardware industry, has revenues that are increasing at a five year compounded rate of 85 percent and income increasing at a 67 percent rate from 1985 to 1990.[1] For fiscal year 1991, Sun's revenues were $3.2 billion and net income was $190 million.[2] The company's rapid growth rate has severely drained its cash resources.

Chairman and CEO of Sun Microsystems

Scott McNealy, the current chairman of Sun, is a native of Detroit and grew up on the fringes of the U.S. automobile industry. Originally rejected by both Harvard and Stanford Business Schools, he graduated from Harvard with a major in economics. In 1981, at the age of 26, McNealy became manufacturing director at Onyx systems, a small minicomputer maker. The company was faced with serious quality problems. In two months, the operation showed drastic improvement as McNealy probed work rules and production bottlenecks, encouraging workers to identify problems and overcome obstacles on the way toward improving workplace efficiency.

In 1982, former Stanford classmates Andy Bechtolsheim and Vinod Khosla asked him to join them as Director of Operations in a new company to be called Sun Microsystems. Two years later, McNealy was chosen by the Board of Directors to be CEO over Paul Ely, now executive vice president of Unisys. During the first month after he became CEO, one of the three cofounders resigned, the company lost $500,000 on $2 million in sales, and two-thirds of its computers didn't work.

He is a workaholic, working from daylight to dark, seven days a week, rarely finding time for recreation activities. The frantic pace at Sun engendered by McNealy is sometimes referred to as Sunburn. There is a tendency for Sun executives to take on too many projects at once, thereby creating tremendous internal pressure and organizational chaos.

McNealy's philosophy can be capsuled in these company sayings[3]:

1. On Decision-making—Consensus if possible, but participation for sure.
2. On Management Cooperation—Agree and commit, disagree and commit, or just get the hell out of the way.
3. On Market Response—The right answer is the best answer. The wrong answer is second best. No answer is the worst.
4. On Individual Initiative—To ask permission is to seek denial.

He has stated that the company is trying to achieve four goals—significant increases in revenue and book value, improved product acceptance, and higher profit margins.

---

[1]John Markoff, "The Smart Alecs at Sun Are Regrouping," *New York Times*, April 28, 1991.
[2]G. Paschal Zachary, "Sun Challenges Microsoft's Hold over Software," *The Wall Street Journal*, September 4, 1991.
[3]"Sun Microsystems Turn on the Afterburners," *BusinessWeek*, July 18, 1988.

Chief Computer Designer

Andreas Bechtolsheim, chief computer designer, was one of Sun's cofounders. At age 35 he has the title of vice president of technology. A native of West Germany, Bechtolsheim designed his first computer in 1980 while still a graduate student at Stanford University. It was a workstation designed for scientists and engineers. However, he was unable to sell the idea to any computer company then in existence. Shortly thereafter, he joined Joy, Khosla, and McNealy in founding Sun Microsystems and the company's first product was based on his machine.

Initially, Bechtolsheim persuaded Sun to use off-the-shelf products to develop its workstations instead of following the usual industry practice of utilizing proprietary components. This meant that company products would be easy for competitors to copy, but it also allowed quick entry into the marketplace. As nonproprietary open systems came to be more widely accepted, competitors such as Apollo, DEC, and IBM encountered problems in keeping pace with product lines that lacked the flexibility and performance of Sun's products. When Steve Jobs formed Next, Inc., and announced the development of a desktop workstation, Bechtolsheim urged Sun officials to build a truly desktop computer. There was considerable resistance to the project, and he almost left the company at that point. Because the company has had a culture based on building bigger boxes, the new sparcstation was widely criticized within the company as being too small. However, Bechtolsheim stubbornly refused to change the specifications and eventually prevailed.

Field Operations Director

Carol Bartz, National Sales Director and the number two executive at Sun Microsystems, has about half of the company's 12,000 employees reporting to her. Bartz attended the University of Wisconsin, receiving a Bachelor of Computer Science degree in 1971. After that, she spent seven years with Digital Equipment Corporation. Since joining Sun in 1983, she has become intimately involved in supervising field support activities and a subdivision that sells to federal governmental agencies. According to Bob Herwick, an investment analyst, Bartz is a very effective problem solver, turning around a sluggish service organization and ensuring that the company fully exploited the market potential in the government market.[4]

Team and Consensus Management at Sun

McNealy, current Sun chairman, attended Cranbrook, a North Detroit prep school. While there, he excelled in a variety of activities including music, tennis, golf, and ice hockey. According to Alan De Clerk, a high school classmate, McNealy developed a strong self-image and competitive spirit as a result of participating in sports activities and competing with two brothers and a sister. Through the years he has approached all activities as if they were team sports.

McNealy's efforts to build consensus among executives before a decision is made have become famous throughout the company. As he has stated, "Give me a draw and I'll make the decision but I won't issue an edict if a large majority is in favor of an alternative proposal."[5] A frequently quoted example occurred in 1988 when he stubbornly resisted changing prices at a time when rapidly increasing memory costs were reducing profit margins. With a consensus arrayed against him, he finally agreed to some product price increases which were en-

[4]Andrew Ould, "Carol Bartz: Star Is Still Rising for Hard Driving Executive," *PC Week*, September 3, 1990.

[5]"Sun Microsystems," op.cit.

EXHIBIT 1   A Comparison of Performance Measures for Major Workstation Makers

Source: J. A. Savage, "Price Takes Backseat with Users," *Computerworld,* September 2, 1991, p. 4.

	Price	Specmarks	Price per Specmark
Hewlett Packard 9000	11,990	55.5	216.00
Sun Sparcstation ELC	4,995	20.1	248.50
IBM RS/6000	13,992	32.8	426.50
Sun Sparcstation IPX	13,495	24.2	557.60

acted without reducing sales. In fact, he has a hard time saying no to any project pushed by one or more company groups. He demands complete loyalty within his concept of teamwork and becomes very angry if he believes that individuals or teams have let him down.[6]

Product Line Focus

The Sparcstation I was introduced in April 1989 at a stripped down price of $9,000. A lower priced version was introduced in May of 1990, costing $5,000. The machine processes data at 12 mips and runs about twice as fast as personal computers. Sun expected the lower price to facilitate sales to large companies who base computer purchases on quantity discounts. However, the low end sparcstation does not have disk drives, color monitors, or add-in slots. Therefore, it must be networked and cannot be used as a standalone unit.

An improved version of Sparc I was introduced in the summer of 1990 with an improved graphical interface, a color monitor, and sales price of $10,000. Sun has asserted that a personal computer with the same characteristics as the IPC would cost $15,000 to $20,000 and would have only about one third the processing power of this workstation model. The Sparcstation is now Sun's top seller among all its product lines and Sparcstation products produce 80 to 90 percent of total company revenues.

Exhibit 1 shows prices and specmarks (a measure of processing power and speed) for two Sun models as well as for the latest Hewlett Packard and IBM workstation models. From this table, the relative performance of the Sun computers in terms of computing power per dollar can be compared with its major competitors.

Company Strategy

Early on, Sun executives believed that they only had a short time to focus on growing demand for computer workstations from scientists and engineers before large companies such as IBM, DEC, and Hewlett Packard would aggressively move into that market niche. Therefore, company strategy was designed to emphasize gaining market share, concentrating on all out sales growth, no matter what the cost. At one point, the organization was adding more than 300 employees and a new sales office each month. Company engineers developed a steady stream of innovative but sometimes impractical prototypes. Products were sold largely by word of mouth with virtually no formal sales promotion programs.

As part of the market share focus, in the mid-80s the company began creating autonomous divisions to develop and market its products. This policy allowed rapid movement into such market areas as sales to government agencies, universities, and financial institutions. The autonomous groups did create unnecessary duplication and contributed to development costs that were almost twice the industry average. When attempts were made to consolidate functions, fierce turf battles resulted and top executives were forced to step in and referee the conflicts.

[6]Ibid.

The market share/sales growth emphasis created many unexpected problems. Needed investments in customer service and data processing activities had to be postponed. The existence of independent, autonomous divisions caused numerous difficulties for both sales and manufacturing activities. At one point, the company had more than 10,000 computer and option combinations to keep track of. Three different product lines based on three different microprocessors—Sparc, Motorola 68000, and Intel 386—required excessive investment and extensive coordination to ensure that they all worked on the same network. Overlaps and duplications in marketing and finance made forecasting all but impossible. At its current size the company can no longer scramble madly to meet shipping deadlines at the last minute.

By the summer of 1989, the company was experiencing production bottlenecks as discounted sales of older products mushroomed. Demand for newer products also increased faster than expected. Large backlogs of sales orders were not being entered in the inventory control system, preventing the company from knowing how many or what kinds of products it needed to produce.

In the last quarter of 1989, Sun experienced a $20 million loss due to misjudging consumer demand for its new Sparcstation and incurring parts shortages. A new management information system produced inaccurate parts forecasts which contributed to order snafus and lower earnings. However, it posted a $5 million profit in the first quarter of 1990. Sun produced revenues of $2.5 billion in fiscal 1990 and expected to achieve revenues of $3.3 billion in 1991.[7] Sun is now changing its approach to place more emphasis on profitability and less on growth, on expanding customer service and hiring fewer employees. Sun President McNealy has recently tied executive pay to before tax return on investment. In the 1989 annual report he stated that he desired performance to be judged on the basis of significant increases in revenues, acceptance of new products, improvements in profit margins, and increases in book value.

McNealy was one of the early pioneers pushing open systems which would allow computers of many different manufacturers to be linked together in networks. In fact, Sun has actually encouraged competition with itself through its focus on open systems development and invited the industry to build Sparc based clones in order to expand the position of the workstation industry. As the percentage of total Sparc based computers sold by Sun has begun to decline, Sun appears to be changing its position on clones. Recently, it told its own dealers they would incur Sun's displeasure if they sold Sun clones along with Sun workstations. Many of these dealers are angry at what they perceive to be Sun's arrogance.

Sun has consistently maintained a narrow product line focus. It has gradually phased out all microprocessors except Sparc and has concentrated on low-end workstations with the greatest market share growth possibilities. It has avoided entering markets for higher priced lines and the personal computer segment with emphasis on low price and compactness. However, recently Sun announced plans to move into high end workstation markets where processing speed and power requirements necessitate linking a series of microprocessors and using sophisticated software. Sun may encounter problems in this market similar to those it experienced in product upgrades of its lower level models, since it does not have a good record in managing product introductions.

As workstations become more powerful and less expensive, workstation manufacturers face a serious challenge in maintaining profit margins. Current models now combine high functionality with high volume, in contrast to an earlier focus on producing highly functional units in small quantities. Extensive use of application specific integrated circuits with fewer components reduces system size, increases reliability, and lowers product costs. Sun and other companies increasingly follow the practice of involving manufacturing representatives in the design process as early as possible in order to minimize manufacturing problems. Increased attention is also being paid to maintaining product quality and improving product testing before systems are shipped.

[7]Kathy Rebello, "Sun Microsystems on the Rise Again," *USA Today*, April 20, 1990.

In past years, Sun's strategies have included focusing on lower prices, well developed marketing programs and third party software development. From 1,500 to 2,000 applications are available for the Sun Sparcstation compared to approximately 1,000 for Hewlett Packard and DEC. The company is licensing its Sparc chip to third party clone companies with the desire of expanding the installed RISC computer base. The overall company goal is to deliver a complete processing solution, including graphics, input/output, software, and networking.

Distribution Channels and Customer Service

Workstation makers have traditionally sold their units using manufacturers' sales forces and specialized hardware resellers, who repackage specialized software with other companies' workstations. Sun has about 300 VARS (i.e., value added resellers) compared to more than 500 for Hewlett Packard with Digital and IBM falling somewhere in between. Some authorities think the majority of VARs are not capable of selling workstations.[8] Sun is now considering the possibility of selling some of its models through retailers such as Microage in a manner similar to personal computer sales now made by IBM, COMPAQ, and Apple. Such a move would reduce selling and inventory costs but is meeting initial resistance from dealers unaccustomed to handling complex workstation models.

Sun still sells a large number of workstations through its 1,000 person salesforce. In July 1990, Sun selected 200 dealers from three retail chains and gave them training in selling workstations. The company expects to sell $30 million of workstations through retail dealers in fiscal 1990, but a full-fledged dealer network may require several years to develop. Because of the higher average selling prices and greater product differentiation and uniqueness of workstations compared to personal computers, many PC vendors are expressing interest in handling workstations in spite of the small volumes generated.

One area of concern has been Sun's field service organization, which has not been very effective in supporting customer software. Bartz has stated that the company wants to improve on customer service without making large monetary expenditures or building a dinosaur service group.[9] In line with this, Sun has announced plans to start using company trained, third party service personnel who can be dispatched to customer locations on demand.

Customer Categories

The workstation market for engineers and scientists is rapidly becoming saturated. About one-third of Sun's customers now come from the commercial side, up from only 10 percent several years ago. The company is now concentrating more of its efforts on airlines, banks, insurance and finance companies, trying to persuade users to utilize Sun workstations to solve new problems. Sun Vice-President Eric Schmidt says that Sun tends to get early adopters of new technology.[10] Often, by starting with a pilot program that proves successful, workstations can be expanded to other areas in a customer's operations. Eastman Kodak began using Sun workstations in engineering design and soon expanded their use of marketing databases and mailroom operations.

Sun machines are being used by Wall Street firms Merrill Lynch, Shearson/Lehman/Hutton and Bear/Sterns on the trading floor. Northwest Airlines uses 500 workstations in Minneapolis to monitor ticket usage, checking the correctness of air fare charges and the impact of flight delays or cancellations on revenues and profits. To

[8]Susan E. Fisher, "Vendors Court Reseller Partners as Workstations Go Mainstream," *PC Week*, July 30, 1990.

[9]Jonathan B. Levine, "High Noon for Sun," *BusinessWeek*, July 24, 1989, pp. 71, 74.

[10]Julie Pitta, "The Trojan Horse Approach," *Forbes*, April 15, 1991.

increase customer satisfaction, Sun has had to change product designs, to make its machines easier to install, and to improve understandability of product manuals. As Sun has discovered, commercial customers need more help than engineers.

Dataquest says that by 1994, 29.1 percent of workstation sales will be made to commercial users as opposed to scientific/engineering users in a market expected to reach $22 billion.[11] Workstation makers are moving into the personal computer area by offering Unix versions that will run on both workstations and on personal computers. Workstations provide much greater computing power at a lower cost than would be required to enhance a personal computer so that it possessed the equivalent capability of a typical workstation. Workstations seem to be making their biggest inroads into CPU intensive applications formerly done on mainframes (e.g., stock transactions, airline reservations).

Sun's first major TV advertising effort occurred in April 1991 and took the form of a 30-second commercial seen on CNN, ESPN, and the three major TV networks. The commercial was not directed specifically at a consumer audience, but instead was an attempt to get broad exposure for a new message beamed at the business market. Sun expected the advertisement to reach 59 percent of U.S. households and 42 percent of the target market of senior level corporate and computer executives. The campaign also included an eight-page insert in *The Wall Street Journal.*

Sun's advertising budget of approximately $4.6 million in 1990 was spent on computer and general interest business publications. Sun's advertising budget is only about 0.25 percent of sales revenues compared to 1.0 to 1.5 percent spent by its major competitors. Some observers have questioned the cost-effectiveness of a high priced TV advertisement by a company which sells high priced computers to a limited group of customers.

Software Developments

Availability of software still remains a major problem in expanding sales of workstations. Only about 5 to 10 percent of UNIX based software is designed for business and commercial applications. Sun is trying to sign up software developers to produce UNIX based versions of many common personal computer products. It now has UNIX based versions of popular PC software, including Lotus 1–2–3 and DBASE IV. It hopes the increased availability of software plus the narrowing cost gap between low end workstations and high end personal computers will help it penetrate the personal computer market. However, it must sell users on the benefit/cost performance of workstations compared to personal computers and also needs to expand its existing base of software developers.

The type of software to be run is often the determining factor in deciding between a personal computer or workstation. For productivity and business applications, PCs can be more cost efficient. For technical and graphics applications, workstations are more appropriate. Differences in costs are no longer a differentiating factor.

An entrenched personal computer MS/DOS operating system base and lack of commercial workstation software have hampered a switch from high end personal computers to workstations. MS/DOS based computers appear adequate for a majority of user needs, especially with the advent of the Windows operating environment. PC users are more likely to change if complex applications such as multimedia, integrated data base, or windowing become desirable rather than on the basis of price alone. Workstations may become less attractive if 80846-based personal computers with considerably more computing power than today's systems become more widely available.

Product/price performance is no longer as important a differentiating factor as it used to be. Software availability and usability are increasing in importance. In recognition of this, Sun has formed two software subsidiaries—one for application software and one to con-

[11]"Getting Down to Business," *Information Week,* January 14, 1991.

EXHIBIT 2
Computer
Workstation Market
Shares

Company	1989	1990
Sun Microsystems	30.4%	38.8%
Hewlett Packard	26.1	20.1
Digital Equipment	26.6	17.0
Intergraph	7.0	3.8
IBM	1.2	4.5
Silicon Graphics	5.1	2.6
Sony	—	3.3
Next	—	2.6
Other	3.6	7.0
Total	100.0%	100.0%

centrate on improvements in the Unix operating system. The Open Look Graphical Interface has been added to make Sun products more user friendly. The key to maintaining market position seems to be improving systems software and selling software developers and users on the benefits of workstations over other hardware options.

Sun has announced that it will release a new version of its operating system designed to run on Intel based personal computers. Some analysts say that Sun will face a stiff test in competing with Microsoft's DOS/Windows combination and that it is a defensive move, made in realization that Sun no longer can generate enough revenue from its own machines to meet its growth goals. McNealy denies that the Sun announcement is defensive, saying that high powered PC owners will move to Sun's operating systems to take advantage of advanced capabilities (e.g., running multiple programs simultaneously) which is something that has been vaguely promised by Microsoft's Windows new NT versions.[12] McNealy has sharply criticized Windows NT version, referring to it as illusionary or not there.

Sun's Solaris operating system will not be available until mid-1991, and will work on both Intel's X86 series and Sun's Sparc processors. The new operating system will make it easier for Sun's customers to link Sun workstations with other computers in a network and increase the number of Sun users. Sun hopes that this will encourage independent software houses to write new programs for Sun OS. So far, approximately 3,500 application programs are available for Sun OS compared with more than 20,000 for IBM-compatible personal computers.[13]

Competition in the Marketplace

Although still the market leader, Sun is facing increasing competition from much larger computer companies. Sun shipped 146,000 workstations in 1990 (39 percent of the market) out of a total of 376,000 and is expected to ship 200,000 in 1991.[14] Having fully absorbed Apollo into its organization, Hewlett Packard is selling about two-thirds as many workstations as Sun, with about 20 percent of the market, and DEC, which has completely reworked its product lines, has about 17 percent of the workstation market. Hewlett Packard has also introduced a new workstation model comparable in price to the sparcstation, which runs about twice as fast as Sun's current model. Exhibit 2 shows the 1989 and 1990 market shares for the major firms in the workstation market.

IBM has made a significant comeback in the workstation market with the RS/6000, after its first workstation model proved to be a slow seller. In 1990, IBM shifted more than 25,000 workstations, producing revenue of 1 billion dollars and attaining a market share of

[12]Zachary, op.cit.
[13]Robert D. Hof, "Why Sun Can't Afford to Shine Alone," *BusinessWeek*, September 9, 1991.
[14]Andrew Ould, "IBM Challenges Sun in Workstation Market," *PC Week*, February 28, 1991.

EXHIBIT 3   Revenues, Expenses, and Income for Five Years (Billions of $)

Source: Adapted from 1990 Annual Report.

	1990	1989	1988	1987	1986
Net revenues	2,466	1,765	1,052	538	210
Cost of sales	1,399	1,010	550	273	102
Gross profit	1,067	755	502	265	108
R&D outlays	302	234	140	70	31
Selling, adm. & general expenses	588	433	250	127	57
Total	890	667	390	197	88
Operating income	177	88	111	68	20
Interest income	(23)	(10)	(302)	834	369
Income taxes	43	17	44	33	9
Net income	111	61	66	36	11
Net income/sales	4.5%	3.4%	6.3%	6.8%	5.3%
Net income/share	1.21	0.76	0.89	0.55	0.21
Book value/share	9.82	7.77	4.75	3.57	2.04
Unit shipment (000'S)	118.3	80.7	48.4	24.6	9.9
Revenue/unit shipped (000'S)	20.8	21.9	21.7	21.8	21.2

6.6 percent or more than double its 1989 market share.[15] In 1991, some analysts estimate IBM will sell between $2 and $3 billion of workstations. IBM has a stated goal of overtaking Sun by 1993, achieving a 30 percent market share, although some experts predict it is more likely to achieve a 15 percent market share by that date.[16]

With the workstation market expected to exceed 20 billion dollars by the mid-1990s, competition is expected to be fierce. IBM's late entry, entrenched positions of competitors in the market, lack of a low-priced entry level model, and the use of nonstandard operating and graphics environments are likely to hamper its efforts to achieve a market share much above 15 percent.[17] IBM's service and sales reputation, its large reseller base, and strong position in commercial markets should give the company leverage to enter the fast growing markets for network servers and small or branch office multiuser systems. However, if IBM focuses its efforts on penetrating these markets with its RS/6000, it runs a serious risk of undercutting sales of the AS/400.

Cost no longer seems to be the primary factor in decisions to acquire workstations. Workers must become more accustomed to graphic as opposed to character based systems before adoption by current PC users becomes more widespread. Some companies feel that workstations have yet to demonstrate significant productivity advantages over personal computers. The biggest shortcomings of workstations are lack of application software and integration difficulties.

Financial Analysis

Exhibit 3 shows revenues, expenses, and income for the five-year period 1986 to 1990. Revenues have increased at a more rapid rate than net income during the period being considered. Return on sales has declined significantly to 4.5 percent from the peak of al-

[15]Ibid.

[16]Bob Francis, "Big Blue's Red Hot Workstation," *Datamation*, October 15, 1990.

[17]Andrew Ould, "What's Behind Lower Workstation Prices," *UNIX World*, July 1990.

EXHIBIT 4 **Computer Industry Data for Years 1989 and 1990**

Source: *BusinessWeek,* 1000 Companies, 1991, 1990.

Company	Sales Growth		Income Growth		Asset Growth		Net Inc./Sales		Mkt. Value/ Equity	
	1990	1989	1990	1989	1990	1989	1990	1989	1990	1989
Apple	1.07	1.21	1.14	1.05	1.12	1.24	8.7	8.2	4.81	3.21
Compaq	1.25	1.39	1.36	1.31	1.30	1.31	12.6	11.6	3.26	3.31
Dec	1.01	1.05	0.00	0.72	1.03	1.10	−.72	6.8	1.21	1.13
Hew Pck	1.10	1.20	0.95	0.97	1.09	1.31	5.7	6.6	1.83	1.98
Intrgrph	1.21	1.07	0.79	0.80	1.06	0.97	6.0	9.2	1.79	1.73
IBM	1.10	1.05	1.60	0.68	1.30	1.06	8.7	6.0	1.75	1.62
NCR	1.06	0.99	0.90	0.94	1.01	0.95	5.9	6.9	3.54	3.40
Silgrphs	1.41	1.73	1.97	1.94	1.37	0.94	8.3	5.9	3.57	4.30
Sun Mcrs	1.34	1.41	318.	0.40	1.49	1.50	5.5	1.8	2.72	1.41
Wang	0.87	0.90	0.00	0.00	0.72	0.87	−6.7	−13.9	1.27	0.87
Avg.	1.14	1.20	32.7	0.88	1.15	1.12	5.4	4.9	2.58	2.37

EXHIBIT 5 **Computer Industry Data for Years 1989 and 1988**

Source: *BusinessWeek* 1000 Companies, 1991; Innovation in America, Special *Business Week* Issues, 1990, 1988.

Company	Sales/ Assets		Sales/ Employee		Adv. Exps./ Sales		R&D Exps./ Sales		R&D Exps./ Employee	
	1990	1989	1989	1988	1989	1988	1989	1988	1989	1988
Apple	1.82	1.91	364	377	7.34	8.30	8.0	6.7	28,937	25,233
Compaq	1.32	1.38	303	289	1.75	2.87	4.6	3.6	13,945	10,849
Dec	1.13	1.15	101	94	1.38	1.01	12.0	11.4	12,123	10,753
Hew Pck	1.22	1.21	125	113	2.69	2.35	10.7	10.4	13,358	11,713
Intrgrph	1.20	1.07	105	110	1.00	1.00	10.6	11.1	11,157	12,216
IBM	0.79	0.81	164	154	1.17	0.44	8.3	7.4	13,572	11,415
NCR	1.38	1.32	106	100	1.06	0.53	7.5	7.0	7,964	6,940
Silgrphs	1.22	1.19	180	105	1.00	1.00	11.9	15.8	21,150	21,908
Sun Mcrs	1.27	1.41	172	148	1.00	0.74	13.3	13.3	22,934	19,733
Wang	1.35	1.12	109	97	1.00	1.02	9.8	8.7	10,543	8,510
Avg.	1.27	1.26	173	159	2.64	1.93	9.7	9.5	15,568	14,027

most 7 percent in 1987 with revenue per shipment also declining in 1990 compared to 1989 and 1988. Book value per share and unit shipments have increased significantly during the five years.

Exhibit 4 indicates that Sun's sales, income and asset growth are higher than the industry average in 1990 and 1989 with the market value/equity ratio also above the industry average. However, the net income/sales ratio was below the industry average in 1989 and slightly above the industry average in 1990. As Exhibit 5 indicates, Sun appears to be very close to the industry average in terms of two common productivity measures, sales/assets and sales/employee. In reviewing the common leverage measures, Sun is well above the industry average for R&D expenses/revenues and R&D expenses/employee.

Case
Group F

Social and Ethical Issues in Marketing Management

Case

25

Notetakers Company: Selling Class Notes and Instructional Notes to Students

S. J. Garner and Judy Spain *Eastern Kentucky University*

Company Background

Kevin and Jennifer own a business called Notetakers which is located in a strip mall near the campus of a major midwestern university. They started their business a year ago with start-up funds of $5,000. The small storefront contains a counter, a price board, a leased copier, a cabinet full of copier paper, a telephone and three file cabinets. Their product? Class notes.

This case was written by Professors Garner and Spain of Eastern Kentucky University, Department of Management and Marketing.

Each semester, Kevin and Jennifer recruit honor students who are enrolled in large auditorium sections of popular general education classes and some business courses such as beginning marketing and beginning management. The honor students are paid to take and transcribe notes of the classes in which they are enrolled. Each student receives $50 for each "module" of class notes which are delivered to Notetakers one week before a course exam is scheduled. Most courses contain three or four modules (each of which is several weeks long). The honor students also receive a royalty of five percent of the gross sales of each module.

Kevin and Jennifer make copies of the class notes and sell them to students enrolled in the classes. Each module sells for six to ten dollars, depending on the length of the notes. Each module is printed with a cover sheet containing the name of the university, the name and section number of the course, room number, professor's name and time that the class meets. Copies are also included of any handouts given by that particular professor in class.

Kevin originally had the idea for this service because he is dyslexic and had difficulty taking coherent notes when he was in school. He had also noticed that students with ADD (attention deficit disorder) had similar problems. Jennifer estimates that thirty to forty percent of the note copies they sell are to disabled students. Students who have missed class due to illness or for other reasons also purchase note modules.

Notetakers offers no guarantee as to the accuracy of the notes they sell. They do place a written notice on each module warning students that they should compare the notes to others taken in class and the textbook materials.

Modules are available for around thirty-six classes currently. But more are added as honor students are recruited and class sizes increase. Currently, each notetaker makes around $300 per course per semester.

The business is open from 8:00 to 5:00 five days a week. Kevin and Jennifer split the counter duties, each spending approximately four and a half hours a day receiving, copying and selling notes. They currently have 20 honor students employed as notetakers.

Business expenses include storefront rental, utilities, supplies, copier lease costs, royalties and base payments to employee notetakers. These expenses total 55 percent of gross receipts. The other 45 percent is split between Kevin and Jennifer.

Notetakers has relied on two promotional methods during its first year of operation. Promotional flyers, designed by Jennifer, are handed out to students visiting the strip center during the first two weeks of class. Kevin and Jennifer merely stand in the door of their shop and hand the flyers to passing students. Secondly, as a condition of their shop lease, they have the strip center's permission to place their flyers on every car parked at the center which has a university parking tag hung on its mirror. So far, these two methods have generated some word-of-mouth among the student population.

Kevin feels that some additional promotion would increase their store traffic and also assist them in recruiting more notetakers to cover more classes. He feels that an advertisement in the student newspaper would be cost-effective and generate maximum exposure to their specific target market without adding waste circulation. Jennifer has designed a six inch by two column ad for use in the newspaper (see Exhibit 1). Kevin has discovered that the base rate for black and white ads is four dollars per column inch for a single insertion. Each insertion will therefore cost $48. (Two columns $\times$ six inches $\times$ $4 = $48.)

Kevin plans to insert the advertisement four times during the coming semester in the weekly college newspaper. The first two insertions will be during the first two weeks of class, the third insertion will be the week before midterm exams and the fourth the week before final exams take place. He has written a check for the first two insertions and mailed it along with a camera ready copy of the ad to the student newspaper.

EXHIBIT 1
Notetakers
Newspaper Ad

Miss a few classes?
Have trouble taking notes?

Let
NOTETAKERS
help!!!

We have notes available for over 36 auditorium section classes. All our notes are taken and transcribed by currently enrolled honor students. Call today for prices and sections available.

NOTETAKERS
31 Oak St. in the Campus Strip Center
8–5 Monday through Friday
555 - 706 - NOTE

Bad News Arrives

A week after mailing the ad to the student newspaper, Notetakers received the following letter in the mail.

Dear Owners of Notetakers:

I am returning your check and advertisement. It is my feeling that the service you provide has the effect of encouraging students to cut classes and thus miss a large part of their education. I do not feel it is ethical for you to provide this service and I certainly do not feel it would be ethical of me to allow this ad to be run in the student newspaper.

Sincerely,

Bob Richardson
Retail Advertising Manager

Kevin showed the letter to Jennifer and said, "This isn't fair at all! I've seen ads for beer and adult movies and videos in the newspaper—why are they picking on us? To say our business is unethical is very hypocritical!" Jennifer replied, "It was probably the faculty advisor who rejected the ad. Why don't you call and ask to speak with the advisor. Maybe you can change his mind."

Two days later Kevin told Jennifer that he had spoken to the newspaper's faculty advisor. The advisor told Kevin that he had not banned the ad. He left the decision up to the newspaper advertising manager and told him that he would have to stand behind his own decision. He also said that this was not the first ad to be rejected by the newspaper. Other ads which had been turned down included one from a group that wanted people to appear in a documentary "debunking" the Holocaust as a myth and another for a "stripper" pen featuring a woman who disrobed whenever the pen was tilted.

Kevin went on to say that the advisor also told him that he thought that Notetakers was doing a disservice to students by selling these notes, that it is a well-known fact that students who attend class learn more and make better grades and that Notetakers was encouraging negative behavior. To top it all off, the advisor said he had sent a copy of the Notetakers ad to the university lawyers to see if they could do anything to prevent Notetakers from stealing the intellectual property of the professors teaching these classes and using the name of the university!

More Bad News Arrives

Four weeks after the rejection letter arrived, Jennifer called Kevin at home and said, "You better get down here in a hurry to meet with our lawyer. We're being sued! The university just had us served with papers. As near as I can tell, they are saying we have infringed on their trademarks by having the name of the university, the course numbers, sections and dates on our covers. There is also something about some of the professors who teach the courses we have notes for having contracts with publishers to produce study guides based on their class notes. The publishers hold the copyrights on these materials. What are we going to do?"

Kevin and Jennifer met with their attorney, Steve King. Steve reviewed the advertisement, the cover sheet, and samples of the note packets. He told Kevin and Jennifer that the university was alleging a violation of the Lanham Trade-Mark Act of 1964, 15 U.S.C. sec. 1125(a).

The Lanham Act prohibits anyone from engaging in misrepresentation of origin and deceptive advertising regarding the origin of the notes. Specifically, Steve stated that the university is contending that because Notetakers used the course number, name, etc., on the cover sheet, it created confusion as to the actual source of the notes.

After talking to the attorney, Kevin and Jennifer were really confused. What should they do? Should they stop producing the notes and close their business? Were they really in violation of the law? If not in violation of the law, were they really acting unethically as the Advertising Manager said?

26

Nintendo versus SEGA: Sex, Violence, and Videogames

Romuald A. Stone *James Madison University*

Violence in America in 1994 was considered by many people to have reached epidemic proportions. All across the United States—in cities and towns large and small—citizens were increasingly fearful and concerned that violence was out of control. What was causing this violent behavior? There was no easy answer. But many experts said that the pervasive violence in television programming, films, and videogames was one seed that promoted physical aggression in some individuals and helped create a culture tolerant of violence.

Just as television emerged as a powerful social and cultural force in the early 1950s, videogames were said to be emerging as a potentially powerful influence on children's behavior in the 1990s. While the impact of the growing violence in videogames was debatable, the years of research on violence in television programming provided instructive warning. According to Parker Page, president of the Children's Television Resource and Education Center, "years of research indicate that children who watch a steady diet of violent programming increase their chances of becoming more aggressive towards other children, less cooperative and altruistic, more tolerant of real life violence and more afraid of the world outside their homes."[1] The advent of virtual reality technology in videogame programming led Page to express a special concern in his testimony before a joint Senate subcommittee hearing held in December 1993.

> Mortal Kombat is simply the first in a new generation of video games that allows software designers to combine high levels of violence with fully digitalized human images. No more cute hedge hogs or cartoonish Super Mario Brothers—increasingly, the characters that a young player beheads, disembowels or crushes will look more and more like the kids at school, the neighbor who lives down the street or the young woman heading for aerobics class.[2]

Alarmed by the violent content of many videogames, parents and concerned citizens started lobbying for a comprehensive, industrywide videogame rating system that would give parents

---

[1]U.S. Senate, *Violence in Videogames: Joint Hearing of the Judiciary Subcommittee on Juvenile Justice and Government Affairs Subcommittee on Regulation and Government Information* (testimony of Parker Page, PhD.), 103rd Cong., 1993.

[2]Ibid.

the information they needed to make informed choices. To address these concerns, Senators Lieberman and Kohl sponsored legislation to establish the National Independent Council for Entertainment in Video Devices as an independent agency of the federal government to oversee the development of "voluntary" standards to alert parents to the content of videogames. In his testimony before the hearing, Robert Chase, vice president of the National Education Association, expressed the collective concern of educators, children's advocates, and parents:

> America's children are faced with a bewildering set of messages from television, movies, music, electronic games, and print media. Too often, the almost unrelenting assault on the senses encouraging aggression and irresponsibility are in direct opposition to the values families hope to instill and the mores our society struggles to preserve. Parents, social scientists, and the community at large share deep trepidation about the fruits of this ever widening dispersal of negative images. The explosion of media in the latter half of this century has made the problem all the more pervasive and the challenges for parents and community leaders all the more difficult.[3]

At the same hearing, the Software Publishers Association (SPA) provided a counter argument:

> In our attempt to protect our children from those relatively few video games which contain unacceptable violence, however, we must not lose sight of the fact that the vast majority of videogames are appropriate for children, and have the potential for developing many important and socially desirable skills. As stated so eloquently by Bob Keeshan, otherwise known as Captain Kangaroo, "Video games . . . provide the potential for heretofore unknown opportunities for information, education and delightful entertainment. . . . The technology is to be encouraged because, used appropriately, such games can be a tool for education as well as entertainment."[4]

The SPA indicated in its testimony that the software entertainment industry was committed to moving quickly and decisively on this issue. The SPA was in the process of working with a coalition of concerned parties to establish a rating system that would be easy for consumers to understand and one that the industry could implement. Nintendo and SEGA had also initiated moves toward a rating system.

Nintendo's Position

When Nintendo entered the U.S. videogame industry in 1985, the company established written Game Content Guidelines requiring games marketed under the Nintendo Seal of Quality to meet the following standards:

- No sexually suggestive or explicit content.
- No sexist language or depictions.
- No random, gratuitous, or excessive violence.
- No graphic illustration of death.
- No domestic violence or abuse.
- No excessive force in sports games.
- No ethnic, racial, religious, or sexual stereotypes.
- No profanity or obscenity.
- No use of drugs, smoking materials, or alcohol.
- No subliminal political messages or overt political statements.

As an example of Nintendo's pledge to control and monitor its game content, the company insisted that one of its largest licensees, Acclaim Entertainment, remove objectionable material from the controversial arcade game "Mortal Kombat." In its original form, the

[3]Ibid. (testimony of Robert Chase).
[4]Ibid. (testimony of Ilene Rosenthal).

game included scenes in which characters' heads were ripped off, their spines were pulled out, they were impaled on spikes, and they spurted blood when hit. All of these graphics were deemed unacceptable and removed from the Nintendo version of the game. SEGA released the game in its entirety.

Some games had been simply rejected outright, since no amount of modification would make them acceptable to Nintendo. One such game was "Night Trap," which contained full motion videos of young, scantily clad females being attacked by hooded men who drilled holes in their bodies to suck out blood.

Howard Lincoln, Nintendo's then senior vice president (and later chairman), reiterated his company's continued commitment to wholesome family entertainment that was both challenging and exciting to youth while remaining nonoffensive to parents:

> This will remain our philosophy despite the fact we have been criticized by both video game players and others in our industry for taking what we feel is the only responsible approach . . . we believe our game guidelines have served us and our customers well for the past eight years. And we have no intention of abandoning this approach.[5]

However, Nintendo apparently decided to moderate its position following a raft of angry letters from users. Nintendo's 1994 holiday season new version of the "Mortal Kombat" game was just as gruesome as the arcade version.

Sega's Position[6]

In 1993, SEGA established a three-pronged approach designed to help parents determine the age-appropriateness of its stable of interactive video software. It included a rating classification system, a toll-free hotline, and an informational brochure. Building on the motion picture industry model, the SEGA rating system applied one of three classifications to each interactive video program it released:

GAF   For general audiences.

MA-13   For mature audiences age 13 and over.

MA-17   Adult appropriate, not suitable for those under age 17.

SEGA's toll-free hotline was staffed by professionals who could supplement the rating classification by informing parents about the specific content of each SEGA product. SEGA also offered its "Everybody Wins" brochure that provided additional information to shoppers at more than 2,800 retail stores. In addition, SEGA formed an independent Videogame Rating Council consisting of experts in the areas of psychology, sociology, cinema, and education to evaluate games and assign appropriate rating classifications. By the end of 1993, 173 SEGA titles had been rated with the following distribution: 86 percent rated for general audiences (GA); 10 percent earned an MA-13 rating; and only 4 percent were targeted for exclusively adult (MA-17) audiences. To make SEGA's rating system work, the company decided that products bearing the MA-17 label should not be distributed to retail toy stores.

Progress Report[7]

In July 1994, the U.S. Senate subcommittee endorsed rating guidelines issued by an industry trade group, the Interactive Digital Software Association (IDSA)—see Exhibit 1. The IDSA ratings provided age guidance with five categories similar to those used by the Mo-

---

[5]Ibid. (testimony of Howard C. Lincoln).

[6]Ibid. (testimony of William White, vice president, SEGA of America Inc.).

[7]M. Moran, "Retailers See Videogame Ratings as a Helpful Guide," *Video Business* 14, no. 32 (1994), pp. 12, 16.

EXHIBIT 1   Rating Guideline

Source: *The Washington Post.*

Interactive Digital Software Association (IDSA) is using five categories by age to rate video game cartridges such as Nintendo, Sega, Atari. They are:

- Early childhood, ages 3 and up
- Kids to adult, ages 6 and up
- Teen, ages 13 and up
- Mature, ages 17 and up
- Adults only

The Software Publishers Association (SPA) is using a label that shows the level of violence, sex, and strong language used in a computer software or CD-ROM game. Games with no offensive material receive a "Suitable for all audiences" label.

tion Picture Association of America. The ratings were expected to appear on videogame packages by mid-November, in time for the holiday season. Retailers who rent games planned to adhere to the ratings guidelines. Some mass merchants (Sears, Wal-Mart, Toys 'R' Us) had vowed to carry only rated videogames. An informal survey of retailers, however, revealed that large numbers of unrated games were on retailers' shelves for the 1994 seasonal buying rush.[8] Although the IDSA had rated more than 280 titles, the ratings were apparently completed after game packages were printed.

The SPA encountered similar problems. At the end of 1994, only 40 CD-ROM and other software game titles had been rated. Exhibit 1 depicts SPA rating guidelines. Ken Wasch, executive director of the SPA, commented: "I wish more had been rated, but it took longer than we expected to get products submitted, to get them rated, and to get them out to the stores."[9]

There was no agreement among game producers on an industrywide rating system. Some observers believed the existence of several rating systems would confuse consumers. There also appeared to be a debate emerging whether widespread dissemination of rated products would ultimately hurt or help sales.

[8]P. Farhi, "A Waiting Game for Rating Games," *The Washington Post,* December 24, 1994, p. D1.
[9]Ibid.

E. & J. Gallo Winery

A. J. Strickland III and Daniel C. Thurman *The University of Alabama*

In the mid-1980s, alcohol consumption in the United States had been declining in virtually every category except low-priced wines. A number of producers in the wine industry did not believe they should be producing what they called skid-row wines (wines fortified with additional alcohol and sweetener and sold in screwtop, half-pint bottles). Richard Maher, president of Christian Brothers Winery in St. Helena, California, who once was with E. & J. Gallo Winery, said he didn't think Christian Brothers should market a product to people, including many alcoholics, who were down on their luck. "Fortified wines lack any socially redeeming values," he said.

Major producers of the low-end category of wines, called "dessert" or "fortified" (sweet wines with at least 14 percent alcohol), saw their customers otherwise. Robert Hunington, vice president of strategic planning at Canandiaqua (a national wine producer whose product, Wild Irish Rose, was the number one low-end wine), said 60 percent to 75 percent of its "pure grape" Wild Irish Rose was sold in primarily black, inner-city markets. Hunington described Wild Irish Rose's customer in this $500 million market as "not super-sophisticated," lower middle-class, and low-income blue-collar workers and mostly men. However, Canandiaqua also estimated the annual national market for dessert category wine to be 55 million gallons; low-end brands accounted for 43 million gallons, with as much as 50 percent sold in pints (typically the purchase choice of winos—alcoholics with a dependency on wine). Daniel Solomon, a Gallo spokesman, said Gallo's Thunderbird had lost its former popularity in the black and skid-row areas and was consumed mainly by retired and older people who didn't like the taste of hard distilled products or beer.[1]

Tony Mayes, area sales representative for Montgomery Beverage Company, Montgomery, Alabama, said one-third of the total revenue from wine sales in the state of Alabama was from the sale of one wine product—Gallo's Thunderbird. Sales crossed all demographic lines. According to Mayes, a consumer developed a taste for wine through an education process that usually began with the purchase of sweet wines from the dessert category. He attributed the high sales of Thunderbird to the fact that the typical wine drinker in Alabama was generally not the sophisticated wine drinker found in California or New York.

Prepared by Daniel C. Thurman, doctoral student, under the supervision of A. J. Strickland III, both of The University of Alabama.

[1] Alix M. Freedman, "Misery Market—Winos & Thunderbird Are a Subject Gallo Doesn't Like to Discuss," *The Wall Street Journal,* February 25, 1988, pp. 1, 18.

Company History and Background

The E. & J. Gallo Winery, America's biggest winery, was founded by Ernest and Julio Gallo in 1933. More than 55 years later, the Gallo Winery was still a privately owned and family-operated corporation actively managed by the two brothers. The Gallo family had been dedicated to both building their brands and the California wine industry.

The Gallos started in the wine business working during their spare time in the vineyard for their father, Joseph Gallo. Joseph Gallo, an immigrant from the Piedmont region in northwest Italy, was a small-time grape grower and shipper. He survived Prohibition because the government permitted wine for medicinal and religious purposes, but his company almost went under during the Depression. During the spring of 1933, Joseph Gallo killed his wife and chased Ernest and Julio with a shotgun. He killed himself following their escape. Prohibition ended that same year, and the Gallos, both in their early '20s and neither knowing how to make wine, decided to switch from growing grapes to making wine. With $5,900 to their names, Ernest and Julio found two thin pamphlets on wine-making in the Modesto Public Library and began making wine.[2]

The Gallos had always been interested in quality and began researching varietal grapes in 1946. They planted more than 400 varieties in experimental vineyards during the 1950s and 1960s, testing each variety in the different growing regions of California for its ability to produce fine table wines. Their greatest difficulty was to persuade growers to convert from common grape varieties to the delicate, thin-skinned varietals because it took at least four years for a vine to begin bearing and perhaps two more years to develop typical, varietal characteristics. As an incentive, in 1967, Gallo offered long-term contracts to growers, guaranteeing the prices for their grapes every year, provided they met Gallo quality standards. With a guaranteed long-term "home" for their crops, growers could borrow the needed capital to finance the costly replanting, and the winery was assured a long-term supply of fine wine grapes. In 1965, Julio established a grower relations staff of skilled viticulturists to aid contract growers. This staff still counsels growers on the latest viticultural techniques.[3]

Private ownership and mass production were the major competitive advantages contributing to Gallo's success. Gallo could get market share from paper-thin margins and absorb occasional losses that stockholders of publicly held companies would not tolerate. Gallo was vertically integrated, and wine was its only business. While Gallo bought about 95 percent of its grapes, it virtually controlled its 1,500 growers through long-term contracts. Gallo's 200 trucks and 500 trailers constantly hauled wine out of Modesto and raw materials in. Gallo was the only winery to make its own bottles (2 million a day) and screw-top caps. Also, while most of the competition concentrated on production, Gallo participated in every aspect of selling its product. Julio was president and oversaw production, while Ernest was chairman and ruled over marketing, sales, and distribution. Gallo owned its distributors in about a dozen markets and probably would have bought many of the more than 300 independents handling its wines if laws in most states had not prohibited it.

Gallo's major competitive weakness over the years had been an image associated with screw tops and bottles in paper bags that developed because of its low-end dessert wine, Thunderbird.[4] There were stories, which Gallo denied, that Gallo got the idea for citrus-flavored Thunderbird from reports that liquor stores in Oakland, California, were catering to the tastes of certain customers by attaching packages of lemon Kool-Aid to bottles of white wine to be mixed at home.[5]

[2]Jaclyn Fierman, "How Gallo Crushes the Competition," *Fortune,* September 1, 1986, pp. 24–31.
[3]"The Wine Cellars of Ernest & Julio Gallo, a Brief History," a pamphlet produced by Ernest & Julio Gallo, Modesto, Calif.
[4]Fierman, "How Gallo Crushes the Competition."
[5]Freedman, "Misery Market."

Thunderbird became Gallo's first phenomenal success. It was a high-alcohol, lemon-flavored beverage introduced in the late 1950s. A radio jingle sent Thunderbird sales to the top of the charts on skid rows across the country: "What's the word? Thunderbird. How's it sold? Good and cold. What's the jive? Bird's alive. What's the price? Thirty twice." Thunderbird has remained a brand leader in its category ever since. In 1986, Ernest Gallo poured $40 million into advertising aimed at changing Gallo's image to one associated with quality wines.

Information on Gallo's finances was not publicly available, and the brothers maintained a tight lid on financial details. In a 1986 article, *Fortune* estimated that Gallo earned at least $50 million a year on sales of $1 billion. By comparison, the second leading winery, Seagram's (also the nation's largest distillery), had approximately $350 million in 1985 wine revenues and lost money on its best-selling table wines. *Fortune* stated that several of the other major Gallo competitors made money, but not much.[6]

Gallo produced the top-selling red and white table wines in the country. Its Blush Chablis became the best-selling blush-style wine within the first year of its national introduction. Gallo's award-winning varietal wines were among the top sellers in their classification. The company's Carlo Rossi brand outsold all other popular-priced wines. Gallo's André Champagne was by far the country's best-selling champagne, and E & J Brandy has outsold the number two and three brands combined. Gallo's Bartles & Jaymes brand was one of the leaders in the new wine cooler market.[7]

The U.S. Wine Industry

Wine sales in the United States grew from about 72 million gallons in 1940 to over 600 million gallons, accounting for retail sales in excess of $9 billion (see Exhibit 1). This retail sales volume had exceeded such major established grocery categories as detergents, pet foods, paper products, and canned vegetables. While wine consumption had grown at an astonishing rate, trends toward moderation and alcohol-free life-styles made this growth rate impossible to maintain. Nevertheless, annual growth was projected to be 3.2 percent through 1995.

Per capita consumption of wine was low in the late 1950s and early 1960s because wine drinking was perceived as either the domain of the very wealthy or the extreme opposite. "Fortified" dessert wines were the top-selling wines of the period. The first surge in consumption in the late 1960s was the result of the introduction of "pop" wines, such as Boones Farm, Cold Duck, and Sangrias. These wines were bought by baby boomers, who were now young adults. Their palates were unaccustomed to wine drinking and these wines were suited to them. By the mid-1970s, the pop wine drinkers were ready to move up to Lambruscos and white wine "cocktails," and per capita consumption increased (see Exhibit 2). The wine spritzer became the trend, still the alternative to more serious wines for immature palates. Just as this surge began to wane, wine coolers were introduced in 1982 and exploded on the market in 1983. Wine coolers were responsible for a 5 percent market surge in 1984 and experienced four consecutive years of very high growth rates, rising 6 percent in 1987 to 72.6 million nine-liter cases.

The imported wines category enjoyed an upward growth rate from 6.6 percent of the market in 1960 to a high of 27.6 percent in 1985 (see Exhibits 3 and 4). The category lost market share to 23.1 percent in 1986 primarily because of the shift from Lambruscos to wine coolers. Additional factors were the weakening dollar and an overall improved reputation for domestic wines.

---

[6]Fierman, "How Gallo Crushes the Competition."
[7]"Gallo Sales Development Program," a pamphlet produced by Ernest & Julio Gallo, Modesto, Calif.

EXHIBIT 1
**The National Wine
Market (1977–86)**

Source: *National Beverage
Marketing Directory,* 10th ed.,
1988.

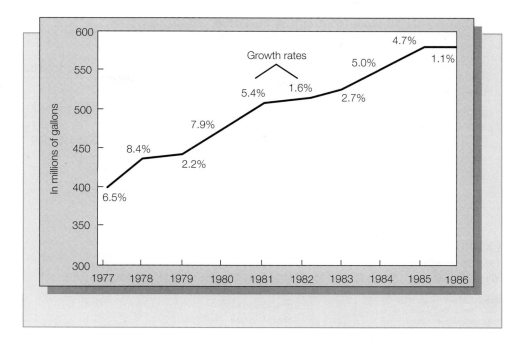

EXHIBIT 2
**Per Capita
Consumption of Wine
in the U.S.**

Source: *National Beverage
Marketing Directory,* 10th ed.,
1988.

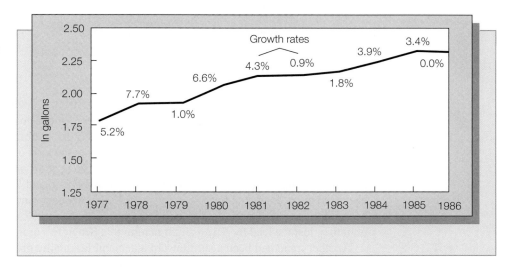

EXHIBIT 3   **Wine Production by Place of Origin (Millions of nine-liter cases)**

Source: *Impact* 17, no. 11 (June 1, 1987), p. 4.

Origin	1970	1975	1980	1985	1986	Average Annual Compound Growth Rate			Percent Change
						1970–75	1975–80	1980–85	1985–86
California	82	115	139.5	133.2	133.3	7.0%	3.9%	−0.9%	−0.1%
Other states*	18	19	18.7	16.9	17.3	1.4	−0.3	−2.0	2.4
United States	100	134	158.2	150.1	150.6	6.1	3.3	−1.0	0.3
Imports	13	21	43.1	57.2	45.3	10.5	15.8	5.8	−20.8

*Includes bulk table wine shipped from California and blended with other state wines.

Note: Addition of columns may not agree because of rounding.

EXHIBIT 4   **Market Share Trends in Wine Production**

Source: *Impact* 17, no. 11 (June 1, 1987), p. 4.

Place Produced	1970	1975	1980	1985	1986	Share Point Change 1970–80*	1980–85	1985–86
California	73%	74%	69.3%	64.3%	68.0%	4	−5.0	3.8
Other states	16	12	9.3	8.2	8.8	−7	1.1	0.7
United States	88	86	78.6	72.4	76.9	−10	−6.2	4.5
Imports	12	14	21.4	27.6	23.1	9	6.2	−4.5
Total†	100%	100%	100.0%	100.0%	100.0%	—	—	—

*1980 based on unrounded data.

†Addition of columns may not agree because of rounding.

EXHIBIT 5

1985 Share of U.S. Wine Market

Source: Jaclyn Fierman, "How Gallo Crushes the Competition," *Fortune,* September 1, 1986, p. 27.

Company	Percent
E. & J. Gallo Winery	26.1%
Seagram & Sons	8.3
Canandiaqua Wine	5.4
Brown-Forman	5.1
National Distillers	4.0
Heublein	3.7
Imports	23.4
All others	24.0
Total	100.0%

There were about 1,300 wineries in the United States. *Fortune* identified the major market-share holders in the U.S. market in a September 1986 article. It showed Gallo as the clear leader, nearly outdistancing the next five competitors combined (see Exhibit 5).

A number of threats had faced the wine industry, not the least of which had been the national obsession with fitness and the crackdown on drunken driving. Americans drank 6.5 percent less table wine in 1985 than in 1984 (see Exhibits 6 and 7), and consumption was projected to be down another 5 percent in 1986. The industry answer to this problem had been introduction of wine coolers. Gallo's Bartles and Jaymes Coolers were number one until they lost the lead by only a slight margin to a Seagram's brand in 1987.

Another trend had been a shift toward a demand for quality premium wines made from the finest grapes. Premium wines increased market share from 8 percent in 1980 to 20 percent in 1986. Again, Gallo had sold more premium wine than any other producer, but Gallo's growth had been limited by its lack of snob appeal.[8]

Although more than 80 percent of the U.S. adult population enjoyed wine occasionally, Gallo's research indicated most Americans were still infrequent wine drinkers by global standards. Only about one in four Americans drank wine as often as once a week. Per capita consumption in the United States was less than 2.5 gallons per year, compared to about 20 gallons in some Western European countries.[9]

Though the health-consciousness and alcohol-awareness of the 1980s had a moderating influence on wine growth patterns as consumers traded up in quality and drank less, long-term growth was expected to be steady but slower than that of the 1970s and early 1980s. Exhibit 8 provides drinking patterns for 1986. Personal disposable income was ex-

[8]Fierman, "How Gallo Crushes the Competition."

[9]"Gallo Sales Development Program."

EXHIBIT 6   Shipments of Wine Entering U.S. Trade Channels by Type (Millions of nine-liter cases)

Source: *Impact* 17, no. 11 (June 1, 1987), p. 3.

Type	1970	1975	1980	1984	1985	1986	Average Annual Compound Growth Rate 1970–75	1975–80	1980–85	Percent Change* 1985–86
Table	55.9	88.9	150.8	170.9	159.2	147.1	9.9%	11.2%	1.1%	−7.4%
Dessert	31.1	28.2	19.1	15.5	14.3	14.7	−2.0	−7.5	−5.7	3.2
Vermouth	4.2	4.2	3.7	3.0	2.9	2.7	—	−2.5	−4.8	−6.9
Sparkling	9.3	8.4	12.7	19.7	19.4	18.7	−1.9	8.6	8.6	−4.5
Special natural	11.8	24.0	13.6	10.9	10.7	10.9	15.3	−10.7	−4.7	1.9
Imported specialty†	0.3	1.0	1.5	1.0	0.9	1.8	25.4	8.1	−9.7	104.7
Total‡	112.6	154.7	201.3	220.1	207.3	195.9	6.6%	5.4%	0.6%	−5.5%

*Based on unrounded data.

†Imported fruit wines and wine specialties (includes sangria and fruit-flavored wines).

‡Addition of columns may not agree because of rounding.

EXHIBIT 7   Share of Market Trends in Shipments of Wine Entering U.S. Trade Channels, by Type

Source: *Impact* 17, no. 11 (June 1, 1987), p. 3.

Type	1970	1975	1980	1984	1985	1986	Share Point Change 1970–80*	1980–85	1985–86
Table	50%	57%	74.9%	77.2%	76.8%	75.1%	25	1.9	−1.7
Dessert	28	18	9.5	7.0	6.9	7.5	−18	−2.6	0.6
Vermouth	4	3	1.8	1.4	1.4	1.4	−2	−0.4	‡
Sparkling	8	5	6.3	9.0	9.4	9.5	−2	3.0	0.2
Special natural	10	16	6.8	5.0	5.2	5.6	−3	−1.6	0.4
Imported specialty	‡	1	0.7	0.5	0.4	0.9	+	−0.3	0.5
Total†	100%	100%	100.0%	100.0%	100.0%	100.0%	—	—	—

*1980 based on unrounded data.

†Addition of columns may not agree because of rounding.

‡Less than 0.05%.

pected to grow in the United States through 1995; busy lifestyles contributed to more dining out; and sale of wine in restaurants was expected to increase. As the aging baby boomers grew in number and importance, their wine purchases were expected to increase. All these factors contributed to the projected average yearly increase in growth rate of 3.2 percent through 1995.[10]

The Dessert Wine Industry

Dessert wine represented a 55 million-gallon, $500 million industry. The dessert wine category, also called fortified wines, included wines that contained more than 14 percent alcohol, usually 18 percent to 21 percent. They were called fortified because they usually contained added alcohol and additional sugar or sweetener. This category included a group of low-end priced brands that had been the brunt of significant controversy. Canandiaqua's

[10]"Coolers Providing Stable Growth," *Beverage Industry Annual Manual,* 1987.

EXHIBIT 8   Beverage Consumption Patterns

Source: *Impact* 17, no. 18 (September 15, 1987), pp. 3–4.

1986 National Beverage Consumption by Gender (Percent of volume):

Gender	Malt Beverages	Wine	Distilled Spirits	Coolers	Total Nonalcoholic Beverages	Total Beverages
Male	80.8%	51.6%	62.6%	44.9%	51.1%	52.7%
Female	19.2	48.4	37.4	55.1	48.9	47.3
Total	100.0%	100.0%	100.0%	100.0%	100.0%	100.0%

1986 National Alcoholic Beverage Consumption by Household Income (Percent of volume):

Household Income	Malt Beverages	Wine	Distilled Spirits	Coolers	Total Alcoholic Beverages
Under $15,000	26.1%	11.7%	19.7%	22.3%	26.5%
$15,000–$24,999	19.1	13.9	18.1	19.5	21.3
$25,000–$29,999	10.8	14.2	6.6	10.9	12.1
$30,000–$34,999	11.7	9.9	14.7	7.9	10.3
$35,000 & over	32.3	50.3	40.9	39.4	29.8
Total	100.0%	100.0%	100.0%	100.0%	100.0%

1986 National Beverage Consumption by Time of Day (Percent of volume):

Time of Day	Malt Beverages	Wine	Distilled Spirits	Coolers	Total Nonalcoholic Beverages	Total Beverages
Breakfast/morning	2.7%	2.1%	4.6%	1.5%	32.7%	30.6%
Lunch	6.8	5.8	4.2	4.4	20.8	19.8
Snack	27.5	19.0	31.9	27.0	10.9	12.0
Dinner	14.2	45.8	15.5	13.7	22.9	22.6
Evening	48.8	27.3	43.8	53.4	12.7	15.0
Total	100.0%	100.0%	100.0%	100.0%	100.0%	100.0%

1986 National Beverage Consumption by Location of Consumption (Percent of volume):

Location	Malt Beverages	Wine	Distilled Spirits	Coolers	Total Nonalcoholic Beverages	Total Beverages
Total home	64.6%	75.8%	61.4%	76.9%	76.1%	75.5%
Total away from home	35.4%	24.2%	38.6%	23.1%	23.9%	24.5%

Wild Irish Rose had been the leading seller in this category, with Gallo's Thunderbird claiming second place, followed by Mogen David Wine's MD 20/20.[11]

Dessert wines had shown a decreasing trend both in amount of wine consumed and in market share from 1970 through 1985. However, the trend changed in 1986 when dessert wine's market share rose six-tenths of a share point to 7.5 percent of the total wine market (see Exhibit 7). The rise was attributed in large measure to the 19 percent federal excise tax increase on distilled spirits. An additional factor in the increase in the dessert wine cat-

[11]Freedman, "Misery Market."

egory was the shift to fruit-flavored drinks, which also affected the soft drink industry and wine coolers.[12]

A number of factors indicated that the growth trend would continue for the $500 million dessert wine category. The desire to consume beverages that contained less alcohol than distilled spirits and were less expensive than distilled spirits, the desire for fruit flavor, and the American trend toward eating out at restaurants more often contributed to the trend toward increased consumption of dessert wines. Additionally, the dessert wine category had survived relatively well with virtually no promotion or advertising. This had been possible because, of the category's 55 million gallons, low-end brands accounted for 43 million gallons, approximately 50 percent of which was sold in half pints; and this market had not been accessible by traditional advertising or promotion.

The dessert wine category had been a profitable venture because many of the wines in this category were made with less expensive ingredients, packaged in less expensive containers, and had usually been sold without promotion. Canandiaqua estimated that profit margins in this category were as much as 10 percent higher than those of ordinary table wines. Gallo said this was not true for its products, but it would not reveal the figures.

The low-end dessert wines were a solid business. *The Wall Street Journal* reported that, of all the wine brands sold in America, Wild Irish Rose was the number six best seller, Thunderbird was 10th, and MD 20/20 was 16th. In contrast to the growth expectations of other brands and categories, sales of these low-end brands were expected to be up almost 10 percent. Yet the producers of these top-selling wines distanced themselves from their products by leaving their corporate names off the labels, obscuring any link to their products. Paul Gillette, publisher of the *Wine Investor,* was quoted in a discussion of this unsavory market as saying: "Makers of skid-row wines are the dope pushers of the wine industry."[13]

[12]"U.S. News and Research for the Wine, Spirits and Beer Executive," *IMPACT* 17, no. 11 (June 1, 1987): and *IMPACT* 17, no. 18 (September 15, 1987).

[13]Freedman, "Misery Market."

Sarah Norton and Wise Research

Ronald L. Coulter, D. Michael Fields, and Mary K. Coulter *All of Southwest Missouri State University*

Rebecca J. Gordon-Runyan *WRG Inc.*

When Jeff Baird knocked on the Dallas motel room door on an early August evening in 1995, he expected to see his bubbling and enthusiastic girlfriend. He expected her to be excited, both because it was her birthday and because she was nearing completion of the first week in a two-week training program for the new job she had recently accepted. Instead, the young woman who answered looked troubled and tired.

"Sarah, you don't look very happy," said Jeff.

"I'm not," explained Sarah. "This week has not gone exactly as I expected, and I am seriously questioning whether or not I should even be here."

Although the tone of the meeting had obviously changed dramatically, Jeff was glad he had made the trip. Sarah was extremely troubled and clearly needed to talk to someone about her concerns. Jeff was happy that he was there to listen as Sarah tried to put in perspective the events of the last four days.

Initiating the Job Search

Sarah Norton was nearing the point where she had just one semester remaining before obtaining her MBA degree from a large state university in Hammonsville, Missouri. She was preparing, with some concern, to begin her job search. Sarah had identified at least three factors that would make finding a job in her field difficult. First, from a general perspective, American industry was still in the process of its most substantial downsizing. Much of the downsizing was at the expense of lower levels of management—which had depressed the hiring environment for MBAs across the nation. Second, Sarah's area of specialization was market research. Although many companies expressed a continued dependence on research in order to be effective in the mature markets that dominated the U.S. marketplace, the research industry was not considered to be a growth industry. This situation was further complicated for MBA students because many undergraduates were in competition for the same jobs and could be employed at lower salaries. Finally, Sarah preferred to remain in Hammonsville. The city of 150,000 was close to her parents, and Jeff was there. The location issue might prove to be particularly limiting because a city of 150,000 would generate a smaller market for researchers. Although the situation was less than encouraging, Sarah still felt that she had some advantages in pursuing and getting a job in her field.

Sarah's Background

Sarah was known to her professors and friends as a mature 32-year-old woman who had grown up in central Missouri in a strong family with loving parents. She had a strong religious background that helped to guide her when she had to make tough personal decisions. She was a very pleasant person to be around, and she was both liked and respected by her colleagues and friends. While her personal philosophy was to respect and treat others as she would like to be treated, she never pushed her moral, ethical, or religious views on others. She was genuine and personable in her relationships and was considered to be a fun person to be around.

Sarah had one younger sister with whom she remained very close. Sarah's first job had been with the state of Missouri in the Professional Registration office of the Board of Healing Arts. She enjoyed working there; the office was operated in a very professional manner, and the employees showed a genuine appreciation for each other. After several years in this job, Sarah realized that she wanted to complete her college degree. At the urging of her sister, Sarah transferred to Hammonsville to work in the local state vocational rehabilitation office. Here Sarah assisted several vocational rehabilitation counselors and took classes at the local state university. Sarah was known for her positive work ethic, strong moral values, and intelligence. She received her undergraduate degree in marketing and management (a double major) and graduated with high honors. During her coursework, Sarah was especially taken with the research classes and decided that she wanted to pursue a career in marketing research.

With this sense of direction, Sarah openly sought opportunities in several research projects with her professors in order to develop her research skills. As a result, she was competent and confident of her ability to do all phases of a research project. She could design questionnaires, input data, analyze and interpret statistical tests, and write reports. She was a proficient statistician. Sarah was also very aware of the importance of collecting and reporting unbiased data. The ethical handling of data had been stressed in her research courses, and such an approach was consistent with her personality and personal values. While no industrywide standards existed for the collection and handling of data, Sarah was aware of the code of ethics developed by the Marketing Research Association, Inc. (see Exhibit 1). This organization consisted of approximately 2,100 members from across the United States. Members used the organization for education and training and for networking opportunities in the field of marketing research.

Sarah knew from her professors' lectures, and from her assigned research readings, that corporations annually spend millions of dollars on research. The results of that research are used to influence multimillion-dollar decisions regarding new product lines, manufacturing employment, and promotional strategies. Sarah was also aware that marketing research conducted by outside research suppliers was a growing industry concern. Articles she had read on the subject reinforced this concern regarding the ethical collection of marketing research data.

When Sarah completed her undergraduate degree in 1994, the job market was particularly tight. Several of her professors suggested that she consider an MBA degree, so Sarah applied to the graduate school and was accepted into the MBA program. This allowed her to

EXHIBIT 1

Code of Ethics of the Marketing Research Association

Source: Used with permission of the Marketing Research Association, Inc., Rocky Hill, CT.

The Code of Professional Ethics and Practices

1. To maintain high standards of competence and integrity in marketing and survey research.
2. To maintain the highest level of business and professional conduct and to comply with federal, state, and local laws, regulations, and ordinances applicable to my business practice and those of my company.
3. To exercise all reasonable care and to observe the best standards of objectivity and accuracy in the development, collection, processing, and reporting of marketing and survey research information.
4. To protect the anonymity of respondents and hold all information concerning an individual respondent privileged, such that this information is used only within the context of the particular study.
5. To thoroughly instruct and supervise all persons for whose work I am responsible in accordance with study specifications and general research techniques.
6. To observe the rights of ownership of all materials received from and/or developed for clients, and to keep in confidence all research techniques, data and other information considered confidential by their owners.
7. To make available to clients such details on the research methods and techniques of an assignment as may be reasonably required for proper interpretation of the data, providing this reporting does not violate the confidence of respondents or clients.
8. To promote the trust of the public for marketing and survey research activities and to avoid any procedure which misrepresents the activities of a respondent, the rewards of cooperation, or the uses of data.
9. To refrain from referring to membership in this organization as proof of competence, since the organization does not so certify any person or organization.
10. To encourage the observance of principles of this code among all people engaged in marketing and survey research.

remain in Hammonsville. She also was given a graduate assistantship in the marketing department which paid her tuition and living expenses. While working on her MBA, Sarah continued to develop her marketing research skills. She took 12 hours in her graduate program specifically in research classes and also worked on several special projects for the College of Business for publication and classroom instruction purposes. She also helped acquire secondary data from the library. Sarah had fully expected to return to her assistantship position in the fall of 1995; she had already been offered the head graduate assistant position.

Sarah had agreed to take on the additional responsibilities of head graduate assistant in her final semester of graduate school in the fall—coordinating the schedules and activities of the five graduate assistants who worked in the marketing department. She was confident that the additional time needed would not interfere with either her preparation for classes or what she considered to be her most important activity—finding an entry-level position in the marketing research field. By mid-summer, Sarah had updated her résumé and was ready to begin aggressively pursuing the job market.

Reacting to the Position Announcement

Sarah had been casually looking through the employment section of the Hammonsville *News Monitor* on Sunday, July 9, 1995, when she noticed a position announcement for a market research manager. She eagerly read the balance of the ad copy to get more details about the opportunity. The advertisement did not give any specific job requirements, but the copy did provide a catchy reference to details, dilemmas, and deadlines as they related to an entry-level management position. The advertisement gave a post office box number in Hammonsville and asked potential applicants to send a cover letter with their résumés. No company name was provided in the advertisement.

Sarah thought long and hard about applying for the position. If she applied and was offered the position, she thought she might get to stay in Hammonsville. She liked the city, and very few managerial positions ever became available in her specialized area of marketing research. She would likely have to wait to finish the last nine hours on her MBA degree, but she could still finish the degree at the university. She would also have to give up her head graduate assistant position. She especially wanted her professors to know what she was contemplating so they could hire a replacement before the fall semester began. The local university had been good to her, and she did not want to do anything that would appear improper to her professors or to herself. She discussed the situation with her major professor, who encouraged her to look seriously at the position. If it did not appear to be the type of position she wanted, she could simply withdraw from the interview process. Sarah agreed and mailed in her résumé and cover letter.

The Initial Response and Sarah's Preparation

Within a week of mailing her application letter, Sarah received a phone call from a woman named Katie. Katie said that Mr. Bill Wise, the company's president, would be arriving in Hammonsville from Dallas to do interviews and that he wanted to interview her. Sarah agreed to meet with Mr. Wise on Thursday, July 27. Sarah inquired as to the name of the organization and was told "Wise Research." A follow-up call was to be made by Katie at a later date to verify the interview time.

Sarah tried to get some background information about the organization so that she could intelligently discuss the company and how she might fit into its plans. She found the company listed in the Hammonsville telephone directory under market research firms. Her professor recommended that she call the number to inquire about the operation prior to the interview, but not to indicate why the call was being made. Sarah called the number and spoke with a young man who said he was the office manager. She asked what type of research they conducted and was informed that the company, located in the Westfield Mall, was strictly involved in fieldwork. The company did not generate any questionnaires, nor did it analyze any of the data it collected. The company simply collected data for other marketing research firms that were providing information to their own clients, such as Procter & Gamble, Ragu, or Campbell's. Sarah, remembering her marketing research text, classified the company as a field service organization (see Exhibit 2); this meant that the firm

EXHIBIT 2 **Types of Marketing Research Service Suppliers**

Customized research services	Companies that work with individual clients from developing the problem/opportunity through the entire research process. They are also referred to as full-service suppliers.
Field research services	These companies concentrate only on collecting data on research projects. They may specialize in various interviewing methodologies such as mail surveys, telephone surveys, personal surveys, focus groups, or mall intercept surveys.
Data analysis research services	These firms specialize in data coding, data editing, and data analysis. They are sometimes referred to as "tab houses," although some specialize in sophisticated data analysis techniques.
Syndicated research services	Companies that routinely collect information to provide to other firms who subscribe to their services.
Branded products research services	These companies have developed specialized data collection and analysis techniques, which are relevant to address specific types of research problems. Their research is branded and marketed like branded products.
Standardized research services	Firms which do marketing research projects conducted in a standard, prespecified manner; the results are then supplied to several different clients.

concentrated on collecting data for research projects. The office manager also indicated that the staff at his facility were not college educated.

The manager, who sounded apprehensive, then asked Sarah why she was interested in this information. Sarah truthfully answered that the president of the company was coming to Hammonsville to interview her for a position, but she did not have any information about the company. The manager seemed upset that the president of the company was coming to Hammonsville and he had not been notified. Sarah specifically indicated that she did not know anything about the position.

The Interview Process

The Initial Interview

When Katie called several days later to confirm Sarah's interview, she indicated that the interviews were to be held at a local hotel in Hammonsville. Sarah was somewhat surprised because she had expected to be interviewed at the local office in the mall. When she arrived at the hotel, she dialed the extension number Katie had provided. Karen Wise, Bill Wise's wife, answered the phone. She indicated that she also worked at Wise Research. Karen Wise came to the hotel lobby and gave Sarah an application to complete. This was a standard form with a space for annual salary requirement. Sarah responded $25,000–$35,000, knowing that it was a high request for the local market conditions.

After completing the application, Sarah went upstairs to the Wises' hotel room. The interview with Mr. and Mrs. Wise was informal and was held at a small table set in the center of a large room. Mr. Wise sat on one side, his wife sat on his side of the table but more to the end, and Sarah sat on the other side. Mr. Wise was dressed in a lightweight, short-sleeve shirt without a tie or jacket, and Mrs. Wise wore a dress. Sarah did not get the impression from their appearance or the interview process that either of them had much formal education or training. Both were very pleased with the sample paperwork Sarah had brought.

Sarah brought with her a copy of a marketing plan she had done as a student and three questionnaires she had developed to collect data for various projects. During her interview she discussed her data-entry skills and her knowledge of various statistical packages to analyze data. She also discussed her work on several special projects with professors in the College of Business. She explained that for the past year she had been employed as a graduate assistant in the marketing department. She indicated that she had expected to return to this position in the fall since she had already been offered the head graduate assistant position. She also discussed her undergraduate employment at a popular local restaurant where she had been responsible for operations in the absence of the owner. She had often managed the restaurant when the owner was away for several days.

The Wises discussed the deadlines necessary for different projects and how the manager might sometimes have two projects going one day and eight working the next. They gave Sarah a short history of the company. The organization had been in business for about 25 years and operated five mall research offices. Three of the offices were located in Dallas; one was located in Tulsa; and the Hammonsville office was the newest, having been in existence for about 10 years.

Sarah was then told that the local manager was being let go because he was unable to achieve the required production levels. The person the Wises chose would be trained in Dallas for two weeks and then returned to Hammonsville where he or she would be responsible for the Westfield Mall office. The interview was spent primarily discussing the job requirements. Sarah was given the impression that while there would be some contact between the Dallas office and the Hammonsville office, the manager they hired would have direct contact with the clients and autonomy to work with the employees as he or she saw fit.

Sarah's next question was about validating surveys. Survey validation is a procedure where supervisors, or other objective individuals, recontact a small random sample of respondents to check the accuracy of the fieldwork being done. Validation is particularly needed when the temptation for interviewer cheating may be present. Sarah was told that the clients did the validations and that the supervisor also did some. The context of the interview led Sarah to believe that the Wises' organization was contracting to provide valid survey data. Sarah was then told that callbacks for second interviews would be made that afternoon.

The Second Interview

Karen Wise called and left Sarah a message on her answering machine that Thursday evening. Sarah returned the call later in the evening. Karen told Sarah that the pay was $11 per hour with time and a half paid for any overtime work. Sarah specifically asked if it was 40 hours per week, and Karen replied in the affirmative. Karen Wise said this would come out to be $25,000 per year with benefits that Bill Wise would tell her about the next day. Sarah accepted the second interview and then calculated that it would take about 42.5 hours per week to make $25,000 per year.

The second interview was held in the same hotel and was as casual as the first interview. The Wises told Sarah that they were leaving on vacation as soon as they were done in Hammonsville. Again, no mention was made of touring the local Hammonsville facilities or of meeting the staff. The benefit package presented to Sarah included health insurance premiums paid on a plan of Sarah's choice, up to the amount that the company paid for Dallas employees. This was done because the Wise Research insurance plan did not cover Missouri employees. One week of vacation was offered after one year of employment. A performance review would be scheduled after three months, and then another review would be held nine months later. Mr. Wise stated that it didn't behoove them to give raises in that interim.

In preparation for the second interview, Sarah had compiled a list of 17 questions that she considered to be important. Much of the second interview consisted of Sarah's questions and the corresponding answers (see Exhibit 3), as she sought to gain more information about the research firm.

After completing the interview, the Wises indicated that they would make their decision later that afternoon. They also told Sarah they would call her either that afternoon or the following Monday.

Karen Wise called Sarah from her car phone later that afternoon and offered Sarah the position. Sarah accepted the position and indicated that she could fly out on Monday, August 7, 1995, for training in Dallas. The following week Sarah withdrew from her fall graduate program courses, informed the marketing department that she would not be returning for the fall semester, wrapped up her summer work as a research assistant, and prepared her personal calendar to be in Dallas from August 7 to August 21, 1995.

The Dallas Training

Sarah arrived at the Dallas Love Field airport around noon on Monday, August 7, and was picked up at the gate by Mark Wise, the son of Mr. and Mrs. Wise. Mark, who was in his early 20s, was very personable and open about the organization. He also spoke very highly of Cindy Brewster, the supervisor with whom Sarah was to train. Mark did bring up the fact that someone had called their Hammonsville office and asked about the position; he was very curious. The first time he discussed it, Sarah let it go without response. He brought the subject up again during the drive and at lunch. He mentioned that they had received a résumé from another employee in the Hammonsville office. They were confused as to how

EXHIBIT 3

**The Second Job
Interview: Sarah
Norton's Questions
and Her Notes on
Wise Research's
Answers**

1. How is the staff paid?

   The staff was paid on an hourly basis.

2. Is there a budget for incentives?

   No, but they were considering one on a trial basis and would possibly use the Hammonsville office to try out a new program. They felt there were problems with incentives based just on completions of surveys as some people screen potential respondents while others actually do the interviews. The Wises seemed to be concerned with the fairness of this method.

3. Are paychecks distributed from Dallas?

   The paychecks come from Dallas (verified at a later date).

4. Are the staff paid weekly or monthly?

   Twice a month.

5. What are the benefits? Health insurance? Profit sharing? Bonuses for production?

   Insurance was provided by the company; there was no profit sharing plan; and bonuses for production might include a pizza party on the company for all the employees, but no specific program was in place.

6. If the Hammonsville office was extremely busy and needed more production, could the manager help do the fieldwork?

   Yes.

7. How do you support your managers?

   Sarah never specifically asked this question but tried to discern information from her conversations. The Wises seemed supportive of their managers. Frequent communication between offices was discussed. They felt that the open lines for assistance from other mall managers would help. Overall, Sarah felt that they would support their managers regarding decisions and actions as long as they were keeping up production.

8. How often are performance reviews done? 3 months? 6 months?

   Reviews were done after the third month and then again at one year.

9. What is the average overtime for a manager?

   No specific time was given, but the Wises did feel that there would be plenty of overtime opportunities. It was mentioned that if the manager frequently had excessive overtime that they would look for either inefficiencies or the need for an additional assistant. Requests for overtime were required prior to actually working. Approval was mandatory.

10. How are the employees trained? Does the manager have latitude in the content of employee training?

    No specific training program had been designed and Sarah would be responsible for how the Hammonsville employees were trained within some guidelines.

11. How does Wise Research get its referrals?

    Companies come to them, and much of their business is repeat. If a mall office does a good job, the client may again specifically ask for that office. The client and mall manager will be able to communicate directly without going through the Dallas office every time. It was mentioned that Hammonsville had a bad reputation and that many clients did not want to use them. The Wises felt this problem could be overcome with time and a new manager.

12. If Sarah increased production in the Hammonsville office, would Wise Research have enough business to keep the office busy?

    Yes, the Wises did not feel that this would be any problem.

13. Would Sarah have autonomy and authority over her office (to set up an evaluation system, to tie bonuses to performance, to specify dress, approach, etc.)?

    The Wises would not directly answer this question. Sarah did not feel that the Wises were willing to let the manager operate completely and independently. The manager did have the authority over his or her office to a certain extent, with the final word coming from Dallas.

14. Were any promotion dollars budgeted to raise the image of the Hammonsville office?

    In preparing for the interview, Sarah had spoken to a variety of Hammonsville people about being interviewed in the mall. The typical first response she received was always negative toward mall interviewers. They were viewed as interruptive, and most people did not like to talk with them. Sarah felt that some efforts to change people's perceptions about the interviewers' work would enable the Hammonsville office to raise production. The Wises indicated that their organization does not budget for any self-promotion efforts.

(continued)

EXHIBIT 3
(Concluded)

15. Where in the mall can interviewers go?
    Interviewers are allowed to go anywhere in the original section of the mall. This is quite a large area, but most interviewers were staying primarily by the research office. Interviewers were typically not going farther into the mall because interviews were typically conducted in the research office and the original section of the mall was so large that it could be a long trip back to the office. The people Sarah talked with often tried to avoid the original mall areas where the interviewers typically stood. The Wises did want to see the interviewers branch out further into the mall.

16. How are focus group participants solicited?
    A file of willing participants was maintained to be used when needed.

17. During the Dallas training what would Sarah be provided with?
    The Wises indicated that the company would provide a room close to the mall, and they would provide a rental car if needed. Airfare would be provided from Hammonsville, and Sarah would also receive reimbursement for her expenses.

that could have happened because they had just listed a post office box number in the advertisement. Sarah simply commented that Hammonsville was a small town in many respects, even though the population was around 150,000, and that it would not be unusual for word to get around.

Mark also commented that his parents were tired of the Hammonsville situation. They were determined to hire someone who could make the office work, and they wanted to keep that person in Hammonsville no matter what it required. Mark said that the company had received a large number of résumés, and he thought they had interviewed nearly 100 applicants. When Sarah looked at him in disbelief, he quickly added that his statement might not be exactly accurate, but that they had interviewed for two days. He also stated that they felt happy with their decision and excited about her employment.

Sarah and Mark also had a conversation about her educational background. Mark was interested in research and said what he really wanted to know was how to design the questionnaires in order to get the data they wanted. Sarah briefly discussed some of the aspects of questionnaire design and data collection. It seemed very odd to Sarah that Mark had very little understanding of the research process as a whole, but she chalked it up to his being the younger son who did not work full-time at the company.

Mark took Sarah to lunch and then to a car rental agency where the Wises' other son had rented a car for Sarah to use during her two-week training program. Sarah was lodged in a hotel across the parking lot from a shopping mall which housed the research office where she would be training. Mark then took Sarah to the hotel and on to the mall where he gave her an envelope containing $200 in cash and a handwritten note, asking for her signature to indicate that she had received the $200 for expenses.

At the Chesterfield Mall, Sarah was introduced to the office supervisor, Cindy Brewster, and Mark left to return to the main office. Cindy immediately informed Sarah that she had been instructed by the main office not to disclose why Sarah would be in their office for two weeks. Cindy had told the employees that Sarah was an auditor and monitor who would be watching her. Cindy had Sarah complete another standard personnel form, which again requested simple information such as name, address, emergency contact, and salary. Upon completion of the form, Cindy faxed it to the main office.

Cindy then took Sarah on a tour of the facility. It soon struck Sarah that she had seen no evidence of a computer or typewriter. Later she did see a computer sitting on a shelf in the storage room. Sarah asked if they were computerized, and Cindy replied no. Cindy added that only the main office had computers.

In further conversations with Cindy, Sarah discovered that Wise Research considered 37.5 hours as a full-time week. Katie, the office manager at the main office, had sent an envelope for Sarah which Cindy gave to her. Sarah was surprised the front of the envelope was marked For Cindy's Eyes Only and Top Secret. The envelope contained copies of the routine paperwork that supervisors were responsible for completing. Cindy then mentioned that someone had called the Hammonsville office for information about the position. Again, Sarah did not reveal any information, but it seemed very peculiar to Sarah that the organization was so concerned about this incident, particularly if they had interviewed as many people as Mark had indicated.

Sarah and Cindy also discussed the story that Cindy had been ordered to tell her employees concerning Sarah's presence in the office. Cindy said that Wise Research had not yet notified the Hammonsville manager that he was being released, and she asked Sarah if that bothered her. Sarah was vague in her response, and Cindy made it clear that it *did* bother her. Cindy said that if the organization could treat the Hammonsville manager that way, they would also likely do it to her.

Day Two

Work began on Tuesday at 9 A.M. Sarah was told to carry her time card in her purse so no one would know that she was clocking in and out. To do this, Sarah arrived before the other employees. Cindy began by showing Sarah the paperwork that was to be completed before 10 A.M. At 10 A.M. Cindy held a briefing where the interviewers were brought up to speed on the outstanding projects and were taken through the steps of preparing for new projects. Cindy introduced Sarah as the auditor and monitor that she had told them about.

As the week progressed, Sarah was shown how to check the completed questionnaires and how to report daily progress to the client. When Wise Research began a project, each interviewer received a sheet that contained (1) an estimate of how many completed questionnaires they should be able to get per hour; (2) what percent of people they would approach (called *net incidence*) who would be eligible to respond based on general criteria, such as age or job; and (3) criteria which were specific (called *category incidence*) to the survey, such as "Do you use body shampoo?" Clients were sent a daily report, and Sarah was told that, in preparing this report, supervisors started with the actual production numbers and worked from them. For example, if interviewers were expected to complete two questionnaires per hour and four were actually completed in one day, the supervisor reported that two hours were worked on the job. This way budgeted hours always matched actual hours. They then took the number four and applied the net incidence and category incidence percentages to come up with a fictional number of people they screened out during the day so the final number showed four completions. This total was then distributed over the categories purely at supervisor discretion. They would just manipulate the data until the numbers totaled those estimated by the client. This report was then faxed to the client. Sarah asked Cindy about this practice, and Cindy said it was the way that everyone did it. She then told Sarah a story about how Karen Wise once was discussing one of the numbers with her and Cindy asked her why it bothered her because the numbers were all fabricated anyway. Karen said she was right, and they both had a good laugh. Cindy indicated that she did feel that it was wrong, though, and Sarah questioned how clients could make good decisions based on potentially biased data.

Sarah learned that the actual jobs each office worked on could vary from a home placement of body shampoo (where the client would use the product and then evaluate it) to a mall taste test of liqueurs. Sarah was concerned by some of these practices, so she asked Cindy what would happen if it appeared that a survey was not going to be completed on time. Cindy replied that first you would call the main office for more time. If that wasn't possible, they were often told to get it done no matter what it takes. This might involve calling uncles, nieces, or anyone demographically acceptable to provide the required data. The main office was also likely to tell the supervisor to write it up. Cindy later told Sarah that some of the other mall offices had interviewers who had been caught so many times with invalidated surveys that they were working under three or four different names so the clients would not recognize them.

Day Three

As training continued, another incident occurred that concerned Sarah. Cindy received a call from another mall supervisor. The other mall supervisor heard Sarah's voice in the background and immediately asked if Karen Wise had brought in the new Hammonsville supervisor for training. Cindy immediately denied that Sarah was the new manager, as she had been instructed to do from the main office. The comment from the other mall supervisor seemed strange to Sarah, since each office has four to six, primarily female, interviewers scheduled per day. She realized that there was a high rate of turnover for interviewers, but it seemed suspicious that the other mall supervisor immediately asked if Sarah was a new supervisor instead of an interviewer. Sarah questioned Cindy about this, and they talked about the grapevine that was in place at Wise Research. Sarah asked if the grapevine was used mainly for information or power within the organization. Cindy's reply was "For both."

Day Four

By Thursday of the first week, Sarah was directing the briefings on new projects for the interviewers. Cindy sat back and supervised Sarah's efforts. As they went through the questionnaire, one of the interviewers asked about the coding numbers. This led to a discussion about data entry, and one of the interviewers asked Sarah what would happen if a question was not answered. Sarah indicated they would leave it blank when inputting that response and then continue. Sarah explained that one blank response would not invalidate the entire interview. This seemed very annoying to the interviewers, and again Sarah was surprised at the lack of knowledge the employees had about the whole data collection process.

Throughout the daily training sessions, Cindy and Sarah had discussed the culture of the Wise Research organization and again, on Thursday, they began another conversation. Cindy recounted examples of her experiences. She believed that when she was hired for the supervisor's position, Bill Wise had known that she badly needed the job. She had been out of work for several months and her elderly mother needed care, so an income was imperative. Cindy's background was in psychology, and she had worked for mental health institutions prior to being out of work.

They also discussed many of the things that Cindy's boss had told her to do, such as being dishonest with her employees. Cindy told Sarah that there were things that she had been asked to do that she had refused. Sarah was very concerned about Cindy's comment and asked what those things were. Sarah felt that if Cindy had been asked to do these things then she would probably be asked to do them, too. Sarah was becoming upset at the thought of so much dishonesty in the office. What else could they want? Cindy was not specific in her response to Sarah's direct question and implied other things *were* currently happening, but that she had chosen not to be a part of those activities.

In her supervisory position, which she had held for over eight months, Cindy immediately stood out as a Wise Research leader. She was educated and perceived by the interviewers as a fair supervisor. But Cindy was bothered: although she had received notification of her three-month raise earlier, Wise Research had withheld the monetary rewards until just a few weeks before Sarah's arrival. Cindy had made attempts to gain raises for herself and for her assistant, but her attempts had been ignored. When the main office informed Cindy that she was going to receive a pay increase, she was happy, but she also wondered what the Wises might be wanting from her. When she was told she would be supervising Sarah's training, Cindy felt she understood the timing of her raise.

Cindy was aware of Sarah's training benefits. Sarah had been flown in for two weeks and provided with a car, a nice hotel, and $200 in cash for spending money. When Sarah's personnel records were completed and returned to Cindy, she commented on Sarah's starting pay. Apparently, Sarah's starting pay was more than Cindy was receiving even after having been with the company for more than eight months. Cindy explained that when she was hired, training was provided in Dallas-area malls and that she was responsible for all transportation costs. Every single weekday for what was supposed to be one month and ultimately turned into three, Cindy drove 85 miles round trip for her training. She admitted to feeling slighted by the company when Sarah was being treated so well.

By now Sarah did not have the positive feeling that she had when she first accepted her new position with Wise Research. The final straw came when Sarah and Cindy were discussing pay, and Cindy shared an experience she'd had on the Monday morning of Sarah's arrival. Apparently Cindy and others had worked the previous Saturday and had been loaned a couple of interviewers from another Dallas-area mall. One of Cindy's interviewers had been befriended by one of these women, and a conversation had ensued about how long each had been with the company and what salary was made per hour. On Monday, the visiting interviewer had gone back to work and complained that Cindy's employee made more money than she did although Cindy's employee had been with the company a shorter time. Cindy had received a phone call from Katie at the main office. Katie told her that she was to fire her interviewer because the interviewer had discussed her salary with another employee. Sarah asked Cindy if the employee had known about this rule or had been shown an employee handbook where this rule was stated. Cindy said that only supervisors and their assistants had employee handbooks and, to her knowledge, her assistant had never seen one. She did say that she felt that discussion of wages was inappropriate, and Sarah stated that she did not feel that way. Sarah said that her salary was hers, it was based on her skills, and that she should be able to discuss it with whomever she wanted.

Cindy had called the employee into the office, told her about the main office's stand, and told the employee that she must be fired. The interviewer began to cry and tried to change Cindy's mind. Cindy explained that it was not her decision and that she had been ordered to do this. The employee asked to talk with someone in the main office; Cindy felt that she should be able to do that, so she placed the call. When she told Katie that the employee wanted to talk with her, Katie responded that she did not know what more could be said but that she would speak to the employee.

The employee was crying and asked to keep her job. Cindy indicated that she literally said, "I beg you for my job." Cindy then heard the employee say that she would talk to Cindy. This surprised Cindy because she'd had no say in the firing. When the employee got off the phone, Cindy told her that she did not have to beg her for her job. She would have to formally write her up, but that she could still work. When Cindy called Katie back to tell her what she had done, she was asked why. Cindy explained that the woman worked several jobs to support a husband who didn't work and three children and that she needed the income. Katie responded that it wasn't their problem. Apparently, however, the interviewer was allowed to remain because she was still working when Sarah was in training.

Sarah had only been in the office for four days, but her winning personality and sincerity had made an impression on other employees. Sarah felt comfortable with Cindy and her staff. Thursday was also Sarah's birthday, and she received a fax from the main office and a card from Cindy. Cindy also said that her brother was making Sarah a handcrafted gift and that it would be done before she left town. One of the interviewers brought Sarah a cupcake, which might not have been so unusual had it not been the employee's day off. However, the kindness shown by the employees of the Chesterfield Mall research office was being overshadowed by concerns that engulfed Sarah.

Sarah's Dilemma

Thursday night was Sarah's chance to evaluate the events of the last four days. After another week of training, Sarah would be returning to her hometown. She would return to Hammonsville to take over the research office in the Westfield Mall. She had already sacrificed her graduate assistantship and would now have to complete her MBA degree at a later time. Even though she felt the new company was pleased with her efforts and knowledge, Sarah wondered if she had made a mistake in accepting the position.

This was Sarah's mindset as she anxiously awaited Jeff's arrival. As she waited, she began to consider her options. Should she resign immediately and return to Hammonsville? Would her concerns likely be alleviated in the second week of her training? Should she complete her training, report to the Hammonsville office, attack her work, and simply refuse to do anything that she considered to be unethical? Or, was she simply overreacting to a normal situation in which a company's culture sometimes conflicts with an individual's personal moral philosophies? Sarah was glad that Jeff was coming to Dallas that evening. He could help her sort through her emotions and decide what action would be in her best interest in the long run. The knot in her stomach signaled a sense of urgency in working through her concerns and arriving at a decision sometime before she reported to work the next morning.

29

Philip Morris Companies

Keith Robbins *George Mason University*

Philip Morris (PM) is best known as a manufacturer and marketer of cigarettes. In fact, PM is the largest cigarette company in the United States, with a 42 percent share of the $70 billion industry.[1] However, over the past 30 years the company has been pursuing such a systematic diversification strategy that, in addition to cigarettes, the company now ranks as the second largest beer brewer in the United States and the second largest food processing company in the world.[2] The company's brands include Clark Chewing Gum, Louis Kemp Seafood, Miller, Miller Lite, Lowenbrau, Jell-O, Oscar Mayer, Sealtest, Maxwell House, Oroweat Baked Goods, Light Touch Desserts, and Marlboro, Virginia Slims, Bucks, Benson & Hedges, Merit, and Parliament (see Exhibit 1).

Philip Morris Companies was incorporated in Virginia on March 1, 1985, as the holding company for the diverse businesses of Philip Morris, Inc.[3] Today, the company is the largest private employer in Richmond.[4,5] The company's ambition has been and remains to be the most successful consumer packaged goods company in the world.[6]

This ambition is reflected in the company's mission statement presented in its 1991 annual report to shareholders: "We are a global consumer products company, manufacturing and marketing tobacco, food, and beer brands around the world. Our broad-based operations generate strong and growing returns for investors by answering consumer needs with low-priced, high-volume, quality products. We are committed to the highest standards of ethics and fairness in all of our activities and operations."

Current CEO Michael Miles (the first nonsmoking CEO at Philip Morris in 145 years) describes the company's strategy for meeting its goal as developing new products to meet emerging consumer trends, expanding geographically, and manufacturing and marketing

This case was prepared by Keith Robbins of the School of Business Administration at George Mason University. Development of this case was made possible by a grant from the Funds for Excellence Program of the State Council of Higher Education in Virginia.

[1]Standard & Poor's, *Industry Survey,* 1992.

[2]P. Sellers, "Can He Keep Philip Morris Growing?" *Fortune* 125, no. 7 (1992), pp. 86–92.

[3]Moody's *Industrial Manual,* 1991.

[4]"The Forbes 500 Ranking," *Forbes* 149, no. 9 (April 29, 1992), pp. 190–396.

[5]"The Fortune 500 Largest Industrial Corporations," *Fortune* 125, no. 8, 1991.

[6]PM, annual report, 1991.

EXHIBIT 1
PM Brands

Cigarettes: *Philip Morris U.S.A., Philip Morris International*
  Marlboro Brands
  Virginia Slims
  Benson & Hedges
  Merit
  Parliament
Beer: *The Miller Brewing Company*
  Miller Lite
  Miller High Life
  Milwaukee's Best
  Lowenbrau
  Sharp's
Food: *Kraft General Foods, Kraft International, General Foods International*
  Kraft Cheeses
  Maxwell House Coffees
  Louis Rich Turkey
  Oscar Mayer Luncheon Meats, Hot Dogs, and Bacon
  Louis Kemp Seafood Products
  Post Cereals
  Jell-O Brand Gelatin
  Kool-Aid
  Sealtest Dairy Products
  Breyers Dairy Products
  Light'n Lively Dairy Products
Financial: *Philip Morris Capital Corporation*
  Major equipment leasing programs for customers and suppliers

globally.[7] The strategy appears to be working, as PM remains the largest and most profitable consumer products company in the world. In 1990, Philip Morris had risen to seventh on *Fortune*'s list of largest U.S. manufacturers, with sales approaching $50 billion.[8]

A History of Diversification Via Acquisition

The company has a distinct heritage among U.S. tobacco companies; it is the only major company that was not formed when the Supreme Court broke up the James Duke American Tobacco Trust in 1912.[9] Since its inception in England, Philip Morris has emphasized growth through acquisitions (see Exhibit 2). The success of Philip Morris in growing the purchased companies into industry leaders is legendary.

In 1957, Philip Morris was sixth and last in the U.S. cigarette market. Under the leadership of Joseph F. Cullman III and by emphasizing the Marlboro brand, the company climbed to first place by the end of 1983. In 1970, it bought Miller Brewing, which at the time ranked seventh among U.S. brewers. By 1977, the company had leapfrogged up to second place behind Anheuser-Busch.[10]

Philip Morris has been able to fund its numerous acquisitions through its high-margin tobacco products, which continue to contribute a disproportionate share of corporate earnings.

[7] Ibid.

[8] "The Fortune 500."

[9] R. Levering, M. Moskowitz, and M. Katz, *The 100 Best Companies to Work for in America* (Reading, Mass.: Addison-Wesley, 1984).

[10]Ibid.

EXHIBIT 2
PM's History of Acquisitions

Source: Moody's Industrial Manual, 1991.

June 1944	Purchased cigarette-producing assets from Axton-Fisher Tobacco Company, Louisville, Kentucky, for $8.9 million cash.
Feb. 1945	Acquired 99% interest in Benson & Hedges through common stock exchange on a share-for-share basis.
Dec. 1959	Acquired an interest in C.A. Tabacalera Nacional Venezuela.
Dec. 1963	Acquired a substantial interest in Fabriques de Tabac Reunies, S.A., Swiss cigarette manufacturer and licensee.
April 1967	Acquired an interest in Kwara Tobacco Company, Ilorin, Nigeria.
June 1969	Purchased 53% interest in Miller Brewing Company for $130 million.
Jan. 1970	Acquired control of Mission Viejo, Cal., new city and land developer for $20 million.
Feb. 1977	Acquired Wisconsin Tissue Mills, Menasha, Wis., for 314,000 shares of common stock.
Feb. 1977	Purchased 97% of common stock of The Seven-Up Company, a soft-drink extract manufacturer, for $520 million.
June 1978	Purchased the international cigarette business of Liggett Group, Inc., (consisting of rights to sell L&M, Lark, Chesterfield, Eve, and Decade outside of United States) for $45 million.
Nov. 1985	Purchased General Foods Corporation for $5.6 billion.
Dec. 1988	Acquired, through merger with a subsidiary, Kraft, Inc., for approximately $12.9 billion.
Aug. 1990	Acquired Swiss-based coffee and confectionery company Jacobs Suchard AG for $4.1 billion.

According to U.S. Labor Department statistics, retail tobacco prices have increased on average 10 percent over the past 11 years. This rate of increase exceeds that of any other product, including hospital rooms and prescription drugs, over this period.[11],[12] Cigarette manufacturers have found demand for tobacco to be price inelastic—smokers do not seem to decrease consumption despite price increases.

The acquisition spree has been motivated by the company's desire to lessen its dependence on tobacco. Many senior executives openly express concern about the company's heavy dependence on tobacco.[13] Thus, the central issue facing management at Philip Morris is the careful selection of the correct portfolio of consumer packaged goods that will allow the company to protect and build upon global operations. This mixture of businesses must smooth the transition away from tobacco dependence to avoid adverse consequences in an increasingly hostile environment.

Industry Segments

Philip Morris's significant industry segments consist of tobacco products, food products, beer, and financial services, including real estate. Operating revenues and operating profits for each of the segments over the past three years are detailed in Exhibit 3.

The company's dependence on tobacco is evidenced by the fact that tobacco revenues account for 41 percent of the company's revenue and 68 percent of its income, though this dependence has lessened somewhat recently. Tobacco's profits represented 72 percent of the company's operating income in 1989. Food products accounted for approximately 27 percent of the company's operating profit in 1990, compared with 23 percent in 1989.

---

[11]J. Dagnoli, "Philip Morris Keeps Smoking," *Advertising Age* 61, no. 48 (1990), p. 20.
[12]E. Giltenan, "Profits Keep Rollin' in . . . ," *Forbes* 146, no. 1 (1992), pp. 152–53.
[13]Sellers, "Can He Keep."

EXHIBIT 3

Company Income and Revenue Contribution by Industry Segment (In millions of dollars)

	1990	1989	1988
Operating revenues:			
Tobacco	$21,090 (41%)	$17,849 (40%)	$16,576 (53%)
Food	26,085 (51)	22,373 (51)	10,898 (35)
Beer	3,534 (7)	3,342 (7)	3,177 (10)
Financial services	460 (1)	516 (2)	622 (2)
Total operating revenues	$51,169	$44,080	$31,273
Operating profit:			
Tobacco	$ 5,596 (67%)	$ 5,063 (72%)	$ 3,846 (84%)
Food	2,205 (27)	1,580 (23)	392 (9)
Beer	285 (4)	226 (3)	190 (4)
Financial services	196 (2)	172 (2)	162 (3)
Total operating revenues	$ 8,282	$ 7,041	$ 4,590

In 1990, beer accounted for 7 percent of company revenues and 4 percent of income from operations.[14]

Tobacco Products

Philip Morris U.S.A. is responsible for the manufacture, marketing, and sale of tobacco products in the United States (including military sales), and Philip Morris International is responsible for the manufacture, marketing, and sale of such products outside the United States and for tobacco product exports from the United States.

Domestic Tobacco

Philip Morris sold 220.5 billion units of cigarettes in 1990, an increase of 1 billion units over 1989. Industry sales decreased 0.3 percent in 1990, compared to 1989. Over the past three years, Philip Morris has increased its sales and market share in the United States even though industry revenues have declined:

Year	Industry (billions of units)	Philip Morris	Market Share (%)
1990	522.1	220.5	42.2%
1989	523.9	219.5	41.9
1988	558.1	219.3	39.3

Source: Wheat, First Securities, Inc.

The major industry rivals in domestic tobacco are American Brands; RJR Nabisco, Inc.; B.A.T. Industries (parent of Brown and Williamson); Loews Corporation (parent of Lorillard); and the Liggett Group. The tobacco companies typically are operated as a subsidiary of diverse parent corporations. American Brands, in addition to its Pall Mall and Carlton cigarettes, markets Titleist golf balls, Jim Beam whiskey, and Master Locks. RJR Nabisco, in addition to its Winston, Salem, and Camel cigarettes, markets Oreos cookies, Planter's Peanuts, Del Monte Fruits, and Grey Poupon mustard. Loews Corporation, in addition to its Newport, Kent, and True cigarettes, owns CNA Financial Services, Inc.; Loews' theaters and hotels; and the Bulova Watch Company.

Philip Morris is the overwhelming leader in domestic market share, achieving 1.5 times the sales of its closest rival, RJR Nabisco (see Exhibit 4).

The Maxwell Consumer Report issued by Wheat, First Securities, Inc., has ranked Philip Morris U.S.A. as the leading cigarette company in the United States market since

[14]Moody's *Industrial Manual,* 1990, 1991, and 1992.

EXHIBIT 4
Domestic Cigarette Producers' Market Shares (Percentage of industry units sold)

Source: Standard & Poor's *Industry Surveys*, 1991.

Company	1990	1989	1988	1987
Philip Morris	42.0%	42.2%	39.3%	37.8%
Reynolds	28.9	28.7	31.8	32.5
Brown & Williamson	10.8	11.4	10.9	11.0
Lorillard	7.8	7.1	8.2	8.2
American	6.8	7.0	7.0	6.9
Liggett	3.7	3.4	2.8	3.6

EXHIBIT 5
Top 10 Domestic Cigarette Brands, 1990

Sources: Moody's, Standard & Poor's.

Rank	Brand	Company	Units (billions)	Mkt. Share
1	Marlboro	Philip Morris	135.6	26%
2	Winston	Reynolds	46.4	9
3	Salem	Reynolds	32.0	6
4	Kool	Brown & Williamson	32.0	6
5	Newport	Lorillard	25.1	5
6	Camel	Reynolds	21.2	4
7	Benson & Hedges	Philip Morris	20.5	4
8	Merit	Philip Morris	20.3	4
9	Doral	Reynolds	19.2	4
10	Virginia Slims	Philip Morris	16.8	3

1983. The company's best-selling brands are Marlboro, Benson & Hedges, Merit, Virginia Slims, and Cambridge. Philip Morris produces 4 of the top 10 selling brands in the United States, including best-selling Marlboro, which garnered 26 percent of the market in 1990 (see Exhibit 5).

Cigarette Industry Segments
Premium and Discount Brands

Philip Morris premium brands consist of top 10 performers Marlboro, Benson & Hedges, Merit, and Virginia Slims. In the summer of 1991, PM spent a record $60 million to advertise Marlboro Medium, the first spinoff from the Marlboro brand in 20 years.[15] According to Marlboro VP Nancy Brennan Lund, the brand's 26 percent domestic market share should increase, though its volume probably will not.

A growing industry segment consists of the discount brands. After initially rejecting the idea of selling less-profitable brands, Philip Morris decided to enter the discount segment in 1985. This was prompted by the realization that many of its customers were switching to cheap cigarettes.[16,17] By 1991, Philip Morris became the market leader in the low-priced segment. Now, 17 percent of PM's U.S.A. sales are discount brands, such as Cambridge, Alpine, Bristol, and Bucks.

Industrywide discount brand sales have risen from 11 percent of sales in 1989 to 25 percent today and are expected to double again over the coming five years. Although Philip Morris is performing well in the discount segment, it is unable to put its formidable advertising might behind these brands for fear of cannibalizing its higher-margin premium brands. Recently tobacco companies have raised prices on the discount brands—for example, PM increased its prices by 20 percent on the discount brands.

[15]Sellers, "Can He Keep."
[16]C. Leinster, "Is Bigger Better for Philip Morris?" *Fortune* 119, no. 10 (1989), pp. 66–68+ .
[17]A. Farnham, "From Soup to Nuts," *Fortune* 119, no. 1 (1989), pp. 43–47.

According to industry analysts,[18,19,20] William Campbell, CEO of Philip Morris U.S.A., is determined to compete in every major cigarette category. The result is that the company now produces low-profit generic cigarettes. Generics, sometimes referred to as *black and whites,* are sold in places like Wal-Mart bearing such names as Best Buy, Basic, and Gridlock: The Commuter's Cigarette—a California brand. Campbell's predominant goal is to increase PM's domestic market share a point a year.

Low Tar

The low tar segment of the market consists of cigarettes delivering 15 milligrams (mg) or less of "tar" per cigarette. In 1990 and 1989, this market accounted for 57.4 percent and 55.5 percent of U.S. industry sales, respectively.[21,22] Philip Morris's low tar brands comprised 42.1 percent of the low tar market in 1990 and 42.8 percent in 1989. The low tar market includes a subsegment referred to as *ultra-low tar* that consists of brands that deliver 6 mg. or less of tar per cigarette. Ultra-low tar brands accounted for 11.3 percent of industry sales in 1990, compared with 10.8 percent in 1989. Philip Morris's ultra-low tar brands garnered 32.9 percent of this market in 1990 and 33.4 percent in 1989.

The low tar and ultra-low tar segments are growing, whereas the industry is in general decline. Philip Morris must ensure that its brands competing in these segments are able to achieve market share positions at least commensurate with its non-low tar cigarettes. This is currently not the case in the rapidly expanding ultra-low tar category, where Philip Morris lost market share during 1990.

International Tobacco

Worldwide tobacco industry sales have been growing at approximately 2 percent per year for the past several years. The United States exported $5 billion of tobacco products in 1990.[23] Philip Morris International's share of this market was 7.6 percent in 1990, compared with 6.7 percent in 1989. Marlboro is the leader. Its sales increased 13.2 percent in 1990. Its 206.9 billion units accounted for over 4.3 percent of the non-United States cigarette market. In particular, Philip Morris International has strong market share positions in Argentina, Australia, Finland, France, Germany, Hong Kong, Italy, Mexico, Saudi Arabia, and Switzerland, holding at least a 15 percent market share position in each.

Philip Morris is the leading cigarette exporter. Total cigarette exports to 111 foreign countries in 1990 were valued at $4.75 billion. The leading destinations were Asian (58 percent) and European (38 percent) countries. Two factors were primarily responsible for the growth in international sales: the lowering of trade barriers in Japan, Taiwan, and South Korea, and the weakened dollar.[24]

The market for cigarettes outside the United States in 1980 was 3.9 trillion units, with only 40 percent open to Western companies. Currently, international (non-U.S.) consumption stands at 4.9 trillion cigarettes a year, and Western companies now can deal with 95 percent of this market. PM sold 640 billion, or 11.6 percent of the world's cigarettes last year. That places PM second behind the Chinese government (1.5 trillion) in terms of total cigarette sales.

---

[18]S. Chakravraty, "Philip Morris Is Still Hungry," *Forbes* 145, no. 7 (1990).

[19]J. Dagnoli, "CEO Miles Sees International Growth for Philip Morris," *Advertising Age* April 8, 1991.

[20]Sellers, "Can He Keep."

[21]Moody's *Industrial Manual,* 1990 and 1991.

[22]S&P's *Industry Surveys,* 1990 and 1991.

[23]M. Levin, "U.S. Tobacco Firms Push Easily into Asian Markets," *Marketing News* 25, no. 2 (January 21, 1991), pp. 2, 14.

[24]Sellers, "Can He Keep."

It is interesting that the company's global perspective largely resulted from its inability to penetrate domestic markets. When it was No. 6 among U.S. tobacco companies during the '50s, PM was the first U.S. manufacturer to begin selling its products in duty-free shops in foreign countries. It focused on those countries most frequented by U.S. travelers. Because many of these markets were closed to imports, the company was forced to license the sale of its cigarettes in the areas. The company reasoned that foreign-domestic managers could best oversee these foreign operations. As a result of this early emphasis on international operations, PM's management is more globally diverse than most: Miles and Mayer are Americans, Maxwell is a Scot, Campbell is Canadian, David Dangoor (PM U.S.A. marketing head) is Iranian. Two of the three bosses Miles vied with for the CEO position are Australian; the third is German.[25]

Though many foreign markets recently have opened access to U.S. firms, many protectionist policies are mitigating penetration. Many governments control prices, levy huge taxes, and even market state-owned brands (Taiwanese government's Long Life cigarettes; Japan's Dean cigarettes). Last year in Hong Kong, a 200 percent tax increase on imported cigarettes effectively doubled the price of a pack of Marlboros and cut PM's sales by 80 percent. The government later cut the tax in half after Philip Morris International employees and friends gathered 75,000 signatures.

In Italy, the company was implicated in a government investigation of cigarette imports that illegally avoided Italian taxes. Consequently, Italy imposed a one-month ban on Marlboro, Merit, and Muratti, a popular local blend.

International tobacco's profit margins are half those of the United States. These margins are improving—they rose 24 percent in 1991 on a 14 percent increase in revenues. In the European community, sales volume has risen 25 percent during the past three years. PM management views Turkey as the "gateway to the east," particularly the former Soviet Union and Central Asia. PM recently broke ground on a $400 million cigarette factory there.[26]

In 1990, PM bought three deteriorating East German factories that churn out the leading local cigarette, F6. In a recent year, PM shipped 22 billion cigarettes to the former Soviet Union.[27]

Food

CEO Miles was formerly head of Kraft General Foods (KGF), which was formed after PM bought Kraft. He was instrumental in the successful implementation of Hamish Maxwell's diversification strategy. Miles's promotion to chief executive helped ease the tension between PM and General Foods that had existed since the latter's hostile takeover. Miles's insight into the food business permitted him to ignore pessimistic forecasts for traditionally strong brands, such as Maxwell House and Post. Many insiders felt that these brands could expect, at best, marginal increases in volume. Miles reemphasized growth and, as a consequence, sales of such leading products as Kool-Aid, Jell-O, and Grape Nuts cereal are expanding again.[28,29] Operating profits in General Foods exceeded $700 million in 1991, versus $433 million in 1989.

Kraft's cheese division has not fared as well. Sales have stagnated. Analysts blame this on Miles's continued price hikes in the face of stable prices for private label cheeses. During 1991, Kraft began cutting prices in an attempt to regain lost market share from the private labels. However, the retailers—who profit quite nicely off their own private label

[25]Ibid.

[26]Moody's *Industrial Manual,* 1992.

[27]PM, annual reports, 1991 and 1992.

[28]Dagnoli, "CEO Miles Sees."

[29]Sellers, "Can He Keep."

brands—were naturally reluctant to pass the cuts on down to the consumers.[30] The division experienced a shortfall of $125 million between anticipated and realized cheese profits. The problems of the cheese division also have resulted from increased health consciousness among consumers. Cheese products are notoriously high in saturated fat and cholesterol. As more consumers become sensitive to nutritional guidelines espoused by leading health agencies, overall demand for cheese likely will continue to decline. Kraft's products in general and cheese products in particular typically are not purchased by health conscious consumers due to their high fat content.

Richard Mayer, president and CEO of KGF, has two primary ideas for stimulating the food division: (1) to get market research and computer people working in teams with brand managers to make better use of scanner-generated sales data and (2) to distribute all KGF products within a particular region from a single warehouse location to serve customers better.[31] Presently, grocers buy 10 percent of all their grocery items from KGF but draw from many warehouses. These strategies should help KGF respond more expeditiously to market trends and competitors' moves.

Philip Morris as an Employer

Philip Morris consistently is ranked as one of the more progressive employers in the United States. Levering, Moskowitz, and Katz included PM among their listing of *The 100 Best Companies to Work for in America.*

According to James Bowling, director of public relations and public affairs, caring about its employees is what distinguishes Philip Morris: "everybody bought tobacco competitively at auction; manufactured cigarettes in Kentucky, Virginia, and North Carolina; used essentially the same machinery; paid the same union wages; and sold through the same wholesalers and retailers. Therefore, they said that, if there is going to be a difference, it will have to be in the people. As simplistic and corny as that seems, it has been the guiding principle here since that day. We have always tried to treat our people better—by being the first or among the first with amenities and working pleasantries."

One survey of senior managers conducted by an independent auditor, showed very high satisfaction with the company. The benefits package includes long- and short-term disability compensation. Employees automatically are insured for twice their annual salary, and there is a survivor income benefit that, in the event of employee death, would start paying, after four years, 25 percent of last base pay to surviving spouses every month plus 5 percent of your last base pay to each surviving child. There is an employee stock ownership plan and employees who smoke—and the majority do—are entitled to one free carton of cigarettes per week.[32]

Philip Morris was one of the first companies to employ blacks in sales positions. One out of every four persons who works for the company is a minority-group member—and minorities hold 14 percent of positions classified as "officials and managers."[33]

The Richmond cigarette factory is a futuristic plant completed in 1974 at a cost of over $200 million—at the time the largest capital investment in the company's history. The plant boasts of parquet floors and floor-to-ceiling windows overlooking elaborate ornamental gardens.[34]

---

[30]Ibid.

[31]Dagnoli, "CEO Miles Sees."

[32]Levering et al., *The 100 Best.*

[33]PM, annual report, 1991.

[34]Levering et al., *The 100 Best.*

EXHIBIT 6   Philip Morris Companies, Inc: Consolidated Income (In millions of dollars)

	1991	1990	1989	1988	1987
Operating revenues	$56,458	$51,169	$44,080	$31,273	$27,650
Cost of sales	25,612	24,430	21,868	13,565	12,183
Excise taxes on products	8,394	6,846	5,748	5,882	5,416
Gross profit	22,452	19,893	16,464	11,826	10,051
Marketing, admin., & research	13,331	11,499	9,290	7,304	5,956
Amortization of goodwill	499	448	385	125	105
Operating income	8,622	7,946	6,789	4,397	3,990
Interest & other debt expense	1,651	1,635	1,731	670	646
Earnings before income taxes	6,971	6,311	5,058	3,727	3,344
Provision for income taxes	3,044	2,771	2,112	1,663	1,502
Earnings before cumulative effect of acct. change	3,927	3,540	2,946	2,064	1,842
Cumulative effect of acct. change for income taxes	(921)			273	
Net earnings	3,006	3,540	2,946	2,337	1,842
Retained earnings (B.O.Y.)	10,960	9,079	7,833	6,437	5,344
Common dividends	(1,765)	(1,432)	(1,159)	(941)	(749)
Four-for-one stock split			(478)		
Exercise of stock options	(172)	(218)	(63)		
Other	9	(9)			
Retained earnings (E.O.Y.)	12,038	10,960	9,079	7,833	6,437

1991 Performance and Future Prospects

Philip Morris currently sells more than 3,000 items. The value of the shares of stock outstanding reached $74 billion in December 1991 (trading at $75 per share) exceeding the value of all other U.S. companies except Exxon. Among the 1991 highlights: revenues increased 10 percent to $56.5 billion; operating income grew 14 percent to $9.9 billion; unit sales increased nearly 200 million in the United States over 1990, whereas U.S. industry volume decreased by 13 billion units.

Despite many bright spots, particularly in fat-free products, beverages, and breakfast cereals, overall results in North American food businesses were lower than expected. Volume in the brewing business grew 0.4 percent despite a doubling of the federal excise tax at the beginning of the year. Performance in 1991 allowed the company to increase dividends by 22.1 percent to an annualized rate of $2.10 per share, the 24th consecutive year of dividend increases.[35]

According to Miles, the company will throw off free cash of more than $21 billion. This is the excess after capital expenditures, dividends, and taxes—and Philip Morris can use it either to pay for acquisitions or to buy back stock, or both. The company currently realizes $15 billion annually from international operations (more than Coca-Cola, PepsiCo, and Kellogg combined). Marlboro is especially strong internationally in Asia, Eastern Europe, and the former Soviet Union.[36]

As portrayed in the company's consolidated income statement (Exhibit 6), Philip Morris U.S.A.'s sales went up 9 percent to $9.4 billion in 1991, and operating profits rose even faster to reach $4.8 billion. Operating margin rose a fabulous 51 percent, up from 42 per-

[35]PM, annual report, 1992.
[36]Sellers, "Can He Keep."

EXHIBIT 7   **Comparative Consolidated Balance Sheet as of December 31 (in millions of dollars)**

	1991	1990	1989	1988	1987
Assets					
Consumer products:					
Cash & equivalents	$ 126	$ 146	$ 118	$ 168	$ 90
Receivables, net	4,121	4,101	2,956	2,222	2,065
Inventories	7,445	7,153	5,751	5,384	4,154
Other current assets	902	967	555	377	245
Total current assets	12,594	12,367	9,380	8,151	6,554
Property, plant, & equipment	15,281	14,281	12,357	11,932	9,398
Less accum. depreciation	5,335	4,677	3,400	3,284	2,816
Property account net	9,946	9,604	8,951	8,648	6,582
Other assets	20,306	20,712	17,251	16,992	5,411
Total consumer products assets	42,846	42,683	35,588	33,791	18,547
Total financial & real estate assets	4,538	3,886	3,440	3,169	2,890
Total assets	$47,384	$46,569	$39,028	$36,960	$21,437
Liabilities					
Total current liabilities	11,824	11,360	8,943	7,969	5,164
Total consumer products liabilities	31,344	31,460	26,108	26,664	12,234
Total financial & real estate assets	3,528	3,162	2,849	2,617	2,330
Stockholders' Equity					
Common stock ($1, par)		935	935	240	240
Additional paid-in capital				252	272
Earnings reinvested in business		10,960	9,079	7,833	6,437
Currency translation adj.		561	143	117	146
Net stockholders' equity	12,512	11,344	9,871	8,208	6,803
Total	$47,384	$45,956	$38,828	$37,489	$21,367

cent seven years ago. Philip Morris's gains in market share are impressive, too—43.3 percent of total U.S. cigarette sales today, versus 35.9 percent in 1985.

The primary objective at Philip Morris traditionally has been to achieve 20 percent annual earnings growth. Hamish Maxwell hit the mark each of the last five years, but Miles is facing a more maleficent marketplace.

The company is in a very solid financial position as it remains one of the more liquid U.S. companies. It often is referred to as the "King of Cash" (see Exhibit 7).

Threats To Philip Morris's Traditional Level of Performance

The Declining American Cigarette Industry

Domestic cigarettes contributed $4.8 billion in operating income last year, roughly half the corporate total. But the American cigarette industry is declining 2 to 3 percent per year. Additionally, the trend is toward budget brands with smaller profit margins and away from premium products, such as Marlboro, Merit, Virginia Slims, and Benson & Hedges. According to industry analysts, the bargain brands—including those marketed by Philip Morris—pose more of a threat to the 20 percent target than the product liability litigation now pending Supreme Court review.[37]

[37]S&P's *Industry Survey,* 1992.

Slowing Processed Food Sales

Recession intensifies price elasticity, so shoppers are moving toward less-costly private label brands. Increasing consumer awareness of ingredients has invited comparison between the private labels and national brands, such as Kraft General Foods (KGF). In many cases, there is no substantive difference. KGF's North American revenues rose only 1 percent last year. Excluding special charges, operating income increased a disappointing 8 percent.

Antismoking Litigation and Legislation

Investors remain concerned about tobacco's legal status. This hinged on a Supreme Court ruling expected during the summer of 1992. The court will decide whether the federally mandated warning labels on cigarette packs—required since 1966—insulate tobacco companies from liability claims in state courts.

Smoking and Health Related Issues

Since 1964, the Surgeon General of the United States and the Secretary of Health and Human Services have released reports alleging a correlation between cigarette smoking and numerous physical maladies, including cancer, heart disease, and chronic diseases of the respiratory system. Recent reports continue to emphasize the health warnings from the earlier studies and additionally focus on the addictive nature of smoking and the demographics of smokers. In particular, the prevalence and growth rates of smoking among women and African-Americans have received much publicity.[38]

Federal law requires marketers of cigarettes in the United States to include one of four warnings on a rotating basis on cigarette packages and advertisements:

> SURGEON GENERAL'S WARNING: Smoking Causes Lung Cancer, Heart Disease, Emphysema, and May Complicate Pregnancy.
> SURGEON GENERAL'S WARNING: Quitting Smoking Now Greatly Reduces Serious Risk to Your Health.
> SURGEON GENERAL'S WARNING: Smoking by Pregnant Women May Result in Fetal Injury, Premature Birth, and Low Birth Weight.
> SURGEON GENERAL'S WARNING: Cigarette Smoke Contains Carbon Monoxide.

In addition to the warnings, federal regulations require that cigarettes sold in the United States disclose the average tar and nicotine deliveries per cigarette.

A more recent concern has been the alleged health risks to nonsmokers from what is most often referred to as *passive smoking* or *environmental tobacco smoke* (ETS). In 1986, the U.S. Surgeon General issued a report claiming that nonsmokers were at increased risk of lung cancer and respiratory illness due to ETS. The Environmental Protection Agency is currently at work on a report detailing the risks of ETS. The findings concerning ETS have been instrumental in the passage of legislation that restricts or bans cigarette smoking in public places and places of employment.

Television and radio advertising of cigarettes has been prohibited in the United States since 1971. Since this time, regulatory agencies have acted to further restrict or prohibit smoking in certain public places, on buses, trains, and airplanes, and in places of employment.

Such restrictions are not exclusive to the United States. Many foreign countries have restricted or prohibited cigarette advertising and promotion, increased taxes on cigarettes, and openly campaigned against smoking. Thailand, Hong Kong, France, Italy, and Portugal

[38]Ibid.

all have implemented cigarette advertising bans. This virtually precludes successful introduction of new brands in these countries. The European Economic Community (EEC) is contemplating a ban on tobacco advertising in newspapers, magazines, and billboards.[39] More recently, the Asian Consultancy on Tobacco Control, a 14-nation consortium, has been formed to combat smoking in this region. Thus, some countries have tighter restrictions than the United States.

Litigation

Approximately 50 court cases are pending, wherein plaintiffs are seeking damages from leading United States cigarette manufacturers. The litigation involves alleged cancer and other health maladies directly resulting from cigarette smoking. Philip Morris was a defendant in 23 actions pending as of March 1, 1991, compared with 24 at the same point in 1990 and with 32 in 1989. The number of court cases appears to have stabilized.

Philip Morris's primary defense tactic has been based on seeking a preemption of liability based on the Federal Cigarette Labeling and Advertising Act. Five federal courts have ruled that the cigarette labeling act does protect cigarette manufacturers from some liability claims. Conversely, the Supreme Court of New Jersey and one of the Texas appellate courts ruled that the cigarette labeling act does not limit the liability of the cigarette manufacturers.

As with any court case the outcome is uncertain. A finding in favor of the plaintiff would have the effect of denying preemption of liability on the basis of the existence of the cigarette warning labels. This could entice additional litigation against cigarette manufacturers. Philip Morris remains confident that, even in this worst-case scenario, the lawsuits will not pose a substantive threat to its overall financial health.

The Company's Position

No tobacco company has ever lost a liability case or paid a penny to settle; juries thus far have ruled that smokers have been adequately warned cigarettes can ruin their health. According to John McMillin of Prudential Securities: "A Supreme Court ruling against the industry has limited downside for the stock because worries have already pulled down the price. A tobacco victory could mean the end of major litigation risk and take Philip Morris's stock up 15 to 20 percent."

Tobacco use is one of the most widely discussed health issues around the world. The company's position was stated by CEO Miles in a letter to shareholders in 1992: "Given the general availability of information concerning the health issue, we regard smoking as a voluntary lifestyle decision that need not be subjected to new marketing or use restrictions."

He added: "While we believe that consumers are aware of the claimed health risks of smoking, nonetheless in February 1992 we took actions to begin placing the U.S. Surgeon General's health warning on all our cigarette packages worldwide where warnings are not currently required. This initiative applies to brands manufactured in the United States for export, as well as to those produced overseas by our affiliates and affected licensees. We are taking these steps because the lack of warning on a relatively small number of packages—approximately 10 percent of our volume—has become an issue out of proportion to its importance."

Continuing, Miles stated: "Moreover in the United States we are acting to increase awareness and enforcement of minimum age purchase restrictions on our tobacco products through multimillion-dollar programs involving advertising, trade relations, and family education."

---

[39]P. Engardio, "Asia: A New Front in the War on Smoking," *BusinessWeek* (Industrial/Technical Edition), no. 3201 (February 25, 1991), p. 66.

Future Prospects

According to Miles, the company has no plans to diversify outside of packaged goods. Since acquisition opportunities in tobacco are limited, most analysts predict a major food acquisition, probably in Western Europe within the coming year or so. In 1990, PM bought one of Europe's largest coffee and chocolate companies, Jacobs Suchard, well known for Toblerone candy bars. The $4.1 billion deal made PM the third-largest food marketer in Europe, behind Nestlé and Unilever. The company's European revenues today are approaching $10 billion in food. Nestlé has about $15 billion in European sales but, with acquisitions, PM figures it will grow faster.

There is much speculation centered on acquisition targets. One is rumored to be H. J. Heinz, a European powerhouse. PepsiCo is not considered a likely target but Cadburry Schweppes is. Another suspected target is Paris-based BSN, which would help PM penetrate the lucrative French cheese market with its Velveeta, Cracker Barrel, and Kraft Natural brands.

For Miles to meet the company's goals, PM must reach $85 billion in sales by 1995, with net income of $9 billion.[40] The future of the tobacco industry, particularly domestically, is cloudy. With numerous product liability lawsuits pending and increasing antismoking sentiments, PM must face the increasingly realistic possibility that cigarette smokers will become virtually nonexistent. As pessimistic as this may sound, a more threatening though less-likely scenario exists: cigarette manufacturing could be banned by the FDA. Within the coming five years, Miles must reposition the firm so it may withstand the effects of declining tobacco income.

[40]Sellers, "Can He Keep."

30

Black Diamond Equipment, LTD.

Steven J. Maranville *University of St. Thomas*

Madeleine E. Pullman *Colorado State University*

Jeff Jamison looked above at the glistening ice and snow of the frozen waterfalls. He had waited three weeks for the ice to get to this perfect condition, thick enough to support his weight, and the correct consistency for holding the picks of the two axes in his hands and the tooth-covered crampons on his feet. On this Saturday in early January of 1993, he was trying out a new axe, the Black Prophet, a state-of-the-art climbing tool with a light weight, composite handle, and innovative head design produced by Black Diamond Equipment, Ltd. Everyone in the mountaineering world was talking about the Black Prophet's novel design and waiting for the tool to enter the stores in the coming months. Jeff was lucky enough to have a connection with one of Black Diamond's sales representatives and thus had access to the new Black Prophet before its formal release to the market.

At the top of the last pitch of the climb, he sank the Black Prophet in the ice and suddenly felt a disconcerting snap. Jeff watched with disbelief as pieces of the broken axe plummeted thousands of feet to the canyon floor. As he fought off panic, Jeff realized that he would be forced to descend with only one axe, a doable but challenging feat. During the long, arduous descent, all Jeff could think about was how a tool like that one could have left Black Diamond's factory.

The following Monday, January 4, 1993, Mellie Abrahamsen, Black Diamond's new quality assurance manager, a recent MBA graduate from the University of Utah, entered her office and turned on her computer to scan her e-mail. The news of the axe incident was echoing throughout the plant. Research and Development, Production, Customer Service, Marketing, and the president were all demanding an explanation and a plan. With all the excitement over the new design, preseason orders for the Black Prophet had exceeded expectations. Although the tool was on back order for many customers, the first production run of the axe had already been shipped to mountaineering stores throughout the world. Highlighted at the top of Abrahamsen's e-mail listing was a priority message from Peter Metcalf, president of Black Diamond, calling an emergency meeting with all department heads to develop a plan for handling the crisis.

Monday Morning Meeting

By 9:00 A.M. Black Diamond's top management team was huddled around the square butcher-block table that filled the center of Metcalf's congested corner office. As Mellie Abrahamsen approached, she could see into Metcalf's office through the two large windows that faced the shop floor. Because she was new to the company, many of the artifacts peculiar to Black Diamond still caught her attention.

Metcalf's office walls were decorated with framed photographs of mountain-climbing and skiing adventures. The management team members sitting around the table were dressed casually; many were wearing Black Diamond sportswear—T-shirts and sweaters with the Black Diamond insignia. Abrahamsen squeezed through the office and found a seat next to Metcalf, from which she had a view out the windows.

Metcalf spoke anxiously to the group: "This incident is a devastating blow. Thank goodness the guy didn't get hurt; but now every one of our axes out there is suspect. If we have to issue a recall on the product, that will kill our axe business. If we have to discontinue our axe program, all the European competitors will step in and copy the technology that we worked so long to perfect. Yet think of the liability implications of an accident from this tool! How could this have happened? I thought this axe had the latest and greatest technology! We've never had problems like this with our regular mountaineering axes."

Maria Cranor, the marketing manager, added to Metcalf's fervent speech: "If customers see this axe as being of poor quality, we'll be forced to cease the axe program. But worse, if customers think Black Diamond is a company that markets unsafe products, our whole business is in jeopardy! Black Diamond must not lose its leadership image."

"My sales representatives are having a fit," Stan Smith, manager of customer service, proclaimed loudly. "They have huge back orders for the axe, and the retail shops have several customers a day asking about the tool. You folks know how this industry is—rumors about tool failures and accidents get around fast."

In a despondent tone, the designer of the Black Prophet, Chuck Brainard, said, "I can't believe this nightmare. Just as we were sitting on top of the world with the most innovative design to enter the market in years—all the competition taken by surprise, and a good ice-climbing season ahead—a major stroke of bad luck hits."

"I can't help but think," said Stan Brown, the production manager, "that the cause of the axe's failure is in its design. It's great to be innovative, but I think the design is so innovative that it just doesn't work."

"Now wait a minute, Stan," Metcalf interjected. "I don't want this to deteriorate into finger pointing."

Brainard spoke up. "No, no, that's all right, Peter. Stan might be right. Maybe we did go too far."

Metcalf went on: "We don't know all the facts. So let's stay focused and not jump to conclusions. This is a companywide problem."

Trying to refocus the group, Cranor said, "We tried to cut the lead time on this project so that we would have at least a year of sales before the French, Swiss, and other U.S. competitors could copy our concept and steal our market share. We have a reputation as a high-quality and innovative design company. This incident is potentially very damaging to our reputation as the market leader for innovation."

"We've got to nip this one in the bud and find a way to reassure our customer base," contended Smith. "I need an answer as soon as possible."

John Bercaw, manager of research and development, said, "Stan, I appreciate the urgent need that you're feeling with regard to handling customer concerns, but we need more than a quick fix. We need to find out why the failure occurred and to put systems in place to prevent this from happening again."

"I agree," Metcalf said. "As I said, this is a companywide problem."

Brainard attempted to clarify the situation. "As I see it, the possible sources of the failure are design, materials, and/or assembly."

"I can speak about the development phase of the project," stated Bercaw. "We worked hard to develop this axe and cut down on the lead time between the conceptualization and production of the final tool. Peter, you know we've been under tremendous pressure to have this new axe into the production phase and on the market in under two years."

Metcalf nodded. "That's been our strategy," he said, "being the 'firstest with the mostest.'"

Bercaw continued. "This project has been a real struggle: we've been working with all sorts of new technologies, like composite construction and modular tool design. The vendors normally don't make tools for these types of applications. They've had a hard time meeting our specifications, and many of the vendors don't want to work on our products because of potential liability implications."

"What about the assembly?" asked Metcalf.

Brown answered, "Well, the shop worked like crazy to get those axes out for the winter season and I put my best people on the rush assembly. The shop has been really taxed, what with the increasing growth rate for all our climbing and mountaineering products. We're always scrambling to meet the back orders. We need more people and new machines to keep up with this demand and improve our quality."

Metcalf persisted. "Do you know of anything in particular that may have been out of the ordinary during assembly?"

Brown replied, "I'd have to talk to Brian, our lead assembler, to see if he has any clues about why that axe could have failed in the field."

Metcalf turned to his left, where Black Diamond's newest management team member was sitting. "I realize that this is all new to you and that you came in after the fact, so I doubt the Quality Assurance Department can do much about this situation now."

Caught somewhat by surprise, Abrahamsen pulled her thoughts together and said, "Since this job is a newly created position, I wasn't here during the design development and testing phase. I would like to see the procedures and testing information on the production lot of axes. Black Diamond wants to be ISO 9000-certified, and we would need to have all those documents for ISO 9000 certification anyway, so this is a good starting place. Meanwhile, I think we should bring all the field axes back for inspection to reinforce customer confidence and prevent what happened on Saturday from happening again."

Looking out of his office's windows, Metcalf pointed to the shop floor and remarked, "Isn't that Brian walking through the shop? Ask him to come in."

Brian Palmer, the lead assembler, entered Metcalf's office. There was no place to sit, so he remained standing. Metcalf explained to Brian the purpose for bringing him into the meeting. Brian indicated that he had heard about the climbing incident involving the Black Prophet.

Metcalf continued. "Brian, we're not on a witch hunt; we're trying to understand the full range of factors that could have contributed to the tool's failure. What can you tell us about the assembly?"

Brian spoke frankly: "I personally put together all of those axes. We didn't have any procedures, because it was the first time we had made a production lot. Normally when we work on a new product, we go through a learning curve trying to figure out the best assembly method. We make so many different types of products in the shop, it's really like a craft shop. And I'm not even sure if I have the most up-to-date prints right now. The vendor had a lot of trouble casting all those parts to the exact dimensions. But I was able to find enough parts that seemed to fit, and with a little extra elbow grease, I hammered the pieces together. I had to work overtime to meet the deadline and get all the preliminary orders out to the customers. But that's what matters—pleasing the customer."

"But is creating a defective axe really pleasing the customer?" questioned Abrahamsen. "What good is it to be first to market if the product fails in the field? Sure, we have to get to market fast; but we also have to make the axe right the first time. The way we deal in the short term with the Black Prophet situation will have some long-term implications for Black Diamond's strategy. I think we should examine the new-product introduction process as well as the ongoing production processes to see how we can prevent this type of thing from happening in the future."

The Market for Mountaineering Equipment

The established customer for mountaineering products, including mountaineering skis, had traditionally been the serious international mountaineer—professionals as well as expert amateurs. Some dedicated mountaineers worked as professional guides and explorers; nonprofessionals had other jobs, but both professionals and amateurs spent their vacations and weekends climbing in their local areas and traveling throughout the world attempting to conquer remote peaks. This traditional customer base had been primarily in North America, eastern and western Europe, Japan, and Korea, although limited numbers of participants were from other countries.

Mountaineering was as popular in Europe as basketball was in the United States, with mountaineering stars earning high incomes through competitions, product endorsements, and other media exposure. Because of the long history of climbing in Europe, the European market was the biggest segment in the world climbing market, with 10 percent of the market in France alone. Not only did the adult urban European population prefer to spend vacations in mountain villages, but increasingly younger generations of Europeans were forsaking crowded beaches for mountain holidays revolving around mountain sports.

Starting in the 1980s, media exposure had brought mountain sports to previously ignored market segments throughout the world. Rock climbing and mountaineering images had become popular for advertising many types of products and for adding "color" to music videos and movie plots. Because of this exposure, teenage and recreational customers—predominantly in the U.S. market—represented high-growth segments, with the noticeable growth rate in the mid-1980s erupting into an explosive rate of 40 percent in the early 1990s. Customers in this growing market segment had no intention of traveling the world looking for untouched and ever more challenging peaks; instead, they climbed and skied purely for fun in their local and national resort areas.

Customarily, people wishing to learn mountain sports would employ guide services and schools for acquiring the necessary skills. The newer converts, however, were bypassing this conventional route by going to indoor climbing gyms or learning skills from friends. Many industry experts speculated that the breakdown of the conventional training methods would contribute to an increased lack of knowledge regarding mountaineering safety and lead to increased accident rates. In turn, accidents would increase the chances of litigation for all firms involved in the industry. These trends concerned mountain-sports firms worldwide.

Competition in the Mountaineering Equipment Industry

Located in Salt Lake City, Utah, Black Diamond Equipment, Ltd., was a major player in the burgeoning international mountaineering industry, on both domestic and global fronts. Black Diamond manufactured and distributed a full range of products for mountain sports, from rock-climbing gear to mountaineering and backcountry skis, and faced few domestic or global competitors whose business was on a similar scale. (Exhibit 1 offers a company/product profile of the mountaineering industry.)

The industry that served the mountaineering market consisted of three groups: retailers, wholesalers, and manufacturers.

EXHIBIT 1

Comparative Market Shares of Mountaineering Industry Competitors, by Product

Source: Estimates of industry representatives.

Product Category	Manufacturers	National Market Share %	International Market Share %
Carabiners	Black Diamond	50	10
	Omega	10	3
	SMC	10	3
	Wild Country	10	20
	DMM	10	20
	Petzl	5	30
	MSR (REI)	5	4
Climbing protections	Black Diamond	50	20
	Metolius	20	10
	Lowe	10	10
	Wild Country	10	25
	DMM	10	25
Harnesses	Black Diamond	45	10
	Petzl	20	50
	REI	20	
	Blue Water	10	10
	Wild Country	5	20
Plastic boots	Scarpa*	40	30
	Merrell	25	5
	Koflach	25	40
	Lowe	15	5
Adjustable ski poles	Black Diamond	60	5
	Life Link	40	5
Mountaineer skis	Rossignol	30	50
	Hagen*	20	10
Climbing accessories	Black Diamond	55	15
	Omega	25	10
	Petzl	20	75
Gloves	Black Diamond	50	5
Axes			
Snow climbing	Charlie Moser	50	10
	Black Diamond	20	5
Ice climbing	Black Diamond	30	10
	Charlie Moser	30	16
	DMM	25	30
	Grivel	15	30
Rock shoes	Scarpa*	25	20
	Sportiva	25	35
	Boreal	25	35
	Five Ten	15	5
Ropes	Mamutt	30	50
	PMI*	20	40
	New England	20	0
	Blue Water	20	10

*European manufacturers producing Black Diamond designs.

Retailers

The retail businesses serving the market's diverse variety of mountaineering customers were one of three types. The first group, the "core" mountaineering shops, were small retail operations specializing in products specific to mountaineering such as ropes, climbing protection, climbing axes, expedition clothing, packs, harnesses, and information guides for local and national sites. Because these shops were usually located in mountain areas such as the Rocky Mountains or the Alps, the shop personnel were experts in the special tools and applications for their regions. In addition, these employees often had personal knowledge of other locations around the world.

Mountaineering shops usually carried products made in their region with specialized products from other countries. The core shops competed on the basis of the expertise of their personnel and their stock of technically appropriate tools. These retailers specialized in high-quality, cutting-edge-technology products. Prices were relatively high. The majority of their customers were highly skilled mountaineers. Black Diamond operated a small retail shop in this category located next to its Salt Lake City manufacturing facility. Black Diamond's full product range sold well in its own shop as well as in other core shops.

Because of their remote locations, many core shops made effective use of catalogs as a direct-marketing tool. Several mail-order companies, including Black Diamond's mail-order division, competed in this core area, selling products both nationally and internationally.

The second group, mom-and-pop stores, were also small retail outlets, but they sold all types of equipment, from camping and backpacking equipment to bikes and skis. The product mix varied depending on the geographical location. Most of these stores carried a limited assortment of climbing products—usually ropes, harnesses, and carabiners (small clips used in all climbing applications to attach the climber to rock or snow). The personnel in mom-and-pop stores usually had limited technical knowledge of the products being sold.

The third group consisted of sporting goods and department store chains, ranging in size from regional chains such as Eastern Mountain Sports (seven stores) to national chains such as Recreational Equipment Inc. (REI) (40 stores). These stores, which were located in major cities with access to mass markets, had extensive outdoor clothing departments, tents, stoves, canoes and kayaks, sleeping bags, bikes, skis, and so on. Products in each category were selected for volume sales. Thus, in the climbing department, the product line covered the needs of entry-level or intermediate recreational climbers. The expertise of department store personnel was, however, generally limited.

In the United States, REI was the dominant firm in this group of retailers. REI operated department stores in Seattle, Boston, Los Angeles, and Washington, DC, with limited national competition on this level. Because of its large size and wide scope, REI could buy in volume for all its stores and could offer very competitive prices. The Canadian retailer Mountain Equipment Co-op (MEC) served a similar market in Canada, with a large store in each of Canada's major cities. In France, Au Vieux Campeur owned multiple department stores in major French cities, serving a broad customer base.

Wholesalers

Retail outlets bought their product lines from wholesalers during semiannual outdoor equipment shows held throughout the world. The wholesaler category of firms consisted of (1) companies that either manufactured their own products or subcontracted the manufacturing of their designs and distributed their own product lines, (2) companies licensed to distribute the products of other companies in certain geographic areas, and (3) companies that represented various combinations of the two types. Black Diamond was in this last category. The company distributed equipment designed and manufactured in its Utah plant, equipment manufactured for Black Diamond by other firms, and merchandise designed by Black Diamond and distributed under other manufacturers' names. In all, Black Diamond offered over 250 different items, covering most mountain sports (see Exhibit 2).

EXHIBIT 2
Black Diamond's
Product Line

Climbing Protection	**Ropes and Rope Bags**
Camming devices	**Packs**
Nuts	Hip packs
Stoppers	Backpacks
Pitons	**Tents**
Piton hammers	**Snow and Ice Tools**
Slings	Axes
Runners	Crampons
Daisy chains	Ice screws and hooks
Etriers	**Ski Tools**
Webbing	Skis
Belay devices	Bindings
Carabiners	Poles
Harnesses	**Climbing Clothing**
Sport climbing	T-shirts
Alpine mountaineering	Sweatshirts
Big wall	Shorts
Footwear	Pants
Mountaineering boots	Hats
Ski boots	Belts
Rock-climbing shoes	Chalk bags

REI was Black Diamond's biggest wholesale customer, making up almost 10 percent of Black Diamond's total sales. The next biggest customer, Lost Arrow—Japan, was a Japanese distributor comprising 5 percent of Black Diamond's sales. The other major wholesale customers were North American outdoor sports department store chains, mail-order companies, and Black Diamond's own retail shop and mail-order business. Combined, the top 20 percent of Black Diamond's retail customers—roughly 60 companies—accounted for about 80 percent of total sales.

Domestically, Black Diamond's wholesaling competition came from Omega Pacific, which manufactured and distributed its own metal products, and Blue Water, which wholesaled its own lines of ropes and harnesses. Neither of these companies, however, carried a product line as extensive as Black Diamond's.

The international wholesaling segment included strong competition from two British firms, Denny Morehouse Mountaineering and Wild Country, and a French company, Petzl. These firms wholesaled a full range of mountaineering products manufactured by companies with strong international reputations. Additional competition came from regional firms. Most countries had several smaller manufacturers of specific products such as carabiners or climbing axes that were successful in wholesaling their own products.

Several issues influenced sales in the international marketplace. First, the International Organization for Standardization had mandated that by 1997 "personal protective equipment" would have to meet ISO 9000 quality certification standards in order to be sold in Europe. Companies that had been granted certification stamped their products with a symbol showing that the product's manufacturer had met the relevant ISO 9000 standards. The certification was intended to give consumers more confidence in a product's quality. Most of the European mountaineering manufacturers had initiated the certification process and were well on their way to obtaining certification. In contrast, very few American companies had even begun the certification process. Black Diamond had begun the process but was not yet near completion. (Exhibit 3 provides an overview of the ISO 9000 standards.)

Second, some European countries had a long history of climbing and mountaineering, and certain manufacturers, Grivel, for example, dated back to the late 1800s. Although several European companies had well-established worldwide reputations for quality and

EXHIBIT 3
ISO 9000 Standards

The ISO 9000 standards provide the requirements for documenting processes and procedures. The intent of the standards is to ensure that organizations "do what they say and say what they do." The standards offer three quality system models—ISO 9001, ISO 9002, and ISO 9003—with increasing levels of stringency. ISO 9003 covers documentation and procedure requirements for final inspection and testing, ISO 9002 adds production and installation, and ISO 9001 includes design and development. An organization chooses the appropriate standard depending on the strategically important functional areas requiring quality procedures. In most cases, manufacturers use ISO 9001 for covering all areas.

In order to receive ISO 9000 certification, a company will spend several years complying with the requirements in the standards. This compliance usually requires extensive documentation of the company's existing quality program and training for all employees involved in processes related to quality. Individual auditors, who work for the international ISO registration organization, evaluate the company for requirement compliance. The certified companies are reevaluated every two years to ensure continuing compliance.

The following is a brief overview of the ISO 9001 requirements:

- The entire quality system must be defined and documented to ensure that each product meets specifications.
- The contractual requirements for quality between the company and the customer must be defined and documented.
- Procedures are required to ensure that critical processes are under control.
- Procedures are required for inspection at all levels and for identification of nonconforming parts or products.
- Procedures are required to prevent nonconforming parts from getting damaged in storage, delivery, or packing.
- Training is required for all personnel affecting quality.
- The quality system must be audited internally to ensure effectiveness and compliance.

innovative products, others relied on home-country support, producing relatively low-quality, low-priced products. All mountainous European countries had small factories for carabiners, skis, axes, or shoes that produced, at relatively low cost, simple products in high volume for domestic consumption.

Third, the European market was predominantly ethnocentric in purchasing behavior. French climbers preferred to buy French products, while German climbers preferred German products. Because of the risks involved in climbing and mountaineering, customers chose equipment they knew the most about and had the most confidence in. Usually, these products were from the buyers' respective countries.

Manufacturers

As a manufacturer, Black Diamond faced both domestic and international competition. Domestic manufacturing firms ran the gamut from small garage operations to large machine shops with 50 or more employees, and most produced either "software" or "hardware." The software firms worked with textile products such as ropes and harnesses. The majority of the software firms, including Blue Water, Sterling Rope, and Misty Mountain, were located in the southeastern United States. These more specialized manufacturing firms expanded their market by catering to the needs of nonmountaineering industries, such as construction safety, military applications, and spelunking. The hardware group manufactured or assembled metal products such as carabiners and other climbing tools and protection. This group of manufacturers included Friends, Rock Hardware, and Rock Exotica. These firms had reputations as producers of innovative and high-quality equipment.

REI had recently started up a small manufacturing facility for carabiners. The manager of the facility had many years of engineering experience with Boeing Aircraft and had designed a highly automated manufacturing system capable of both production and quality testing.

Because Black Diamond had begun as a machine shop, the company had strong capabilities in metalworking. Specifically, the Salt Lake City facility manufactured cold-forged metal parts associated with carabiners, axes, and other climbing accessories and protection. Hot-forging and casting were subcontracted by Black Diamond to manufacturers specializing in this area. Black Diamond was beginning to expand into simple soft goods, such as slings and other webbing products, and intended to continue developing its in-house sewing capabilities.

Black Diamond had plans to become vertically integrated. Management believed that in-house performance of operations related to core products would enhance Black Diamond's competitiveness. Consequently, Black Diamond had started reviewing some of its subcontracting practices to determine what functions could be brought in-house. In particular, the company wanted to bring in-house all sewing of climbing gear and some metal treatments such as heat-treating.

Other products, such as skis, ski poles, foot gear, and ropes, required very specific technologies, production skills, and economies of scale for competitive pricing and quality. Black Diamond entered into subcontracting agreements with international manufacturers to design and manufacture such products. The company also subcontracted the production of its harnesses to a technically sophisticated harness manufacturer located next door to the Salt Lake City facility that made the harnesses on a semiautomated assembly line. This process required minimal human involvement, in contrast to a "garment industry" sewing process by which one person sews the complete harness from start to finish.

By the late 1980s, European competition was becoming a more significant factor in the U.S. market. In particular, Petzl, a French company with a full range of products, had taken an aggressive position in the U.S. market. Like several of the European competitors, Petzl had a well-established reputation as a producer of high-quality, innovative products. Petzl had set up a manufacturing facility in the United States within 60 miles of Black Diamond's manufacturing facility and had sponsored several professional U.S. climbers. Black Diamond, of course, was making efforts to sell its own products in Europe, but faced the problem of ISO 9000 certification.

Some international manufacturing activity went on in Korea and Japan. Products produced by these manufacturers were marketed and distributed through other international companies. The majority of these products were low-cost, mass-produced items such as carabiners.

The continuing growth of copyright violations and product piracy—especially prevalent within international markets—added a further dimension to global competition. Several U.S. and European companies had used machine shops in Korea and Japan as subcontractors, supplying dies and other technological know-how. Consequently, unlicensed clones of more expensive items were expected to appear soon in the international market.

Black Diamond's Operations

Black Diamond Equipment, Ltd., opened for business in 1989 after a group of former managers, with employee support, bought the assets of Chouinard Equipment from Lost Arrow Corporation during Chapter 11 bankruptcy proceedings. The bankruptcy resulted from four lawsuits related to climbing equipment accidents during the 1980s. Chouinard Equipment was the first U.S. company to develop and manufacture rock-climbing gear. From its inception and for the following decade, Chouinard Equipment had a reputation for innovation and quality unmatched by any national competitors.

After the purchase, the new owners chose a new name for the company that would reflect its roots yet would project a fresh beginning. Chouinard Equipment's previous logo had been a diamond. The new company decided to keep the diamond image and chose the name Black

EXHIBIT 4
Black Diamond Logo

Diamond because of the different associations the name might evoke: diamond in the rough, rogue, bad boy, unusual. (See Exhibit 4 for the Black Diamond logo.) Furthermore, a black diamond was used to identify the most difficult type of run in ski areas, and the company owners hoped the name would appeal to the "extreme" athlete, their primary targeted customer base. Black Diamond's management believed that "if you target the extremists, the recreational customers will follow."

The mission of Black Diamond was "to design, manufacture, and bring to market, in a profitable and on-time manner, innovative and technical products of high quality, high performance, and exemplary durability that are targeted toward our primary customers—climbers and backcountry skiers." The company was committed to 10 guiding principles:

1. Being the market leader, synonymous with the sports we serve and are absolutely passionate about;
2. Having a truly global presence;
3. Supporting the specialty retailer;
4. Creating long-term partnerships with companies we do business with;
5. Being very easy to do business with;
6. Being a fierce competitor with the highest ethical standards;
7. Developing sustainable, competitive advantage;
8. Sharing the company's success with its employees;
9. Creating a safe, personally fulfilling work environment for all employees;
10. Championing the preservation of and access to our mountain environments.

In 1991, the owner-employees relocated the business from Ventura, California, to Salt Lake City, Utah, where they would be closer to the targeted customer. Black Diamond began operations with a staff of roughly 40, covering all functional areas. (See Exhibit 5 for Black Diamond's organizational structure.) Black Diamond was 50 percent owned by employees; the remaining 50 percent of the stock was held by outside investors, predominantly distributors, customers, and friends and family of the main employee stockholders. Of the 50 percent that was employee owned, 75 percent was held by Peter Metcalf, the CEO; Maria Cranor, head of marketing; and Clark Kawakami, the chief financial officer.

In 1993, Black Diamond's annual sales were expected to be approximately $12 million, with a gross profit margin of about 40 percent (around $4.8 million) and a net profit margin of about 10 percent (around $1.2 million). From 1990 through 1993, the climbing industry had experienced tremendous sales growth of 20 to 40 percent per year. The market demanded more innovative products and faster delivery. Black Diamond struggled to keep

EXHIBIT 5   Black Diamond Organizational Structure

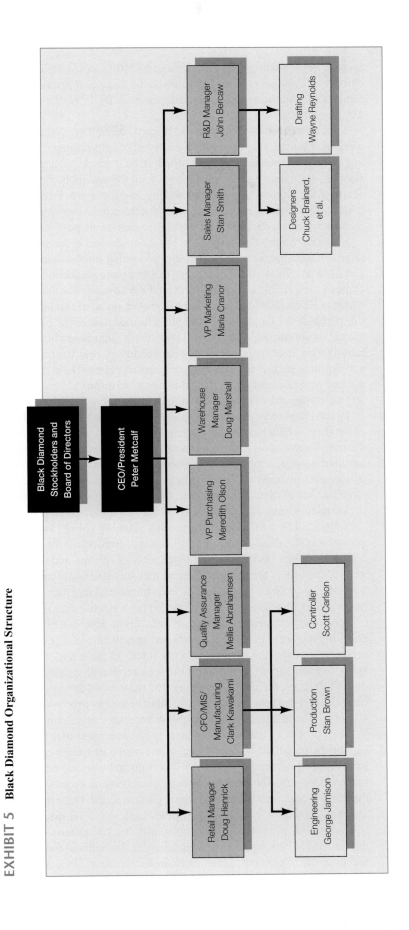

up with the exploding customer demand by hiring more employees and upgrading shop machinery to increase productivity. Slowly, the original machinery was being replaced by automated machining centers and testing devices. By 1993, the company employed more than 100 people.

Like other metalworking shops, Black Diamond specialized in certain types of metalworking; its areas of specialization consisted of cold-forging metal parts, stamping and forming, computer numerically controlled (CNC) machining, and assembly or fabrication. Forging, stamping, and forming, along with the assembly processes, had been done for 20 years by the original Chouinard company, and these processes were considered to be Black Diamond's technical core. These core processes used the same multiton presses that forced metal stock into a die or mold to obtain the desired shape.

Since moving to Salt Lake City, the company had expanded into CNC machines—large programmable machine tools capable of producing small-to-medium-sized batches of intricate parts—in an effort to reduce costs and to move more production processes in-house. These machines were expensive, but they provided the advantages of capacity and product flexibility. Many of Black Diamond's processes, however, required machinery that was too costly to justify purchase for the manufacturing of a limited number of parts. Consequently, Black Diamond subcontracted with other vendors for aluminum hot-forging, investment casting, laser-cutting steel, preshearing metals, anodizing, heat treating, welding, screw machining, wire forming such as springs, and aluminum extrusion. These processes were subcontracted to achieve economies of scale (e.g., aluminum extrusion) or because the specialized equipment and skills required were beyond Black Diamond's capabilities (e.g., hot-forging).

Black Diamond's production facility was divided into several functional areas: the machine shop, which built prototypes and constructed and maintained tool and die apparatus; the punch press room, where parts were pressed out at a rate of one per second by several multiton presses; a room with assorted machines (including CNC machines), each operated by one person doing drilling, milling, or grinding; a tumbling and polishing room, where large batches of parts were polished; the assembly room, where parts were assembled by individuals or teams; and, finally, a room for materials and shipping.

Supported by a material requirements planning (MRP) system, materials were ordered several months in advance for a full batch of products—for example, 5,000 carabiners or 500 axes. When fairly common parts such as springs and aluminum rod stock were involved, the orders arrived on time and met standard quality requirements. The more complex and customized parts, such as investment-cast axe parts, were difficult for vendors to make to specifications and thus often did not meet the assembly deadline.

When the parts arrived in the materials supply area, one person was responsible for spot-checking the order to see if the parts met specifications. For example, when 500 axe heads arrived, the inspector would randomly select 15 parts and would measure 20 key dimensions on each part to determine if the tolerances met specifications. If one dimension was out of tolerance, the quality manager was summoned for an evaluation. Depending on how much impact the flaw would have on other assembly processes, a larger meeting, involving all potentially affected parties, might be necessary to determine a course of action.

Most of Black Diamond's products began as a sheet of steel or aluminum rod. After receiving the metal, the incoming inspector would pull a sample to check hardness and dimensions. When production on an order was ready to begin, the metal was moved from a hallway to the press room. The press operator would receive an order for 5,000 parts and would set up the press to begin cutting and smashing parts to shape. Once the dies were in place, the operator would smash a few sample parts and check with an inspector for approval.

As the dies wore down, the parts might turn out to have excess metal, or the logo engraving might be substandard. Depending on the demand for the parts, the inspector might feel pressure to pass on cosmetically imperfect parts. Once approval was given, the operator would proceed to press out as many parts as possible in the shortest time. Often chips of metal would settle in the die and become imbedded in many parts before being discovered by the operator. When this occurred, thousands of parts needed to be scrapped.

After the smashing process, the parts were usually sent out for heat-treating to harden the metal. The heat-treatment plant was located in California, so this procedure had a turn-around time of several weeks. When the parts returned, they went to the tumbling and drilling rooms for further processing. When color was needed, the parts would be shipped out again for anodizing, an electrolytic process by which metal is covered with a protective and/or decorative oxide film.

Finally, when the main body of a product was finished, the materials department would issue batches of all the other components needed to finish that product. All of these parts would proceed to a group of assemblers, seated around tables, who were responsible for putting together the final product. The assembly room was the epitome of a craft shop en-vironment. Large and expensive products such as axes were assembled in small batches by one individual, while products such as carabiners were assembled in larger batches by teams of people who often rotated jobs. The finished products would go through individual testing and inspection before passing to the shipping area. One inspector might evaluate thousands of parts in a day.

Originally, the company had one employee who was responsible for quality assurance and several shop employees who performed quality control functions. The quality assur-ance person worked for the R&D department and focused on testing new products, proto-types, and work in production. As the company grew and ISO 9000 certification loomed in the future, several members of the management team decided that quality issues needed more prominent attention. Black Diamond needed not only testing but also a plantwide pro-gram to ensure that defects did not occur in the first place.

Black Diamond's original quality assurance officer had left the company to guide climb-ing expeditions, after which Black Diamond's management created a stand-alone quality assurance department and hired Mellie Abrahamsen as the manager. At the time of Abra-hamsen's hiring, the members of R&D and the shop functioned along craft-shop lines. Product designers built prototypes on the shop floor, iterating between field testing and lab testing until they felt the design was ready. When the new design went into production, the shop personnel used trial and error to develop an assembly procedure. Out-of-tolerance parts were often accepted by shop personnel, who invented creative ways of adapting the parts or the procedures for assembling the products.

Implementing a quality control program would mean introducing formal testing and as-sembly procedures for both designers and shop workers. As Andrew McLean, a head de-signer, said, "We are like artists here, and you just can't restrain or rush creativity and get good results." Chuck Brainard complained, "If we have to write procedures for every step of production, we'll be changing those things a million times."

Like most machine-shop workers, Black Diamond's shop employees labored under com-paratively unglamorous working conditions, involving, for example, noise, grease, and mo-notony. Many shop workers lacked a high school education and some could not read or write in English. Although the shop workers were the lowest-paid employees at Black Diamond, the company offered them a generous profit-sharing bonus and tried to involve them in monthly meetings concerning the financial performance of the company. Despite these measures, the shop had a high rate of employee turnover.

Because quality control programs require procedure writing, blueprint reading, and statisti-cal techniques, the shop employees needed elementary math and language training so that they could learn the more complicated subjects. Stan Brown acknowledged that the workers needed training, but said, "I can't let those people miss too much work for training. We really need everyone working nonstop to get products out the door."

Many of the professional employees at Black Diamond were avid climbers and users of the products, taking great pride in trying to make the very best products available.

Marketing was concerned about keeping up the company's innovative image with new products every season. Production worried about vendor costs, delivery of parts, and the shop's ability to meet sales forecasts. R&D attempted to simultaneously develop buildable new products, reduce lead time for new-product development, and improve existing products. Customer service tried to keep retailers pacified with partial deliveries and promises.

Finally, the new quality assurance department was charged with implementing quality control procedures, conducting training, testing products, and resolving problems attributed to parts or products not meeting specifications. All functional areas faced the problems inherent in trying to achieve the simultaneous goals of meeting customer demand and ensuring the highest-quality products, and the different areas often clashed on the best means and methods of achieving these goals.

The Black Prophet

The concept for the Black Prophet axe was originally developed to round out Black Diamond's product line of axes. The product line had two other axes: the Alpamayo, a glacier-walking and snow-climbing axe; and the X-15, a versatile axe for both snow and ice climbing. The Black Prophet was designed specifically for ice climbing and incorporated an innovative ergonomic shape to reduce arm fatigue, a composite, rubber-bounded shaft construction for gripability and weight reduction, and interchangeable modular components that allowed the use of different types of tools—a hammer head, picks, or an adze—for miscellaneous ice applications. (Exhibit 6 is a drawing of the Black Prophet and its component parts.)

Designing and producing the axe entailed several years of working with different vendors to develop the appropriate production process for each component. The axe was designed as a prototype and field-tested with different constructions until R&D agreed on a specific configuration. This configuration was then reviewed by sales representatives considered to be mountaineering experts and by other company members at the quarterly meetings. If the tool did not pass the scrutiny of those examiners, R&D would begin a new phase of prototype development and field tests. This development process would continue until a companywide consensus was reached.

The axe required five parts: shaft, head, hammer, pick, and adze. Three parts were cast metal, requiring a casting subcontractor with the ability to meet strict specifications. The composite shaft was produced by a composite and bonding manufacturer, and the pick was manufactured in Black Diamond's plant. Black Diamond received the parts from each vendor, inspected them for conformance to specifications, and assembled the axes.

The Black Prophet, which cost approximately $80 to produce, sold at retail for $200; the wholesale price was $140. The initial shipment of Black Prophets for the winter season of 1993 comprised approximately 200 axes. Management expected the Black Prophet to be one of Black Diamond's top 10 selling winter products, with yearly sales projected to be at least 2,500 units. The entire company regarded it as a very big image item on the world mountaineering scene. Every competitor in the industry had an axe for glacier walking; axes were especially popular in Europe, where Black Diamond foresaw superb potential for its new offering.

The axe had been well received at the previous year's outdoor product show. At that time, no other axe like it was in the wings, and the climbing industry anticipated the Black Prophet's arrival with great excitement. All of the major U.S. and European industry magazines had published articles about the Black Prophet, and famous mountaineers had called Black Diamond requesting Black Prophets for their upcoming expeditions.

EXHIBIT 6
The Black Prophet

(a) Components Parts

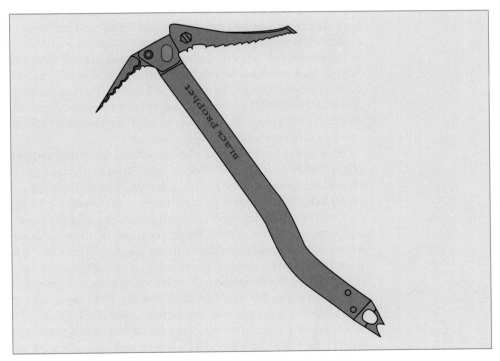

(b) Complete Unit

The Dilemma

As the Monday morning meeting continued, Black Diamond's top management team struggled to find answers to the questions raised by the axe crisis. They knew that the situation required both short- and long-term solutions. In the short term, management needed to address the pressure for immediate delivery confronting customer service. Should management recall all the Black Prophet axes currently on the market? A recall would come with high shipping, testing, and opportunity costs. Or should Black Diamond ignore the incident, assuming the accident was a one-time freak, and continue to sell the axes while refuting any rumors about the product's questionable performance? The possibility of lawsuits had to be considered. For any accident causing injury, legal fees could be expected to run $500,000, and a catastrophic accident could bring a suit for several million dollars. While Black Diamond's insurer would pay legal expenses and any settlement involved, with a cap of $1 million, Black Diamond could expect to pay at least $25,000—the company's insurance deductible—for each legal action. In addition, there would be the costs of lost time for those employees who had to go to court (such costs might involve one or two managers' salaries for a year—at $40,000 to $60,000 per person). Several catastrophic accident cases won by the plaintiffs in a single year could put the company into bankruptcy.

Another option was to continue the sale of Black Prophets—including the axes already released as well as those in production—but to require all units to be sold with a cautionary label. Still another was to just quietly and quickly sell those Black Prophets already in retail outlets and undertake a critical review only of the axes still in production.

Management's response to the short-term issue of customer service would have major implications for Black Diamond's competitive strategy. Would Black Diamond be able to meet the market's rapidly growing demand for all products while improving—or at the very least maintaining—product quality? Would Black Diamond be able to maintain an image as the recognized industry leader in the manufacture of innovative tools and equipment? Would Black Diamond be able to balance the realities of increased risk associated with innovative product design and of increased liability corresponding to the greater potential for accidents, while still establishing a dominant competitive position? Even though various members held strong—and in some cases, divergent—opinions, the management team was willing to consider enterprising alternatives.

Nevertheless, management also knew that a more long-term plan needed to be put into place. "When crises strike," Metcalf said, "there will always be some degree of needing to react to the surprise of the situation. But we need to institute a system of managing crises proactively—that means organizing the business to prevent the preventable crises."

Even though the management team thought the quality assurance department should be a constructive resource in this long-term effort, the department was so new that no one had a clear idea of its role. Abrahamsen also questioned her role: "I was hired to implement a plantwide quality control program and to specifically work on ISO 9000 certification. Representing QA, I'm supposed to improve the efficiency of the company by reducing or eliminating defects in the whole production chain, but I'm not sure that a TQM (total quality management) approach will completely solve Black Diamond's problems. Perhaps the whole process of new-product development and ongoing operations would be more effective if a BPR (business process reengineering) approach were used. Either way, my challenge is to get all these other employees and departments to change the way they do things so they're both more efficient and effective."

(Black Diamond's Web address is www.bdel.com.)

Section VI

Strategic Marketing Cases

Note to the Student

The cases in this section emphasize the role of marketing in developing successful business or organizational strategies. While marketing is critical in these cases, successful analysis and strategy formulation will often involve other areas in the organization as well.

The knowledge and skills you've developed in the analysis of the cases in the previous section provide a useful foundation for analyzing the cases in this section. However, these cases are intended to broaden your knowledge of marketing and your skills at analyzing various strategic problems.

1

Yahoo! Inc.

Ben Elgin and Ronald Grover *BusinessWeek*

When Terry S. Semel walked into the Sunnyvale (Calif.) headquarters of Yahoo! Inc. for his first day as chief executive on May 1, 2001, he faced an unenviable task. Ad sales at the Internet icon were plummeting, and the new CEO was replacing the well-liked Timothy Koogle, who had been pushed aside by the company's board. Worse, leery employees quickly saw that Semel, a retired Hollywood exec, didn't know Internet technology and looked stiffly out of place at Yahoo's playful, egalitarian headquarters. Would this guy tour the Valley in the purple Yahoo car, as Koogle did, or play a Yahoo kazoo? Fat chance. And instead of bunking in nearby Atherton or Palo Alto, like other Silicon Valley execs, he rode off every evening in a chauffeured SUV to a luxury suite at San Francisco's Four Seasons Hotel.

Two years after taking control as chairman and CEO, Semel has silenced the doubters. By imposing his buttoned-down management approach on Yahoo, the 60-year-old has engineered one of the most remarkable revivals of a beleaguered dot-com. Once paralyzed by management gridlock and written off as another overhyped has-been, Yahoo is roaring back. The company earned $43 million on revenues of $953 million in 2002, compared with a $93 million loss in 2001 on $717 million in sales. And Yahoo's momentum is growing. Net income hit $47 million in this year's first quarter as revenues powered ahead 47%. Analysts predict that this year's profits will quadruple, to more than $200 million, while sales climb 33%, to $1.3 billion. "What he has done is just phenomenal," says Hollywood pal Barry Diller, CEO of USA Interactive Inc., a Yahoo competitor.

Semel has done nothing less than remake the culture of the quintessential Internet company. The new Yahoo is grounded by a host of Old Economy principles that Semel lugged up the coast from Los Angeles. The contrast with Yahoo's go-go days is stark. At Terry Semel's Yahoo, spontaneity is out. Order is in. New initiatives used to roll ahead following free-form brainstorming and a gut check. Now, they wind their way through a rugged gauntlet of tests and analysis. Only a few make the grade. It's a wrenching change. But Semel's self-effacing style, honed over years of navigating through the towering egos of Hollywood, helps soften the shock.

Yahoo's newfound success does, too. Semel has used the dealmaking skills that made him a legend in the movie business to land crucial acquisitions and partnerships that are producing rich new revenues for Yahoo (Exhibit 1). A deal with phone giant SBC Communications Inc. launched Yahoo into the business of selling broadband access to millions of American homes—which should add $70 million in revenue this year. The buyout of HotJobs.com last year put Yahoo into the online job-hunting business, adding $80 million

Source: "Yahoo! Act Two," *BusinessWeek*, June 2, 2003, 70–76.

EXHIBIT 1   Yahoo's Game Plan

Can CEO Semel lift Yahoo to greatness? The nine-year-old company is poised to notch its best-ever sales and profits in 2003. But Semel must accomplish even more to justify Yahoo's nosebleed market valuation, including a p-e of 79. Here are his biggest bets:

Paid Search

Revenues for selling links on its search-results pages rocketed from zilch to $130 million in 2002. With the overall paid-search market expected to grow 40% to 50% annually, paid search may be Yahoo!'s jet fuel in coming years.

2003 Projected Revenue

   $230 million   ▲ 77%

Outlook

   Excellent This is the Internet's growth market, and few are positioned as well as Yahoo.
   Possible spoiler: Google.

Internet Advertising

Life is creeping back into Yahoo's longtime mainstay, traditional online advertising, which should top $600 million in 2003 sales. Yahoo expects to double the industry growth rate, with annual growth of at least 5% to 10% for the next several years.

2003 Projected Revenue

   $615 million   ▲ 18%

Outlook

   Good The market is coming back, and Yahoo! has learned the hard way what works.

Paid Subscriptions

Only 1% of Yahoo's 232 million online users pay the company for services. Yahoo is working to bring in more cash outlays by offering a host of premium services, including online personals and supersize e-mail accounts.

2003 Projected Revenue

   $251 million   ▲ 25%

Outlook

   Fair This is Yahoo's Achilles' heel. The potential is rich, but turning free Web surfers into paying subscribers is proving tough.

Broadband Access

A partnership with SBC Communications makes Yahoo a broadband player, generating fees and establishing Yahoo as a high-speed home page. But its failure to link up with other telecoms limits the offering, for now, to SBC's region.

2003 Projected Revenue

   $70 million   ▲ 900%

Outlook

   Good Yahoo can grow with broadband, which is gaining 30% annually. The risk: It hinges on partnerships that could prove fragile.

Online Careers

Yahoo acquired Hotjobs.com in late 2001, which contributed $80 million to Yahoo's top line in 2002. But growth is slow in the stagnant U.S. employment market, and Yahoo trails job-search leader Monster.com

2003 Projected Revenue

   $80 million   ▲ 0%

Outlook

   Good Online recruiting is expected to grow 18% a year for the next five years. Yahoo should grab a growing share.

in revenue. Most important, a partnership with Overture Services Inc. to carry ads on Yahoo's search-results pages is gushing some $230 million in revenue this year. The upshot? Semel's new businesses should make up half of Yahoo's top line in 2003. "We planted a lot of seeds a year and a half ago, and some are beginning to grow," he says (Exhibit 2).

Semel's strategy is gaining fans on Wall Street—and stoking new fears of a mini-Internet bubble. The company's shares have soared 200% in the past eight months, to $26. Sure, Yahoo's market capitalization is a mere 13% of its giddy all-time high of $127 billion in early 2000. But today's price-earnings ratio of 79 is triple that of heavyweight Microsoft Corp. and more than eBay Inc.'s 67, despite the online auctioneer's heftier revenues, profits, and growth projections. "Yahoo's valuation is a tough case to make," concedes Firsthand Funds Chief Investment Officer Kevin Landis, who nonetheless has bought 50,000 Yahoo shares in the past eight months based on the portal's turnaround and brighter industry trends.

Investors are betting on Semel to follow up his bold debut with a sizzling encore. Call it Act Two. For this next stage of growth, Semel envisions building Yahoo into a digital Disneyland, a souped-up theme park for the Internet Age. The idea is that Web surfers logging on to Yahoo's site, like customers squeezing through the turnstiles in Anaheim, will find themselves in a self-contained world full of irresistible offerings.

EXHIBIT 2
Yahoo's Turnaround

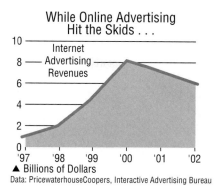

While Online Advertising Hit the Skids . . .

Internet Advertising Revenues

▲ Billions of Dollars
Data: PricewaterhouseCoopers, Interactive Advertising Bureau

. . . Yahoo Rekindled Sales by Diversifying . . .

Yahoo Quarterly Revenues

▲ Millions of Dollars
Data: Company reports

. . . Giving Investors Reason to Applaud

Stock Price

▲ Dollars
Data: Yahoo!

In the past, Yahoo attracted visitors with free services such as stock quotes and headlines and drew 90% of its revenue from online ads. Now, Semel is trying to charge for many services, coaxing Web surfers to spend hard cash on everything from digital music and online games to job listings and premium e-mail accounts with loads of extra storage. Already, he pulls in one-third of revenue from such offerings and hopes to drive it up to 50% by 2004. To do that, analysts say, he's likely to cut deals to add online travel and classified ads for cars.

But nothing is more key to Semel's strategy than his push into broadband. Lots of the services he's banking on, such as music and interactive games, are data hogs that appeal mostly to customers with high-speed links. Plus, broadband is always on, so many of Yahoo's customers will be lingering in Semel's theme park for hours on end, day after day. "The more time you spend on Yahoo, the more apt you are to sample both free and paid services," he says.

If Semel can pull it off, the new Yahoo could become one of the few enduring powerhouses on the Net. Customers who pay for its services could more than triple, to 10 million in 2005 from 2.9 million in 2003, analysts predict. Profits could soar 75% over the next two years, to $350 million, and sales could surge 30%, to $1.7 billion, analysts say. "Yahoo has emerged as a durable digital franchise," says Alberto W. Vilar, president of Amerindo Investment Advisors Inc., which has an undisclosed stake. "If you take the long view, this stock could still double or triple."

But Semel doesn't have a monopoly on digital theme parks. AOL Time Warner Inc. and Microsoft's MSN are pushing nearly identical agendas—and both boast advantages over Yahoo. AOL, despite its merger headaches, can tap into popular content from the world's largest media company, from CNN to Warner Music. MSN benefits from the software muscle and cash hoard of Microsoft, as well as broadband partnerships that cover 27% more lines into homes and businesses than Yahoo's SBC deal. It also may have an easier time getting Web surfers to pay for new offerings. "Yahoo's brand is built on free information services," says MSN Group Product Manager Lisa Gurry. She says coaxing Yahoo customers to pull out their wallets will be "very challenging."

An even greater challenge is coming from a newer competitor, Google Inc. In just four years, Google has turned a global sensation and is now widely regarded as the preeminent search engine on earth. The risk to Yahoo is that the search king will give birth to a more potent business model. Instead of flocking to flashy theme parks such as Yahoo's, consumers are already starting to rely on Google's uncluttered search to find everything they need. Already, some online advertisers are moving their ad dollars to search engines. "We're shifting our emphasis away from portals [such as Yahoo, AOL, and MSN]," says Alan Rimm-Kaufman, vice-president for marketing at electronics retailer Crutchfield Corp. "The people stealing these ad dollars are [companies] like Google."

Hot competition in the search business could force Semel's next big move. His partnership with Overture, a company that delivers Internet advertising, is producing some 20% of Yahoo's revenues. Microsoft's MSN has a similar deal with Overture that also is paying off richly. Analysts say Semel could make an offer for Overture—if he thinks it's necessary to preempt a Microsoft acquisition. He is already sitting on $2.2 billion in cash, 50% more than the likely price tag for Overture. Still, Semel likely won't make a bid unless he's pushed into it because of the distractions of such a large merger. Yahoo and Overture declined comment on a possible deal.

Distraction is something Yahoo can ill afford as it adapts to the changes ahead. To date, Semel has honed the company's execution—cutting costs, filtering out iffy ideas, pursuing sure things, and making money. It's the perfect model for today's sickly market. But when the slump ends, new ideas will likely make a dramatic comeback. These could define the next generation of the Internet. The question is whether Yahoo, with its careful and laborious vetting process for new projects, risks losing out to Google or getting blindsided by a nimble newcomer.

Can Semel innovate, beat back the rising tide of competition, and live up to the latest round of great expectations for Yahoo? If he plays his cards right, yes. Despite the advantages of AOL and MSN, Yahoo has kept its position as the most popular site on the Web, according to Nielsen/Net Ratings. Yahoo claims 232 million monthly visitors. Semel is demonstrating the skills to turn this large chunk of humanity into paying customers, boosting the customer count eightfold, from 375,000 when he arrived two years ago. To combat Google, Semel is hurrying to beef up Yahoo's search capabilities. He closed a $290 million deal for search company Inktomi in March, and the marketing campaign to promote it blasted off in New York's Times Square on May 19. "Yahoo has reemerged as a potent force," says Derek Brown, an analyst at Pacific Growth Equities. "It's well-positioned to leverage its massive global user base and dominant brand."

The CEO's low-key approach has worked quiet magic through a 40-year career. When Brooklyn-born Semel arrived as a sales trainee at Warner Bros. in 1965, the 22-year-old accountant had little relevant experience but an understated confidence in himself. In an industry brimming with ego, Semel stayed offstage and worked to shine the light on others. It paid dividends. As he moved from Warner Bros. to Buena Vista and back again, Semel rose to the top on a vast network of friends and allies. He used these, along with his formidable negotiating skills, to create a giant. In a two-decade partnership as co-CEO with Bob Daly, Semel turned Warner Bros. from a $1 billion studio to an $11 billion behemoth, producing megahits such as *The Matrix.*

Through his retirement in 1999, Semel kept up the winning formula, making friends and minting millions. He says that in their two decades together, he and Daly never fought. If such a smooth track record is rare in high tech, it's even more uncommon in Hollywood. "When you're releasing 20 or 25 movies a year, you're navigating a minefield every weekend," says Barry M. Meyer, chairman and CEO of Warner Bros. Entertainment Inc. and a longtime Semel colleague. "His success at Yahoo does not surprise me at all."

It was Yahoo co-founder Jerry Yang who nudged Semel toward Yahoo in 2001. The two had met two years earlier at a media conference and had hit it off. By the spring of 2001, Yahoo was reeling from the falloff in Net advertising and needed a major overhaul. The question was whether the wealthy Semel, who was already dabbling in online entertainment companies, would dive into one of the biggest of them all at a time of crisis. Semel signed on with the proviso that Koogle step down as chairman.

When the new chief arrived, he ran into a few troubling surprises. Semel was shocked early on to learn that Yahoo did not have the technology in place to handle surging demand for services such as online personals, say two former executives. That spelled months of delay before Semel could push premium offerings.

Then there were the cultural challenges. Initially, Semel balked at the company's "cubicles only" policy, finally settling into a cube adjacent to a conference room so he could make phone calls in private. He stayed free of the Valley social scene, spending weeknights at the hotel in San Francisco and flying his private jet home to his swanky Los Angeles neighborhood of Bel Air on weekends.

Morale was also an issue. Compared with his predecessor, the relaxed and chatty Koogle, known by the troops as T.K., Semel came off at first as cold and rough. He chopped down the 44 business units he inherited to 5, stripping many execs of pet projects. Veteran Yahoo execs prodded Semel to mingle more with the rank and file and pushed him into grabbing lunch more often at the campus cafeteria. Still, such forays often fell flat. "T.K. was just one of the guys," says a former Yahoo manager. "When Semel talked to you, it felt like he was consciously making an effort to talk to employees."

Soon, Semel's strengths started to shine through. With his focus and dealmaking savvy, he appeared to have the tools to rescue Yahoo. Employees, with loads of underwater stock options, increasingly cheered him on. "People don't always agree with the direction they're getting, but they're happy the direction is there," says a current Yahoo manager who requested anonymity.

Walk through Yahoo's headquarters, past the purple cow in the lobby, the acres of cubicles, the workers in jeans, and you might think T.K. was still running the place. But sitting across from Semel, the change is evident. His voice quiet and steady, his language cordial yet deliberate, Semel seems incapable of the hype that once vaulted companies such as Yahoo into the stratosphere. This is the voice of the post-dot-com era. He steers attention to his colleagues. "I love [my managers] to do their homework," he says. "I love them to help make decisions, and they do. Somewhere in that process, I'll include myself—or they'll include me."

Semel's not kidding about the homework. In the old days, Yahoo execs would brainstorm for hours, often following hunches with new initiatives. Those days are long gone. Under Semel, managers must prepare exhaustively before bringing up a new idea if it's to have a chance to survive.

It's a Darwinian drama that takes place in near-weekly meetings of a group called the Product Council. Dreamed up by a couple of vice-presidents and championed by Semel and his chief operating officer, Daniel Rosensweig, a former president of CNET Networks Inc., the group typically includes nine managers from all corners of the company. It's chaired by Geoff Ralston and often includes key lieutenants such as Jeff Weiner and Jim Brock, all senior vice-presidents. The group sizes up business plans to make sure all new projects bring benefits to Yahoo's existing businesses. "We need to work within a framework," says Semel. "If it's a free-for-all … we won't take advantage of the strengths of our company."

For years, managers built up their own niches around the main Yahoo site. No one, say former and current execs, appeared to be thinking about the portal as a whole, much less how the various bits and pieces could work together. "Managers would beg, borrow, and steal from the network to help their own properties," says Greg Coleman, Yahoo's executive vice-president for media and sales.

Semel wants to stitch it all together. He calls the concept "network optimization" and says it's a key goal for 2003. The idea is that every initiative should not only make money but also feed Yahoo's other businesses. It's the painstaking job of establishing these interconnections that eats up much of the time at council meetings. And the winnowing process is brutal. Of the 79 current ideas for premium services at some stage of planning inside Yahoo, only a few will launch in 2003, predicts Rosensweig.

Although some critics worry that innovative ideas may never see the light of day under Semel's tight control, he dismisses the prospect. Semel stresses instead the potential payoff: less clutter and a handful of high-performance services that feed each other. For a success story, he points to the company's recently relaunched search capabilities. Search for "pizza" and type in your area code, and Yahoo culls its Yellow Pages site to return addresses and driving maps to nearby pizza joints. Yahoo is the only heavyweight portal that integrates content this deeply with its search features.

Such smart execution was in dangerously short supply at Yahoo in the past. At the height of the Net bubble, Yahoo came off as arrogant. Its attitude, recalls Jeff Bell, a marketing vice-president at DaimlerChrysler Corp., was "Buy our stuff, and shut up." Semel has turned that around, hiring traditional media sales veterans and introducing more flexibility. The payoff: As the online ad market has recovered, advertisers are flocking back to Yahoo. Daimler's Bell says his Yahoo ad budget has doubled over the past two years.

Entertainment companies are joining the rush to buy key Yahoo ad space. Some 42 movies advertised on Yahoo in the first quarter, up from zilch in the first quarter of 2001. "Getting a presence on Yahoo's home page is huge," says Sarah Beatty, a senior marketing vice-president at USA Network, which was running seven ad campaigns on Yahoo in 2003.

Semel has supplemented Yahoo's ad revenues with dealmaking in other businesses. Consider the SBC pact to market broadband Net access. SBC pays Yahoo about $5 out of the $40 to $60 customers pay each month for service. Revenues from the deal should jump from $70 million this year to $125 million in 2004.

Still, Yahoo remains vulnerable in broadband. MSN has cut similar deals with Verizon Communications and Qwest Communications International Inc., which have 75 million lines to homes and businesses, vs. SBC's 59 million. Semel's efforts to land other broadband deals have come up short. More worrisome is the fragile nature of these partnerships. If SBC concludes that the Yahoo brand isn't a big draw, it could cut Yahoo out and save itself millions. An SBC spokesman says it is "happy" with Yahoo.

Of all Semel's deals, none shines brighter than the partnership with Overture Services. The companies team up to sell ads near Yahoo's search results, a business known as "paid search." If a user searches for "cookware," for instance, advertisers from Macy's to Sur La Table can bid to showcase their links near the results. Overture delivers the advertisers and forks over roughly two-thirds of the revenue. While Yahoo had debated such a partnership for years under Koogle, Semel drove it through in a hurry.

Just in time for paid search to blossom into the latest Web sensation. The partnership notched Yahoo more than $130 million in revenues last year—14% of its business. Analysts expect revenues from the partnership to increase 75% in 2003, accounting for nearly 20% of Yahoo's revenues.

That assumes that Goggle won't spoil Yahoo's fun. The wildly popular search engine has emerged as the fourth-most-trafficked site on the Internet, with an estimated $700 million in 2003 revenues. And the world may be heading Google's way. Industry analysts say that as Web surfers gain expertise, they visit general-interest sites such as Yahoo less and instead cut to the chase by typing in keywords on a search engine. According to analytics firm Web-SideStory, the percentage of Web site visitors arriving via search engines doubled in the past year, to 13%.

Google's strength puts Semel in a bind. He licenses Google's search engine, which is popular among Yahoo's users. Trouble is, by keeping Google on Yahoo, he publicly endorses a rival. His likely goal, say analysts, is to replace Google soon with Inktomi, the search engine he acquired in March. That would save $13 million a year in licensing and pull the plug on Yahoo's apparent backing of Google. The danger? If Yahoo's Google-loving customers balk at switching to Inktomi, they could ditch Yahoo and surf straight to the Google site.

His answer is a national marketing campaign to boost Yahoo as a search brand. It kicked off on May 19 in New York's Times Square with the unveiling of a huge computer-screen ad featuring live searches on the Yahoo site. At street level in New York, teams of Yahoo's costumed "searchers" paraded among the crowds waving five-foot-long search bars.

It's all part of the growing buzz at Yahoo. Using his mix of discipline, sales, and deal-making, Terry Semel has pulled off a stunning revival. But can he pull off Act Two and build Yahoo into the digital theme park of his dreams? If he does, Semel will be one of the biggest winners: When he took the helm, he bought 1 million shares of Yahoo at $17 apiece. Those shares are up 60%. The fact that Yahoo shares are banging on the ceiling and not the floor is a vivid sign that Semel's turnaround may be just getting started.

Case 2

Yum! Brands, Pizza Hut, and KFC

Jeffrey A. Krug *Appalachian State University*

Yum! Brands, Inc., was the world's largest fast-food company in 2004. It operated more than 33,000 KFC, Pizza Hut, Taco Bell, Long John Silver's, and A&W restaurants worldwide. It was the market leader in the chicken, pizza, Mexican, and seafood segments of the U.S. fast-food industry. Yum! Brands also operated more than 12,000 restaurants outside the United States. KFC and Pizza Hut accounted for more than 96 percent of the company's international restaurant base and managed restaurants in 116 countries. Among the first fast-food chains to go international in the late 1950s and 1960s, KFC and Pizza Hut were two of the world's most recognizable brands. Both KFC and Pizza Hut expanded through the 1990s by growing their restaurants into as many countries as possible. However, Yum! Brands realized that different countries offered different opportunities to contribute to the company's worldwide operating profits.

By 2004 Yum! Brands began to focus more attention on portfolio management in individual countries. It increasingly focused its international strategy on developing strong market share positions in a small number of high-growth markets such as Japan, Canada, the United Kingdom, China, Australia, Korea, and Mexico. It also hoped to build strong positions in continental Europe, Brazil, and India. Consumer awareness in these markets, however, was still low and neither KFC nor Pizza Hut had strong operating capabilities there. China and India were appealing markets because of their large populations. From a regional point-of-view, Latin America was appealing because of its close proximity to the United States, language and cultural similarities, and the potential for a future World Free Trade Area of the Americas, which would eliminate tariffs on trade within North and South America. The most important long-term challenge for Yum! Brands was to strengthen its position in a set of core international markets while also developing new markets where consumer awareness and operating capabilities were weak.

Company History

Kentucky Fried Chicken Corporation

Fast-food franchising was still in its infancy in 1952 when Harland Sanders began his travels across the United States to speak with prospective franchisees about his "Colonel Sanders Recipe Kentucky Fried Chicken." By 1960, "Colonel" Sanders had granted Kentucky Fried Chicken (KFC) franchises to more than 200 take-home retail outlets and restaurants across the United States. Four years later, at the age of 74, he sold KFC to two Louisville businessmen for $2 million. In 1966 KFC went public and was listed on the New York Stock Exchange. In 1971 Heublein, Inc., a distributor of wine and alcoholic beverages, successfully approached KFC with an offer and merged KFC into a subsidiary. Eleven years later, R.J. Reynolds Industries, Inc., (RJR) acquired Heublein and merged it into a wholly owned subsidiary. The acquisition of Heublein was part of RJR's corporate strategy of diversifying into unrelated businesses such as energy, transportation, food, and restaurants to reduce its dependence on the tobacco industry. In 1985 RJR acquired Nabisco Corporation in an attempt to redefine RJR as a world leader in the consumer foods industry. As RJR refocused its strategy on processed foods, it decided to exit the restaurant industry. It sold KFC to PepsiCo, Inc., one year later.

Pizza Hut

In 1958 two students at Wichita State University—Frank and Dan Carney—decided to open a pizza restaurant in an old building at a busy intersection in downtown Wichita. To finance their new business, they borrowed $500 from their mother. They called the restaurant the "Pizza Hut," a reference to the old tavern beside the market that they renovated to open the new business. They opened four more restaurants during the next two years. The Pizza Hut concept was so well received by consumers that they were soon licensing the concept to franchises. By 1972 the Carneys had opened 1,000 restaurants and listed the firm on the New York Stock Exchange. In less than 15 years, Pizza Hut had become the number one pizza restaurant chain in the world in terms of sales and number of units. Internationally, they opened their first restaurant in Canada in 1968 and soon established franchises in Mexico, Germany, Australia, Costa Rica, Japan, and the United Kingdom. In 1977 they sold the business to PepsiCo, Inc. Pizza Hut's headquarters remained in Wichita and Frank Carney served as Pizza Hut's president until 1980. (It is interesting to note that Frank opened a Papa John's Pizza franchise in 1994. Today he is one of Papa John's largest franchisees).

PepsiCo, Inc.

PepsiCo believed the restaurant business complemented its consumer product orientation. The marketing of fast food followed many of the same patterns as soft drinks and snack foods. Pepsi-Cola and Pizza Hut pizza, for example, could be marketed in the same television and radio segments, which provided higher returns for each advertising dollar. Restaurant chains also provided an additional outlet for the sale of Pepsi soft drinks. In 1978 PepsiCo acquired Taco Bell. After acquiring KFC in 1986, PepsiCo controlled the leading brands in the pizza, Mexican, and chicken segments of the fast-food industry. PepsiCo's strategy of diversifying into three distinct but related markets created one of the world's largest food companies.

In the early 1990s, PepsiCo's sales grew at an annual rate of more than 10 percent. Its rapid growth, however, masked troubles in its fast-food businesses. Operating margins at Pepsi-Cola and PepsiCo's Frito-Lay division averaged 12 and 17 percent, respectively. Margins at KFC, Pizza Hut, and Taco Bell, however, fell from an average of 8 percent in 1990 to 4 percent in 1996. Declining margins reflected increasing maturity in the U.S. fast-food industry, intense competition, and the aging of KFC and Pizza Hut restaurants. PepsiCo's restaurant chains absorbed nearly one-half of PepsiCo's annual capital spending but generated less than one-third of its cash flows. Cash had to be diverted from PepsiCo's soft drink and snack food businesses to its restaurant businesses. This reduced PepsiCo's corporate return on assets, made it more difficult to compete effectively with Coca-Cola, and hurt its stock price. In 1997 PepsiCo decided to spin off its restaurant businesses into a new company called Tricon Global Restaurants, Inc.

Yum! Brands, Inc.

The spin-off created a new, independent, publicly traded company that managed the KFC, Pizza Hut, and Taco Bell franchises. David Novak became Tricon's new CEO. He moved quickly to create a new culture within the company. One of his primary objectives was to reverse the long-standing friction between management and franchisees that was created under PepsiCo ownership. Novak announced that PepsiCo's top-down management system would be replaced by a new management emphasis on providing support to the firm's franchise base. Franchises would have greater independence, resources, and technical support. Novak symbolically changed the name on the corporate headquarters building in Louisville to "KFC Support Center" to drive home his new philosophy.

The firm's new emphasis on franchise support had an immediate effect on morale. In 1997, the year of the divestiture, the company recorded a loss of $111 million in net income. In 2003 it recorded net income of $617 million on sales of $7.4 billion, a return on sales of 8.3 percent. In 2002 Tricon acquired Long John Silver's and A&W All-American Food Restaurants. The acquisitions increased Tricon's worldwide system to almost 33,000 units. One week later, shareholders approved a corporate name change to Yum! Brands, Inc. (Exhibit 1). The acquisitions signaled a shift in the company's strategy from a

EXHIBIT 1   **Yum! Brands, Inc.: Organizational Chart, 2004**

focus on individual to multibranded units. Multibranding combined two brands in a single restaurant such as KFC and Taco Bell, KFC and A&W, Pizza Hut and Taco Bell, and Pizza Hut and Long John Silver's. Multibranded units attracted a larger consumer base by offering them a broader menu selection in one location. By 2004 the company was operating more than 2,400 multibrand restaurants in the United States.

Fast-Food Industry

The National Restaurant Association (NRA) estimated that U.S. food service sales increased by 3.3 percent to $422 billion in 2003. More than 858,000 restaurants made up the U.S. restaurant industry and employed 12 million people. Sales were highest in the full-service, sit-down sector, which grew 3.3 percent to $151 billion. Fast-food sales rose at a slower rate, 2.7 percent to $119 billion. The fast-food sector was increasingly viewed as a mature market. As U.S. incomes rose during the late 1990s and early 2000s, more consumers frequented sit-down restaurants that offered better service and a more comfortable dining experience. Together, the full-service and fast-food segments made up about 64 percent of all U.S. food service sales.

Major Fast-Food Segments

Eight major segments made up the fast-food segment of the restaurant industry: sandwich chains, pizza chains, family restaurants, grill buffet chains, dinner houses, chicken chains, non-dinner concepts, and other chains. Sales data for the leading chains in each segment are shown in Exhibit 2. Most striking is the dominance of McDonald's, which had sales of more than $22 billion in 2003. McDonald's accounted for 14 percent of the sales of the top 100 chains. To put McDonald's dominance in perspective, the second largest chain—Burger King—held less than a 5 percent share of the market.

Sandwich chains made up the largest segment of the fast-food market. McDonald's controlled 35 percent of this segment, while Burger King ran a distant second with a 12 percent share. Sandwich chains struggled through early 2003 as the U.S. recession lowered demand and the war in Iraq increased consumer uncertainty. U.S. consumers were also trending away from the traditional hamburger, fries, and soft drink combinations and demanding more healthy food items and better service. Many chains attempted to attract new customers through price discounting. Instead of drawing in new customers, however, discounting merely lowered profit margins. By mid-2003 most chains had abandoned price discounting and began to focus on improved service and product quality. McDonald's, Taco Bell, and Hardee's were particularly successful. They slowed new restaurant development, improved drive-through service, and introduced a variety of new menu items. McDonald's and Hardee's, for example, introduced larger, higher-priced hamburgers to increase value perceptions and ticket prices. The shift from price discounting to new product introductions increased average ticket sales and helped sandwich chains improve profitability in 2004.

Dinner houses made up the second-largest and fastest-growing fast-food segment. Segment sales increased by almost 9.0 percent in 2003, surpassing the average increase of 5.5 percent in the other segments. Much of the growth in dinner houses came from new unit construction in suburban areas and small towns. Applebee's, Chili's, Outback Steakhouse, Red Lobster, and Olive Garden dominated the segment. Each chain generated sales of more than $2 billion in 2003. The fastest-growing dinner houses, however, were newer chains generating less than $700 million in sales, such as P. F. Chang's China Bistro, the Cheesecake Factory, Carrabba's Italian Grill, and LongHorn Steakhouse. Each chain was increasing sales at a 20 percent annual rate. Dinner houses continued to benefit from rising household incomes in the United States. As incomes rose, families were able to move up from quick-service restaurants to more upscale, higher-priced dinner houses. In addition,

EXHIBIT 2   Top U.S. Fast-Food Restaurants (Ranked by 2003 sales, $ millions)

Source: *Nation's Restaurant News*. Sales rankings for contract and hotel chains not included.

Sandwich Chains	Sales	Change	Dinner Houses	Sales	Change
McDonald's	$22,121	8.9%	Applebee's	$ 3,520	10.6%
Burger King	7,680	–2.8	Chili's	2,505	11.8
Wendy's	7,315	5.2	Outback Steakhouse	2,456	7.1
Subway	5,690	8.8	Red Lobster	2,315	–1.9
Taco Bell	5,346	2.8	Olive Garden	2,165	11.6
Arby's	2,710	0.6	TGI Friday's	1,791	2.6
Jack in the Box	2,360	5.4	Ruby Tuesday	1,450	14.8
Sonic Drive-In	2,359	7.0	Romano's	699	9.4
Dairy Queen	2,165	–1.1	Cheesecake Factory	689	20.6
Hardee's	1,662	–2.3	Hooter's	670	6.5
Other Chains	3,934	9.4	Other Chains	5,277	10.7
Total Segment	$63,342	5.2%	Total Segment	$23,537	8.8%
Pizza Chains			**Chicken Chains**		
Pizza Hut	$ 5,033	–1.3%	KFC	$ 4,936	2.8%
Domino's	3,003	2.6	Chick-fil-A	1,534	11.8
Papa John's	1,719	–2.4	Popeyes	1,274	1.6
Little Caesars	1,200	4.3	Church's	700	–2.5
Chuck E. Cheese's	476	3.5	Boston Market	646	0.8
CiCi's Pizza	380	13.9	El Pollo Loco	396	8.7
Round Table Pizza	378	1.1	Bojangles'	375	8.0
Total Segment	$12,189	0.7%	Total Segment	$ 9,861	3.8%
Family Restaurants			**Other Dinner Chains**		
Denny's	$ 2,132	0.6%	Panera Bread	$ 908	32.0%
IHOP	1,676	14.7	Long John Silver's	777	2.8
Cracker Barrel	1,480	5.3	Disney Theme Parks	707	0.4
Bob Evans	954	9.0	Old Country Buffet	548	–4.5
Waffle House	789	2.7	Captain D's Seafood	506	1.7
Perkins	787	–1.3	Total Segment	$ 3,446	7.0%
Other Chains	2,162	1.2	**Non-dinner Concepts**		
Total Segment	$ 9,980	4.3%	Starbucks	$ 3,118	25.8%
Grill Buffet Chains			Dunkin' Donuts	2,975	10.2
Golden Corral	$ 1,247	7.8%	7-Eleven	1,410	5.6
Ryan's	814	0.2	Krispy Kreme	957	24.0
Ponderosa	537	–2.1	Baskin-Robbins	510	–2.5
Total Segment	$ 2,598	3.2%	Total Segment	$ 8,970	14.9%

higher incomes enabled many professionals to purchase more expensive homes in new suburban developments, thereby providing additional opportunities for dinner houses to build new restaurants in unsaturated areas.

Increased growth among dinner houses came at the expense of sandwich chains, pizza and chicken chains, grill buffet chains, and family restaurants. "Too many restaurants chasing the same customers" was responsible for much of the slower growth in these other fast-food categories. Sales growth within each segment, however, differed from one chain to another. In the family segment, for example, Denny's (the segment leader in sales), Shoney's, Perkins, and Big Boy shut down poorly performing restaurants. At the same time, IHOP, Bob Evans, and Cracker Barrel expanded their bases. The hardest-hit segment was grill buffet chains. Declining sales caused both Sizzlin' and Western Sizzlin' to drop out of

EXHIBIT 3
Leading Pizza, Chicken, and Sandwich Chains, 2003

Source: *Nation's Restaurant News.*

Pizza Chains	Sales ($ millions)	Growth Rate (%)	Units	Growth Rate (%)	Sales per Unit ($000s)
Pizza Hut	$ 5,033.0	(1.3)%	7,523	(1.0)%	$ 665.7
Domino's Pizza	3,003.4	2.6	4,904	1.2	616.0
Papa John's Pizza	1,718.5	(2.4)	3,035	(0.4)	661.5
Little Caesars Pizza	1,200.0	4.4	2,593	(0.2)	395.1
Chuck E. Cheese's	476.2	3.5	485	5.1	1,070.1
CiCi's Pizza	380.4	13.9	465	11.5	862.6
Round Table Pizza	378.4	1.1	456	(5.6)	757.6
Total	$12,189.9	3.1%	19,461	1.5%	$718.3
Chicken Chains					
KFC	$ 4,936.0	2.8%	5,524	1.0%	$ 897.8
Chick-fil-A	1,534.4	11.8	1,235	4.9	1,394.3
Popeyes Chicken	1,274.0	1.6	1,447	3.8	896.9
Church's Chicken	700.0	(2.5)	1,235	(1.0)	564.1
Boston Market	646.0	0.8	630	(3.1)	1,009.4
El Pollo Loco	395.7	8.7	314	2.6	1,276.5
Bojangles'	374.8	8.0	320	9.6	1,224.8
Total	$ 9,860.9	4.5%	10,705	2.6%	$1,037.7
Sandwich Chains					
McDonald's	$22,121.4	8.9%	13,609	0.9%	$1,632.6
Burger King	7,680.0	(2.8)	7,656	(3.1)	987.1
Wendy's	7,315.0	5.2	5,761	3.8	1,293.5
Subway	5,690.0	8.8	16,499	13.6	366.8
Taco Bell	5,346.0	2.8	5,989	(2.9)	879.7
Arby's	2,710.0	0.6	3,303	1.6	827.1
Jack in the Box	2,360.0	5.4	1,947	4.6	1,239.2
Total	$53,222.4	4.1%	54,764	2.6%	$1,032.3
Long John Silver's	777.0	2.8	1,204	(1.4)	640.8
A&W Restaurants	200.0	NA	576	(13.4)	NA
Yum! Brands Total	16,292.0	NA	20,822	(1.4)	NA

Note: Sales per unit are calculated based on a mathematical equation of annual systemwide sales growth and changes in the number of operating units.

the list of Top 100 chains, leaving only three chains in the Top 100 (Golden Corral, Ryan's, and Ponderosa). Each of these three chains shut down restaurants in 2003. Dinner houses, because of their more upscale atmosphere and higher-ticket items, were better positioned to take advantage of the aging and wealthier U.S. population.

Yum! Brands: Brand Leadership

Exhibit 3 shows sales and restaurant data for the pizza, chicken, and sandwich segments. Yum! Brands generated U.S. sales of $16.3 billion across its five brands. It operated close to 21,000 U.S. and 12,000 non-U.S. restaurants, or more than 33,000 restaurants worldwide. Four of its brands—Pizza Hut (pizza), KFC (chicken), Taco Bell (Mexican), and Long John Silver's (seafood)—were the market leaders in their segments. Taco Bell was the third most profitable restaurant concept behind McDonald's and Starbucks. Profitability at McDonald's was primarily driven by volume; each McDonald's restaurant generated an annual average of $1.6 million in sales compared to an industrywide average of $1.0 million. Starbucks, in contrast, generated less revenue per store—about $660 million each year—but premium pricing for its specialty coffee drinks drove high profit margins. Taco Bell was able to generate greater overall profits because of its lower operating costs. Products such as tacos, burritos, gorditas, and chalupas used similar ingredients. In addition, cooking machinery was simpler, less costly, and required less space than pizza ovens or chicken broilers.

Pizza Hut controlled the pizza segment with a 41 percent share, followed by Domino's (25 percent) and Papa John's (14 percent). As the pizza segment became increasingly mature, the traditional pizza chains were forced to close old or underperforming restaurants. Only relatively new pizza chain concepts such as CiCi's Pizza, which offered an inexpensive all-you-can-eat salad and pizza buffet, and Chuck E. Cheese's, which focused on family entertainment, were able to significantly grow their restaurant bases during 2003. Most chains could no longer rely on new restaurant construction to drive sales. Another problem was the proliferation of new diets. Many Americans were eating pizza less often as they pursued the Atkins Diet (low carbohydrates), "The Zone" (balanced meals containing equal parts of carbohydrates, protein, and unsaturated fat), or a traditional low-fat diet. Each diet discouraged users from eating pizza, which was high in both fat and carbohydrates.

Operating costs were also rising because of higher cheese and gasoline prices. Pizza chains were forced to develop unique strategies that attracted more customers but protected profit margins. Some chains raised pizza prices to offset higher-priced ingredients or raised home delivery charges to offset higher gasoline costs. Most chains, however, responded with new product introductions. Pizza Hut introduced a low-fat "Fit 'n Delicious" pizza that used one-half the cheese of normal pizzas and toppings with lower fat content. It also introduced a "4forAll" pizza that contained four individually topped six-inch square pizzas in the same box. Domino's introduced a Philly cheese steak pizza, its first new product introduction since 2000. Papa John's introduced a new barbeque chicken and bacon pizza. In addition, it began a campaign that allowed customers to choose one of three free DVDs with the purchase of a large pizza. By matching pizza and movies, Papa John's hoped to encourage customers to eat pizza more often. Pizza Hut quickly responded with its own offer for a free DVD with the purchase of any pizza at the regular price.

KFC continued to dominate the chicken segment with sales of $4.9 billion in 2003, more than 50 percent of sales in the chicken segment. Its nearest competitor, Chick-fil-A, ran a distant second with sales of $1.5 billion. KFC's leadership in the U.S. market was so extensive that it had fewer opportunities to expand its U.S. restaurant base. Despite its dominance, KFC was slowly losing market share as other chicken chains increased sales at a faster rate. Sales data indicated that KFC's share of the chicken segment fell from a high of 64 percent in 1993, a 10-year drop of 14 percent. During the same period, Chick-fil-A and Boston Market increased their combined share by 11 percent. On the surface, it appeared that these market share gains came by taking customers away from KFC. The growth in sales at KFC restaurants, however, had generally remained steady during the last two decades. In reality, the three chains competed for different market groups. Boston Market, for example, appealed to professionals with higher incomes and health-conscious consumers who didn't regularly frequent KFC. It expanded the chicken segment by offering healthy, "home-style" alternatives to nonfried chicken in a setting resembling an upscale deli. Chick-fil-A concentrated on chicken sandwiches rather than fried chicken and most of its restaurants were still located in shopping mall food courts.

The maturity of the U.S. fast-food industry intensified competition within the chicken segment. As in the pizza segment, chicken chains could not rely on new restaurant construction to build new sales. In addition, chicken costs, which represented about one-half of total food costs, increased dramatically in 2004. A boneless chicken breast, which cost $1.20 per pound in early 2001, cost $2.50 per pound in 2004, an increase of more than 100 percent. Profit margins were being squeezed from both the revenue and cost sides. All chains focused on very different strategies. KFC added new menu boards and introduced new products such as oven roasted strips and roasted twister sandwich wraps. Boston Market experimented with home delivery and began to sell through supermarkets. Chick-fil-A continued to build freestanding restaurants to expand beyond shopping malls. Church's focused on adding drive-through service. The intensity of competition led chicken chains to implement very different strategies for differentiating their product and brand.

Trends in the Restaurant Industry

A number of demographic and societal trends influenced the demand for food eaten outside the home. Rising income, greater affluence among a larger percentage of American households, higher divorce rates, and the marriage of people later in life contributed to the rising number of single households and the demand for fast food. More than 50 percent of women worked outside the home, a dramatic increase since 1970. This number was expected to rise to 65 percent by 2010. Double-income households contributed to rising household incomes and increased the number of times families ate out. Less time to prepare meals inside the home added to this trend. Countering these trends, however, was the slower growth rate of the U.S. population and a proliferation of fast-food chains that increased consumer alternatives and intensified competition.

Baby boomers (ages 35 to 50) constituted the largest consumer group for fast-food restaurants. Generation Xers (ages 25 to 34) and the "mature" category (ages 51 to 64) made up the second and third largest groups, respectively. As consumers aged, they became less enamored of fast food and were more likely to trade up to more expensive restaurants such as dinner houses and full-service restaurants. Sales for many Mexican restaurants, which were extremely popular during the 1980s, began to slow as Japanese, Indian, and Vietnamese restaurants became more fashionable. Ethnic foods were rising in popularity as U.S. immigrants, who constituted 13 percent of the U.S. population in 2004, looked for establishments that sold their native foods.

Labor was the top operational challenge of U.S. restaurant chains. Restaurants relied heavily on teenagers and college-age workers. Twenty percent of all employed teenagers worked in food service, compared to only 4 percent of all employed men over the age of 18 and 6 percent of all employed women over age 18. As the U.S. population aged, fewer young workers were available to fill food service jobs. The short supply of high school and college students meant they had greater work opportunities outside food service. Turnover rates were notoriously high. The National Restaurant Association estimated that about 96 percent of all fast-food workers quit within a year, compared to about 84 percent of employees in full-service restaurants.

Labor costs made up about 30 percent of a fast-food chain's total costs, second only to food and beverage costs. To deal with the decreased supply of employees in the age 16 to 24 category, many restaurants were forced to hire less reliable workers. This affected service and restaurant cleanliness. To improve quality and service, restaurants hired elderly employees who wanted to return to the workforce. To attract more workers, especially the elderly, restaurants offered health insurance, noncontributory pension plans, and profit-sharing benefits. To combat high turnover rates, restaurants turned to training programs and mentoring systems that paired new employees with experienced ones. Mentoring systems were particularly helpful in increasing the learning curve of new workers and providing better camaraderie among employees.

The Global Fast-Food Industry

As the U.S. market matured, more restaurants turned to international markets to expand sales. Foreign markets were attractive because of their large customer bases and comparatively little competition. McDonald's, for example, operated 48 restaurants for every one million U.S. residents. Outside the United States, it operated only one restaurant for every five million residents. McDonald's, Pizza Hut, KFC, and Burger King were the earliest and

EXHIBIT 4   The World's 35 Largest Fast-Food Chains in 2004

Source: Case author's research.

Franchise	Corporate Headquarters	Home Country	Number of Countries with Operations
1. McDonald's	Oak Brook, Illinois	U.S.	121
2. KFC	Louisville, Kentucky	U.S.	99
3. Pizza Hut	Dallas, Texas	U.S.	92
4. Subway Sandwiches	Milford, Connecticut	U.S.	74
5. TCBY	Little Rock, Arkansas	U.S.	67
6. Domino's Pizza	Ann Arbor, Michigan	U.S.	65
7. Burger King	Miami, Florida	U.S.	58
8. TGI Friday's	Dallas, Texas	U.S.	53
9. Baskin-Robbins	Glendale, California	U.S.	52
10. Dunkin' Donuts	Randolph, Massachusetts	U.S.	40
11. Wendy's	Dublin, Ohio	U.S.	34
12. Chili's Grill & Bar	Dallas, Texas	U.S.	22
13. Dairy Queen	Edina, Minnesota	U.S.	22
14. Little Caesars Pizza	Detroit, Michigan	U.S.	22
15. Popeyes	Atlanta, Georgia	U.S.	22
16. Outback Steakhouse	Tampa, Florida	U.S.	20
17. A&W Restaurants	Lexington, Kentucky	U.S.	17
18. PizzaExpress	London	U.K.	16
19. Carl's Jr.	Anaheim, California	U.S.	14
20. Church's Chicken	Atlanta, Georgia	U.S.	12
21. Taco Bell	Irvine, California	U.S.	12
22. Hardee's	Rocky Mount, North Carolina	U.S.	11
23. Applebee's	Overland Park, Kansas	U.S.	9
24. Sizzler	Los Angeles, California	U.S.	9
25. Arby's	Ft. Lauderdale, Florida	U.S.	7
26. Denny's	Spartanburg, South Carolina	U.S.	7
27. Skylark	Tokyo	Japan	7
28. Lotteria	Seoul	Korea	5
29. Taco Time	Eugene, Oregon	U.S.	5
30. Mos Burger	Tokyo	Japan	4
31. Orange Julius	Edina, Minnesota	U.S.	4
32. Yoshinoya	Tokyo	Japan	4
33. IHOP	Glendale, California	U.S.	3
34. Quick Restaurants	Brussels	Belgium	3
35. Red Lobster	Orlando, Florida	U.S.	3

most aggressive chains to expand abroad beginning in the 1960s. This made them formidable competitors for chains investing abroad for the first time. Subway, TCBY, and Domino's were more recent global competitors. By 2004 each was operating in more than 65 countries. Exhibit 4 lists the world's 35 largest restaurant chains.

The global fast-food industry had a distinctly American flavor. Twenty-eight chains (80 percent of the total) were headquartered in the United States. U.S. chains had the advantage of a large domestic market and ready acceptance by the American consumer. European firms had less success developing the fast-food concept because Europeans were more inclined to frequent midscale restaurants where they spent several hours enjoying multicourse meals in a formal setting. KFC had trouble breaking into the German market during the 1970s and 1980s because Germans were not accustomed to buying takeout or ordering food over the counter. McDonald's had greater success in Germany because it

EXHIBIT 5
Yum! Brands, Inc.—
Largest International
Markets, 2004

Source: Yum! Brands, Inc.

	KFC	Pizza Hut	Taco Bell	Long John Silver's	A&W	Yum! Brands
			Number of Restaurants			
United States	5,524	7,523	5,989	1,207	579	20,822
International	7,354	4,560	249	31	183	12,377
Worldwide	12,878	12,083	6,238	1,238	762	33,199
International Total (%)	57.1%	37.7%	4.0%	2.5%	24.0%	37.3%
Top Foreign Markets						
1. Japan	1,167	327	24			1,518
2. Canada	733	353	84			1,170
3. U.K.	591	556				1,147
4. China	979	127	1			1,107
5. Australia	516	319	7			842
6. Korea	209	299				508
7. Malaysia	329	106	32	6	26	499
8. Mexico	309	180	1		1	491
9. Thailand	299	77	28		28	432
10. Indonesia	198	85	69		74	426
11. South Africa	360	3				363
12. Philippines	128	113	6		6	253
Other Latin America						
Puerto Rico	95	60	32			187
Ecuador	45	20	4			69
Costa Rica	15	41	11			67
Brazil	3	63				66
Chile	30	28				58
Other Asia						
Taiwan	132	111				242
Singapore	73	34	24	24		155
Other Selected Markets						
France	24	126				150
Germany	45	77				122
Saudi Arabia	50	92	9		9	160
India	2	65				67

made changes to its menu and operating procedures to appeal to German tastes. German beer, for example, was served in all of McDonald's restaurants in Germany. In France, McDonald's used a different sauce that appealed to the French palate on its Big Mac sandwich. KFC had more success in Asia and Latin America where chicken was a traditional dish.

Yum! Brands operated more than 12,000 restaurants outside the United States (see Exhibit 5). The early international experience of KFC and Pizza Hut put them in a strong position to exploit the globalization trend in the industry. A separate subsidiary in Dallas—Yum! Brands International—managed the international activities of all five brands. As a result, the firm had significant international experience concentrated in one location and a well-established worldwide distribution network. KFC and Pizza Hut accounted for almost all of the firm's international restaurants. Yum! Brands planned to open 1,000 new KFC and Pizza Hut restaurants outside the United States each year, well into the future. This came at a time when both KFC and Pizza Hut were closing units in the mature U.S. market.

Of the KFC and Pizza Hut restaurants located outside the United States, 77 percent were owned by local franchisees or joint venture partners who had a deep understanding of local language, culture, customs, law, financial markets, and marketing characteristics. Franchising allowed firms to expand more quickly, minimize capital expenditures, and maximize return on invested capital. It was also a good strategy for establishing a presence in smaller markets like Grenada, Bermuda, and Suriname where the small number of consumers only allowed for a single restaurant. The costs of operating company-owned restaurants were prohibitively high in these markets. In larger markets such as China, Canada, Australia, and Mexico, there was a stronger emphasis on building company-owned restaurants. Fixed costs could be spread over a larger number of units and the company could coordinate purchasing, recruiting, training, financing, and advertising. This reduced per unit costs. Company-owned restaurants also allowed the company to maintain tighter control over product quality and customer service.

Country Evaluation and Risk Assessment

International Business Risk

Worldwide demand for fast food was expected to grow rapidly during the next two decades as rising per capita income made eating out more affordable for greater numbers of consumers. International business, however, carried a variety of risks not present in the domestic market. Long distances between headquarters and foreign franchises made it more difficult to control the quality of individual restaurants. Large distances also caused servicing and support problems, and transportation and other resource costs were higher. In addition, time, cultural, and language differences increased communication problems and made it more difficult to get timely and accurate information.

During the 1970s and 1980s, KFC and Pizza Hut attempted to expand their restaurant bases into as many countries as possible—the greater the number of countries, the greater the indicator of success. By the early years of the 21st century, however, it became apparent that serving a large number of markets with a small number of restaurants was a costly business. If a large number of restaurants could be established in a single market or region, then significant economies of scale could be achieved by spreading fixed costs of purchasing, advertising, and distribution across a larger restaurant base. Higher market share, as a result, was typically associated with greater cash flow and higher profitability.

Country analysis was an important part of the strategic decision-making process. Few companies had sufficient resources to invest everywhere simultaneously. Choices had to be made about when and where to invest scarce capital. Country selection models typically assessed countries on the basis of market size, growth rates, the number and type of competitors, government regulations, and economic and political stability. In an industry such as fast food, however, an analysis of economic and political variables was insufficient. As mentioned earlier, KFC had trouble establishing a presence in Germany because many consumers there didn't accept the fast-food concept. An analysis of Germany's large, stable economy would otherwise have indicated a potentially profitable market.

An important challenge for multinational firms was to accurately assess the risks of doing business in different countries and regions in order to make good choices about where to invest. A useful framework for analyzing international business risk was to separate risk into factors of country, industry, and firm. Country factors, for example, included risks associated with changes in a country's political and economic environment. These included political risk (e.g., war, revolution, changes in government, price controls, tariffs, and government regulations), economic risk (e.g., inflation, high interest rates, foreign exchange rate volatility, balance of trade movements, social unrest, riots, and terrorism), and natural risk (e.g., rainfall, hurricanes, earthquakes, and volcanic activity).

Industry factors addressed changes in industry structure that inhibited a firm's ability to compete successfully in its industry. These included supplier risk (e.g., changes in supplier quality and supplier power), product market risk (e.g., consumer tastes and the availability of substitute products), and competitive risk (e.g., rivalry among competitors, new market entrants, and new product innovations).

Last, firm factors examined a firm's ability to control its internal operations. They included labor risk (e.g., labor unrest, absenteeism, employee turnover, and labor strikes), supplier risk (e.g., raw material shortages and unpredictable price changes), trade secret risk (e.g., protection of trade secrets and intangible assets), credit risk (e.g., problems in collecting receivables), and behavioral risk (e.g., control over franchise operations, product quality and consistency, service quality, and restaurant cleanliness). Each of these factors—country, industry, and firm—had to be analyzed simultaneously to fully understand the costs and benefits of international investment.[1]

Country Risk Assessment in Latin America

Latin America is comprised of some 50 countries, island nations, and principalities that were settled by the Spanish, Portuguese, French, Dutch, and British during the 1500s and 1600s. Spanish is spoken in most countries, the most notable exception being Brazil where the official language is Portuguese. Despite commonalities in language, religion, and history, however, political and economic policies differ significantly from one country to another.

Mexico

Many U.S. companies considered Mexico to be one of the most attractive investment locations in Latin America in the 1990s. Its population of 105 million was more than one-third as large as the United States, and three times larger than Canada's population of 32 million. Prior to 1994, Mexico levied high tariffs on many goods imported from the United States. As a result, many U.S. consumers purchased less expensive products from Asia or Europe. In 1994 the North American Free Trade Agreement (NAFTA) was signed. NAFTA eliminated tariffs on goods traded between the United States, Canada, and Mexico. It created a trading bloc with a larger population and gross domestic product than the European Union. The elimination of tariffs led to an immediate increase in trade between Mexico and the United States. By 2004, 85 percent of Mexico's exports were purchased by U.S. consumers. In turn, 68 percent of Mexico's total imports came from the United States.

Most Mexicans (70 percent) lived in urban areas such as Mexico City, Guadalajara, and Monterrey. Mexico City's population of 18 million made it one of the most populated areas in Latin America. Many U.S. firms had operations in or around Mexico City. The fast-food industry was well developed in Mexico's cities. The leading U.S. fast-food chains already had significant restaurant bases in Mexico, most importantly KFC (274 restaurants), McDonald's (261), Pizza Hut (174), Burger King (154), and Subway (71). Mexican consumers readily accepted the fast-food concept. Chicken was also a staple product in Mexico and helped explain KFC's wide popularity. Mexico's large population and ready acceptance of fast-food represented a significant opportunity for fast-food chains. Competition, however, was intense.

Brazil

Brazil, with a population of 182 million, was the largest country in Latin America and the fifth largest country in the world. Its land base was almost as large as the United States and bordered 10 countries. It was the world's largest coffee producer and largest exporter of

[1]For an in-depth discussion of international business risk, see Miller, Kent D., 1992, A framework for integrated risk management in international business, *Journal of International Business Studies*, 21 (2): 311–31.

EXHIBIT 6 Latin America: Selected Economic and Demographic Data

Source: U.S. Central Intelligence Agency, 2002, *The World Factbook.* Demographic data is 2003 estimate; economic data as of year-end 2002.

	United States	Canada	Mexico	Colombia	Venezuela	Peru	Brazil	Argentina	Chile
Population (millions)	290.3	32.2	104.9	41.7	24.7	28.4	182.0	38.7	15.7
Growth rate (%)	0.9%	0.9%	1.4%	1.6%	1.5%	1.6%	1.5%	1.1%	1.1%
Population Data: Origin									
European (non-French origin)	65.1%	43.0%	9.0%	20.0%	21.0%	15.0%	55.0%	97.0%	95.0%
European (French origin)		23.0%							
African	12.9%			4.0%			6.0%		
Mixed African and European				14.0%	10.0%		38.0%		
Latin American (Hispanic)	12.0%								
Asian	4.2%	6.0%							
Amerindian or Alaskan native	1.5%	2.0%	30.0%	1.0%	2.0%	37.0%			
Mixed Amerindian and Spanish			60.0%	58.0%	67.0%	45.0%			3.0%
Mixed African and Amerindian				3.0%					
Other	4.3%	26.0%	1.0%			3.0%	1.0%	3.0%	2.0%
Total	100.0%	100.0%	100.0%	100.0%	100.0%	100.0%	100.0%	100.0%	100.0%
GDP ($ billions)	$10,400	$ 923	$ 900	$ 268	$ 133	$ 132	$1,340	$ 391	$ 151
Per capita income (US$)	$37,600	$29,400	$9,000	$6,500	$5,500	$4,800	$7,600	$10,200	$10,000
Real GDP growth rate	2.5%	3.4%	1.0%	2.0%	-8.9%	4.8%	1.0%	-14.7%	1.8%
Inflation rate	1.6%	2.2%	6.4%	6.2%	31.2%	0.2%	8.3%	41.0%	2.5%
Unemployment rate	5.8%	7.6%	3.0%	17.4%	17.0%	9.4%	6.4%	21.5%	9.2%
Literacy rate	97.0%	97.0%	92.2%	92.5%	93.4%	90.9%	86.4%	97.0%	96.2%

sugar and tobacco. In addition to its abundant natural resources and strong export position in agriculture, Brazil was a strong industrial power. Its major exports were airplanes, automobiles, and chemicals. Its gross domestic product of $1.3 trillion was larger than Mexico's and the largest in Latin America (see Exhibit 6). Some firms viewed Brazil as one of the most important emerging markets, along with China and India.

The fast-food industry in Brazil was less developed than in Mexico or the Caribbean. This was partly the result of the structure of the fast-food industry that was dominated by U.S. restaurant chains. U.S. chains expanded further away from their home base as they gained experience operating in Latin America. As firms gained a foothold in Mexico and Central America, it was a natural progression to move into South America. McDonald's understood the importance of Brazil. It opened its first restaurant in 1979 and by 2004 was operating 1,200 restaurants, ice-cream kiosks, and McCafés there. Many restaurant chains such as Burger King, Pizza Hut, and KFC built restaurants in Brazil in the early- to mid-1990s but eventually closed them because of poor sales. Like Germany, many Brazilians were not quick to accept the fast-food concept.

One problem facing U.S. fast-food chains was eating customs. Brazilians ate their big meal in the early afternoon. In the evening, it was customary to have a light meal such as soup or a small plate of pasta. Brazilians rarely ate food with their hands, preferring to eat with a knife and fork. This included food like pizza, which Americans typically ate with their hands. They also were not accustomed to eating sandwiches; if they did eat sandwiches, they wrapped the sandwich in a napkin. U.S. fast-food chains catered to a different kind of customer who wanted more than soup but less than a full sit-down meal. U.S. fast-food chains were more popular in larger cities such as São Paulo and Rio de Janeiro where business people were in a hurry. Food courts were well developed in Brazil's shopping malls but included sit-down as well as fast-food restaurants. U.S. restaurant chains were, therefore, faced with the challenge of changing the eating habits of Brazilians or convincing Brazilians of the attractiveness of fast-food, American style.

Risks and Opportunities

Yum! Brands faced difficult decisions surrounding the design and implementation of an effective international strategy over the next 20 years. Its top seven markets generated more than 70 percent of its international profits. As a result, it planned to continue its aggressive investments in its primary markets. It was also important, however, to improve brand equity in other regions of the world such as continental Europe, Brazil, and India where consumer acceptance of fast food was still weak and the company had limited operational capabilities. Latin America as a region was of particular interest because of its geographic proximity to the United States, cultural similarities, and NAFTA. The company needed to sustain its leadership position in Mexico and the Caribbean but also looked to strengthen its position in countries such as Brazil, Venezuela, and Argentina. Limited resources and cash flow limited KFC's ability to aggressively expand in all countries simultaneously. Country evaluation and risk assessment would be an important tool for developing and implementing an effective international strategy.

Case 3

Caterpillar, Inc.

Sara L. Pitterle and J. Paul Peter *University of Wisconsin–Madison*

After a record year in 1988, Caterpillar's profits declined steadily, culminating in a $404 million loss ($4.00 per share of common stock) in 1991. The loss was attributed to a number of factors, including a prolonged global recession and one-time charges associated with facility closings, consolidation, and employment reductions. These cutbacks were designed to reduce Caterpillar's manufacturing costs over the long term. On April 23, 1992, Caterpillar announced a $132 million loss for the first quarter. Although a strike by the United Auto Workers had disrupted production for the entire quarter, management attributed the loss solely to lower sales. (Appendix A contains a summary of Caterpillar's recent financial performance.)

These losses were incurred by a company which had made unprecedented changes over the past decade in response to the changing industrial equipment market. These changes include a multibillion dollar plant modernization program begun in 1985 and a company reorganization undertaken in 1990. These two changes were designed to ensure Caterpillar's profitability for the 1990s and beyond. However, the 1991 and 1992 profit results led management to wonder whether the changes would be successful.

History

Caterpillar is a multinational corporation headquartered in Peoria, Illinois, that competes in three principal business segments. The company designs, manufactures, and markets engines for a wide range of applications including electrical power generation systems, on-highway trucks, and industrial machinery. The company also designs, manufactures, and markets earthmoving, construction, and materials-handling machinery. (See Appendix B for a complete listing of Caterpillar equipment.) In addition, Caterpillar provides financial products to assist customers in purchasing Caterpillar and noncompetitive related equipment.[1] The company has manufacturing facilities and/or marketing offices in fifteen countries besides the United States.[2]

Caterpillar, the largest manufacturer of engines and construction equipment in the world, traces its origins to two inventors, Daniel Best and Benjamin Holt, who in the late 1800s independently developed mechanized agricultural equipment. In February 1889,

This case was prepared by Sara L. Pitterle, Nielson Fellow at the University of Wisconsin–Madison, under the supervision of J. Paul Peter.

[1]Caterpillar, Inc. Annual Report for 1991.

[2]Taken from speech by Ed Terrel, Manager of Human Resources for Caterpillar, Inc., at the University of Wisconsin–Madison, September 23, 1992.

Daniel Best introduced the first steam-powered harvester, replacing the 40-horse-drawn combine with an 8-man, 11-ton, self-propelled tractor using wheels eight feet in diameter. Around the same time, Benjamin Holt began field testing the first crawler-type equipment, built simply by replacing the wheels on existing equipment with new "track" structures—pairs of treads comprised of wooden slats linked loosely together.

The two companies prospered, driven by increasing demand in agriculture, road building, military equipment, and industrial construction. The introduction of the internal-combustion engine provided yet another boost for the evolving heavy-equipment industry. In 1925, the Holt and Best companies merged to form Caterpillar Tractor Company, setting the stage for several decades of uninterrupted growth through technological leadership and a commitment to total quality.

In 1931, the first Caterpillar diesel tractor was introduced. This product initiated a six-year sales growth from $13 million to $63 million and launched the track-type tractor into prominence as the single largest user of diesel power. Caterpillar's growing reputation for industry leadership and technological superiority was further strengthened during World War II by U.S. government defense contracts. These contracts included demand for both existing equipment (e.g., bulldozers and graders) and special government requests for revolutionary and sophisticated equipment such as air-cooled diesel engines for advanced military operations.

Throughout the postwar years, and into the 1970s, Caterpillar generally concentrated on the development of large industrial-sized machines and engines. During this time the company purchased the Trackson Company of Milwaukee to produce hoists, pipe layers, and hydraulically operated tractor shovels for Caterpillar crawlers. Later, Towmotor Corporation was acquired to continue the company's expansion into heavy equipment with forklift trucks and straddle carriers for a wide range of materials-handling applications. By the early 1970s, Caterpillar had achieved at least foothold positions in a variety of heavy equipment product lines, with the objective of achieving industry leadership in each of the new areas.

In 1977, Caterpillar unveiled the single largest, most technologically advanced tractor in the world—the D-10. Foremost among its advantages were an elevated drive sprocket and modular-designed major components. The elevation of the drive sprocket removed it from high-wear and shock-load areas, reduced overall stress on the undercarriage, and produced a smoother ride. The modular design of major components not only permitted faster and more efficient servicing, but also provided the opportunity to pretest components before final assembly. Modular designs thereby reduced repair and overall downtime in some cases by as much as 80 percent.[3] Caterpillar rapidly introduced other new products which incorporated the modular design concept.

In the early 1980s, after 50 years of uninterrupted profits, Caterpillar appeared to be invincible because of its ability to continually introduce technologically superior machines that became the industry standard. The company built the biggest and the best equipment in the world for which customers were willing to pay hefty premiums. Then, during 1982, in the words of past Caterpillar chairman and chief executive officer George Schaefer, "Almost overnight the world changed for us."[4]

The construction industry collapsed. Oil and other commodity prices fell, eliminating demand for Caterpillar equipment in mining, logging, and other heavy equipment markets. The dollar strengthened against the yen, giving Japanese equipment makers, especially Komatsu, an opportunity to aggressively pursue the United States' equipment market with cost advantages of up to 40 percent.[5] If these factors were not enough to

---

[3]Donald Eckrich, "Caterpillar Tractor Company," in J. Paul Peter and James H. Donnelly, Jr., *Marketing Management: Knowledge and Skills,* 3rd ed. (Homewood, IL: Richard D. Irwin, 1991), pp. 702–4.

[4]Ronald Henkoff, "This Cat Is Acting Like a Tiger," *Fortune,* December 19, 1988, p. 72.

[5]Allan J. Magrath, "Eight Ways to Avoid Marketing Shock," *Sales & Marketing Management,* April 1989, p. 55.

disrupt the "profits as usual" pattern at Caterpillar, the United Auto Workers, Caterpillar's largest union, went out on strike for seven months during 1982. After making record profits of $579 million in 1981, the company lost $953 million over the next three years.

Realignment Strategies

Some of Caterpillar's financial problems during the early '80s were a result of management's failure to react to the changing world environment. Caterpillar was increasing its plant capacity at a rate of 5 percent a year as late as 1982, even though expansion in the world heavy-equipment market ended in 1980. In fact, Caterpillar had pursued expansion until less than half of existing capacity was needed. As a result of this overcapacity, the company reduced plant space by one-third, closing 10 plants (8 in the United States) between 1983 and 1987. During this same time period, 28 percent of the company's equity and 40 percent of its labor force, more than 30,000 jobs, were eliminated.[6]

New Products

With the realization that world demand for large heavy equipment would expand only marginally in the future, the company began to consider other market opportunities. The company recognized that it had been ignoring small contractors who did not need such massive equipment, but who represented a growing market segment. The company responded by introducing new multipurpose products for the owner/operator or small construction contractor. These products included tractor mounted backhoes, front-end loaders, and even farm tractors.[7] While Caterpillar has gained market share in these segments quite successfully (11 percent by 1987), these smaller products also have smaller profit margins and more competition from both domestic manufacturers, such as Deere & Company and Tenneco's J. I. Case, and Japanese companies such as Komatsu, Kawasaki, and Kubota.[8]

Price Changes

Because of Caterpillar's leadership position in product quality and innovation, the company was able to obtain a premium price for its equipment. However, when Komatsu began offering comparable equipment at a 40 percent lower price in the early 1980s, Caterpillar was forced to cut prices to match those of a competitor for the first time in its history. The company decided to sacrifice profits to protect market share and ensure the company's long-term survival. Even using this strategy, Caterpillar's North American market share dropped 11 points from 1981 to 1986. Most analysts agree the figures would have been worse had the company not slashed prices and profits in response to its competitors.[9]

In addition, Caterpillar recognized that pricing was just one part of the overall revenue-generating strategy for the corporation. Caterpillar pursued other strategies to generate income. For example, the company capitalized on its recognized strength in distribution of products, and sold logistic services to a variety of corporations including Land Rover and Chrysler.[10]

[6]Robert S. Eckley, "Caterpillar's Ordeal: Foreign Competition in Capital Goods," *Business Horizons,* March–April 1989, p. 80.

[7]Henkoff, p. 73.

[8]Kathleen Deveny, "For Caterpillar, the Metamorphosis Isn't Over," *Business Week,* August 31, 1987, p. 73.

[9]Henkoff, p. 72.

[10]Allan J. MaGraph, "Ten Timeless Truths about Pricing," *Journal of Consumer Marketing,* Winter 1991, pp. 5–13.

Production Changes

In response to Japanese competition, Caterpillar also broke with its traditional policy of manufacturing everything it sells. The company's paving equipment, sold under the Cat name, was manufactured by CMI Corp. Caterpillar also began a joint venture with Mitsubishi Heavy Industries Ltd. to make excavation equipment in Japan, as well as light construction equipment and forklifts for the U.S. market. In addition, almost all of the equipment sold with the Caterpillar name in the Pacific Rim was manufactured jointly with Mitsubishi.

Plant with a Future Program

Although Caterpillar was profitable in 1985, management had no illusions about the company's ability to remain profitable for the long term with its historically high cost structure. For this reason, the company decided to concentrate on driving costs down and improving quality standards. To achieve these objectives, Caterpillar completed a massive six-year, $1.2 billion plant modernization program called *Plant with a Future (PWAF)*. At the heart of PWAF were automation, new factory layouts, and continuous work flow. The program meant a complete remake of Caterpillar's tooling and manufacturing methods, as well as a change to global sourcing to achieve the lowest possible costs on components.

The first priority for the Plant with a Future program was to simplify and integrate assembly-line processes. This objective was accomplished using a cell manufacturing concept in which plants and equipment are arranged to process families of components from start to finish. For example, machining, welding, heat treating, and painting might all be functions within a single cell. Work flow is continuous because all cells feed the assembly line just in time. Thus, the entire plant requires just-in-time (JIT) delivery schedules.

For Caterpillar to integrate just-in-time delivery to each cell, computer integrated manufacturing (CIM) was utilized. CIM links self-contained manufacturing cells (independent islands of automation) to a material tooling and information network. The program allows and enhances electronic communication between engineering, logistics, and the factory floor. At the completion of the modernization program, interplant communication flowed through a corporate information center coupled with global marketing and financial databases. All systems, from the plant's host computer to personal computers on the shop floor, were linked—resulting in unprecedented coordination and optimization of all manufacturing functions.

An example of what Plant with a Future accomplished can be found at the East Peoria, Illinois, transmission factory. Modernization took five years and cost $200 million. While workers put together gears and clutch assemblies, construction crews worked to build an underground chamber the size of a high school gymnasium. The chamber became a computer-controlled heat treatment system, just one part of the modernization program that touched every corner of this 20-acre factory. Transmission assembly, formerly performed in five different buildings, has been consolidated under one roof. Nearly every one of the 500 machine tools has been moved or replaced, and all of this modernization was accomplished without slowing down production lines.

Efficiency at the East Peoria plant increased even during modernization. By installing a computerized inventory control system, the time it took to run components through the plant was cut dramatically. The parts for a clutch housing used to take 20 days to assemble and ship under the old system. With the new system, this same process took just four hours. Quality standards were maintained by shifting quality-control responsibilities to the workers themselves. Costs at this plant were expected to drop 19 percent.[11]

---

[11]Henkoff, p. 74.

Company Reorganization

In addition to the plant modernization program, Caterpillar tried to reduce costs and maintain a competitive advantage by restructuring the entire company. In 1990, the company announced a plan to change the company from its functional structure to a modern product orientation. The new matrix revolves around 13 profit centers spread throughout the world. Each profit center is divided into specific product groups and four service divisions. This new structure has streamlined processes to such an extent that the company has been able to eliminate 1,000 positions that were no longer necessary.[12]

Caterpillar's new structure tied the entire company much more closely to its customers. For example, although Caterpillar has always had an impressive global dealer network, the old structure required countless phone calls to multiple functional areas in order to receive assistance from the company. Under the new structure, customers and dealers are able to contact each product group directly. The ability to effectively communicate with dealers and customers enabled Caterpillar to guarantee delivery of replacement parts in 48 hours or there was no charge.

This enhanced ability to communicate directly with customers and dealers enabled Caterpillar to respond to customer suggestions more rapidly, and allowed the company to exploit product niches. Under the new structure, decisions were pushed down to lower level management throughout the company. This simplification of the decision making chains enabled the company to introduce new models every two years instead of every five as it had under the old system.[13]

Labor Agreements

Caterpillar's responses to foreign competitors and sliding market share in the '80s assumed that personnel, both salaried and hourly, would give full support to each new program. The plant-modernization program and the company's reorganization into strategic profit centers required unequivocal labor support to be successful. Caterpillar assumed personnel support through these changes. The company endured a decade of tumultuous relations with its largest union, the United Auto Workers.

The company weathered two prolonged strikes, a seven-month strike in 1982 and a five-month strike beginning in late 1991. In between these strikes, the company managed to increase its production flexibility by winning union approval to cut the number of union job classifications from 418 to 150 in 1986.

During the 1991 strike, Caterpillar steadfastly refused to accept another "pattern agreement" with the United Auto Workers as it has done since 1950.* The company maintained that such pattern agreements provided Japanese competitors with a 25 percent wage cost-advantage. While the union never accepted this position, the strike was broken when Caterpillar announced plans to replace all striking workers. The company hoped to gain productivity increases by avoiding job security clauses that were traditionally part of union contracts.

By breaking the union's strike, Caterpillar had an opportunity to negotiate favorable wage and benefit terms but also had to manage a disgruntled and disheartened workforce. The company, at this writing, has not been able to regain workers' trust. In November 1992, the union cancelled all worker involvement programs. These worker involvement programs had been a successful and critical part of both the factory modernization and company re-

[12]Tracy E. Benson, "Caterpillar Wakes Up," *Industry Week,* May 20, 1991, p. 33.

[13]Gary Slutsker, "Cat Claws Back," *Forbes,* February 17, 1992, p. 46.

*Pattern bargaining is a potent negotiating tactic for the United Auto Workers, although it was abandoned long ago by unions in other industries like communications and steel. Under pattern bargaining, a union negotiates a new contract with one company and that contract then becomes the pattern for contracts with the company's competitors. In Caterpillar's case, its UAW contract would be patterned on contracts negotiated with both Deere and Tenneco's J. I. Case.

organization programs. At a single plant in Aurora, Illinois, the worker involvement programs had saved the company in excess of $4 million. Now, many workers view these programs as management's attempt to weaken the influence of the UAW at Caterpillar.[14]

Dealers

While Caterpillar substantially changed its manufacturing systems, philosophy, and corporate structure, the company did not change its distribution system. Caterpillar's channel involved a network of independent dealers. Caterpillar's dealer network handled all sales and service worldwide, with the exception of direct sales to the U.S. government, the Soviet Union, and the People's Republic of China. Caterpillar's 215 independent dealers represented an enterprise almost as large as the company itself; it included operating, sales, parts, and service outlets in more than 140 countries, and employed approximately 72,000 people. A typical dealership sold and serviced Caterpillar equipment exclusively and was likely to be in a second- or third-generation affiliation with the company. Caterpillar's dealer network has long been recognized as the strongest in the industry.

In the early '80s, Caterpillar responded to Komatsu's entrance into the U.S. market by capitalizing on the area where it had a strong competitive advantage—its extensive global dealer network. Caterpillar chose to compete with a total product concept by providing the services that customers deemed most important, which included postsales support and responsiveness to equipment malfunction. Typically, the purchaser of industrial equipment can expect to spend three to four times the original investment on repair and maintenance costs over the life of the machine. While equipment breakdown is a normal part of using this equipment, customers expect quick service and replacement parts for machinery; downtime is extremely costly for them. Caterpillar, through its dealers, has been able to provide unequaled postsales service to the end users.

Caterpillar expects its dealers to be experts in the industry in which they compete. The dealers must know which Caterpillar equipment is required by what market segments and how best to reach these market segments in their own territories. Dealers decide on the best marketing strategy to reach potential customers in their territory. Dealers can elect to reach their customers through direct-mail campaigns, electronic media, trade shows, or some unique combination of the above. The company supports each dealer's marketing plans through merchandising plans, inventory plans, and assistance in pricing and advertising.

Caterpillar recognizes that to sustain its competitive advantage in the industry, it must provide an aggressive program of ongoing training and support for its dealers. Caterpillar provides training for dealership personnel, both sales and service, to make them more responsive to the market and to improve total product image. As the company's product line broadens and deepens, it has to ensure that dealers are aware of each new product and its potential market. In 1985, Caterpillar initiated a program known as the *Sales Team Development System (STDS)*. The aim of the program was to provide professional assistance in utilizing all the resources that are available through Caterpillar. The results from STDS were impressive: 80 percent of the participating dealers felt they significantly improved their planning skills, product/technical knowledge, and general marketing sales skills. Dealers participating in the program increased their net revenues by 102 percent during a time of contraction in global markets.[15]

[14]Robert L. Rose and Alex Kotlowitz, "Strife between UAW and Caterpillar Blights Promising Labor Idea," *The Wall Street Journal,* November 23, 1992, Section A: p. 1.

[15]S. Tamer Cavusgil, "The Importance of Distributor Training," *Industrial Marketing Management,* February 1990, p. 5.

Caterpillar also increased its support for dealers through improved information flow and communications. The company modernized its communications capabilities with the purchase of advanced computer equipment that allowed for more accurate record and inventory keeping. During the 1991 strike at Caterpillar's U.S. plants, the ability to communicate effectively with dealers enabled Caterpillar to meet the needs of the majority of customers. Equipment was moved between dealers as needed, and some used equipment was leased to customers until new equipment could be made available. Domestic dealers, who normally received most of their inventory from manufacturing plants in the United States, received equipment from Japan, Belgium, and Brazil to meet their customers' orders. Caterpillar management stated repeatedly that they could not identify a single sale lost due to the strike.[16]

Caterpillar's distinct advantage lies not only in its control of the largest market share in the United States, but also in having the most extensive and competent dealership organization in the industry. Its customer offering goes beyond the equipment to a complete package of unique benefits. Caterpillar was able to break away from the competition because of its stronger distribution network. Caterpillar's dealers compete directly and effectively with competitors' dealers, especially Komatsu's and Deere's, by being able to respond to individual customer needs more effectively.

Competition

Caterpillar is striving to remain the dominant manufacturer in a mature industry that has many competitors. One competitor, Japan's Komatsu, has aggressively pursued Caterpillar for the last decade. Its motto has been "Encircle Cat."[17] Long before the crisis in the early 1980s, management had identified Komatsu as deadly serious in its quest to become the new industry leader. While management had identified the risk, it failed to act upon this information. In 1982, Komatsu began to aggressively pursue market share in the United States. The strong dollar allowed Komatsu to offer prices 40 percent below Caterpillar's prices and still remain profitable.

In 1983, Komatsu continued its aggressive entry into Caterpillar's home market by adding five lines to the crawler tractor and loaders already being sold in the United States. Two years later, the company established a manufacturing plant in Tennessee and bought an old Caterpillar plant in England. In 1988, Komatsu and Dresser formed a 50/50 joint venture for their operations in the United States, Canada, and Latin America. The joint venture combined the two companies' manufacturing, financial, and distribution functions but maintained the companies' separate product lines. The joint venture did not change the dealership network of either company. Komatsu dealers still competed with Dresser dealers in most territories.

Komatsu's surge in the U.S. market slowed in 1987 when it lost its price advantage. Komatsu began to lose market share in the following year, and by 1991 its market share in the United States had fallen from a high of 20 percent to 18 percent. During this same period, Caterpillar increased its market share from 34.5 percent to 36.4 percent.[18]

In addition to losing its price advantage, Komatsu had problems with the Dresser joint venture from the beginning. After the joint venture was established, Dresser executives felt left out of decision making, and most U.S. employees could not understand the work

---

[16]Robert L. Rose, "Caterpillar Reports First-Quarter Loss Plays Down Strike," *The Wall Street Journal,* April 23, 1992, Section A: p. 6.

[17]Robert L. Rose and Masayoshi Kanabayashi, "Corporate Focus: Komatsu Throttles Back on Construction Equipment; Japanese Company, Lagging Rival Caterpillar, Eyes Other Areas for Growth," *The Wall Street Journal,* May 13, 1992, Section B: p. 4.

[18]Ibid.

ethic or culture of Japanese personnel. Another major problem for the Komatsu-Dresser venture was that the dealers of both companies struggled against each other for sales, instead of focusing on the major competition from Caterpillar dealers. As a solution to this problem, Komatsu-Dresser began encouraging dealers to combine operations and sell both lines of equipment. Currently, over 50 percent of dealers have combined operations. Komatsu-Dresser's sixty independent U.S. and Canadian dealers have a net worth of $300 million. In comparison, Caterpillar's 65 full-line U.S. dealers have a net worth of $1.72 billion.[19]

Komatsu reported its first annual loss of $14.4 million in 1990. It was followed by a $74 million operating loss in 1991. Both of these losses were attributed to low sales volume as a result of a severe recession. Komatsu began to diversify away from construction equipment, which accounted for 63 percent of the company's total sales. Company executives said publicly that they were no longer trying to overtake Caterpillar as industry leader and that Komatsu's future lies in robotics and machine tools. To underline this shift away from construction equipment, the bulldozer was removed from atop the corporate headquarters in Tokyo.[20]

While Komatsu states that it is no longer going head-to-head with Caterpillar, the companies are still arch rivals in all markets. Although Komatsu has lost many of its competitive advantages, the company has been able to maintain a better relationship with blue-collar workers in its North American factories. In addition, its per unit labor costs are lower than Caterpillar's. In the international market arena, when Caterpillar was constrained by U.S. foreign policy from selling to many former communist countries, Komatsu was able to develop strong trading relationships with them. For example, when Caterpillar was prohibited by the Carter administration from making sales to the Soviet Union, Komatsu was able to provide the necessary equipment.

Major Domestic Competitors

While Caterpillar and Komatsu battle for the number one and two positions in the heavy equipment market around the world, Caterpillar also competes with a number of domestic manufacturers. These include Deere & Company and Tenneco's J. I. Case in selected product lines. While Deere is more commonly known for its major share of the farm equipment market, it does manufacture and market a line of industrial equipment. Caterpillar has met more competition from Deere & Company since introducing backhoes and front-end loaders for smaller construction companies. These are areas that have traditionally been serviced by Deere and others.

Deere & Company has gone through a turbulent decade much the same as Caterpillar. The company has survived strikes by its largest union and a decade-long slump in its farm-equipment markets. Deere responded by trimming its payroll by 29,000 jobs, which included both salaried and hourly positions. The company restructured and modernized its manufacturing facilities to be able to react more quickly and efficiently to changing customer requirements. Deere expects to compete aggressively in all market segments, but sees its best growth potential in the farm equipment segment of its business.

Tenneco's J. I. Case was primarily a manufacturer of tractors and industrial equipment until it acquired International Harvester and Steiger Tractor Company. Case now has a full line of agricultural equipment and has the number two position for the farm equipment market behind Deere & Company. Case competes with Caterpillar primarily in the smaller construction lines and the farm equipment segment.

---

[19]Kevin Kelly, "A Dream Marriage Turns Nightmarish," *Business Week,* April 29, 1991, p. 94.

[20]Robert L. Rose and Masayoshi Kanabayashi, "Corporate Focus: Komatsu Throttles Back on Construction Equipment; Japanese Company, Lagging Rival Caterpillar, Eyes Other Areas for Growth," *The Wall Street Journal,* May 13, 1992, Section B: p. 4.

International Sales

Caterpillar has traditionally sold approximately 50 percent of its products in countries other than the United States. Sales outside of the United States are projected to increase in the future. Many of Caterpillar's greatest opportunities lie in developing countries that are not able to pay for products in hard currency. Caterpillar established the Caterpillar World Trade Corporation in response to these payment difficulties. The World Trade Corporation negotiates payment for Caterpillar equipment in commodities or other finished goods that are then resold to obtain hard currency.

An example of how the World Trade Corporation facilitates Caterpillar's equipment sales can be seen in a recent sale of mining equipment to a Brazilian corporation. Instead of paying for the equipment in an agreed-upon currency, the Brazilian company traded iron ore for it. Caterpillar's World Trade Corporation sold the iron ore to a company in Hungary for men's suits. These suits were then sold in London for hard currency. Although this is a complex means of receiving payment for construction equipment, it allows Caterpillar to take advantage of opportunities in developing countries.[21]

Africa

Caterpillar is one of the largest exporters to Africa. The company has been successful on this continent because it has exploited the expertise of its local dealers. In addition, the company has been extremely flexible in arranging sales terms. The company will sell to governments under existing international loans programs, or establish long-term leasing arrangements. Counter-trade options have also been used with success.* The company has met with success on this continent on its own terms. The company, while adopting the local business practices, will not indulge in bribery or other kickbacks, which are a common means of facilitating business exchanges in many parts of this continent. In the future, Africa is expected to be an area of continued growth for mining equipment because of the continent's mineral wealth.

Brazil

The decline in the company's overall profits during 1990 was due in large part to difficulties in the Brazilian unit. The unit was profitable through 1989 and the first quarter of 1990, but incurred an operating loss for the year overall. The Brazilian government, in March 1990, introduced austerity programs that curtailed government spending and reduced sales volume for Caterpillar. The Brazilian currency weakened substantially, which meant that sales that were finalized translated into fewer dollars for the parent company.[22] In 1991, due to continuing economic turmoil in Brazil, Caterpillar Brasil S.A. announced the planned closing of its facility in São Paulo and the consolidation of all operations in Piracicaba. Business conditions are expected to continue to be affected by political and economic factors in the short term.

Eastern Europe and Countries of the Former Soviet Union

While there are definite opportunities for industrial equipment manufacturers in the countries that made up Eastern Europe and the former Soviet Union, in all these countries some means of payment for imported equipment must be established. Counter-trade arrangements and international loan programs are expected to play a major role in these countries.

---

[21]Taken from speech by Ed Terrel, manager of human resources for Caterpillar Inc., at the University of Wisconsin–Madison, September 23, 1992.

*Counter-trade options are defined as the selling company accepting commodities in lieu of cash payment. Caterpillar's World Trade Corporation specializes in counter-trade options.

[22]James P. Miller, "Caterpillar Shares Tumble as Firm Says Profit Will Drop Substantially in 1990," *The Wall Street Journal,* June 26, 1990, Section C: p. 15.

Caterpillar pursued these opportunities with caution because of continued political instability. The company has tried to extend its distribution network into these countries. However, establishing dealerships in these countries is difficult because most interested parties do not meet Caterpillar's criteria, which include a stable financial position and the ability to do business with Caterpillar in English.

Southeast Asia, China, and Pacific Rim Countries

Caterpillar has been quite successful in pursuing opportunities in these countries. The company has established a special Far East trading company to focus on the opportunities and special problems associated with transacting business in many of these countries. Caterpillar already has a manufacturing plant in Indonesia and has been successful in selling heavy equipment in China. To take advantage of many of these sales, the company has had to establish complex counter-trade arrangements. In the future, there should be additional opportunities in Cambodia if the recently signed peace agreement is successful.

Counter trade has not been necessary when dealing with the developed countries of Australia and New Zealand. Caterpillar had been extremely successful in selling equipment, particularly large mining equipment, in these two countries. Recently, environmental concerns in both these countries have reduced sales. In Australia, large new mining developments in the Northern Territory have been rejected because of environmental concerns and complaints from indigenous people. In addition, the government has been prohibiting the expansion of even existing mining operations in all regions of the country.

Caterpillar's Future

Slow growth in the industrial equipment market is projected for the short term because of continued global recession. In the United States, industrial equipment market growth is closely linked to expansion in the national economy. The need to upgrade and maintain the public infrastructure in older cities is expected to increase and stimulate growth in the construction equipment segment of this market. In addition, highway and bridge repair may continue to provide a major source of market demand, as will the continued construction of new power plants and water supply facilities.

Environmental issues are affecting the demand of industrial equipment. Demand for products used primarily in large mining operations will be most affected by the increased awareness of environmental issues. The world's recent focus on the environment has forced many existing mining operations to downsize, and in some countries, mining projects which would utilize industrial equipment are not being approved.

The equipment market is expected to be stimulated by the growing versatility of products in which attachments are designed to be changed quickly. For example, excavators can now be equipped with bucket or rock-breaker attachments for a wide range of applications. In addition, higher productivity is being achieved through computerized power transmissions that automatically control the engine speed and hydraulic output to maximize productivity and achieve fuel savings. These product improvements promote higher product-replacement rates in the near term.[23]

Caterpillar responded to the challenges of the 1980s better than many other U.S. manufacturers. The company made unprecedented changes and learned from previous mistakes. Even with all these changes, the company still recorded losses in recent years and continues to be troubled by severe labor problems. The company must decide whether there is a profitable future for it as a U.S.–based manufacturer of heavy construction equipment and diesel engines.

[23]1991 U.S. Industrial Outlook.

APPENDIX A   Four-Year Financial Summary (Dollars in millions except per share data)*

Years Ended December 31				
	1991	**1990**	**1989**	**1988**
Sales and revenues	$ 10,182	$ 11,436	$ 11,126	$ 10,435
Sales	9,838	11,103	10,882	10,255
Percent inside U.S.	41%	45%	47%	50%
Percent outside U.S.	59%	55%	53%	50%
Revenues	344	333	244	180
Profit (loss)	(404)	210	497	616
As a percent of sales and revenue	(4.0%)	1.8%	4.5%	5.9%
Profit (loss) per share of common stock	(4.00)	2.07	4.90	6.07
Dividends per share of common stock	1.05	1.20	1.20	.86
Return on average common stock equity	(9.4%)	4.7%	11.6%	16.0%
Capital expenditures:				
Land, buildings, etc.	653	926	984	732
Equipment leased to others	121	113	105	61
Depreciation and amortization	602	533	471	434
R&E expense	441	420	387	334
As a % of sales and revenue	4.3%	3.7%	3.5%	3.2%
Provision (credit) for income taxes	(152)	78	162	262
Wages, salaries, and employee benefits	3,051	3,032	2,888	2,643
Average number of employees	55,950	59,662	60,784	57,954
Total receivables:				
Trade and other	2,133	2,361	2,353	2,349
Finance	2,145	1,891	1,498	1,222
Inventories	1,921	2,105	2,120	1,986
Total assets:				
Machinery and engines	9,346	9,626	9,100	8,226
Financial products	2,696	2,325	1,826	1,460
Long-term debt due after one year:				
Machinery and engines	2,676	2,101	2,561	1,428
Financial products	1,216	789	491	525
Total debt:				
Machinery and engines	3,136	2,873	2,561	2,116
Financial products	2,111	1,848	1,433	1,144
Ratios—excluding financial products:				
Ratio of current assets to current liabilities	1.74 to 1	1.67 to 1	1.78 to 1	1.76 to 1
Percent of total debt to total debt and stockholders' equity	43.7%	38.8%	36.4%	34.0%

*Data taken from Caterpillar's 1991 Annual Report, pp. 28–29.

APPENDIX B
Caterpillar Product Line

Source: Tabulated from Caterpillar's 1991 Annual Report.

Type of Equipment	Number of Models
Wheel loaders	10
Integrated tool carriers	4
Backhoe loaders	5
Pavement profilers	4
Asphalt pavers	5
Road reclaimer/soil stabilizer	2
Compaction equipment	15
Wheel tractors	3
Compactors	2
Landfill compactors	4
Track loaders	10
Track-type tractors	22
Motor graders	6
Excavators	18
Pipelayers	4
Scrapers	12
Trucks	6
Tractors	4
Articulated trucks	8
Forest machines	4
Skidders	4
Engines	7
Lift trucks	8

Harley-Davidson, Inc. —Motorcycle Division

J. Paul Peter *University of Wisconsin–Madison*

Harley-Davidson, Inc., is a diversified company with corporate headquarters at 3700 Juneau Avenue, Milwaukee, Wisconsin. Its three major business segments include (1) motorcycles and related products, (2) transportation vehicles including both recreational and commercial vehicles, and (3) defense and other businesses. In 1990, the company experienced another record year of growth. In the *BusinessWeek 1,000* ranking of the top U.S. companies, Harley-Davidson, Inc., with a market value of $515 million, moved from the 973rd to the 865th largest U.S. company. Richard F. Teerlink, president and chief executive officer of the company, offered the following introduction to the company's 1990 annual report:

> Fellow Shareholder: I am again pleased to announce a record year at Harley-Davidson, Inc. in terms of revenues, profits and earnings. I'm especially proud this year because we were able to deliver very impressive results despite the fact that 1990—the third and fourth quarters, especially—was tough on most American manufacturers.
>
> Revenues for 1990 totaled $864.6 million, an increase of 9.3 percent over 1989. Net income was $37.8 million, a 14.8 percent increase and net earnings per share increased 11.0 percent to $2.12. Since 1987, revenues, net income, and net earnings per share have increased 33.8, 78.3, and 29.3 percent, respectively. Considering where we were as recently as five years ago, these are tremendous results.

Indeed, these were tremendous results given that the company is the only U.S. motorcycle manufacturer still in business, although there were once more than 140 competitors. In addition, the company had tremendous difficulties surviving the 1970s and early '80s and few analysts thought it would survive. In fact, the company would have gone bankrupt in 1985 had it not gotten refinancing with only days to spare.

Company Background and Operations

Harley-Davidson was established in 1903 and had a virtual monopoly on the heavyweight motorcycle market by the 1960s.[1] In the early '60s Japanese manufacturers entered the marketplace with lightweight motorcycles that did not directly compete with Harley-Davidson. The influx of the Japanese products backed by huge marketing programs caused the demand for motorcycles to expand rapidly.

Recognizing the potential for profitability in the motorcycle market, American Machine and Foundry (AMF, Inc.) purchased Harley-Davidson in 1969. AMF almost tripled production to 75,000 units annually over a four-year period to meet the increases in demand. Unfortunately, product quality deteriorated significantly as over half the cycles came off the assembly line missing parts and dealers had to fix them up in order to make sales. Little money was invested in improving design or engineering. The motorcycles leaked oil, vibrated, and could not match the excellent performance of the Japanese products. While hard-core motorcycle enthusiasts were willing to fix up their Harleys and modify them for better performance, new motorcycle buyers had neither the devotion nor skill to do so. If Harley-Davidson was to remain in business, it desperately needed to improve quality and update its engine designs. Japanese manufacturers also moved into the heavyweight motorcycle market and began selling Harley look-alike motorcycles. Yamaha was the first company to do so and was soon followed by the three other major Japanese manufacturers, Honda, Suzuki, and Kawasaki. Their products looked so similar to Harley's that it was difficult to tell the difference without reading the name on the gas tank. The Japanese companies also copied the style of the Harley advertisements. As one Harley executive put it, "We weren't flattered."

In late 1975, AMF appointed Vaughn Beals in charge of Harley-Davidson. He set up a quality control and inspection program that began to eliminate the worst of the production problems. However, the cost of the program was high. For example, the company had to spend about $1,000 extra per bike to get the first 100 into shape for dealers to sell at around $4,000. Beals along with other senior managers began to develop a long-range product strategy—the first time the company had looked 10 years ahead. They recognized the need to upgrade the quality and performance of their products to compete with the faster, high-performance Japanese bikes. However, they also recognized that such changes would require years to accomplish and a huge capital investment.

In order to stay in business while the necessary changes in design and production were being accomplished, the executives turned to William G. Davidson, Harley's styling vice president. Known as "Willie G." and a grandson of one of the company founders, he frequently mingled with bikers, and with his beard, black leather, and jeans was well accepted by them. Willie G. understood Harley customers and stated that:

> They really know what they want on their bikes: the kind of instrumentation, the style of bars, the cosmetics of the engine, the look of the exhaust pipes, and so on. Every little piece on a Harley is exposed, and it has to look just right. A tube curve or the shape of a timing case can generate enthusiasm or be a total turnoff. It's almost like being in the fashion business.[2]

---

[1]This section is based on "How Harley Beat Back the Japanese," *Fortune,* September 25, 1989, pp. 155–64.

[2]Ibid., p. 156.

Willie G. designed a number of new models by combining components from existing models. These included the Super Glide, the Electra Glide, the Wide Glide, and the Low Rider. Each model was successful and other Harley executives credit Davidson's skill with saving the company. One senior executive said of Willie G., "The guy is an artistic genius. In the five years before we could bring new engines on-stream, he performed miracles with decals and paint. A line here and a line there and we'd have a new model. It's what enabled us to survive."

Still, Harley-Davidson was losing market share to its Japanese competitors, who continued to pour new bikes into the heavyweight market. By 1980, AMF was losing interest in investing in the recreational market and decided to focus its effort on its industrial product lines. Since AMF could not find a buyer for Harley-Davidson, it sold the company to 13 senior Harley executives in an $81.5 million leveraged buyout financed by Citicorp on June 16, 1981.

In 1982 things turned worse than ever for Harley-Davidson. Overall demand for motorcycles dropped dramatically and Harley's market share of this smaller market also continued to drop. The company had a large inventory of unsold products and could not continue in business with its level of production and expenses. Production was cut drastically, and more than 1,800 of the 4,000 employees were let go.

The Japanese manufacturers continued producing and exporting to the United States at rates well above what the market could endure. Harley-Davidson was able to prove to the International Trade Commission (ITC) that there was an 18-month finished-goods inventory of Japanese motorcycles that fell well below fair market value and asked for protection. The ITC can offer protection to a U.S. industry being threatened by a foreign competitor. In 1983, President Reagan increased the tariffs on large Japanese motorcycles from 4.4 percent to 49.4 percent, but these would decline each year and be effective for only five years. While this did decrease the imports somewhat and gave Harley some protection, Japanese manufacturers found ways to evade most of the tariffs, for example, by assembling more of their heavyweight bikes in their U.S. plants. Harley-Davidson's market share in the 1983 heavyweight motorcycle market slipped to 23 percent, the lowest ever, although it did earn a slight profit. By 1984, it had sales of $294 million and earned $2.9 million; it has continued to increase sales and profits through the early 1990s.

Manufacturing Changes

From the late 1970s Harley-Davidson executives recognized that the only way to achieve the quality of Japanese motorcycles was to adopt many of the manufacturing techniques used by them. The manufacturing systems changes that were instituted included a just-in-time manufacturing program and a statistical operator control system.[3]

The just-in-time manufacturing program was renamed MAN which stood for Materials As Needed. When the program was discussed with managers and employees at the York, Pennsylvania manufacturing facility, many of them reacted in disbelief. The York plant already had a modern computer-based control system with overhead conveyors and high-rise parts store and the new system would replace all of this with push carts! However, the MAN system eliminates the mountains of costly parts inventory and handling systems, speeds up set-up time, and can solve other manufacturing problems. For example, parts at the York facility were made in large batches for long production runs. They were stored until needed and then loaded on a 3.5 mile conveyor that rattled endlessly around the plant. In some cases, parts couldn't be found, or when they were, they were rusted or damaged. In other cases, there had been engineering changes since the parts were made and they simply no longer fit. The MAN system consists of containers that travel between the place where

---

[3]This section is based on Thomas Gelb, "Overhauling Corporate Engine Drivers Winning Strategy," *Journal of Business Strategy,* November/December 1989, pp. 8–12.

the parts are made and where they are to be used. The containers serve as a signal at each end to either "feed me" or "empty me." This system is credited with reducing work-in-process inventory by $22 million.

The statistical operator control (SOC) system allows continuous process improvements to reduce costs. The system involves teaching machine operators to use simple statistics to analyze measurements taken from parts to determine dimensional accuracy and quality. The system helps identify problems that occur during production early enough that they can be corrected before many parts are produced.

Human Resource Changes

In designing the new manufacturing processes, Harley executives recognized the importance of employee involvement.[4] In 1978 the company was among the first in the United States to institute a companywide employee involvement program. Harley-Davidson was the second U.S. company to begin a quality circles program which permits employees to contribute their ideas, solve problems, and improve the efficiency and quality of their work. Prior to these changes, engineers would figure out how to improve the manufacturing process and then tell operating employees what changes they needed to make. Naturally, the engineering plans were not flawless but the operating employees would not lift a finger to help solve the problems and would simply blame the engineers for screwing up again.

The changes in manufacturing and human resource strategy were credited with a 36 percent reduction in warranty costs; a 46 percent increase in defect-free vehicles received by dealers since 1982; inventory turnover up 500 percent; and productivity per employee up 50 percent.

Marketing Changes

By 1983 Harley executives recognized that they had become too internally-oriented and needed to pay greater attention to customers.[5] They recognized that they would not be able to compete effectively with the Japanese manufacturers by offering a complete product line of motorcycles but rather would have to find a niche and defend it successfully. They decided to focus all of their efforts on the superheavyweight motorcycle market (850cc or greater) and adopted a "close-to-the-customer" philosophy. This involved several unique marketing strategies. First, Harley executives actively sought out and discussed motorcycle improvement issues with customers. Second, it started the Harley Owner Group (HOG) to bring together Harley riders and company management in informal settings to expand the social atmosphere of motorcycling. The club is factory sponsored and is open to all Harley owners. It sponsors national rallies and local events and gives customers a reason to ride a Harley and involves them in a social group whose main activities revolve around the product.

Third, it began a Demo Ride program in which fleets of new Harleys were taken to motorcycle events and rallies and licensed motorcyclists were encouraged to ride them. This program was felt to be critical for convincing potential new customers that Harley-Davidson motorcycles were of excellent quality and not the rattling, leaking bikes of the 1970s. The program was renamed SuperRide and $3 million was committed to it. A series of TV commercials was purchased to invite bikers to come to any of Harley's over 600 dealers for a ride on a new Harley. Over three weekends, 90,000 rides were given to 40,000 people, half of whom owned other brands. While sales from the program did not immediately cover costs, many of the riders came back a year or two later and purchased a Harley.

Fourth, the company invited several manufacturing publications to visit the plant and publish articles on quality improvement programs. These articles reached the manufacturing trade audience and the national media as well. Finally, recognizing that many dealers

[4]Ibid.
[5]Ibid.

viewed their business as a hobby and did not know how to sell, the company increased its sales force by 50 percent to give sales representatives more time to train dealers in how to sell Harleys.

Financial Changes

Although Harley-Davidson was improving its quality, reducing its breakeven point, catching up with competitors in the superheavyweight market, and marketing more aggressively, Citicorp was concerned about the economy and what would happen to Harley-Davidson when the tariffs on Japanese bikes were lifted in 1988.[6] The bank decided it wanted to recover its loans and quit being a source of funds for the company. After a number of negotiations, Citicorp took a $10 million write-off which might have facilitated Harley obtaining new financing. However, other bankers felt that the company must have been in really bad shape if Citicorp took a write-off and refused financial assistance. While lawyers were drawing up a bankruptcy plan, Harley executives continued to seek refinancing. Finally, several banks did agree to pay off Citicorp and refinance the company with $49.5 million.

Harley-Davidson went public with a stock sale on the American Stock Exchange in 1986. The company hoped to raise an additional $65 million and obtained over $90 million with the sale of common stock and high-yielding bonds. It then was in an excellent cash position and purchased Holiday Rambler Corporation, at that time the largest privately held recreational vehicle company in the United States. Holiday Rambler is similar to Harley-Davidson in that it is a niche marketer that produces premium-priced products for customers whose lives revolve around their recreational activities. In 1987 the company moved to the New York Stock Exchange and made two additional stock market offerings. Selected financial data for Harley-Davidson is contained in Exhibits 1 through 4.

By 1987, Harley-Davidson was doing so well that it asked to have the tariffs on Japanese bikes removed a year ahead of schedule. On its 85th birthday in 1988, the company held a huge motorcycle rally involving over 40,000 motorcyclists from as far away as San Francisco and Orlando, Florida. All attenders were asked to donate $10 to the Muscular Dystrophy Association and Harley memorabilia was auctioned off. The event raised over $500,000 for charity. The final ceremonies included over 24,000 bikers whose demonstration of product loyalty is unrivaled for any other product in the world.

Motorcycle Division—Early 1990

Exhibit 5 shows the motorcycle division's growth in unit sales. In 1990, Harley-Davidson dominated the superheavyweight motorcycle market with a 62.3 percent share while Honda had 16.2 percent, Yamaha had 7.2 percent, Kawasaki had 6.7 percent, Suzuki had 5.1 percent, and BMW had 2.5 percent. Net sales for the division were $595.3 million with parts and accessories accounting for $110 million of this figure. Production could not keep up with demand for Harley-Davidson motorcycles although a $23 million paint center at the York, Pennsylvania plant was nearing completion and would increase production to 300 bikes per day.[7]

Approximately 31 percent of Harley-Davidson's 1990 motorcycle sales were overseas. The company worked hard at developing a number of international markets. For example, anticipating the consolidation of Western European economies in 1992, a European parts and accessories warehouse was established in Frankfurt, Germany, in 1990. After

[6]Ibid.

[7]Harley-Davidson, Inc. Annual Report 1990, p. 12.

EXHIBIT 1 **Harley-Davidson, Inc., Selected Financial Data (In thousands, except share and per share amounts)**

Source: Harley-Davidson, Inc., Annual Report 1990, p. 29.

	1990	1989	1988	1987	1986
Income statement data:					
Net sales	$864,600	$790,967	$709,360	$645,966	$295,322
Cost of goods sold	635,551	596,940	533,448	487,205	219,167
Gross profit	229,049	194,027	175,912	158,761	76,155
Selling, administrative, and engineering	145,674	127,606	111,582	104,672	60,059
Income from operations	83,375	66,421	64,330	54,089	16,096
Other income (expense):					
Interest expense, net	(9,701)	(14,322)	(18,463)	(21,092)	(8,373)
Lawsuit judgment	(7,200)	—	—	—	—
Other	(3,857)	910	165	(2,143)	(388)
	(20,758)	(13,412)	(18,298)	(23,235)	(8,761)
Income from continuing operations before income taxes and extraordinary items	62,617	53,009	46,032	30,854	7,335
Provision for income taxes	24,309	20,399	18,863	13,181	3,028
Income from continuing operations before extraordinary items	38,308	32,610	27,169	17,673	4,307
Discontinued operation, net of tax	—	3,590	(13)	—	—
Income before extraordinary items	38,308	36,200	27,156	17,673	4,307
Extraordinary items	(478)	(3,258)	(3,244)	3,542	564
Net income	$ 37,830	$ 32,942	$ 23,912	$ 21,215	$ 4,871
Weighted average common shares outstanding	17,787,788	17,274,120	15,912,624	12,990,466	10,470,460
Per common share:					
Income from continuing operations	$ 2.15	$ 1.89	$ 1.70	$ 1.36	$ 0.41
Discontinued operation	—	0.21	—	—	—
Extraordinary items	(.03)	(.19)	(.20)	0.28	0.05
Net income	$ 2.12	$ 1.91	$ 1.50	$ 1.64	$ 0.46
Balance sheet data:					
Working capital	$ 50,152	$ 51,313	$ 74,904	$ 64,222	$ 38,552
Total assets	407,467	378,929	401,114	380,872	328,499
Short-term debt, including current maturities of long-term debt	23,859	26,932	33,229	28,335	18,090
Long-term debt, less current maturities	48,339	74,795	135,176	178,762	191,594
Total debt	72,198	101,727	168,405	207,097	209,684
Stockholders' equity	198,775	156,247	121,648	62,913	26,159

In December 1986, the company acquired Holiday Rambler Corporation. Holiday Rambler Corporation's results of operations are not included in the income statement data for 1986.

entering a joint venture in 1989 with a Japanese distributor, the company bought out all rights for distribution in Japan in 1990. Revenue from international operations grew from $40.9 million in 1986 to $175.8 million in 1990.

Product Line

For 1991, Harley-Davidson offered a line of 20 motorcycles shown in Exhibit 6. Other than the XLH Sportster 883 and XLH Sportster 883 Hugger which had chain drives, all models were belt driven; all models had a five speed transmission. Three of the Sportster models had an

EXHIBIT 2 **Harley-Davidson, Inc., Consolidated Statement of Income (in thousands except per share amounts)**

Source: Harley-Davidson, Inc., Annual Report 1990, p. 34.

Years Ended December 31	1990	1989	1988
Net sales	$864,600	$790,967	$709,360
Operating costs and expenses:			
Cost of goods sold	635,551	596,940	533,448
Selling, administrative, and engineering	145,674	127,606	111,582
	781,225	724,546	645,030
Income from operations	83,375	66,421	64,330
Interest income	1,736	3,634	4,149
Interest expense	(11,437)	(17,956)	(22,612)
Lawsuit judgment	(7,200)	—	—
Other-net	(3,857)	910	165
Income from continuing operations before provision for income taxes and extraordinary items	62,617	53,009	46,032
Provision for income taxes	24,309	20,399	18,863
Income from continuing operations before extraordinary time	32,610	27,169	38,308
Discontinued operation, net of tax:			
Income (loss) from discontinued operation	—	154	(13)
Gain on disposal of discontinued operation	—	3,436	—
Income before extraordinary items	38,308	36,200	27,156
Extraordinary items:			
Loss on debt repurchases, net of taxes	(478)	(1,434)	(1,468)
Additional cost of 1983 AMF settlement, net of taxes	—	(1,824)	(1,776)
Net income	$ 37,830	$ 32,942	$ 23,912
Earnings per common share:			
Income from continuing operations	$ 2.15	$ 1.89	$ 1.70
Discontinued operation	—	.21	—
Extraordinary items	(.03)	(.19)	(.20)
Net income	$ 2.12	$ 1.91	$ 1.50

883cc engine and one had a 1200cc engine; all of the remaining models had a 1340cc engine. The first five models listed in Exhibit 6 were touring models while the remaining bikes were standard and cruising types. All of the models exhibited impressive painting and classic styling attributes visually reminiscent of Harley-Davidson motorcycles from the '50s and '60s.

Motorcycle magazine articles commonly were favorable toward Harley-Davidson products but pointed out weaknesses in various models. For example, a review of the XLH Sportster 1200 in the December 1990 edition of *Cycle* reported that

> But Harley undeniably has its corporate finger on the pulse of Sportster owners, and knows what they want. All of the complaints—poor suspension, high-effort brakes, awkward riding position, short fuel range, engine vibration, and poor seat—have echoed through the halls of 3700 Juneau Ave. for more than a decade, yet have had seemingly little effect on XL sales. H-D sold 24,000 Sportsters over the past two years, and these complaints have been common knowledge to anyone who's cared enough to listen.[8]

The article, however, was very complimentary of the newly designed engine and new five speed transmission and concluded that "This is the best Sportster ever to roll down an assembly line."

A review of the same model in *Cycle World's 1991 Motorcycle Buyer's Guide* pointed out a number of the same problems but concluded that

[8]"Harley-Davidson 1200 Sportster," *Cycle,* December 1990, p. 90.

EXHIBIT 3 Harley-Davidson, Inc., Consolidated Balance Sheet (In thousands except share amounts)

Source: Harley-Davidson, Inc., Annual Report 1990, p. 33.

December 31	1990	1989
Assets		
Current assets:		
Cash and cash equivalents	$ 14,001	$ 39,076
Accounts receivable, net of allowance for doubtful accounts	51,897	45,565
Inventories	109,878	87,540
Deferred income taxes	14,447	9,682
Prepaid expenses	6,460	5,811
Total current assets	196,683	187,674
Property, plant and equipment, net	136,052	115,700
Goodwill	63,082	66,190
Other assets	11,650	9,365
	$407,467	$378,929
Liabilities and Stockholders' Equity		
Current liabilities:		
Notes payable	$ 22,351	$ 22,789
Current maturities of long-term debt	1,508	4,143
Accounts payable	50,412	40,095
Accrued expenses and other liabilities	72,260	69,334
Total current liabilities	146,531	136,361
Long-term debt	48,339	74,795
Other long-term liabilities	9,194	5,273
Deferred income taxes	4,628	6,253
Commitments and contingencies (Note 6)		
Stockholders' equity:		
Series A Junior Participating preferred stock, 1,000,000 shares authorized, none issued	—	—
Common stock, 18,310,000 and 9,155,000 shares issued in 1990 and 1989, respectively	183	92
Additional paid-in capital	87,115	79,681
Retained earnings	115,093	77,352
Cumulative foreign currency translation adjustment	995	508
	203,386	157,633
Less:		
Treasury stock (539,694 and 447,091 shares in 1990 and 1989, respectively), at cost	(771)	(112)
Unearned compensation	(3,840)	(1,274)
Total stockholders' equity	198,775	156,247
	$407,467	$378,929

Yet the bike's appeal is undeniable. A stab at the starter button rumbles it into instant life, and as the engine settles into its characteristically syncopated idle, the bike is transformed into one of the best platforms anywhere from which to Just Cruise. And that means everything from cruising your immediate neighborhood to cruising (with appropriate gas and rest stops) into the next state.

This the bike is more than willing to do, with its premium tires and seemingly bullet-proof reliability. The important thing is to not ask the Sportster 1200 to be something it isn't. What it is, is a Sportster, much as Sportsters always have been.

This is merely the best one yet.[9]

[9]"Harley-Davidson Sportster 1200—Improving on Tradition," *Cycle World 1991 Motorcycle Buyer's Guide,* April–May 1991, p. 27.

EXHIBIT 4   Harley-Davidson, Inc., Business Segments and Foreign Operations

Source: Harley-Davidson, Inc., Annual Report 1990, p. 43.

A. Business Segments (in thousands)			
	1990	**1989**	**1988**
Net sales:			
Motorcycles and related products	$595,319	$495,961	$397,774
Transportation vehicles	240,573	273,961	303,969
Defense and other businesses	28,708	21,045	7,617
	$864,000	$790,967	$709,360
Income from operations:			
Motorcycles and related products	$ 87,844	$ 60,917	$ 49,688
Transportation vehicles	825	12,791	20,495
Defense and other businesses	2,375	2,236	755
General corporate expenses	(7,699)	(9,523)	(6,608)
	83,375	66,421	64,330
Interest expense, net	(9,701)	(14,322)	(18,463)
Other	(11,057)	910	165
Income from continuing operations before provision for income taxes and extraordinary items	$ 62,617	$ 53,009	$ 46,032

	Motorcycles and Related Products	Transportation Vehicles	Defense and Other Businesses	Corporate	Consolidated
1988					
Identifiable assets	$180,727	$215,592	$2,863	$1,932	$401,114
Depreciation and amortization	10,601	6,958	3	396	17,958
Net capital expenditures	14,121	6,693	66	29	20,909
1989					
Identifiable assets	192,087	176,813	7,018	3,011	378,929
Depreciation and amortization	9,786	7,282	1,125	1,814	20,007
Net capital expenditures	18,705	3,524	1,190	200	23,619
1990					
Identifiable assets	220,656	177,498	7,163	2,150	407,467
Depreciation and amortization	13,722	6,925	1,166	618	22,431
Net capital expenditures	34,099	2,547	1,257	490	38,393

There were no sales between business segments for the years ended December 31, 1990, 1989, and 1988.

B. Foreign Operations			
	1990	**1989**	**1988**
Assets	$25,853	$18,065	$ 6,557
Liabilities	17,717	15,814	3,761
Net sales	82,811	39,653	22,061
Net income	5,555	2,281	1,941

Export sales of domestic subsidiaries to nonaffiliated customers were $93.0 million, $75.4 million and $56.8 million in 1990, 1989, and 1988, respectively.

EXHIBIT 5

Harley-Davidson Motorcycle Unit Sales 1983–1990

Source: Adapted from Harley-Davidson, Inc., Annual Report 1990, p. 20.

Year	Total Units	Domestic Units	Exports Units	Export Percentage
1990	62,458	43,138	19,320	30.9
1989	58,925	43,637	15,288	25.9
1988	50,517	38,941	11,576	22.9
1987	43,315	34,729	8,586	19.8
1986	36,735	29,910	6,825	18.6
1985	34,815	29,196	5,619	16.1
1984	39,224	33,141	6,083	15.5
1983	35,885	31,140	4,745	13.2

EXHIBIT 6

Harley-Davidson, Inc., 1991 Product Line and Suggested Retail Prices

Source: Adapted from *Cycle World 1991 Motorcycle Buyer's Guide*, pp. 76–82.

Model	Suggested Retail Price
FLTC Tour Glide Ultra Classic	$13,895
FLHTC Electra Glide Ultra Classic	$13,895
FLTC Tour Glide Classic	$11,745
FLHTC Electra Glide Classic	$11,745
FLHS Electra Glide Sport	$10,200
FXDB Sturgis	$11,520
FLSTC Heritage Softail Classic	$11,495
FLSTF Fat Boy	$11,245
FXSTS Springer Softail	$11,335
FXSTC Softail Custom	$10,895
FXLR Low Rider Custom	$10,295
FXRT Sport Glide	$10,595
FXRS Low Rider Convertible	$10,445
FXRS SP Low Rider Sport Edition	$10,295
FXRS Low Rider	$10,195
FXR Super Glide	$ 8,995
XLH Sportster 1200	$ 6,095
XLH Sportster 883 Deluxe	$ 5,395
XLH Sportster 883 Hugger	$ 4,800
XLH Sportster 883	$ 4,395

Pricing

The suggested retail prices for 1991 Harley-Davidson motorcycles are also shown in Exhibit 6. These products were premium-priced although the low-end XLH Sportster 883 and XLH Sportster 883 Hugger were less so in order that new motorcyclists could buy them and then trade up at a later time to larger, more expensive models. In fact, in 1987 and 1988, the company offered to take any Sportster sold in trade on a bigger Harley-Davidson at a later time.

The prices for Harleys can be compared with competitive products.[10] For example, the three 1991 Honda Gold Wing touring models with larger 1520cc engines had suggested retail prices of $8,998, $11,998 and $13,998. A Harley look-alike, the Kawasaki Vulcan 88, had a 1470cc engine and a suggested retail selling price of $6,599; a Kawasaki Voyager XII with a 1196cc engine had a suggested retail selling price of $9,099. Another Harley look-alike, the Suzuki Intruder 1400, had a 1360cc engine and a suggested retail selling price of

[10]All prices are taken from the same reference as footnote 9.

$6,599. The Yamaha Virago 1100, another Harley look-alike, had a 1063cc engine and also had a suggested retail selling price of $6,599.

Promotional Activities

Kathleen Demitros, vice president of marketing for the Motorcycle Division, discussed a problem in designing advertising for Harley-Davidson motorcycles:

> One of the problems was that we had such a hard-core image out there that it was turning off a lot of people, even though people basically approved of Harley-Davidson. We had to find a way to balance our image more, without turning it into 'white bread' and making it bland. Our goal was to get as close to our Harley riders as possible and communicate with them very personally.[11]

In addition to print advertising in general magazines, and Harley's own quarterly magazine, called *Enthusiast,* Harley has its own catalogs with full color pictures and descriptions of each model and discussions of Harley-Davidson products. For example, following is an excerpt from the 1991 Harley-Davidson catalog:

> To the average citizen, it's a motorcycle. To the average motorcyclist, it's a Harley. To the Harley owner, it's something else entirely, something special. Once you've got your Harley, it's much more than a piece of machinery or a way to get around. In a sense, it actually owns you. It occupies you even when you're not riding it. It's part of your life. And while you might not ever be able to explain it to anyone who doesn't know, you know; the trip certainly doesn't end after the road does. Different? Most wouldn't have it any other way.

In 1990 the Harley Owner Group had 650 chapters and 134,000 members with expected growth in 1991 of 15 percent and an additional 55 chapters.[12] In addition to national, regional, and state rallies and other events, meetings between HOG members and Harley management continued to provide suggestions for product improvements. HOG groups have "adopted" various scenic highways and have taken responsibility for their upkeep. In the 10 years Harley-Davidson and its owner groups have been involved, they have raised over $8.6 million for the Muscular Dystrophy Association.

Dealer Improvements

Several years earlier Harley-Davidson instituted a Designer Store program to improve the appearance, image, and merchandising of its products at the retail level. By the end of 1990, more than 310 of the company's 851 domestic and international motorcycle dealerships had completed major store renovation projects or had agreed to do them in 1991. Some dealers reported receiving full return on the renovation investment within 12 to 18 months due to increased sales brought about by a more inviting shopping environment.

Market Information

The traditional U.S. motorcyclist is an 18- to 24-year-old male.[13] Since 1980, the number of men in this age group has declined from 42.4 million to 35.3 million. By 2000 the number is expected to be only slightly higher, at 36.1 million. Women are buying motorcycles in increasing numbers and sales to them have doubled. However, they still account for only 6 percent of the total motorcycles purchased. Motorcycle manufacturers have responded to this market, however, by designing bikes that are lower slung and easier for

---

[11]Kate Fitzgerald, "Kathleen Demitros Helps Spark Comeback at Harley-Davidson," *Advertising Age,* January 8, 1990, p. 3.

[12]This discussion is based on Harley-Davidson, Inc., Annual Report 1990, pp. 15–26.

[13]This discussion is based on Doron P. Levin, "Motorcycle Makers Shift Tactics," *New York Times,* September 16, 1989.

EXHIBIT 7 U.S. Motorcycle Market Shares for Major Manufacturers

Source: R. L. Polk & Co., as reported in "That 'Vroom!' You Hear Is Honda Motorcycles," *BusinessWeek,* September 3, 1990, p. 74.

Company	1985	1987	1989
Honda	58.5	50.8	28.9
Yamaha	15.5	19.8	27.7
Kawasaki	10.2	10.2	15.6
Suzuki	9.9	11.6	14.2
Harley-Davidson	4.0	6.3	13.9

women to ride. The Harley-Davidson XLH Sportster 883 Hugger was designed in part for this market.

The sale of motorcycles, including three- and four-wheel off-road vehicles, peaked in 1984 at 1,310,240 units. Five years later sales had dropped to 483,005 units. Sales dropped in all categories, although dirt bikes had the largest sales losses. Sales of larger motorcycles, which tend to be purchased by older buyers for use on highways, represented 12.2 percent of sales in 1984 but increased to 21.3 percent of sales five years later.

As less affluent young men have drifted away from motorcycling, the sport has been taken up by professionals and businesspeople in their 40s and 50s. Likely, the late Malcolm S. Forbes, motorcycle enthusiast and wealthy magazine publisher, influenced this market which is older, more conservative, and often rides long distances with their spouses on luxury vehicles.

There is some evidence that many motorcycle owners do not use their bikes very often, some only for a ride or two in the summer. Although the number of fatal accidents involving motorcycles declined 9 percent in a recent year, this decrease was likely because of decreased usage. The Insurance Institute for Highway Safety reported that in a crash, a person was 17 times more likely to die on a motorcycle than in a car.

Competition

Exhibit 7 shows changes in overall market share percentages for the five major competitors in the U.S. motorcycle market.[14] Honda clearly lost the greatest share and its sales decreased from $1.1 billion in fiscal 1985 to $230 million in fiscal 1990. However, motorcycle sales represent less than 1 percent of Honda's worldwide revenues.

Honda's plan to battle its sagging sales involved the introduction of more expensive, technologically-advanced bikes. However, with an increase in the value of the yen from 250 to the dollar in 1987 to 120 by 1988, all Japanese competitors had to raise prices. Honda had to raise their prices even more to cover their new expensive models and became less price competitive. In fact, nearly 600 Honda motorcycle dealers went out of business since 1985, leaving the company with 1,200 dealers in North America. Honda's Maryville, Ohio, plant had so much excess capacity that executives considered transforming much of it to production of auto parts.

Honda's 1990 strategy included cutting back prices and a $75 million advertising campaign to reintroduce the "wholesome" angle of cycling to reach new market segments. Promotional emphasis was also given to encouraging Americans to use motorcycles for commuting as an alternative to cars as is done in Europe and the Far East. High levels of air pollution, increased traffic, and rising fuel costs supported Honda's strategy. The advertising campaign was oriented less to selling individual products than to selling the idea that motorcycling is fun. Honda also offered free rides in shopping malls, sponsors races, and paid for Honda buyers to be trained at Motorcycle Safety Centers throughout the country.

[14]This discussion is based on "That 'Vroom!' You Hear Is Honda Motorcycles," *BusinessWeek,* September 3, 1990, pp. 74, 76.

In 1991, Honda's motorcycle product line included 25 models with displacements from 49 to 1520cc's including sportbikes, touring, cruisers, standards, and dual purpose types. It also included four models of 4-wheel all terrain vehicles (ATVs). Kawasaki's line included 23 motorcycle models in a variety of types and four 4-wheel models. Suzuki offered 24 models of motorcycles and 8 4-wheel models. Yamaha offered 25 motorcycle models and 7 4-wheel models. Other smaller competitors in the U.S. market included ATK, BMW, Ducati, Husqvarna, KTM, and Moto Guzzi.

The Future

Rich Teerlink and the other Harley executives have much to be proud of in bringing back the company to a profitable position. However, they must also plan for the future, a future that is uncertain and fraught with problems. For example, the company faces much larger, well-financed competitors in the industry. The company faces increasing legislation on motorcycle helmet use and noise abatement laws that could decrease industry sales.

The company clearly recognizes the fact that the motorcycle industry has contracted greatly since the mid-1980s. It faces the problem of judging how much to increase supply of Harley-Davidson motorcycles given that it is a mature product whose future is uncertain. It faces decisions concerning how much should be invested in such an uncertain market and what marketing approaches are the most appropriate given this situation.

5

L. A. Gear, Inc.

A. J. Almaney, S. Green, S. Slotkin, and H. Speer *DePaul University*

Overview

In February 1989, Robert Y. Greenberg stood on the floor of the New York Stock Exchange and watched as the letters "LA" flashed across the ticker tape for the very first time after L. A. Gear was listed on the Big Board. "It was my proudest moment. It was my dream," Greenberg said. "You see, I always wanted to be the president of a company on the New York Stock Exchange,"[1] he added.

For over 14 years, L. A. Gear promoted the Southern-California lifestyle with attractively styled shoes designed primarily for women. Later, however, the company altered its focus to include products that appealed to the men's performance athletic market. The company continued to produce fashion shoes for women, but its core business became the performance athletic market where sales were not as dependent on swings in consumer tastes. The company achieved its position as the number three brand maker of footwear products when it surpassed Converse, Inc. in 1989. Greenberg set his sights at the number one position in the industry by challenging Nike and Reebok.

However, L. A. Gear began to experience financial difficulties in 1991. Its market share dropped from a high of 12 percent in 1990, to 8 percent in 1991, and to 5 percent in 1992. And its net sales declined from $820 million in 1990, to $619 million in 1991, and to $430 million in 1992. The company incurred losses of $45 million in 1991 and $72 million in 1992. As a result, L. A. Gear was unable to obtain credit from its lenders. To enhance its credit rating, L. A. Gear managed to lure a new investor, Trefoil Capital Investors L.P. who, in September 1991, paid $100 million for a 34 percent stake in the company.

Since the Trefoil deal, L. A. Gear's internal operations underwent major restructuring. As part of the restructuring, the Trefoil team replaced L. A. Gear's top management—including the company's founder, Robert Y. Greenberg. Stanley P. Gold, managing director of Trefoil Capital Investors L. P., and Mark R. Goldston, former Reebok executive, took over. Gold succeeded Greenberg as the company's new chairman and chief executive officer, and Goldston was appointed president and chief operating officer.

[1]"L. A. Gear," *Los Angeles Magazine,* December 1991, p. 116.

Gold and Goldston developed a survival strategy to nurse the ailing L. A. Gear back to health. At the core of the turnaround strategy was a new advertising campaign built around the theme, "Get in Gear." In an effort to create a clear identity for L. A. Gear, Goldston reorganized product lines into three groups: athletic, lifestyle, and children. The new management also launched a restructuring program aimed at paring the company's costs.

In their letter to the shareholders, Gold and Goldston stated, "We believe that the accomplishments of the past year have laid the groundwork upon which we can build to achieve our ultimate objective—to make L. A. Gear a leader in the footwear industry and one of the most admired companies in America." But, will they be able to accomplish their objective in this highly competitive industry?

History

Robert Y. Greenberg, L. A. Gear's founder, had a knack for selling. First, it was wigs. Later it was roller skates and jeans for the trendy residents of Venice Beach, California. Then it was sneakers. As one analyst described him, "Greenberg is the quintessential salesman."[2]

Greenberg's story is a 1980s financial fairy tale with a 1990s climax: A streetsmart shoemaker who always feared being poor would create a pair of sneakers that brought him fortune. As a kid working in the Brooklyn's family produce business and reading his father's copies of *Forbes* magazine, Greenberg set his sights on starting his own company. He took his first step toward that goal by enrolling in a beauty school. After graduation, he opened a chain of hair salons in Brooklyn in the mid-1960s. Later, he started a wig-importing business. As that venture petered out, Greenberg spotted another trend—fashion jeans—and began importing them from South Korea. By 1979, the jeans business had started to fade, and Greenberg decided to pack up for Southern California.

His next inspiration came soon after his arrival in Los Angeles, as he waited three hours at Venice Beach to rent roller skates for his wife and kids. "I figured the guy must be taking in $4,000 to $5,000 a day," he said. So, Greenberg walked out of that skate shop and immediately plunked $40,000 into his own, which soon expanded to nine locations. Not only did he sell skates through the stores, but he established a skate-manufacturing business. The market for skates quickly soured, though. As a result, Greenberg opened a clothing store on Melrose Avenue which he named L. A. Gear. By 1985, the L. A. Gear store was losing money.

Greenberg started looking for the next trend to ride. Having watched Reebok storm the market a year earlier with its fashionable aerobics shoes, Greenberg went chasing after Reebok with his own candy-colored sneakers, all aimed at a market he knew: trend-conscious teenage girls. In what proved to be a brilliant marketing strategy, he opted to sell his shoes not just to sporting-goods stores but to big department stores like Nordstrom, May Co, and Bullock's. L. A. Gear's big break came the following year, 1987, when Reebok underestimated the demand for its wildly popular black-and-white athletic shoes. Greenberg stepped in to meet the demand by marketing "The Workout," a simple canvas shoe that became the flagship of the company.

During Greenberg's Venice Beach tenure, he had become friends with Sandy Saemann, who was making skating safety equipment while Greenberg was hawking skates. After Saemann launched his own advertising agency, Greenberg brought him into the company to help craft L. A. Gear's frothy image of sun and sex.

The Greenberg-Saemann combination worked. L. A. Gear soon became a highly profitable operation. Sales mushroomed from $200,000 per month at the beginning of 1985 to 1.8 million per month by mid-year. As the company grew to an operation of 51 employees,

[2]"L. A. Gear Calls in a Cobbler," *BusinessWeek,* September 16, 1991, p. 78.

it needed outside funds for more development and opted for an initial public offering which was completed on July 1, 1986.

The company used the $16.5 million in proceeds from the offering to fund its growing working capital requirements and to fund a hefty advertising and promotion budget. The initial single style of footwear developed into 150 styles, and L. A. Gear's preeminence in the youth market expanded to include footwear for customers of all ages. In 1986, L. A. Gear launched lines for men, children, and infants and expanded its women's line to include athletic shoes for basketball, aerobics, and crosstrainers.

In 1989, sales rocketed to $617 million from $71 million in 1987, and the company surpassed Converse Inc. to become the nation's third-largest seller of athletic shoes. In 1989, L. A. Gear's stock switched from trading in the over-the-counter market to the Big Board. L. A. Gear's stock price in 1988 was $10.94 with $224 million in sales. By early December 1989, L. A. Gear's stock had climbed more than 178 percent, more than any Big Board stock.[3] *The Wall Street Journal, BusinessWeek,* and *Fortune* named L. A. Gear the best performing stock on the New York Stock Exchange in 1989. Greenberg boasted that he would push L. A. Gear past Reebok and Nike by 1991. Mark R. Goldston, L. A. Gear's current president, described the company's early success as a phenomenon achieved by innovative styling and a unique ability to have their ear to the market and respond quickly.

In 1990, however, the company's stock price started to decline, and investors became concerned that L. A. Gear was losing its appeal to fashion-conscious young women. Some analysts marked the beginning of L. A. Gear's troubles with the failure of its Michael Jackson shoes.[4] In 1989, Sandy Saemann, executive vice president, signed a $20 million contract with Michael Jackson for endorsement of a line of black, silver-buckled shoes. But the shoes proved to be a failure. Other signs of trouble included reports of stock selling by insiders as well as the Justice Department's investigation of alleged underpayment of custom duties.[5]

In April 1991, L. A. Gear posted a fiscal first-quarter loss of $12.5 million. Sales fell 8.8 percent to $171 million from $187 million. L. A. Gear posted a tangible net worth of $193 million as of February 28, 1991.[6]

In May 1991, L. A. Gear agreed to sell a 30 percent stake to Roy E. Disney's Trefoil Capital Investors L.P. for $100 million. Under the agreement, Trefoil would also receive three seats on L. A. Gear's board of directors and the opportunity to have first option to buy shares of Greenberg's 3.5 million in common shares should Greenberg decide to sell. L. A. Gear also agreed to hire Disney's Shamrock Capital Advisors Inc. as consultants for three years, paying fees of $500,000 the first year, $600,000 the second year, and $700,000 the third year.

Shortly after the Trefoil agreement was initiated, Sandy Saemann—a flamboyant, gold-chain decked executive vice president—resigned. Saemann was the architect of L. A. Gear's sexy marketing campaign which often featured scantily clad models. He was also credited with gathering celebrity endorsers for L. A. Gear. Saemann agreed to provide consulting services to L. A. Gear for 2.5 years. Analysts said Saemann resigned because his flamboyant personality conflicted with the Trefoil team.[7] Kevin Ventrudo, 32, senior vice president of administration and a board member, also resigned. Mark R. Goldston succeeded Robert Greenberg as president. Greenberg remained chairman and chief executive.

[3]"L. A. Gear +184.6%," *Institutional Investor,* March 1990, pp. 52, 53.

[4]"L. A. Gear Co-Founder Saemann Quits in Wake of Firm's Deal with Trefoil," *The Wall Street Journal,* June 13, 1991, p. B1.

[5]"The Best and Worst Stocks of 1989," *Fortune,* January 29, 1990, p. 114.

[6]"L. A. Gear Inc.," *The Wall Street Journal,* April 4, 1991, p. B1.

[7]"L. A. Gear Co-Founder Saemann Quits in Wake of Firm's Deal with Trefoil," *The Wall Street Journal,* June 13, 1991, p. B1.

EXHIBIT 1
L. A. Gear's Board of Directors

Source: L. A. Gear, 1992 Annual Report, p. 29.

Stanley P. Gold
Chairman of the Board and Chief Executive Officer
L. A. Gear, Inc.
President and Managing Director
Trefoil Investors, Inc. and Shamrock Capital Advisors, Inc.

Mark R. Goldston
President and Chief Operating Officer
L. A. Gear, Inc.

Richard W. Schubert
General Counsel and Secretary
L. A. Gear, Inc.

Alan E. Dashling
Chairman of the Board and Chief Executive Officer
Sterling West Bancorp.

Willie D. Davis
President and Chief Executive Officer
All-Pro Broadcasting

Stephen A. Koffler
Executive Vice President and Director of Investment Banking
Sutro & Co., Inc.

Ann E. Meyers
Sports Commentator
KMPC Radio, Prime Ticket, ESPN, Sportschannel, and ABC

Clifford A. Miller
Chairman
The Clifford Group, Inc.

Robert G. Moskowitz
Managing Director
Trefoil Investors, Inc. and Shamrock Capital Advisors, Inc.

R. Rudolph Reinfrank
Executive Vice President
Shamrock Holdings, Inc.

Vappalak A. Ravindran
Chief Executive Officer
Paracor Company
President
Elders Finance, Inc.

On January 27, 1992, Robert Greenberg, L. A. Gear's founder, was eased out as chairman and chief executive and a director, along with Gil N. Schwartzberg, vice chairman. Stanley P. Gold, 50, managing director of Trefoil, was appointed as the new chairman and chief executive officer of L. A. Gear.

Board of Directors

As shown in Exhibit 1, the board of directors was composed of 11 members. Three of them were insiders, while the others were outsiders. One of the outside directors was a woman, Ann E. Meyers, who worked as a sports commentator. The chairman of the board was Stanley P. Gold who also served as the chief executive officer (CEO) of the firm. The board carried out its duties through the Executive and Nominating Committees. The Executive Committee consisted of Stanley Gold, R. Rudolph Reinfrank, and Mark Goldston. Reinfrank served as chairman of the Executive Committee. The Nominating Committee consisted of Stephen A. Koffler, Robert G. Moskowitz and Mark Goldston. Koffler served as the chairman of the Nominating Committee.

Top Management

L. A. Gear's top management underwent major changes since the consummation of Trefoil's $100 million investment in the company. Below is a profile of each of the key executives.

Stanley P. Gold   Stanley Gold, 50 years old, succeeded Greenberg as chairman and chief executive officer of L. A. Gear, Inc. Formerly, he was president and chief executive officer of Shamrock Holdings, Inc., a Burbank, California-based company wholly owned by the Roy Disney Family. Gold was considered to be a turnaround expert. He proved himself by helping revive Walt Disney Co., oil driller Enterra, and soybean processor Central Soyal.

Prior to assuming his positions at Shamrock, Gold was a managing partner of Gange, Tyre, Ramer & Brown, Inc., a prominent Los Angeles law firm he joined in 1968. For a number of years, he specialized in corporate acquisitions, sales, and financing. Earlier in his legal career, he served as a trial lawyer in major corporate and civil litigation.[8]

A native of Los Angeles, California, Gold first studied at the University of California at Berkeley and subsequently graduated from the University of California at Los Angeles with an A.B. degree in political science. After receiving his J.D. degree from the University of Southern California Law School in 1967, he did postgraduate work at Cambridge University in England.[9] Gold's professional and civic affiliations included the American Bar Association and the Copyright Society. He served as a guest lecturer at the Wharton School at the University of Pennsylvania. He was Chairman of the Board of Governors of Hebrew Union College, a Trustee of the Center Theater Group in Los Angeles, the George C. Marshall Foundation, and a member of the USC Law Center Board of Councilors.

Mark R. Goldston   Mark Goldston, 38 years old, succeeded Robert Y. Greenberg, the company's founder, as president and chief operating officer. Greenberg was also eased out as chairman, chief executive, and a director at a board meeting in an apparent effort by the company's largest investor, Trefoil Capital Investors L.P., to bury the "old" L. A. Gear.[10] Despite Greenberg's assertions that "the company is left in great hands," the ouster capped a four-month battle between the laid-back Greenberg and the buttoned-down Trefoil team for the soul of L. A. Gear.[11]

Goldston was a principal of Odyssey partners, a leverage buyout and investment firm. At Odyssey, Goldston was part of an internal operating unit that supervised the management of certain portfolio companies. His responsibilities included the development, execution, and management of operating plans and the evaluation of strategic alternatives for those portfolio companies. Prior to joining Odyssey, Goldston was senior and chief marketing officer of Reebok International, Ltd. where he spearheaded the marketing effort for "The Pump," a $500 million line of athletic footwear products. As one of the inventors of the Reebok "Visible Energy Return System Technology," Goldston was on the U.S. patent for that technology. Additionally, Goldston was involved in the development of the Hexalite and Energaire product lines for Reebok. Prior to joining Reebok, Goldston was president of Faberge USA, Inc., a cosmetics and personal care products company. During his tenure there, the company's U.S. sales increased about 50 percent.

Goldston was on the J. L. Kellogg Graduate School of Management Dean's Advisory Board at Northwestern University. In addition, he sat on the board of directors of Revel/Monogram, Inc., ABCO Markets, and Collection Clothing Corp. Goldston's book, entitled *The Turnaround Prescription,* detailing a step-by-step blueprint for effecting a corporate marketing turnaround, was published in 1992.[12]

In his new position as president and chief operating officer, Goldston brought in fresh talent by hiring former Reebok employees—Gordie Nye, Robert Apatoff and Christopher Walsh. Gordie Nye, Vice President of Marketing Athletic Footwear, joined the company in December 1991. Previously, he was at Reebok where he was Senior Director of Fitness Marketing, with responsibility for marketing men's and women's fitness products.

---

[8]"Stanley P. Gold L. A. Gear Chairman & Chief Executive Officer," L. A. Gear Press Release, January 24, 1992.

[9]Ibid.

[10]"L. A. Gear Inc. Investor Steps in With New Team," *The Wall Street Journal,* January 27, 1992, pp. B1, B5.

[11]Ibid.

[12]"L. A. Gear Inc. Investor Steps in With New Team," *The Wall Street Journal,* January 27, 1992, pp. B1, B5.

Christopher Walsh   Christopher Walsh was 43 years old. He joined L. A. Gear as senior vice president of operations in December 1991. Previously, he was vice president of production at Reebok for three years, where he was in charge of worldwide supply sources. Prior to joining Reebok, he spent two years at Toddler University, a children's shoe manufacturer, as vice president of operations. Prior to that, he worked as a senior consultant for Kurt Satmon Associates for two years, focusing on strategic planning. Earlier in his career, he worked at Nike for ten years in production and sourcing.[13]

William L. Benford   William L. Benford, 50 years old, was appointed chief financial officer in September 1991.[14] Prior to that, he was senior vice president and chief financial officer of Central Soya company. Before that he was vice president and treasurer of Dekalb, Inc. He was also affiliated with Shamrock Holdings, Inc., an investment company for the Roy E. Disney Family. Shamrock Holdings, Inc., bought Central Soya company in 1985, turned it around, and sold the company two years later at a profit of about $125 million.

Mission

L. A. Gear defined its mission as follows:

> The Company's principal business activity involves the design, development, and marketing of a broad range of quality athletic and casual/lifestyle footwear. Since its inception, the Company has expanded its product line from its original concentration on fashionable women's footwear to diversified collections of footwear for men, women, and children. The Company is organized into two primary marketing divisions: Athletic (including men's and women's basketball, fitness, walking, tennis, and aerobics) and Lifestyle (casual footwear styles intended for non-athletic use). All of the Company's footwear products are manufactured to its specifications by independent producers located primarily in South Korea, Indonesia, Taiwan and the People's Republic of China.[15]

Objectives and Strategies

L. A. Gear's short-term objective was to streamline its operations over the next two years. In the long-term, the company would attempt to achieve the following objectives:

- To provide a broad range of quality athletic and casual/lifestyle footwear, primarily in the "mid" price range (i.e., $30 to $65 retail).
- To improve relations with, and increase shelf space at, full-margin retailers.
- To improve production and quality control practices.
- To increase international sales and profitability.

In attaining these objectives, L. A. Gear adopted a retrenchment/turnaround strategy that involved a comprehensive restructuring of its operations. Thus, in 1992 the company's staff was reduced by 613 employees, or about 45 percent. In addition, the company reduced its occupancy of about 200,000 square feet of leased office space in five buildings to about 116,000 square feet in two buildings. Further, the general and administrative expenses were reduced in 1992 by $42.7 million, or 21.2 percent, to $158.7 million from $201.4 million in 1991. The company also discontinued its apparel marketing and design operations which had a pre-tax operating loss of $14.2 million in 1991.

---

[13]Ibid.

[14]"L. A. Gear, Several Changes at Senior Level," *The Wall Street Journal,* September 17, 1991, p. A22.

[15]L. A. Gear, Form 10-K, 1991, p. 2.

The company's restructuring was augmented with a product development strategy. The product strategy involved developing a broad range of innovative new products for the athletic, lifestyle, and children's line. Grouping products into three well identified divisions was well received by analysts of the footwear industry. Bob McAllister, West Coast market editor for *Footwear News,* said, "In the past, there was no rhyme or reason to L. A. Gear's different styles. Now, the company has introduced new lines that are cleanly divided into athletic, lifestyles and kids."[16]

The company also sought to differentiate its products from its competitors. Goldston was confident that L. A. Gear would increase its market share by using materials in a unique way to carve a specific niche for its products. According to Goldston, "L. A. Gear is committed to designing shoes that do not resemble its competition."[17] While pursuing retrenchment and product development strategies, L. A. Gear launched a marketing campaign that focused on projecting a consistent brand image across varying retail price points and distribution channels.

Production

L. A. Gear's footwear was manufactured to its specifications by independent producers located primarily in The People's Republic of China, Indonesia, South Korea, and Taiwan. In 1992, manufacturers in these countries supplied 34, 32, 30, and 4 percent of total pairs of footwear purchased by the company respectively.

The footwear products imported into the United States by the company were subject to customs duties, ranging from 6 to 48 percent of production costs. Duty rates depended on the construction of the shoe and whether the principal component was leather or some other material.

The use of foreign manufacturing facilities subjected the company to the customary risks of doing business abroad, including fluctuations in the value of currencies, export duties, import controls, trade barriers, restrictions on the transfer of funds, work stoppage, and political instability. Thus far, these factors, however, did not seem to have had an adverse impact on the company's operations.

Products

L. A. Gear's product lines were organized into three marketing categories: Athletic, Lifestyle, and Children's. Athletic footwear included fitness, walking, tennis, crosstraining, and basketball shoes, as well as the recently introduced Light Gear CrossRunner and Dance Training shoes. These products were marketed under two brand names: L. A. Gear, with suggested domestic retail prices under $70; and L.A. Tech, the newly released, which were a higher priced premium brand.

The Lifestyle lines included men's and women's casual footwear styles that included the Street Hiker, Vintage Series, and Fashion Athletic and Casual Collections. The Children's footwear incorporated features from the Athletic and Lifestyle lines plus products specifically developed for children. L. A. Lights, lighted shoes for children introduced in June 1992, became one of the largest selling children's shoes in the company's history. The age of the company's target market for the adult products was 14 to 35 years, and for children 5 to 13.[18] Some of L. A. Gear's products and the technologies incorporated in the Athletic, Lifestyle, and Children's lines are described in Exhibit 2.

---

[16]Ibid.

[17]Ibid.

[18]L. A. Gear Inc., 1990 Annual Report (Los Angeles, CA: L. A. Gear Inc.), p. 7.

EXHIBIT 2
L. A. Gear's Products and Their Technologies

Source: L. A. Gear, 1992 10-K Form, p. 4.

Athletic	Description
Catapult	A midsole system consisting of a carbon graphite spring to provide cushioning and shock absorption
Encapsole Air	A cushioning system which uses air chambers built into the outsole to provide shock absorption
Light Gear	Shoes incorporating battery-powered lights in the outsole that flash upon impact
Lifestyle	
Street Hiker	A lightweight casual hiking shoe
Vintage Series	Footwear based on classic athletic styles
Children's	
L. A. Gear (Galactica for boys; L. A. Twilight for girls; Nightcrawlers for infants)	Shoes incorporating motion activated battery-powered lights in the outsole that flash with movement
Regulator	Shoes with an adjustable fit and support system using an air inflation device to cushion the foot over the midfoot area
Bendables	Flexible shoes for infants
Clear Gear	Shoes with a clear outsole in flexible plastic with an assortment of designs printed on the midsole

Product Quality

In 1990, L. A. Gear committed a grave marketing blunder in the process of launching its new line of basketball shoes. In a scramble to launch the new shoes, the company outfitted the Marquette University team with handmade pairs, since molds were not completed yet for the large sizes the team members required. As TV cameras zeroed in on one player, the bottom of his sneaker peeled away from the top. This and other cases of poor quality served to seriously tarnish the company's brand image. In an effort to improve quality, L. A. Gear reduced the number of foreign manufacturers from 44 in 1991 to 29 in 1992, retaining only those known for their quality products. The company also engaged a "sourcing" agent with the responsibility of inspecting finished goods prior to shipment by the manufacturer, supervising production management, and facilitating the shipment of goods.

Advertising

Sandy Saemann, Greenberg's second in command, was the architect of L. A. Gear's early advertising campaign. His success in signing such celebrities as Paula Abdul and Kareem Abdul-Jabbar was responsible for the phenomenal increase in the company's sales between 1985 and 1990. Saemann fit the image of the laid-back California executive perfectly—right down to the silver necklace. And his flamboyant vision proved perfect for peddling flashy sneakers. Saemann represented L. A. Gear's brash, entrepreneurial roots by producing virtually all of the company's ads and commercials himself without the help of Madison Avenue. However, L. A. Gear's tumble began, ironically, with its biggest advertising deal ever. In 1989, Saemann was able to sign megastar Michael Jackson in what was described as the largest endorsement contract ever: $20 million. L. A. Gear had hoped to time the release of a new line of shoes to an upcoming Michael Jackson greatest-hits album, but the album never materialized. Teenagers everywhere thumbed their noses at the black, buckle-laden shoes. The company was eventually forced to discontinue the entire line, taking a loss of several million dollars.

Since the failure of the Michael Jackson advertising campaign, L. A. Gear stopped contracting for the endorsement of its products by entertainment celebrities. Instead, the company chose to contract endorsements with athletic stars such as Karl "The Mailman" Malone of the Utah Jazz, Hakeem Olajuwon of the Houston Rockets, and Joe Montana of the San Francisco Forty-Niners. A new slogan, "Get in Gear," was used in the campaign.

Under the new management, L. A. Gear changed the focus of many of its advertising campaigns from promoting a fashionable shoe to promoting a performance shoe. Performance was emphasized with the advertisement tag line for the Catapult performance shoe, "It's not just a shoe, it's a machine."[19] L. A. Gear's most successful commercial was the use of the tag line "Anything else is just hot air" to promote the Catapult shoe, with its high-tech, carbon-fiber soles. The ad was an indirect attack at Nike who made the Air Jordan shoes, endorsed by Chicago Bulls' star Michael Jordan. NBC refused to run the television ads, and the ensuing exposure received by coverage of NBC's refusal was worth millions to L. A. Gear.[20] In promoting the $110 Catapult shoe, the new management decided to drop the L. A. Gear logo, believing that the L. A. Gear name was a liability in performance shoes.

The new management team subdivided the marketing of the company's products on the basis of price. Shoes costing less than $70 per pair retained the L. A. Gear name and logo, and shoes priced over $70 per pair carried the L.A. Tech name. L. A. Gear's management believed that the L.A. Tech name would help establish the line as a high-technology and performance product. The lowest-cost L. A. Gear shoe retailed for approximately $30 per pair, whereas the top of the line L.A. Tech shoe, the Catapult, topped out at about $150 per pair.[21] L. A. Gear's budget amounted to between 10 and 15 percent of total sales.

Research and Development

In designing its products, L. A. Gear conducted comprehensive market research, using a variety of conventional research techniques. Primarily, the company depended on focus groups, product testing, and interviews with consumers and retailers. These methods allowed the company to accurately gauge the image and reputation of L. A. Gear's products and to incorporate changes demanded by the public.

Sales

The phenomenal rise in L. A. Gear's sales between 1985 and 1990 was due to Greenberg's ability to create a clear-cut image for the company with brightly colored shoes and sexy ads aimed at teenage girls. The company's spectacular success led Greenberg to set a higher objective for the company, $1 billion in sales. To achieve this objective, Greenberg tried to challenge Nike and Reebok directly by adding a line of men's performance shoes. The move was too much, too fast. Venturing into men's performance shoes blurred L. A. Gear's image. According to one analyst, "When L. A. Gear moved into the performance side, it lost its way." Greenberg, however, was unwilling to lay the company's problems on the men's shoes. Instead, he maintained that "in any battle you're gonna get a little bruised or battered. And we're playing with a couple of billion-dollar companies that don't need us around."

The rapid growth also placed an enormous strain on the company. Employees had to push hard to attain the new growth objective. As a result, the company's internal controls got out of hand. A shareholders' class action lawsuit called those controls "chaotic and virtually nonexistent."

[19]B. Horivitz, "Some Companies Find They Get More," *Los Angeles Times,* February 5, 1991, p. D6.
[20]"L. A. Gear Says High Inventories May Affect 1992 Earnings," *Bloomberg News,* March 3, 1992.
[21]Ibid., p. B5.

EXHIBIT 3   **Net Sales (dollars in thousands)**

Source: L. A. Gear, 1992 10-K Form, p. 5.

	1992		1991		1990	
	$	%	$	%	$	%
Domestic footwear						
Women's	112,990	26	178,481	29	285,709	35
Men's	104,593	24	176,238	28	196,969	24
Children's	90,997	21	134,485	22	174,486	21
Other	2,688	1	2,517	—	4,217	1
Total domestic net sales	311,268	72	491,721	79	661,381	81
International footwear	118,926	28	127,454	21	158,220	19
Total net sales	430,194	100	619,175	100	819,601	100

As a result of the relentless push for fast growth, product-quality problems, and the attendant bad publicity, L. A. Gear saw its share of the overall athletic shoe market drop from a high of 12 percent in 1990 to 5 percent in 1992. The company net sales, as shown in Exhibit 3, declined from $820 billion in 1990 to $619 billion in 1991 and to $430 in 1992. The 1992 sales figure represented a 31 percent decline from 1991. The company incurred losses of $72 million in 1992 and $45 million in 1991. Net international sales, which accounted for about 28 percent of the company's total net sales, decreased by 6.7 percent from 1991.

According to management, the overall decline in net sales for 1992 was principally due to a drop in the number of pairs sold worldwide resulting from decreased customer demand, and, to a lesser extent, to an average decrease of $1.52 in the selling price per pair. The decline was also due to the continuing effects of the recession and price reductions by the company's principal competitors, which resulted in increased competition at lower prices.

Another factor that contributed to the drop in the 1992 sales volume was delivery delays. As part of its restructuring program in 1992, the company changed the manufacturers from which it purchased products. These changes contributed to the company's difficulties in meeting its delivery deadlines on orders for its back-to-school season.

International Strategy

In recent years, sales of athletic and casual/lifestyle footwear in many international markets grew at a faster rate than in the United States. However, L. A. Gear's own sales in the international market declined from $158 million in 1990, to $127 million in 1991, and to $119 million in 1992.

In an effort to stem this decline in sales, L. A. Gear decided to increase its investment in the international market through joint ventures, acquisitions of distributors, and the creation of wholly owned foreign subsidiaries. By selling its products directly abroad (as opposed to the company's historical reliance on independent distributors in those markets), the company sought to increase sales by adopting more competitive marketing and distribution programs. In March 1992, the company established its first foreign subsidiary to conduct direct sales of its products in France.

L. A. Gear also began to focus on Asia for its potential as a retail sales market. "We see Asia as a huge market. You have basically got two billion pairs of feet out here," said Goldston. Consequently, the company began investigating promotional alliances and equity partnerships with Asian companies.

Distribution

L. A. Gear distributed its products out of a one million square foot warehouse/distribution center in Ontario, California. The company's products were sold in the U.S. to about 4,000 distributors that included department, sporting goods, athletic footwear and shoe stores, and wholesale distributors.

In recent years, L. A. Gear relied on extensive distribution through wholesale distributors who sold into deep-discount outlets. This policy tarnished the company's image and, as a result, several key retail accounts ceased or reduced their business with the company in 1991. To improve relations with full-margin retailers, the company began to distribute its products through specific channels, using what it called the "Gear Strategy Classification System." In line with this system, distribution channels were grouped in terms of "Image," "Mainstream," "Volume," and "Value." The Image channels were used to market the most technologically advanced and expensive high-performance products such as the L.A. Tech. The Mainstream and Volume channels were used to market "2nd Gear" and "1st Gear" products which incorporated fewer technological and aesthetic features. The Value channels were intended only for the distribution of inventory that could not be sold through the other channels. As part of the Value channels, the company planned to open a limited number of outlet stores.

Under Greenberg, the company maintained a next-day (at once) open stock system, where retailers could order products and have them shipped within 24 hours. This system forced inventory expenses to skyrocket. To mitigate this problem, the company also adopted a "futures" ordering system which provided discounts to retailers who ordered products four to six months in advance of shipment. It was hoped that the new program would enable the company to improve inventory management.

Internationally, L. A. Gear distributed its product in about 60 countries, primarily through agreements with independent distributors. The distribution agreements were intended to maintain a consistent product offering and brand image throughout the world. However, this arrangement afforded the company little or no control over the ultimate retail price of its footwear. It also restricted both profit and growth potential.

Research and Development

L. A. Gear maintained close ties with firms that conducted basic materials research. For example, L. A. Gear had an alliance with U.T.I. Chemicals Corporation of California. U.T.I. developed a new outsole material known as Z-thane which was a patented plastic compound that outlasted similar materials already in the marketplace.[22] L. A. Gear also applied older materials to their shoe lines, such as the innovative use of carbon fiber heel protectors in its performance shoes. With the Catapult, L. A. Gear hoped to challenge the high performance image of Nike and Reebok by luring the performance oriented buyer away from these market leaders.

L. A. Gear, however, lagged behind its competitors in product innovation. For example, the company introduced a "pump" style shoe almost two years after Nike and Reebok introduced their versions of this technology. Ironically, former CEO Robert Greenberg once boasted that the company spent a fraction of what its competition spent on research and development.[23] The company's "catch-up" R&D practices damaged its relations with retailers. For example, one shoe buyer to a large department store chain said: "We saw Nike and Reebok 1993 spring lines in May or June of 1992 and started committing for product in July. We didn't see L. A. Gear's product until mid-August."[24]

---

[22]L. A. Gear Inc., 1990 Annual Report (Los Angeles, CA: L. A. Gear Inc.), p. 8.

[23]"The Goldston Prescription," *Footwear News*, January 27, 1992, pp. 11–12.

[24]"L. A. Gear Still Looks Like an Also-Ran," *BusinessWeek*, December 21, 1992, p. 37.

Human Resources

L. A. Gear employs 753 full-time employees. In 1991, the company embarked on a restructuring program to reduce its workforce. By 1992, 613 employees ceased employment with the company, 152 of whom were associated with the company's discontinued apparel design and marketing operations. This represented a 45 percent reduction in staff and reduced the company's monthly payroll expense from $4.8 million in 1991 to $3.4 million in 1992. The company's employees were not covered by any collective bargaining agreement, but management considered the company's relations with its employees to be satisfactory. The company offered its employees 401(k) retirement savings programs and had an employee stock option plan (ESOP) in place. The ESOP program was instituted as an incentive program for employees and management.

Communication and Corporate Culture

As L. A. Gear grew bigger, it had to hire more employees to handle the new functions. In 1985, 50 people turned out the product; by 1992, that figure swelled to 1,200. As a result, the company which was characterized by an informal communication system and corporate culture, splintered into departmental fiefdoms scattered in several buildings. The new structure eroded the informal relationships that existed among L. A. Gear's management and employees. In the early days, for instance, Greenberg and Saemann worked just across the hall from each other, and their basic form of communication was to yell back and forth. Greenberg, who had a passion for tropical fish and kept a large tank in his office, would often march across the hall to see Saemann with a dripping net in one hand and a new sneaker design in the other.

The new management brought with it buttoned-down seriousness. Coats and ties were now a regular sight at L. A. Gear. Gone were the days when Greenberg would slip each of his employees $100 bills in pink envelopes whenever the company turned a profit. Now, employees carried around black coffee mugs that read ATTACK BUSINESS COSTS.

Legal Issues

In 1990 and 1991, three class action lawsuits were brought against L. A. Gear by shareholders. The shareholders claimed that the company violated the U.S. securities laws by inflating sales by tens of millions of dollars in 1990 when it counted as revenues merchandise that was being stored in L. A. Gear's warehouses and docks. In settling these lawsuits, the company recorded a $23 million pre-tax charge against its 1992 earnings.

In October 1992, L. A. Gear reached an agreement with the U.S. Attorney for the District of Massachusetts regarding the resolution of all customs claims arising from the importation of footwear from Taiwan in 1986 and 1987. Accordingly, L. A. Gear entered a guilty plea with respect to two counts of charging underpayment of duties on such shipments. A sentencing hearing was scheduled in 1993. In addition, the company paid $1.3 million in settlement of all potential civil claims arising from underpayment of duties on the 1986 and 1987 shipments from Taiwan.

In November 1992, L. A. Gear settled a patent infringement lawsuit brought against it by Reebok International Ltd, alleging that certain footwear products marketed by the company infringed on a patent issued to Reebok covering "inflatable bladder" shoe technology. L. A. Gear paid Reebok $1 million to settle the lawsuit. As part of the settlement, L. A. Gear entered into a license agreement under which Reebok granted the company a four-year non-exclusive worldwide license to manufacture, use, and sell footwear utilizing the "inflatable bladder." The license agreement, however, did not grant L. A. Gear access to Reebok's technology.

Another legal issue involved L. A. Gear's relationship with entertainer Michael Jackson. In September 1992, the company filed a complaint against Jackson alleging, among other things, fraud, breach of contract, and breach of good faith. The company's claims arose from contracts between the company and the defendant which granted the company the exclusive right to use Jackson's name and likeness in advertising and promoting the company's shoes and apparel as well as the right to develop and market a Michael Jackson athletic shoe line. Michael Jackson countered with a lawsuit, alleging fraud and breach of good faith on the part of the company. No settlement of this dispute has been reached yet.

Finance and Accounting

L. A. Gear's gross profit declined from $286 million in 1990, to $170 million in 1991, and to $109 million in 1992. While the company earned a net income of $31 million in 1990, it lost $66 million and $72 million in 1991 and 1992 respectively.

Because of an imbalance between inventory purchases and sales, L. A. Gear accumulated inventory greater than that necessary for its business. The introduction of the company's new product lines also resulted in a greater number of styles being discontinued than would otherwise have been the case. As a result, as part of an inventory reduction program, the company sold inventory at significant discounts resulting in lower margins. As was the custom in the footwear industry, substantial changes to the current product lines were made at least twice a year (i.e., for the spring and back-to-school seasons). As a result, a certain number of styles were usually discontinued.

In September 1991, Trefoil Capital Investors, L.P. invested $100 million in L. A. Gear in the form of a new issue of Series A Cumulative Convertible Preferred Stock, the net proceeds of which were used to repay indebtedness. In November 1992, the company had cash and cash equivalent balances of $84 million. In addition, the company expected to receive income tax refunds in 1993 of about $25 million.

Industry

The U.S. general footwear market was valued at about $12 billion. The athletic shoe market comprised about $6 billion. According to *Footwear News,* the domestic retail shoe market was expected to continue to grow at a rate of 5.5 percent at least until the year 2000.[25]

A 1987 Census of Manufacturers conducted by the U.S. Bureau of the Census revealed that over 100 companies participated in the men's and women's footwear industries.[26] During 1992 there were two dozen companies competing in the U.S. branded footwear market.[27] Domestically, the two largest athletic shoe makers were Nike and Reebok with a combined share of the market totaling 50 percent.[28] Although Nike and Reebok, as well as L. A. Gear, were headquartered in the U.S., the majority of their products was manufactured in Asian, European, and South American countries. A shoe that retailed for $100 cost the company between $20 and $25 if manufactured in foreign countries. Markups to the retailer and consumer were nearly 100 percent.

The footwear industry was not cyclical but did show some seasonality with back-to-school sales in August and September. Although profitability and sales for footwear

[25]"Footwear (Men's, Women's, Boys' and Girls')," *Fairchild Fact File,* 1990, pp. 5–9.

[26]Ibid., pp. 5–9.

[27]F. Meeds, "The Sneaker Game," *Forbes,* October 22, 1990, p. 114.

[28]J. Schlax, "The Shoe as Hero," *Forbes,* August 20, 1990, p. 77.

companies fluctuated, these fluctuations were attributable not to economic cycles but to changes in advertising expenditures, price, product quality, and overall market trends such as consumer preferences for fashion versus performance shoes.

Entry into the footwear industry was rather difficult. This was due to the fact that success in this industry depended to a great extent on heavy advertising, brand awareness, and intensive research and development. In the high-performance athletic shoe market, advertising was critical to footwear producers as a means of promoting new styles and creating brand awareness. Footwear companies spent vast sums to get popular athletes to endorse certain shoes. Nike and Reebok, for example, spent $200 million on advertising and promotion in 1992. This medium was cost prohibitive to smaller firms whose revenues were often too small to mount effective marketing campaigns. Another barrier to entry was brand awareness. Consumers purchased shoes based on either how well they perceived a brand to perform or on its fashion characteristics. On the average, when selecting a shoe, men tended to look at sole cushioning and how well an inner structure supported the foot—not fashion or style. Women's purchases, however, were determined more by the design or style of the shoe.[29]

An even greater entry barrier in the footwear industry was the excessive capital required for research and development. Nike, Reebok, and L. A. Gear allocated large budgets toward R&D. Each of the top three competitors had a highly advanced technology. Nike had its Air Jordan; Reebok had the Pump and Insta Pump; and L. A. Gear had its Catapult and Regulator shoes that incorporated high-tech carbon fiber soles.

In the highly competitive discount-athletic footwear market, barriers to entry were less formidable. Volume companies (mass producers) tended to carve out a niche through brands they licensed or created on their own. According to *Footwear News,* "the mass market usually followed where the better-grade merchandise had already beaten a path. Volume sources capitalized on the consumer appetite for branded-athletic footwear generated by the sophisticated marketing of companies such as Nike, Reebok, and L. A. Gear." According to the Sporting Goods Manufacturers Association, discount stores commanded $3.4 billion of the athletic shoe market.[30]

The U.S. footwear industry was maturing and analysts expected that consumers would purchase more non-athletic footwear than athletic footwear. With the domestic market maturing, many footwear companies began expanding overseas where the market was expected to grow at a rate of 23 percent a year in the next decade.[31]

The appeal of overseas markets to U.S. footwear companies stemmed not only from their sheer size but also from the cheap advertising common in such markets. Furthermore, a growing number of consumers overseas were becoming increasingly interested in U.S. sports generally and in basketball in particular. Actually, U.S. basketball was now a close second to soccer in worldwide popularity.[32] As a result, footwear companies discovered that their big endorsers, like Michael Jordan for Nike, translated well across borders.

Competitors

The athletic and athletic-style footwear industry was highly competitive in the United States and on a worldwide basis. L. A. Gear's competitors included both specialized athletic shoe companies and companies with diversified footwear product lines. The company's primary competitors in the domestic athletic and athletic-style markets were Nike

---

[29]K. Kerwin, "L. A. Gear Is Going Where the Boys Are," *BusinessWeek,* June 19, 1989, p. 54.

[30]Ibid., p. 52.

[31]M. Grimm, "To Munich and Back with Nike and L. A. Gear," *Adweek's Marketing Week,* February 18, 1991, p. 21.

[32]Ibid., p. 22.

and Reebok. These companies were more established than L. A. Gear and had greater financial, distribution, and marketing resources, as well as greater brand awareness, than the company. Internationally, L. A. Gear's major competitor was Adidas. Below is a brief profile of each of L. A. Gear's major competitors.

Nike

Nike was a publicly held sports and fitness company with a 26 percent share of the domestic market. Nike was the first company in the sports and fitness industry to exceed $2 billion in U.S. revenues and $3 billion worldwide. The company accomplished this in 1991. The diversity of Nike's product lines was far reaching. The company designed and marketed athletic footwear, apparel, and related items for competitive and recreational uses. To promote this breadth of product line, Nike was successful with advertisements that used high-profile athletes. Nike had an impressive stable of endorsers with Michael Jordan, Bo Jackson, David Robinson, and Andre Agassi. The success of these advertising campaigns enabled Nike to command a higher price for its shoes than its competitors.

To add to their image as one of the premier athletic footwear companies, Nike began to open a series of high-tech futuristic looking, company-owned outlets around the world called Nike Town. This outlet was a tribute to Nike's innovative flair and marketing genius.[33] The design concept incorporated sports, fitness, entertainment, history, and product innovation.

Nike spent more than its competitors on research and development. Nike learned the hard way to push its technology. In 1987, Nike was surpassed by rival Reebok as the number one domestic footwear company. At this time, Nike was concentrating on marketing its apparel and fashion shoes instead of promoting its air cushioning system. Within eighteen months of being surpassed by Reebok, Nike regained the number one spot by marketing its Nike Air Jordan shoes. Now, Nike's engineers began to call the shots—not its fashion designers.

Reebok

Reebok International Ltd. was a designer and marketer of active lifestyle and performance products, including footwear and apparel. Reebok held 24 percent of the domestic footwear market. According to industry sources, Reebok was the company best positioned to take advantage of the developing worldwide sneaker market.[34] Reebok announced in early 1992 that it had established a new worldwide sports marketing unit and that it would spend 25 percent more on advertising. Additionally, international sales soared 75 percent to $832.6 million from $475.2 in 1990. The sports marketing unit worked in conjunction with the fitness and casual units to deliver the best products and programs to consumers and retailers worldwide.

In 1988, Reebok acquired Avia and Rockport—two fast-growing companies. Paul Fireman, chairman and chief executive officer, believed that Avia and Rockport exemplified a "sense of aliveness" which was a characteristic of Reebok.[35] In 1991, Avia's sales rose 4.3 percent to $161 million, and Rockport's sales grew 8.5 percent to $251.3 million. Rockport produced products primarily for the walking shoe market while Avia competed directly with the Reebok brand for the athletic footwear market.

Reebok replaced its ineffective advertising with a cause-related campaign aimed at supporting philanthropic organizations while promoting its own products. In 1990, industry sources noted that Reebok was lacking a winning advertising campaign. In that year, two

---

[33]M. Wilson, "Nike Town Goes Back to the Future," *Chain Store Age Executive*, February, 1991, pp. 82–83.

[34]M. Tedeschi, "Reebok Splits U.S. Int'l Setups," *Footwear News*, November 26, 1990, p. 12.

[35]S. Gannes, "America's Fastest-Growing Companies," *Fortune*, May 23, 1988, p. 37.

consecutive advertising campaigns flopped. In 1991 and 1992, Reebok reversed this trend with its cause-related advertising. Practitioners maintained that cause-related advertising could be risky, but when handled carefully, could supply the best of all promotional worlds: higher visibility, a unique image niche resulting from association with worthy projects, and stronger ties to the community.[36] As part of its cause-related marketing, Reebok gave financial support to Amnesty International's Human Rights Now tour. Angel Martinez, vice president of business development at Reebok's Los Angeles office, said that "the tour was an extension of our value system as a company. We believe in freedom of expression and wanted to do something of importance, beyond selling sneakers."[37] Reebok's President, Joseph LaBonte, added: "We both believe very strongly in the freedom to do what you want."

To remain competitive with Nike, Reebok also planned to contract endorsements with high-profile athletes. Even though the Insta-Pump would not be available to consumers until January 1993, Reebok hoped to get a lot of promotional mileage by putting the shoes on several Olympic track-and-field stars at the 1992 summer games in Barcelona, Spain.

Adidas and Puma

A decade ago, most athletic shoes sold in Europe were made by Adidas or its smaller rival, Puma. For years, the two German companies controlled about 75 percent of Europe's athletic shoe and apparel market, and they were also strong in the U.S. Things changed, however. Now, Nike and Reebok, and to a lesser degree L. A. Gear, made spectacular inroads in Europe. Although Adidas continued to be No. 1 with $1.6 billion in revenues, Nike ranked second with $500 million and Reebok ranked third with $380 million. L. A. Gear's sales were less than $119 million.

Both Nike and Reebok profited from long-term problems at Adidas and Puma. In the past five years, both German companies reported steady streams of losses because of unfocused marketing, high costs, and a glut of products. At Adidas, the confusion was acute: In footwear alone, it had 1,200 different variations and styles. "We had everything," said Michel Perrauding, Adidas' manager for logistics, "even shoes for left-handed bowlers."

Adidas' poorly coordinated marketing in Europe angered many distributors who started to desert to Nike and Reebok. And in the United States where Adidas was once No. 1 in athletic shoes, chronic delivery problems and a failure to spot the trend to more comfortable shoes led to huge losses and a dramatic drop in market share.

Nike and Reebok, however, might have to confront the possibility that Adidas and Puma might fight back. A Swedish company took full control of Puma and planned to pump cash into it. At Adidas, a new French owner slashed its product range in shoes and apparel to several hundred from several thousand, retired hundreds of employees, and started a network of more efficient purchasing and production facilities in Asia. Adidas launched a new line, Equipment, featuring no-frills shoes for such sports as soccer, tennis, and track. There was also a new Adidas series of hiking and outdoors shoes. Nevertheless, Adidas and Puma lacked the deep pockets of Nike and Reebok to enable them to spend as much on advertising as the two U.S. companies.

Customers

L. A. Gear sold to retail stores, specialty shoe stores, and sporting goods stores but their ultimate customer was the individual retail consumer. L. A. Gear's customers historically were young fashion minded girls. Under Greenberg, the company promoted the young

---

[36]A. Shell, "Cause-Related Marketing: Big Risks, Big Potential," *Public Relations Journal,* July, 1989, pp. 8, 13.

[37]Ibid., p. 8.

Southern-California lifestyle. Its advertisements were of young blondes on the beach in stylish L. A. Gear shoes. Under the new management, the company repositioned itself. Former CEO Robert Greenberg said that they knew that in order to grow they would eventually have to enter the men's market and that meant more technically-oriented footwear.[38] Fashion athletics was now only a part of L. A. Gear.

Government Regulations

In 1990, the U.S. Congress passed the Textile, Apparel, and Footwear Trade Act (the "Textile Act") which would have set highly restrictive global quotas on imported textile, apparel, and footwear products. This legislation was vetoed by President Bush, and the veto was sustained by the House of Representatives.

There was a possibility that a similar legislation would be proposed in the future. If such a legislation was enacted into law, L. A. Gear could face restrictions on its ability to import into the U.S. its footwear products manufactured abroad.

In 1992, the U.S. placed L. A. Gear's suppliers in Taiwan, China, Indonesia, and South Korea on a "priority watch list" for engaging in unfair trade practices. If such countries were proved to be engaged in unfair trade practices, the U.S. might retaliate against them, which could result in increases in the cost, or reductions in the supply, of footwear generally and L. A. Gear's footwear in particular.

Demographics

The U.S. population, which totaled 250 million in 1990, was expected to reach 283 million by the year 2010. That was an increase of about 13 percent. Perhaps more significant to the footwear industry was the rise in the size of the baby boom generation, born between 1946 and 1964. A prime target of footwear companies, this segment, which comprised 18 percent of the population in 1990, was expected to grow by about 9 percent by the year 2010.

Culture

Lifestyle changes in the United States, as well as in many other countries, were propitious for footwear producers. An increasing segment of the population was becoming more health conscious, engaging in athletic activities such as jogging and walking. Because of the increasing popularity of walking, the walking-shoes market was expected to be the largest growth segment of the footwear industry. According to industry sources, 75 percent of the walking-shoes market consisted of women in their mid-30s and up.[39]

Economy

In 1991 and 1992, the Federal Reserve Board laid the groundwork for an economic recovery by keeping prime interest rates low and gradually expanding the money supply. The Fed was able, at the same time, to keep inflation at less than 4 percent. Depressed consumer confidence in economic recovery, however, continued to be a major obstacle to increased consumer and business spending. The slow start of President Clinton's economic program served only to slow a long-awaited growth in the nation's economy.

[38]M. Rottman, "L. A. Gear Catapults into Technology," *Footwear News,* February 18, 1991, pp. 12, 14.
[39]D. McKay, "Walk This Way," *Footwear News,* September 9, 1991, pp. 14–15.

Technology

Counterfeiting is the perennial enemy of brand-name producers in Asia. Recognizing the danger to his company's technology, Goldston, L. A. Gear's president said, "The major focus of our agreements with new manufacturers is on integrity. Our technology innovation will be protected."[40] However, an L. A. Gear executive said the means available to foreign shoe manufacturers for protecting patents were limited. As a result, athletic-shoe makers could find their most nagging competitors were not each other but the companies who filled their orders. Such companies as L. A. Gear "tend to stumble when faced with competition, and this time it will come from say, . . . a factory in Indonesia that has acquired the technology to make a good jogging shoe."[41]

Politics

With political changes occurring in Eastern Europe and the Soviet Union, markets that were previously closed to Western companies were now fairly wide open.

The enactment of NAFTA (North American Free Trade Agreement) among the U.S., Canada, and Mexico, was likely to strengthen U.S. exports. According to estimates made by the U.S. Trade Representative, the tariff reductions alone, if undertaken by all countries, could raise U.S. real GNP by 3 percent by the year 2000.[42]

Conclusion

As they implement their turnaround strategy, Gold and Goldston have their work cut out for them. What should they do next? And will their strategic moves be sufficient to restore L. A. Gear to its heyday or will they cause the company to disappear?

---

[40]"L. A. Gear President Says Shoe Maker Will Recover and Will Focus on Asia," *The Wall Street Journal*, October 16, 1992, p. B7.

[41]Ibid.

[42]OECD Economic Survey, United States, 1990/1991, pp. 60–65.

APPENDIX A   L. A. Gear, Inc. Consolidated Balance Sheet, as of November 30 (in thousands)

Source: L. A. Gear, 1992 Annual Report, p. 17.

	1992	1991
Assets		
Current assets:		
Cash and cash equivalents	$ 55,027	$ 1,422
Collateralized cash	28,955	—
Accounts receivable, net	56,369	111,470
Inventories	61,923	141,115
Prepaid expenses and other current assets	2,557	8,506
Refundable income taxes	25,269	22,795
Deferred income taxes	—	11,763
Total current assets	230,100	297,071
Property and equipment, net	17,667	26,869
Other assets	1,735	1,631
Total assets	$249,502	$325,571
Liabilities, Mandatorily Redeemable Preferred Stock and Shareholders' Equity		
Current liabilities:		
Borrowing under line of credit	$ —	$ 20,000
Accounts payable and accrued liabilities	49,753	55,856
Dividends payable on mandatorily redeemable preferred stock	7,746	—
Costs related to discontinued operations	4,552	18,000
Total current liabilities	62,051	93,856
Mandatorily redeemable preferred stock:		
7.5% Series A Cumulative Convertible Preferred Stock, $100 stated value; 1,000,000 shares authorized, issued and outstanding; redemption value of $100 per share	100,000	100,000
Shareholders' equity:		
Common stock, no par value; 80,000,000 shares authorized; 22,898,182 shares issued and outstanding at November 30, 1992 (19,542,513 shares issued and outstanding at November 30, 1991)	127,714	92,331
Preferred stock, no stated value; 9,000,000 shares authorized; no shares issued	—	—
Retained earnings (accumulated deficit)	(40,263)	39,384
Total shareholders' equity	87,451	131,715
Commitments and contingencies	—	—
	$249,502	$325,571

APPENDIX B L. A. Gear, Inc. Consolidated Statements of Cash Flows, as of November 30 (in thousands)

Source: L. A. Gear, 1992 Annual Report, p. 17.

	1992	1991	1990
Operating activities:			
Net income (loss)	$(71,901)	$(66,200)	$31,338
Adjustment to reconcile net income (loss) to net cash provided by (used in) operating activities: Shareholders' litigation settlements	17,075	—	—
Depreciation and amortization	7,107	7,182	3,394
Provision for loss on discontinued operations	—	18,000	—
Loss on sale or abandonment of property and equipment	1,871	4,146	—
Issuance of shares to employee stock savings plan	233	382	—
(Increase) decrease in: Accounts receivable, net	55,101	44,431	(52,969)
Inventories	79,192	19,553	(21,152)
Prepaids and other assets	6,343	1,565	(998)
Refundable and deferred income taxes	8,791	(26,174)	(3,795)
Increase (decrease) in:			
Accounts payable and accrued liabilities	(6,103)	(8,222)	3,143
Costs related to discontinued operations	(8,343)	—	—
Net cash provided by (used in) operating activities	89,366	(5,337)	(41,039)
Investing activities-capital expenditures	(4,881)	(14,188)	(18,939)
Financing activities:			
Net proceeds from issuance of mandatorily redeemable preferred stock	—	92,511	—
Payment of dividends on mandatorily redeemable preferred stock	—	(1,265)	—
Exercise of stock options and warrants	1,986	414	908
Tax benefits arising from the disposition/exercise of incentive stock options	2,089	356	5,408
Proceeds from issuance of common stock	14,000	—	—
Net borrowing (repayment) under line of credit agreement	(20,000)	(74,000)	56,600
Net cash provided by (used in) financing activities	(1,925)	17,656	62,916
Net increase (decrease) in cash and cash equivalents	82,560	(1,869)	2,938
Cash at beginning of year	1,422	3,291	353
Cash and cash equivalents at end of year, including collateralized cash	$83,982	$ 1,422	$ 3,291

6

Kikkoman Corporation in the Mid-1990s: Market Maturity, Diversification, and Globalization

Norihito Tanaka *Kanagawa University*

Marilyn L. Taylor *University of Missouri at Kansas City*

Joyce A. Claterbos *University of Kansas*

In early 1996 Mr. Yuzaburo Mogi, president of Kikkoman Corporation, faced a number of challenges. Analysts indicated concern with Kikkoman's slow sales growth and noted that the company's stock had underperformed on the Nikkei Exchange in relation to the market and to its peers for several years. Throughout the world ongoing changes in taste preferences and dietary needs presented threats to the company's traditional food lines. The company marketed its branded products in 94 countries and had to consider which products and

Reprinted by permission from the Case Research Journal, volume 21, issue 3. Copyright 2001 by Norihito Tanaka, Marilyn Taylor, Joyce A. Claterbos, and the North American Case Research Association. All rights reserved.

The authors express deep appreciation to Kikkoman Corporation, which provided encouragement to this study, including access to the U.S. manufacturing and marketing facilities in addition to time in the corporate offices in Japan. The authors also gratefully acknowledge the support for this study provided by the Japanese Department of Education and the Institute for Training and Development in Tokyo. Quotes and data in this case study were drawn from a variety of personal interviews in the United States and Japan, company documents, and public sources. Documents and public sources appear in the list of references at the conclusion of the case.

markets to emphasize as well as which new markets to enter. As Mr. Mogi described the company's focus, ". . . we are now concentrating on further enhancing our ability to serve consumers in Japan and overseas. The basic keynotes of this effort are expansion of soy sauce markets, diversification and globalization."

In Japan, Kikkoman had long dominated the soy sauce market, and its mid-1990s market share position of 27 percent was well beyond the 10 percent of its next closest competitor. However, its share of the soy sauce market had continued to decline from its high of 33 percent in 1983, falling from 28 percent in 1993 to 27.2 percent in 1994. Further, although the company's worldwide sales had increased slightly overall from 1994 to 1995, sales of soy sauce in Japan had decreased over 1 percent during that period.

The U.S. market had provided significant opportunity in the post–World War II period. However, the company's U.S. market share for soy and other company products was essentially flat. In addition, three competitors had built plants in the United States beginning in the late 1980s. Mr. Mogi was aware that Kikkoman's choices in the U.S. market would provide an important model for addressing higher income mature markets.

With a market capitalization of nearly ¥160 billion,[1] Kikkoman Corporation was the world's largest soy sauce producer, Japan's nineteenth largest food company, and also Japan's leading soy sauce manufacturer. The company was the oldest continuous enterprise among the 200 largest industrials in Japan. The company began brewing shoyu, or naturally fermented soy sauce, in the seventeenth century and had dominated the Japanese soy industry for at least a century. The company held 50 percent of the U.S. soy sauce market and 30 percent of the world market. Kikkoman had 13 manufacturing facilities in Japan and one each in the United States, Singapore, and Taiwan. The company was one of the few traditional manufacturers to successfully establish a presence worldwide. (Exhibits 1 and 2 have the locations of and information on the company's principal subsidiaries. Exhibits 3 and 4 list the consolidated financial statements.)

Kikkoman in Japan

The Beginnings in Noda

In 1615, the widow of a slain samurai warrior fled 300 miles from Osaka to the village of Noda near Edo (now called Tokyo). With her five children the widow Mogi embarked upon rice farming and subsequently began brewing shoyu, or soy sauce. The quality of the Mogi family's shoyu was exceptional almost from its beginnings. At the time, households produced shoyu for their own use, or local farmers made and sold excess shoyu as a side enterprise to farming. As more people moved to the urban areas in the seventeenth and eighteenth centuries, there was increased demand for non-home production. Households developed preferences for the product of a particular brewer. (See Appendix A: The Making of Soy Sauce.)

Shoyu had come to Japan with the arrival of Buddhism in the sixth century. The teachings of Buddhism prohibited eating meat and fish. Residents of the Japanese islands turned from meat-based to vegetable-based flavorings. One of the favorites became a flavorful seasoning made from fermented soy beans. A Japanese Zen Buddist priest who had studied in China brought the recipe to Japan. The Japanese discovered that adding wheat gave the sauce a richer, more mellow flavor.

---

[1] In early 1996, the exchange rate was about 95 yen per U.S. dollar. Thus, in U.S. dollars, Kikkoman's market value was about $1.7 billion. Sales at year end 1995 for the consolidated company were 203 billion yen, or slightly less than $2 billion (See Exhibits 2 and 3 for consolidated financial data and Exhibits 8, 9, and 11 for parent company and domestic versus non-Japan revenues plus other selected financial information.)

EXHIBIT 1 **Locations of Principal Subsidiaries**

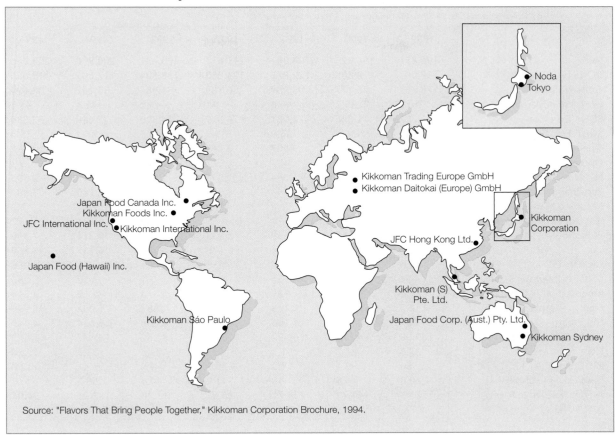

Source: "Flavors That Bring People Together," Kikkoman Corporation Brochure, 1994.

EXHIBIT 2 **Consolidated Subsidiaries as of FY 1995**

Source: Table 4: Consolidated Subsidiaries, UBS Securities Limited, May 28, 1996, as reported by *Investext*.

Subsidiary	Country	Paid-In Capital ((Y)m/$m)	Kikkoman Equity (%)
Japan Del Monte	Japan	900	99.7
Mann's Wine	Japan	900	100
Pacific Trading	Japan	72	66.7
Morishin	Japan	30	66.7
Kikkoman Foods, Inc.	US	US$6	100
Kikkoman International	US	US$3.5	92.6
JFC International	US	US$1.2	98
Kikkoman Trading Europe	Germany	DM1.5	75
Kikkoman Pte	Singapore	S$7.5	100
Kikkoman Trading Pte	Singapore	S$.4	100
Tokyo Food Processing	US	US$.02	100
Hapi Products	US	US$.05	100
Rex Pacific	US	US$1.5	100

EXHIBIT 3   Consolidated Profit and Loss Statement ((Y) m)

Sources: Table 9: UBS Securities Limited, May 28, 1996; *The World Almanac*, 1998 (original source: IMF).

	1989	1990	1991	1992	1993	1994	1995
Sales	195,851	196,925	206,861	211,671	203,491	200,976	203,286
COGS	117,062	118,808	122,872	124,882	118,504	117,809	119,656
Gross Profit	78,789	78,117	83,989	86,789	84,987	83,167	83,629
Gross Profit Margin (%)	40.2	39.7	40.6	41	41.8	41.4	41.1
SG&A Expenses	71,227	71,876	74,181	76,019	74,320	72,689	72,836
SG&A Exp. (%)	36.4	36.5	35.9	35.9	36.5	36.2	35.8
Operating Profit	7,562	6,240	9,807	10,769	10,666	10,477	10,792
Operating Margin (%)	3.9	3.2	4.7	5.1	5.2	5.2	5.3
Net Non-Op. Income	−572	−1,042	−1,564	−1,895	−2,282	−2,197	−2,305
Recurring Profit	6,990	5,197	8,243	8,873	8,384	8,280	8,487
Recurring Margin (%)	3.6	2.6	4	4.2	4.1	4.1	4.2
Net Extraordinary Income	181	1,165	1,317	59	108	1,434	−1,177
Pretax Profit	7,170	6,363	9,559	8,932	8,493	9,714	7,310
Tax	3,327	3,299	4,726	5,178	4,597	4,157	3,569
Tax Rate (%)	46.4	50.7	49.4	58	54.1	42.8	48.8
Minority Interest	56	78	37	34	1	−52	46
Amortization of Consol. Dif.	0	0	−35	1	5	0	−314
Equity in Earnings	1,097	1,464	1,188	1,245	887	1,002	996
Net Profit	4,697	4,694	6,166	4,928	4,688	6,614	4,447
Shares Outstanding (m)	169.08	169.71	169.97	178.61	187.62	187.77	197.2
EPS	27.8	27.7	31.3	25	23.8	33.5	22.6
EPS Change (%_)	80	−0.4	13.3	−20.2	−4.9	41	−32.8
Cash Flow per Share	20.8	46.5	48	41.9	44.4	58.5	46.8
Average Exchange Rate (yen/USD)	137.96	144.79	134.71	126.65	111.20	102.21	94.06

Over the eighteenth century, Noda became a major center for shoyu manufacturing in Japan. Shoyu's major ingredients, soybeans and wheat, grew readily in the rich agricultural Kanto plain that surrounded Noda. The trip to the major market of Edo took only one day on the Edo River. The various shoyu-producing families in the Noda area actively shared their knowledge of fermentation. The Mogi family and another Noda area family, the Takanashi family, were especially active in the industry. By the late eighteenth century, the two families had become interrelated through marriage. Their various enterprises made considerable investment in breweries, and family members began ancillary enterprises such as grain brokering, keg manufacture, and transportation.

Japan's Shoyu Distribution System and Industry Structure

Japan's neophyte and fragmented shoyu industry had two distribution systems during this time. In the rural areas the shoyu breweries sold their products directly to households. In the cities, urban wholesalers distributed shoyu, vinegar, and sake. The wholesalers purchased bulk shoyu and established their own brands. The wholesalers controlled pricing, inventory, distribution, and marketing knowledge. They would distribute branded shoyu only on consignment. During the 1800s, the wholesalers formed alliances that gave them near monopolistic power over the Tokyo market. As the shoyu manufacturers became more efficient, they found it impossible to lower prices or make other adjustments to increase their market share.

The Mogi and Takanashi families took several steps to counteract the wholesalers' dominance. The Takanashi family had diversified into wholesaling some years prior and were

EXHIBIT 4 **Consolidated Balance Sheet ((Y) m)**

Source: Nikkei Needs as reported in Table 12: Consolidated Balance Sheet, UBS Securities Limited, May 28, 1996.

	1990	1991	1992	1993	1994	1995
Current Assets	81,611	88,092	89,705	103,152	105,220	107,339
Cash and Deposits	13,254	17,570	18,261	28,826	36,381	37,366
Accounts Receivable	43,579	44,661	44,503	46,009	44,246	44,439
Securities	315	1,012	1,316	3,310	3,306	3,307
Inventories	21,769	21,300	22,484	21,469	18,579	19,258
Fixed Assets	94,631	97,999	105,231	113,940	112,183	119,411
Tangible Assets	52,087	53,254	59,276	67,649	65,795	72,684
Land	11,768	12,011	11,910	15,156	15,613	11,540
Investments	26,371	29,597	31,771	33,051	34,083	35,006
Total Assets	177,583	187,316	195,955	218,561	218,805	228,308
Liabilities and Owner's Equity						
Current Liabilities	48,040	52,626	54,014	50,272	46,663	63,400
Short-Term Borrowings	18,846	18,908	19,046	17,462	14,838	15,741
Fixed Liabilities	58,374	58,850	62,351	85,532	85,143	71,710
Long-Term Borrowings	4,457	4,549	4,723	3,274	3,091	2,312
Bonds and CBs*	26,565	26,346	26,231	46,170	44,776	29,921
Minority Interest	1,223	1,166	1,157	1,103	1,024	427
Total Liabilities	107,638	112,643	117,522	136,909	132,832	135,538
Shareholders' Equity	69,945	74,673	78,434	81,651	85,973	92,770
Total Liabilities and Equity	177,583	187,316	195,955	218,561	218,805	228,308

*There were two CBs issued Jan. 90 exercisable at (Y) 1,522. The other two were issued July 93 and were exercisable at (Y) 969. With the share price at approximately (Y) 100, the total dilution factor was about 18 percent, with 80 percent of that dependent on the two CBs exercisable at (Y) 969. Of 228 ((Y) m) in 1995, about 170 belonged to the parent (i.e., Japan corporation) company.

part of the wholesalers' alliance. One Mogi family intermarried with a wholesaler's family—a traditional strategy in Japan for cementing strategic alliances. In addition, the Mogi and Takanashi families worked to increase brand recognition and dominance. In 1838, Mogi Saheiji applied for and received the shogunate's recognition of his family's premier brand, named Kikkoman. He aggressively promoted the brand by sponsoring professional storytellers and sumo wrestlers, embossing paper lanterns and umbrellas with the Kikkoman trademark, and putting ornate gold labels from Paris on his Kikkoman shoyu kegs. In the latter part of the nineteenth century, Kikkoman shoyu won recognition in several world's fairs.

In reaction to depressed market prices and fluctuating costs of inputs, a number of the Noda shoyu brewers formed the Noda Shoyu Brewers' Association in 1887. The association purchased raw materials, standardized wages, and regulated output quality. The members' combined efforts resulted in the largest market share at the time, 5 to 10 percent of the Tokyo market, and widespread recognition of the high quality of Noda shoyu.

Noda brewers, and especially the Mogi and Takanashi families, began research and development activities early. The Japanese government encouraged the Noda shoyu brewers to conduct research in the recovery and processing of the two by-products of shoyu manufacture, shoyu oil and shoyu cake. In the early 1900s, the association began to fund a joint research and development laboratory.

The Shoyu Industry in the Twentieth Century

In 1910, there were still 14,000 known makers of shoyu in Japan. However, a number of changes led to consolidation. Manufacturing shifted from a small-batch, brewmaster-controlled production process to a large-batch, technology-controlled process. Mogi families in Noda invested in modernized plants, and a fifth-grade Japanese geography reader featured a state-of-the-art Kikkoman facility. A national market also developed, thanks to the development of a railway system throughout most of the country. In addition, consumer tastes shifted to the Tokyo-style shoyu produced by eastern manufacturers such as the Noda Shoyu Brewers' Association.

Consumers also began to purchase shoyu in smaller glass bottles rather than in the traditional large wooden barrels that sometimes leaked and were expensive to build and difficult to store. Raw materials also became more expensive as the brewers increasingly sought higher quality imported soybeans (from Manchuria, China, and Korea) and salt (from England, Germany, and China). The association members controlled costs by purchasing in bulk and demanding high-quality materials from suppliers.

The Noda Shoyu Company: 1918–1945—A Family Zaibatsu[2]

In 1918, seven Mogi families and a related Takanashi family combined their various enterprises into a joint stock holding company called the Noda Shoyu Company. The merger was in reaction to the market upheaval caused by World War I. The new company was a small zaibatsu with nearly a dozen companies in manufacturing fermented grain-based products, transportation, and finance. Unlike early shoyu manufacturing where ownership, management, and operations were clearly separated, the Mogi and Takanashi families owned, managed, and operated their firm. Initially the family produced 34 different brands of shoyu at various price points. The Kikkoman brand had a history of heavy promotion for over 40 years, greater Tokyo market share, and a higher margin than the company's other brands. The Kikkoman brand became the company's flagship brand. The new corporation continued its long-standing emphasis on research and development and aggressively pursued new manufacturing processes, increased integration, and acquired other shoyu companies.

After the Mogi Takanashi coalition, the company aggressively pursued a strong nationwide sole agent system and direct distribution. The combined company also continued Kikkoman's well-known advertising activities. Kikkoman had carried out the first newspaper advertising in 1878. In 1922, the company carried out the firm's first advertising on the movie screen.

During the 1920s, the company aggressively modernized with machines such as hydraulic presses, boilers, conveyors, and elevators. The company's modernization efforts were emulated by competitors, and the results were increased supply and heightened industry competition. The changes brought about by increased automation led to severe labor unrest. One particularly long strike against the Kikkoman company in the late 1920s almost destroyed the participating labor union. After the strike ended, Kikkoman rehired about a third of the striking employees. The company centralized and reorganized the work processes to accommodate improved technology, restructured work practices, and established methods to monitor and reward workers for their performance. However, the company also established efforts to improve the identity of the workers with the company. Internal communications carried the message that all employees were members of one family, or ikka, united in a common purpose, i.e., the production of shoyu. The Noda Shoyu Company was also heavily involved in the city of Noda and supported many of its cultural and charitable activities as well as the local railroad, bank, town hall, cultural center, library, fire station, elementary school, hospital, recreation facilities and association, and much of the city's water system.

---

[2]*Zaibatsu:* Industrial and financial combines dissolved by occupation fiat after World War II, but which have reemerged as somewhat weaker entities. Some of these *zaibatsu* have developed into large conglomerates such as Mitsubishi. However, they should be distinguished from *keiretsu* (of which Mitsubishi is also one of the largest). *Keiretsu* are informal enterprise group-based associations of banks, industrials, and so forth.

Kikkoman's International Activities

Kikkoman's initial export activities began in the late seventeenth century with Dutch and Chinese traders. The Dutch began to export shoyu to Holland and the rest of Europe, while the Chinese served the southeast Asian markets. The shoyu brewers relied on agents for these early export transactions. During the nineteenth century, one Mogi patriarch opened a factory in Inchon, Korea. Demand for the increasing export, marketing, and direct investment continued to come primarily from Japanese and other peoples living abroad whose traditional cuisines called for shoyu. In 1910, the Noda city brewers' international activities were recognized when the Japanese government selected Noda shoyu to appear in a public relations publication introducing Japan's industries overseas.

Noda Shoyu Company continued to expand internationally between World War I and World War II. Acquisition of raw materials from abroad continued. The company added a manufacturing facility for shoyu and miso in Manchuria and two shoyu factories in North America. Other facilities in Japan were expanded or updated to support increasing international sales.

The company established sales offices in China and Korea to market shoyu, miso, and sake. By the late 1930s, the company exported 10 percent of its output, about half to the Asian region—especially Korea, China, and Indonesia—and half to Hawaii and California. Almost all of the exports were the Kikkoman brand and were sold through food import/ export firms to the company's traditional customers.

Post–World War II Kikkoman in Japan

At the end of World War II, Kikkoman operated only in Japan. Activities elsewhere had been closed. To meet the need for capital, Kikkoman issued publicly-traded stock in 1946, reducing family ownership markedly. (Exhibit 5 shows the changes in ownership from 1917 to 1993.) The post–World War II period brought a number of social changes to Japanese society. Japanese families began the change to nuclear rather than extended-family formation. Food tastes changed leading, among other trends, to a decline in per capita consumption of shoyu. Compared with other industries, demand for soy sauce grew very slowly. In 1942, demand for soy sauce in Japan was 1.7 times greater than in 1918. Demand in the 1960s was expected to be 2.2 times greater than that in 1918. However, modernization led to increased output.

Kikkoman had received considerable recognition for its advertising efforts prior to World War II. After the war, the company began to market even more aggressively in Japan. These efforts included establishing the company's strong nationwide distribution system throughout Japan; mounting aggressive activities in marketing research, advertising, and consumer education; and changing to a new and more Western image. As a result

EXHIBIT 5   Noda Shoyu Company and Kikkoman Corporation Ownership

Sources: W. Mark Fruin, *Kikkoman—Company, Clan, and Community* (Cambridge, MA, Harvard, University Press, 1983), pp. 98, 121, 249, *Japan Company Handbook*, Toyo Keizai, Inc., 1993, p. 207.

Shareholder Name	Holdings (% of total shares or assets)			
	1917	1925	1955	1993
Mogi-Takanashi-Horikiri Brewing Families	100%[a]	34.6%	15.0%[b]	2.3%
Senshusha Holding Company		62.0%	3.1%	3.4%
Insurance and Banking Companies			9.9%[c]	20.5%[c]
All Others		3.6%	71.1%	73.6%

[a]Eight holdings ranging from 1.4 percent to 29.3 percent.
[b]Five holdings ranging from 1.5 percent to 4.4 percent.
[c]In 1955 and 1993, including Meiji Mutual Insurance Co, Mitsubishi Trust Bank; in 1955, including Kofukan Foundation and Noda Institute of Industrial Science; in 1993, including Nitsuit Trust Bank, Nippon Life Insurance, Sumitomo Trust, and Yasuda Trust.

EXHIBIT 6
National Output and Company Market Share of Shoyu (in kiloliters)[a]

Source: W. Mark Fruin, *Kikkoman—Company, Clan, and Community* (Cambridge, MA, Harvard University Press, 1983), pp. 40–41.

Year	National Output (Japan)	Noda Shoyu Share
1893	230,360	3.5%
1903	317,500	4.5%
1913	430,435	6.1%
1923	624,764	5.1%
1933	576,026	10.1%
1943	680,955	12.0%
1953	822,179	14.1%
1963	1,051,730	21.4%
1973	1,277,887	31.4%
1983	n.a.	33.0%
1993	n.a.	28.0%[c]
1994	1,323,529[b]	27.2%[c]

[a]1 kiloliter = 264 gallons.
[b]Derived from Kikkoman's production of 360,000 kl and its 27.2 percent market share. Residents of Japan consumed about 2.6 gallons of soy sauce per capita yearly. In contrast, U.S. citizens consumed about 10 tablespoons.
[c]As reported by UBS Securities Limited, May 28, 1996 in *Investext*. This source also reported that demand for soy sauce was flat in Japan and production between 1984 and 1994 had declined about 5.1 percent.

of Kikkoman's marketing efforts, the company's market share rose sharply. (Exhibit 6 shows the national output of shoyu and the company's market share from 1893 to 1994.) By 1964 the company officially changed its name to Kikkoman Shoyu and in 1980 became Kikkoman Corporation. The word *Kikkoman* is a combination of "kikko" (the shell of a tortoise) and "man" (10,000). It was taken from an old Japanese saying, "A crane lives a thousand years and a tortoise 10,000 years." (Implying , in other words, "May you live as long!") In essence, the Kikkoman brand connotes a long-lasting living thing. Kikkoman had become well-known for its advertising skill in Japan and had found that the word *Kikkoman* was easy for Americans to pronounce.

The company also diversified its product line using its expertise in shoyu manufacture, fermentation, brewing, and foods marketing. This diversification included a 1963 venture to market Del Monte products in Japan. In 1990, the company bought the Del Monte assets and marketing rights for the Del Monte brand name in the Asia–Pacific region. (Exhibit 7 shows Kikkoman Corporation's product lists as of 1949, 1981, and 1993.) Kikkoman's R&D expertise led to activities in biotechnology and products such as enzymes, diagnostic reagents, and other biologically-active substances used to test for microorganisms in water samples in hospitals, food processing factories, and semiconductor plants. The company also developed a number of patents at home and overseas. The company became involved in both the import and export of wines. It also undertook activities in food processing machinery. In spite of the diversification, Kikkoman's domestic sales were still about 55 percent soy-sauce related.

In the 1990s, soy sauce continued as a perennial favorite in Japan's cuisine, although demand was essentially flat. Among the remaining 3,000 shoyu companies in Japan, Kikkoman produced 360,000 kl in Japan, or about 27 percent of the country's output. (Exhibit 6.) The company faced price pressures especially on its base product of soy sauce, mainly due to the competitive pressures at the retail level in Japan and the aggressive introduction of private brands. Sales in the Del Monte line also decreased in the early 1990s. To improve performance, Kikkoman began to reduce its product line from a high of 5,000 items to an expected eventual 2,500. One bright spot was the growth in wines and spirits. In addition, Kikkoman also introduced successful new soy-sauce related products in 1993, 1994, and 1995 in the form of two soup stocks and Steak Soy Sauce. Profit increases in the early 1990s came primarily from higher priced luxury products. (Exhibits 8 and 9 display the parent company financial statements.) The company recognized that continuing success in

EXHIBIT 7   Kikkoman Corporation Products and Product Lines

Sources: W. Mark Fruin, *Kikkoman—Company, Clan, and Community* (Cambridge, MA, Harvard University Press, 1983), pp. 275–276; "Flavors That Bring People Together," Kikkoman Corporation Brochure, 1994.

1949	1981	1994
Kikkoman Brand soy sauce, sauce, memmi and tsuyu (soup bases)	**Kikkoman Brand** soy sauce, mild soy sauce (lower salt, 8%), light color soy sauce (usu-kuchi), teriyaki barbecue marinade and sauce, Worcestershire sauce, tonkatsu sauce, memmi and tsuyu (soup bases), sukiyaki sauce, instant soy soup mix, instant osumono (clear broth soup mix)	**Kikkoman Brand** soy sauce, mild soy sauce (lower salt, 8%), light color soy sauce (usu-kuchi), teriyaki sauce, Worcestershire sauce, tonkatsu sauce, memmi (soup base), sukiyaki sauce, sashimi soy sauce, lemon flavored soy sauce, mirin (sweet rice wine), Aji-Mirin, plum wine, instant miso (soybean paste) soups, egg flower soup mixes, rice crackers, tofu, neo-genmai (puffed brown rice), genmai soups, oolong tea, tsuyudakono (soup base), ponzu soy sauce, soy sauce dressing, oyster sauce, bonito stock
Manjo Brand mirin (sweet rice wine), sake, shochu, whiskey	**Manjo Brand** mirin (sweet rice wine), shochu, plum wine	**Manjo Brand** triangle, komaki
	Yomonoharu Brand sake	**Yomonoharu Brand**
	Del Monte Brand tomato ketchup, juice, puree, paste, chili sauce, Mandarin orange juice	**Del Monte Brand** tomato ketchup, juice, fruit drinks, Mandarin orange juice
	Disney Brand fruit juice (orange, pineapple, grape), nectar (peach, orange)	
	Mann's Brand[a] wine and sparkling wine, brandy	**Mann's Brand** koshu, koshu (vintage), zenkoji, blush, brandy
	Higeta Brand shoyu, tsuyu, Worcestershire sauce	
	Ragu Brand spaghetti sauces	
	Kikko's Brand tomato ketchup	**Beyoung** protein powder, wheat germ
	Monet Brand cognac	**Imported wines** aujoux, chateau tatour, borie-manoux, franz reh and sohn, pol roger

[a]The company established its Mann Wine subsidiary in 1964.

EXHIBIT 8
Parent Company Revenues by Product Line
((Y) m)

Source: Table 5: UBS Securities Limited, May 28, 1996, as available on *Investext*.

	1994	1995	Percent Change	1996E	Percent Change
Soy Sauce	74,666	73,843	−1.1	75,000	1.6
Food	15,091	16,310	8.1	18,500	13.4
Del Monte	24,692	19,857	−19.6	19,000	−4.3
Alcohol	24,993	25,925	3.7	27,000	4.1
Others	4,159	4,285	3	4,500	5
Total	143,601	140,220	−2.4	144,000	2.7

EXHIBIT 9
Parent Company
Balance Sheet ((Y) m)

Source: UBS Securities Limited, May 28, 1996. Table 11 as reported by *Investext*.

	1993	1994	1995
Current Assets	78,463	81,805	80,749
Fixed Assets	88,007	86,029	89,599
Total	166,802	168,000	170,348
Short-Term Liabilities	33,469	32,033	46,762
Long-Term Liabilities	79,898	79,527	66,567
Equity	53,434	56,440	57,019
Total Liabilities and Equity	166,802	168,000	170,348

its mature domestic market would depend on continuous development of new applications and variations of its older products as well as development of new products.

Kikkoman in the United States in the Post–World War II Era

U.S. Market Potential

The various Mogi family branches and Noda Shoyu Company had expanded company efforts beyond Japan since the early 1800s. By the end of World War II, the various family enterprises and the Noda Shoyu Company had ended all activities outside Japan. Japanese expatriates living in various countries and other peoples whose traditional cuisine used shoyu comprised the company's primary pre–World War II markets. In 1949, Kikkoman started to export soy sauce, mainly to the United States. In the 1950s, consumption of soy sauce began to decline in Japan. Noda Shoyu Company made the decision to invest heavily in expanding the international sales of Kikkoman brand shoyu to overseas markets. Prior to World War II, Noda Shoyu's major overseas markets were Asia and Hawaii. After the war, the company decided to focus on the mainland United States because (1) political and economic conditions in Asia were very unstable, (2) the Japanese community in Hawaii had re-learned shoyu brewing during World War II, and there were many small Hawaiian shoyu breweries that would have made competition intense in that market, and (3) the United States had a healthy and rapidly growing economy.

Several changes in the U.S. market made that market attractive to Noda Shoyu Company. First, Americans who had been in Asia during or just after World War II developed a taste for Japanese goods, including food. Second, the company expected that as Asians in the United States became more Americanized, their consumption of traditional foods including soy sauce would decline. Third, American eating habits were shifting to more natural foods and to food that could be prepared quickly. Noda Shoyu Company moved to target both Asians and non-Asians in its marketing efforts.

During the 1956 U.S. presidential elections, Noda Shoyu bought air time to advertise Kikkoman brand products. Yuzaburo Mogi, son of the head of the company's planning department, urged this move to U.S. television advertising.

U.S. Distribution Activities

During the years immediately after World War II, Japanese companies in general relied on a small group of internationalized and entrepreneurial Japanese and Japanese-American individuals. Sale of food products in the United States involved a complex distribution system with heavy reliance on food brokers as promoters to local wholesalers and retailers. Food brokers required careful training by a knowledgeable sales team in how to use the product, especially where the product was unusual or unfamiliar to consumers. Food brokers marketed the product to wholesalers and large retailers, took orders for the product, and relayed the orders to the manufacturer or, in the case of foreign manufacturers, the manufacturer's agent. The manufacturer or agent then made delivery of the product to the wholesaler or retailer and handled all billing and accounts, paying the broker a commission for his/her marketing representation. The food broker was an important link between the manufacturer and the wholesaler or retailer. Food brokers were evaluated based on their ability to persuade retailers and wholesalers to carry products and to feature them prominently.

In 1957, the company formed Kikkoman International, Inc. (KII), a joint venture between Noda Shoyu Company in Japan and Pacific Trading of California. KII was incorporated in San Francisco to serve as the marketing and distribution center for Kikkoman products in the United States. Most of the products were produced by Noda Shoyu Company, but some were purchased from other manufacturers and sold under the Kikkoman label.

Over the next 10 years, sales grew 20 to 30 percent a year. In 1960, the Safeway grocery store chain agreed to have some of its stores carry Kikkoman Soy Sauce. Noda Shoyu opened regional sales offices for KII in Los Angeles (1958), New York City (1960), Chicago (1965), and Atlanta (1977). Retail marketing activities included in-store demonstrations, advertising campaigns in women's magazines that emphasized soy sauce use in American cuisine, and limited television commercials. The company used brokers as their distribution channels to supermarkets and wholesalers for the small oriental retail stores. The company encouraged food brokers through contests and training. For the food service and industrial market segments, the company carried out industrial magazine ad campaigns and special educational programs. The company also formed partnerships with the American Veal Manufacturers' Association and the Avocado Association to feature Kikkoman Soy Sauce in their product advertisements.

Other major international companies had to modify their products for the United States. However, Kikkoman marketed the same soy sauce in the United States as in Japan. The company's experience in its campaign to "westernize" soy sauce for the Japanese market applied to the campaign in the United States. In the United States Kikkoman provided the traditional, low-sodium preservative-free, and dehydrated soy sauce. The company also marketed tailor-made sauces, other food extracts, and agents.

Exploration of Potential U.S. Manufacturing Capacity

As early as 1965, Kikkoman Corporation began to explore the possibility of manufacturing in the United States. However, the company determined that sales in North America were insufficient to support the economies of scale required for a minimum efficient scale production facility. Instead, in 1968 Kikkoman Corporation contracted with a subsidiary of Leslie Salt Company of Oakland, California, to bottle the Kikkoman soy sauce shipped in bulk from Japan and to blend and bottle teriyaki sauce, a major ingredient of which was soy sauce. These bottling efforts constituted Kikkoman's first post–World War II manufacturing efforts in the United States. Bottling in the United States reduced customs and tariff costs. However, moving goods back and forth from the United States and Japan added considerably to the company's costs. In the mid 1980's Japan imported 95 percent and 88 percent of its soybeans and wheat respectively. The United States was Japan's major source of supply. Transportation of raw materials (e.g., soybeans and wheat) to Japan was between 5 percent and 20 percent of preproduction costs; transportation costs of brewed soy sauce from Japan to the United States was 25 percent of production costs. Various import/export restrictions and tariffs increased the risk and expense of importing raw materials to Japan and exporting finished goods to the United States.

The North American market was potentially much larger than the Japanese market, and Kikkoman had a greater share of the North American market than the company had in Japan. Yuzaburo Mogi hired a Columbia University classmate as a consultant, and the company formed a team to work with him to consider a U.S. plant. By 1970, the analyses, in spite of higher U.S. labor costs, favored construction of a U.S. manufacturing facility. As Yuzaburo Mogi put the company's motivation, "We made a decision to go after the American consumer."

Selection of Walworth, Wisconsin

The team considered over 60 potential sites in the east, west, and midwest. The team chose the midwest because of its central location and crop production. Ultimately, the team selected a 200-acre dairy farm site in Walworth, Wisconsin. Walworth provided the best fit with the five criteria established by the company: (1) access to markets (proximity to Milwaukee and Chicago, as well as the geographic convenience of a midway point between the east and west coasts made shipping relatively efficient); (2) ample supplies of wheat and soybeans (soybeans came from Wisconsin, wheat from North Dakota, and salt from Canada); (3) a dedicated workforce, (4) a strong community spirit; and (5) an impeccable supply of water. Kikkoman also appreciated Wisconsin's emphasis on a clean environment.

Walworth, Wisconsin, was situated about 2 hours northwest of Chicago and about 1 hour west of Milwaukee. A community of about 1,100, Walworth was surrounded by some of the most productive farmland in the United States. The area included a number of other smaller communities whose economies depended primarily on farming and summer vacation home residences. The company hired a local consultant, lawyer Milton Neshek, who ultimately became general counsel of Kikkoman Foods, Inc. Mr. Neshek described the original reaction to Kikkoman's purchase of prime farmland as mixed, "with a small faction on the town board opposed to the company coming in." Yuzaburo Mogi described the opposition as strong. Residents of the small, rural, close-knit farming community expressed concerns about the impact of a large, especially foreign, corporation in a small community, potential inflation of land values, and the possibility of industrial pollution.

One of Neshek's partners, Thomas Godfrey, visited Kikkoman facilities in Noda City, Japan. "When Kikkoman called me in 1971," said Godfrey, "and asked me to create a Wisconsin corporation for them so they could make soy sauce, I didn't even know what the hell soy sauce was. Nobody else around here did either." Walworth's plant manager, Bill Wenger, recalled his introduction to the company. In 1972, he was stationed with the U.S. Marines in Hawaii. His mother sent a newspaper clipping about the soy sauce plant, suggesting that it might be a good place to begin his return to civilian life. Wenger and his wife didn't know what soy sauce was either, but his wife went to the local grocery store and bought a bottle. As Wenger described it, the purchase was ". . .some horrible local Hawaiian brand. She brought it home and opened it. We looked at one another and said, '*@& . . ., this stuff is terrible.' " Another of the three American production managers employed at the plant had a similar tale. The production manager said, "The first year I worked here, we never had any soy sauce in my home. My wife wouldn't buy it, wouldn't even allow it in the house. I finally brought home a bottle and put it on some meatloaf. Now we use it on just about everything. I put it on peaches. And we even have a local minister who puts it on his ice cream . . . I do too. It's good."

No other Japanese-owned manufacturing facility had been constructed in the United States at the time. Neshek's partner, Godfrey, visited Noda because as he put it, "I had to see for myself what it was they were talking about. I had to make sure the factory wasn't going to pollute the air and water and stink up the place." Local Kikkoman representatives met with organizations such as the Local Grange, Farm Bureau groups, church groups, Rotary, and ladies' clubs. Wisconsin's governor, Patrick Lucey, came to one of the seven town meetings held to discuss the plant and explain the state's role and position. Yuzaburo Mogi described the process as "removing the fears of the local people and local council about the building of the new factory." The company was able to convince area residents that Kikkoman would not pollute the environment and would use local labor and other resources. The final vote of the county zoning board was 53 for, 13 against. The town board declined to oppose the zoning board's action. Among other issues, Kikkoman put a great deal of effort into reducing potential pollution. In talking about this process of "nemawashi" or root tending, Mr. Mogi emphasized the importance of a prosperous coexistence between the company and the local community. He said, "We've been doing business in Noda for 360 years. We learned a long time ago that to survive you need to coexist with the surrounding community."

Opening the New Plant

In January 1971, Kikkoman executives along with Japanese, Walworth, and Wisconsin officials held a ceremonial groundbreaking on the 200-acre site. A Cleveland, Ohio, design and construction firm built the plant. Other American companies, many located in the region, built many of the critical components. The initial investment in the 10,000 kiloliter facility was $8 million, and the plant was finished just in time to avoid the 1973 American embargo on the sale of soybeans to Japan. Kikkoman's Walworth plant was the first Japanese investment in production capacity in the United States in the post–World War II period and the first plant Kikkoman built outside Japan after World War II. Opening ceremonies included dignitaries and officials from Wisconsin, Kikkoman, Japan, and the United States. The 700 invited guests heard the texts of telegrams from the Japanese Prime Minister and President Richard Nixon. President Nixon referred to the plant as a ". . . visionary step (that) will mean meaningful trade relations and balance of trade and will enhance further friendships between our two countries."

From its opening in 1972 through the mid-1990s, the company expanded the Walworth facility eight times to 500,000 square feet. Kikkoman invested in facilities or equipment every year with production increasing 8 to 10 percent per year. Originally, the plant produced two products, soy sauce and teriyaki sauce. In the mid-1990s, the plant produced 18 products, including regular and light soy sauce, teriyaki steak sauce, sweet and sour sauce, and tempura dip. All but one used a soy base. The company had been very careful about pollution, treating its wastewater carefully so that there was no threat to nearby popular Lake Geneva. The Walworth town clerk said, "There's no noise, no pollution. I live about three-quarters of a mile from them, and once a day, I get a whiff of something that's like a sweet chocolate odor. It's no problem." The company marketed the plant's output in all 50 states plus Canada and Mexico. Soy sauce was shipped in many varieties, including bottles ranging from 5 to 40 ounces, 1- to 5-gallon pails, and sometimes in stainless steel tank trucks for large customers. McDonald's, for example, used soy sauce in one of the Chicken McNuggets condiments.

Management of the Walworth Plant

The company maintained a state-of-the-art laboratory at the Walworth facilities. However, plant management pointed out that the most accurate test during production was the human nose. "Our people have worked with the product for so long, a whiff can tell them something is not quite right," said one Kikkoman director. The venture was described as "a prime example of the best combination of Japanese and American business and industrial savvy." As the plant's general manager, Michitaro Nagasawa, a Ph.D in Biochemistry from the University of Wisconsin, put it, "The productivity of this plant is the highest of all our plants. . . . It's an exceptional case in Kikkoman history. We took the sons and daughters of farmers, trained them and taught them about total quality management. They were raw recruits with no experience in making soy sauce. People with farm backgrounds are very diligent workers. They will work seven days a week, 24 hours a day if necessary. They understand what hard work is."

The plant opened with 50 employees. Originally, 14 Japanese Kikkoman employees and their families came to Walworth to train employees and get the plant functioning. The Japanese families scattered in groups of two or three to settle in Walworth and various nearby communities. Local women's community organizations "adopted" the Japanese wives, formed one-to-one friendships, and helped the Japanese wives become acclimated to the communities, including learning to drive, using the local supermarkets, and hiring baby-sitters for their children. The Japanese husbands joined local service clubs. "That helped achieve an understanding between the Americans and Japanese and helped them to assimilate faster. It exposed Japanese people to a farming town that had had no Asian people before," noted Bill Nelson, Kikkoman Foods Vice President. Kikkoman established the practice of rotating its Japanese employees back to Japan after an average of 5 years in the United States. In the mid-1990s, only seven Japanese families remained in the Walworth area, still spread throughout the local communities.

Community Contributions

Kikkoman Foods, Inc., was an active and contributing member of the community. The company donated time and funds on three levels. At the local level the company established Kikkoman Foods Foundation in 1993. The foundation, which was to be ultimately funded at the $3 million level, was formed to support area charitable activities. The company supported as many as 30 local projects a year, including college scholarships for area students, local hospital activities, a vocational program that assisted people in developing employment-related skills, and a nearby facility that preserved circus-related items. As Walworth's town clerk put it, "They sponsor just about everything—Community Chest (an organization similar to the United Way), Boy Scouts, Girls Scouts, all the way down the line. They're very good neighbors." The clerk treasurer from a nearby town said, "You see their name in the paper almost every week helping out some organization."

At the state level, Kikkoman Foods, Inc., supported the University of Wisconsin educational system, established up to four Beloit College scholarships to honor Governor Lucey at his alma mater, and funded a Mogi Keizaburo scholarship at the Milwaukee School of Engineering. Members of the board of directors served on several public service boards and commissions. At the national level, Kikkoman Corporation, through its U.S. subsidiary Kikkoman Foods, Inc., supported Youth for Understanding exchange programs. At the fifth anniversary celebration, Kikkoman's chairman reported that the plant had developed better than had been anticipated. At the tenth anniversary celebration of the Kikkoman plant, the local Walworth paper reported, "In the 10 years that Kikkoman Foods, Inc., has been located here, it has become an integrated part of the community. The company has truly become a part of the Walworth community, and not only in a business sense." In 1987, reflecting Kikkoman's contributions, Wisconsin's governor appointed Yuzaburo Mogi as Wisconsin's honorary ambassador to Japan.

Kikkoman's Japanese–American Management in the United States

In the mid-1990s, Kikkoman operated its U.S. activities through two subsidiaries, Kikkoman Foods, Inc. (KFI), and Kikkoman International, Inc. (KII). KFI owned and operated the Walworth manufacturing plant. KII in San Francisco, California, undertook marketing responsibilities, including wholesaler and distributor activities throughout the United States. The boards of directors for both subsidiaries had several members from the parent corporation but were primarily Americans from among local operations officers or local Walworth citizens (for KFI) or the broader U.S. community (for KII). The KFI board met as a whole once a year and rotated the site of its annual stockholders' meeting between Japan and Wisconsin. An executive committee met monthly to consider operational decisions. The executive committee included Yuzaburo Mogi, who attended two to three meetings in the United States every year, and the head of Kikkoman Corporation's International Division. The remaining members of the executive committee included American and Japanese officers from the U.S. corporation. The KII Board operated in a similar manner but met only in the United States.

Yuzaburo Mogi believed that a long-term commitment was essential for international success. A 1961 alumnus of Columbia University's Graduate School of Business, Mr. Mogi was the first Japanese to graduate from a U.S. university with an MBA degree. In the years following graduation, he worked in various departments in Kikkoman, including accounting, finance, computers, long-range planning, and new product development. In time, he took on other roles, including member of Kikkoman's board of directors (1979), managing director of the company (1982), executive management director (1989), and executive vice president (1994). The seventeenth generation of his family to brew soy sauce, Mr. Mogi had become Kikkoman's president in early 1995. He explained his view regarding the necessity of a long-term perspective: "We should do business from a longer range viewpoint. It will be very difficult to expect fruitful results in the short run under different and difficult circumstances. Failure will be inevitable in foreign countries if one proceeds with a short-range view. In fact, it took Kikkoman 16 years to become established in the United States."

Of the five senior managers at the Walworth facility, three were Japanese and two were American. The plant manager, the finance manager, and the laboratory manager were Japanese. It was expected that these three positions would continue to be Japanese appointments. One American manager described the situation, "We know we will only attain a certain level, but that's OK, though. I can accept that. Soy sauce has been made in Japan for centuries. It's their product, their technology. They have the history, the research."

The general manager, i.e., plant manager, was the most senior person in authority at the plant and was responsible directly to headquarters in Japan. The appointment would be a person who had been with the company for many years. The finance manager's position required someone who was familiar with Japanese accounting systems and who was steeped in the Japanese emphasis on long-range profits. Japanese corporate headquarters controlled their foreign branches through their accounting and finance sections.

Mr. Mogi explained the Japanese appointment to the position of laboratory manager, "The production of soy sauce is very sophisticated. Normally, we recruit graduates with a master's degree in Japan who have gone to universities that have specialized programs in soy sauce production. In America, there is no university that teaches soy sauce production techniques, so it is difficult to promote Americans into general manager positions." As Dr. Magasawa, general manager at the Walworth plant, put it in explaining the discriminating tastes the Japanese have developed since childhood, "The sensory system, passion, feeling, or sensitivity can't transfer. That is based on just experience. Our vice president is a kind of god in this plant because he recognizes (even) a slight difference . . . I don't have that. That's why I can't be manufacturing vice president. I am a general manager—nothing special. I am a biochemist (with) 39 years in Kikkoman, mostly in research."

Decisions at the Walworth plant, when possible, were made by consensus. KFI vice president Bill Nelson described the plant management as American in content and Japanese in style, with decisions arrived at from the bottom up and most matters of importance needing a consensus of employees. "It's hard, really, to get at because of the fact that nothing . . . here should run in an American style or a Japanese style or what have you. It was just simply—let's see what happens when you have both parties participate," he said. Nelson gave the example of an idea for changing summer working hours to start at 7 A.M. instead of 8 A.M. so that workers could leave earlier and enjoy more daylight. It was, Nelson, pointed out, unusual for a company to even entertain the idea. Nelson explained the process: "Instead of simply exploring it on a management level, here we started the process of asking individual employees what personal inconvenience would be experienced if the hours were changed."

Milton Neshek observed that Japanese management and the middle management at the Walworth plant worked well together with long-range budgeting and strategic planning carried out by the Japanese executive team. He described the situation, "Our 30 employees feel like part of our family. That makes management more responsive to employees. Decisions, whenever possible, are made by consensus." The fact that the plant has no labor union was no surprise to Nelson. As he put it, a union "has never been an issue here."

Yuzaburo Mogi summarized Kikkoman's approach to its U.S. operations and, in particular, its Walworth plant as a five-point approach:

> Kikkoman has been successful doing business in the United States by adapting to American laws, customers, and most importantly, its culture . . . (An) important matter to consider, especially when establishing a manufacturing plant in a foreign country, is the maintenance of what has come to be called "harmony" with society and the local community. A foreign concern should try to prosper *together* with society and the local community. . . . It is important to try to localize the operation. . . . (Our). . . first commitment is the employment of as many local people as possible. Second we try to participate in local activities . . . trying to be a good corporate citizen (in Wisconsin) and contributing to society through our business activities. Third, we have been trying to avoid the so-called "Japanese-village" . . . by advising our people from Japan not to live together in one single community, but to spread out and live in several separate communities in order to become more familiar with the local people. Fourth, we try to do business with American companies. The fifth commitment is our practice of delegating most authority to local management in order to better reflect local circumstances. Through this process we are better able to make the most responsible decision. If we have an opinion, for example, we discuss it with other members at a local meeting in our American plant before reaching a decision. Kikkoman attempts to avoid a remote-control situation with letters or telephone calls from Japan. . . . If we have an opinion, we discuss it with other members at a local meeting in our American plant before reaching a decision.

The plant did encounter intercultural issues, however. For example, plant manager Bill Wenger pointed out "Communication can be a problem sometimes. The language barrier is one reason. Then there's the problem of saving face. If a mistake is made, the Japanese tend to cover up for one another so the person who made the mistakes doesn't lose face."

The company was a popular local employer in Walworth. Local unemployment was phenomenally low at 2 percent, but the Walworth plant had over 1,000 active applications on file for the plant's total 136 positions. However, turnover among plant employees was negligible. "No one quits unless it is a move by a spouse. Our absenteeism is minimal and as for tardiness—we just don't have it. We offer competitive wages and good benefits . . . employees feel like part of our family," said general counsel Neshek. Company officials stated that they paid about 10 percent more than the state average of $9.71 per hour, and employees did not have to contribute to the cost of their health insurance. As the company's vice president Shin Ichi Sugiyama put it, "In management, our primary concern is always the employee." The employees reported, "We feel like they listen to us. Our opinion counts, and we have the ability to make change, to better the company."

Mr. Sugiyama pointed out that the Walworth plant's productivity and quality had been about equal to that of Japanese plants. Productivity improved following the plant opening and by 1993 was actually the best of all the company's plants.

The U.S. Market in the 1990s[3]

U.S. Demand in the 1990s

After the opening of the Walworth plant, Kikkoman's U.S. sales growth slowed somewhat. However, Ken Saito, Kikkoman's brand manager for the midwest, summarized the company's hopes: "Americans are more adventurous than Japanese when it comes to trying new

---

[3]Information on the market and competitors was drawn primarily from InfoScan.

foods. That's why we have developed some products only for the American market. But most Americans still are not familiar with how to use soy sauce." Thus, the company developed a number of non-oriental recipes that call for soy sauce and other Kikkoman products, for example, teriyaki chicken wings and Pacific Rim pizza with sweet and sour sauce, beef and chicken fajitas, and grilled salmon with confetti salsa flavored with "lite" soy sauce. Kikkoman clearly expected Americans to increasingly use soy sauce for applications beyond oriental foods and expected significant growth in the company's base product in the United.States. According to Saito, "We figure the market in the United States will increase 100 times in the next decade." Kikkoman marketing coordinator, Trisha MacLeod, articulated the goal as ". . . to get consumers to realize soy sauce is the oldest man-made condiment, and that it can also be used in meatloaf, barbecue—across the spectrum."

MacLeod pointed out, "Americans eat a lot more soy sauce than they realize." However, America's per capita consumption was barely 10 tablespoons, translating into $300 million in North American sales. In contrast, Japanese per capita consumption was about 10.5 quarts per person, which translated into about $1.4 billion in annual sales in Japan.

The population of Asian immigrants and families of Asian descent was projected to grow significantly in the United States. The California population increased 127 percent to 2.8 million during the 1980s. The total population of Asian-Americans in the United States was estimated at 7.3 million in 1990, up 108 percent over the 1980s. Asian peoples represented the traditional mainstay market for oriental foods. Asians had higher income and educational levels than any other ethnic groups in the United States. However, each country represented a different cuisine, and the different Asian ethnic groups required different marketing approaches. Asian populations had spread throughout many parts of the United States, and retail outlets were learning how to highlight and display oriental foods to spur sales. Restaurants greatly influenced American food-buying habits. One industry executive observed that almost all U.S. restaurant kitchens in the 1990s had soy sauce. A 1996 National Restaurant Association study indicated that ethnic foods were increasing in popularity. Thus, oriental food manufacturers and distributors expected that oriental food sales would increase sharply.

Some information in the mid-1990s suggested strong and increasing popularity for oriental foods. U.S. sales of oriental foods had slowed considerably. The most recent aggregate information regarding the demand for oriental food in the United States in the mid-1990s is shown in Exhibit 10.

By the late 1980s consumers began to indicate dissatisfaction with canned entrees, at $81 million in sales the second largest subcategory of oriental foods. Sales of this subcategory had declined as much as 10 percent (1991 to 1992) and showed no signs of abating. Competition was intense, with a third of all products sold on the basis of feature, price, and/or display promotion.

U.S. Major Competitors

Kikkoman's two major competitors in the United States were Chun King and LaChoy. Both companies made soy sauce by hydrolyzing vegetable protein. This European derived method was faster and less expensive than the six-month fermentation process Kikkoman used. By 1971, Kikkoman had surpassed Chun King in supermarket sales of soy sauce, becoming #2 in the American marketplace. In 1976, Kikkoman outsold LaChoy brand soy

EXHIBIT 10   U.S. Oriental Food Sales ($000,000)

Year	1992	1993	1994
Sales	$275	$305	$301

Source: Information Resources, Inc., Chicago, IL.

sauce and became the #1 retailer of soy sauce in the United States, a position it continued to hold in the mid-1990s. However, the company faced strong competitors in the oriental foods category and in the sauces and condiments subcategory.

The new consumer focus was on oriental food ingredients that individuals could add to home-cooked dishes. "People are cooking more oriental foods at home," said Chun King's vice president of marketing, "Over 40 percent of U.S. households stir-fry at least once a month. Sauces are an opportunity to get away from the canned image." Indeed, sauces were the only growth area on the oriental food category, with 1992 sales rising 11 percent over the previous year. Rivals Chun King and LaChoy were flooding the oriental foods aisle in American supermarkets with new products. LaChoy had about 40 percent of the shelf products in oriental foods and Chun King had about 20 percent.

However, there were more changes than just new products. In the early 1990s, LaChoy and Chun King had revved up their marketing efforts under new ownership. LaChoy was owned by ConAgra's Hunt-Wesson division. Among other initiatives, ConAgra, a major U.S. food company, hired a new advertising firm for LaChoy.

A Singapore-based firm purchased Chun King in 1989 and brought in a new management team. As one observer put it, "The brand had really been neglected as part of Nabisco (its previous owner). It was just a small piece of a big pie." The new management team introduced a line of seasoned chow mein noodles and another of hot soy sauces. The firm's marketing plan included consumer promotions and a print ad campaign in women's magazines. Chun King's 1992 oriental food sales were estimated at $30 million. In mid-1995, ConAgra purchased Chun King from the Singapore company and added the brand to its Hunt-Wesson division. ConAgra was no stranger to the Chun King brand. The large U.S. competitor had purchased Chun King's frozen food line in 1986 from Del Monte. It was expected that Hunt-Wesson would eventually consolidate manufacturing but continue to aggressively advertise the two brands separately. As a Hunt-Wesson executive put it, "They're both established leaders in their field, and they both have brand strength."

LaChoy advertised itself as "the world's largest producer of oriental foods created for American tastes." The company led the oriental foods category with sales (excluding frozen) of $87 million in 1992 and $104.4 million in 1994. Its products included chow mein noodles, bamboo shoots, sauces, and miscellaneous foods. About $28 million of the 1992 sales came from sauce and marinade sales. LaChoy's manager of corporate communications indicated that the Chicago-based firm planned no increase in marketing spending in reaction to the new Chun King initiatives. However, the company did plan to advertise two new lines—Noodle Entrees and Stir-Fry Vegetables 'N Sauce. The company expected to expend most of its marketing support for the latter product line, a set of vegetables in four sauces formulated for consumers to stir-fry with their choice of meat.

Kikkoman and Other Competitors

Kikkoman remained the one bright spot in the oriental food category of sauces and marinades. Kikkoman controlled $63 million of the $160 million sauces/marinades segment and supported its position with a moderate amount of advertising—$3.2 million in 1992, about the same as 1991. In its major product lines, Kikkoman controlled about two-thirds of the California market and had about one-third market share in other major U.S. sales regions. The company was test-marketing a new line of sauces for addition to the consumer's own vegetables and meat.

Kikkoman also had to consider recent moves by several other competitors. Yamasa Shoyu Co., Ltd., Japan's second-largest soy sauce maker, had announced plans to build a factory in Oregon in mid-1994. This multigenerational company was founded in 1645 in Choshi City, Japan. Estimates on the cost of the Oregon factory ranged from $15 million to $20 million, and the plant was expected to eventually employ 50 workers. Yamasa intended to produce soy sauce for the U.S. market by using soybeans shipped from the midwest. It took Yamasa 4 years to select the final site for its new plant. The company produced a number of products in addition to soy sauce, including other food and drugs made from biological raw materials such as soybean protein and wheat starch.

Hong Kong–based Lee Kum Kee was a producer and importer of Chinese-oriented sauces and condiments. Lee Kum Kee had opened a sauce manufacturing plant in Los Angeles in 1991 to keep up with rising U.S. demand and to reduce dependence on imports thus avoiding payment of import duties, which could be as high as 20 percent. The company was a Hong Kong subsidiary of one of Japan's leading soy sauce brewers. Lee Kum Kee retailed its sauces in big supermarket chains in all 50 states. Historically, the company imported its soy sauce through an independent U.S.-based importer of the same name. The U.S. importer also imported about 40 other food products, mostly marinades, curries, and sauces from the East. Lee Kum Kee found its sales propelled by the population doubling of Americans of Asian or Pacific Island descent.

Competitor San-J International of the San-Jirushi Corporation of Kuwana, Japan, built a soy sauce plant in Richmond, Virginia in 1988. Hawaiian competitor Noh Foods of Hawaii innovated a line of oriental dried seasonings and powdered mixes. In reaction, other manufacturers, including Kikkoman, produced copycat products. Noh Foods distributed its products in the United States, Europe, and Australia through distributors and trade show activities.

Kikkoman's International Position

The Kikkoman Vision

In the mid-1990s, Kikkoman manufactured in four countries and marketed its brand products in over 90 countries. (Exhibit 11 shows the comparison of domestic and non-Japan sales and operating profits.) Of the company's 3,200 employees, over 1,000 were in international subsidiaries, and only 5 percent of those were Japanese. The company saw at least part of its mission as contributing to international cultural exchange. Yuzaburo Mogi explained,

> Kikkoman believes that soy sauce marketing is the promotion of the international exchange of food culture. In order to create a friendlier world, I believe we need many types of cultural exchanges. Among these, there is one that is most closely related to our daily lives—the eating of food. Soy sauce is one of the most important food cultures in Japan. Hence, the overseas marketing of soy sauce means the propagation of Japanese food culture throughout the world.

As one U.S. scholar who had studied the company extensively in the 1980s put it, "There is an evident willingness on the part of Kikkoman to experiment with new products, production techniques, management styles, and operational forms in the international arena." Yuzaburo Mogi put it similarly when he said, "It should be understood that adjustment to different laws, customs, and regulations is imperative, instead of complaining about those differences."

EXHIBIT 11

Consolidated Results FY 1995 ((¥) m)

Source: UBS Securities Limited, May 28, 1996. Table 7 as reported by *Investext*.

	Domestic	Non-Japan
Sales	162,426	40,860
Operating Profit	6,640	4,152
Operating Margin	4.0	10.1

Kikkoman in Europe

Kikkoman began its marketing activities in Europe in 1972. Kikkoman found Europeans more conservative and slower to try new tastes than Americans. The firm found Germany the least conservative and opened restaurants there in 1973. By the early 1990s, the company had opened six Japanese steak houses in Germany. The restaurants gave their customers, over 90 percent of whom were non-Asian, the opportunity to try new cuisine. The Kikkoman trading subsidiary in Germany was the company's European marketing arm. Said the managing director for Kikkoman's European marketing subsidiary located in Germany, "Germany and Holland are big business for us, as both countries are very much into interesting sauces and marinades." Kikkoman's managing director of Europe made it clear that he had aggressive plans to grow sales both by increasing the sales of soy sauce as well as extending the markets in which the company operated. The massive ready-made meal business in both the United States and Europe had huge potential for Kikkoman. The firm would need to market to end consumers at the retail level as well as to food manufacturers.

The company established its second overseas manufacturing facility in 1983. This facility supplied soy sauce to Australian and European markets. By the early 1990s, Kikkoman had about 50 percent of the Australian soy sauce market. The United Kingdom brand debut occurred in 1986, and the 1992 U.K. market was estimated at 1 billion pounds. In 1993, the firm opened a 25,000-square-foot warehouse in London. With $1.66 billion (U.S.) in sales, Kikkoman had come a long way with "just" soy sauce. Overall, analysts noted that the United States had experienced about 10 percent annual growth in soy sauce demand and expected Europe to expand similarly.

Kikkoman in Asia

In Asia, the company opened a production facility in Singapore in 1983 and incorporated a trading company in 1990. Industry observers expected the company to enter the soy sauce market in China in the near future. In addition, other Asian countries offered various opportunities in sauces, condiments, and foods.

Kikkoman—The Challenges

The company the Mogi family had headed for nearly 400 years confronted a number of challenges on the global stage in the latter part of the 1990s. Kikkoman executives realized that the company's future could depend primarily on its mature domestic market. The multi-generation family firm would have to change its image as a maker of a mature product. As Mr. Mogi stated "We . . . take pride in our ability to contribute to the exchange of cultures by using some of the world's most familiar flavors. We are now concentrating on further enhancing our ability to serve consumers in Japan and overseas. Kikkoman continues as a company that is proud of its heritage, but nevertheless willing and able to adapt to the constantly evolving requirements of our customers and markets."

References

Allen, Sara Clark. "Kikkoman, a Good Neighbor in Wisconsin," *Business,* Tuesday, June 11, 1996.

Bergsman, Steve. "Patience and Perseverance in Japan," *Global Trade,* Vol. 109, Issue 8 (August 1989), pp. 10, 12.

Campbell, Dee Ann. "Del Monte Foods to See European Foods Business," *Business Wire,* April 17, 1990.

Demestrakakes, Pan. "Quality for the Ages," *Food Processing,* Vol. 70, No. 6 (September 1996).

"Fireflies Help Kill Germs," *Times Net Asia,* January 1, 1996.

Forbish, Lynn. "Grand Oriental Celebration Held for Opening of Kikkoman Foods," *Janesville Gazette,* June 18, 1973.

Forrest, Tracy. "Kikkoman: a Way of Life," *Super Marketing,* January 28, 1994.

Fruin, W. Mark. *Kikkoman: Company, Clan, and Community* (Cambridge, Massachusetts: Harvard University Press, 1983).

Hewitt, Lynda. "Liquid Spice," *Food Manufacture,* February, 1993, p. 23.

Hostveldt, John. "Japan's Kikkoman Corp. Brews Success Story in Walworth," *Business Dateline: The Business Journal—Milwaukee,* Vol. 3, No. 31, Sec. 3 (May 19, 1986), p. 17.

"In-Store: Happy New Year's Feast," (Article on Kikkoman's In-Store Promotion), *Brandsweek,* Vol. 37 (January 1, 1996), pp. 14–15.

Jensen, Debra. "Kikkoman Executive Lauds Wisconsin, Lucey," *Gazette,* January 13, 1989, p. 1B.

Jensen, Don. "A Stainless Success Story," *Kenosha News,* Business Section, August 1, 1993.

Jensen, Leah. "Kikkoman Spices Up Walworth's Quality of Life," *Janesville Gazette,* January 21, 1984.

Kikkoman Corporation: Flavors That Bring People Together (Company Brochure).

Kinugasa, Dean. "Kikkoman Corporation," 1979 (Private Translation by Norihito Tanaka and Marilyn Taylor, 1994).

LaChoy's Homepage (www.hunt-wesson.com/lachoy/main/mission/).

LaGrange, Maria L. "RJR Sells Del Monte Operations for $1.4 Billion," *Los Angeles Times,* Vol. 108, Issue 297, September 26, 1989, p. 2.

Mogi, Yuzaburo. "*Masatsunaki Kokusai Senryaku,*" (Tokyo, Japan: Selnate Publishing Co., Ltd., 1988—in English Translation).

Mogi, Yuzaburo. "The Conduct of International Business: One Company's Credo—Kikkoman, Soy Sauce and the U.S. Market," (Available from Company).

Ostrander, Kathleen. "Kikkoman's Success Tied to Proper Blend," *Business Datelines (Wisconsin State Journal),* March 1, 1992, p. 29.

Plett, Edith. "Kikkoman Foods Marks Fifth Year," *Janesville Gazette,* January 26, 1979.

Redman, Russell. "Hunt-Wesson Acquires Chun King," *Supermarket News,* Vol. 45, No. 19 (May 8, 1995), p. 101.

SBA Homepage, Wisconsin Gallery.

Schoenburg, Lorraine. "Governor Supports Kikkoman," *Janesville Gazette,* September 14, 1989.

Shima, Takeshi. "Kikkoman's Thousand-Year History," *Business JAPAN,* January, 1989, p. 65.

"The Joy of Soy: How a Japanese Sauce Company Found a Happy Home in Walworth, Wisc.," *Chicago Tribune Magazine,* January 31, 1993, p. 13.

Wilkins, Mira. "Japanese Multinational in the United States: Continuity and Change, 1879–1990," *Business History Review,* Vol. 64, Issue 4 (Winter 1990), pp. 585–629.

Yates, Ronald E. "Wisconsin's Other Brew," *Chicago Tribune Magazine,* January 31, 1993, p. 14.

In addition to personal interviews in Tokyo, Walworth, Wisconsin, and San Francisco, information and quotations were also drawn from these references. This list is part of a much broader set of sources that the authors consulted.

The Making of Soy Sauce

The Chinese began making jiang, a precursor of soy sauce, about 2,500 years ago. The most likely story of soy sauce's origins relates how Kakushin, a Japanese Zen priest who studied in China, returned to Japan in the middle of the thirteenth century and began preparing a type of miso, or soybean paste produced through fermentation, that became a specialty of the area. By the end of the thirteenth century, the liquid was called *tamari* and sold commercially along with the miso. Experimentation with the raw ingredients and methods of fermentation began. Vegetarianism also became popular in Japan during this time, and people were eager for condiments to flavor their rather bland diet. Soldiers also found the transportability of the seasonings useful.

Soy sauce evolved from tamari and miso by adding wheat to the soybean fermentation mash. The Japanese modified the shoyu to include wheat to gentle the taste so that it did not overwhelm the delicate flavors of Japanese cuisine. Most households made their shoyu during the slack time in agricultural cycles. Families harvested grains in the fall and processed them into mash. The mash fermented beginning in October–December to January–March when the shoyu was pressed from the mash.

Regional differences among the soy sauces developed depending upon the mix of soybean, wheat, and fermentation techniques. Even in the last decade of the twentieth century, there were hundreds of local varieties of soy sauce available commercially in Japan.

Produced in the traditional way, soy sauce was a natural flavor enhancer. In the latter part of the twentieth century, ingredient-conscious consumers shied away from artificial flavor enhancers. Soy sauce responded to the challenge of finding ingredients to flavor foods. For vegetarian manufacturers, the "beefy" taste provided by the soy sauce without any meat extract was highly desirable.

There were two methods of manufacturing soy sauce—the traditional fermentation process used by Kikkoman and the chemical method.

Soy Sauce through Fermentation— Kikkoman's Traditional Method

Kikkoman's process was the traditional one and involved processing soy and wheat to a mash. Kikkoman had developed an innoculum of seed mold that the company added. The seed mold produced a growth, the development of which was controlled by temperature and humidity. The resulting mash (koji) was discharged into fermentation tanks where selected microorganism cultures and brine were added. The product (moromi mash) was aerated and mixed, then aged. During this process, enzymes formed in the cells of the koji and provided the characteristics of the brewed sauce. The soybean protein changed to amino acid, and the enzymatic reaction that occurred between the sugar and amino acids produced the taste and color. Enzymes changed the wheat starch to sugars for sweetness, and a special yeast developed changing some of the sugars to alcohol. Fermentation changed other parts of the sugars to alcohol that produced tartness. The brewing process determined flavor, color, taste, and aroma. The brine added to the koji mixture stimulated the enzymes and produced the reddish brown liquid mash. This process resulted in umami—or flavor-enhancing—abilities, as well as the brewed flavor components. The final mash was pressed between layers of cloth under constant pressure. After a pasteurization process to intensify color and aromas, the shoyu was filtered again and bottled. There were no flavorings, coloring, additives, or artificial ingredients in the product. According to produce developers, these complex flavors were not present in brewed soy sauce.

Chemically Produced Soy Sauce

Nonbrewed soy sauce could be made in hours. Soybeans were boiled with hydrochloric acid for 15 to 20 hours. When the maximum amount of amino acid was removed from the soybeans, the mixture was cooled to end the hydrolysis action. The amino acid liquid was then neutralized, mixed with charcoal, and finally purified through filtration. Color and flavor were introduced via varying amounts of corn syrup, salt, and caramel coloring. The resulting soy sauce was then refined and bottled.

Case

7

The Black & Decker Corporation

John E. Gamble *University of South Alabama*

Arthur A. Thompson *University of Alabama*

In 2000 Black & Decker Corporation was still struggling to get out from under the array of financial and strategic problems stemming from the company's $2.8 billion acquisition of Emhart Corporation in 1989. Black & Decker had long been the world's leading producer and marketer of power tools and power tool accessories. But it had begun a program of diversification in the 1980s that had produced mixed results for shareholders. The company's foray into small household appliances had been a success originally, but the small-appliance division acquired from General Electric in the early 1980s had recently been divested because of its drag on B&D's growth. The follow-on acquisition of Emhart, a conglomerate with very diverse business interests, had proved to be a significant impairment to the company's earnings and cash flow as well as a management burden, and during the past 11 years Black & Decker had achieved success in only a few of the businesses it obtained in the Emhart acquisition.

Black & Decker described itself as a diversified global manufacturer and marketer of household, commercial, and industrial products. Going into 2000, the company was the world's largest producer of power tools, power tool accessories, security hardware, and electric lawn and garden products. The company's Price Pfister kitchen and bathroom faucets subsidiary, a business acquired in the Emhart deal, had gained market share for 11 consecutive years to become the third largest brand of plumbing fixtures in North America. Black & Decker was also the worldwide leader in the market for certain types of mechanical fastening systems used in automobile assembly and in other industrial applications—fasteners had been one of Emhart's businesses as well. But while Black & Decker's business portfolio included a lineup of several competitively strong brands, the company's stock price had been a ho-hum performer throughout the unprecedented bull market of the 1990s, substantially lagging behind the performance of well-known indexes like the Dow Jones Industrials Average and the Standard & Poor's 500 Index. A graph of Black & Decker's stock performance between 1985 and January 2000 is presented in Exhibit 1. Exhibit 2 provides an 11-year summary of Black & Decker's financial performance.

EXHIBIT 1 **Market Performance of Black & Decker's Common Stock, by Quarter, 1985–January 2000**

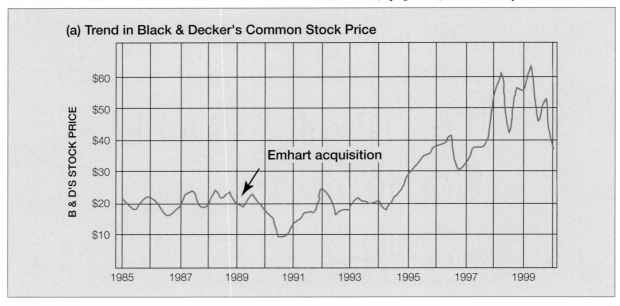

(a) Trend in Black & Decker's Common Stock Price

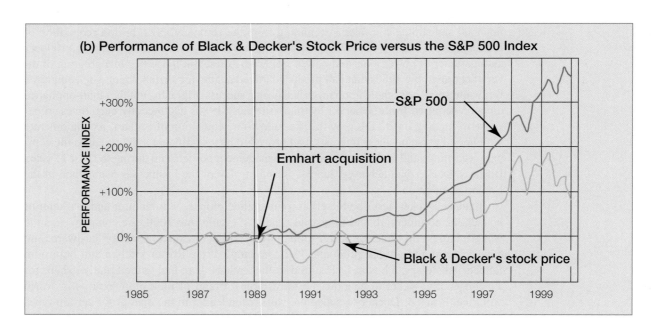

(b) Performance of Black & Decker's Stock Price versus the S&P 500 Index

The Expectation of Better Times for Black & Decker

In late 1998 Black & Decker management celebrated the completion of an almost decade-long effort to divest nonstrategic businesses gained through its 1989 acquisition of Emhart Corporation and expected the company to enter a long-awaited period of growth as its entire management attention was refocused on its core power tools, plumbing, and security hardware businesses. Black & Decker's CEO, Nolan Archibald, told Wall Street analysts in

EXHIBIT 2 **Summary of Black & Decker's Financial and Operating Performance, 1989–99 (In millions of dollars except per share and employee data)**

Source: The Black & Decker Corporation annual reports.

	1999	1998	1997	1996	1995	1994	1993	1992	1991	1990	1989
Sales	$4,520.5	$4,559.9	$4,940.5	$4,914.4	$4,766.1	$4,365.2	$4,121.5	$4,045.7	$3,952.6	$4,313.2	$3,172.5
Operating income	536.3	(466.2)	489.3	356.9	426.1	351.9	302.7	177.1	365.2	458.1	259.2
Operating income excluding restructuring and goodwill amortization*	536.3	509.2	552.6	514.5	494.5	424.9	364.4	391.3	436.0	524.1	284.5
Income taxes	141.0	166.5	122.3	43.5	9.0	62.7	60.7	44.3	54.5	72.4	32.9
Earnings data:											
Earnings (loss) from continuing operations	300.3	(754.8)	227.2	159.2	216.5	89.9	64.1	(95.3)	16.1	19.7	30.0
Discontinued operations	—	—	—	70.4	38.4	37.5	31.1	22.0	36.9	31.4	—
Extraordinary item	—	—	—	—	(30.9)	—	—	(22.7)	—	—	—
Cumulative effects of accounting change	—	—	—	—	—	—	(29.2)	(237.6)	—	—	—
Net earnings (loss)	300.3	(754.8)	227.2	229.6	224.0	127.4	66.0	(333.6)	53.0	51.1	30.0
Total assets	4,012.7	3,852.5	5,360.7	5,153.5	5,545.3	5,264.3	5,166.8	5,295.0	5,456.8	5,829.7	6,258.1
Long-term debt	847.1	1,148.9	1,623.7	1,415.8	1,704.5	1,723.2	2,069.2	2,108.5	2,625.8	2,754.7	2,629.7
Total debt	1,243.5	1,360.6	1,862.5	1,705.8	2,351.7	2,393.3	2,564.6	2,563.8	2,870.3	3,266.2	4,057.5
Stockholders' equity	801.1	574.0	1,791.4	1,632.4	1,423.2	1,169.4	1,048.9	1,074.0	1,027.1	920.7	720.7
Capital expenditures	171.1	146.0	203.1	196.3	203.1	181.5	190.3	167.7	94.9	103.1	112.1
Depreciation and amortization	160.0	155.2	214.2	214.6	206.7	195.4	182.4	188.3	187.1	197.8	131.0
Number of employees	22,100	21,800	28,600	29,200	29,300	29,200	30,500	32,300	31,900	35,900	38,600
Number of shares outstanding	88.4	91.8	96.5	96.1	94.4	85.3	84.5	76.3	62.6	61.4	59.6
Dividends per share	$0.48	$0.48	$0.48	$0.48	$0.40	$0.40	$0.40	$0.40	$0.40	$0.40	$0.40

*For 1998 this figure also excludes goodwill write-off and gain on sale of businesses.

early 1998 that the pending elimination of nonstrategic businesses that manufactured and marketed such products as True Temper golf club shafts and Emhart glass-making machinery would allow the company to position itself for greater growth in 1999 and 2000. "This [portfolio restructuring] will allow us to focus on core operations that can deliver dependable and superior operating and financial results."[1] However, with the exception of a brief run up to $60 per share in mid-1999, the portfolio restructuring had done little to improve the market performance of the company's securities. In January 2000 Black & Decker's common shares traded at a 52-week low and at a price below the high for 1996 and 1997. Nevertheless, management continued to express confidence that the company's streamlined business portfolio would allow Black & Decker to achieve revenue and earnings growth that the market would find impressive. In commenting on the company's year-end 1999 financial performance, Nolan Archibald said, "We are extremely pleased with Black & Decker's performance this past year, which resulted in record earnings and clearly indicates that the strategic repositioning we undertook in 1998 has been successful."[2]

Company Background

Black & Decker was incorporated by Duncan Black and Alonzo Decker in 1910 and initially produced milk cap machines and candy dippers. In 1916 the company introduced its first power tool—a portable half-inch electric drill that was eventually placed on display in the Smithsonian Institution. Over the next 40 years, Duncan Black and Alonzo Decker undertook a number of actions that established the company as the dominant name in power tools and accessories. Black & Decker introduced the first portable screwdriver in 1922, the first electric hammer in 1936, finishing sanders and jigsaws in 1953, and the Dustbuster handheld vacuum in 1978. The company expanded internationally in 1919 when it began sales operations in Russia, Japan, and Australia and opened a production facility in Canada in 1922. The company eventually became known worldwide for its power tools, particularly so in Europe. Black & Decker was managed by the two partners until they died—Black in 1951 and Decker in 1956. As managers, Black and Decker achieved growth by adding to the company's lineup of power tools and accessories and by increasing its penetration of more and more foreign markets. The company maintained a corporate growth strategy tied exclusively to product-line extensions and international expansion until the mid-1980s.

Diversification into Small Household Appliances

Black & Decker began to pursue diversification in the 1980s because of growing maturity of its core power tools business. In 1984 Black & Decker acquired General Electric's housewares business for $300 million. GE's brands had about a 25 percent share of the small-appliance market and generated annual revenues of about $500 million. GE sold its small-appliance division, despite its number one market position, because of the division's low profitability. GE's strong suit was in irons and toaster ovens, where its share was close to 50 percent; sales of GE irons alone totaled about $250 million. Among the other 150 GE products acquired by Black & Decker were coffeemakers, hair dryers and hair curlers, food mixers and processors, toasters, electric skillets, can openers, waffle irons, and blenders. Also in 1984, Black & Decker purchased three European tool manufacturers to fill in product gaps and strengthen its manufacturing base; the acquisition involved a Swiss manufacturer of portable electric woodworking tools for professional users, the leading European manufacturer of drill bits, and a German producer of hobby and precision power tools.

---

[1] As quoted in *Knight-Ridder/Tribune Business News,* January 28, 1998.
[2] As quoted in PR Newswire, January 27, 2000.

The acquisition of GE's housewares division launched Black & Decker on a course to transform the company from a power tools manufacturer into a consumer products company. In early 1985, the firm changed its name from Black & Decker Manufacturing Company to Black & Decker Corporation to reflect its new emphasis on "being more marketing driven" rather than being merely engaged in manufacturing.

Black & Decker's CEO—Nolan D. Archibald

The chief architect of Black & Decker's foray into diversification was Nolan D. Archibald. Black & Decker hired Archibald as president and chief operating officer in 1985, shortly after the acquisition of GE's small household appliance business. Prior to joining Black & Decker, Archibald was president of the $1.7 billion consumer durables group at Beatrice Companies, where he was responsible for such business units as Samsonite luggage, Culligan water treatment products, Del Mar window coverings, Stiffel lamps, and Aristocraft kitchen cabinets. At the time he was hired, Archibald was 42 years old; he was chosen from a pool of some 50 candidates for the position and turned down offers to be president at two other companies to take the B&D job. Archibald had been at Beatrice since 1977 and was successful in engineering turnarounds in three of Beatrice's businesses. Prior to that, he had headed a turnaround of Conroy Inc.'s Sno-Jet Snowmobile business. Archibald spent two years of his youth winning converts as a Mormon missionary, was an All-American basketball player at Utah's Dixie College, became a standout player at Weber State College in Utah, earned his MBA degree at Harvard Business School, and tried out (unsuccessfully) for the Chicago Bulls professional basketball team. Corporate headhunters rated Archibald as a good strategic thinker who was personable, versatile, and sensitive to people.

Archibald's Early Successes at B&D

According to one Black & Decker dealer, prior to when Archibald took over as president in September 1985 "Black & Decker had been coasting along for quite a few years like a ship without a captain."[3] Archibald wasted little time in reorganizing Black & Decker's worldwide manufacturing operations. Within three months, Archibald initiated a restructuring plan to close older, inefficient plants and boost factory utilization rates by consolidating production within B&D's newest and biggest plants. Approximately 3,000 jobs were eliminated, including a number of high-level managerial jobs. In 1985, B&D took a $215 million write-off for plant shutdowns and other cost-saving reorganization efforts.

Prior to 1985, the company had pursued a decentralized, multicountry strategy. Each geographic area had its own production facilities, its own product-design centers, and its own marketing and sales organizations to better cater to local market conditions. Over the years, this had resulted in short production runs at scattered production sites, reduced overall manufacturing efficiency, and prevented achievement of scale economies—for example, there were about 100 different motor sizes in B&D's product line. Archibald set the company on a more globalized approach to product design and manufacturing, with much greater communication and coordination between geographic operating units. Production at plants was organized around motor sizes, the number of product variations was reduced, and production runs were lengthened. From 1984 to 1989 seven plants were closed and nearly 3,000 employees were let go. Archibald also insisted more emphasis be put on quality control—during the early 1980s, B&D's reputation in power tools had been tarnished by shoddy product quality.

Meanwhile, Archibald put additional resources into new product development and redesign of the company's power tools and small-appliance lines. Archibald set a goal for the tool division to come up with more than a dozen new products each year—more than B&D had introduced in the five years before his arrival. He also created panels of dealers to

[3]As quoted in *BusinessWeek,* July 13, 1987, p. 90.

suggest new products and features that consumers desired. The company introduced a number of highly successful products such as its Snakelight flashlights; a line of cordless power tools; Macho rotary hammers that could punch holes in stone, brick, and concrete; DeWalt professional power tools; and VersaPak rechargeable batteries that fit both Black & Decker power tools and household appliances.

One of Archibald's biggest marketing challenges was transferring consumers' brand loyalty for GE small appliances over to Black & Decker. Some observers believed Black & Decker would have trouble because B&D's traditional customers were men, and buyers of houseware products were usually women—as a *Wall Street Journal* article headline put it, "Would You Buy a Toaster from a Drillmaker?" B&D executives believed, however, that many women were familiar with the Black & Decker name because they bought power tools as gifts for men and because B&D had pioneered the development of household appliances powered by rechargeable batteries. Black & Decker's handheld DustBuster vacuum cleaner was the market leader, with a 45 percent share. B&D also had been marketing a cordless rotary scrub brush, a cordless rechargeable shoe shiner, and a rechargeable flashlight. Even before acquiring GE's housewares business, B&D had planned to introduce a line of cordless kitchen appliances, but gaining ample retail shelf space was often a hit-or-miss proposition. What made the GE acquisition attractive to B&D was the extra clout that being able to offer retailers a full line of housewares would have in competing for shelf space.

Black & Decker's competitors in small appliances saw the brand-name transition from GE to Black & Decker as an opportunity to gain market share that once was GE's. Sunbeam Appliance quadrupled its 1985 ad budget to $42 million because it wanted to replace GE as the best-known brand in small appliances. Norelco launched a new line of irons and a handheld can opener powered by rechargeable batteries to wrest share away from GE/Black & Decker. Hamilton Beach introduced a battery-operated carving knife. Nearly all small-appliance producers were rumored to be trying to develop cordless adaptations of irons, coffee makers, handheld mixers, and electric carving knives.

Archibald responded to the brand transfer challenge with a series of actions. Since Black & Decker had until 1987 to put its own name on all the GE products it acquired, it led off the transfer process by first putting its name on GE's innovative, expensive, high-margin Spacemaker products, which were designed to be mounted under kitchen cabinets—a line that was not as strongly identified with the GE name. Then B&D introduced a new iron (invented by GE) that shut off automatically when it sat too long or was tipped over; B&D's TV ads for the iron showed an elephant walking away from an iron that had been left on, with a tag line: "Even elephants forget." The brand transfer was accomplished product by product, in each case accompanied by heavy advertising. Under Archibald, Black & Decker spent approximately $100 million during the 1985–87 period to promote the brand transition. The company also organized a large team of brand transition assistants to hang paper tags on display models of newly rebranded products in about 10,000 retail stores across the United States—the tags stated that GE previously sold products now made by Black & Decker. Most analysts regarded Archibald's brand transfer program as successful; a Harvard Business School professor stated, "It is almost a textbook example of how to manage a brand transition."[4]

Archibald was promoted to chairman, president, and chief executive officer in 1986. He was listed among *Fortune* magazine's 10 Most Wanted Executives that year and was named as one of the Six Best Managers of 1987 by *BusinessWeek*. By year-end 1988, Archibald was widely credited with engineering another impressive turnaround, having boosted Black & Decker's profits to $97.1 million—up sharply from the loss of $158.4 million posted in 1985. Archibald was also the recipient of the American Marketing Association's 1996 Edison Achievement Award for his accomplishments as Black & Decker chief executive.

[4]Ibid.

Failed Acquisition Attempts

In early 1988 Black & Decker began an unsolicited takeover bid for American Standard Inc., a diversified manufacturer of bathroom fixtures, air conditioning products, and braking systems for rail and automotive vehicles. American Standard had revenues of $3.4 billion and earnings of $127 million in 1987 (compared to revenues of $1.9 billion and earnings of almost $70 million for Black & Decker). After several months of negotiations, the takeover effort failed and B&D withdrew from the battle.

In January 1989, Black & Decker negotiated a deal with Allegheny International to purchase its Oster/Sunbeam appliance division for about $260 million. Oster/Sunbeam was a leading manufacturer and marketer of small household appliances—blenders, can openers, food mixers, electric skillets, steam irons, and other kitchen items. However, in February, Allegheny International backed out of the sale and merged with another company instead.

The Emhart Acquisition

A month later, in March 1989, Black & Decker agreed to acquire Emhart Corporation for $2.8 billion, rescuing the firm from a hostile takeover bid. Emhart had 1988 sales of $2.8 billion, earnings of $127 million, assets of $2.4 billion, and shareholders' equity of $971 million. Emhart was a diversified manufacturer of industrial products (1988 sales of $1.6 billion), information and electronic systems (1988 sales of $654 million), and consumer products (1988 sales of $547 million). Approximately 40 percent of Emhart's sales and earnings came from foreign operations, the majority of which were concentrated in Europe. Exhibit 3 provides a profile of Emhart's business portfolio. Exhibit 4 provides data on the financial performance of Emhart's business units.

In the days following the announcement of Black & Decker's friendly plan to acquire Emhart, B&D's stock price dropped about 15 percent. There was considerable skepticism over the wisdom of the acquisition, both from the standpoint of whether Emhart's businesses had attractive strategic fit with B&D's businesses and whether B&D could handle the financial strain of making such a large acquisition. Emhart was significantly larger than Black & Decker:

1988 Financials	Emhart	Black & Decker
Sales revenues	$2.76 billion	$2.28 billion
Net earnings	126.6 million	97.1 million
Assets	2.43 billion	1.83 billion
Stockholders' equity	970.9 million	724.9 million
Long-term debt	$674.3 million	$277.1 million

The acquisition agreement called for Black & Decker to purchase 59.5 million shares (95 percent) of Emhart Corporation common stock at $40 per share—a price almost three times book value per share ($14.32). Altogether, Black & Decker had to secure $2.7 billion in financing to acquire Emhart. To come up with the funds, Black & Decker entered into a credit agreement with a group of banks that consisted of term loans due 1992 through 1997 and an unsecured revolving credit loan of up to $575 million. The loans carried an interest rate of ¼ percent above whatever the prevailing prime rate was. Scheduled principal payments on the term loans were as follows:

1992	$201,217,000
1993	274,287,000
1994	275,221,000
1995	743,923,000
1996	401,318,000

EXHIBIT 3 **Emhart Corporation's Business Portfolio in 1989 (At the time of the company's acquisition by Black & Decker)**

Business and Product Categories	Trademarks/Names	Primary Markets/ Customers
Industrial Businesses (1988 sales of $1.6 billion)		
Capacitors, audible signal devices	Emhart, Mallory, Sonalert, Arcotronica	Telecommunications, computer, automotive, and electronic components industries
Electromechanical devices, solid-state control systems, hydrocarbon leak detection systems	Emhart, Mallory, Pollulert	Appliance, automotive, and environmental controls manufacturers
Commercial door hardware, electronic locking systems	Emhart, Carbin, Russwin	Commercial, institutional building construction, and original equipment manufacturers
Footwear materials (insoles, toe puffs, shanks, eyelets, tacks, and nails)	Emhart, Texon, Aquiline	Manufacturers of footwear
Fastening systems (rivets, locknuts, screw anchors, adhesive systems, sealants, and grouts)	Emhart, Molly, Warren, Gripco, Bostik, Kelox, Dodge, Heli-Coil, POP	Appliance, construction, electronics, furniture/ woodwork, packaging, automotive, and other transportation industries
Glass container machinery	Emhart, Hartford, Powers, Sundsvalls	Producers of glass containers for beverage, food, household, and pharmaceutical products
Printed circuit board assembling machinery	Emhart, Dynapert	Electronics industry
Information and Electronic Systems (1988 sales of $654 million)		
Technology-based systems and services (including computer-based systems), scientific research services, program management	Emhart, PRC, Planning Research Corp., PRC System Services, PRC Environmental Management, PRC Medic Computer Systems, Nova, Stellar	Governmental units and agencies, real estate multiple listing services, group medical practices, and public utilities
Consumer Products Businesses (1988 sales of $547 million)		
Door hardware, including lock sets, high-security locks, and locking devices	Emhart, Kwikset	Residential construction
Nonpowered lawn and garden equipment, landscape lighting	Garden America, True Temper	Do-it-yourself homeowners
Underground sprinkling and watering systems	Lawn Genie, Drip Mist, Irri-trol	Landscape specialists, do-it-yourself consumers
Golf club shafts, bicycle-frame tubing	True Temper, Dynamic Gold, Black Gold	Golf club manufacturers
Bathroom and kitchen faucets	Price Pfister, The Pfabulous Pfaucet with the Pfunny Name	Residential and commercial construction
Adhesive, sealants	Bostik, Thermogrip	Residential and commercial construction, do-it-yourself consumers
Fasteners, staplers, nailers	Blue-Tack, POP, Molly	Residential and commercial construction

EXHIBIT 4
Financial Performance of Emhart's Business Groups, 1986–88 (In millions of dollars)

Source: Emhart 1988 annual report.

	1988	1987	1986A*	1986B
Revenues				
Industrial				
Components	$ 641.8	$ 671.9		$ 653.9
Fastening systems	640.5	638.8		576.3
Machinery	279.0	291.1		419.2
	$1,561.3	$1,601.8	_____	$1,649.4
Information and electronic systems	653.7	438.3		39.3
Consumer	547.5	414.4		405.6
Total	$2,762.5	$2,454.5	_____	$2,094.3
Operating Income (Loss)				
Industrial				
Components	$ 63.8	$ 65.7	$ 48.2	$ (5.4)
Fastening systems	74.8	78.7	68.3	24.8
Machinery	42.7	34.1	44.4	3.9
	$ 181.3	$ 178.5	$160.9	$ 23.3
Information and electronic systems	37.2	22.3	2.0	2.0
Consumer	84.8	68.3	60.4	51.7
	$ 303.3	$ 269.1	$223.3	$ 77.0
Corporate expense	(35.0)	(32.9)	(30.3)	(34.0)
Total	$ 268.3	$ 236.2	$193.0	$ 43.0
Identifiable Assets				
Industrial				
Components	$ 457.8	$ 472.0		$ 400.3
Fastening systems	428.4	428.2		409.7
Machinery	167.8	164.8		297.2
	$1,054.0	$1,065.0	_____	$1,107.2
Information and electronic systems	546.7	361.3		334.5
Consumer	702.7	225.1		266.1
	$2,303.4	$1,651.4		$1,707.8
Corporate	123.2	378.5		148.9
Total	$2,426.6	$2,029.9	$000.0	$1,856.7

*1986 before provision for restructuring.

The credit agreement included covenants that required Black & Decker to achieve certain minimum levels of cash flow coverage of its interest obligations and not to exceed specified leverage (debt-to-equity) ratios during the term of the loan:

Fiscal Year	Maximum Leverage Ratio	Minimum Cash Flow Coverage Ratio
1992	3.25	1.35
1993	2.75	1.50
1994	2.25	1.55
1995 and thereafter	1.50	1.60

Note: The leverage ratio was calculated by dividing indebtedness, as defined by the credit agreement, by consolidated net stockholders' equity. The cash flow coverage ratio was calculated by dividing earnings before interest, taxes, depreciation, and amortization of goodwill minus capital expenditures by net interest expense plus cash income tax payments and dividends declared.

Other covenants in the credit agreement limited Black & Decker's ability to incur additional indebtedness and to acquire businesses or sell assets.

Black & Decker also entered into factoring agreements with financial institutions where it sold its receivables at a discounted rate to avoid waiting 30 to 60 days to collect on its invoices. The company ended its sale of receivables program in December 1997 when it became able to meet its liquidity requirements without factoring receivables.

Black & Decker recorded the excess amount of its purchase price for Emhart over the book value of Emhart's net assets as goodwill to be amortized on a straight-line basis over 40 years. This resulted in Black & Decker's having increased depreciation and amortization charges of about $45 million annually.

Initial Divestitures of Emhart Businesses

Senior management at Black & Decker realized early on that as much as $1 billion of Emhart's business assets would have to be sold to reduce B&D's interest expenses and debt obligations and enable it to meet its covenant agreements. According to accounting rules, these assets had to either be sold within a year or be consolidated with the rest of B&D assets—a move that could cause B&D to fail to meet its maximum leverage covenant. The Emhart businesses that were identified for sale within one year from the acquisition date included footwear materials, printed circuit board assembly equipment (Dynapert), capacitors, chemical adhesives (Bostik), and the entire information and electronic systems business unit (PRC). During 1989 and early 1990, Black & Decker sold the Bostik chemical adhesives division to a French company for $345 million, the footwear materials business to the United Machinery Group for approximately $125 million, and its Arcotronics capacitors business to Nissei Electric of Tokyo for about $80 million; the net proceeds from these sales were used to reduce debt. In early 1990, when the one-year period expired, Black & Decker was forced to consolidate about $566 million of the unsold assets, boosting the goodwill on its balance sheet by $560 million, raising annual amortization charges by $14 million. To keep from violating the maximum debt/equity ratio allowed under its credit schedule, Black & Decker was forced to issue $150 million in new preferred stock, $47 million of which was purchased from its 401(K) employee thrift plan when no other buyers came forward.

Throughout 1991 Black & Decker continued to struggle to meet its covenant agreements. The company divested Emhart's Garden America business unit and the Mallory Controls operations in North America and Brazil for a combined total of about $140 million. The company also sold its True Temper Hardware unit, its PRC Medic unit, and its U.S. Capacitors business for a combined total of nearly $110 million. The prices B&D got for the Emhart businesses it sold were generally below management's expectations, partly because oncoming recessionary effects reduced what buyers were willing to pay.

Nonetheless, these divestitures (described by B&D management as "nonstrategic assets") and the sale of $150 million in preferred stock, allowed Black & Decker to reduce its total debt from a peak of $4 billion following the Emhart acquisition in April 1989 to $2.9 billion at year-end 1991. Even so, Black & Decker was still hard pressed to generate enough cash to meet its debt repayment schedule, a problem compounded by the 1990–91 recession, which hit the company's tool and household goods businesses fairly hard. The company's stock price fell from the mid-20s at the time of the Emhart acquisition to a low of $11–$12 in early 1991—many observers believed that the fundamental cause of B&D's financial plight was that it had paid too much for Emhart. There was also concern about whether there was enough strategic fit between Emhart and B&D. By early 1992, the stock price had recovered to the low 20s, partly because a decline in the prime rate from 10 percent to 6.5 percent had lowered B&D's interest burden substantially. (The credit agreement pegged the interest rate B&D paid at ¼ percent above the prevailing prime rate.)

Subsequent Divestitures: 1993–96

During the next six years, Black & Decker's corporate management sought to find buyers for several nonstrategic businesses acquired as part of the Emhart deal. Three were sold between 1993 and 1996.

Dynapert

The Dynapert business unit provided automated equipment for assembling printed circuit boards to electronics customers around the world. The equipment was among the most complex computer-controlled machinery being used in any industrial application. Dynapert had two manufacturing plants (one in the United States and one in England) and sales and service facilities throughout the world. The unit had launched a total quality program and implemented just-in-time manufacturing techniques.

Sales were made directly to users by an employee sales force and independent sales representatives. Dynapert faced competition from both U.S. and foreign manufacturers. Competition centered on technological and machine performance features, price, delivery terms, and provision of technical services. The Dynapert division, which generated 1991 sales of about $180 million, had been put on the market shortly after the Emhart acquisition, and was sold two years later to Dover Corporation's Universal Instrument division for an undisclosed amount.

Corbin Russwin

Emhart's Corbin Russwin manufactured locks and door hardware for the European commercial security hardware market. The unit employed 550 people at its plant in Berlin, Germany. Yale and Valour, Inc., the British manufacturer of Yale locks, purchased the Corbin Russwin unit from Black & Decker in 1994 for $80 million. Black & Decker recorded a gain of $18 million on the combined sales of the Corbin Russwin and Dynapert units.

PRC Information Systems and Services

This segment consisted of a single business unit known as PRC, Inc., headquartered in McLean, Virginia. PRC and its predecessors had been in business since the mid-1970s. A majority of PRC's business came from contracts with various agencies and units of the federal government. Approximately 40 percent of PRC's 1991 revenues were from contracts with the Department of Defense. In addition, PRC was the leading provider of (1) online printed residential real estate multiple listing systems and (2) computer-aided emergency dispatch systems. The types of services PRC provided were highly competitive, and strategic defense expenditures were expected to decline given the improvement of foreign relations. Many of PRC's competitors were large defense contractors with significantly greater financial resources. As the Department of Defense's expenditures for weapons programs continued to decline, these large contractors were expected to bid more aggressively for the types of contract work done by PRC. PRC had also been put on the market for sale following the Emhart acquisition. In 1991, PRC had sales of $684 million and pretax operating earnings of $32.3 million. In mid-1991 B&D appointed a new person to head PRC; shortly thereafter, PRC launched an initiative to pursue new markets. The objective was to shift PRC's business mix so that half came from U.S. customers and half from overseas customers. However, PRC management had great difficulty developing new nongovernment customers and was only growing at about one-third the rate of its closest competitors under Black & Decker ownership.

Black & Decker had little success in locating interested buyers for the PRC unit until 1995, when PRC Realty Systems and PRC Environmental Management, Inc., were sold for $60 and $35.5 million, respectively. Litton Industries agreed to purchase the remaining PRC operations in 1996 for $425 million. Prior to its sale to Litton, when it appeared that finding a buyer was becoming increasingly unlikely, Black & Decker management had considered a spinoff of the unit in 1992. The spinoff was never finalized because Wall Street showed little interest in a $350 million public offering of PRC stock. PRC's 1995 sales and after-tax earnings were $800 million and $38.4 million, respectively.

Black & Decker's 1998 Divestitures

Black & Decker again initiated portfolio restructuring in 1998 when it divested its household products business and two businesses gained through the Emhart acquisition.

Household Products

Black & Decker's household products business had established itself as a worldwide leader in products used for home cleaning, garment care, cooking, and food and beverage preparation by 1990. It had the largest market share of any full-line producer of household appliance products in the United States, Canada, Mexico, and Australia and a growing presence in Europe, Southeast Asia, and Latin America. The household products division was using the worldwide distribution network and brand-name recognition that had been established by the tools division to gain greater global penetration in household appliances. However, by 1996, the company had lost substantial market share in almost every housewares product category. Its Toast-R-Ovens and irons were the only remaining Black & Decker products that held leading shares of their respective markets. (See Exhibit 5 for market shares of the major competitors by product category for 1990, 1993, and 1996.)

Like the market for power tools, the market for small household appliances was both mature and cyclical. Growth opportunities existed mainly in the form of creating innovative new products and in increasing market penetration in the countries of Eastern Europe and other developing nations where household appliance saturation rates were low. It was difficult to grow sales in the United States without introducing innovative new products since most small appliances had very high household saturation rates. In 1996 blenders were found in 80 percent of U.S. households, coffeemakers had a 74 percent saturation rate, and toasters were found in 90 percent of U.S. households. Many consumers clearly had both a toaster and toaster oven, since toaster ovens had a 42 percent U.S. household saturation rate.

Black & Decker's housewares business unit had been successful at launching new products that might entice a consumer into replacing an existing small appliance for one offering more features or better performance. The company's SnakeLight flexible flashlight was introduced in 1994 and quickly became one of the most popular small appliances ever developed by the company. In 1996 the company introduced a revamped Quick 'N Easy line of irons with a new Sure Steam system, and in 1998 it improved the glideability of its irons with a new proprietary coated soleplate. The company also introduced cordless products such as the ScumBuster, a submersible scourer and scrubber, and the FloorBuster, an upright vacuum cleaner that achieved rapid sales increases.

In late 1997 the company launched a designer line of small kitchen appliances, Kitchentools, which won five Industrial Design Excellence Awards in 1998. The Kitchentools line carried premium pricing; the stand mixer had a suggested retail price of $289.99, the thermal coffeemaker listed at $159.99, the blender was priced at $139.99, the food processor was priced at $229.99, the hand mixer's retail price was $69.00, and the Kitchentools can opener carried a suggested retail price of $34.99. Even though the Kitchentools line was praised for its quality and innovative styling, it did not sell as well as Black & Decker management had expected. The company also had some difficulty manufacturing the products and getting them to market by the planned launch date.

Black & Decker had lost substantial market share in recent years and had seen its profit margins erode despite its best efforts to maintain efficient operations. Between 1995 and 1997 the company had completely overhauled its supply chain management to reduce finished goods inventory and improve customer service and production planning. The company had eliminated $150 million from logistics costs during that time period but still only averaged about 2 percent profit margins on its housewares products. The business unit was identified for divestiture by Nolan Archibald in January 1998 and was sold to Windmere-Durable in May 1998 for $315 million. The agreement allowed Black & Decker to retain its DustBuster, FloorBuster, ScumBuster, and SnakeLight product lines. In June 1998 Black & Decker announced the sale of its housewares operations in New Zealand and Australia to Gerard Industries, an Australian electrical products manufacturer. The company had also sold its consumer glue gun and stapler business to Longwood Industries for an undisclosed amount in July 1998.

EXHIBIT 5
Unit Volume for Selected Small Appliances and Market Shares of Leading Producers, 1990, 1993, and 1996 (Unit volume in thousands)

Source: Compiled by case researchers from data presented in *Appliance,* April 1991 and April 1997.

Product/Leading Brands	1990	1993	1996
Can openers	6,200	6,380	6,910
Rival	33%	27%	26%
Hamilton Beach/Proctor Silex	13	15	24
Black & Decker	26	28	13
Oster/Sunbeam	11	13	13
Coffeemakers	17,740	14,390	15,000
Mr. Coffee	28%	31%	32%
Hamilton Beach/Proctor Silex	19	18	24
West Bend	—	3	9
Black & Decker	20	17	8
Food processors	4,760	1,916	1,525
Hamilton Beach/Proctor Silex	21%	19%	40%
Cuisinart	Unknown	13	18
Black & Decker	25	21	10
Oster/Sunbeam	18	19	8
Hand mixers	4,400	5,060	5,280
Hamilton Beach/Proctor Silex	14%	18%	24%
Black & Decker	34	28	15
Oster/Sunbeam	25	18	13
HPA/Betty Crocker	—	—	11
Irons	16,950	17,460	15,600
Black & Decker	50%	50%	38%
Hamilton Beach/Proctor Silex	24	30	29
Oster/Sunbeam	17	10	17
Rowenta	—	—	7
Toaster ovens	2,800	3,340	3,670
Black & Decker	57%	56%	56%
Toastmaster	13	16	17
Hamilton Beach/Proctor Silex	19	20	11
HPA/Betty Crocker	—	—	6
Toasters	8,900	9,850	10,760
Hamilton Beach/Proctor Silex	35%	50%	37%
Toastmaster	27	31	30
Rival	—	—	17
HPA/Betty Crocker	—	—	5
Black & Decker	16	13	4

Recreational Outdoor Products

In 1998 B&D's True Temper Sports business unit was the leading global designer, manufacturer, and marketer of steel golf club shafts; with over a 60 percent market share in the steel shaft segment, it was three times as large as its closest rival. True Temper also manufactured graphite shafts but had a very limited market share in that segment since it focused on the premium end of the market. The division supplied more than 800 golf club manufacturers around the world, including such industry leaders as Callaway Golf, Ping, Titleist, and Taylor Made. The sales of this unit had grown at a compounded annual rate of 12 percent between 1995 and 1997. True Temper Sport's growth rate reflected the overall growth in the golf equipment industry. The unit also manufactured specialty tubing for the bicycle and sporting goods industries. Many of the bicycles and kayak paddles used by U.S. Olympians were manufactured from True Temper precision tubing.

Black & Decker sold the business to Cornerstone Equity Investors in June 1998 for $178 million. The new owners stated that they intended for True Temper to remain the leader in golf club shafts and that they intended to expand into new product categories requiring specialty tubing. True Temper's president said that the new company would develop precision tubing products for such sporting goods industries as down-hill skiing and archery.

Glass-Container-Forming Machinery

In 1998 B&D's Emhart glass-container-forming machinery division was considered the global leader and offered the world's most complete line of glass-container-making equipment. Important competitive factors were price, technological and machine performance features, product reliability, and technical and engineering services. An increasing worldwide preference for plastic and other nonglass containers had led to a slowing growth rate for glass-container-forming equipment and inspection equipment. There was little seasonal variation in industry demand. Glass-container-making equipment was in 24-hour use in virtually all plants worldwide, creating a predictable need for servicing and rebuilding; nearly two-thirds of the unit's revenues came from rebuilding and repair services and technology upgrades. In January 1998 the business was identified as a nonstrategic asset that was to be divested; it was sold to Bucher Holding AG of Switzerland in September 1998 for $178 million.

Black & Decker's Business Portfolio in 2000

In 2000 Black & Decker Corporation was a diversified multinational enterprise with a business portfolio consisting of

* Power tools and accessories for both do-it-yourselfers and professional tradespeople.
* Lawn and garden equipment.
* Security hardware for residential markets in the United States and residential and commercial hardware in certain European countries.
* Cleaning and lighting products.
* Plumbing products.
* Commercial fastening systems.

Exhibit 6 provides a detailed listing of the products produced and marketed by B&D in these business areas. Exhibit 7 provides 1997–99 financial performance data by business group. A brief description of each business group follows.

Power Tools and Accessories

Black & Decker was the world's largest manufacturer, marketer, and servicer of power tools and accessories. The company's products were available at almost all retail outlets that sold power tools in the United States, Europe, and other developed countries. In fact, Black & Decker products were so popular in the United Kingdom that many British do-it-yourselfers referred to home improvement projects as "Black & Deckering." Black & Decker was named as the top-performing hardware brand by 6 out of every 10 U.S. retailers included in a 1997 survey conducted by *Discount Store News*. Other brands that were highly rated by hardware retailers were Stanley, General Electric, Skil, Rubbermaid, Makita, and Dutch Boy. Black & Decker's products were also highly rated in terms of performance by consumers, and most of its products carried a two-year warranty.

Industry Growth and Competition

Demand for power tools and accessories was regarded as mature and cyclical. Volume was influenced by residential and commercial construction activity, by consumer expenditures for home improvement, and by the overall level of manufacturing activity. (A number of manufacturers used power tools in performing certain production tasks—automotive and aerospace firms, for example, were heavy users of power tools.) Worldwide sales of power

EXHIBIT 6
Black & Decker's
Business Portfolio at
Year-End 1999

Power tools and accessories
(1999 sales: $3.21 billion)

- Drills
- Screwdrivers
- Saws
- Sanders
- Grinders
- Tabletop saws
- Drill bits
- Screwdriver bit
- Saw blades
- Cleaning and lighting products

Hardware and home improvement
(1999 sales: $882 million)

- Lock sets
- Deadbolts
- Master keying systems
- Faucets and fixtures
- Lawn and garden care products

Fastening and assembly systems
(1999 sales: $498 million)

- Rivets and riveting tools
- Threaded inserts
- Stud welding fastening systems
- Lock nuts
- Self-drilling screws
- Construction anchors

tools were an estimated $10 billion in 1999. The North American market for power tools was estimated at $3.5 billion, European sales were estimated at $4.0 billion, Asia/Pacific sales were an estimated $2.0 billion, and Latin American sales of power tools were approximately $500 million. The global market for power tools failed to grow significantly between 1997 and 1999, but was expected to grow at low- to mid-single-digit annual rates between 2000 and 2002. The industry's worldwide demand plateau during the late 1990s was attributable in large part to Asian financial and economic troubles. During 1998 and 1999 North America was the fastest-growing market for power tools as cordless and professional-grade power tools gained in popularity with consumers. Demand in Europe grew more slowly than in the United States during the late 1990s and was expected to continue to lag behind U.S. demand in the near future. Worldwide, the biggest percentage growth during the early and mid-1990s occurred in emerging Asian countries, where the use of power tools was quickly replacing the use of hand tools. Healthy demand for power tools was expected to return to Asian markets once the region had fully recovered from the effects of financial and economic instability that began in late 1997.

Market Segments

There were two distinct groups of buyers for power tools: professional users and do-it-yourselfers. Professional users included construction workers, electricians, plumbers, repair and maintenance workers, auto mechanics, and manufacturing workers. Professional users were very conscious of quality and features; they tended to buy only those tools that were durable, functional, dependable, and capable of precision. They also tended to be very knowledgeable compared to do-it-yourselfers, many of whom were first-time buyers and used power tools infrequently.

Because the needs of professional users and do-it-yourself consumers tended to be sharply different, some manufacturers had a heavy-duty professional line and a consumer/do-it-yourself line and others catered to just one of the two segments. Professional users tended to purchase their tools through jobbers, contractor supply firms, industrial supply houses, building supply centers, and some home improvement centers. Tools for the

EXHIBIT 7   **Black & Decker's Financial Performance by Business Segment, 1997–99**

Source: Black & Decker annual reports.

	Power Tools and Accessories	Hardware and Home Improvement	Fastening and Assembly Systems	All Others	Currency Translation Adjustments	Corporate Adjustments and Eliminations	Consolidated
1999							
Sales to unaffiliated customers	$3,209.3	$881.8	$497.7	—	($68.3)	$ —	$4,520.5
Operating income before restructuring and exit costs, write-off of goodwill, and gain on sales of businesses	377.3	124.0	84.3	—	(6.9)	(42.4)	536.3
Depreciation and amortization	87.7	31.1	15.4	—	(1.8)	27.6	160.0
Identifiable assets	1,836.0	508.2	273.2	—	2,617.4	1,395.3	4,012.7
Capital expenditures	$ 109.1	$ 38.3	$ 26.9	—	($ 3.5)	$ 0.3	$ 171.1
1998							
Sales to unaffiliated customers	$2,946.4	$851.1	$463.0	$333.6	($34.2)	$ —	$4,559.9
Operating income before restructuring and exit costs, write-off of goodwill, and gain on sales of businesses	293.4	125.2	76.6	16.5	(4.4)	(23.3)	484.0
Depreciation and amortization	88.2	27.1	13.4	—	(1.1)	27.6	155.2
Identifiable assets	1,631.3	507.8	246.7	—	1,471.3		3,852.5
Capital expenditures	$ 79.1	$ 36.5	$ 16.2	$ 13.3	($ 1.1)	$ 2.0	$ 146.0
1997							
Sales to unaffiliated customers	$2,936.4	$804.8	$451.3	$718.1	$29.9	$ —	$4,940.5
Operating income before restructuring and exit costs, write-off of goodwill, and gain on sales of businesses	290.7	121.3	69.7	61.7	(2.3)	(51.8)	489.3
Depreciation and amortization	87.5	24.7	11.9	24.4	(0.3)	66.0	214.2
Identifiable assets	1,635.4	476.5	248.2	438.6	8.0	2,554.0	5,360.7
Capital expenditures	$ 113.2	$ 47.3	$ 15.4	$ 25.3	($ 0.2)	$ 2.1	$ 203.1

consumer segment were sold at home improvement centers, building materials centers, mass merchandisers (Sears), discount chains (Wal-Mart, Kmart), and hardware stores.

Until the late 1980s, the consumer tool segment was growing at a faster clip than the professional segment. But narrowing price differentials and a rising interest on the part of gung-ho do-it-yourselfers in professional-quality tools had, in the U.S. market, spurred demand for heavy-duty professional tools. The sales of both consumer-grade and professional-grade cordless products were also becoming increasingly popular, with a compound annual growth rate of over 10 percent during the mid- and late 1990s.

Competition

Power tool manufacturers competed on such variables as price, quality, product design, product innovation, brand-name reputation, size and strength of retail dealer networks, and after-sale service. All makers were working to bring out new products that were lightweight, compact, cordless, quiet, less prone to vibration, strong, and easy to manipulate. The major manufacturers had sales forces whose main task was to expand and strengthen the network of retail dealers carrying their line of tools. Salespeople signed on new dealers and called on major accounts—wholesale distributors, discount chains, home improvement centers, and other mass merchandisers—to win better access to shelf space in their retail outlets, help with promotion and display activities, and upgrade dealers' product knowledge and sales skills. Some manufacturers offered training seminars and provided training videos to dealers/distributors. Manufacturers that concentrated on the professional segment engaged in limited advertising and promotion activities, spending their dollars for trade magazine ads, trade shows, and in-store displays. Those that concentrated on the consumer segment, like Black & Decker, spent comparatively heavily for TV and magazine ads and also for co-op ad programs with dealers.

Black & Decker's Global Competitive Position in Power Tools

In 2000 Black & Decker was the overall world leader in the world power tool industry, followed by Bosch/Skil Power Tools, a division of Robert Bosch Corporation (one of Germany's leading companies), and Japanese brands Makita and Hitachi. Other competitors were Atlas/Copco, Delta/Porter Cable, Hilti, Ryobi, and Electrolux. For most of the company's history, Black & Decker's greatest strength was in the consumer tools segment (see Exhibit 8); it was the market leader in the United States, Europe (where it had had a presence since the 1920s), and many other countries outside Europe. No other manufacturer came close to matching B&D's global distribution capabilities in the do-it-yourself segment. Makita and Ryobi were the leaders in Japan and several other Asian countries. Bosch was strongest in Europe.

In consumer tools Black & Decker's strongest U.S. competitor was Sears, which marketed tools under the Sears Craftsman label. Sears's longtime supplier of tools was Ryobi, which supplied Sears with 75 percent of its tool requirements. Skil's strength was in power saws; its 1992 joint venture with Robert Bosch Power Tools was contrived to give the two brands more clout in gaining shelf space and greater global coverage capabilities. Black & Decker's consumer-grade power tools were also carried by Sears, and the company had developed a new Quantum line of power tools sold exclusively by Wal-Mart. Quantum was an intermediate line that was more durable than typical consumer lines but did not meet the performance of the company's professional power tools. Black & Decker's Mouse sander, WoodHawk circular saws, and FireStorm drills, along with its products that used the VersaPak interchangeable battery, were among the company's best-selling consumer tools.

Although surveys showed that consumers associated the Black & Decker name with durable power tools, trade professionals viewed Black & Decker products as products for

EXHIBIT 8

Estimated U.S. Sales and Market Shares of Power Tool Manufacturers, 1979, 1991, and 1997 ($ millions)

Source: Compiled by the case researchers from a variety of sources, including telephone interviews with company personnel; data for 1979 are based on information in Skil Corporation, Harvard Business School, case #9–389–005.

	1979		1991		1997	
	Dollar Sales	Percent Share	Dollar Sales	Percent Share	Dollar Sales	Percent Share
Consumer Tools						
Black & Decker	$169	44.5%	$325	39.7	$460	43.1%
Sears/Ryobi	107	28.2	280	34.0	305	28.5
Milwaukee	6	1.5	4	0.5	6	0.6
Makita	2	0.5	43	5.2	32	3.0
Porter Cable	—	—	—	—	—	—
Delta	—	—	—	—	—	—
Skil	52	13.7	82	10.0	165	15.4
Others	44	11.6	86	10.6	102	9.4
Total	$380	100.0%	$820	100.0%	$1,070	100.0%
Professional Tools						
Black & Decker	$205	42.1%	$125	17.9%	$918	36.7%
Sears/Ryobi	9	1.8	50	7.1	285	11.4
Milwaukee	89	18.2	145	20.7	436	17.4
Makita	22	4.5	160	22.9	304	12.2
Porter Cable	NA	NA	50	7.1	240	9.6
Delta	NA	NA	40	5.7	209	8.4
Skil	54	11.1	40	5.7	32	1.3
Others	109	22.3	90	12.9	76	3.0
Total	$488	100.0%	$700	100.0%	$2,500	100.0%
Total Tools						
Black & Decker	$374	43.1%	$450	29.6%	$1,378	38.6%
Sears/Ryobi	116	13.4	330	21.7	590	16.5
Milwaukee	95	10.9	149	9.8	442	12.4
Makita	24	2.8	203	13.4	336	9.4
Porter Cable	NA	NA	50	3.3	240	6.7
Delta	NA	NA	40	2.6	209	5.9
Skil	106	12.2	122	8.0	197	5.5
Others	153	17.6	176	11.6	210	9.4
Total	$868	100.0%	$1,520	100.0%	$3,570	100.0%

NA = not available

do-it-yourselfers. During the late 1980s, the company's charcoal-gray professional tools line was not seen by professional users as sufficiently differentiated from B&D's traditional black line of consumer tools. Professionals preferred tools made by Makita, Skil, and Milwaukee (a U.S. tool manufacturer with a reputation for quality, heavy-duty tools). During the 1970s and 1980s, Makita had steadily increased its share of the professional segment and by 1991 had captured 53 percent of the U.S. professional handheld power tool segment.

In 1991 B&D executives formed a team, headed by the president of B&D's power tools division, to come up with a new strategy for the professional market segment. The team elected to create an entirely new line of industrial-grade tools for professional users under the DeWalt brand, a name borrowed from a 65-year-old maker of high-quality stationary saws acquired by B&D in 1960. The team changed the tools' color from gray to industrial yellow because the latter was easy to see, signaled safety, and was distinct from other leading brands of professional power tools. Every product in B&D's professional line was redesigned based on input from professionals, dealers, and B&D engineers. The redesigned versions were all tested by professional users; every item had to meet or beat Makita's tools in user tests before going into production. The new DeWalt line was introduced in March 1992. As part of the introduction of the DeWalt line, B&D created "swarm teams" of 120 young, high-energy marketers that visited construction sites to demonstrate DeWalt tools in their bright yellow-and-black Chevy Blazers. DeWalt swarm teams also promoted DeWalt tools at NASCAR events, vocational clubs, union apprenticeship programs, and retail locations. The company intended to double the number of swarm team members in the United States between 1998 and 1999. In 1996 De-Walt swarm teams invaded Europe with a fleet of yellow-and-black Range Rover Defenders with the charge of making DeWalt a leading brand on that continent. The company also instituted a policy of offering professional users the loan of a DeWalt power tool when waiting for their equipment to be fixed at any of the company's 135 U.S. service centers. There were also DeWalt demonstration booths at each of the service centers.

Initial response to the DeWalt line was excellent. As the brand began to gain in popularity with professional users, Black & Decker developed additional DeWalt tools. In 1997, newly introduced DeWalt products were awarded two Industrial Design Excellence Awards from the Industrial Designers Society of America. The success of the new DeWalt line exceeded Black & Decker management's expectations and surpassed its $200 million sales volume objective for 1995 by over $100 million. In 1999 DeWalt was one of the leading power tool brands for professionals and serious do-it-yourselfers.

Black & Decker was also the world leader in the market for such accessories as drill bits, saw blades, and screwdriver bits. Vermont American, Irwin Hanson/American Tool, Bosch, Freud, and Wolfcraft were B&D's closest competitors in the accessories market, but no other company had as broad a product line or geographic coverage as Black & Decker. Most of the company's growth in accessory sales was accounted for by accessory lines developed for the DeWalt brand and a line of new premium woodworking saw blades. The company intended to maintain its market leadership by expanding into more woodworking supply and industrial/construction distribution channels and continuing to introduce innovative products.

In 1998 Black & Decker launched a series of initiatives intended to strengthen its competitive position in power tools and accessories. First, it introduced a corporatewide six sigma quality program to bring about improvements in costs, defect rates, product quality, and customer satisfaction. Second, the company took a $164 million restructuring charge that involved the elimination of 2,900 positions; worldwide plant rationalization that resulted in plant closings in Canada, Singapore, and Italy; a reorganization of its European operations; and various reengineering projects in all plants. Third, it initiated a restructuring of its supply chain management to improve customer service while reducing inventories. Although Black & Decker's restructuring program cut across all business units, it was primarily focused on its global power tools business and was expected to yield more than $100 million annually in cost savings. Additional cost savings were achieved through the integration of Black & Decker's cleaning and lighting products like its DustBuster vacuum cleaner, ScumBuster wet scrubber, and SnakeLight flashlight with its power tool businesses after the sale of the housewares division to Windmere in 1998.

The April 21, 1999, exit of Joseph Galli, Black & Decker's president of its Worldwide Power Tools and Accessories group, shocked analysts and investors and caused a one-day 8 percent decline in the company's share price. Galli, age 41, was a rising star at Black & Decker and was thought to be the leading candidate to succeed Archibald as CEO. There was a widely held belief in the power tools industry that much of the DeWalt brand's success was attributable to Galli's strategic leadership and that Galli had been forced out of B&D as a result of his desire to become the company's CEO within the near future. Archibald, who had no immediate retirement plans, commented that Galli had "expressed an interest in advancing his management career to a higher level, and we have agreed it makes sense for him to pursue this goal outside of Black & Decker."[5] In June 1999 Joe Galli become president and chief operat-

[5]As quoted in the *Baltimore Sun,* April 22, 1999.

ing officer of Amazon.com. Even though there was some initial concern by investors over Galli's departure, B&D's Power Tools and Accessories group continued to perform well in his absence; its sales increased by 11 percent and operating profit increased by 27 percent during the fourth quarter of 1999. The business unit's annual sales and operating profits increased by 9 percent and 29 percent, respectively, over 1998 sales and operating profits.

Lawn and Garden Equipment

Black & Decker's lawn and garden tools like Groom 'N' Edge, Vac 'N' Mulch, and Leaf-Buster were distributed through the same channels as the company's power tools. In addition, the buyers of B&D's hedge trimmers, string trimmers, lawn mowers, edgers, and blower/vacuums could get the items repaired at B&D's 150 company-owned service centers worldwide and several hundred other authorized service centers operated by independent owners. Where feasible, B&D's lawn and garden products had a global design. The company had recently begun to offer cordless electric string trimmers and hedge trimmers in North America and Europe. The cordless hedge trimmer could run continuously for about 30 minutes, and the cordless string trimmer could trim hard-to-reach areas from a half-acre lawn on a single battery charge. As of 2000, Black & Decker marketed its cordless lawn mowers only in Europe.

Security Hardware

B&D's security hardware business was the leader in the $2 billion global market for door hardware for homes and businesses. The company had developed good-better-best product lines that covered all major residential price points. The Kwikset brand was positioned as an affordable product targeted to do-it-yourselfers; B&D had boosted Kwikset's sales by providing retailers with a videotape that took the mystery out of changing household locks. Kwikset Plus was a midrange product, and the company's TITAN products were designed for the fine home market. TITAN NightSight handsets and deadbolts featured lighted keyways, and the TITAN AccessOne keyless entry deadbolt and handset systems allowed homeowners to use a remote control to unlock the door from as far away as 30 feet. The TITAN line also included the Society Brass Collection of solid brass designer door hardware. All TITAN products boasted a lifetime finish that was protected against tarnishing, rust, and corrosion.

This business, acquired from Emhart, had achieved significant cost savings by integrating its purchasing, distribution, and marketing activities with B&D's other consumer products businesses. B&D's worldwide distribution network was also providing the hardware group wider geographic sales opportunities. In many instances, door hardware was sold in the same retail channels as B&D's power tools and accessories. Black & Decker's restructuring and six sigma quality initiatives, begun in 1998, also affected its security hardware business—products and facilities were rationalized, high-cost operations were restructured, and automation was used where feasible. Black & Decker's major competitors in the North American security hardware market included Schlage, Weiser, Weslock, and a variety of Asian exporters. Major competitors in Europe included Williams, Assa Abloy, Cisa, Keso, and Abus.

Plumbing Products

B&D's plumbing products business, Price Pfister, had gained market share since the Emhart acquisition to become the third largest manufacturer and marketer of plumbing fixtures in North America by 2000. Price Pfister had benefited from access to B&D's retail distribution network by gaining more shelf space in home improvement centers. Price Pfister had also introduced fashionable, but affordably priced, new designs and new lines that had become popular with plumbing wholesalers and plumbing contractors. Price Pfister had increased its brand recognition through in-store merchandising activities and with TV ads using the theme

"The Pfabulous Pfaucet with the Pfunny Name" in the early 1990s and "The Pfabulous Pfaucet. Pforever. No Drips, No Tarnish, No Worries" theme in the late 1990s.

Price Pfister's major competitors in the $1.9 billion North American market for sink, tub, shower, and lavatory plumbing hardware were American Standard, Kohler, Delta, and Moen. The industry had grown at a slow rate of 2 to 3 percent since 1995 and was expected to grow at a comparable rate over the next few years. Plumbing products with new styles and features were in the highest demand. Black & Decker expected new decorative faucets like Price Pfister's Georgetown and Roman lines, introduced during the late 1990s, to account for 20 percent of the unit's annual sales. Price Pfister expected to improve its performance with the addition of innovative and attractive new lines, better in-store merchandising, improved manufacturing efficiency, and better supply chain management.

Commercial Fastening Systems

Black & Decker was among the global leaders in the $2 billion fastening and assembly systems market. This business unit marketed fastening products under 26 different brands and trademarks to automotive, electronics, aerospace, machine tool, and appliance companies in the United States, Europe, and the Far East. The industry's recent growth rate had ranged between 3 and 5 percent, and future growth was expected to remain within that range. Some emerging markets did generate higher growth rates as new industries and companies emerged and plant capacity was added.

Products were sold directly to users and also through distributors and manufacturers' representatives. Competition centered on product quality, performance, reliability, price, delivery, and ability to provide customers with technical and engineering services. Competition came from many manufacturers in several countries. Major competitors included Textron, TRW, Eaton, and such regional companies as Raymond, Gesipa, Huck, and Fukui. Black & Decker was the global leader in commercial blind riveting and automotive stud welding systems, and its other fastening system categories held strong positions in various geographic regions. Black & Decker management intended to maintain its leadership in the automotive stud welding category with new product innovations. More than 30 percent of the unit's 1999 sales were accounted for by products introduced within the past five years. Black & Decker intended to improve the performance of the division through implementation of its six sigma quality initiative, reengineered operations, and plant rationalizations.

Black & Decker's Future Prospects

The year 2000 marked the beginning of Black & Decker's second year of operations with its streamlined portfolio of businesses following the 1998 divestiture of its small-appliance, True Temper recreational products, and Emhart glass-forming machinery businesses. Black & Decker had sold the three businesses for more than management's expected $500 million and was able to reduce operating expenses by more than $100 million annually, primarily as a result of the elimination of 3,000 jobs from its payroll. In addition, the series of divestitures had cut the company's amortization of goodwill associated with the Emhart acquisition by about $30 million annually for the next 30 years.

This last round of divestitures, coupled with the sale of businesses in earlier years, completed the divestiture of the nonstrategic Emhart assets gained in the 1989 acquisition. Price Pfister and Kwikset were two of the Emhart businesses that initially captured the attention of Black & Decker management and were now among the three remaining Emhart businesses still included in Black & Decker's portfolio. So far, the 1998 divestitures had not produced steady increases in the company's stock price, but Nolan Archibald was confident that the company's ability to focus solely on power tools and other closely aligned businesses would allow the company to begin to provide its shareholders with above-average returns.

Krispy Kreme Doughnuts in 2005: Are the Glory Days Over?

Arthur A. Thompson *University of Alabama*

Amit J. Shah *Frostburg State University*

We think we're the Stradivarius of doughnuts.

—*Scott Livengood, president, chairman, and CEO of Krispy Kreme*

In early 2004, Krispy Kreme's prospects appeared bright. With 357 Krispy Kreme stores in 45 states, Canada, Great Britain, Australia, and Mexico, the company was riding the crest of customer enthusiasm for its light, warm, melt-in-your-mouth doughnuts. During the past 4 years, consumer purchases of Krispy Kreme's doughnut products had taken off, with sales reaching 7.5 million doughnuts a day. Considerable customer excitement—approaching frenzy and cult status—often surrounded the opening of the first store in an area. When a new Krispy Kreme opened in Rochester, New York, in 2000, more than 100 people lined up in a snowstorm before 5:00 AM to get some of the first hot doughnuts coming off the conveyor line; within an hour there were 75 cars in the drive-through lane. Three TV stations and a radio station broadcast live from the store site. The first Krispy Kreme store in Denver, which opened in 2001, grossed $1 million in revenues in its first 22 days of operation; commonly had lines running out the door with a one-hour wait for doughnuts, and, according to local newspaper reports, one night had 150 cars in line for the drive-through window at 1:30 AM. Opening day was covered by local TV and radio stations, and off-duty sheriff's deputies were brought in to help with traffic jams for a week following the store's grand opening.

The first Minnesota store, just outside of Minneapolis, had opening-week sales of $480,693—the company record for fiscal 2002. In July 2003, the first store to open in the Massachusetts market—in Medford, outside Boston—had a record opening-day revenue of

$73,813 and a record opening-week sales volume of $506,917. Sales exceeded $2 million in the first seven weeks. At the June 2003 opening of the company's first store in Australia, in the outskirts of Sydney, some customers camped overnight in anticipation of the opening and others waited in line for hours to experience their first Krispy Kreme hot doughnut. The store, about an hour from downtown Sydney, attracted more than 500,000 customers from Sydney in its first six months of operations. In South Bend, Indiana, one exuberant customer camped out in the parking lot for 17 days to be the first in line for the grand opening of that city's first Krispy Kreme store.

To capitalize on all the buzz and customer excitement, Krispy Kreme had been adding new stores at a record pace throughout 2002–2003. The company's strategy and business model were aimed at adding a sufficient number of new stores and boosting sales at existing stores to achieve 20 percent annual revenue growth and 25 percent annual growth in earnings per share. In the just-completed 2004 fiscal year, total company revenues rose by 35.4 percent, to $665.6 million, compared with the $491.5 million in the fiscal 2003. Net income in fiscal 2004 increased by 70.4 percent, from $33.5 million to $57.1 million. Krispy Kreme's stock price had increased eightfold since the company went public in April 2000, giving the company a high profile with investors and Wall Street analysts. In February 2004, Krispy Kreme stock was trading at 30 times the consensus earnings estimates for fiscal 2005, a price/earnings ratio that was justified only if the company continued to grow 20 to 25 percent annually.

A number of securities analysts doubted whether Krispy Kreme's strategy and growth potential would continue to push the company's stock price upward. According to one analyst, "The odds are against this stock for long-term success." Another commented, "I think the market is overly optimistic about the long-term opportunities of the growth of the doughnut business." A third said, "Single-product concepts only have so many years to run." Indeed, restaurants with quick-service products presently had the slowest revenue growth of any restaurant type. The Krispy Kreme bears were particularly concerned about reports from franchisees that, as the number of Krispy Kreme stores expanded in choice markets, average-store sales were slowing and newly opened stores were not performing as well as the first one or two stores. After the initial buying frenzy at high-profile store openings in a major market, the buzz tended to fade as the fourth, fifth, and sixth outlets opened; moreover, new stores started to cannibalize sales from existing stores, thus moderating the potential for new stores to boost overall sales. Several franchisees in California, Michigan, New York, Canada, and a few other places were said to be in financial difficulty because of overexpansion and disappointing sales at newly opened stores.

Company Background

In 1933, Vernon Rudolph bought a doughnut shop in Paducah, Kentucky, from Joe LeBeau. His purchase included the company's assets and goodwill, the Krispy Kreme name, and rights to a secret yeast-raised doughnut recipe that LeBeau had created in New Orleans years earlier. Several years thereafter, Rudolph and his partner, looking for a larger market, moved their operations to Nashville, Tennessee; other members of the Rudolph family joined the enterprise, opening doughnut shops in Charleston, West Virginia, and Atlanta, Georgia. The business consisted of producing, marketing, and delivering fresh-made doughnuts to local grocery stores. Then, during the summer of 1937, Rudolph decided to quit the family business and left Nashville, taking with him a 1936 Pontiac, $200 in cash, doughnut-making equipment, and the secret recipe; after some disappointing efforts to find another location, he settled on opening the first Krispy Kreme Doughnuts shop in Winston-Salem, North Carolina. Rudolph was drawn to Winston-Salem because the city was developing into a tobacco and textiles hub in the Southeast, and he thought a doughnut shop would make a good addition to the thriving local economy. Rudolph and his two partners, who accompanied him from Nashville, used their last $25 to rent a building across from Salem College and Academy. With no money left to buy ingredients, Rudolph convinced a local grocer to lend them what they needed, promising payment once the first doughnuts were sold. To deliver the doughnuts, he took the backseat out of the 1936 Pontiac and installed a delivery rack. On July 13, 1937, the first Krispy Kreme doughnuts were made at Rudolph's new Winston-Salem shop and delivered to grocery retailers.

Soon afterward, people began stopping by the shop to ask if they could buy hot doughnuts. There were so many requests that Rudolph decided to cut a hole in the shop's wall so that he could sell doughnuts at retail to passersby. Krispy Kreme doughnuts proved highly popular in Winston-Salem, and Rudolph's shop prospered. By the late 1950s, Krispy Kreme had 29 shops in 12 states, with each shop having the capacity to produce 500 dozen doughnuts per hour.

In the early 1950s, Vernon Rudolph met Mike Harding, who was then selling powdered milk to bakeries. Rudolph was looking for someone to help grow the business, and Harding joined the company as a partner in 1954. Starting with six employees, the two began building an equipment department and a plant for blending doughnut mixes. They believed the key to Krispy Kreme's expansion was to have control over each step of the doughnut-making process and to be able to deliver hot doughnuts to customers as soon as they emerged from the frying and sugar-glazing process. In 1960, they decided to standardize all Krispy Kreme shops with a green roof, a red-glazed brick exterior, a viewing window inside, an overhead conveyor for doughnut production, and bar stools—creating a look that became Krispy Kreme's trademark during that era.

Harding focused on operations, while Rudolph concentrated on finding promising locations for new stores and getting bank financing to support expansion into other southeastern cities and towns. Harding became Krispy Kreme's president in 1958, and he became chief executive officer when Rudolph died in 1973. Under Rudolph and then Harding, Krispy Kreme's revenues grew from less than $1 million in 1954 to $58 million by the time Harding retired in 1974. Corporate headquarters remained in Winston-Salem.

In 1976, Beatrice Foods bought Krispy Kreme and proceeded to make a series of changes. The recipe was changed, and the company's script-lettered signs were altered to produce a more modern look. As customers reacted negatively to Beatrice's changes, business declined. A group of franchisees, led by Joseph McAleer, bought the company from Beatrice in 1982 in a $22 million leveraged buyout. The new owners quickly reinstated the original recipe and the original script-lettered signs. Sales rebounded, but with double-digit interest rates in the early 1980s, it took years to pay off the buyout debt, leaving little for expansion.

To grow revenues, the company relied mainly on franchising "associate" stores, opening a few new company-owned stores—all in the southeastern United States—and boosting store volume through off-premise sales. Associate stores operated under a 15-year licensing agreement that permitted them to use the Krispy Kreme system within a specific geographic territory. They paid royalties of 3 percent of on-premise sales and 1 percent of all other branded sales (to supermarkets, convenience stores, charitable organizations selling doughnuts for fund-raising projects, and other wholesale buyers); no royalties were paid on sales of unbranded or private-label doughnuts. The primary emphasis of the associate stores and many of the company stores was on wholesaling both Krispy Kreme doughnuts and private-label doughnuts to local groceries and supermarkets. Corporate revenues rose gradually to $117 million in 1989 and then flattened for the next six years.

New Leadership and a New Strategy

In the early 1990s, with interest rates falling and much of the buyout debt paid down, the company began experimenting cautiously with expanding under Scott Livengood, the company's newly appointed president and chief operating officer. Livengood, 48, joined Krispy Kreme's human relations department in 1978 three years after graduating from the University of North Carolina at Chapel Hill with a degree in industrial relations and a minor in psychology. Believing strongly in the company's product and long-term growth potential, he rose through the management ranks, becoming president and chief operating officer in 1992, a member of the board of directors in 1994; president and CEO in 1998; and president, CEO, and chairman of the board in 1999.

Shortly after becoming president in 1992, Livengood became increasingly concerned about stagnant sales and shortcomings in the company's strategy: "The model wasn't working for us. It was more about selling in wholesale channels and less about the brand." He and other Krispy Kreme executives, mindful of the thousands of "Krispy Kreme stories" told by passionate customers over the years, concluded that the emphasis on off-premise sales did not adequately capitalize on the enthusiasm and loyalty of customers for Krispy Kreme's doughnuts. A second shortcoming was that the company's exclusive focus on southeastern U.S. markets unnecessarily handcuffed efforts to leverage the company's brand equity and product quality in the rest of the U.S. doughnut market. The available data also indicated that the standard 7,000-plus-square-foot stores were uneconomic to operate in all but very high-volume locations.

By the mid-1990s, with fewer than 100 franchised and company-owned stores and corporate sales stuck in the $110–$120 million range for six years, company executives determined that it was time for a new strategy and aggressive expansion outside the Southeast. Beginning in 1996, Krispy Kreme began implementing a new strategy to reposition the company, shifting the focus from a wholesale bakery strategy to a specialty retail strategy that promoted sales at the company's own retail outlets and emphasized the "hot doughnut experience" so often stressed in customers' Krispy Kreme stories. Doughnut sizes were also increased. The second major part of the new strategy was to expand the number of stores nationally using both area franchisees and company-owned stores. In preparing to launch the strategy, the company tested several different store sizes, eventually concluding that stores in the 2,400- to 4,200-square-foot range were better suited for the company's market repositioning and expansion plans.

The franchising part of the strategy called for the company to license territories, usually defined by metropolitan statistical areas, to select franchisees with proven experience in multi-unit food operations. Franchisees were expected to be thoroughly familiar with the local area market they were to develop and also to have the capital and organizational capability to open a prescribed number of stores in their territory within a specified period. The minimum net worth requirement for franchise area developers was $750,000 per store or $5 million, whichever was greater. Area developers paid Krispy Kreme a franchise fee of $20,000 to $40,000 for each store they opened. They also were required to pay a 4.5 percent royalty fee on all sales and to contribute 1.0 percent of revenues to a company-administered advertising and public relations fund. Franchisees were expected to strictly adhere to high standards of quality and service.

By early 2000, the company had signed on 13 area developers operating 33 Krispy Kreme stores and committed to open another 130 stores in their territories within five years. In addition, the company was operating 61 stores under its own management. Sales had zoomed to $220 million, and profits were a record $6 million.

After a decision was made to take the company public in April 2000, Krispy Kreme spent much of late 1999 and early 2000 preparing for an initial public offering (IPO) of the company's stock. The old corporate structure, Krispy Kreme Doughnut Corporation, was merged into a new company, Krispy Kreme Doughnuts, Inc. The new company planned to use the proceeds from its IPO to remodel or relocate older company-owned stores, to repay debt, to make joint venture investments in franchised stores, and to expand its capacity to make doughnut mix.

The IPO of 3.45 million shares was oversubscribed at $21 per share, and when the stock began trading in April under the ticker symbol KREM, the price quickly rose. Krispy Kreme was the second-best-performing stock among all IPO offerings in the United States

EXHIBIT 1   **Financial Statement Data for Krispy Kreme Doughnuts, Fiscal Years 2000–2004 (Dollar amounts in thousands, except per share data)**

	Fiscal Years Ending				
	Jan. 30, 2000	Jan. 28, 2001	Feb. 3, 2002	Feb. 2, 2003	Feb. 1, 2004
Statement of operations data					
Total revenues	$220,243	$300,715	$394,354	$491,549	$665,592
Operating expenses	190,003	250,690	316,946	381,489	507,396
General and administrative expenses	14,856	20,061	27,562	28,897	36,912
Depreciation and amortization expenses	4,546	6,457	7,959	12,271	19,723
Arbitration award	—	—	—	9,075	(575)
Income from operations	10,838	23,507	41,887	59,817	102,086
Interest expense, (income), net, and other adjustments	1,232	(276)	(659)	5,044	7,409
Income (loss) before income taxes	9,606	23,783	42,546	54,773	94,677
Provision for income taxes	3,650	9,058	16,168	21,295	37,590
Net income	$ 5,956	$ 14,725	$ 26,378	$ 33,478	$ 57,087
Net income per share:					
Basic	$0.16	$0.30	$0.49	$0.61	$0.96
Diluted	$0.15	0.27	0.45	0.56	0.92
Shares used in calculation of net income per share:					
Basic	37,360	49,184	53,703	55,093	59,188
Diluted	39,280	53,656	58,443	59,492	62,388
Balance sheet data					
Current assets	$ 41,038	$ 67,611	$101,769	$141,128	$138,644
Current liabilities	29,586	38,168	52,533	59,687	53,493
Working capital	11,452	29,443	49,236	81,441	85,151
Total assets	104,958	171,493	255,376	410,487	660,664
Long-term debt, including current maturities	22,902	—	4,643	60,489	137,917
Total shareholders' equity	$ 47,755	$125,679	$187,667	$273,352	$452,207
Cash flow data					
Net cash provided by operating activities	$ 8,498	$ 32,112	$ 36,210	$ 51,036	$ 95,553
Net cash used for investing activities	(11,826)	(67,288)	(52,263)	(94,574)	(186,241)
Net cash provided by (used for) financing activities	(398)	39,019	30,931	53,837	79,514
Cash and cash equivalents at end of year	3,183	7,026	21,904	32,203	21,029

Source: Company SEC filings and annual reports.

in 2000. The company's stock began trading on the New York Stock Exchange in May 2001 under the symbol KKD.

Between early 2000 and early 2004, the company increased the number of Krispy Kreme stores from 144 to 357, boosted doughnut sales from an average of 3 million a day to an average of 7.5 million a day, and began the process of expanding internationally— opening its first factory store in Europe, located in the world-renowned department store Harrods of Knightsbridge, London (with plans for another 25 stores in Britain and Ireland by 2008), and continuing expansion in Australia, Canada, and Mexico. In fiscal 2004, Krispy Kreme captured an estimated 30.6 percent of the market for packaged doughnut sales, compared with 23.9 percent in fiscal 2003 and 6.4 percent in fiscal 2002.

Exhibit 1 presents a summary of Krispy Kreme's financial performance and operations for fiscal years 2000–2004.

EXHIBIT 2   Krispy Kreme's Performance by Business Segment, Fiscal Years 2000–2003 (In thousands)

	Fiscal Years Ending				
	Jan. 30, 2000	Jan. 20, 2001	Feb. 3, 2002	Feb. 2, 2003	Feb. 1, 2004
Revenues by business segment					
Company store operations	$164,230	$213,677	$266,209	$319,592	$441,868
Franchise operations	5,529	9,445	14,008	19,304	23,848
KK Manufacturing and Distribution	50,484	77,593	114,137	152,653	193,129
Total	$220,243	$300,715	$394,354	$491,549	$665,592*
Operating income by business segment (before depreciation and amortization)					
Company store operations	$ 18,246	$ 27,370	$ 42,932	$ 58,214	$ 83,724
Franchise operations	1,445	5,730	9,040	14,319	19,043
KK Manufacturing and Distribution	7,182	11,712	18,999	26,843	39,345
Total	$ 10,838	$ 23,507	$ 41,887	$ 59,817	$ 102,086*
Unallocated general and administrative expenses	$ (16,035)	$ (21,305)	$ (29,084)	$ (30,484)	$ (38,564)
Depreciation and amortization expenses					
Company store operations	$ 3,059	$ 4,838	$ 5,859	$ 8,854	$ 14,392
Franchise operations	72	72	72	108	173
KK Manufacturing and Distribution	236	303	507	1,723	3,006
Corporate administration	1,179	1,244	1,521	1,586	1,653
Total	$ 4,546	$ 6,457	$ 7,959	$ 12,271	$ 19,723*

*Totals include operations of Montana Mills, a business that was acquired in April 2004 and divested during fiscal 2005.
Source: Company SEC filings and annual reports.

EXHIBIT 3
Estimated Krispy Kreme Store Economics as of 2001

Store revenues	$3,600,000
Cash flow (after operating expenses)	960,000
Cash flow margin	27%
Owner's equity investment to construct store	$1,050,000
Cash flow return on equity investment	91%

Source: As estimated by Deutsche Bank Alex. Brown.

Krispy Kreme's Business Model and Strategy

Krispy Kreme's business model involved generating revenues and profits from three sources:

- Sales at company-owned stores.
- Royalties from franchised stores and franchise fees from new store openings.
- Sales of doughnut mixes, customized doughnut-making equipment, and coffees to franchised stores.

Exhibit 2 shows revenues, operating expenses, and operating income by business segment. The company was drawn to franchising because it minimized capital requirements, provided an attractive royalty stream, and put responsibility for local store operations in the hands of successful franchisees who knew the ins and outs of operating multi-unit chains efficiently. Krispy Kreme had little trouble attracting top-quality franchisees because of the attractive economics of its new stores (see Exhibit 3).

Krispy Kreme had developed a vertically integrated supply chain whereby it manufactured the mixes for its doughnuts at company plants in North Carolina and Illinois and also manufactured proprietary doughnut-making equipment for use in both company-owned and franchised stores. The sale of mixes and equipment, referred to as "KK manufacturing and distribution" by the company, generated a substantial fraction of both revenues and earnings (Exhibit 2).

Many of the stores built prior to 1997 were designed primarily as wholesale bakeries, and their formats and site locations differed considerably from the newer stores being located in high-density areas where there were lots of people and high traffic counts. In order to improve on-premise sales at these older stores, the company was implementing a program to either remodel them or close and relocate them to sites that could better attract on-premise sales. In new markets, the company's strategy was to focus initial efforts on on-premise sales at its stores and then leverage the interest generated in Krispy Kreme products to secure supermarket and convenience store accounts and grow packaged sales.

So far, the company had spent very little on advertising to introduce its product to new markets, relying instead on local media publicity, product giveaways, and word of mouth. In almost every instance, local newspapers had run big features headlining the opening of the first Krispy Kreme stores in their area; in some cases, local radio and TV stations had sent news crews to cover the opening and conduct on-the-scene interviews. The grand opening in Austin, Texas, was covered live by five TV crews and four radio station crews (there were 50 people in line at 11:30 PM the night before the 5:30 AM store opening). At the first San Diego store opening, there were five remote TV trucks on the scene; radio reporters were out interviewing customers camped out in their pickup trucks in the parking lot; and a nationally syndicated radio show broadcast "live" at the site. It was common for customers to form lines at the door and at the drive-through window well before the initial day's 5:30 AM grand opening, when the HOT DOUGHNUTS NOW sign was first turned on. In a number of instances, there were traffic jams at the turn in to the store—a Buffalo, New York, traffic cop said, "I've never seen anything like this . . . and I mean it." As part of the grassroots marketing effort surrounding new-store openings, Krispy Kremes were typically given away at public events as a treat for participants—then, as one franchisee said, "the Krispy Kremes seem to work their own magic and people start to talk about them."

Krispy Kreme had originally financed its expansion strategy with the aid of long-term debt. However, the April 2000 IPO raised enough equity capital to completely pay off the long-term debt outstanding as of fiscal 2001. Since then the company had borrowed about $50 million on a long-term basis to help fund its rapid growth during 2002–2004. When the company went public, it ceased paying dividends to shareholders; currently all earnings were being retained and reinvested in growing the business.

Company Operations

Products and Product Quality

Doughnuts

Krispy Kreme produced nearly 50 varieties of doughnuts, including specialty doughnuts offered at limited times and locations. By far the biggest seller was the company's signature "hot original glazed" doughnut made from Joe LeBeau's original yeast-based recipe. Exhibit 4 shows the company's doughnut varieties as of September 2003. Exhibit 5 indicates the nutritional content for a representative selection of Krispy Kreme doughnuts.

Company research indicated that Krispy Kreme's appeal extended across all major demographic groups, including age and income. Many customers purchased doughnuts by the dozen for their office, clubs, and family. According to one enthusiastic franchisee:

EXHIBIT 4
Varieties of Krispy Kreme Doughnuts

- Original Glazed
- Chocolate Iced
- Chocolate Iced with Sprinkles
- Maple Iced
- Chocolate Iced Creme Filled
- Glazed Creme Filled
- Traditional Cake
- Apple Fritter
- Powdered Strawberry Filled
- Chocolate Iced Custard Filled
- Raspberry Filled
- Lemon Filled
- Cinnamon Apple Filled

- Powdered Blueberry Filled
- Chocolate Iced Cake
- Dulce de Leche
- Sugar Coated
- Glazed Cruller
- Powdered Cake
- Glazed Devil's Food
- Chocolate Iced Cruller
- Cinnamon Bun
- Glazed Blueberry
- Glazed Sour Cream
- Caramel Kreme Crunch

Source: www.krispykreme.com, September 22, 2003.

EXHIBIT 5 **Nutritional Content of Selected Varieties of Krispy Kreme Doughnuts**

Product	Calories	Calories from Fat	Total Fat		Saturated Fat		Carbohydrates		Sugars (grams)
			Grams	% Daily Value*	Grams	% Daily Value*	Grams	% Daily Value*	
Original Glazed	200	110	12	18	3	15	22	7	10
Chocolate Iced Glazed	250	110	12	19	3	15	33	11	21
Maple Iced Glazed	240	110	12	18	3	15	32	11	20
Powdered Blueberry Filled	290	150	16	25	4	21	32	11	14
Chocolate Iced Creme Filled	350	190	21	32	5	25	39	13	23
Glazed Creme Filled	340	180	20	31	5	24	39	13	23
Traditional cake	230	120	13	20	3	15	25	8	9
Glazed Cruller	240	130	14	22	3.5	17	26	9	14
Cinnamon Bun	260	140	16	24	4	20	28	9	13
Glazed Devil's Food	340	160	18	28	4.5	21	42	14	27

*Based on a 2,000-calorie diet.
Source: www.krispykreme.com, September 22, 2003.

We happen to think this is a very, very unique product which has what I can only describe as a one-of-a-kind taste. They are extremely light in weight and texture. They have this incredible glaze. When you have one of the hot original doughnuts as they come off the line, there's just nothing like it.

In 2003, Krispy Kreme ranked number one in Restaurants and Institutions' Choice in Chains category, beating number-two-ranked Starbucks.

The company received several thousand e-mails and letters monthly from customers. By all accounts, most were from customers who were passionate about Krispy Kreme products, and there were always some from people pleading for stores to be opened in their area. Exhibit 6 presents sample comments from customers and franchisees. According to Scott Livengood:

You have to possess nothing less than a passion for your product and your business because that's where you draw your energy. We have a great product . . . We have loyal customers, and we have great brand equity. When we meet people with a Krispy Kreme story, they always do it with a smile on their faces.

EXHIBIT 6   Sample Comments from Krispy Kreme Customers and Franchisees

Customer comments:

* "I ate one and literally it brought a tear to my eye. I kid you not."
* "Oh my gosh, this is awesome. I wasn't even hungry, but now I'm going to get two dozen."
* "We got up at 3 o'clock this morning. I told them I would be late for work. I was going to the grand opening."
* "They melt in your mouth. They really do."
* "Krispy Kreme rocks."
* "It's hot, good and hot. The way a doughnut should be."
* "The doughnut's magnificent. A touch of genius."
* "I love doughnuts, but these are different. It's terrible for your weight because when you eat just one, you feel like you've barely tasted it. You want more. It's like popcorn."*
* "When you bite into one it's like biting into a sugary cloud. It's really fun to give one to someone who hasn't had one before. They bite into one and just exclaim."†

Franchisee comments:

* "Krispy Kreme is a 'feel good' business as much as it is a doughnut business. Customers come in for an experience which makes them feel good—they enjoy our doughnuts and they enjoy the time they spend in our stores watching the doughnuts being made."
* "We're not selling doughnuts as much as we are creating an experience. The viewing window into the production room is a theater our customers can never get enough of. It's fun to watch doughnuts being made and even more fun to eat them when they're hot off the line."
* "Southern California customers have responded enthusiastically to Krispy Kreme. Many of our fans first came to Krispy Kreme not because of a previous taste experience but rather because of the 'buzz' around the brand. It was more word of mouth and publicity that brought them in to sample our doughnuts. Once they tried them, they became loyal fans who spread the word that Krispy Kreme is something special. . . We witness the excitement everyday, especially when we're away from the store and wearing a hat or shirt with the Krispy Kreme logo. When people see the logo, we get the big smile and are always asked. 'When will we get one in our neighborhood?' . . . The tremendous local publicity coupled with the amazing brand awareness nationwide has helped us make the community aware of our commitment to support local charities. Our fund-raising program, along with product donations to schools, churches, and other charitable organizations have demonstrated our real desire to give back. This commitment also impacts our employees who understand firsthand the value of supporting the needy as well as the worthy causes in our neighborhoods."
* "In all my many years of owning and operating multiple food franchise businesses, we have never been able to please—until Krispy Kreme—such a wide range of customers in the community. Its like an old friend has come to town when we open our doors: we're welcomed with open arms . . . Quite frankly, in my experience, publicity for Krispy Kreme is like nothing I have ever seen. It is truly unprecedented."

*As quoted in "Winchell's Scrambles to Meet Krispy Kreme Challenge," *Los Angeles Times,* September 30, 1999, p. C1.
†As quoted in Greg Sukiennik, "Will Dunkin' Donuts Territory Take to Krispy Kreme?" The Associated Press State & Local Wire, April 8, 2001.

Source: Krispy Kreme's 2000 and 2001 annual reports, except for two quotes noted above.

Coffee

Krispy Kreme had recently launched strategic initiatives to improve the caliber and appeal of its on-premise coffee and beverage offerings, aligning them more closely with the hot doughnut experience in its stores. The first move came in early 2001 when Krispy Kreme acquired Digital Java, Inc., a small Chicago-based coffee company that sourced and roasted premium quality coffees and that marketed a broad line of coffee-based and noncoffee beverages. Scott Livengood explained the reasons for the acquisition:

> We believe the Krispy Kreme brand naturally extends to a coffee and beverage offering that is more closely aligned with the hot doughnut experience in our stores. Vertical integration of our coffee business provides the capability to control the sourcing and roasting of our coffee. Increasing control of our supply chain will help ensure quality standards, recipe formulation, and roast consistency. With this capability, one of our first priorities will be the research and benchmarking necessary to develop premier blends and roasts of coffee which will help make Krispy Kreme a coffee destination for a broader audience. Beyond coffee, we intend to offer a full line of beverages including espresso-based drinks and frozen beverages. We be-

lieve we can substantially increase the proportion of our business devoted to coffee specifi- cally and beverages generally by upgrading and broadening our beverage offering.

Since the acquisition of Digital Java, coffee sales at Krispy Kreme stores had increased nearly 40 percent due to expanded product offerings and upgraded quality. In 2003, Krispy Kreme was marketing four types of coffee: Smooth, Rich, Bold, and Robust Decaf—all us- ing coffee beans from the top 5 percent of the world's growing regions. Beverage sales ac- counted for about 10 percent of store sales, with coffee accounting for about half of the beverage total and the other half divided among milk, juices, soft drinks, and bottled water. In the years ahead, Krispy Kreme hoped to increase beverage sales to about 20 percent of store sales.

Store Operations

Each store was designed as a "doughnut theater" where customers could watch the dough- nuts being made through a 40-foot glass window (see Exhibit 7). New stores ranged in size between 2,400 and 4,200 square feet. Stores had a drive-through window and a dining area that would seat 50 or more people—a few of the newer and larger stores had special rooms for hosting Krispy Kreme parties. Store decor was a vintage 1950s look with mint green walls and smooth metal chairs; some of the newest stores had booths (see Exhibit 8). A typ- ical store employed about 125 people, including about 65 full-time positions. Approxi- mately half of on-premise sales occurred in the morning hours and half in the afternoon and evening. Many stores were open 24 hours a day, with much of the doughnut making for off- premise sales being done between 6:00 PM and 6:00 AM. Production was nearly always un- der way during peak in-store traffic times. In several large metropolitan areas, however, the doughnut making for off-premise sales was done in a central commissary specially equipped for large-volume production, packaging, and local-area distribution.

Each doughnut took about one hour to make. After the ingredients were mixed into dough, the dough was rolled and cut. The pieces went into a 12-foot-tall machine where each piece rotated on a wire rack for 33 minutes under high humidity and a low heat of 126 degrees to allow the dough to rise. When the rising process was complete, the doughnuts moved along a conveyor to be fried on one side, flipped, fried on the other side, and drained. Following all this came inspection. Doughnuts destined to be glazed were directed through a waterfall of warm, sugary topping; the others were directed to another part of the baking section to be filled and/or frosted. Exhibit 8 depicts the mixing, rising, frying, drain- ing, and glazing parts of the process. Depending on store size and location, a typical day's production ranged between 4,000 and 10,000 dozen doughnuts.

Each producing store featured a prominent HOT DOUGHNUTS NOW neon sign (Exhibit 8) signaling customers that freshly made original glazed doughnuts were coming off the bakery conveyor belt and were available for immediate purchase. Generally, the signs glowed from 6:00 to 11:00 AM and then came on again during the late afternoon into the late-night hours.

Depending on the store location, Krispy Kreme's original glazed doughnuts sold for 60 to 75 cents each, or $4.50 to $7.50 per dozen; a mixed dozen usually sold for about 50 cents extra. Some stores charged a small premium for hot doughnuts coming right off the pro- duction line. Customers typically got a $1.00-per-dozen discount on purchases of two or more dozen.

Stores generated revenues in three ways:

- On-premise sales of doughnuts.
- Sales of coffee and other beverages.
- Off-premise sales of branded and private-label doughnuts to local supermarkets, conve- nience stores, and fund-raising groups. Krispy Kreme stores actively promoted sales to schools, churches, and civic groups for fund-raising drives.

EXHIBIT 7   Making the Doughnuts

Mixing Ingredients

Rising

Frying and Flipping

Inspection and Draining

Drying and Entering Glazing

Inspection and Draining

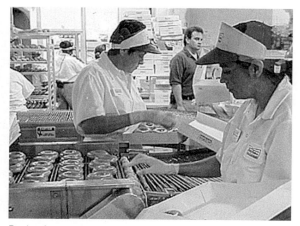

Packaging

EXHIBIT 8   Representative Krispy Kreme Stores and Store Scenes

The company had developed a highly effective system for delivering fresh doughnuts, both packaged and unpackaged, to area supermarket chains and convenience stores. Route drivers had the capability to take customer orders and deliver products directly to retail accounts where they were typically merchandised either from Krispy Kreme–branded displays or from bakery cases (as unbranded doughnuts). The popularity of Krispy Kreme's stores had prompted many area supermarkets to begin stocking a selection of Krispy Kreme products in either branded display cases or in dozen and half-dozen packages.

The franchisee for Krispy Kreme stores in San Francisco had arranged to sell a four-pack of Krispy Kremes for $5 at San Francisco Giant baseball games at Pacific Bell Park—Krispy Kreme sold out of 2,100 packs by the third inning of the first game and, despite increasing supplies, sold out again after the fourth and sixth innings of the next two games; stadium vendors were supplied with 3,450 four-packs for the fourth game. The franchisee of the Las Vegas stores had a Web site that allowed customers to place orders online before 2:00 PM and have them delivered to their place of work by a courier service.

A Texas franchisee built a new 18,000-square-foot production and distribution center to supply Metroplex supermarkets, convenience stores, and other area retailers with Krispy Kreme 12-packs because newly opened Krispy Kreme stores did not have the baking capacity to keep up with both on-premise and off-premise demand; there were similar franchiser-operated wholesale baking and distribution centers in Nashville, Cincinnati, Atlanta, Chicago, and Philadelphia. Several of these centers had established delivery capability to supply Krispy Kremes to retailers in outlying areas deemed too small to justify a stand-alone Krispy Kreme store.

In 2004, about 20,000 supermarkets, convenience stores, truck stops, and other outside locations sold Krispy Kreme doughnuts. A growing number of these locations had special Krispy Kreme display cases, stocked daily with trays of different varieties for shoppers to choose from; these stand-alone cases could be placed in high-traffic locations at the end of an aisle or close to the check-out register.

The cost of opening a new store was around $2 million (including the standard package of equipment purchased from Krispy Kreme), but new store construction could range as high as $2.5 million in locations with high land and/or building costs. The initial franchise fee per unit was $40,000. Site selection was based on household density, proximity to both daytime employment and residential centers, and proximity to other retail traffic generators. A record number of new stores were opened in fiscal 2004—28 company-owned stores and 58 franchised stores (the net gain in stores was only 81 because 5 older stores were closed). Plans were in place to open 75 new stores in the upcoming fiscal 2005 year.

Weekly sales at newly opened stores could run anywhere from $100,000 to $500,000 the first couple of weeks a new store was open. Weekly sales tended to moderate to around $40,000 to $50,000 after several months of operation, but Krispy Kreme management expected new stores to have annual sales averaging more than $3 million in their first year of operation. In fiscal 2003, sales at all of the company's 276 stores (which included those open less than a year) averaged $2.82 million. In fiscal 2004, sales at all 357 stores averaged $2.76 million—slightly lower than in 2003, chiefly because of the larger number of new store openings (roughly half of the 86 new stores were open less than six months). Exhibit 9 provides data on store operations.

Krispy Kreme Manufacturing and Distribution

All the doughnut mix and equipment used in Krispy Kreme stores was manufactured and supplied by the company, partly as a means of ensuring consistent recipe quality and doughnut making throughout the chain and partly as a means of generating sales and profits from franchise operations. Revenues of the Krispy Kreme Manufacturing and Distribution (KKM&D) unit had averaged about 30 percent of total Krispy Kreme revenues for the past three years and contributed 38 to 45 percent of annual operating income (Exhibit 2). The

EXHIBIT 9   **Store Operations Data, Krispy Kreme Doughnuts, Fiscal Years 1998–2004**

	1998	2000	2001	2002	2003	2004
Systemwide sales	$203,439	$318,854	$448,129	$621,665	$778,573	$984,895
Number of stores at end of period:						
Company-owned	58	58	63	75	99	141
Franchised	62	86	111	143	177	216
Systemwide total	120	144	174	218	276	357
Increase in comparable store sales:						
Company-owned	11.5%	12.0%	22.9%	11.7%	12.8%	13.6%
Franchised	12.7%	14.1%	17.1%	12.8%	11.8%	10.2%
Average weekly sales per store:						
Company-owned (000s)	$42	$54	$69	$72	$76	$73
Franchised (000s)	$23	$38	$43	$53	$58	$56

Source: Company annual reports and 10K reports.

company's line of custom stainless-steel doughnut-making machines ranged in capacity from 230 to 600 dozen doughnuts per hour. Franchisees paid Krispy Kreme about $770,000 for the standard doughnut-making equipment package in 2003–2004 (up from about $500,000 In the late 1990s); the price Increase was due partly to Increased equipment capacity and partly to longer equipment durability. Increased doughnut sales at franchised stores also translated into increased revenues for KKM&D from sales of mixes, sugar, and other supplies to franchisees.

Krispy Kreme had recently opened a state-of-the-art 187,000-square-foot manufacturing and distribution facility in Effingham, Illinois, dedicated to the blending and packaging of prepared doughnut mixes and to distributing mixes, equipment, and other supplies to stores in the Midwest and the western half of North America. This facility had significantly lowered Krispy Kreme's unit costs and provided triple the production capacity of the older plant in Winston-Salem.

Training

Since mid-1999, Krispy Kreme had invested in the creation of a multimedia management training curriculum. The program included classroom instruction, computer-based and video training modules, and in-store training experiences. The online part of the training program made full use of graphics, video, and animation, as well as seven different types of test questions. Every Krispy Kreme store had access to the training over the company's intranet and the Internet; employees who registered for the course could access the modules from home using their Internet connection. Learners' test results were transferred directly to a Krispy Kreme human resources database; learners were automatically redirected to lessons where their test scores indicated that they had not absorbed the material well on the first attempt. The online course was designed to achieve 90 percent mastery from 90 percent of the participants and could be updated as needed.

The course for managers had been recast into a program suitable for hourly employees. The course could also be divided into small pieces and customized to fit individual needs. In 2003, Krispy Kreme intensified its focus on leadership development by establishing the Learning Initiative Program as well as the Performance Management System. In 2003, 18 employees attended the Krispy Kreme Leadership Institute to increase their capacities in senior management areas.

Growth Potential

In 2003 and continuing into early 2004, Krispy Kreme management expressed confidence that the company was still in its infancy. The company's highest priority was on expanding into markets with over 100,000 households; management believed these markets were attractive because the dense population characteristics offered opportunities for multiple store locations, gave greater exposure to brand-building efforts, and afforded multi-unit operating economies. However, the company believed that secondary markets with fewer than 100,000 households held significant sales and profit potential—it was exploring smaller-sized store designs suitable for secondary markets. In 2002, Krispy Kreme CEO Scott Livengood stated, "We are totally committed to putting full factory stores in every town in the U.S." Krispy Kreme's management further believed the food-service and institutional channel of sales offered significant opportunity to extend the brand into colleges and universities, business and industry facilities, and sports and entertainment complexes. Management had stated that the company's strong brand name, highly differentiated product, high-volume production capability, and multichannel market penetration strategy put the company in a position to become the recognized leader in every market it entered.

Expansion into Foreign Markets

In December 2000, the company hired Donald Henshall, 38, to fill the newly created position of president of international development; Henshall was formerly managing director of new business development with the London-based Overland Group, a maker and marketer of branded footwear and apparel. Henshall's job was to refine the company's global strategy, develop the capabilities and infrastructure to support expansion outside the United States, and consider inquiries from qualified parties wanting to open Krispy Kreme stores in foreign markets. Outside of the United States, Krispy Kreme stores had opened in Canada, Australia, Mexico, and Great Britain. Krispy Kreme and its franchisees planned to open 39 new stores in Canada, 30 in Australia and New Zealand, 20 in Mexico, and 25 in Great Britain and Ireland in the coming years. So far, sales had been very promising at the foreign locations that had been opened, and franchise agreements were in the works for further global expansion.

As of May 2001, the company had stopped accepting franchise applications for U.S. locations, indicating that there were no open territories. By 2003, it had stopped accepting franchise applications in Canada, Mexico, Western Europe, and Australia, indicating that franchise contracts were already under way and that Krispy Kreme would be opening in these areas soon. According to Scott Livengood, "Krispy Kreme is a natural to become a global brand. Looking at our demographics, we appeal to a very broad customer base. We receive lots of interest on a weekly basis to expand into international locations and we are confident our brand will be received extremely well outside the U.S."

The Montana Mills Acquisition

Krispy Kreme's chief strategic move in 2003 was to acquire Montana Mills Bread Company, a Rochester, New York–based bakery operation with 11 retail locations. The acquisition price was 1.2 million shares of Krispy Kreme stock (worth roughly $50 million). The Montana Mills chain of neighborhood bakeries featured fresh stone-ground flour, a highly visual presentation of the baking process in full view of the customer, and customer sampling with large slices of a variety of fresh-baked breads. In explaining why the acquisition was made, Scott Livengood, Krispy Kreme's Chairman and CEO, said:

> This acquisition is a natural outgrowth of the development of Krispy Kreme over the past five years. As I have indicated previously, we view Krispy Kreme Doughnuts, Inc., first and foremost as a set of unique capabilities which include the abilities to explore and nurture our customers' passion for and connection to a brand, create an effective franchise network, vertically integrate to provide a complete range of products and services to a system-wide store network serving flour-based, short shelf life products, and deliver these products daily

across multiple channels. Applying these core organizational competencies to the development of a second concept has the potential to create significant leverage.

The opportunity to create a wholesome, fresh-baked bakery and café concept the "Krispy Kreme way" is obviously unique to Krispy Kreme. I have long considered how to capitalize on this opportunity. In Montana Mills, we found the perfect foundation for this new concept—passionate bread bakers who have created a fiercely loyal customer following around a wide variety of fresh-baked goods, bread-baking theater, and sampling of large slices of bread. I have personally observed this passion that each Montana Mills employee carries for their customers and their breads. This is a great platform on which to build. We will work closely with the Montana Mills team as we try to add value to an already outstanding concept.

I expect we will spend in the range of two years fully developing the concept I described. As we have indicated regarding our international expansion, we will always try to prepare for any type of expansion well before we need the growth. We want the time to do it right. For this concept, I think that time is now.

In fiscal 2004, Montana Mills generated revenues of $6.7 million and had operating expenses of $8.7 million, thus resulting in operating loss of $2.0 million.

Industry Environment

By some estimates, the U.S. doughnut industry was a $5 to $6 billion market in 2003–2004. Americans consumed an estimated 10 to 12 billion doughnuts annually—over three dozen per capita. In 2002, doughnut industry sales rose by about 13 percent. According to a study done by Technomic, a marketing research specialist in foods, doughnut shops were the fastest-growing dining category in the country in 2002–2003.

In 2002, estimated sales at outlets specializing in doughnuts rose by about 9 percent, to about $3.6 billion. Growth in packaged doughnut sales at supermarkets, convenience stores, and other retail outlets had been quite small in the past five years. The proliferation of bakery departments in supermarkets had squeezed out many locally owned doughnut shops and, to some extent, had constrained the growth of doughnut chains. Doughnuts were a popular item in supermarket bakeries, with many customers finding it more convenient to buy them when doing their regular supermarket shopping as opposed to making a special trip to local bakeries. Doughnut aficionados, however, tended to pass up doughnuts in the grocery store, preferring the freshness, quality, and variety offered by doughnut specialty shops. Most patrons of doughnut shops frequented those in their neighborhoods or normal shopping area; it was unusual for them to make a special trip of more than a mile or two for doughnuts.

Small independent doughnut shops usually had a devoted clientele, drawn from neighborhood residents and regular commuters passing by on their way to and from work. A longtime employee at a family-owned shop in Denver said, "Our customers are very loyal to us. Probably 80 percent are regulars."[1] Owners of independent shops seemed to believe that new entry by popular chains like Krispy Kreme posed little competitive threat, arguing that the market was big enough to support both independents and franchisers, that the Krispy Kreme novelty was likely to wear off, and that unless a doughnut franchiser located a store close to their present location the impact would be minimal at worst. A store owner in Omaha said, "Our doughnut sales increased when Krispy Kreme came to town. We benefit every time they advertise because doughnuts are as popular as ever."[2]

As of early 2004, there was little indication the low-carbohydrate, weight-watching craze that had swept the United States and other countries in recent years had cut much into

[1]As quoted in "Dough-Down at the Mile High Corral," *Rocky Mountain News,* March 25, 2001, p. 1G.
[2]As quoted in "Hole-ly War: Omaha to Be Battleground for Duel of Titans," *Omaha World Herald,* September 7, 1999, p. 14.

sales. Industry observers and company officials attributed this in part to doughnuts being an affordable indulgence, easy to eat on the run, and in part to the tendency of many people to treat themselves occasionally. Doughnuts were readily available almost anywhere.

The three leading doughnut chains were Krispy Kreme; Dunkin' Donuts, with worldwide 2002 sales of $2.7 billion, 5,200 outlets worldwide (3,600 in the United States), and close to a 45 percent U.S. market share based on dollar sales volume; and Tim Hortons (160 outlets and 2002 U.S. sales of $115 million, plus 2,300 Canadian outlets with 2002 sales of $536 million).

Krispy Kreme's Chief Competitors

Dunkin' Donuts

Dunkin' Donuts was the largest coffee and baked-goods chain in the world, selling 4.4 million donuts and 1.8 million cups of coffee daily. The quick-service restaurant chain was owned by British-based Allied Domecq PLC, a diversified enterprise whose other businesses included the Baskin-Robbins ice cream chain, ToGo's Eateries (sandwiches), and an assortment of alcoholic beverage brands (Kahla, Beefeater's, Maker's Mark, Courvoisier, Tia Maria, and a host of wines). In 2004, Allied Domecq's Dunkin' Donuts chain had total sales approaching $4 billion, almost 6,200 franchised outlets in 40 countries (including 4,418 in the United States), and comparable store sales growth of 4.4 percent in the United States. About 83 percent of the chain's total sales were in the United States. In New England alone, Dunkin' Donuts operated 1,200 stores, including 600 in the Greater Boston area, where the chain was founded in 1950. Starting in 2000, Dunkin' Donuts franchisees could open co-branded stores that included Baskin Robbins and ToGo. Dunkin' Donuts ranked 9th in *Entrepreneur* magazine's annual Franchise Top 500 for 2005.

The key thrust of Dunkin' Donuts' strategy was to expand into those geographic areas in the United States where it was underrepresented. In areas where there were clusters of Dunkin' Donuts outlets, most baked items were supplied from centrally located kitchens rather than being made on-site. Despite its name, Dunkin' Donuts put more emphasis on coffee and convenience than on doughnuts. According to one company executive, "People talk about our coffee first. We're food you eat on the go. We're part of your day. We're not necessarily a destination store." Roughly half of all purchases at Dunkin' Donuts included coffee without a doughnut.[3] Dunkin' Donuts menu included doughnuts (50 varieties), muffins, bagels, cinnamon buns, cookies, brownies, Munchkins doughnut holes, cream cheese sandwiches, nine flavors of fresh coffee, iced coffees, and a lemonade Coolatta.

In 2004, Coolatta was being promoted in collaboration with MTV in a campaign called "Route to Cool." Dunkin' Donuts also had a new "express donuts" campaign to promote the sale of boxed donuts—12-packs containing the top six flavors. This campaign was being supported by advertising based on the theme "Who brought the donuts?" In addition, the chain was emphasizing coffee sales by the pound and had recently broadened its coffee offerings to include cappuccino, latte, espresso, and iced coffees.

The nutritional content of Dunkin' Donuts' 50 doughnut varieties ranged between 200 and 340 calories, between 8 and 19 grams of fat, between 1.5 and 6 grams of saturated fat, and between 9 and 31 grams of sugars; its cinnamon buns had 540 calories, 15 grams of fat, 4 grams of saturated fat, and 42 grams of sugars. Whereas Krispy Kreme's best-selling original glazed doughnuts had 200 calories, 12 grams of fat, 3 grams of saturated fat and 10 grams of sugar, the comparable item at Dunkin' Donuts had 180 calories, 8 grams of fat, 1.5 grams of saturated fat, and 6 grams of sugar. Several Dunkin' Donuts customers in the

---

[3]According to information in Hermione Malone, "Krispy Kreme to Offer Better Coffee as It Tackles New England," *Charlotte Observer,* March 16, 2001.

Boston area who had recently tried Krispy Kreme doughnuts reported that Krispy Kremes had more flavor and were lighter.[4]

Dunkin' Donuts had successfully fended off competition from national bagel chains and Starbucks. When national bagel chains, promoting bagels as a healthful alternative to doughnuts, opened new stores in areas where Dunkin' Donuts had stores, the company responded by adding bagels and cream cheese sandwiches to its menu offerings. Dunkin' Donuts had countered threats from Starbucks by adding a wider variety of hot and cold coffee beverages—and whereas coffee drinkers had to wait for a Starbucks barista to properly craft a $3 latte, they could get coffee and a doughnut on the fly at Dunkin' Donuts for less money. Quick and consistent service was a Dunkin' Donuts forte. Management further believed that the broader awareness of coffee created by the market presence of Starbucks stores had actually helped boost coffee sales at Dunkin' Donuts. In markets such as New York City and Chicago where there were both Dunkin' Donuts and Krispy Kreme stores, sales at Dunkin' Donuts had continued to rise. In commenting on the competitive threat from Krispy Kreme, a Dunkin' Donuts vice president said:

> We have a tremendous number of varieties, a tremendous level of convenience, tremendous coffee and other baked goods. I think the differentiation that Dunkin' enjoys is clear. We're not pretentious and don't take ourselves too seriously, but we know how important a cup of coffee and a donut or bagel in the morning is. Being able to deliver a great cup of coffee when someone is on their way to something else is a great advantage.[5]

In 2003, Couche-Tard, Canada's largest convenience store operator, bought control of the Dunkin' Donuts name in Quebec as well as the 104 Dunkin' Donuts outlets located there. Couche-Tard planned to double the number of outlets within five years to better compete with Tim Hortons and Krispy Kreme.

Tim Hortons

Tim Hortons, a subsidiary of Wendy's International, was one of North America's largest coffee and fresh-baked-goods chains, with almost 2,400 restaurants across Canada and a steadily growing base of 200 locations in key markets within the United States. In April 2004, Tim Hortons acquired 42 Bess Eaton coffee and doughnut restaurants throughout Rhode Island, Connecticut, and Massachusetts, which it planned to convert to the Tim Hortons brand and format. Tim Hortons had systemwide sales of around $3.0 billion in 2003, equal to annual sales of about $1.3 million per store. Same-store sales were up about 4.7 percent in 2003 and, during the first nine months of 2004, were up 10.1 percent in the United States and 7.7 percent in Canada. In Canada, the Tim Hortons chain was regarded as something of an icon—it was named for a popular Canadian-born professional hockey player who played for the Toronto Maple Leafs, Pittsburgh Penguins, and Buffalo Sabers; Horton was born in 1930, started playing hockey when he was five years old, and died in an auto accident while on the Buffalo Sabers. A recent survey of Canadian consumers rated Tim Hortons as the best managed brand in Canada.

The Tim Hortons division of Wendy's relied heavily on franchising—only 57 of the 2,527 Tim Hortons outlets at year-end 2003 were company-owned. Franchisees paid a royalty of 3 to 6 percent of weekly sales to the parent company, depending on whether they leased the land and/or buildings from Tim Hortons and on certain other conditions; in addition, franchisees paid fees equal to 4 percent of monthly gross sales to fund advertising and promotional activities undertaken at the corporate level. Franchisees were also required to purchase such products as coffee, sugar, flour and shortening from a Tim Hortons subsidiary; these

[4]"Time to Rate the Doughnuts: Krispy Kreme Readies to Roll into N.E. to Challenge Dunkin' Donuts," *Boston Globe,* February 21, 2001, p. D1.

[5]As quoted in Malone, "Krispy Kreme to Offer Better Coffee."

products were distributed from five warehouses located across Canada and were delivered to the company's Canadian restaurants primarily by its fleet of trucks and trailers. In the United States, both company and franchised stores purchased ingredients from a supplier approved by the parent company.

Tim Hortons used outside contractors to construct its restaurants. The restaurants were built to company specifications as to exterior style and interior decor. The standard Hortons restaurant being built in 2003–2004 consisted of a freestanding production unit ranging from 1,150 to 3,030 square feet. Each included a bakery capable of supplying fresh baked goods throughout the day to several satellite Tim Hortons within a defined area. Tim Hortons locations ranged from full standard stores with in-store baking facilities, to combo units with Wendy's and Tim Hortons under one roof, to carts and kiosks in shopping malls, highway outlets, universities, airports, and hospitals. Most full-standard Tim Hortons locations offered 24-hour drive-through service. Tim Hortons promoted its full-standard stores as neighborhood meeting places and was active in promoting its products for group fund-raisers and community events.

The menu at each Tim Hortons unit consisted of coffee, cappuccino, teas, hot chocolate, soft drinks, soups, sandwiches, and fresh baked goods such as doughnuts, muffins, pies, croissants, tarts, cookies, cakes, and bagels. In recent years, the chain had expanded its lunch menu to include a bigger variety of offerings. One of the chain's biggest drawing cards was its special blend of fresh-brewed coffee, which was also sold in cans for customers' use at home. About half of the purchases at Tim Hortons included coffee without a doughnut. Tim Hortons had the number one in market share in Canada during breakfast, was number one in the afternoon/early evening snack category, and had a strong number two position at lunch with a menu featuring six sandwiches.

Executives at Tim Hortons did not feel threatened by Krispy Kreme's expansion into Canada and those parts of the United States where it had stores (Michigan, New York, Ohio, Kentucky, Maine, and West Virginia). According to David House, Tim Hortons president, "We really welcome them. Anyone who draws attention to doughnuts can only help us. It is a big market and a big marketplace. I would put our doughnut up against theirs any day."[6] A Canadian retailing consultant familiar with Tim Hortons and Krispy Kreme said, "This is the Canadian elephant and the U.S. mouse. Listen, if there's anything where Canadians can kick American butt, it is in doughnuts."[7] Another Canadian retailing consultant said, "It [Krispy Kreme] is an American phenomenon. These things are sickeningly sweet."[8]

Canada was reputed to have more doughnut shops per capita than any other country in the world. Aside from Tim Hortons, other chains in Canada featuring doughnuts included Dunkin' Donuts, Robin's Donuts, Country Style, and Coffee Time. Tim Hortons management had a goal of opening 500 Tim Hortons stores in the United States over the next three years, mostly in the Northeast and Great Lakes regions, and a longer-term goal of growing to about 3,500 outlets in Canada.

Winchell's Donut House

Winchell's, founded by Verne Winchell in 1948, was owned by Shato Holdings, Ltd., of Vancouver, Canada. In 2000, there were approximately 600 Winchell's units located in 10 states west of the Mississippi River, along with international franchises in Guam, Saipan, Korea, Egypt, Saudi Arabia, and New Zealand. Since then, Winchell's Doughnut House had lost steam and closed two-thirds of its locations. In 2003, there were 200 units in 12 states, plus locations in Guam, Saipan, New Zealand, and Saudi Arabia. Winchell's was the largest doughnut chain on the West Coast. To combat Krispy Kreme's entry into Southern Califor-

---

[6]As quoted in "Can Krispy Kreme Cut It in Canada?" *Ottawa Citizen,* December 30, 2000, p. H1.

[7]As quoted in ibid.

[8]As quoted in ibid.

nia, where Winchell's had a brand awareness of 97 percent, Winchell's had launched a Warm 'n Fresh program for all outlets in 2000. The program entailed having fresh glazed doughnuts in display cases that were replaced every 15 to 20 minutes between 6:00 and 9:00 AM daily. A flashing red light on display cases signaled that a fresh batch of glazed doughnuts was available. Winchell's was offering customers a Warm 'n Fresh doughnut between 6:00 and 11:00 AM daily.

As of September 2003, a "Winchell's dozen" of 14 doughnuts sold for $5.99 and a double dozen (28) sold for $9.99. A single donut sold for about 60 cents, and many stores regularly ran a special of two donuts and a cup of coffee for $1.99. Winchell's bakery offerings included 20 varieties of doughnuts and 14 flavors of muffins, as well as croissants, bagels (breakfast bagel sandwiches were available at select locations), eclairs, tarts, apple fritters, and bear claws. It served three varieties of its "legendary" coffees—Dark Roast Supreme, Legendary Blend, and Legendary Decaf—all using only 100 percent arabica beans (considered by many to be the finest coffee beans in the world). Other beverages included regular and frozen cappuccino, soft drinks, milk, and juices.

Winchell's corporate goal for the next five years was to triple its sales. In 2003–2004 it was actively seeking franchisees in 14 western and midwestern states. Winchell's charged a franchise fee of $7,500 and required franchisee's to be able to invest $75,000 of unborrowed funds; the cost of new stores depended on such factors as store size, location, style of decor, and landscaping. A 5 percent royalty and a 3 percent advertising fee were charged on net sales.

LaMar's Donuts

Headquartered in Englewood, Colorado, LaMar's was a small, privately held chain that had 32 corporate-owned and franchised doughnut shops open or under development in 10 states; 8 stores were in the Denver area. Ray LaMar opened the original LaMar's Donuts in 1960 on Linwood Avenue in Kansas City and quickly turned the shop into a local institution. On a typical day, lines started forming before 6:00 AM and, by closing time about 11,000 donuts would be sold. Based on the doughnut shop's success and reputation, Ray and his wife, Shannon, decided in the early 1990s to franchise LaMar's. Hundreds of LaMar's devotees applied for the limited number of franchises made available in the Kansas City area; 15 were granted over a few months. But little became of the initial franchising effort and, in 1997, Franchise Consortium International, headed by Joseph J. Field, purchased a majority interest in LaMar's Franchising, renamed the company LaMar's Donuts International, moved the company's headquarters to a Denver suburb, and began laying the groundwork for a national expansion program.

LaMar's stores were typically located along neighborhood traffic routes. Average unit sales were $500,000 in 2003, and management expected that the average would increase to $750,000 in a few years. At one point, Fields expressed an objective of having 1,200 stores in operation by 2013, but so far LaMar's expansion was far slower than had been anticipated.

LaMar's utilized a secret recipe to produce "artisan quality" doughnuts that were handmade daily with all-natural ingredients and no preservatives. Day-old doughnuts were never sold at the shops but were donated at day's end to the needy. In addition to 75 varieties of doughnuts, LaMar's menu included gourmet coffee and cappuccino. LaMar's had recently partnered with Dazbog Coffee Company in Denver, Colorado, and created over a dozen customized specialty coffee blends under the LaMar's Old World Roast label. Beans were hand-picked from Costa Rica and then slow-roasted in an authentic Italian brick fire oven. Coffee products at LaMar's shops included cappuccinos, espressos, lattes, iced coffee drinks, and chai teas.

The company used the tag line "Simply a better doughnut." Joe Fields said, "People come in and try the product and they are surprised. They are wowed, in a very different way than Krispy Kreme. They say, 'Oh my God, this is the best doughnut I've had in my life.'" The Zagat Survey, a well-known rater of premier dining spots nationwide, described

LaMar's doughnuts as "extraordinary; fit for kings." *Gourmet* magazine, in search of the country's favorite doughnut, conducted a nationwide poll; the winner was a LaMar's doughnut. LaMar's Donuts has been named Best in the Country by the John Walsh Show, a one-hour daily nationally syndicated television program. Several newspapers had named LaMar's doughnuts as tops in their market area.

Unexpected Developments at Krispy Kreme in 2004

In March 2004, Krispy Kreme's management announced that it expected the company to have diluted earnings per share of $1.16 to $1.18 for fiscal 2005 (up from $0.92 in fiscal 2004) and systemwide comparable store sales growth in the mid-to-high single digits. Executives estimated that systemwide sales would increase approximately 25 percent in fiscal 2005 (ending January 29, 2005) and that approximately 120 new stores would be opened systemwide, including 20 to 25 smaller doughnut-and-coffee-shop stores, during the next 12 months. But as 2004 progressed, Krispy Kreme's business prospects went from rosy to stark within a matter of months.

Developments at Krispy Kreme in May 2004

In a May 7, 2004, press release that caught investors by surprise, CEO Scott Livengood said:

> For several months, there has been increasing consumer interest in low-carbohydrate diets, which has adversely impacted several flour-based food categories, including bread, cereal and pasta. This trend had little discernable effect on our business last year. However, recent market data suggests consumer interest in reduced carbohydrate consumption has heightened significantly following the beginning of the year and has accelerated in the last two to three months. This phenomenon has affected us most heavily in our off-premises sales channels, in particular sales of packaged doughnuts to grocery store customers.

Sales at Krispy Kreme's franchised stores were approximately evenly split between on-premises and off-premises sales, while approximately 60 percent of company-owned store sales were off-premises. As a consequence of the falloff in sales at external outlets, sales at Krispy Kreme stores open at least 18 months grew only 4 percent, well below the 9 percent realized in the preceding quarter. Due to the lower-than-expected off-premise sales at company stores, Livengood said the company was lowering its earnings guidance for the first quarter of fiscal 2005 to about $0.23 per share, down from about $0.26 per share. The company went on to announce in the same press release that it was

- Divesting its recently acquired Montana Mills operation. The plan was to close the majority of the Montana Mills store locations, which were underperforming, and pursue a sale of the remaining Montana Mills stores. Management indicated the Montana Mills divesture would entail write-offs of approximately $35 to $40 million in the first quarter on its Montana Mills investment and would likely involve further write-offs of $2 to $4 million in subsequent quarters.

- Closing six underperforming factory stores—four in older retail locations in below-average retail trade areas and two commissaries.

- Lowering its guidance for fiscal 2005 diluted earnings per share from continuing operations, excluding asset impairment and other charges described below, to between $1.04 and $1.06, approximately 10 percent lower than prior forecasts. Including the Montana Mills charges, diluted earnings per share from continuing operations were estimated to be between $0.93 and $0.95 for fiscal 2005.

In the hours following the announcement, the company's stock price was hammered in trading—dropping about 20 percent.

On May 25, 2004, Krispy Kreme reported a $24.4 million loss for the first quarter of fiscal 2005, blaming (1) trendy low-carb diets such as Atkins and South Beach for a decline in its sales in grocery stores and (2) a $34 million write-off of its investment in Montana Mills. The stock price was down 37 percent since the May 7 lower earnings announcement and was trading at about $20.

At the company's annual stockholders' meeting on May 26, 2004, executives said the company was slowing down expansion plans and had plans to counter consumer interest in low-carbohydrate foods by adding a sugar-free doughnut to its product lineup. Management also announced that the company would soon (1) introduce a chocolate-flavored glazed doughnut; mini rings that were 40 percent smaller than regular doughnuts; and crushed-ice drinks in raspberry, latte, and double chocolate flavors and (2) begin selling bags of the company's own brand of coffee in whole-bean and ground form in grocery stores alongside Krispy Kreme doughnut displays. The company said it planned to go forward with overseas expansion. The overseas expansion was concentrated in Asia; 25 new stores were being planned for South Korea, and on the horizon were stores in Japan, China, Indonesia, the Philippines, and the Persian Gulf.

Developments at Krispy Kreme in July–August 2004

In late July 2004, the company announced that the U.S. Securities and Exchange Commission was launching an inquiry into the company's accounting practices regarding certain franchise buybacks. A *Wall Street Journal* article in May had detailed questionable accounting in the $32.1 million repurchase of a struggling seven-unit franchise in Michigan that was behind on its payments for equipment, ingredients, and franchise fees, along with questionable accounting for another reacquired franchise in southern California.

In late August 2004, Krispy Kreme reported its second-quarter fiscal 2005 results:

- Systemwide sales increases of 14.8 percent as compared with the prior year's second quarter.

- An 11.5 percent increase in company revenue to $177.4 million (versus $159.2 million in the second quarter of the prior year)—company store sales increased 18.7 percent to $123.8 million, revenues from franchise operations grew 13.7 percent to $6.8 million, and KKM&D revenues decreased 4.1 percent to $46.9 million (principally because of lower equipment sales to franchisees opening new stores).

- Very small comparable store sales increases—sales at company-owned increased 0.6 percent, and systemwide sales (at both company-owned and franchised stores) increased only 0.1 percent.

- A decline in operating income from continuing operations for the second quarter of fiscal 2005 to $6.2 million, or $0.10 per diluted share, versus $13.4 million, or $0.22 per diluted share, in the second quarter of fiscal 2004.

- Twenty-two new Krispy Kreme factory/retail stores in 12 new markets, and 10 new doughnut-and-coffee-shop stores. Six company-owned factory/retail stores and three doughnut-and-coffee shops were closed during the quarter.

Commenting on the Krispy Kreme's second quarter performance, Scott Livengood, said:

> Although we are disappointed with the second-quarter financial results, we are optimistic about the long-term growth potential of the business. We are focusing our efforts and resources on initiatives that improve long-term business prospects. We have core strategies with supporting initiatives, a leading consumer brand and great people to address the current challenges. Krispy Kreme has proven over its 67-year history an ability to overcome challenges, and I am confident in our ability to restore our business momentum.[9]

[9] Company press release, August 26, 2004.

EXHIBIT 10   Quarterly Operating Performance of Krispy Kreme Stores, Fiscal Years 2004–2005

	Fiscal Year 2004				Fiscal Year 2005		
	Q1	Q2	Q3	Q4	Q1	Q2	Q3
Average sales per week							
Company stores	$77.4	$74.4	$73.0	$69.1	$67.9	$63.1	$58.4
Area developer stores	58.0	61.2	60.3	58.7	59.2	54.3	49.9
Associate stores	52.4	48.7	45.9	42.6	46.7	43.9	41.7
Franchised store average	56.2	57.3	56.3	54.3	56.0	51.6	47.9
Systemwide average	64.1	63.7	62.7	60.1	60.7	56.3	52.2
Change in comparable store sales							
Company stores	15.4%	15.6%	13.3%	10.7%	5.2%	0.6%	−6.2%
Systemwide	11.2%	11.3%	9.5%	9.1%	4.0%	0.1%	−6.4%
Increase in systemwide sales	24.4%	27.6%	28.6%	25.5%	24.2%	14.8%	4.7%

Source: Company press releases of quarterly earnings results.

EXHIBIT 11   Financial Statement Data for Krispy Kreme Doughnuts, First Nine Months of Fiscal 2004 versus First Nine Months of 2005 (Dollar amounts in thousands, except per share)

	Nine Months ending November 2, 2003	Nine Months ending October 31, 2004
Statement of operations data		
Total revenues	$475,598	$531,941
Operating expenses	359,820	430,613
General and administrative expenses	27,362	34,928
Depreciation and amortization expenses	13,473	19,496
Arbitration award	(525)	—
Impairment charge and store closing costs	—	14,865
Income from operations	$ 75,468	$ 32,039
Interest expense, (income), net, and other expenses and adjustments	6,410	5,424
Income (loss) from continuing operations before income taxes	69,058	26,615
Provision for income taxes	27,488	11,543
Income from continuing operations	41,570	15,072
Discontinued operations	(907)	(36,741)
Net income (loss)	$ 40,663	$ (21,669)
Diluted earnings (loss) per share		
Income (loss) from continuing operations	$0.67	$0.24
Discontinued operations	(0.01)	(0.58)
Net income (loss) per share	$0.66	$(0.34)
Diluted shares outstanding	61,975	63,441
Balance sheet data		
Cash and cash equivalents	$ 39,287	$ 17,213
Receivables	62,454	73,416
Inventories	29,717	32,287
Payables and accrued expenses	52,101	67,820
Long-term debt and other long-term obligations, including current maturities	149,142	170,509
Total assets	$629,431	$675,897
Total shareholders' equity	$428,188	$437,568

Source: Company press releases, November 21, 2003, and November 22, 2004.

EXHIBIT 12   **Krispy Kreme's Performance by Business Segment, First Nine Months of Fiscal 2004 versus First Nine Months of 2005 (In thousands)**

	Nine Months ending November 2, 2003	Nine Months ending October 31, 2004
Revenues by business segment		
Company store operations	$317,158	$369,593
Franchise operations	17,555	20,060
KK Manufacturing and Distribution	140,885	142,288
Total	$475,598*	$531,941
Operating income by business segment (before depreciation and amortization)		
Company store operations	$ 61,969	$ 41,797
Franchise operations	13,721	14,694
KK Manufacturing and Distribution	27,824	26,706
Total	103,514*	83,197
Unallocated general and administrative expenses	$ (28,571)	$(36,293)

*Totals do not include operations of Montana Mills, a business which was acquired in April 2004 and divested during fiscal 2005; nine-month revenues for Montana Mills were $4,481,000, and the operating loss at Montana Mills was $1,408,000.

Source: Company press releases, November 21, 2003, and November 22, 2004.

Top management indicated that systemwide sales should grow approximately 15 percent for fiscal 2005 and approximately 10 percent in the last two quarters of the year but declined to provide updated earnings estimates. The company said it had scaled back expansion plans and would only open approximately 75 new stores systemwide (60 factory/retail stores and 15 doughnut-and-coffee shops) during fiscal 2005.

Developments at Krispy Kreme in November–December 2004

In November 2004, Krispy Kreme reported that the company lost $3.0 million in the third quarter of fiscal 2005. Total revenues for the quarter, which included sales from company stores, franchise operations and KKM&D, were up only 1.4 percent to $170.1 million (versus $167.8 million in the third quarter of fiscal 2004). Third-quarter systemwide sales at both company-owned and franchised stores were up 4.7 percent over the third quarter of fiscal 2004. The sales increases were well below the 10 percent gains that management had forecast in August.

During the quarter, 13 company-owned factory/retail stores and two doughnut-and-coffee shop stores were opened, and seven company owned factory/retail stores and two doughnut-and-coffee shop stores were closed. There were total 429 Krispy Kreme stores systemwide at the end of October 2004, consisting of 393 factory/retail stores and 36 doughnut-and-coffee shops. There were plans to open approximately 10 new stores systemwide in the fourth quarter of fiscal 2005.

Exhibit 10 shows the declining performance of Krispy Kreme's stores during the first three quarters of fiscal 2005. Exhibits 11 and 12 shows selected financial statistics for Krispy Kreme Doughnuts during the first nine months of fiscal 2005 compared to the first nine months of fiscal 2004.

Management declined to provide systemwide sales and earnings guidance for the fourth quarter of fiscal 2005 and withdrew its previous estimates of 10 percent systemwide sales growth made in August. Commenting on the company's performance, Scott Livengood said, "Clearly we are disappointed with our third-quarter results. We are focused on addressing the challenges facing the Company and regaining our business momentum." Early in the fourth fiscal quarter, Krispy Kreme sold its remaining Montana Mills assets for what management described as "a modest amount."

In December 2004, Krispy Kreme announced that it had identified accounting errors related to its acquisition of two franchises that could reduce net income for fiscal 2004 by 2.7 percent to 8.6 percent. It was as yet unclear whether the company would have to restate its fiscal year 2004 results. A special committee of the company's board of directors was investigating the accounting problems. The company's outside auditor, Pricewaterhouse-Coopers LLP, said it refused to complete reviews of Krispy Kreme's financial performance for the first six months of 2005 until the special committee completed its probe of the book-keeping problems.

In late December 2004, Krispy Kreme's stock was trading in the $10–$13 range, well below the $40 high attained in March 2004.

Case

9

Campbell Soup Company

John E. Gamble *University of South Alabama*

Arthur A. Thompson, Jr. *University of Alabama*

As the new millennium began, Campbell Soup's CEO, Dale Morrison, was wrestling with how to get the company's underperforming business portfolio back on track and satisfy shareholder expectations of a steadily rising stock price. Morrison was the third CEO in recent years to struggle to develop a diversification strategy for Campbell that could produce attractive growth in revenues and profits. Under two prior CEOs, George McGovern and David Johnson, Campbell's business portfolio had been revamped, but the gains in performance had proved temporary and the overall results somewhat disappointing. Now the challenge to restore luster to Campbell's business lineup and build shareholder wealth rested with Dale Morrison.

Going into 2000 Campbell Soup Company was one of the world's leading manufacturers and marketers of branded consumer food products, with approximately 24,500 employees, 1999 revenues of $6.4 billion, 30 manufacturing plants in six nations, and over 2,000 products on the market. Its major brands in the United States were Campbell's flagship red-and-white label canned soups, Prego spaghetti sauces, Godiva chocolates, Pepperidge Farm baked goods, V8 vegetable juices, Swanson broths, Franco-American canned pastas, and Pace Mexican salsas. Arnott's baked goods and Home Pride sauces were the best-selling Campbell brands in various international markets.

Company Background

The company was founded in 1869 by Joseph Campbell, a fruit merchant, and Abram Anderson, an icebox maker, and was originally known for its jams and jellies. In 1891 it was incorporated as the Joseph Campbell Preserve Co. in Camden, New Jersey. John T. Dorrance, a brilliant 24-year-old chemist with a PhD from the Massachusetts Institute of Technology, was hired by the company in 1894 and three years later developed a process for canning soup in condensed form. The new process took water out of the soup during the canning process and thus dramatically reduced production and distribution costs. Soups made with the new production process were awarded the gold medal at the 1900 Paris Exhibition and by 1905 were selling at the rate of 40,000 cases per week. John T. Dorrance purchased the company in 1900, and it was entirely owned by his family until 1954. It was reincorporated as the Campbell Soup Company in 1922.

When John Dorrance died in 1930, he left an estate of over $115 million—the nation's third largest at that time. He also left a company devoted to engineering, committed to providing good products (in recessions it would rather shave margins than cut back product quality or raise price), and obsessed with secrecy. His successor, John T. Dorrance Jr., headed the company for the next 24 years (1930–54) and few, if any, important decisions were made at Campbell without his approval. In 1954, the company went public, with the Dorrance family retaining majority control. In 1999, the Dorrance family still owned about 50 percent of Campbell's stock and, despite having relinquished direct management control, still exerted considerable shareholder influence. Four of Campbell Soup's 16 board members were grandchildren of John T. Dorrance Sr.

Over the years Campbell had diversified into a number of businesses—Swanson frozen dinners, Pepperidge Farm bakery products, Vlasic pickles, Franco-American spaghetti products, Recipe pet food, various fast-food restaurant chains, Godiva chocolates, and even retail garden centers. However, canned soup had always remained Campbell's core business. The company had had three chief executive officers over the last 20 years, and its corporate strategy had evolved with each change in leadership. The company's diversification strategy and new investment priorities had shifted as each new CEO pursued a course to build value for Campbell Soup Company's shareholders.

The Gordon McGovern Era: 1980–89

Gordon McGovern was in business school when Margaret Rudkin, founder of Pepperidge Farm, spoke to his class. She told how she had built her bread company from scratch in an industry dominated by giants. McGovern was impressed. He wrote to Rudkin for a job, received it in 1956, and began his climb through Pepperidge Farm's ranks. When Campbell acquired Pepperidge Farm in 1961, it had sales of $40 million and had only reached $60 million when McGovern became Pepperidge Farm's president in 1968. When McGovern was named president of Campbell in 1980, Pepperidge Farm's annual sales had grown to $300 million under his leadership. McGovern implemented several key elements of Pepperidge Farm's strategy when he took over at Campbell: creativity and a willingness to experiment, emphasis on new product development, and building strong competencies in marketing.

McGovern's Corporate Strategy as Campbell's CEO

During the McGovern years, Campbell's strategic focus was on the consumer. The consumer's "hot buttons" were identified as nutrition, convenience, low sodium, attractive price, good quality, and unique products—and managers were urged to press those buttons. Business unit managers were expected to be responsive to consumer perceptions, needs, and demands regarding nutrition, safety, flavor, and convenience. Key business unit strategies included (1) improving operating efficiency, (2) developing new products to capitalize on consumer trends, (3) updating advertising for new and established products, and (4) continuing Campbell's long-standing emphasis on high production standards and premium-quality products.

Early in his tenure, McGovern developed a five-year plan that featured four financial performance objectives: a 15 percent annual increase in earnings, a 5 percent increase in volume, a 5 percent increase in sales (plus inflation), and an 18 percent return on equity by 1986. The two cornerstones of McGovern's growth strategy were (1) developing and introducing new products and (2) making acquisitions every two years that would bring in $200 million in annual sales. Campbell's acquisition strategy was to look for small, fast-growing food companies strong in product areas where Campbell had no presence and companies on the fast track that were in rapidly growing product categories or industries. Under Mc-Govern, Campbell made a number of acquisitions:

1982

- Mrs. Paul's Kitchens, Inc., a processor and marketer of frozen prepared seafood and vegetable products, with annual sales of approximately $125 million (acquired at a cost of $55 million).
- Snow King Frozen Foods, Inc., engaged in the production and marketing of a line of uncooked frozen specialty meat products, with annual sales of $32 million.
- Juice Bowl Products, Inc., a Florida producer of fruit juices.
- Win Schuler Foods, Inc., a Michigan-based producer and distributor of specialty cheese spreads, flavored melba rounds, food service salad dressings, party dips, and sauces, with annual sales of $6.5 million.
- Costa Apple Products, Inc., a producer of apple juice retailed primarily in the eastern United States, with annual sales of $6 million.

1983

- Several small domestic operations, at a cost of $26 million, including:
  —Annabelle's restaurant chain of 12 units in the southeastern United States.
  —Triangle Manufacturing Corp., a manufacturer of physical fitness and sports medicine products.

1984

- Mendelson-Zeller Co., Inc., a California distributor of fresh produce.

1985

- Continental Foods Company SA and affiliated companies, which produced sauces, confectioneries, and other food products in Belgium and France; the cost of the acquisition was $17 million.
- A 20 percent ownership interest in Arnott's Ltd., an Australian producer of cookies and crackers.

1988

- Freshbake Foods Group, a British producer of baked goods.

Campbell's Business Portfolio under McGovern

During the McGovern era, Campbell Soup Company was organized into six business units—Campbell U.S., Pepperidge Farm, Vlasic Foods, Mrs. Paul's Kitchens, Other United States, and International. Sales and profit performance by division are shown in Exhibit 1.

The Campbell U.S. Business Unit

In 1989 the Campbell U.S. division was the company's largest operating unit, accounting for just over 50 percent of corporate revenues. The Campbell U.S. division was divided into eight profit centers: soup, frozen foods, grocery, beverage, food service, poultry, fresh produce, and pet foods. Exhibit 2 shows the brands Campbell had in this division and the major competitors each brand faced during most of the 1980s.

The soup business group alone accounted for more than 25 percent of the company's consolidated sales (as compared to around 50 percent in the 1970s). Campbell's flagship brands of soup accounted for 80 percent of the $1 billion–plus annual canned soup market; in 1989, Campbell offered grocery shoppers over 50 varieties of canned soups. Heinz was the second largest soup producer, with 10 percent of the market. Heinz had earlier withdrawn from producing Heinz-label soups and shifted its production over to making soups

EXHIBIT 1   **Performance of Campbell's Divisions under Gordon McGovern, 1980–89 ($ millions)**

Source: Campbell's annual reports.

	1989	1988	1987	1986	1985	1984	1983	1982	1981	1980
Campbell U.S.										
Sales	$2,776	$2,584	$2,445	$2,507	$2,500	$2,282	$1,987	$1,773	$1,678	$1,608
Operating earnings	175	272	284	302	292	278	250	211	190	205
Pepperidge Farm										
Sales	548	495	459	420	426	435	433	392	329	283
Operating earnings	54	58	54	46	39	35	43	41	35	29
Vlasic Foods										
Sales	441	353	283	263	199	193	168	149	137	130
Operating earnings	39	30	22	24	16	14	13	12	10	8
Mrs. Paul's Kitchens										
Sales	140	150	153	141	138	126	108	—	—	—
Operating earnings	0.4	(4)	10	8	11	14	10	—	—	—
Other United States*										
Sales	—	—	59	76	81	84	64	56	27	35
Operating earnings	—	—	(2)	(7)	(3)	(2)	(1)	(1)	(1)	1
International										
Sales	1,527	1,037	898	766	716	624	599	643	694	512
Operating earnings	($ 81)	$ 58	$ 69	($ 61)	$ 35	$ 34	$ 33	$ 46	$ 46	$ 33

*Division eliminated in 1988 and replaced with a new division named Campbell Enterprises.

for sale under the private labels of grocery chains; Heinz was the leading private-label producer of canned soup, holding almost an 80 percent share of the private-label segment.

Although the soup business was relatively mature (McGovern preferred to call it underworked), Campbell's most ambitious consumer research took place in this unit. McGovern opted to grow Campbell's soup sales by turning out a steady flow of new varieties in convenient packages: "Ethnic, dried, refrigerated, frozen, microwave—you name it, we're going to try it."[1] In 1985, Campbell entered the $290 million dry-soup-mix market dominated by Thomas J. Lipton Inc., a business unit of Unilever. Dry-soup sales in the United States were growing faster than sales of canned soup. Lipton's aggressive response to test marketing of an early Campbell dry-soup product resulted in Campbell's rushing a six-flavor line into national distribution ahead of schedule.

In 1982 McGovern caused a stir when he announced publicly that Campbell's Swanson TV-dinner line was "junk food": "It was great in 1950, but in today's world it didn't go into the microwave; it didn't represent any variety or a good eating experience to my palate."[2] Over the past five years, Swanson's sales volume had slipped 16 percent. He maintained that consumers had discovered better-quality options to the TV-dinner concept. Campbell's frozen foods group answered the challenge by creating a new frozen gourmet line, LeMenu. Campbell committed about $50 million in manufacturing, marketing, and trade promotion costs when initial market tests of the LeMenu line proved encouraging.

LeMenu products—packaged on round heatable plates and featuring such selections as chicken cordon bleu, al dente vegetables, and sophisticated wine sauces—produced 21 per-

[1]As quoted in *Business Week,* December 24, 1984, p. 67.
[2]Ibid.

EXHIBIT 2 **The Campbell U.S. Division: Products, Rival Brands, and Competitors as of 1985**

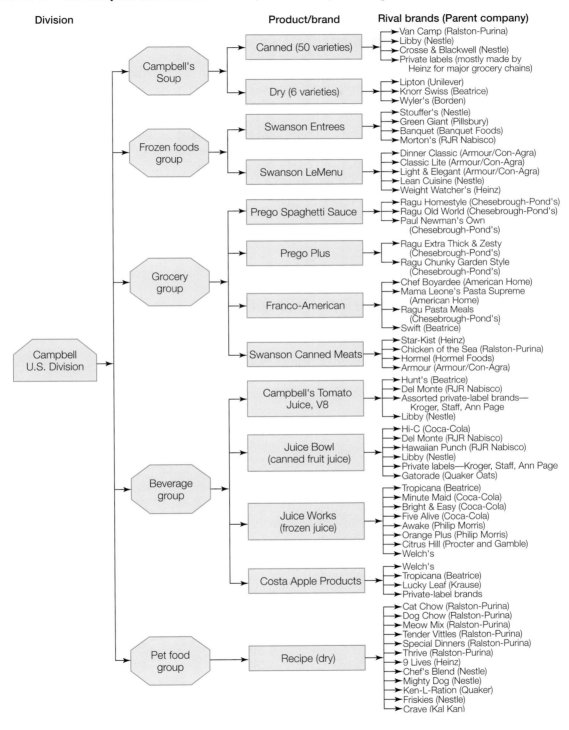

Division

Product/brand

Rival brands (Parent company)

Campbell U.S. Division

- **Campbell's Soup**
  - Canned (50 varieties)
    - Van Camp (Ralston-Purina)
    - Libby (Nestle)
    - Crosse & Blackwell (Nestle)
    - Private labels (mostly made by Heinz for major grocery chains)
  - Dry (6 varieties)
    - Lipton (Unilever)
    - Knorr Swiss (Beatrice)
    - Wyler's (Borden)
- **Frozen foods group**
  - Swanson Entrees
    - Stouffer's (Nestle)
    - Green Giant (Pillsbury)
    - Banquet (Banquet Foods)
    - Morton's (RJR Nabisco)
  - Swanson LeMenu
    - Dinner Classic (Armour/Con-Agra)
    - Classic Lite (Armour/Con-Agra)
    - Light & Elegant (Armour/Con-Agra)
    - Lean Cuisine (Nestle)
    - Weight Watcher's (Heinz)
- **Grocery group**
  - Prego Spaghetti Sauce
    - Ragu Homestyle (Chesebrough-Pond's)
    - Ragu Old World (Chesebrough-Pond's)
    - Paul Newman's Own (Chesebrough-Pond's)
  - Prego Plus
    - Ragu Extra Thick & Zesty (Chesebrough-Pond's)
    - Ragu Chunky Garden Style (Chesebrough-Pond's)
  - Franco-American
    - Chef Boyardee (American Home)
    - Mama Leone's Pasta Supreme (American Home)
    - Ragu Pasta Meals (Chesebrough-Pond's)
    - Swift (Beatrice)
  - Swanson Canned Meats
    - Star-Kist (Heinz)
    - Chicken of the Sea (Ralston-Purina)
    - Hormel (Hormel Foods)
    - Armour (Armour/Con-Agra)
- **Beverage group**
  - Campbell's Tomato Juice, V8
    - Hunt's (Beatrice)
    - Del Monte (RJR Nabisco)
    - Assorted private-label brands—Kroger, Staff, Ann Page
    - Libby (Nestle)
  - Juice Bowl (canned fruit juice)
    - Hi-C (Coca-Cola)
    - Del Monte (RJR Nabisco)
    - Hawaiian Punch (RJR Nabisco)
    - Libby (Nestle)
    - Private labels—Kroger, Staff, Ann Page
    - Gatorade (Quaker Oats)
  - Juice Works (frozen juice)
    - Tropicana (Beatrice)
    - Minute Maid (Coca-Cola)
    - Bright & Easy (Coca-Cola)
    - Five Alive (Coca-Cola)
    - Awake (Philip Morris)
    - Orange Plus (Philip Morris)
    - Citrus Hill (Procter and Gamble)
    - Welch's
  - Costa Apple Products
    - Welch's
    - Tropicana (Beatrice)
    - Lucky Leaf (Krause)
    - Private-label brands
- **Pet food group**
  - Recipe (dry)
    - Cat Chow (Ralston-Purina)
    - Dog Chow (Ralston-Purina)
    - Meow Mix (Ralston-Purina)
    - Tender Vittles (Ralston-Purina)
    - Special Dinners (Ralston-Purina)
    - Thrive (Ralston-Purina)
    - 9 Lives (Heinz)
    - Chef's Blend (Nestle)
    - Mighty Dog (Nestle)
    - Ken-L-Ration (Quaker)
    - Friskies (Nestle)
    - Crave (Kal Kan)

cent growth in the frozen meal unit, with sales of $150 million during its first year of national distribution (1984), double Campbell's sales projection. In addition, the Swanson line of TV dinners was overhauled to put in less salt and more meat stock in gravies, add new desserts and sauces, and create new packaging and a redesigned logo.

The grocery business unit's star was Prego spaghetti sauce. By 1984 the Prego brand had captured 25 percent of the still-growing spaghetti sauce market, becoming the number two sauce, behind Ragu. A Prego Plus spaghetti sauce line was introduced in 1985.

Pepperidge Farm

Pepperidge Farm was Campbell's third largest division in 1989, with 10 percent of the company's consolidated sales. Although the division was one of Campbell's best performers during the late 1970s (with sales rising at an average compound rate of 14 percent), by the mid-1980s growth had slowed and a number of newly introduced products had produced disappointing results (Star Wars cookies, Vegetables in Pastry). To remedy the division's weak performance, a number of steps were taken:

- The Costa Apple Products unit, acquired in 1982, was transferred to the Campbell U.S. beverage group.
- Pepperidge Farm divested itself of operations that no longer fit into its strategic plan, including Lexington Gardens, Inc., a garden center chain.
- Deli's Vegetables in Pastry went back into research and development to improve quality.
- A new management team was put in place and a comprehensive review of each product was initiated.

Exhibit 3 shows Pepperidge Farm's product portfolio during the 1980s.

EXHIBIT 3
The Pepperidge Farm Division: Products, Rival Brands, and Competitors in 1985

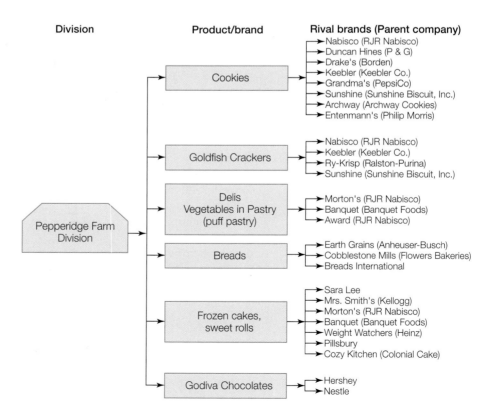

Vlasic Foods

Vlasic, Campbell's fourth largest division, was the leading producer and marketer of pickles and relishes in the United States, with a 31 percent market share. During the 1982–84 period, Vlasic also had responsibility for Win Schuler Foods, a Michigan-based maker of cheese spreads, melba rounds, party dips, sauces, and salad dressings. Win Schuler was purchased in 1982, and its products were marketed in several states in the upper Midwest. When sales of the Win Schuler unit flattened in 1984, partly due to a sagging Midwest economy, McGovern transferred the unit to the refrigerated foods group in the Campbell U.S. business division.

In 1985 Vlasic implemented new labels that used color bands and a new flavor scale to help consumers find their favorite tastes quickly on the supermarket shelf. Following up on marketing research indicating consumer desires for new and interesting flavors, Vlasic had introduced Zesty Dills and Bread and Butter Whole Pickle lines in 1985. Heinz was Campbell's leading national competitor in this area, but there were a number of important regional and private-label brands that competed with Heinz and Vlasic for shelf space.

Mrs. Paul's Kitchens

The Mrs. Paul's business unit produced frozen fish entrees, frozen breaded vegetables, and frozen chicken nuggets. When Campbell acquired Mrs. Paul's in 1982, it was rumored that Heinz and Pillsbury, among others, were considering the same acquisition. In 1983, the Mrs. Paul's division responded to consumer preferences for convenience seafood products that were nutritious, low in calories, microwavable, and lightly coated by introducing Light & Natural Fish Fillets. Quality improvements were also made in existing products, and a promising new product line, Light Seafood Entrees, was introduced in 1984. Market share increased about 25 percent over 1983, and Light Seafood Entrees went national in 1985. This line, which featured seven varieties of low-calorie microwavable seafood dishes, accounted for 11 percent of 1985's volume. However, sales of the company's established product lines of breaded seafood items eroded in the years following acquisition because these items had to be fried in cooking oil prior to serving. Revenues had dropped in both 1988 and 1989, and the division was barely profitable in 1989 (see again Exhibit 1).

Campbell's Other United States Business Unit

Grouped into the Other United States business division were Triangle Manufacturing Corporation, a health-and-fitness products manufacturer; Campbell Hospitality, a restaurant unit that operated 59 Pietro's restaurants, 15 Annabelle's restaurants, and 6 H. T. McDoogal's restaurants; and Snow King Frozen Foods, Inc., a manufacturer of frozen specialty meat products. Triangle's best-known product line was The Band wrist and ankle weights, which had the number two position in its market category, with a market share of 14 percent. Triangle was trying to build on its strength by entering the exercise equipment market and by selling its products internationally. The Campbell Hospitality division struggled through most of the 1980s to sustain sales and earnings growth. Snow King was also a weak performer. In 1988, this division was reorganized and renamed Campbell Enterprises; it included Triangle Manufacturing; Godiva International; V8 and Campbell Juices; Campbell Food Services; Snow King Frozen Foods; and Pietro's, Annabelle's, and H. T. McDoogal's restaurant chains. All three restaurant chains were divested in 1989.

Campbell's International Business Unit

The International business unit was Campbell's second largest division throughout the 1980s and accounted for about one-fifth of corporate revenues in 1989. Campbell International had subsidiaries in about 12 foreign countries as of 1989 and had plans to expand further. The division was reorganized in 1985 to build a more solid base for sales and earnings growth. McGovern's goal was for the International division to contribute 25 percent of Campbell's corporate sales and earnings. His strategy was to develop and strengthen Campbell's presence in international markets and to make Campbell a premier international company.

A number of acquisitions were completed in 1989 to strengthen Campbell's international competitive position. The Habitant soup and pickle brands, the Laura Secord brand of jams, and a refrigerated distribution company were all acquired by Campbell's Canadian subsidiary. In Europe, Campbell acquired a German specialty food importer and an Italian producer of institutional foods. Also during 1989, the company increased its ownership in Australia's leading cookie company, Arnott's Ltd., to 32 percent; acquired 50 percent ownership in an Australian juice manufacturer; and obtained complete ownership of Melbourne Mushrooms. The International division's three biggest profit contributors in 1989 were Campbell Soup Canada, the European food and confectionery group, and the operations in Australia.

Even though the company had a number of successes internationally, Campbell management had encountered some difficulties. Campbell's Italian business suffered losses during 1989 as a result of excessive costs brought on by an aggressive and poorly controlled attempt to build market share. Campbell was also having difficulty with making its recently acquired Freshbake Foods unit profitable. The UK food processing company was struggling to absorb a number of acquisitions it had made prior to its acquisition by Campbell in 1988. Campbell management found it necessary to institute an extensive restructuring process at Freshbake, including closing a number of plants.

McGovern's Approach to Managing Campbell's Business Portfolio

Every Saturday morning McGovern did his family's grocery shopping, stopping to straighten Campbell's displays and inspect those of competitors, studying packages and reading labels, and trying to learn all he could about how and what people were eating. He encouraged his managers to do the same. Several board meetings were held in the backrooms of supermarkets so that afterward directors could roam the store aisles interviewing customers about Campbell products.

McGovern decentralized Campbell management to facilitate entrepreneurial risk taking and new product development, devising a new compensation program to reward these traits. He restructured the company into some 50 autonomous units, each with the leeway to develop new products even if the new product ideas were closely related to another business unit's products. Thus, the Prego spaghetti sauce unit—not the frozen food group—initiated frozen Mexican dinners. And although it wasn't his job, the director of market research created Today's Taste, a line of refrigerated entrees and side dishes. "It's like things are in constant motion," the director said. "We are overloaded but it's fun."[3]

McGovern believed the new structure encouraged managers of business units, who had to compete for corporate funding, to be more creative and venturesome in developing promising products:

> These business divisions allow the company to really get its arms around chunks of the business. The managers are answerable to the bottom line—to their investments, their hiring, their products—and it's a great motivation for performance.[4]

As part of this motivation, Campbell began annually allotting around $30 to $40 million to support new ventures and the creation of new product families; it often took $10 million to

[3]As quoted in *The Wall Street Journal,* September 17, 1984, p. A10.
[4]*Advertising Age,* January 3, 1983, p. 38.

develop and test new products. In addition, it took $10 to $15 million in advertising and couponing to launch a new brand. McGovern believed a special new product venture fund was needed to encourage managers to think big in terms of new product development. He emphasized that it was no disgrace to fail if the effort was a good one. High failure rates were common in the industry—only about 20 percent of new products lasted more than one year on the market—but Campbell's failure rate on new product introductions was running even higher. In fact, during the 1980s, only about one out of eight new Campbell products reaching the market was successful.

Every Friday morning McGovern held meetings to discuss new products. The fact-finding sessions were attended by financial, marketing, engineering, and sales personnel. Typical McGovern questions included: "Would you eat something like that?" "Why not?" "Have you tried the competition's product?" "Is there a consumer niche?"[5]

McGovern's New Product Development and Marketing Strategies

McGovern instituted a number of internal changes to make Campbell's product development strategy produce the desired results. Much revolved around efforts to enhance the sophistication of Campbell's corporate marketing strategies and approach to marketing research. Under McGovern, Campbell's market research unearthed several findings and projections that drove the company's product development effort:

- Women comprised 43 percent of the workforce (with a level of 50 percent projected by 1990).
- Two-income marriages represented 60 percent of all U.S. families and accounted for 60 percent of total family income.
- Upper-income households would grow 3.5 times faster than the total household formations.
- More than half of all households consisted of only one or two members; 23 percent of all households contained only one person.
- More and more consumers were exhibiting a growing preference for refrigerated and fresh produce over canned and frozen products.
- The percentage of meals eaten at home was declining.
- Nearly half of the adult meal planners in the United States were watching their weight.
- Poultry consumption had increased 26 percent since 1973.
- Ethnic food preparation at home was increasing, with 40 percent, 21 percent, and 14 percent of households preparing Italian, Mexican, and Oriental foods, respectively, at home from scratch.
- There was a growing consumer concern with food avoidance: sugar, salt, calories, chemicals, cholesterol, and additives.
- The "I am what I eat" philosophy had tied food into lifestyles that embraced exercise machines, hot tubs, jogging, racquetball, backpacking, cross-country skiing, and aerobic dancing.

In response to growing ethnic food demand, Campbell began marketing ethnic selections in regions where consumer interests for particular food types were strong. For instance, it marketed spicy Ranchero Beans only in the South and Southwest, and its newly acquired Puerto Rican foods only in New York City and Florida (which had sizable Puerto Rican populations).

---

[5]*The Wall Street Journal*, September 17, 1984, p. A10.

Campbell's product-development guidelines emphasized convenience, taste, flavor, and texture. The strategic themes McGovern stressed were these:

* Concentrate on products that represent superior value to consumers and constantly strive to improve those values.
* Develop products that help build markets.
* Develop products that yield a fair profit to Campbell.

In pursuing these guidelines, Campbell adopted several operating practices:

* Using ongoing consumer research to determine eating habits. It included checking home menus, recipes, and food preparation techniques to learn which food items were served together.
* Studying meal and snack occasions to learn which household members participated so that preliminary estimates of volume potential could be made for possible new products and product improvement ideas.
* Testing new or improved products in a large enough number of households across the United States that reliable national sales projections could be made. Once a product met pretest standards, testing in a sample of supermarkets and sales outlets was conducted.
* Rolling out the new products on a regional or national plan and using test-market data to establish the sequence in which area markets should be entered.

By 1983 McGovern's strategy had turned Campbell into the biggest generator of new products in the combined food and health-and-beauty aids categories, with a total of 42 new products. Prego spaghetti sauce, LeMenu frozen dinners, Great Starts breakfasts, and Chunky New England Clam Chowder were among the leading products introduced by Campbell Soup during the early 1980s. Meanwhile Campbell's marketing budget grew from $275 million in 1982, to $488 million in 1985, and to $552 million in 1989. Ad expenditures jumped from $67 million in 1980 to $197 million in 1989. Prior to McGovern, Campbell often trimmed ad spending at the end of a quarter to boost earnings.

In 1982 McGovern was named *Advertising Age*'s Adman of the Year for his efforts in transforming Campbell into "one of the most aggressive market-driven companies in the food industry today."[6] *Advertising Age* cited the company's emphasis on nutrition and fitness as opposed to the former "mmm, mmm, good" emphasis on taste. Print ads featured government studies concerning soup's nutritional values and a new slogan, "Soup is good food."

Production, Quality, and Cost Considerations during the McGovern Era

Gordon McGovern also stressed the importance of high production quality; a 1984 article in *Savvy* quoted him as saying, "I want zero defects. If we can't produce quality, we'll get out of the business." That same year, Campbell held its first Worldwide Corporate conference dedicated to quality. Hundreds of Campbell managers from all levels and most company locations spent three days at this conference. Management believed that the ultimate test of quality was consumer satisfaction, and the company's goal was to instill a strong quality consciousness among employees in every single operation throughout the company.

Before McGovern took over, Campbell used to adjust the design of new products so that they could be produced with existing equipment and plant facilities. For example, a square omelet was specified for Swanson's breakfasts because it was what the installed machine would make. After McGovern's appointment, although low-cost production was still a strategic factor, market considerations and consumer trends—not existing machinery and

---

[6]*Advertising Age,* January 3, 1983, p. 38.

production capabilities—were deciding factors in production, packaging, and labeling. Still, the company spent between $150 million and $300 million annually throughout the 1980s for improved equipment, new plants and plant expansions, better packaging technology, and distribution facilities.

Campbell executives believed the company's key strengths during the 1985–89 period were (1) a worldwide system for obtaining ingredients; (2) a broad range of food products that could be used as a launching pad for formulating, producing, and marketing new products; and (3) an emphasis on low-cost production.

Campbell's Performance under Gordon McGovern

McGovern's campaign for renewed growth via new product introduction and acquisition produced good results early on. By year-end 1984 sales were up 31 percent—to $3.7 billion—and earnings had risen by 47 percent—to $191 million. During McGovern's 10-year reign as CEO, Campbell introduced 922 new items—more than any other food-processing company. By the late 1980s however, there were signs that Campbell's brand managers had become so involved in new product development that they had neglected the old stand-by products as well as slighting cost-control and profit margin targets. According to one Campbell executive:

> We became fat cats. We said, "We can't fail." We began to throw things against the marketplace that had long paybacks and were in processes, packaging, and distribution that we didn't understand.[7]

Campbell's growth in operating earnings for fiscal years 1985–89 fell short of McGovern's 15 percent target rate, and McGovern in 1989 initiated several internal restructuring moves to eliminate many of the inefficiencies and cost excesses that had crept into the company's operations and new product development efforts. A summary of Campbell Soup's financial performance between 1989 and 1999 is presented in Exhibit 4.

McGovern's Resignation and the Recruitment of a Replacement

Beginning in the late 1980s, the heirs of John T. Dorrance began to show frustration with Campbell Soup's industry-lagging performance and began to openly criticize McGovern's approach to running the company. Quaker Oats management believed that the Dorrance family might be interested in a merger between the two companies and approached Campbell's chairman of the board, Robert Vlasic, in March 1989 to explore the issue. The Dorrance heirs were split on the prospect of a merger, with one faction publicly announcing its intent to sell its shares and another vying to block a merger at all costs. The heirs supporting Campbell Soup's independence successfully prevented a merger but were unable to bring prompt reconciliation among the family.

Disenchanted with the family squabble and stung by outspoken criticism of his performance by family members, Gordon McGovern resigned as CEO and took early retirement in November 1989. Campbell's search for a replacement, spearheaded by Ippy Dorrance and Robert Vlasic, quickly focused on Gerber's CEO, David Johnson, as the best candidate to replace McGovern. A native of Australia, David Johnson had a bachelor's degree in economics from the University of Sydney and an MBA from the University of Chicago. Starting out as a management trainee with the international division of Colgate-Palmolive in Australia, he moved up through the ranks to become managing director of Colgate's South

[7]As quoted in *Financial World*, June 11, 1991, p. 53.

EXHIBIT 4 Financial Summary, Campbell Soup Company, 1989–99 (In millions, except per share amounts)

Source: Campbell annual reports.

	1999	1998	1997	1996	1995	1994	1993	1992	1991	1990	1989
Net sales	$6,424	$6,696	$7,964	$7,678	$7,250	$6,664	$6,577	$6,263	$6,204	$6,205	$5,672
Earnings before taxes	1,097	1,073	1,107	1,179	1,042	963	520	779	667	179	107
Earnings before cumulative effect of accounting change	1,097	1,062	713	802	698	630	257	491	402	4	13
Net earnings	724	660	713	802	698	630	8	491	402	4	13
Taxes on earnings	373	384	394	395	344	333	263	309	266	175	93
Interest—net	173	175	165	126	115	64	74	87	90	94	56
Earnings per share	1.63	1.46	1.51	1.61	1.40	1.26	0.02	0.97	0.79	0.01	0.03
Dividends per share	0.89	0.82	0.75	0.67	0.61	0.55	0.46	0.36	0.28	0.25	0.23
Wgt. avg. shares outstanding	445	460	472	498	498	501	504	504	508	518	518
Capital expenditures	297	256	331	416	391	421	371	362	371	397	302
Depreciation and amortization	255	261	328	326	294	255	242	216	209	201	192
Assets	5,522	5,633	6,459	6,632	6,315	4,992	4,897	4,353	4,149	4,115	3,932
Stockholders' equity	$ 235	$ 874	$1,420	$2,742	$2,468	$1,989	$1,704	$2,027	$1,793	$1,691	$1,778

African operations in 1967. In 1973, he moved to Hong Kong as president of Warner-Lambert/Parke Davis Asia; there, exposed to the Orient's fundamentally different customs and approaches, he came to appreciate that if managers were creative enough to look beyond accepted solutions to business problems, it was easy to find innovative answers. Looking back on his Hong Kong experiences, Johnson observed that he gained "an elasticized mind, opened to a greater run of possibilities than I'd ever known before."[8] Warner-Lambert brought Johnson to the United States in 1976 as president of its personal products division; a year later, he was promoted to president of the company's American Chicle division. When Warner-Lambert acquired Entenmann's in 1979, Johnson took over as head; he then moved to General Foods when GF acquired Entenmann's from Warner-Lambert in 1982. As Entenmann's chief executive from 1979 to 1987, he engineered the company's drive from a regional to a national provider of bakery products, more than quadrupling sales and profits. In 1987, Johnson left Entenmann's to become CEO of Gerber Products, a company whose performance had been lackluster for several years. He proceeded to craft a turnaround strategy for Gerber that involved divesting seven business divisions (toys, furniture, trucking) and refocusing Gerber's attention on its core baby-foods business. By 1990, 27 months after Johnson became CEO, Gerber's sales were up 30 percent, profits were up 50 percent, and the stock price had tripled. With the Dorrance family's blessing, Campbell lured Johnson away from Gerber as McGovern's successor.

The David Johnson Era: 1990–97

When David Johnson became chairman and CEO of Campbell Soup Company in January 1990, he saw his first priority as crafting a strategy for Campbell that would grow earnings and win the confidence of the Dorrance heirs. While at Gerber, Johnson viewed Campbell, a competitor of Gerber's in some product categories, as an underperforming company that was a likely target for corporate raiders, once even commenting, "Boy, that's a troubled company. I could really run that one."[9] In interviewing for the job at Campbell, Johnson determined that the arguments and differences between the Dorrance family and Campbell's prior management were more a function of "poor results" than of activist family members wanting to meddle in company affairs or the desire of some to sell out their stake and invest their inheritance elsewhere. Johnson deemed the challenge worthy for several reasons:

> It was a company that was founded on incredible strength on which you could build. I knew that it had excellent R&D. I knew it had terrific brands. It had lost its direction, lost its focus, was underperforming, and I knew that it could be refocused and reorganized within six months, and that we could really get it going very quickly.[10]

Johnson immediately embarked on a course of boosting Campbell's performance quickly, not only to pacify disgruntled shareholders but also to get the company's stock price high enough to discourage would-be acquirers from launching a takeover attempt:

> Under those circumstances, when you come in, it's not the pretties of "Here is my vision. Let me explain the principles from the book." When you move in, you've got to do it in an exciting fashion, lay down the challenge—Boom! Strike! Crash! It's short-term focus. You know that dirty word we're all accused of? "Short term." Isn't it terrible? Under those circumstances, if you don't win the first year, if you don't win in the short term, you're dead.[11]

[8]Jeffrey Zygmont, "In Command at Campbell," *Sky Magazine,* March 1993, p. 60.

[9]As quoted in *Fortune,* September 9, 1991, p. 143.

[10]As quoted in *Sky Magazine,* March 1993, p. 54.

[11]As quoted in *Fortune,* December 14, 1992, p. 112.

Johnson's Turnaround Strategy

To spur Campbell's managers and give them something to shoot for in rejuvenating the company's performance, Johnson set financial objectives of 20 percent earnings growth, 20 percent return on equity, and 20 percent cash return on assets: "I used to say, if perfect human vision is 20–20, then perfect business vision is 20–20–20, which was shorthand for earnings, return and cash."[12] This was followed by the establishment of four corporate-level strategic principles to guide the creation of business and functional strategies in each divisional unit:

- The primary purpose of the corporation is to *build shareholder wealth.* It is imperative to provide dividend growth and long-term stock appreciation to reward the stockholders of the corporation.
- Campbell must exploit its *brand power.* Campbell's strong brands have been the basis of the company's strength's over the past 90 years and should be the focal point for the future.
- Campbell's ability to sustain its brand power and build on its powerful brands is only possible through *people power.* The company's employees have to be responsible for maintaining the existing brands, for building on these brands, and for finding new markets for these brands. Campbell should encourage individual risk-bearing and teamwork with rewards linked to results.
- It is important to *preserve the company's independence.* Management needs to preserve the heritage of Campbell Soup Company and resist any outside thrust for control through delivery of superior performance on building long-term shareholder wealth.

Johnson disagreed with McGovern's view that Campbell's growth should come primarily from the acquisition of small, fast-growing food companies and from the introduction of new products that served some niche of the food industry. Instead, Johnson believed that Campbell Soup should concentrate on growing sales of its best-known brands—the red-and-white soup line, Prego, Pepperidge Farm, Vlasic, and Swanson—and to increase its U.S. market share in these product categories. During the 1980s, for example, Campbell's tonnage in canned soups had risen a paltry 1 percent annually and Campbell's market share of the U.S. soup market, according to Wall Street estimates, had slipped from a lofty 80 percent in the 1950s and 1960s to 70 percent in the mid-1980s to around 65 percent in 1990. Johnson also decided to press harder and faster than McGovern had to gain increased penetration of foreign markets.

While McGovern had pursued ways to reduce costs and eliminate inefficiencies during his 1989 restructuring, Johnson saw opportunities to achieve further economies and better profit margins, principally by eliminating unprofitable and slow-selling items from Campbell's product lineup and by divesting peripheral lines of businesses that did not complement the company's strengths or bolster the market power of its flagship brands. Consequently, the strategy Johnson crafted to boost Campbell's performance incorporated six major initiatives:

- Divesting poorly performing and nonstrategic business units and reorganizing Campbell's six divisions.
- Eliminating weak items from the company's product lineup.
- Requiring that new product introductions exploit Campbell Soup's strengths, core competencies, and organizational capabilities as well as have the potential to achieve the three 20–20–20 financial performance targets.

---

[12]Ibid.

EXHIBIT 5

Divested Campbell Soup Company Businesses, 1990–96

Source: Campbell annual reports and 10-Ks.

- Fried chicken plant in Sumpter, South Carolina
- Salmon Farms
- Snow King Frozen Foods—frozen meat products
- Triangle Manufacturing Corporation—a health-and-fitness products manufacturer
- Mushroom farms
- Mendelson-Zeller, Inc.
- Recipe Pet Food
- D. Lazzaroni Cookie Company (Italy)
- Win Schuler Foods, Inc.
- Juice Bowl
- Juice Works
- The fresh produce and frozen vegetable portions of the UK Freshbake Foods Group—the frozen entree portion of Freshbake was retained.
- Campbell Chilled Foods, Ltd. (United Kingdom)
- Mrs. Paul's frozen seafood
- Poultry processing operations
- Marie's salad dressings
- Beeck-Feinkost GmbH chilled foods (Germany)
- Beef farms in Argentina
- Durkee and Early California olives
- Groko BV frozen vegetable processing (Holland)

- Focusing on the global marketing of the company's competencies and capabilities.
- Installing and expanding low-cost business systems at the corporate level to support the operations of the business divisions.
- Improving utilization of assets to maximize the return to stockholders.

Exhibit 5 shows the business lines that were divested—Johnson saw all of them as either nonstrategic and unrelated to Campbell's core competencies or as chronic money losers or low-return businesses. This pruning of Campbell's portfolio resulted in the sale of 8 plants and the shutdown of 12 plants worldwide plus a workforce reduction of 8,000 people during Johnson's first 18 months as CEO. As the remaining plants bid to absorb the production of the closed plants, overall capacity utilization rose from 60 to 80 percent; Campbell's Maxton, North Carolina, plant was able to increase its output 50 percent and become Campbell's first canned-soup plant to drive manufacturing costs below 50 percent of the retail price of its products. Included among the initial plant closings was the company's 131-year-old Camden, New Jersey, plant with its distinctive water towers painted to look like giant Campbell Soup cans.

Johnson's restructuring continued throughout his tenure, with major initiatives approved by the board in 1993 and 1996. The 1993 restructuring program identified six plants and 14 businesses that were to be sold. In 1996 the board approved an additional restructuring that eliminated not only additional plants and businesses but also 2,100 administrative and operational positions at various Campbell Soup facilities. Both restructuring programs were intended to shift production from underutilized or inefficient production facilities to more cost-effective locations and eliminate nonstrategic poor-performing businesses from the portfolio. Under Johnson, Campbell Soup went on to divest a total of 26 businesses that had an average net profit margin of 1 percent. Campbell Soup also closed a total of 10 older and inefficient plants between 1990 and 1997 to boost capacity utilization.

Once Johnson assessed that the turnaround was well under way, he complemented the divestitures with 20 acquisitions of higher-margin business with ample growth potential to complete the portfolio restructuring initiative. In 1996 David Johnson commented on the

EXHIBIT 6

Businesses Acquired by Campbell Soup, 1994–97

1994 (acquisitions totaled $14 million)

- Dandy mushrooms (Australia)
- Fray Bentos canned meats (Australia)

1995 (acquisitions totaled $1.26 billion)

- Pace Foods—the leading salsa brand in the United States, with annual sales of $700 million. The company was purchased for $1.12 billion.
- Increase in share ownership of Arnott's Ltd. to 65 percent.
- Fresh Start Bakeries—maker of buns and English muffins for quick-service restaurants in the United States, Europe, and South America. At the time of the acquisition, the company had approximate annual sales of $75 million, 480 employees, and had been a supplier to McDonald's for more than 30 years. The business was integrated into Campbell's Food Service unit.
- Stratford-upon-Avon Foods—a food-service company operating in the United Kingdom with annual sales of $60 million. The business manufactured, marketed, and distributed canned baked beans, vegetable and fruit products, and branded and private-label pickles.
- Greenfield Healthy Foods—U.S. manufacturer of all-natural, low-fat cakes and cookies. The company provided Pepperidge Farm with new resources to enter the $800 million healthy-snack category.
- Homepride sauces—the best-selling cooking sauce in the United Kingdom. The business, purchased for an estimated $93 million, allowed Campbell to build gravy and sauce sales in the United Kingdom.

1996 (acquisitions totaled $186 million)

- Joint venture began between Arnott's Ltd. and Helios Foods, one of Indonesia's most prominent food companies—thereby providing Arnott's with biscuit manufacturing capability in Asia.
- Joint venture began in Malaysia with Cheong Chan that provided manufacturing facilities for canned soups, ketchup, and soy sauces in Southeast Asia. Campbell Soup also acquired a minority interest in Cheong Chan.
- Joint venture between Godiva and J. Osawa Ltd. to immediately open 33 retail stores and outlets for Godiva chocolates. An additional 20 stores were planned to open by the year 2000.
- Increase in share ownership of Arnott's Ltd. to 70 percent.

1997 (acquisitions totaled $228 million)

- Erasco Group—the leading wet-soup brand in Germany, with annual sales of $223 million and 900 employees. The business was purchased for approximately $210 million. Campbell management believed that the acquisition would accelerate the company's growth throughout Germany and the European Union.
- Kettle Chip Company—salty-snack company operating in Australia and acquired for $18 million.

strategy of moving Campbell from a position of "best in class" to "best in show," the contribution of the newly acquired businesses, and the company's prospects for growth:

> We begin this new attack from a position of great strength. Our balance sheet and cash flow are strong. Since 1990, we have divested non-strategic and low-margin businesses with approximately $800 million in sales and acquired strategic, higher-margin businesses with more than $1.2 billion in sales, including Mexican sauce leader Pace Foods. Our management team has transformed Campbell into a place where results count and where the bar is constantly raised . . . We are poised for breaking away from our competitors in the food industry. This strategic growth plan is designed to vault our company into the ranks of the world's renowned consumer goods companies, in terms of financial profile and market multiple.[13]

Exhibit 6 presents a listing and description of business acquisitions initiated by David Johnson. By year-end 1996 the new businesses Johnson had added to Campbell's portfolio achieved an average net profit margin of 12 percent.

[13]As quoted in PR Newswire, September 5, 1996.

Many of Johnson's acquisitions were intended to add brands and infrastructure that were necessary for the growth of Campbell's international business. The acquisition of Pace Foods was one of the few acquisitions not specifically aimed at growing international food sales. Pace Foods, the leading U.S. producer and marketer of Mexican salsa, was Campbell's biggest acquisition ever. The $1.12 billion purchase price represented five times Pace's sales and 20 times its earnings. A number of companies, including Heinz and Lea & Perrin, had been attempting to buy Pace for a number of years, but owner Kit Goldsbury was not interested. The chief operating officer of Pace Foods stated that Goldsbury agreed to the sale to Campbell because Goldsbury could identify with and liked Campbell's management team.[14]

As a product category, salsa (a spicy blend of jalapeños, tomatoes, onion, and garlic) surpassed ketchup in 1991 as the nation's best-selling condiment. The salsa category grew at just under a 13 percent compound annual growth rate from 1988 to 1993 as sales increased from $325 million to $700 million. The rapid growth in sales of salsa products was attributed to its spicy flavor and low fat content (a jar of Pace salsa contained no fat and only 70 calories), to the excellent way it complemented such snack foods as tortilla chips, to growing consumer popularity of Mexican dishes, and to a fast-increasing Hispanic population.

Johnson's Revised New Product Development and Marketing Strategies

David Johnson instituted a more cautious approach to new product development and challenged Campbell marketers to become more aggressive in marketing the company's products. Johnson was quick to comment, "There's no such thing as mature markets, only tired marketers,"[15] when told that low industry growth rates were obstacles to growth. New product ideas were more heavily researched and tested before they were put on the market. Moreover, new products were expected to provide quicker paybacks on investment; potential products that held little promise for near-term profitability and for meeting the 20–20–20 financial performance standards were tabled.

The search for new product ideas was limited to areas where Campbell had production and marketing expertise; as one executive put it, "We want to be in areas we know we are good at and in processes we are good at."[16] Despite the more conservative approach to new product development, Campbell introduced nearly 300 new products during Johnson's first three years as the company's chief executive. Johnson committed between $77 million and $88 million annually to R&D during his last three years as CEO to improve existing products and to develop new products that would be successful in U.S. and international markets. New items included cream of broccoli soup (which became the first new soup since 1935 to rank in the top five best-selling soups), Joseph A. Campbell premium-quality ready-to-serve soups, cheese tortellini soup, Light 'n Tangy V8, Swanson Kids Fun Feast frozen dinners, Vlasic Sandwich Stackers, Prego pizza sauce, and more varieties of Pepperidge Farm products. Johnson suggested that the company's new approach to product development had been successful in developing products that consumers desired and had allowed the company to achieve sales growth in traditionally mature markets: "Innovations and breakthroughs are so simple, but they come only if you're immersed in your field and determined to make the necessary connections. For instance, take our Stackers, which are pickles sliced to lay flat on a sandwich. A simple idea, but it took off: The overall Stackers market grew 55% last year. In addition, we're

---

[14]*The Wall Street Journal,* November 29, 1994, p. A3.

[15]As quoted in *Chief Executive,* November 1996.

[16]As quoted in *Financial World,* June 11, 1991, p. 53.

tapping into growing consumer segments, such as the healthy food category. For example, our new line of cream soups is 98% fat free."[17]

Johnson's Corporate Reorganization

Johnson's reorganization effort aimed at capturing strategic-fit benefits among related products and product families. Johnson concluded that McGovern's 50 autonomous units had resulted in lack of communication and cooperation between the different business units. For example, the U.S. soup division once ran a promotion with Nabisco crackers even though Pepperidge Farm produced a competing product. Also, U.S. tomato paste plants did not share technology with Mexican tomato paste plants since the Mexican plants were in a different division. A three-division structure was established during Johnson's first year as Campbell CEO to improve communication and technology sharing between businesses in similar product categories and geographies (see Exhibit 7). This initial structure was modified three times over the next five years. Each shuffling of businesses within the three-division structure was directed at improving the strategic fit within the portfolio of businesses. The series of new alignments also helped Campbell Soup put more emphasis on the company's international businesses.

Johnson's International Push

Johnson was convinced that a sizable fraction of Campbell Soup's growth should come from international expansion because the world market for processed food products was projected to grow over twice as fast as the 1 percent growth rate projected for the $200 billion U.S. food-processing industry. By 2000, Johnson wanted at least one-third of Campbell's revenues to come from outside of the United States. Johnson saw such companies as Coca-Cola and Gillette, whose international operations contributed 70 to 80 percent of total sales, as prototypes for Campbell Soup's future:

> Clearly, we're not going to be a Coca-Cola or Gillette in two years, but we're inching toward that aim as we go into the next century . . . We're expanding in the United Kingdom, Canada, and Australia, and trying to establish more beachheads in Asia Pacific. Our acquisition of Germany's Erasco increases our total international soup sales to 21 percent of total soup sales. We bought an operation in Malaysia called Cheong Chan, where we're now making the investments that will enable us to produce soup instead of importing it. We're looking for ventures in China and growing in Taiwan.

Campbell marketed its soups in Mexico, Canada, Argentina, Poland, Hong Kong, and China, and its baked goods in Europe and Asia Pacific. In 1993 Campbell increased its 33 percent share of Australia's Arnott's Ltd. to 58 percent to gain an organizational base for increasing its long-term presence in baked goods in the Pacific Rim and Asia. Johnson increased Campbell's ownership of Arnott's further to 65 percent in 1995 and to 70 percent in 1996. To help familiarize himself with Campbell's international operations and to better gauge the company's potential for foreign expansion, Johnson had all of Campbell's top international executives report directly to him for the first 12 months he was at Campbell.

International marketing of prepared foods was not easy. Taste preferences varied significantly from country to country (and sometimes within countries), prompting international producers to employ multicountry strategies to gear product characteristics to local preferences and eating habits. Campbell's 1988 acquisition of Britain's Freshbake Foods Group never performed up to expectations partly because Campbell management didn't cater adequately to the taste preferences of British consumers. Also, Campbell's penetration of the European soup market had proved more difficult than originally expected because the predominant forms of store-bought soups on the continent were dry soups and ready-to-serve soups; demand for

---

[17]As quoted in *Chief Executive,* November 1996.

EXHIBIT 7 Comparison of Campbell's Business Unit Structure under Gordon McGovern and David Johnson

Source: Campbell annual reports.

Campbell's Structure under Gordon McGovern		Campbell's Structure under David Johnson		Campbell's Structure under Dale Morrison	
Division	Example Brands/Services	Division	Example Brands/Services	Division	Example Brands/Services
Campbell U.S.		**U.S.A.**		Soups and Sauces	All worldwide dry and canned soups, Franco American pastas, V8 Campbell's tomato juice
• Soup Group	Red-and-white, Healthy Request, Chunky	• U.S. Soup Group	Dry and canned soup, Franco-American		
					Prego spaghetti sauces, Pace salsas Swanson broths,
• Frozen Food Group	Swanson, LeMenu	• Beverage Group	V8, Campbell's tomato juice		
• Grocery Group	Prego, Franco-American, Swanson canned meats	• Meal Enhancement Group	Open Pit barbecue sauce, Pace salsas, Vlasic, Prego, food service		Erasco, Cheong Chan, Home Pride, Leibig, Stockpot
• Beverage Group	Campbell's tomato juice, V8, Juice Bowl, Juice, Works	• Frozen Foods Group	Swanson	Biscuit and Confectionery	Arnott's Ltd., Pepperidge Farm, Godiva Chocolatier, Kettle Chips
• Pet Food Group	Recipe				
Pepperidge Farm	Pepperidge Farm breads, cookies, Godiva chocolates, Costa apple juice, Deli's frozen entrees	Bakery and Confectionery	Arnott's Ltd., Pepperidge Farm, Delacre, Godiva Chocolatier, Lami Lutti confections, Kettle Chips		
Vlasic	Pickles and relishes				
Mrs. Paul's	Frozen fish, frozen chicken, frozen vegetables				
Other U.S.	Triangle Manufacturing Corp.—fitness products Campbell Hospitality— restaurants Snow King Frozen Foods—frozen meats			Away from Home	Distribution and Campbell soups, Pace salsas, and specialty kitchen entrees to food-service markets
Campbell International	Soup—Canada and Mexico Fresh Bake Foods Group (Britain)—baked goods	International Grocery	Red-and-white canned soup, Erasco, Cheong Chan, Home Pride		
		• International Soup Group			
		• International Specialty Foods	Stratford-upon-Avon, Fray Bentos, Swift		

EXHIBIT 8   **Sales and Earnings of Campbell Soup Company, by Geographic Region, 1991–99 ($ millions)**

Source: Campbell annual reports.

	1999	1998	1997	1996	1995	1994	1993	1992	1991
United States									
Net sales	$4,808	$4,850	$5,495	$5,332	$5,012	$4,639	$4,744	$4,649	$4,496
Earnings before taxes	1,196	1,124	1,155	1,123	957	854	715	809	695
Europe									
Net sales	630	859	1,201	1,122	1,143	1,041	1,050	1,043	1,149
Earnings before taxes	32*	36*	50	71	74	64	(170)	45	49
Other countries									
Net sales	1,054	1,044	1,408	1,347	1,179	1,011	917	652	656
Earnings before taxes	$ 121	$ 123	$ 122	$ 172	$ 171	$ 154	$ 99	$ 70	$ 55

*Earnings before interest and taxes.

Campbell's mainstay condensed soups was virtually nonexistent in Europe, and consumers had to be persuaded of the merits of switching to a different preparation technique.

Campbell management opened a Hong Kong taste kitchen as part of the company's effort to ensure that the products it introduced would appeal to Asia's 2 billion consumers, whose average per capita soup consumption averaged six bowls per week. The Hong Kong kitchen proved to be a success, having a role in creating such popular sellers as scallop, watercress, duck-gizzard, and ham soups. The kitchen was experimenting with other soup varieties made from pork, dates, figs, and snake.

Campbell had been successful in Mexico with spicy soups such as Creama de Chile Poblano and had captured 10 percent of Argentina's $50 million soup market within one year of introducing nine varieties of its red-and-white canned soup. A summary of Campbell Soup's geographic performance between 1991 and 1998 is displayed in Exhibit 8.

The Dale Morrison Era Begins: Mid-1997

When David Johnson's five-year contract expired and he elected to step aside as Campbell Soup Company's CEO in July 1997, the company announced that 48-year-old Dale Morrison would become its new chief executive officer effective July 15, 1997. Morrison joined Campbell Soup in June 1995 as president of Pepperidge Farm, where he was largely responsible for a turnaround of the business that had averaged 2 to 3 percent sales growth between 1990 and 1995. Prior to joining Campbell Soup's management, Morrison spent 14 years with PepsiCo, where he held management positions with both Frito-Lay and Pepsi-Cola. Dale Morrison also coordinated the merger of British snack foods companies while at Frito-Lay. Morrison held a number of positions with General Foods from 1972 to 1981, marketing such brands as Tang, Post cereals, and Kool-Aid.

David Johnson agreed to remain on as chairman of Campbell's board of directors through July 1999 from which he could aid Morrison in an advisory role. Johnson announced, "My priority is to ensure that we continue our relentless commitment to building shareowner wealth. I will assist Dale in exploring the strategies needed to achieve Campbell's vision of becoming the best consumer products company in the world."[18]

[18]As quoted in *Milling & Baking News,* July 8, 1997, p. 14.

Morrison's Accomplishments at Campbell Soup Prior to His Appointment as CEO

When he arrived at Pepperidge Farm, Dale Morrison initiated a number of cost-cutting programs that freed up resources and gave the division enough gross margin leeway to spend additional sums on marketing and product promotion. Such products as Pepperidge Farm Goldfish crackers and Milano cookies benefited from increased advertising and marketing innovations like Goldfish milk-carton-style packaging, which was easier for children to manage than the previous paper-bag-style packaging. Morrison also made a point of visiting all Pepperidge Farm plants and met with the company's independent distributors, whom Morrison reclassified as sales development associates. Morrison's strategies resulted in a 10 percent sales increase in 1996, a 13 percent sales increase in 1997, and a 20 percent earnings increase in both years.

In recognition of his success at Pepperidge Farm, David Johnson gave Morrison added responsibilities at Campbell Soup. Morrison was appointed president of Campbell's International Specialty Foods in November 1996, putting him in charge of Campbell's international grocery, food-service, frozen and specialty foods, and bakery and confectionery businesses.

Recent Trends in the Performance of Campbell Soup's Stock Price, 1990–2000

Exhibit 9 shows Campbell Soup's market performance relative to the Dow Jones Industrial Index and the Dow Jones composite of other food-processing companies since 1990. The company's stock performance mirrored that of many of its processed food competitors, which averaged a 30 percent decline in their share prices and had collectively seen over $160 billion in market value disappear during 1999. Some of Campbell Soup's share price decline after January 2000 was attributable to a number of class-action lawsuits brought against Campbell Soup that claimed the company misrepresented its revenue from its condensed soup sales between November 1997 and January 1999. The complaints alleged that, in an attempt to meet analysts' quarterly earnings estimates, the company claimed to have sold product to major distributors and resellers when in actuality Campbell never shipped the product to customers. When asked about the suits' allegations by a *Wall Street Journal* reporter, Campbell's chief financial officer retorted, "Campbell Soup does not make and has not made sham shipments of its products. We do not make and have not made false or misleading statements."[19]

Morrison's Strategy for Campbell Soup

Morrison's strategies to improve Campbell Soup's performance were, for the most part, a continuation and refinement of Johnson's initiatives. Morrison agreed with David Johnson that Campbell Soup should become more like Coca-Cola, with faster sales growth in international markets and a tighter focus on the core business. Morrison wanted to increase Campbell Soup Company's annual sales growth to 8 to 10 percent and believed that the company's greatest opportunity for rapid growth lay in focusing on its premium brands, which were differentiated from competing brands in terms of taste, perceived quality, and image. Morrison wanted growth to come more from volume increases rather than price increases and intended to allocate greater resources to advertising some of the company's more highly differentiated brands like Joseph A. Campbell premium-quality ready-to-serve soups, Pepperidge Farm Goldfish crackers, and Milano cookies. The centerpiece of Morrison's plan for boosting unit sales was to increase advertising expenditures from 3.5 percent of sales to 8 percent of sales. Morrison also launched initiatives to enhance Campbell products' differentiated image in international

[19]As quoted in *The Wall Street Journal Interactive Edition,* February 17, 2000.

EXHIBIT 9   Campbell Soup Company's Stock Performance, 1990–March 2000

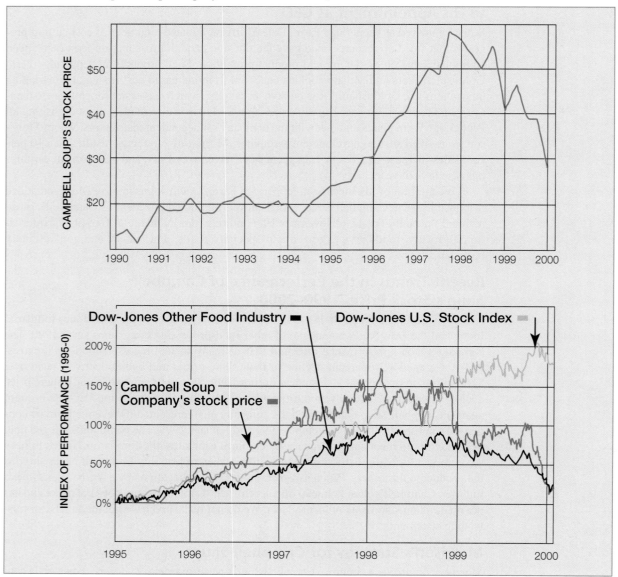

markets. In Japan, for example, the decision was made to upgrade the quality of its soup cans and to redesign the labels on the cans; Japanese consumers were drawn to products with high-quality packaging.

Morrison's Portfolio Restructuring Efforts

In September 1997 Dale Morrison announced the spinoff of seven low-growth businesses with combined sales of $1.4 billion—about 18 percent of Campbell Soup Company's 1997 sales. The spinoff was a carryover of strategic initiatives that David Johnson had announced in September 1996. Under the plan, Vlasic Foods International would become a stand-alone company with operations in the United States, Europe, and South America and over 9,000 employees. The new company's shares would be distributed tax-free to Campbell share-holders, and upon the completion of the spinoff the new company would be ranked 21st among 32 publicly traded food companies. Campbell's Swanson frozen food business in the United States and Canada and its frozen food lines in the United Kingdom would make up Vlasic Foods International's frozen food division. The grocery division would include Campbell's Vlasic retail and food-service products, Swift Armour meats in Argentina, Open Pit barbecue sauces, Stratford-upon-Avon's retail and food-service pickle and canned vegetable businesses in the United Kingdom, Gourmet Specialty Foods in Germany, and the U.S. fresh mushroom business.

Morrison commented at the time of the announced spinoff that shareholders would benefit greatly by a separation of Campbell Soup businesses:

> This is a watershed day for Campbell Soup Company and its shareowners. Spinning off these businesses allows us to focus on our most profitable businesses with the highest growth potential. Our core businesses have gross margins in excess of 45%. Net sales for these businesses grew 10% and earnings grew 15% in fiscal 1997. This is an outstanding platform to drive significant volume growth while continuing to deliver top-quartile earnings. The creation of this new company gives great brands like Vlasic and Swanson tremendous opportunities for growth under a dedicated management team. In both cases, shareowners will reap the rewards of highly focused companies.[20]

Some Wall Street analysts were not as optimistic that the new company would become a strong competitor in the processed-food industry. One portfolio manager suggested that the spinoff would allow Campbell to achieve higher growth rates in terms of sales and earnings, but Vlasic Foods International would find growth difficult: "Whenever a company spins off the crummy parts, it's always good for what's left. What they're spinning off didn't have the value or the growth rate of the other divisions."[21] Another analyst commented on the attractiveness of frozen food, where over the last 10 years the size of the market had declined and margin points were gained only through price cuts: "There is not going to be a mad rush to own this [new] food company. Swanson has been a stagnant brand at best, though I suppose it's a bit better than Schlitz beer."[22]

Even though the frozen foods category was highly competitive and had become commodity-like after the 1980s, Vlasic Foods International did include a number of popular brands and products. Swanson was the originator of the TV dinner in 1954 and continued to maintain category leadership with products like Hungry Man dinners, Great Start breakfasts, and Fun Feast kids' meals. Vlasic was the leader in U.S. pickle sales, with a 36 percent market share, and approximately 35 percent of Vlasic's sales came from products introduced within the previous five years. In addition, Swift was Argentina's largest exporter of beef, Open Pit was the number one barbecue sauce in the midwestern United States, Gourmet Specialty Foods was Germany's number one specialty foods company, and the company's mushroom business was the largest in the world. The new company's third- and fourth-quarter sales and earnings fell below projections, and sales of pickles and frozen foods were down about 10 percent for the year. The company's stock closed at $22¾ on the first day of trading in March 1998, but was trading in the $13 to $15 range within four months of the spinoff. The market performance of Vlasic Foods' common stock following its spinoff is depicted in Exhibit 10.

Morrison continued to restructure Campbell's portfolio during 1998 and 1999 to allow the company to focus on core brands and activities directly related to either product quality or image. Continental Sweets was sold to a Dutch venture capital fund in 1998. Continental Sweets made and distributed sugar and chocolate confectionery; its facilities were located in France and Belgium. Campbell Soup also sold its European-based Delacre

[20]Securities and Exchange Commission, Form 8-K, September 9, 1997.

[21]*Knight-Ridder/Tribune Business News,* September 10, 1997.

[22]As quoted in *The New York Times,* September 10, 1997, p. D1.

EXHIBIT 10   **Vlasic Foods International's Stock Performance, by Week, March 1998–March 2000**

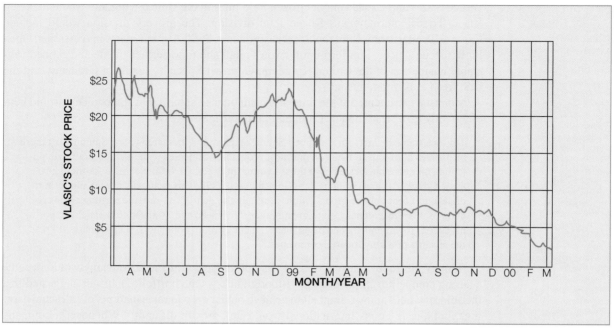

premium biscuit business and Australian-based Melbourne Mushrooms and Spring Valley beverages in 1998.

The company's Fresh Start Bakeries, a supplier of English muffins and buns to quick-service restaurants, was sold to a joint venture between Berkshire Partners and Fresh Start's management in May 1999. Morrison also chose to divest the company's can-making assets to Silgan Holdings—a supplier of food cans with annual sales of approximately $1.5 billion. The can-making operations were sold for $123 million, and the transaction included a 10-year supply agreement between Campbell Soup and Silgan that called for can purchases by Campbell totaling over $200 million each year. The company also took restructuring charges of $262 million and $41 million in 1998 and 1999, respectively, related to streamlining its production and administrative facilities in North America and Europe. The restructuring programs merged certain Canadian and U.S. administrative functions and attempted to maximize capacity utilization among its production facilities by combining operations whenever possible. For example, Campbell closed its Pace salsa plant in San Antonio, Texas, and shifted production of Pace products to Campbell's Paris, Texas, plant, which produced Prego spaghetti sauce, Franco-American gravies, and an assortment of soups. Campbell Soup management expected the restructuring program to reduce the company's operating expenses by $221 million annually.

The spinoff and divestitures allowed Campbell Soup to implement a $2 billion share buyback plan to repurchase 8 percent of the company's 451 million outstanding shares of stock between 1999 and 2001. The strategy to boost earnings per share and return on stockholders' equity was a continuation of an ongoing Johnson strategy of repurchasing 2 percent of the company's outstanding shares annually. Morrison also retained a Johnson-devised strategy of repurchasing shares in addition to the $2 billion buyback plan to offset per share dilution resulting from incentive compensation programs.

To boost Campbell's growth potential, Morrison initiated a number of new acquisitions during 1997 and 1998. In 1997 the company purchased the remaining 30 percent of

EXHIBIT 11

Sales and Earnings of Campbell Soup Company, by Division, 1995–99 ($ millions)

Source: Campbell annual reports.

	1999	1998	1997	1996	1995
Soups and Sauces					
Sales	$4,423	$4,434	$4,156	$3,742	$3,415
Operating earnings	1,082	1,109	1,012	978	863
Biscuits and Confectionery					
Sales	1,430	1,522	1,546	1,459	1,348
Operating earnings	215	206	154	183	164
Away from Home					
Sales	507	453	459	418	345
Operating earnings	57	53	62	55	40
Other					
Sales	126	334	1,904	2,149	2,204
Operating earnings	(5)	(85)	99	150	135
Interdivision					
Sales	($ 62)	($ 49)	($ 101)	($ 90)	($ 62)

Arnott's outstanding shares for $290 million, giving Campbell 100 percent ownership of the Australian biscuit company. The company also acquired Leibig soups in 1997 for $180 million. Leibig was France's leading producer of wet soups, with annual sales of approximately $75 million. In June 1998 Campbell Soup acquired privately held Fortun Foods for $105 million. Fortun's Stockpot brand of fresh, chilled soup was distributed to restaurants, supermarkets, and convenience stores in over 20 countries and was the market leader in premium refrigerated soups, with about 50 percent market share of the rapidly growing category and annual sales of $40 million. Campbell Soup had tried unsuccessfully a number of times since the 1980s to develop freshly made chilled soup without preservatives. Fortun's manufacturing process transferred hot soup from the kettle to a vacuum-sealed bag that was then immediately refrigerated. The company's proprietary process allowed Stockpot soups to stay fresh for about 120 days.

Morrison's acquisitions and divestitures prompted a realignment of Campbell Soup divisions and business units. Morrison created a Soups and Sauces division, which included all soup and sauce brands marketed globally. The Biscuit and Confectionery division was reorganized to include all global brands of baked goods, and the makeup of the Away from Home food-service division was adjusted to include all businesses that were dedicated to supplying the growing quick-service restaurant industry. A special division titled Campbell's Other was temporarily formed to handle the details of transferring the divested businesses to the new owners and report the historical performance of divested businesses.

Morrison believed that cross-business skills transfer would be more readily achieved by abandoning Campbell's previous geographically based divisions and placing all businesses sharing common R&D, production, and marketing activities in a common division (see again Exhibit 7, which presents a comparison of business divisions and units under Gordon McGovern, David Johnson, and Dale Morrison). Exhibit 11 provides the sales and operating earnings for Morrison's divisions from 1995 to 1999. The 1995 and 1996 financial data shown in the exhibit have been reorganized to match Campbell Soup Company's divisional structure in 1997–99.

Campbell Soup in 2000

Soups and Sauces Group

The Soups and Sauces division was Campbell's largest operating unit, accounting for about two-thirds of the company's total consolidated sales. The U.S. and international markets for canned soup were mature and possibly entering into a declining stage. The U.S. wet-soup category had grown at low single-digit rates during the late 1990s and was not expected to grow at a faster rate during 2000–2001. The maturity of the U.S. soup segment was attributable to the increased popularity of fresh foods, a 40 percent decrease in the usage of cooking soups in recipes, and an overall reduced tendency of consumers to purchase canned products. The slow growth in international markets was primarily related to the preference for homemade soups in many regions. During most of the 1990s consumption of Campbell's soups grew at 2 to 3 percent annually, but U.S. consumption of Campbell's wet soups declined by about 1 percent in 1998 and by 8 percent in 1999. Campbell's worldwide soup sales grew by 3 percent during 1998, but declined by 4 percent in 1999. The company's 1997 acquisition of Liebig helped Campbell Soup increase its international wet-soup volume by 7 percent in 1999.

Campbell's market share in the condensed soup category had declined from 80 percent in 1993 to 74 percent in 1997. In an attempt to regain lost market share, the company forwent its usual 3 to 7 percent annual price increases in 1998 since much of its lost market share was being captured by lower-priced private-label brands. The level pricing failed to recapture enough lost market share to offset the impact of smaller margins on the division's 1998 revenues. In 1999 the company's U.S. sales of canned soup declined by 8 percent after Campbell management eliminated quarter-end promotions to retailers.

The division implemented a plan to increase advertising spending by 18 percent in 1998 and intended to eventually increase the advertising budget for Campbell soups and sauces from 3.5 percent of sales to 8 percent of sales. Dale Morrison believed that increased advertising was necessary to support new products and newly packaged products and to promote soup in appealing ways to children. Campbell's fastest growing soup and sauce products during the late 1990s were Swanson broths and V8 Splash juices. Swanson's 20 percent annual growth was in large part a result of new 32-ounce recloseable aseptic packaging and its positioning as a 100 percent fat-free seasoning alternative that could be used in a number of recipes. Recent product introduction V8 Splash, a beverage combining carrot and tropical fruit juices, helped the V8 brand grow by more than 10 percent in 1998, and the 1999 introduction of new packaging (e.g., kid-sized juice boxes), new flavors, and a greater availability throughout the world helped V8 Splash become Campbell's most successful new product introduction in more than a decade.

Campbell introduced additional products after Morrison became the company's CEO to improve the sales volumes of products like tomato soup. Its new 32-ounce recloseable plastic ready-to-serve Campbell Tomato Soup allowed consumers to pour a single serving or use what was called for by a recipe and then store the remaining portion in the refrigerator for later use. Campbell marketers believed that having soup in the refrigerator would lead to higher consumption since most people opened the refrigerator more often than the pantry. Campbell Soup added a line of Select Soups, packaged in metal cans, as was the company's Classic line of soups that included tomato, cream of broccoli, and cream of mushroom, but the Select Soups line included more unique varieties of soups. Select Soups used distinctive combinations of ingredients to create flavorful soups like chicken and pasta with roasted garlic—a blend of chicken, penne and rotini pasta, and vegetables with roasted garlic in a chicken broth. Campbell Soup also introduced a Soups-to-Go line of ready-to-serve microwavable single-serving bowls that achieved volume gains in 1999. Joseph A.

Campbell premium-quality soups had not experienced the sales gains expected by Campbell management; the line was rebranded Simply Home in 1998 and achieved volume gains in 1999. Campbell's Chunky line was also one of the company's faster-growing lines of canned soup in the late 1990s.

Even though the company had been largely successful with its new product introductions in recent years, Campbell management still believed in David Johnson's commitment to thoroughly assessing a product's potential on the market prior to its launch. Robert Bernstock, president of Campbell's U.S. Grocery division, explained, "In the early 1990s we were launching two new, single SKU products with more than $10 million in sales a year. We're now launching more than 20 a year. Tremendous up-front discipline is the key. We spend 12–18 months in rigorous testing."[23]

Biscuits and Confectionery Group

Campbell's Biscuits and Confectionery business unit had 1999 sales of $1.4 billion and operating earnings of $215 million. The division included Pepperidge Farm in North America; Godiva chocolates in North America, Europe, and Asia; Arnott's in the Pacific Rim/Asia; and Kettle Chips in Australia. Such products as Goldfish crackers, Swirl bread, and Milano cookies helped the Biscuits and Confectionery division achieve a sales increase of 5 percent in 1998 prior to the impact of exchange rates. The division had a sales decline of 6 percent in 1999, but Godiva grew its U.S. sales volume by more than 10 percent in 1998 and made some headway in increasing penetration of European and Asian markets. Campbell management expected the business to continue to increase its strength in Asia as more Godiva retail outlets were opened in the region. The company also opened additional free-standing boutiques in shopping malls and Godiva departments in upscale department stores throughout the United States.

Pepperidge Farm continued the transformation begun by Dale Morrison in 1995 with continued increases in sales volume. The company's increased promotion of Goldfish crackers allowed sales of the product to grow 25 percent in 1996 and 40 percent in 1997. New varieties such as Goldfish Grahams contributed to sales volume increases for Goldfish products in 1999. Other market-leading Pepperidge Farm products included Milano cookies, which grew by 35 percent in 1997, Dessert Classics frozen cakes, and frozen garlic bread, which grew more than 40 percent after being moved adjacent to frozen pasta in grocery freezers. Pepperidge Farm management had established a "2 × 2" program with the objective of doubling sales between 1997 and 2000. The program called for Pepperidge Farm to achieve its growth objective by developing several innovative new products, lowering operating costs by eliminating costs that did not provide value to the customer, and purging waste.

Campbell management believed that a controlling interest in Arnott's Ltd. would yield a competitive advantage in the $3 billion Asian cookie-and-cracker market. The 132-year-old Arnott's was one of Australia's best-known food companies, had access to low-cost ingredients, and had efficient manufacturing processes. Arnott's Australian location also provided a shipping-cost advantage for products exported to the entire Asian/Pacific Rim region. The biscuit and confectionery division introduced popular Pepperidge Farm products to international markets in 1999 when Arnott's Goldfish were launched in Australia.

Away from Home Group

Dale Morrison, like David Johnson, realized the importance of Campbell's food-service unit, Away from Home, in growing corporate sales and earnings. In 2000, U.S. consumers were projected to eat approximately 46 percent of all meals away from home and spend an

[23]As quoted in *Prepared Foods,* September 1997, p. 14.

estimated $342 billion in restaurants. On an average day, almost 140 million meals were eaten in U.S. restaurants and cafeterias. In addition, nearly 21 percent of U.S. households used some form of takeout or delivery each day. Campbell Soup management intended for the company to make Campbell products readily available to both consumers who purchased food for home preparation and those who chose to dine away from home. Morrison believed that Campbell Soup should position itself to provide soups and other processed foods to consumers in their homes and other locations: "If you look at the U.S. soup business, you could say we have an 80% share of the condensed and ready-to-serve market, and where do we go from there? But if you look at soup consumption in total. . . we really have a 38% share. Under that frame of reference, there's real opportunity."[24]

In 1999 the sales of the Away from Home division reached $507 million—a 12 percent increase over 1998. The division provided pot pies to Kentucky Fried Chicken, soups to roughly one-third of McDonald's restaurants, and a wide variety of Prego entrees and Campbell soups to various restaurants and cafeterias. V8 Splash beverages and Pace Mexican salsas were also distributed to restaurants, delicatessens, and cafeterias. The company had introduced serve-your-own soup vending machines in convenience stores and soup kettles in college cafeterias and had also provided complete meals to supermarket delis and cafeterias that included entrees and side dishes packaged in 5.5- and 2.5-pound aluminum trays. The company also tested the popularity of soup kiosks in airports and sports arenas. Campbell's 1998 acquisition of Stockpot soups allowed the company to expand its branded soup presence in the food-service market for soups because of Stockpot's proprietary manufacturing process that allowed soups to be shipped fresh and without preservatives.

Events at Campbell Soup in Early 2000

Campbell Soup Company was ranked number four among *Fortune* magazine's 1999 and 2000 listings of the most admired food companies; it also was ranked as the third most profitable food company among the Fortune 500. However, Campbell Soup's financial and market performance fell considerably short of being rated "best in show" (a David Johnson objective). In his letter to the stockholders in the company's 1999 annual report, Dale Morrison stated his belief that even though the processed-food industry was confronted by a variety of challenges and Campbell Soup had failed to outperform the overall stock market, it was still feasible for Campbell Soup to deliver an attractive return to its shareholders:

> Campbell Soup Company's primary commitment has been, and always will be, to build shareowner wealth. For many years, we succeeded brilliantly in doing so. Lately, however, much has been said and written about the challenges facing our industry and our company—challenges relating, for example, to changing consumer habits and the pace and prospects for growth. Over the past several years, the food industry has underperformed the overall market. And as we are all aware, this year, in a painful departure from our recent track record, Campbell disappointed our investors as well. Our stock price declined 19 percent in the [1999] fiscal year. So I believe our shareowners today are entitled to ask, "What does the future hold for Campbell Soup Company?"
>
> The answer begins with our central business—soup. For millions of people, the Campbell's name is synonymous with quality, wholesomeness, and the best moments of family life.
>
> Beyond soup, we compete in categories that offer abundant opportunities to grow with changing consumer preferences and lifestyles—sauces, beverages, biscuits and confectionery. Campbell brings significant brand power to these categories with favorites like V8 and V8 Splash, Pace, Prego, Franco-American, Pepperidge Farm, Arnott's and Godiva.[25]

[24]Ibid.

[25]Campbell Soup Company 1999 annual report.

Mounting Problems

Despite Morrison's optimism about the company's growth prospects, Campbell's stock price continued to slide from its all-time high of $63 per share in early 1998. During the first nine months of 1999, the stock price traded mostly in the $40 to $45 per share range. Then in late fall of 1999 it began a steep slide, falling below $30 as the company was hit by (1) a series of shareholder lawsuits alleging that company documents misled shareholders about revenues, (2) a February 2000 recall of 109,000 pounds of canned vegetable soup in 13 states after consumers found long pieces of metal in the soup, and (3) forecasts of slow growth for Campbell's brands by both Wall Street analysts and Campbell's executives. Campbell Soup had reported slightly better-than-expected second-quarter earnings for the period ending December 1999, but several Wall Street analysts expected full-year earnings for fiscal year 2000 (ending July) to be $1.86, rising to perhaps $1.99 at the end of fiscal year 2001.

On March 22, 2000, Dale Morrison resigned as president, CEO, and a director of the company. He was replaced by David Johnson, the company's previous CEO, who agreed to serve while the company's board of directors searched for a permanent replacement. The closing stock price on March 22, 2000, was $29^{11}/$_{16}$, off $1^{7}/$_{16}$.

10

Dell, Inc., in 2005: A Winning Strategy?

Arthur A. Thompson *University of Alabama*

John E. Gamble *University of South Alabama*

In 1984, at the age of 19, Michael Dell invested $1,000 of his own money and founded Dell Computer with a simple vision and business concept—that personal computers (PCs) could be built to order and sold directly to customers. Michael Dell believed his approach to the PC business had two advantages: (1) bypassing distributors and retail dealers eliminated the markups of resellers, and (2) building to order greatly reduced the costs and risks associated with carrying large stocks of parts, components, and finished goods. Between 1986 and 1993 the company worked to refine its strategy, build an adequate infrastructure, and establish market credibility against better-known rivals. In the mid and late 1990s, Dell's strategy started to click into full gear. By 2003, Dell's sell-direct and build-to-order business model and strategy had provided the company with the most efficient procurement, manufacturing, and distribution capabilities in the global PC industry and had given Dell a substantial cost and profit margin advantage over rival PC vendors. And by late 2004 Dell seemed well on its way to solidifying its market standing as the global leader in PCs.

Dell had a market-leading 33 percent share of PC sales in the United States in the first nine months of 2004, comfortably ahead of Hewlett-Packard (19.5 percent), IBM (5.1 percent), and Gateway (4.7 percent). Dell had moved ahead of IBM into second place during 1998 and then overtaken Compaq Computer as the U.S. sales leader in the third quarter of 1999. Its market share leadership in the United States had widened every year since 2000. Dell had overtaken Compaq as the global market leader in 2001. But when HP, the third-ranking PC seller in the world, acquired Compaq, the second-ranking PC vendor in 2002, Dell found itself in a tight battle with HP for the top spot globally. Dell was the world leader in unit sales in the first and third quarters of 2002, and HP was the sales leader in the second and fourth quarters. However, Dell opened a clear market share gap over HP in 2003–2004. In the United States, Dell had the number one PC market share in every customer segment in the three months ending October 2004. However, Dell trailed HP in PC sales outside the United States; HP's non-U.S. share had been in the 12.5 to 13.8 percent range since late 2001, with Dell's share climbing from about 7.5 percent in late 2001 to 11 percent in 2004. Exhibit 1 shows the shifting domestic and global sales and market share rankings in PCs during 1998–2004.

Since the late 1990s, Dell had also been driving for industry leadership in servers. In 2004 Dell was the number one domestic seller of servers, with close to a 33 percent market share (up from about 3–4 percent in the mid-1990s). It was number two in the world in server shipments, with a 24.5 percent share in the third quarter of 2004, within striking distance of global market leadership. Dell was the leader in servers in the three largest server markets—the United States, Japan, and China. In the mid-to-late 1990s, a big fraction of the servers sold were proprietary machines running on customized Unix operating systems and carrying price tags ranging from $30,000 to $1 million or more. But a seismic shift in server technology, coupled with growing cost-consciousness on the part of server users, produced a radical shift away from more costly, proprietary, Unix-based servers during 1999–2004. In 2003–2004, about 8 out of 10 servers sold carried price tags below $10,000, were based on standardized components and technology, and ran on either Windows or Linux operating systems. The overall share of Unix-based servers shipped in 2003–2004 was under 10 percent, down from about 18 percent in 1997. Dell's rise to prominence in servers came from its focus on low- and mid-range servers that used standard technology.

In addition, Dell was making market inroads in other product categories. Its sales of data storage devices had grown to over $2 billion annually, aided by a strategic alliance with EMC, a leader in the data storage. In 2001–2002, Dell began selling low-cost data-routing switches—a product category in which Cisco Systems was the dominant global leader. In late 2002 Dell introduced a new line of handheld PCs—the Axim X5—to compete against the higher-priced products of Palm, HP, and others; the Axim offered a solid but not trend-setting design, was packed with features, and was priced roughly 50 percent below the best-selling models of rivals. Starting in 2003, Dell began marketing Dell-branded printers and printer cartridges, product categories that provided global leader HP with the lion's share of its profits—the company was on track to sell over 5 million printers and generate more than $1 billion in imaging and printing revenues in 2004. Also in 2003, Dell began selling flat-screen LCD TVs and retail-store systems, including electronic cash registers, specialized software, services, and peripherals required to link retail-store checkout lanes to corporate information systems. Dell's recently introduced MP3 player, the Dell DJ, was number two behind the Apple iPod. Dell added plasma screen TVs to its TV product line in 2004. Since the late 1990s, Dell had been marketing CD and DVD drives, printers, scanners, modems, monitors, digital cameras, memory cards, data storage devices, and speakers made by a variety of manufacturers.

So far, Dell's foray into new products and businesses had proved to be profitable. According to Michael Dell, "We believe that all our businesses should make money. If a business doesn't make money, if you can't figure out how to make money in that business, you shouldn't be in that business."[1] In 2003 and 2004, Dell earned a profit in each of its product categories, customer segments, and geographic markets. Dell products were sold in more than 170 countries, but sales in 60 countries accounted for about 95 percent of total revenues.

---

[1]As quoted in "Dell Puts Happy Customers First," *Nikkei Weekly,* December 16, 2002.

EXHIBIT 1   U.S. And Global Market Shares of Leading PC Vendors, 1998–2004

A. U.S. Market Shares of the Leading PC Vendors, 1998–2003

2003 Rank	Vendor	First Nine Months of 2004		2003		2002	
		Shipments (in 000s)	Market Share	Shipments (in 000s)	Market Share	Shipments (in 000s)	Market Share
1	Dell	14,011	33.1%	16,319	30.9%	13,324	27.90%
	Compaq*	—	—	—	—	—	—
2	Hewlett-Packard*	8,256	19.5	10,851	20.6	8,052	16.8
3	IBM	2,170	5.1	2,748	5.2	2,531	5.3
4	Gateway	1,991	4.7	1,987	3.8	2,725	5.7
5	Apple	n.a.	n.a.	1,675	3.2	1,693	3.5
	Others	15,954	37.6	19,158	36.3	19,514	40.8
	All vendors	42,382	100.0%	52,739	100.0%	47,839	100.0%

B. Worldwide Market Shares of the Leading PC Vendors, 1996–2003†

2003 Rank	Vendor	First Nine Months of 2004		2003		2002	
		Shipments (in 000s)	Market Share	Shipments (in 000s)	Market Share	Shipments (in 000s)	Market Share
1	Dell	22,999	18.4%	25,833	16.9	20,672	15.2%
	Compaq*	—	—	—	—	—	—
2	Hewlett-Packard*	19,796	15.8	25,009	16.4	18,432	13.6
3	IBM	7,478	6.0	9,000	5.9	7,996	5.9
4	Fujitsu Siemens	5,142	4.1	6,375	4.2	5,822	4.3
5	Toshiba	n.a.	n.a.	5,080	3.3	n.a.	n.a
	Others	69,753	55.7	81,271	53.3	78,567	57.8
	All vendors	125,168	100.0%	152,568	100.0%	136,022	100.0%

n.a. = Not available.

*Compaq was acquired by Hewlett-Packard in May 2002. The 2002 data for Hewlett-Packard include both Compaq-branded and Hewlett-Packard-branded PCs for the last three quarters of 2002 plus only Hewlett-Packard-branded PCs for Q1 2002. Compaq's worldwide PC shipments during Q1 2002 totaled 3,367,000 units; its U.S. PC shipments during Q1 2002 totaled 1,280,000 units.

†Includes branded shipments only and excludes original equipment manufacturer (OEM) sales for all manufacturers; shipments of Compaq PCs for last three quarters of 2002 included in 2002 figures for Hewlett-Packard.

Source: International Data Corp.

Company Background

At age 12, Michael Dell was running a mail-order stamp-trading business, complete with a national catalog, and grossing $2,000 a month. At 16 he was selling subscriptions to the *Houston Post,* and at 17 he bought his first BMW with money he had earned. He enrolled at the University of Texas in 1983 as a premed student (his parents wanted him to become a doctor), but he soon became immersed in computers and started selling PC components out of his college dormitory room. He bought random-access memory (RAM) chips and disk drives for IBM PCs at cost from IBM dealers, who at the time often had excess supplies on hand because they were required to order large monthly quotas from IBM. Dell resold the components through newspaper ads (and later through ads in national computer magazines) at 10–15 percent below the regular retail price.

By April 1984 sales were running about $80,000 per month. Michael decided to drop out of college and form a company, PCs Ltd., to sell both PC components and PCs under

A. U.S. Market Shares of the Leading PC Vendors, 1998–2003

2001		2000		1999		1998	
Shipments (in 000s)	Market Share	Shipments (in 000s)	Market Share	Shipments (in 000s)	Market Share	Shipments (in 000s)	Market Share
10,817	23.5%	9,645	19.7%	7,492	16.6%	4,799	13.2%
5,341	11.6	7,761	15.9	7,222	16	6,052	16.7
4,374	9.5	5,630	11.5	3,955	8.8	2,832	7.8
2,461	5.3	2,668	5.5	3,274	7.2	2,983	8.2
3,219	7.0	4,237	8.7	4,001	8.9	3,039	8.4
1,665	3.6	n.a	n.a.	n.a	n.a.	n.a.	n.a.
23,509	51.0	18,959	38.8	19,248	42.6	16,549	45.6
46,051	100.0%	48,900	100.0%	45,192	100.0%	36,254	100.0%

B. Worldwide Market Shares of the Leading PC Vendors, 1996–2003†

2001		2000		1999		1998	
Shipments (in 000s)	Market Share	Shipments (in 000s)	Market Share	Shipments (in 000s)	Market Share	Shipments (in 000s)	Market Share
17,231	12.9%	14,801	10.6%	11,883	10.5%	7,770	8.5%
14,673	11	17,399	12.5	15,732	14	13,266	14.5
9,309	7	10,327	7.4	7,577	6.7	5,743	6.3
8,292	6.2	9,308	6.7	9,287	8.2	7,946	8.7
6,022	4.5	6,582	4.7	n.a.	n.a.	n.a.	n.a.
n.a.	n.a.	n.a.	n.a.	n.a.	n.a.	n.a.	n.a.
73,237	54.9	80,640	58	62,258	55.2	50,741	55.5
133,466	100.0%	139,057	100.0%	112,726	100.0%	91,442	100.0%

the brand name PCs Limited. He obtained his PCs by buying retailers' surplus stocks at cost, then powering them up with graphics cards, hard disks, and memory before reselling them. His strategy was to sell directly to end users; by eliminating the retail markup, Dell's new company was able to sell IBM clones (machines that copied the functioning of IBM PCs using the same or similar components) about 40 percent below the price of IBM's best-selling PCs. The discounting strategy was successful, attracting price-conscious buyers and generating rapid revenue growth. By 1985, the company was assembling its own PC designs with a few people working on six-foot tables. The company had 40 employees, and Michael Dell worked 18-hour days, often sleeping on a cot in his office. By the end of fiscal 1986, sales had reached $33 million.

During the next several years, however, PCs Ltd. was hampered by growing pains—specifically, a lack of money, people, and resources. Michael Dell sought to refine the company's business model; add needed production capacity; and build a bigger, deeper management staff and corporate infrastructure while at the same time keeping costs low.

The company was renamed Dell Computer in 1987, and the first international offices were opened that same year. In 1988 Dell added a sales force to serve large customers, began selling to government agencies, and became a public company—raising $34.2 million in its first offering of common stock. Sales to large customers quickly became the dominant part of Dell's business. By 1990 Dell Computer had sales of $388 million, a market share of 2–3 percent, and a research and development (R&D) staff of over 150 people. Michael Dell's vision was for Dell Computer to become one of the world's top three PC companies.

Thinking its direct sales business would not grow fast enough, in 1990–93, the company began distributing its computer products through Soft Warehouse Superstores (now CompUSA), Staples (a leading office products chain), Wal-Mart, Sam's Club, and Price Club (now Price/Costco). Dell also sold PCs through Best Buy stores in 16 states and through Xerox in 19 Latin American countries. But when the company learned how thin its margins were in selling through such distribution channels, it realized it had made a mistake and withdrew from selling to retailers and other intermediaries in 1994 to refocus on direct sales. At the time, sales through retailers accounted for only about 2 percent of Dell's revenues.

In 1993, further problems emerged: Dell reportedly lost $38 million in a risky foreign-currency hedging, quality difficulties arose with certain PC lines made by the company's contract manufacturers, profit margins declined, and buyers were turned off by the company's laptop PC models. To get laptop sales back on track, the company took a charge of $40 million to write off its laptop line and suspended sales of laptops until it could get re-designed models into the marketplace.

Because of higher costs and unacceptably low profit margins in selling to individuals and households, Dell did not pursue the consumer market aggressively until sales to individuals at the company's Internet site took off in 1996 and 1997. It became clear that PC-savvy individuals, who were buying their second and third computers, wanted powerful computers with multiple features; did not need much technical support; and liked the convenience of buying direct from Dell, ordering exactly what they wanted, and having it delivered to their door within a matter of days. In early 1997, Dell created an internal sales and marketing group dedicated to serving the individual consumer segment and introduced a product line designed especially for individual users.

By late 1997, Dell had become a low-cost leader among PC vendors by wringing greater and greater efficiency out of its direct sales and build-to-order business model. Since then, the company had continued driving hard to reduce its costs and, by late 2004, was considered the lowest-cost producer among all the leading vendors of PCs and servers. The company was a pioneer and an acknowledged world leader in incorporating e-commerce technology and use of the Internet into its everyday business practices. Michael Dell's goal was to stitch Dell's business together with its supply partners and customers in real time such that all three appeared to be part of the same organizational team.[2]

In its fiscal year ending January 30, 2004, Dell Computer posted revenues of $41.4 billion, up from $3.4 billion in the year ending January 29, 1995—a nine-year compound average growth rate of 32 percent. Over the same period, profits were up from $140 million to $2.62 billion—a 38.5 percent compound average growth rate. Dell expected to achieve close to $50 billion in sales in its fiscal year ending January 2005. A $100 investment in Dell's stock at its initial public offering in June 1988 would have been worth about $52,000 in December 2004. Based on 2003 data, Dell ranked number 31 on the Fortune 500, number 93 on the Fortune Global 500, and number 6 on the Fortune Global "most admired" list. In late 2004, Dell Computer had over 53,000 employees worldwide, up from 16,000 at

---

[2]Joan Magretta, "The Power of Virtual Integration: An Interview with Dell Computer's Michael Dell," *Harvard Business Review,* March–April 1998, p. 75.

year-end 1997; over 50 percent of Dell's employees were located in countries outside the United States, and this percentage was growing. The company's headquarters and main office complex was in Round Rock, Texas (an Austin suburb). The company changed its name from Dell Computer to Dell, Inc., in 2003 to reflect the company's growing business base outside of PCs. Exhibits 2 and 3 provide information about Dell's financial performance and geographic operations.

Michael Dell

In the company's early days Michael Dell hung around mostly with the company's engineers. He was so shy that some employees thought he was stuck up because he never talked to them. But people who worked with him closely described him as a likable young man who was slow to warm up to strangers.[3] He was a terrible public speaker and wasn't good at running meetings. But Lee Walker, a 51-year-old venture capitalist brought in by Michael Dell to provide much-needed managerial and financial experience during the company's organization-building years, became Michael Dell's mentor, built up his confidence, and was instrumental in turning him into a polished executive.[4] Walker served as the company's president and chief operating officer during the 1986–1990 period; he had a fatherly image, knew everyone by name, and played a key role in implementing Michael Dell's marketing ideas. Under Walker's tutelage, Michael Dell became intimately familiar with all parts of the business, overcame his shyness, learned to control his ego, and turned into a charismatic leader with an instinct for motivating people and winning their loyalty and respect.

When Walker had to leave the company in 1990 because of health reasons, Dell turned to Morton Meyerson, former CEO and president of Electronic Data Systems, for advice and guidance on how to transform Dell Computer from a fast-growing medium-sized company into a billion-dollar enterprise. Though sometimes given to displays of impatience, Michael Dell usually spoke in a quiet, reflective manner and came across as a person with maturity and seasoned judgment far beyond his age. His prowess was based more on an astute combination of technical knowledge and marketing know-how than on being a technological wizard. In 1992, at the age of 27, Michael Dell became the youngest CEO ever to head a Fortune 500 company; he was a billionaire at the age of 31.

By the late 1990s, Michael Dell had become one of the most respected executives in the PC industry. Media journalists had described him as "the quintessential American entrepreneur" and "the most innovative guy for marketing computers." He was a much-sought-after speaker at industry and company conferences. His views and opinions about the future of PCs, the Internet, and e-commerce practices carried considerable weight both in the PC industry and among executives worldwide. Once pudgy and bespectacled, in early 2005, 40-year-old Michael Dell was physically fit, considered good-looking, wore contact lenses, ate only health foods, and lived in a three-story 33,000-square-foot home on a 60-acre estate in Austin, Texas, with his wife and four children. He owned about 9 percent of Dell's common stock, worth over $9 billion.

Michael Dell was considered a very accessible CEO and a role model for young executives because he had done what many of them were trying to do. He delegated authority to subordinates, believing that the best results came from turning "loose talented people who can be relied upon to do what they're supposed to do." Business associates viewed Michael Dell as an aggressive personality, an extremely competitive risk taker who had always played close to the edge. He spent about 30 percent of his time traveling to company operations and meeting with customers. In a typical year, he would make two or three trips to Europe and two trips to Asia.

---

[3]"Michael Dell: On Managing Growth," *MIS Week,* September 5, 1988, p. 1.
[4]"The Education of Michael Dell," *BusinessWeek,* March 22, 1993, p. 86.

EXHIBIT 2   Selected Financial Statement Data for Dell Inc., Fiscal Years 1998–2004
(In millions, except per share data)

	Fiscal Year Ended	
	January 30, 2004	January 31, 2003
Results of operations		
Net revenue	$41,444	$35,404
Cost of revenue	33,892	29,055
Gross margin	7,552	6,349
Operating expenses:		
Selling, general and administrative	3,544	3,050
Research, development and engineering	464	455
Special charges	—	—
Total operating expenses	4,008	3,505
Operating income	3,544	2,844
Investment and other income (loss), net	180	183
Income before income taxes, extraordinary loss, and cumulative effect of change in accounting principle	3,724	3,027
Provision for income taxes	1,079	905
Net income	$ 2,645	$ 2,122
Earnings per common share:		
Basic	$1.03	$0.82
Diluted	$1.01	$0.80
Weighted average shares outstanding:		
Basic	2,565	2,584
Diluted	2,619	2,644
Cash flow and balance sheet data		
Net cash provided by operating activities	$ 3,670	$ 3,538
Cash, cash equivalents, and investments	11,922	9,905
Total assets	19,311	15,470
Long-term debt	505	506
Total stockholders' equity	$ 6,280	$ 4,873

*Includes effect of $59 million adjustment due to the cumulative effect of a change in accounting principle.

Source: Dell, Inc., 2004 10-K and 1999 annual report.

In mid-2004, Michael Dell, the company's first and only CEO, transferred his title of CEO to Kevin Rollins, the company's president and chief operating officer. Dell remained as chairman of the board. Dell and Rollins had run the company for the past seven years under a shared leadership structure. The changes were primarily ones of title, not of roles or responsibilities.

Dell Computer's Strategy

The core of Dell Computer's strategy during 2002–2004 was to use its strong capabilities in supply chain management, low-cost manufacturing, and direct sales capabilities to expand into product categories where it could provide added value to its customers in the form of lower prices. Its standard pattern of attack was to identify an IT product with good margins; figure out how to build it (or else have it built by others) cheaply enough to be able to

Fiscal Year Ended				
February 1, 2002	February 2, 2001	January 28, 2000	January 29, 1999	February 1, 1998
$31,168	$31,888	$25,265	$18,243	$12,327
25,661	25,455	20,047	14,137	9,605
5,507	6,443	5,218	4,106	2,722
2,784	3,193	2,387	1,788	1,202
452	482	374	272	204
482	105	194	—	—
3,718	3,780	2,955	2,060	1,406
1,789	2,663	2,263	2,046	1,316
(58)	531	188	38	52
1,731	3,194	2,451	2,084	1,368
485	958	785	624	424
$ 1,246	$ 2,177*	$ 1,666	$ 1,460	$ 944
$0.48	$0.84	$0.66	$0.58	$0.36
$0.46	$0.79	$0.61	$0.53	$0.32
2,602	2,582	2,536	2,531	2,631
2,726	2,746	2,728	2,772	2,952
$ 3,797	$ 4,195	$ 3,926	$ 2,436	$ 1,592
8,287	7,853	6,853	3,181	1,844
13,535	13,670	11,560	6,877	4,268
520	509	508	512	17
$ 4,694	$ 5,622	$ 5,308	$ 2,321	$ 1,293

significantly underprice competitive products; and then market the new product to Dell's steadily growing customer base and watch the market share points, incremental revenues, and incremental profits pile up.

Dell management believed it had the industry's most efficient business model. The company's strategy was built around a number of core elements: a cost-efficient approach to build-to-order manufacturing, partnerships with suppliers aimed at squeezing cost savings out of the supply chain, direct sales to customers, award-winning customer service and technical support, pioneering use of the Internet and e-commerce technology, and product-line expansion aimed at capturing a bigger share of the dollars its customers spent for IT products and services.

Cost-Efficient Build-to-Order Manufacturing

Dell built its computers, workstations, and servers to order; none were produced for inventory. Dell customers could order custom-equipped servers and workstations based on the

EXHIBIT 3   **Dell's Geographic Area Performance, Fiscal Years 2000–2004 (In millions of dollars)**

	Fiscal Year Ended				
	January 30, 2004	January 31, 2003	February 1, 2002	February 2, 2001	January 28, 2000
Net revenues					
Americas					
Business	$21,888	$19,394	$17,275	$18,969	$15,160
U.S. consumer	6,715	5,653	4,485	3,902	2,719
Total Americas	28,603	25,047	21,760	22,871	17,879
Europe	8,495	6,912	6,429	6,399	5,590
Asia-Pacific-Japan	4,436	3,445	2,979	2,618	1,796
Total net revenues	$41,444	$35,404	$31,168	$31,888	$25,265
Operating income					
Americas					
Business	$ 2,124	$ 1,945	$ 1,482	$ 1,999	$ 1,800
U.S. consumer	400	308	260	253	204
Total Americas	2,594	2,253	1,742	2,252	2,004
Europe	637	388	377	347	359
Asia-Pacific-Japan	313	203	152	169	94
Special charges	—	—	(482)	(105)	(194)
Total operating income	$ 3,544	$ 2,844	$ 1,789	$ 2,663	$ 2,263

Source: Dell, Inc., 10-K reports, 2004 and 2001.

needs of their applications. Desktop and laptop customers ordered whatever configuration of microprocessor speed, random-access memory, hard disk capacity, CD or DVD drives, fax/modem/wireless capabilities, graphics cards, monitor size, speakers, and other accessories they preferred. The orders were directed to the nearest factory. In 2004 Dell had assembly plants in Austin, Texas; Nashville, Tennessee; Limerick, Ireland; Xiamen, China; Penang, Malaysia; and El Dorado do Sul, Brazil; a seventh manufacturing plant was being constructed in North Carolina. At all locations, the company had the capability to assemble PCs, workstations, and servers; Dell assembled its data storage products at its Austin, Limerick, and Penang plants. In 2002–2004, typical orders were built and delivered in three to five days.

Until 1997, Dell operated its assembly lines in traditional fashion with workers performing a single operation. An order form accompanied each metal chassis across the production floor; drives, chips, and ancillary items were installed to match customer specifications. As a partly assembled PC arrived at a new workstation, the operator, standing beside a tall steel rack with drawers full of components, was instructed what to do by little red and green lights flashing beside the drawers. When the operator was finished, the drawers containing the used components were automatically replenished from the other side, and the PC chassis glided down the line to the next workstation. However, Dell had reorganized its plants in 1997, shifting to "cell manufacturing" techniques whereby a team of workers operating at a group workstation (or cell) assembled an entire PC according to customer specifications. The shift to cell manufacturing reduced Dell's assembly times by 75 percent and doubled productivity per square foot of assembly space. Assembled computers were first tested and then loaded with the desired software, shipped, and typically delivered five to six business days after the order was placed.

At Dell's newest plant on its Austin manufacturing campus, the cell manufacturing approach had been abandoned in favor of an even more efficient assembly-line approach.

Workers at the new plant in 2004 could turn out close to 800 desktop PCs per hour on three assembly lines that took half the floor space of the older cell manufacturing process, where production had run about 120 units per hour. Although the new Austin plant was originally designed for production of 400 units per hour, management believed that it would be able to boost hourly production to 1,000 units per hour. The gains in productivity were being achieved partly by redesigning the PCs to permit easier and faster assembly, partly by innovations in the assembly process, and partly by reducing the number of times a computer was touched by workers during assembly and shipping by 50 percent. At both Dell's Austin plant and its plant in Ireland, workers could assemble a PC in two to three minutes. Moreover, just-in-time inventory practices that left pallets of parts sitting around everywhere had been tweaked to just-in-the-nick-of-time delivery by suppliers of the exact parts needed every couple of hours; double-decker conveyor belts moved parts and components to designated assembly points. Newly assembled PCs were routed on conveyors to shipping, where they were boxed and shipped to customers the same day.

Dell was regarded as a world-class manufacturing innovator and a pioneer in how to mass-produce a customized product—its methods were routinely studied in business schools worldwide. Most of Dell's PC rivals—notably IBM and HP/Compaq—had given up on trying to produce their own PCs as cheaply as Dell and shifted to outsourcing their PCs from contract manufacturers. Dell management believed that its in-house manufacturing delivered about a 6 percent cost advantage versus outsourcing. Dell's build-to-order strategy meant that the company had no in-house stock of finished goods inventories and that, unlike competitors using the traditional value chain model, it did not have to wait for resellers to clear out their own inventories before it could push new models into the marketplace—resellers typically operated with 30 to 60 days inventory of prebuilt models (see Exhibit 4). Equally important was the fact that customers who bought from Dell got the satisfaction of having their computers customized to their particular liking and pocketbook.

Quality Control

All assembly plants had the capability to run testing and quality control processes on components, parts, and subassemblies obtained from suppliers, as well as on the finished products Dell assembled. Suppliers were urged to participate in a quality certification program that committed them to achieving defined quality specifications. Quality control activities were undertaken at various stages in the assembly process. In addition, Dell's quality control program included testing of completed units after assembly, ongoing production reliability audits, failure tracking for early identification of problems associated with new models shipped to customers, and information obtained from customers through its service and technical support programs. All of the company's plants had been certified as meeting ISO 9002 quality standards.

Partnerships with Suppliers

Michael Dell believed that it made much better sense for the company to partner with reputable suppliers of PC parts and components than to integrate backward and get into parts and components manufacturing on its own. He explained why:

> If you've got a race with 20 players all vying to make the fastest graphics chip in the world, do you want to be the twenty-first horse, or do you want to evaluate the field of 20 and pick the best one?[5]

Dell management evaluated the various makers of each component; picked the best one or two as suppliers; and then stuck with those suppliers as long as they maintained their leadership in technology, performance, quality, and cost. Management believed that long-term

[5]As quoted in Magretta, "The Power of Virtual Integration," p. 74.

EXHIBIT 4   Comparative Value Chain Models of PC Vendors

Traditional Build-to-Stock Value Chain Used by Hewlett-Packard, IBM, Sony, and Most Others

| Manufacture and delivery of PC parts and components by suppliers | Assembly of PCs as needed to fill orders from distributors and retailers | Sales and marketing activities of PC vendors to build a brand image and establish a network of resellers | Sales and marketing activities of resellers | Purchases by PC users | Service and support activities provided to PC users by resellers (and some PC vendors) |

Build-to-Order, Sell-Direct Value Chain Developed by Dell Computer

| Manufacture and delivery of PC parts and components by supply partners | Custom assembly of PCs as orders are received from PC buyer | Sales and marketing activities of PC vendor to build brand image and secure orders from PC buyers | Purchases by PC users | Service and support activities provided to PC users by Dell or contract providers |

Close collaboration and real-time data sharing to drive down costs of supply chain activities, minimize inventories, keep assembly costs low, and respond quickly to changes in the makeup of customer orders

partnerships with reputable suppliers had at least five advantages. First, using name-brand processors, disk drives, modems, speakers, and multimedia components enhanced the quality and performance of Dell's PCs. Because of varying performance among different brands of components, the brand of the components was quite important to customers concerned about performance and reliability. Second, because Dell partnered with suppliers for the long term and because it committed to purchase a specified percentage of its requirements from each supplier, Dell was assured of getting the volume of components it needed on a timely basis even when overall market demand for a particular component temporarily exceeded the overall market supply. Third, Dell's long-run commitment to its suppliers made it feasible for suppliers to locate their plants or distribution centers within a few miles of Dell assembly plants, putting them in position to make deliveries daily or every few hours, as needed. Dell supplied data on inventories and replenishment needs to its suppliers at least once a day—hourly in the case of components being delivered several times daily from nearby sources.

Fourth, long-term supply partnerships facilitated having some of the supplier's engineers assigned to Dell's product design teams and being treated as part of Dell. When new products were launched, suppliers' engineers were stationed in Dell's plants; if early buyers called with a problem related to design, further assembly and shipments were halted while the supplier's engineers and Dell personnel corrected the flaw on the spot.[6] Fifth, long-term partnerships enlisted greater cooperation on the part of suppliers to seek new ways to drive costs out of the supply chain. Dell openly shared its daily production schedules, sales forecasts, and new model introduction plans with vendors. Dell also did a three-year plan with each of its key suppliers and worked with suppliers to minimize the number of different stock-keeping units of parts and components in its products and to identify ways to drive costs down.

Commitment to Just-in-Time Inventory Practices

Dell's just-in-time inventory emphasis yielded major cost advantages and shortened the time it took for Dell to get new generations of its computer models into the marketplace. New advances were coming so fast in certain computer parts and components (particularly microprocessors, disk drives, and wireless devices) that any given item in inventory was obsolete in a matter of months, sometimes quicker. Moreover, rapid-fire reductions in the prices of components were not unusual—for example, Intel regularly cut the prices on its older chips when it introduced newer chips, and it introduced new chip generations about every three months. In 2003–2004, component costs declined an average of 0.5 percent weekly.[7] Michael Dell explained the competitive and economic advantages of minimal component inventories:

> If I've got 11 days of inventory and my competitor has 80 and Intel comes out with a new chip, that means I'm going to get to market 69 days sooner. In the computer industry, inventory can be a pretty massive risk because if the cost of materials is going down 50 percent a year and you have two or three months of inventory versus eleven days, you've got a big cost disadvantage. And you're vulnerable to product transitions, when you can get stuck with obsolete inventory.[8]

For a growing number of parts and components, Dell's close partnership with suppliers was allowing it to operate with no more than two hours of inventory.

Dell's supplier of CRT monitors was Sony. Because the monitors Sony supplied with the Dell name already imprinted were of dependably high quality (a defect rate of fewer than 1,000 per million), Dell didn't even open up the monitor boxes to test them at its Reno, Nevada, monitor distribution center.[9] Utilizing sophisticated data exchange systems, Dell arranged for its shippers (Airborne Express and United Parcel Service) to pick up computers at U.S. assembly plants, then pick up the accompanying monitors at its Reno distribution center and deliver both to the customer simultaneously. The savings in time and cost were significant. Dell had been working hard for the past several years to refine and improve its relationships with suppliers and its procedures for operating with smaller inventories.

In fiscal year 1995, Dell averaged an inventory turn cycle of 32 days. By the end of fiscal 1997 (January 1997), the average was down to 13 days. In fiscal 1998 Dell's inventory averaged 7 days, which compared very favorably with Gateway's 14-day average, Compaq's 23-day average, and the estimated industrywide average of over 50 days. In fiscal years 1999 and 2000, Dell operated with an average of six days' supply in inventory; the average dropped to five days' supply in fiscal year 2001, four days' supply in 2002, and three days' supply in 2003 and 2004.

---

[6]Ibid., p. 75.

[7]Speech by Michael Dell at University of Toronto, September 21, 2004; posted at www.dell.com and accessed December 15, 2004.

[8]Ibid., p. 76.

[9]Ibid.

Dell's Direct Sales Strategy and Marketing Efforts

With thousands of phone, fax, and Internet orders daily and ongoing field sales force contact with customers, the company kept its finger on the market pulse, quickly detecting shifts in sales trends, design problems, and quality glitches. If the company got more than a few of the same complaints, the information was relayed immediately to design engineers who checked out the problem. When design flaws or components defects were found, the factory was notified and the problem corrected within a few days. Management believed Dell's ability to respond quickly gave it a significant advantage over PC makers that operated on the basis of large production runs of variously configured and equipped PCs and sold them through retail channels. Dell saw its direct sales approach as a totally customer-driven system, with the flexibility to transition quickly to new generations of components and PC models.

Dell's Customer-Based Sales and Marketing Focus

Whereas many technology companies organized their sales and marketing efforts around product lines, Dell was organized around customer groups. Dell had placed managers in charge of developing sales and service programs appropriate to the needs and expectations of each customer group. Up until the early 1990s, Dell operated with sales and service programs aimed at just two market segments—high-volume corporate and governmental buyers, and low-volume business and individual buyers. But as sales took off in 1995–97, these segments were subdivided into finer, more homogeneous categories that by 2000 included global enterprise accounts, large and midsize companies (over 400 employees), small companies (under 400 employees), health care businesses (over 400 employees), federal government agencies, state and local government agencies, educational institutions, and individual consumers. Many of these customer segments were further subdivided—for instance, in education, there were separate sales and marketing programs for K–12 schools; higher education institutions; and personal-use purchases by faculty, staff, and students.

Dell's largest global enterprise accounts were assigned their own dedicated sales force—for example, Dell had a sales force of 150 people dedicated to meeting the needs of General Electric's facilities and personnel scattered across the world. Dell's sales to individuals and small businesses were made by telephone, fax, and the Internet. It had call centers in the United States, Canada, Europe, and Asia with toll-free lines; customers could talk with a sales representative about specific models, get information faxed or mailed to them, place an order, and pay by credit card. The Asian and European call centers were equipped with technology that routed calls from a particular country to a particular call center. Thus, for example, a customer calling from Lisbon, Portugal, was automatically directed to a Portuguese-speaking sales rep at the call center in Montpelier, France.

Dell in Japan

With a market share of about 10 percent, Dell was the number three provider of computer systems in Japan (behind NEC and Toshiba); in 2002 Dell had the fifth highest dollar market share, at 7.7 percent. Other competitors in Japan included Sony, Fujitsu, Hitachi, IBM, Sharp, and Matshusita. Counting units sold, however, Dell was number one in business desktop computers and was number two in entry-level and midrange servers. Dell's 2004 sales in Japan were up about 30 percent, in a market where overall sales were flat. Dell's technical and customer support for PCs, servers, and network storage devices was ranked the best in Japan in 2002 and 2003. Dell had 1,100 personnel in Japan and was tracking Japanese buying habits and preferences with its proprietary software. The head of Dell's consumer PC sales group in Japan had installed 34 kiosks in leading electronics stores around Japan, allowing shoppers to test Dell computers, ask questions of staff, and place orders—close to half the sales were to people who did not know about Dell prior to visiting the kiosk. Dell believed that it was more profitable than any other PC-server vendor selling in the Japanese market. Dell's profit margins in Japan were higher than those in the U.S. market, and sales were rising briskly.

Dell in China

Dell Computer entered China in 1998 and achieved faster growth there than in any other foreign market it had entered. The market for PCs in China was the third largest in the world, behind the United States and Japan, and was on the verge of being the second largest. PC sales in China were growing 20–30 percent annually and, with a population of 1.4 billion people (of which some 400 million lived in metropolitan areas where computer use was growing rapidly), the Chinese market for PCs was expected to become the largest in the world by 2010.

The market leader in China was Lenovo, a local company formerly called Legend, which had a 26.4 percent share in 2004. Other major local PC producers were Founder (10.3 percent share) and Great Wall (8.7 percent share). Dell had an 8.1 percent share and expected to overtake Great Wall and move into third place in 2004. Dell's shipments in China rose 60 percent in fiscal 2004 (four times the rest of the industry) and its revenues were up 40 percent, making China Dell's fourth largest market. Other competitors in China included IBM, Hewlett-Packard, Toshiba, Acer, and NEC Japan. All of the major contenders except Dell relied on resellers to handle sales and service; Dell sold directly to customers in China just as it did elsewhere.

Dell's primary target market in China consisted of large corporate accounts. Management believed that many Chinese companies would find the savings from direct sales appealing, that they would like the idea of having Dell build PCs and servers to their requirements and specifications, and that—once they became a Dell customer—they would like the convenience of Internet purchases and the company's growing array of products and services. Dell recognized that its direct sales approach put it at a short-term disadvantage in appealing to small business customers and individual consumers. According to an executive from rival Lenovo, "It takes two years of a person's savings to buy a PC in China. And when two years of savings is at stake, the whole family wants to come out to a store to touch and try the machine."[10] But Dell believed that over time, as Chinese consumers became more familiar with PCs and more comfortable with making online purchases, growing numbers of small business customers and consumers would become comfortable with placing Internet and telephone orders. In 2002, about 40 percent of Dell's sales in China were over the Internet.

Dell in Latin America

In 2002 PC sales in Latin America exceeded 5 million units. Latin America had a population of 450 million people. Dell management believed that in the next few years PC use in Latin America would reach 1 for every 30 people (one-tenth the penetration in the United States), pushing annual sales up to 15 million units. The company's plant in Brazil, the largest market in Latin America, was opened to produce, sell, and provide service and technical support for customers in Brazil, Argentina, Chile, Uruguay, and Paraguay.

Using Dell Direct Store Kiosks to Access Individual Consumers

In 2002 Dell began installing Dell Direct Store kiosks in a variety of retail settings. The kiosks did not carry inventory, but customers could talk face-to-face with a knowledgeable Dell sales representative, inspect Dell's products, and order them on the Internet while at the kiosk. The idea for using kiosks had begun in Japan, where Dell sales reps were

---

[10]Quoted in Neel Chowdhury, "Dell Cracks China," *Fortune,* June 21, 1999, p. 121.

encountering resistance to Dell's direct sales approach from individual buyers—Japanese consumers were noted for wanting to carefully inspect different PC brands in stores before making a purchase. When kiosks were installed in Japanese retail settings, they proved quite popular and helped generate a big boost in Dell's share of PC sales to consumers in Japan. The success of kiosks in Japan had inspired Dell to try them in the United States. About 60 kiosks were in place at U.S. locations during the 2002 holiday sales season. Dell began placing Dell Direct Store kiosks in selected Wal-Mart and Sears stores in 2003 and had a total of 80 kiosks at various locations in December 2004.

Customer Service and Technical Support

Service became a feature of Dell's strategy in 1986 when the company began providing a year's free onsite service with most of its PCs after users complained about having to ship their PCs back to Austin for repairs. Dell contracted with local service providers to handle customer requests for repairs; on-site service was provided on a next-day basis. Dell also provided its customers with technical support via a toll-free phone number and e-mail. Dell received 500,000 to 600,000 e-mail messages and 6 to 8 million phone calls annually requesting service and support. Dell was aggressively pursuing initiatives to enhance its online technical support tools and reduce the number and cost of telephone support calls. The company was adding Web-based customer service and support tools to make a customer's online experience pleasant and satisfying. In 2003–2004, over 50 percent of Dell's technical support activities were conducted via the Internet.

Bundled service policies were a major selling point for winning corporate accounts. If customers preferred to work with their own service provider, Dell supplied the provider of choice with training and spare parts needed to service customers' equipment. Recently, Dell had instituted a First Call Resolution initiative to strengthen its capabilities to resolve customer inquiries or difficulties on the first call; First Call Resolution percentages were made an important measure in evaluating the company's technical support performance.

Value-Added Services

Dell kept close track of the purchases of its large global customers, country by country and department by department—and customers themselves found this purchase information valuable. Dell's sales and support personnel used their knowledge about a particular customer's needs to help that customer plan PC purchases, to configure the customer's PC networks, and to provide value-added services. For example, for its large customers Dell loaded software and placed ID tags on newly ordered PCs at the factory, thereby eliminating the need for the customer's IT personnel to unpack the PC, deliver it to an employee's desk, hook it up, place asset tags on the PC, and load the needed software from an assortment of CD-ROMs and diskettes—a process that could take several hours and cost $200–$300.[11] While Dell charged an extra $15 or $20 for the software-loading and asset-tagging services, the savings to customers were still considerable—one large customer reported savings of $500,000 annually from this service.[12]

Premier Pages

Dell had developed customized, password-protected Web sites called Premier Pages for close to 50,000 corporate, governmental, and institutional customers worldwide. These Premier Pages gave customers' personnel online access to information about all Dell products and configurations the company had purchased or that were currently authorized for purchase. Employees could use Premier Pages to (1) obtain customer-specific pricing for what-

[11]Magretta, "The Power of Virtual Integration," p. 79.
[12]"Michael Dell Rocks," *Fortune,* May 11, 1998, p. 61.

ever machines and options the employee wanted to consider, (2) place an order online that would be electronically routed to higher-level managers for approval and then on to Dell for assembly and delivery, and (3) seek advanced help desk support. Customers could also search and sort all invoices and obtain purchase histories. These features eliminated paper invoices, cut ordering time, and reduced the internal labor customers needed to staff corporate purchasing and accounting functions. Customer use of Premier Pages had boosted the productivity of Dell salespeople assigned to these accounts by 50 percent. Dell was providing Premier Page service to thousands of additional customers annually and adding more features to further improve functionality.

www.dell.com

Dell operated one of the world's highest-volume Internet commerce sites, with nearly 8 billion page requests annually at 81 country sites in 28 languages/dialects and 26 currencies. Dell began Internet sales at its Web site (www.dell.com) in 1995, almost overnight achieving sales of $1 million a day. By early 2003, over 50 percent of Dell's sales were Web-enabled—and the percentage was increasing, especially for sales to small businesses and consumers. Dell's Web site sales exceeded $60 million a day in 2004, up from $35 million daily in early 2000 and $5 million daily in early 1998. Its Web site averaged over 6 million visits weekly in the third quarter of 2004.

At the company's Web site, prospective buyers could review Dell's entire product line in detail, configure and price customized PCs, place orders, and track orders from manufacturing through shipping. The closing rate on sales at Dell's Web site was 20 percent higher than that on sales inquiries received via telephone. Management believed that enhancing www.dell.com to shrink transaction and order fulfillment times, increase accuracy, and provide more personalized content resulted in a higher degree of "e-loyalty" than traditional attributes like price and product selection.

On-Site Services

Corporate customers paid Dell fees to provide technical support, on-site service, and help with migrating to new IT technologies. Services were one of the fastest-growing part of Dell, accounting for almost $4 billion in sales in 2002 and close to $6 billion in fiscal 2003. Dell's service business was split about 50–50 between what Michael Dell called close-to-the-box services and management and professional services—but the latter were growing faster, at close to 25 percent annually. Dell estimated that close-to-the-box support services for Dell products represented about a $50 billion market, whereas the market for management and professional services (IT life-cycle services, deployment of new technology, and solutions for greater IT productivity) was about $90 billion. IT consulting services were becoming more standardized, driven primarily by growing hardware and software standardization, reduction in on-site service requirements (partly because of online diagnostic and support tools, growing ease of repair and maintenance, increased customer knowledge, and increased remote management capabilities), and declines in the skills and know-how that were required to perform service tasks on standardized equipment and install new, more standardized systems.

Dell's strategy in services, like its strategy in hardware products, was to bring down the cost of IT consulting services for its large enterprise customers. The providers of on-site service, technical support, and other types of IT consulting typically charged premium prices and realized hefty profits for their efforts. According to Michael Dell, customers who bought the services being provided by Dell saved 40 to 50 percent over what they would have paid other providers of IT services.

Top management expected services to play an expanding role in the company's growth. Kevin Rollins, Dell's president and CEO in 2004, indicated the company's business model "isn't just about making cheap boxes, it's also about freeing customers from overpriced relationships" with such vendors as IBM, Sun Microsystems, and Hewlett-Packard.[13] While a number of Dell's corporate accounts were large enough to justify dedicated on-site teams of Dell support personnel, Dell generally contracted with third-party providers to make the necessary onsite service calls. Customers notified Dell when they had problems; such notices triggered two electronic dispatches—one to ship replacement parts from Dell's factory to the customer sites, and one to notify the contract service provider to prepare to make the needed repairs as soon as the parts arrived.[14] Bad parts were returned so that Dell could determine what went wrong and how to prevent such problems from happening again. Problems relating to faulty components or flawed components design were promptly passed along to the relevant supplier for correction.

Customer Forums

In addition to using its sales and support mechanisms to stay close to customers, Dell periodically held regional forums for its best customers. The company formed Platinum and Gold Councils composed of its largest customers in the United States, Europe, Japan, and the Asia-Pacific region; regional meetings were held every six to nine months.[15] Some regions had two meetings—one for chief information officers and one for technical personnel. At the meetings, which frequently included a presentation by Michael Dell, Dell's senior technologists shared their views on the direction of the latest technological developments, what the flow of technology really meant for customers, and Dell's plans for introducing new and upgraded products over the next two years. There were also breakout sessions on topics of current interest. Dell found that the information gleaned from customers at these meetings assisted the company in forecasting demand for its products.

Pioneering Leadership in Use of the Internet and E-Commerce Technology

Dell was a leader in using the Internet and e-commerce technologies to squeeze greater efficiency out of its supply chain activities, to streamline the order-to-delivery process, to encourage greater customer use of its Web site, and to gather and use all types of information. In a 1999 speech to 1,200 customers, Michael Dell said:

> The world will be changed forever by the Internet . . . The Internet will be your business. If your business isn't enabled by providing customers and suppliers with more information, you're probably already in trouble. The Internet provides a dramatic reduction in the cost of transactions and the cost of interaction among people and businesses, and it creates dramatic new opportunities and destroys old competitive advantages. The Internet is like a weapon sitting on a table ready to be picked up by either you or your competitors.[16]

Dell's use of its Web site and various Internet technology applications had proved instrumental in helping the company become the industry's low-cost provider and drive costs out of its business. Internet technology applications were a cornerstone of Dell's collaborative efforts with suppliers. The company provided order-status information quickly and conveniently over the Internet, thereby eliminating tens of thousands of order-status inquiries coming in by phone. It used its Web site as a powerful sales and technical support tool. Few

---

[13]Quoted in Kathryn Jones, "The Dell Way," *Business 2.0,* February 2003.

[14]Kevin Rollins, "Using Information to Speed Execution," *Harvard Business Review,* March–April 1998, p. 81.

[15]Magretta, "The Power of Virtual Integration," p. 80.

[16]Keynote speech given on August 25, 1999, in Austin, Texas, at Dell's DirectConnect Conference and posted at www.dell.com.

companies could match Dell's competencies and capabilities in the use of Internet technology to improve operating efficiency and gain new sales in a cost-efficient manner.

Expansion into New Products

Dell's recent expansion into data storage hardware, switches, handheld PCs, printers, and printer cartridges represented an effort to diversify the company's product base and to use its competitive capabilities in PCs and servers to pursue revenue growth opportunities. Michael Dell explained why Dell had decided to expand into products and services that complemented its sales of PCs and servers:

> We tend to look at what is the next big opportunity all the time. We can't take on too many of these at once, because it kind of overloads the system. But we believe fundamentally that if you think about the whole market, it's about an $800 billion market, all areas of technology over time go through a process of standardization or commoditization. And we try to look at those, anticipate what's happening, and develop strategies that will allow us to get into those markets. In the server market in 1995 we had a 2 percent market share, today we have over a 30 percent share, we're number 1 in the U.S. How did that happen? Well, first of all it happened because we started to have a high market share for desktops and notebooks. Then customers said, oh yes, we know Dell, those are the guys who have really good desktops and notebooks. So they have servers, yes, we'll test those, we'll test them around the periphery, maybe not in the most critical applications at first, but we'll test them here. [Then they discover] these are really good and Dell provides great support . . . and I think to some extent we've benefited from the fact that our competitors have underestimated the importance of value, and the power of the relationship and the service that we can create with the customer.
>
> And, also, as a product tends to standardize there's not an elimination of the requirement for custom services, there's a reduction of it. So by offering some services, but not the services of the traditional proprietary computer company, we've been able to increase our share. And, in fact, what tends to happen is customers embrace the standards, because they know that's going to save them costs. Let me give you an example . . . about a year ago we entered into the data networking market. So we have Ethernet switches, layer 2 switches. So if you have PCs and servers, you need switches; every PC attaches to a switch, every server attaches to a switch. It's a pretty easy sale, switches go along with computer systems. We looked at this market and were able to come up with products that are priced about 2 1/2 times less than the market leader today, Cisco, and as a result the business has grown very, very quickly. We shipped 1.8 million switch ports in a period of about a year, when most people would have said that's not going to work and come up with all kinds of reasons why we can't succeed.[17]

As Dell's sales of data-routing switches accelerated in 2001–2002 and Dell management mulled whether to expand into other networking products and Internet gear, Cisco elected to discontinue supplying its switches to Dell for resale as of October 2002. Dell's family of PowerConnect switches—simple commodity-like products generally referred to as layer 2 switches in the industry—carried a price of $20 per port, versus $70–$100 for comparable Cisco switches and $38 for comparable 3Com switches.

Michael Dell and Kevin Rollins saw external storage devices as a growth opportunity because the company's corporate and institutional customers were making increasing use of high-speed data storage and retrieval devices. Dell's PowerVault line of storage products had data protection and recovery features that made it easy for customers to add and manage storage and simplify consolidation. The PowerVault products utilized standardized technology and components (which were considerably cheaper than customized ones), allowing Dell to underprice rivals and drive down storage costs for its customers by about 50 percent. Dell's competitors in storage devices included Hewlett-Packard (HP) and IBM.

---

[17]Remarks by Michael Dell, Gartner Fall Symposium, Orlando, Florida, October 9, 2002; posted at www.dell.com.

Some observers saw Dell's 2003 entry into the printer market as a calculated effort to go after HP's biggest and most profitable business segment and believed the Dell offensive was deliberately timed to throw a wrench into HP's efforts to resolve the many challenges of successfully merging its operations with those of Compaq. One of the reasons that Dell had entered the market for servers back in 1995 was that Compaq Computer, then its biggest rival in PCs, had been using its lucrative profits on server sales to subsidize charging lower prices on Compaq computers and thus be more price-competitive against Dell's PCs—at the time Compaq was losing money on its desktop and notebook PC business. According to Michael Dell:

> Compaq had this enormous profit pool that they were using to fight against us in the desktop and notebook business. That was not an acceptable situation. Our product teams knew that the servers weren't that complicated or expensive to produce, and customers were being charged unfair prices.[18]

Dell management believed that HP was doing much the same thing in printers and printer products, where it had a dominant market share worldwide and generated about 75 percent of its operating profits. Dell believed HP was using its big margins on printer products to subsidize selling its PCs at prices comparable to Dell's, even though Dell had costs that were about 8 percent lower than HP's. HP's PC operations were either in the red or barely in the black during most of 2003–2004, while Dell consistently had profit margins of 8 percent or more on PCs. Dell's entry and market success in printer products had put pricing pressure on HP in the printer market and had helped erode HP's share of the printer market worldwide from just under 50 percent to around 46 percent. Kevin Rollins believed that Dell's decision to enter the printer market as a head-to-head rival of HP served two purposes:

> Any strategist is going to try to develop a strategy that is going to help them and hurt competitors. Our whole vision here was to do both: improve the revenues and profits of our own business, and at the same time put our competitors at a disadvantage.[19]

To further keep the pricing pressure on HP in 2003, Dell had priced its new Axim line of handheld PCs at about 50 percent less than HP's popular iPaq line of handhelds, and Dell's storage and networking products also carried lower prices than comparable HP products. Dell management believed the company's entry into the printer market would add value for its customers. Michael Dell explained:

> We think we can drive down the entire cost of owning and using printing products. If you look at any other market Dell has gone into, we have been able to significantly save money for customers. We know we can do that in printers; we have looked at the supply chain all the way through its various cycles and we know there are inefficiencies there. I think the price of the total offering when we include the printer and the supplies . . . can come down quite considerably.[20]

When Dell announced it had contracted with Lexmark to make printers and printer and toner cartridges for sale under the Dell label beginning in 2003, HP immediately discontinued supplying HP printers to Dell for resale at Dell's Web site. Dell had been selling Lexmark printers for two years and since 2000 had resold about 4 million printers made by HP, Lexmark, and other vendors to its customers. Lexmark designed and made critical parts for its printers but used offshore contract manufacturers for assembly. Gross profit margins on printers (sales minus cost of goods sold) were said to be in single digits in 2002–2004, but

---

[18]Remarks by Michael Dell at the University of Toronto, September 21, 2004; posted at www.dell.com.

[19]Quoted in Adam Lashinsky, "Where Dell Is Going Next," *Fortune,* October 18, 2004, p. 116.

[20]Quoted in the *Financial Times* Global News Wire, October 10, 2002.

the gross margins on printer supplies were in the 50–60 percent range—brand-name ink cartridges for printers typically ran $25 to $35.

Dell's Entry into the White-Box PC Segment

In 2002 Dell announced it would begin making so-called white-box (i.e., unbranded) PCs for resale under the private labels of retailers. PC dealers that supplied white-box PCs to small businesses and price-conscious individuals under the dealer's own brand name accounted for about one-third of total PC sales and about 50 percent of sales to small businesses. According to one industry analyst, "Increasingly, Dell's biggest competitor these days isn't big brand-name companies like IBM or HP, it's white-box vendors." Dell's thinking in entering the white-box PC segment was that it was cheaper to reach many small businesses through the white-box dealers that already served them than by using its own sales force and support groups to sell and service businesses with fewer than 100 employees. Dell believed its low-cost supply chain and assembly capabilities would allow it to build generic machines cheaper than white-box resellers could buy components and assemble a customized machine. Management forecast that Dell would achieve $380 million in sales of white-box PCs in 2003 and would generate profit margins equal to those on Dell-branded PCs. Some industry analysts were skeptical of Dell's move into white-box PCs because they expected white-box dealers to be reluctant to buy their PCs from a company that had a history of taking their clients. Others believed this was a test effort by Dell to develop the capabilities to take on white-box dealers in Asia and especially in China, where the sellers of generic PCs were particularly strong.

Other Elements of Dell's Business Strategy

Dell's strategy had two other elements that assisted the company's drive for industry leadership: R&D and advertising.

Research and Development

Dell's R&D focus was to track and test new developments in components and software, ascertain which ones would prove most useful and cost-effective for customers, and then design them into Dell products. Management believed that it was Dell's job on behalf of its customers to sort out all the new technology coming into the marketplace and help steer customers to options and solutions most relevant to their needs. The company talked to its customers frequently about "relevant technology," listening carefully to customers' needs and problems, and endeavoring to identify the most cost-effective solutions.

Dell was a strong advocate of incorporating standardized components in its products so as not to tie either it or its customers to one company's proprietary technology and components, which almost always carried a price premium and increased costs for its customers. Dell actively promoted the use of industrywide standards and regularly pressed its suppliers of a particular part or component to agree on common standards. Dell executives saw standardized technology as beginning to take over the largest part of the $800 billion spent annually on IT—standardization was particularly evident in servers, storage, networking, and high-performance computing. One example of the impact of standardized technology was at the University of Buffalo, where Dell had installed a 5.6 teraflop cluster of about 2,000 Dell servers containing 4,000 microprocessors that was being used to decode the human genome. The cluster of servers, which were the same as those Dell sold to its business customers, had been installed in about 60 days at a cost of a few million dollars and represented the third most powerful supercomputer in the world. High-performance clusters of PCs and servers were replacing mainframe computers and custom-designed supercomputers because of their much lower cost. Amerada Hess, attracted by Dell's use of standardized and upgradable parts and components, installed a cluster of several hundred Dell workstations and allocated about $300,000 a year to upgrade and maintain it; the cluster had replaced an IBM supercomputer that cost $1.5 million a year to lease and operate. Studies conducted by Dell indicated that, over time, products incorporating standardized technology delivered about twice the performance per dollar of cost as products based on proprietary technology.

Dell's R&D group included over 3,000 engineers, and its annual R&D budget was $450 to $470 million. The company's R&D unit also studied and implemented ways to control quality and to streamline the assembly process. About 15 percent of Dell's 800 U.S. patents were ranked "elite."

Advertising

Michael Dell was a strong believer in the power of advertising and frequently espoused its importance in the company's strategy. His competitive zeal resulted in the company's being the first to use comparative ads, throwing barbs at Compaq's higher prices. Although Compaq won a lawsuit against Dell for making false comparisons, Michael Dell was unapologetic, arguing that the ads were very effective: "We were able to increase customer awareness about value."[21] He insisted that the company's ads be communicative and forceful, not soft and fuzzy. The company regularly had prominent ads describing its products and prices in such leading computer publications as *PC Magazine* and *PC World,* as well as in *USA Today, The Wall Street Journal,* and other business publications.

Dell's Performance in 2004

During the first nine months of 2004, Dell's revenues and unit shipments grew 2–3 times faster than the industry average. Despite steadily eroding average selling prices—$1,540 in fiscal 2004, down from $1,640 in 2003; $1,700 in 2002; $2,050 in 2001; $2,250 in 2000; and $2,600 in 1998—Dell's revenues were climbing as the company gained volume and market share in virtually all product categories and geographic areas where it competed. Worldwide revenues, which reached $35.7 billion in the first nine months of fiscal 2005, were expected to run about 20 percent higher than fiscal 2004 levels and total about $48–$50 billion for the full year. Dell's sales increases were strongest in Europe and in notebook PCs.

During the November 2002–January 2003 period (the fourth quarter of Dell's 2003 fiscal year), the company posted its best-ever quarterly product shipments, revenues, and operating profits. Management indicated that Dell's global market share in PCs in the last quarter of fiscal 2003 was almost 3 points higher than in its fiscal 2002 fourth quarter, and its U.S. share was 5 points higher—in servers, Dell's market share was over 3 points higher. Unit shipments were up by 25 percent, and shipments in China, France, Germany, and Japan increased a combined 39 percent, with server sales in those countries up by 47 percent.

Market Conditions in the Information Technology Industry in Late 2004

Analysts expected the $800 billion worldwide IT industry to grow roughly 10 percent in 2004, following a single-digit increase in 2003, a 2.3 percent decline in 2002, and close to a 1 percent decline in 2001—corporate spending for IT products accounted for about 45 percent of all capital expenditures of U.S. businesses. From 1980 to 2000, IT spending had grown at an average annual rate of 12 percent and then flattened. The slowdown in IT spending reflected a combination of factors: sluggish economic growth worldwide that was

---

[21]"The Education of Michael Dell," p. 85.

EXHIBIT 5
Worldwide Shipments of PCS, 1980–2005

Year	PCs Shipped (in millions)	Year	PCs Shipped (in millions)
1980	1	1999	113
1985	11	2000	139
1990	24	2001	133
1995	58	2002	136
1996	69	2003	153
1997	80	2004*	177
1998	91	2005*	195

*Forecast data.

Source: International Data Corp.

prompting businesses to delay IT upgrades and hold on to aging equipment longer, overinvestment in IT in the 1995–99 period, declining unit prices for many IT products (especially PCs and servers), and a growing preference for lower-priced, standard-component hardware that was good enough to perform a variety of functions using off-the-shelf Windows or Linux operating systems (as opposed to relying on proprietary hardware and customized Unix software). The selling points that appealed most to IT customers were standardization, flexibility, modularity, simplicity, economy of use, and value.

Exhibit 5 shows actual and projected PC sales for 1980–2005 as compiled by industry researcher International Data Corporation (IDC). According to Gartner Research, the billionth PC was shipped sometime in July 2002; of the billion, an estimated 550 million were still in use. Nearly 82 percent of the 1 billion PCs that had been shipped were desktops, and 75 percent were sold to businesses. With a world population of 6 billion, most industry participants believed there was ample opportunity for further growth in the PC market. Computer usage in Europe was half of that in the United States, even though the combined economies of the European countries were a bit larger than the U.S. economy. Growth potential for PCs was particularly strong in China, India, several other Asian countries, and portions of Latin America. Forrester Research estimated that the numbers of PCs in use worldwide would approach 1.3 billion by 2010, up from 575 million in 2004, with the growth being driven by the emerging markets in China, India and Russia. IDC had predicted that notebook PC sales would grow from 26.9 percent of PC shipments in 2003 to 37.3 percent in 2007.

Currently, there was growing interest in notebook computers equipped with wireless capability; many businesses were turning to notebooks equipped with wireless data communications devices to improve worker productivity and keep workers connected to important information. The emergence of Wireless Fidelity (Wi-Fi) networking technology, along with the installation of wireless home and office networks, was fueling the trend. Wi-Fi systems were being used in businesses, on college campuses, in airports, and other locations to link users to the Internet and to private networks. Three other devices—flat-panel LCD monitors, DVD recorder drives, and portable music players like Apple's iPod—were also stimulating sales of new PCs.

The Server Market

At the same time, forecasters expected full global build-out of the Internet to continue, which would require the installation of millions of servers. But since 2000 IT customers had been switching from the use of expensive high-end servers running customized Unix operating systems to the use of low-cost servers running on standardized Intel/Windows/Linux technologies; the switch to stands-based servers had caused a slowdown in dollar revenues from server sales despite rapidly increasing unit volume. A number of industry observers believed that the days of using expensive, proprietary Unix-based servers were numbered.

The Unix share of the server operating system market (based on unit shipments) was said to have decreased by nearly 50 percent over the past five years, whereas Windows and Linux servers had tripled in use. As of the third quarter of 2004:

- IBM held the number one spot in the worldwide server systems market based on dollar revenues, with a 31.7 percent market share. HP had the number two spot, with a 26.8 percent share.
- Sun and Dell tied for third place in server revenues, with 10.2 percent and 10.1 percent shares, respectively. Dell had experienced strong 14.1 percent year-over-year revenue growth while Sun's revenues were flat.
- In terms of unit shipments, HP was the number one vendor worldwide and Dell was number two, with a 24.5 percent share. HP had been the unit volume leader in server shipments for 10 consecutive quarters, but Dell had narrowed the gap considerably.
- HP had the number one spot in Linux servers, with a 26.9 percent market share based on revenue, while IBM was second, with 20.5 percent, and Dell was third, with 17.4 percent. Overall, 31.7 percent of the servers shipped in the third quarter of 2004 were Linux-based.

Competing Value Chain Models in the Global PC Industry

When the personal computer industry first began to take shape in the early 1980s, the founding companies manufactured many of the components themselves—disk drives, memory chips, graphics chips, microprocessors, motherboards, and software. Subscribing to a philosophy that mandated in-house development of key components, they built expertise in a variety of PC-related technologies and created organizational units to produce components as well as handle final assembly. While certain noncritical items were typically outsourced, if a computer maker was not at least partially vertically integrated and produced some components for its PCs, then it was not taken seriously as a manufacturer. But as the industry grew, technology advanced quickly in so many directions on so many parts and components that the early personal computer manufacturers could not keep pace as experts on all fronts. There were too many technologies and manufacturing intricacies to master for a vertically integrated manufacturer to keep its products on the cutting edge.

As a consequence, companies emerged that specialized in making particular components. Specialists could marshal enough R&D capability and resources to either lead the technological developments in their area of specialization or else quickly match the advances made by their competitors. Moreover, specialist firms could mass-produce the component and supply it to several computer manufacturers far cheaper than any one manufacturer could fund the needed component R&D and then make only whatever smaller volume of components it needed for assembling its own brand of PCs. Thus, in the early 1990s, such computer makers as Compaq Computer, IBM, Hewlett-Packard, Sony, Toshiba, and Fujitsu-Siemens began to abandon vertical integration in favor of a strategy of outsourcing most components from specialists and concentrating on efficient assembly and marketing their brand of computers. They adopted the build-to-stock value chain model shown in the top section of Exhibit 4. It featured arm's-length transactions between specialist suppliers, manufacturer/assemblers, distributors and retailers, and end users. However, a few others, most notably Dell and Gateway, employed a shorter value chain model, selling directly to customers and eliminating the time and costs associated with distributing through independent resellers. Building to order avoided (1) having to keep many differently equipped models on retailers' shelves to fill buyer requests for one or another configuration of options and components, and (2) having to clear out slow-selling models at a discount before introducing new generations of PCs (for instance, HP's retail dealers had an average of 43 days of HP products in stock as of October

2004). Direct sales eliminated retailer costs and markups (retail dealer margins were typically in the range of 4 to 10 percent).

Because of Dell's success in using its business model and strategy to become the low-cost leader, most other PC makers in 2002–2004 were endeavoring to emulate various aspects of Dell's strategy, but with only limited success. Nearly all vendors were trying to cut days of inventory out of their supply chains and reduce their costs of goods sold and operating expenses to levels that would make them more cost-competitive with Dell. In an effort to cut their assembly costs, IBM, HP, and several others had begun outsourcing assembly to contract manufacturers and refocused their internal efforts on product design and marketing. Virtually all vendors were trying to minimize the amount of finished goods in dealer/distributor inventories and shorten the time it took to replenish dealer stocks. Collaboration with contract manufacturers was increasing to develop the capabilities to build and deliver PCs equipped to customer specifications within 7 to 14 days, but these efforts were hampered by the use of Asia-based contract manufacturers—delivering built-to-order PCs to North American and European customers within a two-week time frame required the use of costly air freight from Asia-based assembly plants.

While most PC vendors would have liked to adopt Dell's sell-direct strategy for at least some of their sales, they confronted big channel conflict problems: if they started to push direct sales hard, they would almost certainly alienate the independent dealers on whom they depended for the bulk of their sales and service to customers. Dealers saw sell-direct efforts on the part of a manufacturer whose brand they represented as a move to cannibalize their business and to compete against them. However, Dell's success in gaining large enterprise customers with its direct sales force had forced growing numbers of PC vendors to supplement the efforts of their independent dealers with direct sales and service efforts of their own. During 2003–2004, several of Dell's rivals were selling 15 to 25 percent of their products direct.

Profiles of Selected Competitors in the PC Industry

This section presents brief profiles of three of Dell's principal competitors. Exhibit 6 summarizes Dell's principal competitors in the various product categories where it competed and the sizes of these product markets.

Hewlett-Packard

In one of the most contentious and controversial acquisitions in U.S. history, Hewlett-Packard shareholders voted by a narrow margin in early 2002 to approve the company's acquisition of Compaq Computer, the world's second largest full-service global computing company (behind IBM) and a company with 2001 revenues of $33.6 billion and a net loss of $785 million. Compaq had passed IBM to become the world leader in PCs in 1995 and remained in first place until it was overtaken by Dell in late 1999. Compaq had acquired Tandem Computer in 1997 and Digital Equipment Corporation in 1998 to give it capabilities, products, and service offerings that allowed it to compete in every sector of the computer industry.[22] When Compaq purchased it, Digital was a troubled company with high operating costs, an inability to maintain technological leadership in high-end computing, and a nine-year string of having either lost money or barely broken even.[23]

The acquisitions gave Compaq a product line that included PCs, servers, workstations, mainframes, peripherals, and such services as business and e-commerce solutions, hardware and software support, systems integration, and technology consulting. In 2000,

[22]"Can Compaq Catch Up?" *BusinessWeek,* May 3, 1999, p. 163.
[23]More information on Digital's competitive position can be found in "Compaq-Digital: Let the Slimming Begin," *BusinessWeek,* June 22, 1998.

EXHIBIT 6   **Dell's Principal Competitors and Dell's Estimated Market Shares by Product Category, 2004**

Product Category	Dell's Principal Competitors	Estimated Size of Worldwide Market, 2003–2004 (in billions)	Dell's Worldwide Share, 2004
PCs	Hewlett-Packard (maker of both Compaq and HP brands); IBM, Gateway, Apple, Acer, Sony, Fujitsu-Siemens (in Europe and Japan), Legend (in China)	$175	18.5%
Servers	Hewlett-Packard, IBM, Sun Microsystems, Fujitsu	50	~10
Data storage devices	Hewlett-Packard, IBM, EMC, Hitachi	40	~10
Networking switches and related equipment	Cisco Systems, Enterasys, Nortel, 3Com	58	2–3
Handheld PCs	Palm, Sony, Hewlett-Packard, Toshiba, Casio	4	~2–3
Printers and printer cartridges	Hewlett-Packard, Lexmark, Canon, Epson	~50	~7
Cash register systems	IBM, NCR, Wincor Nixdorf, Hewlett-Packard, Sun Microsystems	4 (in North America)	~1–2
Services	Accenture, IBM, Hewlett-Packard, many others	350	~2–3

Source: Compiled by the case authors from a variety of sources, including International Data Corp. and www.dell.com.

Compaq spent $370 million to acquire certain assets of Inacom Corporation that management believed would help Compaq reduce inventories, speed cycle time, and enhance its capabilities to do business with customers via the Internet. Carly Fiorina, who became HP's CEO in 1999, explained why the acquisition of Compaq was strategically sound:

> With Compaq, we become No. 1 in Windows, No. 1 in Linux and No. 1 in Unix . . . With Compaq, we become the No. 1 player in storage, and the leader in the fastest growing segment of the storage market—storage area networks. With Compaq, we double our service and support capacity in the area of mission-critical infrastructure design, outsourcing and support . . . Let's talk about PCs . . . Compaq has been able to improve their turns in that business from 23 turns of inventory per year to 62—100 percent improvement year over year—and they are coming close to doing as well as Dell does. They've reduced operating expenses by $130 million, improved gross margins by three points, reduced channel inventory by more than $800 million. They ship about 70 percent of their commercial volume through their direct channel, comparable to Dell. We will combine our successful retail PC business model with their commercial business model and achieve much more together than we could alone. With Compaq, we will double the size of our sales force to 15,000 strong. We will build our R&D budget to more than $4 billion a year, and add important capabilities to HP Labs. We will become the No. 1 player in a whole host of countries around the world—HP operates in more than 160 countries, with well over 60 percent of our revenues coming from outside the U.S. The new HP will be the No. 1 player in the consumer and small- and medium-business segments . . . We have estimated cost synergies of $2.5 billion by 2004 . . . It is a rare opportunity when a technology company can advance its market position substantially and reduce its cost structure substantially at the same time. And this is possible because Compaq and HP are in the same businesses, pursuing the same strategies, in the same markets, with complementary capabilities.

However, going into 2005 the jury was still out on whether HP's acquisition of Compaq was the success that Carly Fiorina had claimed it would be. The company's only real bright spot was its $24 billion crown jewel printer business, which still reigned as the unchallenged world leader (largely because of a highly productive $1 billion investment in printer R&D). But the rest of HP's businesses were underachievers. Its PC and server businesses

EXHIBIT 7 **Performance of Hewlett-Packard's Four Major Business Groups, Fiscal Years 2001–2004** (In billions of dollars)

	Printing and Imaging	Personal Computing Systems*	Enterprise Systems*	HP Services
2004 (fiscal year ending October 31)				
Net revenue	$24,199	$24,622	$16,074	$13,778
Operating income (loss)	3,847	(210)	28	1,263
2003 (fiscal year ending October 31)				
Net revenue	$22,623	$21,228	$15,379	$12,305
Operating income (loss)	3,570	19	(54)	1,372
2002 (fiscal year ending October 31)*				
Net revenue	$20,447	$21,895	$16,194	$12,326
Operating income (loss)	3,345	(372)	(664)	1,369
2001 (fiscal year ending October 31)*				
Net revenue	$19,602	$26,710	$20,205	$12,802
Operating income (loss)	2,103	(728)	(579)	1,617

*Results for 2001 and 2002 represent the combined results of both HP and Compaq Computer.

Source: 2003 10-K report and company press release, November 16, 2004.

were struggling, losing money in most quarters and barely breaking even in others—and HP was definitely losing ground to Dell in PCs and low-priced servers. In servers, HP was being squeezed on the low-end by Dell's low prices and on the high-end by strong competition from IBM. Most observers saw IBM as overshadowing HP in corporate computing—high-end servers and IT services. In data storage and technical support services, HP had been able to grow revenues but profit margins and total operating profits were declining. While HP had successfully cut annual operating costs by $3.5 billion—beating the $2.5 billion target set at the time of the Compaq acquisition, the company's operating margins in the first nine months of 2004 were a skimpy 5.3 percent, well below the 8–10 percent targets expected when the Compaq deal was finalized.[24] And the company had missed its earnings forecasts in 7 of the past 20 quarters.

With the company's stock price stuck in the $18–$23 price range, impatient investors had recently begun clamoring for the company to break itself up and create two separate companies, one for its printer business and one for all the rest of the businesses (PCs, servers, storage devices, digital cameras, calculators, and IT services). A Merrill Lynch analyst had estimated that the total value of HP's business would be 25–45 percent greater if split into printing and nonprinting operations.[25] In fact, HP's board of directors was actively considering breaking up the company into smaller pieces, but so far had taken no action. Carly Fiorina had expressed opposition to a breakup, arguing that HP's broad product/business lineup paid off in the form of added sales and lower costs. In an August 2004 speech, she said, "We think we have a unique opportunity, because we have leadership positions and intellectual property at every stage of the value chain."[26]

HP reported total revenues of $79.9 billion and net profits of $3.5 billion for fiscal 2004, versus total revenues of $73.1 billion and earnings of $2.5 billion in 2003. However, a substantial portion of the increase in net earnings in 2004 was due to cutbacks in R&D spending and a lower effective tax rate. Moreover, the company's EPS of $1.16 in 2004 was substantially below the EPS of $1.80 reported in 2000. Exhibit 7 shows the performance of HP's four major business groups.

[24]Ben Elgin, "Carly's Challenge," *BusinessWeek,* December 13, 2004, p. 101.

[25]Ibid.

[26]Ibid., p. 102.

IBM

IBM was seen as a "computer solutions" company and had the broadest and deepest capabilities in customer service, technical support, and systems integration of any company in the world. IBM's Global Services business group was the world's largest information technology services provider, with sales of $42.6 billion in 2003. In addition to its IT services business, IBM had 2003 hardware sales of $28.2 billion and software sales of $12.2 billion. IBM conducted business in 170 countries and had total sales of $89 billion and earnings of $7.6 billion in 2003. Once the world's undisputed king of computing and information processing, IBM was struggling to remain a potent contender in PCs, servers, storage products, and other hardware-related products. Since the early 1990s, IBM had been steadily losing ground to competitors in product categories it had formerly dominated. Its recognized strengths—a potent brand name, global distribution capabilities, a position as the longtime global leader in mainframe computers, and strong capabilities in IT consulting services and systems integration—had proved insufficient in overcoming buyer resistance to IBM's premium prices. Many of its former customers had turned to lower-priced vendors—the old adage "No one ever got fired for selecting IBM products" no longer applied. IBM's revenues had hovered in the $81 to $89 billion range for the past five years. The company's only remaining strength in IT hardware was in high-end servers.

IBM's Troubles in PCs

IBM's market share in PCs was in a death spiral—it had lost more market share in the 1990s than any other PC maker. Once the dominant global and U.S. market leader, with a market share exceeding 50 percent in the late 1980s and early 1990s, IBM was fast becoming an also-ran in PCs, with a global market share of only 6 percent in 2004 (see Exhibit 1). Its last stronghold in PCs was in laptop computers, where its ThinkPad line was a consistent award winner on performance, features, and reliability. The vast majority of IBM's laptop and desktop sales were to large enterprises that had IBM mainframe computers and had been long-standing IBM customers. IBM's PC group had higher costs than rivals, making it virtually impossible to match rivals on price and make a profit. IBM distributed its PCs, workstations, and servers through reseller partners, but used its own sales force to market to large enterprises. IBM competed against rival hardware vendors by emphasizing confidence in the IBM brand and the company's longstanding strengths in software applications, IT services and support, and systems integration capabilities. IBM had responded to the direct sales inroads Dell had made in the corporate market by allowing some of its resellers to economize on costs by custom-assembling IBM PCs to buyer specifications.

The Sale of IBM's PC Business to Lenovo in Late 2004

In December 2004, IBM agreed to sell its PC business to Lenovo Group Ltd., the number one computer maker in China, in a $1.75 billion business deal that made Lenovo the world's third biggest PC maker, with a global market share of about 8.7 percent, and that also gave IBM an 18.9 percent ownership interest in Lenovo. The head of IBM's PC operations was slated to become CEO of Lenovo, with Lenovo's current CEO (who did not speak English) assuming the role of chairman. Lenovo announced it would move its corporate headquarters from Beijing to New York City.

The new company was expected to have about $12 billion in annual sales and about 20,000 employees, including about 10,000 IBM employees who would be a part of the new company—about 2,500 of the IBM employees scheduled to become part of Lenovo were in North Carolina, about half were in China, and the rest were scattered around the world. Prior to the deal, Lenovo had annual sales of about $3 billion and IBM's PC business had annual sales close to $9 billion; IBM's PC business lost $258 million in 2003. IBM had about a 6 percent share of the PC market in China. The new company had the rights to use the IBM name on its PCs for a maximum of five years, but Lenovo indicated it would consider co-branding after 18 months. The new company planned to continue to sell its PCs through the efforts of an internal sales force for large accounts and its network of distributors and retail outlets.

Lenovo had little reputation for innovation, and it usually followed the technology lead of Intel and Microsoft, the PC industry's standard setters. It was regarded as a made-in-China-for-China producer of PCs. It had previously tried to enter the PC market outside China without success and was under competitive pressure in its home market, particularly from Dell (which was said to have lower costs). However, the company's original parent, the government's Chinese Academy of Sciences, was still a major shareholder, which gave Lenovo access to loans from state banks.

Some observers believed that one of management's major challenges would be integrating the cultures of the operations. Twice daily at Lenovo's headquarters, the sound system broadcast "Number Six Broadcast Exercises," a set of stretches and knee bends—participation was voluntary but highly encouraged.[27] The company song was played every morning at eight o'-clock and sung by workers at the start of widely attended meetings. Lenovo employees who were late to meetings had to stand behind their chairs for one minute (as an attempt to humiliate them into being punctual). Employees' activities were strictly monitored; time spent outside the work area during work hours had to be accounted for, and deductions were made from employees' paychecks if the explanations were unsatisfactory. Most employees were young and had worked at Lenovo since graduating from college; few spoke English and most had never met a foreigner.

Gateway

Gateway, a San Diego–based company (recently relocated from South Dakota), had 2003 revenues of $3.4 billion (down from $4.2 billion in 2002) and a net loss of $515 million (bigger than the loss of $298 million in 2002). It was the fourth largest seller of PCs in the U.S. market and one of the top 10 sellers worldwide. However, as shown in Exhibit 1, its unit sales and market share had been sliding since 2000. Gateway's all-time peak revenues were $9.6 billion in 2000 and its peak-year profits were $428 million.

In 2001–2002, Gateway's top management tried to reverse the company's deteriorating market position; the turnaround initiatives included:

- Closing its retail stores in Canada, Europe, the Middle East, Africa, and the Asia-Pacific region, along with 70 underperforming U.S. retail locations.

- Combining its consumer and business sales organization into a single unit.

- Focusing its sales and marketing efforts on consumers, small and medium-sized businesses, educational institutions, and government.

- Consolidating its manufacturing operations and call center operations to pave the way for a 50 percent cutback in its workforce in 2001. Manufacturing operations in Ireland and Malaysia were closed, and all production was moved to the company's two existing plants in South Dakota and Virginia. Further cutbacks to reduce the workforce from 14,000 to 11,500 employees were announced in early 2002.

- Supplementing its sell-direct distribution strategy by stocking a limited inventory of pre-built Gateway PCs in its retail stores that customers could take home immediately.

- Improving its offering of digital cameras, music, and videos and actively marketing broadband Internet services to its customers via alliances with a number of cable broadband Internet access providers.

[27]Julie Chao, "Chinese Computer Maker Lenovo Shoots for Leadership in the World," *Atlanta Journal-Constitution*, December 14, 2004, pp. F1, F8.

- Introducing a sleek new line of desktop and notebook PCs with industry-leading features.
- Refreshing its spotted-cow box logo, used since 1998.
- Selling consumer electronics products made by other manufacturers in its retail stores, including digital cameras, MP3 players, and high-end plasma-screen TVs.

The 2001–2002 initiatives failed to reverse the decline. In 2003, further efforts were made to stem Gateway's slide in the marketplace (which was mainly due to stiff competition from Dell):

- The entire product line was refreshed and expanded, with 118 Gateway-branded products in 22 categories being introduced.
- The company concentrated its sales efforts in PCs on the government and education segments.
- Back-office operations were streamlined to reduce costs.

Then in January 2004, Gateway acquired eMachines, Inc., for 50 million shares of Gateway common stock and $30 million in cash. A $1.1 billion producer of low-end computers, eMachines had distribution capabilities in Japan, Great Britain, and parts of western Europe. The two companies had combined sales of $4.5 billion in 2003. Gateway management believed the eMachines acquisition would allow Gateway to better compete in the low end of the PC market and also give it the resources and competitive strength to reenter markets outside the United States. As part of the deal, the founder and CEO of eMachines, Wayne Inouye, became the CEO of Gateway, with Ted Waitt, Gateway's founder and former CEO, functioning as chairman.

Gateway's revenue decline continued in the first half of 2004. The company had a net loss of $561 million on sales of $2.6 billion during the first nine months of 2004, but management expected that the company to become profitable in the fourth quarter on sales of about $1 billion. Gateway sold 931,000 units in the third quarter of 2004, its highest volume in 14 quarters. Management had forecast sales of $4 billion in 2005 and earnings of $50–$60 million.

Dell's Future Prospects

In a February 2003 article in *Business 2.0,* Michael Dell said, "The best way to describe us now is as a broad computer systems and services company. We have a pretty simple system. The most important thing is to satisfy our customers. The second most important thing is to be profitable. If we don't do the first one well, the second one won't happen."[28] For the most part, Michael Dell was not particularly concerned about the efforts of competitors to copy many aspects of Dell's build-to-order, sell-direct strategy. He explained why on at least two separate occasions:

> The competition started copying us seven years ago. That's when we were a $1 billion business . . . And they haven't made much progress to be honest with you. The learning curve for them is difficult. It's like going from baseball to soccer.[29]

> I think a lot of people have analyzed our business model, a lot of people have written about it and tried to understand it. This is an 18½-year process . . . It comes from many, many cycles of learning . . . It's very, very different than designing products to be built to stock . . . Our whole company is oriented around a very different way of operating . . . I don't, for any sec-

[28]*Business 2.0,* February 2003; posted at www.business2.com.
[29]Comments made to students at the University of North Carolina and reported in the *Raleigh News & Observer,* November 16, 1999.

ond, believe that they are not trying to catch up. But it is also safe to assume that Dell is not staying in the same place. You know, this past year we've driven a billion dollars of cost out of our supply chain, and certainly next year we plan to drive quite a bit of cost out as well.[30]

On two other occasions, Michael Dell spoke about the size of the company's future opportunities:

> When technologies begin to standardize or commoditize, the game starts to change. Markets open up to be volume markets and this is very much where Dell has made its mark—first in the PC market in desktops and notebooks and then in the server market and the storage market and services and data networking. We continue to expand the array of products that we sell, the array of services and, of course, expand on a geographic basis. The way we think about it is that there are all of these various technologies out there . . . What we have been able to do is build a business system that takes those technological ingredients, translates them into products and services and gets them to the customer more efficiently than any company around.[31]

> This year [2004], we're roughly a $50 billion business. We have only six percent market share in an $800 billion market. There are enormous opportunities for us to grow across multiple dimensions in terms of products, with servers, storage, printing and services, representing a huge realm of expansion for us. There's geographic expansion and market share expansion back in the core business. The primary focus for us is picking those opportunities, seizing on them, and making sure we have the talent and the leadership growing inside the company to support all that growth. We have the goal of reaching $60 billion and we're tracking about a year ahead of plan. And there's also a network effect here. As we grow our product lines and enter new markets, we see a faster ability to gain share in new markets versus ones we've previously entered. Printing is a great example; it's also a great example of a market where people are either underestimating us or wondering if we'll succeed. In the U.S. market where all-in-one inkjets are the fastest growing part of the market, we already have 20 percent of the market. We just introduced color laser printers. You can pay only $449 for a color networked laser printer that offers industry-leading price performance for both the hardware and printing supplies. That's a huge new opportunity for us that's highly-related to computing. Our first full year in [the printer] business, we hit a billion dollars of revenue— that's pretty good for a startup.[32]

Going into 2005, Dell Computer had a war chest of over $12 billion in cash and liquid investments that it could deploy in its pursuit of attractive revenue growth opportunities.

[30]Remarks by Michael Dell, Gartner Fall Symposium, Orlando, Florida, October 9, 2002; posted at www.dell.com.

[31]Remarks by Michael Dell, MIT Sloan School of Management, September 26, 2002, and posted at www.dell.com.

[32]Remarks by Michael Dell, University of Toronto, September 21, 2004, and posted at www.dell.com.

Section VII

Developing Marketing Plans

Section I
Essentials of Marketing
Management

Section II
Analyzing Marketing
Problems and Cases

Section III
Financial Analysis for
Marketing Decisions

Knowledge
Enhancement

Section VII
Developing
Marketing Plans

Skill
Development

Section IV
Internet Exercises and
Sources of Marketing
Information

Section V
Marketing Management
Cases

Section VI
Strategic Marketing
Cases

Imagine this scenario. After receiving your bachelor's or master's degree in marketing, you are hired by a major consumer goods company. Because you've done well in school, you are confident that you have a lot of marketing knowledge and a lot to offer to the firm. You're highly motivated and are looking forward to a successful career.

After just a few days of work you are called in for a conference with the vice president of marketing. The vice president welcomes you and tells you how glad the firm is that you have joined them. The vice president also says that, because you have done so well in your marketing courses and have had such recent training, he wants you to work on a special project.

He tells you that the company has a new product, which is to be introduced in a few months. He also says, confidentially, that recent new product introductions by the company haven't been too successful. Suggesting that the recent problems are probably because the company has not been doing a very good job of developing marketing plans, the vice president tells you not to look at marketing plans for the company's other products.

Your assignment, then, is to develop a marketing plan for the proposed product in the next six weeks. The vice president explains that a good job here will lead to rapid advancement in the company. You thank the vice president for the assignment and promise that you'll do your best.

How would you feel when you returned to your desk? Surely, you'd be flattered that you had been given this opportunity and be eager to do a good job. However, how confident are you that you could develop a quality marketing plan? Would you even know where to begin?

We suspect that many of you, even those who have an excellent knowledge of marketing principles and are adept at solving marketing cases, may not yet have the skills necessary to develop a marketing plan from scratch. Thus, the purpose of this section is to offer a framework for developing marketing plans. In one sense, this section is no more than a summary of the whole text. In other words, it is an organizational framework based on the text material that can be used to direct the development of marketing plans.

Students should note that we are not presenting this framework and discussion as the only way to develop a marketing plan. While we believe this is a useful framework for logically analyzing the problems involved in developing a marketing plan, other approaches can be used just as successfully.

Often, successful firms prepare much less detailed plans because much of the background material and current conditions are well known to everyone involved. However, our review of plans used in various firms suggests that something like this framework is not uncommon.

We would like to mention one other qualification before beginning our discussion. Students should remember that one important part of the marketing plan involves the development of a sales forecast. While we have discussed several approaches to sales forecasting in the text, we will detail only one specific approach here.

A Marketing Plan Framework

Marketing plans have three basic purposes. First, they are used as a tangible record of analysis so the logic involved can be checked. This is done to ensure the feasibility and internal consistency of the project and to evaluate the likely consequences of implementing the plan. Second, they are used as roadmaps or guidelines for directing appropriate actions. A marketing plan is designed to be the best available scenario and rationale for directing the firm's efforts for a particular product or brand. Third, they are used as tools to obtain funding for implementation. This funding may come from internal or external sources. For

FIGURE 1
A Marketing Plan Format

- Title page.
- Executive summary.
- Table of contents.
- Introduction.
- Situational analysis.
- Marketing planning.
- Implementation and control of the marketing plan.
- Summary.
- Appendix: Financial analysis.
- References.

example, a brand manager may have to present a marketing plan to senior executives in a firm to get a budget request filled. This would be an internal source. Similarly, proposals for funding from investors or business loans from banks often require a marketing plan. These would be external sources.

Figure 1 presents a format for preparing marketing plans. Each of the 10 elements will be briefly discussed. We will refer to previous chapters and sections in this text and to other sources where additional information can be obtained when a marketing plan is being prepared. We also will offer additional information for focusing particular sections of the plan as well as for developing financial analysis.

Title Page

The *title page* should contain the following information: (1) the name of the product or brand for which the marketing plan has been prepared—for example, Marketing Plan for Little Friskies Dog Food; (2) the time period for which the plan is designed—for example, 2005–2006; (3) the person(s) and position(s) of those submitting the plan—for example, submitted by Amy Lewis, brand manager; (4) the persons, group, or agency to whom the plan is being submitted—for example, submitted to Lauren Ellis, product group manager; and (5) the date of submission of the plan—for example, June 30, 2006.

While preparing the title page is a simple task, remember that it is the first thing readers see. Thus, a title page that is poorly laid out, is smudged, or contains misspelled words can lead to the inference that the project was developed hurriedly and with little attention to detail. As with the rest of the project, appearances are important and affect what people think about the plan.

Executive Summary

The *executive summary* is a two- to three-page summary of the contents of the report. Its purpose is to provide a quick summary of the marketing plan for executives who need to be informed about the plan but are typically not directly involved in plan approval. For instance, senior executives for firms with a broad product line may not have time to read the entire plan but need an overview to keep informed about operations.

The executive summary should include a brief introduction, the major aspects of the marketing plan, and a budget statement. This is not the place to go into detail about each and every aspect of the marketing plan. Rather, it should focus on the major market opportunity and the key elements of the marketing plan that are designed to capitalize on this opportunity.

It is also useful to state specifically how much money is required to implement the plan. In an ongoing firm, many costs can be estimated from historical data or from discussions with other executives in charge of specific functional areas. However, in many situations (such as a class project), sufficient information is not always available to give exact costs for every aspect of production, promotion, and distribution. In these cases, include a rough estimate of total marketing costs of the plan. In many ongoing firms, marketing cost elements are concentrated in the areas of promotion and marketing research, and these figures are integrated with those from other functional areas as parts of the overall business plan.

Table of Contents

The *table of contents* is a listing of everything contained in the plan and where it is located in the report. Reports that contain a variety of charts and figures may also have a table of exhibits listing their titles and page numbers within the report.

In addition to using the table of contents as a place to find specific information, readers may also review it to see if each section of the report is logically sequenced. For example, situational analysis logically precedes marketing planning as an activity, and this ordering makes sense in presenting the plan.

Introduction

The types of information and amount of detail reported in the *introduction* depend in part on whether the plan is being designed for a new or existing product or brand. If the product is new, the introduction should explain the product concept and the reasons it is expected to be successful. Basically, this part of the report should make the new idea sound attractive to management or investors. In addition, it is useful to offer estimates of expected sales, costs, and return on investment.

If the marketing plan is for an existing brand in an ongoing firm, it is common to begin the report with a brief history of the brand. The major focus here is on the brand's performance in the last three to five years. It is useful to prepare graphs of the brand's performance that show its sales, profits, and market share for previous years and to explain the reasons for any major changes. These exhibits can also be extended to include predicted changes in these variables given the new marketing plan. A brief discussion of the overall strategy followed in previous years also provides understanding of how much change is being proposed in the new marketing plan.

Also useful in the introduction is to offer a precise statement of the purpose of the report as well as a roadmap of the report. In other words, tell readers what this report is, how it is organized, and what will be covered in the following sections.

Situational Analysis

The *situational analysis* is not unlike the analysis discussed in Chapter 1 and Section II of this text. The focus remains on the most critical and relevant environmental conditions (or changes in them) that affect the success or failure of the proposed plan. While any aspect of the economic, social, political, legal, or cooperative environments might deserve considerable attention, there is seldom if ever a marketing plan in which the competitive environment does not require considerable discussion. In fact, the competitive environment may be set off as a separate section called *industry analysis*. The strengths and weaknesses of major competitors, their relative market shares, and the success of various competitive strategies are critical elements of the situation analysis.

Section V of the text offers some sources of information for analyzing the competitive environment, such as the *Audits and Surveys National Total-Market Index* and the *Nielsen Retail Index*. In addition, trade association publications, *Fortune, Business Week,* and *The Wall Street Journal* frequently have useful articles on competitive strategies. Firms' annual reports often provide considerable useful information.

Marketing Planning

Marketing planning is, of course, a critical section of the report. As previously noted, it includes three major elements: marketing objectives, target markets, and the marketing mix.

Understanding an industry and the actions of competitors is critical to developing success-ful marketing plans. Below is a list of some questions to consider when performing com-petitive analysis. Thinking about these questions can aid the marketing planner in developing better marketing strategies.

1. Which firms compete in this industry and what are their financial position and marketing capability?
2. What are the relative market shares of various brands?
3. How many brands and models does each firm offer?
4. What marketing strategies have the market leaders employed?
5. Which brands have gained and which have lost market share in recent years, and what factors have led to these changes?
6. Are new competitors likely to enter the market?
7. How quickly do competitive firms react to changes in the market?
8. From which firms or brands might we be able to take market share?
9. What are the particular strengths and weaknesses of competitors in the industry?
10. How do we compare with other firms in the industry in terms of financial strength and marketing skills?

Marketing Objectives

Marketing objectives are often stated in plans in terms of the percentage of particular out-comes that are to be achieved: for example, 80 percent awareness of the brand in particular markets, increase in trial rate by 30 percent, distribution coverage of 60 percent, or increase in total market share by 3 percent over the life of the plan. Similarly, there may also be ob-jective statements in terms of sales units or dollars or increases in these. Of course, the rea-sons for selection of the particular objectives and rationale are important points to explain.

Target Markets

The *target markets* discussion explains the customer base and rationale or justification for it. An approach to developing appropriate target markets is contained in Chapter 5 of this text, and a useful source of secondary data for segmenting markets is the *National Purchase Diary Panel*.

This section also includes relevant discussion of changes or important issues in con-sumer or organizational buyer behavior: for example, what benefits consumers are seeking in this products class, what benefits does the particular brand offer, or what purchasing trends are shaping the market for this product. Discussions of consumer and organizational buyer behavior are contained in Chapters 3 and 4 of this text.

Marketing Mix

The *marketing mix* discussion explains in detail the selected strategy consisting of product, promotion, distribution and price, and the rationale for it. Also, if marketing research has been done on these elements or is planned, it can be discussed in this section.

Product   The *product* section details a description of the product or brand, its packaging, and its attributes. Product life-cycle considerations should be mentioned if they affect the proposed plan.

Of critical importance in this discussion is the competitive advantage of the product or brand. Here it must be carefully considered whether the brand really does anything better than the competition or is purchased primarily on the basis of brand equity or value. For example, many brands of toothpaste have fluoride, yet Crest has the largest market share primarily through promoting this attribute of its brand. Thus, does Crest do anything more than other toothpastes, or is it Crest's image that accounts for sales?

Discussion of product-related issues is contained in Chapters 6 and 7, and services are discussed in Chapter 12 of this text. For discussion of marketing plans for products marketed globally, see Chapter 13.

Promotion   The *promotion* discussion consists of a description and justification of the planned promotion mix. It is useful to explain the theme of the promotion and to include some examples of potential ads as well as the nature of the sales force if one is to be used. For mass-marketed consumer goods, promotion costs can be large and need to be considered explicitly in the marketing plan.

Discussion of promotion-related issues is contained in Chapters 8 and 9 of this text. Secondary sources, such as *Standard Rate and Data, Simmons Media/Market Service, Starch Advertising Readership Service,* and the *Nielsen Television Index,* provide useful information for selecting, budgeting, and justifying media and other promotional decisions.

Distribution   The *distribution* discussion describes and justifies the appropriate channel or channels for the product. This includes types of intermediaries and specifically who they will be. Other important issues concern the level of market coverage desired, cost, and control considerations. In many cases, the channels of distribution used by the firm, as well as competitive firms, are well established. For example, General Motors and Ford distribute their automobiles through independent dealer networks. Thus, unless there is a compelling reason to change channels, the traditional channel will often be the appropriate alternative. However, serious consideration may have to be given to methods of obtaining channel support, for example, trade deals to obtain sufficient shelf space.

Discussion of distribution-related issues is contained in Chapter 10 of this text. Useful retail distribution information can be found in the *Nielsen Retail Index* and the *Audits and Surveys National Total-Market Index.*

Price   The pricing discussion starts with a specific statement of the price of the product. Depending on what type of channel is used, manufacturer price, wholesale price, and suggested retail price need to be listed and justified. In addition, special deals or trade discounts that are to be employed must be considered in terms of their effect on the firm's selling price.

Discussion of price-related issues is contained in Chapter 11. In addition to a variety of other useful information, the *Nielsen Retail Index* provides information on wholesale and retail prices.

Marketing Research   For any aspect of marketing planning, there may be a need for marketing research. If such research is to be performed, it is important to justify it and explain its costs and benefits. Such costs should also be included in the financial analysis.

If marketing research has already been conducted as part of the marketing plan, it can be reported as needed to justify various decisions that were reached. To illustrate, if research found that two out of three consumers like the taste of a new formula Coke, this information would likely be included in the product portion of the report. However, the details of the research could be placed here in the marketing research section. Discussion of marketing research is contained in Chapter 2.

Implementation and Control of the Marketing Plan

This section contains a discussion and justification of how the marketing plan will be implemented and controlled. It also explains who will be in charge of monitoring and changing the plan should unanticipated events occur and how the success or failure of the plan will be measured. Success or failure of the plan is typically measured by a comparison of the results of implementing the plan with the stated objectives.

For the direction-setting purpose of objectives to be fulfilled, objectives need to meet five specifications:

1. An objective should relate to a single, specific topic. (It should not be stated in the form of a vague abstraction or a pious platitude—"we want to be a leader in our industry" or "our objective is to be more aggressive marketers.")
2. An objective should relate to a result, not to an activity to be performed. (The objective is the result of the activity, not the performance of the activity.)
3. An objective should be measurable (stated in quantitative terms whenever feasible).
4. An objective should contain a time deadline for its achievement.
5. An objective should be challenging but achievable.

Consider the following examples:

1. Poor: Our objective is to maximize profits.
    Remarks: How much is "maximum"? The statement is not subject to measurement. What criterion or yardstick will management use to determine if and when actual profits are equal to maximum profits? No deadline is specified.
    Better: Our total profit target in 2006 is $1 million.

2. Poor: Our objective is to increase sales revenue and unit volume.
    Remarks: How much? Also, because the statement relates to two topics, it may be inconsistent. Increasing unit volume may require a price cut, and if demand is price inelastic, sales revenue would fall as unit volume rises. No time frame for achievement is indicated.
    Better: Our objective this calendar year is to increase sales revenues from $30 million to $35 million; we expect this to be accomplished by selling 1 million units at an average price of $35.

3. Poor: Our objective in 2006 is to boost advertising expenditures by 15 percent.
    Remarks: Advertising is an activity, not a result. The advertising objective should be stated in terms of what result the extra advertising is intended to produce.
    Better: Our objective is to boost our market share from 8 percent to 10 percent in 2000 with the help of a 15 percent increase in advertising expenditures.

4. Poor: Our objective is to be a pioneer in research and development and to be the technological leader in the industry.
    Remarks: Very sweeping and perhaps overly ambitious; implies trying to march in too many directions at once if the industry is one with a wide range of technological frontiers. More a platitude than an action commitment to a specific result.
    Better: During the 2000–2010 decade, our objective is to continue as a leader in introducing new technologies and new devices that will allow buyers of electrically powered equipment to conserve on electric energy usage.

5. Poor: Our objective is to be the most profitable company in our industry.
    Remarks: Not specific enough by what measures of profit—total dollars, or earnings per share, or unit profit margin, or return on equity investment, or all of these? Also, because the objective concerns how well other companies will perform, the objective, while challenging, may not be achievable.
    Better: We will strive to remain atop the industry in terms of rate of return on equity investment by earning a 25 percent after-tax return on equity investment in 2000.

Source: Adapted from Arthur A. Thompson, Jr., and A. J. Strickland, *Strategic Management: Concepts and Cases,* 5th ed. (Burr Ridge, IL: Irwin/McGraw-Hill, 1990), pp. 23–34.

Knowledge of consumers is paramount to developing successful marketing plans. Below is a list of questions that are useful to consider when analyzing consumers. For some of the questions, secondary sources of information or primary marketing research can be employed to aid in decision making. However, a number of them require the analyst to do some serious thinking about the relationship between brands of the product and various consumer groups to better understand the market.

1. How many people purchase and use this product in general?
2. How many people purchase and use each brand of the product?
3. Is there an opportunity to reach nonusers of the product with a unique marketing strategy?
4. What does the product do for consumers functionally and how does this vary by brand?
5. What does the product do for consumers in a social or psychological sense and how does this vary by brand?
6. Where do consumers currently purchase various brands of the product?
7. How much are consumers willing to pay for specific brands and is price a determining factor for purchase?
8. What is the market profile of the heavy user of this product and what percentage of the total market are heavy users?
9. What media reach these consumers?
10. On average, how often is this product purchased?
11. How important is brand equity for consumers of this product?
12. Why do consumers purchase particular brands?
13. How brand loyal are consumers of this product?

For a marketing plan developed within an ongoing firm, this section can be quite explicit, because procedures for implementing plans may be well established. However, for a classroom project, the key issues to be considered are the persons responsible for implementing the plan, a timetable for sequencing the tasks, and a method of measuring and evaluating the success or failure of the plan.

Summary

This *summary* need not be much different than the executive summary stated at the beginning of the document. However, it is usually a bit longer, more detailed, and states more fully the case for financing the plan.

Appendix—Financial Analysis

Financial analysis is a very important part of any marketing plan. While a complete business plan often includes extensive financial analysis, such as a complete cost breakdown and estimated return on investment, marketing planners frequently do not have complete accounting data for computing these figures. For example, decisions concerning how much overhead is to be apportioned to the product are not usually made solely by marketing personnel. However, the marketing plan should contain at least a sales forecast and estimates of relevant marketing costs.

Sales Forecast

As noted, there are a variety of ways to develop sales forecasts. Regardless of the method, however, they all involve trying to predict the future as accurately as possible. It is, of

FIGURE 2

A Basic Approach to Sales Forecasting

Total number of people in target markets (*a*)	*a*
Annual number of purchases per person (*b*)	× *b*
Total potential market (*c*)	= *c*
Total potential market (*c*)	*c*
Percent of total market coverage (*d*)	× *d*
Total available market (*e*)	= *e*
Total available market (*e*)	*e*
Expected market share (*f*)	× *f*
Sales forecast (in units) (*g*)	= *g*
Sales forecast (in units) (*g*)	*g*
Price (*h*)	× *h*
Sales forecast (in dollars)(*i*)	= *i*

course, necessary to justify the logic for the forecasted figures, rather than offer them with no support.

One basic approach to developing a sales forecast is outlined in Figure 2. This approach begins by estimating the total number of persons in the selected target market. This estimate comes from the market segmentation analysis and may include information from test marketing and from secondary sources, such as *Statistical Abstracts of the United States*. For example, suppose a company is marketing a solar-powered watch that is designed not only to tell time but also to take the pulse of the wearer. The product is targeted at joggers and others interested in aerobic exercise. By reviewing the literature on these activities, the marketing planner, John Murphy, finds that the average estimate of this market on a national level is 60 million persons and is growing by 4 million persons per year. Thus, John might conclude that the total number of people in the target market for next year is 64 million. If he has not further limited the product's target market and has no other information, John might use this number as a basis for starting the forecast analysis.

The second estimate John needs is the annual number of purchases per person in the product's target market. This estimate could be quite large for such products as breakfast cereal or less than one (annual purchase per person) for such products as automobiles. For watches, the estimate is likely to be much less than one since people are likely to buy a new watch only every few years. Thus, John might estimate the annual number of purchases per person in the target market to be .25. Of course, as a careful marketing planner, John would probably carefully research this market to refine this estimate. In any event, multiplying these two numbers gives John an estimate of the *total potential market,* in this case, 64 million times .25 equals 16 million. In other words, if next year alone John's company could sell a watch to every jogger or aerobic exerciser who is buying a watch, the company could expect sales to be 16 million units.

Of course, the firm cannot expect to sell every jogger a watch for several reasons. First, it is unlikely to obtain 100 percent market coverage in the first year, if ever. Even major consumer goods companies selling convenience goods seldom reach the entire market in the first year and many never achieve even 90 percent distribution. Given the nature of the product and depending on the distribution alternative, John's company might be doing quite well to average 50 percent market coverage in the first year. If John's plans call for this kind of coverage, his estimate of the total available market would be 16 million times .5, which equals 8 million.

A second reason John's plans would not call for dominating the market is that his company does not have the only product available or wanted by this target market. Many of the people

Below is a brief list of questions about the marketing planning section of the report. Answering them honestly and recognizing both the strengths and weaknesses of the marketing plan should help to improve it.

1. What are the key assumptions that were made in developing the marketing plan?
2. How badly will the product's market position be hurt if these assumptions turn out to be incorrect?
3. How good is the marketing research?
4. Is the marketing plan consistent? For example, if the plan is to seek a prestige position in the market, is the product priced, promoted, and distributed to create this image?
5. Is the marketing plan feasible? For example, are the financial and other resources (such as a distribution network) available to implement it?
6. How will the marketing plan affect profits and market share and is it consistent with corporate objectives?
7. Will implementing the marketing plan result in competitive retaliation that will end up hurting the firm?
8. Is the marketing mix designed to reach and attract new customers or increase usage among existing users or both?
9. Will the marketing mix help to develop brand-loyal consumers?
10. Will the marketing plan be successful not just in the short run but also contribute to a profitable long-run position?

who will purchase such a watch will purchase a competitive brand. He must, therefore, estimate the product's likely market share. Of all the estimates made in developing a sales forecast, this one is critical because it is a reflection of the entire marketing plan. Important factors to consider in developing this estimate include (1) competitive market shares and likely marketing strategies; (2) competitive retaliation should the product do well; (3) competitive advantage of the product, such as lower price; (4) promotion mix and budget relative to competitors; and (5) market shares obtained by similar products in the introductory year.

Overall, suppose John estimates the product's market share to be 5 percent, because other competitive products have beat his company to the market and because the company's competitive advantage is only a slightly more stylish watch. In this case, the sales forecast for year one would be 8 million times .05, which equals 400,000 units. If the manufacturer's selling price was $50, then the sales forecast in dollars would be 400,000 times $50, which equals $20 million.

This approach can also be used to extend the sales forecast for any number of years. Typically, estimates of most of the figures change from year to year, depending on changes in market size, distribution coverage, and expected market shares. The value of this approach is that it forces an analyst to carefully consider and justify each of the estimates offered, rather than simply pulling numbers out of the air.

Estimates of Marketing Costs

A complete delineation of all costs, apportionment of overhead, and other accounting tasks are usually performed by other departments within a firm. All of this information, including expected return on investment from implementing the marketing plan, is part of the overall business plan.

However, the marketing plan should at least contain estimates of major marketing costs. These include such things as advertising, sales force training and compensation, channel

Implementation and control of a marketing plan require careful scheduling and attention to detail. While some firms have standard procedures for dealing with many of the questions raised below, thinking through each of the questions should help improve the efficiency of even these firms in this stage of the process.

1. Who is responsible for implementing and controlling the marketing plan?
2. What tasks must be performed to implement the marketing plan?
3. What are the deadlines for implementing the various tasks and how critical are specific deadlines?
4. Has sufficient time been scheduled to implement the various tasks?
5. How long will it take to get the planned market coverage?
6. How will the success or failure of the plan be determined?
7. How long will it take to get the desired results from the plan?
8. How long will the plan be in effect before changes will be made to improve it based on more current information?
9. If an ad agency or other firms are involved in implementing the plan, how much responsibility and authority will they have?
10. How frequently will the progress of the plan be monitored?

development, and marketing research. Estimates may also be included for product development and package design.

For some marketing costs, reasonable estimates are available from sources such as *Standard Rate and Data.* However, some cost figures, such as marketing research, might be obtained from asking various marketing experts for the estimated price of proposed research. Other types of marketing costs might be estimated from financial statements of firms in the industry. For example, Morris's *Annual Statement Studies* offers percentage breakdowns of various income statement information by industry. These might be used to estimate the percentage of the sales-forecast figure that would likely be spent in a particular cost category.

References

The *references* section contains the sources of any secondary information that was used in developing the marketing plan. This information might include company reports and memos, statements of company objectives, and articles or books used for information or support of the marketing plan.

References should be listed alphabetically using a consistent format. One way of preparing references is to use the same approach as is used in marketing journals. For example, the format used for references in *Journal of Marketing* articles is usually acceptable.

Conclusion

Suppose you're now sitting at your desk faced with the task of developing a marketing plan for a new product. Do you believe that you might have the skills to develop a marketing plan? Of course, your ability to develop a quality plan will depend on your learning experiences during your course work and the amount of practice you've had; for example, if you developed a promotion plan in your advertising course, it is likely that you could do a better job on the promotion phase of the marketing plan. Similarly, your experiences in analyzing cases should have sharpened your skills at recognizing problems and developing solutions to them. But inexperience (or experience) aside, hopefully you now feel that you understand the process of developing a marketing plan. You at least know where to start, where to seek information, how to structure the plan, and some of the critical issues that require analysis.

Additional Readings

Cohen, William A. *The Marketing Plan.* 4th ed. New York: John Wiley & Sons, 2005.

Cravens, David W., and Nigel F. Piercy, *Strategic Marketing,* 7th ed. Burr Ridge, IL: McGraw-Hill/Irwin, 2003, pp. 499–523.

Hiebing, Roman G., and Scott W. Cooper. *The Successful Marketing Plan,* 2nd ed. Lincolnwood, IL: NTC Business Books, 1997.

Lehmann, Donald R., and Russell S. Winer. *Analysis for Marketing Planning.* 5th ed. Burr Ridge, IL: McGraw-Hill/Irwin, 2002.

Parmerlee, David. *Preparing the Marketing Plan.* Chicago: NTC Business Books/American Marketing Association, 2000.

Chapter Notes

Section 1

Chapter 1

1. See Reinhard Angelmar and Christian Pinson, "The Meaning of Marketing," *Philosophy of Science,* June 1975, pp. 208–14.

2. "Marketing Redefined," *Marketing News,* September 15, 2004, p. 1.

3. Much of this section is based on J. H. Donnelly, Jr., J. L. Gibson, and J. M. Ivancevich, *Fundamentals of Management,* 9th ed. (Burr Ridge, IL: Irwin/ McGraw-Hill, 1998), Chap. 7.

4. The process may differ depending on the type of organization or management approach, or both. For certain types of organizations, one strategic plan will be sufficient. Some manufacturers with similar product lines or limited product lines will develop only one strategic plan. However, organizations with widely diversified product lines and widely diversified markets may develop strategic plans for units or divisions. These plans usually are combined into a master strategic plan.

5. For a discussion of this topic, see Gerald E. Ledford, Jr., Jon R. Wendenhof, and James T. Strahely, "Realizing a Corporate Philosophy," *Organizational Dynamics,* Winter 1995, pp. 4–19; and Stephan Cummings and John Davies, "Mission, Vision, Fusion," *Long Range Planning,* December 1994, pp. 147–50.

6. Philip Kotler and Gary Armstrong, *Principles of Marketing,* 6th ed. (Englewood Cliffs, NJ: Prentice Hall, 1994), Chap. 2.

7. Philip Kotler, *Marketing Management: Analysis, Planning, Implementation and Control,* 8th ed. (Englewood Cliffs, NJ: Prentice Hall, 1994), Chap. 3.

8. Norton Paley, "A Sign of Intelligence," *Sales & Marketing Management,* March 1995, pp. 30–31.

9. Peter Drucker, *Management: Tasks, Responsibilities, Practices* (New York: Harper & Row, 1974), pp. 77–89; Kotler, *Marketing Management,* Chap. 3.

10. Much of the following discussion is based on Drucker, *Management,* pp. 79–87.

11. Noel B. Zabriskie and Alan B. Huellmantel, "Marketing Research as a Strategic Tool," *Long Range Planning,* February 1994, pp. 107–18.

12. Originally discussed in the classic H. Igor Ansoff, *Corporate Strategy* (New York: McGraw-Hill, 1965).

13. For complete coverage of this topic, see Michael E. Porter, *Competitive Advantage: Creating and Sustaining Superior Performance* (New York: The Free Press, 1985). Material in this section is based upon discussions contained in Steven J. Skinner, *Marketing,* 2nd ed. (Boston: Houghton Mifflin Co., 1994), pp. 48–50; and Thomas A. Bateman and Carl P. Zeithaml, *Management Function & Strategy,* 2nd ed. (Burr Ridge, IL: Irwin/ McGraw-Hill, 1993), pp. 152–53.

14. For a complete discussion of this topic, see Michael Treacy and Fred Wiersema, *The Discipline of Market Leaders* (Reading, MA: Addison-Wesley, 1995); and Michael Treacy and Fred Wiersema, "How Market Leaders Keep Their Edge," *Fortune,* February 6, 1995, pp. 88–98.

15. Philip Kotler, *Marketing Management,* p. 13.

16. For a discussion of this issue and other mistakes marketers frequently make, see Kevin J. Clancy and Robert S. Shulman, "Breaking the Mold," *Sales & Marketing Management,* January 1994, pp. 82–84.

17. George S. Day and David B. Montgomery, "Diagnosing the Experience Curve," *Journal of Marketing,* Spring 1983, pp. 44–58.

18. P. Rajan Varadarajan, Terry Clark, and William M. Pride, "Controlling the Uncontrollable: Managing Your Market Environment," *Sloan Management Review,* Winter 1992, pp. 39–47.

19. Reed E. Nelson, "Is There Strategy in Brazil?" *Business Horizons,* July–August 1992, pp. 15–23.

20. Peter S. Davis and Patrick L. Schill, "Addressing the Contingent Effects of Business Unit Strategic Orientation on the Relationship between Organizational Context and Business Unit Performance," *Journal of Business Research,* 1993, pp. 183–200.

21. J. Scott Armstrong and Roderick J. Brodie, "Effects of Portfolio Planning Methods on Decision Making: Experimental Results," *International Journal of Research in Marketing,* January 1994, pp. 73–84.

22. Michel Roberts, "Times Change but Do Business Strategies?" *Journal of Business Strategy,* March–April 1993, pp. 12–15.

23. Donald L. McCabe and V. K. Narayanan, "The Life Cycle of the PIMS and BCG Models," *Industrial Marketing Management,* November 1991, pp. 347–52.

Chapter 2

1. Based on Peter D. Bennett, ed., *Dictionary of Marketing Terms,* 2nd ed. (Chicago: American Marketing Association, 1995), p. 77.

2. Gilbert A. Churchill, Jr., and J. Paul Peter, *Marketing: Creating Value for Customers,* 2nd ed. (Burr Ridge, IL: Irwin/McGraw-Hill, 1998), p. 116.

3. For a discussion of some general problems in marketing research, see Alan G. Sawyer and J. Paul Peter, "The Significance of Statistical Significance Testing in Marketing Research," *Journal of Marketing Research,* May 1983, pp. 122–33.

4. This section is based on Churchill and Peter, *Marketing,* pp. 114–16.

Chapter 3

1. Richard P. Coleman, "The Continuing Significance of Social Class to Marketing," *Journal of Consumer Research,* December 1983, pp. 265–80.

2. See William O. Bearden and Michael J. Etzel, "Reference Group Influence on Product and Brand Purchase Decisions," *Journal of Consumer Research,* September 1982, pp. 183–94; and Terry L. Childers and Akshay R. Rao, "The Influence of Familial and Peer-Based Reference Groups on Consumer Decisions," *Journal of Consumer Research,* September 1992, pp. 198–211.

3. See Rosann L. Spiro, "Persuasion in Family Decision Making," *Journal of Consumer Research,* March 1983, pp. 393–402.

4. See Janet Wagner and Sherman Hanna, "The Effectiveness of Family Life Cycle Variables in Consumer Expenditure Research," *Journal of Consumer Research,* December 1983, pp. 281–91. Also see Charles M. Schanninger and William D. Danko, "A Conceptual and Empirical Comparison of Alternative Household Life Cycle Models," *Journal of Consumer Research,* March 1993, pp. 580–94.

5. Russell W. Belk, "Situational Variables and Consumer Behavior," *Journal of Consumer Research,* December 1975, pp. 156–64. Also see Jacob Hornik, "Situational Effects on the Consumption of Time," *Journal of Marketing,* Fall 1982, pp. 44–55; C. Whan Park, Easwer S. Iyer, and Daniel C. Smith, "The Effects of Situational Factors on In-Store Grocery Shopping Behavior: The Role of Store Environment and Time Available for Shopping," *Journal of Consumer Research,* March 1989, pp. 422–33; and Mary Jo Bitner, "Servicescapes: The Impact of Physical Surroundings on Customers and Employees," *Journal of Marketing,* April 1992, pp. 57–71.

6. J. Paul Peter and Jerry C. Olson, *Consumer Behavior and Marketing Strategy,* 7th ed. (Burr Ridge, IL: Irwin/McGraw-Hill, 2005), Chap. 4.

7. A. H. Maslow, *Motivation and Personality* (New York: Harper & Row, 1954); also see James F. Engel, Roger D. Blackwell, and Paul W. Miniard, *Consumer Behavior,* 8th ed. (Fort Worth, TX: Dryden Press, 1995), Chap. 5, for further discussion of need recognition.

8. For a detailed review of research on external search, see Sharon E. Beatty and Scott M. Smith, "External Search Effort: An Investigation across Several Product Categories," *Journal of Consumer Research,* June 1987, pp. 83–95. Also see Narasimhan Srinivasan and Brian T. Ratchford, "An Empirical Test of a Model of External Search for Automobiles," *Journal of Consumer Research,* September 1991, pp. 233–42; and Julie L. Ozanne, Merrie Brucks, and Dhruv Grewal, "A Study of Information Search Behavior during the Categorization of New Products," *Journal of Consumer Research,* March 1992, pp. 452–63.

9. For further discussion of information processing, see J. Paul Peter and Jerry C. Olson, *Consumer Behavior and Marketing Strategy,* 7th ed. (Burr Ridge, IL: Irwin/McGraw-Hill, 2005), Chap. 3.

10. For a summary of research on attitude modeling, see Blair H. Sheppard, Jon Hartwick, and Paul R. Warshaw, "The Theory of Reasoned Action: A Meta-Analysis of Past Research with Recommendations for Modification and Future Research," *Journal of Consumer Research,* December 1988, pp. 325–43.

11. For further discussion of postpurchase feelings, see Richard L. Oliver, "Cognitive, Affective, and Attribute Bases of the Satisfaction Response," *Journal of Consumer Research,* December 1993, pp. 418–30; and Haim Mano and Richard L. Oliver, "Assessing the Dimensionality and Structure of the Consumption Experience: Evaluation, Feeling, and Satisfaction," *Journal of Consumer Research,* December 1993, pp. 451–66.

Chapter 4

1. This discussion is based on Gilbert A. Churchill, Jr., and J. Paul Peter, *Marketing: Creating Value for Customers,* 2d ed. (Burr Ridge, IL: Irwin/McGraw-Hill, 1998), pp. 182–84. Also see Michele D. Bunn, "Taxonomy of Buying Decision Approaches," *Journal of Marketing,* January 1993, pp. 38–56.

2. This discussion is based on Eric N. Berkowitz, Roger A. Kerin, Steven W. Hartley, and William Rudelius, *Marketing,* 4th ed. Irwin/McGraw-Hill (Burr Ridge, IL: 1994), p. 184.

3. For research on influence strategies in organizational buying, see Gary L. Frazier and Raymond Rody, "The Use of Influence Strategies in Interfirm Relationships in Industrial Product Channels," *Journal of Marketing,* January 1991, pp. 52–69; and Julia M. Bristor, "Influence Strategies in Organizational Buying," *Journal of Business-to-Business Marketing,* 1993, pp. 63–98.

4. For research on the role of organizational climate in industrial buying, see William J. Qualls and Christopher

P. Puto, "Organizational Climate and Decision Framing: An Integrated Approach to Analyzing Industrial Buying Decisions," *Journal of Marketing Research*, May 1989, pp. 179–92.

Chapter 5

1. Russell I. Haley, "Benefit Segmentation: A Decision-Oriented Research Tool," *Journal of Marketing*, July 1968, pp. 30–35; Russell I. Haley, "Benefit Segmentation—20 Years Later," *Journal of Consumer Marketing*, 1983, pp. 5–13; and Russell I. Haley, "Benefit Segments: Backwards and Forwards," *Journal of Advertising Research*, February–March 1984, pp. 19–25.

2. Roger J. Calantone and Alan G. Sawyer, "The Stability of Benefit Segments," *Journal of Marketing Research*, August 1978, pp. 395–404; also see James R. Merrill and William A. Weeks, "Predicting and Identifying Benefit Segments in the Elderly Market," in *AMA Educator's Proceedings*, eds. Patrick Murphy et al. (Chicago: American Marketing Association, 1983), pp. 399–403; Wagner A. Kamakura, "A Least Squares Procedure for Benefit Segmentation with Conjoint Experiments," *Journal of Marketing Research*, May 1988, pp. 157–67; and Michel Wedel and Jan-Benedict E. M. Steenkamp, "A Clusterwise Regression Method for Simultaneous Fuzzy Market Structuring and Benefit Segmentation." *Journal of Marketing Research*, November 1991, pp. 385–96.

3. John L. Lastovicka, John P. Murry, Jr., and Eric Joachimsthaler, "Evaluating the Measurement Validity of Lifestyle Typologies with Qualitative Measures and Multiplicative Factoring," *Journal of Marketing Research*, February 1990, pp. 11–23.

4. This discussion is taken from J. Paul Peter and Jerry C. Olson, *Consumer Behavior and Marketing Strategy*, 7th ed. (Burr Ridge, IL: Irwin/McGraw-Hill, 2005), pp. 384–5.

5. See Al Ries and Jack Trout, *Positioning: The Battle for Your Mind* (New York: Warner Books, 1981); and Al Ries and Jack Trout, *Marketing Warfare* (New York: McGraw-Hill, 1986).

Chapter 6

1. Material for this section is based on discussions contained in Louis E. Boone and David L. Kurtz, *Contemporary Marketing*, 8th ed. (Fort Worth, TX: Dryden, 1995), Chap. 2; Gilbert A. Churchill, Jr., and J. Paul Peter, *Marketing: Creating Value for Customers* (Burr Ridge, IL: Irwin/McGraw-Hill, 1995), Chap. 1, p. 634; James H. Donnelly, James L. Gibson, and John M. Ivancevich, *Fundamentals of Management*, 9th ed. (Burr Ridge, IL: Irwin/McGraw-Hill 1995), p. 501; Joseph M. Juran, "Made in the U.S.A.: A Renaissance in Quality," *Harvard Business Review*, July–August 1993, pp. 42–47, 50; and

Valerie A. Zeithaml, "Consumer Perceptions of Price, Quality, and Value: A Means End Model and Synthesis of Evidence," *Journal of Marketing*, April 1988, pp. 35–48.

2. For a discussion on this topic, see Andrew J. Bergman, "What the Marketing Professional Needs to Know about ISO 9000 Series Registration," *Industrial Marketing Management*, 1994, pp. 367–70.

3. The material for this section comes from Glenn L. Urban and Steven H. Star, *Advanced Marketing Strategy* (Englewood Cliffs, NJ: Prentice Hall, 1991), Chap. 16.

4. For a detailed discussion of this topic, see Anne Perkins, "Product Variety beyond Black," *Harvard Business Review*, November–December 1994, pp. 13–14; and "Perspectives: The Logic of Product-Line Extensions," *Harvard Business Review*, November–December 1994, pp. 53–62.

5. Mats Urde, "Brand Orientation—A Strategy for Survival," *Journal of Consumer Marketing*, 1994, pp. 18–32.

6. James Lowry, "Survey Finds Most Powerful Brands," *Advertising Age*, July 11, 1988, p. 31.

7. Peter H. Farquhar, "Strategic Challenges for Branding," *Marketing Management*, 1994, pp. 8–15.

8. Peter D. Bennett, ed., *Dictionary of Marketing Terms*, 2nd ed. (Chicago: American Marketing Association, 1995), p. 27.

9. Terance Shimp, *Promotion Management and Marketing Communications*, 2nd ed. (Hinsdale, IL: Dryden Press, 1990), p. 67.

10. David A. Aaker and Kevin Lane Keller, "Consumer Evaluations of Brand Extensions," *Journal of Marketing*, January 1990, pp. 27–41.

11. Ibid.

12. For a detailed discussion of brand equity, see David Aaker, *Managing Brand Equity* (New York and London: Free Press, 1991).

13. For a complete discussion of this topic, see Geoffrey L. Gordon, Roger J. Calantone, and C. A. Di Benedetto, "Brand Equity in the Business-to-Business Sector: An Exploratory Study," *Journal of Product & Brand Management*, 1993, pp. 4–16.

14. Jeffrey D. Zbar, "Industry Trends Hold Private-Label Promise," *Advertising Age*, April 3, 1995, p. 31.

15. Karen Benezra, "Frito Bets 'Reduced' Pitch Is in the Chips," *Brandweek*, January 23, 1995, p. 18.

16. Thomas Hine, "Why We Buy," *Worth*, May 1995, pp. 80–83.

17. For a discussion of problems related to this issue, see Geoffrey L. Gordon, Roger J. Calantone, and C. Anthony Di Benedetto, "Mature Markets and Revitalization Strategies: An American Fable," *Business Horizons*, May–June 1991, pp. 39–50.

18. Barry L. Bayus, "Are Product Life Cycles Really Getting Shorter?" *Journal of Product Innovation Management*, September 1994, pp. 300–308.

19. The discussion on benchmarking is based on Stanley Brown, "Don't Innovate—Imitate," *Sales & Marketing Management,* January 1995, pp. 24–25; Charles Goldwasser, "Benchmarking: People Make the Process," *Management Review,* June 1995, pp. 39–43; and L. S. Pryor and S. J. Katz, "How Benchmarking Goes Wrong (and How to Do It Right)," *Planning Review,* January–February 1993, pp. 6–14.

Chapter 7

1. "Face Value: The Mass Production of Ideas, and Other Impossibilities," *The Economist,* March 18, 1995, p. 72.

2. Greg Erickson, "New Package Makes a New Product Complete," *Marketing News,* May 8, 1995, p. 10.

3. Zina Mouhkheiber, "Oversleeping," *Forbes,* June 15, 1995, pp. 78–79.

4. The material on the five categories of new products is from C. Merle Crawford and Anthony Di Benedetto, *New Products Management,* 6th ed. (Burr Ridge, IL: McGraw-Hill/Irwin, 2000), Chap. 1.

5. H. Igor Ansoff, *Corporate Strategy* (New York: McGraw-Hill, 1965), pp. 109–10.

6. Richard Stroup, "Growing in a Crowded Market Requires Old and New Strategies," *Brandweek,* August 22, 1994, p. 19.

7. These two examples came from Justin Martin, "Ignore Your Customers," *Fortune,* May 1, 1995, pp. 121–26.

8. "Where Do They Get All Those Ideas?" *Machine Design,* January 26, 1995, p. 40.

9. This section is based on Daryl McKee, "An Organizational Learning Approach to Product Innovation," *Journal of Product Innovation Management,* September 1992, pp. 232–45.

10. The discussion on risk is from Thomas D. Kuczmarski and Arthur G. Middlebrooks, "Innovation Risk and Reward," *Sales & Marketing Management,* February 1993, pp. 44–51.

11. For a more complete discussion on the advantages and disadvantages of strategic alliances, see Richard N. Cardozo, Shannon H. Shipp, and Kenneth J. Roering, "Proactive Strategic Partnerships: A New Business Markets Strategy," *Journal of Business and Industrial Marketing,* Winter 1992, pp. 51–63; and Frank K. Sonnenberg, "Partnering: Entering the Age of Cooperation," *Journal of Business Strategy,* May/June 1992, pp. 49–52.

12. James Quinn, "Managing Innovation: Controlled Chaos," *Harvard Business Review,* May–June 1985, pp. 73–84; and Hirotaka Takeuchi and Ikujiro Nonaka, "The New New Product Development Game," *Harvard Business Review,* January–February 1986, pp. 137–46.

13. For a discussion of this issue, see Eric M. Olson, Orville C. Walker, Jr., and Robert W. Ruekert,

"Organizing for Effective New Product Development: The Moderating Role of Product Innovativeness," *Journal of Marketing,* January 1995, pp. 48–62; and Cristopher Meyer, "How the Right Measures Help Teams Excel," *Harvard Business Review,* May–June 1994, pp. 95–97.

14. For a detailed discussion on these stages, see Karl T. Ulrich and Steven D. Eppinger, *Product Design and Development* (New York: McGraw-Hill, 1995); and Glen Rifken, "Product Development: Emphatic Design Helps Understand Users Better," *Harvard Business Review,* March–April 1994, pp. 10–11.

15. Patricia W. Meyers and Gerald A. Athaide, "Strategic Mutual Learning between Producing and Buying Firms during Product Innovation," *Journal of Product Innovation Management,* September 1991, pp. 155–69.

16. For a discussion of this issue, see Christina Brown and James Lattin, "Investigating the Relationship between Time in Market and Pioneering Advantage," *Management Science,* October 1994, pp. 1361–69; Robin Peterson, "Forecasting for New Product Introduction," *Journal of Business Forecasting,* Fall 1994, pp. 21–23; and Tracy Carlson, "The Race Is On," *Brandweek,* May 9, 1994, pp. 22–27.

17. For a discussion of reasons why products fail, see Betsy Spellman, "Big Talk, Little Dollars," *Brandweek,* January 23, 1995, pp. 21–29.

Chapter 8

1. This discussion is adapted from material contained in Gilbert A. Churchill, Jr., and J. Paul Peter, *Marketing: Creating Value for Customers,* 2nd ed., (Burr Ridge, IL: Irwin/McGraw-Hill, 1998), Chap. 18.

2. Material for this section is largely based on the discussion of advertising tasks and objectives contained in William Arens and Courtland BovÈe, *Contemporary Advertising,* 5th ed. (Burr Ridge, IL: Irwin/McGraw-Hill, 1994), Chap. 7.

3. For more comprehensive coverage of this topic, see George E. Belch and Michael A. Belch, *Advertising and Promotion: An Integrated Marketing Communications Perspective,* 5th ed. (Burr Ridge, IL: Irwin/McGraw-Hill, 2001), Chap. 12.

4. For a fuller explanation of the pros and cons associated with push marketing strategies, see Betsy Spellman, "Trade Promotion Redefined," *Brandweek,* March 13, 1995, pp. 25–34; and John McManus, "'Lost' Money Redefined as 'Found' Money Won't Connect the Disconnects," *Brandweek,* March 25, 1995, p. 16.

5. This discussion is based on Donald R. Glover, "Distributor Attitudes toward Manufacturer-Sponsored Promotions," *Industrial Marketing Management,* August 1991, pp. 241–49.

6. For a discussion of this topic, see Murray Raphel, "Frequent Shopper Clubs: Supermarkets' Newest Weapon," *Direct Marketing,* May 1995, pp. 18–20; Richard G. Barlow, "Five Mistakes of Frequency Marketing," *Direct Marketing,* March 1995, pp. 16–17; and Alice Cuneo, "Savvy Frequent-Buyer Plans Build on a Loyal Base," *Advertising Age,* March 20, 1995, pp. S10–11.

Chapter 9

1. Warren Keegan, Sandra Moriarty, and Thomas Duncan, *Marketing,* 2nd ed. (Englewood Cliffs, NJ: Prentice Hall, 1994), p. 654.

2. Material for this discussion came from Ronald B. Marks, *Personal Selling: An Interactive Approach,* 5th ed. (Boston, MA: Allyn and Bacon, 1994), pp. 12–13.

3. Material for the discussion of objectives is adapted from Joel R. Evans and Barry Berman, *Marketing,* 6th ed. (New York: Macmillan, 1994), pp. 640–42.

4. Unless otherwise noted, the discussion on the relationship-building process is based largely on material contained in Barton A. Weitz, Stephen B. Castleberry, and John F. Tanner, Jr., *Selling: Building Partnerships,* 3rd ed. (Burr Ridge, IL: Irwin/McGraw-Hill, 1998); and Rolph Anderson, *Essentials of Personal Selling: The New Professionalism* (Englewood Cliffs, NJ: Prentice Hall, 1995). For an in-depth discussion of this topic, readers should consult these references.

5. The discussion of aftermarketing is based on the work of Terry Vavra, *Aftermarketing: How to Keep Customers for Life through Relationship Marketing* (Burr Ridge, IL: McGraw-Hill, 1995).

6. Ibid.

7. The discussion on national account management is from James S. Boles, Bruce K. Pilling, and George W. Goodwyn, "Revitalizing Your National Account Marketing Program," *Journal of Business & Industrial Marketing,* no. 1 (1994), pp. 24–33.

8. Based on a survey by the National Industrial Conference Board: "Forecasting Sales," *Studies in Business Policy,* no. 106.

9. Much of the discussion in this section is based on material contained in Gilbert A. Churchill, Jr., Neil M. Ford, and Orville C. Walker, Jr., *Sales Force Management,* 4th ed. (Burr Ridge, IL: Irwin/McGraw-Hill, 1993); and William J. Stanton, Richard H. Buskirk, and Rosann L. Spiro, *Management of a Sales Force,* 9th ed. (Burr Ridge, IL: Irwin/McGraw-Hill, 1995), pp. 319–20.

10. For a complete discussion of the skills and policies used by successful sales leaders in motivating salespeople, see David W. Cravens, Thomas N. Ingram, Raymond W. LaForge, and Clifford E. Young, "Hallmarks of Effective Sales Organizations," *Marketing Management,* Winter 1992, pp. 57–66; Thomas R.

Wortruba, John S. Mactie, and Jerome A. Colletti, "Effective Sales Force Recognition Programs," *Industrial Marketing Management,* February 1991, pp. 9–15; and Ken Blanchard, "Reward Salespeople Creatively," *Personal Selling Power,* March 1992, p. 24.

Chapter 10

1. Peter D. Bennett, *Dictionary of Marketing Terms,* 2nd ed. (Chicago: American Marketing Association, 1995), p. 242.

2. For further discussion of relationship marketing, see Jan B. Heide, "Interorganizational Governance in Marketing Channels," *Journal of Marketing,* January 1994, pp. 71–85; Robert M. Morgan and Shelby D. Hunt, "The Commitment-Trust Theory of Relationship Marketing," *Journal of Marketing,* July 1994, pp. 20–38; and Manohar U. Kalwani and Narakesari Narayandas, "Long-Term Manufacturer-Supplier Relationships: Do They Pay Off for the Supplier Firm?" *Journal of Marketing,* January 1995, pp. 1–16.

3. This section is based on Donald J. Bowersox and M. Bixby Cooper, *Strategic Marketing Channel Management* (New York: McGraw-Hill, 1992), pp. 104–7; Bert Rosenbloom, *Marketing Channels: A Management View,* 4th ed. (Hinsdale, IL: Dryden Press), pp. 440–65; and Roger A. Kerin, Eric N. Berkowitz, Steven W. Hartley, and William Rudelius, *Marketing,* 7th ed. (Burr Ridge, IL: Irwin/McGraw-Hill, 2003), pp. 409–11.

4. This section is based on Gilbert A. Churchill, Jr., and J. Paul Peter, *Marketing: Creating Value for Customers,* 2nd ed. (Burr Ridge, IL: Irwin/McGraw-Hill, 1998), pp. 392–98.

5. This section is based on Churchill and Peter, *Marketing: Creating Value,* pp. 414–18.

6. This classification is taken from Michael Levy and Barton A. Weitz, *Retailing Management,* 3rd ed. (Burr Ridge, IL: Irwin/McGraw-Hill, 1998), Chap. 3.

7. For an excellent discussion of electronic exchange, see David W. Stewart and Qin Zhao, "Internet Marketing, Business Models, and Public Policy," *Journal of Public Policy & Marketing,* Fall 2000, pp. 287–96.

Chapter 11

1. Kent B. Monroe, "Buyers' Subjective Perceptions of Price," *Journal of Marketing Research,* February 1973, pp. 70–80; also see Donald R. Lichtenstein and Scot Burton, "The Relationship between Perceived and Objective Price—Quality," *Journal of Marketing Research,* November 1989, pp. 429–43.

2. For research concerning the effects of price and several other marketing variables on perceived product quality, see Akshay R. Rao and Kent B. Monroe, "The Effect of Price, Brand Name, and Store Name on Buyers'

Perceptions of Product Quality: An Integrative Review," *Journal of Marketing Research,* August 1989, pp. 351–57; and William B. Dodds, Kent B. Monroe, and Dhruv Grewal, "Effects of Price, Brand, and Store Evaluations on Buyers' Product Evaluations," *Journal of Marketing Research,* August 1991, pp. 307–19.

3. For further discussion of price elasticity, see Stephen J. Hoch, Byung-Do Kim, Alan L. Montgomery, and Peter Rosi, "Determinants of Store-Level Price Elasticity," *Journal of Marketing Research,* February 1995, pp. 17–29.

4. For further discussion of legal issues involved in pricing, see Louis W. Stern and Thomas L. Eovaldi, *Legal Aspects of Marketing Strategy* (Englewood Cliffs, NJ: Prentice Hall, 1984), Chap. 5.

5. For more detailed discussions, see Frederick E. Webster, *Marketing for Managers* (New York: Harper & Row, 1974), pp. 178–79; also see Thomas T. Nagle and Reed K. Holden, *The Strategy and Tactics of Pricing* (Englewood Cliffs, NJ: Prentice Hall, 1995); and Kent B. Monroe, *Pricing: Making Profitable Decisions,* 3rd ed. (Burr Ridge, IL: McGraw-Hill/Irwin, 2003).

Chapter 12

1. Much of the material for this introduction came from Ronald Henkoff, "Service Is Everybody's Business," *Fortune,* June 27, 1994, pp. 48–60; and Tim R. Smith, "The Tenth District's Expanding Service Sector," *Economic Review,* Third Quarter 1994, pp. 55–66.

2. Peter D. Bennett, ed., *Dictionary of Marketing Terms,* 2nd ed. (Chicago: American Marketing Association, 1995), p. 261.

3. The material in this section draws from research performed by Leonard L. Berry, Valerie A. Zeithaml, and A. Parasuraman, "Quality Counts in Services, Too," *Business Horizons,* May–June 1985, pp. 44–52; A. Parasuraman, Valerie A. Zeithaml, and Leonard L. Berry, "A Conceptual Model of Service Quality and Its Implications for Future Research," *Journal of Marketing,* Fall 1985, pp. 41–50; Leonard L. Berry, A. Parasuraman, and Valerie A. Zeithaml, "The Service-Quality Puzzle," *Business Horizons,* September–October 1988, pp. 35–43; Stephen W. Brown and Teresa A. Swartz, "A Gap Analysis of Professional Service Quality," *Journal of Marketing,* April 1989, pp. 92–98; Leonard L. Berry, Valerie A. Zeithaml, and A. Parasuraman, "Five Imperatives for Improving Service Quality," *Sloan Management Review,* Summer 1990, pp. 29–38; A. Parasuraman, Leonard L. Berry, and Valerie A. Zeithaml, "Understanding Customer Expectations of Service," *Sloan Management Review,* Spring 1991, pp. 39–48; and Leonard L. Berry, *On Great Service: A Framework for Action* (New York: Free Press, 1995).

4. Rick Berry, "Define Service Quality So You Can Deliver It," *Best's Review,* March 1995, p. 68.

5. Material for this section is drawn from John T. Mentzer, Carol C. Bienstock, and Kenneth B. Kahn, "Benchmarking Satisfaction," *Marketing Management,* Summer 1995, pp. 41–46; and Alan Dutka, *AMA Handbook for Customer Satisfaction: A Complete Guide to Research, Planning and Implementation* (Lincolnwood, IL: NTC Books, 1994). For detailed information on this topic, readers are advised to consult these sources.

6. Much of the material for this section was taken from Karl Albrecht and Ron Zemke, *Service America* (Burr Ridge, IL: Irwin/McGraw-Hill, 1985); and Ron Zemke and Dick Schaaf, *The Service Edge 101: Companies That Profit from Customer Care* (New York: New American Library, 1989).

7. Chip R. Bell and Kristen Anderson, "Selecting Super Service People," *HR Magazine,* February 1992, pp. 52–54.

8. James A. Schlesinger and James L. Heskett, "Breaking the Cycle of Failure in Services," *Sloan Management Review,* Spring 1991, pp. 17–28.

9. Leonard L. Berry and A. Parasuraman, "Services Marketing Starts from Within," *Marketing Management,* Winter 1992, pp. 25–34.

10. Ibid.

11. Leonard L. Berry and A. Parasuraman, "Prescriptions for a Service Quality Revolution in America," *Organizational Dynamics,* Spring 1992, pp. 5–15.

12. Bob O'Neal, "World-Class Service," *Executive Excellence,* September 1994, pp. 11–12.

13. This example is from David E. Bowen and Edward E. Lawler III, "The Empowerment of Service Workers: What, Why, How, and When," *Sloan Management Review,* Spring 1992, pp. 31–39.

14. Howard Schlossberg, "Study: U.S. Firms Lag in Using Customer Satisfaction Data," *Marketing News,* June 1992, p. 14.

15. Andrew E. Serwer, "The Competition Heats Up in Online Banking," *Fortune,* June 26, 1995, pp. 18–19.

16. John Labate, "Chronimed," *Fortune,* February 20, 1995, p. 118.

17. Elaine Underwood, "Airlines Continue Flight to E-Ticketing," *Brandweek,* May 8, 1995, p. 3.

18. Peter L. Ostrowski, Terrence V. O'Brien, and Geoffrey L. Gordon, "Determinants of Service Quality in the Commercial Airline Industry: Differences between Business and Leisure Travelers," *Journal of Travel & Tourism Marketing* 3, no. 1 (1994), pp. 19–47.

Chapter 13

1. Jason Vogel, "Chicken Diplomacy," *Financial World,* March 14, 1995, pp. 46–49.

2. For a full explanation on cultural differences, see Rose Knotts, "Cross-Cultural Management: Transformations

and Adaptations," *Business Horizons,* January–February 1989, pp. 29–33.

3. Claudia Penteado, "Pepsi's Brazil Blitz," *Advertising Age,* January 16, 1995, p. 12.

4. Karen Benezra, "Fritos 'Round the World,'" *Brandweek,* March 27, 1995, pp. 32, 35.

5. Material for this section is from Craig Mellow, "Russia: Making Cash from Chaos," *Fortune,* April 17, 1995, pp. 145–51; and Peter Galuszka, "And You Think You've Got Tax Problems," *Business Week,* May 29, 1995, p. 50.

6. Mir Magbool Alam Khan, "Enormity Tempts Marketers to Make a Passage to India," *Advertising Age International,* May 15, 1995, p. 112.

7. This section was taken from James F. Bolt, "Global Competitors: Some Criteria for Success," *Business Horizons,* January–February 1988, pp. 34–41.

8. This section is based on George S. Yip, Pierre M. Loewe, and Michael Y. Yoshino, "How to Take Your Company to the Global Market," *Columbia Journal of World Business,* Winter 1988, pp. 37–48.

9. Ibid.

10. The introductory material on foreign research is based on Michael R. Czintoka, "Take a Shortcut to Low-Cost Global Research," *Marketing News,* March 13, 1995, p. 3.

11. Donald B. Pittenger, "Gathering Foreign Demographics Is No Easy Task," *Marketing News,* January 8, 1990, pp. 23, 25.

12. This discussion is based on John Burnett, *Promotion Management* (Boston: Houghton-Mifflin Co., 1993), Chap. 19.

13. The material for this section on market entry and growth approaches is based on Philip R. Cateora, *International Marketing,* 8th ed. (Burr Ridge, IL: Irwin/McGraw-Hill, 1993), pp. 325–34; Charles W. L. Hill, *International Business: Competing in the Global Marketplace* (Burr Ridge, IL: Irwin/McGraw-Hill, 1994), pp. 402–8; and William M. Pride and O. C. Ferrell, *Marketing: Concepts and Strategy,* 9th ed. (Boston: Houghton-Mifflin Co., 1995), pp. 111–14.

14. Bruce A. Walters, Steve Peters, and Gregory G. Dess, "Strategic Alliances and Joint Ventures: Making Them Work," *Business Horizons,* July–August 1994, pp. 5–10.

15. Material in this section is based on Subhash C. Jain, "Standardization of International Marketing Strategy: Some Research Hypotheses," *Journal of Marketing,* January 1989, pp. 70–79.

Section II

1. Michael E. Porter, *Competitive Strategy* (New York: Free Press, 1980). Also see Michael E. Porter, *Competitive Advantage: Creating and Sustaining Superior Performance* (New York: Free Press, 1985); and Michael E. Porter, *The Competitive Advantage of Nations* (New York: Free Press, 1990).

Section III

1. For methods of estimating the cost of capital, see Charles P. Jones, *Introduction to Financial Management* (Burr Ridge, IL: Irwin/McGraw-Hill, 1992), Chap. 14.

2. See Eugene F. Brigham, *Fundamentals of Financial Management* (Hinsdale, IL: Dryden Press, 1986).

3. It is useful to use average inventory rather than a single end-of-year estimate if monthly data are available.

4. For a discussion of ratio analysis for retailing, see Joseph B. Mason and Morris L. Mayer, *Modern Retailing: Theory and Practice,* 6th ed. (Burr Ridge, IL: Irwin/McGraw-Hill, 1993), Chap. 8.

Index

NAME INDEX

SUBJECT INDEX